The Handbook of Morphology

The Handbook of Morphology

Edited by

Andrew Spencer and Arnold M. Zwicky

WILEY

Published by John Wiley & Sons, Hoboken, NJ

For general information on our other products and services, please contact our Customer Care Department within the United States at 800-762-2974, outside the United States at 317-572-3993 or fax 317-572-4002.

For more information about Wiley products, visit our website at www.wiley.com.

ISBN: 978-0-631-22694-9

Contents

Contributors

FRANK ANSHEN
Department of Linguistics
State University of New York at Stony Brook

MARK ARONOFF
Department of Linguistics
State University of New York at Stony Brook

WILLIAM BADECKER
Department of Cognitive Science
The Johns Hopkins University

ROBERT BEARD
Department of Modern Languages, Literatures and Linguistics
Bucknell University

HAGIT BORER
Department of Linguistics
University of Southern California

ALFONSO CARAMAZZA
Department of Psychology
Harvard University

ANDREW CARSTAIRS-MCCARTHY
Department of English
University of Canterbury
New Zealand

EVE V. CLARK
Department of Linguistics
Stanford University

GREVILLE G. CORBETT
Department of Linguistic and International Studies
University of Surrey

ANNE CUTLER
Max Planck Institute
Nijmegen

DANIEL L. EVERETT
Department of General Linguistics
University of Pittsburgh

NIGEL FABB
Department of English Studies
University of Strathclyde

JAMES FIFE

DONNA B. GERDTS
Department of Linguistics
Simon Fraser University
British Columbia

JOHN HAIMAN
Macalester College
St Paul, Minnesota

AARON L. HALPERN
Los Alamos National Laboratory/Santa Fe Institute

RICHARD J. HAYWARD
Africa Department
School of Oriental and African Studies
University of London

BRIAN D. JOSEPH
Department of Linguistics
Ohio State University

EDWARD L. KEENAN
Department of Linguistics
University of Southern California

ALEKSANDR E. KIBRIK
Philology Faculty
Moscow State University

FERENC KIEFER
Linguistics Institute
Hungarian Academy of Sciences

GARETH KING

BETH LEVIN
Department of Linguistics
Northwestern University

JOHN J. McCARTHY
Department of Linguistics
University of Massachusetts

JAMES M. McQUEEN
Max Planck Institute
Nijmegen

SAM A. MCHOMBO
Department of Linguistics
University of California at Berkeley

IRINA A. MURAVYOVA
Faculty of Theoretical and Applied Linguistics
Russian State University for the Humanities

MARIA POLINSKY
Department of Linguistics
University of California at San Diego

ALAN S. PRINCE
Department of Linguistics
Rutgers University

MALKA RAPPAPORT HOVAV
Department of English
Bar Ilan University

KEREN RICE
Department of Linguistics
University of Toronto

LOUISA SADLER
Department of Language and Linguistics
University of Essex

JANE SIMPSON
Department of Linguistics
University of Sydney

ANDREW SPENCER
Department of Language and Linguistics
University of Essex

RICHARD SPROAT
Linguistics Research Department
AT&T Bell Laboratories

JOSEPH PAUL STEMBERGER
Department of Communication Disorders
University of Minnesota

GREGORY T. STUMP
Department of English
University of Kentucky

JINDŘICH TOMAN
Department of Slavic Languages and Literatures
University of Michigan

ARNOLD M. ZWICKY
Department of Linguistics
Ohio State University and Stanford University

Abbreviations

1σ	monosyllabic
2D	second daughter
2P	second position (clitic)
2σ	disyllabic
2W	second word (clitic)
A	adjective
AAM	Augmented Addressed Morphology
ABL, abl.	ablative
ABS, abs.	absolutive
ACC, acc.	accusative
act.	active
ADJ, adj.	adjective
AFF	affix
AFFPRT	affirmative particle
AG	agreement marker
Agr	agreement
AgrP	Agreement Phrase
ALL, all.	allative
AOR, aor.	aorist
appl.	applicative
arg.	argument
art.	article
ASL	American Sign Language
asp.	aspect
assoc.	associative
ATR	Advanced Tongue Root
AUGM	augmentative
AUX, aux.	auxiliary
ben.	Benefactive
Bg.	Bulgarian

C	consonant
C, COMP	complementizer
CAUS, caus.	causative
circ.	circumstantial
cit.	citation
CL	classifier
cl	clitic
cond.	conditional
CONN, cn.	connective, connector
CP	complementizer phrase
CSLI	Center for the Study of Language and Information (Stanford)
Cz.	Czech
D	determiner
DAT, dat.	dative
DEF	definite
dem.	demonstrative
det.	determiner
DIM	diminutive
DIST	distributive
DM	Distributed Morphology
DO	direct object
DP	Determiner Phrase
DR	default rule
DS	'different subject' (switch reference)
du.	dual
DUR	durative
ECP	Empty Category Principle
emph.	emphatic
EP	European Portuguese
ERG, erg.	ergative
ex.	external (argument)
excl.	exclusive
F., FEM, fem.	feminine
foc.	focus
Fr.	French
Ft	foot
FUT, fut.	future
FV, fv	final vowel
GB	Government and Binding (theory)
GEN, gen.	genitive
GF	grammatical function
Gr.	Greek
H	heavy (syllable), high (tone)
hab.	habitual
HMC	Head Movement Constraint

HPSG	Head-Driven Phrase Structure Grammar
IA	Item-and-Arrangement
IC	intrinsic classification, Inherent Classification
IMPER, imper.	imperative
IMP(F), impf.	imperfect
INC	incorporated
inc.	(generalized) incorporation
INCH, inch.	inchoative
incl.	inclusive
indef.	indefinite
INDIC, indic.	indicative
INF	infinitive
INFL, infl.	'Inflection' node (Government Binding theory)
INST	Instrumental
int.	internal (argument)
inter.	interrogative
INTPRT	interrogative particle
intr.	intransitive
IO	indirect object
IP	Infl. phrase (Government Binding theory)
IP	Item-and-Process
irr.	irrealis
L	light (syllable), low (tone)
LCS	Lexical Conceptual Structure
LF	Logical Form
LIH	Lexical Integrity Hypothesis
LMT	Lexical Mapping Theory
LOC, loc.	locative
LRS	lexical relational structure
m., MASC, masc.	masculine
m/frp/p	masculine/feminine realis past/present
max	maximal (projection)
med.	medial
MinWd	minimal word
MS	Morphological Structure (Distributed Morphology)
n.	neuter
N, n.	noun
n.s.	noun suffix
NEG, neg.	negation
NEGPRT	negative particle
NEUT, neut.	neuter
NHG	New High German
NM	Natural Morphology
nm.	nominal
NOM, nom.	nominative, nominalization, nominalizer

NP	noun phrase
nrp/p	neuter realis past present
NUM	number
OBJ	object
OBL	oblique
OFr.	Old French
OHG	Old High German
OM	object marker
P	preposition
Pa.	Pashto
p.c.	personal communication
PAS	Predicate Argument Structure
PASS, pass.	passive
PER	person
perf.	perfect
PF	Phonological (Phonetic) Form (Government Binding theory)
PIE	proto-Indo-European
PL, pl.	plural
pos.	possessor, possessive
POSS, poss.	possessor, possessive
PPT	Principles and Parameters Theory
pred.	predicate
PREP, prep.	prepositional (case)
PRES, pres.	present
PRO, pro.	pronoun
prog.	progressive
prox.	proximal
PRT, prtc.	particle
PrWd	prosodic word
PSC	paradigm structure condition
p.t.	potential topic
punct.	punctual
Q	question (interrogative element)
QR	Quantifier Raising
recip.	reciprocal
Red.	Reduplication
redup.	reduplicated
REFL, reflex.	reflexive
REL, rel.	relative
rem.	remote
rev.	reversative
rf	realis future
RHR	Right-hand Head Rule
rp/p	realis past/present
S	subject

SCr.	Serbo-Croat
sec. asp.	secondary aspect
SG, sg.	singular
sgt.	singulative
SLI	Specific Language Impairment
SM	subject marker
SOV	Subject–Object–Verb (word order)
Sp.	Spanish
SPE	*The Sound Pattern of English* (Chomsky and Halle, 1968)
Spec	Specifier
SS	'same subject' (switch reference)
SS	S-structure (Government Binding theory)
STAT, stat.	stative
SUB, sub.	subject
SUBJ	subject, subjunctive
subjun.	subjunctive
subord.	subordinator
SUFF	suffix
TNS, tns	tense
TP	Tense Phrase
tr., trans.	transitive
UAH	Universal Alignment Hypothesis
UG	Universal Grammar
UTAH	Uniform Theta Assignment Hypothesis
V	vowel, verb
V2	verb second
VIC	verbal inflectional clitic
VOS	Verb–Object–Subject (word order)
VP	verb phrase
VR	verb root/radical
WF	West Flemish, Word Formation
WL	Wackernagel's Law
Y/N	Yes/No (question)

Introduction

ANDREW SPENCER AND
ARNOLD M. ZWICKY

Morphology is at the conceptual centre of linguistics. This is not because it is the dominant subdiscipline, but because morphology is the study of word structure, and words are at the interface between phonology, syntax and semantics. Words have phonological properties, they articulate together to form phrases and sentences, their form often reflects their syntactic function, and their parts are often composed of meaningful smaller pieces. In addition, words contract relationships with each other by virtue of their form; that is, they form paradigms and lexical groupings. For this reason, morphology is something all linguists have to know about. The centrality of the word brings with it two important challenges. First, there is the question of what governs morphological form: how is allomorphy to be described? The second is the question of what governs the syntactic and semantic function of morphological units, and how these interact with syntax and semantics proper.

There is a less enviable aspect to this centrality. Morphology has been called 'the Poland of linguistics' – at the mercy of imperialistically minded neighbours. In the heyday of American structuralism, morphology and phonology were the principal objects of study. Monographs entitled 'The Grammar of L', for some language L, would frequently turn out to consist of the phoneme system of L and its morphology. However, the study of morphology in generative linguistics was largely eclipsed by phonology and syntax in the early days (though it is up to historians of linguistics to say exactly why). Ultimately, it came to be that when morphology was considered at all, it was regarded as essentially either a part of phonology or a part of syntax. True, there were a number of important works on morphology, mainly inflectional morphology, such as Kiefer's (1973) work on Swedish, Bierwisch's (1967) study of German and Warburton's (1973) paper on Greek inflection; but it was not until Halle's (1973) short programmatic statement that linguistics at large began to appreciate that there was a vacuum in linguistic theory where morphology should be. This was followed in 1974 by two particularly influential MIT dissertations, later published as Aronoff (1976) and Siegel (1979), proposing radically different approaches to the subject.

Siegel's theory of Level Ordering brought with it a new way of looking at the phonology–morphology interface, which ultimately grew into Kiparsky's (1982a) Lexical Phonology. Siegel argued that those affixes in English which never affect stress (and which do not trigger other lexical phonological alternations) such as -*ness* are attached after stress rules have applied. These are the # boundary affixes of *SPE* (Chomsky and Halle 1968), renamed Class II. The + boundary (Class I) affixes are those which do affect stress, such as -*ity*, and they are attached before the stress rules. This led to an interesting prediction about the linear order of affixes: Class I affixes appear nearer the root than Class II affixes. This generalization is largely true, though it has been regularly pointed out since Aronoff (1976) that it is not entirely true. Fabb (1988) has argued that even if it is true, the Level Ordering Hypothesis is not sufficient to explain affix ordering in its entirety, and that alternative conceptions which do give reasonably broad coverage can also handle the Level Ordering phenomena.

Lexical Phonology is generally associated with Level Ordering (though a number of lexical phonologists have distanced themselves from it; cf. Booij and Rubach 1987). However, the leading ideas of the model do not actually require Level Ordering. The main thrust of Kiparsky's theory is to emphasize the traditional distinction between morphophonemic alternations and automatic alternations. The morphophonemic alternations are generally mappings from sets of phonemes into sets of phonemes (Structure Preservation), apply in contexts which are not defined in purely phonological terms, often have lexical exceptions, can be 'cancelled' by native speakers (e.g. in loan phonology), and generally apply only within words. The automatic alternations are generally allophonic (non-Structure Preserving), speakers are generally not aware of them, they apply to monomorphemic forms, and they often apply across words. Kiparsky argued that morphophonemic alternations are actually triggered by morphological operations of affixation. As an affix is added (or a cycle of affixation with a level is completed), the battery of lexical phonological rules applies. This gives rise to various types of cyclic effect, and accounts for a good many of the properties of the two types of rule.

This innovation was more significant for the development of phonology than for that of morphology, except that it (a) began to draw the attention of phonologists to morphology, and (b) tended to strengthen the view that morphology was the poor relation to phonology. Lexical Phonology retains the assumptions of *SPE* that every microgram of phonological regularity has to be squeezed out of the system before we have to throw in the towel and admit that it's 'mere allomorphy'. As a result, there have been very few attempts to examine the extent to which the alternations might themselves have a morphological function. To some extent this is addressed in Spencer's chapter, MORPHOPHONOLOGICAL OPERATIONS and also in Carstairs-McCarthy's PHONOLOGICAL CONSTRAINTS ON MORPHOLOGICAL RULES.

While Chomsky's original syntactic theorizing overturned structuralist thinking about that discipline, seminal studies in morphology from MIT served to strengthen structuralist assumptions. McCarthy (1979) showed that root-and-pattern morphology could be handled very nicely as a kind of affixation by adopting the then new theory of Autosegmental Phonology. Lieber (1980) built a theory of the lexicon in which affixes are almost exactly like fully-fledged lexical items, with a phonology, a meaning, a syntactic category and a subcategorization frame. At the same time, Selkirk (1982) and E. Williams (1981b) were arguing that word structure is very much like phrase structure, by applying X-bar syntax to words. This very influential approach is reviewed in Toman's chapter, WORD SYNTAX.

Central to the debate over the relationship between phonology and morphology is a long-standing question in structuralist linguistics, whether morphology is best thought of in terms of Item-and-Process or Item-and-Arrangement. In an IA approach, a word is made out of a string (or tree) of objects; that is, word formation is the concatenation of morphemes, conceived of as mini-lexemes. In an IP approach, forms of a word are the outputs of processes applied to a lexeme. This idea has been revivified in various ways. Categorial grammar has been co-opted to develop a formal way of describing the idea that affixation be viewed as a process (Hoeksema 1985). In a different vein, and working from a different tradition, McCarthy and Prince have studied the way in which non-concatenative effects are obtained by parsing out various phonologically defined subparts of words and stems before applying affixation (or other operations) to them, and this work is summarized in their chapter PROSODIC MORPHOLOGY.

However, the structuralist idea that words are just like phrases, and that the same set of principles applies to both domains, is very attractive, especially to non-morphologists, and it is a theme which runs through much of the research on the morphology–syntax interface over the past two decades. Its most obvious application is in compounding where almost everyone accepts that words have some kind of constituent structure. Somewhat more controversial is the view that derivational morphology is like phrase syntax, a thesis that is being explored in the domain of argument structure by Hale and Keyser (1993). This assumption was challenged by Aronoff (1976), and has more recently been attacked by Anderson (1992), for whom all non-compounding morphology is 'a-morphous'. Anderson's strong position is, perhaps, extreme (see Carstairs-McCarthy 1992 for a telling critique). However, the idea that morphemes are something other than just very short words which happen to be bound is particularly influential amongst morphologists. Many theorists view word formation not as the concatenation of two things to form a headed syntax-like structure , but as an operation on a lexeme. For such theorists, affixation tends to be thought of as just one type of morphophonological operation among several, and not a privileged syntactic process of concatenation. Word formation in Aronoff (1976) is accomplished by Word Formation Rules (WFRs), and this leads to a radically different conception of word structure. For one thing it opens the way to separating the phonological form of an affix from the morphological function or meaning of which it is an exponent. This is the content of the Separation Hypothesis (Beard 1988). It is widely assumed in works on inflection, but Beard argues it for derivation too, and surveys a number of the arguments in his chapter, DERIVATION.

The domain where separationism has been most popular is inflection. Following Matthews's (1972) detailed critique of the structuralist notion of morpheme in inflection, Anderson (1977b) began a programme of research which took inflections to be the result of word formation rules much like those proposed by Aronoff (1976) for derivation, but with complex interactions. This work is summarized in Stump's chapter, INFLECTION.

In Principles and Parameters syntax the importance of functional categories, which include inflectional categories, was being stressed throughout the 1980s. At the same time, Baker's dissertation (written in 1985 and revised as Baker 1988a) developed an extremely influential view of valency alternations based on the idea of incorporation, coded as syntactic head-to-head movement. This meant that, for example, the causative form of a verb was treated as a syntactic compound of two verbs, one of them a causative. This led to the view that inflectional morphology could be handled in the same way, and that an inflectional piece, say, a third-person singular subject in the past tense, was syntactically a compound consisting of the verb, an Agreement head, Agr^0, bearing the features [3sg] and a Tense head, T^0, bearing the feature [+Past] (cf. Pollock 1989). Some general problems with this account are discussed in Borer's chapter, MORPHOLOGY AND SYNTAX, and a number of morphologists have pointed out problems with the full-blown version of the approach, mainly from allomorphy (Carstairs-McCarthy 1992, Joseph and Smirniotopoulos 1993, Spencer 1992). However, more recently, Halle and Marantz (1993) have attempted to combine the separationist tradition in inflection with the functional head-movement approach, arguing that only in this way can we capture certain alleged homologies between morphological structure and syntactic structure. Their model is discussed in Stump's contribution. In addition, Rice shows how the complex and arbitrary-looking structure prefix of Slave (Athabaskan) none the less reflects syntactic structure to an interesting degree.

One of the traditional problems in morphology and lexicology has been defining what is meant by 'word'. There are various criteria based on form (which tend to be equivocal) and others based on behaviour and function (which tend to be even more equivocal). One symptom of this is the existence of elements which bear some of the hallmarks of words and also important features of affixes, namely, clitics. Ever since Zwicky's (1977) preliminary typology, there has been interest in this problem, and for many phonologists and syntacticians, as well as morphologists, it is an urgent practical matter, since both phonology and syntax appeal regularly to the distinction between 'proper' words and other elements. The issues are surveyed in Halpern's chapter, CLITICS.

One of the alleged criterial properties of words is 'integrity': words are 'islands' to syntactic and other processes, which are unable to 'see inside' words; in this way words contrast with phrases. There is a great deal of appeal to distinguishing words from phrases in this way (see Bresnan and Mchombo 1995 for a defence of lexical integrity and a catalogue of advantages), but lexical integrity has been denied by many linguists. The head-movement approach to word structure is a clear case in point, as is the approach of Hale and Keyser (1993) to argument structure. One traditional problem related to lexical integrity is the distinction between compounding (morphology) and phrase formation (syntax). In many (if not most) languages with compounding, the distinction is far from clear (half of the annual *Yearbook of morphology 1989* was given over to this: Booij and van Marle 1990). Compounding is surveyed in Fabb's chapter, COMPOUNDING.

The kinds of phenomena which tend to raise questions of integrity most keenly are serial verb constructions, light verb contructions, and, most notoriously, incorporation. The most studied type of incorporation is noun incorporation, in which a verb stem forms a morphological compound with a noun apparently functioning, say, as its direct object. Other sorts of incorporation are also found, as in Chukchee, where a noun may incorporate its modifiers (adjectives, determiner-like elements and so on; see Muravyova's sketch of the language and also Spencer 1995). Gerdts's contribution, INCORPORATION, discusses these issues, suggesting that there might be types of incorporation effectively midway between genuine phrase formation and *bona fide* compounding.

Cliticization and noun incorporation can both be thought of as instances of a kind of structural mismatch. Thus, in a sentence such as *John's here* the *'s* of *John's* is phonologically simply the last phoneme of the first word, but syntactically it corresponds to the main verb, which doesn't even form a constituent with the first word, *John*. Likewise, in a language in which object incorporation is possible and we can say *John bear=killed*, meaning *John killed a bear*, we seem to have a single word, *bear=kill*, functioning as a transitive VP $[_{VP}[_V kill]$ $[_{NP} bear]]$. In both cases we have a mismatch between form and function over what we expect in the 'canonical' case.

Such mismatches occur elsewhere, most famously in so-called bracketing paradoxes.[1] These are instances in which the apparent constituent structure of a word is at odds with some other aspect of its form or function. The mismatch in *John's* would be a case in point. In some cases, the paradoxes are in effect theory-internal. Thus, a frequently discussed case is that of *ungrammaticality*. Semantically, this is a nominalization of the adjective *ungrammatical*, entailing a constituent structure [[*un + grammatical*] *ity*]. However, in the theory of Level Ordering, *-ity* is a Class I suffix and *un-* is a Class II prefix. The order of affixation should therefore give rise to a constituent structure [*un* [*grammatical + ity*]]. Similarly, some theories of English synthetic compounds such as *truck driver* would have them derived by suffixing *-er* to a noun-incorporated form of the verb, [[*truck drive*] *er*], even though morphologically the compound is clearly made up of *truck* and *driver*.

However, there are structures which are anomalous under any reasonable description. English personal nouns provide numerous examples (see Beard 1990, Spencer 1988b, Stump 1991, Zwicky 1988, amongst many references). A transformational grammarian is not (necessarily) a grammarian who is transformational; the bracketing appears to be [[*transformational grammar*] *ian*]. More extreme examples are *moral philosopher* (derived from, or at least motivated by, *moral philosophy*) and, with apparent truncation of a suffix, *monumental mason* (*monumental masonry*), *electrical engineer* (*electrical engineering*) and *theoretical linguist* (*theoretical linguistics*). The direction of motivation is clear from the semantics (the personal noun has to inherit all the semantic idiosyncrasies of the abstract noun) and from the fact that only established fixed terms can motivate such personal nouns (witness the absence of **abstract linguist* from the purely compositional, non-lexicalized phrase *abstract linguistics*, cf. Spencer 1988b). Clearly, conundrums such as these have to be handled in anybody's theory, but a number of linguists have paid particular attention to such questions. Sadock (1991), in particular, has developed an integrated theory of the mismatches caused by incorporation and cliticization processes. This and other approaches are summarized in Sproat's contribution, MORPHOLOGY AS COMPONENT OR MODULE.

The interface between morphology and syntax also surfaces in a number of ways. One area of great interest for both syntacticians and morphologists is that of agreement morphology, and it is an area where any specialist needs to have a careful eye on both subdisciplines. Corbett's chapter, MORPHOLOGY AND AGREEMENT, provides a clear, morphologist's view of the matter, informed by his extensive experience as a typologist. An area which stands at the crossroads between morphology, syntax and semantics concerns the way in which grammatical relations such as subject and object are realized and the types of alternations in valency that are found. This has led to an investigation of notions of argument structure. The semantic prerequisites are laid down in Levin and Rappaport Hovav's chapter, MORPHOLOGY AND LEXICAL SEMANTICS, which asks such questions as 'What semantico-syntactic relations can be packaged up inside a single lexeme?' Sadler and Spencer's contribution, MORPHOLOGY AND ARGUMENT STRUCTURE, then explores the idea raised by Levin and Rappaport Hovav that there might be a specific level of representation at which argument structure is encoded.

Levin and Rappaport Hovav's chapter can also be seen as an investigation of the relations between morphology and semantics. This is also explored, though from a different perspective, in Beard's chapter, DERIVATION. Recent research has been uncovering the ways in which semantic principles underly the organization of much of the lexicon, and this has an impact, of course, on the way that derivational morphology works. Finally, we must not forget that morphology can also serve as the exponent of pragmatic functions, and this is summarized in Kiefer's MORPHOLOGY AND PRAGMATICS.

So far in this introduction we have stressed the interface questions which are raised by morphology. These have not been the traditional concern of the discipline, of course, and to a certain extent the autonomy of morphology has been overshadowed by research at the interfaces (as well as being denied by a fair number of syntacticians and a smaller number of morphologists). However, as Aronoff (1994) has recently reminded us, there is a good deal to say about 'morphology by itself'. One of Aronoff's most significant claims is that inflectional paradigms can be autonomous with regard to syntax, semantics or phonology, and thus motivate a separate component, module or some kind of level of representation. This set of questions is summarized in Carstairs-McCarthy's INFLECTIONAL PARADIGMS AND MORPHOLOGICAL CLASSES. Aronoff (1994) also argues that the existence of stems provides evidence for the autonomy of morphology. He points out that in Latin a verb has three stems (which may be idiosyncratic or derived by regular and productive operations), but that it is not possible to say that a given stem has a meaning as such. It functions as part of a morphological system, but as a pure phonological form – a further instance of separationism. The stem as such has no meaning, but contributes non-compositionally to the meaning of the whole word form. An illustration of stem autonomy in Sanskrit (recently discussed by Stump) is given in Spencer's chapter MORPHOPHONOLOGICAL OPERATIONS. Finally, another aspect in which words are different is the fact that words, unlike (most) phrases, have to have some component which is listed. This leads to the tricky question of productivity, an issue at the border between linguistics proper and psycholinguistics. The chapter by Aronoff and Anshen surveys these matters.

Part IV of the Handbook is devoted to what we may call 'hyphenated linguistics'. Joseph, in DIACHRONIC MORPHOLOGY, summarizes recent advances in historical morphology, another Cinderella subject which is undergoing something of a rebirth. The rest of this part is devoted to various aspects of psycholinguistics in which particularly important advances have been made of late. Clark summarizes recent research into first-language acquisition of morphology. While the acquisition of morphology has not received quite the same attention as the acquisition of syntax from linguists in recent years, it has none the less assumed considerable importance. In part, this is because of provocative and extremely challenging claims from researchers working in the field of connectionism, to the effect that the facts of acquisition, especially of inflection, can be handled by associationist networks without the mediation of linguistic rules, or indeed, of conventional linguistic representations. Another interesting recent development has been in the study of selective language impairment (SLI). Pioneering work by Gopnik and her collaborators, as well as other groups, has provided controversial evidence in support of a biologically defined innate predisposition for language in the form of language impairments, principally to the morphological system, which appear to be inherited genetically.

Psycholinguistic research of the mental lexicon, and the way in which morphological structures are perceived and produced, has been pursued intensively since the beginning of modern psycholinguistics. One of the challenges here is to reconcile the kinds of models which seem necessary to interpret the psycholinguistic data with the most plausible linguistic models of word structure, and with the facts of word structure across the world's languages unearthed in morphological research. One important question is: How do we identify words in the speech stream? And in particular, how can we do this in such a way as to be able to incorporate words into a syntactic parsing? An important constraint on models of on-line processing is the fact that words have to be recognized and parsed as they are spoken (i.e. in a left-to-right fashion). McQueen and Cutler's chapter, MORPHOLOGY IN WORD RECOGNITION, presents an overview of recent findings in this field.

One of the most powerful tools for investigating the workings of an on-line mechanism is to examine the patterns of errors that mechanism produces. Word production studies, which often involve the careful analysis of large corpora of speech errors, have generated a number of sophisticated models, including connectionist-inspired ones. These are surveyed in Stemberger's chapter, which includes a convenient summary of the issues raised by connectionism for morphology. A further important source of informative errors has been provided by victims of language impairment due to brain injury or disease, giving rise to aphasias or, in the case of reading and writing, dyslexias. Study of these language disturbances has provided ample opportunity to investigate the way in which processes of word recognition and production 'fractionate' into their component subprocesses. This work is surveyed in Badecker and Caramazza's chapter, MORPHOLOGY AND APHASIA.

The Handbook closes with a collection of morphological sketches. These are written by linguists who have both a specialist interest in some aspect of morphology and a detailed knowledge of the language sketched, in some cases being native speakers. We have selected a group of languages which illustrate as many as possible of the phenomena we believe to be of interest to the widest circle of morphologists.

Among the phenomena surveyed which show interesting features in certain of the languages are the following (where a language appears in parentheses, the phenomenon is either restricted or only identifiable under certain theoretical interpretations of the facts):

non-concatenative morphology	Qafar
vowel harmony	Chichewa, Chukchee, Wari'
consonant mutation	Celtic, (Malagasy), (Slave)
apophony	Archi, Hua, Qafar
stress marking gender	Qafar
tone marking inflection	Chichewa
reduplication	Chichewa, Chukchee, Malagasy, Warumungu
infixation	Archi, Hua, Malagasy, Qafar
compounding	Chukchee, Malagasy, Qafar, Slave, Wari'
genitive complement	Malagasy
incorporation	Chukchee, Malagasy
clitics	Archi, Malagasy, Qafar, Slave, Wari', Warumungu

phonologically conditioned allomorph selection	Wari', Qafar
preverbs	Slave, Wari', Warumungu
conjugation classes	Archi, Qafar
agreement	
by prepositions	Celtic
inverse	(Chukchee), Warumungu
possessive	Archi, Hua, Qafar, Slave, Wari'
switch reference	Hua
with objects	Archi, Chichewa, Chukchee, Hua, Qafar, Slave, Wari', (Warumungu)
gender	Archi, Chichewa, Qafar
singulative	Qafar
diminutive	Chichewa, Chukchee, Slave
augmentative	Chichewa, Chukchee, Slave
case	Archi, Celtic, Hua, Qafar, Warumungu
ergative	Chukchee, Hua, Warumungu
localization	Archi
marked nominative	Qafar
multiple case marking	Archi, Warumungu
valency alternations and grammatical roles	
antipassive	Archi, Chukchee
applicative	Chichewa, (Chukchee)
autobenefactive	Qafar
causative	Archi, Chichewa, Malagasy, Qafar, Slave, Warumungu
comitative	Chukchee, Malagasy
inchoative	Malagasy, Qafar, Warumungu
passive	Malagasy
reciprocal	Chichewa, Malagasy
reflexives	Chichewa, Malagasy, Warumungu
reversive	Chichewa
stative	Chichewa
light verbs	Archi, Hua, Qafar ('compound conjugation'), (Chukchee)
predicate nominal	Chukchee, Hua, Qafar
proper names	Hua
aspect	Archi, Chukchee, Slave,
mood	
admirative	Archi
associated motion	Warumungu
commentative	Archi
continuality	Archi
evidential	Archi, Hua, Qafar, Slave
focus	Qafar

inconsequential	Hua
inferential	Archi
interrogative	Archi, Hua
negation	Archi, Chichewa, Chukchee, Qafar, Slave, Wari'
requestive	Qafar
topic (potential)	Hua
nominalization	Archi (masdar), Chichewa, Chukchee, Malagasy, Qafar, Slave, Wari', Warumungu
agentive	Chichewa, Chukchee, Malagasy, Warumungu
relativizer	Hua
gerund	Archi, Chukchee

NOTE

1 To refer to such phenomena as 'paradoxical' is a misnomer, of course, though the term has tended to stick.

Part I The Phenomena

1 Inflection

GREGORY T. STUMP

1 The logic of inflection

The notion of inflection rests on the more basic notion of lexeme. A *lexeme* is a unit of linguistic analysis which belongs to a particular syntactic category, has a particular meaning or grammatical function, and ordinarily enters into syntactic combinations as a single word; in many instances, the identity of the word which realizes a particular lexeme varies systematically according to the syntactic context in which it is to be used. Thus, English has a verbal lexeme meaning 'cantāre' which enters into syntactic combinations as either *sing*, *sings*, *sang*, *sung*, or *singing*, depending on its syntactic context; this lexeme might be given the arbitrary label SING.[1] The words realizing a given lexeme can be conceived of both as units of form (i.e. as *phonological words*, such as /sæŋ/) and as units of grammatical analysis (i.e. as *grammatical words*, such as 'the past tense of SING'); the full set of words realizing a particular lexeme constitutes its *paradigm*.

The structure of paradigms in a given language is determined by the inventory of morphosyntactic properties available in that language. Given a lexeme L of category C, the structure of L's paradigm is determined by the set S of morphosyntactic properties appropriate to C and by the co-occurrence restrictions on these properties: for each maximal consistent subset of S, there is a corresponding *cell* in the paradigm of L. For instance, in a language in which the set S of morphosyntactic properties appropriate to category C is the set {PER:1, PER:2, PER:3, NUM:sg, NUM:pl, TNS:pres, TNS:past} and in which distinct specifications of the same feature are forbidden to co-occur, the maximal consistent subsets of S are those in (1). Accordingly, a lexeme L of category C has (in this language) a paradigm with twelve cells, one for each of the sets in (1); each of these cells is occupied by a particular word realizing L.

(1) {PER:1, NUM:sg, TNS:pres}   {PER:1, NUM:sg, TNS:past}
     {PER:2, NUM:sg, TNS:pres}   {PER:2, NUM:sg, TNS:past}

{PER:3, NUM:sg, TNS:pres}	{PER:3, NUM:sg, TNS:past}
{PER:1, NUM:pl, TNS:pres}	{PER:1, NUM:pl, TNS:past}
{PER:2, NUM:pl, TNS:pres}	{PER:2, NUM:pl, TNS:past}
{PER:3, NUM:pl, TNS:pres}	{PER:3, NUM:pl, TNS:past}

A lexeme's *root* is that unit of form from which its paradigm of phonological words is deduced (e.g. the phonological words /sɪŋ/, /sɪŋz/, /sæŋ/, /sʌŋ/, and /sɪŋɪŋ/ are all deduced from the root /sɪŋ/ by principles of English morphology). Some lexemes have more than one root: French ALLER, for example, has the root *all-* in *allons* 'we go', but the root *i-* in *irons* 'we will go'. A root also qualifies as a *stem*, as does any form which is morphologically intermediate between a root and a full word (such as the perfect stem *dūk-s-* in Latin *dūk-s-ī* 'I led').

Once the existence of lexemes is assumed, two different uses of morphology can be distinguished. On the one hand, morphological devices can be used to deduce the words constituting a lexeme's paradigm from that lexeme's root(s); for instance, a very general rule of English morphology entails that the verbal lexeme SING (root /sɪŋ/) has a third-person singular present indicative form /sɪŋz/ in its paradigm. On the other hand, morphological devices can be used to deduce new lexemes from existing lexemes; thus, another rule of English morphology deduces an agentive nominal lexeme SINGER (root /sɪŋr/) from the verbal lexeme SING. Morphology put to the former, paradigm-deducing use is *inflection*; morphology put to the latter, lexeme-deducing use has traditionally carried the (potentially misleading) label of *word formation*, which encompasses both derivation and compounding (see Beard, DERIVATION; Fabb, COMPOUNDING).

2   Empirical criteria for distinguishing inflection from other things

However clear the logic of this distinction might be, it can be difficult, in practice, to distinguish inflection from word formation, particularly from derivation; by the same token, inflection – a morphological phenomenon – is not always easily distinguished from cliticization – a syntactic phenomenon. Various empirical criteria have been invoked in drawing these distinctions.

2.1   Inflection vs derivation

At least five criteria are commonly used to distinguish inflection from derivation. These criteria are, to a considerable extent, logically independent of one another; a priori, one wouldn't necessarily expect each of the five criteria to divide morphological phenomena into the same two groups. The boundaries which these criteria actually entail coincide to a remarkable degree, but not perfectly, as we shall see.

Consider first the criterion of *change in lexical meaning or part of speech*:

(2)   Two expressions related by principles of derivation may differ in their lexical meaning, their part-of-speech membership, or both; but two expressions belonging to the same inflectional paradigm will share both their lexical meaning and their part of speech – that is, any differences in their grammatical behavior will stem purely from the morphosyntactic properties that distinguish the cells of a paradigm.

By this criterion, the rule of agentive nominalization which produces SINGER from SING must be derivational, while the rule of pluralization which produces *singers* from *singer* need not be.

The diagnostic utility of criterion (2) obviously depends on the precision with which one can articulate the principles for determining an expression's part of speech (for which see e.g. Schachter 1985) and the principles for distinguishing lexicosemantic properties from morphosyntactic ones (see section 3). But even if such principles are clearly delineated, the usefulness of criterion (2) is inherently limited, for two reasons. First, a change in lexical meaning is not always accompanied by a change in part of speech – that is, some derivation is category-preserving, e.g. the derivation of REREAD from READ; thus, category change is not a necessary property of derivation, but is at most a sufficient property. Second, synonymous pairs such as *cyclic/cyclical* suggest that derivational morphology need not change lexical meaning; that is, change of lexical meaning is at most a sufficient property distinguishing derivational morphology from inflection.

To complicate matters even further, criterion (2) is not fully consistent with the other criteria, since there are morphological phenomena which are otherwise arguably inflectional but which involve a change in part of speech; for instance, a verbal lexeme's past participle is traditionally seen as an integral part of its paradigm, yet past participles are, in many languages, unmistakably adjectival in character.

Now consider the criterion of *syntactic determination*:

(3)   A lexeme's syntactic context may require that it be realized by a particular word in its paradigm, but never requires that the lexeme itself belong to a particular class of derivatives.

Thus, if the lexeme SING is to head the complement of the auxiliary verb HAVE, it must assume its past participial form: *They have *sing/*sings/*sang/sung /*singing several sea shanties.* By contrast, there is no syntactic context which requires agentive nominalizations such as SINGER and therefore excludes simplex (synchronically underived) lexemes such as FAN: *a singer/fan of sea shanties.* This criterion is the intended content of the slogan "inflectional morphology is what is relevant to the syntax" (Anderson 1982: 587), but of course not all inflectional morphology is directly relevant to syntax; for instance, inflectional expressions of conjugation- or declension-class member-ship (e.g. the distinct theme vowels of Latin *laud-ā-mus* 'we praise' and *mon-ē-mus* 'we remind') need not be – that is, they may be *morphomic* (Aronoff 1994). Nevertheless, the logic of inflection entails that distinct members of a lexeme's paradigm carry distinct sets of morphosyntactic properties; in the context of a fully articulated theory of syntax in which such properties are by definition syntactically relevant, it follows that inflectional morphology must itself be syntactically relevant in the indirect sense that it spells out a para-digm's syntactically contrasting word-forms. Here again, the diagnostic utility of the criterion depends on the precision of one's principles for distinguishing lexicosemantic properties from morphosyntactic ones (cf. section 3).

A third criterion is that of *productivity*:

(4)   Inflection is generally more productive than derivation.

In English, for instance, an arbitrarily chosen count noun virtually always allows an inflected plural form; by contrast, an arbitrarily chosen adjective may or may not give rise to a related causative verb (e.g. *harden, deafen,* but **colden, *braven*). Thus, inflectional paradigms tend to be complete, while deriva-tional relations are often quite sporadic.

Criterion (4) is sometimes inconsistent with the others. On the one hand, there are highly productive morphological phenomena which (by the other criteria) are derivational; in English, for example, virtually every nonmodal verb has a gerund (a nominal derivative identical in form to the present par-ticiple). On the other hand, one occasionally encounters groups of forms which (by the other criteria) constitute inflectional paradigms, but which are *defective* in that some of their cells are left empty; for instance, the paradigm of the French verb *frire* 'to fry' lacks a number of expected forms, including those of the subjunctive, the imperfect, the simple past, the plural of the present indicative, and the present participle.

Not all defective paradigms need be seen as instances of unproductive inflection, however. Defective paradigms are often systematically complemented by sets of *periphrastic* forms; in classical Sanskrit, for example, many vowel-initial roots consisting of a metrically heavy syllable lack an inflected perfect, but a periphrastic perfect formation (comprising the accusative singular form of the verb's nominal derivative in -*ā́* and a perfect form of the auxiliary verb KR̥ 'make' or AS 'be') makes up for this (Whitney 1889: §1071). If the cells of an inflectional paradigm admit periphrastic formations as well as individual inflected words (as Börjars et al. 1997 argue), then defectiveness is not as widespread a phenomenon as it might first appear to be. Nevertheless, once periphrastic formations are admitted into inflectional paradigms, criteria must be established for distinguishing systematically complementary periphrasis from mere coincidence of meaning; for instance, should *more alert* (cf. **alerter*) be assumed to figure in the paradigm of ALERT, given the coexistence of *more muddy* and *muddier*?

A fourth criterion is that of *semantic regularity*:

(5)   Inflection is semantically more regular than derivation.

Thus, the third-person singular present-tense suffix -*s* in *sings* has precisely the same semantic effect from one verb to the next, while the precise semantic effect of the verb-forming suffix -*ize* is somewhat variable (*winterize* 'prepare (something) for winter', *hospitalize* 'put (someone) into a hospital', *vaporize* '(cause to) become vapor'). This difference might be attributed to a difference in lexical listing:

(6)   Assumption: The lexicon lists derivative lexemes, but not inflected words.

On this assumption, the fact that derived lexemes are listed in the lexicon frees their meanings to "drift" idiosyncratically, while the fact that regularly inflected forms are not listed requires their meanings to remain rule-regulated. The semantic "drift" typical of derivation need not be understood in dia-chronic terms: it is not clear, for example, that the meaning of *winterize* has, through time, been drifting away from an original, less idiosyncratic meaning. Rather, it seems that, in this case and many others, the meaning of a derived form is not fully determined by the grammar, but depends on the intentions and inferences of language users at the moment of its first use (the moment at which the form and meaning are first "stored"); that is, the semantic idio-syncrasy of many derived lexemes follows not from the fact that their mean-ings are lexically listed, but from the fact that their meanings are inevitably shaped by pragmatic inferences at the very outset of their existence (and are therefore in immediate need of lexical listing). The opposite is true in instances of inflection: given the meaning of a lexeme L, the meaning associated with each cell in L's paradigm is in general fully determinate. This is not to say, of course, that it is the *form* of an inflected word that determines its meaning. On the contrary, an inflected word's form frequently underdetermines its morpho-syntactic properties (i.e. its membership in a particular cell), hence its mean-ing; indeed, there are often blatant mismatches between an inflected word's morphology and its semantics (as e.g. in the case of Latin deponent verbs). An inflected word's meaning is instead generally a function of the lexeme which it realizes and the cell which it occupies in that lexeme's paradigm (Stump 1991).

Criterion (5) is occasionally inconsistent with the other criteria. On the one hand, there are (rare) instances of semantic idiosyncrasy involving forms which (by the other criteria) are inflectional (cf. the discussion of (8d) below); on the other hand, classes of derived lexemes are sometimes quite regular in mean-ing (e.g. English verbal derivatives in *re*-). Facts such as these suggest that, contrary to assumption (6), listedness is neither a necessary nor a sufficient correlate of the inflection/derivation distinction (a conclusion that is in any event necessitated by the existence of highly productive classes of derived forms and irregular or defective paradigms of inflected forms).

A final, widely assumed criterion for distinguishing inflection from derivation is that of *closure*:

(7)   Inflection closes words to further derivation, while derivation does not.

In English, for example, a privative adjective cannot be derived from a noun's inflected plural form (**socksless*), but can be derived from a noun's uninflected root, whether or not this is itself derived (*sockless, driverless*). A corollary of this criterion is that in words containing both inflectional and derivational affixes, the inflectional affixes will always be further from the root than the derivational affixes (except in cases of infixation). This criterion has been used to motivate a principle of grammatical organization known as the Split Morphology Hypothesis (Perlmutter 1988; cf. Anderson 1982; Thomas-Flinders (ed.) 1981), according to which all derivation takes place in the lexicon, prior to lexical insertion, while all regular inflection is postsyntactic.

Evidence from a variety of languages, however, suggests that neither criterion (7) nor the Split Morphology Hypothesis can be maintained. To begin with, it is actually quite common for category-preserving derivational morphology to appear "outside of" inflectional morphology: for instance, Russian *stučát'-sja* 'to knock purposefully' (a derivative of *stučát'* 'to knock') inflects internally (*stučím-sja* 'we knock purposefully', *stučát-sja* 'they knock purposefully', etc.); the plural of the Breton diminutive noun *bagig* 'little boat' is *bagoùigoù*, in which one plural suffix *-où* appears before the diminutive suffix *-ig* while the other appears after it; and so on. Moreover, it is even possible for category-changing derivation to appear "outside of" inflection: in Breton, for example, plural nouns can be converted to verbs from which a variety of derivatives are then possible (e.g. *pesk-ed* 'fish-PL' gives rise to *pesketa* 'to fish', whence the agentive nominalization *pesketer* 'fisherman'); they can give rise to privative adjectives (*ler-où* 'sock-PL', *dileroù* 'without socks'); and so on. For discussion of the evidence against the Split Morphology Hypothesis, see Bochner 1984; Rice 1985; Booij 1993; and Stump 1990a, 1993a, 1995b.

2.2 Is the distinction between inflection and derivation illusory?

In its simplest form (unadorned by such supplementary assumptions as (6) or the Split Morphology Hypothesis), the logic of inflection does not entail that the five criteria discussed in section 2.1 should partition morphological phenomena along the same boundary; the extent to which the criteria do coincide therefore suggests that a number of independent morpholexical principles are sensitive to (if not categorically constrained by) the distinction between inflection and derivation. This conclusion has, however, been questioned: it has sometimes been asserted (Lieber 1980: 70; Di Sciullo and Williams 1987: 69ff; Bochner 1992: 12ff) that the distinction between inflection and derivation has no real empirical motivation, and therefore has no place in morphological theory. According to Bochner (1992: 14),

> The basic argument in any theory for treating inflection and derivation in a unified fashion is that they involve the same sorts of formal operations. Operations such as prefixation, suffixation, reduplication and infixation all have both inflectional and derivational uses in the world's languages.

But nothing in the logic of inflection excludes the possibility that inflection might involve the same sorts of formal operations as derivation; indeed, nothing excludes the possibility that the very same operation might serve a derivational function in some instances and an inflectional function in others. Breton furnishes an example of just this sort (Stump 1990b: 219ff): in Breton, the suffixation of *-enn* yields feminine nouns. In many cases, this operation serves a transparently derivational function: *bas* 'shallow (adj.)', *basenn* 'shoal'; *koant* 'pretty', *koantenn* 'pretty girl'; *lagad* 'eye', *lagadenn* 'eyelet', *c'hoant* 'want (n.)', *c'hoantenn* 'birthmark' (cf. French *envie*). But when *-enn* is suffixed to a collective noun, it yields the corresponding singulative: *buzug* 'worms', *buzugenn* 'worm'; *sivi* 'strawberries', *sivienn* 'strawberry'. Such singulative/collective pairs are syntactically indistinguishable from ordinary singular/plural pairs. Thus, *-enn* suffixation allows the root of one lexeme to be deduced from that of another, but it likewise fills the singular cell in a collective noun's inflectional paradigm; and this fact is in no way incompatible with the logic of inflection. As Aronoff (1994: 126) observes, "derivation and inflection are not kinds of morphology but rather uses of morphology: inflection is the morphological realization of syntax, while derivation is the morphological realization of lexeme formation." (See Beard 1995, where the implications of this fact are explored in detail.)

The theoretical appropriateness of the inflection/derivation distinction will be definitively established only through the comparison of carefully constructed formal analyses of ambitious scope for a typologically diverse range of grammatical systems. Only by this means can the fundamental question be addressed: Does a theory that incorporates this distinction furnish simpler (more learnable) grammars than one that doesn't? A theory must naturally provide some means of accommodating such exceptional morphological phenomena as category-changing inflection and defective paradigms, but it is the unexceptional phenomena – which are vastly more numerous – whose properties will likely weigh most heavily in the resolution of this issue.

2.3 *Inflections vs clitics*

Because of their syntactic relevance, inflectional affixes ᵢ
to distinguish from *clitics*, elements which exhibit an ᵃ

dependency on a neighboring word but whose syntax is word-like. Zwicky and Pullum (1983a: 503f) propose the following six criteria for distinguishing affixes from clitics:

(8) (a) "Clitics exhibit a low degree of selection with respect to their hosts while affixes exhibit a high degree of selection with respect to their stems."
  (b) "Arbitrary gaps in the set of combinations are more characteristic of affixed words than of clitic groups."
  (c) "Morphophonological idiosyncrasies are more characteristic of affixed words than of clitic groups."
  (d) "Semantic idiosyncrasies are more characteristic of affixed words than of clitic groups."
  (e) "Syntactic rules can affect words, but cannot affect clitic groups."
  (f) "Clitics can attach to material already containing clitics, but affixes cannot."

Consider, for example, the Breton preposition *da* 'to'. On the one hand, *da* may inflect for agreement with a pronominal object, as in (9); on the other hand, it may host the first-person singular clitic *-m* and the second-person singular clitic *-z*, as in (10).

(9)	din	'to me'	(10)	dam zad	'to my father'
	dit	'to thee'		dam gweloud	'to see me'
	dezañ	'to him'		daz tad	'to thy father'
	dezi	'to her'		daz kweloud	'to see thee'
	deom	'to us'			
	deoc'h	'to you'			
	dezo	'to them'			

This difference in status between the person/number markers in (9) and (10) is revealed quite clearly by the criteria in (8). Although *-m* and *-z* impose a rather severe prosodic requirement on their host (it must be a codaless monosyllable), they are otherwise quite indifferent to its category (criterion (8a)): it may be a preposition (as in (10)), a preverbal particle (e.g. *ne-m selaouez ket* 'you (sg.) aren't listening to me'), a subordinating conjunction (*pa-m magit* 'because you feed me'), or a coordinating conjunction (*ma c'hoar ha-m breur* 'my sister and my brother'). By contrast, object-agreement paradigms comparable to (9) are found with only a subclass of prepositions in Breton (e.g. *araog* 'before' inflects, but *kent* 'before' does not); exactly which prepositions inflect is apparently a matter of arbitrary lexical stipulation.

The expected combinations of *-m* or *-z* with a (prosodically appropriate) host are uniformly possible (criterion (8b)), but some inflecting prepositions (including *da*) have defective paradigms lacking the so-called indefinite form; contrast *dirag* 'in front of', whose indefinite form is *dirazer* 'in front of one'.

The result of concatenating -*m* or -*z* with its host exhibits no morpho-phonological peculiarities (criterion (8c)); by contrast, inflecting prepositions are often quite idiosyncratic in form (e.g. the first singular and third singular feminine forms of *ouz* 'against' are *ouzin* and *outi*, while those of *a* 'of' are *ac'hanon* and *anezi*).

Whereas inflected prepositions can be "stranded" by principles of anaphoric ellipsis (criterion (8e)), clitic groups with -*m* or -*z* cannot: *Da biou eo al levr-se? Din.* 'To whom is this book? To me.' *Da beseurt mestr eo al levr-se? *Dam.* 'To which teacher is this book? To mine.'

The person/number inflections in (9) cannot attach to prepositions that are already marked with -*m* or -*z* to express meanings such as that of *aux miens* 'to my ones'; nevertheless, criterion (8f) is not particularly revealing here, since Breton happens not to have any clitics which attach before or after the clitics -*m* and -*z* (but cf. English *I'd've*). Criterion (8d) is likewise relatively unhelpful, for although the clitics -*m* and -*z* are regularly interpreted (as possessive pronouns in prenominal contexts and as object pronouns in preverbal contexts), the inflected prepositions are also regular in their interpretation. Nevertheless, inflected forms occasionally have unexpected meanings. For instance, Breton nouns with suffixal plurals sometimes also allow "double plural" forms with two plural suffixes; but the exact nuance expressed by a double plural varies idiosyncratically from noun to noun: while the simple plural *preñv-ed* 'worm-s' and its double plural counterpart *preñv-ed-où* differ in that the former refers to an undifferentiated mass of worms and the latter to a number of individually distinguishable worms, the simple plural *merc'h-ed* 'girl-s' differs from its double plural *merc'h-ed-où* in that the latter conveys a sense of affectionate scorn (Trépos 1957: 264).

Notwithstanding the ease with which the criteria in (8) allow the inflections in (9) to be distinguished from the clitics in (10), there are many cases which are much less clear. A well-known example is that of bound pronouns in French: criteria (8a, e) imply that they are affixes (cf. Auger and Janda 1994), while criteria (8b–d) are compatible with the (traditional) assumption that they are clitics (see Halpern, Clitics).

3 The functions of inflection

As was seen above (section 2.1), the distinction between inflection and derivation presupposes a well-delineated distinction between morphosyntactic properties (such as 'plural' and 'nonfinite' in English) and lexicosemantic properties (such as 'agentive' and 'stative' in English). Fundamentally, the latter distinction is one of function: morphosyntactic properties are phrase-level properties to which syntactic relations such as agreement and government (in the traditional sense) are sensitive; a word's lexicosemantic properties, by contrast, simply determine the manner in which it enters into the semantic composition of larger constituents. 'Plural' is a morphosyntactic property in English because (e.g.) the subject and the predicate of a finite clause in English agree with respect to this property; 'nonfinite' is a morphosyntactic property because verbs such as *condescend* require that their clausal complement assume a nonfinite form. By contrast, English expressions are never required to agree with respect to agentivity, nor to assume a 'stative form' in a particular syntactic context. Thus, the distinction between inflection and derivation is first and foremost one of function: while derivation serves to encode lexicosemantic relations within the lexicon, the function of inflection is to encode phrase-level properties and relations. Typically, a phrase's morphosyntactic properties are inflectionally encoded on its head (but see section 5.2).

3.1 Agreement properties

Agreement is asymmetrical in the sense that one member of an agreement relation can be seen as depending on the other member for some or all of its morphosyntactic properties. This asymmetry is particularly clear in cases involving a property which is invariably associated with one member of the relation; in French, for instance, adjectives and nouns covary in number (*petit animal*, pl. *petits animaux*) but not in gender – rather, the adjective must be seen as conforming to the invariant gender of the noun it modifies. Even where there is covariation, there is evidence of asymmetry. Thus, even though French adjectives and nouns covary in number, the adjective is clearly the dependent member of the relation of number agreement: whereas adjectives exhibit number inflection purely as an effect of their participation in this sort of relation, nouns exhibit number inflection wherever they appear, whether or not there is an agreeing expression. A word's *agreement properties* are those morphosyntactic properties which it possesses by virtue of being the dependent member of an agreement relation.

Languages vary widely with respect to the range of syntactic relations they encode by means of agreement morphology. Some familiar relations include the agreement of a modifier or specifier with the head of the encompassing phrase (as the article and the adjective agree in number and gender with the nominal head in *la petite souris*, or as certain Maori adverbs agree in voice with the verb they modify (K. Hale 1973a: 417)); the agreement of a predicate with one or more of its arguments (as an English verb agrees in person and number with its subject, or as many Welsh prepositions agree with their object in person, number, and (in the third person) gender – *yno i* 'in me', *ynot ti* 'in thee', *ynddo fe* 'in him', *ynddi hi* 'in her', etc.); the agreement of an anaphoric expression with its antecedent (as *kile* 'that one' agrees in noun class with its antecedent *kisu* 'knife' in the Swahili example in (11)); and the agreement of a complementizer with the subject of its complement (as West Flemish *dat* agrees in person and number with the subject of the finite clause which it introduces (Haegeman 1992: 47ff)).

(11) Wataka ki-su   ki-pi?   Nataka ki-le.
      you.want NOUN.CL-*knife* NOUN.CL-*which* I.*want* NOUN.CL-*that.one*
      'Which knife do you want? I want that one.'

Among languages that exhibit verb–argument agreement, a range of patterns is found. In an *accusative* agreement system, subjects are encoded differently from direct objects. In Swahili verbs, for instance, third-person singular personal subject agreement is encoded by a prefix *a-* (which precedes the tense prefix, as in *a-li-soma* 's/he read', *a-li-ni-ona* 's/he saw me'), while third-person singular personal object agreement is expressed by a prefix *m(w)-* (which follows the tense prefix, as in *ni-li-mw-ona* 'I saw her/him'). In an *ergative* agreement system, by contrast, subjects of transitive verbs are encoded differently from direct objects and subjects of intransitive verbs, which are themselves encoded alike. In vernacular Hindustani, for example, perfective/preterite verb forms are marked identically for agreement with direct objects and intransitive subjects, and are not overtly marked for agreement with transitive subjects:

(12) (a) 'aurat chal-ī.   (b) mard chal-ā.
           woman went-FEM.SG   *man went*-MASC.SG
           'The woman went.'   'The man went.'

(13) (a) 'aurat-nē ghōṛī   (b) 'aurat-nē ghōṛā
           woman-ERG *mare*   *woman*-ERG *horse*
           mār-ī.   mār-ā.
           struck-FEM.SG   *struck*-MASC.SG
           'The woman struck   'The woman struck
           the mare.'   the horse.'

These two sorts of system may appear side by side; in Hindustani, for example, verbs outside of the perfective/preterite exhibit an accusative pattern of agreement. In some languages, moreover, it is an intransitive verb's lexicosemantic properties that determine whether its subject is encoded in the same way as a direct object or a transitive subject. Thus, in an *active* agreement system, the subject of an active intransitive verb is encoded in the same way as the subject of a transitive verb, while the subject of a stative intransitive verb is encoded in the same way as the object of a transitive verb; the Choctaw verb forms in (14) and (15) (from Davies 1986) illustrate this.

(14) (a) Hilha-li-tok.   (b) Sa-hohchafo-h.
           dance-1SG-PAST   1SG-*hungry*-PREDICATIVE
           'I danced.'   'I am hungry.'

(15) (a) Chi-bashli-li-tok.   (b) Ano is-sa-hottopali-tok.
           2SG-*cut*-1SG-PAST   *I*   2SG-1SG-*hurt*-PAST
           'I cut you.'   'You hurt me.'

Agreement relations vary widely with respect to the set of morphosyntactic properties that agreeing constituents are required to share. This is true of distinct agreement relations in the same language; in French, for instance, adjective–noun agreement is sensitive to number and gender, while subject–verb agreement is sensitive to number and person. It is likewise true of comparable agreement relations in distinct languages: in Swahili, for example, the relation of verb–object agreement is sensitive to properties of person, number, and gender (which receive simultaneous expression in the Swahili system of noun-class inflections); in Maithili, verbs agree with their objects in person and honorific grade but not number; in Lardil, nonimperative verbs and their objects agree in tense (K. Hale 1973a: 421ff); in Hungarian, verbs agree with their objects in definiteness; and so on. The diversity of agreement relations in natural language presents an imposing challenge for syntactic theory: besides providing a means of representing such relations, an adequate theory must furnish a principled delimitation of the range of possible agreement relations (see Corbett, MORPHOLOGY AND AGREEMENT).

3.2 *Governed properties*

Although an asymmetrical dependency exists between the members of an agreement relation, agreement is nevertheless symmetrical in the sense that the members of an agreement relation share the properties to which the relation is sensitive. It is this latter sort of symmetry that distinguishes agreement from government: in a relation of government, the governing member imposes specific restrictions on the morphosyntactic properties of the governed member, but does so without (necessarily) sharing any of its properties. A word's *governed properties* are those morphosyntactic properties which are constrained by a governing expression in this way.

A wide range of government relations can be found; typically, the governing member is the head of a phrase, and the governed member is its complement or specifier. A verb or preposition may govern the case of its nominal object (as German *helfen* 'to help' and *mit* 'with' govern the dative case, while *sehen* 'to see' and *ohne* 'without' govern the accusative); a verb or complementizer may govern the mood or finiteness of its clausal complement (as French *craindre* requires a subjunctive complement, or as English *that* requires a finite complement); a numeral may govern the case and number of the enumerated noun (as nominative and accusative forms of Russian *tri* 'three' require the enumerated noun to appear in the genitive singular); an auxiliary may determine the inflection of its associated verb (as the English progressive auxiliary *be* requires that its associated verb appear as a present participle); and so on.

Languages with case systems vary in their patterns of case government. In an *accusative* system of case marking, the subject of a finite verb has the same (nominative) case whether the verb is transitive or intransitive, and the object of a transitive verb has a distinct (accusative) case; in an *ergative* system, by contrast, the subject of an intransitive verb and the object of a transitive verb exhibit the same (absolutive) case, while the subject of a transitive verb exhibits a distinct (ergative) case.[2] Systems of the two sorts may serve complementary functions in a single language; in the Australian language Pitjantjatjara, for instance, nouns exhibit ergative case marking, while pronouns show the accusative pattern, as the examples in (16) (from Bowe 1990: 10f) show.

(16) (a) Tjitji   a-nu.
          child(ABS) go-PAST
          'The child went.'

   (b) Ngayu-lu a-nu.
          1SG-NOM   go-PAST
          'I went.'

   (c) Tjitji-ngku ngayu-nya
          child-ERG   1SG-ACC
          nya-ngu.
          see-PAST
          'The child saw me.'

   (d) Ngayu-lu tjitji
          1SG-NOM   child(ABS)
          nya-ngu.
          see-PAST
          'I saw the child.'

Languages with case systems also show considerable variation in the number of cases they distinguish: English has only three, while Sanskrit has eight, Finnish fifteen, and so on.

A government relation and an agreement relation may be sensitive to the same morphosyntactic property. In German, for instance, the government relation between preposition and object and the agreement relation between determiner and noun are both sensitive to properties of case; thus, in the expression *gemäß den Vorschriften* 'according to the rules', the dative case is a governed property of the object noun phrase (hence also of its head *Vorschriften*) as well as an agreement property of the determiner *den*.

3.3 *Inherent properties*

Morphosyntactic properties which are neither agreement properties nor governed properties are said to be *inherent* (cf. Anderson 1985a: 172). From a morpholexical perspective, inherent properties are of two types. On the one hand, an inherent property may be associated with some but not all words in a lexeme's paradigm. In German, for example, plural number is associated with some words in a nominal lexeme's paradigm but not others; plural number might therefore be characterized as a *word property* in nominal paradigms. On the other hand, a property may be invariably associated with the words in a lexeme's paradigm; thus, feminine gender might be characterized as a *lexeme property* in the paradigms of feminine nouns in German.

The properties to which an agreement relation is sensitive are, in general, either governed properties or inherent properties of its controlling member. Inherent properties do not always figure in agreement relations, however. In Amharic, for example, definiteness is an inherent property of noun phrases.

The inflection is situated on the head of the first constituent of the noun phrase (Halpern 1992: 204ff):

(17)   (a)   məSɪhaf-u   (b)   tɪnnɪš-u məSɪhaf
              *book-*DEF   *small-*DEF *book*
              'the book'   'the small book'

In Amharic, definiteness is irrelevant to the expression of agreement (a verb e.g. agrees with its subject in person, number, and sometimes gender, but not in definiteness) and is not imposed by a governing head. Nevertheless, the exponence of case is sensitive to definiteness: as the examples in (18) show, definite objects carry the suffix *-(ı)n* while indefinite objects do not.

(18)   (a)   and məSɪhaf yasayyu-ñ.   (b)   məSɪhaf-u-n yasayyu-ñ.
              one book   show-me   *book-*DEF-OBJ *show-me*
              'Show me one book.'   'Show me the book.'

The boundary between inherent properties and governed properties is in some instances rather cloudy, since the same property can sometimes seemingly be either inherent or governed according to its syntactic context. In French, for instance, the indicative mood is to all appearances an inherent property of verbs in main clauses; yet, it is a governed property of verbs in conditional clauses introduced by *si* 'if'. Properties of mood (section 4.2) are particularly prone to exhibit this sort of variability.

4 Inflectional categories

A language's *inflectional categories* are the categories of morphosyntactic properties which are expressed in its inflectional system. Languages vary considerably in their inflectional categories. An exhaustive enumeration of the inflectional categories found in human language is beyond the scope of the present discussion; nevertheless, some widely recurring categories can be noted.[3]

4.1 *Some inflectional categories of nouns*

Many languages exhibit gender and number as inherent inflectional categories of nouns. *Gender* is a category of morphosyntactic properties which distinguish classes of nominal lexemes: for each such class of lexemes, there is a distinct set of inflectional markings for agreeing words. In many languages, a noun's gender is overtly expressed only through the inflection of agreeing words; in French, for example, the feminine head noun of *la petite souris* 'the little mouse' does not carry any overt inflection for feminine gender, but the agreeing article and adjective both do. Often, however, a noun's membership in a particular declension class implies that it belongs to a particular gender; in Sanskrit, for example, nouns in the *ā* declension (e.g. SENĀ 'army') are virtually always feminine. Moreover, in languages with noun-class systems, nouns ordinarily carry an overt inflectional marking simultaneously expressing gender and number; thus, in the Kikuyu noun phrase *mū-ndū mū-kūrū* 'old person' (pl. *a-ndū a-kūrū*), both the noun and its agreeing modifier carry an overt gender/ number marker. Languages vary widely in the number of genders they encode: French, for example, has two genders (masculine and feminine), while Kikuyu has ten (A. R. Barlow 1960: 14A). Correlations may exist between the meanings of nouns and the genders to which they belong (thus, in French, nouns which refer exclusively to females are generally feminine); such correlations need not involve the sex of a noun's referent (in Plains Cree e.g. the genders instead correlate with an animate/inanimate distinction). Correlations of this sort are, however, virtually never perfect; that is, membership in a particular gender is most often a matter of arbitrary stipulation. In French, for instance, *bête* 'beast' is feminine, while *animal* 'animal' is masculine; Plains Cree *nitās* is animate with the meaning 'my pants', but inanimate with the meaning 'my gaiter' (Wolfart 1973: 22); and so on.

Number is a category of morphosyntactic properties used to distinguish the quantity to which a noun phrase refers. Many languages distinguish only two number properties (singular and plural); others additionally distinguish a dual and (rarely) a trial. In Sanskrit, for example, nouns have three distinct nominative forms, a singular, a dual, and a plural: *aśvas* 'horse', *aśvāu* '(two) horses', *aśvās* '(more than two) horses'.

Another inherent inflectional category of nouns in many languages is that of *(in)definiteness* – a category of morphosyntactic properties distinguishing noun phrases according to whether their reference in a given context is presumed to be uniquely identifiable. In the Syrian Arabic noun phrase *l-madīne l-ʔkbīre* 'the large city', for example, the definite prefix *l-* on the head and its agreeing modifier implies that the city in question is uniquely identifiable – an implication absent from the indefinite noun phrase *madīne kbīre* 'a large city'.

Case is a category of morphosyntactic properties which distinguish the various relations that a noun phrase may bear to a governing head. Some such relations are fundamentally syntactic in nature – for example, the subject, direct object, indirect object, and genitive relations; cases used to encode relations of this sort (the so-called *direct* cases) include the nominative, the accusative, the ergative, the absolutive, the dative, and the genitive. Other cases – the *oblique* cases – encode relations which are instead fundamentally semantic; these include the instrumental case (e.g. Sanskrit *tena aśvena* 'by/with that horse'), the ablative (*tasmāt aśvāt* 'from that horse'), and the locative (*tasmin aśve* 'at that horse'), among many others.

A noun may also inflect as the dependent member of an agreement relation with a possessor noun phrase. In Uyghur, for example, a noun agrees in person (and number, in the nonthird persons) with a possessor noun phrase – *Nuriyi-niŋ yoldiš-i* 'Nuriyä's husband' [Nuriyä-GEN husband-3RD.PERSON.POSSESSOR];

unsurprisingly, possessor agreement allows pronominal possessors to be omitted (*u-niŋ yoldiš-i* ~ *yoldiš-i* 'her husband').

It is sometimes claimed (e.g. by Anderson 1982: 586; 1985a: 177) that evaluative properties such as 'diminutive' and 'augmentative' constitute an inflectional category of nouns in some languages. Consider, for instance, the situation in Kikuyu. Every Kikuyu noun belongs to a particular gender. A noun's gender and number are cumulatively realized as a noun-class inflection, so a gender can be thought of as a pairing of a singular noun class with a plural noun class; for instance, *-raatũ* 'shoe' belongs to gender 7/8, exhibiting the class 7 prefix *kĩ-* in the singular and the class 8 prefix *i-* in the plural. Rather than inflect for its proper gender, a noun may exhibit the class 12 prefix *ka-* in the singular and the class 13 prefix *tũ-* in the plural; when it does, it takes on a diminutive meaning (*ka-raatũ* 'little shoe', pl. *tũ-raatũ*) and requires agreeing constituents to exhibit the appropriate class 12/class 13 concords. Should "diminutivity" be regarded as an inherent inflectional category on a par with number and gender in a system of this sort? It is not clear that it should. Morphosyntactically, the pairing of classes 12 and 13 behaves like an ordinary gender, not like a morphosyntactic property of some separate category; moreover, there are members of gender 12/13 that are not diminutives of nouns from other genders (e.g. *ka-raagita* 'tractor', pl. *tũ-raagita*). One might just as well assume that the pairing 12/13 is simply a gender, and that the category of diminutives arises by means of a highly productive derivational rule whose effect is to shift nouns to this gender.

4.2 *Some inflectional categories of verbs*

Inherent inflectional categories of verbs include tense, aspect, polarity, voice, and (in some uses) mood.[4] *Tense* is a category of morphosyntactic properties distinguishing a finite verb's temporal reference. In Latin, for instance, verbs inflect for three tenses: past, present, and future (*laudābam* 'I praised', *laudō* 'I praise', *laudābō* 'I will praise'). Despite the conceptual naturalness of this three-way distinction, it is far from universal: inflectionally speaking, English has two tenses, past and nonpast (J. Lyons 1968: 306); Kikuyu has six (far past, yesterday past, today past, present, near future, far future – Bennett et al. 1985: 138f); and so on.

Aspect is a category of morphosyntactic properties distinguishing the various senses in which an event e can be situated at a particular time interval i. In Kikuyu, six such properties are distinguished in the present affirmative (Bennett et al. 1985: 139ff): the continuous aspect (e.g. *tũraagũra nyama* 'we are buying meat') indicates that e is in progress throughout i; the habitual aspect (*tũgũraga nyama* 'we buy meat') indicates that events of kind e are customary at i; the projected aspect (*tũũkũgũra nyama* 'we are going to buy meat') indicates an intention at i for e to take place; the completive aspect (*twagũra nyama*, roughly 'we have bought meat') indicates that e has just come to completion at i; the initiative aspect (*tūgūrīīte nyama*, also roughly 'we have bought meat') indicates that the state resulting from the completion of e holds true at i; and the experiential (*twanagūra nyama* 'we have (at some point) bought meat') identifies e as having happened at some indefinite (and potentially remote) time interval prior to i. Often, there is a kind of conceptual overlap between the categories of aspect and tense; for instance, an event which is described in aspectual terms as having come to completion by a particular time can likewise be described in temporal terms as a past event relative to that time. In view of such cases, the boundary between aspect and tense is sometimes elusive.

Polarity is a category of morphosyntactic properties distinguishing affirmative sentences from negative sentences. In Kikuyu, for instance, a verb's affirmative form is unmarked for polarity, while a verb's negative form is marked by a prefix *ti-* (in subordinate clauses, *ta-*): *tū-kaagwata* 'we will take hold', *tū-ti-kaagwata* 'we will not take hold' (in subordinate clauses, *tū-ta-kaagwata*). The expression of mood and polarity sometimes intersect; thus, Sanskrit verbs exhibit a special prohibitive (negative imperative) inflection (Whitney 1889: §579).

Voice is a category of morphosyntactic properties distinguishing the various thematic relations that may exist between a verb and its subject. In Sanskrit, for instance, a verb appears in the active voice if its subject is the agent but not the beneficiary of the action it describes (*odanam āpnoti* 's/he obtains porridge (for someone else)'), in the middle voice if its subject is both agent and beneficiary (*odanam āpnute* 's/he obtains porridge (for herself/himself)'), and in the passive voice if the subject is the theme rather the agent (*odana āpyate* 'porridge is obtained').

Mood is a category of morphosyntactic properties which, as inherent properties (section 3.3), distinguish the ways in which a proposition may relate to actuality (in the speaker's mind). In classical Sanskrit, for example, there are three principal moods: the indicative mood (e.g. *bhavāmi* 'I am') is used to assert a proposition as fact; the optative mood (*bhaveyam* 'would that I were') is used to express propositions whose reality is wished for; the imperative mood (*bhavāni* 'I will be!') is used to command that a proposition be realized. The boundaries between distinct moods can be quite fluid; for instance, the expression of a wish can have the illocutionary force of a command. Moreover, the boundary separating mood from tense and aspect is itself sometimes hazy; future tense, for example, is inherently nonactual. As noted earlier (section 3.3), properties of mood behave, in some uses, as governed rather than inherent properties; thus, certain English verbs (e.g. *require*) mandate that a finite complement be in the subjunctive mood.

Another category for which a verb may inflect under the influence of a governing head is that comprising the morphosyntactic properties 'finite' and 'nonfinite', which distinguish verbs according to whether they are inflected for tense; in French, for example, the verb *devoir* 'to have to' requires its clausal complement to be nonfinite, while *vouloir* 'to want to' allows either a finite or a nonfinite complement.[5] Similarly, verbs in many languages exhibit a special set of forms for use in subordinate clauses: in Plains Cree, for example, the set of verbal affixes used to mark agreement (in person, number, gender, and obviation) in main clauses is distinct from that used in dependent clauses (Wolfart, 1973, p. 41); in Swahili, relative verb forms (i.e. those bearing an affix encoding the relativized argument) exhibit a smaller range of tense inflections than ordinary indicative verb forms, and inflect differently for negation; and so on.

A syntactic relation in some ways akin to government is encoded by verbal inflections in systems of *switch reference*. Choctaw furnishes an example of this sort of system: in coordinate clauses, the verb in the first clause inflects to indicate whether its subject is identical in reference to that of the second clause (Davies 1986: 9); in (19a), for instance, the first verb carries the same-subject suffix -*cha* (glossed 'ss'), while in (19b), the first verb carries the different-subject suffix -*na* (glossed 'ds').

(19) (a)   Tobi apa-li-cha oka   ishko-li-tok.
            bean eat-1SG-SS water drink-1SG-PAST
            'I ate beans and drank water.'

      (b)   Wa:k nipi ish-awashli-na oka   ishko-li-tok.
            cow   flesh 2SG-fry-DS   water drink-1SG-PAST
            'You fried the beef, so I drank water.'

As the dependent member of an agreement relation, a verb may inflect for a number of categories; instances of verb agreement in person, number, gender, honorificity, and definiteness have been alluded to above. In many languages, verbs inflected for *person* exhibit special subsidiary distinctions (which likewise tend to be expressed in pronominal inflection). In Plains Cree, for example, verb forms marked for agreement with a nonthird-person plural argument show a three-way distinction (Wolfart 1973: 16): *exclusive* first-person agreement encodes an argument referring to a group which includes the speaker(s) but excludes the addressee(s); exclusive second-person agreement encodes an argument referring to a group which excludes the speaker(s) but includes the addressee(s); and *inclusive* agreement encodes an argument referring to a group which includes both the speaker(s) and the addressee(s). Moreover, Plains Cree verb forms marked for agreement with a third-person argument show a distinction in obviation: *proximate* agreement encodes an argument whose referent is "the topic of discourse, the person nearest the speaker's point of view, or the person earlier spoken of and already known" (Bloomfield 1962: 38, cited by Wolfart 1973: 17), while *obviative* agreement encodes an argument whose referent lacks these characteristics. The inter-penetration of agreement categories in a language's system of verb inflection can be quite complex; for instance, a verb may exhibit more honorific grades in the second person than in the third (as in Maithili); a verb may inflect for gender in the second-person plural but not the second-person singular (as in Kabyle Berber); and so on.

4.3 *Some inflectional categories of adjectives*

Degree is an inherent inflectional category of adjectives; the morphosyntactic properties which it comprises serve to distinguish the extent to which a referent evinces some quality. The English adjective TALL, for instance, has three degrees. The positive degree *tall* specifies the quality of tallness without reference to the extent to which it is exhibited; the comparative degree *taller* specifies the extent of one referent's tallness relative to that of some other referent; and the superlative *tallest* specifies extreme tallness relative to some class of referents.

An adjective may exhibit distinct attributive and predicative forms, depending upon its syntactic relation to the controlling noun; in Russian, the feminine nominative singular of NOVYJ 'new' is *nóvaja* in attributive uses (*nóvaja kníga* 'new book') but *nová* in predicative uses (*kníga nová* 'the book is new').

As the dependent member of an agreement relation, an adjective may inflect for the properties possessed (either inherently or as an effect of government) by the controlling noun. In the Russian noun phrase *nóvaja kníga* 'new book', for instance, the dependent adjective is feminine, nominative, and singular, matching the controlling noun in gender, case, and number; contrast *nóvyj dom* 'new house' (where the gender is instead masculine), *nóvuju knígu* (where the case is instead accusative), and *nóvye knígi* (where the number is instead plural). Similarly, adjectives may agree in (in)definiteness (e.g. Syrian Arabic *l-madīne l-ʔkbīre*, lit. 'the-town the-large', cited above), and so on.

5 The realization of inflection

Languages show extraordinary variation in the morphological realization of their inflectional categories; two dimensions of variation are particularly salient.

5.1 *Inflectional exponence*

An *exponent*[6] of a morphosyntactic property in a given word is a morphological marking expressing that property in that word; thus, the property 'plural' has *-s* as its exponent in *girls* and a vowel modification (of [ʊ] to [ɪ]) as its exponent in *women*. Very frequently, a single marking serves simultaneously as an exponent of two or more morphosyntactic properties; in Latin, for instance, the suffix *-ibus* in Latin *rēgibus* 'to kings' is simultaneously an exponent of dative case and plural number. In this particular example, the simultaneous exponence of case and number is a reflection of a more general fact: namely, that in Latin declensional morphology, the exponents of case and number always coincide; that is, the categories of case and number exhibit *cumulative exponence* in Latin declension. Not all simultaneous exponence is cumulative, however. For instance, voice and subject agreement are simultaneously realized in second-person plural verb forms (by *-tis* in *laudātis* 'you praise', by *-minī* in *laudāminī* 'you are praised') but not in third-person plural forms (e.g. *laudant* 'they praise', *laudantur* 'they are praised', where *-nt* expresses subject agreement while *-ur* expresses passive voice); thus, voice and subject agreement are merely said to exhibit *overlapping exponence* in Latin verb inflection. A morphosyntactic property may also exhibit *extended exponence*: that is, it may exhibit more than one exponent in a single word; thus, in Latin *laudāvī* 'I have praised', both *-v* and *-ī* are exponents of the perfect. (Because *-ī* additionally expresses first-person singular subject agreement and present tense, *laudāvī* is also another example of overlapping exponence.)

Inflectional systems employ a variety of different kinds of exponents. These include concatenative operations of suffixation (*girl*, pl. *girl-s*), prefixation (Kikuyu *mū-rūūthi* 'lion', pl. *mī-rūūthi*), and infixation (Oaxaca Chontal *kwepoʔ* 'lizard', pl. *kwe-ł-poʔ*), quasi-concatenative operations of partial or total reduplication (Papago *bana* 'coyote', *kuna* 'husband', pl. *baabana, kuukuna*; Indonesian *babi* 'pig', pl. *babibabi*), and an array of nonconcatenative operations, from vowel modifications (*woman*, pl. *women*) and consonant gradation (Fula *yiite* 'fire', pl. *giite*) to modifications of accent (Russian *oknó* 'window (nom. sg.)', nom. pl. *ókna*) and tone (Somali *èy* 'dog' (with falling tone), pl. *éy* (with high tone)). One can even find instances in which subtraction serves an inflectional function; in Huichol, for example, a verb's completive form arises from its stem through the loss of its final syllable (*pïtiuneika* 'he danced', completive *pïtiunei*). Naturally, these different sorts of exponence are often intricately interwoven within a single paradigm.

In many languages, stem choice may serve as an exponent of some morphosyntactic property. In Latin, for example, there is a special stem (Aronoff (1994: 59) calls it the *b stem*) which is formed by suffixing *-b* to the present stem (with concomitant lengthening of its final vowel). The *b* stem is used to form the imperfect of verbs in all conjugations, as well as the future of verbs in the first and second conjugations. In view of this fact, the *-b* suffix in *laudāb-* (the *b* stem of the first-conjugation verb *laudāre* 'praise') cannot, in and of itself, be seen as an exponent of any morphosyntactic property; its (purely morphomic) status is simply that of a *b* stem-forming suffix. Nevertheless, the choice of *laudāb-* from among the range of available stems must count as one of the exponents of the imperfect in *laudābam* 'I praised' and as one of the exponents of the future in *laudābō* 'I will praise'.

In the simplest cases, stems are inflected without regard to their internal morphological structure. Nevertheless, category-preserving derivation gives rise to stems which are *headed*, and some such stems inflect through the inflection of their head. In Russian, for example, the verb *stučát'-sja* 'to knock purposefully' is headed by the verb *stučát'* 'to knock' and inflects on its head (*stučím-sja, stučát-sja*, etc., noted above); Sanskrit *ni-pat-* 'fly down' inflects on its head *pat-* 'fly' (*ni-patati* 's/he flies down', *ny-apatat* 's/he flew down', etc.); English *undergo* inflects on its head *go* (whose suppletive past-tense form is therefore faithfully preserved in *underwent*); and so on. The phenomenon of head marking has numerous implications for morphological theory (see Hoeksema 1985, Stump 1995b, for discussion).

Quite separate from the (morphological) fact that some headed stems inflect on their head is the (syntactic) fact that a phrase's morphosyntactic properties are ordinarily realized through the inflection of its head. In English, for example, the plural number of the noun phrase *her favorite books* is manifested only in the inflection of the head noun. In some cases, however, a phrase's morphosyntactic properties are realized by inflectional markings situated on a constituent other than the head of the phrase. In many such cases, the inflected constituent is at the periphery of the phrase. In English, for example, a possessive noun phrase has the inflectional suffix -*'s* on its final constituent, whether or not this is the head of the phrase: *someone else's (hat)*, *the King of England's (hat)*; the possessive suffix has therefore been characterized as an *edge inflection* (Zwicky 1987; cf. also Lapointe 1990, Miller 1992, Halpern 1992). But inflections which aren't realized on a phrase's head aren't necessarily realized at its periphery. In Bulgarian, for example, noun phrases are inflected for definiteness on the head of their first constituent: the inflected word need not be the head of the noun phrase itself; nor does it have to be at any phrasal periphery (Halpern 1992: 193ff).

5.2 *Inflectional "templates"*

Many languages exhibit what has come to be known as *template morphology* – systems in which inflectional affixes are apparently organized into a number of *position classes* such that the members of any given class are mutually exclusive but occupy the same sequential position, or *slot*, relative to members of other classes within a given word form. For instance, Swahili verb inflections are (pretheoretically) organized according to the following template:

(20) The Swahili verb "template" (cf. Schadeberg 1984: 14ff)

SLOT	CONTENTS
1	negative affix *ha-* (nonrelative, indicative forms; optionally in the conditional)
2	subject agreement prefixes; infinitive affix *ku-*; habitual affix *hu-*
3	negative affix *si-* (relative, subjunctive, and imperative forms; optionally in the conditional)
4	tense and mood prefixes; negative infinitive affix *to-*
5	relative agreement prefixes (tensed or negative forms)
6	metrically motivated empty affix *ku-* (Ashton 1947: 142f, Schadeberg 1984: 14)
7	object agreement prefixes
Stem	(= verb root + theme vowel -*a*, -*i*, or -*e*)
8	affix -*ni* encoding a plural addressee; relative agreement suffixes (tenseless affirmative forms)

Systems of this sort raise an important question: how, if at all, does "template" morphology differ from ordinary inflection?

Simpson and Withgott (1986) propose the following criteria for distinguishing "template" morphology from what they call "layered" morphology:[7]

(i)   The absence of any affix in a particular slot may, in a "templatic" system, contrast paradigmatically with the presence of any given affix in that slot; in Swahili, for example, the absence of any slot 2 prefix is what distinguishes the imperative form *si-pige* 'don't you (sg.) beat!' from the subjunctive form *u-si-pige* 'that you (sg.) may not beat'.

(ii) "Template" morphology yields a form whose morphosyntactic properties cannot all be attributed to a single one of its parts. For example, Swahili *tu-li-wa-ona* 'we saw you (pl.)' has the morphosyntactic properties 'first-person plural subject', 'past tense', and 'second-person plural object'; the first of these is associated with the prefix *tu-*, the second with *li-*, the third with *wa-*.

(iii) "Template" morphology presents cases in which the exponence of one property is sensitive to the presence of another property whose principal exponent is nonadjacent (in violation of the Adjacency Constraint – M. Allen 1978, Siegel 1978); thus, in Swahili verbs, the choice between the slot 3 negative prefix *si-* and the slot 1 negative prefix *ha-* is conditioned by the presence of the property 'subjunctive mood', whose principal exponent (the theme vowel *-e*) is not structurally adjacent to either slot.

(iv) "Template" morphology presents cases in which a property's exponence is sensitive to the presence of another property whose principal exponent is more peripheral (in violation of the so-called No Lookahead Constraint): in finite verb forms in Swahili, the principal exponents of negation are peripheral to those of tense, yet the exponence of past tense as *li-* or *ku-* is sensitive to negation (*tu-li-taka* 'we wanted', but *ha-tu-ku-taka* 'we didn't want').

(v)   Finally, systems of "template" morphology typically allow a verb to agree with more than one of its arguments (as in the Swahili example in (ii)).

Simpson and Withgott (1986) assert that "layered" morphology possesses none of these characteristics. The clearest cases of "layered" morphology, however, are instances of category-changing derivation. The question therefore arises as to whether a distinction can be drawn between "templatic" inflection and "layered" inflection. Stump (1997) argues that such a distinction is unmotivated – that all inflection is in fact "templatic." Inflectional systems generally behave like "template" morphology with respect to criteria (i) and (ii), and although inflection does not behave uniformly with respect to criteria (iii)–(v), these are at most sufficient and not necessary properties of "template" morphology. Stump nevertheless rejects the notion (implicit in the unfortunate template metaphor) that "template" morphology is regulated by positive morphological output conditions (whose postulation is otherwise unmotivated), arguing instead that "templates" take the form of paradigm function schemata (section 6.3), whose existence is independently motivated by the phenomena of head marking (Stump, 1995b).

6 Theoretical approaches to inflection

Although there is considerable consensus on which phenomena are inflectional and which are not, there is considerable disagreement about the theoretical status of inflection. Here, I will briefly discuss four contrasting points of view.

6.1 The lexicalist approach to inflection

In one widely pursued approach to inflection (see e.g. Di Sciullo and Williams 1987, Lieber 1992, Selkirk 1982) an affix is assumed to have much the same status as a word: it has a lexical listing which specifies its phonological form, its semantic content (if any), its subcategorization restriction, and its morphosyntactic properties. On this view, the suffix *-s* in *sing-s* has a lexical entry something like (21):

(21) (a) Phonology: /z/
     (b) Semantics: $\varnothing$
     (c) Subcategorization: $[_vV\_\_\_]$
     (d) Morphosyntactic properties: PER:3
                                     NUM:sg
                                     TNS:pres
                                     MOOD:indic

The subcategorization restriction (21c) allows *-s* to combine with the verbal stem *sing* to yield the third-person singular present indicative form *sing-s*; a mechanism of feature percolation guarantees that *sing-s* is (like *sing*) a verb and carries (like *-s*) the morphosyntactic properties in (21d).

Whatever intuitive appeal it may have, this lexicalist approach is subject to a wide range of criticisms. Because it accords affixes the special status of lexical items, it entails a fundamental grammatical difference between affixal exponence and nonconcatenative varieties of inflectional exponence; for instance, it entails that the manner in which *played* comes from *play* is, in theoretical terms, quite separate from the manner in which *sang* comes from *sing*. This distinction, however, is poorly motivated; there is no clear empirical obstacle to assuming that the process of affixation by which *play* → *played* is on a theoretical par with the process of substitution by which *sing* → *sang*.[8] The assumption that an inflected word's morphosyntactic properties are assembled from those of its component morphemes by a percolation mechanism is highly dubious, since a word's morphosyntactic properties are often underdetermined by its form; as Stump (1993e: 488f) shows, this fact can only be reconciled with the lexicalist approach through the postulation of zero affixes, a device whose theoretical legitimacy has rightly been questioned (Matthews 1972: 56ff). Moreover, the phenomena of overlapping and extended exponence pose an enormous technical obstacle to the formulation of a structure-based percolation mechanism (Stump 1993d). The assumption that an affix's distribution is regulated by a subcategorization restriction is similarly problematic: as Stump (1992, 1993c) shows, subcategorization frames are inherently incapable of capturing certain kinds of generalizations about the distribution of inflectional affixes.

6.2 *The functional head approach to inflection*

A second, more recent approach to inflectional morphology has its origins in the proposals of Pollock (1989). Assuming a version of the 'Principles and Parameters' approach to syntax, Pollock argues that INFL, the syntactic locus of tense, subject agreement, and negation in English and French, should be broken down into three distinct functional categories, each of which heads its own maximal projection. Pollock demonstrates that this idea affords a unified account of several subtle syntactic differences between French and English (relating, specifically, to the syntax of adverb placement, negation, verb fronting, quantifier floating, and quantification at a distance). At the core of Pollock's discussion is the assumption that verbs generally acquire their inflectional properties by moving from one head position to the next, as in the derivation of the sentence *Kim isn't afraid* in (22).

(22)

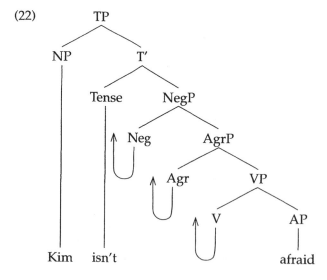

Developing this assumption, a number of researchers (e.g. Rivero 1990, Speas 1990, Mitchell 1991) have proposed that the order of inflectional formatives in a verb's morphology arises through a gradual accretion of affixes during a verb's movement from one functional head to the next; on this view, the order of inflectional markings follows the sequence in which functional categories are nested in syntactic structure. Thus, Rivero (1990: 137) proposes that the Modern Greek verb form *plí-θ-ik-a-n* 'they were washed/they washed themselves' arises by head movement, as in (23).

(23)

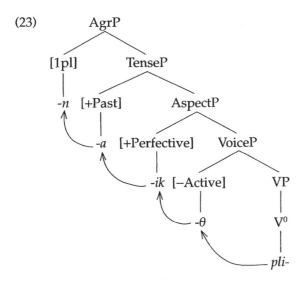

This approach to verb structure suggests that inflection is not a morphological phenomenon at all, but rather a syntactic one; indeed, it calls into question the very claim that morphology exists as an autonomous grammatical component in natural language.

Compelling reasons for rejecting this approach to inflectional morphology are abundant. Joseph and Smirniotopoulos (1993) demonstrate that the segmentation of morphemes presumed by Rivero's analysis of Modern Greek verb inflection is fundamentally incompatible with the surface morphology of the language – that here and elsewhere, the frequent incidence of overlapping and extended exponence relations simply excludes the possibility of reducing inflectional morphology to head movement. Janda and Kathman (1992) observe, in addition, that the head-movement approach requires the ordered nesting of functional categories to be stipulated on a language-specific basis (note e.g. the contrasting affix orderings in Latin *amā-ba-m* 'love-IMPF-1SG' and Welsh Romany *kamá-v-as* 'love-1SG-IMPF'), and that it affords no credible account of nonconcatenative morphology, nor of affix orderings which are sensitive to nonsyntactic properties (such as the fact that in Qafar, a stem's initial sound determines whether subject agreement is realized suffixally, as in *bah-t-é* 'bring-she-PERFECT', or prefixally, as in *t-okm-é* 'she-eat-PERFECT').

Moreover, Bresnan and Mchombo (1995) discuss five tests of lexical integrity and demonstrate that in the Bantu languages words exhibiting noun-class inflections generally pass these tests; as they show, a head-movement approach to Bantu noun-class inflections affords no explanation for this fact. None of these considerations militate against the postulation of abstract functional heads whose existence is syntactically motivated;[9] it does, however, cast serious doubt on the assumption that functional heads are concrete pieces of morphology whose combination with a given stem is effected by head movement. That is, they favor the lexicalist view of Chomsky (1995b: 195), according to which words are already fully inflected at the time of their insertion into syntactic structures (cf. Borer, MORPHOLOGY AND SYNTAX).[10]

Both the lexicalist approach and the functional head approach to inflection are based on the assumption that in the inflection of a stem X, a morphosyntactic property P is associated with X only through the addition of an exponent of P to X. This is not a necessary assumption, however; in particular, one might instead assume that in the inflection of a stem X, an exponent of P is added to X only if X is, by prior assumption, associated with P. This latter hypothesis has been pursued by proponents of two (otherwise very different) approaches to inflection: the Word-and-Paradigm approach and Distributed Morphology.

6.3 *The Word-and-Paradigm approach to inflection*

Under the Word-and-Paradigm approach to inflection (Robins 1959; Matthews 1972; Anderson 1977b, 1992; Zwicky 1985), a word's inflectional markings are determined by a set of inflectional rules. The markings introduced by these rules may be affixal or nonconcatenative; a rule's applicability to a stem X is conditioned by the set of morphosyntactic properties associated with X, by X's phonological form, by X's membership in a particular morphological class, or by some combination of such factors. For example, the suffix -*s* in *sing-s* is introduced by a rule such as (24); where /X/ is any verb stem carrying specifications for third person, singular number, present tense, and indicative mood, (24) applies to /X/ to yield /X-z/.

(24)   V
$$\begin{bmatrix} \text{PER:3} \\ \text{NUM:sg} \\ \text{TNS:pres} \\ \text{MOOD:indic} \end{bmatrix}$$
        /X/ $\rightarrow$ /X-z/

In the Word-and-Paradigm approach, inflectional rules are assumed to be organized into blocks such that rules belonging to the same block are mutually exclusive in their application. A central question concerns the factors which determine this mutual exclusivity: where one member of a rule block overrides another member, can this override relation always be predicted as the effect of universal principles, or are some such overrides a matter of sheer stipulation? Anderson (1992: 128ff) argues for the latter conclusion. A second question concerns the sequencing of rule blocks. Anderson (1992: 123ff) shows that this must be, at least in part, a matter of language-specific stipulation. But a language's rule blocks cannot be assumed to adhere to a fixed linear sequence, since the sequencing of rule blocks may vary according to the set of morphosyntactic properties being realized (Stump 1993c). This is one kind of evidence favoring the introduction of paradigm functions. Thus, suppose that σ is a cell in the paradigms of lexemes belonging to some class C, and that the *paradigm function* for cell σ is that function f_σ such that for each $L \in C$, f_σ applies to the root of L to yield the word form occupying σ; one can then say that the sequence of rule blocks in a language may vary according to the definition of its individual paradigm functions.

The Word-and-Paradigm approach to inflection has a number of virtues: it doesn't presume an unmotivated theoretical boundary between affixal and nonconcatenative exponence; it is fully compatible with the incidence of extended and overlapping exponence and with the fact that a word's form may underdetermine its morphosyntactic properties; and it does not entail nonoccurring interactions between morphology and syntax.

6.4 Distributed morphology

Halle and Marantz (1993) argue for an approach to inflection which they call Distributed Morphology. The salient properties of this theory are as follows:

(i) At the superficial level of syntactic structure known as S-structure (SS), morphemes exist as terminal nodes associated with bundles of morphosyntactic feature specifications but lacking any association with phonological feature specifications.

(ii) Intermediate between the levels of SS and Phonological Form (PF) is a level of Morphological Structure (MS) at which "vocabulary insertion" takes place; it is through the process of vocabulary insertion that the abstract morphemes supplied by the syntax acquire their phonological feature specifications.

(iii) In the mapping from SS to MS, the abstract morphemes may undergo various kinds of modifications: the relation of linear ordering is, for instance, introduced as a part of this mapping, which may also involve the addition of new morphemes (e.g. the introduction of agreement morphemes), the adjunction of one morpheme to another (e.g. the attachment of tensed INFL to an adjacent V), the merging of two morphemes into one, the splitting of one morpheme into two, and so on.

(iv)   Vocabulary insertion is assumed to be constrained by the Elsewhere Condition, so that when two morphs are both insertable into a given morpheme, it is the more narrowly specified morph that wins.

(v)   Once vocabulary insertion has taken place, the inserted morphs are subject to a battery of readjustment rules.

Under this approach, the past-tense form *play-ed* arises as follows: in the mapping from SS to MS, tensed INFL gets adjoined to an adjacent V node, producing M-structures of the form [$_v$ V INFL]; on the assumption that INFL carries the specification [+Past], the process of vocabulary insertion then inserts the suffix *-ed* into INFL from its vocabulary entry (25).

(25)   *ed*, [+Past].

Numerous arguments against this approach to inflection have been raised (Pullum and Zwicky 1992, Spencer 1996). Consider, for instance, the following problem: why doesn't the suffix *-ed* in (25) appear in the past-tense form of SING? According to Halle and Marantz (1993), this is because there is a zero suffix whose vocabulary entry is as in (26):

(26) $\emptyset_1$, [+Past]. Contextual restriction: Y + ____, where Y = *sing, drive*, etc.

By virtue of its contextual restriction, -$\emptyset_1$ is more narrowly specified than *-ed*, and is therefore chosen for insertion into INFL in those instances in which the preceding verb stem is *sing*. As for the change from [ɪ] to [æ] in *sang*, this is effected by a readjustment rule:

(27)   vowel → /æ/ in the context 'X____Y + [+Past]', where X-vowel-Y = *sing, sit*, etc.

By the very same reasoning, the failure of the default plural suffix *-s* in (28a) to appear in the plural of TOOTH would be attributed to the existence of the more narrowly specified zero suffix in (28b), and the change from [u] to [i] in *teeth* would be attributed to the readjustment rule in (28c); likewise, the failure of the Breton default plural suffix *-où* in (29a) to appear in the plural of DANT 'tooth' would be attributed to the more narrowly specified zero suffix in (29b), and the change from [a] to [ɛ] in *dent* 'teeth' would be attributed to the re-adjustment rule in (29c); and so on. Both within and across languages, instances of this same general character appear again and again.

(28)   (a)   *s*, [+Plural].
       (b) $\emptyset_2$, [+Plural]. Contextual restriction: Y + ____, where Y = *tooth, man*, etc.
       (c)   vowel → /i/ in the context 'X____Y + [+Plural]', where X-vowel-Y = *tooth, foot*, etc.

(29) (a) *où*, [+Plural].
     (b) $\emptyset_3$, [+Plural]. Contextual restriction: Y + ____, where Y = *dant, maout* 'sheep', etc.
     (c) vowel → /ɛ/ in the context 'X____Y + [+Plural]', where X-vowel-Y = *dant, sant* 'saint', ect.

These facts highlight some of the problems with Halle and Marantz's approach. First, their approach forces them to assume that in a very large class of cases, a default inflectional affix is prevented from appearing by a more narrowly specified affix whose own appearance is never prevented by anything narrower and whose form is zero; yet they portray this state of affairs as an accident of piecemeal stipulation in the vocabulary entries of language after language. Zero affixes are purportedly just like other, overt affixes in their theory, but it is clear that they actually serve a special, homogenizing function by allowing words which are different in structure to be assigned structural representations which are alike; for instance, they allow both *play-ed* and *sang* to be treated as stem + suffix structures. (This special status can be seen especially clearly by imagining an overt phonetic sequence such as [ba] in place of the zeroes entailed by Halle and Marantz's assumptions: *sangba, sungba, teethba, worseba*, Breton *dentba*, etc. An overt affix with that sort of distribution – within and across languages – would be an unprecedented find.) Moreover, their theory portrays the frequent pairing of zero affixes with readjustment rules (such as (27), (28c), and (29c)) as still another coincidence.

The Word-and-Paradigm approach affords a much more natural account of such cases: that of dispensing with zero affixes and assuming that the "readjustment" rules with which they are paired are in fact simply morphological rules whose narrower specification causes them to override default rules of affixation (so that the past tense of SING lacks *-ed* because the rule replacing [ɪ] with [æ] belongs to the same rule block as the rule of *-ed* suffixation and overrides it, and so on).

A further problem with Distributed Morphology is that it unmotivatedly allows an inflectional affix to be associated with morphosyntactic properties in two different ways. Consider, for instance, the Kabyle Berber form *t-wala-ḍ* 'you (sg.) have seen', in which *t-* is an exponent of second-person agreement (cf. *t-wala-m* 'you (masc. pl.) have seen', *t-wala-m-t* 'you (fem. pl.) have seen') and *-ḍ* is an exponent of second-person singular agreement. How should the M-structure of *t-wala-ḍ* be represented, given the assumptions of Distributed Morphology? One might assume either the M-structure in (30a) (in which case the affixes *t-* and *-ḍ* would have the vocabulary entries in (31a, b)) or that in (30b) (in which case *ḍ-* would instead have the entry in (31c)).

(30) (a) [2nd person] V [2nd person, −Plural]
     (b) [2nd person] V [−Plural]

(31) (a) *t*, [2nd person]. Contextual restriction: ___ + V.
      (b) *ḍ*, [2nd person, –Plural]. Contextual restriction: V + ___.
      (c) *ḍ*, [–Plural]. Contextual restriction: [2nd person] V + ___.

The choice between (30a) and (30b) is, in effect, a choice between treating the property [2nd person] as a part of -*ḍ*'s feature content and treating it as part of -*ḍ*'s contextual restriction. Considerations of pattern congruity are of no help for making this choice, since Berber person agreement is sometimes only marked prefixally (e.g. *i-wala* 'he has seen', *n-wala* 'we have seen') and sometimes only suffixally (*wala-γ* 'I have seen', *wala-n* 'they (masc.) have seen'). The choice here, however, is merely an artifact of Halle and Marantz's assumptions: in the Word-and-Paradigm approach to inflection, for instance, no such choice even arises, since the morphosyntactic properties associated with an affix (or rule of affixation) are not artificially partitioned into properties of content and properties of context.

As the foregoing discussion suggests, the theoretical status of inflectional morphology is hardly a matter of current consensus. Nevertheless, a unifying characteristic of much recent inflectional research has been its heightened attention to the properties of inflectional paradigms, including such properties as syncretism (Carstairs 1987: 87ff, Zwicky 1985, Stump 1993b, Noyer, in press, Spencer 1996), periphrasis (Börjars et al. 1997), defectiveness (Morin 1996), suppletion (Plank 1996), limits on the diversity of a language's paradigms (Carstairs-McCarthy 1994), the theoretical status of the notion of "principal parts" (Würzel 1989), and so on. It seems likely that work in this domain will turn up important new criteria for the comparative evaluation of theories of inflection (see Carstairs-McCarthy, INFLECTIONAL PARADIGMS AND MORPHO-LOGICAL CLASSES).

NOTES

1 Throughout, I follow Matthews's (1972: 11, n. 3) practice of representing lexemes in small caps.

2 In many instances, a language's systems of case marking and verb agreement coincide in the sense that they are either both ergative or both accusative; there are, however, languages in which an ergative system of case marking coexists with an accusative system of verb agreement (Anderson 1985a: 182).

3 For more extensive discussion, see J. Lyons 1968: 270ff, Anderson 1985a, Bybee 1985: 20ff, and Beard 1995: 97ff.

4 For detailed discussion of the categories of tense, aspect, and mood, see Chung and Timberlake 1985.

5 Note the fundamental difference that exists between finiteness and tense: although finiteness is a governed property, properties of

tense are inherent (rather than governed) properties of finite verbs.

6 The terminology given in italics in this paragraph is that of Matthews (1972).

7 The Swahili illustrations in (i)–(v) are from Stump (1997).

8 Recent psycholinguistic findings (Bybee and Newman 1995) suggest that there is no significant difference in the ease with which the human brain processes affixal and nonconcatenative morphology.

9 But see Janda 1994 and E. Williams 1996 for syntactic arguments against "exploded INFL".

10 See Spencer 1992 for additional arguments against the functional head approach.

2 Derivation

ROBERT BEARD

1 Derivation versus inflection

Unlike inflectional morphology, which specifies the grammatical functions of words in phrases without altering their meaning, *derivational morphology* or *word formation* is so named because it usually results in the derivation of a new word with new meaning. This traditional definition, however, has failed to secure a distinction between the two types of morphology, and the reasons for this failure have become matters of considerable discussion. Before proceeding to the question of what is derivational morphology, therefore, it makes sense to first attempt to locate the inflection–derivation interface.

2 The derivation–inflection interface

Chomsky (1970) proposed a sharp modular distinction between lexical and syntactic processes, known widely under the rubric of *Lexicalism*.[1] According to the Lexicalist position, words are derived in the lexicon and emerge with an internal structure to which syntax has no access (*Lexical Integrity Hypothesis*, Postal 1969). Sentences like *I speak Russia$_i$n though I've never been there$_i$* are thereby ruled out, since the pronoun *there* is syntactically coindexed with a lexeme-internal morpheme, *Russia*, which has no independent status in the syntax. Sentences, on the other hand, are generated by the principles of syntax, to which lexical operations have no access. This rules out phrasally based lexical items such as *over-the-counter* in *over-the-counter sales*, widely held to be extragrammatically generated.[2]

Lexicalism entails a set of diagnostics which distinguish derivation from inflection. First, if inflection is relevant only to syntax, the output of inflectional rules cannot be listed lexically. Derivation, on the other hand, is purely lexical, so the output of a derivation rule is a new word which is subject to lexical listing. Listing allows lexical but not inflectional derivates to semantically idiomatize or lexicalize. Even though *went* has been phonologically lexicalized for centuries, semantically it has remained no more than the past tense of *go*. *Terrific*, on the other hand, has lost all semantic contact with its derivational origins in *terror* and *terrify*, despite its residual phonological similarity.

Second, if lexical operations precede syntactic ones, and if derivational operations map isomorphically onto marking operations (see section 6 for alternatives), inflectional markers will always occur outside derivational markers, as in Russian *lët-čik-a* fly-AGENT-GEN 'the flyer's (pilot's)', where the derivational agentive marker *-(š)čik* precedes the inflectional case marker *-a*. Third, since inflection is purely syntactic, it cannot change the lexical category of a word; derivation can. The agentive suffix in this example changes the verbal base to a noun, but the case ending does not affect that nominal status.

Finally, since inflection specifies syntactic relations rather than names semantic categories, it should be fully productive. If an inflectional stem is susceptible to one function of a paradigm, it is susceptible to them all. No verb, for example, should conjugate in the singular but not the plural, or in the present but not the past tense. The productivity of derivation, however, is determined by semantic categories, and we would expect derivation to be constrained by less predictable lexical conditions.

Unfortunately, each of the Lexicalist diagnostics is vexed by some aspect of the data. Derivation does change the meanings of words so as to allow the derivate to become a lexical entry in the lexicon. Case functions, however, also lexicalize. In Russian, for example, the Instrumental never marks punctual time with the odd exception of instances involving temporal nouns which form natural quadruplets – for example, *utr-om* 'in the morning', *dn-em* 'in the afternoon', *večer-om* 'in the evening', and *noč'-ju* 'at night'. There is simply no way to derive punctuality from the major or minor functions of the Instrumental: that is, manner, means, vialic, essive. Punctuality is productively marked by *v* 'in' + ACC in Russian, e.g. *v to vremya* 'at that time'. The instrumental time nouns apparently must be lexically marked, even though punctuality is a case function.

Under most current grammatical theories, lexical selection occurs prior to agreement operations and the amalgamation of functional categories under INFL. If derivation is a lexical process, inflectional operations must apply subsequent to lexical ones. Assuming again an isomorphic relation between form and function, it follows that inflectional markers will emerge in surface structure outside all derivational markers. However, inflectional markers occur widely inside derivational markers. For example, the derivation of verbs by *preverbs*, prefixes which often share the form of an adverb or adposition, is considered derivational, since these derivates often lexicalize semantically. In English these derivations are marked with *discontinuous morphemes*: for example, *bring* (someone) *around*. In Sanskrit, however, similar derivations prefix the base: for example, *pari=ṇayat*, literally 'around he.leads', the present active for 'he marries'. The imperfect is derived by inserting a marker between the idiomatized prefix and stem: that is, *pary=a-ṇayat*. Georgian exhibits a similar tendency: for example, *mo=g-ḳlav-s* Preverb=2Obj-KILL-3Sub 'He will kill you'.

The third entailment of lexicalism, that derivation changes the category of a stem while inflection does not, also faces a variety of problems. The first is a practical one: a dearth of research on lexical and grammatical categories. Whether N, V, A, for example, are lexical or syntactic categories has never been resolved. It has been common to presume that they are both and to ignore the fact that this presumption violates the strict modularity of lexicalism. Assuming that these categories are lexical, they are not changed by derivations like *violin : violinist, cream : creamery, zip : unzip*. A diminutive does not alter the referential category of its base, even though it changes its sense, very much as does inflection. Thus Russian *dožd'* 'rain' : *dožd-ik* 'a little rain' : *dožd-ič-ek* 'a tiny little rain' – all refer to rain, even though they might express varying judgments and attitudes of the speaker towards a particular instance of rain.

There are also ostensible inflectional functions which belong to categories other than that of the base. Participles like English *talking* and *raked*, for instance, freely reflect the inflectional categories of aspect, tense, and voice, as in *John is **talking*** and *the leaves have been **raked***. They also serve the relational adjectival function of attribution – for example, *the talking boy, the raked leaves* – and agree adjectivally in languages requiring agreement – for example, Russian *govorjašč-ij mal'čik* 'talking boy', but *govorjašč-aja devuška* 'talking girl'. The diagnostics of lexicalism, therefore, remain fragile until contradictions like these are resolved. Nonetheless, an intelligible picture of derivation emerges from the data underlying them.

3 The nature of derivation

Three accounts of derivation have emerged in the recent literature.[3] The first considers derivation simply a matter of lexical selection, the selection of an affix and copying it into a word-level structure. Others see derivation as an operation or set of operations in the same sense that Matthews and Anderson see inflection. A derivational morpheme on this view is not an object selected, but the processes of inserting or reduplicating affixes, vocalic apophony, etc. Finally, Jackendoff and Bybee argue that derivation is a set of static paradigmatic lexical relations. In light of the lack of agreement on the subject, a brief examination of each of these three accounts would seem appropriate.

It is common to assume that the lexical entries (*lexemes*) upon which derivational rules operate comprise at least three types of features: a phonological matrix, a grammatical subcategorization frame, and a semantic interpretation, all mutually implied. For future reference, let us illustrate these relations with the hypothetical entry for English *health* in (1).

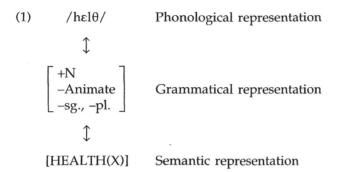

(1)   /hɛlθ/   Phonological representation

$$\begin{bmatrix} +N \\ -Animate \\ -sg., -pl. \end{bmatrix}$$ Grammatical representation

[HEALTH(X)]   Semantic representation

There is general agreement on these three constituents of a lexical representation, and that they mutually imply each other in the Saussurean sense; that is, no one such representation occurs without the other two, as indicated by the double-headed arrows in (1). Current disagreement centers on whether lexemes comprise only open open-class morphemes (N, A, V stems) or whether they include grammatical (functional) morphemes as well. We will return to this issue further on.

3.1 Derivation as lexical selection

Advocates of *Word Syntax*, including Selkirk (1982), Lieber (1981, 1992), Scalise (1984), and Sproat (1985), reduce derivation to the selection of an affix from the lexicon (see Toman, WORD SYNTAX). This particular view of derivation is dependent upon the existence of word-internal hierarchical structure: that is, below the X_0 level. Lieber (1992) claims that this structure in no way differs from syntactic structure, so that words contain specifiers, heads, and complements, just as do clauses. If words contain their own structure, and if affixes are regular lexical entries like stems, then derivation, compounding, and regular lexical selection may all be accomplished by a single process: lexical selection. (2) illustrates how compounds and derivations might share the same structure.

(2) (a)   (b)   (c)

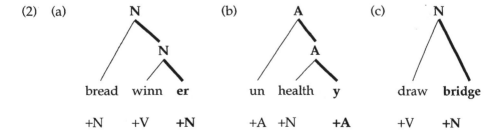

bread winn er   un health y   draw bridge

+N   +V   +N   +A +N   +A   +V   +N

Derivational affixes are not distinguished from stems, but share the same classification, *morpheme*, defined as a classical linguistic sign. That is, derivational morphemes have the same mutually implied phonological, grammatical, and semantic representations as do lexemes. According to Lieber, the grammatical representation contains the category and subcategorization of the affix, plus any diacritics, such as its *Level Order*, the level at which an affix applies under Lexical Phonology (Kiparsky 1982b). The semantic representations of the stems and affixes in (2), for example, compose under the scope conditions provided by the structural hierarchy and the head-dominance principles. In (2), the rightmost lexical item dominates and assigns the grammatical and semantic categories to the derivate or compound, as indicated by the boldface branches. The simplicity of the Word Syntax theory of derivation is achieved by the assumption that affixes are regular lexical items, and as such may serve as heads of derivates. However, morphology involves far more types of marking than simple affixation, and most of these types represent problems for Word Syntax.

3.2 *Derivation as morphological operations*

Anderson (1992), Aronoff (1976, 1994), and Beard (1981) have extended the notion of grammatical morphemes as operations developed in Matthews's WORD-AND-PARADIGM (see Stump, INFLECTION) theory to derivation. Process morphology addresses first and foremost those types of morphology other than external affixation. For example, both inflectional and derivational morphology are characterized by *reduplication*. Reduplication is a process which copies all or part of the phonological representation of a stem as an affix: for example, the Dakota de-adjectival verbalization: *puza* 'dry' : *puspuza* 'be dry', *čʰepa* 'fat' : *čʰepčʰepa* 'be fat'. Notice that reduplication presupposes the prior existence of some lexeme, making it difficult to classify this process as a lexical item as Marantz (1982) proposes. Whatever reduplication is, it must take place subsequent to lexical selection, and hence cannot be accounted for by lexical selection itself, unless that process is enhanced in an ad hoc fashion.

In addition to external affixation, languages also widely exhibit *infixation*. The inchoative de-adjectival verb in Tagalog infixes the base; for example, *ganda* 'beautiful' : *gumanda* 'become beautiful', *gising* 'awake' : *gumising* 'awaken'. Processual morphology handles infixation with the same sort of rules employed in accounting for external affixation. Structures like (2) cannot adequately explain infixation without special phonological rules which determine the position of infixes but not prefixes and suffixes. The issue between Word Syntax and process morphology then reduces to the question of whether such special operations differ qualitatively from other phonological operations.

Whether affixes are copied from stems to which they are attached, or whether they are written external or internal to the lexical base, are matters of indifference if affixation is a process, rather than the selection of a lexeme. This interpretation of derivation distinguishes operations on the grammatical representation of the lexical base from phonological modifications of the base such as affixation. (3) illustrates how affixation is realized on the derived base for *unhealthy* on this hypothesis.

(3)   *un*   *health*   *y*   Phonological representation

$$\llcorner\ \begin{bmatrix} +\text{Neg} \\ +\text{Adj} \\ +\text{Poss(Y)} \\ +\text{N} \end{bmatrix} \rbrace \Big\rbrace \quad$$ REALIZATION RULES

Grammatical representation

Affixation applies after morpholexical and morphosyntactic rules have provided the base with derivational features. Since no grammatical or semantic operations are involved, affixation becomes a set of purely phonological modifications of the phonological representation of the base conditioned by the grammatical features. The head of such derivations is the lexical base. The crucial factor determining the order of affixes is not structural relations, but the order in which they are attached. Scope relations are determined by autonomous semantic operations which follow the order of grammatical features in the base.

3.3 *Derivation as lexical relations*

Jackendoff (1975) and Bybee (1988) have argued that derivation is simply a static set of lexical relations. Jackendoff argued that all derivates must be listed in the lexicon since they are subject to lexicalization. Derivational rules are *redundancy rules*, rules which state the single redundant relation "is lexically related." The nominalization rule for assigning *-ion* to Latinate verbs would then have the form (4):

(4) $\begin{bmatrix} /y+ \text{ ion}/ \\ +\text{N} \end{bmatrix} \leftrightarrow \begin{bmatrix} /y/ \\ +\text{V} \end{bmatrix}$

Separate semantic rules are similar in that they express the same redundancy relation between the meanings of the base and the affix.

(5) $\begin{bmatrix} +\text{N} \\ +[\text{NP}_1\text{'s }((\text{P})\text{NP}_2)] \\ \text{ABSTRACT RESULT OF} \\ \text{ACT OF NP}_1\text{'s Z -ING} \\ \text{NP}_2 \end{bmatrix} \leftrightarrow \begin{bmatrix} +\text{V} \\ +[\text{NP}_1\text{\_\_\_\_ }((\text{P})\text{NP}_2)] \\ \text{NP}_1 \text{ Z NP}_2 \end{bmatrix}$

Jackendoff proposed that such rules as (4) and (5) could be applied generatively in speech to create neologisms; however, generation is not their purpose in the competence model. Jackendoff also left open the question of how such regularities arise in the lexicon in the first place if they are lexically superfluous. Bybee offers a psychological answer to that question.

Bybee argues for a connectionist theory of morphology, inflectional and derivational, based on the theory of parallel distributed processing by Rumelhart and McClelland (1986). In her view, lexical rules have no status "independent of the lexical items to which they are applicable. Rather, rules are highly reinforced representational patterns or schemas." Schemas are abstractions from memorized lexical items which share semantic or phonological properties. One such schema results from the association of verb pairs like *cling* : *clung*, *sling* : *slung*, *sting* : *stung*.[4] A derivation rule on Bybee's account is simply a relationship which is more strongly represented, where "strongly" refers to the number of representations a pattern has in long-term memory. In the instance just cited, the phonological relation /ɪŋ/ : /ʌŋ/ is more strongly represented than /kl/ : /sl/ or /sl/ : /st/. The more recurrent phonological relation is therefore more likely to be associated with the past tense than the less frequent ones.

When speakers add the past tense innovatively, they simply search their memories for phonological relations associated with the past tense and choose one analogically. Following recent connectionist theories, the most highly reinforced relation is most likely to be selected for the neologism. The relation /ɪŋ/ : /ʌŋ/, for instance, will not be as strongly represented in the semantic schema for past tense as ø : /d/. Speakers are therefore more likely to add /d/ to a neologism than to replace a stem vowel /ɪ/ with /ʌ/. If the neologism ends in /ŋ/, however, the probability that this method will be selected increases.

Bybee's suggestion has the advantage of conflating derivation and derivational acquisition. A derivational rule reduces to the arrangement of memorized items in mental storage. Without derivation rules, all morphology may be confined to the lexicon as in Word Syntax, and only one rule, lexical selection, is required to account for morphology in syntax. Moreover, morphological creativity reduces to the general cognitive process of analogy which is commonly used in categorization. So far, however, many of the processes vital to Bybee's model remain undefined, so it is not currently possible to determine this theory's efficacy in accounting for the derivational data.

4 Derivational heads

If affixes are regular lexical items which may be selected for word structures as fully derived words are selected for phrase structures, they should be able to serve as heads, as do fully derived words. If affixes are the results of processes, however, they cannot be lexical heads, and the traditional assumption that stems represent morphological heads regains credibility. This issue has been a central concern of recent morphological research, so is next on the agenda.

4.1 Affixes as heads

If derived words are structured, the question naturally arises as to whether word structure is the same as syntactic structure. Lieber and Sproat claim that not only are the two types of structure identical, but the principles for composing words are precisely those of X-bar syntax. It follows that morphology may be dispensed with altogether, resulting in yet another major theoretical economy under Word Syntax. A major contention of modern X-bar theory is that the head of a phrase (*X*) determines the category of the whole phrase (*XP*). A sound test of Word Syntax, therefore, is whether the head of a derived word determines the category of the whole word. Since the outermost affix of a word is often associated with the category of the whole word, it might be possible to mount a case for affixes serving as the heads of derived words.

E. Williams (1981b) advanced the simplest account of affixes as heads of words: the head of a word is its rightmost element. Thus the head of *bread-winner* in (2a) would be -*er* which, under the premise that affixes are lexical items, is a noun in the same sense that *bridge* in *drawbridge* (2c) is a noun. Both -*er* and *bridge* are nouns which determine the category of *bread-winner* and *drawbridge*. The heads of *redraw* and *unhealthy* (2b), on the other hand, are the bases *draw* and *healthy*, since prefixes in IE languages tend not to change the category of the derivates to which they adhere.

Some features, however, must be raised from nonheads. Diminutives, for example, usually bear the features of the base rather than the affix. In Russian, for example, both *sobaka* 'dog' and its diminutive, *sobač-k-a*, are feminine; *jazyk* 'tongue' and its diminutive, *jazyč-ok*, are both masculine. This contrasts with German diminutives, which are all consistently neuter: for example, *der Brief* : *das Briefchen* 'letter', *die Lampe* : *das Lämpchen* 'lamp'. To redress this problem, Di Sciullo and Williams (1987) proposed that feature inheritance relativizes the head; that is, features of categories present in the stem but not in the affix determine the lexical categorization of the final derived word. This new variation presumes that affixes, like Russian diminutive suffixes, are unmarked for certain features such as gender; this allows gender features from the next highest node to be inherited by the derivate. The German suffix -*chen*, on the other hand, does bear an inheritable gender valuation, neuter, and so passes this feature on to the derivate.

Unfortunately, relativizing morphological heads renders them radically different from phrasal heads, which are always absolute and never relative. Derived words differ greatly from derived phrases, where *face* is just as good a noun phrase as *a strange face peering through the door*. *Ist* is not just as good a noun as *violinist*. Relativizing morphological heads then defeats the original purpose of postulating affixal heads. This difference between word and phrase heads nonetheless must be characterized in an adequate model of grammar, even though it impedes the reduction of morphology to syntax.

4.2 Head operations

There is another clue to the question of morphological heads. The phonological structures of a wide range of derivations do not isomorphically parallel their semantic structures. English, for example, restricts the comparative suffix *-er* to monosyllabic adjectives or disyllabic stems ending on a weak vowel: for example, *quick : quicker, hateful : *hatefuller* but *happy : happier* (see Sproat, MORPHOLOGY AS COMPONENT OR MODULE, for further details). Trisyllabic stems are wholly excluded from the distribution of this suffix, with one exception: disyllabic stems prefixed with *un-: unhappier*. This exception is obviated on the assumption that *-er* attaches to *happy* before *un-*; however, the semantic reading of such terms is not 'not happier' but 'more unhappy'. The morphological and semantic structures of such forms are hence "mismatched."

To circumvent exceptional treatment of such MORPHOSEMANTIC MISMATCHES, Hoeksema (1985) proposed that every rule of derivation has a correlate that applies specifically to heads, but is in all other respects a context-free rewrite rule. Stump (1991) argues that this correlate is the default. English derived verbs exhibit the effect of a head operation in maintaining their conjugations even when serving as a base in a derivate. The past tense of *understand* is *understood*, and that of *overdrive* is *overdrove*. This seems to indicate that although past tense has scope over the entire derivation (or compound) in these instances, morphology applies strictly to *stand* and *drive*, respectively; otherwise, we might expect the past tense to be the productive **understanded* and **overdrived*.

Morphosemantic mismatches like *unhappier* are susceptible to the same interpretation; the morphology of the negative adjective applies to the head of the derivate, *happy*, even though the scope of comparison extends to the entire word *unhappy*. Head operations may also be extended to instances of inflection occurring inside derivation, such as the Sanskrit perfect mentioned above, *pari=ṇayat* 'he marries' : *pary=a-ṇayat* 'he married', and to diminutives like the Hebrew loan *xaxom-im-l-ex* 'smart little people' in Yiddish and Breton *bag-où-ig-où* 'little boats' (Stump 1991), assuming that diminutive suffixes are grammatically empty and that the stem is the head. On this account the Sanskrit perfect inflection is added to the head (stem) inside the preverb, because the preverb is a phrasal head clitic or semi-discontinuous morpheme. The Hebrew and Breton plural mark both their scope and the head of the derivation, for reasons undetermined.

Head operations remain exceptional so long as affixes may be heads, since semantic evidence indicates that affixes are never themselves affixed. No language exhibits scope ambiguities such that the plural of a locative nominalization like *bakeries* would refer either to an aggregate of places, only some of which are devoted to baking (head marking, the affix the head), or to an aggregate of baking places (scope marking). The scope of all derivational functions is the entire word to which it is added, derived or underived; the only variation is in the placement of affixes marking them. This situation, combined with the failure of theories of affixal heads, endorses the traditional assumption that the morphological head of a word is its root or stem. Morpholexical and morphosyntactic feature operations seem to apply concatenatively to the base lexeme; the distribution of affixes, on the other hand, seems to be determined by language-dependent rules of spellout.

5 Synthetic compounds and derivation

If affixes are not morphological heads, the question arises as to whether compounds and derivations are at all related as (2) implies. If they are, it is doubtful that their relation is structural. It is common to distinguish *analytic* from *synthetic compounds* by the presence of affixation. *Drawbridge, redhead, houseboat* are thereby analytic compounds, while *truck-driver, truck-driving, red-headed* are all synthetic. There is little evidence that most analytical compounds are related to derivation. Rather, other analytic compounding appears to be a simple process of combining lexemes. The head of those compounds composed of constituents belonging to different categories determines the category of the compound. The right constituent determines the category of English compounds, so that a *houseboat* is a boat while a *boathouse* is a house. However, this description excludes prepositions, since compounds with prepositional modifiers are often adjectives (*inland, between-class, outboard*), and those with prepositional heads may be anything but prepositions (*sit-in, hold-out, run-away*). Even most P + P compounds fail the head test: *without* does not imply *out*, and *in* and *on* would seem to be the heads of *into* and *onto*, respectively. The evidence from compounding hence suggests that adpositions are not lexemes in the sense that N, V, A stems are.

The distinction between analytic and synthetic compounds is nevertheless imperfect at best. Synthetic compounds do resemble simple derivations in several respects. For example, they share the same derivational categories often marked by the same affixes: *bearded : gray-bearded, driver : truck-driver, driving : truck-driving*. Analytic *Bahuvrihi* compounds, like *redhead, long-hair, hardhead*, for instance, share their derivational function with possessional adjectives like *red-headed, long-haired, hardheaded*. Indeed, the same possessional function ("having *N*") emerges in simple derivations like *headed* and *hairy*. Parallels like these suggest that synthetic compounding is derivation which allows an optional modifier. Affixation, however, is not a reliable indicator of the distinction between compounds and derivations, since the zero morphology, which is available to simple derivations, is also available to compounds. Indeed, Booij (1988) has shown that synthetic compounds, whose structure is presumed to be [*truck-driv*]ing, may be explained with equal cogency as analytic compounds with the structure [*truck*][*driving*], given a semantic level capable of resolving morphosemantic mismatches.

Until research better clarifies the subject, it is best to assume that analytic compounds represent an independent lexical means of derivation; however, it is doubtful that those bearing adpositions are compounds (see also Fabb, COMPOUNDING). Analytic compounds in this sense should not be confused with zero-marked Bahuvrihi compounds. Like synthetic compounds, bahuvrihis may be interpreted as derivations with optional modifiers. This area of research is very fluid, however, and Booij has shown how all compounds may be reduced to analytic concatenation.

Morphosemantic mismatches raise another important issue in morphology: the fact that derivational meaning and the affixation marking it are not always isomorphic. Karcevskij (1929) called this phenomenon *morphological asymmetry*. It is an attribute of morphology whose importance is only now being appreciated.

6 Morphological asymmetry

Karcevskij noted that while several endings mark the genitive in Russian – *-i, -a, -u* – each of these endings also has multiple functions. The ending *-a*, for example, also marks feminine nominative singular and neuter plural. The ending *-i* marks feminine and masculine nominative plural, as well as genitive, dative, and locative singular in declension III. In other words, it is common for grammatical morphemes to be *cofunctional* (*-i, -a, -u* above) and *multifunctional* (*-i*), to use the terms of Szymanek (1989). In addition to cofunctionality and multifunctionality, Matthews (1972) identified *extended* and *cumulative exponence* as morphological asymmetries. In the Latin word *rēxistī* [*re:k-s-is-ti:*] 'you (sg.) ruled', for example, the suffix *-ti:* cumulatively (simultaneously) marks second person, singular, and perfective. The remaining markers, *-s* and *-is* are empty extensions of *-ti*, redundantly marking the perfective, too. The same phenomena characterize derivation. In the adjective *dram-at-ic-al*, *-at* and *-al* are empty extensions of *-ic*; cf. *theatr-ic*. The German suffix *-er* in *Lehr-er* 'teacher' cumulatively marks [+subjective], [+masculine], and [declension I]. Finally, *zero* (null) *morphology* reflects morphological asymmetry. While most non-count modalic (instrumental) nominals require either the suffix *-er* (*conditioner*, *softener*) or *-ant* (*stimulant, relaxant*), many require no suffix at all: for example, *a rinse, a wash, a spray*. Again, the relationship between the grammatical and phonological levels is nonisomorphic.

Bazell (1949, 1952) argued that these phenomena collectively indicate a fault in structuralist morphology, which he dubbed the *Correspondence Fallacy*, the assumption that an analysis at one linguistic level will isomorphically map onto analyses at other levels. Bazell argued that the phonological analysis of a word need not correspond to its semantic analysis; however, it does not follow from this that no analysis is possible. It is quite conceivable that each level is defined in its own terms, and that mapping from one level to another involves more sophisticated relations than the isomorphic relation of the classical linguistic sign.

To obviate the correspondence fallacy, Beard (1966, 1976), Kiefer (1970), and Leitner (1973) proposed what was subsequently called the *Separation Hypothesis*, the claim that the functional and spelling operations of derivation are discrete and autonomous. The Separation Hypothesis assumes that lexical items are restricted to N, V, and A stems, all of which are perfect signs comprising mutually implied phonological, grammatical, and semantic representations, as in (1). It then provides a set of abstract lexical operations on the grammatical representation of a lexical item discrete from operations on the phonological and semantic representations. Algorithms in an autonomous morphological spelling component like those proposed by Matthews (1972) then modify the phonological representation of grammatically and semantically derived stems. By the same token, compounding operations which combine words like *truck* and *driving* mentioned above need not establish the semantic scope of compound constituents. This can be accomplished by autonomous principles of composition based on the argument structure of the phrasal head, in this case, *drive*.

The separation of grammatical and phonological operations allows for a simple account of all morphological asymmetry. Cumulative exponence results from a single-stem modification conditioned by several grammatical features, while extended exponence is the collective marking by several stem modifications of a single feature. Cofunctionality and multifunctionality are explained similarly. Finally, zero morphology is simply derivation without affixation, while empty morphemes result from affixation without derivation.

Morphosemantic mismatches like those in *unhappier*, those in compounds like *truck-driving* on Booij's interpretation, and those in head operation constructions may be resolved by a similar separation of derivation and semantic composition. The asymmetry explored by Karcevskij and Matthews, on the other hand, is more a *morphophonological mismatch* between derivation and phonological realization. The ultimate implication of asymmetry, therefore, is that semantics, derivation, and affixation represent three distinct levels of morphological operations, which require two distinct mapping systems.

7 Types of derivation

We have surveyed the general attributes of derivation and the major accounts of them. We may now turn to the particular properties of derivation: the types of derivation and the types of affixation marking them. In its broadest sense, *derivation* refers to any process which results in the creation of a new word. However, the output of some morphological operations is far more principled than the output of others. The derivations in (6), for example, form a sort of lexical paradigm which holds for many other bases:

(6)

$$\text{LASER}\begin{cases} \text{re-laser, out-laser, over-laser, ...} \\ \text{laser-er} \rightarrow \text{laser-er-s, laser-er-'s} \\ \text{laser-ing} \rightarrow \text{laser-ing-s, laser-ing-'s} \\ \text{(un)laser-able} \rightarrow \text{(un)laser-abil-ity} \end{cases}$$

Some types of derivation do not fit into derivational paradigms like (6). It is well known that words may be misanalyzed when a phonological sequence identical with that of an affix is misperceived as that affix. The result is that a previously nonexistent underlying base is extracted and added to the permanent lexical store via a process known as *back formation*. *Sculptor*, for example, was borrowed as an integral base into English. However, because the final phoneme cluster /ər/ is identical with an agentive marker in English, and since *sculptor* is an agentive noun, a verbal base, *to sculpt*, has been extracted and added to the stock of English verbs. Consequently, *sculptor* changes from a lexical base to a derivate.

Several facts obstruct the conclusion that back formation is a derivational process. First, in order to use back-formed words, we must be familiar with them. While some potentially back-formed words are used, far more may not be. It is not possible, for instance, to say that a butcher **butches* or that a barber **barbs*, even though these verbs are potential back derivates as legitimate as *sculpt*. There is no grammatically definable constraint preventing this; it simply is not acceptable to do so. Second, we do not find positions for back derivates in lexical paradigms like (6). Take the back derivate of *laser* itself: *to lase*, for example. It generates exactly the same paradigm as (6). Thus, in those dialects which use *lase*, one may say *relase, outlase, overlase, laser, lasing, (un)lasable, (un)lasability* – all with the same sense as the corresponding zero-derived verb in (6). In other words, rather than forming a derivational relationship with a lexical base, back-formed words create a new base, expanding the underived lexical stock in a way that regular derivations do not. This characterization partially fits several other types of word formation which need to be distinguished from regular, grammatically determined derivation.

7.1 Lexical stock expansion

Clipping (telephone : phone), blends (smoke + fog = smog), acronymization (aids), and *analogical formation (workaholic)* all conform to the description of back formation in significant ways. Back formation generates a base which the lexicon lacks. Clipping, on the other hand, produces a redundant base, but a new one all the same. With rare exceptions (e.g. *caravan : van*), the input and output of clipping rules are semantically identical, and both remain active in the lexicon. Both *telephone* and *phone* have the same range of grammatical derivations, all with the same meaning: *(tele)phoner, (tele)phoning*, etc. Notice, too, the irregularity of clipping. It usually reduces a polysyllabic word to a monosyllabic one; however, this may be accomplished by removing the initial syllables (*phone*), the final syllables (*rep*), or the initial and final syllables (*flu*).

Blending, acronymization, and analogical formation also tend to be conscious operations, unlike grammatical derivation. Words like *smog, motel*, and *tangelo* are created intentionally by a logical rather than grammatical process: if the reference is part A and part B, then the word referring to it should comprise parts of the words for A and B. Acronyms like *laser, scuba, aids*, have been converted from phrases to the initial letters of the words in those phrases, which are not part of grammar, then the initials have been phonologically interpreted. *Acquired immune deficiency syndrome*, for example, provides *aids*, which is rendered pronounceable by applying English spelling rules in reverse. The process hence requires considerable conscious activity outside the bounds of grammar. As in the case of clipping, the phrase and the acronym are synonymous, and both remain in the language.

Analogical forms like *workaholic, chocaholic* and *cheeseburger, fishburger, chickenburger* differ from regular derivations in that they require prosodic identity. Genuine suffixes like *-ing* may be added to stems of any length or prosodic structure. Pseudo-derivates like *chocaholic*, however, must additionally fit the prosodic template of their analog, in this case, *alcoholic*: the output must contain four syllables with penultimate accent. Thus *chocolaholic, shoppingaholic*, and *handiworkaholic* do not work as well as *chocaholic, shopaholic*, and *workaholic*. When we begin to find acceptable violations of this extragrammatical principle like *chickenburger*, we usually find that the remainder, in this case *burger*, has become an independent back-formed word capable of undergoing regular compounding.

This does not exhaust the catalogue of lexical stock expansion processes. That catalogue also contains *borrowing* (*troika, detente, thug*), *commonization* (*quisling, aspirin*), *semantic narrowing* (*percolator, escalator*), *loan translation* (German *Einfluß* 'influence', *Mitleid* 'compassion'), *folk etymology* (*craw[l]fish* from Old French *crevise*), and perhaps others. The point is that these processes tend to be conscious, extragrammatical, and hence grammatically irregular. Rather than filling a position in some lexical paradigm, they create new lexical bases which then generate their own paradigms. To better understand the difference, let us now examine the regular derivation types.

7.2 *Lexical derivation*

Four distinct types of regular grammatical derivation have been described in the literature; *featural derivation, functional derivation, transposition*, and *expressive derivation*. While all the details of the properties of these types of derivation and their interrelations have not been refined, their basic nature and functions may be broadly described.

7.2.1 Featural derivation Featural derivation does not change the category of the underlying base, but operates on the values of inherent features. An obvious candidate for such a rule is natural gender, as described by Jakobson

(1932, 1939) in connection with his concept *markedness*.[5] In most languages which support natural gender, the default or unmarked form is masculine. A convenient technical notation of the fact that unmarked masculine nouns may refer to males or females is [+Feminine, +Masculine]. This requires a Jakobsonian principle of markedness whereby in cases of conflict, the surface realization will default to that of the unmarked category, masculine. Thus the Russian noun *student* 'student' may refer to females or males, but all grammatical agreement will be the same as purely masculine nouns like *brat* 'brother', *otec* 'father', which cannot refer to females.

Default masculines like *student* differ from pure masculines in that they are susceptible to feminization. This requires some rule on the order of *student(ø)* → *student-k(a)* which converts the default masculine noun into a purely feminine one and marks this fact by transferring the base from declension I, marked in the nominative by -ø, to declension II, marked in the nominative by -a. All that is required grammatically and semantically of this rule is the toggling of the masculine feature from positive to negative: that is:

(7)   [+Feminine, +Masculine] → [+Feminine, −Masculine]

(7) converts the lexical description of the base from unmarked masculine to marked feminine like the purely feminine nouns *sestra* 'sister' and *mat'* 'mother', which may refer only to females and not to males. The addition of any feature [+Feminine] would be inappropriate since (7) applies only to nouns with natural gender: that is, those which inherently (lexically) possess lexical gender features.

7.2.2 Functional derivation   Kuryłowicz (1936) first distinguished rules which add features to the underlying base from those which merely change its category. Consider (8), for example:

(8)   (a)   recruit : recruit-er
      (b)   recruit : recruit-ee
      (c)   bake : bak-ery

Kuryłowicz referred to this type of derivation as "dérivation lexicale," because the derivate differed semantically from its base. In the middle of this century, several European linguists, among them Belić (1958: 140–1, 148–50), noted a similarity between the functions of these derivations and those of the case system. The traditional names of nominals like *recruiter* and *recruitee*, "agentive" and "patientive," suggest that the functions of this type of derivation are semantic. However, many "agentive" forms are not animate as the name implies (*breaker, floater, sparkler*), and many are not even active (*riser, marker, divider*). The same is true of patientives: alongside *employee, recruitee, draftee*, we find inanimate "patientives" of resultative verbs like *painting, carving, writing*. The suffixal distinction does not change the fact that a painting is an object painted in just the same sense that an employee is an object employed. It therefore seems more likely that this type of derivation is based on case functions: for example (nominative of) subject, (accusative of) object, (locative of) place (*bakery, fishery*), (genitive of) possession (*dirty, forested*) and material (*oaken, woolen*), (ablative of) origin (*American, Brazilian*), (dative of) purpose (*roofing, siding*), (instrumental of) means (*cutter, defoliant*).

Languages with rich morphologies have dozens of such derivations, including those just mentioned. Even in Serbian and Polish all these derivations are still quite productive, and all their functions serve as pure case functions expressed without adpositions in some language. Basque has a locative of locus, *mendi-an* = mountain-Loc 'on the mountain'; Serbian exhibits the possessional (qualitative) genitive: *čovek plav-ih oči-ju* 'a man of (with) blue eyes'; Turkish marks origin and material with the ablative, *Ankara-dan* = Ankara-ABL 'from Ankara', *taş-tan bir ev* = stone-ABL one house 'a house of stone'; and Latin has a dative of purpose: *castr-īs locum* = camp-DATSG place-AccSG 'a place for a camp'. All languages express these functions with case endings, adpositions, or a combination of both. Few verbs and no nouns are subcategorized for these argument relations, yet they are widely available to functional lexical derivation in languages with rich morphological systems like Serbian, Inuit, and Chukchee.[6]

If the ultimate constraint on functional derivations is the set of case functions, the question becomes why some functions seem to be missing and why subject and object relations are more productive and diachronically stable than others. Some omissions are obvious: the (ablative) absolute relation is missing because it is purely a syntactic relation, that of sentential adverbs; the same applies to the (ablative of) distinction, used to mark comparatives in many languages: for example, Turkish *Halil'-den tembel* = Halil-ABL lazy 'lazier than Halil'. The reason why we find more subjective and objective nominalizations than others is, no doubt, high pragmatic demand. This is an area which has received little attention historically, and thus no definitive answers to these questions are available.[7] However, it is clear that functional derivations involve far more functions than the argument functions found in the base, yet few if any productive derivational functions fall outside those found in the inflectional system.

7.2.3 Transposition Another type of derivation which reflects a simple change of category without any functional change is *transposition*, illustrated in (9):

(9) (a) walk : walk-ing (V → N)
    (b) new : new-ness (A → N)
    (c) budget : budget-ary (N → A)

Kuryłowicz called derivations like those of (9) "dérivation syntaxique," but Marchand (1967) used the more distinctive term, "transposition."

Transposition introduces no argument structure, but simply shifts a stem from one category to another, sometimes marking the fact affixally, sometimes not. The definition of *dryness* must coincide with that of *dry* in all essential respects, since, unlike *bake* and *baker*, its reference is identical to that of its base. The same is true of all the relations represented in (9). Whether transpositions are marked by real or zero affixation is a separate issue, bound up with the general issue of the nature of zero morphology.

7.2.4 Expressive derivation   Expressive derivation does not change the referential scope of its input; however, expressive derivation also does not change the lexical category of the base. As mentioned in section 2, the reference of the three grades of the Russian word for 'rain', *dožd'*, *doždik*, and *dožd-ič-ek*, all refer to the same conceptual category. The formal variation reflects subjective perceptions of the speaker: whether he perceives the rain to be relatively light, beneficial, or pleasant. For this reason, expressive derivation may be recursive, applying to its own output as in the Russian example. In addition to diminutive and augmentative expressive derivation, pejorative and affectionate forms also occur: for example, Russian *kniga* : *knižonka* 'damned book' (cf. *knižka* 'little book') and *papa* 'daddy' : *papočka*.

There is no obvious means of relegating expressive derivation to any of the other three types. The categories involved are not found elsewhere in grammar as are functional categories, nor are they inherent lexical categories like gender. Since expressive derivation does not involve a category change, it cannot be a form of transposition. It therefore remains mysterious in many respects.

8 Realization and productivity

The types of phonological realization (stem modification) which express derivation are by and large the same as those which express inflection. The glaring exception seems to be that derivation is not expressed by *free morphemes*: those which are not modifications of stems, but which stand alone. This would follow from the assumption that only inflection is syntactic. Since free morphemes require a structural position, this type of realization would be ruled out for lexical derivation by the Lexicalist Hypothesis.

Evidence indicates, however, that the bound phonological realization of derivational and inflectional morphology is provided by a single component (see also the discussion of the Split Morphology Hypothesis in Stump, INFLECTION). The English suffix *-ing*, for example, may be attached to verb stems to generate inflectional forms like the progressive (*is painting*), the present participle (*painting machine*), as well as derivational forms like the objective nominalization (*a painting*). The same is true of *-ed*, which productively marks the past tense and participles (*John (has) annoyed Mary*), as well as derivations like the possessional adjective: for example, *two-headed, forested*. The important point is that derivation seems to be an abstract process independent of the various means of phonological realization and of the means of semantic interpretation.

Two specific types of marking, *subtraction* and *metathesis*, weakly represented in inflection, apparently do not mark derivation. Papago, for example, seems to derive perfective verbs from imperfective ones by deleting the final consonant if there is one, *him* 'walking' : *hi:* 'walked (sg.)', *hihim* 'walking (pl.)' : *hihi* 'walked (pl.)' (Anderson 1992). However, aspect is probably inflectional, though the matter remains unclear. Metathesis for the most part is an allomorphic change effected by affixation, as in the case of the Hebrew reflexive prefix, *hit-*, whose final segment metathesizes with initial voiceless stridents: for example, *xipes* 'seek' : *hitxapes*, but *silek* 'remove' *histalek*.

8.1 Discontinuous morphemes

Evidence suggests that one type of verbal derivation is marked by *discontinuous morphemes*, morphemes which may be loosened or removed from their base. The English correlate of *preverbs*, a type of verbal prefix expressing a closed set of adverbal functions, is a particle which is written separately and may appear either immediately following the verb or the VP. Consider the Russian examples and their English counterparts in (10) for example:

(10) (a) Ivan vy-vel sobaku   'John brought [out] his dog [out]'
     (b) Ivan v-vel sobaku   'John brought [in] his dog [in]'
     (c) Ivan so-stavil plan   'John put [together] a plan [together]'

Because verbs with preverbs form notoriously irregular patterns and are equally notorious for idiomatizing (e.g. *pri* 'to' + *pisat* 'write' = *pripisat* 'attribute'), they are considered lexical derivates. How, then, may their markers appear a phrase away from the stem which they mark?

Preverbs are in fact often loosely attached to their stem as the examples above from Sanskrit (*pari=a-ṇayat* = Around=Imp-lead 'he married') and Georgian (*mo=g-klav-s* Prvb=2Obj-KILL-3Sub 'He will kill you') illustrate. These preverbs attach to the outside of the fully inflected verb, the head of the VP. One possible account of these morphemes is that they are clitics, defined in terms of attachment to either the phrasal head or periphery, depending on the morphological conditions of specific languages. The important point is that their position is morphologically predictable by Anderson's general theory of affixation (see *affixation* in section 8.2.1 below), and requires no syntactic projection as do lexemes and free morphemes. Hence it is possible to explain these derivations without violating the Lexicalist Hypothesis, given the Separation Hypothesis.

8.2 Other types of stem modification

8.2.1 Affixation   Affixation (prefixation, suffixation, and infixation) is the most productive means of marking derivation. Anderson (1992: ch. 8) points out that affixation may be defined in the same terms as cliticization, assuming that the peripheral element of a word is its initial or final segment or syllable and its head is the accented syllable. That is, affixes may attach only to the inside or outside of the initial or final phoneme or syllable, or to either side of the head, the accented syllable.[8] This purely morphological definition of affixation is far more accurate than structural descriptions, and does not require word structure or any sort of affix movement. *Circumfixation*, such as Indonesian *ke . . . -an* as *besar* 'big' : *ke-besar-an* 'bigness, greatness', is merely extended exponence involving a prefix and a suffix simultaneously.

8.2.2 Apophony (stem mutation, revoweling)   This type of stem modification is well attested in Semitic languages. Lexical items in those languages comprise consonants only, and vowels are used to mark morphological functions. The (Algerian) Arabic stem for 'write' is **ktb-*, and the derivate for 'book' is *ktaab*, while that for 'writer' is *kaatəb*. This type of morphological modification, like subtraction and metathesis, raises the question of the limits on modification of the phonological representation of the base: to what extent may the base be corrupted before it becomes unrecognizable? This is another open question in morphology.

8.2.3 Conversion   Transposing a lexeme from one category to another without affixation is sometimes called *conversion*. The evidence weighs against a separate operation of conversion, however, for we find precisely the same semantic relations between conversional pairs as between derivational pairs. Thus for every conversion *to dry, to wet, to empty* we find at least an equal number of affixed derivates with the same relation: *to shorten, to normalize, to domesticate*. Moreover, precisely those stems which affix are precluded from conversion (*to *short, *normal, *domestic*), and precisely those which convert are precluded from affixation: *to *endry, *wetten, *emptify*.[9] The simpler account of such forms is that those without affixation are null marked variants of the same derivation which is otherwise marked by a variety of affixes.

8.2.4 Paradigmatic derivation   A common means of marking lexical derivation is shifting the base from one nominal declension class to another, with or without a derivational marker. Thus, in Swahili, diminutives are formed by shifting nouns to noun class 3: for example, *m-lango* 'door' (class 2) : *ki-lango* 'little door' (class 3), *m-lima* 'mountain' : *ki-lima* 'hill'. Feminine agentives in Russian are usually derived from masculines of declension I (= noun class 1) by adding a declension II (= noun class 2) suffix: for example, *učitel'* 'teacher' : *učitel'-nic-a*, where the final *-a* indicates declension II. However, the processes of adding the suffix and changing the declensional paradigm must be independent, since the latter may apply without the former: *rab* (masc., declension I) : *rab-a* (fem., declension II) 'slave', *suprug* (masc., declension I) : *suprug-a* (fem., declension II) 'spouse'.

8.2.5 Prosodic modification A derivational function may be marked by simply shifting the accent of a word or modifying the intonation, perhaps a variant of apophony. Thus, in English, it is common to indicate the objective (resultative) nominalization by shifting accent from the stem to the prefix: for example, *survéy : súrvey, suspéct : súspect*. The process is productive with verbs prefixed by *re-*: *rewríte : réwrite, remáke : rémake*. The morpheme here seems to be the process of shifting the accent from one syllable to another.

8.2.6 Reduplication In addition to attaching phonologically specified affixes to a stem, derivation is often marked by the full or partial reduplication of a part of the stem attached to it. Indonesian forms adverbs from all categories by completely reduplicating them: *kira* 'guess' : *kira-kira* 'approximately', *pagi* 'morning' : *pagi-pagi* 'in the morning'. Reduplication may be combined with various types of affixation as in Indonesian *anak* 'child' : *ke-anak-anak-an* 'childish'.

8.3 Productivity and allomorphic variation

Proponents of *Natural Morphology* (NM) have long noted that not all the modes of stem modification surveyed in the previous section are equally productive (Dressler et al. 1987); some means of morphological marking are more productive than others. Aronoff (1976) first noted that affixes such as the English suffixes *-ing* and *-ness* (e.g. *deriding, kindness*), which are *transparent*, in that they involve no allomorphy, tend to be more productive and more predictable than those which do induce allomorphy: for example, *-ion* and *-ity* (e.g. *deride : derision*, but *ride : *rision; curious : curiosity*, but *spurious : *spuriosity*).

NM argues that the isomorphic linguistic sign is the linguistic ideal, and that the further a morpheme deviates from this ideal, the more difficult it is for languages to sustain it. If the subjective nominalization changes or adds semantic material to the underlying base, it should add phonological material to the stem iconically and transparently. English derivates like *bak-er, resid-ent, escap-ee* then are more natural, and thus more likely to be productive, than unmarkered derivates like (a) *cook, guide, bore*. Opaque affixes which cause or require phonological adjustments such as the Latinate suffixes mentioned above should be less productive inter- and intralinguistically. Zero and empty morphology should be rare, and subtractive morphology nonexistent for the same reasons.

NM offers a means of uniting Word Syntax and processual morphology. Notice that while NM offers the isomorphic morpheme as the ideal, it implicitly admits the sorts of asymmetrical variations that processual morphology is designed to explain. Processual morphology, however, holds that this ideal is restricted to lexemes in the lexicon. Moreover, it has no inherent account of why transparent, symmetrical markers seem to be more productive than asymmetrical ones. If the predictions of NM hold, they could make a major contribution toward unifying the two major approaches to derivational morphology discussed in this chapter.

9 Conclusion

Derivational morphology differs from inflectional morphology in that it provides new lexical names for objects, relations, and properties in the world. Lexical names may be combined in syntactic constructions to generate descriptions of the real world in speech, or may be used to label objects in the real world: for example, *bakery, careful, occupied, slippery, gentlemen*. The grammatical relations upon which derivation operates seem to be the same as those found in inflection; the difference is that these relations hold between the derivate and its base in derivation, rather than between two different phrases in syntax. Consider *the cookie-baker bakes cookies*, for instance. The noun *cookie-baker* exhibits internal subject and object relations between the derivate and its constituent parts. The same relations hold in the sentence between the subject, *cookie-baker*, the object, *cookies*, and the verb. The semantic difference between the two uses is that *cookie-baker* is the name of a semantic category while the sentence is a description of a specific event. We would expect inflectional means of marking the subject and object relations in the sentence but derivational means of marking it in the derived compound.

Evidence supports the conclusion that morpholexical derivation and phonological realization are two discrete processes executed by autonomous components. Lexical rules apparently provide for derivation, and either the phonological component or a separate morphological component is responsible for phonological realization. The Split Morphology Hypothesis notwithstanding, it is possible that a single autonomous spellout component accounts for inflectional and derivational morphological realization. If the lexicon and syntax appropriately distinguish morpholexical features and morphosyntactic features, derivation and inflection may be distinguished despite the fact that both operate over the same morphological categories, realized phonologically by the same spellout component.

NOTES

1 Bybee (1985) is one of several morphologists to take issue with the Lexicalist position itself. She argues that derivational and inflectional processes form a scale along which rules are more or less derivational and inflectional. A rule's position along this scale is determined by its

generality and *relevance*. Tense, for example, is more general than the functions of prefixes like *trans-* and *re-* since it applies to all verbs. Tense, on the other hand, is more relevant to verbs than is person, since it directly modifies the meaning of the verb, while person simply denotes an argument of the verb. The less general and more relevant the meaning of a morphological operation, the more "derivational" it is; the more general and less relevant, the more "inflectional" it is. Tense by this measure is less derivational than verbal prefix functions, but more so than person. No strict division between the two may be made, however, according to Bybee.

2 Beard (1995: 286–9) offers a contemporary account of phrasal adjectives as an extragrammatical phenomenon.

3 Chomsky's Minimalist Program (Chomsky 1995b) as of the moment provides no theory of derivation, hence any comment would be premature. However, since words are copied from the lexicon "fully inflected," it would seem that Minimalism currently makes no distinction between either derivation and inflection or lexemes and grammatical morphemes. To the extent that this observation is accurate, Minimalism is susceptible to the problems with these assumptions discussed here.

4 Although Bybee exemplifies her hypothesis with inflectional categories, she makes it clear that she intends it to extend to derivation, which, in her view,

is merely the other end of the same continuum (see n. 1).

5 Note that the following discussion does not apply to *grammatical gender*, which amounts to no more than *lexical class* (Halle 1989).

6 Only two accounts of the parallel between inflectional and derivational categories have been suggested. According to Botha's *Base Rule Theory* (Botha 1981, Beard 1981), both lexical and syntactic rules operate on deep structures, which must contain these functions. Borer (1988) argues for a single word formation component which operates at two levels, deep and surface structure. At present it is not clear whether these two approaches differ in any essentials.

7 Beard (1993) argues that higher productivity is also facilitated by "dual origin." Subjective and objective nominalization e.g. may be derived either by functional derivation or by transposition. The semantic interpretation is identical in either case; however, if the desired output is blocked for any reason via one derivational type, another means of derivation, which may not be blocked, is available in these cases.

8 Clitics may be attached at correlate points of a phrase, i.e. either side of the phrasal head or either side of a peripheral word or constituent (see Halpern, CLITICS).

9 A few sporadic examples of derivation–"conversion" pairs may be found, e.g. *to clear* : *clarify*, *winter* : *winterize*. However, such pairs are rare and semantically unpredictable, and may be explained as easily in terms of zero morphology.

3 Compounding

NIGEL FABB

1 Overview

A compound is a word which consists of two or more words. For example, the Malay compound *mata-hari* 'sun' is a word which consists of two words: *mata* 'eye' and *hari* 'day'. Compounds are subject to phonological and morphological processes, which may be specific to compounds or may be shared with other structures, whether derived words or phrases; we explore some of these, and their implications, in this chapter. The words in a compound retain a meaning similar to their meaning as isolated words, but with certain restrictions; for example, a noun in a compound will have a generic rather than a referential function: as Downing (1977) puts it, not every man who takes out the garbage is a *garbage man*.

1.1 Structure and interpretation

The meaning of a compound is usually to some extent compositional, though it is often not predictable. For example, *popcorn* is a kind of corn which pops; once you know the meaning, it is possible to see how the parts contribute to the whole – but if you do not know the meaning of the whole, you are not certain to guess it by looking at the meaning of the parts. This lack of predictability arises mainly from two characteristics of compounds: (a) compounds are subject to processes of semantic drift, which can include metonymy, so that a *redhead* is a person who has red hair; (b) there are many possible semantic relations between the parts in a compound, as between the parts in a sentence, but unlike a sentence, in a compound, case, prepositions and structural position are not available to clarify the semantic relation.

1.1.1 Endocentric and exocentric compounds Compounds which have a head are called 'endocentric compounds'. A head of a compound has similar characteristics to the head of a phrase: it represents the core meaning of the constituent, and it is of the same word class. For example, in *sneak-thief*, *thief* is the head (a sneak-thief is a kind of thief; *thief* and *sneak-thief* are both nouns). Compounds without a head are called 'exocentric compounds' or 'bahuvrihi compounds' (the Sanskrit name). The distinction between endocentric and exocentric compounds is sometimes a matter of interpretation, and is often of little relevance; for example, whether you think *greenhouse* is an endocentric or exocentric compound depends on whether you think it is a kind of house. The major interest in the head of a compound relates to the fact that where there is a clear head, its position seems to be constrained; endocentric compounds tend to have heads in a language systematically on either the right (e.g. English) or left (e.g. Vietnamese, French).

1.1.2 Co-ordinate compounds There is a third kind of compound, where there is some reason to think of both words as equally sharing head-like characteristics, as in *student-prince* (both a student and a prince); these are called 'appositional' or 'co-ordinate' or 'dvandva' (the Sanskrit name) compounds. Co-ordinate compounds can be a combination of synonyms (example from Haitian):

toro-bèf   (*bull-cow*) 'male cow'

a combination of antonyms (example from French):

aigre-doux   (*sour-sweet*)

or a combination of parallel things (example from Malayalam):

acchanammamaaīə   (*father-mother-pl.*) 'parents'

Co-ordinate compounds can have special characteristics in a language. For example, in Mandarin, co-ordinate compounds behave differently in terms of theta-assignment from (endocentric) resultative verb compounds. And in Malayalam, co-ordinate compounds are not affected by gemination processes which other compounds undergo (see section 5.2).

1.1.3 The semantic relations between the parts The semantic relations between the parts of a compound can often be understood in terms of modification; this is true even for some exocentric compounds like *redhead*. Modifier–modifiee relations are often found in compounds which resemble equivalent phrases; this is true, for example, of English AN%N[1] compounds and many Mandarin compounds (see Anderson 1985b). It is not always the case, though; the French compound *est-allemand* (East German) corresponds to a phrase *allemand de l'est* (German from the East). In addition, many compounds manifest relations which can be interpreted as predicator–argument relations, as in *sunrise* or *pull-chain*. Note that in *pull-chain, chain* can be interpreted as an argument of *pull*, and at the same time *pull* can be interpreted as a modifier of *chain*.

1.1.4 Transparency: interpretive and formal   The transparency and predictability of a compound are sometimes correlated with its structural transparency. For example, in languages with two distinct types of compound where one is more interpretively transparent than the other, the less interpretively transparent type will often be subject to greater phonological or morphological modification. A diachronic loss of transparency (both formal and interpretive) can be seen in the process whereby a part of a compound becomes an affix, as in the development of English -*like* as the second part of a compound to become the derivational suffix -*ly*.

1.2 Types of compound

Accounts of compounds have divided them into classes. Some of these – such as the exocentric, endocentric and appositional types, or the various interpretive types (modifier–modifiee, complement–predicator, etc.) – are widespread across languages. Then there are compound types which are language- or language-family-specific, such as the Japanese postsyntactic compounds (4.3), Hebrew construct state nominals (4.2), or Mandarin resultative verb compounds (4.1). Other types of compounds are found intermittently; these include synthetic compounds (section 1.2.1), incorporation compounds (section 1.2.2) and reduplication compounds (section 1.2.3).

1.2.1 Synthetic (verbal) compounds   The synthetic compound (also called 'verbal compound') is characterized by a co-occurrence of particular formal characteristics with particular restrictions on interpretation. Not all languages have synthetic compounds (e.g. English does, but French does not). The formal characteristic is that a synthetic compound has as its head a derived word consisting of a verb plus one of a set of affixes (many writers on English restrict this to agentive -*er*, nominal and adjectival -*ing*, and the passive adjectival -*en*). Thus the following are formally characterized as synthetic compounds:

> expert-test-ed
> checker-play-ing (as an adjective: a checker-playing king)
> window-clean-ing (as a noun)
> meat-eat-er

(There is some disagreement about whether other affixes should also be included, so that *slum-clear-ance* for example would be a synthetic compound.) Compounds with this structure are subject to various restrictions (summarized by Roeper and Siegel 1978), most prominent of which is that the left-hand member must be interpreted as equivalent to a syntactic 'first sister' of the right-hand member. We discuss this in section 3.2. There have been many accounts of synthetic compounds, including Roeper and Siegel 1978, Selkirk 1982, Lieber 1983, Fabb 1984, Botha 1981 on Afrikaans, and Brousseau 1988 on Fon; see also section 2.1.2. Many of the relevant arguments are summarized in Spencer 1991.

1.2.2 Incorporation compounds In some languages, incorporation words resemble compounds: for example, both a verb and an incorporated noun may exist as independent words. Bybee (1985) comments on this, but suggests that even where the two parts may be independently attested words, an incorporation word may differ from a compound in certain ways. This includes phonological or morphological differences between incorporated and free forms of a word. (In fact, as we have seen, this is true also of some compound processes; e.g. segment loss, which is found in Tiwi incorporation words, is found also in ASL compounds.) Another difference which Bybee suggests may distinguish incorporation from compounding processes is that the incorporation of a word may depend on its semantic class. For example, in Pawnee it is mainly body part words which are incorporated, while various kinds of name are not (such as personal names, kinship terms, names of particular species of tree, etc.). It is possible that compounding is not restricted in this way; as we will see, semantic restrictions on compounding tend to be in terms of the relation between the parts rather than in terms of the individual meanings of the parts.

1.2.3 Repetition compounds Whole-word reduplication is sometimes described as a compounding process, because each part of the resulting word corresponds to an independently attested word. Steever (1988), for example, describes as compounds Tamil words which are generated through reduplication: *vantu* 'coming' is reduplicated as *vantu-vantu* 'coming time and again'. In another type of Tamil reduplicated compound, the second word is slightly modified: *viyāparam* 'business' becomes *viyāparam-kiyāparam* 'business and such'. English examples of this type of compound include words like *higgledy-piggledy*, *hotchpotch*, and so on.

1.3 Compounds which contain 'bound words'

In a prototypical compound, both parts are independently attested as words. However, it is possible to find words which can be parsed into an independently attested word plus another morpheme which is not an independently attested word but also does not appear to be an affix (see Aronoff 1976). Here are some examples from English (unattested part italicized):

church-*goer*   iron*monger*   *tele*vision   *cran*berry

The part which is not attested as an isolated word is sometimes found in other words as well; in some cases it may *become* an attested word: for example, *telly*

(= television). These parts fail to resemble affixes morphologically (they are relatively unproductive compared to most affixes), and there is no good evidence on phonological grounds for considering them to be affixes. They are also unlike affixes semantically; judging by their contribution to the word's meaning, they have lexical rather than grammatical meanings. A similar example from standard Tamil (Steever 1988) is the form *nāḷ* 'goodness', which is not independently attested, but can be found in compound nouns such as *nalla-nāḷ* 'good-day'.

2 The structure of compounds

One thing that is reasonably clear about the structure of compounds is that they contain two words, and the distinctness of these two components is visible to various rules. Other aspects of structure are not so obvious, however: in the order of the parts regulated by rules 2.1, are their word classes visible to any rules 2.2, and are three-word compounds hierarchically structured (2.3)?

2.1 Directionality

A compound can be 'directional' in two senses. One sense involves the position of the head: whether on the right or the left. The other sense involves the direction of the relation between the parts of the compound: the direction of modification in a noun–noun compound (e.g. in *log cabin* modification is rightwards) or the direction of complementation in a verb-based compound (e.g. in *push-bike* complementation is rightwards). Notice that the two senses of directionality can be independent, because a compound can have internal modification or complementation without having a head: *killjoy* has no head, but it does have a predicator–complement order. This is an important descriptive issue; some accounts assume that a modifier–modifee or predicator–argument relation inside a compound is itself evidence that part of the compound is a head. To the extent that there are any useful claims about directionality of the head to be made, it is probably best to focus on the narrowest definition of head (which involves a semantic link between head and whole); see Brousseau 1988 for arguments to this effect.

2.1.1 The location of the head   In English, the head of an endocentric word is on the right. In French, the head is on the left (as in *bal masqué*, 'masked ball'). It has been argued (e.g. by DiSciullo and Williams 1987) that all true endocentric compounds are right-headed, and that any left-headed compounds should be considered as exceptions – for example, as phrases which have been reanalysed as words. This is not a widely accepted account (it is based on the controversial Right-Hand Head rule of Williams 1981b).

2.1.2 *An argument about directionality and synthetic compounds*

Brousseau suggests that the direction of relations inside a compound is responsible for determining whether a language is able to have synthetic compounds. She suggests that in a synthetic compound, the non-head must modify the head, and be a complement of the head. This means that the direction of modification must be opposite to the direction of complementation:

> —modifies→
>   meat-eater
> ←takes as complement—

Because in English, the directions of complement taking and modification are opposed, synthetic compounds are possible (the same is true of Fon). In French and Haitian (a Fon–French creole), on the other hand, both modification and complementation are leftward, and so the particular conditions which allow a synthetic compound are absent – hence there are no synthetic compounds in these languages.

2.2 *The word classes of the component words*

Another question which must be asked about the structure of compounds is whether the class of the component words is relevant, or whether word class is lost when the words are formed into a compound. 'Relevant' would mean, for example, visibility of word class to a class-sensitive phonological or morphological rule. Little attention has been focused on this question; clearly some compound-internal affixation rules are class-sensitive (but this might be because they are added before the compound is formed).

Most of the attention to word class in a compound has focused on the attested word-class structures of compounds in a language. For example, in Punjabi (Akhtar 1992) there are large numbers of compounds involving a combination NN, AN, AA, NV and VV, but none with a structure VA, and very few with a structure VN. Selkirk (1982) suggests that these facts about a language are best expressed by compound-specific rewriting rules analogous to phrase-structure rules. This approach has been adopted by many people, and is useful as a descriptive device. However, there are some fundamental differences between structure-building rules for compounds and structure-building rules for phrases:

(a)   There is no true equivalent of X-bar theory as a constraint on compound-building rules. Most obviously, compounds need not have a head. More generally, it is hard to find structural generalizations across compound structures analogous to the generalizations expressed by X-bar theory for phrases.

(b)   Compound-building rules would rarely be recursive. In English, for example, the only clearly recursive type is the NN%N combination.

(c)   There is a problem about productivity. Phrase-structure rules are fully productive; each rule can underlie an infinite number of phrases (partly because of recursion). But some rules for building compounds are manifested by very few actual compounds. Selkirk recognizes this, and distinguishes rule-built compounds from non-rule-built compounds. Perhaps, though, there is an alternative way of explaining the prevalence of certain compound types along functional rather than formal lines. Thus, in English, the prevalence of NN%N and AN%N types might be because of a functional need for compound nouns before other word classes, and because these have a modifier–modifee structure which is easily interpreted. This is a complex problem which requires metatheoretical decisions about the place of functional considerations and the meaning of productivity.

2.3 *Subconstituency in three (or more) word compounds*

Where compounds consist of three or more words, the compound can sometimes be interpreted by breaking it down into subconstituents. This is true, for example, of *chicken-leg-dinner*, which is interpreted by taking *chicken-leg* as a subcompound within the larger compound. In some cases, ambiguity arises from the possibility of two alternative groupings of words, as in *American history teacher* (a history teacher who is American or a teacher of American history). This fact about interpretation raises the question of whether three-or-more-word compounds might perhaps have a subconstituent (hierarchical) structure like a phrase (i.e. (b) or (c) rather than the flat structure (a)).

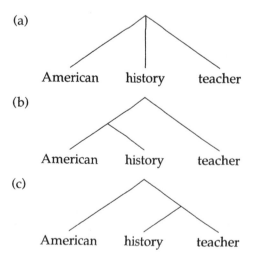

It is not obvious that the interpretive facts alone demonstrate the presence of a complex structure. The interpretive rules might simply pick any pair of adjacent units and make them into a unit, taking a 'syntactic' structure like (a) and building a 'semantic' structure like (b) or (c). Compare hierarchical *phrase* structure, which pre-exists any interpretive strategy, as can be shown by the sensitivity of syntactic processes (such as binding theory) to constituent structure. But compounds are relatively inert compared to syntactic constituents (no movement, anaphoric coindexing, etc.), so it is harder to find supporting evidence for complex constituent structure.

As we will see (section 5.1.1), there is some evidence in English from the stressing of four-word compounds that the compound-specific stress rules are sensitive to a subconstituent structure, and hence that such structure exists outside the interpretive component. Turkish also presents evidence for sub-constituent structure in hierarchically interpreted compounds (Spencer 1991). The 'indefinite izafet compound' has the structure Noun + Noun-poss. when it consists of two words. The three-part compound has one of two types of structure, each corresponding to a different interpretation of its hierarchical structure (as bracketed):

[Noun + Noun-poss.] + Noun-poss.
Noun + [Noun + Noun-poss.]

Here the placement of the possessive affix is sensitive to hierarchical structure.

Most of the multiple-word compounds which are cited (particularly those cited as hierarchical compounds) tend to be combinations of nouns. This suggests that if there are structure-building rules for compounds, as discussed in the previous section, they are not generally recursive.

Note that sometimes a compound can be interpreted as having an internal subconstituency, without that subconstituent being an attested word. An example from Fon (Brousseau 1988) is:

gàn-ɡɔ̀-kɛ̀n   NNN%N money-stomach-cord = money belt

This compound is presumably interpreted as N[NN], but the [NN] sub-constituent does not exist as an independent word. This is not necessarily a strong argument against a hierarchical structure in this case, however, because there are also many examples of two-word compounds where one 'word' is not independently attested.

Note that some multiple-word compounds are not interpreted as having a hierarchical structure; this is true particularly of dvandva compounds such as the following from Tamil:

vīra-tīra-cakacaṅ-kaḷ (*courage-bravery-valour-pl.*) 'courage, bravery and valour'

An example of a compound which mixes non-hierarchical with hierarchical interpretation is the following, from Mandarin:

jī-yā-yú-ròu = 'animal foodstuffs' (i.e. chicken-duck-fish-meat)

Interpretively the structure is [[chicken + duck + fish] meat].

2.3.1 Hierarchies which include non-word components   A three-member compound need not contain three words. For example, a morpheme may appear between two words in a compound or at one end of a compound. It has been argued by a number of writers that in (English) synthetic compounds, the suffix is a third constituent of the compound; synthetic compounds on this analysis have a hierarchical structure such as [[meat-eat]-er].

3 The interpretation of compounds: interpretive gaps

Extensive descriptive work has been undertaken on the semantic relations holding between the components of English compounds (see e.g. Levi 1978, Warren 1978). An interesting theme that arises from some of this work is the possibility that there are certain gaps: semantic relations between the parts of a word which are possible in principle, but are not attested in practice. In this section we look at two such gaps in English compounds.

3.1 The missing goal

One of the commonest kinds of compound in English is the NN%N type. Many different relations can be interpreted as holding between the two members of such a compound. The interesting question in these cases is whether any relationships are not attested; in surveys of NN%N compounds, both Downing (1977) and Warren (1978) found that while source (something moved away from) was attested, goal (something moved towards) was only marginally attested. Warren found only fourteen potential examples out of 3,994 compounds, and suggests that these may not even be true examples of 'goal' compounds. In her list of relations between the parts of nominal compounds, Levi (1978) has 'from' (e.g. *store-clothes*) but not 'to'.

The same gap can be seen in other compounds; for example, while we find VN%N compounds like *print-shop* (a shop where printing takes place), there are no compounds like *go-place* (meaning a place to which someone goes). This gap also appears in synthetic compounds: *heaven-sent* can be interpreted only as sent *from* heaven, not sent *to* heaven. Note that apparent goal compounds like *church-goer* actually mean 'someone who attends church' (not someone who moves towards church); similarly, *sea-going* means 'going on the sea' (not *to* the sea).

3.2 Synthetic compounds in English: the absence of 'subject'

In a synthetic compound, the crucial interpretive restriction is that the left-hand word (a noun, adverb or adjective) must be interpretable as a complement of the right-hand word (and must *not* be interpretable as an external argument or subject). In effect, synthetic compounds with *-ing* or *-er* are like reversed active verb phrases with equivalent components (play checkers > checker-playing), while synthetic compounds with passive *-en* are like reversed passive verb phrases (tested by experts > expert tested). Synthetic compounds thus differ from other compounds (sometimes called 'root compounds'); hence while **bird-singing* is excluded, there is a compound *bird-song* where the left-hand member is interpretable as the subject of the right-hand member.

Synthetic compounds are interesting because the rules for their interpretation seem to be related to rules for building the meaning of sentences (e.g. the assignment of thematic roles to particular positions in a sentence, depending on the active or passive nature of the verb).

3.3 Ways of explaining interpretive gaps

Interpretive gaps in compounds could in principle be explained in one of three ways:

(a)   Constrain the compound-building rules to make them sensitive to interpretation-relevant aspects such as thematic relations. Levi (1978) takes this approach within a Generative Semantics framework, for compound nouns. This is also the approach taken by Roeper and Siegel (1978) in an Extended Standard Theory framework; they build synthetic compounds by a special (transformational) rule which takes a combination of a verb and a subcategorized complement as input. The gaps exist because there is no possibility of building synthetic compounds which have a verb combined with a non-subcategorized argument such as its subject. But Roeper and Siegel's approach (in particular) runs into a problem. Consider, for example, the compound *bird-singing*. This cannot be built by the synthetic-compound-building rule, because it combines the verb with a non-subcategorized argument (its subject). But nothing stops it being built by an alternative rule – the root-compound-building rule, which takes two nouns and combines them (*bird + singing*). This rule is not subject to thematic constraints, as can be seen in subject–predicate compounds like *sunrise*. So whatever rules out *bird-singing* <u>as a root compound</u> is clearly not associated with the compound-building rules.

(b)   Instead, it may be that the subject is ruled out by some filter which looks at the compound, and if it has the structure of a synthetic compound, applies certain constraints on interpretation to it. This would differentiate root from synthetic compounds not in how they are built, but in their surface form.

(c)   A third possible approach would be to explain interpretive gaps in compounds in terms of general constraints on the possible meanings of a word (see Carter 1976). Such an approach does not necessarily require that compound-internal thematic relations be specified, because these relations are not explicitly referred to. This approach might provide an explanation of the 'goal' gap. Note that this gap is found also in non-compound word formation: Hale and Keyser (1992) point out that while there is a verb *shelve*, meaning 'put on a shelf', there is no verb *church*, meaning 'go to church'. It may be that a meaning of 'movement towards' is incompatible with some aspect of possible word meaning. For example, Downing (1977) comments that 'unambiguously fortuitous or temporary relationships' are ruled out in favour of generic or habitual relationships. Perhaps 'movement towards' is ruled out in general because it is not usually a generic or habitual relationship: in this light, it is interesting to compare 'source' (movement from) with 'goal' (movement towards). The source of something remains a stable and permanent property of that thing; the goal of something is its goal only while it is travelling towards it.

4 Compounds and syntax

In this section we look at some language (or language-family)-specific compound types which have an internal structure open to syntactic manipulation and visible to syntactic processes. Incorporation compounds are a clear example, and synthetic compounds have also been argued to have such a structure (e.g. by Fabb 1988). There are two complicating factors when considering the 'syntactic' aspects of compounds.

One is that compounds tend to have relatively fixed meanings, so that it is difficult, for example, to modify them; the question of syntax vs morphology may be irrelevant here. Thus, for example, the ASL compound 'blue-spot' (= bruise) cannot be morphologically modified to '*darkblue-spot' (?= bad bruise); and the French compound *garde-malade* (= nurse) cannot be syntactically modified to *garde-bien-malade* (?= good nurse).

The second problem relates to the possibility that some compounds are the result of lexicalization of phrases. Thus, while in English it is generally impossible to have *the* inside a compound, there is a word *middle of the road* which looks like a compound but may best be analysed as a lexicalized phrase; the same can be said for many French compounds such as *pomme-de-terre* (= potato) or *trompe-l'œil* (= illusion), both of which contain typically syntactic components, the preposition *de* or the article *l'*. Compounds containing *and*, such as *foot-and-mouth disease* may perhaps be dealt with by claiming lexicalization of a phrase; or it may simply be that co-ordination can involve parts of words with no syntactic implications (see Sproat 1985 and Bates 1988 for different positions on this).

4.1 *Mandarin resultative verb compounds*

Y-F. Li (1990) discusses resultative verb compounds in Mandarin, which have a VV%V structure:

Baoyu qu-lei-le ma
Baoyu ride-tired-asp horse
'Baoyu rode a horse (and as a result it/Baoyu got) tired'

The resultative verb compound here is *qu-lei*. The first verb describes an action 'ride'; the second verb characterizes the result of that action as a state, 'tired', of the compound verb's subject (Baoyu) or object (that horse). The compound verb thus inherits theta-role-assigning properties from the component verbs. This is one reason for thinking that the internal structure of the compound may be visible in the syntax. Another reason comes from the fact that the first verb can be duplicated and followed by the object, so that the above sentence has this as an alternative form:

Baoyu qu ma qu-lei-le

A third reason for assuming syntactic visibility is that it is possible to modify the compound by inserting *de* or *bu* between the two verbs; the particles add the meaning 'can' or 'cannot' respectively (see Anderson 1985b).

Li suggests that the identification of the first verb as the head of the resultative verb compound has important consequences. He compares the resultative verb compound with a co-ordinate VV%V compound type. In the resultative verb compound, only the first verb must assign its external argument to the subject of the sentence, because only the first verb is the head of the compound word; the second word is free to assign its external argument to the subject or the object in the sentence, resulting in the ambiguity illustrated above. In a co-ordinate compound, however, both verbs must assign their external argument to the subject of the sentence, because they are both heads of the compound word (hence the ambiguities found in the resultative verb compound are not available to co-ordinate compounds).

4.2 *Hebrew construct state nominals*

Borer (1988) distinguishes two kinds of multi-word words in Hebrew, construct state nominals:

ca9if ha-yaldá   (*scarf the-girl*) 'the girl's scarf'

and compounds:

beyt xolím   (*house sicks*) 'hospital'

The two kinds of word can be seen as two kinds of compound. Both kinds of compound have word-like phonology (e.g. both have a single primary stress) and morphology (e.g. both are pluralized in the same way). Neither compound can be extracted from. The difference between them is that construct state nominals are more transparent interpretively and syntactically than other compounds; for example, definiteness and plurality on the components of a construct state nominal are taken into account by sentence-interpretation rules. Borer argues that the distinction should be achieved by having word-formation rules in the lexicon (to build ordinary compounds) or in the syntax (to build construct state nominals). A word built in the syntax will have its components visible to syntactic processes.

4.3 Japanese post-syntactic compounds

Shibatani and Kageyama (1988) argue that Japanese has lexical and postsyntactic compounds. A postsyntactic compound is 'postsyntactic' because it appears to consist of the turning of syntactic material into a compound: it consists of a noun phrase followed by a verbal noun which takes it as a complement (i.e. the compound is subject to a kind of first-sister constraint, and so cannot take a scrambled sentence as input). Here is an example of such a compound:

zikken-syuuryoo-go
experiment-finish-after = 'after the experiment was completed'

Postsyntactic compounds are interpretively transparent. They are also transparent to syntactic processes such as anaphoric co-reference, and they can contain demonstratives and honorifics. They do not have the tonal pattern associated with lexical words. Despite these syntactic characteristics, Shibatani and Kageyama argue that the constituents as a whole are words (i.e. compounds), because the case particle (following the NP) is omitted, there is no tense on the verbal element, and the compound cannot be interrupted by an adverb. Like Borer, they thus allow compounds to be built at different levels (in this case, lexicon and PF).

5 Phonological and morphological processes and compounds

Compounds resemble derived words in some ways, and resemble phrasal combinations in other ways. This is true also of the phonological and morphological processes which apply to compounds. For example, some phonological processes group compounds with derived words; others group compounds with phrases; and others isolate compounds as a distinct class. Most recent discussions of these groupings have been in a Lexical Morphology/Phonology framework, and have been used to argue for a level-ordering of morphological and phonological processes (see section 5.2 for an illustration).

5.1 Suprasegmental processes

5.1.1 Stress One of the most commonly cited compound-specific phonological rules is stress assignment. Compounds may be subject to a rule which places heavier stress on one word. In English, for example, the compound *big-foot* (the name of a monster) is differentiated from the phrase *big foot* by the heavier stressing of *big* relative to *foot* in the compound. (In English and Danish, the first word is stressed; in Italian and Spanish, the second word.) Even where there is not a compound-specific stress rule, compounds can still show interesting stress properties. For example, Anderson (1985b) shows that in Mandarin, contrastive stress 'sees' a compound as a single word, so there is only one place in the compound where contrastive stress can be placed; by comparison, a two-word phrase can have contrastive stress on either word.

The stress pattern of English compounds has been the source of extensive analysis. It is relevant primarily in three areas:

(a) The stress pattern of compounds may indicate the presence of hierarchical structure inside the compound. Since most versions of the compound stress rule apply to two-word compounds, it is interesting to see what happens to the stress in larger compounds. In these, there seems to be clear evidence that stress assignment recognizes internal subcomponents; for example, in a four-word compound like *student essay récord book*, the greatest stress is on *record* because a rule recognizes the presence of a subconstituent *record book* and places extra stress here. Note that a different hierarchical structure (corresponding to a different hierarchy of interpretation) involves a different stress pattern, as in *American hístory teacher association*. This is one of the few pieces of evidence that multi-word compounds in English have a complex internal formal structure.

(b) Compounds must be handled by some system of rules for stress assignment in English. Accounts vary in the extent to which they have rules specific to compounds. Chomsky and Halle (1968) have a separate Compound Rule. Breaking with this tradition, Liberman and Prince (1977) adapt the Lexical Category Prominence Rule so that it applies to derived words and compounds; similarly Halle and Vergnaud (1987) draw attention to the close similarity between rules for compounds and rules for derived words. The question of which rules apply to stress in compounds is relevant to questions of ordering in the lexicon (e.g. level-ordering). This extends beyond English: Shaw (1985) shows that the Dakota 'syntactic compounds' have two major stresses, while the 'lexical compounds' have one major stress; she explains this by having the compounds formed at different levels in a level-ordered lexicon, with stress rules also level-ordered.

(c)   English compounds do not all have initial stress; examples of level- and final-stressed compounds are *knee-déep* and *apprentice-wélder* respectively. This opens up the possibility that there are structural (or interpretive) characteristics of compounds, which stress rules are sensitive to. Bates (1988), for example, develops an analysis in which the English compound stress rules are sensitive to whether an initial adjective is predicative (initial stress) or not (final stress). Analyses along these lines provide potential evidence for internal structure in a compound (evidence which is otherwise sparse, see section 2.3). Note that the initial/final stress issue is in some cases a matter of dialectal difference; compare British English *ice-créam* and *hot dóg* with American English *íce-cream* and *hót dog*.

5.1.2 Other suprasegmental processes   While stress is the most commonly cited compound-specific suprasegmental process, other such processes may differentiate compounds from derived words or phrasal combinations. In many Mandarin Chinese compounds the second element loses stress because it first loses its tone (Anderson 1985b). In Fon, nasalization occurs in a suffix, but not in the second word in a compound (Brousseau 1988). And Klima and Bellugi (1979) argue that in American Sign Language, temporal rhythm is analogous to stress; a compound word and a simple word take more or less the same amount of time to produce, because in a compound word, the first word is made significantly more quickly. Hence there is a compound-specific temporal reduction rule (cited in Liddell and Johnson 1986).

5.2 Phonological processes between the two words

Segmental phonological processes will tend to happen between two morphemes – either a word and an affix, or two words. There are examples of such processes which distinguish compounds from other combinations. In English, some phonological rules apply within derived words but not within compounds; M. Allen (1978) shows this for *beauty-parlour* vs *beauti-ful*. In Dakota (Shaw 1985) a different alliance can be found, with compounds patterning with derived words rather than phrases: 'lexical compounds' are subject to an epenthesis rule adding *a* to the end of the first word, which then feeds a continuant voicing rule; this rule is found also in derived words, but not in 'syntactic compounds'.

Malayalam (Mohanan 1982) provides a particularly complex picture of the visibility of compound structures to different phonological processes. Stem-final nasal deletion and stem-final vowel lengthening apply just to compounds. Other rules apply to both compounds and derived words (but not to sequences of words in a phrase), such as a vowel sandhi rule where two adjacent vowels are merged into one. A further complexity is that some rules apply only to a subset of the compounds: stem-final and stem-initial gemination of obstruents in Dravidian stems occurs in compounds with a modifier–modifiee structure ('subcompounds') but not in co-ordinate compounds. Mohanan uses these facts as evidence for a theory of level-ordered lexical phonology/morphology, along the following lines:

stratum	morphological processes	vowel sandhi	vowel lengthening	nasal deletion	gemination
1	derivation	yes			
2	subcompounding	yes	yes	yes	yes
3	co-compounding	yes	yes	yes	
4	inflection				

5.3 Segment loss

American Sign Language compounds tend to undergo more radical formal restructuring than most spoken language compounds, with loss of segments being a common feature of compound formation. For example, the compound translated as 'black-name' (meaning bad reputation) involves loss of one of the segments of the word for 'name' (which on its own consists of a sequence of two identical segments). Liddell and Johnson (1986) comment that in ASL 'the average compound has the same number of segments as the average simple sign'.

5.4 Morphemes and compounds

5.4.1 Compound-specific morphemes In some languages, a morpheme (with no independent meaning) may be inserted between the two words. This morpheme may bear a historical relation to some affix, but is synchronically found only in compounds. In German, for example, *s* or *en* may be inserted:

Schwan-en-gesang 'swan song'

5.4.2 Inflectional morphology There have been two lines of research focusing on whether an inflectional morpheme (e.g. marking plurality, case or tense) can be found on a component word inside a compound.

One approach (e.g. Kiparsky 1982b) focusing on the question of level-ordering of morphological processes, looks at the distinction between regular and irregular inflectional morphology, and asks whether irregular morphology is more likely to appear on a compound-internal word (because it precedes the compounding process) than regular morphology (which comes later than the compounding process). The evidence from English is not particularly clear. As predicted, regular inflection is lacking in some compounds like *footprints* (compare **foots-prints*), where irregular inflection is present in corresponding compounds like *teeth-marks*. But, *contra* predictions, sometimes regular inflection is present as in *arms race* where irregular inflection is missing as in *out-putted*.

The second line of enquiry focuses on the implications of having any inflection on a part of a compound, and whether this means that the internal structure of compounds is visible to the syntax (the answer to this depends on one's theory of inflection). For further discussion, see Anderson 1992: ch. 11. Questions about the visibility of inflection relate also to questions about the visibility of theta-assigning properties of subparts (as e.g. in Mandarin resultative compounds) and what this implies about the visibility of compound structure in syntax.

5.4.3 Derivational processes and compounds   Compounds on the whole tend not to undergo derivational processes. However, there are some fairly clear examples such as English *bowler-hatted*, which can only be interpreted as *bowler-hat + ed*. It may be that English synthetic compounds are the result either of a verb-final compound being affixed with *-ing*, *-er*, etc., or of a combination of derivation and affixation (as in Roeper and Siegel's (1978) compound formation rule). There has also been discussion of compounds such as *transformational grammarian*, which on interpretive grounds would seem to involve suffixation of *transformational grammar*; there are, however, other ways of dealing with these 'bracketing paradoxes' (see Spencer 1988b, e.g.). Liddell and Johnson (1986) show that in ASL a reduplication process adds the meaning of 'regularly' to a verb; this process reduplicates all of a compound verb (though this may be an inflectional process).

5.4.4 Clitics and compounds   Dakota postverbal clitics are attached in the lexicon (Shaw 1985). They attach to the first member of syntactic compounds, but not to the first member of lexical compounds.

6 Conclusion

Comparatively little theoretical work has been done on compounds. This is because compounds tend to be less phonologically or morphologically active than derived words, and less syntactically active than phrases: compounds are relatively inert. My view is that the three most interesting questions about compounds are as follows:

(a)   If there are compound-building rules, what form do they take? Are they recursive (i.e. building hierarchical structure), and do they take word class into account? Are compound-building rules based on a universally available rule type (i.e. is 'compound' a universal?).

(b) How do compound-building rules interact with other rules – or, put slightly differently, what aspects of compound structure are visible to what other processes, whether syntactic, morphological or phonological? It is particularly important here to show that a certain structural fact about a compound is visible to two distinct rules (e.g. Bates (1988) argues that compound stress rules and interpretive rules both 'see' that a particular modifier in a compound is predicative rather than attributive). The question of the interaction of compound-building rules with other rules has been discussed particularly in the level-ordered systems of lexical phonology and morphology.

(c) Are there interpretive gaps? Are some sorts of meaning not creatable by putting compounds together – and if so, is this because of compound-specific rules, or because of more general principles of possible word meaning?

NOTE

1 XY%Z is to be interpreted as: [XY] is a compound of word class Z.

4 Incorporation

DONNA B. GERDTS

1 Incorporation

Incorporation is the compounding of a word (typically a verb or preposition) with another element (typically a noun, pronoun, or adverb). The compound serves the combined syntactic function of both elements. This chapter focuses on noun incorporation, on which there exists a substantial literature. Much less is known about pronoun incorporation, due largely to the difficulty of distinguishing incorporation from agreement or cliticization. (See Halpern, CLITICS.) Other types of incorporation are rare. (See Muravyova, CHUKCHEE (PALEO-SIBERIAN) for various examples.)

Noun incorporation is the compounding of a noun stem and a verb (or adjective) to yield a complex form that serves as the predicate of a clause (Kroeber 1909, 1911; Sapir 1911; Mithun 1984). Compare sentences (1a), (2a), and (3a), where the object nominals are free-standing noun phrases, with sentences (1b), (2b), and (3b), where they are incorporated into the verb stem.

(1) Nahuatl (Sapir 1911)
    (a) ni-c-qua in nacatl.   (b) ni-*naca*-qua.
         I-it-eat   the flesh   *I-flesh-eat*
         'I eat the flesh.'   'I eat flesh.'

(2) Onondaga (H. Woodbury 1975)
    (a) waʔhahninú?   ne?   oyɛ́ʔkwaʔ.
         tns-he:it-buy-asp. nm. prtc. it-tobacco-n.s.g.
         'He bought the tobacco.'

    (b) waʔhayɛʔ*kwa*hní:nuʔ.
         tns-he:it-tobacco-buy-asp.
         'He bought (a kind of) tobacco.'

(3) Chukchee (Comrie 1992)
    (a) kupre-n nantəvatgʔan.   (b) *kopra*-ntəvatgʔat.
        net-ABS set   *net-set*
        'They set the net.'   'They set the net.'

The incorporated noun in each of the (b) sentences is clearly part of the same word as the verb stem. In (1b) and (2b) the noun appears between the agreement prefixes and the verb. In (3b) the noun undergoes word-level vowel harmony (*kupre* > *kopra*). The above examples also demonstrate that a noun stem, not a word, is incorporated. In Nahuatl the absolute suffix *-tl* appears on free-standing nouns (1a) but not incorporated nouns (1b). In Onondaga the nominal prefix *o-* and the final glottal stop appear only on free-standing nouns (2a). Furthermore, all of the above examples show that the incorporated noun does not take a determiner or case marker.

Pairs of examples like those above raise the question: when does a language use a free-standing noun and when does it use an incorporated noun? The noun + verb compound is used to express habitual or general activities or states. The noun is frequently generic and nonspecific in reference, although some languages, such as Southern Tiwa, allow specific nouns to be incorporated:

(4) Southern Tiwa (Allen et al. 1984)
    ti-seuan-mū-ban.
    1sg.:A-man-see-past
    'I saw the man.'

These nouns are nevertheless devoid of discourse focus. Thus, we see that incorporated nouns in most languages have a different discourse role from free-standing nouns. See Hopkins 1988, Merlan 1976, and Mithun 1984 for discussion of the discourse properties of noun incorporation.

Languages exhibiting noun incorporation place many restrictions on the nouns that can be, or must be, incorporated. H. Woodbury (1975) shows that only nouns that can be stripped down to a simple root can incorporate in Onondaga. Cross-linguistically we find that nouns that arise through nominalization or compounding do not incorporate. The constraints on object noun incorporation in Southern Tiwa (Allen et al. 1984) serve to illustrate the relevance of the semantic class of the nominal. Proper nouns do not incorporate in Southern Tiwa. Mardirussian (1975) posits this as a universal characteristic of noun incorporation. In contrast, inanimate nouns in Southern Tiwa must incorporate. Also, plural nonhuman animate nouns must incorporate. Singular nonhuman animate nouns and plural human nouns must incorporate if they are not modified. Singular human nouns obligatorily incorporate if there is a third-person subject. The above restrictions show that inanimate nouns incorporate more readily than animate nouns, and that nonhuman animate nouns incorporate more readily than human nouns. This hierarchy reflects the general cross-linguistic tendency for nouns that are higher in animacy to be more central to the discourse. The more salient a noun is, the less likely it is to be incorporated.

In some instances, the meaning of these noun + verb compounds may drift from a simple compositional one; that is, they are idiomatic:

(5)   Mohawk (Hopkins 1988)
      tehanuhwarawv́:ye
      du-MA-brain-stir-stat
      'He's crazy.'

Such considerations lead to the conclusion that the noun + verb compound in a clause with incorporation is not a simple paraphrase of the same verb with a free-standing noun phrase.

We see, then, that it is not always possible to have two corresponding clauses, with and without noun incorporation. This is due to special discourse meaning assigned to incorporated nouns, restrictions on what cannot, can, or must incorporate, and the development of idiomatic meanings. Even when there are two corresponding clauses which seem to be propositionally equivalent, we see that they are not usually in free variation. In most languages, incorporation serves the function of making the nominal less salient in the discourse. In some languages, such as Southern Tiwa, it also seems to serve the function of reducing the number of free-standing nouns in a clause.

2 Syntactic conditions on incorporation

Kroeber (1909) and others have observed that the most common type of incorporation is where the incorporated noun serves as the notional object of the clause. The examples b in (1–3) above show this kind of incorporation. In addition, an incorporated noun can also serve as the notional subject of the clause in most languages:

(6)   Onondaga (H. Woodbury 1975)
      kahsahe?tahíhwi.
      it-bean(s)-spill-caus.-asp.
      'Beans are spilled.'

(7)   Southern Tiwa (Allen et al. 1984)
      I-k'uru-k'euwe-m.
      B-dipper-old-pres.
      'The dipper is old.'

(8) Koryak (Bogoras 1917)
imtilɪ-ntatk-ɪn.
strap-break.off-pres.
'The strap breaks off.'

In all of the above examples, the predicates hosting the incorporated noun are intransitive predicates that can be characterized as inactive: that is, process verbs, stative verbs, or adjectives. Active verbs generally do not allow incorporation of their subjects. (However, see Axelrod 1990 and Polinsky 1990.)

Sapir (1911) notes that some languages also allow the incorporation of obliques, such as instruments (9) or passive agents (10):

(9) Huahtla Nahuatl (Merlan 1976)
ya' ki-kočillo-tete'ki panci.
3SG 3SG:it-knife-cut bread
'He cut the bread with it (the knife).'

(10) Southern Tiwa (Allen et al. 1984)
Khwienide Ø-kan-ēdeure-ban.
dog   A-horse-kick:pass-past
'The dog was kicked by the horse.'

In summary, incorporated nouns are typically related to objects or to subjects of inactive predicates, and rarely to locatives, instruments, or passive agents. They do not generally correspond to subjects of active intransitives or transitives, to indirect objects, or to benefactives. In this respect, noun incorporation appears to be like other cases of compounding. (See Fabb, COMPOUNDING.)

Since incorporation is prototypically limited to objects, and since most clauses contain only one object, examples with more than one incorporated noun are rare. One place where multiple incorporation is found is in morphological causatives:

(11) Alyutor (Koptjevskaja-Tamm and Muravyova 1993)
gəmmə t-akka-n-nalgə-n-kuww-at-avə-tk-ən.
I:ABS   1SG.S-son-CAUS-skin-CAUS-dry-SUFF-SUFF-PRES-1SG.S
'I am making a son dry a skin/skins.'

(12) Southern Tiwa (Allen et al. 1984)
Ti-seuan-p'akhu-kumwia-'am-ban wisi te-khaba-'i.
1sg.:A-man-bread-sell-cause-past   two 1sg.:C-bake-subord.
'I made the man sell the two breads I baked.'

Here we see that two objects are incorporated: the object of the lexical verb and the object of the causative (the causee).

3 The effect of incorporation on the clause

Incorporation, as defined above, is not a simple case of compounding. In standard cases of compounding, new words are produced, are assigned a category label in the lexicon, and, like simple words, are used in the syntax accordingly. In noun incorporation, however, the stem that results from the compounding of a noun stem and a verb serves a dual role in the clause: it is both the verb and one of the arguments of the verb.

This fact is seen most clearly in languages where clauses with and without incorporation have different valence. In such languages, when the incorporated noun corresponds to the object, the clause is syntactically intransitive. In Nahuatl, for example, the incorporated object does not determine object agreement (cf. (1b) above). In Chukchee, an ergative language, the subject of a clause with an incorporated object appears in the absolutive case, not the ergative:

(13)   Chukchee (Polinsky 1990)
    (a)   ətləg-e   qoraŋə   təm-nen.
        father-ERG reindeer (ABS) kill-AOR.3SG:3SG
        'The father killed a/the reindeer.'

    (b)   ətləg-ən   qaa-nmə-gʔe.
        father-ABS reindeer (INC)-kill-AOR.3SG
        'The father killed a reindeer.'

This led Mardirussian (1975) to suppose that detransitivization is a universal property of object incorporation.

However, we do not see this effect in all languages. For example, in Southern Tiwa the incorporated noun determines object agreement (for person, number, and class):

(14)   Southern Tiwa (Allen et al. 1984)
    (a)   Ti-shut-pe-ban.   (b)   Te-shut-pe-ban.
        1sg.:A-shirt-make-past   *1sg.:C-shirt-make-past*
        'I made the/a shirt.'   'I made (the) shirts.'

Also, in some ergative languages – for example, Rembarnga (McKay 1975), the subject of a clause with an incorporated object appears in the ergative case, the case used for subjects of transitive clauses:

(15)   Rembarnga (McKay 1975)
    . . . piri-r̩ut-maṇinʔ-miɲ   munaŋa-yiʔ.
    3sg.obj+3pl.trans.sub+Rel-road-build-past.punct. white.man-ERG
    '. . . where the white men built the road'

Therefore, we find that in some languages the incorporation of the object nominal seems to have no effect on the clause valence.

Subject incorporation behaves similarly. In some languages – for example, Onondaga (6) and Southern Tiwa (7) – the incorporated subject determines agreement on the verb. In other languages, however, the incorporated noun does not determine agreement. Instead, there is no agreement, as in Koryak (8), or there is indefinite agreement:

(16) Huahtla Nahuatl (Merlan 1976)
   tla-a·-weci-Ø-Ø.
   indef.-water-fall-pres.-SG
   'It is raining.'

Facts like the above lead to the conclusion that it is necessary to distinguish at least two types of noun incorporation (Hopkins 1988, Mithun 1984, Rosen 1989b, H. Woodbury 1975). These will be referred to here as "compounding incorporation" and "classifying incorporation." In compounding incorporation the valence of the clause is decreased, but in classifying incorporation the valence of the clause is not affected. Many languages with incorporation consistently use only one type. However, as Hopkins (1988) and Mithun (1984) have shown, some languages have both types.

3.1 Modification and doubling

Classifying incorporation can be viewed as simply a presentational device: that is, a means for expressing a nominal within the predicate rather than as a free-standing noun, thereby shifting the burden of lexicalization from the noun phrase onto the predicate. In languages with classifying incorporation, it is also possible to have free-standing material in the object position when a noun is incorporated. For example, determiners (17), numerals (18), and other modifiers (19, 20) can appear in the object position of the clause. (A, B are class designations.)

(17) Southern Tiwa (Allen et al. 1984)
   Yedi bi-musa-tuwi-ban.
   those 1sg.:B-cat-buy-past
   'I bought those cats.'

(18) Wisi bi-musa-tuwi-ban.
   two 1sg.:B-cat-buy-past
   'I bought two cats.'

(19) Wim'a-tin ti-musa-tuwi-ban.
   one-only 1sg.:A-cat-buy-past
   'I bought only one cat.'

(20)   Mohawk (Mithun 1984)
       Kanekwarúnyu wa'-k-akya'tawi'tsher-ú:ni.
       it.dotted.DIST   PAST-1sg.-dress-make
       'I made a polka-dotted dress.' ('I dress-made a polka-dotted one.')

Such data show that the incorporated nominal should not be regarded as a noun phrase, but rather as the *head* of a noun phrase.[1]

Furthermore, a full noun phrase can appear in the object position when there is an incorporated noun:

(21)   Gunwinggu (Oates 1964)
       . . . bene-ṛed-naŋ   redgereŋeni.
       they.two-camp-saw camp.new
       '. . . they saw a camp which was freshly made.' ('. . . they saw a new camp.')

(22)   . . . bene-dulg-naŋ mangaralalymayn.
       they.two-tree-saw   cashew.nut
       '. . . they saw a cashew tree.'

(23)   Mohawk (Mithun 1984)
       Tohka niyohserá:ke   tsi nahe' sha'té:ku nikú:ti rabahbót
       several so.it.year.numbers so it.goes eight   of.them bullhead
       wahu-tsy-ahní:nu ki   rake'níha.
       he-fish-bought   this my.father
       'Several years ago, my father bought eight bullheads.'

In this case, the free-standing object must be semantically related to the incorporated noun. It is either a double of the incorporated noun, as in (21), or a more specific noun phrase referring to the same element as the incorporated noun, which is often of a generic nature, as in (22) and (23).

Examples like these have led Di Sciullo and Williams (1987) to claim that it is unreasonable to propose that noun incorporation arises through a transformation that takes the head of the noun phrase and moves it into the predicate (Baker 1988a, Postal 1979, Mardirussian 1975). While it may be possible to account for examples like (21) by allowing the noun to leave a copy of itself *in situ*, such a proposal does not accommodate data like (22) and (23), where the external position is occupied by a more specific coreferential noun phrase. (See Spencer 1991: ch. 7, for an evaluation of this debate.)

3.2 Other nominals in clauses with incorporation

In many languages, nominals other than the patient can appear as the grammatical object – for example, benefactives, locatives, and possessors. We find that this is also the case in many languages with incorporation. In the following examples, the patient is incorporated, while the benefactive (24, 25) or locative (26) serves as the grammatical object:

(24) Classical Nahuatl (J. R. Andrews 1975)
ni-quin-xōchi-tēmo-lia.
1sg.-3pl.-flower-seek-for
'I seek flowers for them.'

(25) Chukchee (Polinsky 1990)
tumg-e   ekək   kayŋə-nmə-nen.
friend-ERG son (ABS) bear-kill-AOR.3SG:3SG
'The friend killed the bear for his son.'

(26) Chukchee (Polinskaja and Nedjalkov 1987)
ətləg-e   kawkaw   mətqə-rkele-nen
father-ERG bread (ABS) butter-spread on-AOR.3SG:3SG
'The father spread the butter on the bread.'

That a semantically oblique nominal is the grammatical object is evidenced by the fact that it determines object agreement (24) or appears in the absolutive case (25, 26).

More commonly, the incorporated noun corresponds to a possessed nominal: that is, the head of a possessive phrase. When a possessed body part is incorporated, the possessor assumes the function of object in the clause, and hence determines object agreement.

(27) Tupinambá (Rodrigues, n.d.)
(a) s-oβá a-yos-éy.   (b) a-s-oβá-éy.
his-face I-it-wash   *I-him-face-wash*
'I washed his face.'   'I face-washed him.'

(28) Blackfoot (Frantz 1971)
Nít-ssik-o'kakín-aw óma nínaawa.
I-break-back-him   that man
'I broke the man's back.'

(29) Gunwinggu (Oates 1964)
namegbe biru-dur-aynbom.
that (man) he/him-heart-speared
'He speared that man in the heart.'

In many languages, constructions like the above are limited to cases of part–whole possession. However, in some languages, alienably possessed nouns can also be incorporated, and, as above, the possessor assumes the object function.

(30)   Southern Tiwa (Allen et al. 1984)
       Ka-kuchi-thã-ban.
       1sg.:2sg.|A-pig-find-past
       'I found your pig.'

(31)   Classical Nahuatl (J. R. Andrews 1975)
       ni-mitz-cac-tohtoma.
       1sg.-2sg.-shoe-undo
       'I take off your shoes.'

Instances of possessors assuming the role of the possessive noun phrase are not limited to object function. As noted above, most languages allow the incorporation not only of a noun corresponding to the object of a transitive verb, but also of a noun corresponding to the sole argument of an inactive intransitive predicate. If this argument is a possessed body part, the body part is incorporated, and the possessor takes on the subject function in the clause, and hence determines subject agreement.

(32)   Blackfoot (Frantz 1971)
       Nit-á-istts-o'kakíni.
       I-DUR-pain-back
       'I have a backache.'

As in the case of possessed objects, some languages also allow alienably possessed subjects to be incorporated:

(33)   Southern Tiwa (Allen et al. 1984)
       In-shut-k'euwe-m.
       1sg.|A-shirt-old-pres.
       'My shirt is old.'

(34)   Alyutor (Koptjevskaja-Tamm and Muravyova 1993)
       gəmmə tə-sejnik-av-∅-ək.
       I:ABS   1SG.S-tea.pot-have.a.hole-AOR-1SG.S
       'I have a hole in my tea-pot.' (Approx. 'I am tea-pot-broken.')

4 Incorporation compared to other similar phenomena

The properties of noun incorporation can be summarized as follows:

(i)   An element that can otherwise exist as a noun stem and an element that can otherwise exist as a verb stem are compounded into a single word.

(ii)   This word serves as the predicate of the clause, and the incorporated noun stem corresponds to one of the arguments of the verb.

(iii)   Prototypically, the incorporated noun stem corresponds to the object of a transitive predicate or the subject of an inactive intransitive predicate. In many languages, an incorporated noun may also correspond to an oblique nominal, such as a locative, instrument, or passive agent.

(iv)   Two types of incorporation exist across languages (and sometimes within a single language): compounding incorporation, which decreases the valence of the clause, and classifying incorporation, which does not decrease the valence of the clause.

(v)   Languages with classifying incorporation allow the modification or doubling of the incorporated element.

(vi)   In both types of incorporation, when the incorporated noun corresponds to the head of a possessive phrase, the possessor assumes a grammatical function – subject or object – in the clause.

If we look beyond the strict definition of incorporation in (i), we find that many languages exhibit phenomena that share many of the properties of noun incorporation. Several of these phenomena are discussed in the following sections.

4.1 Noun stripping

One phenomenon that closely resembles noun incorporation is noun stripping (Miner 1986, 1989), also known as composition by juxtaposition (Mithun 1984). As seen in (35b), a "stripped" noun does not have the usual case marking associated with its grammatical function.

(35)   Tongan (Churchward 1953)

     (a)   Na'e inu 'a   e   kavá 'e   Sione.
          PAST drink ABS CONN kava ERG John
          'John drank the kava.'

     (b)   Na'e inu kava 'a   Sione.
          PAST drink kava ABS John
          'John kava-drank.'

Noun stripping differs from incorporation, however.[2] Incorporation is morphological: the two elements involved are part of the same word in surface structure. In noun stripping, the two elements remain as separate words according to phonological criteria such as stress placement. However, surface adjacency of the noun and verb is required. For example, in Kusaiean, adverbs can appear between a verb and an object (36a) but not between a verb and a stripped noun (36b).

(36)   Kusaiean (K. Lee 1975)
 (a) Sah el twem upac mitmit sac.
   Sah he sharpen diligently knife the
   'Sah is sharpening the knife diligently.'

 (b) Sah el twetwe mitmit upac.
   Sah he sharpen knife diligently
   'Sah is diligently knife-sharpening.'

The motivation for noun stripping may be simple: languages prefer to represent generic and nonspecific nouns with as little morphological marking as possible. We can observe, however, that noun stripping does more than simply delete the case marking or determiners of the noun phrase; the valence of clauses with noun stripping is also decreased. For example, the subject in (35b) is in the absolutive case, indicating that it is the subject of an intransitive clause. In this respect, noun stripping is like compounding incorporation. As is the case in compounding incorporation, stripped nouns may not be modified:

(37)   Kusaiean (ibid.)
  *Nga twetwe mitmit sahfiht sac.
  I sharpen knife dull the
  'I am knife-sharpening the dull ∅.'

Miner (1986, 1989) points out other similarities between incorporation and noun stripping. Like incorporation, noun stripping is almost always limited to objects and to subjects of inactive verbs. Prototypical stripped nouns are indeterminate and inanimate, though animate nouns may be stripped in some languages. The stripping of possessed nouns is rare.[3]

Thus, noun stripping is very much like incorporation, particularly compounding incorporation. The sole difference is that in true incorporation the noun and verb form a single word. Noun stripping can thus be seen as a precursor of noun incorporation. If the language tolerates complex morphology, over time noun stripping can develop into incorporation.

4.2 *Lexical suffixes*

Salish languages, Wakashan languages, and other northwestern Native American languages are well known for their lexical suffixes. These suffixes have substantival meaning, but bear little, if any, resemblance to free-standing nouns with the same or similar meaning. Compare some lexical suffixes in Halkomelem Salish with free-standing nouns of similar meaning: *-cəs* versus *céləš* 'hand', *-šən* versus *sx̌én?ə* 'foot', and *-?éx̌ən* versus *t'élu* 'arm, wing'.[4] Most Salish languages have around one hundred lexical suffixes denoting body parts ('hand', 'foot', 'heart', 'nose'), environmental concepts ('earth', 'fire', 'water', 'wind', 'tree', 'rock', 'berry'), cultural items ('canoe', 'net', 'house', 'clothing', 'language'), and human terms ('people', 'spouse', 'offspring'). Lexical suffixes are widely used in complex nominals:

(38) Halkomelem (Musqueam dialect, Wayne Suttles, p.c.)
      qá?-li?c   'water box' (water + container)
      táx̣ʷac-əłp   'yew tree' (bow + plant)
      xiləx̣-áwəł   'battleship' (make war + vessel)
      t'íwəyəł-éwtxʷ   'church' (worship + building)

They also appear on verbs, and in this case they have the same syntactic and semantic properties as incorporated nouns. First, the lexical suffixes correspond to the same range of relations typical of noun incorporation: objects (39a), subjects of inactive predicates (39b), and obliques such as locatives (39c) and instruments (39d), but not subjects of active verbs, goals, or benefactives.

(39) Halkomelem (Musqueam dialect, ibid.)
    (a)   θék̓ʷ-əl'yən   'pull a net' (pull + net)
           məƛ'-é:l-ze?   'to return wealth' (return + hide)
           səẉq̓-iẉs   'search for a lost person' (seek + body)
           łəc̓-ə́l-qən   'shear wool' (cut + hair)

    (b)   yəqʷ-əl?cəp   'fire burns' (burn + firewood)

    (c)   q̓ət-á-θən   'walk along (a shore etc.)' (go along + mouth)
           p̓á:-l'-cəp   'blow on a fire' (blow + fire)

    (d)   k̓ʷc-áləs   'see with one's own eyes' (see + eye)
           q̓ə-xín-t   'accompany him' (accompany + foot + transitive)

Second, we see the same sort of transference of argument structure in cases of lexical suffixation that we saw with incorporation. When the lexical suffix is notionally equivalent to a possessed noun, the possessor assumes a clausal argument position:

(40) ni   łic'-áqʷ-t-əs   lə   sɬeni? kʷθə swiw?ləs.
     aux. cut-head-tr.-3erg det. woman det. boy
     'The woman cut the boy's hair.'

(41) ni   cən k'ʷəs-cəs.
     aux. 1sub. burn-hand
     'I burned my hand.'

In general, Salish lexical suffixes parallel compounding incorporation. First, we can see that when the lexical suffix refers to the object, the clause is intransitive, since the subject determines absolutive rather than ergative agreement:

(42)   ni   yəqʷ-əlʔ-cəp(*-əs).
       aux. burn-cn.-firewood(-3erg)*
       'He made a fire.'

Furthermore, external modification is usually not possible:

(43)   ni   ləkʷ-əl-wíl-t-əs   (*(kʷθə) łíx̌ʷ) kʷθə John.
       aux. break-cn-rib-tr.-3erg.   det. three det. John
       'He broke (*three of) John's ribs.'

Finally, the lexical suffix usually cannot be doubled with a free-standing noun
of the same or more specific meaning:

(44)   qʷs-iẏən   (*tə-ṅ   swəltən)
       go into water-net det.-your net
       'set your net'

(45)   ni   tší-ʔqʷ-t-əs   (*kʷθə sx̌áləməs-s)   łə   stálʔəs-s.
       aux. comb-head-tr.-3erg.   det. white hair-3pos. det. spouse-3pos.
       'He combed his wife's (*white) hair.'

The above data show that lexical suffixation parallels compounding incorporation. We see that lexical suffixes, just like incorporated nouns, have the
syntactic characteristics of a nominal in an argument or adjunct position in the
clause. And while we have no direct evidence that the lexical suffix should
be assigned the categorial status of a noun, we note that it does block a free-
standing noun of the same or more specific meaning from occurring in the
clause.

In addition, a small subset of lexical suffixes in each Salish language can
serve as numeral classifiers. For example, there are thirteen classifiers in
Halkomelem, including *-as* 'round or spherical objects', *-aqʷ* 'head' (e.g. of
cabbage, animals), *-eʊtxʷ* 'building', and *-xʷəł* 'canoe, conveyance'. This type
of lexical suffixation parallels classifying incorporation. In the case of numerals,
the classifier is usually doubled with an elaborating nominal:

(46)   łixʷ-əqən   lisék
       three-containers sack
       'three sacks'

(47)   teʔcs-élə   kʷθə nə   meʔmənə.
       eight-people det. 1pos. children
       'I have eight children.'

Also, in rare examples, classificatory suffixes attached to a lexical verb can
double with a free-standing nominal:

(48)   Halkomelem (Musqueam dialect, Wayne Suttles, p.c.)
       ẋs-əléʔc-t   tə nə́wək̓ʷaʔ
       nail-container-tr. det. coffin
       'nail up the coffin'

(49)   wə-náy kʷs ẋəx̌-wil-t   ct   tə lepát ʔi tə láʔθən.
       only   det. wash-vessel-tr. 1pl.sub. det. pot   and det. dishes
       'We only wash pots and plates.'

Data like the above are quite suggestive of noun incorporation. However, Sapir (1911: 251–2) says that the Salish lexical suffixes should not be considered to be noun incorporation. He claims that "it is clear that verbal affixes that refer to nouns . . . are not instances of noun incorporation if they are etymologically unrelated to the independent nouns or noun stems with which they seem logically connected." This point of view has been taken by Mithun (1984) and others (see e.g. Anderson 1985b, Hagège 1978) as rationale for excluding lexical suffixes from discussions of noun incorporation.[5] However, it has been claimed that lexical suffixes originated as nominals that commonly occurred as the second element in compounds (Carlson 1989). They were phonologically reduced, and eventually became bound forms. Once these shortened forms took on a generic meaning, new, longer, free-standing forms with more precise meaning were invented. From this viewpoint, lexical suffixes can be regarded as incorporated nouns that have lost their status as free-standing nominals.

4.3 Denominal verbs

In some languages we see a phenomenon that is the reverse of lexical suffixation. A noun stem that can be an independent word is compounded with a verbal affix that does not otherwise appear as a free-standing verb:

(50)   Greenlandic (Sadock 1980)
       Qimmeqarpoq.
       dog-have-INDIC-3sg.
       'He has a dog.'

Sadock (1980) estimates that there are roughly two hundred verbal affixes that can be attached to nouns in Greenlandic. These include -*qar*- 'to have', -*nngor*- 'to become', and -*lior*- 'make for'. Although such examples have been referred to as noun incorporation, a more appropriate label would be "denominal verbs." (See Mithun 1986 and Sadock 1986.)

Denominal verb constructions show interesting properties that at first glance may seem to parallel noun incorporation. First, like classifying incorporation, they allow external modification:

(51)   Greenlandic (Sadock 1980)
       Kusanartunik   sapangarsivoq.
       beautiful-NOM-PL-INST bead-get-INDIC-3sg.
       'He bought beautiful beads.'

Second, the verbalized nominal can correspond to the head of a possessed noun phrase.

(52)   Greenlandic (ibid.)
       (a)   Tuttup   neqaanik   nerivunga.
             reindeer-REL meat-3sg.-INST eat-INDIC-1sg.
             'I ate reindeer meat.'

       (b)   Tuttup   neqitorpunga.
             reindeer-REL meat-eat-INDIC-1sg.
             'I ate reindeer meat.'

Note, however, that unlike the cases of noun incorporation discussed above, the possessor does not take on the object role in the clause when the head appears predicate-internally. Rather, it remains in its usual case, the relative/ ergative. The Greenlandic data also differ from noun incorporation with respect to the complexity of the nominals involved. In some examples, the noun to which the verbal suffix is attached is not a bare noun stem, but rather bears case and other inflectional suffixes:

(53)   Greenlandic (ibid.)
       Palasip   illuanukarpoq
       priest-REL house-3sg.-ALL-go-INDIC-3sg.
       'He went to the priest's house.'

Finally, the Greenlandic denominal verb construction differs from noun incorporation with respect to the grammatical relation of the participating noun. In noun incorporation, it is usually objects, subjects of inactive verbs, or obliques that incorporate. The Greenlandic data seem to involve objects (50) or obliques (53), but not subjects.[6] Sadock (1980) also gives examples involving predicative nominals:

(54)   Palasinngorpoq.
       priest-become-INDIC-3sg.
       'He became a priest.'

The above examples show that what has been called noun incorporation in Greenlandic differs from core cases of noun incorporation in other languages. However, these data provide strong evidence that the predicate-internal nominal must be the head of the noun phrase in the syntax. Thus the derivational process of compounding the noun and the verb, whatever it is called, must occur in a postsyntactic level of structure (Sadock 1980).[7]

5 Conclusion

True noun incorporation, where a noun stem compounds with a verb, is a typologically rare phenomenon, though it appears in languages in many areas of the world. Noun incorporation is exhibited in some of the language families of the Americas (Algonquian, Athapaskan, Caddoan, Iroquoian, Muskogean, Siouan, Takelma, Tanoan, Tsimshian, Tupinambá, Uto-Aztecan, Yana), in Paleo-Siberian languages (Alyutor, Chukchee, Koryak), in Australian languages (Gunwinggu, Rembarnga), in a Munda language (Sora), in Oceanic languages, and in Turkish. (See Mardirussian 1975, Mithun 1984, and de Reuse 1992.)

In addition, several languages have constructions that might be analyzed as either noun stripping or noun incorporation: for example, Mayan, Zuni, and several Austronesian languages (Miner 1986). Noun stripping, where a noun (usually the object) is stripped of its case marking and positioned next to the verb, can be viewed as a precursor of incorporation or as the equivalent of incorporation in analytic languages. Lexical suffixes, which probably originated through incorporation, can be found in northwestern Native American languages, including the Salishan and Wakashan languages. What has been called "noun incorporation" in Greenlandic (Sadock 1980) is best regarded as a denominal verb (Mithun 1986).

However these various constructions are labeled, they all present an interesting challenge to theories of morphosyntax. In each case, a noun (or nominal affix) combines with a verb (or verbal affix) to form a complex predicate. In the case of noun incorporation, lexical suffixation, and denominal verbs, the complex predicate is a single word by morphological and phonological criteria. Thus, two syntactic constituents combine to form a single word that satisfies both the predicate function and some argument function (usually object) of the clause. This mixture of properties has led Mithun (1984) to call noun incorporation "the most nearly syntactic of all morphological processes."

NOTES

1   Alternatively, the incorporated noun could be coreferential with a phonologically null head.

2   Miner (1986) argues that noun stripping and noun incorporation are distinct processes by showing that both exist in Zuni.

3   Japanese and Korean exhibit a phenomenon sometimes referred to as noun incorporation, but probably more accurately classified as noun stripping, where nouns preceding the verbs meaning 'do' are stripped of their case marking. Either nominative or accusative case can be stripped, depending on the valence of the clause. Modifiers, including possessors, which appear in the genitive case if the head noun is marked with case, cannot appear in the genitive case if

the noun is stripped. Rather, the modifier is marked nominative or accusative, depending on the valence of the clause.

4   Unless otherwise specified, the data in this section are from the Island dialect of Halkomelem Salish (Gerdts, field-notes).

5   Hagège's discussion hinges on the contrast between lexical suffixation and another construction that he calls noun incorporation. However, this latter construction is more appropriately classified as a denominal verb construction (see section 4.3).

6   As Sadock (1980) argues, the denominal verb construction is based on an intransitive construction. (See (52a) for example.) The notional object normally appears in the instrumental case. This accounts for the instrumental marking of modifiers, as in (51).

7   Alternatively, a theory of grammar such as Autolexical Syntax (Sadock 1985), in which morphological structure and syntactic structure exist independently but are cross-referenced with each other, could capture these facts.

5 Clitics

AARON L. HALPERN

1 Introduction

While the distinction between independent words or phrases on the one hand and affixes on the other is often fairly clear, many languages have various formatives which are hard to classify as one or the other. Such formatives are often called clitics.[1] As we shall see, the various elements which are called *clitics* form a heterogeneous bunch, at least superficially, and exactly what is meant by "clitic" varies from study to study, though there are two predominant senses.

In some uses, "clitic" denotes any prosodically weak (unaccented) element which is not a canonical inflectional or derivational affix.[2] This is the sense in which the term is usually used in the discussion of phonological issues. Whether such a clitic lacks independent accent inherently or because of some reduction process, it must be incorporated into the accentual structure of an adjacent word or phrase, the clitic's *host*, since in order to be pronounced, a formative (word, affix, etc.) needs to be part of an accentual unit. This dependency leads to one of the common diagnostics used to distinguish clitics from independent words: they may not constitute an utterance on their own. Clitics which form a prosodic unit with a host on their left are *enclitics*, while those forming a unit to their right are *proclitics*.

Cliticization in this strictly phonological sense need not entail any syntactic consequences. An unstressed word which is otherwise unexceptional is known as a *simple clitic*, after Zwicky (1977); for example, a simple clitic which is a preposition will head a prepositional phrase and be followed by its complement; the resulting phrase will have the distribution of any other PP in the language. In contrast to this prosodic definition of the clitic, syntactic discussions usually use the term to refer to the sort of weak pronoun found in modern Romance languages which appears in a special position in the clause (generally immediately before the verb). However, the syntactic and morphological issues raised by such *special clitics* extend to elements with other functions and other distributions, as we shall see in later sections.

In the remainder of this chapter, I will focus primarily on the behavior of special clitics, but it will be instructive to examine simple clitics first, since some of the apparently distinctive properties of special clitics may result purely from their prosodic weakness rather than anything to do with syntax or morphology (section 2). In sections 3, 4, and 5, we will examine in some detail the behavior of various types of special clitic and the descriptive and theoretical issues they raise. In the final section, we will return to some proposals which aim to provide a general theory of the distribution of clitics.[3]

2 Simple clitics – accentless words

Reduced auxiliaries and pronouns in English are often cited as examples of simple clitics; they lack stress, and are pronounced as a single unit with the preceding word, while their distribution is essentially a subset of that which the corresponding unreduced forms occupy. Various function words in most if not all languages may be reduced in this fashion, or perhaps be listed in the lexicon without an inherent accent (see Kaisse 1985 for discussion of these alternatives).

(1)   <u>She will</u> have to find a new job soon. [šiwɪl]/[šil̩]/[šl̩]

(2)   Jonathan <u>saw him</u>. [sɔhɪm]/[sɔm̩]/[sɔm]

Simple clitics often do not have the full range of distribution of an independently accented word of the same category, but the restrictions seem to reflect a filtering of the structures permitted by the syntax, rather than some special syntactic status. For instance, fully reduced (i.e. vowel-less) forms of auxiliaries other than *is* and *has*, which are subject to looser constraints, are available only immediately after a subject pronoun, and not after a nonpronominal subject, a nonsubject, or even after a pronoun if the pronoun is part of a coordinate subject.

(3)   <u>He'll</u> have to go now. [hl̩]

(4)   <u>Mary'll</u> have to go now. [mærɪl̩]/*[mærl̩]

(5)   Mary and <u>he'll</u> have to go now. [hɪl̩]/*[hl̩]

Perhaps more surprisingly, reduced auxiliaries are also sensitive to the following context, being ungrammatical before the site of various elisions, though they are phonologically enclitic.

(6)   John's tired, and Mary is too/*Mary's ___ too.

(7)   John's as tall as you are/*you're ___ wide.

These limits on the distribution of reduced auxiliaries have received a good bit of attention (Kaisse 1985, Selkirk 1984), with the nature of the elements to which the constraints must refer – syntactic or prosodic – being the primary theoretical question.[4] Regardless, we may say that the syntax per se, as opposed to postlexical/postsyntactic phonological rules or filters, does not need to give special treatment to reduced auxiliaries.[5]

Regarding the attachment of a clitic to its host, there is considerable debate as to its nature. It is commonly accepted that, for simple clitics, it is of a nonsyntactic nature. Zwicky and Pullum (1983a) consider syntactic irrelevance an important way of distinguishing cliticization from affixation, one of several which have become a standard set of diagnostics.[6] This can be made sharper by contrasting reduced auxiliaries with *n't*, the reduced form of *not*, which does behave like a part of the preceding auxiliary, as illustrated by the fact that it may accompany the auxiliary in subject-auxiliary inversion contexts.

(8) Isn't/*Is not Regina going to come to practice tonight?

(9) Is Regina not/*n't going to come to practice tonight?

Various authors have proposed that cliticization involves the formation of a morphological constituent, making it affix-like in this sense, though not syntactically (see esp. Sadock 1991). This is motivated by the fact that cliticization can lead to phonological interactions between a clitic and its host which are not seen between two independent words. However, the phonology and morphology of cliticization is generally not entirely that of an affix. For instance, like suffixes, enclitics in Latin affect the location of stress on their host; independent words, on the other hand, generally do not affect the stress of an adjacent word. Yet, the effect of an enclitic is not the same as the effect of a suffix (Nespor and Vogel 1986: 115–16; Steriade 1988). The addition of a suffix causes stress to shift so that it is located as follows: stress is on the penultimate syllable if that syllable is heavy, but on the antepenultimate syllable if the penult is light, as shown in (10a, b). The addition of a clitic, however, causes stress to appear on the penultimate syllable of the host + clitic sequence regardless of the weight of that syllable, as shown in (10c, d):

(10) (a) stomachôsus   'irritated'
      (b) homúncŭlus   'little man'
      (c) rosá=que   'and the rose (nom.)'
      (d) rosá=que   'and the rose (abl.)'

Simple clitics are also notably lacking in irregularities in their combinations with their hosts; they are not involved in suppletion, and do not generally enter into morphologically conditioned alternations with their hosts. Several explanations of this phonologically and morphologically intermediate behavior have been advanced, including treating clitics as an outer layer of affixation within a level-ordered morphology (Klavans 1983, Kanerva 1987, Booij and Rubach 1987), treating clitic + host as a *clitic group* – a unique prosodic constituent between the phonological word and the phonological phrase (Hayes 1989a, b; Nespor and Vogel 1986), treating clitics as being adjoined to phonological words or other prosodic constituents (Inkelas 1990, Zec and Inkelas 1991, Lapointe 1991, A. Woodbury 1996).

To sum up, it is quite common for stressless function words to behave in a syntactically normal fashion while being prosodically bound to an adjacent word. Ways in which such a simple clitic differs from a nonclitic may be derived from the surface conditions or filters which the clitic imposes, plausibly reducing to requirements related to the incorporation of a clitic into its host.

3 Verbal clitics

In contrast to, say, weak pronouns in English, which occupy essentially the same position as stressed pronouns and nonpronominal NPs, weak pronouns in French do not behave like other noun phrases. Consider the following examples:[7]

(11) (a)   Jean <u>le</u> vois. (Fr)
              Jean it sees
              'Jean sees it.'

      (b)   *Jean vois <u>le</u>.

(12) (a)   Jean vois <u>le</u> <u>livre</u>.
              Jean sees the book
              'Jean sees the book.'

      (b)   *Jean <u>le livre</u> vois.

While nonclitic objects follow the tensed verb in a simple finite clause, clitics must precede it. Similar behavior for weak pronouns is observed in many languages, including nearly all of the modern Romance dialects and several Balkan languages (Greek, Macedonian, Albanian). Their special distribution and other ways in which they differ from independent words distinguish them from simple clitics. At least superficially, there are a variety of types of such special clitics, and I will refer to the type illustrated above as *verbal clitics*.

Kayne (1975) pointed out several respects in which verbal clitics are like inflectional affixes.[8] To begin with, they always appear adjacent to a verb and attach morphologically or phonologically to it.[9] They are also subject to various language-specific co-occurrence conditions which are similar to conditions on the co-occurrence of inflectional affixes; these conditions are often expressed in terms of a *template* which separates clitics into groups which are associated with an ordered set of slots.[10] A given slot will generally contain at most one clitic, drawn from the relevant group. The classes of clitics associated with a given slot are defined according to a variety of properties, grammatical function and grammatical person being common factors, but phonological shape may also play a role (Schachter 1973, Tegey 1978). Such templates are also known in systems of complex inflectional morphology, as in the Athabaskan languages. Consider the following examples (where '1', '2', '3' means '1st', '2nd', '3rd' person):

(13)   Bulgarian: NEG < FUT < AUX < IO < DO < 3SG.AUX

(14)   French: 1/2.PRO < 3ACC.PRO < 3DAT.PRO < *y* < *en*

(15)   Ngiyambaa: PRT* < 1PRO < 2PRO < 3NOM.PRO < 3GEN.PRO < 3ABS.PRO
        (Donaldson 1980)

(16)   Tagalog: 1σ.PRO < PRT* < 2σ.PRO*

Phonologically speaking, certain nonautomatic alternations are observed between two special clitics and, perhaps less commonly, between special clitics and their host. For instance, Simpson and Withgott (1986: 167) note the arbitrary insertion of [z] in dialectal French *donnez-moi-z-en* 'give me some'. See also Akmajian et al. (1979: 5ff). Morphologically, we also find portmanteau clitics, and clitics whose interpretation depends on the presence or absence of other clitics (Steele et al. 1981: 24ff, Perlmutter 1971, Simpson and Withgott 1986).

Based on such observations, it is generally accepted that verbal clitics are syntactically adjoined to the verb or to a functional head which incorporates the verb. Indeed, they are often assumed to be types of inflectional affixes themselves, perhaps simply agreement markers. This *base generation* approach is a relatively traditional view; within the generative literature, it has been defended within a variety of frameworks (Rivas 1978; Lapointe 1980; Borer 1984; Stump 1980; Jaeggli 1982, 1986b; Suñer 1988; Dobrovie-Sorin 1990; P. Miller 1992). However, despite these similarities between clitics and inflections, there are also several respects in which clitics are not like canonical agreement affixes.

Agreement is usually a local relationship between a head and one of its arguments, and applies obligatorily regardless of the nature of the argument. Inflectional affixes are generally fixed in position with respect to a stem; and object-agreement affixes are generally internal to (or, closer to the stem than) tense, aspect, and subject agreement (Bybee 1985). Finally, inflection often involves a high degree of irregularity, involving selection of particular allomorphs or stem forms, and may sometimes be expressed via a suppletive form. In contrast, a typical special clitic is either in complementary distribution with an overt nonclitic argument or may co-occur with a nonclitic only under restricted circumstances. The ungrammaticality of (17) illustrates that in

French complementarity is obligatory; we will return to contexts where co-occurrence is possible below. Verbal clitics are observed to attach to verbs which are not the source of the theta role to which the clitic is associated, a phenomenon known as *clitic climbing*, and they have greater *mobility* with respect to the verb stem than canonical inflections, in the sense that they may be preverbal in one context but postverbal in another; these points are illustrated in (18)–(20).

(17)   *Jean <u>le</u> voit le livre. (Fr.) (cf. (11) and (12))

(18)   Je <u>l'</u>ai   fait   manger aux   enfants.
        I it-have made eat.INF   to.the children
        'I made the children eat it.'

(19)   J'<u>en</u> ai   bu   deux verres.
        I-of.it have drunk two   glasses
        'I have drunk two glasses of it.'

(20) (a)   Luis trató de comer -<u>las</u>. (Sp.)
            Luis tried DE to.eat -them
            'Luis tried to eat them.'

      (b)   Luis <u>las</u> trató de comer.

As for morphological considerations, clitics are generally external to any (other) inflectional affixes.[11] Finally, while they are known to interact with their hosts in somewhat irregular fashions, this is clearly true to a lesser degree than with inflectional affixes: they seldom if ever select for particular stem forms; nor are they sensitive to the morphology of the host, and they are not involved in suppletion.[12]

These are not necessarily fatal blows to the view that clitics are inflectional affixes. We will discuss the complementarity between clitics and other arguments shortly. As for the long distance character of clitic climbing, there are also cases of agreement applying long-distance (Spencer 1991, P. Miller 1992). For both clitics and clear cases of agreement, this probably reflects some sort of *restructuring*, the formation of a complex predicate in which the semantic arguments of one verb act like the syntactic arguments of another (Kayne 1975; Rizzi 1982; Borer 1984a; Jaeggli 1982, 1986b; P. Miller 1992; Manning 1992). Fulmer (1991) and Noyer (1994) have documented cases of mobility of affixes similar to that observed with verbal clitics. As for the peripheral position of clitics, it is clear, even in light of recent suggestions as to how to make syntax more accountable for the structure of words (Baker 1988a and much subsequent work), that syntax cannot completely account for affix ordering; if nothing else, clitic templates clearly involve purely morphological conditions. The limited degree of interaction between verbal clitics and their hosts is matched by that of various affixes, such as English *-ing*, which is fully regular.

These considerations suggest that the theory of inflectional morphology probably has to be powerful enough to accommodate the behavior of verbal clitics. However, there remains some question as to whether verbal clitics should be reduced to inflections, for there remains a difference, if not in absolute (non)attestedness, then in the markedness of the various characteristics: what is marked for a clitic is unmarked for an inflection, and vice versa.

These observations have led to an alternative view of verbal clitics according to which they are generated in a deep-structure argument position just like a nonclitic pronoun and are subsequently adjoined to the position occupied by the verb.[13] This is known as the *movement* approach to clitic placement.

Whereas clitic climbing, the complementarity between clitics and independent noun phases in, for example, French, and the exterior morphological position of clitics are all complications for a base-generation account, they are the sort of behavior one would expect from the movement approach. However, the ability to explain the complementarity in (17), which is one of the clearest successes of the movement approach, is also one of its greatest stumbling blocks. Unlike standard French, many languages allow clitics and nonclitics serving the same function to co-occur, as in the following Spanish examples. This is known as *clitic doubling*; the nonclitic phrase is sometimes referred to as the clitic's double.

(21) (Le) puso comida al canario/a un perro. (Sp.)
      to-him put.3SG food to-the canary/to a dog
      'S/he gave food to the canary/to a dog.'

(22) (%La) oían a Paca/a la niña.
      her listened.3PL to Paca/to the girl
      'They listened to Paca/to the girl.'

Clitic doubling presents the movement approach with a problem which has not really received adequate treatment. The most common tactic is to treat the double as an adjunct rather than an argument (Aoun 1985, Jaeggli 1982).[14] However, several arguments have been made against this view (Borer 1984a, Everett 1987, Jaeggli 1986b, Suñer 1988), and it seems unlikely to provide a universal account of doubling.[15] Nevertheless, most approaches to clitic doubling have made a related assumption: namely, that some clitics do have some argument-like property which prevents the expression of a separate nonclitic argument (and perhaps simultaneously satisfies the subcategorization or theta-role requirements of the verb so that no other argument is necessary). The relevant property is often assumed to be case absorption.[16] This was originally motivated by the *Kayne–Jaeggli generalization*: namely, that doubling is possible only if the double is accompanied by an independent case assigner. In Spanish, doubling is possible only if the double is an indirect object or an animate direct object, both of which are accompanied by the preposition *a*. Inanimate direct objects, which are not accompanied by *a*, may not be doubled:

(23)   *L̲o̲ compró   el   libro. (Sp.)
       it   bought.3SG the book
       'S/he bought the book.'

Similar facts are observed in connection with the genitive clitics in the Hebrew Construct State, in which doubles must be preceded by the preposition *šel* (Borer 1984a). Consequently, several early works assumed that clitic pronouns always absorb case: for example, Jaeggli 1982, Borer 1984a. However, the presence of an overt case marker, or even overt case marking, is not universal in cases of doubling – see Berent 1980, Joseph 1988, and Everett 1987 for discussion of Macedonian, Modern Greek, and Pirahã respectively.[17] This has suggested that whether or not a clitic absorbs case is a parameter of variation (Jaeggli 1986b, Everett 1990): case-absorbing clitics do not permit doubling (or require doubles to be accompanied by an independent case assigner), while clitics which don't absorb case permit, and in fact require, doubling.

Doubling also turns out to be sensitive to properties of the double; for instance, while Spanish clitics are generally optional in the presence of a nonclitic object, they are obligatory with pronominal objects, as in (24). Another common factor is specificity, as shown in (25) and (26): nonspecific direct objects often can not be doubled. (Examples from Suñer 1988.) Similar specificity effects are observed in Romanian, Macedonian, and Greek (Steriade 1980, Berent 1980, Kazazis and Pentheroudakis 1976). Dobrovie-Sorin (1990) proposes an account of the specificity effect based on the assumption that clitics are base-generated case absorbers in combination with the idea that nonspecific phrases are subject to quantifier raising at LF; however, it is not clear that the account can deal with variation in obligatoriness of doubling such as that which distinguishes Macedonian from Romanian or Spanish.

(24)   Ellos *(l̲a̲) llamaron a ella. (Sp.)
       they   her   called.3PL A her
       'They called her.'

(25)   Diariamente, (l̲a̲) escuchaba a una mujer que cantaba tangos.
       daily   her listened.3SG to a   woman who sang   tangos
       'S/he listened daily to a woman who sang tangos.'

(26)   (*L̲a̲) buscaban   a alguien que los   ayudara.
       her   searched.for.3PL A somebody who them could-help.SUBJ
       'They were looking for somebody who could help them.'

To summarize, common to most approaches to verbal clitics is the view that they in some sense form a morphological or syntactic unit with a verb (or with an inflectional head). Whether they are attached in the lexicon or in the syntax, and if the latter, whether they are base-generated or moved (or copied) from some other position, remains in question. The peripheral position of clitics is probably the most convincing argument against treating them as inflectional affixes, though this is only an argument if one adheres to a strongly syntactic theory of affix ordering. On the other hand, the facts surrounding doubling suggest strongly that they are not generated in the position of a nonclitic argument.

4 Second-position clitics

While verbal clitics have dominated discussion in the syntactic literature, there is a growing appreciation of the fact that several other types exist. The other most commonly discussed type is the *second-position* (2P) clitic, also sometimes known as a *Wackernagel's Law* (WL) clitic, after Wackernagel (1892). As a first approximation, second-position clitics must appear second in the relevant domain.[18] Consequently, they are not attached to a host of any particular category, and do not (necessarily) form a syntactic or semantic constituent with their host. For example, the words in the Serbo-Croatian sentence in (27a) may be rearranged in any order, so long as the clitics (as a group) are second; placing them elsewhere is ungrammatical. In this way they contrast with corresponding full forms: compare the position of *mu* with that of *njemu* in (27b).

(27) (a) Marija   =<u>mu</u> =je dala knjigu. (SCr.)
           Maria.NOM to.him AUX gave book.ACC
           'Maria gave him a book.'

       (b) Njemu =je Marija   dala knjigu.
            to.him AUX Maria.NOM gave book.ACC
            'Maria gave HIM a book.'

Note that the clitic *je* is an auxiliary. This illustrates another salient fact about 2P clitics: they may serve a variety of functions other than pronominal, including that of auxiliary, voice marker, discourse particle, and so on. Serbo-Croatian has 2P clitics which function as object pronouns, auxiliaries, and a Y/N question particle. In the ancient Indo-European languages, various Australian languages, Tagalog, and so on, we find a large set of discourse "particles" – markers of voice and mood, discourse connectives, and adverbials – which occupy 2P. Indeed, Kaisse (1982, 1985) suggested that nonpronominal 2P clitics are a prerequisite to pronominal 2P clitics; in support of this, we find that in languages which have both, they are often inseparable. In Serbo-Croatian for instance, pronominal clitics, interrogative *li*, and weak auxiliaries all have to appear in a string and, like verbal clitics, in a fixed order:

(28) Kad <u>li</u> ćeš   <u>joj</u> <u>ih</u> dati? (SCr.)
      when Q FUT.2SG.AUX to.her them give.INF?
      'When will you give them to her?'

Li itself is plausibly treated as a complementizer, based on its function and its distribution. Furthermore, we find that in embedded clauses the other clitics must immediately follow a complementizer, just as they follow *li*.

(29)   Mama odgovara da <u>su</u> one u ormaru. (SCr.)
       mama answers   that are they in armoire
       'Mama answers that they are in the wardrobe.'

Due in part to such observations and in part to analogy to the treatment of verbal clitics, it has been suggested that these clitics occupy some head in the syntax, usually C^0 (Progovac 1996), with the pronominal and auxiliary clitics adjoining to this position. If we assume that the various particle clitics of other languages are also generated in C^0 and that pronominal and auxiliary clitics are adjoined to this position, then we have a partial reconstruction of Kaisse's claim. This analysis in connection with the view that verbal clitics adjoin to a lower head suggests that perhaps all special clitics occupy a head position, with the difference being the choice of the head. Additional intuitive support for this interpretation of the behavior of 2P clitics comes from the analogy to *verb second* (V2) constructions.[19]

However, this conclusion is less plausible in other languages. We find that in various languages (Sanskrit, Ancient Greek, Tagalog), both particle and pronominal clitics may appear in 2P together in most situations, as in (30), but they may or must be separate in certain contexts, as in (31).

(30)   ou p̄ō pote <u>moi</u> to krēguon eipas. (Gr.)
       not yet ever to-me the good   spoke
       'You have never yet spoken a good thing to me.' (*Iliad*, 1.106)

(31)   tôn   <u>d'</u> állōn há   <u>moi</u> ésti thoēi para nēi melainēi
       the.GEN PRT others which me   are swift beside ship black
       'of the others which are with me beside the swift black ship' (*Iliad*, 1.300)

Given this, we clearly cannot assume that pronominal clitics and particle clitics always occupy the same position in these languages (Hale 1987, Garrett 1990, Taylor 1990). Freeze (1992) and Halpern and Fontana (1994) present other reasons for doubting that all clause-level 2P clitics are adjoined to C^0. One argument in favor of this view is that no cases of clitics which are proclitic to a complementizer (or other element in C^0) have been documented – compare (29); given that the preverbal position is the unmarked case for verbal clitics, this strongly suggests that 2P clitics are not adjoined to C^0.

Another thing which (31) illustrates is that some 2P clitics follow the first (phonological) word of a clause, while, as we shall see, others follow the first syntactic daughter (Browne 1974, K. Hale 1973b). I refer to these options as *2W* (for "second word") and *2D* (for "second daughter") respectively. In some languages, the choice between 2D and 2W is fixed, while in others there is either free or conditioned variation. Particle clitics in Ancient Greek follow a single (phonological) word, as just illustrated. The following examples illustrate that

Serbo-Croatian allows alternation between the two, while Czech clitics must appear in 2D.

(32) (a) [Taj čovek]$_{NP}$ joj ga je   poklonio. (2D) (SCr.)
           that man   her it AUX presented
           'That man presented her with it.'

      (b) Taj joj ga je čovek poklonio. (2W)

(33) (a) Ten básník mi   čte   ze   své knihy. (Cz.)
           that poet   to.me reads from his book
           'That poet reads to me from his book.'

      (b) *Ten mi básník čte ze své knihy.

It has been noted that many languages which allow 2W placement of clitics permit extensive discontinuous constituency (Klavans 1982, Nevis 1988, Kaisse 1985), suggesting that 2W may ultimately reduce to 2D. In support of this, several languages which allow for 2W placement in some circumstances require 2D placement in others, as illustrated in (34)–(36) for Serbo-Croatian. Crucially, those constructions which require 2D placement of clitics are also more resistant to discontinuous expression. See Kroeger 1993 for discussion of this with respect to Tagalog, and Progovac 1996 for Serbo-Croatian.

(34) (a) Prijatelji moje   sestre   su upravo stigli. (SCr.)
           friends   my.GEN sister.GEN AUX just   arrived
           'My sister's friends have just arrived.'

      (b) *Prijatelji su moje sestre upravo stigli.

(35) (a) Studenti iz   Beograda su upravo stigli.
           students from Belgrade AUX just   arrived
           'Students from Belgrade have just arrived.'

      (b) *Studenti su iz Beograda upravo stigli.

(36) (a) Lav Tolstoj je   veliki ruski   pisac.
           Leo Tolstoj AUX great   Russian writer
           'Leo Tolstoj is a great Russian writer.'

      (b) %*Lav je Tolstoj veliki ruski pisac.

However, there are certain problems with this view as a general approach to 2W. For one thing, some speakers apparently accept (36b) without allowing for more extensive discontinuous constituency (Browne 1975: 113–14). More generally, 2W is possible in languages or constructions where there is no other possibility for discontinuous constituency (Steele 1976: 610, Halpern 1995: 48–52). Another problem is that while considerable discontinuous constituency is possible in the ancient Indo-European languages, such an approach doesn't explain the fact that the relevant clitics never appear at the end of a multi-word constituent. Treating 2P clitics in these languages as following a full syntactic daughter of the clause would force us to claim that there is some special syntactic construction which allows only constituents comprised of a single (phonological) word to be fronted (Schäufele 1991, Taylor 1992). Indeed, similar arguments can be made with respect to Tagalog, where clitics must follow the first word of certain sorts of constituents. Thus, while some apparent cases of 2W placement may reduce to 2D with discontinuous constituency, there are other cases where clitics may truly be located with respect to a prosodic constituent (the first phonological word) rather than a syntactic one.

Another approach to 2W which has been pursued by several authors (Sadock 1985, 1991; Marantz 1988, 1989; Sproat 1988; M. Hale 1987, 1996; Taylor 1990, 1992, 1996; Halpern 1995) is to assume that, syntactically, 2W clitics are initial within their domain, perhaps adjoined to an entire phrasal constituent, but that their requirement for a preceding host triggers metathesis of the clitic and the syntactically following phonological word, an effect we might refer to as *prosodic inversion*. For instance, particle clitics in Ancient Greek could be treated as being left-adjoined to CP (or as heads which take CP as their complement), but surfacing after the first word of the CP because of their enclitic status. Assuming that prosodic inversion takes place only if necessary to provide the clitic with a host, we may account for the placement of Sanskrit pronominal clitics by assuming that they are syntactically adjoined to IP, with inversion taking place when they are adjoined to a bare IP (to put them in 2W of a simple clause), but not when other material from the same clause precedes the IP, such as a complementizer or a wh-word.[20]

(37)

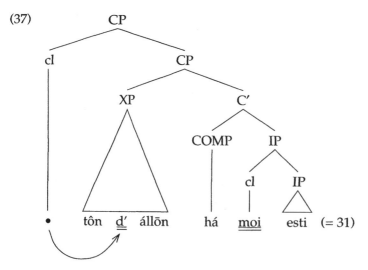

Similarly, 2D clitic placement would presumably result if the initial constituent is outside the domain of the clitic; for instance, we might propose that clitics in Czech are adjoined to IP, and that the initial constituent in a main clause occupies SpecCP.

(38)

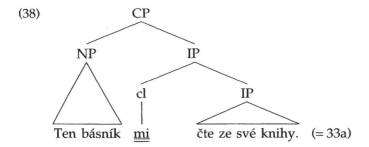

One final point about 2P clitics is that in perhaps all languages with 2P clitics, certain sentence-initial constituents have to be ignored for the purpose of determining the second position, as illustrated in (39). Such *skipping* is generally assumed to indicate that the skipped constituents are in some sense invisible to the clitic, or outside the domain relevant for the calculation of second position. Studies differ as to the notion of domain which is relevant, whether it is syntactic (e.g. phrases outside CP don't count) or prosodic (e.g. phrases outside the intonational phrase containing the verb don't count). See, for instance, Fontana 1993 for the syntactic approach, and Radanovíc-Kocić 1988 and Hock 1992, 1996, for the prosodic approach.

(39) (a) *Ove godine*, taj pesnik <u>mi</u> je napisao knjigu (SCr.)
          this year   that poet   me ＡUX wrote   book
          'This year that poet wrote me a book.'

     (b) *Ove godine*, taj <u>mi</u> <u>je</u> napisao knjigu.

5 Other special clitics

In this section, I will briefly mention some additional types of special clitics. One interesting case to begin with is that of clitics in Old French, especially in the earliest texts (de Kok 1985, Cardinaletti and Roberts, to appear), and Bulgarian (Hauge 1976, Ewen 1979). Like verbal clitics, clitics in OFr. and Bg. are always adjacent to a verb; however, the choice of pre- or postverbal positioning is determined as follows: they are preverbal unless this would make them 'sentence-initial', in which case they are postverbal, regardless of the finiteness or mood of the clause. This is known, within the Romance tradition, as the *Tobler–Mussafia Law*.

(40) (a) Az <u>mu</u> <u>go</u> dávam. (Bg.)
          I   to.him it give.1sg
          'I give it to him.'

     (b) Dávam <u>mu</u> <u>go</u>.

(41)   Včera   v gradinata Daniela <u>mu</u>   <u>gi</u>   dade.
       yesterday in the.garden Daniela to.him them gave
       'Yesterday in the garden Daniela gave them to him.'

(42)   Falt <u>me</u>   li   cuer. (OFr.)
       lack to.me the heart
       'I lack the courage.' (*Eneas*, 1274)

(43)   [L]essiez <u>le</u>   et   <u>me</u> prennez.
       leave   him and me take
       'Leave him and take me.' (*Mort Artu*, 41, 126)

This mobility of the clitics suggests that the connection between the verb and the clitic is not as direct as in the mainstream modern Romance languages.[21] The specific pattern suggests that the clitics require some constituent to precede them, much like 2P clitics.[22] Lema and Rivero (1989) suggest that this requirement can force the verb to raise exceptionally to a position above a clitic if nothing else precedes it; see also Cardinaletti and Roberts, to appear. Alternatively, Halpern (1995: 26–32) suggests that clitics are syntactically preverbal in these languages, but may undergo prosodic inversion to avoid being sentence-initial – see Rivero 1993 for additional evidence for something like prosodic inversion in Bulgarian. As with second-position clitics, we must refine the notion 'sentence-initial' to allow for certain fronted constituents to be skipped.

(44)   Ivan, vidjah <u>go</u> včera.   (Bg.)
       Ivan, saw.1sg him yesterday.
       'Ivan, I saw him yesterday.'

European Portuguese offers another interesting variation on the verbal clitic in that the choice of pre- and postverbal conditioning is sensitive to a wider range of factors than in the standard modern Romance paradigm. Here, clitics are preverbal in embedded clauses, but may appear before the verb in a main clause only if preceded by certain types of constituents: negation, a universally quantified subject, a wh-phrase, or a focused constituent.

(45)   (a)   O   Pedro encontrou -<u>a</u>.   (EP)
             the Peter   met   her
             'Peter met her.'

       (b)   Dizem que o Pedro <u>a</u>   encontrou.
             say.3PL that the Peter her met
             'They say that Peter met her.'

       (c)   Onde <u>a</u>   encontrou o   Pedro?
             where her met   the Peter
             'Where did Peter meet her?'

(46) (a) Todos los rapazes <u>me</u> ajudaram.
  all   the boys   me helped
  'All the boys helped me.'

  (b) Alguns rapazes ajudaram -<u>me</u>.
  some   boys   helped   me
  'Some boys helped me.'

Spencer (1991) and Barbosa (1996) suggest that this pattern results from the same sort of skipping which is observed with 2P clitics in Old French and Bulgarian; the difference between Portuguese and Old French/Bulgarian would have to do with the syntactic conditions on the skipped constituents. See Manzini 1994 for an alternative based on differences in the order of movement of clitics and the inflected verb to their surface position.

Several recent studies (Pintzuk 1991; Cardinaletti 1992; Cardinaletti and Roberts, to appear; Zwart 1993, 1996; Haegeman 1992; Fontana 1993; Halpern and Fontana 1994) have suggested that weak pronouns in various Germanic and Old Romance languages are closely related to the behavior of second-position clitics, despite substantial superficial divergence from this pattern. For instance, in West Flemish, clitics are third (postverbal) in V2 main clauses, but second (immediately after the complementizer) in embedded clauses and V1 main clauses, as illustrated in (47). Assuming that verb-second in West Flemish involves the verb occupying C^0 with a topic occupying SpecCP, the clitic pronouns may be assumed to occupy the same position as those of the ancient Indo-European languages (see above). One analysis is schematized in (48).

(47) (a) Gisteren ee <u>ze</u> Marie gekocht. (WF)
  yesterday has them Mary bought
  'Yesterday Mary bought them.'

  (b) da <u>et</u> Marie gisteren gekocht eet
  that it Mary yesterday bought has
  'that Mary bought it yesterday'

(48)

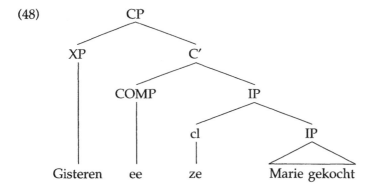

Still other types of special clitics have been documented which are less well understood. Polish pronouns and past tense (preterite) markers have considerable distributional freedom, but show signs of being clitics (Sussex 1980, Booij and Rubach 1987, Spencer 1991). Other cases are interesting because they contrast different types of clitics within a single language; Pashto (Tegey 1978) and Bulgarian (Hauge 1976, Ewen 1979) distinguish a set of 2P clitics from a set of verbal clitics, as illustrated in the following examples, suggesting that verbal clitics and 2P clitics should not be reduced to a single source. On the other hand, various Ngumpin languages (McConvell 1978, 1996) suggest precisely the opposite conclusion, as pronominal clitics in these languages may alternate between 2P and verbal placement.

(49)   Nova-ta <u>li</u> riza <u>ti</u>   podari Krasi? (Bg.)
       new-DEF Q shirt to.you gave   Krassi
       'Did Krassi give you the new shirt?'

(50)   Nen <u>me</u> dafter <u>pe</u>   pak ke.   (Pa.)
       today I   office with-him   cleaned
       'I made him clean the office today.'

Other distributions are known as well. Phrase-final locative clitics which apparently undergo climbing are discussed by Kaufman (1974); other phrase-final clitics are discussed in Zwicky 1977. Possible cases of second-to-last clitics (the mirror image of 2P clitics) in Nganhcara and Modern Greek are discussed by Klavans (1985: 104–5) and Sadock (1991: 171), but see Marantz (1988: 268) and Halpern (1995: 34–6) for critical assessments of these examples.

6 Prospects for a unified theory of clitics?

We have seen that there are various ways in which clitics may be distributed. Ultimately, evaluating approaches to clitics amounts as much to deciding which cases deserve a unified treatment as it does getting the facts of particular examples correct. So far, I have focused on the behavior of certain individual types of clitics, and on primarily syntactic accounts of their behavior. In the last fifteen years, several general theories of the behavior of clitics which seek to provide a unified (parametric) account of the different types have been proposed.

Klavans (1980, 1985) was perhaps the first to suggest that the distribution of all clitics could be accounted for by a limited set of parameters. (Verbal clitics may not be part of this system – Klavans 1985: 100.) In addition to the specification that a given formative is a clitic and that it has a certain domain, she proposed that they be specified for the following three parameters:

(51)   P1: Initial/Final
       P2: After/Before
       P3: Proclitic/Enclitic

The specification for P1 indicates whether a clitic should be positioned with respect to the first or last (syntactic) daughter of the domain; P2 specifies whether it should appear before or after this daughter; and P3 specifies whether it is enclitic or proclitic. This theory predicted that there should be eight basic types of clitics, corresponding to the eight ways of setting these parameters. For example, one type would involve an enclitic which appeared before the first constituent of its domain. A classic example of this are the Kwakwala case-marking determiners: syntactically part of the following noun phrase, they are phonologically part of the preceding word. This example also illustrates one of the points of Klavans's work which has gained the widest acceptance: namely, the independence of syntactic affiliation and phonological/morphological attachment of clitics. The attachment is thus viewed as something which is syntactically irrelevant, the behavior of verbal clitics aside.

Subsequent work in the same general vein (Marantz 1988; Sadock 1985, 1991; Sproat 1988; Taylor 1990; Pintzuk 1991; Halpern 1995; Fontana 1993) has led to certain alternative proposals in both the distribution and the attachment. One common change is to assume that the work of P1 and P2 should be reduced to independent syntactic principles. Regarding P3, the attachment parameter, some recent work concurs with Klavans in assuming that cliticization is simply a matter of stray-adjoining clitics to adjacent material (Nespor and Vogel 1986, Anderson 1993), while other theories assume that the attachment may effect an adjustment in the surface position of the clitic, as per the discussion of prosodic inversion above; more dramatic versions of this (Marantz 1988, 1989; Sadock 1991) allow a clitic which is associated to an entire phrase in the syntax to incorporate into the head of that phrase in the morphology/phonology.

Of these latter approaches, Sadock's proposal is the most thoroughly worked out. It is based on the central idea of Autolexical Theory that there are several levels of grammatical representation which must be put in correspondence with one another according to certain constraints. For clitics and certain other phenomena (e.g. noun incorporation), it is the morphological and syntactic representations which are relevant. Both the syntactic and the morphological representation encode linear order, but the orders involved may diverge when necessary to satisfy the requirements of each level. The divergence, however, must satisfy the following conditions (Sadock 1991: 103; cf. also Sproat MORPHOLOGY AS COMPONENT OR MODULE):

(52)   Linearity constraints

       (a)   Strong: The associated elements of morphological and syntactic representations must occur in the same linear order.

(b) Weak: The associated elements of morphological and syntactic representations must occur in as close to the same linear order as the morphological requirements of the lexemes allow.

Constructional integrity constraints

(a) Strong: If a lexeme combines with a phrase P in the syntax and with a host in the morphology, then the morphological host must be associated with the head of the syntactic phrase P.

(b) Weak: If a lexeme combines with a phrase P in the syntax and with a host in the morphology, then the morphological host must be associated with some element of the syntactic phrase P.

A given association between morphology and syntax must either satisfy the strong version of one of the constraints or satisfy at least the weak version of both constraints (Sadock 1991: 104). See Lapointe (1991: 149–50) and A. Woodbury (1996) for proposed revisions within the basic autolexical framework, especially the question of whether the behavior of clitics involves morphological or prosodic conditions.

Anderson (1992, 1993) argues for a conceptually very distinct approach to special clitics, according to which they are the result of an entirely different mechanism: namely, the application of morphological spellout rules applied to a phrase. (Simple clitics, in contrast, are syntactic words which are phonologically stray-adjoined to adjacent material.) The range of possible spellouts for a clitic, given in (53), is entirely parallel to that of word-level spellouts except for the nature of the input (the phrase as opposed to the word).

(53) The distribution of special clitics (quoted from Anderson 1992):
(a) The clitic is located in the scope of some syntactic constituent (S, VP, NP, etc.: probably only X^{max} but perhaps e.g. V′ as well) which constitutes its domain.
(b) The clitic is located by reference to the {FIRST VS LAST VS HEAD element} of the constituent in which it appears.
(c) The clitic {PRECEDES VS FOLLOWS} this reference point.

In favor of this treatment, which is essentially the extension to the phrasal domain of his treatment of (inflectional) morphology, Anderson points out that there is a strong parallel between the properties of clitics on the one hand and affixes on the other. Similar generalizations can be drawn about their distributions – abstracting away from the difference in their domains (i.e. affixes being related to wards, and clitics being related to phrases).

All such general theories of clitics run the risk of over-generalizing. For instance, several authors have questioned whether indeed all eight types predicted by Klavans are attested. Specifically, proclitics appearing after the first constituent of their domain, proclitics appearing after the last constituent of their domain, proclitics before the last constituent of their domain, and enclitics before the last constituent of their domain are all at best questionably attested (Marantz 1988, Sadock 1991, Halpern 1995). The lack of so many types of proclitics suggests that perhaps independent factors conspire against procliticization, much as suffixation is more common than prefixation. However, at least at its simplest articulation, there is a problem with this: there are certainly plenty of simple clitics which attach to the beginning of their domain (proclitic determiners, prepositions, complementizers, etc.), and procliticization is in fact the norm rather than the exception with verbal clitics. In contrast, sentence-initial special clitics (pronominal or particle) are virtually unknown – though see Pintzuk 1991: ch. 4 for a discussion of Old English clitic pronouns, which could appear sentence-initially. This is a fact which remains unexplained in any framework to my knowledge.

Another sort of approach to clitics which we have discussed indirectly throughout the chapter would treat all clitics as being syntactically incorporated into a head. Everett (1996) argues for a particularly strong version of this view, according to which all clitics and inflectional affixes are syntactically the same type of element, differing only in their requirements for morphological or phonological support. We have seen ways in which simple versions of the view that clitics are adjoined to a head are problematic (e.g. 2P clitics need not adjoin to an overt head at all; the split between 2P clitics and verbal clitics mentioned above for Pashto and Bulgarian indicates that these must be differently represented in the syntax). It is likely that the problems may be overcome by appeal to a sufficiently rich theory of functional heads. Whether such a theory of heads can be independently motivated remains to be seen.

In this chapter, we have reviewed various characteristic properties of clitics. We have also seen that there is significant variation from clitic to clitic which resists reduction to a single invariant characterization, though parametric approaches are highly promising for certain subsets of clitics. Determining the nature of these parameters ultimately depends not only on the behavior of individual cases, but also on deciding which phenomena deserve a unified treatment. We must ask whether there is a significant split between simple and special clitics, between verbal clitics and other (special) clitics, between clitics and affixes, or between clitics and independent words. It is my sense that answers to these questions go hand in hand with a theory of the distinction between independent words and affixes. Consequently, the behavior of clitics is a problem which any theory of grammar must face; but we also expect that our theory of grammar will help us understand the behavior of clitics, as indeed many of the works reviewed above have done.

ACKNOWLEDGEMENTS

This chapter was written during a year on a University postdoctoral fellowship at the Ohio State University and revised at the Santa Fe Institute; I thank both institutions for their support. I would like to thank Arnold Zwicky for discussion of various issues. The views expressed here are, however, my sole responsibility, as are any errors.

NOTES

1   I use the term "formative" here rather than "morpheme" or the like because various clitics seem to be at least partially segmentable into meaningful parts. The question of whether clitics may be morphologically complex has received a certain amount of attention. See Inkelas, 1990: 302 for the view that clitics – like function words – must be simplex, but see also Klavans 1985: 115 for an example which is arguably complex.

2   While clitics may in some cases come to bear stress, they do so only by forming a unit with an adjacent element.

3   Due to the scope of this chapter, many interesting topics pertaining to clitics will have to be given cursory treatment. In addition to the original sources cited throughout the chapter, the reader is urged to consult Nevis et al. 1994.

4   The conditions on auxiliary reduction, and on the distribution of other simple clitics, are very similar to those which affect the application of postlexical phonological (external sandhi) rules, and raise similar issues regarding the correct formulation of syntactic conditions on phonological or prosodic processes.

5   But see Kaisse 1985: 43, for some respects in which reduced auxiliaries are syntactically exceptional as well.

6   Other tests include selectivity with respect to the host, morphological conditioning on the interaction between bound form and host, idiosyncrasies in interpretation, peripherality of attachment.

7   I will use a double underscore to identify special clitics throughout. This is a variation on the usual use of '=' between a clitic and its host. In various cases, it is unclear from the literature whether a given clitic is an enclitic or a proclitic, or the language allows some variation – see e.g. de Kok 1985: 152ff on the attachment of clitics in Old French. Moreover, cases have been reported of words which have the distribution of a special clitic but do not seem to be phonologically dependent on an adjacent host – for instance, Warlpiri clitic sequences involving a disyllabic base (K. Hale 1973b: 312), various adverbials in Finnish (Nevis 1988).

8   Ironically, some of Kayne's more influential arguments may have more to do with clitics' prosodic dependency than any particular syntactic status: he noted that verbal clitics in French, like affixes, cannot be modified, conjoined, used in isolation, or emphasized; but this turns out to be true of reduced auxiliaries and pronouns in English as well, which are much less plausibly affixes, making these points rather weak arguments for affixal status.

9   There are limited, unproductive exceptions to this claim, of the sort in *en bien parler*, which I ignore here.

10 See Perlmutter 1971, Schachter 1973, Bonet 1991, Stump 1993c, Inkelas 1993, Halpern 1995, for various approaches to formalizing the notion of the template.

11 Various exceptions arise; e.g. in both Greek and Portuguese, clitics may come between the verb stem and certain tenses (see Joseph 1988, Spencer 1991). At least in the Portuguese case, this seems to reflect the fact that the morphemes expressing these tenses became verbal affixes more recently, if indeed one can claim them to be fully affixal at this point.

12 See Poser 1985, Nevis 1988, Zwicky 1987, Lapointe 1991, P. Miller 1992, and Halpern 1995, for discussion of some problems with this generalization which either require clitics to interact in nonautomatic fashions with their hosts, or require a more flexible theory of the distribution of inflectional affixes than is generally assumed.

13 Kayne (1975) suggested that verbal clitics were generated as pronouns and were subsequently adjoined to a verb to yield the structure [$_v$ cl V]. More recent formulations have proposed adjoining clitics not to the verb but to some higher functional head (Kayne 1990, 1991).

14 There are a couple of variants of the movement approach worth mentioning, though they fare little better in accounting for the full complexity of doubling. One is to assume that clitics are not pronouns but, rather, some functional head generated inside the noun phrase but subsequently incorporated into the verb. The other would be to decompose movement into two operations: copying and deletion, with doubling resulting from the application of the former only. Regarding the first of these, it is

not clear what position the clitic could be assumed to originate in. There seems to be no language in which verbal clitics are in complementary distribution with some noun-phrase-internal function words; furthermore, this makes it all the more surprising that clitics are obligatory with pronominal objects in Spanish, where pronouns are cross-linguistically not usually accompanied by other nominal heads (determiners, etc.). Regarding the second option, two problems arise. First, the conditions on deletion which would effect the variability of doubling would be completely ad hoc. Second, in many cases it is unclear what could be being copied, aside from a set of features; the common similarity between the shape of definite articles and pronominal clitics suggests that the article itself is being copied, and that such clitics are generally a type of definite article, but examples such as (25) where an indefinite noun phrase is doubled then become problematic.

15 See Bresnan and Mchombo 1987 for some cases which do seem best analyzed by treating the double as an adjunct.

16 See ibid. for an alternative view.

17 Indeed, Suñer (1988: 399ff) discusses dialects in which this constraint does not hold.

18 We will only consider clitics which are in second position with respect to the clause here; however, there are also examples of clitics in second position within other domains, such as possessive pronouns or determiners in 2P of the noun phrase, prepositions in 2P of the prepositional phrase, etc.

19 This analogy between 2P and V2 has also been noted in connection with very different proposals, as in

Anderson 1993, but also as far back as Wackernagel 1892.

20 The view that 2P clitics are adjoined to phrases treats them like adverbs distributionally, a connection also noted by Nevis (1988).

21 In other old Romance languages, clitics are still less connected to the verb, and may indeed be separated from it (Ramsden 1963, Wanner 1987). In the literature on Old Romance, the separation of clitics from the verb has been viewed as the marked case and is known as *interpolation*.

22 Interestingly, it appears that this is true even when the clitics are attached to a following host – see de Kok (1985: 152ff), Ewen (1979: 5). This suggests that clitics may impose constraints independent from their host requirement, a hypothesis which is reinforced by the behavior of reduced auxiliaries discussed in connection with (6) and (7).

6 Morphophonological Operations

ANDREW SPENCER

1 Introduction

This chapter describes the manipulations of the morphophonological shape of roots, stems and words which are found in morphological systems. It will be first and foremost a typological survey, but I will also argue for a particular view of the place of allomorphy in the grammar. I shall adopt the perspective that morphophonological operations of various sorts can be the exponents, or at least the partial exponents, of morphological properties.

Chomsky's work in generative morphosyntax, despite undergoing radical changes of emphasis and philosophy, has retained two key related assumptions throughout its history, both of them derived from its structuralist antecedents. The first is that morphemes are listed lexical items, and the second is that they subtend syntax-like structural relationships within word forms (see Halle and Marantz 1993 for a recent defence of this). In other words, much work in generative grammar presupposes a concatenative, 'Item-and-Arrangement (IA)' approach (cf. Hockett 1958). On this conception, a morpheme is a thing, and morphology is simply the concatenation of these things, so is viewed as formally agglutinative. The plural *cat-s* of *cat* is then viewed as a kind of compound, but one in which there are highly restricted privileges of occurrence of the second 'lexeme', the plural morpheme *-s*. Cases of non-concatenativity, such as the alternation between singular *man* and plural *men*, are not treated as special types of deviation from this scheme, but are accommodated by appeal to greater abstraction in the forms of morphemes, and to morphological triggering of phonological operations. This position was inherited in generative phonology (*SPE*, Chomsky and Halle 1968). In more recent frameworks, we might, for instance, say that the plural morpheme was a floating palatal feature, which docked on to the /a/ of /man/ to give /men/ (see Wiese 1996 for a detailed analysis of the much more systematic case of German umlaut in these terms).

However, a distinct tradition, associated with Sapir (1921) in American linguistics, holds that morphology should be regarded as a set of processes acting on stems or words to produce new stems, words or word forms. In this 'Item-and-Process (IP)' framework (Hockett 1958), *men* is derived from *man* by a vowel-changing process, while *cats* is derived from *cat* by a process of attaching a formative or phoneme (sequence) -*s*. On this conception only the stems or words can be thought of as pairings of form and meaning. The morphological property of plural for the lexeme *man* is then realized as the difference in the two vowels. In effect, the property of plural is a paradigmatic relationship between forms, not a thing listed in the lexicon. Clearly, both perspectives have little difficulty in providing an adequate description of *cats*. The differences revolve around the extent to which we regard examples like *men* as indicative of an important type of morphological operation or just a more abstract instance of concatenation.

One consequence of an IP view is that we do not have to picture affixes as lexical entries, because they do not have to be listed form–meaning correspondences. Rather, affixation can be thought of as the result of an operation, such as Aronoff's (1976) Word Formation Rules for derivation or Hoeksema's (1985) head operations (see Beard, DERIVATION). A radical version of this view is Beard's Separation Hypothesis (ibid.), some form of which is widely assumed in inflectional morphology (see Stump, INFLECTION). However, this does not, of course, prevent us from assuming that the concrete formatives themselves (such as the -*s* affix of *cats*) can have their own phonological properties. The question that is raised by the IP perspective is simply this: are there operations over phonological form, or equivalently, alternations in phonological form, which can be regarded as the exponent, or at least the partial exponent, of a morphological property? In a strict Item-and-Arrangement model the answer would be 'no', and all phonological variation would be ascribed to perhaps rather abstract underlying phonological properties of the affixes and stems. On an IP perspective we can answer the question positively, thus giving substance to the notion of 'morphologized phonology'.

In many instances, no doubt, a good case might be made for treating a superficially processual phenomenon as underlyingly the result of concatenation of things in tandem with the application of purely (or perhaps 'essentially') phonological processes and phonologically defined constraints. Infixation in languages such as Tagalog is arguably of this type (see section 2.2). Indeed, Stonham (1994) argues in detail that all of the most processual phenomena discussed in the literature are susceptible to such analyses. He, in common with many phonologists, views this as an advantage, in that it means that there is only one morphological operation, that of concatenation. This is then supposed to lead to a more constrained theory (of morphology, presumably), on the assumption that all the phonological operations are independently motivated phenomena of Universal Grammar.

To see what is at stake, consider a case of morphologically triggered allomorphy in English, the famous case of Velar Softening. In *SPE* a rule system was proposed for capturing the lexical relatedness of pairs such as *critic ~ criticize, analog ~ analogy*. The /k ~ s/ and /g ~ ʤ/ alternations were the result of a palatalization rule triggered by a high front vowel. This meant that the suffix *-ize* had to be furnished with an underlying vowel /I/ (a tense /i/) which later underwent a battery of changes, the Great Vowel Shift, to become /aɪ/. The palatalization process itself had to be split into several subprocesses, because /s/ is not what one would expect phonetically from adding a palatal element to /k/. The upshot is that the relatedness can be expressed in the vocabulary of phonology, and all the roots and affixes can be given a single underlying form. In an IP model it is open to us to argue that the consonant alternations are triggered purely by the morphological affixation process, and serve to partially identify that process. This can be coded as a process which replaces /k/ with /s/ in tandem with affixation, or as a set of relations between listed stem allomorphs, with the affix marked to select the 'softened' allomorph. The crucial point is that there is an explicit recognition that Velar Softening is a *part of* the affixation process, and not just an accidental by-product of it.

Now, the *SPE* analysis of Velar Softening is a modified recapitulation, of course, of a set of historical changes (in English and Norman-French). As is typical in such analyses, the cost is a battery of rules, extrinsically ordered, operating over underlying forms which are often strikingly distant from the surface forms. Even with the more recent technology of autosegmental multi-tiered representations and phonological operations triggered by constraints, a detailed analysis of a single language within this framework of assumptions retains essentially all the properties of the original *SPE* model. A good example of this is Rubach's (1993) meticulous description of Slovak (though unfortunately, the point is not so obvious, because detailed studies such as Rubach's, while indispensable for testing phonological models, are rather rare).

Among many morphologists and a good many phonologists, the assumption remains that a common underlier must be assumed for all alternants and that phonological determinants must be factored out at all costs. However, for present purposes, there are several reasons for retaining a perspective closer to IP. In subsequent discussion I shall refer to the phonological alternations which realize morphology as 'operations'. However, it is not crucial to the thesis that the alternations in phonological form be coded in the grammar as explicit operations, as opposed to, say, redundancy rules relating allomorph types. The crucial point is that there should be cases in which morphology is not realized affixally, where the phonological form of stem is the principal exponent of some morphological property. Under this conception the use of a particular prosodic template as the exponent of a given category would count as a non-affixal realization (see Aronoff 1994: ch. 5 for a detailed discussion of such cases). There are several reasons for adopting such a perspective here.

First, it will be convenient to view morphological exponence in terms of the operations 'visible' at the surface for purely expositional reasons, in order to bring out the rich variety of formal relationships which morphology can commandeer for its semiotic and grammatical purposes. This can be of practical value to the descriptive linguist working on little-known languages, for whom highly abstract investigation might be premature.

Second, the phonologically driven approach treats as a surface accident any correspondence between allomorph selection and morphological function. This means that allomorphy can never be viewed as a (partial) exponent of a morphological property. Typologically, then, we would be saying that languages are permitted to list floating features as morphemes (which may, of course, be true), but we would not be allowed to say that languages are permitted to signal a difference in morphological property by means of a paradigmatic relationship between singular and plural allomorphs. Now, it is quite possible that nothing of interest will come of the IP research programme which asks such questions, so it is feasible that the 'phonology first' strategy will ultimately prove correct. However, suppose that the IP view is, after all, correct. By ruling out that possibility from the outset, we will never discover the error of our ways. The IP programme would not, however, impinge on phonological research, to the extent that the devices which phonologists appeal to are really phonological, so there could be no corresponding methodological catastrophe awaiting phonology. Thus, from a purely methodological standpoint, it is better to make the richer set of assumptions embodied in the IP view.

In a related vein, there is a strong methodological reason for rejecting the phonology-first approach and adopting an IP perspective, based on considerations of learnability. Item-and-Arrangement theorists (often tacitly) assume that restricting all morphological operations to simple concatenation makes grammatical theory more constrained. This is then supposed to have beneficial consequences for the child acquiring language. Actually, as far as I can tell, such talk is almost invariably empty. This is because learnability considerations have to be computed over the whole of the relevant portions of the grammatical system. In order for considerations of 'restrictiveness' to have any meaning at all, what has to be shown is one of two things: either that the formal class of languages permitted under one conception leads to learnability problems, and that these are absent under the other conception, or that the best available theory of language learning is compatible with one conception and not the other.

Needless to say, no one has even attempted to make a case of either sort. Worse than this, no one has ever demonstrated that learnability considerations based on 'restrictiveness' are even relevant to morphology. The point here is that in syntax a case can be made for the existence of highly abstract universals on the basis of the 'poverty of the stimulus' argument (cf. Chomsky 1980). This argument gains much of its strength from the observation that syntax is an unbounded system, and, at a more practical level, that language users show evidence of linguistic knowledge which is underdetermined by the primary data. Now, although morphological systems can be very large and can occasionally show recursion, it is far from clear that they pose any 'poverty of the stimulus' problems. On the contrary, a characteristic of morphological systems is that they are subject to idiosyncratic restrictions, indicating that storage, rather than generation, is the key device. But this would suggest that there are no learnability-theoretic reasons for wishing to impose some notion of restrictiveness. On the other hand, at a more practical level, learnability considerations are, indeed, relevant where analyses require highly abstract underlying forms and complex interactions. This is because in many cases the 'correct' analysis can be obtained only from a fairly detailed survey of the entire system, with some crucial examples appearing only in vocabulary which is normally learnt fairly late in acquisition. Now, when the language learner has yet to be exposed to all the relevant data, s/he will presumably have to construct a grammar which is ultimately inadequate and will have to be overhauled. The simplest strategy is memorization of allomorphic variants, and given that we are dealing with lexemes or finite lists of affixes, this strategy will presumably be successful. Moreover, for the language use system (perception and production) storage of small sets of alternations is not likely to be disadvantageous compared to on-line production. Thus, it is difficult to see why any language learner should bother to project the more abstract, phonologically driven analyses.

An objection to this strategy is to say that it leaves unconstrained the space of possible operations that can be posited. This may be true, but then it is unclear why we should need to constrain that space. Children can learn language games which involve reversing the order of phonemes or syllables of a word. However, no natural language described hitherto has been shown to employ this strategy for grammatical purposes. But this does not mean that such a possibility is excluded by Universal Grammar; rather, it means that the chances of a language developing such a strategy, given the way that language change occurs, are minutely small (though theoretically possible, say, as a development from an adolescent language game). It may also mean that the learning strategies adopted by small children would deter them from positing such a rule. Finally, within the perspective of Optimality Theory, Universal Grammar must countenance a completely arbitrary set of operations over strings (the Gen function of McCarthy and Prince 1993a: 86). The effects of these operations are filtered out by ranked constraints, but in principle the theory permits a very wide spectrum of operation types to surface.

The rest of the chapter surveys the most common processual phenomena that can be seen as helping to realize a morphological property.

2 Concatenation

As we have seen, even the concatenation of concrete forms is often associated with morphophonological operations which serve as partial morphological exponents. This is true both of compounding and of affixation.

2.1 Compounding

Compounding is canonically characterized as the concatenation of two words to form another word. This is arguably the simplest type of morphology, and one from which many types of affixation derive historically. In practice, it can be extremely difficult to distinguish this from syntactic phrase formation. However, when compounded types become fossilized, the head of the compound may turn into an affix. At intermediate stages it might be very difficult to decide which type it falls into. This is also a problem in languages in which (bound) roots are compounded, for we are not then dealing with the formation of a word from other words. Neoclassical compounding in English poses such problems: is the *hypo-* of *hyponym* a prefix or a bound root compounded with another bound root (notice the stress shift in *hyponymy*, something more characteristic of affixes than compounded elements in English)? The type of compounding seen in incorporating languages (e.g. Chukchee; see Muravyova, CHUKCHEE (PALEO-SIBERIAN)) is also frequently a type of root compounding, in which a new stem, rather than a new word, is formed.

On the periphery of genuine word formation and word creation are so-called stub compounds in Russian and a number of other languages. Here, we concatenate some phonological subpart of each compounded element (in Russian this is generally a bimoraic syllable, which effectively means a closed syllable). Some examples are shown in (1) (I have separated the elements by = for ease of reading):

(1) (a)   zarabotnaja plata   zar=plata
            'earned payment'   'salary'

    (b)   kollektivnoe xozjajstvo   kol=xoz
            'collective farm'   'collective farm'

    (c)   Gos=sort=sem=fond
            Gossudarstvennyj Fond Sortovyx Semjon
            state collection specialist.GEN.PL seed.GEN.PL
            'State Specialist Seeds Collection'

    (d)   NIIN=Avto=sel^j xoz=maʃ
            Nautʃno-Issledovatel^i skij Institut Informacii po Avtotraktornomu
            scientific-research institute of-information on tractor
            i Sel^i skoxozjajstvennomu Maʃinostroeniju
            and farming machine-construction
            'Research and Information Institute for Tractor and Farm Machinery Construction'

In (1d) we see an abbreviation incorporated into the compound, which allies the construction with non-morphological (non-linguistic?) means of word creation such as acronyms. In addition, the component *sel^j xoz* is constructed from the compound adjective *selʲ-sk-o-xozjaj-stv-ennyj, village-ADJ-o-husbandry-NOM-ADJ* (where *-o-* is a meaningless intermorph) by taking the CVC initial of the two lexical elements, *selʲskij* 'pertaining to the village' and *xozjajstvennyj* 'pertaining to husbandry'. Note, too, that this compound is effectively headless, because the element that would correspond to a head, *institut* 'institute', is incorporated into the abbreviated first component *NIIN-*. In (1c), on the other hand, we observe that the element order of the compound is different from that of the full name, in that it seems that the compound is headed by its semantic head, *fond* 'collection', and its modifiers precede it. This is interesting, because genuine pre-head modification in root compounds is very rare in Russian (indeed, genuine root compounding is limited).

2.2 *Affixation*

The most important affixal operations are prefixation and suffixation.[1] These operations may be combined to conjointly realize a single process by means of a circumfix. Prefixation and suffixation do not invariably entail that the prefix/suffix appears on the far left/right of the word or stem, however. Prosodic considerations may demand that the affix appears inside the stem to which it is attached, in which case we have an infix. This is discussed in detail by McCarthy and Prince, PROSODIC MORPHOLOGY.

An intriguing puzzle is presented by circumfixation, in which a given morphological property is signalled by a simultaneous prefixation and suffixation process. In most cases both prefix and suffix are independently attested, usually with rather different meanings or functions. This is true of the two types of Comitative case in Chukchee (Muravyova, CHUKCHEE (PALEO-SIBERIAN)). However, the negative form of the verb in Chukchee is formed by a circumfix *e- . . . -ke*, neither part of which occurs elsewhere except in the privative circumfix added to nouns *e- . . . -ki*. The latter is almost identical to the negative circumfix, and is presumably closely related to it.

The term 'infixation' is properly applied to the insertion of an affix within some other morpheme (and not, for instance, simply between two other morphemes). Thus, we might wish to say that the plural form *mothers-in-law* is derived from the singular *mother-in-law* by inserting the plural formative *-s* between *mother* and *in*, but this would not count as infixation (for discussion of such cases see Stump 1995b). Genuine examples are provided by the Tagalog examples (taken from McCarthy and Prince 1993a: 101, in which an affix *um-* creates verb forms). When the verb stem is vowel-initial, *um-* appears as a prefix. When the stem begins with a consonant (or consonants), *um-* shifts to the right of the onset of the first syllable:

(2) aral   um-aral   'teach'
     sulat   s-um-ulat   'write'   *um-sulat
     gradwet   gr-um-adwet   'graduate'   *um-gradwet

In other words, the prefix is aligned as far to the left as possible, provided it doesn't create a coda.

Particularly interesting cases from Ulwa are shown in (3) (McCarthy and Prince 1993a: 109–10; *idem,* Prosodic Morphology):

(3) bás   'hair'   bás-ka   'his hair'
     ásna   'clothes'   ás-ka-na   'his clothes'
     arákbus   'gun'   arák-ka-bus   'his gun'

Here the suffix *-ka* is placed immediately after the stressed syllable; that is, it is aligned to the right of the stress foot of the stem. The interaction between morphological positioning of the affix and phonological constraints has been extensively explored with Optimality Theory, and the reader is referred to McCarthy and Prince 1993a, 1995b and Prosodic Morphology).

Reduplication is a morphological operation which, since Marantz 1982 has been fruitfully analysed as a species of affixation of a prosodic template to a stem, followed by copying of that stem and association to the template. More recent conceptions are discussed in McCarthy and Prince (1995b and Prosodic Morphology). The simplest type is simple copying of an entire root, as in the Japanese examples (4) and (5) (from Tsujimura 1996: 152, 107). In (4) we see examples of mimetics (similar to onomatopoeic words):

(4) pota-pota   'dripping'
     hena-hena   'weak'
     pitya-pitya   'splashing'

In (5) we see cases of Renyookei reduplication, which creates a particular verb stem in conjugation:

(5) nak-   'cry'   nakinaki
     tabe-   'eat'   tabetabe
     yorokob-   'rejoice'   yorokobiyorokobi

In more complex cases reduplication is only partial. Tagalog, for instance, has (in addition to whole form reduplications) reduplications of the sort shown in (6):

(6) (a) sulat   'writing'   su-sulat   'will write'
          trabaho   'working'   ta-trabaho   'will work'

     (b) magpa-sulat causative   magpa-pa-sulat 'will cause to write'

     (c) basa   'reading'
          mambasa   infinitive mam-ba-basa   nominalization

Notice that the reduplication can affect a root which has already been prefixed (6b), and may even appear to affect part of the prefix itself (6c).

In other cases, part of the reduplicated affix is pre-specified. This was true in Ancient Greek, for instance, where the first consonant is reduplicated in the prefect prefix, but the vowel is always /e/ (cf. Spencer 1991: 150):

(7) ly:o: 'I release'   le-lyka   'I have released'
     grapho: 'I write'   ge-grapha   'I have written'

Finally, we sometimes find that the reduplicated portion is introduced within the morpheme (i.e. as an infix). A simple example is Samoan, in which certain verb forms are the result of reduplicating the first syllable of the main stress foot of the word (which effectively means reduplicating the penultimate, stressed syllable; cf. ibid. 151):

(8) alofa 'love (sg.)'   a-lo-lofa (pl.)

Cliticized elements may be reanalysed over time as affixes, and this is probably the commonest source of inflectional affixes. Zwicky and Pullum (1983a) have argued that this has happened to the English negation formative -*n't* (as in *hasn't*), and that this is now an inflection. The transition can be seen in midstream in the reflexive clitic/affixes of some Scandinavian languages and of Russian. In (9) we see examples of the Russian reflexive formative -*sja/s^j* with various verb forms:

(9) myt^j 'to wash'   myt^j-sja   'to wash oneself'
     moju   'I wash'   moju-s^j 'I wash myself'
     mojem   'we wash'   mojem-sja   'we wash ourselves'
     myl   '(he) washed'   myl-sja   'he washed himself'
     myla   '(she) washed'   myla-s^j 'she washed herself'
     mojuʃʧij   '(one who is)   mojuʃʧiesja   '(ones who are) washing
                 washing'   themselves'

The reflexive formative -*sja/s^j* is always the rightmost element. In general, we find the -*sja* allomorph after consonants and -*s^j* after vowels; but this is not true of the present participles, where we find -*sja* even after a vowel (*mojuʃʧiesja*). Such phonologically unmotivated deviation is typical of an affix. In addition, the reflexive formative is regularly used to form a passive voice form from imperfective verbs. This suggests that we are dealing with an inflectional suffix (though it is typologically unusual for passive morphology to be outside agreement morphology).

On the other hand, the -*sja* formative is often simply a part of the lexeme without any identifiable meaning of its own, and certainly without any inflectional function, as in *uʧit^j-sja* 'to learn' (cf. *uʧit^j* 'to teach') or *loʒit^j-sja* 'to lie down' (imperfective) (cf. *leʧ^j*, which is the perfective form of the same lexeme, without any 'reflexive' morphology). In *loʒit^{j}sja* the tense and agreement markers occur inside the -*sja* formative, just as in the case of a genuine reflexive:

(10) loʒ-u-s^j loʒi-l-a-s^j
      lie-1sg.PRES-SJA *lie-PAST-FEM.SG-SJA*
      'I lie down' 'she lay down'

The problem here is that we must say we have a case of 'internal' inflection if we regard the *-sja* as part of the lexeme itself. Moreover, this internal inflection is identical to the external inflection we get from an ordinary verb. The situation is readily understandable if we think of the *-sja* formative as a clitic. It is noteworthy that in most other Slav languages the cognate formative is still very clearly a clitic. Thus, by some criteria *-sja* is a suffix, and by others a clitic.[2]

3 Morphophonemic processes (often accompanying affixation)

3.1 Apophony

The most well known cases of apophony (ablaut) serving as a morphological exponent come from the Semitic languages, though it is also found in other Afroasiatic languages, including Cushitic (cf. Hayward, QAFAR (EAST CUSHITIC)). Haiman (HUA (PAPUAN)) describes a particularly interesting case in the Papuan language Hua. Thus, the basic (default) shape of a perfective active verb stem in Modern Standard Arabic is CaCaC – for example, *katab-a* 'he wrote'. Verbs of this class form their passive by replacing the vocalism with *u-i*: *kutib-a* 'it was written'. Many nouns in Arabic, including recent borrowings, have a 'broken plural', in which both the vocalism and the disposition of vowels with respect to consonants may be altered. Thus, one class of nouns behaves like the word *film* 'film', which has the plural *aflaam* (see McCarthy and Prince 1990a for detailed discussion). These systems have been discussed in great detail in the wake of the work of McCarthy (1979), who provided an IA analysis within an autosegmental framework. Within the framework of Prosodic Morphology a more processually oriented account has been proposed by McCarthy and Prince (e.g. PROSODIC MORPHOLOGY).

Semitic provides abundant cases in which the consonantism of a stem is manipulated for morphological purposes, though this is widespread in certain Penutian languages of California (e.g. Yokuts, Miwok; cf. Archangeli 1983, N. Smith 1985). Though not traditionally referred to as apophony, this is a comparable type of operation. See below on consonant gemination in Amharic. McCarthy and Prince (PROSODIC MORPHOLOGY) provide more extensive discussion.

A relatively common type of apophony involves a nasal prosody. In (11) we see examples from Terena (Spencer 1991: 157), in which the nasalization is the exponence of 1sg:

(11) (a) emoʔu 'his word' emõʔu 'my word'
    (b) owoku 'his house' õwõ^{n}gu
    (c) piho 'he went' ^{m}biho 'I went'

In (11a) the nasalization affects all the sonorants in the word (skipping the glottal stop). In (11b, c) we see that the nasalization moves from left to right until the first plosive, giving a prenasalized stop.

3.2 C-mutation

It is very frequently the case that affixes induce phonological changes in the final consonant (or consonants) of their bases and that these alternations then become morphologized. At this stage we can say that the alternations cease to be part of the productive phonological system, but remain as signals of the affixation operation and hence as partial exponents of the morphological process.

When consonantal alternations take place word-initially, we speak of (initial) consonant mutation, which we could also call left-edge mutation. This is described fully for the Celtic languages in Fife and King (CELTIC (INDO-EUROPEAN)), and is also well known from the West African language Fula and its relatives, and from the Siberian language isolate Nivkh. Such mutation often arises historically from the effects of prefixes which induce phonological alternations but which are then lost. Initial consonant mutation has been analysed in terms of the effects of a floating autosegment (cf. Lieber 1987), mirroring diachronic change to some extent, though the alternations are sometimes such as to require phonetically unmotivated derivations. Keenan and Polinsky (MALAGASY (AUSTRONESIAN)) discuss a similar kind of left mutation which is triggered by certain types of compounding process in Malagasy, somewhat reminiscent of the mutation found in certain types of Welsh compound. In these cases there is no synchronic purely phonological source for the consonant alternations.

Typologically speaking, we could easily use the term 'mutation' to refer to non-automatic consonant alternations occurring when the affix is still overtly present. Similarly, (and more commonly) we could speak of right-edge mutation when a suffix induces a morphologized change. Slavic palatalizing suffixes provide a rich source of examples of such right-edge mutations (cf. Rubach 1984 on Polish, Rubach 1993 on Slovak). Note that many phonologists within structuralist as well as generative paradigms propose quasi-phonological treatments of such phenomena, which generally require rather abstract derivational analyses appealing to various types of rule-ordering convention.

A rather intriguing case of right-edge mutation without synchronic suffixation is found in the West Nilotic Kenyan language DhoLuo. Nouns form their singular construct forms (used for expressing possession) by mutation, which in some cases has the effects of a feature-switching operation, in that a basic voiced sound may become voiceless, while a basic voiceless sound may be voiced (Stafford 1967) (these examples also show Advanced Tongue Root vowel alternations):

(12) | Singular | Singular construct | Meaning |
| --- | --- | --- |
| gɔt | god | 'hill' |
| lʊθ | luð | 'stick' |
| kɪdo | kit | 'appearance' |
| lwɛdo | luet | 'hand' |
| puoðo | puoθ | 'garden' |
| ʧogo | ʧok | 'bone' |
| buk | bug | 'book' |
| kɪtabu | kɪtap | 'book' |
| gowi | gop | 'debt' |
| barua | barup | 'letter' |
| sɪgana | sɪgand | 'story' |
| bul | bund | 'drum' |
| lwɛɲ | luɛɲdʒ | 'war' |
| ʧɔŋ | ʧoŋg | 'knee' |
| ʧiemo | ʧiemb | 'food' |
| ndara | ndaʧ | 'road' |
| taya | taʧ | 'lamp' |
| wɪʧ | wi | 'head' |
| agulu | aguʧ | 'pot' |

A similar alternation is found with accompanying suffixation in the plural and plural construct forms. This feature switching is sometimes cited as an instance of an exchange rule, and has been cited as the kind of phenomenon which poses difficulties for purely concatenative morphology (e.g. Anderson 1992: 43). Stonham (1994) points out that several cases (including DhoLuo) involve singular/plural alternations, and suggests that in some words it is the plural stem which is basic. However, this doesn't explain other cases; nor does it help to explain why in DhoLuo the (singular) construct form also participates in the alternation.

Consonants between vowels often undergo lenition (or less commonly, fortition) processes, depending on prosodic, especially syllabic, structure. Since syllable structure is often affected by affixation, such alternations can easily become morphologized. Such word-medial alternations are generally referred to as (consonant) gradation. A well-known instance of this occurs in Finnish (Karlsson 1987: 30f), where long consonants in open syllables alternate with short consonants in closed syllables (length is shown as a doubling of the letter in the orthography; I have used a hyphen in these examples to separate a suffix from its stem):

(13) (a) kaappi 'cupboard'   kaapi-ssa 'in the cupboard'
    (b) matto 'mat'   mato-lla 'on the mat'
    (c) kukka 'flower'   kuka-n 'of the flower'

This is morphologized, as shown by three facts. The alternation is not entirely regular phonologically. First, the alternants of original short vowels undergo gradation which cannot be captured as a natural phonological process:

(14) (a) tupa 'hut'   tuva-ssa 'in the hut'
    (b) katu 'street'   kadu-lla 'on the street'
    (c) jalka 'foot'   jala-n 'of the foot'
    (d) kenkä 'shoe'   kengä-n 'of the shoe' [=keŋŋän]
    (e) polke- 'trample'   polje-n 'I trample'
    (f) särke- 'break'   särje-n 'I break'
    (g) puku 'dress'   puvu-n 'of the dress'

Secondly, the phonological context of being in a closed syllable is not sufficient to determine when gradation will take place. Some suffixes do not trigger the process. Thus possessive suffixes, even if they close the syllable, never trigger gradation:

(15) katto 'roof'   kato-lle   'on to the roof'
             katto-mme 'my roof'   [*kato-mme]

Thirdly, gradation does not take place before a long vowel:

(16) renkaa- 'ring'   renkaa-n 'of a ring' [*rengaa-n]

However, it does generally take place before a diphthong: for instance, one formed by the plural suffix -*i*:

(17) kato-lle 'on to the roof'   kato-i-lle 'on to the roofs'

But if the stem ends in a long vowel underlyingly, as in the case of *renkaa-* in (16), then gradation is still blocked, even though vowel length in diphthongs is neutralized:

(18) renkaa- 'ring'   renka-i-lta 'from the rings' [*renga-i-lta]

3.3 Tone

Innumerable languages make use of tonal alternations as exponents of grammatical categories. A straightforward example is again provided by DhoLuo. In (19) we see the imperfective and perfective forms of the phrase 'taste soup':

(19)   Imperfective   Perfective

    1sg.   á ! bíló kàdò   à bílò kàdò
    2sg.   í ! bíló kàdò   ì bílò kàdò
    3sg.   ó ! bíló kàdò   ò bílò kàdò
    1pl.   wá ! bíló kàdò   wà bílò kàdò
    2pl.   ú ! bíló kàdò   ù bílò kàdò
    3pl.   gí ! bíló kàdò   gì bílò kàdò

(The raised exclamation mark (!) indicates downstep, an acute accent means high tone, and a grave accent means low tone.)

3.4 Stress

Although stress, like tone, is an extremely common phonological feature used for distinguishing lexemes, it is not, perhaps, used morphologically as much as tone is. However, it isn't difficult to find examples of languages in which derivational or inflectional forms are distinguished solely by stress, and stress is regularly an important concomitant of affixation and compounding. An often cited case of stress apparently being used for derivation is that of English *contrást* (verb) versus *cóntrast* (noun), and there are a fair number of similar examples. However, it is probably better to relate this to a general difference between the stress patterns of nouns and verbs: nouns exhibit what is often called Noun Extrametricality, under which the final syllable is ignored for stress purposes. Verbs do not show this property. Hence, given some principle placing stress on the final syllable of verbs with Latinate prefixes such as contrast, we would in any case expect the stress to shift back by one syllable after the verb had undergone conversion to a noun. Interestingly, no such stress alternation is shown when a verb arises by conversion from a noun. Thus, the verb (and adjective) *abstráct* has end stress, and the noun *ábstract* has initial stress; but the verb derived from the noun *abstract* meaning 'to write an abstract of an article' (i.e. produce an abstract of) has the same stress as the noun: *ábstract* (cf. Kiparsky 1982a).

Stress is often used to mark membership of particular cells of inflectional paradigms, and many authors speak about 'paradigmatic stress' in this context. Thus, in Spanish the first- and third-person singular forms of the preterite of verbs are given end stress, in violation of the usual pattern for vowel-final words, which is to have penultimate stress. This can give rise to minimal pairs as in *háblo* 'I speak' (1sg. pres.) versus *habló* 'he spoke' (3sg. preterite).

Phonologists regularly analyse such cases in terms of stress assignment rules or principles triggered by various morphosyntactic features. However, some alternations are not necessarily easy to analyse in such a quasi-phonological fashion. One such example comes from Russian. The overwhelming majority of monosyllabic, neuter noun stems in -*o*/-*e* exhibit a curious stress exchange in the singular and plural paradigms. In one class the singular is ending-stressed throughout and the plural stem-stressed, while in the other class it is the plural that is ending-stressed and the singular which has stress on the stem. In (20) we see two such nouns, *okno* 'window' and *mesto* 'place', inflected for all their cases:

(20)	Case	Singular	Plural	Singular	Plural
	nominative	oknó	ókna	mésto	mestá
	accusative	oknó	ókna	mésto	mestá
	genitive	okná	ókon	mésta	mest
	dative	okné	óknam	méste	mestám
	instrumental	oknó	óknami	méstom	mestámi
	locative	okné	óknax	méste	mestáx

This could be taken as another instance of an 'exchange rule' (cf. discussion of DhoLuo mutation above).[3]

3.5 *Vowel length*

In Slovak the genitive plural of (mainly feminine) nouns in the -*a* class and the (neuter) -*o* class has no suffix, but usually has a lengthened final syllable (depending on details of phonological form). This applies to the syllabic liquids /l, r/ as well as vowels, and often manifests itself as a diphthongal vowel: for example, *e* ~ *ie*, *o* ~ *ô* (=/ᵘo/):

(21)	kladivo	'hammer'	kladív
	mesto	'town'	miest
	srdce	'heart'	sŕdc
	stopa	'trace'	stôp
	vlna	'wave'	vĺn

Despite the apparently processual nature of this alternation, Rubach (1993) argues for an analysis in which it is triggered phonologically, by an affix consisting of an 'abstract' lax vowel with no associated skeletal slot (a 'yer'). When final, such yers regularly trigger lengthening of the vowel of the previous syllable. All word-final yers are then deleted. This gives rise to what phonologists call an 'opaque' derivation, in that there can never be a surface form in which the triggering suffix (the yer) ever materializes. There is thus some pressure on proponents of such analyses to demonstrate that the system is learnable, compared to more surface-oriented alternatives.

Just as it is possible to see paradigmatic stress alternations, so vowel length may shift systematically across a paradigm. In (22) we see noun paradigms of certain nouns, *vrána* 'crow' and *jáma* 'pit', in Czech (this is not a regular phenomenon, only a feature of certain limited lexical classes; regular nouns do not exhibit any length alternations):

(22) Case   Singular Plural   Singular Plural

     nominative   vrána   vrány   jáma   jámy
     genitive   vrány   vran   jámy   jam
     dative   vráně   vranám   jáměř   jámám
     accusative   vránu   vrány   jámu   jámy
     locative   vráně   vranách   jáměř   jámách
     instrumental vránou   vranami   jámou   jámami

(NB: an accent here indicates a long vowel, not stress!)

3.6 Consonant length

Length alternations can affect consonants, too. A particularly interesting use of gemination is found in the verb system of Amharic, a Semitic language of Ethiopia.[4] As in other Semitic languages, the lexeme is built on a consonantal root (usually three in number, giving a 'triliteral root'). In many verbs we find gemination of the penultimate of these consonants: that is, the second for a triliteral root, the third for a quadriliteral (four-consonant) root. This is found throughout the inflectional and derivational system, including the formation of the stems for the perfect, imperfect, imperative, jussive, infinitive, instrumental, gerund and agentive (Type B). In other verbs, Type A, gemination is only found in the perfect (regarded as the basic stem form for Amharic verbs). Other verbs have gemination in the perfect and imperfect, Type C. Finally, a few verbs lack gemination. Examples of Type A (*mäkkärä* 'advise') and Type B (*fällägä* 'want') are given in (23):

(23)   mäkkärä   fällägä

    perfect   mäkkärä   fällägä
    imperfect   yəmäkral   yəfälləgal
    gerund   mäkro   fällǝgo
    imperative   məkär   fälläg
    jussive   yəmkär   yəfälläg
    infinitive   mæmkær   mæfællæg
    agentive   mäkari   fällagi
    instrumental mämkärya   mäfällägya

3.7 Metathesis

Metathesis is the reordering of phonemes, as when in child speech or certain dialects the verb *ask* is pronounced /aks/. Metathesis often accompanies affixation (when it is frequently little more than a phonological repair of an illicit phonotactic combination resulting from the affixation), but on occasion it gives the impression of being the sole exponent of a morphological property. Clearly, if it could be demonstrated that metathesis was a morphological exponent, this would demonstrate that a purely concatenative, affixal theory of morphology was inadequate.

A case that has been the subject of some discussion is that of the derivation of the 'actual' (essentially an imperfective) form of a verb from its 'non-actual' (perfective) form in certain Salishan languages, notably Saanich. The data in (24) are taken from Stonham 1994: 172:

(24)   Non-actual   Actual

    (a) se   se-ʔ   'send'
          wéqəs   wé-ʔ-qəs   'yawn'

    (b) t'sə   t'əs   'break something'
          q'k'ʷə   q'ək'ʷ   'straighten something'
          sc'ə   səc'   'whip something'

In the (a) examples the actual form is derived from the non-actual by infixation of -ʔ after the first nucleus of the stem. In the (b) forms we have metathesis of the second consonant and the vowel. Stonham points out that this CV metathesis occurs only with roots beginning with a cluster. He argues that the actual is formed by adding a mora to the first syllable. In the (a) cases this is achieved by closing the syllable with -ʔ. In the (b) cases a 'simpler' solution is to assume that consonants and vowels are segregated (cf. McCarthy 1989); in effect, that the linear ordering of vowels with respect to consonants is not fully determined. The non-actual forms are monomoraic, which means that the vowel must be syllable-final. However, the actual forms are bimoraic. This means that, instead of closing the syllable with -ʔ, the root can simply assign its second consonant to the second mora (note that there are no long vowels in the language).

This is an ingenious solution which skilfully appeals to phonological constraints apparent elsewhere in the language. However, even if this type of solution allows us to dispense with metathesis as a primitive operation, it does not dent the thesis that non-segmental phonological shape can be used as the exponence of a morphological property. First, suppose we grant that the Saanich lexicon contains a prefix consisting of just a single mora serving as the exponent of the 'actual' category. (How exactly you 'list' a mora in the lexicon is a question that needs investigating, but we will pass this by for the present.) We must then ensure that the grammar selects the metathesis solution for (24b) over glottal stop insertion. In Optimality Theory there are various plausible possibilities. For example, we could say that the constraints against epenthetic consonants and against onset clusters outrank the constraint against codas. However, Stonham points out that minimal words in Saanich are bimoraic (as is frequently the case cross-linguistically). Therefore, given the claim that vowels and consonants are segregated, and that their relative ordering is determined by syllable phonotactics, there must be a constraint in the morphology stating that non-actual roots lacking vowels must not be bimoraic. But this is itself an instance of a morphological property being realized by purely phonological exponence – there is no way to characterize this in terms of addition of an affix.

3.8 Subtractive morphology

Another phenomenon which is very hard to analyse in terms of the addition of affixes is subtractive morphology, under which a form is derived from another form by deleting material. Dressler (1987) has discussed a number of such cases. A simple example is provided by agentive nouns in Russian derived from Latinate names of sciences or profession: *biologija* 'biology' *biolog* 'biologist', *agronomija* 'agronomy' *agronom* 'agronomist'. Here, a portion of the stem is deleted, *-ija*. Dressler points out that there is no justification for assuming the opposite direction of derivation.

3.9 Truncation

Related to subtractive morphology is the sort of shortening which is very widespread in evaluative morphology, as in the formation of diminutives of personal names: *Michael – Mike, Patricia – Trish*. This can regularly be analysed as the fitting of the original phoneme string of the word to a prosodically defined template. In this respect it is reminiscent of many forms of reduplication, in which it is the reduplicant which is often analysed as fitting over a template. Opinion is divided as to whether such evaluative formations reflect genuine morphological phenomena and processes (see Zwicky and Pullum 1987 for a dissenting view). Of potential relevance is the fact that such formations often reflect spelling pronunciations, as in *spec* (from *specification*) or *Ameslan* (from American Sign Language).

3.10 Replacive morphology

In structuralist morphemics the alternation between singular *man* and plural *men* would often be handled in terms of the replacement of part of a morpheme by another phoneme string, in this case /a/ by /e/. However, there are a good many ways in which such apophonic alternations might be handled. More interesting are cases in which there appears to be a paradigmatic relationship between affixes. Consider the case of *-ist* and *-ism* suffixation. We could take the forms *Marxist* and *Marxism* to be derived by adding either *-ist* or *-ism* to *Marx*. However, this would miss the point that a Marxist is not just someone with some arbitrary relationship to Marx, but rather one who practises Marxism. Thus, semantically at least, we can say that *Marxist* is motivated by

Marxism, not by *Marx*. But this would mean saying that *Marxist* is derived by replacing *-ist* with *-ism*.

4 Stem indexing

A final aspect of the morphological use of phonology is the way in which different stem forms of a word are used to signal morphological relations. Though not strictly speaking an instance of a morphological property realized as a morphophonological operation, it represents essentially the same kind of relationship. Lieber (1980) argued that it was possible to do without purely morphological diacritical markings on Latin verb stems, and that conjugation class membership could be established purely on the basis of the phonology of the main stem allomorph (listed in the lexical entry). She then concluded that morphological diacritics of this sort were universally unnecessary. This position was criticized by Spencer (1988a), and a much more detailed demonstration of the need for purely morphological indexing of stems has been made by Stump (1995a) from Sanskrit.

Many Sanskrit stems occur in three forms, depending on the nature of the vowel of the final syllable of the stem (an instance of ablaut). These are known traditionally as the vrddhi grade, guna grade and zero grade. The precise phonological shape assumed in these grades depends on a complex phenomenon involving vowel coalescence, sonorant vocalization and so on, but the basis is that the vrddhi grade has a long *-a:*, the guna grade has a short *-a*, and the zero grade has no *-a* vocalism. An example using the verb lexeme *pat* 'fall' is given in (25), and one involving a nasal alternation from the masculine declension of the possessive adjective *bhagavant* 'fortunate, blessed' is shown in (26) (ignoring accent):

(25)	*pa:t*	pa-pa:t-a	3sg. perf. act.		'has fallen'	vrddhi
	pat	pat-ati	3sg. pres. indic. act.		'falls'	guna
	pt	apa-pt-at	3sg. aor. act.		'fell'	zero

(26)	*bhagavant-*	bhagavant-as	nom. pl.		guna
		bhagavant-a:u	nom./acc. du.		
	bhagavat-	bhagavat-as	abl./gen. sg. or acc. pl.		zero
		bhagavat-os	gen./loc./ du.		

At the same time, various morphological properties or categories make appeal to different types of stem. In nominals, for instance, declensional forms are regularly built on two stems, referred to as Strong and Middle. Thus, in the possessive adjective *bhagavant*, the Strong stem is found in the nominative forms and in accusative singular and dual (but not plural) forms, with the Middle stem occurring elsewhere. Notice that this cannot be defined purely in terms of the phonology of the case/number/gender suffixes, since formally identical suffixes may select different stems, as is seen with *-as* 'nom. pl.' (Strong) and *-as* 'abl./gen. sg. or acc. pl.' (Middle).

In (26), the Strong stem is the guna form, and the Middle stem is the zero form. However, this correspondence between morphologically defined stem type and ablaut type (vrdhhi, guna, zero) doesn't always hold. The Strong stem of the neuter noun *na:man* 'name', for instance, is in the vrddhi grade, not the guna, as seen in (27):

(27)   na:ma:n-i   'nom./acc. pl.'   na:ma:n-   vrddhi
      na:mn-a: 'instr. sg.'   na:mn-   zero

Some nominals have a third stem form, called 'Weakest'. In some adjectives the Weakest stem is suppletive, while in others it is the zero grade. In the noun *ahan* 'day', however, the Weakest stem is zero grade, the Strong stem is vrddhi, and the Middle stem is suppletive. In present and future active participles, the Strong stem is in the guna grade, while both Middle and Weakest are in zero grade (with differences in accent).

These kinds of data illustrate that it is not in general possible to predict the stem type from the morphophonology. Stump concludes that stems in general need to be indexed for the morphological function they fulfil. Where there is a regular relationship between morphophonological form and function, this can be stated as part of the stem-indexing rule, but in general such rules have to be kept separate from the morphophonological stem-formation rules. Such indexing rules may take the form shown approximately in (28) (where 'Class (V)' is an arbitrary feature I have created for labelling nominals such as *na:man* or *ahan*):

(28)   For lexeme L:
      where L is in Class (V), $\text{Stem}_{\text{Strong}}$ =   vrddhi(L)
      $\text{Stem}_{\text{Strong}}$ =   guna(L)
      $\text{Stem}_{\text{Middle}}$ =   zero(L)
      $\text{Stem}_{\text{Weakest}}$ =   zero(L)

The point here is that purely morphological properties within the organization of the inflectional system such as Strong, Middle and Weakest stem are realized by a complex interaction between phonological shape and purely morphological indexing in a fashion that cannot be handled in terms of affixation. Given that languages clearly have to appeal to such non-affixal relationships between stems, it should not come as any great surprise to find that stem allomorphy can be extended to include inflectional or derivational forms, giving rise to situations in which morphological properties which are normally expressed affixationally are realized as systematic morphophonological relationship, without the intermediary of affixation.

ACKNOWLEDGEMENT

I am grateful to Greg Stump for helpful comments on an earlier draft.

NOTES

1 Throughout I shall use examples predominantly from inflection. For examples in derivational morphology of some of the operations discussed here see Beard, DERIVATION.

2 Interestingly, there seem to be no cases of infixation of true clitics (endoclitics; see Nevis 1984).

3 Brown et al. 1996, provides a defence of the paradigmatic approach to Russian stress, though it does not treat the alternations seen in (20) as a unitary phenomenon. It thus remains to be seen whether the behaviour of monosyllabic neuter (for Brown et al., 'Class IV') roots is systematic or accidental.

4 The data, though not the terminology, are based on Titov 1971: 99f. I am grateful to Dick Hayward for discussion of the examples and for explaining the standard terminology to me.

7 Phonological Constraints on Morphological Rules

ANDREW CARSTAIRS-MCCARTHY

Pieces of morphological material, when strung together or combined, can affect each other phonologically, as Spencer (MORPHOPHONOLOGICAL OPERATIONS) makes clear. But phonology can have a more radical influence on morphology than that, in that it can determine whether some pieces of morphological material are combinable at all. This is because some morphological processes (of affixation, reduplication or whatever) are restricted to bases with certain phonological characteristics, and cannot apply to bases without those characteristics, even if they are appropriate on other grounds (syntactic, morphological and semantic).

Phonological constraints of this sort can be found in both derivation and inflection. Here are some derivational examples:

(1) The English suffix *-al* which forms abstract nouns from verbs, as in *arrival, committal, referral, refusal*, is restricted to bases with main stress on the final syllable. Evidence for this is the non-existence of nouns such as **abolishal, *benefital, *developal, *examinal* (Marchand 1969: 236–7; Siegel 1979). (One apparent exception is the noun *burial*.) The restriction does not apply to the adjective-forming suffix *-al*, as is shown by the acceptability of *occasional, procedural, fanatical*, etc. This shows that such restrictions need not reflect any general phonological characteristic of the language in question, unlike many of the morphophonological operations described by Spencer.

(2) The English suffix *-en* which forms verbs from adjectives, as in *blacken, dampen, redden, loosen, stiffen*, is restricted to bases ending in obstruents. Evidence for this is the non-existence of verbs such as **coolen, *greyen, *thinnen, *puren* (Marchand 1969: 271–3; Siegel 1979). Again, this restriction does not reflect any general phonological characteristic of English, because it does not apply to the adjective-forming suffix *-en* (as in *woollen*), or to the past participle, or passive, suffix *-en* (as in *swollen*).

(3) The Turkana suffixes for forming abstract nouns from intransitive verbs of state are distributed mainly on the basis of stem shape; for example, the suffix *-(i)si* (and its vowel-harmonic variants) seems to be productively attachable only to verbs with the stem shape CVC (Dimmendaal 1983: 270).

Here now are some inflectional examples:

(4) The English comparative and superlative suffixes *-er* and *-est*, as in *redder*, *calmer*, *happiest*, are restricted to short bases. Among two-syllable adjectives, individual speakers differ over precisely which examples are acceptable, but nearly all adjectives of three or more syllables consistently lack these forms: for example, **curiouser*, **sensitivest*, **motherlier*.

(5) The Hungarian second-person singular present indicative indefinite suffix *-(a)sz* [-ɒs], as in *ír-sz* 'you write', *mond-asz* 'you speak', cannot be attached to bases (verb stems) ending in [s, z, ʃ] (coronal strident segments). Hence a form such as **olvas-asz* ['olvɒʃɒs] 'you read' is unacceptable (Bánhidi et al. 1965: 87).

(6) In Classical Attic Greek, perfect stems of verbs were regularly formed from a base identical with the present stem, by reduplicating the first consonant and inserting *-e-*. Examples are *pe-paideu-* from *paideu-* 'train' and *te-ti:me:-* from *ti:ma:-* 'honour'. Reduplication could not, however, apply to bases beginning with a vowel or certain consonants including *r* and *h*, and was avoided with stems beginning with consonant clusters, especially *sC-* clusters. Forms such as **se-spa-* from *spa-* 'draw (sword)' and **he-haire-* from *haire-* 'take' were therefore unacceptable (Smyth 1956: 147; Schwyzer 1939: 649–50).

(7) In Classical Attic Greek, the third-person plural perfect indicative passive suffix *-ntai*, as in *pe-paideu-ntai* 'they have been trained', was not added to consonant-final bases. From a perfect stem such as *te-tag-* 'have (been) drawn up' we find forms such as first-person singular *te-tag-mai*, third-person singular *te-tak-tai*, etc., but we do not find a form such as third-person plural **te-tag-ntai* 'they have been drawn up' (Smyth 1956: 132).

These phonological restrictions leave morphological 'gaps' which may or may not be filled in other ways. We can distinguish three situations:

(a) The gap is usually filled morphologically, but in unsystematic fashion.
(b) The gap is filled morphologically in systematic fashion.
(c) The gap is filled in systematic fashion by a syntactic periphrasis.

In (1)–(7) we find all three of these situations exemplified: (a) by (1) and (2), (b) by (3), (5) and (6), and (c) by (4) and (7).

Examples of situation (a) (where gap filling is not systematic) are:

(1')   Most English verbs whose phonology prevents the attachment of noun-forming -*al* have corresponding abstract nouns formed in other ways: for example, *abolition, benefit, development, examination.* As these examples show, however, there is no single alternative for -*al*; nor is there a set of alternatives with a clearly systematic distribution. But that is not surprising, given that corresponding to any one English verb there may be several abstract nouns, formed in different ways and differing more or less subtly in meaning. For example, corresponding to *commit* we find not only *committal* (formed with the suffix in question) but also *commission* and *commitment.*

After this paragraph, there is an indented continuation:

The lack of any overall system in English deverbal abstract noun formation is confirmed by the existence of arbitrary gaps. That is, for some verbs there is no corresponding abstract noun at all with the expected meaning 'act of Ving' or 'state of being Ved' (apart from a 'gerundive nominal' in -*ing*, which is available for every English verb). This is true both of some verbs which appear to meet the phonological condition for the -*al* suffix, such as *ignore*, and of some which do not, such as *edit.* (The nouns *ignorance* and *edition* do exist, but they do not have the expected meanings 'act of ignoring' and 'act of editing'.)

(2')   Many of the adjectives which do not meet the conditions for the suffixation of -*en* can be used as verbs without any morphological change, thus illustrating 'zero-derivation' or 'conversion'. Examples are *cool, grey, thin.* Some use another verb-forming suffix: for example, *purify.* Alongside three adjectives which reject -*en* (viz. *long, strong, high*) there is a verb in -*en* formed from a corresponding noun which happens to end in an obstruent and therefore meets the phonological condition for -*en* suffixation: *lengthen, strengthen, heighten.* Nevertheless, some adjectives, whether or not they could appropriately take -*en*, arbitrarily lack any corresponding verb: for example, *cold, limp* 'not stiff', *tall, wild*; and some which could take -*en* have corresponding verbs formed by other means: for example, *wet* (verb *wet*, not **wetten*) and *hot* (verb *heat*, not **hotten*).

Examples of situation (b) (where gap filling is systematic and morphological) are:

(3')   In Turkana, every intransitive verb of state (including many items which would be glossed in English as adjectives) has a corresponding abstract noun (Dimmendaal 1983: 270–4). These nouns are formed through a variety of processes, distributed largely on the basis of the phonology of the verb stem, as follows (Dimmendaal 1987: 206):

Stem shape	Suffix	Example
-CVC	-isi *or* -ɪsɪ	a-rɛŋ-ɪsɪ 'goodness'
-CV$_i$CV$_i$C$_i$	-V$_i$C$_i$	a-sɔlɔb-ɔb 'disorder'
-C$_i$V$_i$C$_i$V$_i$C	-u	a-lilim-u 'coldness'

Thus, for any verb which is polysyllabic and is therefore phonologically inappropriate for the *-isi* suffix, some other suffix will be available, and its choice is likely to be phonologically determined.

(5′) All Hungarian verbs whose stem ends in a coronal strident fricative and which therefore cannot take *-(a)sz* in the second-person singular present indicative indefinite take the suffix *-ol* instead: for example, *olvas-ol* 'you read'. The suffix *-ol* is therefore in systematic complementary distribution with *-(a)sz*. Historically, *-ol* belonged to a minority inflection class of verbs which, in modern colloquial Hungarian, is merging with the majority class in all forms except the third-person singular. So the distribution of *-(a)sz* and *-ol*, which was once based at least partly on inflection class, irrespective of stem phonology, has now acquired a purely phonological rationale (Sauvageot 1951: 70–2).

(6′) Attic Greek verbs whose phonology prevents the formation of a perfect stem by means of reduplication regularly form perfect stems by two other means. If there is an initial vowel or *hV*- sequence, the vowel is lengthened, with or without a change in quality, as in *e:ukse:-* 'have (been) increased' and *he:ire:-* 'have (been) taken' from *auks(-an)-* and *haire-* respectively. If there is an initial *r-*, *sC*- cluster or *z-* (probably pronounced [zd-]), then *e-* is prefixed, as in *e-spa-* 'have (been) drawn' from *spa-*, *e-zeug-* 'have (been) yoked together' from *zeug-*. This is sometimes found, instead of reduplication, with other consonant clusters too.

It is clear from comparison with other Indo-European languages that reduplication for perfect stem formation was an old feature, and that it was not originally restricted from applying to *sC*- clusters; thus, we find the Latin perfect stem *spo-pond-* corresponding to non-perfect *spond(-e)-* 'pledge', and Gothic *(ga-)stai-stald-* corresponding to *(ga-)stald-* 'possess'. It is also clear that *e*-prefixation (traditionally called the 'syllabic augment') was originally characteristic of other, non-perfect verb forms, where it is also still found in Attic Greek. What has happened in Attic, therefore, is that a stem-formation process from elsewhere in the verb system (the augment) has had its domain extended to fill the gap left by a new phonological constraint on perfect-stem reduplication which is peculiar to Greek (Smyth 1956: 145–9; Schwyzer 1939: 649–50). (Steriade 1990 offers an explanation for the Attic reduplication 'gaps' in terms of sonority and syllabification.)

Examples of situation (c) (where gap filling is systematic but not morphological) are:

(4')   For those English adjectives which reject the comparative and superlative suffixes *-er* and *-est*, there is always available a periphrasis with *more* and *most*, as in *more curious, most sensitive, more motherly*.

(7')   In the earlier stages of Ancient Greek, a third-person plural suffix *-atai* appeared on those consonant-final perfect passive stems which rejected *-ntai*, as in *te-takh-atai* 'they have been drawn up'. Etymologically these two suffixes are related, and synchronically too one might well regard them as alternants of the same suffix, related morphophonologically. But in Classical Attic Greek the *-atai* form came to be replaced by a periphrasis involving the perfect passive participle in *-men-* and the third-person plural present indicative form (*eisí*) of the copula *eînai* 'be', as in *te-tag-mén-oi eisí* 'they have been drawn up' (Smyth 1956: 132, 183; Schwyzer 1939: 812).

It is notable that for the gaps resulting from all the examples which we have classified as inflectional, (4)–(7), there exists a systematic filler, whether purely morphological or not. On the other hand, of the gaps classified as derivational, (1)–(3), only one is systematically filled. This reflects the importance of the paradigmatic dimension in inflection (see Stump, INFLECTION; Carstairs-McCarthy, INFLECTIONAL PARADIGMS AND MORPHOLOGICAL CLASSES).

Inflected forms fill 'cells' in a paradigm of related word forms appropriate to different grammatical contexts; consequently, if some morphological process is debarred phonologically from applying to some lexeme in some cell, there will be pressure to fill that cell in some other way, so as to avoid the risk that there may be some grammatical contexts from which the lexeme in question is excluded, just for want of an appropriate word form. This pressure to fill 'cells' is not felt in most areas of derivational morphology, though there is evidence that it is felt in some (Carstairs 1988); the Turkana example in (3) above may be one such instance, unless it is classified as inflectional.

Facts of the kind discussed here have recently become more prominent in theoretical debate within the framework of Optimality Theory (e.g. McCarthy and Prince (1993a; *idem*, PROSODIC MORPHOLOGY).

Part II Morphology and Grammar

8 Morphology and Syntax

HAGIT BORER

Introduction

The interaction between syntax and word formation has always been a battle-ground, on which many important linguistic wars have been fought. In the late 1960s and early 1970s, disagreements involving the nature of the Word Formation (WF) component and the Lexicon provided the background for the emergence of two radically different trends within generative grammar: that of Generative Semantics, on the one hand, and Lexicalism, on the other hand. At stake at the time was the appropriate constraining of the grammar, and whether an independent, list-like lexicon is more or less costly than an extremely powerful syntax, in which transformations could derive varying syntactic and morphological structures from unique semantic representations.

To a large extent this issue, which has been inert within the Extended Standard Theory during the late 1970s and early 1980s, has reemerged in the mid-1980s, albeit in a slightly different guise. Work done on the lexicon during that decade has resulted in important structural insights into the nature of word formation, thus strengthening the claim that morphology is an autonomous module, on a par with the phonological and the syntactic modules, and that it should be understood in these terms. On the other hand, work done in syntax during that same decade resulted in the emergence of syntactic systems capable of handling word-formation operations in a more restricted way, thereby avoiding many of the pitfalls encountered by earlier, less constrained such work.

It is within this enhanced understanding of both syntax and word formation that the same question is now raised again: is word formation an independent module, subject to restrictions all its own, or should it be subsumed under syntax, obeying syntactic restrictions which are independently motivated? For those who believe in the existence of an independent word-formation component, another question must be resolved: how is the interaction between such an independent word-formation component and the syntax to be characterized?

on of these questions is an empirical issue. Proponents of an
ord-formation component must show that such a component
ions and constraints which cannot be reduced to independently
ictic conditions. They must further show that an independent
...; component with its accompanying restrictions allows for a
range of phenomena that cannot otherwise be accounted for. Proponents of an
exclusively syntactic word formation, on the other hand, must do the opposite: they must provide a way of accounting for the richness of WF phenomena,
without appealing to any syntactic processes which are not otherwise motivated. An illustrative example: if in order to allow word formation in the
syntax one has to introduce constituent structures which are only attested in
word formation, never induced for non-word-formation syntactic operations,
this would not represent any simplification of the grammar. It would simply
allow a modified specialized syntax for generating words, differing in crucial,
principled ways from that needed for generating syntactic phrases.

Below, I will review very briefly some of the answers that have been given
to these two questions in recent studies, pointing out the strengths as well as
the weaknesses of those positions. Section 1 reviews a lexicalist, pre-syntactic
approach to WF. In section 2, I review approaches attempting to reduce WF
to syntax. In section 3 I turn to a formal comparison of morphological and
syntactic structures, while section 4 reviews briefly issues concerning morphology and argument structure. Section 5 focuses on the existence, or non-
existence, of isomorphism between morphosyntactic and morphophonological
representations. Finally, section 6 is devoted to a review of some "mixed systems," those which cannot be easily described as syntactic or lexicalist in nature.

1 Linear models

Much of the work on word formation in the 1970s and the early 1980s has
been informed by the assumption that not only is there an independent word-
formation component, but its interaction with the syntax is severely limited by
some version of Lapointe's (1980) Lexical Integrity Hypothesis (LIH). Di Sciullo
and Williams (1987) formulate this principle as the Atomicity Thesis in (1):

(1)   The Atomicity Thesis: Words are 'atomic' at the level of phrasal syntax
      and phrasal semantics. The words have 'features,' or properties, but these
      features have no structure, and the relation of these features to the internal
      composition of the word cannot be relevant in syntax.

The way in which LIH is enforced in many of these models is by assuming
that the WF component, as a block of rules, is ordered with respect to the
syntax. The WF component and the syntax thus interact only in one fixed

point. Such ordering entails that the output of one system is the input to the other. This notion of the autonomy of the syntax and the WF component, and the restricted interaction between them, thus mimics the notion of autonomy developed for the interaction between the syntax and the phonology, where it is the output of the former which interacts with the latter. I will refer to this class of models as linear models.

One possible ordering for the WF component is prior to D-structure: that is, prior to the availability of any syntactic operations. Such ordering entails that the output of the WF component is the input to the syntax. Oversimplifying, this model may be schematized as in (2):

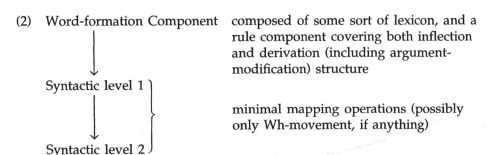

(2)   Word-formation Component   composed of some sort of lexicon, and a rule component covering both inflection and derivation (including argument-modification) structure

Syntactic level 1

Syntactic level 2

minimal mapping operations (possibly only Wh-movement, if anything)

Another possible ordering would entail a separation between the lexical and word-formation components which precedes the syntax, and some morphophonological component which follows it. Within such approaches, lexical insertion and WF involve the combination of categories and features (e.g. V+NOM), and it is the morphophonological component which is responsible for assigning actual phonological value to these combinations. Such an approach is depicted in (3):

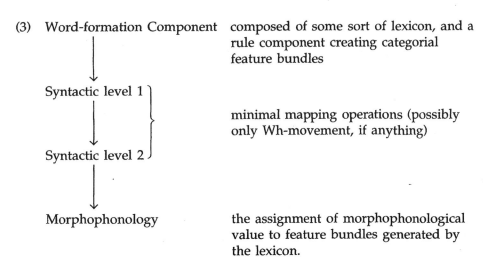

(3)   Word-formation Component   composed of some sort of lexicon, and a rule component creating categorial feature bundles

Syntactic level 1

Syntactic level 2

minimal mapping operations (possibly only Wh-movement, if anything)

Morphophonology   the assignment of morphophonological value to feature bundles generated by the lexicon.

As an illustration of the distinction between (2) and (3), consider a case of suppletion, as in, for example, the *sing–sang* pair. In type (2) models, the phonological string /*sang*/ is generated by the lexicon and inserted at D-structure. It is lexically specified as [+past], a feature that percolates to the root of the word, thereby becoming syntactically visible. On the other hand, in type (3) models the past tense of *sing* is generated by the WF component exactly on a par with the past tense of *walk*: both consist of [V+past] feature bundles. It is only at a later stage, when the morphophonological component is reached, that [SING+past] is given the phonological representation /*sang*/, while [WALK+past] is given the phonological representation /*walked*/.

Note that while the Atomicity Thesis may hold for (3), only the model in (2) actually *requires* it to be correct. If, indeed, the phonological string /*sang*/ is inserted as such under V, the fact that it is past tense must be associated with the entire word, rather than with any internal segment of it, for the word as a whole is clearly morphologically opaque. In other words, for supporters of model (2), there could not be a discrete [past] morpheme associated with /*sang*/ which is syntactically visible. On the other hand, this is not the case for (3). Here, a discrete morpheme [past] is associated in an identical fashion with both [SING+past] and [WALK+past], regardless of their phonological spellout, making it possible, at least in principle, for the syntax to refer to such a morpheme. I will return in section 5 below to some further ramifications of this distinction.

Proponents of an independent word formation, LIH, and the D-structure insertion of word-formation output typically support a strongly lexicalist approach to syntax, where much of the syntactic tree is base-generated as is, and the power of syntactic movement operations to modify the tree is greatly reduced. This correlation, while not logically necessary, is nevertheless not accidental. Within such models, it is assumed that there is a pre-syntactic independent word-formation component, with a set of well-defined properties and formal operations associated with it. Among the properties we find typically lexical ones such as subregularities, accidental gaps, suppletion, semantic drift, and blocking. Among the formal operations we find, depending on particular models, rewrite schemata, subcategorization frames for affixes, heads-of-words and percolation, level ordering, etc.[1] Crucially, now, these properties and operations characterize both derivational morphology and inflectional morphology. Halle (1973) has already pointed out that inflectional morphology shares its formal properties with derivational morphology: both exhibit accidental gaps, semantic drift, and blocking, and both can be characterized by the same formal mechanisms. In the work of Kiparsky (1982c) it is further shown that, morphologically speaking, regular inflectional morphology and irregular inflectional morphology do not form a natural morphological class, thus casting serious doubt on the validity of any formal morphological distinction between derivation and inflection.[2]

Proponents of linear models thus assume the existence of an independent WF component which encompasses both inflection and derivation, and whose internal structure, in accordance with (1) or a similar principle, is syntactically opaque. It thus follows that inflectional morphological structures, although they typically interact with syntactic structures, may not be derived by a post-lexical syntax but, rather, must be derived lexically and pre-syntactically, forcing the introduction into the lexicon of richly annotated lexical entries where syntactic information is abundant. Now, having given so much formal power to the WF component, and having incorporated so much syntactic information into it already in order to allow the derivation of inflectional forms, it is only natural to attempt to bank on the resulting formal richness, and to try to restrict the syntax so as to leave in it only those mapping operations which cannot be encoded lexically at all.

Consider a concrete example. In much work done in the early 1990s, and much inspired by Pollock's (1989) adaptation of Emonds (1978), it is assumed that V moves from its original position to the functional heads Tns and Agr, thereby becoming inflected for tense and agreement. A scheme of such a movement is illustrated in (4) for the French form *mangera* 'eat-fut.-3-sg.' (irrelevant details omitted):

(4)

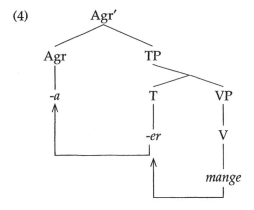

If, however, /*mangera*/ is base-generated already as is, specified as future and third person, the *morphological* motivation for the movement in (4) disappears. It can no longer be derived from the need for a host for the affixes heading TP and AgrP respectively, as has been argued by Baker (1988a) and Ouhalla (1991), among others.[3]

This rationale, note, carries over to supporters of type (3) models as well. Here, the verb would be inserted at D-structure as [STEM+Future+Agreement], and although phonological representation is delayed, head-to-head movement is not necessary for the stem to accumulate the necessary inflectional affixes.

Even more important, support for a strong lexicalist model, of type (2) or (3), comes from a massive redundancy present in models which assume the existence of syntactic movement alongside operations which modify argument structures lexically. Consider, for instance, the classical GB account of verbal and adjectival passives (cf. Freidin 1978, Chomsky 1981, Marantz 1984a). In these accounts, the burden of explaining verbal passives is divided between the lexicon and the syntax. First, in the lexicon, some sort of de-thematization of the external argument takes place. The resulting participle is then inserted into D-structure having, essentially, the structure of an unaccusative verb. Subsequent NP movement then moves the internal argument to its surface subject position to receive Case. This highly modularized account of passive is schematized in (5) (where the underlined theta role is the external argument):

(5)   Passive:

   (a)   WF operation: [*wash*]   ⇒   [*washed*]
                 $<,\underline{\theta}_1\theta_2>$ $<\theta_2,(,\theta_1),>$

   (b)   D-structure insertion and NP movement:

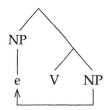

Yet within the same approach, adjectival passives are derived without NP movement, by a WF operation which takes the participle derived in (5a) as its input, and further lexically externalizes the internal argument, and (possibly) eliminates the original external argument altogether, as is schematized by (6a) (cf. Levin and Rappaport 1986). The resulting D-structure is (in essence) as in (6b), where the structure of adjectival passives (in predicative contexts) is in essence like that of unergative verbs:[4]

(6)   (a)   WF operation: $[_v$ *washed*$]$ ⇒ $[_A[_v$ *washed*$]]$
                     $<,\underline{\theta}_1,\theta_2>$ $<\underline{\theta}_2>$

   (b)

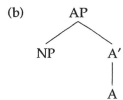

While empirical data lend some support to the representation of verbal passives as unaccusatives and adjectival passives as unergatives, from a conceptual point of view the following question arises: if lexical operations are allowed to modify argument structure, to eliminate external arguments, and to externalize internal arguments, as in adjectival passives, what, in principle, prevents a lexical operation that will externalize an internal argument in passive participles, thereby giving rise to a "lexical" verbal passive? Without an appropriate constraining of the WF component, such an operation cannot be ruled out in principle. In eliminating NP movement and restricting argument-structure modification to the WF component, proponents of strong lexicalist models, such as Lexical Functional Grammar (see Bresnan 1982a, Bresnan and Kanerva 1989), thus carry to its logical conclusion the research program launched by Chomsky (1970).

2 Syntactic models

In contrast with so-called linear models, much research from the mid-1980s onwards (notably inspired by Baker 1985, 1988a) can be characterized as an attempt to deny (much of) WF its status as an independent module. The thrust of the argumentation in these works is to show that WF phenomena adhere to syntactic constraints and interact with syntactic rules, and hence are best characterized as syntactic phenomena, not WF-specific phenomena. Most recently, this research program has been explicitly articulated in Lieber 1992:

> The conceptually simplest possible theory would . . . be one in which all morphology is done as a part of a theory of syntax . . . A truly simple theory of morphology would be one in which nothing at all needed to be added to the theory of syntax in order to account for the construction of words. (p. 21)

As Lieber (1992) herself points out, "no one has yet succeeded in deriving the properties of words and the properties of sentences from the same basic principles of grammar" (and I return to Lieber's own attempt shortly), but the desirability of this result continues to inform much current morphosyntactic research. Most of this research, however, continues to concentrate on a rather narrow range of phenomena, and the expansion of its results to a general explanatory model of syntactic WF is not clearly tenable.[5] In fact, with the recent exception of Lieber (1992), most researchers who have attempted to construct a model explicitly reducing (at least some of) WF to syntax have concluded that the task is impossible and quite possibly an undesirable one.[6]

Syntactically speaking, much of the work done by Baker (1988a) and subsequent work utilizes the notion of head-to-head movement, first proposed by Travis (1984). Head-to-head movement is the possibility of moving a Y^0 projection by Move-α and adjoining it to a governing X^0, thereby creating the adjunction structure in (7):[7]

(7) X^0

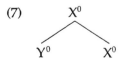

The availability of a syntactic operation which creates X^0 projections under well-defined conditions sets the stage for forming words syntactically. The case for syntactic WF is a formal one: if syntactic operations may form words, then the formal necessity for an autonomous WF component is weakened considerably. The reader should note, however, that the availability of syntactically derived X^0 projections does not entail that words as such are derived in the syntax, unless it is actually assumed that, *by definition*, all adjunction-created X^0 projections are *words* in the morphological sense: that is, if it is already assumed that morphological structures and syntactic structures are identical. It is in fact entirely compatible with existing syntactic assumptions to claim that the structures generated by head-to-head movement are *not* words in the morphological sense, but rather, nonmaximal phrases with some well-defined range of syntactic (rather than morphological) properties.

In general, work attempting to reduce morphological representations and operations to the syntactic configuration in (7) is divided into two groups, roughly corresponding to the traditional distinction between inflectional and derivational morphology. The first centers on the derivation of complex inflected forms from movement of lexical items through a succession of functional heads occupied by inflectional affixes. A typical example is shown in (4) above. It is an explicit assumption of most of these studies (see Belletti 1990 and subsequent work) that the representation in (4) is not just a syntactic one, in which nodes such as Tns and Agr are bundles of functional and possibly syntactic features, but that, specifically, these nodes dominate actual morphophonological strings, and that the head-to-head movement depicted in (4) has the effect of affixing to a verb specific morphemes, resulting in a structure which is a morphophonological word, as depicted in (8):

(8)

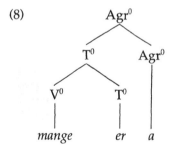

Furthermore, the formation of a complex inflected word adheres to Baker's (1985) Mirror Principle:

(9)   The Mirror Principle: Morphological derivations must directly reflect syntactic derivations (and vice versa). (Baker 1985: 375)

Given the Head Movement Constraint, the order of morphemes in a derived form must reflect the syntactic structure. Thus, if the morpheme /er/ corresponding to FUTURE appears closer to the stem than the morpheme /a/ representing third person, it follows that the syntactic node which dominates tense markers is lower in the tree than the syntactic node which dominates agreement markers.

A historical note is of some interest here. Pollock (1989), in arguing for the existence of two functional projections above the VP (but below CP), uses exclusively syntactic argumentation. Given the placement of negation, adverbials, tensed verbs, and infinitives in French, he argues for the existence of two possible X^0 landing sites for the verb outside the VP, and hence for the existence of two maximal projections above the VP. The labeling of these nodes as 'Tense' and 'Agreement', with the former dominating the latter, is not directly argued for by Pollock; nor is this labeling a crucial part of his argumentation. The claim that these projections are morphological in nature was first put forth by Belletti (1990), who linked the syntactic structure proposed by Pollock with the Mirror Principle, suggesting that since agreement morphemes in Italian occur outside tense morphemes, the Mirror Principle requires postulating AgrP over TP. It is worthwhile noting here that Baker's (1985) Mirror Principle was a claim specifically about the syntactic representation of argument-structure-changing morphology, not about the order of inflectional morphemes, and extending the Mirror Principle to structures such as those in (4) is by no means a logical necessity.

On the other hand, the possibility of deriving morphophonological strings by syntactic movement, coupled with a research program seeking to reduce WF to syntactic operations, resulted immediately in the emergence of what Laka (1990) refers to as the "Inflectional Big Bang." If, indeed, syntactic head-to-head movement is the only device for forming (8), the projection, as a full syntactic phrase, of every inflectional piece of morphophonology is inevitable. Further, as languages do not always display the same order of affixes with respect to the stem (i.e. some have tense markings outside agreement markings), the model requires the parameterization of the order of functional projections in a syntactic tree, allowing it to differ from one language to the next.[8] The system further necessitates postulating language-specific, and sometimes affix-specific, direction of adjunction. For a review of the problematicity of these results and attempts to constrain the system, see, in particular, Laka 1990 and Speas 1991a.

Before considering further implications of syntactic versus nonsyntactic WF, let us turn briefly to a comparison of the formal structures proposed for WF with syntactic structures.

3 Morphological vs syntactic structures

From the late 1970s onwards, work on WF typically utilizes notions such as head, projection, and subcategorization, all terms used in current syntactic theories. But are morphological structures one and the same as syntactic ones? Let us briefly consider some of these alleged parallelisms.

3.1 Headedness and hierarchical structures in morphology

A review of the rewrite schemata and hierarchical structures proposed for morphology reveals immediately that they are systematically incompatible with notions of phrase structure and tree structure proposed for syntax.[9] Considering, specifically, proposals made by Selkirk (1982), note that her re-write schemata cannot be reduced to a categorial projection from the lexicon, as is customarily assumed for syntax (nor was it intended to achieve this goal). Second, there is no way to reduce it to X'-theory. Selkirk proposes rules such as WORD ⇒ STEM; STEM ⇒ ROOT, etc., where notions such as WORD, STEM, and ROOT are morphological primitives with a host of morphological and phonological properties, in order to represent cyclical domains for the application of morphological and phonological rules. An attempt to translate this terminology into syntactic phrase structure would require postulating that X^{max} be formally distinct from X', each representing a syntactically distinct primitive undergoing fundamentally distinct syntactic operations, a perspective implicitly and explicitly rejected in syntax (for an explicit argument against this perspective see esp. Speas 1990, as well as Kayne 1994, Chomsky 1995a).[10] Clearly, there is no sense in which Selkirk's rewrite schemata give rise to maximal or nonmaximal projections in the X'-theoretic sense.

Heads and maximal projections of sorts are explicitly proposed for morphological structures by E. Williams (1981). Specifically, it is proposed that the rightmost element in a morphological string determines the categorial type of the projection dominating it (the Right-hand Head Rule). As such, the notion of head proposed for morphological structures is similar to that proposed for syntax: it is proposed that in branching hierarchical structures, branches may differ in their relations to the root node, and that some constituents may be more prominent or more closely related to the root than others. Note, however, that this generalization is true not only of syntax and morphology, but also of phonology, specifically in representations of syllable structure, where the vowel is more prominent than either the onset or the coda. This, then, may represent an inherent property of grammatical hierarchical structures across the board, and does not argue for reducing the morphology to the syntax any more than it argues for the reduction of the phonology to the syntax, or vice versa. Rather, what needs to be explored is whether the sense in which some subconstituent in a hierarchical structure is more prominent than others is identical in morphological representations and syntactic ones.

As a case at hand, consider the Right-hand Head Rule. Putting aside the question of its empirical adequacy, note that this is a very different type of relation from the one proposed for syntactic projections: it is relativized to a linear order. The head, rather than being a terminal projection of the same type as its dominating category, as it is in syntax, is identified by its position. Considering, for instance, a strict SOV language, it is unlikely that the presence of a Y constituent to the right of the verb in such a language would result in interpreting that Y constituent as a head. Rather, a movement would be assumed to derive that configuration, and the head would continue to be the X^0 terminal which projects the X^{max}. As a particularly striking illustration, consider a recent proposal of Kayne's (1994), according to which UG only provides for [Specifier[Head Complement]] word orders at D-structure. At first sight, the mandated left-headedness of such a proposal appears similar to the Right-hand Head Rule, postulating a strict correlation between linearity and hierarchical order. Upon closer scrutiny, however, the similarity disappears. Thus, when confronted with a typical SOV language in the Kayne model, the null syntactic hypothesis would still be that the noncanonical position of the verb (or more accurately, the position of the object to the left of it) is the result of some movement operation, and that a closer investigation would, in fact, reveal the effects of such movement. It is rather unlikely that because of its location to the left of the final constituent, the structure would designate the object as the head and the verb following it as the complement. Yet, this is precisely the proposal made by E. Williams (1981) for all morphological structures, and by Lieber (1980) for the structure of English compounds, assuming that the determination of headedness of morphological structures is computed strictly from linearity.[11] Note, interestingly, that while the head of a word is assumed to be the rightmost constituent, heads of phrases according to Kayne (1994) are always generated in the leftmost periphery of X′, rendering the unification of these two notions of head *prima facie* implausible.[12]

Lieber (1980), rather than defining heads and projections as such, defines a set of percolation relations in morphological binary-branching structures. At times these are relations between affixes and the binary structure which dominates them. The term 'affix' in her system is a derivative, rather than a primitive notion: it is the element that has a subcategorization frame. For compounds, on the other hand, percolation is directionally determined.

While Lieber's (1980) notions of affix, binary structure construction, and percolation come closest to the notions of projection from the lexicon used in syntax, they still show a range of properties which are clearly distinct from those attested for syntactic heads. First, head affixes may be on the right periphery (*-ation*, *-ment*, etc.) or the left periphery (*en-*, *be-*). Second, headedness for compounds remains strictly directional. Third, while syntactic structures give rise to trees in which heads are dominated by projections with an increased number of bars, morphological representations are typically recursive, and a morphological head X is typically dominated by a formally identical X. Thus, in a representation such as (10) an identical bar-level projection, N^0, is associated with the verb *transform* and with the adjectival affix *-al*:

(10)

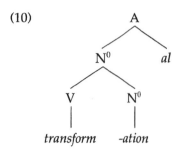

As Lieber (1992) points out, a simple solution in terms of introducing a sub-zero projection is problematic, in that it would require *happy* to be dominated by A^0 when occurring independently, but by A^{-1}, when occurring affixed, as in *unhappy*. In turn, however, Ackema (1995) suggests that the problem is only apparent, if it is assumed that *happy* is ambiguous between being a phrasal head and a morphological head. As a phrasal head, it is A^0. However, as a morphological head, it is A^{-2}. The structure of *happy* is thus as in (11a), while the structure of *unhappy* is as in (11b):

(11)   (a) A^2 maximal phrasal projection   (b) A^2

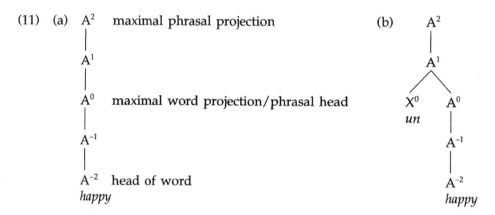

While the solution proposed by Ackema is certainly attractive formally, note that it crucially requires the assumption of projection levels dedicated to subword structures and the postulation, within a single maximal projection, of two distinct heads and two distinct maximal projections, phrasal and word respectively. Further, syntactic heads and phrasal maximal projections are subject to distinct formal conditions from heads of words and maximal projections of words. On the other hand, Ackema (1995), quite explicitly, does not try to reduce WF to syntax. Rather, he claims that there is a distinct morphological component which is governed by principles which are identical to those of the syntax, but which is nevertheless distinct from the syntax.[13]

Interestingly, Lieber's (1980) notion of projections is not too different from that put forth in Chomsky's (1995a) Bare Phrase Structure. Here, as well, notions such as X^0 and X' are no longer basic; nor is a typical node composed of the sequence $X''–X'–X^0$. Rather, a phrase is conceived as a succession of identical nodes dominating each other, as in $[_{cat}\ [_{cat}\ [_{cat}\ cat]]]$, where the lowest, the terminal, is interpreted as X^{min} and the highest as X^{max}. To draw a parallelism with a morphological structure, in a string such as $[_A\ un\ [_A\ happy]]$, *happy* would be A^{min}, while *unhappy* would be A^{max}.

In her own attempt to unite the hierarchical representation of words and phrases, and being fully aware of the syntactic incompatibility of previous accounts, Lieber (1992) proposes a modification of the (syntactic) X' schema, adapting it to both morphological and syntactic needs. Such an attempt can only be successful, however, if in doing so, Lieber does not merely create a set of hierarchical structures and conditions on them which apply exclusively to word formation. Examining her proposed modification, it appears that she does precisely that. Specifically, she argues for the following modifications to the X'-schema:

(12) (a) Specifiers must be allowed to appear within the X' level.
      (b) Recursion is allowed within the X^0 level.
      (c) Nonheads need not be maximal projections.

It is not clear that the modifications proposed in (12) have any independent syntactic justification. Concerning (12a), Lieber relies on a comment by Stowell (1981), proposing that in Japanese and German specifiers are generated under X'. Research since then has seriously challenged this claim. Nor does Lieber provide any evidence for the independent necessity of (12b) in syntactic (i.e. nonmorphological) representations. Finally, proposals quoted by Lieber as evidence for (12c) are extremely limited in scope, and center on a very narrow range of properties. Specifically, even if structures such as (13) are, according to some phrase-structural approaches, attested syntactically,[14] the question is why structures such as (14), which Lieber predicts to exist freely, are rare for morphological units, and not attested at all for syntactic ones:[15]

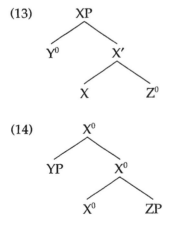

However, the most serious problem for Lieber's (1992) attempt to reduce morphological formalism to a syntactic one concerns her use of specifiers and complement, a point to which I return shortly.

3.2 Subcategorization

Lieber (1980) and others have proposed that morphological selection can be captured by means of a morphological subcategorization frame, or selection. Again, it is tempting to try and subsume this notion of subcategorization, or selection, under the notion of selection familiar from the syntax. Yet, an investigation of the properties of morphological selection reveals that it must be kept entirely distinct from syntactic selection. In order to illustrate this, consider a proposal by Rizzi and Roberts (1989) to encode morphological subcategorization syntactically. They propose that morphological subcategorizations are projected syntactically as adjunction structures with an empty slot into which substitution movement can move heads. Head-to-head movement is further possible without such base-generated structures, creating adjunctions, rather than substituting into base-generated ones. This latter operation does not result in a word. The two structures have distinct properties. Thus excorporation (in the sense of Roberts 1991) is possible from the latter, but not from the former.

Consider some of the consequences of this proposal. First, note that it allows head-to-head movement, and hence the formation of an X^0 projection, which is not a word, when no morphological subcategorization is projected. Thereby, the definition of word is lifted out of the syntax, becoming a purely morphological matter, which is entirely independent of the existence of an X^0 projection. This is especially striking, as, syntactically, the outputs of substitution into a base-generated adjunction structure and adjunction-creating movement are identical. The syntax is thus in principle incapable of distinguishing between these two outputs, and an (independent) morphology must be appealed to, to determine which syntactic configurations correspond to words and which do not.

Second, since the outputs of substitution and adjunction are identical, a configuration is introduced here which is otherwise unattested in syntax, and seems needed only for the purposes of incorporating word formation into the syntax. (Note that this issue is independent of whether or not adjunction structures can be base-generated, as it addresses specifically the possibility of substitution into such structures, if, indeed, they may be base-generated.)

Attempting to address some of these problems, Roberts (1991) proposes that in substitution cases (but not in adjunction cases) a sub-X^0 structure is base-generated, with a null sister, having the structure in (15):

(15)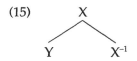

In this structure, substitution is to the empty Y slot. In this way, the structural identity between the outputs of adjunction and substitution is avoided. However, other problems arise. Some issues concerning sub-X^0 projections were reviewed in section 3.1. Note, in addition, that identity of output between adjunction and substitution is avoided here at the cost of introducing a sub-X^0 structure for the manifest purpose of allowing words to have syntactic structures. None but morphological structures would ever have sub-X^0 structure; nor would morphological selection ever be realized anywhere else. Thus the syntactic difficulty here is solved by reinforcing the gap between syntactic selection and morphological selection, not eliminating it.

Second, note that under the standard assumptions that substitution movement is only possible to a specifier position, never to a complement position, we must assume that Y in (15) is a specifier. Under equally accepted assumptions, however, selection may only be realized by complements. We are thus faced with a contradictory situation where Y is selected by X^{-1}, and hence is its complement, but movement to it is possible, thus suggesting that it is a specifier. The problem is compounded by approaches (cf. Speas 1990, Kayne 1994) which obliterate the distinction between specifiers and adjuncts altogether, making the distinction which Rizzi and Roberts (1989) try to draw impossible to state.

This criticism is equally applicable to proposals made by Lieber (1992). In her attempt to reduce morphological representations to syntactic ones, Lieber is clearly faced with the need to explain the persistent right-headedness of English words such as [[*happy*_A] *ness*_N]] [[*monster*_N] *ous*_A]] [[*glory*_N] *ify*_V]]. As -*ness*, -*ous*, -*ify* are clearly heads here, and as the stems to which they are attached appear to their left, Lieber concludes that *happy*, *monster*, and *glory* are specifiers (or possibly modifiers), and not complements of their respective heads. In addition, however, Lieber would still like to maintain that in a meaningful way, -*ness*, -*ous*, -*ify* categorially, and possibly semantically, select *happy*, *monster*, and *glory*. Again, selection according to standard syntactic assumptions may only be realized by complements, leading to a contradiction, or to a system of complements, specifiers, and selection which behaves differently for morphology and for syntax. (The nonstandard aspect of specifiers as sisters of an X^0 projection in Lieber's system was pointed out above.)

Returning to (15) (or, for that matter, to the original structure proposed by Rizzi and Roberts (1989)), and given the D-structure syntactic projection of morphological subcategorization frames, one may ask what actually prevents the base-generation of morphological structures such as (15) with all morphemes in place, preempting movement altogether. The answer is that such base-generation is often not possible as the incorporated element is itself a complement of X which must satisfy a distinct syntactic subcategorization frame at D-structure in order to meet the Projection Principle. The schema of such a structure is given in (16):

(16)

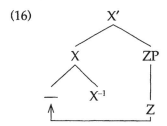

It thus seems that morphological subcategorization frames need not, and indeed, at times may not, be satisfied at D-structure. In fact, it is precisely the conflict between the syntactic subcategorization, which must be satisfied at D-structure, and the morphological subcategorization, which need not be thus satisfied, which gives rise to the movement. It is thus obvious that syntactic subcategorization and morphological subcategorization are distinct, and should be kept as such, to ensure that one must be satisfied at D-structure, while the other need not be.[16]

In conclusion, extending the syntax to cover morphological structures requires a radical modification of our notion of hierarchical structures and selection as they emerge from the X' schema. Notions such as head and selection, when used morphologically, are sufficiently distinct to seriously shake any attempt to reduce them to well-known syntactic mechanisms.

3.3 Incorporation and government

In view of the fundamental problems associated with the formal reduction of morphological structures to syntactic ones, what further support is there for the claim that, for example, noun incorporation as a morphological process is syntactically derived? Baker (1988a) brings forth many empirical arguments for his assumption that noun incorporation must be syntactically derived. However, subsequent work by Di Sciullo and Williams (1987) has shown clearly that none of his empirical arguments actually excludes a lexical derivation. Rather, Baker's argumentation by and large shows noun incorporation to be consistent with a syntactic analysis, rather than incompatible with a lexical one.

A major conceptual argument brought forth by Baker in support of a syntactic derivation for noun incorporation is based on simplicity: some central properties of words can be shown to follow directly from independently motivated syntactic principles if we assume that they are formed by head-to-head movement. The major independently motivated constraint is the Head Movement Constraint (of Travis 1984) and its (possible) reduction to the Empty

Category Principle (see Chomsky 1986). Specifically, the HMC/ECP accounts elegantly for subject–object asymmetries observed in noun incorporation, and groups them together with a wide range of syntactic subject–object asymmetries independently reducible to ECP effects.

This line of argumentation, however, is actually less than conclusive. More than anything else, it is indicative of the prevalence of the notion of government in syntactic models put forth in the 1980s. As is well established, word-formation operations which interact with argument structure are sensitive to selection properties. In particular, internal arguments, the classical "subcategorized" elements, enter word formation with the stem in a way which is not (typically) attested with external arguments. This was observed at least as early as Lees (1960), and has been incorporated in some fashion into WF accounts, be they syntactic (as in Roeper and Siegel 1978) or lexical (as in Lieber 1983).

Under standard assumptions, complements are projected in some minimal domain of the head, while noncomplements, either adjuncts or specifiers, are projected outside that same domain. If we refer to this minimal domain as "government," as is commonly done, it is clear that a statement concerning the incorporability of selected complements and a statement concerning the incorporability of elements governed by V are almost identical.[17]

Configurations of government and configurations of selection do, however, vary. Within phrase structures proposed in the mid-1980s, one area of difference involves Exceptionally Case Marked embedded subjects. Another involves specifiers of complements. As is well known, clitics do incorporate in the former contexts, as the following example from French illustrates. However, there are no documented cases of noun incorporation from such contexts:

(17)   Je le$_2$ considère [$_{AP}$ t$_2$ malade]
       'I him consider   sick'

Baker (1988a) discusses, however, a case in Chichewa where it is clearly not a selected complement which incorporates into the verb, but rather its possessor, which is governed by the verb but is not selected by it:

(18) (a)   Fisi   a- na- dy-a   nsomba za kalulu
            hyena SP-PAST-*eat*-ASP *fish*   *of hare*
            'The hyena ate the hare's fish'

      (b)   Fisi   a- na- dy-er- a   kalulu$_1$ nsomba (t$_1$)
            hyena SP-PAST-*eat*-APPL-ASP *hare*   *fish*

Note that in (18a), the possessor appears as a post-nominal PP, while in (18b) an applicative affix is attached to the verb, and the possessor appears adjacent to it.

Interestingly, on recent assumptions concerning phrase structure, the government asymmetry between complements and subjects disappears. Specifically, if subjects are base-generated as the specifiers of the head selecting them, and that head moves to a higher head, resulting in the configuration in (19), noun incorporation of subjects into the V can no longer be excluded by the HMC:

(19) $[_{FP} \ldots [_{F'} \text{ V} + \text{F} [_{VP} \text{ Subj } t_v \text{ (Obj)}]]]$

Borer (1995) argues that, indeed, the incorporation of specifiers in structures such as (19) is licit, also in construct state nominal configurations such as (20a), exemplified in (20b), where *'axilat-Dan* 'eating Dan' is argued to be an incorporated form (irrelevant details omitted):

(20)   (a) $[_{DP1} \text{ N}_1 \ldots [_{NP} \text{ N}_2 \text{ } t_1 \text{ } [_{XP} \ldots]]]$

     (b)   'axilat Dan 'et   ha-tapuax
         eating Dan acc. the-apple
         'Dan's eating of the apple'

In view of this, one wonders why it is that cliticization and Hebrew construct state allow a type of head-to-head movement which is excluded for noun incorporation.

4 WF and argument structure

Word formation by syntactic means receives its strongest, overwhelming support from the existence of a very powerful pretheoretical approach to the interaction between lexical semantics and syntax. According to this view, closely resembling the Generative Semantics tradition, there should be a direct mapping between thematic roles and syntactic structures, and if such a direct mapping could be established, it would per force favor those formal representations which are compatible with it and exclude others. For proponents of such an approach it thus suffices that syntactic word formation be shown to be empirically adequate. It is not necessary to show that the rival approach, the lexical one, is empirically flawed, since everything else being equal, it is to be dismissed on general, pretheoretical grounds.

In the work of Baker (1988a), this perspective on the interaction of syntax and lexical semantics is formulated as the Uniformity of Theta Assignment Hypothesis given in (21):

(21)   The Uniformity of Theta Assignment Hypothesis: Identical thematic relationships between items are represented by identical structural relationships between these items at the level of D-structure.

UTAH, as utilized by Baker, argues that, for example, active and passive verbs must have the same D-structure; that causative verbs must appear in structure in which the arguments of the source, a noncausative verb, are fully represented, etc. Intuitively, UTAH suggests that for every lexical item there is a unique D-structure, and any further manipulation of argument structure or affixation must be syntactic, the output of movement. In its strongest possible interpretation, a principle such as UTAH not only enables words which interact with argument structure to be formed syntactically, but actually forces them to be formed syntactically.[18]

An illustration of the way in which a principle such as UTAH motivates a derivation is the comparison of the derivation of verbal passive in Chomsky 1981 with the analysis of verbal passive put forth in Baker et al. (1989). Recall (see section 1 for a brief discussion) that in the system of Chomsky (1981), deriving verbal passive is a modular process, having a 'lexical' WF component and a syntactic one. Specifically, for a verb such as *derive*, the WF operation forms the participle *derived* from the source V and suppresses/internalizes the external argument. The internal argument, however, remains intact, and projects as the complement of the participle at D-structure. Syntactic considerations (i.e. the need for Case) now result in that internal argument moving to receive nominative Case.

This derivation, note, is only partially compatible with UTAH. Although the projection of the internal argument remains identical for the lexical entry of *derive* both in its verbal and in its participial form, the projection of the external argument is altered. While for *derive* the external argument is projected as a sister of V' (or, alternatively, as a sister of VP), for the participle *derived* the external argument is not projected at all, or, alternatively, it is internalized, in violation of UTAH. Similarly, proposals put forth by Jaeggli (1986a) are not fully compatible with UTAH. This suggests that the affix *-en* is assigned the external argument. However, that affix is placed internal to the V' constituent, thereby allowing the external argument to be realized in different positions, although its thematic relationship with *derive(d)* is constant.

Baker et al. (1989) address this issue directly. Adopting Jaeggli's (1986a) assumption that the external argument is assigned to the morpheme *-en*, they project that morpheme *external* to the VP, and as its sister. Assuming that the notion "identical structural relations" means for external arguments sisterhood with a maximal projection, the assignment of an external thematic role to a head external to the VP satisfies UTAH. Relevant aspects of the structure proposed by Baker et al. (1989) are given in (22):

(22) $[_{\text{IP}} -en_1 [_{\text{VP}} \textit{derive NP}]]$
     $\theta_{\text{ex.}}$ $\theta_{\text{int.}}$

The ramifications of UTAH for the WF component and its interaction with argument structure are far-reaching and interesting. As has been pointed out often, however, for some argument-structure-changing morphology, a full syntactic representation might turn out to be problematic. A particular problem is presented by the existence of complex morphological forms which are derived from verbs, but which do not preserve the argument of the source verb. This is the case for (some) agentive nominals derived from transitive verbs, which appear to lose their internal arguments (e.g. *killer*); for adjectives derived from verbs, either as adjectival passives (e.g. *the derived structure*) or as *-able* adjectives (e.g. *a derivable structure*), which appear to lose their external arguments; or for derived de-verbal nominals, which, on their result reading, lose both external and internal arguments of the source verb (e.g. *the excavation was successful*). I return, specifically, to the issue of derived nominals in section 6 below.

The necessity of introducing into the syntax all argument-structure-changing morphology follows from a particular set of assumptions concerning the relationship between argument structure and syntax, one which entails, in essence, that D-structure is the canonical level of argument-structure realization, and that the lexical entry is the locus of argument-structure specification. Recent approaches to argument structure, however, have cast doubt on the existence of D-structure as GF-θ, or, more generally, as a level of representation encoding argument structure altogether. Further, currently, the pivotal role played by lexical entries is in question, and models giving more weight in the determination of argument structure to predicates and to functional (rather than lexical) structures are widely entertained (for some current research along these lines, see e.g. van Hout 1992, 1996; Kratzer 1994; Borer 1994, in press; Ghomeshi and Massam 1994; Davis and Demirdash 1995). In view of this, the epistemological advantage of placing in the syntax all argument-structure-changing morphology, as follows from the UTAH research program, is no longer self-evident, leaving the merits and de-merits of syntactic WF to be determined independently of issues concerning argument structure and its projection.

5   Morphophonological/morphosyntactic isomorphism?

5.1   *Projecting phonological strings?*

Interestingly, the so-called Inflectional Big Bang approach shares an important property with type (2) linear models, but not necessarily with type (3) linear models. In both, the syntactic properties of words and the phonological properties of words are assumed to go hand in hand. Proponents of (2), assume that what is inserted at D-structure is the actual phonological string, rather than categorial feature bundles. Likewise, proponents of the derivation in (4) assume that the relevant inflectional heads dominate actual phonological material, and that the structure in (8) is responsible for the formation of an accurate phonological string. Clearly, this is the rationale which drives the positioning of AgrP higher than TP, as discussed in section 2: it is based exclusively on the order of the morphophonological material in forms like /*mangera*/. Likewise, the assumption that grammars may project functional heads in different hierarchical orders is an attempt to derive a morphophonological string by syntactic movement.

Consider, however, the model in (3). Here, what are inserted at D-structure are categorial feature bundles, which are in turn given phonological representation later on. If this is the case, there is no longer any reason to assume that a feature bundle such as [STEM+AFF$_{infl1}$+AFF$_{infl2}$] actually corresponds to any particular morphophonological sequence. And indeed, this point has been made by Marantz (1988), who suggests that there is no necessary isomorphism between feature bundles, lexically or syntactically derived, and the morphophonological representations assigned to them. In other words, it may be that while in Grammar 1 morphophonological considerations would lead to AFF-1 being realized closer to the stem, in Grammar 2 different morphophonological considerations would realize the same syntactic feature bundle differently.

What is at stake here is the following question: are syntactic representations or word structure isomorphic with phonological representations of word structure? Specifically, is there a unified notion of a morpheme, such that it is the true mediator between sound and (syntactic) function? Or, put differently, are morphological operations to be captured through the existence of lexical-like elements, which compose to give rise to the correct combinations, very much as is assumed for syntactic representations? For proponents of type (2) models, as well as for proponents of the Inflectional Big Bang approach, the answer is "Yes." For "lexicalists," this isomorphism is reflected by a lexically derived WF structure, encoding, as a derived unit, all the syntactic information associated with its components. For "movers," on the other hand, it is the syntactic movement which creates, through adjunction, the string which is directly mapped onto phonological representations.

Just as the assumption of morphophonological/morphosyntactic isomorphism has its lexical and syntactic variants, so the assumption of no isomorphism has a lexical and a syntactic variant. Its lexical variant is the model in (3). Consider now its syntactic variant. Returning to the original Pollock (1989) argumentation, one may argue syntactically for the existence of a complex functional structure above the VP, or support the existence of such functional structure on semantic grounds (e.g. the existence of a T head as necessary for the formation of a proposition, and the existence of a D head as necessary for the assignment of reference). Such functional structure may itself dominate a feature bundle to which a stem will be adjoined by syntactic movement. However, the specific ordering of such projections, or their existence, would now be motivated exclusively on syntactic or semantic grounds. As an illustration, consider the following structure, assuming there to be compelling UG reasons to place Agr above T:

(23) (a)

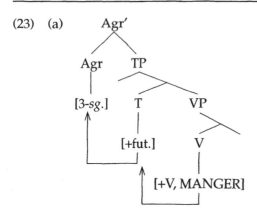

(b) syntactic output:

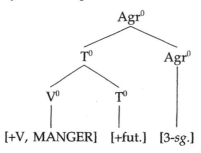

(c) morphological output:
[+V, MANGER][+fut.][3-*sg.*] ⇒ /*mangera*/

For *mangera*, the order of syntactic projections following head-to-head movement and the order of phonological material are the same, thereby leading to an appearance of syntax/phonology isomorphism. Consider, however, the case of agreement and tense morphology in Hebrew, as illustrated in (24). While in the past tense, agreement and tense marking are stem-final, as in (24a), in the future tense, the agreement morpheme is split between a post-stem and a pre-stem position:[19]

(24) (a) qibbəl   -u   (a′) ye-   qabbəl   -u
           receive+past -3pl.   3+fut.-   receive   -pl.

      (b) qibbal   -ti   (b′) 'a-   qabbel
           receive+past -1sg.   1+sg.+fut.- receive

      (c) qibbal   -nu   (c′) ne-   qabbel
           receive+past -1pl.   1+pl.+fut.- receive

Even if one were to grant, as Ouhalla (1991) suggests, that in some languages TP is above AgrP, such an order would not give rise to the correct order of morphemes in Hebrew. First, the division of the agreement morphology in some cases, but not in others, into pre- and post-stem positions is hard to reconcile with a morphophonological/morphosyntactic isomorphism. The fact that in (24a′) a future plural form receives its number specification post-stem, but its person specification pre-stem, while in (24c′) a future plural form receives both its number and its person specification pre-stem could only be reconciled within an isomorphic model by fragmenting the functional representation so as to give a separate, and hierarchically distinct, representation to first person, third person, plural, singular, etc. A theory which does not assume isomorphism faces no such difficulties.

Isomorphic models, be it noted, need not elaborate on the structure of the morphophonological component. That structure is one and the same as the morphosyntactic component. However, proponents of nonisomorphic models must address another issue. Assuming the syntactic aspect of WF to be essentially as in (23b), where (23b) is derived either lexically or through movement, and its hierarchical structure is either syntactic or morphological in nature, what is the nature of the morphophonological component? In other words, what is the model that would give the structure in (23b) the correct phonological representation?

On this issue, we find considerable variation. On the one hand, we find models which assume that the morphophonological component is hierarchical in nature, and that morphemes are coherent phonological units. Typically, in these models the hierarchical structure of (23b), derived lexically or syntactically, is matched with a distinct hierarchical structure which is morphophonological in nature, but which still embodies within it a coherent notion of a morpheme. Such a model is explicitly put forward by Zubizarreta (1985), who proposes that Italian causatives, exhibiting both bi-clausal and mono-clausal properties, do so because their morphosyntactic structure is bi-clausal, but their morphophonological structure is mono-clausal. A similar idea is put forward in Sadock's (1985, 1991) autolexical model, where the output of syntactic trees projects independently as a morphological structure, with co-occurrence conditions restricting the relationship between the two structures and preventing reordering of elements. Most recently, a morpheme-based non-isomorphic model has been proposed by Halle and Marantz (1993) (see also Marantz 1988 on cliticization). This model, Distributed Morphology, derives syntactic structures akin to (23b) through syntactic movement, subsequently assigning to them morphophonological representations. Crucially, in this model it is possible to assign an identical syntactic structure to amalgams in which the order of agreement and tense differs and cannot be derived from the syntactic structure, as is the case in (24), leaving the derivation of the correct (distinct) morphophonological structure to a postsyntactic component. Further, it is capable of assigning the correct phonological string to syntactically regular, but morphophonologically irregular forms, such as /*sang*/. Crucially, within the model there is still a coherent phonological notion of a morpheme, and hence some hierarchical structure associated with complex phonological words.

At the other end of the spectrum, we see the coupling of hierarchical syntactically relevant representations with a phonological component that is explicitly based *not* on discrete morphemes, but rather, on phonological representations of particular operations. The strongest thesis along these lines, labeled appropriately as the "Separation Hypothesis", was proposed by Beard (1976, 1988, 1995). In such a model, the derivation of, for example, /*walked*/ from /*walk*/ is not phonologically or morphologically distinct from the derivation of /*sang*/ from /*sing*/: both involve the mapping of syntactic amalgams to phonology on the basis of paradigmatic representations. A similar model is proposed for inflectional morphology (but not for derivational morphology) by Anderson's (1992) A-morphous Morphology (or, alternatively, the Extended Word-and-Paradigm model), where it is argued that inflectional processes are exclusively phonological in nature, consisting in giving a phonological representation to an abstract entry, comprising, among other factors, syntactic information. Again, there is no necessity in this approach to assume that the hierarchical nature of morphosyntactic representations translates into a morphophonological hierarchical structure or, for that matter, that morphemes are discrete phonological terminals of any sort.

Summarizing, nonisomorphic approaches assume that the hierarchical grammatical properties of words are segregated completely from their phonological realization, and that the term "morpheme," as such, implying, indeed, some phonological-functional isomorphism, is an ill-defined one.[20]

Morphophonological considerations, especially those concerning the representations of suppletive forms, mixed-order forms, and autosegmental forms strongly favor a nonisomorphic approach, be it lexical or syntactic. However, some recent syntactic analyses which depend crucially on the actual projection of morphophonological material in the syntactic tree cannot be captured naturally in a DM-type system. As an illustration, consider recent proposals to account for the restrictions on verb movement by appealing to the "richness" of morphophonological representations. Thus it has been proposed that the existence of V movement in Icelandic, versus its absence in the mainland Scandinavian languages or English, is due to the presence of a "rich," in some sense, inflectional paradigm in the former, and its absence in the latter (see Platzack and Holmberg 1989, Roberts 1985, Rohrbacher 1994). Thus Rohrbacher (1994) proposes that the "rich" inflectional paradigm comprises a full person/ number paradigm in at least one tense. In this system, "rich" paradigms are lexical entries which project as independent heads, thereby requiring the verb to move and attach to them. By contrast, "nonrich" paradigms are not lexical entries; nor are they discrete morphemes at all. Rather, they are the result of phonological stem change of the type advocated in Anderson's (1992) A-morphous Morphology. Syntactically speaking, they do not project, and therefore no (overt) V movement is required. A movement configuration is given in (25a), a nonmovement one in (25b):[21]

(25) (a)

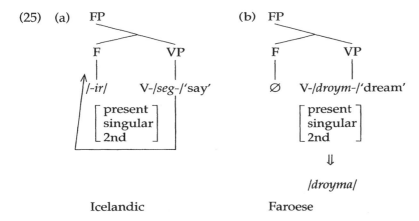

Icelandic   Faroese

Crucially, the notion of richness is based on the properties of actual morpho-phonological strings. From the perspective of a Distributed Morphology model, such a distinction cannot be made. Considering, within a DM model or any other model based on feature bundles, the syntactic structure of English versus that of Icelandic form such as, for example, *receive* in the context of *we receive*, both would have the structure shown in (26), making the statement of any dependence between verb movement and the nature of the inflectional para-digm unstatable (see Rohrbacher 1994, where this point is made explicitly):

(26)

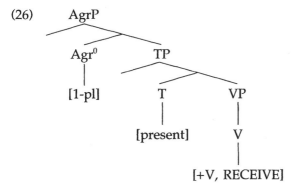

In turn, the result obtained in (25) could be achieved within a DM model by stipulating that in English, but not in Icelandic, Agr is weak, in the sense of Chomsky (1993), thereby making (overt) movement unnecessary. However, within the DM model the weak–strong feature must be formally dissociated from the properties of the morphophonological paradigm, as these are strictly nonpresent in the syntactic structure. The correlation, if such indeed exists, between the "weak–strong" property and morphophonological "richness" thus becomes entirely stipulative in nature.

Similar issues arise concerning accounts of null pronominal subjects which are based on the richness of inflection. Thus, Speas (1994) suggests that English bars null pronominal subjects because Agr must be phonologically licensed, through the presence of phonological material either in its head (a condition met by the classical null-subject languages such as Italian and Spanish) or in its specifier. As Agr does not dominate (sufficiently rich) phonological material in English, the specifier must be filled.[22] Again, it is hard to see how such a notion of phonological licensing can be translated into a DM-type system which utilizes syntactic feature matrices rather than actual phonological material.

5.2 Checking Theory

In what is possibly the strongest departure from the assumption of isomorphism, Chomsky (1993, 1995b) assumes that while (inflectionally-derived) words are well formed only if syntactic head-to-head movement has occurred, syntactic movement and the resulting adjunction are entirely divorced from any morphological properties of such words, be they phonological or syntactic. Thus, for the formation of words, Chomsky adopts, in essence, a linear model of WF, assuming that the output of some WF component consists of fully formed words with a set of properties which may be syntactically relevant, but with an opaque internal structure, thereby, in essence, adopting the atomicity thesis.[23] However, in departure from the spirit, if not the letter, of the atomicity thesis, these outputs of the WF component must move through the syntactic tree, checking their inflectional features through a succession of functional projections marked inflectionally. The input of such movement may be a syntactic structure similar to (4) (cf. (27)), in which head-to-head movement applies, but (27) is specifically *not* the input to WF, and the output of head-to-head movement, as in (28), is specifically *not* morphological in nature, nor do the heads in it dominate actual phonological material, or even bundles of features to be associated with the moved stem, in the sense of Distributed Morphology. Rather, the heads dominate abstract semantic features, such as tense, number, etc., to be matched with the properties of the word as a whole. The movement is thereby entirely divorced from morphological considerations, and the syntax, while equipped with a device for checking the *syntactic* appropriateness of words, is deprived of any role in the building of morphological units, be they phonological, as in isomorphic approaches, or syntactic, as in nonisomorphic ones.

(27)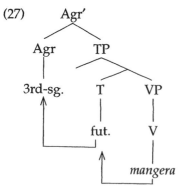

(28)

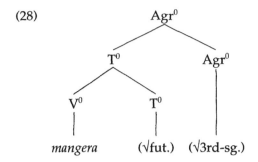

As within Checking Theory, the specific nature of the WF component is not fully explicit; it is not clear whether it entails the insertion of morpho-phonological forms as in (29a) (in essence a type (2) model) or bundles of features as in (29b) (in essence a type (3) model):

(29) (a)

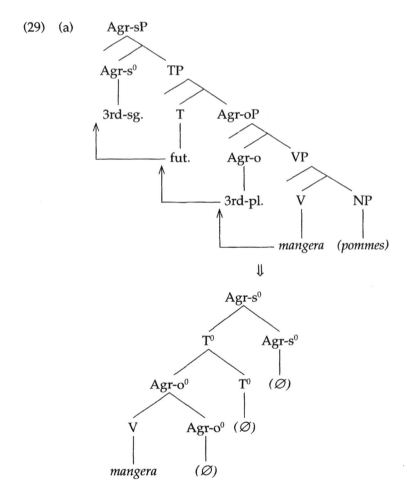

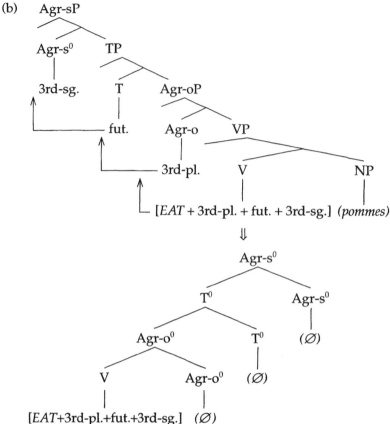

(b)

[EAT+3rd-pl.+fut.+3rd-sg.]   (∅)
where *(∅)* stands for checked off (and hence deleted) feature.

Nor is it entirely clear how properties of derivational morphemes are to be checked. As an illustration of the problems involved, consider the structure of (bi-clausal) synthetic causatives, using as an example Chichewa, as discussed by Baker (1988a). As is well established, (30b) is bi-clausal, on a par with (30a), leading Baker to give it the D-structure in (30c) and the S-structure in (30d) (irrelevant details omitted):

(30) (a) Mtsikana ana-chit-**its**-a   kuti mtsuko   u-**gw**-e
           girl   AGR-do-make-ASP that waterpot AGR-fall-ASP

      (b) Mtsikana anau-**gw-ets**-a   mtsuko
           girl   AGR-**fall-made**-ASP waterpot

      (c) ... [$_{VP1}$ **its** ... [$_{VP2}$ waterpot **gw**]

      (d) ... [$_{VP1}$ [$_{V1}$ [$_{V2}$ **gw**] [$_{V1}$ **its**]] ... [$_{VP2}$ waterpot t$_{v2}$]

In (30), the D-structure configuration, the level at which argument structure is determined, V$_2$, **gw**, 'fall' assigns its thematic roles and projects a well-formed VP. At S-structure, it has incorporated into the matrix a causative verb, forming a morphological unit with it. Consider, however, a potential Checking Theory account of (30b). If all morphological structures are inserted as such at D-structure, to preserve the bi-clausality of (30b), the incorporated causative form **gw-ets** 'make-fall' would have to head the embedded VP at D-structure, as in (31a). In turn, V_2 in (31) would rise to check its causative component. Addressing this issue briefly, and proposing that checking can only be accomplished in functional (non-lexical) heads, Chomsky (1995b) suggests that checking in such structures would be in a superordinate functional V projection. Suppose, then, that the structure is as in (31b), where V_1 adjoins to F dominating VP_1, thereby checking off its **its**-*CAUSE* properties (again, irrelevant details omitted):

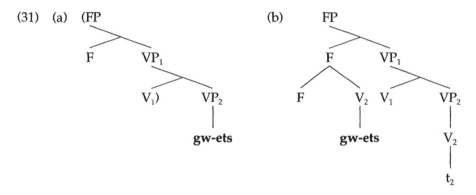

(31) (a) (FP / F VP_1 / V_1) VP_2 / gw-ets)   (b) FP / F VP_1 / F V_2 V_1 VP_2 / gw-ets V_2 / t_2

The structures in (31) give rise to a host of yet to be resolved issues. What is the argument structure associated with **gw-ets** when it heads VP_2 prior to head-to-head movement? At least morphologically, the causative verb **its** is the head of such structures. How, then, is the argument structure of the embedded verb **gw** 'fall' realized in the embedded VP? Further, in order to be checked, **gw-ets** must move and adjoin to F. Does this movement pass through V_1? If yes, how is this movement motivated, given that no features are checked at V_1. If not, how can the movement skip V_1 without violating HMC? Further, does V_1 dominate an abstract *CAUSE* marker? If yes, is this marker an abstract lexical entry, of the sort typically associated with the derivation of causative *break* ($[\emptyset [_v break]]$)? But if V_1 does dominate a lexical entry distinct from **its**, what is the nature of the fully morphologically derived **gw-ets** form? On the other hand, if the abstract *CAUSE* marker generated under V_1 is not an abstract lexical entry, but rather, a semantic feature, on a par with, say, *TENSE*, is VP_1 a regular VP, or rather, is it a functional projection of sorts (e.g. CAUSEP)? Similar questions clearly arise with respect to noun incorporation and synthetic compounding, both morphological structures that have been argued to correspond to syntactically articulated structures.[24]

Leaving the possible resolution of these issues to future research, let us turn now to a more detailed comparison of morphological structures and syntactic structures, asking whether they are the same. Specifically, let us ask whether the notion of head and, consequently, selection (or subcategorization) are unified notions; or, put differently, whether morphological hierarchical structures are identical to syntactic hierarchical structures.

6 "Mixed" models

In sections 1 and 2 of this chapter two types of models were reviewed: LIH models, which assume an independent WF component which does not interact with the syntax, and syntactic models, which attempt to derive internal word structure syntactically. Indeed, it has often been assumed that an independent WF component entails the absence of syntactic interaction with word-internal structure, while syntactic interaction with word-internal structure entails the absence of an independent WF component. For convenience of presentation, this entailment is given as (32):

(32)   Independent WF component ⇔ no syntactic interaction with word internal structure

However, the discussion in section 5 has already indicated the possible existence of models in which the entailment in (32) does not hold. Consider again nonisomorphic models, such as those of Beard (1988, 1995), Sadock (1985, 1991), Anderson (1992), or Halle and Marantz (1993). From the perspective of these proposals, it is not clear that the entailment in (32) can even be stated coherently. In these models (abstracting away from differences between them), the formation of amalgams of functional heads is a nonmorphological task, and its output, in turn, feeds into an independent morphophonological component that is syntactically irrelevant. Recall again that lexicalist versus movement accounts are neutral with respect to this factor. Thus in lexicalist isomorphic models, an output of the WF component, a word, is associated with all the syntactic features, allowing it to interact with the syntax. These features, in turn, are associated with it as a result of the internal structure of the word, as determined by the WF component (see Di Sciullo and Williams 1987). On the other hand, in nonisomorphic models, regardless of the existence or nonexistence of movement, word structure as formed by syntactic or morphological rules is explicitly distinct from morphophonological considerations, and the output of the morphophonological component, in turn, does not have, meaningfully, any syntactic properties. Consider, as an example, the representations given by Zubizarreta (1985) or by Sadock (1985, 1991): the syntactic representation is fully syntactically interactive, while the morphophonological representation is fully syntactically opaque, rendering the entailment in (32) meaningless. Rather, in nonisomorphic systems the relationship between the (independent) morphophonological component and the syntax is either linear, as in (33a), or parallel, as in (33b):

(33)   (a)   Phrasal syntactic structure   →   morphophonological spellout

     (b) $\begin{bmatrix} \text{Phrasal syntactic structure} \\ \text{Morphophonological structure} \end{bmatrix}$

Yet another type of system in which the entailment in (32) does not hold in a straightforward way is that proposed by Laka (1990) and by Rohrbacher (1994) (see section 5 for some discussion), as well as the system proposed by Emonds (1985). Here, WF is partitioned into syntactically active versus syntactically inert components, or in essence, into the two logical possibilities provided by (32). Thus, syntactically active WF is reduced to syntax, while syntactically inert WF is syntactically opaque:

(34)   WF 1: no independent morphological component ⇔ syntactic derivation of word-internal structure

WF 2: independent morphological component ⇔ no syntactic interaction with word-internal structure

Crucially for Rohrbacher (1994) as well as for Laka (1990), there is no principled functional distinction between those operations which fall under WF1 and those which fall under WF2. For Laka (1990), some typically inflectional markings are generated pre-syntactically, while others are projected as heads. For Rohrbacher (1994), it is crucial that while some agreement markers in some languages be projected as independent heads, having their own lexical entries – for example, agreement in Icelandic – the same function in other languages would not constitute an independent lexical entry and would be part of an abstract morphophonological spellout rule – for example, agreement in Danish.[25]

It is in this latter respect that Laka (1990) and Rohrbacher (1994) differ from Emonds (1985). On Emonds's account, WF is partitioned according to the function of the morphology involved. While some morphology remains, in essence, pre-syntactic in accordance with type (2) linear models, other morphological processes, defined specifically as those which are transformationally introduced, are the amalgamation of abstract features through syntactic means, to be spelled out in a post-lexical phonology, in essence along the lines suggested by Anderson's Extended Word-and-Paradigm system. The former, lexical morphology encompasses, in essence, those traditional WF processes classified as derivational (but excluding some argument-structure-changing operations). The latter encompasses, in essence, those WF processes traditionally classified as inflectional. Thus, for Emonds, unlike Rohrbacher (1994), the introduction of agreement morphology at times through direct projections and at other times through a post-syntactic spellout rule, as in the picture in (25), is an impossibility.

While Laka (1990), Rohrbacher (1994), and Emonds (1985) are interested primarily in WF processes which are sensitive to syntactic contexts, systems embodying the duality in (34) have been proposed extensively for derivational processes. Specifically, consider the model proposed by Shibatani and Kageyama (1988) and that proposed by Borer (1984b, 1988, 1991). Like that of Rohrbacher (1994), these models assume that the output of morphological processes may be inserted at D-structure or later on. In accordance with the entailments in (34), these systems further propose that, depending on the level at which the relevant morphological output becomes available, it does, or does not, interact with syntactic representations.[26] In Shibatani and Kageyama 1988 and in Borer 1988 this analysis is articulated with respect to compounds in Japanese and Hebrew respectively. While lexical compounds display idiosyncratic, drifted properties, compounds that are inserted later preserve argument structure (Japanese, Hebrew), allow their nonhead members to be modified (Hebrew), and exhibit word-internal effects of post-syntactic phonology (Japanese), all absent from lexical compounds.[27]

The existence of parallel processes of WF applying pre-syntactically as well as at a later stage, be it the syntax or post-lexical phonology, presents an interesting problem for co-representational models of the type put forth by Zubizarreta (1985) and Sadock (1985, 1991). In these theories, a form could, in principle, have two representations, one syntactic and one morphological, where morphological well-formedness conditions are met on the morphological representations, while syntactic well-formedness is met by the syntactic one. Thus, for Zubizarreta (1985), the morphological representation of causatives is, in essence, flat, while the syntactic one is bi-clausal. What, within such a system, is the fate of forms which are morphologically identical, but syntactically distinct?

As a possible answer to this question, consider Parallel Morphology as proposed by Borer (1991). Here, there is an independent WF component, and its output is, in accordance with the LIH or similar principles, syntactically inert. However, in violation of the spirit, if not the letter, of LIH and the Atomicity Thesis, there is a clear interaction between morphological and syntactic structures. This interaction is dependent on whether morphological structures have a corresponding syntactic one or not. In turn, the presence versus absence of a coexisting syntactic structure depends exclusively on whether the output of WF is inserted at D-structure or at a later level, where it corresponds to the output of syntactic movement. In this model, as in (34), there is no morphological difference between forms derived prior to D-structure and those derived later on. Further, the morphological properties of the output are identical. There are, however, syntactic differences between the derivations, dependent exclusively on the accompanying syntactic structure. As an illustration (with irrelevant details omitted) consider de-verbal derived nominals. Morphologically, a form such as *destruction* has the structure in (35):

(35)

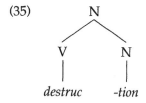

(35) may be inserted as such at D-structure, under N, resulting in the following syntactic structure, where the syntactic properties of *destruction* are not different from those of an underived word such as, for example, *event*:

(36)

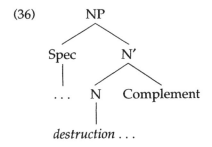

Crucially, however, both *-tion* and *destruc* (= *destroy*) are independent lexical entries, and, as such, may either enter into WF or be projected as heading their own phrases. In the latter case, D-structure is as in (37) (functional structure omitted):

(37)

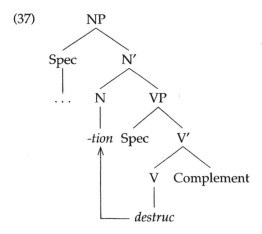

In (37), head-to-head movement adjoins V to N, thereby giving rise to the syntactic structure in (38). In turn, the circled tree segment in (38) could enter WF, resulting in the formation of *destruction*:

(38)

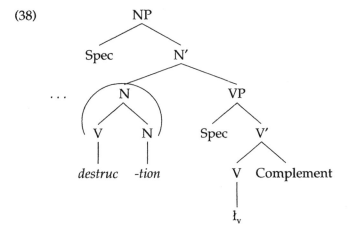

Note that, syntactically, head-to-head movement in (37) is optional, and without it, (37) is still well formed. However, we may assume that (37) is not morphologically well formed, due to the presence of a morphologically free affix, *-tion*. While, morphologically, *destruction* always has the structure in (35), note that the syntactic structures in (36) and (37) are very distinct: (37) contains a VP, while the existence of a V node word-internally in (36) is syntactically irrelevant. It is this syntactic difference, I argue, which results in the so-called process reading associated with (38), versus the result reading associated with (36) (see Grimshaw 1990 for extensive discussion of process versus result nominals).

Interestingly, Hebrew provides some reason to prefer the insertion of concrete phonological material under the heads in (37), rather than bundles of abstract features such as V and NOM. Specifically, it turns out that morphologically complex forms where an actual source V exists allow a process reading, in this account corresponding to a structure with a projected VP, as in (37), alongside a result reading, with the syntactic structure in (36). On the other hand, synonymous forms with no such source V – for example, borrowed words – may only have a result interpretation. A minimal pair is given in (39) and (40):

(39) (a)   ha-transformacia Sel ha-'ir
             the-transformation of the-city

      (b)   ha-Sinui Sel ha-'ir (source verb: *Sina*, 'change')
             the-transformation of the-city

(40) (a)   *ha-transformacia Sel ha-Sita 'al yedey ha-memSala
             the-transformation of the-system by the-government

      (b)   ha-Sinui   Sel ha-Sita 'al yedey ha-memSala
             the-transformation of the-system by the-government

However, as pointed out by Hazout (1990, 1995), the direct projection of morphophonological segments in structures such as (37) faces the typical problems associated with direct phonological projections, already discussed in section 5 above. Thus derived nominals in Hebrew are often morphophonologically deviant, presenting the same problem as is presented by English forms such as /*sang*/ or /*children*/.[28] It is to be hoped that future research will shed additional light on these matters, as well as on other matters concerning the morphophonological/morphosyntactic isomorphism already discussed in section 5.

7 Conclusion

I have surveyed here a number of important issues that have emerged in the attempt to model the relationship between WF and syntax. We have looked at exclusively syntactic models, as well as exclusively lexicalist models, surveying a number of issues that emerge in each. We saw that the lexical/syntactic distinction interacts with another, equally important one: the issue of isomorphism, which cuts across the lexical/syntactic distinction. Finally, we have looked at mixed systems, where solutions to the interaction between morphology and syntax are given in terms of partitioning the morphological component, allowing it to accomplish its task in slightly different ways, depending on the way in which it interacts with the syntax. As is clear from the range of models and possibilities, issues concerning the interaction between WF and syntax are not resolved, and they remain sensitive to theoretical contributions to syntactic theory on the one hand and to WF theory and phonology on the other hand.

NOTES

1   I am referring here, in no particular order, to the work of Halle (1973), Aronoff (1976), Jackendoff (1975), Lieber (1980), Selkirk (1982), E. Williams (1981b), and Kiparsky (1982c), as well as others.

2   Some important work on word formation (notably Jackendoff 1975; Aronoff 1976; M. Allen 1978; Anderson 1982, 1992; and Emonds 1985) does subscribe to the view that inflectional morphology is formally distinct from derivational morphology. In much of this work, however, a model of the interaction of inflectional morphology with the syntax is not proposed in any detail. Excepted from this generalization are the models proposed by Anderson and by Emonds. Emonds (1985) puts forth an explicit theory which distinguishes inflectional morphology and derivational morphology formally. In the theory, inflectional morphology is that morphology which is introduced through syntactic transformations. On the other hand, derivational morphology remains pre-syntactic in the sense discussed in section 1. I return briefly to Emonds 1985 in section 6. For discussion of Anderson 1992, see primarily section 5.

3   The so-called stray affix filter, often attributed to H. Lasnik. Note that regardless of the need for an affix to find a host, there may still remain a *syntactic* motivation for such movement, as e.g. in Chomsky's Checking Theory. See discussion in section 5.2.

4   I am abstracting away here from a number of irrelevant details such as the D-structure position of verbal subjects and the correct representation for modifying (as opposed to predicative) adjectives.

5   As an example, consider Ouhalla 1991, in which a theory of functional heads and inflectional affixation is spelled out in great detail, and where there is an implicit assumption that the reduction of WF representation to syntactic structures is a desirable one. While the workings of inflectional affixation are spelled out in detail, a full, comprehensive

model of the reduction of morphology to syntax is not attempted; nor is it clear what is the fate of affixes which do not have a syntactic representation in the Ouhalla system. Much other research which tries to derive morphological representations and syntactic representations from similar principles, such as Toman 1985 and Walinska de Hackbeil 1986 is, in general, either too vague or utilizes syntactic principles specific to WF. See Lieber 1992 for a recent review.

6   Thus, in a departure from his earlier position stating that "all Grammatical Function changing rules such as passive, causative, and applicative can be eliminated from the grammar [and] their effects can be derived entirely from . . . the result of standard movement rules applying to words rather than to entire phrases" (1985: 10), Baker (1988) has himself moved away from the attempt to reduce *all* grammatical function-changing rules to syntax, allowing at least some of them (notably, adjectival passive) to be derived lexically. See section 6 for some additional discussion.

Other illustrative examples are the system proposed in Rohrbacher 1994 (see section 5.1 below for a brief discussion) and that proposed in Laka 1990, where the inflectional system is divided between the syntax and the morphology, some inflectional markings are added through head-to-head movement, while others are base-generated on the stem. Yet a third type of affix is generated as a syntactic specifier. I return in section 6 to "mixed" systems, which divide the morphological task between different components.

7   In (7), movement is restricted to a governing head so that the resulting structure obeys the Head Movement Constraint (see Travis 1984), possibly reducible to the Empty Category Principle (see Chomsky 1986).

8   Thus Ouhalla (1991) argues that in Arabic TP dominates Agr-SP, unlike French and English, which display the opposite order.

9   For an excellent recent review of the differences between morphological hierarchical structures and syntactic hierarchical structures, which goes beyond the review given here, see Lieber 1992. The discussion in the text incorporates many of her points, as well as independent ones.

10   See directly below for more comments on the implications of Chomsky 1995a for the attempt to integrate morphology into the X'-system.

11   The same observations are applicable to revisions of the Right-hand Head Rule proposed by Selkirk (1982) and Di Sciullo and Williams (1987). See Lieber 1992 for review.

One may argue that the Kayne model is, in fact, identical to the RHR model for morphology, with the added proviso that movement is not available for morphological structures, and hence surface order reflects the base-generated order. However, if, indeed, the morphology is to be reduced to the syntax, which is the purpose of postulating this identity of structure to begin with, the prohibition of movement, rather than accounting for the distinction, just adds to the mystery. Why should it be impossible for the head of a compound, say, to move and adjoin to the left of its complement, creating a left-headed S-structure, although the D-structure was right-headed?

12 For an interesting attempt to apply Kayne's system to morphology, with the assumption that all morphologically right-headed structures are derived by adjunction, see Keyser and Roeper 1994. Roeper argues that if Kayne is correct, and e.g. synthetic compounds are generated syntactically as in (i), in a left-headed structure, the surface right-headed structure is derived by head-to-head movement of the complement:

(i)

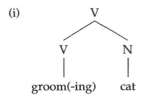

As is clear already from the representation in (i), this proposal, although intriguing, and possibly promising, would need to further elaborate on the derivation of *-ing* forms and the way in which *-ing* comes to be positioned between the V and its complement. Syntactically, *cat* is the complement of *groom*, not *grooming*. On the other hand, *-ing*, if a syntactic functional head, would need to be a sister to the entire *[groom cat]* constituent, thereby predicting the erroneous *[[cat groom$_v$]–ing$_N$]*.

13 That WF and syntax do remain in essence segregated systems in Ackema's (1995) model is further clear when one considers the representation in (i), which, for Ackema, consists of a single projection containing a maximal phrase, a maximal word, a head of phrase, and a head of word, all projected in accordance with the same X'-theoretic principles:

(i) $[_{N_2}[_{N_1}[_{N_0}[_{N_{-1}}[_{N_{-2}} \textit{John}]]]]]$

Formally, however, it is not at all clear in what sense, other than a definitional one, there is a single phrasal maximal projection N^2, which in turn dominates the maximal head projection N^0, in a string such as (i), rather than a maximal phrasal projection with a syntactic head which is distinct from a maximal word projection with a morpheme head as in (ii), given that the well-formedness conditions on N_2 as a maximal projection and N^0 as a maximal projection are distinct anyway:

(ii) Phrasal maximal projection:
$[_{N_2}[_{N_1}[_{N_0} \textit{John}]]]$
Word maximal projection:
$[_{N_0}[_{N_{-1}}[_{N_{-2}} \textit{John}]]]$

14 Note in this context that here Lieber's (1992) proposal is quite different from that put forth by Chomsky (1995a), where a Y^0 specifier would be both maximal and minimal. Kayne (1994) and Chomsky (1995a) allow (13) as a possible syntactic structure (albeit for Chomsky without the X' specification for the intermediate projection), but would specifically exclude the structure in (10). The possibility of generating structures such as (13) syntactically derives directly from the relative definition of maximal and minimal projections, which would render a bare head an X^0 and an X^{max} at the same time. Precisely for that very reason, the $[_x[_x[X]]$ structure in (14) is a syntactic impossibility, rendering the most deeply embedded X^0 by definition X^{min}, and the topmost one, by definition, X^{max}.

15 Lieber (1992) specifically argues that they do exist as morphological units, as in *an ate too much headache* and *the Charles and Di syndrome*.

16   Ouhalla (1991) makes this
     distinction between morphology
     and syntax explicit, arguing that the
     (Generalized) Projection Principle
     applies differently to affixes and to
     syntactic elements, forcing selection
     by the latter, but not the former, to
     be satisfied at D-structure. Clearly,
     such a proposal flies in the face of
     reducing morphological selection to
     a syntactic one.

17   Chomsky (1995b) defines the
     domain of complementation
     without using government. For the
     purposes of this work, however,
     his approach is equivalent, as the
     relevant domain would cover both
     selection and subject–object
     asymmetries.

18   A somewhat similar principle of
     lexical projection sometimes utilized
     is the Universal Alignment
     Hypothesis, due to Perlmutter and
     Postal (1984):

     (i)   The Universal Alignment
           Hypothesis: Principles of UG
           predict the initial relation borne
           by each argument in a given
           clause from the meaning of the
           clause.

     While the claims made by UTAH
     and UAH appear similar in nature,
     they are actually distinct. Unlike
     UTAH, UAH predicts the role
     played by arguments from the
     meaning of the entire clause rather
     than from the properties of
     particular lexical entries. Thus
     UAH is entirely consistent with
     an approach whereby argument
     structure is computed on the basis
     of a predicate, rather than the
     lexical semantics of individual
     entries. As the dominant
     approaches to morpho-syntax
     within the GB model clearly center
     on lexical entries, only UTAH will
     be discussed here. See Pesetsky

     1995 for a lexical-entry-based
     formulation of UAH.

19   An additional complication for the
     morphophonology/morphosyntax
     isomorphism approach is the fact
     that in Semitic languages some of
     the tense morphology is affixal and
     some is autosegmental. Note in
     this context that autosegmental
     morphological systems, such as
     Semitic morphology, present a
     particular problem here, as the
     order of morphemes is sometimes
     an incoherent notion when a
     particular vocalic melody serves
     to give information about a binyan
     (typically derivational information),
     person, and tense, all in one.
     In fact, the existence of such
     portmanteau marking supports the
     approach of Anderson (1992), who
     argues that viewing WF as the
     hierarchical projection of discrete
     morphemes attached to a stem
     (rather than viewing morphology
     as an operation which transforms
     a stem) is empirically problematic.
     See text below for a brief
     discussion.

20   The determination of the formal
     nature of the morphophonological
     component is dependent, to a large
     extent, on the determination of the
     formal property of the phonological
     operations involved. This issue, not
     touched upon here, is reviewed in
     detail in Halle and Marantz 1993,
     as well as in Anderson 1992.

21   Alternatively, Rohrbacher (1994)
     suggests that nonrich markers may
     fail to project, but are nevertheless
     available for pre-syntactic affixation
     processes, resulting in the base-
     generation of a fully inflected form,
     thereby preempting movement.

22   Neither the particular notion of
     richness used by Speas (1994) nor
     the overall workings of her system
     are crucial to the discussion here.

What is of significance is that any system accounting for null subjects by appealing to properties of inflection cannot be naturally captured in DM terms.

23 In a tentative weakening of this claim, Chomsky (1995b) suggests, following Lasnik (1994), that it may turn out that some inflectional affixation is syntactically derived. See n. 25 below for a brief discussion of Lasnik 1994.

24 It could be argued that causatives are light verbs of sorts, and hence functional in nature, thereby avoiding at least some of the problems presented by (31) (although note that licensing the argument structure for both VP_2 and VP_1 remains an issue). However, a similar problem exists for noun incorporation, where a V+N form must be inserted under N. Even if the appropriateness of the form is checked in some functional projection dominating V, it is difficult to see, in this case, how a lexical VP intervening between the inserted form under N and the functional head where it is checked can be avoided.

25 For a similar system, see Lasnik 1994, where it is assumed that the base-generation of inflected forms as well as the projection of inflectional morphemes under functional heads coexists in UG as well as being internal to the grammar of specific languages. Thus in English, auxiliaries are base-generated as inflected forms, as are, perhaps, irregular verbs; but regular past tense /-ed/ may still be projected as an independent functional head under TENSE. Note that in Checking Theory, as assumed by Lasnik (1994), this difference in the formation of, say, /were/ and /walked/ cannot be

syntactically relevant, due to the extreme nonisomorphic nature of Checking Theory, as discussed in section 5.2 above.

26 The possibility of identical affixing existing lexically as well as a result of syntactic movement is also put forth in Baker (1988a), but is not executed in detail.

27 An additional issue concerns the existence of morphological processes at a post-lexical, but pre-phonological stage, i.e. in a direct interaction with syntactic structures. In Borer 1988 it is suggested that these, indeed, exist. Thus *syntactically* formed compounds allow modification of the nonhead member, as well as its binding, as in (ia, b); but a nonhead quantifier embedded in a compound may not take wide scope, plausibly because of the impossibility of LF movement from within a word (compare (iia, b):

(i) (a) **beyt mora** xadaSa
          house teacher new
          'the house of the new teacher'

     (b) Ran₂ hibit be-**tmunat**
          Ran looked at-picture-
          'acmo₂
          himself
          'Ran looked at a picture of himself'

(ii) (a) tmuna Sel SloSa anaSim
          picture of three people
          'one picture showing three people'
          'three pictures, each of a single person'

     (b) **tmunat SloSa 'anaSim**
          picture three people
          'one picture showing three people'
          *'three pictures of a single person each'

If this is indeed the correct interpretation of the data in (i) and (ii), it suggests that the word *tmunat SloSa 'anaSim* has been formed at a level which affects the possibility of further syntactic movement, most plausibly, at S-structure (or spellout).

28   Another problem pointed out by Hazout (1990) in advocating an abstract NOM representation is relevant to attempts to derive de-verbal derived nominals exclusively syntactically. Thus Hazout (1990) points out that in Hebrew the particular (nonexceptional) de-verbal nominalizing affix is determined on the morpho-phonological properties of the stem V. In a system which gives V+N a syntactic representation exclusively, it is not clear how the correct affix would be selected. However, in the parallel system sketched above, V+N has a morphological structure as well. Assuming free (overgenerating) lexical insertion, it may be assumed that morpho-logically inappropriate (although syntactically well-formed) V+N forms simply fail to result in the formation of a word, thereby violating the morphological well-formedness conditions on the affix.

9 Morphology and Agreement

GREVILLE G. CORBETT

1 Definitions

There have been several attempts to define agreement: for instance, Keenan 1978: 167; Lehmann 1982: 203; and Lapointe 1988; but as Anderson (1992: 103) says, 'this is a quite intuitive notion which is nonetheless surprisingly difficult to delimit with precision'. Steele (1978: 610) talks of 'systematic covariance between a semantic or formal property of one element and a formal property of another'. The essential notion is the covariance or matching of feature specifications between two separate elements, such as subject noun phrase and verb. There is then the question as to whether the determination of the form of anaphoric pronouns is a part of agreement. In fact, most mainstream work on agreement uses the term in this wider sense, to include pronouns. Barlow (1988: 134–52; 1991) reviews the literature and concludes that there are no good grounds for distinguishing between agreement and antecedent–anaphora relations. It is generally accepted that, diachronically, pronouns provide a major source of agreement morphology, progressing from full pronouns to clitics to inflections (see Givón 1976; Bynon 1990, 1992; Corbett 1995).[1]

In order to be able to generalize about different types of agreement, we need a set of terms. We call the element which determines the agreement (say the subject noun phrase) the 'controller'. The element whose form is determined by agreement is the 'target'. The syntactic environment in which agreement occurs is the 'domain' of agreement. And when we indicate in what respect there is agreement (agreement in number, e.g.), we are referring to 'agreement features'.[2] As these terms suggest, there is a clear intuition that agreement is directional. In *Mary laughs*, most accept that *laughs* is singular because *Mary* is singular. Some accounts of agreement capture this intuition directly by copying feature specifications from the controller to the target. There are several problems with this approach: the controller may be absent (as in pro-drop languages); or it may be present but underspecified; or the feature specifications on the controller and the target may simply not match.

More recent approaches, particularly that of Generalized Phrase Structure Grammar and its descendants, allow free instantiation of features on controllers and targets. To be grammatical, those structures must meet certain constraints, typically constraints requiring identity of particular feature specifications. The work is done by unification, which provides a matching of feature specifications without copying, but also without directionality of agreement. In Generalized Phrase Structure Grammar the intuitively important notion of directionality is reintroduced by the Control Agreement Principle, which specifies possible controllers and targets, and gives them different statuses (see Gazdar et al. 1985). Since, however, there is no movement of features in such models, it is more accurate to talk of 'asymmetry' of agreement rather than 'directionality'. In Head-Driven Phrase Structure Grammar the asymmetry is captured through 'anchoring'; gender, number and person features are anchored to real-world entities through noun-phrase indices, even though they may be expressed morphologically other than on the noun phrase (see Pollard and Sag 1994: 60–99; cf. Kathol, forthcoming). Unification does not require that feature sets should be fully specified; controllers may be absent or underspecified. Thus agreement can be seen as a matter of cumulating partial information from the controller and the target (see Barlow 1988, Pollard and Sag 1988, Wunderlich 1994).[3]

Traditional accounts treat agreement as a matter of syntax. However, there are well-known cases where the information available to the syntax is inadequate to allow a full account. For instance, plural agreement with *committee*-type nouns in some varieties of English suggests that semantic information is relevant. As a result, and particularly if one starts from English data, there is a temptation to suggest that agreement is instead all a matter of semantics. However, there are serious problems here too: *I'm parked on the hill* is acceptable for *My car is parked on the hill*, but semantic agreement is impossible here: **I is parked* (H. Clarke, cited in Barlow 1988: 227). An adequate theory requires reference both to syntactic and to semantic/pragmatic information (Pullum 1984, Corbett 1994).

What then is the role of morphology? Obviously to mark the agreement information (whether of syntactic or semantic/pragmatic origin) on targets. Given the asymmetric nature of agreement just discussed, this means that agreement morphology will mark on targets information which relates primarily to controllers. Note especially that the morphological part of agreement need not mirror syntax: dependants may agree with their heads, mirroring the syntactic dependency; but, conversely, the syntactic head may bear agreement morphology controlled by its syntactic dependent (Nichols 1985; Zwicky 1993: 298, 303–10). In other words, the agreement controller may be the syntactic dependent.

In the next section we consider the agreement features. Then we look at the forms used to express them (section 3). In section 4 we consider the effect that the target has on agreement in terms of the forms available, while in section 5 we examine its effect on the form to be selected.

2 Agreement features

There are three indisputable agreement features, gender, number and person, which we shall examine in turn.

2.1 *Gender*

Agreement in gender is widespread; for instance, adjectives may agree with their head noun in gender, as in these Russian examples:

(1)   nov-yj   avtomobil'
      new-SG.MASC car
      'a new car'

(2)   nov-aja   mašina
      new-SG.FEM car
      'a new car'

(3)   nov-oe   taksi
      new-SG.NEUT taxi
      'a new taxi'

The adjective selects its form according to (= it agrees with) the noun: in (1) it takes *-yj* because the noun *avtomobil'* 'car' is of masculine gender (we would find a similar agreement form with nouns denoting males); in (2) it takes *-aja* because the alternative word for 'car', *mašina*, is feminine; and (3) shows the neuter ending. Such three-gender patterns are quite common, as are two-gender systems; but languages with four or five genders are not unusual, and larger numbers are found (as in Fula, which has around twenty genders, depending on the dialect). Gender systems may have sex as a component, as in languages with masculine and feminine genders; but equally, sex may be irrelevant – the distinction may be between animate and inanimate, for example (see Corbett 1991 for illustrations).

2.2 *Number*

The Russian examples above also show agreement in number; in each, the adjective is singular, to agree with the singular noun. If we change the noun in (1) to a plural, the form of the adjective must change to match:

(4)   nov-ye avtomobil-i
      new-PL car-PL
      'new cars'

The contrast here is just between singular and plural. Many languages have a third member of the number system, the dual, for two items. More complex systems may also be found: for example, with special forms for three items (the 'trial', as in Larike; see Laidig and Laidig 1990) or for a small but unspecified number of items (the 'paucal', as in Bayso; see Hayward 1979). We return to the question of the interaction between the categories in section 3 below.

2.3 Person

The third agreement feature is person. Systems with three persons, like Russian *ja beru* 'I take', *ty bereš'* 'you take' and *on/ona beret* 'he/she takes', are common. Larger inventories occur in languages which subdivide one or more of these three persons in some way. For example, languages like Quechua subdivide the first-person plural into the first-person inclusive (including the hearer) and exclusive (excluding the hearer). Another type of extended system occurs when the third person is divided into proximate and obviative (for less central participants in the situation), as in Algonquian languages like Cree (Wolfart and Caroll 1981: 25–39). For illustration of person systems see Forchheimer 1953 and Ingram 1978, and for further exemplification of all three features see Moravcsik (1978a: 336–62).

The three features which we called indisputable agreement features are somewhat different in nature. Gender is an inherent feature of the noun. It is found on the target, say the adjective, as a consequence of its presence in the noun (overt or covert). In example (1), the masculine ending on *novyj* has nothing to do with the lexical meaning of the adjective, but results from the fact that the adjective is modifying a masculine noun. A somewhat similar situation obtains for person; in Russian *ja beru* 'I take', person is an inherent feature of the pronoun, but not of the verb. Number is more difficult. It is an inherent feature of some nouns: those which are only singular (like English *watchfulness*) or only plural (like *trousers*) impose this feature value on their modifiers. Typically, however, a considerable proportion of the nouns of a given language can be associated with both (or all) numbers. In straightforward examples involving such nouns, like (4), the number feature appears to relate primarily to the noun; the property denoted by the adjective is not affected by the change in number. The three agreement features are all nominal; they are what Zwicky (1992: 378) calls the 'direct features' of nouns and noun phrases. As Nichols (1992: 160–2) shows, they have an interesting hierarchical relationship: gender is the one which is most prone to be marked only by agreement; number is quite likely to be marked only in this way, but this never occurs with person. Further discussion of the relations between the three features can be found in Bybee 1985: 22–4, 28–33, and Wunderlich 1993.

2.4 Other possible features

Traditional accounts of languages like Russian also discuss agreement in case: all the examples given so far are in the nominative case, as would be appropriate for subject position. If instead we take one in a prepositional phrase, then noun and modifier both take a different form:

(5)   v nov-om   avtomobil-e
      in new-SG.LOC.MASC car-SG.LOC
      'in a new car'

The preposition *v* 'in' governs the locative case, and the adjective, like the noun, stands in this case. While both do indeed stand in the same form, this covariance differs from that found with gender, number or person. Case is not a feature of the noun: it is imposed on the noun phrase by government by some other syntactic element (the preposition in (5)). Thus the noun and adjective in (5) are in the same case because it is imposed equally on both. This is not agreement, if we take seriously the question of asymmetry. On that view, we should not recognize case as an agreement feature, though we should recognize that it interacts strongly with agreement features. Besides the straightforward instances of case being shared within the noun phrase, there are more complex instances of covariance in case between predicate complements and their controllers (for which see Timberlake 1988; Anderson 1992: 115–18; and references in both to earlier work; for other complex patterns of case see Plank (ed.) 1995).

Finally, some consider definiteness to be an agreement feature, since there are languages like Arabic in which definiteness is marked more than once within the noun phrase. But this too is an instance where there is no asymmetry within the noun phrase. Rather, a feature value is imposed on the noun phrase as a whole, and may be indicated at more than one point in the phrase.

3 Forms

In this section we look at the exponents of agreement (section 3.1) and the constraints on the expression of agreement features (section 3.2).

3.1 The exponents of agreement

The examples of agreement so far have involved inflectional affixes; these occur after the stem in our Russian examples, but before the stem in many other languages – in various Bantu languages, for instance. While some languages treat all agreement in the same way, this is not necessary. Thus in

Babanki (a language of the Ring group, part of the Western Grassfields division of Bantu, spoken in north-west Cameroon) agreement may occur as a prefix or as both a prefix and a suffix, depending on the target involved (Hyman 1980: 237).[4]

Agreement may even be found stem-internally. Marind (which belongs to the family of the same name and has about 7,000 speakers in southern Irian Jaya) uses this device; the data, originally from Drabbe 1955, are presented in Foley 1986: 82–3. There are four genders (indicated with Roman numerals):

(6)   e-pe anem e-pe akek ka
      I-the man   I-the light.I is
      'the man is light'

(7)   u-pe anum u-pe akuk ka
      II-the woman II-the light.II is
      'the woman is light'

(8)   e-pe de   e-pe akak   ka
      III-the wood III-the light.III is
      'the wood is light'

(9)   i-pe   behaw i-pe   akik   ka
      IV-the pole   IV-the light.IV is
      'the pole is light'

The forms of the adjective *ak-k* 'light' mark gender by the infixed vowel: -e-/ -u-/-a-/-i-. Infixed agreement is also found in various Pamir languages (Iranian languages of Tadzhikistan and Afghanistan), such as Roshani, but it is restricted to certain adjectives and past-tense intransitive verbs (Payne 1989: 429, 436–8). It appears that all the means of inflectional morphology are available for agreement. And there are difficult boundary cases, when it is not clear whether inflections or clitics are involved (see the references in section 1 above).

It is important to note the possibility of multiple formants (mentioned above in relation to Babanki). Thus in Archi, a Daghestanian (North-east Caucasian) language, we find forms like this (Kibrik 1977a: 127–30, 320):

(10) **d-as̄-a-r-ej-r-u-ĩu-r**   x̌anna
      II-of.me-SELF-II-SUFFIX-II-SUFFIX-ADJ-II wife
      'my own (emphatic) wife'

The initial *d-* signals gender II singular agreement. Next is a pronominal stem. Then, following Kibrik's analysis, there are two complex suffixes for forming reflexives, each with an internal agreement slot: *a-GN-u* and *ej-GN-u* (*GN* = gender/number marker). Both suffixes are used here, with the first *u* dropped before the second suffix. The final suffix *ĩu* derives an adjective, and brings with it an agreement slot (naturally). Thus we have a prefixed gender/number marker (the *d-*), a suffixed form (the final *-r*) and two internal forms (the other occurrences of *r*). The four markers are all the same, in the sense that they mark the same person/number combination for agreement with the same controller. Agreements of this type may be problematic for analyses based on the notion of functional heads, as Spencer (1992: 323–9) shows. We take up the question of multiple formants again in section 4.

3.2 Constraints on the co-occurrence of agreement features

If we return to the Russian examples (1)–(3), which show agreement in gender, we find that the plural for each would be identical: the plural adjective is *novye* 'new'. Thus gender is constrained by number in Russian: gender distinctions are found only in the singular number. This conforms to Greenberg's universal number 37: 'A language never has more gender categories in nonsingular numbers than in the singular' (Greenberg 1966: 112). There are further universal constraints of this type (for which see Greenberg 1966) and some language-specific constraints; both may involve just the agreement features, or they may refer to other features too. For instance, Russian verbs show agreement in gender only when in the past tense.

A rather different type of interaction between the features is found if we look at the formal expression of combinations of features. In the Russian examples, the expression of different features was fusional: in example (2), the inflection *-aja* marks feminine gender and singular number (and nominative case). One such marker may represent different possible combinations of feature values (i.e. it may be an instance of syncretism); the most spectacular examples of this type are provided by polarity. This phenomenon can be found in the Cushitic language Somali (data from Serzisko 1982: 184–6; see also Bell 1953: 12–13 and Saeed 1987: 114–16):

(11)   ìnan-kìi   baa   y-imid
       boy-the.SG.MASC FOCUS.MARKER SG.MASC-came
       'the boy (!) came'

(12)   inán-tii   baa   t-imid
       girl-the.SG.FEM FOCUS.MARKER SG.FEM-came
       'the girl (!) came'

(13)   inammá-dii   baa   y-imid
       boys-the.PL.MASC FOCUS.MARKER PL-came
       'the boys (!) came'

(14)   ináma-hii   baa   y-imid
       girls-the.PL.FEM FOCUS.MARKER PL-came
       'the girls (!) came'

Table 9.1   The definite article in Somali (basic forms)

gender	singular	plural
masculine	kii	tii
feminine	tii	kii

The postposed definite article has various morphophonologically determined variants: after any vowel except *i*, *kii* becomes *hii*, and after any vowel *tii* becomes *dii*. Given this, in the examples above the article used for the masculine plural might be considered the same as that for the feminine singular, while that for the feminine plural is the same as that for the masculine singular. The basic forms are as in table 9.1.

The two markers are exponents of two features (gender and number), and when the value of one feature is changed, the marker changes, but if both values are changed, the form stays the same.[5] The polar opposites are identical, hence the term 'polarity'.

Not surprisingly, we never find complete polarity. For Somali, this is shown by two facts. First, it has polarity only in noun-phrase internal agreement. Examples (11)–(14) show that the verbal agreement forms are different: there the plural for both genders is the same as the masculine singular, which is another type of syncretism. The second restriction in Somali is that not all nouns fall into the pattern shown in (11)–(14). Some masculine nouns form their plural by reduplication, and take the same article in the singular and the plural: for example, *nin-kii* 'the man', *niman-kii* 'the men'. Thus not all targets show polarity; nor are all nouns included in the polarity system. (Conversely, a small number of nouns are exceptional in taking polarity-type agreements for predicate agreement too: see Hetzron 1972; Zwicky and Pullum 1983b.)

4   Effect of the target – the forms available

A simple but not unreasonable view of agreement would have the syntax establish the domains of agreement, the agreement features and their values, and leave the morphology with the apparently simple task of 'spelling out' those feature values. Things are somewhat more complicated, however, since the agreement forms available depend on the agreement target and on its type. In part, the availability of agreement may be syntactically determined: thus, in German, adjectives in pre-nominal attributive position show agreement, while others, particularly those in predicative position, do not. But the restriction frequently depends just on the word class of the target; often we find that, say, adjectives agree in number in a given language, irrespective of their syntactic role.[6]

The question then arises as to the outcome when the demands of the syntax in terms of agreement cannot be met by the morphology. The issue was raised by Huddleston (1975) with respect to verbal agreement in English. Assume that on the basis of present-tense verbs we set up a syntactic rule of agreement. How then do we ensure that the verb *be* will agree when in the past tense, but no other verb will? The usual move is to configure the morphology to match distinct forms (when available) to feature specifications, and to allow for a default form when no distinct forms are available. But this is not the only possible outcome. It is possible for the lack of appropriate agreement morphology to render a syntactic construction ungrammatical; for instance, Addis (1993: 446–52), in a discussion of Basque, claims that ditransitive sentences which would require verbal agreement with a first- or second-person direct object and with an indirect object are ungrammatical and must be reformulated, since the agreement morphology is not available (she indicates similar problems in Georgian (for which see Anderson 1992: 128–32), Southern Tiwa and Spanish). Thus the relation to syntax is more complex than a simple spelling out of feature specifications. We shall therefore consider briefly the inventory of agreeing items, the agreement slots they have available, the agreement features involved, and finally in this section variation within word classes.

The word class of the target has a major effect on agreement. Of course, verbs regularly show agreement, as do adjectives. We also find articles, demonstratives, numerals, possessives (including associative morphemes) and various types of pronoun showing agreement (for examples see Lehmann 1982: 207–15; Corbett 1991: 106–12). We might expect that to be the complete list, but in fact there are several other items which can show agreement. Thus, in West Flemish, and elsewhere in West Germanic, we find agreement of the complementizer (Bennis and Haegeman 1984: 41; cf. Hoeksema 1986 and Zwart 1993a for other examples); adpositions may agree with their noun phrase, as in the North-west Caucasian language Abkhaz (B. G. Hewitt 1979: 113–14, 125–37) and in most of the modern Indic languages (Payne 1995); various languages have agreeing adverbs: for instance, Lak (Daghestanian), Kala Lagaw Ya (the language of the western Torres Straits Islands), Italian to a limited degree (for sources see Corbett 1991: 113) and Gujarati (Hook and Joshi 1991). And in Somali the focus marker can show agreement (Gebert 1988). Several of the Daghestanian languages allow a case-marked noun to take an agreement marker (Kibrik, p.c.). Thus in Lak, the allative marker, which is added to the lative marker, brings with it an agreement slot: *q̄at-lu-wu-n-m-aj* (*house-OBLIQUE-IN-LATIVE-III-ALLATIVE*) 'into the house'. In this example, the *-m-* is a gender III singular marker for agreement (for the possible controllers see Kibrik 1979a: 76). In Dargwa (Lak's closest relative), the essive similarly adds an agreement slot, but has no distinct marker itself; thus the presence of the agreement signals essive case: *bidra-li-če-b* (*bucket-OBLIQUE-SUPER-III*); 'on the bucket'; the *-b* (gender III singular marker in this instance) signals the essive case. Pronouns too may behave in a comparable way. Consider these Archi examples (Kibrik 1972: 124):

(15)   d-ez   buwa k̓anši d-i
       II-me.DAT mother like   II-is
       'I like mother'

(16)   b-ez   dogi   k̓anši b-i
       III-me donkey like   III-is
       'I like the donkey'

Since Archi is an ergative language, the part of the verb which shows agreement agrees with the object of a transitive verb; the different forms in (15) and
(16) correspond to two of the four genders of Archi. With verbs of emotion
and perception, the subject stands in the dative case; in (15) and (16) the subject is a personal pronoun with an agreement slot, and this also agrees with the
object. Evidently, then, languages have different inventories of agreeing items,
and the possible distributions have yet to be fully investigated.

Given that we have an item which can show agreement, we may then ask
how many times it can mark agreement and with how many controllers. The
Russian adjectives we analysed earlier are simple, in that they agree just once
(there is a suffixal position for agreement which is always with a single type
of controller). As we shall see, targets vary both in the number of times they
can mark agreement and in the type of their controller(s). A single target may
have more than one agreement position: in the Archi example (10) we saw
four agreement slots. In this instance they were all for agreement with the
same controller, in respect of the *same features*. Four appears to be the maximum
number of same-controller agreement slots. As a variant of the same-controller
type, the different slots of the target may show agreement with the same controller, but with different morphological patterning (different syncretisms);
this is found in the Daghestanian language Khinalug (Corbett 1991: 119–23).
Then we may find targets with more than one agreement slot, which agree
with a single controller in respect of *different features*. Thus Maltese verbs when
imperfective agree with their subject prefixally in terms of person (and to a
limited extent in gender) and suffixally in terms of number (Fabri 1993: 94).
We also find targets with more than one agreement slot, for agreement with
different controllers. A common example is verbs which agree with both subject and object; for discussion of the handling of such cases by the use of
'layered features' see Anderson 1992: 93–100; an alternative, 'tagged features',
is presented by Zwicky (1986a). Just as the maximum number of slots for same-
controller agreement is four, so, it seems, the same may hold for different-
controller agreement; Anderson (1985a: 196) claims that verbs in the Penutian
language Chinook and North-west Caucasian languages like Adyge can agree
with up to four different noun phrases.[7]

While different slots may correspond one-to-one to different controllers,
this need not be the case. A given slot may take agreement with different controllers under different conditions; for instance, in Dargwa (Chirag dialect), the
verb has a suffixal person marker for the subject if first or second person and

Table 9.2 Agreement of Latin adjectives (nominative singular)

masculine	*feminine*	*neuter*	*gloss*
acer	acris	acre	sharp
facilis	facilis	facile	easy
felix	felix	felix	happy

for the object if third person (see Kibrik 1979b: 28–9).[8] Note that while targets may offer more than one slot for one and the same controller (as in Archi) or for more than one controller in different syntactic positions (as in Georgian), we never find slots for two or more controllers in the same syntactic position.[9] We never find, for instance, a verb with slots available to agree with conjoined subject noun phrases individually, such that if the noun phrases were, say, feminine singular and neuter singular, the verb would have feminine singular and neuter singular agreement. In such circumstances agreement is with just one controller, or with all conjuncts, but the agreement feature values are determined by a resolution rule (Corbett 1991: 261–9).

When we turn to agreement features, we find that these cannot be stated just at the level of the language. We cannot simply say that a particular language has gender agreement. There is likely to be variation among the elements identified as agreement targets, as this example from the West Slavonic language Upper Sorbian shows:

(17) wón je   pisał
      he   is.3SG written.SG.MASC
      'he wrote'

Here the finite verb agrees in number and person, while the participle agrees in number and gender.[10]

While observing differences *between* word classes in respect of the agreements they may show, we have nevertheless treated word classes as internally uniform in respect of their agreement potential. This too is an oversimplification, since there are instances of systematic differences *within* word classes. Thus, as mentioned previously, Russian verbs agree with their subject in person and number, except in the past tense (formerly a participle), which agrees in gender and number. This generalization holds for all verbs. But there are also instances of idiosyncratically different agreement possibilities within word classes. Latin adjectives show this clearly (see table 9.2).

In the nominative singular, *acer* 'sharp' and similar adjectives distinguish three genders; those like *facilis* 'easy' mark neuter as opposed to masculine and feminine; while *felix* 'happy' and adjectives like it do not distinguish gender for this case/number combination.

5 Effect of the target – the form selected

In the last section we saw that, even if we assume a reasonable morphosyntactic representation with the relevant agreement information, the task remaining for the morphology may be quite complex. Nevertheless, these problems could in principle be handled for each agreement target separately, given a full array of morphosyntactic and lexical information. We now turn to examples which appear to pose problems for such a view, since the agreement form selected appears to depend on more complex interactions – typically interactions between agreement targets. In each case, determining the appropriate form to mark agreement requires more information than a 'common sense' view of agreement would lead us to expect.

The first type of example involves agreement of one target requiring information about another. For instance, in the Semitic language Tigre, three types of noun phrase (direct objects, indirect objects and causees) can trigger object agreement. Furthermore, a definite direct object can optionally give rise to an agreeing object clitic. But this is possible, according to Jake (1980: 75–8), only provided another noun phrase triggers object agreement; thus one type of agreement depends on the occurrence of the other. A second example can be found in Somali. Here the focus marker agrees with or does not agree with the subject, according to a set of factors which need not detain us. The relevant point is that when the focus marker does agree, the verb has a reduced agreement paradigm; that is, it makes fewer distinctions (Gebert 1988: 599–600; cf. Saeed 1987: 62–4; 1993: 86–7). In other words, the form of agreement of the verb depends on whether or not the focus marker shows agreement. A third, more familiar example concerns adjectival agreement in German. Adjectives within the noun phrase show agreement in gender and number, but the form of this agreement depends on the agreement information supplied by various types of determiners within the same noun phrase (see Zwicky 1986c for analysis).

The last type of problem involves syncretism. It is common to find different morphosyntactic representations which have a single realization: we saw examples in section 3.2. Occasionally the existence of syncretism, which would appear to be a matter of morphology (the morphology of targets in the cases which interest us here), makes possible a type of agreement which would otherwise be unacceptable. To illustrate this we will consider briefly the problem of gender resolution in the Bantu language Chichewa (for details see Corbett and Mtenje 1987 and Corbett 1991: 276–8). Chichewa has ten genders, which we refer to by the agreements they take in the singular and plural. Thus 7/8 is a gender which includes a wide variety of inanimate nouns. When noun phrases which do not refer to humans are conjoined, the general rule requires that the agreeing verbal predicate will be in the plural of gender 7/8, shown by the prefixed marker *zi-* (irrespective of whether the head nouns belong to that gender or not). However, there is an interesting class of apparent exceptions:

(18) ma-lalanje ndi ma-samba a-kubvunda
    6-orange   and 6-leaf   6-be.rotting
    'the oranges and leaves are rotting'

Here we find noun phrases headed by nouns of the same gender, both plural, and the verb takes the same plural form. This was found fully acceptable, though it is not the form which would be predicted by the rule given. Now consider phrases headed by non-human plural nouns which are of different genders, but whose subject agreement forms happen to coincide.

(19) a-mphaka ndi ma-lalanje a-li   uko
    2-cat   and 6-orange   GN-be there
    'the cats and the oranges are there'

The gender/number marker (GN) on the verb (*a-*) is that corresponding to the plural both of gender 1/2 and of gender 5/6 (the form *zi-*, which would be predicted by the usual rules, may be an alternative). The regularity here is that if noun phrases headed by plural nouns which would take the same target gender form are conjoined, then that target gender form will be the preferred form. There are different ways in which these examples might be analysed. The crucial point, however, is that the agreement form is determined, at least in part, by the fact that particular markers are syncretic. If the forms did not happen to be syncretic, then the regular rule would apply. For further discussion of syncretism in agreement morphology see Zwicky 1991; Gvozdanović 1991; and Carstairs-McCarthy 1992: 202–6.

6 Conclusion

It used to be considered that agreement was primarily a matter of syntax. But several investigations have show that semantics and pragmatics also have a large role. It now seems that morphology too has a more substantial role in the working of agreement than has generally been assigned to it. Indeed, the morphology of agreement is one of the most interesting parts of inflectional morphology.[11] We should be looking to predict which types of language will have agreement, the conditions under which particular agreement features will be expressed, the types of formal expression which will be employed, and the ways in which the target itself may help to determine the form of agreement.

ACKNOWLEDGEMENTS

I would like to thank the following colleagues for helpful comments on earlier versions of this chapter: Dunstan Brown, Andrew Carstairs-McCarthy, Norman Fraser, David Gil, Andrew Hippisley, Aleksandr Kibrik, Marianne Mithun, Edith Moravcsik, Frans Plank and Ivan Sag. Errors are mine. The support of the ESRC (UK) under grant R000236063 and of the British Academy is gratefully acknowledged.

NOTES

1 For the synchronic connection see C. Lyons 1990. It is also important, though sometimes quite difficult, to distinguish pronominal affixes from straightforward verbal agreement. Pronominal affixes are obligatory arguments of the verb; a verb with its pronominal affixes constitutes a full sentence, and additional noun phrases are optional (as e.g. in Barbareño Chumash; see Mithun 1991: 85–6). If pronominal affixes are the primary arguments, then they may be said to agree only in the sense that anaphoric pronouns agree, provided that one accepts that broader definition of agreement (see also Siewierska and Bakker 1996: 116–19 for discussion of the difficulties).

2 We shall treat, say, number as a 'feature' and singular, dual, plural as 'values' of that feature. The features and their values carried by a controller or target are its 'feature specification'. An alternative terminology has number as a 'category' and singular as a 'property' or 'feature' (Matthews 1991: 39–40).

3 For a different approach to the compatibility of feature specifications in agreement see Steele (1990: 90–3). For a critique of the treatment of agreement in unification-based grammars and an account of an approach using Lambek Categorial Grammar see Bayer and Johnson 1995.

4 Several languages of the East Cushitic group have some verbs which mark subject agreement by prefixation, while the majority of verbs use suffixation (Hayward and Orwin 1991).

5 Of course, the case would be more convincing if these basic forms were not subject to variation.

6 A closer tie between syntax and morphology is postulated by Baker (1985), and agreement data form a crucial part of his argument. There are problems, however, for which see Grimshaw 1986 and Anderson 1992: 127–8.

7 Davies (1986: 1) states that 'a Choctaw predicate can agree with up to five arguments in a single clause', but he seems to be referring to potential controllers; it is not clear how many agreement markers can occur on a single target.

8 A complex example is found in verb agreement in Tabassaran, described by Kibrik and Seleznev (1982); see also A. C. Harris 1994; another is Georgian (A. C. Harris 1978; Anderson 1992: 141–56).

9   Foley (1986: 185–6) reports data (originally from Scott 1978) on the Gorokan language Fore. Dependent verbs whose subject differs from that of the independent verb take separate markers showing the person and number of their own subject and the person and number of the subject of the independent verb. Thus a verb can be said to agree with two subjects; but note that they are not in the same syntactic position: one is the subject of a dependent verb, the other is the subject of a different (independent) verb.

10 The target type also influences the form of agreement when there is an agreement option (as e.g. in British English, where *committee* may take a singular or a plural predicate). The distribution of these options is constrained by the Agreement Hierarchy (Corbett 1979, 1991: 225–60; Barlow 1991) and the Predicate Hierarchy (Comrie 1975; Corbett 1983: 42–59, 87–8). Typically, these constraints operate at the level of the corpus – the target type makes one agreement form more or less likely. But these constraints may also operate as a sentence-level constraint (Corbett 1983: 60–9), in which case the choice of form of one target is determined in part by the choice of form for another. Similar considerations apply to stacked constructions (Corbett 1983: 69–74).

11 It is also proving of considerable interest to psycholinguists; see e.g. Kehayia et al. 1990, Bock and Miller 1991, Clahsen and Hansen 1993, Vigliocco et al. 1995.

10 Morphology and Argument Structure

LOUISA SADLER AND ANDREW SPENCER

1 Introduction

In English we can say (1a) or (1b):

(1)　(a)　The peasants loaded hay onto the wagon.
　　　(b)　The peasants loaded the wagon with hay.

However, although we can say (2a), we can't say (2b):

(2)　(a)　The peasants poured water into the tank.
　　　(b)　*The peasants poured the tank with water.

And while we can say (3b), we can't say (3a):

(3)　(a)　*The peasants filled water into the tank.
　　　(b)　The peasants filled the tank with water.

Further, we can say (4a) or (4b):

(4)　(a)　Ira broke the vase.
　　　(b)　The vase broke.

Yet, although we can say (5a), we can't say (5b):

(5)　(a)　Ira cut the bread.
　　　(b)　*The bread cut.

In addition to the contrasts in examples (4) and (5), we have those exhibited by examples such as (6) and (7):

(6)　(a)　Children easily break such vases.
　　　(b)　Such vases are easily broken (by children).
　　　(c)　Such vases break easily (*by children).

(7)　(a)　An ordinary knife will easily cut such bread.
　　　(b)　Such bread is cut easily (with an ordinary knife).
　　　(c)　Such bread cuts easily (with an ordinary knife).

Examples such as these raise the question of how participants which are entailed by the lexical meaning of predicates are made explicit in the morpho-syntactic representation, and whether and under what conditions they may remain implicit: that is, issues of valency. In addition, they raise the question of alternations: that is, where two morphologically related (or even identical) predicates differ in their lexical semantics and in the way participants are realized in the morphosyntax and, in particular, in morphology. This facet of the morphology–syntax interface has come to be referred to as 'argument structure'. This term means different things to different authors, and one of our aims will be to make explicit a number of distinctions between some of the different types of realization and different types of alternation that have fallen under this term.

We begin our discussion with a distinction between two sorts of operation which affect valency. Section 3 goes on to examine the question of linking, the way that grammars describe the associations between semantic and/or argument structure representations and surface grammatical relations. We describe how this is accomplished in two major frameworks: Lexical Functional Grammar and Principles and Parameters Theory. We also discuss the vexed question of unaccusativity and its representation, and conclude the section with brief mention of other frameworks. In the fourth section we provide three case-studies illustrating the architecture we propose: passives/middles in English, reflexives/reciprocals in Bantu, and causatives in Japanese, then close with a brief discussion of noun incorporation and synthetic compounding.

There are several important topics we cannot address for reasons of space. First, we are restricting our attention to verbs, and ignoring the argument structure properties of adjectives, nouns and prepositions. More specifically, we will side-step a number of difficult but important questions about participles and nominalizations, especially the inheritance of argument structure in deverbal nominalizations (cf. Grimshaw 1990: chs 3, 4). We are also unable to delve into the question of light verb constructions (and the related problem of serial verbs). Finally, there are interesting questions surrounding argument structure and derivational morphology (e.g. the argument structure of deverbal adjectives such as *readable* from *read*) which we leave untouched. However, we hope to have provided sufficient foundation in this chapter for the interested reader to investigate the primary literature in those areas with some confidence.

2 Two types of operations

Between them, lexical semantics and morphosyntactic theory must enable us to relate, at some level, the two uses of *load* in (1) and *break* in (4), and the passive voice to the active. There is by now a broad consensus that lexical semantics plays a large role in determining such morphosyntactic realizations, but disagreement as to whether it can all be reduced to semantics. For those who believe that semantics is insufficient on its own, it is necessary to stipulate some other level of representation to account for these phenomena. In addition, we would wish to see evidence that such extra structure is empirically or conceptually necessary.

Any verb will have some number of (optional or obligatory) syntactic dependents, and the lexicon and grammar of a language must therefore include information about these valency requirements. This information may be expressed in a variety of ways, appealing directly to grammatical functions such as subject and object, as in Lexical Functional Grammar (Bresnan 1996) or Relational Grammar (see Blake 1990), or to syntactic configurations, as in Principles and Parameters Theory (Chomsky 1981), or to some combination of grammatical functions and category labels, as in Head-Driven Phrase Structure Grammar (HPSG, Pollard and Sag 1994). In addition, there must be some representation of the linguistic aspects of word meaning: that is, a semantic level of representation characterizing the necessary properties of the semantic arguments of predicates. A number of different proposals have been put forward in the literature concerning the nature, structure and vocabulary of the level of lexico-semantic representation, summarized by Levin and Rappaport Hovav, Morphology and Lexical Semantics.

Given this background, two fundamentally important, and clearly related, issues arise:

(i)   To what extent is syntactic valency idiosyncratic, and to what extent can it be said to be predictable from the lexico-semantic representations associated with individual predicates?

(ii) How can the relationships between different 'uses' of the same word form and between related word forms be captured/predicted in a non-redundant manner?

Our first response to these questions will be to follow a number of authors in drawing a distinction between two sorts of operation 'in' the lexico-semantic/ syntax interface (cf. Levin and Rappaport Hovav, Morphology and Lexical Semantics, for a succinct summary of this claimed distinction). The first, 'meaning-changing' operation alters the semantic content of predicates, and we refer to such operations as 'morpholexical operations'. The second, 'meaning-preserving' operation alters the syntactic manifestation of a given semantic representation, particularly the way that it is mapped on to grammatical relations.

We will refer to these as 'morphosyntactic operations'.[1] In a sense, this division corresponds to the traditional distinction between derivation (lexeme-creating) and inflection (creation of distinct forms of a given lexeme), though it may not always be helpful to push this analogy. The distinction is reminiscent of that found in morphophonology, in which phrasal phonology becomes morphologized by giving rise to morphophonological alternations and ultimately suppletive allomorphy.

2.1 Morpholexical operations

To makes things more concrete, consider (8):

(8) Resultative construction
  (a) The blacksmith hammered the metal.
  (b) The blacksmith hammered the metal flat.

This example illustrates an operation which is appropriate for verbs in certain semantic classes (roughly, the meaning of the verb must be compatible with an eventual change of state), and adds a semantic argument to a predicate. This argument expresses the resultant state, flatness, of the object, *metal*. Evidently, the resultative construction increases the syntactic valency of the predicate – in (8b), *hammer* in the resultative complex *hammer flat* has a surface syntactic valency of three. The claim that result predication is a semantic or morpholexical operation is based on the assumption that the syntactically bivalent predicate illustrated in (8a) expresses a relation between just two semantic arguments, without entailing an end result. That is, (8b) crucially means that the blacksmith flattened the metal by means of hammering activity. Example (9) is a particularly clear case in which the main verb is atelic:

(9) They drank the teapot dry.

Since one cannot drink a teapot, (9) must be interpreted as 'they rendered the teapot dry by drinking (from it)'.

2.2 Morphosyntactic operations

Two constructions in English, dative shift and passive, are often taken to be examples of morphosyntactic operations. These are illustrated in (10) and (11):

(10) Dative shift
  (a) Tom gave a bone to his dog.
  (b) Tom gave his dog a bone.

(11)   Passive
 (a)   Tom broke the vase.
 (b)   The vase was broken (by Tom).

Each operation brings about an alteration in the morphosyntactic manifestation of the semantic dependents of a predicate, but they do not alter the basic
semantics of the predicate itself (though see section 3.3 for discussion of dissenting views).

The first of these alternations, dative shift, appears to involve a simple alternation between two different syntactic manifestations of the same semantic
roles. In (10a) the direct object realizes the Theme role, and in (10b) it realizes
the Recipient. Now, other things being equal, we might expect morphosyntactic
operations to be unconstrained by the semantics of the predicate. This is largely
true of the passive in English, for instance. On the other hand, dative shift is
restricted in applicability to verbs of transfer respecting rather subtle semantic
constraints (see Pinker 1989 for detailed discussion and for examination of
some the consequences of this for learnability).

Turning now to the second alternation, it is common to treat passivization
as a morphosyntactic operation involving the suppression of the external argument, or most prominent argument. If passive is a morphosyntactic operation,
we would expect that the semantics of the predicate would remain constant
across the voice alternation. A consequence of this in English and many other
languages is that the Agent is available semantically, and enjoys a certain presence syntactically without necessarily being syntactically expressed. In many
languages, this suppressed argument may be expressed as an oblique or an
adjunct of some sort, as in the English optional *by* phrase illustrated in (11b).
If the passivization process is simply one of syntactic suppression (as opposed
to downright deletion), we would expect the first argument to be available for
processes which are semantically rather than syntactically governed, and indeed
this seems to be the case. This is discussed in more detail in section 4.1.

A distinction something like that between our morpholexical and morphosyntactic operations is widely assumed, and it is very often taken to motivate
a further (third) notion of dependent and a third level of information. This conceptual level is often known as 'argument structure' or 'predicate–argument
structure' (PAS), and it occupies the interface between the two sorts of operations. The morpholexical operations alter (add, delete, identify) semantic components of predicates and create new semantic representations, LCSs. Each of
these is associated with its own argument structure, PAS. The morphosyntactic operations intervene between PAS and syntactic structures, resulting in a
multiplicity of syntactic realizations for one and the same argument structure.

Argument structure is essentially a syntactic representation: in fact, it is the
syntactic reflex of certain semantic properties. These properties determine the
arity (adicity) of the predicate and the relative prominence of the dependence.
Both these properties will determine the way the arguments project into the
syntax. In a two-place predicate, if no morphosyntactic operations intervene,

the most prominent argument (the more 'agent-like') will map to the subject position, and the less prominent (the more 'theme-like') will map to the object position. In many accounts, the parallel between PAS and constituent syntactic structure proper is increased by distinguishing a special argument position, that of external argument (E. Williams 1980) or most prominent argument (Grimshaw 1990), which always surfaces as the subject. This is the argument of which the entire VP is predicated (hence, it is in a sense external to the verb as such). In a two-place predicate, the remaining argument is often called an internal argument, while a three-place predicate may distinguish a direct internal argument, generally associated with the direct object, and an indirect internal argument, associated with an indirect object. For many purposes it is convenient to assume a further PAS position, denoting events (cf. Higginbotham 1985). This is a position which can be bound by tense operators in the syntax, and to which certain sorts of adverbial may have access.

We give a simplified sketch of this architecture in an essentially theory-neutral fashion. We take examples (11) for illustration, ignoring various complexities such as the precise surface representation of tense elements, participles and so on:

(12) (a) Active form: *Tom broke the vase.*

   $[[x \text{ ACT}] \text{ CAUSE } [\text{BECOME } [\text{BROKEN}(y)]]]$ LCS

   break: $<x <y>>$ PAS

Tom	broke	the vase.	syntax
SUBJECT		OBJECT	

(b) Passive form: *The vase was broken by Tom.*

   $[[x \text{ ACT}] \text{ CAUSE } [\text{BECOME } [\text{BROKEN}(y)]]]$ LCS

   broken: $<(x) <y>>$ PAS

The vase	was broken	(by Tom).	syntax
SUBJECT		OBLIQUE	

In the PAS representations, the external argument is leftmost, the direct internal argument is written in its own set of angle brackets, . . . $<y>$. . . . In the passive representation, the suppression of the external argument is notated by means of parentheses $<(x) . . . >$. The reader must expect to see a number of notational variants on this theme. If we wish to include an event position, we would write the PASS as *break* $<e <x <y>>>$ and *broken* $<e <(x) <y>>>$ (assuming passive participles are 'eventive' in the appropriate sense).

In this section, we have motivated and illustrated Levin and Rappaport's (MORPHOLOGY AND LEXICAL SEMANTICS) distinction between two conceptually different sorts of relations between lexemes or word forms. The morphosyntactic operations are meaning-preserving, but alter the syntactic realization of the predicate. The morpholexical operations are meaning-altering, and add, delete or identify certain components of meaning. They therefore create slightly different lexemes with syntactic realizations different from those of the base predicate. Either type of operation may be, but is not necessarily, morphologically mediated. Morphosyntactic operations regularly arise when fully fledged syntactic processes become morphologized (as when a verb becomes an affix). Not infrequently a morphosyntactic operation becomes a morpholexical operation in historical change (lexicalization). As a result of this, one and the same piece of morphology may realize a morphosyntactic operation in one language/dialect and a morpholexical operation in a closely related language/dialect.

In most of the rest of this paper, we will be turning our attention to morphologically mediated operations of these two sorts. Before doing so, however, we will turn in the next section to the question of how the surface syntactic form (possibly through the mediation of PAS) is related to the LCS representation.

3 Linking

3.1 *Standard cases in LFG and PPT/GB*

In this section we provide a brief sketch of linking theories, within two frame-works, Lexical Mapping Theory (LMT), within Lexical Functional Grammar (LFG) (Bresnan and Kanerva 1989, Bresnan and Moshi 1990), and the Principles and Parameters Theory (PPT, also called Government Binding Theory, GB) of Chomsky 1981.

The lexical semantic representation in LMT uses a set of thematic roles, including Agent, Patient, Theme, Experiencer, Beneficiary, Goal, Instrument, Location.[2] For *break*, this lexical representation, known as the argument structure in LFG, would then be as in (13):

(13)   *break*: <Agent, Patient>

The roles are ordered by the hierarchy given in (14) (Bresnan and Kanerva 1989):

(14)   Agent < Benefactive < Goal/Experiencer < Instrumental < Patient/ Theme < Locative . . .

The argument structure given in (13) is then mapped to a set of sub-categorized grammatical functions, which are syntactic primitives in LFG (SUBJ, OBJ, etc.). These are decomposed into binary distinctive features as shown in (15):

(15) SUBJ [−r, −o]
      OBJ [−r, +o]
      OBJ2 [+r, +o]
      OBL [+r, −o]

Subjects and ordinary objects can express any thematic role, so they are unrestricted, [−r]. Secondary objects and obliques are associated with some specific thematic role, and are hence restricted [+r].[3] Genuine objects are able to complement transitive verbs, but not, say, nouns or adjectives, and these are marked [+o]. Subjects and obliques lack this property. This leads to the classification given in (15).

Mapping is achieved as follows: first, a set of Intrinsic Classification (IC) principles associate thematic roles with particularly syntactic feature values, as exemplified in (16):

(16) Agent   Patient/Theme   Locative
       | | |
      [−o]   [−r]   [−o]

The association of Patient/Theme with [−r] in (16) reflects the fact that Patients or Themes alternate between subject and object functions. Next, a set of Default Rules (DR) apply, filling in redundant values in accordance with (17):[4]

(17) (a) $\hat{\theta}$ (b) θ
             | |
            [−r]   [+r]

The symbol $\hat{\theta}$ stands for the highest thematic role. The effects of these can be seen in (18):

(18) break   <Agent, Patient>
                 −o   −r   IC
                 −r   DR

Notice that the system is monotonic, so it would be impossible for DR (17b) to override the intrinsic specification [−r] on the Patient role. Thus far, (18) guarantees that the Agent is mapped to the SUBJ position. To complete the derivation, we appeal to a principle of Function-Argument Biuniqueness which states that every lexical argument position must be uniquely associated with a grammatical function (and vice versa). This limits the specification for [o] which may be given to the Patient in (18). It cannot be [−o], as that would mean that the clause would have two subjects, thus violating bi-uniqueness. Hence, the Patient must be marked [+o], and therefore maps to OBJ.

Of course, we may find that the lexical form in (18) is altered by a valency-affecting (for us, morphosyntactic) operation such as Passive. In LFG passive is an operation which suppresses the highest thematic role:

(19)   Passive $\hat{\theta}$
                     |
                     $\varnothing$

The morphosyntactic operations apply before the Default Rules, a consequence of the Elsewhere Condition, under which the more specific of two rules in competition applies in preference to the more general (see Stump, INFLECTION, for general discussion of the Elsewhere Condition). The derivation for the passive of *break* (as in *The vase was broken*) would therefore be (20):

(20)   break   <Agent, Patient>
                    −o   −r   IC
                    $\varnothing$ Passive

The Default Rule cannot apply (even vacuously). We now appeal to a further well-formedness condition which states that every clause must have exactly one subject. Thus, the Patient is mapped to the SUBJ function, as required.

These represent very simple cases, of course (the minimal requirement on a successful linking theory). Rather complex problems emerge when we look at more tricky types of predicate, especially those with double objects in some languages (cf. Alsina and Mchombo 1993, Bresnan and Moshi 1990) and, perhaps most notoriously, psychological predicates. The problem with the latter is that there are languages (such as English) which have two types of predicate with roughly the same meaning, as illustrated in (21):

(21)   (a)   Tom fears enclosed spaces.
        (b)   Enclosed spaces frighten Tom.

Suppose we say that these are exactly synonymous, so that the thematic relations borne by *Tom* and *enclosed spaces* are identical in each case: how do we then construct a linking theory which will obtain both mappings? This conundrum has been the subject of much recent debate (see e.g. Belletti and Rizzi 1988, Dowty 1991, Grimshaw 1990, Pesetsky 1995).

We now turn briefly to the second model, in which grammatical relations are not primitive labels or feature bundles, but are positions in a constituent structure. The PAS representation for *break* will be that of (22):

(22)   *break*: <x <y>>

This representation conveys information about arity, just as representation (13) did, but it also contains limited information about prominence. In addition to indicating that there are two syntactically realizable arguments, (22) also specifies the *x* argument as the external argument and *y* as the internal argument. This is obtained by means of rules mapping the LCS to the PAS. The semantic argument of an ACT (or CAUSE) predicate is more prominent than, say, the semantic argument of a stative predicate such as BROKEN (or BECOME[BROKEN]). (This is another way of saying that Agents are more prominent, or higher on a hierarchy, than Themes.) Most of what has been said about the use of a thematic hierarchy can be automatically translated into this framework (including the problems with psychological predicates!), so we will not rehearse this (see Jackendoff 1990 for detailed discussion).

The next question is how (22) is related to a syntactic representation. In the standard Principles and Parameters Theory of Chomsky (1981) there is a D-structure representation, which reflects argument structure very directly, and this is mapped into S-structure by the general rule of Move-α (constrained in various ways). We therefore map the PAS (22) for sentence (11a) into the D-structure shown in (23):

(23)

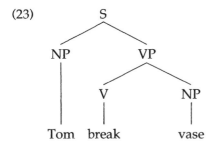

Representation (23) corresponds very closely to the S-structure representation. In PPT, nominals have to be licensed in syntactic form by receiving abstract Case. The subject position receives Nominative Case from I, the position associated with tense marking and subject agreement, while the direct object gets Accusative Case from the verb. These conditions are satisfied in (26), the S-structure derived from (23):

(24)

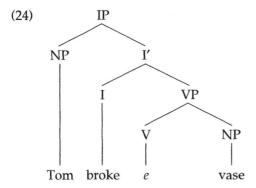

The passive operation is viewed as suppression of the external argument,[5] notated by putting it in parentheses. As in all other theories, there is then a rider permitting this argument to be expressed as an oblique of some kind in many languages. The passivized verb form, which in English is a periphrastic construction involving a participle and auxiliary verb *be* or *get*, is inserted into the D-structure and the internal argument, *vase*, is linked to the object position (technically, the nominal complement governed by the V head of the VP). However, the external argument has been suppressed, and cannot therefore be linked to the subject position. The best it can hope for is to be realized as an optional PP adjunct, as in (25):

(25)
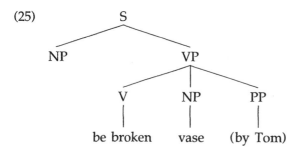

There is a general principle known as Burzio's Generalization, which states that a predicate lacking an external argument cannot assign Accusative Case. This means that passive participles cannot assign Accusative Case and hence cannot license their own objects. This means that *vase* in (25) cannot remain where it is. It is therefore moved to the only landing site where it will receive a legitimate Case: namely, the (currently unoccupied) subject position. Hence, we obtain (26):

(26)
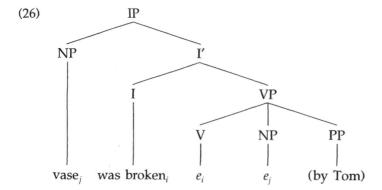

PPT, like LMT, is governed by ancillary assumptions: in particular, that all clauses must have a subject (the Extended Projection Principle) and all lexical argument positions must map on to a structurally defined argument position in the syntax, and vice versa (the Theta Criterion).

It will be seen that although the details of the architecture differ, and a number of theoretical positions contrast starkly (e.g. whether grammatical relations are primitive or not), the two models manipulate very much the same ideas, especially with respect to argument-structure representations.

3.2 *The mapping of intransitive verbs*

As is well known, many languages distinguish morphosyntactically between two types of intransitive verb. In the first type, the unergative, the subject fulfils an active semantic role (such as the traditional Agent), while in the second, the unaccusative, the subject is more passive semantically, and corresponds to a Theme or Patient. The important point here is that there are sometimes morphosyntactic processes which treat the subject of an unaccusative and the direct object of a transitive verb as a single class, distinct from the subject of an unergative verb.[6] An example of this is found in the English resultative construction (seen in (8) and (9) above). We can say *They hammered the metal flat*, and also *The river froze solid*, but we can't say *She ran tired* with a resultative meaning 'she tired herself by running'. This corresponds to the fact that *freeze* has a Theme subject and is thus unaccusative, while *run* has an Agent subject and is thus unergative. In other languages the distinction is said to manifest itself in terms of the auxiliaries selected for certain tense/aspect forms (Italian, French, Dutch, Danish), whether an impersonal passive is permitted (Dutch, German and many other languages), whether a genitive subject is possible under negation (Russian), which argument certain quantificational or aspectual prefixes apply to (Slavic generally), or whether the argument can undergo noun incorporation (Mohawk, Chukchee and many other languages).

In LMT this distinction is coded in terms of the specification of grammatical function features. The Intrinsic Classification presented in (16) above will give us the representations (27) for the unergative and unaccusative verbs *run*, *freeze*:

(27) (a) *run*<Agent>   (b) *arrive*<Theme>
                  −o   −r
           ----------------   ----------------------
                 SUBJ   SUBJ

We can now make those processes diagnostic of unaccusatives sensitive to the presence of a [−r] argument.

In the PPT/GB framework an unaccusative predicate can be character-ized in two ways. First, we could say that it is a one-place predicate with no external argument; second, we could say that it is a one-place predicate whose argument occupies a D-structure object position. In principle, one might even expect to find different processes sensitive to these different characterizations, though such evidence is hard to come by.

The PAS representations for *run* and *freeze* are shown in (28), and the corres-ponding D-structures are given in (29):

(28)   (a)   *run*<x>   (b)   *freeze*<<x>>

Here we follow Grimshaw (1990) in representing the internal argument in double angled brackets. ·

(29)   (a)   *run* – unergative   (b)   *freeze* – unaccusative

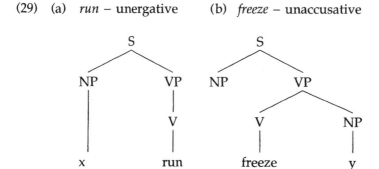

By Burzio's Generalization, the unaccusative predicate cannot assign Accusat-ive Case (because it has no external argument), so the 'y' argument has to move to subject position to receive Nominative Case.

3.3 Alternative approaches to argument structure

This chapter is investigating the idea that argument structure is an independ-ently definable level of representation, and for that reason we have not delved into those approaches under which alternations are the result of head move-ment in the syntax (Baker 1988a, D. G. Miller 1993, Ackema 1995; for review see Carstairs-McCarthy 1992, Spencer 1991). It is not clear how this relates to PAS/LCS representations, especially in a theory such as Baker's which countenances an autonomous morphology module. It is worth mentioning, though, that most approaches to morphological causatives treat them at some level as a kind of complex predicate (see section 4.3), which is reminiscent of Baker's view that they have the morphosyntax of V–V compounds.

An interesting offshoot of Baker's work which links it to the notion of LCS is that of Hale and Keyser (1992, 1993). They propose that argument structure be described in terms of lexical argument structures or lexical relational structures (LRS), essentially a sparse form of LCS built up out of binary-branching syntactic structures and obeying syntactic principles from PPT such as the Empty Category Principle. The idea is that the argument positions are represented by NP or PP complements, and the differences in argument structure associated with various verb types are coded as occurrences of (generally empty) V, A or sometimes P slots in the LRS. Thus, a causative verb is one which has a lexical VP structure headed by a V slot (corresponding roughly to a causative predicate in other frameworks).

Hale and Keyser consider location verbs such as *shelve*, in which the incorporated noun corresponds to a locative prepositional phrase:

(30)   She shelved the books.

Cf.
(31)   She put the books on the shelf.

They argue that the LRS for *shelve* is (32), akin to the syntactic structure corresponding to (31):

(32)

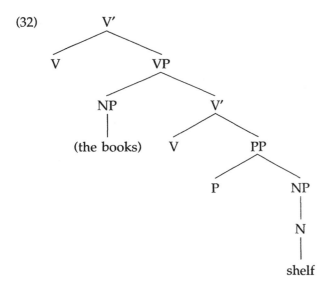

The final verb form is derived by multiple application of head movement of *shelf*, successively through P, V and V:

(33)

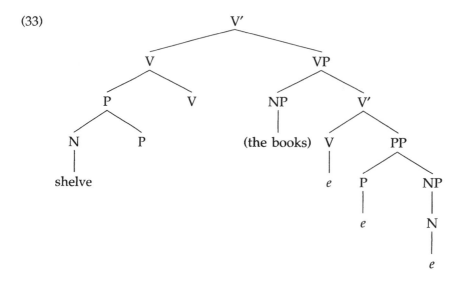

Hale and Keyser argue that similar derivations account for cases such as *saddle* (*Harriet saddled the horse*; cf. *Harriet provided the horse with a saddle*). They claim that syntactic principles explain why this is not possible when the converted noun corresponds to an indirect object. Thus, although we can say *Harriet donated a fortune to the church*, we can't say **Harriet churched a fortune*. They also analyse causative/inchoative pairs in terms of movement of nouns or adjectives through empty V positions (*The gravy thinned, The cook thinned the gravy*). In this theory there appears to be no room for a distinction between morpholexical and morphosyntactic operations. Most of the alternations Hale and Keyser discuss are lexically restricted, and are clearly morpholexical (e.g. conversion from *shelf* to *shelve*).

One very interesting alternative to the two-level architecture presented here is the theory of argument-structure alternations developed by Goldberg (1995) within the framework of Construction Grammar. For Goldberg, an alternation such as dative shift or the locative alternation is the result of fusing the lexical structure of an individual lexical item with a more general frame, the dative shift construction. A construction modulates the original verb entry, and is even capable of adding extra arguments or underlying predicates such as CAUSE. The framework is a particularly attractive way of handling alternations in which a semantic component is added, such as causatives and resultatives. It is less obvious how it handles cases of argument identification (e.g. reflexivization) or suppression (passives, antipassives). There is little scope in such a framework for the LCS/PAS distinction, because all alternations are regarded as on a par.

4 Morpholexical and morphosyntactic operations

Having discussed background notions and general theoretical approaches to argument structure, we will now illustrate our overall typology of operations with specific examples. We will discuss three sets of alternations which are each similar except that one can be regarded as a morpholexical relationship while the other can be viewed as a morphosyntactic operation. In the first morphosyntactic operation, passive, an argument position is suppressed. A similar morpholexical operation (which is not expressed morphologically) is English middle formation. In Chichewa reflexivization we see a process in which one argument position is linked with another referentially. The morphological reciprocal turns out to be morpholexical, however. In productive causatives an argument position is added. This has a drastic effect on the LCS, but in regular cases this is a predictable side-effect of the morphosyntactic change brought about by fusing the argument structure of the base verb with that of the causative. Finally, we look briefly at noun incorporation and at some of the theoretical responses to this phenomenon.

4.1 Passives and middles

In both the passive and the middle alternations in English an argument is lost and fails to be projected in the syntax. Consider (34, 35) (cf. Ackema and Schoorlemmer 1995: 175):

(34) (a) Tom painted the walls.
     (b) The walls were painted (by Tom).   (Passive)

(35)   These kinds of walls paint easily.   (Middle)

The suppressed external argument of the passive is still syntactically 'active' to some extent. It can appear as a *by* phrase more or less irrespective of the semantics of the verb (34b), and it can license agent-oriented adverbials (36), and can control the null subject of purposive clauses (37):

(36) The walls were painted on purpose.

(37) The walls were painted to protect them against the rain.

As is well known, the middle construction imposes semantic constraints: the resulting sentence is interpreted as a stative, and stylistically is preferred, therefore, with a generic subject. In addition, the construction is generally difficult or impossible without adverbial support (in the form of adjuncts referring to ease or difficulty).

An important contrast between passives and middles is that the lost subject is not syntactically available, even where the above felicity conditions are met:

(38) (a) *These kinds of walls paint easily by professional painters.
      (b) *These kinds of walls paint easily on purpose.
      (c) *These kinds of walls paint easily to protect them against the rain.

English passives are possible with a great variety of verb construction types, including raising verbs (39), double object constructions (40) and with idiom chunks, as in (41):

(39) (a) The coach expected Tom to win.
      (b) Tom was expected to win (by the coach).

(40) (a) Tom gave Dick a book.
      (b) Dick was given a book (by Tom).

(41) (a) The used-car salesman took advantage of Tom.
      (b) Tom was taken advantage of by the used-car salesman.
      (c) Advantage was taken of Tom by the used-car salesman.

Middles fail in such cases:

(42) Such committed athletes readily expect to win.

(This is ungrammatical on a reading synonymous with *are readily expected to win*.)

(43) (a) *Such well-educated children give books easily.

(Also *Such books give easily to young children*.)

(44) (a) *Tom takes advantage of easily.
      (b) *Advantage takes easily of Tom.

We will follow Ackema and Schoorlemmer (1995) in assuming that middles are formed by a 'pre-syntactic' – for us a morpholexical – process, whereas passives are formed by a morphosyntactic process. The middle, then, has a single syntactically projectable argument (an external argument, according to Ackema and Schoorlemmer, hence the middle is an unergative form) and no syntactically available implicit argument. This lone argument corresponds to a patient argument in semantic structure (and, of course, corresponds to the patient argument which is associated with the direct internal argument of the ordinary active form of the verb). The passive, however, has an internal argument which is linked to subject position in the syntax, and a suppressed, but implicit, argument corresponding to the external argument of the active form. The existence of such an implicit argument is, for us, a sufficient condition for a morphosyntactic valency-reducing operation.[7]

Given the logic of the overall architecture of grammar which we have taken as our descriptive starting-point, the active and passive alternants of a verb are forms of one and the same lexeme, while the middle form is effectively a closely related lexeme, with slightly different semantics. The difference in syntactic projection in the middle follows from the difference. The fact that there are fairly strict lexical and semantic restrictions on the formation of middles should come as no surprise. However, this is not to say that all verb forms in a given language which behave like the English middle with respect to argument structure necessarily exhibit such restrictions.

In Bantu languages – for instance, Swahili – verbs accept a wide range of suffixes to form new voices or new lexemes. Swahili has a form which is generally referred to as a passive, formed by a suffix *-w-*. Hence, from *pika* 'cook' we have *pikwa* 'be cooked', *funga* 'close', *fungwa* 'be closed'. The Swahili passive permits expression of the suppressed external argument, as in (45):

(45)   Chakul kili-pik-wa na mwanamke yule.
       food   PAST-cook-PASS by woman that
       'The food was cooked by that woman.'

In addition, we find a class of derivates known as 'stative verbs', formed regularly by suffixation of *-k*. Thus, we have verb stems such as the following (Wilson 1985: 63; Ashton 1944: 226–8):

(46)   (a)   vunja   'break'   vunjika   'be broken'
       (b)   pasua   'crack'   pasuka   'be cracked'
       (c)   funga   'close'   fungika   'be closed'
       (d)   fungua   'open'   funguka   'be opened'

Stative verbs refer to a resultant state without any indication of an agent. Thus, we have examples such as (47) and (48) (Ashton 1944: 229, 361):

(47)   Sikuvunja kikombe hiki, kimevunj-ika tu
       NEG.I.broke cup this broke-STAT just
       'I didn't break this cup; it merely broke.'

(48)   Sikufunga mlango, umefungika tu.
       NEG.I.open door open-STAT just
       'I didn't shut the door, it shut of itself.'

The difference between *mlango ulifungwa* 'The door was closed (*passive*)' and *mlango umefungika* 'The door is shut' is essentially the same as in the English translations: the passive refers to an event, the stative to a state (cf. Mchombo's discussion of similar facts, in CHICHEWA (BANTU).

Very intriguingly, the stative form is associated with a potential meaning in addition to the simple intransitive meaning illustrated so far. Thus, the stems *fungika* and *funguka* can also mean 'be closeable/openable' respectively. This is reminiscent of the meaning of the English middle (*This book reads easily* ⟺ *It is easy to read this book*).

Wilson (1985: 65) claims that 'any verb, provided its meaning allows it, can be made into a stative form', by which we take it that the verb's lexical semantics must be such as to imply the possibility of a resultant state. Thus, stative formation is very productive, and arguably part of the paradigm of the verb. However, from the brief descriptions provided here, it would seem to have the same argument structure as the English middle. Here, then, is a case in which we have something akin to English passive and middle constructions, but both are realized by regular and productive suffixation. The difference is that the passive merely suppresses the external argument, leaving it syntactically available, while the stative disposes of that argument altogether.[8]

4.2 *Reflexives and reciprocals*

Many languages have within their inventory of morphological operations a class of processes which may be viewed as deriving reflexive or reciprocal verb forms from transitive verb forms (see e.g. the brief discussion and exemplification in Levin and Rappaport Hovav, Morphology and Lexical Semantics). Syntactically, these operations are valency-reducing, resulting in predicates which do not permit a direct function to be assigned to an NP corresponding to the reflexive or reciprocal affix or clitic, as in the French examples (49):

(49)   (a)   Jean voit l'homme dans le miroir.
              Jean sees the.man in the mirror.
              'Jean sees the man in the mirror.'

        (b)   Jean se voit dans le miroir (*l'homme).
              Jean REFL sees in the mirror (the.man).
              'Jean sees himself in the mirror.'

Levin and Rappaport Hovav (Morphology and Lexical Semantics) suggest that such processes result in a predicate with the same semantic representation as the input predicate, and on this basis we might be tempted to classify all such processes as morphosyntactic. There are a number of issues here. First, although intuitively speaking it is clear that the basic verb and its reflexive or reciprocal form have the same semantics, these operations clearly have a semantic effect: namely, that of identifying the semantics of the fillers of two role slots (and, in the case of reciprocal, placing a constraint on plurality). The question is whether this identification is brought about syntactically (by syntactic binding) or whether it falls purely within the lexical domain. Second, we have argued that the prototypically morphosyntactic processes are simply relation-changing alternations. These operations, of which the best examples are voice alternations, may be viewed as doing nothing more than providing different sets of syntactic prominence arrays for sets of roles, or as mapping between alternative syntactic realizations for the arguments of predicates. In this context, then, we may ask whether reflexivization and reciprocalization are morphosyntactic in the appropriate sense, specifically:

(i)   Do they provide different grammatical function arrays/surface realizations for arguments?

(ii) Does the reflexive or reciprocal 'role' remain accessible in the syntax (in the way that the suppressed argument of a passive remains accessible)?

Both these questions are addressed in Mchombo's (1993a) discussion of reflexives and reciprocals in the Bantu language Chichewa. In Chichewa the object marker (OM) is optional, and Mchombo treats it as an agreement marker (unlike the subject marker, SM, which is ambiguous in status between an agreement marker and an incorporated argument/function). Reflexives are realized by a prefix *-dzi-* occupying the OM slot (FV = 'final vowel'):

(50)   Mkâñgo u-na-dzí-súpul-a
       3-lion 3SM-past-REFL-bruise-FV
       'The lion bruised itself.'

Mchombo offers a most interesting argument for the syntactic 'presence' of the reflexive marker on the basis of ambiguities in comparative clauses. In (51) the reflexive gives rise to strict as well as sloppy identity readings, and also to a comparative object (rather than subject) reading:

(51)   Alenje á-ma-dzi-nyóz-á kupósá asodzi
       2-hunters 2SM-hab.-reflex.-despise-FV exceeding 2-fishermen
       (i)   The hunters$_i$ despise themselves$_i$ more than the fishermen$_i$ (despise themselves$_i$) – sloppy identity reading.
       (ii) The hunters$_i$ despise themselves$_i$ more than the fishermen$_j$ (despise them$_i$) – strict identity reading.
       (iii) The hunters despise themselves more than (the hunters despise) the fishermen – comparative object reading.

The existence of strict identity and comparative object deletion readings points to the presence of a syntactic argument (for Mchombo, in fact, an object) corresponding to the reflexive in the two clauses.

Given Mchombo's reasoning, it follows that at least at PAS, reflexivized predicates have two arguments, so they remain bivalent even if they are not transitive in surface syntax. This indicates that reflexivization in Chichewa is a morphosyntactic operation. If, furthermore, Mchombo is correct that the reflexive really *is* an object, then we have no difference in surface grammatical function, although we do have a difference in surface expression (as an affix rather than an independent NP).

Mchombo presents further data to support this position. In (52) we see that under gapping, the reflexive verb patterns in a way parallel to a normal transitive verb:

(52)   Alenje á-ma-dzi-nyóz-á kupósá asodzi alimi.
       2-hunters 2SM-hab.-reflex.-despise-FV exceeding 2-fishermen 2-farmers
       'The hunters despise themselves more than the fishermen the farmers.'

The essence of Mchombo's claim concerning the Chichewa (and by extension, the Bantu) reflexive is that it is present in the syntax, as an anaphoric syntactic element, subject to syntactic binding. Since the domain of binding is syntax, and this domain is separate from that of the morpholexical rules, reflexivization cannot be a morpholexical rule.

The behaviour of the reflexive morpheme contrasts sharply with that of the reciprocal. The reciprocal marker is a suffix to the verb root, hence part of the verb stem. This means that in contrast to the reflexive marker, the reciprocal participates in the process of vowel harmony, reduplication, nominalization and imperative formation. This puts the reciprocal in the same position as exponents of morphosyntactic operations such as passive, applicative and causative; but this does not mean that it is a morphosyntactic operation itself. To see this, note its behaviour in comparative clauses. As seen in (53), the reciprocal gives rise only to the sloppy identity reading:

(53)   Alenje á-ma-nyoz-án-á kupósá asodzi
       2-hunters 2SM-hab.-despise-recip.-FV exceeding 2-fishermen
       'The hunters$_i$ despise themselves$_i$ more than the fishermen$_j$ (despise themselves$_j$).'

This strongly suggests that the process involved identifies the fillers of the two semantic role slots lexically and not syntactically; that is, we have a (productive) semantic derivation providing a predicate with a slightly altered semantic representation. In parallel fashion, the counterpart of (52) is impossible with reciprocal verbs.[9]

4.3 Causatives

In a causative construction a bare verb, V, an adjective, A, or sometimes a noun stem, N, alternates with a verb meaning 'cause/allow/persuade/help . . . to V' or 'cause/allow/persuade/help . . . to become A/N'. In many genetically and typologically varied languages this is realized morphologically in a completely regular fashion. The causative alternation has been the subject of considerable research, to which we can hardly do justice here. At first blush this would seem to be an instance of the creation of an entirely new lexeme, as in English *They darkened the room* (from adjective *dark*) or *They enslaved the populace* (from noun *slave*). This is because there is an additional semantic component of causation. Moreover, this component often receives subtly different interpretations (as indicated in our glosses above), such as persuasion, instruction ('tell someone to do something') or permission ('allow someone to do something'). However, many researchers regard the morphological causative as an instance of an argument-structure alternation, rather than lexemic derivation proper. This is particularly attractive when the causative is completely productive and lacking in lexical idiosyncrasies.

Japanese has an interesting and well-studied causative morphology. For convenience we will follow the discussion in Tsujimura's (1996) overview of Japanese grammar (cf. also Shibatani 1976). The examples in (54) are adapted from Tsujimura (1996: 247):

(54)　(a)　Hanako-ga arui-ta.
　　　　　　Hanako-NOM walk-PAST
　　　　　　'Hanako walked.'

　　　(b)　Taroo-ga Hanako-o aruk-ase-ta.
　　　　　　Taroo-NOM Hanako-ACC walk-CAUSE-PAST
　　　　　　'Taroo made Hanako walk.'

　　　(c)　Taroo-ga Hanako-ni aruk-ase-ta.
　　　　　　Taroo-NOM Hanako-DAT walk-CAUSE-PAST
　　　　　　'Taroo had Hanako walk.'

The causative morpheme is a suffix taking the form *-(s)ase* (*-sase* occurs after vowel-final stems). As is typical cross-linguistically, the subject of the basic verb *walk* in (54a), *Hanako*, is expressed as a direct object marked by *-o* in the causative version in (54b). This sentence means something like 'Taroo forced Hanako to walk'. In (54c), however, *Hanako* is marked with a dative case marker *-ni*, and the interpretation is closer to 'Taroo persuaded Hanako to walk'.

When a transitive verb is causativized, the embedded subject is always marked with dative case, as in (55):

(55)　(a)　Taroo-ga hon-o yon-da.
　　　　　　Taroo-NOM book-ACC read-PAST
　　　　　　'Taroo read a book.'

　　　(b)　Hahaoya-ga Taroo-ni hon-o yom-ase-ta.
　　　　　　mother-NOM Taroo-DAT book-ACC read-CAUSE-PAST
　　　　　　'His mother made/had Taroo read a book.'

This has been linked to a general prohibition in Japanese against two nominals marked with -*o* in one clause. In other languages it is quite common for the embedded subject of a transitive verb to be marked as an (optional) oblique rather than as a direct object, but Japanese is only accidentally similar to this type.

Morphological causatives in Japanese are very productive, and are relatively free of lexical restrictions or idiosyncrasies. Moreover, there is good evidence (cf. Shibatani (ed.) 1976) that at some level a causativized transitive sentence such as (56) behaves like two clauses, much like the bi-clausal English translation (again, adapted from Tsujimura 1996: 255):

(56)   Taroo-ga Ziroo-o/ni zibun-no heya-de benkyoo-sase-ta.
        Taroo$_i$-NOM Ziroo$_j$-ACC REFL$_{i/j}$-GEN room-in study-CAUSE-PAST
        'Taroo made Ziroo study in his own room.'

Reflexivization in Japanese is subject-oriented, so (56) suggests that both *Taroo* and *Ziroo* correspond to subjects at some level. We can say that, in a certain sense, *Ziroo* is the subject of *study*, while *Taroo* is the subject of CAUSE. Evidence from ambiguities with temporal and subject-oriented adverbs points the same way. We can call a causative construction of this sort 'bi-clausal'.

In what sense is a productive morphological causative a morphosyntactic operation? One viewpoint, which in some ways incorporates the insights of Baker (1988a), is to say that the causative operation comprises the fusion or union of two argument structures. Thus, suppose we take the argument structure of predicates such as *walk* or *hit* as something like (57):

(57)   (a)   walk: <arg. 1>
        (b)   hit: <arg. 1, arg. 2>

Then we can say that the causative will be (58):

(58)   (a)   cause-walk: <arg. 0 <arg. 1>>
        (b)   cause-hit: <arg. 0 <arg. 1, arg. 2>>

To some extent it is immaterial for our typology whether structures such as (58a,b) are the result of an operation 'in the lexicon' or the result of V-movement 'in the syntax'. The point is that it makes sense to say that the operation is defined over an essentially unrestricted set of predicates and results in an argument structure representation along the lines of (58), such that all three of the arguments are syntactically visible in some sense. The operation thus qualifies as morphosyntactic in our sense.[10]

Languages differ in how these three arguments are realized (see Baker 1988a for a detailed study of this). Cross-linguistically, *arg. 1* in (58a) is uniformly realized as a canonical direct object. However, the (58b) structure (where it exists) will sometimes realize *arg. 1* as a direct object, and sometimes *arg. 2* retains the direct object status, depending on the language. When *arg. 1* becomes the derived direct object, *arg. 2* is generally marked as a second object, though this will often be inert to object-oriented processes like passive. Thus, despite the fact that *Taroo-ni* in (55b) is an obliquely marked phrase, it is in fact the direct object of the causative. This is clear when we try to passivize a causative. Consider the data in (59) (cf. Tsujimura 1996: 259):

(59) (a) Ziroo-ga Mitiko-ni kodomo-o home-sase-ta.
          Ziroo-NOM Mitiko-DAT child-ACC praise-CAUSE-PAST
          'Ziroo made Mitiko praise the child.'

     (b) Mitiko-ga Ziroo-ni kodomo-o home-sase-rare-ta.
          Mitiko-NOM Ziroo-DAT child-ACC praise-CAUSE-PASS-PAST
          'Mitiko was made to praise the child by Ziroo.'

Here, *Mitiko-ni* in (59a) has been promoted to subject when (59a) is passivized, while *kodomo-o* 'child-ACC' remains marked as an accusative. However, if we try to passivize on the accusative marked object in (59a), *kodomo-o*, we get an ungrammatical sentence:

(60) *Kodomo-ga Ziroo-ni Mitiko-ni home-sase-rare-ta
       child-NOM Ziroo-DAT Mitiko-DAT praise-CAUSE-PASS-PAST
       'The child was made praised by Mitiko by Ziroo.'

Thus, *kodomo-o* behaves like an inert, or frozen, second object. Such 'freezing' of the second object is typical, though in some languages both objects retain full object properties, including passivization, object agreement marking and so on (see Baker 1988a and Bresnan and Moshi 1990 for discussion of variation in Bantu in this respect).

In other languages *arg. 2* in (58b) is treated as the object of the causative, with *arg. 1* becoming an oblique marked adjunct, generally optional. This is how causatives work in Turkish, for instance. Consider (61) (Comrie 1976: 268):

(61) Dişçi mektub-u müdür-e imzala-t-tı.
      dentist letter-ACC director-DAT sign-CAUSE-PAST
      'The dentist made the director sign the letter.'

Here the object of the basic verb, *letter*, remains the object of the derived causative verb, while the subject of the basic verb, *director*, appears as a Dative marked oblique.

In general, when *arg. 2* is treated as the derived (as well as basic) object, the causative construction behaves syntactically like a single clause. Thus, if the object is a reflexive pronoun, it can only refer back to the surface subject, *arg. 0*, and not to *arg. 1*. In other words, *arg. 1* cannot be treated as a kind of subject for the purposes of reflexivization, and we have a monoclausal causative construction. This is in contrast to the biclausal causative of Japanese.[11]

The semantic effects of the causative operation will differ somewhat from language to language, and, importantly, from construction to construction, so Japanese causatives with -*o* marked objects have the coercive or the adversity reading, while those with the -*ni* object have the permissive reading. However, the basic semantic relationships are the same cross-linguistically.

Japanese also has verb pairs which we can interpret as lexical causatives, often related by non-productive ablaut. Some examples are given in (62) (Tsujimura 1996: 260):

(62)   causative   intransitive

        tomeru   tomaru   'stop'
        ageru   agaru   'rise/raise'
        sageru   sagaru   'lower'
        okosu   okiru   'wake up'
        nekasu   neru   'sleep'

Despite the meanings of these pairs, the causative member does not behave like a morphological causative derived with -*(s)ase*. Thus, with reflexives we get a monoclausal patterning. Compare (63) with (56):

(63)   Taroo-ga Ziroo-o zibun-no heya-no mae-de tome-ta.
      Taroo$_i$-NOM Ziroo$_j$-ACC REFL$_{i/*j}$ room-GEN front-at stop-PAST
      'Taroo stopped Ziroo in front of his room.'

In (63) *Ziroo* is a 'pure' object, and hence cannot be the antecedent to the reflexive. Contrast this with (64), in which the intransitive *toma-* is causativized morphologically, not lexically:

(64)   Taroo-ga Ziroo-o zibun heya-no mae-de tomar-ase-ta.
      Taroo$_i$-NOM Ziroo$_j$-ACC REFL$_{i/j}$ room-GEN front-AT stop-CAUSE-PAST
      'Taroo made Ziroo stop in front of his room.'

Here, *his room* can refer to Taroo or to Ziroo.

Clearly, we want to relate the intransitives to their lexical causatives by means of a morpholexical operation, while we will argue that the morphological causatives (at least in Japanese) are the result of morphosyntactic operations. A further piece of semantic evidence in favour of this is that the lexical causatives signify direct causation, in which the agent must come into direct contact with the patient. Morphological causatives, however, denote indirect causation. Thus, (64) could refer to a situation in which Ziroo is brought to a stop outside Taroo's room by a large obstacle which Taroo has left there. Taroo could be hundreds of miles away when Ziroo is thus halted. Sentence (63) cannot have such an interpretation.

Discussion of how exactly the linking to grammatical functions is achieved would require a separate chapter in itself, and would require a detailed analysis of the morphosyntax of various subject- and object-oriented processes in the languages which have such causatives. However, we must address one question which arises with a morphosyntactic analysis of causatives. Since there is a sharp shift in meaning (the addition of a CAUSE predicate), in what sense can any causative be morphosyntactic: that is, an operation over argument structures? We assume that what is actually happening here is that the causative operation involves addition of an argument structure, consisting minimally of an external argument position and a further argument position corresponding to the embedded proposition. This then 'fuses' or 'merges' with the argument structure of the basic predicate. Language-particular principles dictate exactly what happens to the elements of the embedded PAS. We thus obtain a representation such as (65):

(65)   CAUSE(x, Ev)   [$_{EV}$STOP(y)]

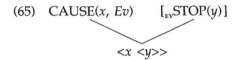

                       <x <y>>

This is a complex predicate, whose overall argument structure is a function of two independent argument structures. However, the fusion takes place at the level of PAS, not LCS. The LCS portion of (65) is what we would see in a syntactic causative, so the causative predicate and clausal semantic argument can behave, to some extent, independently.

In the lexical causatives we simply have a causative LCS which includes the embedded predicate:

(66)   [CAUSE(x)[STOP(y)]]
              |
      <x <y>>

This does not differ significantly from the representation for any (monomorphemic) transitive verb with a causative component.

4.4 *Noun incorporation*

Levin and Rappaport (MORPHOLOGY AND LEXICAL SEMANTICS) illustrate English verbs derived by conversion from nouns, such as *butter* in *to butter toast (with margarine)*. Here the converted noun corresponds to an object in a syntactic construction such as *to spread butter on the toast*. In some languages the conversion is signalled morphologically, by affixation: for example, Dutch *ver-botter-en* from the noun *botter*, Hungarian *meg-vaj-az* from the noun *vaj*. In other languages, we can create a lexical unit akin to the VP *to spread butter* by means of noun incorporation. An example from Chukchee is cited by Gerdts (INCORPORATION), from Polinskaja and Nedjalkov 1987: 240:

(67)   ətləg-e kawkaw mətqə=rkele-nin.
        father-ERG bread.ABS butter=spread.on=AOR.3SG:3SG
        'Father spread the bread with butter.'

This corresponds to (68) without incorporation:

(68)   ətləg-e kawkaw-ək mətqəmət kele-nin.
        father-ERG bread-LOC butter.ABS spread.on=AOR.3SG:3SG
        'Father spread the butter on the bread.'

In the model proposed by Baker (1988a) such an alternation would be the result of movement applying to the head noun of the object NP *butter*, forming a compound verb as in (69):

(69)   (a)

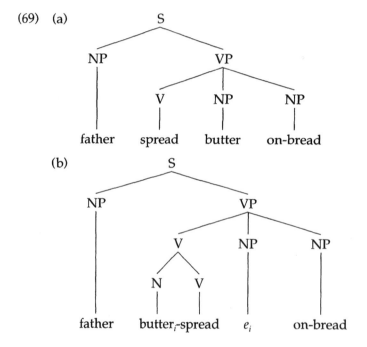

The movement of butter leaves a trace, e_i, which has to be properly governed by the verbal complex. Given this analysis, Baker is able to account for a number of important features of NI, such as the stranding of modifiers in some languages. In this type of approach, the fact that the noun *butter* is interpreted as the direct object of the verb is a consequence of the fact that it is, indeed, the verb's object in the syntactic representation. Further discussion of some of the implications of this type of approach is given in Borer (MORPHOLOGY AND SYNTAX).

A similar kind of analysis is available in principle for an English synthetic compound such as *butter-spreader* (e.g. Roeper 1988, Lieber 1992), though here there are important questions surrounding the fact that the verb is nominal-ized and cannot occur in finite forms, as witnessed by the ungrammaticality of **Tom butter-spreads his toast every morning (with margarine)*. An alternative analysis, which is also open to noun incorporation proper, would say that the incorporated element discharges an argument position, but not in the same way as a syntactic direct object. Sproat (1985) and DiSciullo and Williams (1987) propose rather different solutions, which, however, are alike in not appealing to syntactic movement. This is especially attractive for synthetic compound-ing, in which compounding renders the verb syntactically intransitive: there is no stranding of modifiers, and no 'doubling' is possible: **butter-spreader of bread with rancid e_i*, **butter-spreader of bread with margarine*.

What is the argument-structure status of *butter-spreader*? Here, again, we have a combination of lexemes, which produces what is morphologically more akin to a single word than to a genuine phrase. We can then say that the argument structure of the noun *butter* is somehow 'fused' with that of the verb stem *spread* in such a way that *butter* is interpreted as the direct internal argu-ment of *spread*. If this is a direct operation over the verb argument structure, then presumably we have to say that the nominalizing suffix *-er* is attached after the internal argument is discharged. This means we must assume that the grammar creates an otherwise non-existent verb stem *[butter-spread]* which then triggers discharge of the internal role. Only then does suffixation take place to give *[[butter-spread]er]* (cf. Sproat 1985). On the other hand, we might argue that the argument structure of the verb is in some way inherited by the nominalization. Thus, *[[spread]er]* retains at least the direct internal argument of the verb stem. This argument can then be projected either as an *of* phrase (*a spreader of butter (on bread)*), or as part of the compound to give *[bread [spread-er]]* (cf. DiSciullo and Williams 1987).

Approaches to synthetic compounding which appeal to operations over argument structures leave a number of questions unresolved, of course (see Carstairs-McCarthy 1992 for discussion). One of these is the status of the notion of 'inheritance' of argument structure (see Lieber 1992 for discussion of this). Another concerns the generality of the approach. As stressed by Roeper and Siegel (1978) in an early generative treatment of synthetic compounds, English permits compounds in which an adverbial modifier is incorporated, as in *quick-drying (paint)*, *sun-dried (tomatoes)*, *home-made (cakes)* and many others. Recent discussion has tended to ignore these cases. An approach which appeals solely to the discharge of argument-structure positions has little to say about them.

The situation is rendered more interesting by the fact that incorporation of adverbials is observed in some noun-incorporating languages. Thus, in Chukchee it is possible to say things like *Tom quick-ran* or *The mother tent-sewed the shirt* (i.e. the mother sewed the shirt in the tent) (cf. Muravyova, CHUKCHEE (PALEO-SIBERIAN). The incorporation of adverbials is a distinct embarrassment to the framework of Baker (1988a), which is so constructed as to explicitly exclude such constructions (for extensive discussion of this point see Spencer 1995). It seems to us that there is merit in exploring the idea that incorporative structures of this sort can, in part at least, involve something akin to the complex predicate formation we proposed for morphological causatives. Thus, the Chukchee example in (67) might involve a representation along the lines of (70), in which the verb and its object have distinct LCS representations but at PAS that of the object *butter* is indexed with the verb's internal-argument position, thereby saturating it and preventing it from being realized syntactically:

(70)   [[x ACT] CAUSE [y BECOME-ON z [$_{BY}$ x SPREAD y]] [BUTTER(w)]

spread <x <w, P$_{loc}$ z>>

This can be thought of as the PAS equivalent of syntactic incorporation in such theories as those of Baker (1988a) or Sadock (1991) (for the latter, cf. Sproat, MORPHOLOGY AS COMPONENT OR MODULE). In the relatively rare cases like Chukchee where adverbials can be incorporated, we can adopt a similar analysis, in which the adverbial's argument structure is fused with an event position at PAS.

Noun incorporation in many languages is lexically restricted, non-productive and idiosyncratic, much like noun-to-verb conversion of the type *butter the toast* in English (see Mithun 1984 for extensive discussion of this). For such languages, we would argue that the incorporation takes place at the LCS level, despite being realized morphologically by compounding, giving a representation such as (71):

(71)   [[x ACT] CAUSE [*BUTTER* BECOME-ON z [$_{BY}$ x SPREAD *BUTTER*]]

This could then correspond to any of the PAS representations in (72), depending on the language, corresponding to syntactic structures (73):

(72)   (a)   *spread* <x <P$_{loc}$ z>>
        (b)   *spread* <x <z>>
        (c)   *spread* <x <y, P$_{loc}$ z>>

(73)   (a)   butter=spread on to the toast
        (b)   butter=spread the toast
        (c)   butter=spread margarine on to the toast

5 Summary

We have argued that valency alternations can be of two distinct types: morpholexical operations at a semantic level and morphosyntactic operations at a level of argument structure. The morpholexical operations are likely to be semantically or lexically restricted, and to bring with them semantic changes which cannot always be predicted from the valency shift as such. Morphosyntactic operations are more often semantically unrestricted, and are thus often defined solely in terms of input/output conditions on argument-structure representations, independently of the semantic representation. They generally do not give rise to additional semantic affects (modulo other aspects of the construction). The result of a morpholexical operation tends to behave syntactically in the same way as a corresponding monomorphemic predicate, whereas syntactic processes may have access to the individual parts of the result of a morphosyntactic operation (cf. the difference between morphological and lexical causatives). We illustrated these distinctions by contrasting passives/middles in English (and Bantu), reflexives/reciprocals in Bantu, and morphological/lexical causatives in Japanese. We finally discussed noun incorporation and synthetic compounding as possible instances of complex predicate formation, in which PAS positions (rather than LCS positions) are saturated morphologically.

NOTES

1 The terminology, with essentially this interpretation, is due to Ackerman (1992). We acknowledge that the nomenclature is potentially rather misleading, particularly given that 'morpholexical', which already has a number of unrelated uses in linguistics, is used to refer to both our morpholexical operations and our morphosyntactic operations in the LFG literature.

2 In practice, thematic role labels are used for convenience, not out of theoretical commitment to these labels. It is generally understood that they stand for more complex LCS representations, perhaps of the kind argued for by Jackendoff 1990. Alternatively, some theorists take Dowty's (1991) Proto-roles as their starting-point (cf. Ackerman 1992).

3 Though this is a rather complex matter: see Ackerman 1992, Alsina and Mchombo 1993, Bresnan and Moshi 1990, for discussion.

4 There are various formulations of these operations in the literature.

5 There are languages in which this restriction does not hold: e.g. Turkish, in which unaccusative predicates, including passivized verbs, can be passivized. See Spencer 1991 for brief discussion.

6 This explains in part the alternative term used for unaccusative predicates, 'ergative'. However, this is a rather misleading term, since ergative patterning would lead one to expect objects to pattern with all intransitive subjects. The more appropriate alternative to 'ergative' would therefore be 'inactive', though as far as we know, no one has ever made this terminological proposal.

7 The reader should bear in mind that this conclusion is meant to follow for English passives and English middles. Constructions which are called 'passive' or especially 'middle' in other languages, e.g. French (Levin and Rappaport Hovav, MORPHOLOGY AND LEXICAL SEMANTICS), may well

have different properties from the ones described here (French middles can be eventive, for instance).

In addition, many factors govern whether a semantic argument is accessible to syntactic processes, so absence of an implicit argument cannot be taken as criterial for a morpholexical valency-reducing operation.

8   We haven't investigated the full set of properties of the Bantu passive and stative constructions. Given the level of disagreement over the status of Germanic middles in the recent syntactic literature, a detailed cross-linguistic study of that sort on Bantu might be rather timely.

9   A terminological warning: Mchombo uses the term 'morpholexical', but does not explicitly make our terminological distinction between 'morpholexical' and 'morphosyntactic'.

10   Alsina (1992), to whom the approach here offers a certain debt, provides a detailed analysis of causatives in Chichewa along similar lines, except that for him the arg. 1 position is an argument of the causative itself. It is a matter of considerable debate whether the 'real' argument of causation is a patient ('causee') and an event, or just an event, or whether these represent direct and indirect causation respectively. The matter is tangential to our main concerns here.

11   In some languages of the Japanese type, it is *only* arg. 1 which can be the antecedent of a reflexive in a causative. Japanese allows arg. 0 to serve as antecedent, because its reflexive allows 'long-distance' binding, by the subject of a higher clause.

11 Morphology and the Lexicon: Lexicalization and Productivity

MARK ARONOFF AND FRANK ANSHEN

1 Morphology and the lexicon

According to one widely accepted view (Aronoff 1976, 1982), the morphology of a language, because it is part of grammar and trades in structural matters, deals primarily with the internal structure of the potential-complex words of a language. These words may not all exist, but they all conform to the morphological structure of the language.[1] By contrast, the lexicon of a language is a list of existing items in the language, those that a speaker has to know because they are arbitrary signs: unpredictable in some way. Most of the items on this list are words, though the lexicon also contains larger units like idioms, and maybe also smaller units like affixes. On this view, in which the regular morphology and the irregular lexicon are separate entities, one might imagine the two having very little to do with one another, since the morphology deals only with potential words and the lexicon only with existing words. In fact, the two systems do have a great deal to do with one another, for two simple reasons. The first is that they serve the same role in a language: both provide words. This overlap has even led some linguists to say that morphology is "in the lexicon" (Jensen and Stong-Jensen 1984), although in doing so, these linguists are using the term *lexicon* in a much broader and different sense, to mean the source of all words, actual and potential, rather than in the narrow sense of a list of unpredictable items that we have inherited from traditional grammar and from Bloomfield (Bloomfield 1933, Zwicky 1989, Aronoff 1994). The second reason is that morphology and the lexicon are interdependent. Most centrally, the morphology, which forms words from words, finds the words that it operates on (its bases) in the lexicon. We will explore each of these interrelations in a separate section.

1.1 Morphology versus the lexicon

As with any two entities that share a task, morphology and the lexicon do not always do so happily; they are rivals. This rivalry is not empty, but plays a central role in the larger system of the language. In order to understand its nature, we must consider a single speaker/hearer. When we speak of the lexicon from this perspective, we speak of the individual's mental lexicon, the list of irregular items that the speaker/hearer carries around in his or her head. We may then define the difference between existing words and potential words in terms of this mental lexicon. We will say that any word that is stored in a single speaker/hearer's mental lexicon or list of irregular items is an existing word, and that nothing else is. In particular, a word that meets all the criteria for being a word of the language but that is not in an individual's mental lexicon does not exist for that person, though it may exist for another speaker/hearer. The unlisted word is a potential word, and we will say that morphologically well-formed complex potential words are provided by the morphology, not by the lexicon. Thus, the conventional idea that the existing words of a language – English, for example – comprise all the words in the *Oxford English Dictionary* or some other comprehensive dictionary does not apply in this model of the lexicon and the morphology. The difference between which words exist and which are potential is defined solely in terms of the individual's lexicon and morphology.

Most importantly for our purposes, even if our ideal speaker/hearer has spoken or heard (or read) a particular word before, if that word has not been stored in that person's mental lexicon for some reason, then the word is still a potential word rather than an existing word as far as the mental lexicon is concerned. Which words are stored? In the simplest case, a word will be stored because it contain only one morpheme. Take the word *bamboozle*.[2] It has no morphological structure, so nothing to predict its meaning. Someone who hears this word, even in a context in which its sense is clear, must enter it into memory in order to use it again, so it will enter the hearer's mental lexicon. Similarly, a morphologically complex word must be placed in the lexicon if a piece of it is unknown to the hearer. An example of this type is *hornswoggle*, which is almost synonymous with *bamboozle*. One of its components, *horn*, is recognizable, but the other one, *swoggle*, is not, so that, again, we must memorize the word in its entirety if we wish to reuse it in the same sense, even if we can deduce its sense from the context in which we hear it. Yet again, all the components of a word may be familiar, but its sense may not be deducible from them. Here too we must put the word in our lexicon. An example of this phenomenon is yet a third synonym, *hoodwink*. Both *hood* and *wink* are familiar words, but the sense of the entire word *hoodwink* has little to do with the sense of its parts, so even here our ideal speaker/hearer must resort to lexical storage in order to have a hope of reusing the word. So if a word is unpredictable, it must be stored in the lexicon. By contrast, consider the word *rigidification*, encountered in a journal article recently. The parts of this word are readily apparent: *rigid, ify* (which forms verbs from adjectives and nouns), and *ation* (which forms abstract nouns from verbs), with *ific* being a contextual variant of *ify* that appears regularly before *ation*. Also transparent is its meaning, which can be paraphrased roughly as 'the act or fact or state of making or becoming rigid'. The paraphrase is ambiguous, but which of these senses is meant in a particular instance will generally be clear from the context. Since the actual sense of the word does not diverge from its predicted sense, based on its parts and its morphological structure, there is no need for this word to be listed in the speaker/hearer's lexicon, for the morphological component of the speaker/hearer's grammar is able to process it entirely. The word will therefore be spoken, heard, and most likely discarded by all parties, perhaps to be created and discarded again, but not stored, unless it is used in some special sense that is not predictable from the morphology.[3]

So far, the morphology and the lexicon do not interact. The first creates regular words, and the second stores irregular words. To see how they do interact, we must look at a case where both the lexicon and the morphology are in principle capable of being invoked. We will begin with a simple case, that of the plural of a noun in English. Some plurals come from the lexicon, and some from the morphology. The plural will come from the lexicon in case it is irregular and stored there on account of its irregularity, like *women* or *people,* and it will come from the morphology in case it is regular, like *dogs.* But now a question arises. If a word has an irregular plural stored in the lexicon, why does it not also have a regular plural, which comes from the morphology? In the case at hand, how does a speaker know not to say *womans* instead of or as well as *women*? Or why doesn't the speaker sometimes say one and sometimes the other? Something must be preventing the morphology from producing a regular plural just in case an irregular plural for the same word exists in the lexicon. The same is true of irregular past tenses of verbs. A person who knows that the past tense of *go* is *went* (a fact that must be stored in the lexicon) will not say *goed*, although a young child or someone in the early stages of learning English as a second language might say *goed*, because the child or learner hasn't yet learned the form *went*. The lexicon and the morphology seem to interact in assuring that only one form will be used, but how? Does the speaker/hearer somehow check the lexicon to see if a word is there, and only resort to the morphology if there is none?

A clue to the right answer to this question has been known for centuries: languages tend to avoid synonyms (though not always, as *bamboozle, hornswoggle,* and *hoodwink* reveal). In most cases, the speaker will use a word from his or her lexicon (*women, went*) rather than resort to the morphology to produce a new word with the same meaning. This phenomenon, "the nonoccurrence of one form due to the simple existence of another" (Aronoff 1976: 43), is called *blocking,* and its effects can be seen not only in inflection, but also in derivation, where a word like **furiosity* (formed from *furious*) will be blocked by *fury,* which already exists in a speaker's lexicon. We can tell that blocking is at work in rendering **furiosity* unacceptable, because other words of the same pattern are perfectly acceptable, when there is no already existing word to block them.

Thus, *curiosity*, which is structurally analogous to **furiosity*, is perfectly acceptable, because there is no word **cury* to block it. The effects of blocking are also felt in syntax, where an existing word will sometimes block an entire synonymous phrase, as Hoffman (1982) first noted. We do not, for example, find *this night* used in standard English in a sense parallel to *this morning* or *this evening*, because of the existence of synonymous *tonight*. As the example shows, exact synonymy is crucial, for the expression *this night* can in fact be used, so long as it is not synonymous with *tonight* (e.g. in the question "Why is this night different from all other nights?"). There will also be no blocking without synonymy, so we may find a pair like *brethren* and *brothers*, precisely because the former refers not to actual brothers but rather to fellow members of an organized group of some sort. The most cogent account of why blocking occurs is Horn's (1984, 1993), based on general principles of economy of expression, to which we will return in section 2.3.

Because blocking is a psychological phenomenon, it is subject to the vagaries of the mind: if a person has temporarily forgotten the word *fame*, then that person may in fact use the word **famousness*, which *fame* would otherwise block. This seeming failure of blocking is especially common in children, who coin new words quite freely, because their vocabulary is not as entrenched as that of adults. An articulate child might use words like *famousness* and *liquidize* in conversation without hesitating.

Blocking is also subject to another psychological factor: familiarity or its more easily measurable counterpart, frequency. In general, the more frequently used an irregular form is, both in absolute terms and compared to its base, the more likely it is to block the corresponding regular form (Anshen and Aronoff 1988, Rainer 1988). This effect of frequency can be detected not only experimentally (Pinker and Prince 1991), but also in children's "overregularizations," as Bybee and Slobin (1982) have shown for irregular verbs in English. The effect of frequency can also be seen in morphological regularization over time: in general, the more frequently an irregular form is used, the more resistant it will be to being replaced by a regular form, which is to say, the more likely it is to block the corresponding regular form (Anshen and Aronoff 1988). The most widely accepted models of blocking take frequency into account by translating it into processing speed. According to these models (MacWhinney 1975, Anshen and Aronoff 1988, Pinker and Prince 1991), the search for the proper word can be viewed as a race between the mental lexicon and the morphology. Both operate simultaneously, and the faster one wins. If it is true that the speed of lexical access for individual stored irregular words is proportional to the logarithm of their frequency, then the more frequent an irregular word is compared to its base, the more likely it will be to block the morphology. Note that this general model does not involve any direct interaction between the mental lexicon and the morphology. The two components of the language mechanism can thus be insulated from each other, as far as this one phenomenon is concerned. They interact more closely in the actual operation of the morphology, which we will now explore.

Table 11.1 All words of the form *Xidify* and *Xidification* in a very large word list

Xidify	Xidification
acidify	acidification
deacidify	deacidification
reacidify	reacidification
disacidify	*
rancidify	rancidification
*	lucidification
rigidify	*
*	validification
solidify	solidification
resolidify	resolidification
humidify	humidification
dehumidify	dehumidification
nidify	nidification
renidify	renidification
lapidify	lapidification
fluidify	fluidification

1.2 Morphology based on the lexicon

Morphological patterns are abstract. Returning to the word *rigidification*, we may view it simply as an instantiation of the abstract pattern $[[[X]_A \, ify]_v \, ation]_N$. But if we look more closely at attested words that fit this pattern, we see the effect of the lexicon. Let us narrow our gaze from the general pattern just mentioned to a slightly more particular one, in which the adjective is of the form *Xid* (e.g. *acid, livid, candid*). If the pattern were completely independent of the lexicon, then we might expect to find that any adjective of the form *Xid* could serve as the base of an attested word of the form *Xidification*. We have access to a very large English word list, compiled from eighteen general and technical dictionaries, containing about 400,000 entries. Among these are approximately 1,000 words of the form *Xid*. But there are only 14 words of the form *Xidify*, which indicates that this particular rule is not very productive. Thus, we do not find the following words in the list, though all of them have easily constructible senses: **rabidify, *lividify, *acridify, *stolidify*. There are similarly only 14 words of the form *Xidification*. Remarkably, as table 11.1 shows, in all but two cases in each column, the words of the two forms share a base. We cannot, of course, extrapolate directly from a large dictionary to the mental lexicon, but dictionary data of this type, which can be repeated for many patterns in which one suffix is added to another, suggest that the actual production of morphologically complex words is done largely by applying morphological rules (adding affixes) to actually occurring base words that are stored in a speaker's mental lexicon.

Another indication that morphological rules operate on words in the lexicon is the inheritance of irregularity. The most common type of inherited irregularity is semantic. Complex words often have conventional senses that differ slightly from their predicted sense (see section 2.2). Consider the word *immeasurable*. Judging by its parts, it should mean 'that cannot be measured'. In actual use, it almost always means 'very large'. The adverb formed from it, *immeasurably*, therefore means 'greatly', as in expressions like "I have benefited immeasurably from your assistance." Another example is *naturalize*, which should mean 'to make natural', but which has a number of specialized senses, including 'to confer the rights of citizenship upon (an alien)' and 'to adapt (a plant or animal) to a new environment'. The noun *naturalization* that is derived from this verb has the nominal derivatives of these two as senses, because it is formed on the actual verb in the lexicon with all of its specialized senses. Furthermore, because the most familiar sense of the verb for most people is 'to confer the rights of citizenship upon (an alien)', the most salient sense of the noun for most people is based on this sense of the verb. So, for example, a search of our university library's computerized catalogue under the key word *naturalization* reveals a large number of books having to do with immigration to various countries and no other books (though we might expect a different outcome at a school of horticulture).

The inheritance of the phonological irregularities of words in the lexicon is a little harder to detect, largely because we tend to be less aware of them, but one example that springs to mind is the word *comfortable*, which for many people is pronounced [kəmftə(r)bl]. The adverb is similarly pronounced [kəmftə(r)bli], inheriting the phonological irregularity of the adjective base. By contrast, although *probably* is often pronounced [prabli], *probable* is not pronounced *[prabl], showing that a derived word (*probably*) may deviate phonologically from its base (*probable*) and acquire its own lexical entry.

In conclusion, we have seen that morphology is distinct from the lexicon (at least if by the word *lexicon* we mean a speaker/hearer's mental lexicon of unpredictable forms), and that the morphology and the lexicon are rival sources of words. The morphology depends on the lexicon, however, inasmuch as the bases of morphologically complex words are normally lexical entries.

2 Morphological productivity

2.1 Quantitative and qualitative productivity

Morphological productivity may be defined informally as the extent to which a particular affix is likely to be used in the production of new words in the language. On this view, productivity is a probabilistic continuum that predicts

Table 11.2   Morphologically restricted de-adjectival nominal suffixes

conditioned suffix	example	conditioning suffix	base word
-(c)e	tolerance	-ant	tolerant
"	putrescence	-ent	putrescent
-(c)y	buoyancy	-ant	buoyant
"	latency	-ent	latent
-ity	separability	-able/-ible	separable
"	legibility	"	legible
"	legality	-al/-ar	legal
"	popularity	"	popular
"	toxicity	-ic	toxic
"	stupidity	-id	stupid
"	agility	-ile	agile
"	ferocity	-ous	ferocious

the use of potential words. At one end of the continuum are the dead or completely unproductive affixes, which are not likely to be used at all in coining new words. One example of this from English is the nominal suffix *-th* (as in *truth* or *growth*), which has not been used successfully to form a new word for 400 years, despite valiant attempts at terms like *coolth* (which is attested sporadically, but which just never seems to be able to survive long). At the other end in English are the productive inflectional suffixes *-ed*, *-ing*, and *-s*, which are added whenever syntactic conditions are appropriate and there is no irregular form already in existence to block them, and highly productive derivational suffixes like *-ness* and *-ation*. In the middle, we find the less productive derivational suffixes like *-ity*. Some linguists treat morphological productivity as an absolute notion – a pattern is either productive or unproductive – but there is a good deal of evidence for the existence and utility of intermediate cases, which we will review below, so we will assume in this chapter that affixes may differ continuously in productivity, rather than falling only into the polar categories of completely productive and completely unproductive, to which some linguists have restricted the discussion.

Aside from quantitative considerations, there are qualitative morphological factors that are relevant to productivity. This can best be seen by examining rival affixes, affixes that are very similar in their semantic and syntactic conditions. Consider the several suffixes that form nouns from adjectives in English. Most of them are productive only within a morphologically restricted domain, as shown in table 11.2, which classifies the suffixes according to the preceding suffixes that they generally occur with. The suffix *-ness* is different from those exemplified in table 11.2. It occurs with a wide variety of base adjectives patterns, including monomorphemic words and those of the morphological types included in table 11.2: *dryness, redness, wetness, fetidness,* *prolificness, venerableness, trivialness, obliviousness, recentness, pleasantness.* Being unrestricted, *-ness* operates as the default affix for forming de-adjectival nouns, the affix that is normally used when no additional morphological conditions on the base adjective hold. Linguists have found that one of the members of any similar set of rival affixes or operations will usually be the default, qualitatively unrestricted. This qualitative difference is usually mirrored quantitatively as well: the qualitatively least restricted operation among a set of rivals will most often also be the quantitatively most productive, though cases of the default not being the most productive have been found. Clahsen et al. (1992), for example, have shown that the default plural suffix in German is not the most productive or most common. It is also not always true that the least restricted member of a set of rivals will be totally unrestricted in its distribution. For example, we have shown in earlier work (Anshen and Aronoff 1981, 1988) that *-ness* does not attach at all to words of the form *Xible*, despite being the default for de-adjectival nouns in English.

How can quantitative productivity be measured? Baayen (1992) has developed a number of measures that take advantage of modern computational analysis of large corpora in English and other languages. First of all, productivity is related to growth (the rate at which new words in general are being added to a language). The growth rate of the vocabulary of any language is estimated from a large corpus as the ratio of those words occurring only once in the corpus (*hapax legomena*, henceforth *hapaxes*) to the total number of word tokens in the corpus. For rival operations, a similar measure (the ratio of hapaxes formed by that operation to the total number of tokens of the same morphological type in the corpus) can be used to compute relative growth rates. The English suffixes *-ity* and *-ness*, for example, show growth rates of 0.0007 and 0.0044 in Baayen's calculation (based on a corpus of 18,000,000 words), meaning that *-ness* is six times as productive as *-ity*, regardless of any difference in the qualitative morphological restrictions on the two. Another statistical measure is what Baayen calls global productivity, which depends not only on the likelihood of encountering new words of a given morphological type, but also on the number of words of that type that a speaker already knows. By this measure, *-ness* is not quite three times more productive than *-ity*.

The ratio of hapaxes to tokens in a corpus is clearly associated with a lesser average frequency of types; the lower average frequency of *-ness* formations compared to *-ity* formations has long been noted (Aronoff 1982). Baayen's measures assume that the larger ratio of hapaxes is the cause of the lower average frequency, rather than vice versa. We can thread our way out of this trap if we go back to the original concept of productivity mentioned above, the extent to which a given affix is used in the production of new words in the language. The data presented in table 11.3 show that there are close to twice as many *-ness* words as *-ity* words in the language, but it also shows that the productivity of *-ity* as opposed to *-ness* has shown a steady increase over time (with one exception in the fifteenth century) until the *OED* shows more *-ity* words than *-ness* words coined in the twentieth century. Given the more

Table 11.3 The growth in productivity of *-ity* over the centuries, based on entries in the *OED*

century	-ness	-ity	percent -ness
8th	4	0	100.00
9th	38	0	100.00
10th	67	0	100.00
11th	6	0	100.00
12th	21	0	100.00
13th	63	14	81.82
14th	225	72	75.76
15th	145	91	61.44
16th	610	193	75.97
17th	913	447	67.13
18th	308	196	61.11
19th	506	480	51.32
20th	152	166	47.80
total	3058	1659	64.83

restrictive environments for *-ity* versus *-ness*, the table shows that *-ity* is in fact synchronically more productive in English than *-ness*, at least judging from the dictionary data. The dictionary method and the corpus-based method do not agree. A word of caution is in order, though: dictionaries are not always dependable indicators of actual usage, since the entries in a dictionary are selective rather than inclusive, and since hapaxes are less likely to be seen as meriting dictionary entries. Counts based on actual large corpora of the sort that Baayen employs are generally more reliable, since they measure actual use, rather than being filtered editorially. Thus, it may be that the *-ity* words, though in fact less productively formed, are more likely to be listed in the dictionary, because they are more memorable than the *-ness* words, a point that we will return to in section 2.3.

2.2 Frequency and productivity

Word frequency, which we discussed above in relation to blocking, is also related to productivity: the less productive a morphological pattern is, the more frequent on average its individual members will be. But frequency is also important in the selection of bases: a less productive affix is generally found attached to higher-frequency base words than is a more productive affix (Aronoff 1982). This makes sense in terms of what we know about the connection between frequency and lexical recognition: words with high-frequency bases are more readily recognized than words with similar frequency but low-frequency bases (Laudanna and Burani 1985). If less productive affixes are at a disadvantage to begin with, then they seem to benefit from the boost provided by a more frequent base, although the exact psycholinguistic mechanism behind this pattern is not yet clear.

2.3 *Pragmatics and productivity*

Some scholars have insisted that the study of morphological productivity should confine itself to the study of words that are produced unintentionally (Schultink 1961). This rules out entirely the study of unproductive morphology, which resembles more marginal forms of word creation like the formation of blends (e.g. *smog* as a blend of *smoke* and *fog*) or acronyms (e.g. *laser* formed from the initial letters of the phrase *Light Amplification by Stimulated Emission of Radar*), in being more likely to be intentional or noticed. However, less than fully productive morphological patterns are pervasive in language, and they seem to serve a function that arises from their very unproductivity. When we compare the set of words formed by means of a less productive affix to the set formed by a rival affix in the same morphological environment, we generally find that the meanings of the less productively formed set are less predictable, making the entire set less *coherent* semantically. This difference in coherence carries over to newly coined words: the meaning of a new word formed by means of a less productive affix will be less predictable semantically. For that reason, less productive affixes may easily be used to coin special or narrowly technical terms (Aronoff 1982). For example, the word *specialism* has come into use quite recently in British English in the very restricted sense of 'what a (usually medical) specialist practises'. Similarly, we linguists (and participants in other technical fields like economics) use the technical term *productivity* instead of the more productively formed *productiveness*, because the very unproductiveness of the affix allows it to be used in more specialized senses. Horn (1984, 1993) explains this use of less productive affixes in terms of the interaction of two Gricean pragmatic principles. The principle of relation (say no more than you must) leads the speaker not to use the less productive form in most instances, because the more productive form is more readily available; but the principle of quantity (say as much as you can) will interact with that of relation, and lead the speaker to use the less productive affix in order to make a special point or to call attention to some aspect of the word. What the speaker is usually calling attention to is a special sense, which the less productive affix is more likely to allow. Thus we find that morphology and pragmatics act together to enrich language's expressive potential. In Horn's own words: "there is always (given the Division of Labor) a sufficient reason, but it is not always the same reason." Horn's account also helps us to understand why the productivity of inflectional affixes is generally more polarized: they are likely to be either completely productive or completely unproductive, and there are very few in-between cases resembling *-ity*. In the case of inflection, whose role is the realization of morphosyntactic information, which is always compositional, there is nothing for the speaker to call attention to, and hence less productive morphology has no role. Only productive morphology or lexicalized forms will surface.

NOTES

1 For reasons of simplicity, we will couch our discussion of morphology in terms of affixes throughout this paper. In fact, none of the issues that we discuss here bears heavily on the issue of whether the morphology is organized in terms of affixes or in terms of operations.

2 We will use examples from English for the most part, for ease of exposition, and also because most of the work done on the topics covered here has dealt with English data.

3 There is evidence, though, that some regular words can gain entry into the lexicon simply on grounds of familiarity or frequency (Stemberger and MacWhinney 1986b, 1988).

12 Morphology and Lexical Semantics

BETH LEVIN AND
MALKA RAPPAPORT HOVAV

The relation between lexical semantics and morphology has not been the subject of much study. This may seem surprising, since a morpheme is often viewed as a minimal Saussurean sign relating form and meaning: it is a concept with a phonologically composed name. On this view, morphology has both a semantic side and a structural side, the latter sometimes called "morphological realization" (Aronoff 1994, Zwicky 1986b). Since morphology is the study of the structure and derivation of complex signs, attention could be focused on the semantic side (the composition of complex concepts) and the structural side (the composition of the complex names for the concepts) and the relation between them.

In fact, recent work in morphology has been concerned almost exclusively with the composition of complex names for concepts – that is, with the structural side of morphology. This dissociation of "form" from "meaning" was foreshadowed by Aronoff's (1976) demonstration that morphemes are not necessarily associated with a constant meaning – or any meaning at all – and that their nature is basically structural. Although in early generative treatments of word formation, semantic operations accompanied formal morphological operations (as in Aronoff's Word Formation Rules), many subsequent generative theories of morphology, following Lieber (1980), explicitly dissociate the lexical semantic operations of composition from the formal structural operations of composition, focusing entirely on the latter. Carstairs-McCarthy (1992), following Corbin (1987), calls such theories "dissociative" theories of morphology, while Beard (1990) calls them "separationist." Although attention is often paid to "theta-role" operations, such as the addition, suppression, binding, or merger of "theta-roles," which accompany morphological operations (Baker 1985, 1988a; Bresnan 1982c; Bresnan and Kanerva 1989; Bresnan and Moshi 1990; Grimshaw and Mester 1988; Lieber 1983; Marantz 1984a; S. T. Rosen 1989; E. Williams 1981a; among others), many of these operations are syntactic, rather than semantic, in nature, as we argue in section 3.2.

The lack of attention paid to the relation between lexical semantics and morphology stems in part from the absence of a comprehensive theory of lexical semantic representation that can provide a context in which to study such a relation. Yet, such a study could shed light on lexical semantics as well as morphology (Carstairs-McCarthy 1992). In fact, there have recently been advances in the area of lexical semantics that make it possible to pose initial questions concerning the relation between it and morphology, and to venture initial answers to some.[1]

In section 1, we outline the basic elements of the lexical representation of verbs. We distinguish between the lexical syntactic representation, often called "argument structure," and the lexical semantic representation which, following Hale and Keyser (1986, 1987), has come to be known as the "lexical conceptual structure" (LCS); we then focus on the latter. (See Sadler and Spencer, MORPHOLOGY AND ARGUMENT STRUCTURE, for an overview of the former.) We concentrate solely on the lexical semantic representation of verbs, since verbs have been the focus of most of the lexical semantic research in the generative tradition. (See Pustejovsky 1991a for discussion of the lexical semantic representation of nouns.) In this overview, we stress those aspects of verb meaning that are most likely to be relevant to morphology.

In section 2, we suggest that the relation between lexical semantics and morphology can best be investigated by asking how names are attached to the lexical semantic representations that are made available by a theory of lexical semantics. We show that languages differ systematically in terms of which representations can be associated with names, and also in the morphological composition of such names.

In section 3, we pose some questions that arise in the context of the discussion in sections 1 and 2. Given the nature of the lexical representations described in section 1, it is possible to define different types of relations between the representations of pairs of verbs. We show that certain kinds of relations are systematically instantiated in language. We then ask whether verbs with related lexical representations have morphologically related names, and if so, whether there are any generalizations involved in the assignment of such names. We hypothesize that languages in general distinguish morphemes that signal the relation between verbs with the same LCS but different argument structures from those that signal the relation between distinct, though related, LCSs. We illustrate both types of morphological relations, although we concentrate on the second type, since operations on argument structure are the topic of another chapter (Sadler and Spencer, MORPHOLOGY AND ARGUMENT STRUCTURE). Finally, we speculate that certain types of systematically related meanings are never morphologically encoded.

1 The nature of the lexical semantic representation of verbs

In dealing with the lexical representation of verbs and other argument-taking lexical items, it is important to distinguish between the lexical semantic representation proper, often called a lexical conceptual structure (LCS), and another lexical representation, often called a predicate–argument structure (PAS), or simply an argument structure. There are different conceptions of argument structure, but most share the assumptions that argument structure is syntactic in nature and encodes the "adicity" or "valence" of a predicator – the number of arguments it requires – together with an indication of the hierarchcial organization of these arguments. The example below, which is taken from Rappaport and Levin 1988: 15, illustrates one view of argument structure. This particular representation specifies that the verb *put* takes three arguments, and that one is an external argument, one is a direct internal argument, and one is an argument governed by a locative preposition.

(1) $x <y, P_{loc} z>$

An argument structure does not contain any explicit lexical semantic information about the verb or its arguments (Grimshaw 1990, Rappaport and Levin 1988, Zubizarreta 1987), although it is projected via general principles from the LCS (Carrier and Randall 1992, Grimshaw 1990, Jackendoff 1990, Levin and Rappaport Hovav 1995).[2]

The distinction between LCS and argument structure is an important one, not recognized in all theories of lexical representation. We argue that this distinction finds empirical support in the morphologies of the languages of the world, which in general distinguish between morphemes that signal the relation between words with distinct but related LCSs and morphemes that signal the relation between words with common LCSs but distinct argument structures. This morphological division of labor is all the more striking since, as is well known, affixes tend to be associated with more than one function. Therefore, if the multiple functions associated with a given affix are consistently either of the type that derive new LCSs or of the type that derive new argument structures, this dissociation strongly supports the positing of these two distinct lexical representations. In this section we sketch the elements of LCS in order to explore these issues further.

Much research in lexical semantics has been aimed at elucidating the lexical semantics–syntax interface, and advances in this area have been made possible by exploiting the realization that some aspects of meaning are relevant to the grammar and others are not (Grimshaw 1993; Jackendoff 1990; Levin and Rappaport Hovav 1992, 1995; Pesetsky 1995; Pinker 1989). Research aimed at isolating the grammatically relevant meaning components has focused on those aspects of the syntactic behavior of verbs that seem to be determined by their semantic properties, most prominently, the possible syntactic expressions of arguments.

Many lexical semantic studies have illustrated how the syntactic expression of the arguments of a verb is to a large degree determined by its membership in semantically coherent verb classes (Fillmore 1970, Guerssel et al. 1985, B. Levin 1993, Pinker 1989, among others). However, the verb classes cross-classify in intricate ways with respect to the syntactic behavior of their members. This extensive cross-classification suggests that the verb classes themselves are not primitive; rather, they arise because their members share certain basic components of meaning. Thus, generalizations that involve semantically coherent classes of verbs are probably best formulated in terms of these meaning components, just as phonological rules are stated in terms of the basic building blocks of distinctive features.

Explicit representations of verb meaning have generally been of two types: semantic role lists and predicate decompositions (B. Levin 1994). In a semantic role list approach, the meaning of a verb is reduced to a list of the semantic roles that its arguments bear. For example, the causative change-of-state verb *dry* of *Kim dried the clothes* might receive the representation in (2).

(2)   *dry*: <Agent, Patient>

In a predicate decomposition approach, a verb's meaning is represented using members of a fixed set of primitive predicates together with constants – typically chosen from a limited set of semantic types. The constants either fill argument positions associated with these predicates or act as modifiers to the predicates. A verb's arguments are represented by the open argument positions associated with these predicates. Thus, the causative change-of-state verb *dry* might be given the predicate decomposition in (3); in this decomposition *DRY* is a constant representing the state associated with the verb *dry*, and x and y represent the verb's arguments.[3]

(3)   *dry*: [[x ACT] CAUSE [y BECOME *DRY*]]

The information contained in a semantic role list can be extracted from a predicate decomposition; the semantic roles of a verb's arguments can be identified with particular argument positions associated with the predicates in a decomposition (see Jackendoff 1972, 1987). For example, the Agent could be identified as the argument of ACT and the Patient as the first argument of BECOME (see (3)). It appears, however, that the grammatically relevant components of meaning can be better represented using the predicate decomposition approach than the semantic role list approach; see Gropen et al. 1991, Jackendoff 1987, Pinker 1989, Rappaport and Levin 1988, among others, for discussion.

Typically, predicate decompositions are selected so that verbs belonging to the same semantic class have decompositions with common substructures, including common constant positions filled by constants of a particular semantic type. Such recurring substructures are what Pinker (1989) calls "thematic cores"; we refer to them as "lexical semantic templates." Pinker identifies about a dozen of these templates; they include analogues of certain repeatedly cited combinations of predicates. As an example, causative change-of-state verbs would have the lexical semantic template in (4), where "[ ]$_{\text{STATE}}$" represents the constant that will distinguish one change-of-state verb from another (cf. (3)).

(4)   [[x ACT] CAUSE [y BECOME [ ]$_{\text{STATE}}$]]

Most theories of the lexical semantics–syntax interface include a set of rules that effect the mapping from the LCS to argument structure; following Carter (1976, 1988b), these rules are often called "Linking Rules." The LCSs of verbs are chosen to facilitate the perspicuous formulation of the Linking Rules. Therefore, it is appropriate to describe the lexical semantic templates as determining the syntactic properties of the members of the verb classes. The templates that are most widely cited as defining grammatically relevant semantic classes bear a striking resemblance to the predicate decompositions suggested by Dowty (1979) for representing the lexical aspectual classes of verbs. In fact, Foley and Van Valin (1984), in adopting aspectually motivated decompositions, implicitly claim that these are the grammatically relevant lexical semantic representations of verbs. Tenny (1987, 1992, 1994) goes further, proposing the Aspectual Interface Hypothesis: only aspectual information is relevant to the mapping between lexical semantics and syntax.[4]

Following Vendler (1957), four major lexical aspectual classes of verbs are identified: activities, accomplishments, achievements, and states. Various decompositional representations have been suggested for these four classes (Dowty 1979; Foley and Van Valin 1984; Pustejovsky 1991b, 1995; among others). All take as their starting point Kenny's (1963) insight that achievements embed a state, and that accomplishments are complex events including an activity and an achievement. The representations used by Foley and Van Valin (1984) and more recently by Van Valin (1990, 1993), which are adopted with slight modifications from Dowty (1979), are presented in (5). In these representations **predicate'** represents a state, except in (5c), where it represents an atomic activity (Van Valin 1990: 224; 1993: 35–6).[5]

(5)   (a)   STATE: **predicate'** (x) or (x, y)
      (b)   ACHIEVEMENT: BECOME **predicate'** (x) or (x, y)
      (c)   ACTIVITY (+/–Agentive): (DO (x)) [**predicate'** (x) or (x, y)]
      (d)   ACCOMPLISHMENT: ϕ CAUSE ψ, where ϕ is normally an activity predicate and ψ an achievement predicate

(Van Valin 1990: 224, table 2)

Each of these decompositions specifies the lexical semantic template associated with the members of a particular lexical aspectual class.

Of course, there are more than four grammatically relevant semantic classes of verbs, as a cursory glance at the classes of verbs listed in B. Levin 1993 reveals. It is likely that primitive predicates other than those employed in (5) will have to be introduced, and indeed Jackendoff (1990), in what is perhaps the most fully articulated system of lexical semantic representation today, includes additional predicates. But it is primarily through the use of constants that lexical semantic templates such as those in (5) are further differentiated, and the various grammatically relevant verb classes are defined by constraints on the type of constant that can fill particular argument positions in the decompositions. A few examples will illustrate this point.

Although all accomplishments have the decomposition in (5d), particular subtypes can be derived by choosing constants to fill particular argument positions. For example, denominal verbs such as *pocket* and *butter* have the basic decompositional structure of accomplishment verbs, but differ both in the type of constant and in the positions of the constant within the decomposition, as shown in (6) (Carter 1976; Jackendoff 1983, 1990).[6]

(6) (a) *butter*: [[x ACT] CAUSE [[BUTTER]$_{\text{THING}}$ BECOME P$_{\text{loc}}$ z]]
    (b) *pocket*: [[x ACT] CAUSE [y BECOME P$_{\text{loc}}$ [POCKET]$_{\text{PLACE}}$]]

As the examples in (6) show, the placement of a constant in a particular position derives individual verbs.[7] Classes of such verbs can be defined by more general restrictions on the ontological type of what can fill that position. Thus, the lexical semantic template in (7a) is associated with the class of verbs which includes *butter*, and the one in (7b) with verbs like *pocket*. In these decompositions "[ ]$_{\text{THING}}$" and "[ ]$_{\text{PLACE}}$" indicate the position that is filled by a constant, and specify the ontological type of that constant.

(7) (a) [[x ACT] CAUSE [[ ]$_{\text{THING}}$ BECOME P$_{\text{loc}}$ z]]
    (b) [[x ACT] CAUSE [y BECOME P$_{\text{loc}}$ [ ]$_{\text{PLACE}}$]]

The *butter* and *pocket* verb classes both belong to the more general class called "verbs of putting" by Carter (1976), whose members share the representation in (8):

(8) [[x ACT] CAUSE [y BECOME P$_{\text{loc}}$ z]]

In addition to filling argument positions in LCSs, as in the examples so far, constants may modify predicates, as in the LCS for the verb *walk* in (9):

(9) *walk*:

    ACT(x)
      |
    [WALK]$_{\text{MANNER}}$

In this LCS, the constant *WALK* represents the essence of walking; the vertical line connecting this constant to a predicate indicates that the constant modifies the predicate, and the subscript on the square brackets around the constant specifies the constant's ontological type: it is a manner constant. There is a large class of manner constants that serve to modify an activity predicate in a LCS. The LCSs of *walk* and other verbs of manner of motion such as *jog, run*, and *trot* contain such a constant. They all share the same lexical semantic template, which includes a manner constant; but the particular constant differs for each, since it represents what is distinct about each form of motion. Thus, classes of verbs can be defined according to whether or not particular predicates in their LCSs are modified by constants, just as such classes can be defined according to whether or not particular argument positions in their LCSs are filled by constants. Furthermore, constants of the second type are most likely to be elements representing entities in the world, as in (6); constants of the first type might be what Jackendoff (1990) refers to as "action patterns." See Pinker 1989 and Jackendoff 1983, 1990, 1996, for further discussion of the types of constants found in LCSs.

As pointed out by Carter (1976), the use of constants provides the decompositional approach to lexical semantic representations with much of its power.[8] By allowing constants to fill selected positions in a LCS, it is possible to give a finite characterization of the possible verb meanings in a language, while allowing for the coining of new verbs. A language will have a fixed set of lexical semantic templates, but new verbs can be created through the use of new constants in these templates.

As already mentioned, the hypothesis implicit in work on lexical semantic representation is that the predicates used in decompositions represent the principal grammatically relevant aspects of meaning. What is less often appreciated is that the presence or absence of a certain kind of constant in a decomposition may be relevant to a verb's classification, although the content of the constant itself is not. The content of the constant is, by hypothesis, opaque to the grammar (Grimshaw 1990, Jackendoff 1990, Pinker 1989). For example, the existence of a manner modifier – one type of constant discussed here – in a verb's LCS may affect its syntactic behavior, but its syntactic behavior will not be sensitive to the particular instantiation of the modifier. Thus, there are rules which distinguish verbs of manner of motion from verbs of motion whose meaning does not include a manner specification, such as *arrive, come*, and *go*. For example, only verbs of manner of motion can undergo causativization in English (Levin and Rappaport Hovav 1995); compare *The general marched the soldiers across the field* to **The driver arrived the car in front of the house*. By contrast, we know of no rule that is, say, like the English passive rule, but that applies only to verbs of fast motion. Similar observations about the grammatical "inertness" of the components of verb meaning associated with constants are made by Grimshaw (1993), Jackendoff (1990), and Pesetsky (1995).

With this background, we now turn to the central focus of this chapter: the relationship between lexical semantics and morphology.

2 The pairing of names with meanings

A fully articulated theory of lexical semantic representation should be a generative theory that allows for the characterization of all possible word meanings in a language (Carter 1976; Pustejovsky, 1991a, 1995). Many of the possible meanings are meanings of actual words. Those meanings that are realized need to be associated with a name. In order to study the relation between lexical semantics and morphology, we can ask how names are associated with the available meanings. We continue to restrict our attention to verbs, though comparable questions about possible meanings have been asked and answered with respect to the noun lexicon, and to a lesser extent the adjective lexicon, primarily by psychologists interested in concept formation and word learning (Carey 1994; Landau 1994; Markman 1989, 1994; Waxman 1994; and references cited therein).

Setting sound symbolism aside, the pairing of a morphologically simple phonological form with a particular verb meaning is arbitrary (Saussure 1959); for example, there seems to be no reason why the phonological form of the verb *lend* could not have been paired with the meaning associated with the verb *borrow*, and vice versa. However, one aspect of this pairing does not seem arbitrary: the fact that certain LCSs can be associated with monomorphemic names, while others cannot. There appear to be some absolute constraints on the complexity of the LCSs that can be associated with such names (Carter 1976). For instance, Carter points out that there are no verbs meaning "change from *STATE1* to *STATE2*," unless *STATE1* can be characterized as "not *STATE2*." That is, there is no English verb meaning "change from pink to white," although there is a verb *whiten*, meaning "change from not white to white." Furthermore, as we illustrate below, not all languages allow monomorphemic names to be associated with the same LCSs. The question of which LCSs can receive monomorphemic names may be considered by some not to fall under the purview of morphology, but rather to be part of the study of the lexicon. (See Aronoff 1994 and Carstairs-McCarthy 1992 for an articulation of such a view.) Nevertheless, in order to understand the relationship between lexical semantics and morphology, we need to consider this question.

Let us clarify this question with an example. It has often been noted in the literature on lexical aspect (e.g. Declerck 1979; Dowty 1979; Vendler 1957; Verkuyl 1972, 1993) and unaccusativity (e.g. Hoekstra 1984; Levin and Rappaport Hovav 1992, 1995; L. Levin 1986; Van Valin 1990; Zaenen 1993) that English verbs of manner of motion have a dual aspectual classification. For example, the verb *walk* can be used as an activity verb, as in *Sandy walked* (*for an hour*); or, in the presence of a goal phrase, it can be used as an accomplishment verb, as in *Sandy walked to the store*. There is reason to assume that the meaning of the activity use is more basic than the meaning of the accomplishment use. We can, therefore, take *walk* to have a basic classification as an activity verb and a derived classification as an accomplishment verb in the presence of a goal phrase. This dual aspectual classification is open to all English verbs of manner of motion; *amble, jog, limp, swim,* and *trudge* also have both classifications. Thus, there are two relevant facts about the English verb lexicon: (i) for a given manner of motion both activity and accomplishment meanings are available (the exact nature of the relation between these two meanings still needs to be established), and (ii) the same monomorphemic name can be associated with the lcss associated with both meanings.

There are languages that differ from English in both these respects. As discussed by Carter (1988a), Levin and Rapoport (1988), Schlyter (1978, 1981), Talmy (1975, 1985), Wienold (1995), and others, French does not allow a manner of motion verb to appear with a goal phrase, and hence to receive an accomplishment interpretation. Although (10a) is ambiguous in English, allowing either an activity or an accomplishment interpretation, its French translation (10b) has only the activity interpretation.

(10) (a)   The mouse is running under the table.
      (b)   La souris court sous la table.

As (10b) shows, French does have verbs of manner of motion, but these only have a meaning comparable to the activity sense of English verbs of manner of motion. In French, the sense conveyed by the English accomplishment uses of verbs of manner of motion cannot be expressed by the addition of a goal phrase to a verb of manner of motion. Instead, such meanings must be expressed periphrastically: in (11) and (12) the English (a) sentence could receive the French translation in (b).

(11) (a)   Blériot flew across the Channel.
      (b)   Blériot traversa la Manche en avion.
            'Blériot crossed the Channel by plane.'
            (Vinay and Darbelnet 1958: 105)

(12) (a)   An old woman hobbled in from the back.
      (b)   Une vieille femme arriva en boitant de l'arrière-boutique.
            'An old woman arrived in limping from the back-store.'
            (ibid.)

As these examples illustrate, in French the manner of motion is typically expressed in a subordinate clause or adverbial phrase, and the goal of motion is expressed through the use of the appropriate verb of directed motion as the main verb (Vinay and Darbelnet 1958). The generalization that emerges is that English manner of motion constants can be associated with both activity and accomplishment lexical semantic templates, while French allows such constants to be associated only with activity lexical semantic templates.

Russian differs from both French and English. Although Russian makes both activity and accomplishment meanings available to verbs of manner of motion, the two meanings are not always associated with the same name, although the names are always morphologically related. In Russian, as in French and English, morphologically simple verbs of manner of motion have the activity sense, as in (13).

(13) (a) On begal po komnate.
   he (NOM) ran over room-DAT
   'He ran around the room.'

  (b) On plaval v ozere.
   he (NOM) swam in lake-PREP
   'He swam in the lake.'

Unlike French, Russian also allows an accomplishment sense for verbs of manner of motion; however, unlike English, it uses the morphologically simple verb name only for the activity sense. In the accomplishment sense, the verb's name is morphologically complex, including one of a range of directional prefixes indicating the goal of motion, as in (14) (Talmy 1975, 1985). Many of the prefixes are homophonous with prepositions. For example, in (14a) the prefix *v-* is homophonous with the preposition *v* 'in'; in this example, the goal is further specified in the prepositional phrase.

(14) (a) On v-bežal v komnatu.
   he (NOM) in-ran in room-ACC
   'He ran into the room.'

  (b) On pere-plyl čerez reku.
   he (NOM) across-swam across river-ACC
   'He swam across the river.'

It appears, then, that in Russian, lexical semantic templates of a certain complexity cannot be associated with a monomorphemic name. The complexity of the template is reflected in the morphological makeup of the name.

 Having set the context by introducing our conception of LCSs and having briefly explored the attachment of names to meanings, we return now to the relationship between lexical semantics and morphology.

3 The morphological expression of lexical relatedness

Several types of relations can be defined over the elements of the lexical representations introduced in section 1. In this section we identify these relations and ask whether they are morphologically signaled, and if so, how. First, we examine the morphological relation between verbs with distinct but related

LCSs; then we consider the morphological relation between verbs with a single LCS but distinct argument structures.[9]

3.1 Verbs with distinct but related LCSs

In section 2 we identified two major components of LCSs: the predicates and the constants. Given these elements, there are several possible relations between LCSs. LCSs can be related by virtue of containing a shared constant, though the constant itself is found in different lexical semantic templates. Alternatively, LCSs can be related by a shared lexical semantic template, while differing in the identity of the constant filling a particular position in this template.[10] We consider each possibility in turn, examining whether these relations are reflected in the names associated with the LCSs.

3.1.1 Verbs with a shared constant   We begin with LCSs that involve different lexical semantic templates with a shared constant. A survey of such pairs in languages of the world reveals that there are two dominant patterns concerning the morphological relation between the members of such pairs. Either the two members bear the identical name with no morphological derivational relation between them, or the members have different names which share a common base, where the affixes used to signal the morphological relation between the members are drawn from the class of affixes employed for signaling lexical aspect. We begin with a discussion of the first pattern using English for illustration.

In English the name of a verb often derives from the name associated with the constant in its LCS, as can be seen from the *pocket* and *butter* examples in (6). Given this, when two English verbs have LCSs related by a shared constant, it is most natural for them to share the same name – a name that simply reflects the identity of the constant. In fact, many English verbs follow this pattern. The verb *shovel*, for example, though basically an activity verb (*She shoveled all afternoon*), can be used as a verb of either putting (*shovel the gravel onto the road*) or removing (*shovel the snow off the walk*), showing the properties of an accomplishment in both cases. The names associated with the activity, putting, and removing meanings (or LCSs) are identical, and there is no overt derivational morphological relation between them.

English is notoriously poor in morphology, and the absence of an overt derivational morphological relation between the various senses of *shovel* may reflect nothing more than this property. However, there are other languages with richer systems of verbal derivational morphology than English, where the relations between verbs with different lexical semantic templates and shared constants are not necessarily signaled morphologically. We exemplify this with verbs of manner of motion. As the discussion in section 2 implies, the LCS for the activity and accomplishment uses of a verb of manner of motion such as *walk* involve different lexical semantic templates with a shared constant. Possible LCSs are presented below.[11]

(15) Activity *walk*:
     ACT(x)
     |
     [*WALK*]_{MANNER}

(16) Accomplishment *walk*:
     GO(x,y)
     |
     [*WALK*]_{MANNER}

The constant *WALK*, then, can be associated with more than one lexical semantic template in English. This multiple association is not a property of the verb *walk*; rather, it is a property of the English lexicon that all verbs of manner of motion permit activity and accomplishment uses.[12]

Hebrew, which has a richer system of verbal derivational morphology than English, has the same two meanings available to verbs of manner of motion, and allows the association of a single name with both. That is, in Hebrew, as in English, the relationship between these two meanings is not signaled morphologically, as shown by the examples in (17) and (18).

(17) (a) Hu rakad ba-xeder.
         he danced in.the-room
         'He danced in the room.'

     (b) Ha-saxyan saxa ba-nahar.
         the-swimmer swam in.the-river
         'The swimmer swam in the river.'

(18) (a) Hu rakad el mixuts la-xeder.
         he danced to outside to.the-room
         'He danced out of the room.'

     (b) Ha-saxyan saxa la-gada ha-šniya šel ha-nahar.
         the-swimmer swam to.the-side the-second of the-river
         'The swimmer swam to the other side of the river.'

In the languages in which the relation between the names associated with such pairs of LCSs is morphologically encoded, there seems to be a generalization concerning the morphological device used to signal the relationship. As mentioned in section 1, certain combinations of predicates and constants found in LCSs define lexical aspectual classes of verbs, and most languages have pairs of verbs with different lexical semantic templates but shared constants that belong to distinct aspectual classes, as in the verb of manner of motion examples discussed here. This aspectual relation is reflected in the names associated with the members of these pairs: the members tend to have names with a common base, and one, if not both, members of such pairs have morphologically complex names that involve the morphological devices employed to signal classification with respect to lexical aspect. In fact, the existence of morphemes in some languages that indicate the lexical aspectual classification of verbs can be taken as support for lexical semantic representations such as those in (5). For example, in Russian, an atelic verb is typically morphologically simple, while a telic verb is morphologically complex, consisting of a base (which is often a morphologically simple activity verb with a related meaning) and one of a set of prefixes (Brecht 1985).[13] Thus, compare Russian *pit'* 'drink' with *vypit'* 'drink up'. This suggests that, as a general pattern in Russian, morphological complexity is a reflection of template complexity.

The naming of manner of motion events in Russian also illustrates this point. Manner of motion events that qualify as activities are named by morphologically simple verbs (see (13)), while manner of motion events that qualify as accomplishments have morphologically complex names consisting of the same morphologically simple base as the related activity verb together with a directional prefix, chosen from a set of prefixes which are also used to signal aspectual classification (see (14)). Russian is not the only language to show this pattern; as reported by Harrison (1976) (see also Chung and Timberlake 1985), the Micronesian language Mokilese also distinguishes the accomplishment sense of verbs of manner of motion from the activity sense through the use of a set of suffixes that also serve as aspectual markers. For manner of motion verbs, the generalization seems to be that some languages do not allow a single verb name to be associated with lexical semantic templates differing in lexical aspectual classification. The names of such templates are distinguished morphologically in Russian and Mokilese, while one of the templates simply seems to be lacking in French. It is a matter for further research to see whether this generalization may hold more generally in these and other languages.[14]

Another phenomenon that can be characterized as involving different lexical semantic templates with a shared constant is the locative alternation. This term refers to the two expressions of arguments characteristic of verbs such as *spray*, *load*, *cram*, and *spread*.[15]

(19)   (a)   The farmer loaded hay on the truck.   (locative variant)
     (b)   The farmer loaded the truck with hay.   (*with* variant)

(20)   (a)   I spread butter on my toast.
     (b)   I spread my toast with butter.

The pairs of sentences that typify the locative alternation were originally thought to be derived by syntactic transformations from a common deep structure (Hall 1965). This analysis was abandoned because the alternation does not bear what Wasow (1977) identifies as the hallmarks of syntactic operations (see e.g. Baker, in press). Subsequent accounts took as their starting point the subtle differences in meaning between the variants, as we refer to the alternate expressions of arguments associated with locative alternation verbs. For example, (19b), the *with* variant, implies that the truck is full, while (19a), the locative variant, need not. (See Anderson 1977a, Jeffries and Willis 1984, Schwartz-Norman 1976, among others, for a discussion of this effect.) Pinker (1989) and Rappaport and Levin (1988) note that the verbs in the two variants can be assigned to two independently established semantic classes. Once the two variants are given the appropriate LCSs, the expression of arguments characteristic of each follows from general principles governing argument expression. Possible representations for the two variants of the verb *load* are given in (21):[16]

(21) (a) [[x ACT] CAUSE [y BECOME P_{loc} z] [*LOAD*]$_{MANNER}$]
      (b) [[x ACT] CAUSE [z BECOME [ ]$_{STATE}$ WITH-RESPECT-TO y]
           [*LOAD*]$_{MANNER}$]

On this approach, the locative alternation involves two distinct LCSs related by a shared constant. As in the *walk* example, these LCSs are associated with the same name in English; and again, English is not unique in having the locative alternation or in associating the same name with the verb in both variants, as the following examples show:

(22) French:
      (a) On a chargé beaucoup de colis sur le cargo.
           'One loaded many packages on the cargo ship.'

      (b) On a chargé le cargo avec des colis.
           'One loaded the cargo ship with packages.'
           (Postal 1982: 381, ex. 74a–b)

(23) Japanese:
      (a) kabe ni penki o nuru
           wall on paint ACC smear
           'smear paint on the wall'

      (b) kabe o penki de nuru
           wall ACC paint with smear
           'smear the wall with paint'
           (Fukui et al. 1985: 7, ex. 7a–b)

(24) Kannada:
      (a) ra:ju ṭrakkannu pustakagaḷinda tumbisida.
           Raju (NOM) truck-ACC books-INST filled
           'Raju filled the truck with books.'

      (b) ra:ju pustakagaḷannu ṭrakkinalli tumbisida.
           Raju (NOM) books-ACC truck-LOC filled
           'Raju filled the books in the truck.'
           (Bhat 1977: 368, ex. 5a–b)

(25) Hebrew:
    (a)   Hu he'emis xatzir al ha-agala.
          he loaded hay on the-wagon
          'He loaded hay on the wagon.'

    (b)   Hu he'emis et ha-agala be-xatzir.
          he loaded ACC the-wagon with-hay
          'He loaded the wagon with hay.'

These examples further support the proposal that the relation between LCSs with distinct lexical semantic templates but a shared constant is often not reflected in the morphological shape of the names associated with these LCSs.

It is perhaps less obvious that the two variants of the locative alternation, although both classified as accomplishments,[17] can nevertheless be distinguished aspectually, as shown by Dowty (1991). The variants differ with respect to the argument said to be the "incremental theme," a term Dowty employs to refer to the argument of a telic verb which determines the aspectual properties of the sentence that verb is found in. Thus, as suggested above, each such verb is associated with two lexical semantic templates. It is not surprising, then, that in many languages, for a particular choice of constant the pair of lexical semantic representations associated with the locative alternation is associated not with the same name, but rather with morphologically related names, where the affixes used to establish this morphological relation are chosen from those signaling aspectual classification, as suggested above. In fact, there are languages in which the locative alternation involves morphologically related verbs, and in each of the languages illustrated, the morphemes involved have an aspectual function.

(26) German:
    (a)   Adam schmierte Farbe an die Wand.
          Adam (NOM) smeared paint-ACC at the wall-ACC
          'Adam smeared paint on the wall.'

    (b)   Adam be-schmierte die Wand mit Farbe.
          Adam (NOM) be-smeared the wall-ACC with paint-DAT
          'Adam smeared the wall with paint.'
          (Pusch 1972: 130, ex. 27a, c)

(27) Russian:
    (a)   Krest'jany na-gruzili seno na telegu.
          peasants (NOM) na-loaded hay (ACC) on cart-ACC
          'The peasants loaded hay on the cart.'

    (b)   Krest'jany za-gruzili telegu senom.
          peasants (NOM) za-loaded cart-ACC hay-INST
          'The peasants loaded the cart with hay.'

(28) Hungarian:
    (a)   János rá-mázolta a festéket a falra.
           John onto-smeared.he.it the paint-ACC the wall-onto
           'John smeared paint on the wall.'
    (b)   János be-mázolta a falat festékkel.
           John in-smeared.he.it the wall-ACC paint-with
           'John smeared the wall with paint.'
           (Moravcsik 1978b: 257)

Let us consider the locative alternation in each of these languages in turn. The prefixes in the Russian examples are found on the perfective forms of the locative alternation verbs; the imperfective forms are typically unprefixed.[18] More generally, the same prefixes are used to signal telicity elsewhere in Russian; they also overlap with the prefixes signaling the accomplishment sense of verbs of manner of motion. In German, *be-* is often used to signal the affectedness of the object of the verb to which it is attached (Pusch 1972); thus, as a prefix tied to the determination of telicity, it can be viewed as an aspectual morpheme. In fact, Becker (1971) presents other uses of this prefix that support this view. Furthermore, Dutch, like German, uses the prefix *be-* in the locative alternation, and Hoekstra and Mulder (1990) propose that the Dutch morpheme signals total affectedness. De Groot, in a discussion of the Hungarian locative alternation, points out that although the prefixes found in this alternation are sometimes used in Hungarian to contribute independent meaning in the way that the directional prefixes of Russian can, they also function "as indicators of perfectivity and termination of an action" (De Groot 1984: 138).

3.1.2 Verbs with shared lexical semantic templates

Although LCSs that involve different lexical semantic templates but share the same constant can have the same name, we are not aware of any instances in which a single name is associated with multiple instantiations of a certain combination of predicates that differ simply in which constant fills a particular position.

Interestingly, it is verbs that share a lexical semantic template but differ in the associated constant that form classes whose members show the same expression of arguments. For example, all verbs of manner of motion in their activity sense share the same lexical semantic template and expression of arguments. Specifically, such verbs are unergative (Hoekstra 1984, Levin and Rappaport Hovav 1995, Zaenen 1993, L. Levin 1986, C. Rosen 1984). By contrast, when a single verb name is associated with several LCSs that are based on different combinations of predicates but share the same constant, each pairing of the name with a LCS is associated with a distinct argument expression. For instance, *walk* is unergative when it is an activity verb, but unaccusative when it is an accomplishment verb (Hoekstra 1984, Levin and Rappaport Hovav 1995, L. Levin 1986, Zaenen 1993, among others).

In this context it is appropriate to mention one additional relationship between verb meanings that, to our knowledge, is never morphologically signaled. Morphology is not involved in the cross-field generalizations discussed by Jackendoff (1972, 1978, 1983), building on the work of Gruber (1965). Jackendoff points out that certain parallels are found across apparently unrelated semantic fields, such as the fields of location and possession. For instance, the verb *keep* can be used in a variety of semantic fields, as in (29).

(29)   (a)   Tracy kept the bicycle in the shed.
       (b)   Tracy kept the bicycle.
       (c)   Tracy kept the dog quiet.

This verb is used to describe physical location in (a), possession in (b), and a state in (c), being used in what Jackendoff terms the positional, possessional, and identification fields, respectively. According to Jackendoff, these uses arise because motion and location organize a variety of semantic fields, as articulated in his Thematic Relations Hypothesis (1983: 188). Thus, possession can be conceived of as location or motion within an abstract possessional field, with possessors playing the role of locations in this field, and possessed objects playing the part of physical objects. Similarly, states can be conceived of as locations within an abstract identificational field. When a verb is used in more than one semantic field, Jackendoff associates the same LCS with that verb independent of the field. We know of no language in which the morphological shape of a verb reflects the semantic field it is being used in. More generally, we know of no morphological indication that verbs – or words from other lexical categories for that matter – are being used figuratively or metaphorically.

3.2   Verbs with a shared LCS but distinct argument structures

Having looked at the morphological expression of the relation between verbs with distinct but related LCSs, we turn to the morphological expression of the relation between verbs that have the same LCS but differ in their argument structures. Our contention is that the morphological devices which languages use to signal this kind of relationship are different from those mentioned in the previous section. First, across languages, relationships between argument structures are almost always given morphological expression (in this respect, English is rather unusual). Second, the morphemes used to signal these relationships are not the same as those that signal the relationship between words with distinct, but related, LCSs. We begin by sketching the relations we have in mind.

As mentioned in section 1, the LCS contains variables corresponding to the participants in the event described by the verb. The LCS is not projected directly onto the syntax, however; rather, this mapping is mediated by the argument structure. The argument structure is a lexical representation of the syntactic expression of a verb's arguments. This representation, in effect, specifies which participants will be syntactically expressed and how. In the (morphologically) unmarked case, each variable in the LCS corresponds to a grammatically interpreted variable in argument structure. However, there are operations on argument structure that usually result in a change in the number of grammatically interpreted arguments or in the position of an argument in the hierarchical organization of argument structure.

Two examples of operations which result in a change – specifically, a decrease – in the number of arguments are reflexivization and middle formation, which may be called "valence-reducing operations." Reflexivization essentially identifies two of the variables in a verb's argument structure, indicating that they have the same referent (Grimshaw 1982), thus reducing by one the number of syntactic arguments of a verb. We illustrate reflexivization using French. The (a) sentences in (30) and (31) show nonreflexive uses of the verbs *voir* 'see' and *parler* 'speak'; the (b) sentences show reflexives uses, which are signaled by the reflexive clitic *se*.

(30)　(a)　Jean voit l'homme.
　　　　　　Jean sees the man
　　　　　　'John sees the man.'

　　　(b)　Jean se voit.
　　　　　　Jean REFL sees
　　　　　　'John sees himself.'

(31)　(a)　Il parle à l'homme.
　　　　　　he talks to the man
　　　　　　'He is talking to the man.'

　　　(b)　Il se parle.
　　　　　　he REFL talks
　　　　　　'He is talking to himself.'

Although in terms of meaning reflexive verbs take two arguments, from the perspective of the syntax they are monadic. The examples in (30) and (31) suggest that reflexivization is not sensitive to the semantic roles of a verb's arguments, since the verbs *voir* 'see' and *parler* 'talk' do not take arguments bearing the same semantic roles. This insensitivity would be expected of an operation on argument structure (Grimshaw 1990, Rappapport and Levin 1988, Zubizarreta 1987).

Middle formation also relates a transitive verb to an intransitive one, as illustrated once again using French data:

(32)　(a)　Il a nettoyé ces lunettes.
　　　　　　he has cleaned those glasses
　　　　　　'He cleaned those glasses.'

(b)   Ces lunettes se nettoient facilement.
    those glasses REFL clean easily
    'Those glasses clean easily.'
    (Ruwet 1972: 95, ex. 35a)

The exact nature of this operation is a matter of debate (see Condoravdi 1989; Fagan 1988, 1992; Hoekstra and Roberts 1993; Keyser and Roeper 1984; among others), but it is clear that the external argument of the unmarked transitive verb cannot be expressed in the middle form, as discussed with respect to French by Ruwet (1972).

(33)   *Cela se dit par le peuple.
    that REFL says by the people
    (Ruwet 1972: 110, ex. 100)

Thus, middle formation is also valence-reducing. In fact, in French this process is accompanied by the same reflexive clitic that signals reflexivization.

Valence-reducing operations operate on argument structure.[19] They do not create new LCSs, nor do they relate two different LCSs.[20] It is striking that languages which do not mark the locative alternation and, if they have them, manner of motion pairs morphologically may nevertheless mark operations on argument structure morphologically (e.g. Italian, French, Hebrew). Moreover, as far as we know, none of these languages uses aspectual morphology for this purpose. For example, Russian does not use aspectual prefixes to mark changes in valence. It is also striking that a number of languages use a single morpheme for many, if not all, of the valence-reducing operations (Comrie 1985, Langacker 1976, Langacker and Munro 1975, Marantz 1984a, Nedjalkov and Silnitsky 1973, Shibatani 1985, among others). Thus, as already mentioned, the same morpheme is associated with reflexivization and middle formation in French. Furthermore, the morpheme used in valence-reducing operations may be synchronically or diachronically related to a reflexive pronoun, as in the Romance and Slavic languages.

Additional support for the differentiation of argument-structure-related morphology from LCS-related morphology is provided by Haspelmath (1990), who investigates the multiple functions of the passive morpheme – another valence-reducing morpheme – cross-linguistically, and finds that there is a range of uses for this morpheme that are repeatedly attested across languages. Again, these uses resemble passivization in involving valence-reducing operations; they do not signal relations between LCSs.[21] Moving beyond valence-reducing operations, which have been the focus of this section, there are other morphological operations that are good candidates for being considered operations on argument structure. These include the formation of light verb constructions (Grimshaw and Mester 1988) and causative constructions (Marantz 1984a, S. T. Rosen 1989a, among others).[22]

4 Conclusion

Recent work in lexical semantics provides a framework for investigating the relationship between lexical semantics and morphology, which is clearly a rich, though underexplored, area of study. The morphology of languages provides further support for the existence of two levels of lexical representation, LCS and argument structure, as independently argued in studies of the lexicon. Specifically, the morphemes that signal the relation between verbs with related LCSs are different from those that signal the relation between verbs with common LCSs but distinct argument structures. This morphological division of labor is particularly noteworthy, since in the case-studies we have presented, it is maintained even by affixes with multiple functions. Thus, a particular affix consistently derives either new LCSs or new argument structures. Furthermore, when verbs with different LCSs but the same constant are morphologically related, the morphological devices used to signal such relations are associated with grammatically relevant components of meaning, such as aspectual classification. We hope that the ideas sketched here will serve as a starting point for continued exploration of the relationship between lexical semantics and morphology.

ACKNOWLEDGEMENTS

We thank Mark Baker, Jane Grimshaw, Ken Hale, Boris Katz, Mary Laughren, Mari Olsen, and Maria Polinsky for helpful discussion of issues raised here. Andrew Spencer provided invaluable comments on an earlier draft. We thank the members of the Department of Linguistics at Rutgers University for their hospitality during the writing. We are grateful to Olivia Chang for help with the preparation. The work was supported in part by NSF grant SBR-9221993 to Levin.

NOTES

1   One researcher who has paid attention to the relation between lexical semantics and morphology is Joan Bybee, who asks questions that are similar in spirit to those we address here. In her work, Bybee (1985) attempts to predict the kinds of meanings that are likely to find expression as inflectional morphemes and the degree of fusion between two morphemes based on the meaning relation that obtains between them. A second researcher who has investigated the relation between lexical semantics and morphology is Robert Beard, whose recent book (1995) came to our attention after this was completed.

2 The idea that the argument structure is projected from the LCS reflects the assumption that the syntactic expression of arguments of verbs is predictable from their meaning. This idea is incorporated in varying ways in the work of Bresnan and Kanerva (1989), Dowty (1991), Foley and Van Valin (1984), Hale and Keyser (1993, 1997), among others.

3 The LCSs that we give throughout this paper are chosen to illustrate particular points, and are not intended to present a unified system of lexical semantic representation.

4 See Croft 1991 for an alternative approach to the mapping between lexical semantics and syntax that makes reference to the causal structure of events, as elaborated in the work of Talmy (1976, 1988).

5 In this respect, Foley and Van Valin (1984) and Van Valin (1990, 1993) depart from Dowty (1979), who builds the decompositions of all four lexical aspectual classes on state predicates. See also McClure (1994) for a further elaboration of Dowty's idea that all classes are derived from basic state predicates.

6 We use ACT as the predicate, indicating an unspecified activity; some other work uses the predicate DO. The predicate ACT (or DO) is often used as the activity predicate in the LCS of an accomplishment verb, since accomplishment verbs have a complex LCS that consists of an activity and an achievement (Dowty 1979, Grimshaw and Vikner 1993, Levin and Rappaport Hovav 1995; Pustejovsky 1991b, 1995; among others), but many accomplishments are vague as to the nature of the activity. Thus, the meaning of causative *dry* includes a specification of a particular result

state, but is vague as to which of a number of activities brings this state about.

7 For a different lexical semantic analysis of verbs like *butter* that preserves the distinction between the primitive predicates and constants see Hale and Keyser (1993, 1997) and Kiparsky (1997).

8 A word of clarification is in order concerning the use of the term "constant" to refer to an element that fills a certain argument or modifier position in a verb's lexical semantic template and thus is lexically associated with that position. This term is chosen to contrast with the term "variable," used to refer to those argument positions that are not filled in the LCS, but whose interpretation is determined in the syntax via the association of these positions with overt XPs in the syntax. However, the use of the term "constant" may not be altogether felicitous: there is some variability in the meaning of certain verbs that might be said to involve the same constant within the same lexical semantic template. We suspect that this variability arises because the constant itself may actually be a prototype or a cluster concept. The precise representation of constants is an important question for further study. Jackendoff (1990: 33–4), e.g., proposes that all constants take the form of the "3-D model structures" of Marr and Vaina (1982); these structures provide an interface between visual and linguistic representations. Since this issue is outside the scope of this chapter, we simply adopt the convention of representing a constant by the name of the associated verb in capital italics.

9 We distinguish between the "name" of a verb, which is just a phonological stretch of sound, and two uses of the word *verb*. The first corresponds to Aronoff's notion "lexeme": i.e. all forms of a verb associated with a single LCS; thus, *walk, walks, walking, walked* are all instances of the lexeme *walk*. The second corresponds to what Aronoff (1994) calls the "grammatical word": i.e. a verb with a particular set of morphosyntactic features (e.g. the third-person singular present *walks*). It should be clear in any given context which use of *verb* is intended.

10 There is one other possibility, which is not often observed and which is most easily introduced with an example. Consider the verb *string*. This verb can be used as in *to string beans* (to remove the strings from beans), where the constant is a thing, or as in *to string beads* (to put beads on a string), where the constant is a place. *STRING* is one of a handful of constants that qualify for membership in more than one ontological category, and hence can fill more than one constant position in a combination of predicates; see Kiparsky (1997) for additional examples.

11 The predicate GO in (16) is not meant to be equivalent to the predicate BECOME found in the decomposition of achievements in (5b); specifically, unlike BECOME, it is not meant merely to indicate a transition from one state to another. We introduce this predicate to account for sentences such as *The ball rolled out of the room* and *The car rumbled into the driveway*. It seems inappropriate to use BECOME for these sentences, since there is then no appropriate predicate for the manner constant to modify.

Current analyses give a causative representation to all accomplishments, and analyze sentences such as *Tracy walked out of the room* as having a representation along the lines of "Tracy did something that caused Tracy to become at a place out of the room." Whether or not these examples should receive a causative analysis, it seems fairly clear that the just-cited *roll* and *rumble* examples should not. If there are noncausative accomplishments, then the accomplishment use of a verb like *walk* cannot simply be derived by adding a goal to the representation of the verb in its activity use, as is assumed for example in Pustejovsky (1991b). See Jackendoff 1990: 93–5 for a similar suggestion that a predicate like GO is needed.

12 Due to the unavailability of the accomplishment sense of verbs of manner of motion in some languages and to the existence of morphologically complex names for this sense in others, we suggest that manner of motion constants are basically associated with the activity lexical semantic template. We take the association of the constant with the accomplishment lexical semantic template to be effected by rule. We do not formulate such a rule here, but see Levin and Rappaport Hovav 1995 for further discussion.

13 Due to space considerations we cannot provide a fuller discussion of the Russian aspectual system; for further discussion see Brecht 1985, Chung and Timberlake 1985; C. S. Smith 1991, as well as the papers in Flier and Timberlake (eds) 1985.

14 There is reason to believe that this generalization holds more generally in Russian (see e.g. Brecht 1985), but it remains to be seen to what

extent it holds true of French. As we go on to discuss, French does allow the locative alternation, although the two variants differ aspectually, but it is perhaps significant that both variants still describe accomplishments. Further investigation is needed to determine whether other lexical aspectual shifts which are attested in English are attested in French as well, and if so, whether these shifts are accompanied by any changes in the form of the verb.

15   See Anderson 1971, Dowty 1991, Hoekstra and Mulder 1990, Jackendoff 1990, Pinker 1989, Rappaport and Levin 1988, among others, for discussions of the locative alternation, and B. Levin 1993 and Pinker 1989 for a list of English locative alternation verbs. The locative alternation should be distinguished from what might be called "locative advancement," a process by which a locative adjunct or oblique argument becomes a syntactic object of a verb. Such processes, which are found in some Bantu languages, typically involve a different type of morphology than the locative alternation. See also n. 22.

16   In these representations we have not associated the constant with a specific predicate, because it has proved difficult to determine the exact representation for locative alternation verbs. (See Pinker 1989 and Rappaport and Levin 1988 for two suggestions.) It is likely that what is special about these verbs is that the constant restricts facets of the causing activity, the result state, and the theme argument (i.e. *hay* in (19)).

17   We are simplifying somewhat here. As pointed out by Dowty (1991:

591), some of these verbs do permit an activity interpretation.

18   Due to the complexity of aspectual morphology, a full discussion of these examples cannot be offered here.

19   English does have apparent analogues to the two valence-reducing rules discussed in this section – reflexivization and middle formation – as illustrated by *I dressed quickly this morning* and *The can opened easily*; but again there is no morphology associated with such examples. What is interesting is that these processes are much more restricted in English than they are, say, in French. Reflexivization is found only with verbs of grooming and bodily care (see B. Levin 1993 for a list), while middle formation is subject to a much-discussed affectedness condition (Jaeggli 1986a, Roberts 1987, among others). We suspect that the lack of morphology is responsible for these semantic constraints, although we do not understand precisely why this should be.

20   A word of caution is needed here. A sentence with a middle verb does not report an event in the same way that the corresponding sentence with the nonmiddle form does. In this respect, the semantic representations of the two sentences differ significantly. The middle operator is most likely a sentential operator with modal force (Condoravdi 1989; Doron and Rappaport Hovav 1991), and thus embeds the LCS of the corresponding nonderived verb unchanged. However, see Ackema and Schoorlemmer 1994 for an account of middles that uses an operation on LCS and Sadler and Spencer, MORPHOLOGY AND

ARGUMENT STRUCTURE, for some discussion of the issue of whether middle formation involves an operation on argument structure or LCS.

21 The fact that the passive morpheme is homophonous with the perfect morpheme in some languages does not present a problem for our discussion, as the perfect morpheme is different from the perfective morpheme. It is the perfective morpheme which has the lexical aspectual function, and, as far as we know, languages do not tend to use this morpheme to mark the passive.

22 Applied affixes may be additional candidates, though their status requires further investigation. We believe that they are likely to be associated with operations on argument structure, and that, unlike the Russian directional prefixes found with verbs of manner of motion, they are not indicators of an LCS that shares a constant with another LCS.

13 Morphology and Pragmatics

FERENC KIEFER

1 The notion of morphopragmatics

Pragmatics relates linguistic structure to contextual phenomena. In other words, pragmatics can be defined as the functional perspective on language. '[P]ragmatics . . . [can] be conceived as the study of the mechanisms and motivations behind any of the choices made when using language (at the level of phonology, morphology, syntax, semantics, whether they are variety-internal options or whether they involve regionally, socially, or functionally distributed types of variation)' (Verschueren 1987: 36). The relevant contextual phenomena include (i) time, location, social setting and participants' roles, on the one hand, and (ii) the interlocutors' strategies, plans, goals and intentions, on the other. (i) may be referred to as aspects of the 'speech situation' and (ii) as elements of the 'speech event' (Dressler and Merlini-Barbaresi 1993: 3–4).

Morphopragmatics is the study of the interrelationship between morphology and pragmatics. Morphology is relevant pragmatically in so far as word structure (affixes, clitics) can be taken as an indication of the speech situation and/or of the speech event. Morphopragmatics has to be distinguished from lexical pragmatics, on the one hand, and syntactic pragmatics, on the other. Morphologically complex forms which are lexicalized (e.g. German *hierher* 'over here', *dorthinein* 'in there', also a large number of compounds) and which carry pragmatic information come under the heading of lexical pragmatics. Syntactically relevant morphological categories contribute to pragmatics via the syntactic structure in which they appear (e.g. case and plural marking), and belong thus to syntactic pragmatics.

Morphology falls into two parts. 'Grammatical morphology' is rule-governed, and is thus part of grammar. 'Extragrammatical morphology', on the other hand, does not conform to the rules of grammar. The latter is related to 'expressive morphology' (Zwicky and Pullum 1987; Dressler and Merlini-Barbaresi 1993: 23–6). Both types of morphology may be pragmatically relevant, but in the case of extragrammatical morphology it is difficult, if not impossible, to provide general pragmatic accounts of the phenomena involved.

The situation is different with grammatical morphology, where the essential question to be asked is whether a morphological rule has pragmatic effects, and if so, which ones. In general, pragmatic aspects come into play whenever we have to do with competing realizations of morphological rules, or with morphological rules which do not affect denotative meaning or whose semantic contribution is minimal, or which are not prototypical of the respective domain (e.g. diminutives, augmentatives, comparatives in the case of derivational morphology, suffix-like clitics in the case of inflectional morphology).

Most work on morphopragmatics was carried out in the framework of natural morphology (Dressler and Merlini-Barbaresi 1993 and the references quote therein). A number of works treat morphopragmatics under the heading of semantics (e.g. Wierzbicka 1983, 1984). Mey (1989) pleads for the study of the relationship between morphology and pragmatics, and by way of illustration provides a brief survey of some morphological means for expressing power and solidarity. A description of emotive attitudes expressed by diminutives can be found in Volek (1987). However, Dressler and Merlini-Barbaresi 1993 is the only systematic work on morphopragmatics to date.

2 Pragmatics and inflection

Inflection has primarily a syntactic function: it makes the word conform to whatever is required by syntax. In a number of cases, however, there is a choice available between inflectional categories or between affixes expressing the same inflectional category or categories, which may be determined by pragmatic factors.

2.1 Case marking in Polish

A case in point is case marking in Polish (Wierzbicka 1983). In Polish the nominative plural has several allomorphs conditioned by a number of different factors. For example, human masculine nouns with a hard stem can take one of the following endings: *-i*, *-y* and *-owie*. The first ending is neutral; it has no pragmatic implications. The ending *-y*, however, implies contempt, and the ending *-owie* importance or dignity. Some masculine nouns have a choice between two or sometimes even three of these endings. Thus, for example, an inherently respectful word such as *profesor* or *astronom*, which normally takes the *-y* suffix, can be lowered to a neutral form such as *profesorzy* or *astronomy* (with an underlying *-i* suffix which surfaces as *-y* in certain well-defined phonological contexts), and jokingly even a contemptuous word such as *lobuz* 'rascal' can be raised to a marked neutral form such as *lobuzi*, but not to a respectful form such as *lobuzowie*. Consequently, in addition to phonological and semantic factors, the choice of the nominative plural depends on pragmatic factors, on the intentions and goals of the speaker.

2.2 Inflectional suffixes in Hungarian and stylistic layer

The choice of inflectional suffixes may have stylistic consequences. The stylistic meaning of suffixes may range from 'substandard' to 'formal'. For example, the first-person plural conditional has two variants for the definite conjugation: *-nánk/-nénk* and *-nók/-nōk*. The first variant is neutral; the second one belongs to the 'elevated style', and can be used in an appropriate speech situation only. The same holds true for the two variants of the first- and third-person singular present tense conditional suffixes for the indefinite conjugation (*-nék* and *-nám/ -ném*, *-na/-ne* and *-nék*, respectively). In both cases, the older forms belong to the elevated style, whereas the more recent forms are stylistically neutral. Upcoming forms, on the other hand, are often 'substandard'. For example, in careless colloquial speech the present tense indicative endings are sometimes replaced by the corresponding suffixes of the imperative: thus forms such as *takarít-suk* 'we are tidying up' and *vált-sa* 'he is changing' are used instead of *takarít-juk* and *vált-ja*. This variation is partly conditioned phonologically: it is possible only after stem-final or suffix-final *-t*. The use of the imperative instead of the indicative is typical of certain social settings and age-groups.

2.3 Inflectional suffixes as indicators of the speech event

It also happens that the choice of one inflectional variant rather than the other indicates the strength of illocutionary force. For example, in Hungarian some imperatives appear in two forms: for example, *ad-d* 'give' and *ad-jad*, *mond-d* 'say' and *mond-jad*, both second-person singular imperative. Typically, the shorter forms are used to issue a stronger order, and the longer forms are preferred when the speaker wants to issue an attenuated order.

2.4 Inflectional suffixes and honorifics

In Japanese, which seems to have one of the most complex systems of honorifics, some variants are due to morphology rather than to syntax. For example, from among the three ways of expressing the sentence 'Here is a book': (i) *Koko ni hon ga aru*, (ii) *Koko ni hon ga ari-masu* and (iii) *Koko ni hon ga gozai-masu*, (i) is the most neutral, (ii) the polite and (iii) the super-polite variant (Harada 1976:

553–4). *-masu* is an inflectional suffix, and *gozai* is a suppletive form of the existential verb *aru*. The relevant speech situation may be analysed in terms of the speaker, the hearer, other participants, place, time and topic (Dressler and Merlini-Barbaresi 1993: 48–51). It has been observed, for example, that female speakers use polite *-masu* forms more often than male speakers. As far as the hearer is concerned, the polite *-masu* forms are always used with members of an out-group. Also television and radio speakers and oral announcements in train and subway stations use these forms, because the addressees are considered to be members of an out-group. Furthermore, if the hearer has authority over the speaker (in terms of relative social status, power, age), the *-masu* form must be used. If a bystander is present who is a member of an out-group or whose rank is higher than that of the speaker, again the polite form must be used. The place and the time of the interaction influence the formality of the speech situation, and constitute an overriding factor. For example, funerals, weddings and opening ceremonies demand the use of *-masu*. Also a change of topic may prompt the use of *-masu*: for example, businessmen use *-masu* when their topic switches from personal items to business. Additional factors come into play when the super-polite form is used.

3 Derivational morphology and pragmatics

Derivational processes which affect syntactic structure do not seem to have any direct relevance to pragmatics. Thus, causatives and passives derived from a base verb or deverbal nouns can attain pragmatic relevance only via the syntactic structure into which they enter. Typically, morphopragmatics becomes pertinent with derivational affixes which do not affect syntax. Another area where pragmatic effects may be expected are instances of non-prototypical derivation.

3.1 The Japanese beautificational prefix

Japanese has a derivational beautificational prefix *o-*, which is used to make speech softer and more polite (Harada 1976: 504). For example, by using this prefix, an offer becomes more polite. Compare *Biiru ikaga?* 'How about a beer?' with *O-biiru ikaga?* 'Would you like some beer?'

3.2 Australian depreciatives

A 'depreciative' form constitutes an abbreviation of the standard form combined with a pseudo-diminutive suffix (Wierzbicka 1984: 128–9). Thus, the 'depreciative' form of *present* is *prezzie*, of *mushrooms* is *mushies*, of *barbecue* is *barbie*. Though the pseudo-diminutive suffix *-ie* does not mean smallness, it is not void of semantic meaning. It carries the connotation that the thing denoted by the noun should not be considered a big thing. Pragmatically, depreciatives express informality (hence they cannot be used in formal settings) and solidarity (hence they are inappropriate in speech situations in which solidarity is excluded).

3.3 *Italian diminutives*

Italian has a considerable number of diminutive suffixes. The productive suffixes are *-ino*, *-etto*, *-ello*, *-(u)olo*, *-uccio/-uzzo*, *-otto* and *-onzolo*. For example, *film* – *film-ino*, *verme* 'worm' – *verm-etto*, *mano* 'hand' – *man-uccia*. Pragmatically, diminutives express an evaluation or judgement which depends on the speaker's intentions, perspective and standards of evaluation. The most general pragmatic meaning of diminutives seems to be non-seriousness. That is, by using the diminutive suffix, the speaker evaluates his speech act as being non-serious. Furthermore, in order to minimize the risk of disapproval on the part of the hearer, the propositional content of the speech act is shifted into an imaginary world. For example, *Eh, sono dei bei sold-ini/dollar-ini!* 'Well, they are of the nice moneys-/dollars' – diminutive: 'Well, that's a pretty penny', where the diminutive is used to downgrade the precision of the statement concerning the bigness of the amount. The use of the diminutive can be analysed adequately in terms of (i) speech situations, (ii) speech acts and (iii) regulative factors such as playfulness, emotion, intimacy, understatement, modesty, euphemism, etc. Typical speech situations in which diminutives are used are child-centered, pet-centered and lover-centered speech situations. As to speech acts, the main contribution of diminutives is the modification of the relative strength of a speech act (Dressler and Merlini-Barbaresi 1993: 54–275).

3.4 *Italian intensification (augmentatives)*

Intensification in Italian can be expressed by means of the suffix *-one* as in *porta* 'door' – *port-one*, *mano* 'hand' – *man-one*, *tazza* 'cup' – *tazz-ona*. Like diminutives, augmentatives indicate the fictiveness of the situation at hand. 'The speaker suspends the norms of the real world and makes the norms of his evaluation glide upwards' (ibid.: 291). But, in contrast to the diminutive, where in most cases the semantic meaning of smallness is lost, the augmentative preserves the semantic feature of bigness. Compare the augmentative in (i) with the diminutive in (ii): (i) *Come vorrei essere nel mio lett-one!* 'How I'd like to be in my bed' – augmentative: 'How I'd love to be in my big bed!'; (ii) *Come vorrei essere nel mio lett-ino!* 'How I'd love to be in my snug little bed!' In (ii) the bed is not taken to be small, while in (i) the bed is certainly big in the speaker's imaginary world. The importance of the feature of bigness is responsible, among other things, for the frequent use of augmentatives in overstatements and in exaggerations (ibid.: 275–326).

3.5 *The excessive in Hungarian and Viennese German*

In Hungarian, the excessive is formed by repeating the superlative prefix *leg-*: *leg-es-leg-*, where *es* stands for the conjunction *és* 'and'; or even *leg-es-leg-es-leg*, which is added to the comparative form: *nagy* 'big' – *nagy-obb* 'bigger' – *leg-nagy-obb* 'biggest' – *legesleg-nagy-obb* 'the very biggest'. The corresponding German prefix is *aller-*, preposed to a superlative: *aller-neu-est* 'the most recent of all'. The excessive expresses the absolutely highest possible degree of a property, and it is compared only with items which have this property to a high degree; it is used for emphasis and for impressing the hearer (Dressler and Kiefer 1990: 69–72). The excessive can also be used as a corrective device in discourse: *Das ist sehr schlimm* 'That is very bad' – *Aber das allerschlimmste ist, dass . . .* 'But the very worst of all is that . . .'. Furthermore, it may express the last word on the matter in question. At the end of a TV discussion, the moderator may ask the question *Gibt's noch eine allerletzte Frage?* 'Is there a truly last question?', with the excessive *allerletzte* 'very last' signalling that an extra question is still possible, but that this opportunity must be taken immediately, and that any other question will be totally excluded (Dressler and Merlini-Barbaresi 1993: 373).

4 Compounds

Much less is known about the pragmatics of compounds. Morphopragmatics is concerned with the pragmatic effects of *ad hoc* compounds; lexical compounds with lexicalized meaning fall outside its scope. Compounds have been investigated mainly with respect to their discourse function (Dressler 1982, Brekle 1986). For example, compounds have a special discourse referential function; they are used when a pronoun would not suffice to establish referential identity between two expressions: for example, *die Wahlkampfmannschaft von Strauss – die Strauss-Mannschaft* 'Strauss' election-campaign team' (Brekle 1986: 46). *Apple-juice seat* is an English example for a compound used as a deictic device (Downing 1977: 823). Also, newly coined compounds, in virtue of their innovative nature, have a foregrounding function. This function can be observed particularly well in poetic language, in advertising and in journalism (in headlines). Furthermore, most *ad hoc* compounds are many-ways ambiguous. The inherent ambiguity of compounds is often exploited in poetry, in political discourse and in jokes.

5 Clitic particles

The study of the pragmatic effects of clitic particles may be subsumed under the heading of morphopragmatics, since they behave in many respects exactly like affixes: they are unable to bear stress; they have a fixed position in word structure; and quite often they cannot be attached to just any type of word.

5.1 Evidential clitics

Evidential particles are often expressed by suffixes, and are thus part of word structure. In Wintu, an American Indian language spoken in Northern California, direct evidence is unmarked and assumed to be visual, whereas non-visual sensory evidence and inference from intuition are marked by the suffix *-nthEr*. Both second- and third-hand hearsay evidence is marked by *-kee*, inference from observed results by *-ree*, and inference from previous experience by *-?el* (Willett 1988: 64–5). Evidential markers are pragmatically relevant in so far as they modify or determine the speech act performed. The speaker may assert a statement or a supposition, but he or she may also express emphasis and surprise. The latter seem to arise when the claimed fact is directly observable by both the speaker and the hearer. In Turkish, for example, the evidential suffix *-mış* is used to convey inference and hearsay. But an utterance such as *Ahmet gel-mış* 'Ahmet came' could also be an expression of surprise, even if the speaker has had full, sensory information of Ahmet's arrival. For example, this utterance could be used in a situation in which the speaker hears someone approach from outside and open the door, and sees Ahmet, provided that Ahmet is a totally unexpected visitor. The same particle can also be used to express scorn, irony and compliments (Aksu-Koç and Slobin 1986: 162–3). Moreover, evidentials may influence the strength of assertion. Between the source of information and the strength of assertion the following correlation seems to hold: 'The source of a speaker's information can skew the relation between his/her conception of the truth and the strength of his/her assertion about that situation' (Willett 1988: 86). Thus, emphatic assertion can be based only on attested evidence, doubtful truth only on inference.

Evidential suffixes may even determine the illocutionary force of the utterance. Kashaya, for example, has a pair of performative suffixes, *-wela* and *-mela*, which signify that the speaker knows of what he speaks because he is performing the act himself or has just performed it. These suffixes are often used to introduce a conversation. As a conversational interchange develops from the opening remarks, the performative suffixes are replaced by the factual-visual suffixes *-wa* and *-ya* (Oswalt 1986: 34–6).

5.2 Other clitics

Clitics may also function as illocutionary act indicators. Some clitics in Ngiyambaa (South Australian), for example, are used to express the speaker's beliefs about what he or she is saying, giving performative equivalents like 'I assert that . . .', 'I counter-assert that . . .', 'I guess that . . .' (Donaldson 1980:

253–8). The speaker may also make explicit the source of his or her evidence by means of an evidential suffix. In that case evidential suffixes always follow 'belief' clitics. In Ngiyambaa the suffixes *-ba:*, *-bara* and *-baga:* mark assertions, and *-gila* marks a hypothesis. Plain assertion is expressed by *-ba:*, categorical assertion by *-bara*, counter-assertion by *-baga:*, hypothetical assertion by *-gila*. For example, *guyan-baga:-dhu gara*, shy counter-assert I am, 'But I am shy' used to invalidate a previous pragmatic presupposition ('People are not reticent'). The suffix *-gila* also occurs in boasts, 'whose essence is that they assert the subjective, and not necessarily confirmed, value of what is being boasted about'.

In a Central Australian language, Mparntwe Arrernte (Aranda), clitics are used to indicate the illocutionary force of criticism and/or complaint. These pragmatic effects are functions of the meaning of these clitics, of culture-specific pragmatic factors and speech situation. The relevant particle clitics are *-itanye*, *-iknge*, *-me*, *-kathene* and *kwele* (Wilkins 1986: 577). Of these, only the last one does not exhibit suffix-like behaviour. Criticism or complaint is expressed by *-iknge*: for example, *R-iknge angke-me*, which, depending on the speech situation, may mean either 'He's always speaking?' (When do I get my chance?), '(Poor thing.) He's always having to speak', or 'He never stops speaking' (The big-mouth). The clitic *-kathene* invokes special socio-cultural norms determined by the relationship between the participants in the speech situation. The use of this suffix presupposes the 'full command of the sociocultural knowledge of what obligations various relations entail and what constitutes a breach of those obligations'. The clitic *-me* alludes to unfair expectations of what the speaker should do, and forces the addressee to realize what he or she should normally expect of the speaker, and so how he or she should behave. Finally, *-itanye* is the contrary of the expectation clitic, and expresses surprise (Wilkins 1986: 575–96).

Part III Theoretical Issues

14 Prosodic Morphology

JOHN J. MCCARTHY AND
ALAN S. PRINCE

1 Introduction

Prosodic Morphology is a theory of how morphological and phonological determinants of linguistic form interact with one another in grammatical systems. A core area of investigation is the way in which prosodic structure impinges on templatic and circumscriptional morphology, such as reduplication and infixation. In McCarthy and Prince 1986 and 1990a, three essential claims are advanced about Prosodic Morphology:

(1) Principles of Prosodic Morphology
  (a) Prosodic Morphology Hypothesis
      Templates are defined in terms of the authentic units of prosody: mora (μ), syllable (σ), foot (Ft), prosodic word (PrWd).
  (b) Template Satisfaction Condition
      Satisfaction of templatic constraints is obligatory and is determined by the principles of prosody, both universal and language-specific.
  (c) Prosodic Circumscription
      The domain to which morphological operations apply may be circumscribed by prosodic criteria as well as by the more familiar morphological ones.

In short, this approach to Prosodic Morphology hypothesizes that templates and circumscription must be formulated in terms of the vocabulary of prosody, and must respect the well-formedness requirements of prosody.[1] The commitment to prosody is based neither on simple inductive empirical observations, nor on some kind of hegemonic impulse to extend a favored subdiscipline at the expense of others. Rather, it answers to a fundamental explanatory goal: to reduce or eliminate the descriptive apparatus that is specific to particular empirical domains like reduplication, and instead derive the properties of those domains from general and independently motivated principles. Claims

(1a), (1b), and (1c) assert that prosodic theory is where these independent principles are to be found; but the pursuit of more embracing explanations has led researchers to modify and generalize these initial hypotheses in ways we will discuss.

On the morphological side, the assumptions made within Prosodic Morphology are relatively uncomplicated. The morphological constituents Root, Stem, and Affix form a labeled bracketing, essentially along the lines of Selkirk 1982. Most work in Prosodic Morphology adopts a view of morphology that is morpheme-based, under the broad rubric of item-and-arrangement models, though the (morpheme-based) model of prosodic circumscription in McCarthy and Prince (1990a) is a processual one.

On the phonological side, Prosodic Morphology is based on the Prosodic Hierarchy in (2), evolved from that of Selkirk (1980a, b):

(2)   Prosodic Hierarchy

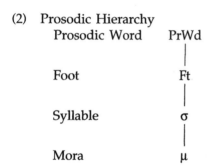

Prosodic Word	PrWd
Foot	Ft
Syllable	σ
Mora	μ

The mora is the unit of syllable weight (Prince 1980, van der Hulst 1984, Hyman 1985, McCarthy and Prince 1986, Zec 1988, Hayes 1989a, Itô 1989, etc.). The most common syllable weight typology is given in (3), where short open syllables like *pa* are light, and long-voweled or closed syllables like *paa* or *pat* are heavy.

(3)   Syllables in Moraic Theory – Modal Weight Typology
      Light (L)   Heavy (H)

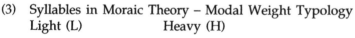

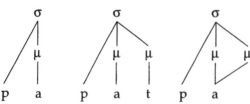

Syllables and syllable weight are fundamental to defining metrical feet. Feet are constrained both syllabically and moraically. The foot inventory laid out in (4) below is proposed in McCarthy and Prince 1986 and Hayes 1987 to account for Hayes's (1985) typological findings. We write L for light syllable, H for heavy syllable:

(4) Foot types Iambic Trochaic Syllabic

                   LH   H, LL   σσ

                   LL, H

Conspicuously absent from the typology are degenerate feet, consisting of just a single light syllable, though they may play a marked role in stress assignment (Kager 1989, Hayes 1995; but see Kiparsky 1992). The following general condition on foot form is responsible for the nonexistence (or markedness) of degenerate feet (Prince 1980; McCarthy and Prince 1986, 1991b, 1993b: ch. 4; Hayes 1995):

(5) Foot Binarity: Feet are binary under syllabic or moraic analysis.

The Prosodic Hierarchy and Foot Binarity, taken together, derive the key notion "Minimal Word" (Prince 1980; Broselow 1982; McCarthy and Prince 1986, 1990a, 1991a, b). According to the Prosodic Hierarchy, any instance of the category prosodic word must contain at least one foot. By Foot Binarity, every foot must be bimoraic or disyllabic. By transitivity, then, a prosodic word must contain at least two moras (or syllables, if all syllables are monomoraic). As we shall see, the Minimal Word is of singular importance in characterizing certain Prosodic-Morphological phenomena, and its role is a matter of continuing study.

2 Exemplification

Reduplicative and root-and-pattern morphology are typical cases where the principles of Prosodic Morphology emerge with full vigor.[2] In reduplicative and root-and-pattern morphology, grammatical distinctions are expressed by imposing a fixed prosodic requirement on varying segmental material. In reduplication, the prosodically fixed material stands as a kind of affix, copying segments of the base to which it is adjoined. In root-and-pattern morphology, broadly construed, the prosodically fixed material is a free-standing stem, to which segments of a root or related word are mapped.

The Ilokano reduplicative plural exemplified in (6) specifies a prefix whose canonical shape is constant – a heavy syllable – but whose segmental content is a (partial) copy of the base to which it is attached:

(6) Ilokano plural reduplication (McCarthy and Prince 1986, 1991a, 1993b; Hayes and Abad 1989)

kaldíŋ	'goat'	*kal*-kaldíŋ	'goats'
púsa	'cat'	*pus*-púsa	'cats'
kláse	'class'	*klas*-kláse	'classes'
jyánitor	'janitor'	*jyan*-jyánitor	'janitors'
róʔot	'litter'	*ro:*-róʔot	'litter (pl.)'
trák	'truck'	*tra:*-trák	'trucks'

We follow the practice of highlighting the copy, called the *reduplicant* (after Spring 1990). The template of the Ilokano plural is a heavy syllable, $\sigma_{\mu\mu}$. Given the independently motivated prosody of the language, a heavy syllable can consist of a diverse set of segmental strings, with simple or complex initial clusters (*kal* vs *klas*) and with a closing consonant or a long vowel (*pus* vs *ro:*, *klas* vs *tra:*). The heavy-syllable template $\sigma_{\mu\mu}$ is the invariant that unites the various forms of the plural in Ilokano. The Prosodic Morphology Hypothesis demands that templates be characterized in just such abstract, prosodic terms; in this way they partake, as the Ilokano template does, of the independently motivated conditions on prosody generally and in the particular language under study.

The Ilokano case also illustrates another significant finding: the fact that the reduplicative template is itself an affix (McCarthy 1979, 1981; Marantz 1982). On the face of it, the idea that reduplication involves affixing a template may seem surprising, since a natural, naive expectation is that reduplication involves an operation like "copy the first syllable," as illustrated in (7):

(7)   "Copy first syllable," hypothetically
      ta.ka   →   *ta*-ta.ka
      tra.pa   →   *tra*-tra.pa
      tak.pa   →   *tak*-tak.pa

Moravcsik (1978c) and Marantz (1982) observe that syllable copying, in this sense, does not occur. Rather, reduplication always specifies a *templatic target* which is affixed to the base, and is satisfied by copying elements of the base.[3]

The Prosodic Morphology Hypothesis, together with the Prosodic Hierarchy, predicts the existence of a range of possible types of reduplicative templates. The heavy syllable $\sigma_{\mu\mu}$ of the Ilokano plural is one of these. Another is the light-syllable template σ_{μ}, which is also used in Ilokano, in other morphological constructions:

(8)   Ilokano $si + \sigma_{\mu}$ 'covered/filled with'
      buneŋ   'buneng'   si-*bu*-buneŋ   'carrying a buneng'
      jyaket   'jacket'   si-*jya*-jyaket   'wearing a jacket'
      pandiliŋ   'skirt'   si-*pa*-pandiliŋ   'wearing a skirt'

Both of these reduplicative patterns are common cross-linguistically. Equally common too is the minimal word (MinWd) template, which consists of a single binary foot, often matching the smallest word-size in the host language. A typical example of this is found in the Australian language Diyari:

(9)   Diyari Reduplication (Austin 1981; Poser 1982, 1989; McCarthy and Prince 1986, 1991a, b, 1994a)
      wiḷa   *wiḷa*-wiḷa   'woman'
      kanku   *kanku*-kanku   'boy'
      kulkuṇa   *kulku*-kulkuṇa   'to jump'

| tʲilparku | tʲilpa-tʲilparku | 'bird species' |
| ŋankaṇṭi | ŋanka-ŋankaṇṭi | 'catfish' |

Reduplicated words of Diyari have various meanings. The formal regularity that unites them is the presence of a prefixed MinWd template. The realization of this template, and of the smallest words in the language as a whole, is a disyllabic trochaic foot, since Diyari does not make distinctions of syllable weight. In fact, the reduplicative prefix of Diyari is a free-standing prosodic word, as shown by the facts that it is vowel-final (like all prosodic words of Diyari) and that both prefix and base bear their own primary word stresses: *kánku-kánku, tʲílpa-tʲílparku*. In effect, then, the prefix + base collocation in Diyari is a compound of a MinWd with a complete PrWd. We will revisit Diyari below, in section 3, with the goal of a better understanding of the relation of MinWd phenomena to general constraints on prosody and morphology.

In root-and-pattern morphology, the prosodic template determines the shape of the whole stem, rather than just an affix. Full-blown systems are found in several widely scattered language families, touched on below. But a particular type of quasi-grammatical root-and-pattern morphology is quite broadly attested: the process of forming a nickname or hypocoristic by mapping a name onto a minimal word template MinWd. This type of prosodic morphology was identified by McCarthy and Prince (1986, 1990a), and is comprehensively surveyed by Weeda (1992). The formation of "proximal vocatives" in Central Alaskan Yup'ik Eskimo is a typical example.

(10) Proximal vocatives in Central Alaskan Yup'ik Eskimo (A. Woodbury 1985; McCarthy and Prince 1986, 1990a)

Name		Proximal vocative
Aŋukaɣnaq		Aŋ ~ Aŋuk
Nupiɣak		Nup ~ Nupix/Nupik
Aŋivɣan		Aŋif
Kalixtuq		Kaɬ ~ Kalik
qətunɣaq	'son'	Qət ~ Qətun
Maɣʷluq		Maχʷ
Aɣnaɣayaq		Aɣən
Nənqəχalɣia		Nənəq
Qakfalɣia		Qak ~ Qakəf ~ Qakfaɬ
Akiuɣalɣia		Akîuk

As is usual in such cases, personal preferences may influence the result. But there is a clear invariant structure amid the alternatives: the shape of a licit vocative is exactly an iambic foot, a single heavy syllable or a light–heavy sequence. This is the minimal prosodic word in a language like Yup'ik, with its pervasive iambic prosody.[4] Hence, the vocative template is MinWd.

Closer to home, the force of this same template can be observed with a certain species of nicknames in English:

(11) English nicknames (McCarthy and Prince 1986)
      Name   Nickname

      Mortimer   Mort, Mortie
      Cynthia   Cynth, Cindy
      Marjorie   Marge, Margie
      Angela   Ange [æñʤ], Angie,
      Francis   Fran, Frank, Frannie, Frankie
      Cyrus   Cy
      Barbara   Bar, Barb, Barbie
      Alfred   Al, Alf, Alfie
      Edward   Ed, Eddie, *Edwie
      Abraham   Abe, Abie, *Abrie
      Jacqueline   Jackie, *Jacquie (=[ʤækwi:])
      Douglas   Doug, Dougie, *Douglie
      Agnes   Ag, Aggie, *Agnie

Again, personal preference is a factor in fixing choices, but the overall scheme is clear: the shape invariant in English nicknames is a bimoraic (heavy) syllable, the minimal word of the language.[5] As in Yupik, the minimal word is the prosodic word that contains a single foot; English is subject to the further restriction that not only the prosodic word but also the foot itself must be minimal, and therefore monosyllabic (McCarthy and Prince 1986, 1991b). By Foot Binarity (5), any single syllable that exhausts a foot must be heavy.

The templatic base of the nickname may be augmented by addition of the external or "Level II" suffix *[i]*, spelled *-y* or *-ie*. That this suffix is prosodically independent of the template is shown by the impossibility of *Edwie* and the other asterisked examples. These all involve a cluster that cannot be mapped to the monosyllabic template, under independently motivated English syllable canons. Because there are no monosyllables *Edw*, *Dougl*, *Abr*, *Agn*, there are no nicknames *Edwie*, *Douglie*, *Abrie*, *Agnie*, and so on, even though such forms are syllabically perfect. The monosyllable base criterion thus limits the segmentism of suffixed hypocoristics in a principled way.[6]

Perhaps the most extensively studied example of this type is found in Japanese:

(12) Hypocoristics in Japanese (Poser 1984, 1990)
      Name   Hypocoristic

      ti   tii-čan
      šuusuke   šuu-čan   *šuusu-čan
      yoosuke   yoo-čan   *yoosu-čan
      taizoo   tai-čan   *taizo-čan
      kinsuke   kin-čan   *kinsu-čan
      midori   mii-čan   *mi-čan
                      mit-čan
                      mido-čan

wasaburoo	waa-čan	*wa-čan
	wasa-čan	
	sabu-čan	
	wasaburo-čan	*wasabu-čan

As usual, personal preferences are a factor; but with complete consistency, any modified hypocoristic stem consists of an even number of moras, usually two.[7] Though prominential stress is not found in Japanese, there is abundant evidence that it has a system of two-mora (probably trochaic) feet (Poser 1990) and that the minimal word is, as expected, bimoraic (Itô 1991). Thus, the template for the hypocoristic can be characterized in prosodic fashion as Ft⁺ (one or more feet) or MinWd⁺, the latter perhaps to be analyzed as a kind of MinWd compound.

Variations on the same theme are played out in a number of other morphological patterns (Itô 1991, Mester 1990, Itô and Mester, 1997; cf. Tateishi 1989, Perlmutter 1992). Strikingly, standard Japanese (the Tōkyō dialect) has a full complement of monomoraic words in the lexicon (cf. e.g. Itô 1991). But no morphological process that demands minimality is ever satisfied by a monomoraic structure. This shows that the notion of MinWd relevant to prosodic morphology is not a simple inductive one, based on the size of attested lexical words in a given language. Rather, the active notion is "minimal *prosodic* word," a unit whose structure is determined by the universal principles of the Prosodic Hierarchy (2) and of Foot Binarity (5).

The Japanese case is particularly notable in the diversity of ways that a bimoraic foot, and therefore a hypocoristic word, can be realized. Long-voweled *tii*, diphthongal *tai*, closed *kin*, and disyllabic *mido* are all licit hypocoristics, and they represent all the canonical types of bimoraic feet to be found in Japanese as a whole. Such diversity defeats any effort to construct a respectable theory that comprehends the template in purely segmental terms, as a sequence of C and V positions. Any such segmentalist effort must painfully recapitulate the vocabulary of foot types within the parochial hypocoristic template. Obviously, any theory with the descriptive richness to do this – say, by basing itself on a Kleene-type regular language notation – will have little or no predictive force. By contrast, the templatic restriction *MinWd* inherits from Universal Grammar a cascade of information about foot and syllable structure. The hypocoristic pattern of many languages is simply *MinWd*; and further independent specification of the foot, syllable, and mora structure in the language determines the details.

Though truncation is usually rather limited in scope, root-and-pattern morphology is an utterly pervasive feature of some morphological systems, particularly in the Afro-Asiatic family, but also in various Penutian languages such as Miwok, Yokuts, and Takelma.[8] These systems are all rather complex and difficult to summarize briefly, but it is possible to get a general feel for the mode of analysis by a brief glance at one of them.

The shapes of canonical nouns in Standard Arabic, analyzed in McCarthy and Prince 1990b, Prince 1991, and McCarthy 1993, illustrate some basic principles.[9] The data are given in (13), based on all the canonical noun stems occurring in the first half of a large dictionary (N ≈ 2400), and classified by syllable-weight pattern (H, L) with a single example of each type:

(13)   The canonical noun patterns in Standard Arabic
    (a) H   (b) LL   (c) LH   (d) HL
        baħr   *badal*   *waziir*   *kaatib*
        33%   7%   21%   12%

    (e) HH   (f) HL   (g) HH
        jaamuus   *xanjar*   *jumhuur*
        2%   14%   11%

These are glosses for the representative examples: 'sea', 'substitute', 'minister', 'writer', 'buffalo', 'dagger', 'multitude'. All patterns are well represented except for (e), which is probably a historical innovation in Arabic.

The classification of nouns in (13) according to the syllable-weight patterns assumes final consonant extraprosodicity, which is independently motivated in Arabic. Modulo this, we observe that the shapes of canonical nouns range from a lower bound at the bimoraic MinWd (H or LL) to an upper bound at the maximal disyllable HH. These observations can be expressed in terms of prosodic conditions on canonical noun stems (Stem$_N$):

(14)   Prosodic conditions on canonicity of Stem$_N$
    (a) Minimally bimoraic   (b) Maximally disyllabic
        Stem$_N$ = PrWd   Stem$_N$ ≤ σσ

Because the morphological category Stem$_N$ is equated with the prosodic category PrWd, a Stem$_N$ must contain a foot, under the Prosodic Hierarchy, and so it is minimally bimoraic, as required by Foot Binarity. The maximality condition is a natural one under general considerations of locality, which impose an upper limit of two on rules that count (McCarthy and Prince 1986); but it can perhaps be given an even more direct prosodic interpretation in terms of conditions on branching (Itô and Mester, 1997) or through an additional foot type, the generalized trochee of Prince (1980), Hayes (1995), and Kager (1992). Details of formulation aside, the minimality and maximality conditions define a family of templates in Arabic, with each member of that family available for particular morphological functions in the nominal system. This shows that the fundamental structural properties of root-and-pattern morphological systems can and should be characterized in prosodic terms.

In the varieties of Prosodic Morphology reviewed so far, the structural constraint falls entirely on the output, characterizing its shape without dependence on any phonological properties of the input. For example, a morphological category can be specified as "MinWd" regardless of whether an input base is itself minimal, supraminimal, or subminimal. There is, however, an important class of cases in which aspects of base shape also play a role in determining output form. These have been analyzed as involving the notion of *prosodic circumscription*.

Typically, affixation is defined on purely *grammatical* entities, adjoining an affix node to morphological categories such as root, stem, or (morphological) word, without regard to their phonological content. The result is ordinary prefixation or suffixation. Under prosodic circumscription, though, affixation or other morphology applies to a phonologically defined prosodic base situated within the grammatical base. The result is often some sort of infix, though there are many applications of prosodic circumscription extending beyond infixation.

Ulwa, a language of the Atlantic coast of Nicaragua, presents a remarkably clear case of infixation by prosodic circumscription (Hale and Lacayo Blanco 1989; Bromberger and Halle 1988; McCarthy and Prince 1990a, 1993a, b). The stress system of Ulwa is iambic, with the main stress falling on the leftmost foot. Remarkably, the possessive morphology of Ulwa is marked by a set of infixes located immediately after the main-stress foot:

(15) Ulwa possessive
    (a) Forms of possessive

sú:lu	'dog'	sú:kinalu	'our (excl.) dog'
sú:kilu	'my dog'	sú:nilu	'our (incl.) dog'
sú:malu	'thy dog'	sú:manalu	'your dog'
sú:kalu	'his/her dog'	sú:kanalu	'their dog'

    (b) Location of infixes (noun + 'his')

        (i) After heavy initial syllable
            bás-ka   'hair'
            kí:-ka   'stone'
            sú:-ka-lu   'dog'
            ás-ka-na   'clothes'
        (ii) After peninitial syllable
            saná-ka   'deer'
            amák-ka   'bee'
            sapá:-ka   'forehead'
            siwá-ka-nak   'root'
            kulú-ka-luk   'woodpecker'
            aná:-ka-la:ka   'chin'
            arák-ka-bus   'gun'
            karás-ka-mak   'knee'

The fundamental idea of prosodic circumscription is that infixes like Ulwa *-ka, -ki, -ma,* . . . are actually suffixes, but suffixes on the *prosodically circumscribed* initial foot within the Ulwa noun stem. The theory of prosodic circumscription aims to make precise and extend this basic idea. The analysis of Ulwa and the (quasi-) formal construction of circumscription theory on which it is based are presented in McCarthy and Prince 1990a; certain aspects of the approach recall earlier proposals in Broselow and McCarthy 1983 and McCarthy and Prince 1986.

Central to the formal development is a parsing function $\Phi(C, E, B)$ which returns the designated prosodic constituent C that sits at the edge E of the base B. The constituent C is thereby circumscribed; the initial foot of Ulwa is an example of exactly such a C. For notational convenience, we will write $\Phi(C, E, B)$ – the result of applying Φ – as B:Φ <C,E>, emphasizing that this is the portion of base B that falls under the description <C,E>. (In line with this usage, we will refer to the parsing function as Φ <C,E>, mentioning only its settable parameters.) In the case of Ulwa *karasmak*, for example, the circumscribed initial foot *karas* would be described as *karasmak*:Φ <Ft,L>.

The function Φ induces a factoring on the base B, dividing it into two parts: one is the *kernel* B:Φ, satisfying the constraint <C,E>; the other is the *residue* B\Φ, the complement of the kernel within B.[10] Assuming an operator "*" that gives the relation holding between the two factors (often left- or right-concatenation), the following identity holds:

(16)   Factoring of B by Φ
        $B = B{:}\Phi * B\backslash\Phi$

Concretely, using Ulwa *karasmak*, we have the following analysis:

(17)   Factoring of the Ulwa noun
        karasmak   =   *karasmak*:Φ *   *karasmak*\Φ
                      =   *karas*   *   *mak*

The word is factored *initial foot + anything else*; that is, kernel + residue, in that order.

In *positive prosodic circumscription*, the specified prosodic constituent B:Φ serves as the base for the morphological operation. Let O be a morphological or phonological operation, so that O[X] is that operation applied to a base X. We can now define 'O:Φ' – the very same operation, but conditioned by positive circumscription of <C,E> – in the following way:

(18)   Operation applying under positive prosodic circumscription
        $O{:}\Phi\ [B] =_{df} O[B{:}\Phi] * B\backslash\Phi$

To apply O to B under positive prosodic circumscription, is, by this definition, to apply O to B:Φ. The result stands concatenated with B\$\Phi$ in the same way ("*") that the kernel B:Φ concatenates with the residue B\$\Phi$ in the base B. In this way, the operation O:Φ inherits everything that linguistic theory tells us about O, except its domain of application.

The Ulwa possessive makes use of a parsing function that picks out the first foot of the base: Φ <Ft, Left>.[11] The morphological operations at issue are those that accomplish suffixation of the possessive markers. Suppose we write SUFFKA for the operation suffixing /ka/ 'possessed by 3psg.'. Appropriately circumscribed, the operation becomes SUFFKA:Φ <Ft, Left>. Suffixation of the possessive now unfolds as follows:

(19) Possessive suffixation under prosodic circumscription

SUFFKA:Φ [*karasmak*]	=	SUFFKA [*karasmak*:Φ]	*	*karasmak*\Φ
	=	SUFFKA [*karas*]	*	*mak*
	=	*karas-ka*	*	*mak*
	=	*karaskamak*		

The initial iambic foot, rather than the whole noun, functions as the base for suffixation of the possessive morpheme, leading to surface infixation. In the limiting case of words consisting of a single iambic foot, like *bas* or *ki:*, the infixes are actual suffixes, since B and B:Φ are identical.

In *negative prosodic circumscription*, the morphological operation is applied to the residue of circumscription, the B\Φ portion, which is what remains when the mentioned constituent C is disregarded. Symmetrically with positive circumscription, we can define an operation circumscribed to apply to the residue:

(20) Operation applying under negative prosodic circumscription

$$O\backslash Φ \; [B] \quad =_{df} \quad B:Φ \; * \; O \; [B\backslash Φ]$$

This formalizes extrametricality. To apply operation O to base B *under extrametricality* is just to apply O to the residue of circumscription, B\Φ. For example, in the prototypical final-syllable extrametricality case of stress rules, a stress rule O applies to B\Φ <σ,R> – the base disregarding the final syllable. Exactly paralleling positive circumscription, the result of applying O to B\Φ stands concatenated with B:Φ in the same way as B\Φ concatenates with the kernel B:Φ in the original base B.

A common type of infixing reduplication requires negative circumscription of an *initial onsetless syllable*, one that starts with a vowel, rather than a consonant. An example of this comes from the Austronesian language Timugon Murut:

(21) Timugon Murut reduplication (Prentice 1971; McCarthy and Prince 1991a, 1993a, 1993b: ch. 7)

bulud	*bu*-bulud	'hill/ridge'
limo	*li*-limo	'five/about five'
ulampoy	u-*la*-lampoy	no gloss
abalan	a-*ba*-balan	'bathes/often bathes'
ompodon	om-*po*-podon	'flatter/always flatter'

The reduplicative template in Timugon Murut is a light syllable, σ_μ. It copies material of the base, minus an initial onsetless syllable, if any. We might therefore characterize it as PREFRED\Φ<σ_v, Left>, where σ_v is a temporary expedient for "onsetless syllable" and PREFRED stands for the operation of prefixing the reduplicative morpheme. Applied to the final example in (21), this schema yields the following result:

(22) Negative prosodic circumscription in Timugon Murut

PREFRED\Φ [ompodon]	=	*ompodon*:Φ	*	PREFRED	[*ompodon*\Φ]
	=	*om*	*	PREFRED	[*podon*]
	=	*om*	*	σ_μ-*podon*
	=	*om*	*	*po-podon*
	=	*ompopodon*

The morphological base *ompodon*, minus its initial syllable *om*, functions as the prosodically circumscribed base to which the operation of prefixing a σ_μ template applies. Crucially, it is the residue of circumscription, rather than the kernel, that is the target of the morphological operation. When the initial syllable has an onset, as in *bulud*, the kernel of circumscription is empty, and the entire base *bulud* is the residue to which the reduplicative template is prefixed.

Prosodic circumscription succeeds in unifying a wide range of phenomena that are sensitive to phonological subdomains, embracing under one theory operations that target a constituent, as in Ulwa, and those that exclude a constituent ("extrametricality"), as in Timugon Murut. The theory situates Prosodic Morphology within broader principles holding for all kinds of phonology and morphology, thereby addressing the fundamental explanatory goal of the enterprise. But Timugon Murut represents a kind of limiting case for prosodic circumscription theory (and, more generally, for its congener, extrametricality). Indeed, the limit appears to have been exceeded, for two reasons. First, the onsetless syllable, though granted the ad hoc symbolization σ_v, is not a legitimate prosodic constituent – on the contrary, it is a *defective* prosodic constituent. So its role in Timugon Murut circumscription contravenes principle (1c), which entails that recognized constituents be employed in circumscription criteria. Second, infixes with the same locus of placement as Timugon Murut are *always reduplicative*, to the best of our knowledge. Reduplicative infixes that go after an initial onsetless syllable are common and widespread, being found also in the Sanskrit aorist and desiderative (Kiparsky 1986, McCarthy and Prince 1986, Janda and Joseph 1986: 89), the Philippine Austronesian language Pangasinán (Benton 1971: 99, 117), and the non-Austronesian languages of Papua New Guinea Yareba (Weimer and Weimer 1970, 1975: 685), Orokaiva (Healey et al. 1969: 35–6), and Flamingo Bay Asmat (Voorhoeve 1965: 51). Ordinary, nonreduplicative infixes never show this distribution. There is an evident interaction: positioning an affix *after an initial onsetless syllable* is dependent upon the affix's being *templatic and reduplicative* rather than segmentally specified. Circumscription theory cannot explain this, because it formally divorces the placement of an affix from the structural nature of the affix. We now turn to work which aims to derive this kind of connection.

3 Recent developments

Much current work in Prosodic Morphology is set within Prince and Smolensky's (1993) Optimality Theory. Optimality Theory asserts that grammars consist of hierarchies of universal constraints that select among candidate output forms; constraint interaction is via this language-particular hierarchy, in which lower-ranking constraints are violated when violation leads to satisfaction of a higher-ranking constraint. Since the constraints are universal (up to the fixing of parameters inherent in the formulation of some constraints), the grammar of a particular language consists of a ranking of the universal constraint set.

The application of Optimality Theory to Prosodic Morphology can be illustrated with a small part of the reduplication system of Axininca Campa (Arawakan, Peru), drawn from the complete treatment in McCarthy and Prince (1993b: ch. 5). (For important earlier work on this system, see Payne 1981, Spring 1990, Black 1991.) The normal pattern in Axininca Campa is total root reduplication (23a), but, under particular phonological circumstances, more or less than the whole root may be reduplicated. In particular, when the root is vowel-initial and long (23b), its first syllable is not reduplicated.

(23) Reduplication of long unprefixed roots in Axininca Campa (Payne 1981, Spring 1990, McCarthy and Prince 1993b)
    (a) Consonant-initial long roots
        /kawosi/   kawosi-*kawosi*   'bathe'
        /koma/   koma-*koma*   'paddle'
        /tʰaaŋki/ tʰaaŋki-*tʰaaŋki* 'hurry'

    (b) Vowel-initial long roots
        /osampi/   osampi-*sampi*   'ask'   *osampi-*osampi*
        /osaŋkina/ osaŋkina-*saŋkina* 'write' *osaŋkina-*osaŋkina*

The constraint responsible for total reduplication of consonant-initial long roots like those cited in (23a) is MAX (McCarthy and Prince 1993b, 1994a, b):

(24) MAX
    Reduplicant = Base.

In total reduplication, there is no templatic requirement to be met (McCarthy and Prince 1986, 1988), so MAX is the sole determining factor. For a form like *kawosi*, MAX imposes a ranking on candidate reduplicants in which the exact copy *kawosi* itself stands at the top, ahead of all partial copies, such as *wosi* or *si*. The optimal candidate reduplicant is therefore *kawosi*. Undominated (and therefore unviolated), MAX will always yield total reduplication – maximal identity between base and reduplicant.

But MAX is crucially dominated in Axininca Campa, as shown by the incomplete reduplication of vowel-initial *osampi* or *osaŋkina* (23b). The reason for the failure of perfect copying in these forms lies with the constraint ONSET, which prohibits onsetless syllables:

(25)   ONSET (formulation from Itô 1989: 223)
     * [$_\sigma$V

Any candidate reduplicant that exactly copied a base shaped /V . . . V/ would have hiatus at the base-reduplicant boundary, violating ONSET, as in **osampi.osampi*. Therefore, the grammar of Axininca Campa must contain the ranking provision ONSET ≫ MAX, compelling less-than-full copying, but satisfying ONSET. The following tableau shows this:[12]

(26)   ONSET ≫ MAX, from /osaŋkina + redup./

	Candidates	ONSET	MAX
(a)	o.saŋkina-.*o.saŋkina*	** !	
(b) ☞	o.saŋkina- *saŋkina*	*	*

Other logical possibilities, such as epenthesis at the base-reduplicant juncture, are barred by additional constraints that are known independently to dominate MAX (see McCarthy and Prince 1993b: ch. 5). The point here is that the reduplicant need not violate ONSET, and in fact it doesn't, at the price of a MAX violation. Since MAX is lower ranking, failure on MAX – that is, partial reduplication – is irrelevant to deciding the outcome.

The same ONSET constraint can also be applied to the problem of Timugon Murut, signaled above in section 2, by recruiting an idea in Prince and Smolensky 1991, 1993. They propose that the prefixal or suffixal positioning of a morpheme can be conceived of as a violable constraint; and one possible way of violating such a constraint is infixation. For a case like Timugon Murut, where the infix is fundamentally a prefix, the constraint responsible is ALIGN-RED-L:

(27)   ALIGN-RED-L
     Align(RED, Left, Stem, Left)
     "The left edge of the reduplicative morpheme RED aligns with the left edge of the Stem."
     i.e. "The reduplicant stands initially, is a prefix."

The formalization comes from McCarthy and Prince (1993a), though details are not relevant here. The point is that obedience to ALIGN-RED-L ensures the absolute prefixal status of RED. However, disobedience can be compelled by higher-ranking constraints. Under general principles of Optimality Theory, any violation of ALIGN-RED-L must be minimal, so that RED will lie *as near as possible* to the initial word edge, given that it maximally satisfies any higher-ranking constraints.

The Timugon Murut reduplicative affix is prefixed to C-initial bases (*bu-bulud*) but infixed in V-initial bases (*om-po-podon*). Simple prefixation runs into problems with ONSET that infixation (i.e. violation of ALIGN-RED-L) success-fully avoids. Reduplicating *ompodon* as **o.ompodon* is syllabically less harmonic than reduplicating it as *om.po.podon* because **o.ompodon* duplicates an ONSET violation.

Formally, this means that ONSET forces violation of ALIGN-RED-L; in terms of ranking, ONSET dominates ALIGN-RED-L in the grammar of Timugon Murut:

(28)   ONSET ≫ ALIGN-RED-L, from /redup. +ompodon/

	Candidates	ONSET	ALIGN-RED-L
(a)	| *o*.om.po.don	** !	
(b)	| *om*.om.po.don	** !	
(c) ☞	| om.*po*.po.don	*	*
(d)	| om.po.*do*.don	*	** !

Ill-alignment (= infixation) spares an ONSET violation. With the ranking ONSET ≫ ALIGN-RED-L, the unaligned *om-po-podon* is optimal. By contrast, in C-initial forms like *bu-bulud*, ONSET is obeyed by even the properly aligned candidate, so infixation is unnecessary – and therefore impossible, since it would involve gratuitous violation of ALIGN-RED-L.[13]

Recall that this infixal locus is observed only with *reduplicative* affixes, and never with segmentally specified (i.e. nonreduplicative) affixes. The proposal here explains why: reduplicating the initial onsetless syllable of *ompodon* would copy the ONSET violation. With segmentally specified affixes, regardless of their shape, the circumstances are different, since they cannot duplicate a violation of ONSET. (For formal analysis, see McCarthy and Prince 1993b: ch. 7.)

This result answers the two objections against a circumscriptional treatment of Timugon Murut raised at the end of section 2. There is no problem here of referring to the onsetless syllable as a type of (defective) prosodic constituent. Rather, the distribution of the infix is determined by the high rank of the con-straint ONSET, an uncontroversial part of the universal theory of the syllable. Equally significantly, the fact that only reduplicative infixes are observed with this distribution is no longer mysterious, but rather follows from the con-straint interaction responsible for this type of infixation.

We have just suggested how Prosodic Morphology within Optimality Theory can provide the first steps toward a real theory of infixability, predicting both what kind of morpheme shapes can be infixed at all and where they can lodge in their hosts. It also sheds further light on the theory of templates, sharpening and extending the predictions made by the Prosodic Morphology Hypothesis (1a). We will focus on the MinWd template, improving on the analysis of Diyari sketched in section 2.

The question raised by Diyari and similar cases is *why* the minimal word should be a possible reduplicative template. Linguistic theory ought to provide more than a heterogeneous list of the reduplicative templates that happen to be observed in various languages. The goal here is to explain why the Diyari reduplicant is identical to the minimal word of the language, without invoking the notion of minimality, or perhaps the notion of *template*. If the argument is successful, the minimality property will be shown to follow from the interaction of the universal constraints on prosodic form, whose status is quite independent of any phenomena of prosodic morphology.

To accomplish this goal, we require some background about a particular aspect of prosodic theory as developed within Optimality Theory (Kirchner 1993, McCarthy and Prince 1993a). The stress pattern of Diyari, illustrated in (29), pairs up syllables into feet from left to right:[14]

(29)   Diyari stress (Poser 1982, 1989)
      (káṇa)   'man'
      (pína)du   'old man'
      (ṇánda)(wàlka) 'to close'

The following constraints are responsible for this stress pattern:

(30)   ALL-FT-LEFT
      Align(Ft, L, PrWd, L)
      "The left edge of every foot aligns with the left edge of some PrWd."
      = "Every foot is initial in the PrWd."

(31)   PARSE-SYLL
      Every syllable belongs to a foot.

With the ranking PARSE-SYLL ≫ ALL-FT-LEFT, the pattern of directional footing observed in Diyari is obtained. According to ALL-FT-LEFT, all feet should be *exactly at* the left edge. This constraint is satisfied when there is just one foot in the entire word. In partial contradiction, the constraint PARSE-SYLL requires that every form be fully footed, demanding multiple feet in longer words.[15] Thus, ALL-FT-LEFT will never be completely satisfied in words longer than three syllables, which will have more than one foot. But under minimal violation of ALL-FT-LEFT, a multifoot form must have its feet *as close to* the beginning of the word as possible. This is the foot-placement effect attributed to left–right directionality.[16]

In a quinquesyllabic form (σσ)(σσ)σ, both PARSE-SYLL and ALL-FT-LEFT are violated. PARSE-SYLL is violated because there is always an unparsed syllable in odd-parity words, because Foot Binarity is undominated. ALL-FT-LEFT is violated because the non-initial foot is misaligned. (See McCarthy and Prince 1993a, elaborating on the proposal of Kirchner 1993, for further development.)

Observe that these constraints are often violated, but are nevertheless consequential even when violated. Both constraints can, however, be obeyed fully. In that case,

Every syllable is footed (PARSE-SYLL is obeyed)
and
Every foot is initial (ALL-FT-LEFT is obeyed).

Only one configuration meets both of these requirements, the minimal word, since it has a single foot that parses all syllables and is itself properly left-aligned:

$[Ft]_{PrWd}$ i.e. $[(\sigma\ \sigma)_{Ft}]_{PrWd}$ *or* $[(\mu\ \mu)_{Ft}]_{PrWd}$

Thus, the minimal word is the most harmonic prosodic word possible, with respect to PARSE-SYLL and ALL-FT-LEFT – indeed, with respect to every form of Ft/PrWd alignment. Of course, the single foot contained within the minimal word is optimally binary, because of FT-BIN. Hence, the most harmonic prosodic word, with respect to these metrical constraints, is a disyllable in any language that does not make syllable-weight distinctions.

Diyari is such a language. Recall that the reduplicant is a free-standing PrWd, as evidenced by its stress behavior and vowel-final status. This is, in fact, *all* that needs to be said about the Diyari reduplicant:

(32)   Templatic constraint
        $R = PrWd$
        "The reduplicant is a prosodic word."

There is no mention of the "minimal word" in this *or in any other* templatic requirement. Rather, minimalization follows from the ranking of PARSE-SYLL and ALL-FT-LEFT, in particular from their domination of MAX, the reduplicative constraint that demands total copy. If the base of reduplication is greater than a minimal word, the reduplicant will contain a less-than-complete copy, violating MAX but obeying high-ranking PARSE-SYLL and ALIGN-FT.

Consider, first, MAX violation under domination by PARSE-SYLL:

(33)   PARSE-SYLL $\gg$ MAX, from /RED + tʲilparku/

		PARSE-SYLL	MAX
(a) ☞	$[(t^{j}ilpa)_{Ft}]_{PrWd} - [(t^{j}ilpar)_{Ft}\ ku]_{PrWd}$	*	***
(b)	$[(t^{j}ilpar)_{Ft}\ ku]_{PrWd} - [(t^{j}ilpar)_{Ft}\ ku]_{PrWd}$	** !	

Form (b) is a perfect copy, as indicated by its success on MAX. But success on MAX is purchased at the intolerable cost of a gratuitous PARSE-SYLL violation. Less-than-full copying is available that avoids this unparsed syllable, and given the dominance of PARSE-SYLL, this is more harmonic, as (a) shows.

The "minimalization" of the reduplicant follows from this ranking. Other seemingly plausible candidates fare no better against (a). Consider these, for example, which violate undominated constraints:

[(t^jil)]-[(t^{j}ilpar)ku]	:	violates Foot Binarity
[(t^jilpar)]-[(t^{j}ilpar)(ku)]	:	violates the requirement, unviolated in Diyari, that all PrWds are V-final.
[(t^jil-t^{j}il)(parku)]	:	violates the constraint R = PrWd.
[(t^jilpar)(ku-t^{j}il)(parku)]	:	violates the constraint R = PRWD.
[t^jil]-[(t^{j}ilpar)ku]	:	contains a footless PrWd, an impossibility under the Prosodic Hierarchy.

The failure of these candidates ensures the validity of the ranking argument just given.

A parallel ranking argument can be constructed for ALL-FT-LEFT and MAX, using a quadrisyllabic root as input. (Unfortunately, no reduplicated quadrisyllables are cited by Austin, so this example is hypothetical.)

(34)   ALL-FT-LEFT ≫ MAX, from (hypothetical) /RED + ŋandawalka/

		ALL-FT-LEFT	MAX
(a) ☞	[(ŋanda)$_{Ft}$]$_{PrWd}$ – [(ŋanda)$_{Ft}$ (walka)$_{Ft}$]$_{PrWd}$	*	*****
(b)	[(ŋanda)$_{Ft}$ (walka)$_{Ft}$]$_{PrWd}$ – [(ŋanda)$_{Ft}$ (walka)$_{Ft}$]$_{PrWd}$	** !	

In (b), the reduplicant fatally violates ALL-FT-LEFT, since it contains an unaligned foot, while (a) avoids that violation by less-than-full copying. Another failed candidate, *(ŋanda)wa-(ŋanda)(walka), incurs a fatal violation of PARSE-SYLL, which also dominates MAX, as was just demonstrated.

Both ALL-FT-LEFT and PARSE-SYLL are fully obeyed by the reduplicant, and this explains why it is minimal-word-sized. There is no need for a minimal-word template; rather, the templatic requirement is simply the prosodic word, with "minimalization" obtained from constraint interaction, via the ranking PARSE-SYLL, ALL-FT-LEFT ≫ MAX.

The success of the accounts of both the Timugon Murut and Diyari examples is inextricably linked with the Optimality-Theoretic principles of constraint ranking and violation. In Timugon Murut, low-ranking ALIGN-RED-L is violated under the compulsion of ONSET. Nonetheless, violation is minimal, as usual in Optimality Theory. More remarkably, even ONSET itself is violated in this language, not only word-initially (*ulampoy, ompodon*) but also medially:

(35)   ONSET violation in Timugon Murut

ambilú.o	'soul'	"two distinct phonetic syllables" (Prentice 1971: 24)
nansú.i	'slanting'	"both vowels are syllabic" (ibid.: 25).
lógo.i	'the price'	"two phonetic syllables" (ibid.)

ONSET is violated when obeying it would run afoul not of RED/Stem alignment, but of *faithfulness* to the underlying segmentism. That is, satisfaction of ONSET cannot be bought at the price of deleting or inserting segments, because faithfulness constraints dominate ONSET. (For various approaches to formalizing these faithfulness constraints, see Prince and Smolensky 1993 and McCarthy and Prince 1994a, b.)

Faithfulness likewise plays a role in Diyari. In contrast to the reduplicant, ordinary stems of Diyari (including the base of reduplication), may violate PARSE-SYLL and/or ALL-FT-LEFT. The reason for this is that ordinary stems must honor the commitment to their underlying segmentism: that is, faithfulness constraints, which require that all input segments be realized in the output, crucially dominate the responsible metrical constraints PARSE-SYLL and ALL-FT-LEFT.

In Optimality Theory, a form is marked with respect to some constraint if it violates it; hence, the universal constraints embody a theory of markedness (Prince and Smolensky 1993, Smolensky 1993). In particular, the constraints ONSET, PARSE-SYLL, and ALL-FT-LEFT constitute part of a theory of prosodic markedness. In both Timugon Murut and Diyari, these constraints stand in the middle of a hierarchy Faithfulness ≫ "Prosodic Markedness" ≫ X. They are crucially dominated by Faithfulness, as shown by the fact that they are freely violated when respecting the input is at stake. Yet they themselves dominate X, a constraint of *morphological* markedness, like ALIGN-RED-L or MAX, that demands a particular structure under morphological conditions. Given this ranking, X must be violated whenever it is possible to achieve a phonologically less marked structure, even though that less marked structure is not consistently observed in the language as a whole. This result, dubbed "emergence of the unmarked" by McCarthy and Prince (1994a), is fundamental to Optimality Theory, since it derives from the theory's intrinsic conception of constraint ranking and its role in linguistic typology.

4 Prospects

As research in Prosodic Morphology proceeds to explore connections between its phenomena and the general principles of phonology and morphology, we expect to find a continuing diminution of dependence on parochial assumptions, and correspondingly greater reliance on independent principles of form, perhaps within the context of Optimality Theory. We will highlight two prospects here.

Under Optimality Theory, where grammars are rankings of interacting constraints, ranking must also be the proper way to characterize phenomena like those studied in Prosodic Morphology. The hypothesis is that all of Prosodic Morphology should be understood in terms of a general ranking schema: "P dominates M" (P ≫ M), where P stands for some prosodic constraint, and M stands for some morphological one (McCarthy and Prince 1993b). To para-phrase, in the analysis of prosodic-morphological phenomena, some phono-logical constraint must dominate some morphological constraint, forcing it to be violated minimally.

The ranking required in Axininca Campa and Timugon Murut conforms to this P ≫ M schema: the P-constraint ONSET dominates the M-constraints MAX and ALIGN-RED-L (respectively), which pertain to the exactness of reduplicative copying and the positioning of the affix with respect to the Stem. Likewise in Diyari, the P-constraints PARSE-SYLL and ALL-FT-LEFT crucially dominate the M-constraint MAX. Interesting questions arise about the full range of P- and M-constraints that may be subsumed under this schema.

Another matter rendered ripe for rethinking is the status of templates in Prosodic Morphology. A striking feature of the analysis of Diyari in section 3 is the relatively minor role played by the template. Instead of stipulating that the template is a foot or minimal word, it is sufficient to say that the reduplic-ant is a prosodic word; other properties of the Diyari reduplicant follow from appropriate ranking of the (quite independent) metrical constraints that specify the character of the most harmonic prosodic word.

It is possible to go still further in reducing the role of templates in Diyari and similar cases (McCarthy and Prince 1994b). The morphological category Stem has a characteristic congeries of phonological properties; in particular, the most harmonic Stem is one that is analyzed as a prosodic word, and appro-priate rankable constraints demand this.[17] We can therefore say that the Diyari reduplicant is a Stem, so the reduplicative formation is a Stem–Stem compound. This is sufficient, with no loss of descriptive accuracy, since the reduplicant's status as a prosodic word – and a minimal prosodic word to boot – will follow from appropriate ranking of the constraints that define the harmony of Stems and prosodic words.

There is, then, no template at all in Diyari or, by extension, in any other case of a minimal-word reduplicant. Rather, the only stipulation in the grammar is that the reduplicative morpheme *is a Stem*. Such a declaration must be present in the lexicon at any rate, regardless of Prosodic Morphology, since it is neces-sary, on most theories of morphology, to specify the morphological status or level of each morpheme.

Pressing the hypothesis to its logical conclusion, we might say that smaller reduplicative morphemes, like the Ilokano examples in (6) and (8), are of the morphological category Affix, looking to independent prosodic properties of Affixes to account for their phonology. If this is successful, then all that is left of the reduplicative "template" is an irreducible minimum of morphological specification – no more than would be required for any morpheme – with the apparatus that is specific to reduplication or Prosodic Morphology essentially eliminated.

NOTES

1 Earlier proposals for including prosody in templatic morphology in various ways include Archangeli 1983, 1984; Broselow and McCarthy 1983; J. Levin 1983; Lowenstamm and Kaye 1986; Marantz 1982; McCarthy 1979, 1981, 1984a, b; Nash 1986: 139; and Yip 1982, 1983. Prosodic Morphology extends this approach to the claim that *only* prosody may play this role, and that the role includes circumscription as well.

2 Treatments of reduplication within Prosodic Morphology include Aronoff et al. 1987; Bagemihl 1991; Bates and Carlson 1992; Black 1993; Chiang 1992; Cole 1991; Crowhurst 1991a, b; Finer 1985; Goodman 1994; Hewitt and Prince 1989; Hill and Zepeda 1992; Kroeger 1989a, b; C. Levelt 1990; McNally 1990; Mutaka and Hyman 1990; Nivens 1992; Noske 1991; Schlindwein 1988, 1991; Shaw 1987, 1992; Spring 1990; Steriade 1988b; Stonham 1990; Weeda 1987; J. Williams 1991; Yin 1989; Yip 1991, 1992.

3 Satisfaction of the $\sigma_{\mu\mu}$ template in Ilokano principally involves MAX and related constraints discussed below in section 3. Particular cases in which the copying is less complete than it could be show the intervention of Ilokano-specific requirements. Words like *ro?ot* reduplicate as *ro:-ro?ot*, rather than **ro?-ro?ot*, because Ilokano bans syllable-final glottal stop. By a further peculiarity of Ilokano, word-final consonants cannot be copied, so forms like *trak* or *nars* 'nurse' also reduplicate with a long vowel.

4 The complexities of the system are extensively explored in Kager 1993; Hayes 1995; Hewitt 1992, 1994; Leer 1985a, b; Rice 1988; A. Woodbury 1987; and others.

5 The bimoraic minimum is clearly evidenced in English by the impossibility of light monosyllables, like [tə] or [ə], except as prosodically dependent function words. The monosyllable minimum is also seen in the system of irregular verbs, all uniformly monosyllabic modulo prefixes (or pseudo-prefixes, as in *believe*). If, indeed, monosyllabicity is an output constraint on the past-tense forms of irregulars, then the lack of -*əd* endings is explained (both -*d* and -*t* are used: *told, lost*). See Pinker and Prince 1988 for recent discussion. Spring 1990, McCarthy and Prince 1991a, b, Black 1993, and Hewitt 1994 deal with some of the issues surrounding subtypes of prosodic minimality.

6 The unsuffixed forms are themselves also subject to additional limitations on their final clusters: **And < Andrew, *Christ < Christine, *Naft < Naftali, *Alb < Albert, *Ald < Aldo*. Contrast *Mort, Walt, Barb*, etc. Evidently, certain consonant sequences are banned, by a restriction that must be imposed after suffixation, since *Andy*, etc., are acceptable. (The markedness of the illicit sequences is evidenced by their inclination to simplify, in English and elsewhere.) Interestingly, certain clusters can appear before -*ie* that are generally banned in the language: *Pengie < Penguin* [attested], *Ambie < Ambrose*

[constructed]. The clusters *ŋg* and *mb* must be admitted by the monosyllable restriction, which therefore refers to general sonority considerations, but they are then disallowed by other constraints of the language, which apply to e.g. [æmb] but not [æmbi]. In short, the monosyllable restriction is a necessary condition on both suffixed and unsuffixed forms, completely eliminating all postvocalic clusters of rising sonority; additional restrictions eliminate other 'marked' clusters of falling sonority from syllable-final position on the surface (Borowsky 1986). For further discussion of this interesting nexus of facts, see McCarthy and Prince 1991a.

7   It is also always possible to attach the hypocoristic suffix *-čan* to the entire original name: hence, *midori-čan*, with three moras in the base; *wasaburoo-čan*, with five. In this case, no prosodic template is at work, and no restriction falls on the base. All short forms invoke the template: contrast licit *wasaburo- < wasaburoo* with illicit **taizo- < taizoo*.

8   References include, for the Afro-Asiatic family: McCarthy 1979, 1981, McCarthy and Prince 1990b, Bat-El 1989, Dell and Elmedlaoui 1992, Hayward 1988, Lowenstamm and Kaye 1986; for Miwok: Freeland 1951, Broadbent 1964, Crowhurst 1991b, Lamontagne 1989, Sloan 1991, N. Smith 1985, 1986, Smith and Hermans 1982; for Yokuts: Newman 1944, Archangeli 1983, 1984, 1991; for Takelma: Sapir 1922, Goodman 1988, B. Lee 1991.

9   *Canonical* nouns are those that are truly integrated into the morphological system, based on their ability to form broken plurals and other criteria. The vast majority

of nouns in Arabic are canonical, but many (such as recent loans like *tilifuun* 'telephone') are not.

10   Some aspects of this approach to formalizing the theory of prosodic specification are influenced by Hoeksema's (1985) notion of a "head operation." Compare also the developments in Aronoff 1988.

11   Alternatively, we might see the target of circumscription in Ulwa as the *head* foot, rather than the leftmost one, allowing the parsing function Φ to refer to the hierarchical notion *head* rather than, or in addition to, left and right edges. This idea is pursued, within an Optimality-Theoretic account, in McCarthy and Prince 1993b: ch. 7).

12   This table observes certain notational conventions: constraints are written (left to right) in their domination order, violations are marked by "*", and crucial violations are also called out by "!." Shading emphasizes the *irrelevance* of the constraint to the fate of the candidate. A loser's cells are shaded after a crucial violation, the winner's when there are no more competitors.

13   Notice that deeper infixation, as in **ompo-do-don*, fares no better on ONSET and even worse on ALIGN-RED-L, so it cannot be optimal. A complete account of the system requires consideration of various other candidates, in which the problem with ONSET is resolved by other means: e.g. deletion or epenthesis. A particularly interesting candidate is the purely prefixal **o.m-om.po.don*, where the reduplicant straddles a syllable boundary. Here the templatic requirement on the reduplicant – that it constitute a syllable – is not met, indicating the dominance of the templatic constraint. For

discussion, see McCarthy and Prince 1993b: ch. 7.

14 Complications arise in polymorphemic words – see Poser 1989.

15 In Diyari, as in many languages, PARSE-SYLL is subject to Foot Binarity (5), which forbids the construction of degenerate feet. FTBIN therefore dominates PARSE-SYLL in Diyari, preventing the complete footing of odd-syllabled words. Indeed, FTBIN is unviolated in the language (except for *ya* 'and'), and therefore undominated.

16 In right-to-left footing, ALL-FT-RIGHT, the symmetric counterpart of ALL-FT-LEFT, is the active constraint.

17 A nearby case is the phonology of Stems with "Level II" affixes in English.

15   Word Syntax

JINDŘICH TOMAN

Introduction

Leafing through older literature on generative grammar, one soon notes that the 1970s mark a beginning of an intensive discussion of word structure in that framework. This was, by and large, for the following reasons. First, Chomsky (1970) argued in the influential "Remarks on nominalization" that word-formation facts cannot be accounted for by means of transformational rules as had until then been assumed. Instead, he suggested, a lexical approach was appropriate, where the term *lexical* essentially means that complex words (such as those formed with derivational affixes) are accounted for in the so-called lexical component of the grammar ("Lexicalism") – in any case not in the syntax. Second, a fundamental theoretical reorientation was beginning to exert its effect in the 1970s, amounting to what can be described briefly as a move from rules to principles. This philosophy of research, in many ways shaping up as early as the 1960s (cf. Ross's 1967 thesis), began to regard grammatical constructions (e.g. passive) as resulting from the interaction of simple elementary principles, rather than as a product of construction-specific rules (e.g. a passive transformation). This approach has guided the development of generative theories to the present day.

Both of these trends, Lexicalism and the abandonment of a construction-oriented transformational grammar, had a perceptible influence on a number of studies, mostly from the early 1980s, that aimed at explaining properties of words by recourse to general grammatical principles rather than word-formation rules. Among them a distinct group of investigations emerged, including Lieber 1980, 1983; Moortgat et al. 1981; Selkirk 1982; Toman 1983; E. Williams 1981a, b; and others. It seems fair to say that Elisabeth Selkirk's (1982) monograph *The Syntax of Words* and a series of articles by Edwin Williams (including his 1981a, b) became the most representative examples of this approach. The interest in this defined perspective continued well into the

1980s and beyond, as witnessed, among others, by *On the definition of word*, a monograph by Anna Maria Di Sciullo and Edwin Williams (1987), and *Deconstructing morphology* by Rochelle Lieber (1992). Alternative approaches to morphology also emerged, mainly in the work of Mark Baker (1988a); despite differences, however, Baker continues the word-syntactic tradition by relying on headed tree structures and employing percolation conventions (see below). In the present chapter, I will review the main tenets of the theory of word syntax that was emerging in the period described. For reasons of space the survey must remain highly selective. I will turn to basic issues only, but will, at a few places, include critical discussion. Inconclusive as this discussion often may be, it should draw the reader's attention to the strategies and possibilities that inhere in the framework presented here. Borer, MORPHOLOGY AND SYNTAX, also discusses some of these trends, from a slightly different viewpoint.

1 Word syntax as a theory of word competence

As pointed out, Chomsky (1970) prompted an increased interest in questions of morphology in generative grammar, and a number of competing concepts of the lexicon emerged as a result. Two basic variants can be noted: one regards the lexicon as nothing more than a list – be it a list of morphemes, or of all nonderived words, or even of all actually occurring words of the given language. Alternatively, the lexicon can be seen as a component which hosts not only lists, but also rules that actually produce words; in this conception the lexicon emerges as an "active" component of the grammar. Most of these approaches claim the label "Lexicalism" for themselves, and, indeed, since Chomsky (1970), a popular opinion, bordering on value-judgement, has emerged, that sees Lexicalism as superior to any other theory that does not explicitly consider the existence of the lexicon (or a lexical component) in the grammar.

In some sense, however, the focus on the lexicon leads away from the classical question of generative theories. In generative syntax, for instance, the declared aim has been a principled representation of the (human) linguistic faculty rather than the study of lists. In view of this, it seems appropriate to recall that some researchers have argued that the lexicon itself is not the primary focus of morphological, or word-formation, theories, especially if understood as a real-time object. Of course, the "real-time" lexicon (Di Sciullo and Williams's (1987) "psychological lexicon") remains a legitimate object of inquiry, as witnessed by numerous psycholinguistic studies; but one cannot presume that list-based mechanisms of storage and retrieval are the basic mechanisms of the human "word-faculty." Discussing this issue, Di Sciullo and Williams have suggested:

> Morphology is more like syntax than heretofore thought. Both of course have
> lists – the list of primes, which are the words in syntax and the morphemes
> in morphology. In syntax there is of course no further list of "actual" versus
> "potential" phrases; the whole theory is about potential objects, though some
> are in fact actual (*How are you, kick the bucket*). In our view *morphology is a the-*
> *ory of potential objects in exactly the same sense.* (Di Sciullo and Williams 1987: 21;
> emphasis added)

Rephrasing this point of view, one can say that a generative theory of word
structure is in the first place a theory of the human word-forming capacity.
Obviously, this approach frees up the investigator to study principles that
govern "the ability to create and understand new words" (Toman 1983: 6)
rather than stick to superficial differences in the material nature of the data
investigated.

2 The internal syntax of words

2.1 Phrase structure morphology

The insight that words can be broken down into subconstituents is probably
as old as the study of words itself. For instance, in the descriptive practice of
American structuralists of the 1940s and 1950s, immediate constituent analysis
proceeded unimpeded right into words. A major step in the understanding of
word structure in early word-syntactic theories has been the apparently triv-
ial idea that word structure can be represented by means of phrase-structure
rules. This "phrase structure morphology," to use D. G. Miller's (1993) term,
stands in contrast to a number of studies characteristic of the classical Lexicalist
period which attempted to make the so-called lexical rules radically dissimilar
from those of syntax. Jackendoff (1975), for instance, developed so-called lexical redundancy rules that were supposed to work in a dual way to actively
create new words and passively assess the cost of irregular formations in the
lexicon. These rules were only minimally concerned with the internal structure of derived words. But Jackendoff himself nearly abandoned this approach
as he was introducing it. In the conclusions to his 1975 article, in which he was
arguing for lexical redundancy rules *sui generis*, he suggested that phrase structure rules are a perfectly viable alternative to morphological redundancy rules
(Jackendoff 1975: 668).

A data domain in which this "tree"-oriented approach has been applied
with notable success is compounding in languages such as English, German,
and the like. Thus Selkirk discusses at length how context-free rewriting rules
should be modified in order to generate English compounds. Following is one
of the variants of her rules for English compounds (Selkirk 1982: 16):

(1)

$$N \rightarrow \left\{ \begin{array}{c} N \\ A \\ V \\ P \end{array} \right\} N \quad \begin{array}{l} \text{mill wheel} \\ \text{smallpox} \\ \text{rattle snake} \\ \text{overdose} \end{array}$$

$$A \rightarrow \left\{ \begin{array}{c} N \\ A \\ P \end{array} \right\} A \quad \begin{array}{l} \text{nationwide} \\ \text{icy cold} \\ \text{underripe} \end{array}$$

$$V \rightarrow P \quad V \quad \text{overdo}$$

Leaving questions of detail aside, we note that this is a simple list of language-particular rules. Among other things, the list is so designed as not to generate structures such as [PP] or [VV]: that is, compound prepositions and compound verbs. This is accomplished by simply stipulating that the requisite rules are not included in the list. While this approach appears to be descriptively correct, a move to a principled analysis is not yet visible – the question of why the English compounding system shows the gaps it shows is not addressed.

Speculating about alternatives, we note that the flavor of arbitrariness inherent in such lists as (1) can be removed by allowing overgeneration and explaining the nonoccurring products by recourse to independent principles. In other words, rather than stating particular rules, we may generalize the above list of rules to a schema such as:

(2) $X \rightarrow YZ$

where X, Y, and Z stand for category variables, and try to explain the non-occurrence of overgenerated forms by recourse to independently motivated principles. Some of such explanations will presumably be universal; some, however, will remain language-particular. We note, for instance, that in Slavic languages compounding is generally not very popular, yet certain subtypes are surprisingly productive. In other words, if a schema such as (2) is assumed for Slavic languages, the burden of explanation actually consists in explaining away the nonexistence of most of its outputs. Although this strategy is in principle straightforward, work of this type has in general been rare, and there is still little understanding even of such basic questions as why certain language types have very productive compounding systems, while others do not.

While word syntax may have benefited initially from thinking about word structure in terms of phrase-structure rules, major progress has consisted in an assimilation of phrase-structure rules for words to the general theory of phrasal architectonics generally known as X-bar theory. (The above suggestion to generalize a list of phrase-structure rules to a structural schema such as (2) is in fact a rudimentary attempt to apply X-bar theory to the structure of words.) A crucial element of X-bar theory is the principle according to which phrases are either uniquely headed, or, perhaps in a special case (such as word-internal coordination – see below), have a level structure. An early version of the principle of headedness for English words (then labeled as a rule) is Williams's:

(3)   Right-hand Head Rule (RHR)
      In morphology we define the head of a morphologically complex word to be the right-hand member of that word. (E. Williams 1981b: 248)

The principle remains domain-specific, though, in that it holds only in morphological structures. One may argue, however, that the problem is just a matter of a historical coincidence, in that the Right-hand Head Rule merely reflects the state of research in syntax prevalent at the point it was proposed. Recall, among other things, that early variants of X-bar theory accepted ternary and higher branching. However, with an X-bar theory in place that permits binary branching only, one can in fact use the left–right distinction – that is, a positional definition of head – in both syntax and word syntax. Naturally, important questions remain: among others, whether binary branching is a primitive or a property to be explained. In the domain of maximal projections – that is, syntax proper – Kayne has suggested that binarity falls out from a principle that is independently needed to determine antecedent–anaphor relations uniquely (Unambiguous Path Principle, Kayne 1984). In word syntax, we may speculate, binarity might also be a consequence of higher-order principles which perhaps do not even have to be typologically comparable to principles like the Unambiguous Path Principle. Note, for instance, that a great number of derivational suffixes can be viewed as operators (functors) that operate on a single domain to form a (derived) single domain upon which another functor can operate. Thus the distinction operator/operans seems to imply binarity to start with.

Other definitions of headedness have been suggested in the word-syntax literature:

(4)   In a word-internal configuration,

      where X stands for a syntactic feature complex, and Q contains no category with the feature complex X, X^m is the head of X^n. (Selkirk 1982: 20)

This, too, is a domain-specific definition proposed largely under the "pressure of facts," mainly the existence of particle verbs in English. Assuming *put up* to be a single unit, (3) identifies *up* as the head, implying that the whole unit is a particle. By contrast, (4) prevents this incorrect conclusion. But again, Selkirk's modification can be evaluated only vis-à-vis a particular analysis of particle verbs, not against unanalyzed facts. That *put up* is a simple word structure is far from clear; for instance, if we accept the analysis of verb–particle combinations in terms of small clauses, the apparently simple verb–particle concatenation will receive a more complex analysis, and it is not clear whether a modification such as (4) will retain its force on an alternative analysis. At any rate, the modified version does not comply with the binarity principle, and seems to hard generalize beyond word syntax.

2.1.1 Uniquely headed structures   Proceeding to other cases, we recall that Germanic compounding has proved to be particularly successful in demonstrating the headedness of words. Thus German *Winternacht* 'winter night', a compound based on *Winter* 'winter' and *Nacht* 'night', is right-headed. This is demonstrated by the fact that the head subconstituent determines the gender of the entire compound (see below for additional discussion). Accordingly, NP-internal concord shows feminine morphology, since it takes *Nacht* (feminine), not *Winter* (masculine), as a point of reference:

(5) (a) eine   stürmische   Winternacht
          'a   stormy   winter night'

     (b) *ein   stürmischer   Winternacht

Moreover, there is a semantic intuition that associates the head with a certain kind of reference. Under the set/subset perspective, a winter night is a kind of night rather than a kind of winter. This semantic intuition may not always be reliable, though, and thus cannot be the exclusive basis of a formal definition. For instance, the intuition as to whether the German derogative compound *Kommunistenschwein* 'Commie pig' denotes a subset of pigs is hazy – I would suggest, rather, the possibility that *Schwein* 'pig' is an epithet of sorts, and that the compound actually denotes a subset of Communists. But whatever semantic subtleties might be involved, morphological data reveal more. Taking NP-internal concord into consideration again, we observe that the adjective agrees in gender with the neuter noun *Schwein*, not with the masculine *Kommunist* in the following constructed examples:

(6) (a) ein   häßliches   Kommunistenschwein
          an (neuter)   ugly (neuter)   Commie-pig (neuter)

     (b) *ein   häßlicher   Kommunistenschwein
          an (masc.)   ugly (masc.)   Commie-pig (neuter)

This is expected under the standard assumptions about headedness of German compounds.

Given the relative success of word syntax in the domain of compounding, it is not altogether surprising that among the strategies pursued in word syntax has been an assimilation of suffixal derivation to compounding. In general, word-syntactic analyses regard what have traditionally been termed "derivational affixes" as bound tokens of parts of speech they in turn derive. Thus *-er* in German *Les-er* 'reader', *-ness* in English *empti-ness*, etc., are essentially interpreted as bound nouns occupying the head position of a complex noun. The reasoning is that it is these elements which provide the relevant morphological properties (Lieber's (1992) categorial signature – see below) of the complex words they appear in. Thus in *Les-er*, the base is a verbal root, but the entire structure is a masculine noun; it is thus reasonable to conclude that the suffix apparently has the relevant nominal features – that is, that it acts as a noun.

While not differing from other, perhaps more prototypical, nouns in having the categorial label "noun", derivational suffixes differ in other respects, though. For instance, their lexical entries include specific subcategorization frames:

(7)   *er*, [V^0 ____]N
       ness, [A^0 ____]N

Suffixes may in addition carry morphophonemic information: for example, about ablaut, accentuation, and other similar properties.

Early work in word syntax, such as Selkirk 1982, was hesitant about analyzing inflectional suffixes as heads. To be sure, the semantic intuitions about headedness discussed above in connection with compounds like *Winternacht* break down when forms such as *hous-es* or *(they) work-ed* are tested. Clearly, the absence of a natural intuition along set/subset lines in these cases is an interesting cognitive fact in and of itself. However, more recent generative studies of the role and structure of so-called functional categories have removed some of the barriers to regarding inflectional suffixes as heads. Staying with verbal forms, we note that they are derived by incorporating the verbal root into the functional head carrying inflectional features by so-called head-to-head movement. In this system (inspired by Pollock 1989) inflected words are thus created in syntax by movement. Outside generative grammar, however, the idea that inflectional formatives are heads remains controversial.

2.1.2 Level structures (coordination)   It is interesting to note that besides the X-bar schema for uniquely headed structures (cf. (2)) the X-bar schema for coordinate structures is also instantiated in word-syntactic structures, although with severe restrictions (cf. Toman 1985). Turning to German again, we observe the following grammaticality judgments:

(8)   schwarz-weißer   Hintergrund
       'black-white   background'

The meaning is that the background is black and white. Among the points to be explained is why only *and* readings are acceptable in such structures; coordinate compounds comparable to disjunctive or negated phrasal coordinations like *black or white*, *neither black nor white*, do not seem to exist.

Other questions arise also. Observing compounds such as:

(9) Kind-Mutter-Beziehung
     'child–mother relationship'

note that the "coordinate subcompound" *Kind-Mutter* is distributable only in the nonhead position of the compound. In other words, the following form cannot appear as a freely distributable compound:

(10) *Mutter-Kind
      'mother-child' (on the attempted reading "mother and child")

By contrast, such compounds are quite acceptable in languages such as Sanskrit and a number of contemporary languages of the Indian subcontinent (cf. Fabb, COMPOUNDING). It is not clear why languages show such restrictions.

3 Operations on base-generated word structure

Once we accept the idea that word structure can be related in a principled manner to the structure of phrases in general, it is natural to ask whether other principles of grammar apply to word structure, or whether word structure remains in some sense autonomous. Below, I will discuss three subtheories that shed some light on this issue. First, I will review word-syntactic literature on percolation, a mechanism claimed to be specific to word syntax. I will speculate on whether percolation could be understood as a general, domain-independent mechanism. Subsequently, I will discuss two subtheories of generative grammar, Case theory and Theta theory, both of which were designed independently of word syntax. I will be mostly interested in whether they also apply to word structure. The reader is referred to other sources for complementary information (D. G. Miller 1993, in particular, contains a discussion structured along similar lines to mine; Lieber 1992 discusses the validity of the theory of Binding in word syntax; and Spencer 1991 discusses questions of argument structure in complex words extensively).

3.1 Percolation

Continuing the discussion of examples such as *Leser* 'reader' from a slightly different angle, we recall that in German the suffix *-er*, traditionally understood as a derivational affix, derives, among other things, agent nouns from deverbal bases (*Les$_v$-er*, *Lehr$_v$-er*). The products of this process are invariably masculine nouns belonging to the so-called strong declension. Positing the tree representation in (11):

(11)

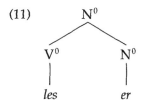

and assuming the approach to suffixes discussed above, it is evident that the properties "masculine" and "strong declension" do not materialize on the mother node in an arbitrary manner. If agent noun spellout proceeded without reference to the suffix, there would be no principled reason why *Leser* could not be a feminine noun, for instance.

As gender and declension features are clearly associated with a particular suffix, one might account for their accessibility either by making them visible *in situ* (where corresponding rules of case affixation and agreement would check them) or by devising a mechanism that copies them on the mother node. The latter analysis implies that the whole word has morphological properties, including gender, while the former implies that this is technically not the case. In general, the traditional position that the entire complex word has morphological properties has been accepted in word syntax, and so-called percolation (or "inheritance") mechanisms have been postulated that make the features of the head visible on the mother node. Lieber's (1983) percolation conventions (first articulated in Lieber 1980) were an early attempt in this direction; Selkirk's (1982) definition seems simpler, however:

(12)   Percolation
    (a)   If a head has a feature specification $[\alpha F_i]$, a $\neq$ u, its mother node must be specified $[\alpha F_i]$, and vice versa.
    (b)   If a nonhead has a feature specification $[\beta F_j]$, and the head has the feature specification $[u F_j]$, then the mother node must have the feature specification $[\beta F_j]$.
    (Here, *u* stands for unspecified feature value.)

(Selkirk 1982: 76)

More recent discussions of percolation revolve, among other things, around the question of what properties can percolate in the first place. The problem has been explicitly addressed by Lieber (1992), who argues that not any feature can percolate. Lieber's definition of percolation principles is based on Selkirk 1982, but introduces some subtle distinctions:

(13)   (a)   *Head percolation*
        Morphosyntactic features are passed from a head morpheme to the node dominating the head. Head percolation propagates the categorial signature.

(b) *Backup percolation*

If the node dominating the head remains unmarked for a given feature after head percolation, then a value for that feature is percolated from an immediately dominated nonhead branch marked for that feature. Backup percolation propagates only values for unmarked features and is strictly local.

(Lieber 1992: 92)

Among the distinctions Lieber is introducing is the notion of "categorial signature": that is, the set of morphosyntactic features that are allowed to percolate. Such feature sets are category- and language-specific:

(14) English nouns: [N, ± plural, ± I, ± II]
(where I and II are person features)

(15) German nouns: [N, ± plural, ± case$_i$, ± case$_j$, ± fem., ± masc., ± I, ± II]
(where the proper setting of case$_i$ and case$_j$ yields the four cases of the German case system)

(based on Lieber 1992: 90)

Lieber argues that diacritic features such as [±L], for "learned" (in French), or [±strong] (as applying to German verbs), are not eligible for percolation; she argues that all German verbs take the same set of past-tense endings, so the desinence is not selected according to whether the verb is weak or strong.

Evaluating percolation conventions and speculating about their status as principles, one may of course wonder whether head percolation mechanisms could not be dropped from word syntax as redundant, on the grounds that they restate a well-formedness condition needed independently in X-bar theory: the head-projection line is categorially uniform in both minimal and nonminimal projections – that is, in both word syntax and phrasal syntax.

Assuming that (12a), or its variant (13a), is dropped from word syntax, percolation from the nonhead branch will attract remaining attention, because no comparable phenomenon is known independently from X-bar theory. In fact, percolation from the nonhead branch is rare in word syntax as well: the best cases are certain types of denominal diminutives that seem to preserve properties such as gender and number of the base noun. This is so in certain cases in Russian (also discussed in Lieber 1992):

(16) (a) travá 'grass' (fem.)   diminutive: tráv-ušk-a (fem.)
        pal'tó 'coat' (neut.)   pal't-íšk-o (neut.)
        krýlo 'wing' (neut.)   krýl-yšk-o (neut.)

   (b) štaný 'pants' (pl.)   štan-íšk-i (pl.)

These words display a diminutive morpheme whose surface forms are *-ušk*, *-išk*, and *-yšk*. On the face of it, the diminutive morpheme seems to be an "interfix" that does not alter gender (16a) or inherent number (16b) of the noun from which the diminutive is formed; if this base noun is feminine, the product is also feminine; if it is neuter, the product is neuter.

One might thus take the position that we are dealing with diminutive suffixes which are "underspecified" for gender (and, in one example, number), and that these features must thus percolate under clause (12b). Although there is some degree of plausibility to such an approach, the scarcity of such instances is striking. Moreover, with clause (12a) eliminated, one might think about getting rid of clause (12b) also, thus simplifying word syntax considerably. Two lines of approach emerge: we either argue that percolation from the nonhead branch is only apparently unique to word syntax, or we reanalyze the cases under discussion so that eventually they do not require percolation from the left branch. Given the available data, it seems plausible to pursue the second approach and assume that the desinence itself is marked for gender. By this token, there is no necessity to supply the head with gender information.

3.2 Case assignment

The question of whether case morphology can appear word-internally, or, in generative terms, whether complex words are a proper domain of Case theory, is difficult both on the descriptive and the theoretical levels. In descriptive terms we observe that *bona fide* straightforward data are relatively scarce; and theoretical discussion has to come to grips with the fact that classical Case theory, outlined by Chomsky (1981), is constantly changing.

Word-internal case morphology is well attested in some languages. Sanskrit compounding is often cited:

(17) (a) ACC   áśva-m$_{ACC}$-isti-   'horse-desiring'
     (b) INST   bhas-á$_{INST}$-ketu-   'bright with light'
     (c) DAT   asm-é$_{DAT}$-hita-   'errand to us'
     (d) GEN   ray-ás$_{GEN}$-káma-   'desirous of wealth'
     (Examples from Miller 1993: 79)

Contemporary languages, both non-Indo-European, such as Finnish (Andrew Spencer, p.c.), and Indo-European, such as Czech, can be quoted also. Turning to Czech, we observe deverbal adjectives that incorporate a case-inflected noun in examples of the following kind:

(18) (a) DAT   ohn-i$_{DAT}$-vzdorný   fire$_{DAT}$-resistant
     (b) DAT   pravd-ě$_{DAT}$-podobný   lit. truth$_{DAT}$-similar, i.e. probable
     (c) GEN   duch-a$_{GEN}$-plný   lit. spirit$_{GEN}$-full, i.e. witty
     (d) GEN   boj-e$_{GEN}$-schopný   fight$_{GEN}$-able, deployable

Finally, we also note German examples such as *Ich-Roman*, literally 'I-novel': that is, a novel written in the first person; *Wir-Gefühl*, literally 'we-feeling': that is, a sense of togetherness. In these cases, the intriguing part is the full form of the personal pronoun that appears fully inflected.

As regards these examples, the main difficulty is to assess clearly whether we are dealing with curiosities or with major patterns. The answer is to some extent easy in the German cases, which are perhaps best analyzed as instances of an incorporated citation form. As far as Sanskrit is concerned, it is my understanding that word-internally inflected forms represent a minor pattern. In other words, Sanskrit compounds typically do not have a case morpheme on the left-hand member (Miller 1993: 79). The Czech examples are similar in this respect, in that they do not represent a major pattern, and often have a literary ring. Assuming, then, that we are really dealing with nonproductive patterns, perhaps historical residues, the question arises as to whether word syntax as a theory of word competence is the appropriate theory to explain these data. I tend to believe it is not.

Recent generative theory rules out the case of word-internal structure as a matter of principle. Under the newer understanding of case, so-called structural cases are assigned under Specifier-Head Agreement by functional categories AgrS and AgrO. These in turn must be licensed by other functional elements such as tense or finiteness. In general, then, the question of word-internal case marking reduces to the question of the distribution of functional categories within words. Put another way, asking why compounds typically do not have word-internal case equals asking why there is no inflection in compounds with a verbal element in the nonhead position. Consider German again:

(19) (a) Miet$_v$-wagen 'rent-car', Schrumpf$_v$-leber 'shrink-liver'
       (b) *Miet-et-wagen,   *Schrumpf-t-leber

These are VN compounds – that is, compounds with a verbal root in the nonhead position – and the *-et*, *-t* affixes in (19b) are attempts to add third-person singular inflections.

Again, assuming that the distribution of finite verbal desinence (cf. *-t*, *-et*) is normally licensed by functional nodes, we see that no such licenser is available word-internally. In other words, in order to be grammatical, the compounds under discussion would contain whole clauses. But this seems generally impossible, primarily on the ground that clauses are semantic objects whose denotation (the truth-value) cannot be incorporated word-internally.

3.3 Operations on argument structure

There is an intuition going back to the ancient Indian grammarians that what we call thematic roles can be assigned inside compounds. Although there is no general consensus about the nature and actual importance of such entities as theta-roles in a generative model that is primarily based on tree geometry, this old intuition has by and large carried over into word syntax. All major studies of word syntax assume Theta theory, a set of component-independent principles, and apply it to words by showing that, and how, subconstituents of words saturate theta-grids (or, alternatively, argument structure) of theta-assigners – that is, mostly of verbs and adjectives. Virtually all principles of theta-role satisfaction maintain that there is a distinction between Theta-roles as regards their saturability in compounds. Much of the pertinent discussion is actually embedded in the discussion of argumenthood. For Selkirk the dividing line falls between the SUBJECT/non-SUBJECT function:

(20)   All non-SUBJ arguments of a lexical category X_i must be satisfied within the first order projection of X_i. (Selkirk 1982: 37)

where first-order projection means 'within the compound' for the purposes of word syntax. This then accounts for such differences as:

(21)   (a)   trash removal by specialists
       (b)   *specialist-removal of trash
       (c)   *Girl-swimming is common.

Spencer (1991: 328) is correct, though, in glossing (20) as the use of "brute force." In view of this, E. Williams's system represents a more principled account, in that it argues that the external argument must not be realized within a compound, since it can be licensed only through predication, a relation that is not available word-internally.

German VN compounds merit some attention in this connection. Note that this rather productive pattern seems to involve theta-roles assigned from the nonhead position to the right, whereby recipients seem to be both internal (22a) and external arguments (22b):

(22)   (a)   Mietwagen   *rent-car*, i.e. 'rented car'
              Rührei   *stir-egg*, i.e. 'scrambled eggs'
              Hackfleisch   *chop-meat*, i.e. 'minced meat'

       (b)   Sprechvogel   *speak-bird*, i.e. 'talking bird'
              Schrumpfleber   *shrink-liver*, i.e. 'shrinking liver'
              Kriechtier   *creep-animal*, i.e. 'reptile'

Clearly, a number of problems remain. (22b) seems to point to the occurrence of external arguments compound-internally. A possible explanation would consist in analyzing the supposedly external arguments as unaccusative – that is, internal arguments. Unfortunately, *Sprechvogel* defies this analysis (cf. Boase-Beier and Toman 1986 for further discussion).

Continuing the discussion of theta-satisfaction, we note that nontransformational analyses in this domain have been the rule. Some researchers, however, resort to movement in certain cases. For instance, Lieber (1992) derives verbal compounds such as *thirst-quencher* by movement:

(23) (a)

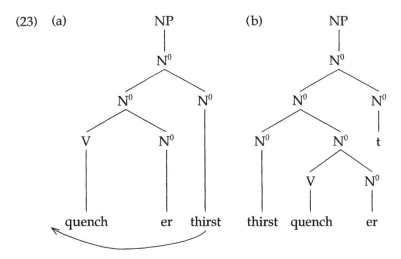

(23a) is the input structure, (23b) the derived structure (adapted from Lieber 1992: 60).

Among the reasons for this analysis is the fact that in verbal compounds of this type the "logical" object precedes the verb, whereas it follows the verb in clausal syntax: that is, (something) quenches thirst. The reason for the clausal distribution of direct objects is assumed to be directionality of case assignment (to the right) and directionality of theta-role assignment (likewise to the right). Clearly, theta-assignment to the right cannot proceed in English compounds under these premises, because the receiving nominal is to the left of the verb (but it would actually be possible in corresponding German forms). Thus the underlying structure (23a) is posited in which the theta-role can be assigned to the right, and the eventual linear order is established by movement (incorporation) – cf. (23b).

The justification for this account does not seem strong, though, mainly because the validity of the premise that theta-role assignment is directional has never been demonstrated. Moreover, the movement is an instance of lowering, a somewhat problematic analysis in view of the fact that traces of lowered material are not c-commanded properly. If we conceive of theta-role assignment as nondirectional, both NV and V NP structures follow naturally: in the former case N receives its theta-role *in situ*, since nothing prevents the theta-assigner from seeking a left-hand recipient; in the latter case, the nondirectionality of theta-role assignment makes it possible to assign the role both to the right and to the left, yielding something like (24):

(24)   (a)   (something) quenches thirst
        (b)   *(something) thirst quenches

but directionality of case assignment, or an equivalent syntactic principle, is sufficient to take care of this: case can be assigned in (24a), but not in (24b).

4 Concluding remarks

As stated at the outset, this survey has been geared towards a discussion, rather than a monolithic statement about a particular doctrine. Given the close dependence of development in word syntax on developments and often radical changes in its "mother theory" – the theory of generative grammar – we can not expect to be able to provide the last word on the subject. Nonetheless, the range of questions and strategies within word syntax, and a certain consensus about them, do exist. Among questions agreed upon is that it is meaningful and theoretically legitimate to discuss the question of whether general principles of grammar hold in word structures. One of the superficial effects of this approach to morphology is that morphology now looks very much like syntax. In some ways this is hardly surprising, since the word-syntactic approach focuses precisely on those aspects of word structure that are not concerned with sound shape. Morphophonemic rules (such as *k/š* alternation in English *logic/logician*) are not assumed to be part of word syntax. On closer inspection, however, we are not obliged to regard morphology as being completely assimilated into syntax. Note that the application of the principles of X-bar theory, theta theory (or a comparable theory of argument saturation), and other sub-theories of generative grammar to the domain of complex words means simply that we have created a single domain in which those particular principles hold. It does not necessarily imply that only syntactic principles apply in the domain of morphology.

Clearly, a number of conceptual and empirical problems remain. To conclude, consider so-called atomicity (Di Sciullo and Williams 1987), a property meant to characterize X^0 structures – that is, words. Words enter syntax as sealed-off "atoms" in the sense that some of their properties, such as their internal structure, are invisible, and hence inaccessible in syntax. Thus Di Sciullo and Williams argue that compounds, although superficially "more phrasal" than words formed by affixation are just as wordlike as affixed forms – for instance, both are islands with respect to Wh-movement, an uncontroversially syntactic phenomenon, as seen in (25) (Di Sciullo and Williams 1987: 52):

(25)   (a)   *[How complete-ness] do you admire?
        (b)   *The who-killer did the police catch?

The unanalyzability of words in syntax has often been stressed in the literature, yet there are counterexamples which come to mind as well. Consider, for instance, the kind of coordination illustrated in the German examples (26) (Toman 1986: 424):

(26) (a) Luft- und Wasserverschmutzung
'air- and water-pollution'

   (b) Wiederaufnahme der Inlands- und des größten Teils der Auslandsflüge
'resumption of domestic, and of the larger part of international, flights'

   (c) rote Seide- und blaue Wollstoffe
'red silk and blue cotton fabrics'

While we might argue that cases such as (26a) are base-generated coordinations, which could thus be accounted for by an extension of the coordination schema to the X^0 domain, examples such as (26b) point to the transparency of words – there must be some process that "sees" the internal structure of compounds.

Di Sciullo and Williams (1987) stress that the atomicity of words is a property to be explained – an *explicandum* rather than an *explicans*. But if atomicity is not a primitive property of words, ample space remains for rethinking the property, and thus the relationship between phrase syntax and word syntax. This, again, illustrates the challenges a word-syntactician must live with. But the benefits of this challenge clearly outweigh its day-to-day frustrations.

16 Paradigmatic Structure: Inflectional Paradigms and Morphological Classes

ANDREW CARSTAIRS-MCCARTHY

1 Introduction

For a language to have inflectional morphology, there must be some words (more precisely, some lexemes) which occur in a variety of forms (or word forms), with the choice between these forms being determined by the syntactic context. Each word form can be thought of as expressing the lexical content of the lexeme plus some morphosyntactic property or combination of morpho-syntactic properties. For example, English *gave* can be thought of as expressing the lexeme GIVE plus the property Past, while *gives* expresses GIVE plus the properties Third Person, Singular and Non-Past.

There are widely differing views of how what we here call 'morphosyntactic properties' should be handled in syntax. Some linguists treat them on a par with lexical stems as occupants of terminal positions in syntactic structures (with or without a phonological shape); others treat them as features of lexical stems which are 'spelled out' outside the syntactic component. The linguists who have devoted most attention to paradigms and inflection classes in recent years have generally preferred the latter approach. In principle, however, the issues discussed here arise independently of the way in which inflection is handled syntactically, and the use of the term 'morphosyntactic property' in this article should not be taken as necessarily implying that entities such as 'Past', 'Third Person' or 'Plural' (or their phonological realizations) can never be syntactic constituents.

Each of the actually or potentially distinct word forms belonging to a lexeme is associated, then, with some morphosyntactic property or combination of properties. (The significance of 'actually or potentially' will be discussed in section 2.) The entire set of these properties or property combinations constitutes the 'paradigm' for that lexeme, and each individual property or property combination within this set can be called a 'cell'. For example, the paradigm for the English lexeme GIVE consists of five cells. Possible labels for these cells, in terms of morphosyntactic properties, are given here alongside the corresponding word forms:

(1) Past   *gave*
     Third-Person Singular Non-Past   *gives*
     Perfective *or* Passive   *given*
     Progressive   *giving*
     Basic (used in all other syntactic contexts) *give*

In the form labelled 'Perfective *or* Passive', comparison with the corresponding forms in other lexemes such as *spoken, taken, eaten* allows us to distinguish a suffix *-en* which is added to the lexical stem. But not all English verbs take *-en* in the form corresponding to this cell; for example, the verb SING, as illustrated here, does not:

(2) Past   *sang*
     Third-Person Singular Non-Past   *sings*
     Perfective *or* Passive   *sung*
     Progressive   *singing*
     Basic (used in all other syntactic contexts) *sing*

This difference between GIVE and SING can be expressed by saying that they conform to the same paradigm, but belong to different morphological classes or 'inflection classes'. An inflection class is a set of lexemes which share a paradigm and whose word forms are alike in respect of the realization of the morphosyntactic properties in every cell.

Before we go further, some comments on terminology are needed. The sense of 'inflection class', as defined here, is well established. It applies to words of any word class; older writers, however, used the term 'declension' (class) for an inflection class of nouns or adjectives and 'conjugation' (class) for an inflection class of verbs. The sense of 'paradigm', as defined here, is also well established, although one also encounters it used in the sense of 'set of inflectional realizations appropriate to a given inflection class' (Carstairs 1987, Matthews 1991). In that sense, GIVE, SING and BAKE will have distinct 'paradigms'. The term 'cell', as defined here, is not yet well established, but there is a clear need for some term with this denotation.

Many questions arise from these introductory definitions and illustrations:

1 Must all lexemes in a given word class share the same paradigm?
2 What morphosyntactic properties typically distinguish the cells in paradigms, and how do these properties interact? For example, do some properties presuppose or exclude others? And do properties of

one morphosyntactic category (e.g. Case or Tense) tend to be realized consistently in the same position relative both to the stem and to properties of other categories, whether in individual languages or cross-linguistically?

3   For any given lexeme, how is the form for any one cell affected by forms for other cells? Do some forms act as the bases from which others are formed? And are there any generalizations to be made about patterns of homonymy or syncretism between forms?

4   How much inflection class proliferation is possible within a language, and how is inflection class membership represented lexically?

These questions will be addressed in sections 2–5 respectively.

2 Paradigm consistency

It is conceivable that some members of a word class might be inflected for one set of morphosyntactic properties while other members of that word class in the same language are inflected for quite a different set of properties. In such a language, there would be two quite distinct paradigms applicable to lexemes of the same word class. But this kind of paradigm inconsistency never, or almost never, arises (Carstairs 1987: 10–11). Instead, all, or nearly all, members of the same word class in a given language are inflected for the same properties. Deviations from this pattern, when they occur, may be of two kinds: a lexeme may unexpectedly lack some forms, or it may possess unexpected 'extra' forms. As regards the first kind of deviation, gaps in the set of word forms associated with certain lexemes nearly always turn out not to be unexpected after all, in that they are attributable to clear-cut semantic or syntactic factors; for example, mass nouns may lack Plural forms, or intransitive verbs may lack Passive forms. In the few lexemes which lack expected word forms without any such motivation, what we find is that the same morphosyntactic properties apply as in the usual paradigm, but that some cells are simply left idiosyncratically unrealized. These are 'defective paradigms' (which in our terminology would more aptly be called 'defective inflection classes'). An example is the archaic English verb QUOTH 'say', used to indicate direct quotations, which has a form only for the Past cell (*quoth*). The second kind of deviation, involving 'extra' forms, will be discussed in section 4.2.

The strong tendency towards paradigm consistency is understandable from a syntactic point of view. If word classes were paradigmatically inconsistent, then there would be a risk that the syntax would need to make available different constructions with the same syntactic function for use with different lexemes. Paradigm consistency also makes it reasonable to allow the same word form to be associated with more than one cell. For example, most English verbs, unlike GIVE and SING, have only four, not five, forms (e.g. *bake, baked, bakes, baking* for the lexeme BAKE), yet we typically ascribe to all English verbs the same paradigm, thus:

(3) Past   *baked*
    Third-Person Singular Non-Past   *bakes*
    Perfective *or* Passive   *baked*
    Progressive   *baking*
    Basic (used in all other syntactic contexts)   *bake*

The Past and Perfective cells are treated as morphosyntactically distinct for all verbs, because the associated word forms, though usually identical, are actually distinct in the small but frequently occurring class of irregular verbs such as GIVE and SING (see (1) and (2)).

The label 'Perfective *or* Passive' illustrates the fact that one word form may realize a disjunction rather than a combination of morphosyntactic properties. The term 'morphome' has been proposed for such disjunctions of properties with consistently shared realizations (Aronoff 1994). It appears that the morphological system of a language may treat certain morphosyntactic properties alike, even if they have no special relationship in the syntax.

3 Morphosyntactic categories and the internal structure of paradigms

In Indo-European languages with relatively elaborate inflectional morphology, nouns typically inflect for the morphosyntactic categories Number and Case, adjectives for Number, Case and Gender, and verbs for Person, Number, Tense, Mood (e.g. Indicative, Imperative, Subjunctive), sometimes Voice and sometimes Aspect (e.g. Imperfective versus Perfective). But how typical are Indo-European languages in this respect? What cross-linguistic generalizations, if any, can be made about the morphosyntactic categories which are relevant to particular word classes? Bybee (1985) studied categories expressed inflectionally in verbs in a sample of fifty languages from different language families and different cultural and geographic areas. She found there to be nine such categories: Valence (relating to the number and role of arguments of the verb), Voice, Aspect, Tense, Mood, Number, Person of subject, Person of object and Gender. Of these, the most frequent is Mood (expressed inflectionally in 68 per cent of the fifty languages), followed by Person (56 per cent), Number (54 per cent), Aspect (52 per cent) and Tense (48 per cent); least frequent are Gender (16 per cent) and Valence (6 per cent). She seeks to explain these figures in terms of the two notions of 'relevance' and 'generality'. The commonest inflectional categories are those which are both highly relevant, in that their semantic content 'directly affects or modifies' the semantic content of the stem (Bybee 1985: 13), and highly general, in that their semantic content is applicable to all or almost all verbs. Gender and Valence are relatively rare as inflectional categories, because they fail this criterion, but in opposite ways. Gender is said to be highly general but low in relevance; Valence is said to be high in relevance but low in generality, because valence-changing operations such as causative formation often alter the meanings of stems so unpredictably that the new form becomes lexicalized, and therefore no longer belongs to the same lexeme as its base.

A similar cross-linguistic survey has yet to be done for nominal and adjectival categories. There are in any case often difficulties in deciding objectively which of two categories, such as Tense and Aspect, has a greater effect on the semantic content of stems. But, independently of these semantic issues, Bybee points out generalizations concerning the order in which the nine categories are realized in relation to each other and to the verb stem. For example, when a language in Bybee's sample has both Aspect and Tense as inflectional categories and their order of realization can be determined (i.e. they are not realized cumulatively), Aspect is realized closer to the stem than Tense; similarly, Tense is nearly always realized closer to the stem than the less 'relevant' property Person (of subject). A related observation concerns stem allomorphy. It is not uncommon for languages to have special stem allomorphs or suppletive stem forms distributed according to Aspect or Tense, but it is very rare for stem allomorphy to be distributed according to Person (Rudes 1980). This tends to support the view that the property contrasts which partition a paradigm are not all equally important; rather, the distinction between cells which differ in Tense or Aspect is more fundamental, in some sense, than the distinction between cells which differ in Person – a less 'relevant' category in Bybee's hierarchy.

If, in general, all the morphosyntactic categories which are manifested in a paradigm were equally fundamental, one might expect to find a cell for every possible combination of the properties belonging to them. The English data in (1)–(3) show this to be wrong, however. There is a non-Past Third-Person Singular cell but no Past Third-Person Singular, and the Tense and Person distinctions do not apply to the Perfective or the Progressive forms. In other languages too it is common for a certain category to be excluded (or for property contrasts within it to be neutralized) when a particular property belonging to some other category is present. For example, adjectives in German and Russian inflect for Number, Case and Gender; however, there are no cells for distinct Gender forms in the Plural. It seems likely that the excluded category will generally be either low in 'relevance' (in Bybee's terms) or realized relatively far from the stem, while the property which imposes the exclusion will be high in relevance or realized relatively close to the stem, or both; but this has not yet been systematically investigated.

Bybee's observations also provoke the question as to whether all the properties of one category are always realized in the same position, or 'slot', relative to the stem. The answer is no; for example, in the Present Tense of Georgian verbs the Person and Number of the subject are sometimes cumulated as a prefix, sometimes cumulated as a suffix, sometimes realized separately, with Number as a suffix -*t*, and sometimes not realized overtly at all:

(4)   Singular   Plural

		Singular	Plural
Person:	1	v-xedav	v-xedav-t
		'I see (him/her/it/them)'	
	2	xedav	xedav-t
	3	xedav-s	xedav-en

Even so, it is more usual for all properties in a category to occupy a consistent position in all or most of the relevant word forms, as in the following Swahili example, where the prefixal positions labelled I, II and III are occupied by object markers, Tense markers and subject markers respectively:

(5)	III	II	I	Stem	
	a-	ta-	ni-	penda	'he will like me'
	a-	ta-	ku-	penda	'he will like you (sg.)'
	a-	li-	ni-	penda	'he liked me'
	a-	li-	ku-	penda	'he liked you (sg.)'
	wa-	ta-	ni-	penda	'they will like me'
	wa-	ta-	ku-	penda	'they will like you (sg.)'
	wa-	li-	ni-	penda	'they liked me'
	wa-	li-	ku-	penda	'they liked you (sg.)'

Detailed consideration of phenomena of this kind has led Stump (1992, 1993c) to re-emphasize the importance in morphological theory of 'position classes', meaning classes of affixes which are mutually exclusive and occupy the same position (or positions) relative to the stem (cf. also Stump, INFLECTION). (Zwicky 1990 mentions the related principle of 'slot competition'.)

In the example at (5), each of the positions is occupied by affixes realizing properties belonging to only one category (subject Person, object Person, or Tense). This is not always so, however; for example, in Georgian the prefix position immediately before the verb stem in the Present tense (see (4)) may be occupied by an object Person marker such as *g-* 'you (sg.)' as well as by the subject marker *v-* 'I'. When the two are in competition for this slot, it is *g-* which wins: *g-xedav* 'I see you (sg.)'. It remains to be seen how tightly the roles of slot competition and position classes can be constrained within morphological theory.

4 Word forms, syncretism and the internal structure of paradigms

Alongside the mutual relationship of the morphosyntactic properties which define the cells of a paradigm, one can consider the mutual relationship of the corresponding word forms. These word forms may simply be distinct, implying no special mutual relationship. On the other hand, one word form may appear to be built on another, or one word form may be identical with another. These situations will be illustrated and discussed in sections 4.1 and 4.2.

One constraint on nominal paradigms has been proposed which relates simply to the number of phonologically distinct exponents (affixes, etc.) available for the properties to be expressed. Plank (1986: 46) suggests that 'the number of exponents potentially available for nominal inflexion in any language is limited to about 30'. It follows that in a language with cumulative exponence of Case and Number (as in Latin), with two Numbers (Singular and Plural) and with two inflection classes for nouns, there can be no more than about seven Cases; on the other hand, a language with agglutinative exponence of Case and Number (as in Hungarian or Turkish) can have twenty or more Cases. Observationally this appears correct, but it is not clear why the crucial limit should be around thirty rather than (say) ten or sixty.

4.1 *Word forms as bases for other word forms*

Word forms which appear to be built on other word forms are common in the nominal inflection of Daghestanian languages such as Archi (Kibrik 1991a and ARCHI (CAUCASIAN – DAGHESTANIAN)). In these languages, each noun typically has an 'oblique' stem, which is used in some but not all Case forms, and which differs between Singular and Plural. The oblique stem may be identical to a particular Case form, such as the Ergative, as in Lezgian (Haspelmath 1993), so that the question arises of whether or not we should analyse this actual Case form as the base on which others are built. Mel'čuk (1986), in contrast to Kibrik (1991), favours this approach, distinguishing 'secondary' Cases whose forms are built on other Case forms from 'primary' Cases whose forms are independent. It is not clear how far the primary–secondary dichotomy, so defined, correlates with any other partitions of the paradigm discussed in this section and section 3. A better-known example of the same kind involves the Future Active Participle forms of Latin verbs, which are sometimes said to be built on the Past Passive Participle forms, as illustrated in (6):

(6)

Present stem	Past Passive Participle stem	Future Active Participle stem
am- 'love'	ama:t-	am-a:t-u:r-
po:n- 'put'	posit-	posit-u:r-
fer- 'carry'	la:t-	la:t-u:r-
rump- 'break'	rupt-	rupt-u:r-

Matthews (1972) describes the formation of the Future Active Participle as 'parasitic' on the Past Passive Participle; on the other hand, Aronoff (1994) argues that both participles have equal status as derivatives from one stem which is itself a purely morphological entity, expressing no morphosyntactic properties.

Bybee (1985) approaches this issue from the point of view of markedness relations between properties within a category. She emphasizes the historical tendency for forms which realize relatively unmarked properties within a category to function as the base for new forms realizing relatively more marked properties. An illustration is the development of Preterite inflection in the modern Charente dialect of Provençal, as shown in (8), from the Old Provençal pattern in (7):

(7) Old Provençal:

		Singular	Plural
Person:	1	améi 'I loved'	amém
	2	amést	amétz
	3	amét	améren

(8) Charente dialect:

		Singular	Plural
Person:	1	cantí 'I sang'	cantétem
	2	cantétei	cantétei
	3	cantét	cantéten

Bybee attributes this to the reanalysis of the Third-Person Singular form. Having been originally a combination of a stem *cant-* and a Tense–Person–Number suffix *-et*, it was reanalysed as Preterite Tense form *cant-ét* with no overt realization of the morphosyntactically unmarked Person–Number combination Third-Person Singular. As such, it came to function as the base for the derivation of a new set of Preterite forms in the Charente dialect (except in the First-Person Singular). In Mel'čuk's terms, one could say that all but the First-Person Singular are secondary forms derived from the primary Third-Person Singular form. Morphosyntactic unmarkedness is one of the factors which, according to Bybee, contribute to the autonomy of certain forms of a lexeme – that is, to the likelihood that they have separate lexical representations. Kuryłowicz (1945–9) discusses similar phenomena, but with different terminology.

4.2 Syncretism

In principle, there could be both factors encouraging and factors inhibiting inflectional homonymy, or syncretism, both at the level of morphosyntactic content and at the level of morphological realization. This yields four possible types of factors. In practice, there is evidence that factors of all four types exist, though there are considerable differences between them as regards strength and theoretical status.

Universal homonymy, for all lexemes, in the realization of two cells in a paradigm is by definition impossible, for in any such purported situation there would be no ground for recognizing those two cells as distinct. Even near-universal homonymy is grounds for suspicion. For example, one might recognize two distinct Locative Singular cells in Russian on the grounds of the distinct forms *lesu* and *lese* of LES 'forest' in *v lesu* 'in the forest' and *o lese* 'concerning the forest', and likewise in a few other nouns, even though for the majority of nouns the corresponding forms are identical. But synchronic descriptions of Russian have tended to say, rather, that for the majority of nouns there is only one Locative Case, thus implicitly attributing to Russian a departure from strict paradigm consistency on the part of the LES class (see section 2).

There are, however, clear-cut instances of inflectional homonymy which cannot be ascribed to paradigm inconsistency, and which are not attributable to phonological factors either. A standard illustration is the Dative–Ablative Plural syncretism in all Latin nouns, adjectives and determiners. Its universality in Latin confirms that it is a systematic feature of the morphological system, and the fact that two phonologically quite distinct affixes, *-i:s* and *-ibus*, realize Dative–Ablative Plural in different lexical contexts shows that this homonymy cannot just be a phonological accident. A second illustration is the Past and Perfective syncretism in regular English verbs, shown in (3). How should morphological theory accommodate such phenomena?

From a naïve common-sense point of view, all inflectional homonymy should impair communicative efficiency by increasing the chance of misunderstanding through ambiguity. In practice, the pragmatic, semantic and lexical context of any utterance nearly always prevents misunderstanding due to homonymy, whether lexical or inflectional. Even so, it has been suggested that there are some inflectional homonymies which are avoided because of the morphosyntactic ambiguity which they create. Plank (1979, 1980) argues that the development in Vulgar Latin of Genitive and Nominative Singular homonymy in certain nouns was inhibited for prototypical possessors (humans) and for certain typical possessees (body parts, etc.) because of the need to maintain an overt distinction between possessor and possessee in constructions with a head noun as possessee and a dependent noun in the Genitive as possessor. The same need is held to explain certain otherwise puzzling patterns of acceptability in German; for example, *Benachteiligungen andersgläubiger Frauen* 'acts of discrimination against heterodox women' is acceptable because the suffix *-er* on *andersgläubiger* 'heterodox' unequivocally marks the phrase *andersgläubiger Frauen* as dependent; on the other hand, **Benachteiligungen Frauen* 'acts of discrimination against women' is not acceptable because there is no overt indication of the roles of the two nouns.

Jakobson (1936: 85–8) proposed for Russian nouns a variety of implicational statements relating to syncretism possibilities, with the conditions expressed in terms of morphosyntactic content; for example, if a noun has distinct forms for the Accusative and the Nominative, then either the Accusative and Genitive or the Dative and Locative must be homonymous. Such conditions can hardly be generalized to other languages, however. Bierwisch (1967) described certain German syncretisms in terms of the sharing of syntactic features between cells. E. Williams (1981b, 1994a) also uses syntactic features to organize hierarchically the paradigm cells for any lexeme class into a branching tree structure, such that forms which are systematically homonymous for any lexeme are all and only those cells dominated by some node on the tree. One may question, however, whether this hierarchical organization is independent of the syncretisms which it is designed to explain; and in any case there are both syncretisms which might occur but do not, and (it has been suggested) some syncretisms which do occur despite the fact that the cells concerned do not form a 'constituent' within the tree structure (Joseph and Wallace 1984). So the search for morphosyntactic-feature configurations which strongly favour syncretism has had only modest success so far.

A characteristic of many syncretisms is that one can distinguish a morphosyntactic property (or properties) which provides the context in which the syncretism occurs. This does not apply to the Past–Perfective syncretism in regular English verbs, for which the conditioning factor is purely lexical (a matter of belonging to the regular inflection class). On the other hand, it does apply to the Latin Dative–Ablative Plural syncretism, where the conditioning factor is morphosyntactic (a matter of being Plural rather than Singular). For such syncretisms, one can investigate the possibility of generalizations concerning the realization of the contextual property in the word forms concerned. Is it, for example, always realized cumulatively with the properties whose expression is rendered homonymous by the syncretism? Carstairs (1987) suggests that the answer to this question is generally yes, and that there is, moreover, a quasi-functional motivation for it. For a lexeme with cumulative inflection, a syncretism reduces the amount of morphological material (affixes, etc.) to be distributed among the cells of the paradigm. On the other hand, for a lexeme with agglutinative inflection, a syncretism does not reduce the amount of this material, and may even increase it; and, in any case, the syncretism will complicate the distribution of this material among the cells, by comparison with a similar pattern without syncretism. Carstairs and Stemberger (1988) show also that syncretism with cumulation is easy to model in a connectionist framework, while syncretism without cumulation is difficult. There remains, however, the problem of the minority of morphosyntactically conditioned syncretisms where the contextual property is not cumulated with the homonymously realized properties. Carstairs (1987) suggests that they are subject to a generalization involving the mutual ranking of the properties in Bybee's relevance hierarchy; but even if this generalization is correct, the reason for it is not clear.

5 Inflection class organization

Two main questions have been asked about inflection class organization in recent years: (a) How is the assignment of a lexeme to its inflection class to be represented grammatically? (b) Are there any constraints on the number of inflection classes which words of a given class in a given language can have? These questions, though seemingly independent, have turned out to have answers (at least provisional ones) which impinge on one another.

Many pedagogical grammars and dictionaries of languages such as Latin and Russian indicate inflection class membership by means of essentially arbitrary labels, such as 'Class I' or 'second declension'. These labels are a shorthand for full sets of inflected forms illustrated by one or more exemplary lexemes for each class. Labels of this kind have been criticized as arbitrary by both generative and non-generative grammatical theorists. In the generative tradition, Lieber (1981) suggested that the full inflectional behaviour of any lexeme might be predictable from its pattern of morpholexical alternation (essentially, its set of stem allomorphs). However, this strong claim cannot be sustained, and another generative linguist, James Harris (1991), reverts to traditional numerical labels to encode lexically the inflectional behaviour of Spanish substantives.

An alternative tradition has been to cite certain word forms, or 'principal parts', for each lexeme, from which its whole inflectional behaviour can be determined by reference to rules. This approach is adopted and refined theoretically by Wurzel (1984, 1987). Wurzel points out that simply to label distinct inflection classes as 'Class 1' etc. obscures three facts: (a) that inflection classes are typically not entirely distinct in their realizations for all cells, but rather resemble each other in some or most cells; (b) that inflection class membership is frequently influenced by extramorphological factors such as Gender, meaning (e.g. animateness) and phonological shape; (c) that within a set of inflection classes whose membership is not influenced by such extramorphological factors and which are therefore in a sense competing for the same pool of lexemes ('complementary classes', in Wurzel's terminology), there is typically one class which is unmarked in the sense that it is the class to which new words are assigned, the class to which words of the other classes are 'wrongly' assigned by infant learners, and the class into which members of the other classes drift in the course of language change. Wurzel seeks to account for these facts by a model of inflection class membership which incorporates 'paradigm structure conditions' (PSCs) and 'reference forms'.

A PSC is a statement to the effect that if a lexeme has characteristic X, then it must have realizations $R_1, \ldots, R_n$ for cells $C_1, \ldots, C_n$. Such conditions are conceived as structuring the implicit knowledge that native speakers of inflectionally complex languages acquire. 'Characteristic X' may be more or less elaborate, and 'cells $C_1, \ldots, C_n$' may cover greater or lesser portions of the paradigm. In the simplest case, characteristic X is membership of a given word class (e.g. verb), and cells $C_1, \ldots, C_n$ extend to the whole paradigm. A PSC of this kind is appropriate for a word class with no inflection class distinctions. But what if there are two or more complementary inflection classes within a word class (or an extramorphologically defined subset of a word class)? Here Wurzel invokes 'reference forms', which are akin to traditional 'principal parts'. Lexemes within the unmarked class have no lexical specification, and obey the dominant PSC for the set of complementary classes – one which specifies realizations for all cells in the paradigm. On the other hand, lexemes within a marked class contain in their lexical specification a reference form for at least one cell in the paradigm, which overrides the dominant PSC in respect of that cell. This reference form may also function as part of 'characteristic X' in a more specific PSC, which, so far as it extends, overrides the dominant condition; for cells not covered by the more specific PSC, however, these lexemes conform to the dominant PSC, which thus constitutes the default PSC for the whole set of complementary classes. The possibility of PSCs being wholly or partly shared by different inflection classes is what accounts for inflection class resemblances in Wurzel's framework, and the drift in membership to unmarked classes is seen as lexical simplification through the loss of reference forms, whereby the lexemes in question become wholly subject to the dominant PSC.

The illustration in (9) shows a hypothetical set of complementary classes for nouns, with Class A assumed to be unmarked and a–h representing distinct inflectional realizations.

(9)

	Class A	Class B	Class C	Class D
Cell 1	a	a	f	f
Cell 2	b	e	e	e
Cell 3	c	c	h	h
Cell 4	d	d	d	g

In (10) we see how this pattern of classes would be represented in Wurzel's framework:

(10)   PSCs: (a)   Noun → {a/1, b/2, c/3, d/4}
　　　　　　　 (b)   g/4 → h/3 → {f/1, e/2}

Reference forms included in lexical specification:

　　　Class A: none
　　　Class B: e/2
　　　Class C: h/3
　　　Class D: g/4

The fact that PSC (a) is dominant follows from the fact that it is more general than PSC (b), being framed so as to apply to all nouns, not just those with a particular reference form; and the fact that Class A is unmarked is represented by the fact that it has no reference form in its lexical specification. PSC (b) incorporates two implications, and so serves for both Class C and Class D. For Class C words, however, only the second implication (h/3 → {f/1, e/2}) has effect, and the form for cell 4 (viz. d) is supplied by PSC (a). Wurzel has applied this sort of analysis to inflection class systems in a variety of mainly Indo-European languages, particularly German, Icelandic and Latin.

Carstairs (1987) asks a different question from Wurzel: What is the largest number of inflection classes which a given array of inflectional resources can be organized into? Looking at (10), one can see that the smallest conceivable number of inflection classes, given the number of distinct realizations available for each cell, is two; on the other hand, the largest conceivable number of inflection classes, given that each of the five cells has two realizations, is 2^5 or 32. Carstairs (1987) proposes a Paradigm Economy Principle to the effect that, subject to certain qualifications, the actual restriction on the number of distinct inflection classes for any word class in any language is very tight: it must be no more than the conceivable minimum. An actual language which had precisely two inflections available for each cell could therefore have no more than two inflection classes, not four, as posited in (9).

It is clear that Carstairs and Wurzel disagree, in that Wurzel's framework can handle without difficulty a pattern, such as (9), which Carstairs claims cannot occur. Carstairs-McCarthy (1991) has suggested that the sort of behaviour allowed by Wurzel's multi-stage PSCs, such as (b) in (10), can be found only in non-affixal inflection (such as stem allomorphy and stress alternation), not in affixal inflection. If correct, this suggests that the two types of inflection are subject to different constraints.

More recently, Carstairs-McCarthy (1994) has suggested that inflection classes are constrained by a principle related to the Principle of Contrast proposed by Clark (1987) for lexical acquisition: every two forms contrast in meaning. As Carstairs-McCarthy applies this to affixal inflection, it has the effect of requiring that each word form should either identify unambiguously the inflection class to which its lexeme belongs or else supply no positive information about inflection class membership at all, exhibiting the sole default, or multi-class, realization for that cell. If correct, this claim would rule out the inflection class organization in (9), but for a different reason from the Paradigm Economy Principle; for cells 1 and 3 each have two realizations neither of which either unambiguously identifies its inflection class or constitutes the sole default realization for that cell.

The outcome of the comparison of Wurzel's and Carstairs-McCarthy's approaches will depend on further detailed study of actual inflection class systems; it seems clear already, however, that inflection class organization is by no means a language-particular free-for-all without interest for the morphological theorist.

17 Morphology as Component or Module: Mapping Principle Approaches

RICHARD SPROAT

1 Introduction

It is common to speak of one or another theory of grammar as being modular. What is meant by a modular theory, of course, is one in which the well- or ill-formedness of an expression is determined not by a single monolithic set of rules, but rather by a set of modules (or components), each formally independent of the other, and each with its own set of rules or principles that must be satisfied. The best-known example of this view of grammar is the so-called Principles and Parameters approach to syntax, which has its origin in the modular Government Binding (GB) theory of Chomsky (1981).

To take a familiar example of how a modular system of grammar is supposed to work, consider a sentence such as (1a), which has a structure roughly like that shown in (1b), on a traditional GB view:

(1) (a)   Mary seems to be intelligent.
    (b)   [Mary$_i$ seems [t$_i$ to be intelligent]]
    (c)   *It seems Mary to be intelligent.

Example (1a) is well formed because it meets the requirements of a number of different modules. For example, it satisfies the Case theory in that the NP *Mary* appears as the subject of an inflected verb (*seems*) and is therefore in a Case-marked position, as is required of overt NPs: non-Case-marked overt NPs are not 'visible', and are ruled ill-formed by a visibility requirement. We see from the structure in (1b) that *Mary* does not appear on the surface in its D-structure position; rather, it has been moved from the position of the subject of the lower clause into the matrix subject position. This movement is licit since (among other things) the relationship between *Mary* and its trace satisfies the Binding theory: in classical GB a trace is an anaphor (functioning like a reflexive such as *herself*, and not like a pronoun like *her*), which must be locally bound by an antecedent in an argument position; the relationship between *Mary* and the trace happens to satisfy this constraint. Finally, *Mary*, being an NP, must be assigned a theta-role by a V or VP. The verb *seem* does not assign a theta-role to its subject (its notional subject is really semantically empty), so *Mary* cannot get one from there. However, since *Mary* is the antecedent of the trace *t*, which is in the subject position of the subject-theta-assigning VP *be intelligent*, *Mary* is able to inherit a theta-role from its trace, and thus the construction satisfies theta-theory. Thus, the construction is ruled in, because it satisfies a set of independent criteria for well-formedness.

Contrariwise, a construction is ill-formed when principles of one or more of the modules are violated. Take the case of (1c), for example. In this case, theta-theory is satisfied since *Mary* appears as the subject of the VP *be intelligent*. Binding theory is simply irrelevant here, since there are no anaphoric relations – at least under simpler versions of GB or Principles and Parameters theories. What is violated relates to Case theory: the overt NP *Mary* is the subject of an infinitival VP, which in English is a non-Case-marked position.

Examples such as those in (1) are typical of the interactions of purely *syntactic* modules in the determination of the well-formedness of a sentence. However, utterances can obviously be unacceptable for reasons that are not syntactic. For example, one of the words in the sentence might be simply morphologically ill-formed, as in (2a) (cf. 2b):

(2) (a) *John edwant to go.
     (b) John wanted to go.

The source of the ill-formedness in (2a) is, obviously, that the English past-tense affix *-ed* is a suffix rather than a prefix, and as such must attach at the end of its base, not the beginning. This restriction is morphological – or at least morphophonological (see section 3).

Now, obviously, anybody's theory of morphology must provide some account of why one cannot say *edwant* in English, and there is therefore a sense in which any morphological theory could be said to function as a module of the grammar, much as the syntactic modules that we have just discussed. However, in many morphological theories, the interaction between morphological principles or rules and the types of syntactic modules described above is not particularly direct. In a typical Lexical Morphology approach, for example, (2a) would be ruled out by simply not allowing the morphology to generate words like *edwant*. So, the sentence in (2a) would not be generated, simply because *edwant* would never be inserted into the sentence. There are, by contrast, views of morphology where morphological principles interact with other principles of grammar in a much more explicit and direct way: broadly speaking, these are theories in which morphology, syntax, and other modules of the grammar have an 'interlocking independence', as Baker (1988b) puts it.

In this chapter, I discuss morphological theories, such as those proposed by Marantz (1984a), Sadock (1985, 1991), and Baker (1985, 1988a, b), in which morphology functions as a module on a par with other modules of the grammar. I will concentrate in particular on the Autolexical Syntax theory as developed by Sadock. Some aspects of this theory will be outlined in section 2. As we shall see, on Sadock's theory, a sentence's morphological structure always differs from, and may actually be nonisomorphic to, the structure assigned by the syntax. There must, therefore, be a *mapping* between the two levels of structure, and this mapping must obey certain principles. Thus the relationship between the morphological component and the syntactic component(s) is rather like the relationship between the S-structure and the Logical Form components in GB theory, which (often) assign nonisomorphic analyses to a given sentence, these analyses to be related by the rule of Quantifier Raising.

So principles of morphology may be viewed as comprising a separate module, and this module, along with assumptions about mapping between modules, is consulted as part of the determination of a sentence's well-formedness. This view can be turned around, however: instead of having separate morphological principles that help determine the well-formedness of sentences, might one not instead assume that the well-formedness of *words* is derivable from principles of *syntax* and other components of the grammar? This opposite view has been argued for by Sproat (1985, 1988), and subsequently by Lieber (1992), and I will outline a few aspects of such approaches in section 3. As we shall see there, despite the oppositeness of such theories in certain respects to that of Sadock, there are also some striking similarities.

2 Sadock's Autolexical Syntax

2.1 *Cliticization in Autolexical Syntax*

To begin with, let us consider a simple case of cliticization in English, involving '*d*, the reduced form of the auxiliary *would* (cf. Sadock 1991: 52ff). From a purely syntactic point of view, '*d* is a separate word, on a parallel with the full form *would*. This consideration would lead us to posit a structure roughly like (3a) for the sentence *He'd have done it*. From a purely morphological point of view, however, '*d* would appear to be attached to the preceding word, namely *he*. This would motivate (3b) as the structure of the sequence *he'd* from a purely morphological point of view, where the subscript w indicates that the sequence counts as a single morphological word:

(3) (a) [He [$_{VP}$ 'd [$_{VP}$ have [$_{VP}$ done it]]]]
    (b) [$_w$ he'd]

The situation with *'d* is typical of clitics (cf. Halpern, Clitics). As Sadock notes, clitics are associated with an array of properties, including being morphologically *bound* morphemes at the same time as being syntactically independent. (Indeed, these two characteristics might be taken as the defining property of clitics.)

In Sadock's approach, *'d* is represented as a lexical entry with two components as follows:

(4)   (a)   morphology = $[_{w[-2]}$ X[–1]____]
      (b)   syntax = $[_{VP[FIN]}$ ____VP[BSE]]

The morphological entry in (4a) states that the clitic attaches to a full word (bar level –1 in Sadock's model), and forms a "somewhat larger" than full-word constituent (cf. the "clitic group" of other theories, such as Nespor and Vogel 1986) – bar level –2 in Sadock's model. The syntactic entry simply states that the clitic subcategorizes syntactically for a VP headed by a bare verb.

So morphological structure may be nonisomorphic with syntactic structure. But just how different may the two structures be? Put another way, given a lexical entry such as that for *'d* in (4), and the requirement that a sentence in which such a morpheme occurs must satisfy both the morphological and the syntactic specifications, what is to stop the morphological and syntactic structures from being arbitrarily nonisomorphic with each other? For example, what is to rule out the sentence **John'd would prefer mole poblano and I prefer it too*, where both the syntactic and morphological requirements of *'d* are satisfied, as indicated by the following structures?

(5)   (a)   Syntactic:
            John would prefer mole poblano, and [I ['d [prefer it too]]]

      (b)   Morphological:
            [John 'd]

One principle that Sadock makes use of is the Cliticization Principle, which is stated as follows (Sadock 1991: 105):

(6)   Cliticization Principle
      If a lexeme combines with an inflected word in the morphology and with a phrase in the syntax, its morphosyntactic association will conform to at least the Weak Linearity Constraint.

The Strong and Weak Linearity Constraints are given as follows:

(7)   (a)   Strong: The associated elements of morphological and syntactic representations must occur in the same linear order.

(b) Weak: The associated elements of morphological and syntactic representations must occur in as close to the same linear order as the morphological requirements of the lexemes allow.

(Sadock's Cliticization Principle is similar in spirit and in predictive power to the Mapping Principle of Sproat 1985, 1988, which I describe later on.) Given this, it is clear why (3) is acceptable whereas (5) is not: in (3) *'d* obeys the Cliticization Principle since, although the word to which *'d* attaches (*he*) is not part of the phrase for which *'d* syntactically subcategorizes, it is immediately adjacent to *'d*, to its left. In this case, the mapping satisfies the Strong Linearity Constraint. Obviously, the same situation does not hold of the intended pairing of (5a) and (5b); not even the Weak Linearity Constraint would be satisfied here, since the phrasal position of *'d* and its morphological position can hardly be said to be 'in as close to the same linear order as the morphological requirements of the lexemes allow'.

2.2 Incorporation in Autolexical Syntax

In Sadock's theory, cliticization is merely one instance of morphology/syntax mismatch – *morphosyntactic mismatch*, as Sadock terms it – which comes about as a result of morphology and syntax being separate modules, with their own principles. Another instance is incorporation. Sadock presents several arguments that noun incorporation in some languages must be viewed as involving nouns which are syntactically separate words, but which are morphologically part of a verb word; thus Sadock's treatment of incorporation is similar in this regard to the approach of Baker (1988a), and differs from that of Mithun (1984) or Di Sciullo and Williams (1987).

Like cliticization, incorporation is governed by three sets of considerations. First, the incorporated element must occur syntactically in a position wherein its syntactic requirements can be met. Secondly, its morphological requirements and the morphological requirements of the other morphemes in the construction into which it is incorporated must be met. Thirdly, the mapping between the syntactic and morphological representations must be licit; in particular, it must obey the Incorporation Principle, as given below (Sadock 1991: 105):

(8) If a lexeme combines with a stem in the morphology and with a phrase in the syntax, its morphosyntactic association will conform to the strong Constructional Integrity Constraint.

The Strong Constructional Integrity Constraint is stated as follows:

(9) If a lexeme combines with a phrase P in the syntax and with a host in the morphology, then the morphological host must be associated with the head of the syntactic phrase P.

Consider, as a simple example, the Greenlandic sentence given in (10a) (Sadock 1991: 94). Following Sadock, in addition to the surface form of the morphologically complex words, I also give the underlying morphological analysis and a morpheme-by-morpheme gloss:

(10) (a)   Marlunnik ammassattorpunga.
            marluk-nik ammassak-tor-punga.
            two-instrumental/pl. sardine-eat-indic./3sg.
            'I ate two sardines.'

      (b)   Ammassannik marlunnik nerivunga.
            ammassak-nik marluk-nik neri-vunga.
            sardine-instrumental/pl. two-instrumental/pl. eat-indic./3sg.
            'I ate two sardines.'

In (10a) the noun *ammassak* 'sardine' is morphologically incorporated into the verb. At the same time, it functions as the head of the object noun phrase meaning 'two sardines'. The *syntactic* structure of (10a) is thus effectively identical to the syntactic structure of (10b), where incorporation of *ammassak* 'sardine' has not taken place, and where the noun functions as a separate word both syntactically and (modulo case/number affixes) morphologically. The syntactic requirements of *ammassak* are thus satisfied in (10a), in that it is functioning as a head of an NP in the syntactic representation, a perfectly legal thing for a noun to be doing. At the same time, the complex verb *ammassattorpunga* is morphologically well formed: in particular, the morpheme glossed as 'eat' in this example, *-tor*, while it functions syntactically as a verb, is morphologically an affix that is marked to attach to nouns. Since *ammassak* is a noun, the morphological construction is licit as far as the morphological requirements on those two morphemes are concerned. Finally, we have to consider the mapping between the two levels of representation, which must satisfy the Incorporation Principle. Clearly the Strong Constructional Integrity Constraint, and thus the Incorporation Principle, is satisfied in this instance, since syntactically *ammassak* functions as the head of an NP, which is itself part of a VP of which *-tor*, the morphological host of *ammassak*, is the head.

The cliticization and noun incorporation examples that we have seen illustrate how, in Sadock's theory, morphology functions as a separate module of the grammar in determining grammatical well-formedness. The syntactic representation of grammatical constructions must satisfy various syntactic principles, and the – possibly nonisomorphic – morphological representations must satisfy morphological principles; and whatever nonisomorphism there may be between the syntactic and morphological representations must obey certain mapping constraints, as we have discussed.

It is important to note that Sadock's model is essentially tripartite, in that in addition to autonomous sets of syntactic and morphological principles and levels of representation, an important role is also played by an autonomous semantic module. Thus, Sadock also argues that one finds mismatches between semantic representations and the other levels of representation; this conclusion is perhaps a little surprising, at least on a compositional semantic theory such as the classic model-theoretic approach presented by Dowty et al. (1981). One instance of a morphology/semantics mismatch is what Sadock terms *morphosemantic incorporation* (Sadock 1991: 170–8). Sadock presents arguments that a Greenlandic example like (11), where the morpheme meaning 'appear, seem' is *morphologically* attached to the morpheme meaning 'love', but where *semantically* 'seem' has scope over the entire phrase headed by 'love', should be considered to be a case of morphosemantic mismatch:

(11)   Kaali-p Amaalia asa-gunar-paa.
       Karl-erg. Amaalia(abs.) love-appear-indic/3sg.
       'Karl seems to love Amaalia.'

(Sadock argues against the alternative analysis that this example should be analyzed as a form of verb incorporation (Baker 1988a), and thus should be counted as *morphosyntactic* mismatch, with the semantics reading directly off the syntactic structure. The reader is referred to Sadock's discussion for details.)

2.3 Summary

To reiterate: Sadock provides a model in which morphology constitutes a separate module of the grammar, where morphological structure may be nonisomorphic with syntactic (or semantic) structure, and where the degree of nonisomorphism is governed by a set of what may be termed *Mapping Principles*.

One assumption that, at least on the face of it, Sadock would appear to subscribe to is that words have but one structure, from a purely morphology-internal point of view. In the next section, I describe relevant aspects of the approach to morphology espoused in Sproat (1985, 1988), where the assumption is made that the representation of words is distributed over different components of the grammar, and thus that the words have more than one structure. Multiple structures for words suggest the possibility of nonisomorphism between those structures, and such nonisomorphism is argued, in fact, to exist. As with Sadock's theory, nonisomorphism is constrained by a Mapping Principle. As we shall see, although the theory to be described starts with a rather different set of data and assumptions than does Sadock, both approaches end up giving a somewhat similar treatment of clitics. On the other hand, the conclusion that words have multiple structures spread across various components of the grammar led Sproat (1985) to argue that there is in fact no specifically *morphological* component, in direct opposition to Sadock's view.

3 Bracketing paradoxes and the mapping principle

3.1 Bracketing paradoxes

Let us start with what is in some ways possibly the simplest (but at the same time probably the most controversial) kind of structural mismatch that has been argued to support multiple structures for words: namely, the kind of *bracketing paradox* exemplified by the words *uneasier* or *unwiser*. As Pesetsky (1979, 1985) first observed, such words are paradoxical in the following way. The English comparative affix *-er*, as well as the superlative affix *-est*, has a phonological restriction on its distribution. Thus, while it may affix to adjectives that are monosyllabic such as those in (12a), or to trochaic disyllabic adjectives such as those in (12b), it does not generally attach to adjectives that do not fit into these categories (12c):

(12) (a)   redder, sadder, wiser, kitscher
     (b)   easier, happier, manlier
     (c)   *ecstaticker, *contenter, *speciouser

At first glance, given the above considerations, adjectives like *uneasier* or *unwiser* would appear to be unproblematic: although the adjectives *uneasy* and *unwise* do not have the right phonological properties to allow for the attachment of the comparative suffix, their bases *easy* and *wise* clearly do. This would lead us to propose the following structures for these two cases:

(13) [un [easy er]]
     [un [wise er]]

But there is a problem here: with these structures the adjectives could not possibly receive the correct interpretation, at least under the most straightforward assumptions (but see e.g. Stump 1991 for a theory under which such structures are not a problem). Pesetsky (1985) noted that structures like those in (13) ought to have the interpretations in (14):

(14) [NOT [MORE EASY]]
     [NOT [MORE WISE]]

Now, the argument is actually a little trickier than that originally presented by Pesetsky. As Sproat (1992) points out, following Horn (1988), *un-*, when attached to scalar adjectives, does not have the contradictory interpretation implied by NOT, but rather the contrary reading OPPOSITE OF. With the examples in (13), however, the difference is of little consequence for the general form of the argument: with Sproat's (1992) considerations taken into account, *uneasier* should mean roughly the same as *harder*, and *unwiser* should mean roughly the same as *more foolish*. Yet the adjectives patently do not have these interpretations. Rather, they are interpreted as the comparative forms of the (idiomatically interpreted) base adjectives *uneasy* and *unwise*. This, in turn, suggests that the structures for these words must actually be as in (15):

(15) [[UN EASY] ER]
      [[UN WISE] ER]

Thus we appear to require two opposing structures for these words. Pesetsky (1985) was the first to suggest that such cases could be viewed as a mismatch between the structural representation of the words at two different levels of the grammar. In his model the two levels were S-structure and Logical Form. As Pesetsky observed, the considerations that force the structures in (13) are basically phonological in nature, since they relate to prosodic restrictions on the affixation of the comparative suffix. Since the so-called Phonetic (or Phonological) Form component in GB syntax was supposed to "read off' S-structure, Pesetsky proposed that the structures in (13) were the S-structure representations of these words. On the other hand, the considerations motivating the structures in (15) – leaving to one side for the moment the question of what *forces* these structures – would clearly appear to be semantic. Since semantic interpretation is computed from LF, Pesetsky proposed that these were the LF representations of the words. The mapping between these two structures was accomplished by Quantifier Raising, applying to the affix *-er*, to raise it out of its internal position in (13) to the position it occupies in (15). There are a number of problems, however, in interpreting the mapping between the two structures as involving QR; there is no space to go into the details here, but the reader is referred to Sproat (1985) and Hoeksema (1987).

Sproat (1985) took a slightly different tack from Pesetsky. Following some earlier suggestions of Marantz (1984b), Sproat proposed that the structures in (15) were actually the *(word-) syntactic* (say, S-structure) representation of the words, whereas those in (13) were the *(word-) phonological* (say, PF) representations of the words. Each of the two structures was licensed by principles applying at the relevant level in the grammar, much as under Pesetsky's proposal, and the two representations were further constrained to be related by what Sproat termed the *Mapping Principle*.

First let us consider the licensing conditions. We have already seen one of these: namely, the prosodic condition that "forces" the structures in (13). This would simply be stated as a prosodic condition on the comparative affix *-er* (and *-est*), and it would be determined in the PF component that the structures in (13) satisfied these conditions. But what principle of (word) syntax might force the (word-)syntactic structures in (15)? Note that these structures were *motivated* on the basis of their meaning. However, a moment's reflection will confirm that there is nothing theoretically wrong with the alternative meanings that we discussed above, which these words happen, in fact, not to have.

Therefore, while one may believe on semantic grounds that the structures in (15) are correct, those structures do not appear to follow from semantic principles. One common suggestion for why these structures are forced is that while *un-* is a derivational affix, *-er* is apparently inflectional. On the assumption that those affixes that are termed inflectional are affixes that are "relevant to the syntax" in a way that derivational affixes are not, various researchers (e.g. Anderson 1982, Perlmutter 1988) have derived the principle that inflectional morphology must occur outside derivation. In Anderson's (1982, 1992) approach, this is encoded by having inflection take place in a later post-syntax part of the grammar than derivation, which feeds into syntax. Alternatively, one might take an approach such as that proposed by Fabb (1984), inter alia, and assume that *-er* is actually attached in the syntax. However this is handled, it seems as if one might be able to derive the semantically desirable structures in (15) on the basis of properties of the affixes involved and their interaction with syntax. So we have the following:

(16) (a) The structures in (13) are motivated on (word-) phonological grounds.
      (b) The structures in (15) are motivated on (word-) syntactic grounds.

In Sproat's (1985) model, morphemes such as *un-*, *easy*, or *-er* were considered to be pairs of phonological and syntactic entities, much as, in Sadock's theory, morphemes have both morphological and syntactic (as well as semantic) frames in their morpholexical entries. Thus, *un-*, for example, was actually a pair of elements <*un-*, $UN_{<A,A>}$>, where the phonological half *un-* was assumed to be labeled as a prefix – in Sproat's model, notions implying linear ordering such as "prefix," "suffix," or "infix" were considered to be relevant only at the *phonological level* of representation – whereas the syntactic half *UN* was marked with various morphosyntactic features, including subcategorization features that mark it as an affix (crucially not a *prefix*) that attaches to adjectives and forms adjectives. The two sets of constraints summarized in (16a) and (16b) apply to representations over, respectively, the phonological halves and the syntactic halves of morphemes.

But, one presumes, there must be some constraints on the relationships between such structures: apparently *uneasier* has two nonisomorphic structures, but surely the nonisomorphism between a word's phonological and syntactic structures cannot be arbitrarily great. This is where the Mapping Principle, stated in (17), comes into play:

(17) If A and B are *sisters* in (word-) syntactic structure, and if B is an affix, then the phonological representation of B, denoted as $\Phi(B)$, *attaches* to the phonological representation of A, $\Phi(A)$.

Phonological attachment is denoted by the *commutative* "phonological attachment" operator *: thus $\Phi(A)^*\Phi(B)$ means simply that the phonological representation of B – for example, the entry *un-* in the pair <*un-, UN$_{<A,A>}$*> – is attached to the phonological representation of A. For a case like *uneasier*, it was assumed that the (linearly unordered) (word-) syntactic structure was as in (18a) (cf. (15)). The phonological mapping of that structure is as given in (18b):

(18) (a) [ER [EASY UN]]
      (b) (-er * (easy * un-))

The phonological structure in (18b) is clearly isomorphic to the (word-) syntactic structure; so how is the nonisomorphic phonologically motivated structure derived? As noted above, in Sproat's 1985 theory it is assumed that properties such as "prefix" or "suffix," which specify relative linear ordering between an affix and its base are purely phonological properties, and it is at the phonological level of representation that considerations of linear ordering become relevant. This is formally encoded by converting the operator * into the *associative* "linear ordering" operator ⌢ whenever the phonological characteristics of particular morphemes dictate a particular ordering. So, from (18b) can be derived (19a), since *un-* is a prefix; similarly, one can then derive (19b), since *-er* is a suffix. Finally, since ⌢ is an associative operator, the structure in (19c) is equivalent to that in (19b): hence this is a licit phonological representation of the word, and since, furthermore, this is the structure that is required by the prosodic restrictions on *-er*, this is the *only* licit structure.

(19) (a) (-er * (un- ⌢ easy))
      (b) ((un- ⌢ easy) ⌢ -er)
      (c) (un- ⌢ (easy ⌢ -er))

It is important to note that while the Mapping Principle, along with the behavior of the operator ⌢, allows mappings like that exemplified by *uneasier*, not all conceivable mappings are licit. For example, there is no way to derive (20b) from (20a):

(20) (a) [RE [MIS ANALYZE]]
      (b) (mis- ⌢ (re- ⌢ analyze))

Similar views of bracketing paradoxes have been presented by subsequent authors. For example, Cohn (1989) argues that certain bracketing paradoxes in Indonesian are best viewed as a consequence of the assumption that words have separate but parallel word-syntactic and prosodic (metrical) structures. So as not to present a completely biased view of the picture, however, it is important to bear in mind that not all scholars have been convinced that examples such as *uneasier* necessitate dual structures for words. Beard (1991, 1995) has argued against this view, and Stump (1991) has presented a particularly comprehensive model of morphology and semantics in which the relevant properties of cases such as *uneasier* can be derived by recourse to only one structure.

3.2 Consequences beyond bracketing paradoxes: parallels between words and phrases

If words have both a (word-) syntactic structure and a (word-) phonological structure (which may furthermore be nonisomorphic), then they are rather like phrases. Work on phrasal phonology – for example, Selkirk 1984, Chen 1987, Pierrehumbert and Beckman 1988, among many others – has largely tended towards the view that prosodic phrasing, while being derivable from syntactic phrasing, is often not isomorphic to it, and that the prosodic representation of a sentence must be considered to be a separate level of representation from its syntactic representation. So just as sentences should be viewed as having representations that are spread over several components of the grammar, including S-structure and PF (where the prosodic representation is presumably relevant), so may words. This particular parallel between words and phrases was implicit in Sproat 1985, and was subsequently made wholly explicit in Inkelas 1990. In that work, Inkelas, like Sproat, argued that words have a (word-) syntactic structure, which is separate from what she termed the "prosodic structure." In her theory, there are different levels in the word-internal prosodic hierarchy (just as there are usually presumed to be different levels in the phrasal prosodic hierarchy, cf. Pierrehumbert and Beckman 1988), and these levels correspond to the strata of the theory of Lexical Phonology (Kiparsky 1982b; Mohanan 1982, 1986). A word such as *nongrammaticality*, which is formed at two different strata – stratum I for *-ity* suffixation, and stratum II for *non-* prefixation – is represented in Inkelas's theory as consisting of two prosodic domains, the inner one spanning just *grammaticality*, the outer one spanning the whole word. Thus, in Inkelas's view, or in the earlier view of Sproat (1985), there are clear parallels between words and phrases.

3.3 Morphology across several components

So let us assume that morphological structure is correctly thought of as being distributed over several components such that there is a syntax-like – "word-syntactic" – representation as well as a prosodic-phrase-like – "word-phonological" – representation. One is then tempted to ask the question as to whether there is any reason to assume that word syntax is really handled in a separate component of the grammar from phrasal syntax? Similarly, is there any reason to assume that word phonology obeys different principles, and must therefore be separated, from phrasal phonology? Simply put, could word syntax be just (a part of) syntax? And is there any reason to make a categorical split between lexical and postlexical phonology?

The major thesis of Sproat (1985), and subsequently of Lieber (1992) (see also e.g. Walinska de Hackbeil 1986), was that the syntax of words is properly a part of syntax, and that there is no reason to draw a categorical distinction between lexical and postlexical phonology. (Note that Fabb 1984 had previously made the somewhat more modest claim that *some* affixation, including derivational affixes such as *-ness*, were added in the syntax, but he stopped short of claiming that all morphology could be subsumed under other components of the grammar.) Sproat attempted to show, for example, that the properties of process nominals such as *destruction* or *categorization*, which had previously been considered to be wholly lexical constructions (cf. Chomsky 1970), could be derived from more general principles of syntax and semantics, given certain assumptions about the properties of the affixes involved. It is fair to say that Sproat's (1985) and Lieber's (1992) views have not gained wide acceptance, though it is equally fair to say that the reasons for insisting that morphology is a separate component from the rest of the grammar have not always been well considered; see my review of Lieber (1992) in Sproat (1993) for some discussion.

(Of course, it needs to be noted that there is a rather basic assumption that must be made before one can even begin to consider a thesis such as that of Sproat (1985): namely, that words can be broken down into morphemes in a more or less item-and-arrangement fashion. Obviously, in a theory such as Anderson's (1992) "A-morphous" morphology, where words are nearly always viewed as being constructed by the application of morphological rules, and where atomic segmentable morphemes have no status, one cannot even begin to make the assumption that word syntax should be considered to be merely a particular type of syntax. The same conclusion follows from Beard's (1995) Lexeme–Morpheme Base Morphology: in this model, only content morphemes have separate lexical entries. Function morphemes, including all affixes, lack separate lexical entries, being introduced rather by word-formation rules, much as in previous theories such as Matthews 1972 and Aronoff 1976. By contrast, Sproat's (1985) theory is based solidly upon the assumption that all morphemes, including affixes, have lexical entries, as proposed by Lieber (1980).

3.4 Other consequences: clitics

The treatment of clitics in the framework of Sproat (1985, 1988) and Marantz (1988) is quite analogous to their treatment in Autolexical Syntax. Let us consider again the English clitic *'d*. In the theory of Sproat (1985, 1988), this clitic would have a representation such as that in (21), where the left-hand portion of the entry says that phonologically *'d* is a suffix, and the right-hand portion claims that syntactically it is a verb:

(21) $'D = <\text{-}d, 'D_v>$

The same Mapping Principle account as was given for bracketing paradoxes such as *unwiser* also extends to examples such as (3a). The syntactic structure would be essentially the same as that assumed in Sadock's theory, given previously in (3a), and repeated here for convenience in (22a). The Mapping Principle, plus the associative property of the linear ordering operator ⌢ allows the desired phonological representation in (22b). Furthermore, since '*d* is phonologically specified as a suffix, and therefore must attach to something to its left in phonological representation, the structure in (3b) is actually forced.

(22)   (a)   [He [$_{vp}$ 'd [$_{vp}$ have [$_{vp}$ done it]]]]
       (b)   [he⌢-d] . . .

So, as we can see, the account given for morphological bracketing paradoxes also extends to clitics. Put slightly differently, simple clitics can be viewed as an instance of the same kind of syntax–phonology mismatch as bracketing paradoxes such as *unwiser*.

4 Summary

In this chapter we have considered two approaches to morphology that are at once rather similar, yet quite different. The similarities lie in the fact that both consider interactions between modules of the grammar, and in particular, the mapping between those modules, as crucial for understanding the place of morphology in the grammar. However, on one view the morphology stands as a fully-fledged module with its own set of principles, whereas on the alternate view the morphology is split across other components of the grammar, and is more or less absorbed into them.

Part IV Morphology in a Wider Setting

18   Diachronic Morphology

BRIAN D. JOSEPH

The various chapters of this Handbook have painted a fairly complete picture of what morphology is, what constructs are needed in the morphological component of a grammar, and how these constructs interact with one another and with other parts of the grammar. For the most part, the perspective taken on these questions has been purely synchronic; yet, as with all aspects of language (and indeed of human institutions in general), a diachronic perspective is possible as well, focusing on what happens to morphology through time. Thus in this chapter, several questions are addressed which are diachronic in their focus:

- What can change in the morphological component?
- What aspects of the morphology are stable?
- Where does morphology come from?
- What triggers change in the morphology?
- Is a general theory of morphological change possible?

Moreover, through the answers given to these questions, especially the first two, several examples of various types of morphological change are presented.

1 What can change? What is stable?

The easy answer here is that just about everything discussed in the previous chapters as constituting morphology is subject to change, especially so once one realizes that regular sound change can alter the shape of morphs without concern for the effect of such a change in pronunciation on the morphological system.[1] Thus, for example, once-distinct case endings can fall together by regular sound change (as a type of "syncretism"), as happened with the nominative plural, accusative plural, and genitive singular of (most) consonant-stem nouns in Sanskrit.[2] Still, morphological change goes beyond change induced merely by sound change, affecting not just the actual realizations of morphemes but also the categories for which these forms are exponents and the processes and operations by which these forms are realized. Thus it is possible to find change in the form taken by the various types of inflectional morphology, such as markings for person, number, gender, agreement, case, and the like, as well as the addition or loss or other alteration of such categories and the forms that express them; in the derivational processes by which stems are created and modified, and in the degree of productivity shown by these processes; in the morphological status (compound member, clitic, affix, etc.) of particular elements; in the overt or covert relationships among morphological elements, and, more generally, in the number and nature of the entries for morphemes and words in the lexicon, etc. Some examples are provided below.[3]

For instance, the category of person in the verbal system of Greek has seen several changes in the form assumed by specific person (and number) endings. Ancient Greek allomorphy between *-sai* and *-ai* for the 2SG.MEDIOPASSIVE.PRESENT ending (generally[4] distributed as *-sai* after consonants, e.g. perfect indicative *tétrip-sai* 'you have (been) rubbed ((for) yourself)', from *tríb-ō* 'rub', and *-ai* after vowels, e.g. present indicative *timâi* 'you honor (for) yourself', contracted from /*timae-ai*/, or *lúēi* 'you are unloosing for yourself', contracted from /*lúe-ai*/) has been resolved (and ultimately, therefore, reduced) through the continuation of a process begun in Ancient Greek (note vowel-stem middle forms like *deíknu-sai* 'you are showing (for) yourself' already in Classical Greek) that resulted, via the extension of one allomorph into the domain of the other, in the generalization of the postconsonantal form into all positions in Modern Greek, giving, for example, *timáse* 'you honor yourself' (as if from earlier *tima-sai). Similarly, in some Modern Greek dialects, the ending for 3PL.MEDIOPASSIVE.IMPERFECTIVE.PAST has innovated a form *-ondustan* from the *-ondusan* found elsewhere; the involvement (via a type of change often referred to as contamination or blending[5]) of the 1PL/2PL endings *-mastan* / *-sastan* is most likely responsible for the innovative form, inasmuch as the innovative form shows the introduction of an otherwise unexpected *-t-* at exactly the same point as in the 1PL/2PL endings. As a final example, from verbal endings but a different language group, there is the case of the West Germanic 2SG.ACTIVE ending; the inherited ending from proto-Germanic was *-iz (as in Gothic *-is*), yet it underwent the accretion of a marker *-t*, giving forms such as Old English *-est*, Old High German *-ist*, which is widely held to be a reflex of an enclitic form of the second-person pronoun *þu*[6] bound onto the end of a verbal form (thus probably the result of cliticization, on which see below).

A change in the realization of number marking alone can be seen in the familiar case of the nominal plural marker /-s/ in English, for it has been spreading at the expense of other plural markers for centuries. For instance, the earlier English form *shoo-n*, as a plural of 'shoe', with the plural ending *-n* still found in *oxen*, has given way to *shoe-s*, with the most frequent, and indeed default, plural ending -*s*; in this case, the marker has not passed from the language altogether, as *oxen* shows, but the domain of a particular marker has come to be more and more restricted, and that of another has expanded. The "battleground" here in the competition between morphemes is constituted by particular lexical items and the markings they select for.[7]

Somewhat parallel to such changes in the form of endings themselves are changes in effects associated with the addition of such endings. The affixation of the plural marker /-s/ in English occasions voicing of a stem-final fricative with a relatively small set of nouns, all inherited from Old English: for example, *loaf* ([lowf]) / *loaves* ([lowv-z], *house* ([haws]) / *houses* ([hawz-əz]), *oath* ([owθ]) / *oaths* ([owð-z]), though the default case now is to have no such voicing, as indicated by the fact that nouns that have entered the language since the Old English period do not participate in this morphophonemic voicing: for example, *class, gaff, gas, gauss, gross, gulf, mass, oaf, puff, safe, skiff.* Many nouns that do show this voicing are now fluctuating in the plural between pronunciations with and without the voicing, so that [owθs] for *oaths*, [(h)worfs] for *wharves*, and [hawsəz] for *houses* can be heard quite frequently.[8] It is likely that the innovative pronunciations will eventually "win out," thereby extending the domain of the default plural marking and essentially assimilating this class of nouns to the now-regular class.[9]

The creation of new markers also represents a change. Thus, when the early Germanic nominal suffix *-es-, which originally was nothing more than a stem-forming element – that is, an extension onto a root to form certain neuter noun stems, as indicated in the standard reconstruction NOM.SG *lamb-iz 'lamb' versus NOM.PL *lamb-iz-ā[10] – was reinterpreted, after sound changes eliminated the final syllable of the singular and plural forms, as a marker of the plural, a change in the marking of (certain) plural nouns in Germanic came about.[11] The ultimate form of this marker, -(e)r with the triggering of umlaut in the root (e.g. OHG nominative singular *lamb* / nominative plural *lembir*, NHG *Wort* / *Wört-er* 'word/words'), reflects the effects of other sound changes and reinterpretations involving umlaut in the root triggered by suffixation.[12]

With regard to case markings, one can note that evidence from unproductive "relic" forms embedded in fixed phrases points to an archaic proto-Indo-European inflectional marker *-s for the genitive singular of at least some root nouns, which was then replaced in various languages for the same nouns as *-es or *-os, affixes which existed as allomorphic variants marking genitive singular already in proto-Indo-European, in use with different classes of nouns. For example, the Hittite form *nekuz* 'of evening' (phonetically [nekʷt-s]) in the fixed phrase *nekuz meḫur* 'time of evening', with its *-s ending, can be compared with Greek *nukt-ós*, Latin *noct-is*, with the innovative endings *-os/-es.[13] Similarly, the genitive ending *-os (as above, with a variant *-es), which can be inferred for *n*-stem nouns such as *óno-ma* 'name' (with -*ma* from *-mṇ)[14] in pre-Greek based on the evidence of Sanskrit *nāmn-as* and Latin *nomin-is* 'of a name',[15] underwent a cycle of changes in historical Greek. It was first altered through the accretion of a -*t*-, giving -*tos* (e.g. *onóma-tos*); although the exact source of this *-t-* is disputed, and although it is found ultimately in other cases, it seems to have arisen earliest with the genitive,[16] and so its appearance perhaps shows some influence from an ablatival adverbial suffix *-tos* found in forms such as Sanskrit *ta-tas* 'then, from there' or Latin *caeli-tus* 'from heaven'. Whatever its source, it at first created a new genitive singular allomorph *-tos*; but later, when this *-t-* was extended throughout the paradigm, giving forms such as the dative singular *onóma-t-i* (for expected **ónomn-i*; cf. Sanskrit locative *nāmn-i*), the *-t-* became a virtual stem extension. At that point, one could analyze *ónoma* as having been "relexicalized" with a different base form /onomat-/, thereby reconstituting the genitive ending again as *-os* for this noun class.

Another relatively common type of change in the realization of case endings involves the accretion of what was originally a postposition onto a case suffix, creating a virtual new case form. This process seems to have been the source of various "secondary local" cases in (Old) Lithuanian (Stang 1966: 175–6, 228–32), such as the illative – for example, *galvôn* 'onto the head', formed from the accusative plus the postposition **nā* (with variant form **na*) 'in' (probably connected with Slavic *na* 'on') – and the allative – for example, *galvôspi* 'to(ward) the head', formed from the genitive plus the postposition **pie* (an enclitic form of *priê* 'at') – where influence from neighboring (or substrate) Balto-Finnic languages is often suspected as providing at least a structural model.[17] Similar developments seem to underlie the creation of an innovative locative form in Oscan and Umbrian – for example, Oscan *húrtín* 'in the garden' (so Buck 1928: 114), where a postposition *en* is responsible for the form of the ending,[18] and may be viewed in progress in the alternation between a full comitative postposition *ile* 'with' in modern Turkish (e.g. *Ahmet ile* 'with Ahmet', *Fatma ile* 'with Fatma') and a bound suffix-like element *-(y)le* (with harmonic variant *-(y)la*), e.g. *Ahmetle, Fatmayla*). It should be noted, however, that though common, the development which these combinations apparently show, from noun-plus-free-postposition to noun-plus-case-suffix, is not unidirectional; Nevis (1986), for instance, has demonstrated that in most dialects of Saame (also known as Lappish) an inherited sequence of affixes **-pta-k-ek/n* marking abessive has become a clitic word (*taga*, with variant *haga*), and more specifically a stressless postposition, while in the Enontekiö dialect, it has progressed further to become a nonclitic adverb *taga*.[19]

As the Turkish example suggests, in Lithuanian and Oscan, there most likely was a period of synchronic variation between alternates before the ultimate generalization of a new case form.[20] There can also be variation of a cross-linguistic sort here, in the sense that what is ostensibly the same development, with a postposition becoming a bound element on a nominal, might not lead to a new case form, if the overall "cut" of the language does not permit the analysis of the new form as a case-marked nominal. For instance, the special first- and second-person singular pronominal forms in Spanish, respectively *migo* and *tigo*, that occur with the preposition *con* 'with' and which derive from Latin combinations of a pronoun with an enclitic postposition – for example, *mē-cum* 'me-with' – could be analyzed as oblique case-marked pronouns. However, they are probably not to be analyzed in that way, since there is no other evidence for such case marking in the language, either with pronouns other than these or with nouns; one could just as easily, for instance, treat the element *-go* as part of a(n admittedly restricted) bipartite discontinuous "circumposition" *con . . . -go*.[21]

As examples involving the creation of new case forms show, inflectional categories – for example, Allative in Old Lithuanian – can be added to a language. Indeed, a typical change involving categories is the addition of a whole new category and the exponents of that category, though sometimes the addition is actually more a renewal or reinforcement of a previously or already existing category, as with the Locative in Oscan. Loss of categories, though, also occurs. For instance, historical documentation reveals clearly that the dual was present as an inflectional category in the verbal, nominal, and pronominal systems of early Greek (cf. the Ancient Greek ending *-methon* noted above), yet there are no traces of the dual in any system in Modern Greek; similarly, a dual category is assumed for the proto-Germanic verb based on its occurrence in Gothic, and is attested for the personal pronouns of earlier stages of the Germanic languages (e.g. Old English *ic* 'I' /*wē* 'we/PL' / *wit* 'we/DU'), yet such pronominal forms are not found in any of the modern Germanic languages, and verbal dual forms occur nowhere else among the older, or indeed the more recent, Germanic languages. Thus, as an inflectional category, one for which paradigmatic forms exist or might be expected to exist, dual number is no longer present in Greek or Germanic. Similarly, there was a loss of a synthetic perfect tense between Ancient Greek and late Koine Greek, so that Ancient forms such as *léluka* 'I have untied' became obsolete relatively early on in the post-Classical period; compare the merging of perfect and simple past tense for some speakers of Modern English, for whom *Did you eat yet?* is as acceptable as *Have you eaten yet?* Actually, though, the reconstitution (and thus addition) of the category "perfect" occurred in the medieval Greek period through the development of a periphrastic (analytic) perfect tense with 'have' as an auxiliary verb out of an earlier 'have' future/conditional tense.[22]

In the case of the Greek perfect, the medieval innovation led to what was a new category, for there had been a period of several centuries in post-Classical times when there was no distinct perfect tense. In some instances, though, it is not so much the creation of a new category as the renewal of the category through new morphological expression. The future in Greek provides a good example, for throughout its history, Greek has had a distinct future tense, contrasting formally and functionally with a present tense and a past tense, but the expression of the future has been quite different at different stages: the synthetic, suffixal, monolectic future in Ancient Greek (e.g. *grápsō* 'I will write') gave way in post-Classical times to a variety of periphrastic futures with infinitives plus auxiliary verbs, first with 'have', later with 'want' (e.g. *thélō grápsein*, lit. 'I-want to-write'), in which the parts maintained some independence (e.g. they could be separated by adverbs or inverted), but which in turn have ultimately yielded a new synthetic, monolectic future formed with a bound inseparable prefixed marker (in Standard Modern Greek, *θa*, as in *θa γrápso* 'I will write').[23]

There can be change as well in the content of a category, which, while in a sense a semantic shift, nonetheless can have morphological consequences, in that the category comes to be realized on elements not originally in its domain. For instance, the Slavic languages have developed a subcategory of "animacy" within the set of nominal gender distinctions, marked formally by the use of genitive forms where accusatives occur for inanimates; in early stages of Slavic (as represented e.g. by the earliest layer of Old Church Slavonic), only certain types of male humans (e.g. adults or freemen, as opposed to children or slaves) participated in such "animacy" marking; while later on, a wider range of nouns came to belong to this subcategory (e.g. in Russian, nouns for females show the animate declensional characteristic in the plural, and in Serbo-Croatian, an animal noun such as *lava* 'lion' follows the animate pattern).[24]

Similar to change in the content of a category is the possibility of change in the function/value of a morpheme: morphology involves the pairing of form with meaning, so it is appropriate to note here as well instances in which there is change in the function of a morpheme, even though that might be better treated under the rubric of semantic change. For instance, the development of the German plural marker *-er* discussed above clearly involves a reassignment of the function of the suffix **-iz-* (→ *-er*) from being a derivational suffix serving to create a particular stem class of nouns to being an inflectional marker of plural number. So also, the polarization of *was/were* allomorphy in some dialects of English to correlate with a positive/negative distinction, so that *were* is more likely to occur with *-n't* than is *was* (Trudgill 1990, Schilling-Estes and Wolfram 1994), shows a reinterpretation of allomorphy that once signaled singular versus plural (or indicative versus subjunctive).

The changes illustrated so far have been fairly concrete, in that they concern the phonological realization of morphological categories or the categories themselves (which need some realization). There can also be change of a more abstract type, and a particularly fruitful area to examine is the matter of lexical relations. The components of grammar concerned with morphology, whether a separate morphological component or the lexicon, reflect the relationships that exist among forms of a language, whether through lexical "linking" rules, lexical redundancy rules, or common underlying forms. Significant changes can occur in the salience of certain relations, to the point where forms that were clearly related at an earlier stage of the language are just as clearly perceived by speakers at a later stage not to be related. Etymological dictionaries[25] provide dozens of examples involving separate lexical items that have lost any trace of a connection except for those speakers who have secondarily acquired knowledge of the relationship: for example, *two* and *twine*, originally a 'double thread' (both from the earlier root for 'two'), or *yellow* and *gall* (both originally from a root for 'shine', but with different original vocalism and different suffixal formations),[26] to name just a few such sets from English. This situation frequently arises with words that are transparent compounds at one stage but lose their obvious composition. For instance, the modern English word *sheriff* derives from an Old English compound *scīrgerēfa*, literally the 'reeve' (*gerēfa*) of the 'shire' (*scīr*), but is not obviously connected in any way with Modern English *shire* or *reeve*; nor is *lord* plausibly connected synchronically with *loaf* or *ward*, the modern continuations of its Old English components (*hlāford*, literally 'bread-guardian', from *hlāf* 'bread' plus *weard* 'guardian'). In these cases, both sound changes, which can obscure the once obvious relationship, as with *l(-ord)* and *loaf*, and semantic changes, as with *(l-)ord* and *ward* (the latter no longer meaning 'guardian'), can play a role in separating lexical items once related synchronically.[27] And borderline cases provide some difficulties for analysis; for instance, are the semantically still compatible words *two* and *twelve* to be synchronically related in Modern English, and if so, does *two* derive from a form with an underlying cluster /tw-/? To a certain degree, the answers to such questions will depend on meta-theoretical concerns, such as a decision on the degree of abstractness to be allowed in morphophonological analyses (on which, see below).

In the face of such examples of change, it is equally important to reflect on what does not or cannot change in the morphology. To the extent that there are well-established principles and constructs that are taken to be part of the basic theoretical framework for morphology – for example, Lexical Integrity, Morphology-free Syntax, disjunctive ordering for competing morphological rules, and the like – presumably these will not change; they are the theoretical building blocks of any account of the morphological component, and thus cannot change diachronically (though they can of course be altered by linguists in their descriptions/accounts if synchronic or diachronic facts make it clear, for instance, that syntax is not morphology-free, or the like).

Among these theoretical building blocks are some that have a significant impact on diachronic accounts of morphology, in particular those that allow for the determination of the borderlines between components of grammar. That is, it is widely recognized that there is interaction at least between morphology and phonology (witness the term *morphophonology* and the possibility of phonological constraints on morphological rules) and between morphology and syntax (witness the term *morphosyntax*). Thus it becomes appropriate to ask how we can tell when some phenomenon crosses the border from "pure" phonology into morphology, or vice versa, or from "pure" syntax into morphology. Although there is a purely synchronic question here of how to characterize a given phenomenon in a given language for a given period of time, the matter of crossing component boundaries is also a diachronic issue. If a once-phonological phenomenon comes to be conditioned completely morphologically, and is considered to be part of the morphological component and not the phonological component, then there has been a change in the grammar of the language with regard to that phenomenon; the surface realization of the forms may not change, but the grammatical apparatus underlying and producing or licensing those surface forms has changed. Thus, when the vowel

fronting induced by a following high vowel (so-called umlaut) in early German
came in later stages of the language, when the phonetic motivation for the
fronting was obscured or absent on the surface, to be an effect associated
with the addition of certain suffixes (e.g. the diminutive -*chen*, the noun plural
-*e*, etc.) or with the expression of certain categories (e.g. plurals of certain
nouns which take no overt suffix, such as *Bruder* 'brother', with plural *Brüder*),
one interpretation is that the umlauting process is no longer phonological in
nature, but rather is a morphological process invoked by certain morphological categories.[28] Similarly, at a stage when the expression of locatives in
(pre-)Oscan was accomplished by a noun plus a postposition, syntactic rules
that license postpositional phrases were responsible for the surface forms;
when the noun fused with the postpositional element to such an extent that
a virtual new case-marker was created, the responsibility for the ultimate
expression of the locative effectively moved out of the realm of syntax and
into the morphological component.

These examples and the relevance of theoretical decisions separating components of grammar point to the need to recognize the impact that the theory
of grammar one adopts has on diachronic analyses. For example, permitting
a degree of abstractness in phonological analyses can often allow for a description that is purely phonological rather than morphological in nature. Umlaut
in German, for instance, could still be considered to be purely phonological if
each suffix or category now associated with umlaut of a stem were represented underlyingly with a high front vowel to act as the triggering segment;
deleting that segment before it could surface would have to be considered to
be allowable abstraction. Similarly, the palatalizations of stem-final velars in
various Slavic languages that accompany the attachment of certain suffixes
(e.g. Russian adjectival -*nyj*, as in *vostoč-nyj* 'eastern' from the noun *vostok*
'(the) east') were once triggered by a suffix-initial short high front vowel (the
"front yer") that was ultimately lost in most positions in all the languages;
thus a synchronic, purely phonological analysis could be constructed simply
by positing an abstract front yer that triggers the palatalization and is then
deleted.[29]

2 Where does morphology come from?

The examples in section 1 show that the primary source of morphology is
material that is already present in the language, through the mediation of
processes of resegmentation and reinterpretation applied in a variety of ways,
as well as by other processes of change – for example, sound changes – that
lead to grammaticalization. In addition, morphology may enter a language
through various forms of language contact.

Thus, examples of blending or contamination involve preexisting material,
as in the case of Greek 1DUAL.MEDIOPASSIVE ending (see n. 5), where a "crossing"

of the 1PL.MEDIOPASSIVE ending *-metha* with the 2DUAL.MEDIOPASSIVE ending *-sthon* yielded *-methon*. In a parallel fashion, when a sequence of elements is resegmented – that is, given a different "parsing" by speakers from what it previously or originally had – material already in the language is given a new life. The English *-ness* suffix, for instance, derives from a resegmentation of a Germanic abstract noun suffix *-assu- attached to *n*-stem adjectives, with subsequent spread to different stem types; thus *ebn-assu- 'equality' (stem: *ebn- 'even, equal') was treated as if it were *eb-nassu-, and from there *-nassu- could spread, as in Old English *ehtness* 'persecution' (from the verb *eht-an* 'to pursue') or *gōdness* 'goodness' (from the adjective *gōd*). The extreme productivity of this new suffix in Modern English, capable of being added to virtually any new adjective (e.g. *gauche-ness*, *uptight-ness*) shows how far beyond its original locus a form can go, and also how the productivity of a morpheme can change, since *-ness* originally had a more limited use.

Other types of reanalysis similarly draw on material present at one stage of a language in one form and transform it at a later stage. In many cases of desyntacticization, for instance, where once-syntactic phrases are reinterpreted as word-level units with affixes that derive from original free words or clitics, as in the Oscan locative discussed above, the same segmental material is involved, but with a different grammatical status. Sometimes, though, such reanalyses are accompanied (or even triggered) by phonological reductions, so that the result is just added segmental material with no clear morphological value; the *-t* of Old English *wit* 'we two', for instance, comes from a phonologically regular reduction of the stem for 'two' in an unstressed position – that is, from *we-dwo – and similar cases involving old compounds – for example, *sheriff* and *lord* – were noted above. Moreover, when sound changes obscure the conditioning factors for a phonologically induced effect, and a new morphological process arises, as with umlaut in German, again what has occurred is the reanalysis of already existing material, in this case the fronting of a stem vowel that accompanies the addition of an affix; the new process is then available to spread into new contexts, having been freed from a connection to a particular phonological trigger.

Sometimes semantic shifts are involved in such reanalyses. The well-known example of the new suffix *-gate* in English is a case in point. This suffix originated from the phrase *Watergate affair* (or *scandal* or the like), referring to the events in the aftermath of a burglary at the Watergate apartment complex that brought down the Nixon administration in the early 1970s, through a truncation of the phrase to *Watergate* (e.g. *Nixon resigned because of Watergate*) and a reanalysis in which the *-gate* part was treated as a suffix and not the compound member it originally was in the place-name *Watergate*. It then spread, giving coinages such as *Irangate* (for a scandal in the 1980s involving selling arms to Iran), *Goobergate* (for a scandal alleged in 1979 to have involved then-President Carter's peanut warehouse), and numerous others.[30] What is especially interesting about this reanalysis is that in the process of *-gate* becoming a suffix, there was a shift in its meaning, so that in *X-gate*, the suffix *-gate* (but not the free word *gate*) itself came to mean 'a scandal involving X', an abbreviation, as it were, for 'a scandal involving X reminiscent of the Watergate scandal'.

Other processes similar to these that create pieces of words produce as well new lexical items, and thus contribute to the morphological component, to the extent that it includes the lexicon. Without going into great detail, one can note active processes of word formation such as compounding, acronymic coinage (e.g. *cpu* (pronounced [sipiyu]) for *central processing unit*, *ram* ([ræm]) for *random-access memory*, *rom* ([ram]) for *read-only memory*), clipping (e.g. *dis* from *(show) disrespect*, *rad* from *radical*, *prep* from *prepare* and from *preparatory*, *vet* from *veteran* and from *veterinarian*), lexical blends (e.g. *brunch* from *breakfast* crossed with *lunch*), phrasal truncations (such as the source of the word *street* via a truncation, with a semantic shift, of Latin *via strāta* 'road (that has been) paved' to simply *strāta*), and so on. It is worth noting here that whereas virtually any piece of a word, even suffixes, can be "elevated" to the status of a free word via clipping, inflectional morphemes seem to be resistant to such an "upgrading"; thus although *ism* as a free word meaning 'distinctive doctrine, system, or theory' (*AHD* 1992) has been extracted out of *communism, socialism*, etc., instances in which suffixes like English *-ed* or *-s* become words for 'past' or 'many' or the like appear not to exist.

One final language-internal path for the development of morphology involves instances in which the conditions for an analysis motivating a sequence of sounds as a morpheme arise only somewhat accidentally. In particular, if a situation occurs in which speakers can recognize a relation among words, then whatever shared material there is among these words can be elevated to morphemic status. This process is especially evident with phonesthemes, material that shows vague associative meanings that are often sensory based, such as the initial sequence *gl-* in English for 'brightly visible', as in *gleam, glitter, glisten, glow*, and the like. Some linguists are hesitant to call these elements morphemes, and terms like quasi-morpheme, submorphemic unit, and others have been used on occasion, even though by most definitions, they fulfill the criteria for being full morphemes. Leaving aside the synchronic issue they pose for analysis, it is clear that they can come to have some systematic status in a grammar, for they can spread and be exploited in new words (e.g. *glitzy*, which, whether based on German *glitzern* 'to glitter' or a blend involving *ritzy*, nonetheless fits into the group of other "bright" *gl-* words). A good example of this process is afforded by the accumulation of words in English that end in *-ag* (earlier [-ag], now [-æg]) and have a general meaning connoting 'slow, tired, or tedious action', specifically *drag* 'lag behind', *fag* 'grow weary', *flag* 'droop', and *lag* 'straggle', all attested in Middle English but of various sources (some Scandinavian borrowings, some inherited from earlier stages of English); at the point at which four words with both a similar meaning and a similar form were present in the language, by roughly the thirteenth century, an analysis was possible of this *-ag* as a (sub-) morphemic element. That it had some reality as such a unit is shown by the fact that these words "attracted" a semantically related word with a different form into their "orbit" with a concomitant change in its form; *sag* 'sink, droop' in an early form (sixteenth century) ended in *-k*, yet a perceived association with *drag/fag/flag/lag* and the availability of *-ag* as a marker of that group brought it more in line with the other members, giving ultimately *sag*.

The example of *-gate* above also shows language contact as a source of new morphology in a language, for it has spread as a borrowed derivational suffix into languages other than English; Schuhmacher 1989 has noted its presence in German, Kontra 1992 gives several instances of *-gate* from Hungarian, and Joseph 1992 provides Greek and Serbo-Croatian examples. Numerous examples of borrowed derivational morphology are to be found in the Latinate vocabulary in English, but it should be noted also that inflectional morphology can be borrowed. Various foreign plurals in English, such as *criteria*, *schemata*, *alumnae*, illustrate this point, as do the occurrence of Turkish plural endings in some (now often obsolete) words in Albanian of Turkish origin – for example, *at-llarë* 'fathers', *bej-lerë* 'landlords' (Newmark et al. 1982: 143)[31] – and the verb paradigms in the Aleut dialect spoken on the island of Mednyj, which show Russian person/number endings added onto native stems – for example, *uŋuči-ju* 'I sit' / *uŋuči-it* '(s)he sits' (Thomason and Kaufman 1988: 233–8). Although it is widely believed that inflectional morphology is particularly resistant to borrowing and to being affected by language contact, Thomason and Kaufman (1988) have shown that what is crucial is the social context in which the contact and borrowing occur. Thus the intense contact and the degree of bilingualism needed to effect contact-induced change involving inflectional morphology simply happen not to arise very often, so that any rarity of such change is not a linguistic question *per se*. Moreover, the spread of derivational morphology across languages may actually take place through the spread of whole words, which are then "parsed" in the borrowing language; the *-gate* suffix in Greek, for instance, occurred first in labels for scandals that followed the English names directly (e.g. "Irangate") before being used for Greek-internal scandals.

3 What triggers change in the morphology?

Historical linguists tend to divide causes of change into those internal to the linguistic system itself and those that are external – that is, due to language contact. The discussion in section 2 shows that language contact is indeed one potential cause of morphological change, and that under the right social conditions for the contact, virtually any morphological element (inflectional, derivational, bound, free, whatever) can be transferred from one language to another. Examining contact-induced morphological change then becomes more a matter – an important one, to be sure – of cataloguing the changes and determining the sociolinguistic milieu in which the contact occurs.[32] There is far more to say, however, about internal forces triggering change in the morphology.

From a consideration of the examples above, it emerges that much morphological change involves "analogy," understood in a broad sense to take in any change due to the influence of one form on another.[33] This process is most evident in blending or contamination, where there is mutual influence, with a part of one form and a part of another combining; but it extends to other types of morphological change as well.

For instance, the spread of *-t-* described above in the stem of Greek neuter nouns in *-ma* involved the influence of the genitive singular forms, the original locus of the *-t-*, over other forms within the paradigm. Such paradigm-internal analogy, often referred to as "levelling," is quite a common phenomenon. An interesting example, to be reexamined below from a different perspective, involves the reintroduction of *-w-* into the nominative of the adjective for 'small' in Latin: in early Latin, the adjective had nominative singular *parw-os* and genitive *parw-ī*, and paradigmatic allomorphy *par-os* versus *parw-ī* resulted when a sound change eliminated *-w-* before a round vowel; paradigm-internal analogical pressures led to the restoration of the *-w-*, giving ultimately the Classical Latin forms *parvus / parvī*.

Analogical influence among forms is not restricted to those that are paradigmatically related. Two elements that mark the same category, but with different selectional properties, can exert analogical pressures, leading to the spread of one at the expense of another. Examples of such analogies include cases across form classes where the elements involved are different morphemes, as with the spread of the *-s* plural in English at the expense of the *-(e)n* plural, discussed in section 1, as well as cases in which one conditioned allomorphic variant extends its domain over another, thereby destroying the once-conditioned alternation, as with the spread of the Greek 2SG.MEDIOPASSIVE ending *-sai*, also discussed above.

Similarly, in cases of folk etymology, speakers reshape a word based on other forms that provide what they see as a semantically (somewhat) motivated parsing for it; for example, *tofu* for some speakers is [tofud], as if a compound with *food*, and *crayfish*, first borrowed from French in the fourteenth century as *crevise*, was remade as if containing the lexeme *fish*. In such cases, which are quite common with borrowings or words that are unfamiliar for reasons such as obsolescence, there is influence from one form being brought to bear on the shape of another. More generally, many cases of reanalysis/reinterpretation involve some analogical pressures, especially when the reanalysis is induced by models that exist elsewhere in the language; for instance, when Middle English *pease*, a singular noun meaning 'pea', was reanalyzed as a plural, allowing for the creation (by a process known as "backformation") of a singular *pea*, the influence of other plurals of the shape [. . . V-z] played a role.

Thus there is a cognitive dimension to (certain types of) morphological change, in the sense that it often involves speakers actively making connections among linguistic forms and actively reshaping their mental representations of forms.[34] Indeed, analogy as a general mode of thinking and reasoning has long been treated within the field of psychology, and studies by Esper (e.g.

Esper 1925 and the posthumous Esper 1973) were an early attempt to determine the psychological basis for analogical change in language.[35] More recently, analogical change has been viewed from the perspective of a theory of signs; Anttila (1972), for instance, has argued that the semiotic principle of "one form to one meaning" drives most analogical change, in that levelings, form-class analogies, folk etymology, and the like all create a better fit between form and meaning, while proponents of Natural Morphology[36] similarly work with the importance of degrees of iconicity in the form–meaning relationship and, for example, evaluate changes in the marking of inflectional categories or derivational relationships in terms of how they lead to a better fit with universal iconic principles. Even the process of grammaticalization has been given a cognitive interpretation; Heine et al. (1991: 150), for instance, have argued that "underlying grammaticalization there is a specific cognitive principle called the 'principle of the exploitation of old means for novel functions' by Werner and Kaplan (1963: 403)," and they note that in many cases grammaticalization involves metaphorical extension from one cognitive domain – for example, spatial relations – to another – for example, temporal relations (as with *behind* in English).[37]

Moving away from these more cognitive, functional, and/or mentalistic views of what causes morphological change, one can find various formal approaches to analogy. The most notable[38] is the generative approach, in which analogy is nothing more than changes in the rule system that generates a given paradigm. The Latin case mentioned above whereby a paradigm of *parw-os* / *parw-ī* yielded *par-os* / *parw-ī* by sound change and finally *parvus* / *parvī* by paradigm leveling could be seen as the addition of a rule of $w \rightarrow \emptyset$ before round vowels (the sound change) operating on an underlying form for the nominative with the *-w-*, and then the loss of that rule giving the underlying stem-final *-w-* a chance to surface once again. What is left unexplained in such an account is why the rule would be lost at all; early generative accounts (e.g. R. King 1969, Kiparsky 1968) simply gave a higher value to a grammar with fewer rules or features in the rules (but then where, as Andersen (1973: 766) asked, would added rules come from, and why would they even be added in the first place?) or unnatural rule orderings, whereas later accounts (especially Kiparsky 1971) gave higher value to grammars that generated paradigm-internal regularity, a condition that tacitly admits that the traditional reliance on the influence of related surface forms had some validity after all. Another type of generative reinterpretation of analogy is that given by Anderson (1988a), who, as observed in footnotes 7 and 9, sees analogies such as the spread of the English *-s* plural or the loss of morphophonemic voicing in certain English plurals as being actually changes in the lexically idiosyncratic specifications for the inflectional markings, derivational processes, and the like selected by particular lexical items.

Finally, any discussion of causes must make reference to the fact that, as is the case with all types of language change, the spread of morphological innovations is subject to social factors governing the evaluation of an innovation by speakers and its adoption by them. Indeed, if one takes the view that true language change occurs only when an innovation has spread throughout a speech community,[39] then the various processes described here only provide a starting point for a morphological innovation, but do not describe ultimate morphological change in the languages in question. The presence of synchronic variation in some of the changes discussed above, as with the loss of morphophonemic voicing in English plurals, shows how the opportunity can arise for nonlinguistic factors to play a role in promoting or quashing an innovation.

4 Is a general theory of morphological change possible?

Over the years, there have been numerous attempts to develop a general theory of morphological change, and the approaches to the causes of morphological change outlined in the previous section actually represent some such attempts. To a greater or lesser extent, there have been successes in this regard. For instance, the recognition of a cognitive dimension to analogy and to grammaticalization has been significant, as has the corresponding understanding of the role of iconicity. The generative paradigm has been embraced by many, but a few further comments about it are in order.

Most important, as noted above, an account of analogical change in paradigms that is based on changes in the rules by which the paradigms are generated does not extend well to analogical changes that cannot involve any rules, such as blends or contamination. As Hock (1991: 256) points out, a development such as Middle English *femelle* (a loan word from French) becoming *female* by contamination with *male* does not involve any generative rules; yet it still took place, and one would be hard-pressed to account for the change in the vocalism of this word without some reference to pressure from the semantically related *male*. Similarly, the change discussed by Anttila (1972: 89), in which the nominative singular of the uniquely inflected word for 'month' in the Elean dialect of Ancient Greek became *meús* (with genitive *mēn-ós*, versus e.g. Attic nominative *meís*), based on the uniquely inflected word for the god Zeus (nominative *Zeús*, genitive *Zēn-ós*), could not involve any generative phonological rules, since both words were the only members of their respective declensional classes, and thus were probably listed in the lexicon rather than rule-governed in terms of their inflection.[40] On the other hand, the semiotic and cognitive views of analogy – for instance, invoking a one-form-to-one-meaning principle – can provide a motivation not only for the putative cases of analogy as rule-change, but also for those that could not involve rule change.[41] Moreover, cases of bi-directional leveling, as presented by Tiersma 1978 with data from Frisian, in which some paradigms involving a particular phonological rule are leveled as if the rule had been lost, while others involving the same rule are levelled as if the rule had been generalized, make it difficult to give any predictive value to a rule-based approach to analogy.[42] Finally, the recognition of paradigm uniformity as a part of the evaluation metric in Kiparsky 1971 is tantamount to recognizing analogy in its traditional sense. As Anttila (1972: 129, 131) puts it: "What rule changes always describe, then, is the before–after relationship. They give a mechanism for description, not a historical explanation . . . Rule change is not a primary change mechanism, but an effect."

This is not to say, however, that traditional analogy is not without some problems. As has frequently been pointed out, it often seems unconstrained, and there is an element of unpredictability about it. When will analogy occur? What direction will leveling take? Which forms will serve as models? And so on. In part to address this uncertainty about the workings of analogy, some scholars have attempted to formulate a set of general tendencies or regularities governing analogy. The two most widely discussed schemes are those of Kuryłowicz (1945–9)[43] and Mańczak (1958). A full discussion of these proposals is beyond the scope of the present chapter,[44] but it is generally held that Kuryłowicz's "laws" are, as Collinge (1985: 252) citing Anttila (1977: 76–80) puts it, more "qualitative and formal" in nature, whereas Mańczak's tendencies are more "quantitative and probabilistic." It can be noted also that some of their specific proposals complement one another, some are contradictory, some are tautologous and thus of little value, but some[45] – for example, Mańczak's second tendency ("root alternation is more often abolished than introduced") and Kuryłowicz's first "law" ("a bipartite marker tends to replace an isofunctional morpheme consisting of only one of these elements") are valuable tools in analyzing analogical changes, as they reflect tensions present in language in general: respectively the need to have redundancy for clarity and the desire to eliminate unnecessary or unmotivated redundancy. Moreover, Kuryłowicz's fourth "law" has, in the estimation of Hock (1991: 230), proved to be "a very reliable guide to historical linguistic research." This "law," which states that an innovative form takes on the primary function and that the older form it replaces, if it remains at all, does so only in a secondary function, can be exemplified by the oft-cited case[46] of English *brethren*; this form, originally a plural of the kinship term *brother*, is now relegated to a restricted function in the meaning "fellow members of a church" or the like, and, significantly, cannot be used in the primary sense of *brothers* as a kinship term.

Other general tendencies of morphological change have been proposed and have proved quite useful. For instance, there is the important observation by C. W. Watkins 1962 that third-person forms are the major "pivot" upon which new paradigms are constituted.[47] However, as with other proposed principles, "Watkins' Law" is also just a tendency; the change of the 3PL past ending in Modern Greek to *-ondustan* discussed in section 1, which shows the effects of pressure from 1PL and 2PL endings on the 3PL, might constitute a counterexample, for instance.

In the end, it must be admitted that much morphological change involves lexically particular developments, and it is significant that even the spread of analogical changes seems to be tied to particular lexical items; thus, unlike sound change, which generally shows regularity in that it applies equally to all candidates for the change that show the necessary phonetic environment, morphological change, especially analogical change, is sporadic in its propagation. Thus, as shown in section 1, even with the vast majority of nouns in English now showing an innovative *-s* plural, a few instances of the older *-(e)n* marker remain in *oxen, children,* and *brethren.*

Thus, it may well be that for morphological change, a general theory – that is, a predictive theory – is not even possible, and that all that can be done is to catalogue tendencies, which, however valid they may be, do not in any sense constitute inviolable predictions about what types of changes will necessarily occur in a given situation. In that sense, accounts of morphological change are generally retrospective only, looking back over a change that has occurred and attempting to make sense of it.

5   Conclusion

Although morphological change in general shows much that is unpredictable, the examples listed herein provide a good overall view of the types of changes that are likely to be encountered in the histories of the languages of the world, the causes underlying these changes, and the ways linguists have gone about explaining the observed changes.

One final observation on the extent of the domain of morphological change is in order. Much morphological change, as described here, involves change in lexical items – in their form, their selectional properties, their relations to other lexical items, and so on – and this is all the more so if inflectional affixes are listed in the lexicon instead of being introduced by morphological rules. It is generally accepted that at least certain types of sound changes involve lexeme-by-lexeme spread (the cases of so-called lexical diffusion – cf. Wang 1969 but especially Labov 1981, 1994), and it seems that in some instances, at least, the impetus for the spread of a pronunciation into new lexical items is essentially analogical in nature.[48] Also, there are many so-called irregular sound changes – for example, metathesis or dissimilation – that apply only sporadically, and thus end up being lexically particular rather than phonologically general. Moreover, at least certain types of changes typically relegated to the study of syntactic change, for instance, changes in agreement patterns, grammaticalization, movement from word to clitic to affix, reduction of once-biclausal structures to monoclausal,[49] and the like – that is to say, much of syntactic change other than word order change – ultimately involves morphology or at least morphosyntax in some way. Thus it is possible to argue that much – perhaps most – language change has a morphological/morpholexical basis, or at least has some morphological involvement. Such a view would then provide some dia-chronic justification for the importance of morphology in language in general, and thus for a morphological component in the grammars of particular languages.[50]

ACKNOWLEDGEMENTS

I gratefully acknowledge a fellowship from the American Council of Learned Societies Joint Committee on Eastern Europe and a sabbatical leave from the College of Humanities, The Ohio State University, both of which enabled me to produce the present piece, an earlier version of which appeared in *Ohio State University Working Papers in Linguistics*, 46 (1995), 16–37. I would like to thank Rex Wallace, Nigel Vincent, and Richard Janda for helpful comments on this chapter. I owe a considerable intellectual debt to Joki Schindler, who opened my eyes some twenty years ago to the wonders of diachronic morphology and whose stimulating lectures provided some of the examples included herein; I dedicate this work to his memory, and hope that it will serve as a lasting monument to his influence in our field.

NOTES

1　This statement conceals a large controversy which cannot be discussed adequately here: viz. whether sound change is a purely mechanical phonetic process that is blind to the specific morphemes and words it operates on, and to their morphological composition, e.g. whether they are morphologically complex or monomorphemic. Thus, in principle, one could imagine that sound changes could be morphologically conditioned, and so could fail to apply in, or could apply only to, certain categories or particular morphemes. The evidence, however, seems to favor viewing sound change as being only phonetically conditioned in its outcome at least, with apparent cases of nonphonetic (so-called grammatical) conditioning being the result of phonetically conditioned sound change followed by analogical (morphological) change. See Hock 1976 for some discussion and relevant literature.

2　These endings all have the form -*as* in Sanskrit, but, as comparisons with other Indo-European languages show, they derive from three different sources (GEN.SG *-os, cf. Greek *pod-ós* 'of a foot'; NOM.PL *-es, cf. Greek *pód-es* 'feet'; ACC.PL *-ns, cf. Greek *pód-as* 'feet').

3　These examples are drawn primarily from the languages I know best and thus am best able to vouch for; they therefore have what might be perceived as an Indo-European bias. However, there is every reason to believe that the same types of examples are to be found in other languages, and that the phenomena illustrated here are not just Indo-European types of changes. See e.g. Bloomfield 1946: §§18–20; Anttila 1972: 91, 97; Robertson 1975; Hock 1991: 200–2; and Dai 1990 for some examples from Algonquian, Estonian, Mayan, Maori, and Mandarin Chinese, respectively, to mention just a few well-established cases from other language families.

4   But see below regarding forms like *deíknusai* that disturb this otherwise regular allomorphic pattern.

5   The Ancient Greek innovative 1DUAL.MEDIOPASSIVE ending -*methon*, which filled a gap in the paradigm (note the absence of a 1DUAL.ACTIVE form) and seems to have arisen as a blend of 1PL.MEDIOPASSIVE ending -*metha* with the 2DUAL.MEDIOPASSIVE ending -*sthon* (note also the 2DUAL.ACTIVE -*ton*), provides another example of a change in a personal ending due to blending/ contamination.

6   The enclitic form, occurring as it does with a stop, presumably reflects a combinatory variant of *pu* after a sibilant.

7   See Anderson 1988a for discussion of the spread of the *s*-plural in English; he argues that the mechanism is one of the elimination of lexically specified idiosyncrasies and the emergence of the default marking; he notes that this interpretation is consistent with, and in fact predicted by, the principle of disjunctive ordering for morphological rules. For a similar example from German, where an -*s* marking for plural is spreading, see Janda 1990.

8   For instance, [owθs] and [(h)worfs] are given in *AHD* 1992 as (innovative) variants; [hawsəz], while common in Central Ohio at

least, has not yet been enshrined in the dictionary.

9   As with the spread of the *s*-plural (see n. 7), this loss of morphophonemic voicing can be seen as the removal of an idiosyncratic specification from the lexical listing of each such noun. See also Anttila 1972: 126–7 for discussion of this example and of parallel ones involving consonant gradation from Baltic Finnic. It should be noted that occasionally the idiosyncratic marking has spread to a noun not originally undergoing this process; e.g. *dwarf* originally had no overt plural marker in Old English, so that the variant plural *dwarves*, alongside the synchronically more regular *dwarfs*, represents a spread of the synchronically irregular pattern.

10   See e.g. Prokosch 1938 for this reconstruction.

11   The situation is actually a bit more complicated, as is clear from the fact that early OHG had -*ir*- in some singular forms, specifically the genitive, the dative, and the instrumental; but as the suffix came to be interpreted purely as a marker of number, as the nominative forms would lead a speaker to surmise, it disappeared from the singular. Still, Salmons (1994: 224–5), in his recent discussion of these facts, notes variability, in particular with regard to -*ir*- less plural forms, throughout the OHG period and dialect space, and concludes that -*ir*- as marking only plurality was not "firmly established in many dialects." See also Anderson 1988a for an interpretation in terms of changes in lexical specifications.

12   Note also that since in earlier stages of Germanic, *Wort* did not have this plural marking (cf. OHG SG *wort*

/ PL *wort*), the extension of this umlaut-plus-*(e)r* plural marking is a process parallel to the example given of the -*s* plural in English; see also nn. 7 and 11.

13 That this archaic inflection is embedded in a fixed phrase (likewise Vedic Sanskrit *dan* 'house/ GEN.SG', from **dem-s*, found in the fixed phrase *patir dan* 'master of the house') is not surprising, for it shows the retention of an older pattern in what is in essence a synchronically unanalyzable expression (like an idiom). From a methodological standpoint in doing historical morphology and morphological reconstruction, it is often useful to look to such expressions for clues as to earlier patterns.

14 The reconstruction of the root for this word is somewhat controversial, and only the stem suffix is at issue here, so no attempt is made to give a complete reconstruction.

15 The **-os/-es* ending in these languages may itself be a late PIE replacement for an earlier simple **-s* ending, based on such forms as the Old Irish genitive singular *anmae* 'of a name', where the ending is from **-men-s* (so Thurneysen 1970: 60); hence the specification "pre-Greek" is used here for the ending, since it may not be the oldest form of this inflectional ending with this noun in PIE.

16 A -*t*- extension is found with several other nominal stem classes in Greek – e.g. the neuter -*as*- stems – but it is not found with all members of the class, and a few specific nouns – e.g. *kréas* 'meat' – show it earliest in the genitive singular (4th century BC), with spread to other case forms coming much later. Even with a noun like

ónoma, which, as noted below, shows the extension of the -*t*- into other case forms, early (Homeric) Greek shows no (metrical) trace of the -*t*- in the dative plural (see Chantraine 1973: 74–5, 82–3).

17 See Thomason and Kaufman (1988: 242–3) for some discussion of the substratum hypothesis, though Stang (1966: 228–9) argues against this view.

18 That this one-time postposition has become a true case ending in Oscan is shown by its appearance on an adjective, in apparent agreement with the noun it modifies; see Buck 1928: 114 for this interpretation. This innovative form presumably replaced an inherited locative, still found to a limited extent in Latin.

19 Within the literature on grammaticalization (e.g. Traugott and Heine (eds) 1991a, b; Hopper and Traugott 1993) there is much discussion of the claim that developments in grammaticalization are subject to a principle of unidirectionality, whereby movement supposedly is always from less grammatical to more grammatical, with meanings always going from concrete to abstract; see Joseph and Janda 1988, Campbell 1991, Janda 1995, and Joseph 1996a for discussion of some counterevidence to this claim.

20 Compare the situation with morphophonemic voicing in English plurals, discussed above (and see n. 8), and note the ongoing variation in the marking of past participles in English, with older -*(e)n* in some verbs giving way to the more widespread -*ed* (as in *sewn / sewed, shown / showed, proven / proved*, etc.).

21 The Spanish example suggests that changes in case-marking systems are not restricted to the distant past,

though the failure of *-go* to spread to other pronouns (indeed, it has retreated somewhat from wider use in older stages of the language) or to be used with other prepositions argues that it is not really a case-marking device. Similarly, the innovative use in certain varieties of written English of *inwhich*, as in *Shopping is a task inwhich one should enjoy*, has led some researchers – e.g. J. R. Smith 1981 and Riley and Parker 1986 – to analyze it as a new case form of the relative pronoun, though Montgomery and Bailey 1991, in an extensive study of the use of the form, argue persuasively against that interpretation. Nonetheless, such examples provide the opportunity to witness the fate of case-like forms that occur in a restricted domain of the grammar, and thus provide some insights into the general processes by which such forms can arise and take hold in a language.

22 Most likely, the path of development was through the conditional tense (past tense of the future) shifting first to a pluperfect (compare the fluctuation in Modern English between a pluperfect form and what is formally a past tense of the future utilizing the modal *would* in *if* clauses – e.g. *If I had only known = If I would have known*), from which a present perfect and other perfect formations could have developed. See Joseph 1983: 62–4; 1996b, for some discussion.

23 The exact path from *thélō grápsein* to *θa γrápso* is a bit convoluted and indirect; see Joseph 1983: 64–7; 1990: ch. 5; 1996a for discussion and further details. The only material that can intervene between *θa* and the verb in Modern Greek is other bound elements, in particular the weak object pronouns.

24 Even in Old Church Slavonic, there was some variability in category membership, and nouns for 'slave', 'child', various animals, etc. showed some fluctuation between animate and nonanimate inflection; see Lunt 1974: 46 and Meillet 1897 for some discussion. The descriptions in Comrie and Corbett (eds) 1993 provide a useful overview of the realization of animacy throughout the various Slavic languages. Thomason and Kaufman (1988: 249–50) suggest that this category may have developed through a Uralic substratum shifting to Slavic.

25 For English, the *American heritage dictionary of the English Language*, 3rd edn (1992), with its "Indo-European Roots Appendix" by Calvert Watkins (see also C. W. Watkins 1985), is an excellent example of such a resource.

26 *yellow* is from Old English *geolu*, from proto-Germanic *gelwaz*; *gall* is from Old English *gealla*, from proto-Germanic *gallōn-*.

27 Note also that words that are etymologically unrelated can come to be perceived by speakers at a later stage as related, perhaps even merged into different meanings of the same word: e.g. the body part *ear* and *ear* as a designation of a piece of corn are etymologically distinct (the former from PIE *ous- 'ear', the latter from *ak- 'sharp'), but they are felt by many speakers to be different meanings of one polysemous lexical item.

28 See Janda 1982, 1983, for a thorough discussion of the relevant facts supporting this analysis of German umlaut. The productivity of umlaut does not in itself argue for it still being phonological; in that sense, the German situation is now similar in nature, though not in scope, to

the very limited umlaut effects still present in English, e.g. in a few irregular plurals (*man/men, foot/feet,* etc.) and verbal derivatives (*drink/ drench,* etc.).

29 Thus there is an important interaction with sound change to note here, for sound change can obscure or remove the conditioning elements for a phonological process, thereby rendering the process opaque from a phonological standpoint and making it more amenable to a morphologically based analysis. Recall also that sound change can play a role in the reduction of compounds to monomorphemic words and of phrasal units, such as noun plus postposition, to monolexemic expressions.

30 Many such *-gate* forms are documented in notes in *American Speech*; see Joseph 1992 for references.

31 Of course, some of these English forms are susceptible, seemingly more so than native plurals, to reanalysis as singular; *criteria* is quite frequently used as a singular, and a plural *criterias* can be heard as well. Similarly, the Albanian plurals in *-llarë/-lerë* show the native plural suffix *-ë* added to the Turkish *-lar/ler* ending, somewhat parallel to forms like *criterias*.

32 The distinction drawn by Thomason and Kaufman (1988) between borrowing and language shift is a crucial one, with the latter situation being the contact vehicle for some of the more "exotic" morphological changes. Their discussion is perhaps the most complete enumeration of the wide range of possible contact-induced changes, including those affecting the morphology. See also n. 24 above concerning a language-shift source for the introduction of

the new animacy subcategory in Slavic.

33 See Anttila 1977 and Anttila and Brewer 1977 for basic discussion and bibliography on analogy in language change.

34 Analogy can also provide direct evidence for the existence of the tight relations among members of clusters of forms that allow for an inference of a (psychologically) real category. For instance, the fact that *drag/fag/flag/lag* could affect [sæk] and draw it into their orbit as *sag* is *prima facie* evidence of the strength of the connections among these four words. Similarly, the dialectal extension of the *-th* nominalizing suffix, which shows limited productivity within the domain of dimension adjectives (cf. *wide/width, deep/depth,* etc.) to *high,* giving [haytθ] (thus also with some contamination from *height* to explain the occurrence of the *-t-*) can be seen as evidence of the subcategory within which the suffix is productive.

35 Another perspective on the cognitive dimension in analogy is provided by Andersen's introduction of the role of abductive reasoning in analogical reanalysis, as discussed most notably in Andersen 1973, 1980.

36 Especially the work by Wolfgang Dressler, Willi Mayerthaler, Wolfgang Wurzel, and others; see e.g. Dressler et al. 1987, Mayerthaler 1981, Wurzel 1984. See also Shapiro 1990 (with references), where a somewhat different view of the role of semiotics in language change, as applied to morphophonemics, can be found.

37 Of course, not all grammaticalization involves morphological change, except insofar as it affects lexical items. The papers in Traugott and Heine

(eds) 1991a, b contain numerous references to the cognitive dimension of grammaticalization; see also Hopper and Traugott 1993 for discussion and references.

38   See also the recent work by Skousen in which an explicit and formal definition of analogy is used to create a predictive model of language structure; among the tests for this approach (in Skousen 1989: ch. 5) is its application to historical drift in the formation of the Finnish past tense.

39   This view has long been associated with William Labov, and is expressed most recently in Labov 1994: 45: "In line with the general approach to language as a property of the speech community, I would prefer to avoid a focus on the individual, since the language has not in effect changed unless the change is accepted as part of the language by other speakers."

40   One could say of course that there has been a change in the morphological rules that introduce the stem variants for 'month', but that still brings one no closer to understanding why the change occurred. Once 'Zeus' and 'month' share the same patterns of alternation, then a generalization over these two forms is possible, allowing for some simplification in the grammar. However, the change cannot have occurred just to simplify the morphological rules for 'Zeus' somewhat by giving them wider applicability, since a greater simplification would have arisen had the stem alternation for this noun been eliminated altogether (as it was in some dialects that innovated a nominative *Zēn*).

41   Thus *female* makes more "sense," and thus is a better fit between form and meaning, when formally paired with its antonym *male*; similarly, providing a "partner" for the unique stem alternations of 'Zeus' makes the *Zeu-/Zēn-* alternation less irregular, and thus more motivated and easier to deal with from a cognitive standpoint.

42   Similarly, note forms such as *dwarves* in English, mentioned above in n. 9, that run counter to the general leveling out of stem differences due to voicing of fricatives in the plural.

43   See Winters 1995 for an English translation, with some commentary, of this important oft-cited yet generally little-read paper.

44   See Vincent 1974; Collinge 1985: 249–53; Hock 1991: ch. 10; and Winters 1995 for more detailed discussion and comparison of the two schemes.

45   The statements of these principles and their comparison are taken from the illuminating account in Hock 1991: ch. 10.

46   See Robertson 1975 for an example of the fourth law from Mayan.

47   See Collinge 1985: 239–40 for discussion and references.

48   For example, a possible scenario for lexically diffuse spread of a sound change is the following: if lexical item X shows variation in pronunciation between X and X', and item Y has some of the same phonological features as item X, speakers may extend, analogically using X as the model, the variant pronunciation X' to Y, so that Y comes to show variation between Y and Y'. If the competition is ultimately resolved in favor of X' and Y', the sound change would have been generalized.

49   See e.g. DeLancey 1991, regarding such clause reduction in Modern Tibetan (discussed in Hopper and Traugott 1993: 198–201).

50 In Joseph and Janda 1988, the claim is advanced that grammars are "morphocentric," and the prevalence noted above in section 1 of diachronic movement into morphology (from syntax and from phonology), as opposed to the relative rarity of movement out of morphology, is taken as diachronic evidence for the centrality of morphology. This claim is based on an assumption that facts from diachrony can have relevance for the construction and evaluation of synchronic grammars, and to the extent that it is valid, provides some support for treating such facts as important.

19 Morphology in Language Acquisition

EVE V. CLARK

1 Language acquisition

Children typically begin to say their first words between twelve and twenty months of age. And they produce systematic morphological modulations of those words within their first year of talking. As they move to more complex expression of their meanings, they add grammatical morphemes – prefixes, suffixes, prepositions, postpositions, and clitics. On nouns, for example, they start to add morphemes to mark such distinctions as gender, number, and case; on verbs, they add markers for aspect, tense, gender, number, and person. Within a particular language, children's mastery of such paradigms may take several years. There are at least three reasons for this: (a) some meaning distinctions appear to be more complex conceptually than others, and so take longer to learn; (b) some paradigms are less regular than others, and they too take longer to learn; and (c) language typology may affect the process of morphological acquisition: suffixes, for instance, are acquired more readily, and earlier, than prefixes.

In order to acquire noun and verb morphology, children must first analyze the structure of words heard in input, identify stems and affixes, map consistent meanings onto them, and then begin to use those stems and affixes in new combinations. This process of analyzing form and assigning meaning is a prerequisite for the acquisition of inflectional morphology. It is also a prerequisite in the acquisition of word formation. Children begin to use some word-formation processes at around the same time as their first inflections. In particular, they produce novel compounds formed from simple stem combinations (often called *root* compounds). Next, during their second year of speech, as some inflectional paradigms become established, they also begin to produce a few derivational affixes in novel word forms. These emerge in greater numbers between ages three and four, in both derived and compound innovations.

1.1 Some issues in acquisition

The acquisition of morphology in inflection and word formation raises a number of questions about both morphology and the process of acquisition. Languages differ in the extent to which they rely on inflectional morphology to mark grammatical distinctions and grammatical relations. In essence, languages range from analytic (with virtually no inflectional morphology, as in Chinese) to synthetic (with fairly extensive reliance on inflections, some for grammatical relations and agreement, and many marking several distinctions at once, as in Spanish), to agglutinative (with highly regular and systematic inflections, each marking a separate distinction, as in Turkish). In word formation, there is just as much variety, with some languages relying almost exclusively on compounding to form new words, others relying mainly on derivation, and many others relying on some mix of the two. Derivation may include both affixal and zero-derived forms, and some affixes commonly appear in compounds too. One issue for acquisition, then, is the extent to which language typology affects the process of learning: Do particular typologies help or hinder?

In acquisition, the domain of morphology is the word. Inflectional affixes are added to words or stems to form words. Each one must be identified and assigned some meaning. But inflections also mark grammatical relations through agreement within or across phrases, so the domain of an inflection may go beyond the word. Take number. Children acquiring English or Spanish must learn that nouns denoting more than one instance of an entity are used in a plural form, with the addition of the relevant inflection. In Spanish, though not in English, any adjective that accompanies that plural noun must also be marked for plural. In addition, if that noun happens to be the grammatical subject, its verb must also be marked for plural. So although children appear to begin with inflections as modulations of the word meaning, they go on to learn the grammatical functions of each inflection, and hence the full domain for each one. Learning inflections ultimately demands attention to both lexical meaning and syntax.

When children learn inflections, they must also learn which words belong to which paradigms. That is, whether a noun takes the regular plural, or which two or three distinct regular plurals, versus an irregular form. In English, this typically amounts to a choice of a regular allomorph (/-s/, /-z/, or /-ɪz/) versus an irregular form – for example, *-en* (as in *ox/oxen*) or a vowel change (as in *tooth/teeth*). Some languages have one highly regular paradigm and a scattering of small irregular ones, as in English plurals. Others may have several regular paradigms, with word membership in each dictated by phonological form, plus some smaller, irregular ones. In each language, children have to learn which paradigm a particular word belongs to for purposes, say, of plural formation. Where children have not yet learnt this, they may regularize some forms by assigning them to a major paradigm. At issue here is the extent to which they learn an inflection like the plural on a word-by-word basis versus a constructional, rule-like basis. That is, once they have extracted the form of the plural affix, when can they add it, as needed, to any unfamiliar stem? Do children shift, at some point in development, from word-by-word acquisition of an inflection to rule-like application? And do all children go through a similar sequence of stages as they learn this?

Some affixes are more complex than others and are typically acquired later. Both meaning and form appear to contribute to their complexity. The complexity of the conceptual distinction underlying the meaning should affect how early and how readily children assign the pertinent conventional meaning to an inflection. In addition, the mapping of meaning onto an inflection may be affected by the complexity of the form itself. If the boundary between stem and affix is obscured by morphophonological rules, children will have a harder time identifying both, and so will acquire the inflection later. If they have to map a particular meaning onto discontinuous elements (e.g. a case ending and a preposition), that form too should take longer to acquire than one where the mapping involves a single element. In short, children must analyze the word forms they encounter, identify stems and potential affixes, and assign meanings to both. Their ability to do this may be taxed by the complexity of the meaning to be assigned, or by the complexity of the form for that meaning, or both. Only after this will they be in a position to produce the pertinent affixes.

Finally, are inflection and word formation treated in a similar way by children acquiring morphology? Inflectional paradigms tend to be complete, and so are generally more regular than word-formational ones. To what extent does this make word formation harder to acquire than inflection? Word formation also involves the construction of new forms to carry new meanings. Is constructing a new word harder than adding an inflection to a familiar or an unfamiliar one? In short, word formation seems to demand attention to, and hence knowledge of, the lexicon as a whole, unlike inflection. It also depends on knowledge of other typological properties of the language.

The discussion that follows will review some of the findings pertinent to these issues, and raise some additional questions about morphology in first-language acquisition. The next section focuses on inflections and their contribution to syntax. The third section takes up morphology in the lexicon through its role in new-word formation.

2 Inflections

Children's acquisition of inflectional morphology has been studied for a variety of different languages. Most of the data come from longitudinal records of children's speech. The data currently available come from a number of language families, including Indo-European (e.g. French, Spanish; English, German, Swedish; Polish), Semitic (Arabic, Hebrew), Uralic (Finnish, Hungarian), Altaic (Japanese, Korean, Turkish), Caucasian (Georgian), Australian (Walpiri),

Niger-Kordofanian (Sesotho), and Sino-Tibetan (Mandarin). For some of these languages, there are also systematic elicitation data available on some topics.

2.1 What is acquired when?

Children start to acquire inflections from their earliest word use on. But they may only produce them after some weeks, or even months. Consistent use of an inflection can be assessed against use in appropriate contexts on the one hand, and against use of other inflections (including use of no inflection) on the other. In highly inflected languages, children may produce their first contrasting inflections within two or three months of beginning to speak (e.g. in Hungarian, Turkish, Polish, Russian). But the production of the first inflections depends on several factors, including complexity and typology.

The typical sequence in the acquisition of an inflection such as the English plural suffix goes as follows: (a) no use at all in contexts that call for a plural form (hence *cat* in lieu of *cats*); (b) sporadic use on a few forms where a plural seems to be called for; followed by (c) general use and over-regularization (the inflection -s applied to *cat* and to words like *foot* and *man*; (d) identification of the relevant limits on use along with acquisition of irregular plural forms (*cat/cats* versus *foot/feet*). Some researchers have proposed that prior to learning the regular inflection for plural, for example, children learn the irregular forms, but then give them up in favor of regularized ones. But such a development seems quite unmotivated. If children have learnt the meaning of a form like *feet*, why drop it again to express the *same meaning* with a different form (*foots*)? An alternative account goes as follows. Children often identify irregular forms as base stems. For example, they may identify both *break* and *broke* as stems, or both *go* and *went*, without realizing, in either case, that these pairs each "belong" to just one verb. On this view, one prediction is that children will add regular inflections to both stems, and that is what they appear to do: they produce both *breaked* and *broked*, as if for two distinct verbs, and they produce both *goed* and *wented* (Clark 1987, Kuczaj 1977). What have not been investigated, though, are the meanings that children who inflect both forms might assign to a pair like *goed* and *wented*.

The order in which children acquire inflections has been studied in some detail for grammatical morphemes in English (R. Brown 1973, Cazden 1968). There, the best predictor of relative order is semantic complexity, with morphemes that are cumulatively more complex being acquired later. A morpheme marking x is acquired before one that marks $x + y$, and so on. This is consistent with Slobin's (1973) identification of conceptual complexity as one major determinant of overall order of acquisition. What has not been established is a general conceptual base for measuring the complexity of specific morphological distinctions within or across languages.

A second major determinant of order of acquisition in production is formal complexity in the expression of a specific meaning. If a language marks x with a single suffix, invariant across noun types, x should be simpler to acquire there than in a language where the same meaning is expressed through a combination of affix and preposition, with the shape of the affix also varying with the gender and number of the noun that it is attached to. Children should acquire the simpler type earlier than the more complex one, and they do. This can be seen in bilingual children's early expression of locative relations in Hungarian (early) versus Serbo-Croatian (late) (Mikeš 1967). In addition, children learn to produce a distinction marked by a regular inflection – where this applies to a large range of stems – earlier than the same distinction marked by a large number of different forms applying to small paradigms. This is the case, for instance, in children's acquisition of plural marking in English versus Egyptian Arabic (Omar 1973, Slobin 1973).

2.2 *Rote learning, rules, and regularization*

Do children need to hear each inflected form before they can use it? Or do they realize, after a time, that unfamiliar forms typically take the same inflections as familiar ones? That is, can they generalize about how to mark plurality, for instance, or past time, and then apply this knowledge to new forms? In 1958, Berko argued that if children learnt inflected forms by rote, they would be unable to add inflections to unfamiliar words. But, as she showed, five- to seven-year-olds readily added different inflectional endings to nonsense words. That is, children were applying a consistent procedure in marking a noun as plural or possessive, or a verb as ongoing or past. These procedures can be represented as rules for constructing the appropriate forms. (Whether such procedures involve templates or internalized procedures analogous to rules is unclear; see further Bybee and Slobin 1982, Clahsen and Rothweiler 1993, MacWhinney 1978, and Marcus et al. 1992.)

Once children have identified an appropriate affix to mark some distinction inflectionally, they can apply it wherever they wish to modulate a stem meaning in that way. They can add a past tense inflection, for instance, to any newly encountered verbs. The problem is that not all such verbs will be regular in form. So addition of the regular inflection will result in an over-regularized form such as English *breaked* or *doed* (for *broke* and *did*), or French *metté* 'put' or *pleuvé* 'rained' (for *mis* and *plu*). Children commonly over-regularize irregular forms during the earlier stages of acquisition. However, the extent, consistency, and contexts of such over-regularizations are in some dispute. Some researchers have observed them at very high rates (from 20 to 50 percent of the time at certain ages), but others, averaging rates across children and ages, have estimated them at no more than 3–10 percent (Kuczaj 1977, Maratsos 1993, Marcus et al. 1992). The issue is the following: do children simply go to a regularized form on those (perhaps rare) occasions when their memory fails, or do they go through a stage, during acquisition, where they assume that irregular forms are actually regular, and only later shift over to the conventional irregular forms? If initial over-regularizations represent a stage in acquisition, they are liable to be more frequent initially for each irregular form and then to taper off as children begin to register that adults never produce the form that they themselves are using.

Which affixes do children identify as "regular"? Children latch on to some affixes very early, and others, with near-equivalent meanings, not until much later. Does frequency play a role here, and if so, do children attend more to token- or to type-frequency in the language they hear? Findings so far show that children attend more to types than to tokens in the input. The first affixes they produce are those that appear on the largest number of types (Guillaume 1927), and typically represent the most widespread paradigms in a language. Once these are established, children begin to acquire affixes marking smaller, irregular, and specially conditioned paradigms. But the latter can take many months or even years to master.

2.3 Case marking

In languages with case marking, children typically begin with just one form of each noun, generally the nominative or the accusative. Contrasting cases on the same noun in some languages begin to appear very early (around twelve to fourteen months), in others a few months later. One determinant appears to be the nature of the case system: where a single affix serves all forms of nouns, children master the case contrasts much faster, even with phonological conditioning, than where the forms of each case ending vary with the gender and number of nouns. Children show much earlier mastery of case marking in languages like Hungarian and Turkish than they do for German or Serbo-Croatian (Slobin (ed.) 1985, 1992).

The first contrast acquired seems to be between the nominative and accusative cases, associated with subject and direct object respectively. Contrasting uses of cases may appear with single-word utterances. In two-word combinations, where word order may offer no clues, case can distinguish the object of a transitive verb from the subject of an intransitive one. As children add other cases such as the dative and genitive, these too serve to distinguish direct objects, for example, from indirect objects (e.g. recipients and possessors) from the two-word stage on. In general, acquisition of nominative and accusative cases is followed by the remaining oblique cases. This may involve only two or three other cases in a language like German, versus many other case forms in one like Finnish.

Several factors make case difficult to learn. The most notable may be the number of forms that children have to deal with in some languages. For example, both gender and number interact with case. In a two- or three-gender language, there are typically multiple affixes for each case. And within each gender, languages may have several noun paradigms, with each paradigm identified by the phonological shape of the root or stem. Children have therefore to deal with several different affixes as they learn how to express each case in a language. When it comes to number, they also have to deal with the fact that some gender distinctions in the singular forms are lost in the plural. In fact, children tend to learn first how to mark case in the singular, and only later in the plural. Languages differ, therefore, in the number of affix shapes to be learnt for each case, as well as in the number of cases – from a minimum of two or three to more than twenty. Where more shapes are associated with a particular case, children are more likely to opt initially for just one affix shape to mark a particular case on every stem. This reliance on a single affix shape, regardless of gender and number, has been dubbed "inflectional imperialism" (Slobin 1973). What this does is allow children to mark case with some consistency prior to the acquisition of gender or of subparadigms within genders. In languages where case affixes are invariable, or vary only, say, with vowel harmony, children acquire adult-like case marking very early, typically before the age of two – for example, in Turkish and Hungarian. In languages where case interacts with gender and number, children acquire the full system of case marking, with all the different affix shapes, much more slowly, and may still make some errors as late as age five or so – for example, in Russian. Adult-like case marking may also take more time in languages where complex morphophonological rules obscure stem–affix boundaries, and so make it harder for children to identify stems and affix shapes. Form, and in particular the range of forms for each affix, depending on gender and noun paradigms within genders, is a major determinant of how long children take to acquire adult-like case marking.

2.4 Person, number, and gender

Verbs are generally marked for person and number, and in some constructions and tenses for gender. The earliest verb forms used are typically third-person singular present, imperative, or infinitive in form. Children may focus on one or more of these as their earliest verb form(s), depending on the language being acquired. For example, in English, the first- or second-person present, the imperative, and the infinitive are all realized as an uninflected or zero-affix form of the stem, while the third-person singular present is marked by -s. Children begin with the uninflected form, and only later mark the third-person verb form in the present. In Portuguese, however, children favor the second- or third-person singular form as their starting point in verb use, and only later produce first-person forms (Simões and Stoel-Gammon 1979). Several factors probably contribute to children's initial choice of a verb form: frequency in adult input and a tendency to make use of third-person forms in self-reference alongside some level of minimal inflection (compared to other verb forms). But the initial form favored by children differs somewhat with language, with choices converging on an imperative form alongside some present-tense form, often in the third person (see languages surveyed in Slobin (ed.) 1985, 1992, 1997).

Number is marked in both verbs and nouns. In verbs, the plural forms are typically learnt some time after their singular counterparts. That is, children usually learn the singular forms for all three persons (first, second, and third) before they master the plural ones in languages that distinguish person and number in the verb. Number is mastered earlier in the noun than in the verb, and typically begins to be marked before age two. The distinction between one versus more than one may be signaled nonconventionally at first through modifiers such as *more* or a numeral (e.g. English *more book* for '(several) books', or *two magnet* for '(many) magnets'). Then children begin to add the regular plural affixes to nouns and to over-regularize irregular plurals. In English, for instance, children add the regular *-s* in lieu of the irregular forms required for nouns like *man, tooth, ox, child*, or *sheep*. In languages where there are a large number of irregular plural forms, children still identify the regular plural forms early and use them when they over-regularize (e.g. Clahsen et al. 1992). But irregular forms may take many years to master, with children continuing to make errors in their plural inflection as late as age twelve, as in Egyptian Arabic (Omar 1973). This shows that the formal complexity, in terms of the number of plural affixes and the conditions on their use, affects the point of acquisition for children. The smaller the number of affixes to be acquired in marking a distinction like plural number, the easier it is for children to master the adult options.

In adult speech, distinctions like plural are often marked redundantly in the sense that "plural" may appear not just on the pertinent noun but also on the accompanying demonstrative (e.g. *those trees*), and in the case of subject noun phrases on the verb (e.g. Those trees have *been cut down* versus That tree has *been cut down*). Three-year-olds acquiring English, for example, do better on a variety of comprehension tasks for the plural when they hear multiple or redundant marking of that distinction (Nicolaci-da-Costa and Harris 1983). This suggests that earlier uses of numerals or *more* may in part also reflect the forms used by adults for marking plurality that children hear in the input.

In mastering plurals, children often have to deal with gender as well, in nouns, and often in verbs too. Here again, factors related to the forms of gender marking appear to be an important determinant of how early and how easily children acquire gender marking. Where gender is marked consistently, with the same affix, for example, on the noun and on any adjective modifying that noun, children seem to find it easier to acquire. The same goes for gender marking in the plural: consistency in the form across nouns of the same gender, plus use of the same affix on adjectives and even verbs marked for that gender, makes for earlier acquisition, as in Hebrew (Levy 1983). But where form offers a less clear guide to gender marking, children take longer to master gender, and may rely initially on semantic rather than formal factors in adding the pertinent affixes, as in Icelandic (Mulford 1985). Similar considerations apply in the acquisition of Sesotho noun-class markers, which are also used on any adjectives or verbs agreeing with the noun (Demuth 1988), and in the acquisition of noun classifiers in a language like Thai (Carpenter 1991).

2.5 Tense and aspect

Several researchers have suggested that children may initially assign an aspectual meaning of completion to past tense markers. One type of evidence is that children appear to be selective in which verbs they first mark with past tense inflections. In both English and Italian, they begin using the past tense on accomplishment (telic) verbs before other verb types (Antinucci and Miller 1976). One interpretation of these data is that children use the past inflection to mark the result or completion of the action referred to by the verb. This does not, of course, imply that aspect is easier to acquire than tense. What it does suggest is that the result or completion of certain action types is highly salient to young children. But in languages where both aspect and tense are marked on the verb, children appear to acquire both forms of inflection at an early age (starting well before two), with no clear ordering of the two (e.g. Weist et al. 1984).

The first tense contrast that children seem to introduce is that between present and nonpresent. The first nonpresent inflections usually mark completed, hence past, actions; but they may also mark future time. (In similar fashion, two-year-olds often use *yesterday* to mark either past or future (e.g. Decroly and Degand 1913, Harner 1975).) Slightly older children, around age four, commonly choose past-tense forms to mark *irrealis*. They do this in pretend play, for example, when assigning roles and planning future series of actions, as in the following exchange which preceded the relevant acting-out (Lodge 1979: 368):

A: I wanted to go.
B: But I wouldn't let you and you argued about it.

After acquisition of the initial present/nonpresent contrast, children add other tense inflections to mark the future and to distinguish past forms for background versus foreground events (typically, imperfect versus perfect forms). Some tenses such as the present perfect may not be fully mastered until age four to five, but the basic present/past/future contrasts are generally well established by around age three.

Aspect marking is acquired early in languages that mark aspect as well as tense through inflections on the verb. In Slavic languages, perfective and imperfective inflections, usually prefixes, appear at the same time as tense marking (Slobin (ed.) 1985). Aspect also appears to interact with the inherent aspectual meanings of verbs (Aktionsart). English-speaking children, for instance, add the limited duration suffix, *-ing*, initially only to activity verbs, and at first apply the past-tense suffix, *-ed*, only to verbs for change of state (e.g. Bloom et al. 1980; Clark 1996).

2.6 Agreement

One basic function of inflectional systems is to indicate which elements in an utterance "go together." One finds agreement in number, person, and sometimes gender, for example, between a subject noun phrase and the verb, and agreement in number and gender between nouns and adjectives that modify them. There can also be agreement between articles or demonstratives and the nouns they go with – in gender, number, and case – and between pronouns (independent, possessive, or relative) and their antecedents – again in gender, number, and case. Agreement markers therefore help group together those elements that belong together for semantic and grammatical purposes. The acquisition of inflections must be measured, therefore, not just by the acquisition of specific paradigms, but also by children's use of agreement more generally.

Overall, children appear to rely on phonological cues to gender and gender agreement. In French, for instance, children omit articles at the one-word stage, and they make some errors in their choices of article early on. But phonological form in French is correlated with gender (masculine or feminine), and children quickly become sensitive to such cues. In one elicitation study, where phonological form and natural gender were correlated, even the youngest children (aged three), having heard an indefinite article, produced the appropriate definite article nearly all the time. With phonological cues only, they did equally well; but with neither phonological clues in the shape of the word nor information about natural gender, they made errors in their choice of definite articles about 20 percent of the time. Where indefinite articles and word shapes conflicted (e.g. a feminine article with a masculine word shape), children up to six would change either the article or the noun shape to make the two agree (e.g. *le bicronne* would be changed to *la bicronne* or *le bicron*). Older children also took account of the natural gender of the dolls being labeled and assigned feminine articles and word shapes for female dolls (Karmiloff-Smith 1979).

Phonological cues to gender agreement also predominate in the acquisition of agreement in other languages. In Hebrew, for example, children rely on word shape in plural formation as they learn to apply *-im* (masculine) or *-ot* (feminine), and they extend these inflections to adjectives for noun–adjective agreement, without apparently taking any account of natural gender (e.g. Levy 1983). Similar observations hold for the acquisition of gender agreement in German, Polish, Russian, and Serbo-Croatian (see Ferguson and Slobin (eds) 1973; Slobin (ed.) 1985). In languages where there are apparently only minimal clues to gender in the actual word shapes, though, children instead seem to rely on semantic criteria, information about natural gender, in interpreting various forms of agreement (e.g. antecedent noun–pronoun). This suggests that children may have recourse to semantic factors in learning gender agreement only when the phonological clues are inconsistent (Mulford 1985).

Finally, in Sesotho, children again seem to focus on phonological cues to word type as they learn gender and agreement. As in other Bantu languages, words in Sesotho belong to one of about fourteen word classes marked by prefixes that appear on the noun and corresponding forms for agreement on verbs, adjectives, demonstratives, and possessive, relative, and full pronouns. Children may begin to mark agreement with the noun on other elements, even before they can produce the noun-prefix reliably. This suggests that they are focusing on the whole noun or verb phrase in the input, so they treat the domain for agreement as some kind of prosodic and grammatical unit (Demuth 1988, Slobin (ed.) 1992). This would be consistent with children's trying to mark linguistic elements as going together if they help pick out the same entity or same activity together with its participants. That is, agreement is not simply an arbitrary set of markings: it has a readily accessible function for the language user.

2.7 *Typology and acquisition*

Children's patterns of acquisition suggest that they can process some kinds of information more readily than others. For example, they consistently learn suffixes before prefixes, even when these express equivalent information. Children learning a prefixing language like Mohawk acquire the inflectional prefixes later than children learning a suffixing language (e.g. Mithun 1989). This asymmetry is consistent with the more general asymmetry among languages: suffixing systems by far outnumber prefixing ones (Hawkins and Cutler 1988). When children are given nonsense prefixes and suffixes to imitate, they find suffixes easier than prefixes (Kuczaj 1979). In short, children seem to find it easier to process information added to the ends of words than to the beginnings.

Children also show a general preference for marking added meaning with an affix. For example, when presented with plural forms that differed from their singular counterparts (a) by the addition of an affix, (b) by subtraction of an affix, or (c) by zero, children prefer option (a), an added affix (Anisfeld and Tucker 1967). This is consistent with Greenberg's (1966) observation that added complexity (of meaning) is typically marked in languages by added morphemes.

Children learning different language types typically follow similar timelines, but several factors make for differences in the acquisition of inflectional morphology: (a) the consistency of the paradigms (Bybee 1991); (b) the nature of the meaning-to-form mapping, with one meaning to one affix shape being the easiest; and (c) the role of each inflection in syntactic constructions. Children exposed to a Semitic language first, for example, take for granted that it is the root consonants that provide the core meaning for each word, while those exposed to an Indo-European or Turkic language take both consonants and vowels into account in identifying words. That is, the effects of typology are relative, so they may be hard to assess. It appears possible, however, in bilinguals with languages of different types. Children growing up with Hungarian and Serbo-Croatian, for example, show that, to express the same meaning, it is easier to use suffixes than a combination of suffixes and prepositions, and that consistency of meaning makes affixes easier to acquire.

3 Word formation

As children learn more words, storing them in memory and producing them themselves, they come to analyze their internal morphological structure. They begin to identify roots and stems inside complex words, in both compound and derived forms, and simultaneously isolate any derivational affixes attached to those roots. Such analysis is a prerequisite for new-word formation. And children do form new words, starting as young as age eighteen months to two years. In English, for example, they construct compounds and form verbs from nouns with no affixation. In the next few months (two and a half to three), they come to use affixes as well in the construction of new words.

Languages differ in the options they offer for coining new words. Some languages rely extensively, or even exclusively, on compounding; others rely mainly on derivation; and others rely on both. Are some options acquired more easily than others? If so, children learning different language types should follow different routes in their acquisition of word formation. The sections that follow review first what is known about children's acquisition of derivational options in word formation, and then their acquisition of compounding. Overall, children begin to use inflectional morphology before they coin new word forms, although there is considerable overlap in some languages. But derivational affixes in general begin to emerge later than inflectional ones.

Lastly, when children coin new words, they fill semantic gaps. Children do not wait until they have learnt the appropriate word before they try to express a particular meaning. Instead, when they need to, they construct a form for the meaning they want to convey. In doing this, they observe two general constraints on the coining of new words. Conventional words – forms that express meanings agreed on by the language community – take priority. If a word is already known to the child for the pertinent meaning, that is the word they use. And there is then no reason to coin another word with the selfsame meaning. New words must therefore contrast in meaning with existing words within any semantic domain (Clark and Clark 1979; Clark 1990, 1993). These two assumptions appear to be observed by both children and adults.

3.1 Derivation

Evidence that children are using derivation comes from their construction of novel words. To use an affix appropriately, for example, requires children to have analyzed that affix in established words and to have assigned it some meaning before they can use it in constructing new words. The first novel derived forms children construct are derived with no affix. Somewhat later, around age three, they begin to produce an increasing number of novel forms with affixes.

Children coin new verbs in English from around age two. They form them mainly from nouns but also, on occasion, from adjectives, as in *to scale* 'weigh', *to key* 'insert a key', *to sand* 'grind', or *to water* 'paddle in water'. Such verbs require no affixation to indicate the change from noun to verb: they need only the appropriate suffixes and syntax (Bowerman 1974, Clark 1982, Maratsos et al. 1987). In effect, children are exploiting a zero-derivation option when they construct new verbs from familiar nouns. This effectively allows them to form new words from words with meanings already known to them, and to do so without having to make any changes in form. Even when they get older, children often omit to palatalize consonants, change vowels, or shift stress where these are required. For example, four-year-olds typically fail to recognize the root *magic* in *magician*, and when asked what they would call someone who does magic, the commonest response is *magic-man*. Equally, in forming an adjective from the noun *volcano*, five- and six-year-olds often construct *volcanic*, without the required change in the stressed vowel. Zero derivation is also favored early on in Hebrew, but there children use it to form new nouns from verbs (Clark and Berman 1984).

Between two and two and a half, children begin to produce derivational affixes, mostly suffixes, but these may be rare before age three. In English, for instance, children start to produce agent and instrument *-er*, though they do not use this suffix consistently until around age four (Clark and Hecht 1982). In other languages, the earliest suffixes to be used to form new words are generally diminutive endings and agent and instrument markers. Children typically show good comprehension of such suffixes for some time before they produce them themselves, and in elicitation tasks will produce other, non-derived forms instead. Finally, children also show distinct preferences for some derived forms over others with closely related meanings. The first agentive suffix they produce, for instance, is normally the one adults favor too (Clark 1993). For example, in English, children misremember novel agentive nouns as using *-er* even when they in fact have *-ist* or *-ian*, or even the non-agentive *-ly*, as a suffix (Clark and Cohen 1984).

These findings suggest that children rely on certain general principles as they analyze word forms and then construct new words themselves. They attend to the *transparency* of the components used; that is, they make use only of elements whose meanings they already know. This would account for why they initially rely on zero derivation, making use of stems or roots of familiar words. Only once they have assigned some meaning to an affix, do they begin to use that too in constructing new words. They also attend to the *simplicity* of the form produced; the fewer the changes to be made in the component elements, the easier it is to construct and produce. This again would lead children to favor zero derivation early on. And they are sensitive to the *productivity* of the affix being used; they follow adult usage in favoring the most productive option first, unless there is some reason not to (Clark 1993).

Finally, there is strong evidence that children analyze affixes and assign some meaning to them some time before they start to produce them themselves. For instance, when asked, they can offer glosses of what novel words might mean well before they will coin words using the same affix. English *-er* and Hebrew *-an*, for example, are readily identified as having agentive meaning by three-year-olds acquiring these languages, but not until age four or later do children produce those suffixes to mark agentive meaning (Clark and Berman 1984, Clark and Hecht 1982).

3.2 Compounding

In some languages, children begin to construct new compounds from as young as one and a half; in others, they make little use of novel compounds before age six or seven. The difference, in general, appears to depend on whether or not compounding is productive within the language. In addition, children are attentive to the *transparency* and *simplicity* of the elements they use in compounding. As a result, their earliest compounds typically consist of combinations of familiar bare nouns which are both transparent in meaning and simple in form (root compounds). It is only later that they begin to use affixes or produce any adjustments in form required for specific types of compounding in the language.

Children learning Germanic languages construct root compounds from an early age, often before age two. They form them mainly from familiar nouns, as in English *crow-bird* (one year, seven, months, for 'crow'), *oil-spoon* (one year, eleven months, 'spoon for cod-liver oil'), or *coffee-churn* (two years, 'coffee-grinder'); German *Korb-wagen* (two years, seven months, 'basket-wagon', for a small doll's pram of woven straw), *Löchern-teller* (two years, nine months, 'hole(s)-plate', for a glass table mat with metal filigree on it), or Icelandic *kubba-bíll* (two years, four months, 'block-car', for a car made of blocks), *flösk-bíll* (same age, 'bottle-car', for a milk-truck), or *fiata-bíll* (same age, 'Fiat-car'). And, by age two to two and a half, children have learnt to identify the modifier and head in such root compounds. In comprehension tasks, children acquiring English consistently identify the second (rightmost) noun as the head and the first as the modifier, while those acquiring Hebrew choose the first (leftmost) noun as the head and the second as the modifier (Berman and Clark 1989, Clark et al. 1985). But children acquiring languages that make less use of compounding do not produce compounds at this age. For example, children acquiring Romance languages produce virtually no root compounds until around age five or later (Clark 1993).

Children acquire synthetic compounds only rather later, and they often make errors in their construction. Elicitation tasks reveal that, in learning the structure of compounds like *button-thrower*, children seem to go through several stages. At around age three, they construct forms like *throw-man* (or, less frequently, *throw-button*) for the agent. They then begin to add the appropriate affix to the verb stem, and now construct *thrower-button*. This form has the affix added to the head, and has incorporated the noun for the generic object affected; but the word order is the head + modifier characteristic of verb phrases (i.e. *throw* preceding *button*), instead of the modifier + head order of compounds. Only around age five do children acquiring English get both affix and order right when asked to coin such compounds. At that point, they begin to construct forms like *button-thrower* or *wagon-puller* with no errors (Clark et al. 1986). Children acquiring other Germanic languages make similar word-order errors, but children learning languages where the verb phrase head and compound head have the same order relative to any modifiers never make these word-order errors (Clark and Berman 1987).

Children rely on transparency and simplicity in their novel compounds just as much as in their derived words. Their earliest compounds are all root compounds, typically forms from two or more 'bare' nouns already known to them. They begin to form novel synthetic compounds only later, after analyzing and assigning some meaning to suffixes such as the English agentive *-er*. This sequence is predicted by both transparency of meaning and simplicity of form. Further evidence for simplicity comes from the sequence observable in the acquisition of Hebrew compounds. In Hebrew, different noun types differ in their bound forms, the ones required in compounds: some make no change; feminine nouns in final *-a* add a *-t*; masculine plural nouns change final *-im* to *-ey*; and so on. In production, three-year-olds favor no change in their compounds, and so make many errors. As children get older, they successively master the final *-t*, then plural *-im* to *-ey*, and, last of all, stem-changing heads. That is, the greater the change required in the form of the head, the longer before it is acquired (Clark and Berman 1987).

Productivity also plays a role in compounding. Children favor the patterns that are more productive over those that are less productive, or no longer productive. This suggests that here too children attend to the relative frequencies of different compound types in the input around them. In level-ordering models of word formation, all compounding is assumed to occur at the same level with all of it productive. But contemporary speakers favor only certain patterns among those possible, and the most productive of those are the ones that children typically acquire first. Frequency, then, presumably makes for accessibility during acquisition.

4 Conclusion

In general, children start to acquire inflections before they begin on novel-word formation. The earliest noun and verb inflections to emerge appear in some languages before age one and a half. Compounding with no affixation emerges soon after the first inflections, but novel derived forms do not emerge until after age two. The first to appear are zero-derived forms with no affix.

Then come some derivational affixes, with sporadic use up to age three, followed by more extensive use from age three or four on. In languages that make little use of compounding or zero derivation, therefore, the first novel-word formations may not appear until age three or later. It is unclear whether typology affects the acquisition of morphology elsewhere. Although it appears easier to process suffixes than prefixes, there are too few data on the acquisition of prefixing languages to see how consistently this holds overall. At the same time, children acquire locative affixes, for example, much earlier in languages that use invariant forms on all stems than in languages that rely on a mix of case marking (varying in form with gender and number) and prepositions. It may be easier in general, then, for children to map inflectional meanings in agglutinative than in synthetic languages.

Overall, the sequence of acquisition for morphology, whether in inflectional systems or in word formation, appears to depend on at least two factors: the complexity of the meaning being expressed – where children have to discover this for each affix – and the complexity of the form to be used – where children have to work out the conditions that govern different allomorphs. However, what counts as easy versus difficult in adjusting the form of a word is not easily measured.

In short, children work with words. Their earliest inflections are typically learnt as parts of words, and only later are analyzed for forms and meanings. Once this is done, children appear able to extend paradigms with rule-like application of an affix to new instances. In doing so, they also regularize irregular forms until they learn to produce the appropriate irregular forms. This holds for both inflections and word formation.

20 Morphology and Aphasia

WILLIAM BADECKER AND ALFONSO CARAMAZZA

The study of acquired language deficits can have one or more of a variety of research goals, but one that is most easily motivated is the use of the observed patterns of impairment (along with other sources of evidence) to motivate particular theories of the normal system. Given certain reasonable assumptions about the consequences of damage to the normal system (e.g. that the derived system will not involve the generation of compensatory mechanisms that themselves had no status in the premorbid condition), the possible patterns of deficit are limited to what could be derived from the normal system under a limited variety of transformations (see Caramazza 1984, Ellis and Young 1988). By identifying the constraints that acquired deficits appear to respect, one can hope to infer the character of the normal system that would impose such constraints. While there are certainly other worthwhile goals that one might wish to pursue using data from aphasia (e.g. to explain a particular language deficit in terms of where and how the language-processing system has broken down, or to use patterns of language deficit and lesion information to deduce how the cognitive mechanisms underlying language processing are anatomically distributed), these goals almost inevitably are intertwined with the first goal that we identified (that of shedding light on the functional organization of the premorbid system). Hence, for most of our discussion of acquired language impairments that appear to affect the comprehension or production of morphologically complex words, we will focus on what insight they can give us into the properties of the normal processing apparatus.

1 Morphological impairments

Morphological paraphasias – for example, producing "walking" for "walked" – are an often observed feature of language impairment. Errors of this type are prominent in the major, clinically defined disorders of sentence production –

agrammatism and paragrammatism (see Bates et al. 1987, Butterworth and Howard 1987, Caplan et al. 1972, Goodglass 1976, Jarema and Kehayia 1992, Kean 1978, Miceli et al. 1989, Saffran et al. 1980, and Tissot et al. 1973 for recent discussions) – and in various disorders of single-word production in reading, writing, and naming (see De Bleser and Bayer 1990, Job and Sartori 1984, Nolan and Caramazza 1982, Patterson 1982; see also papers in Coltheart et al. (eds) 1980). In addition, failure to differentiate among morphologically related forms has been implicated in comprehension impairments (Tyler et al. 1990; Tyler and Cobb 1987). As one might expect, these phenomena are of interest not merely because of their pervasiveness, but also because they offer an opportunity to explore the cognitive mechanisms that underlie lexical processing.

For example, from such errors one might hope to be able to determine whether a speaker's active lexicon is dealt with largely by mechanisms of storage and retrieval of whole-word forms, or whether there are also mechanisms of morphological composition that are invoked during normal processing. Unlike the domain of phrasal processing, where an individual's capacity to produce and comprehend an infinite number of novel and well-formed sentences transparently motivates rule-based processing, the productivity of word formation does not make as clear a case for active word-building operations in the production system. While the need for word-formation rules of one sort or another is necessitated by the capacity to understand and produce word forms that one has never before encountered, the processing issue is when and where these mechanisms come into play. Are they invoked only in order to give structure and content to lexical entries for complex words when they are first learned? Such an arrangement would be compatible with each word of the language having its own, independent entry in a vast lexicon of fully specified forms (see e.g. Butterworth 1983; Bybee 1988, 1995b; Halle 1973; Segui and Zubizarreta 1985). Or are the cognitive mechanisms that underlie lexical production and comprehension rule-based in much the same way that one sees sentence processing to be? As we will show, the study of acquired lexical impairments is an important source of evidence regarding such issues. Other issues that we will discuss relate to evidence from aphasia concerning the relevance of morphological productivity to the issue of compositionality, processing differences relating to the inflection/derivation distinction, and the contribution of morphological processing to the comprehension and production of sentences.

Before we can discuss these issues in detail, though, we must begin by considering the first obstacle one faces in any effort to motivate a deficit that is specific to one or another aspect of morphological processing. The mere existence of morphological paraphasias is not sufficient to show that the locus of the processing impairment actually implicates lexical morphology. One must show, for example, that paraphasias like *darkness* → *darkly* do not result from whole-word substitutions (analogous to errors like *index* → *insect*, or *center* → *cent*) or from sublexical, nonmorphological substitutions (as seen in word and nonword paraphasias like *belt* [bɛlt] → *bell* [bɛl] and *index* [ɪndɛks] → [ɪndɛk]). If morphological errors were the only variety of lexical errors that a patient produced, the argument for a "true" deficit to lexical morphology would be relatively straightforward (although not entirely unproblematic, since even in this case we could conceivably lack any other evidence that these errors arise from a morphological processing deficit). As it is, though, there is a notable absence of such pure cases. Even when morphological lapses are the predominant type of lexical paraphasia, they do not appear to occur as the only variety of lexical error in any reported case. In an ongoing project involving the study of nearly a hundred patients who produce morphological paraphasias in reading and repetition tasks, none presented with a "pure" morphological deficit (in the sense that no other type of lexical error occurred). This may not be a matter of coincidence. Given that lexical morphology embodies the capacity to relate (in a rule-governed fashion) an extended set of lexical meanings to an extended stock of lexical forms, a deficit affecting this capacity may invariably induce semantic and/or phonological and/or orthographic errors as well. In any event, the two most common patterns of performance in reading tasks include the production of morphological errors in conjunction with visual errors (e.g. Job and Sartori 1984, Patterson 1982) or visual and semantic errors (Badecker and Caramazza 1987, Coltheart 1980, Patterson 1980); while two recent cases have been described whose paraphasias are limited to morphological and semantic paraphasias (Caramazza and Hillis 1990a). (Examples of these error types are provided in table 20.1.) Similar cases of acquired

Table 20.1 Error types observed in patients who produce morphological paraphasias in reading tasks

Patient S.J.D.			
halted	→	halts	(morphological substitution)
rustle	→	rustled	(morphological insertion)
frequently	→	frequent	(morphological deletion)
tuber	→	tumor	(phonological error)
excited	→	[ɪnsáysɛst]	(phonological nonword error)
Patient P.B.			
wanted	→	want	(morphological deletion)
cooked	→	cooking	(morphological substitution)
dig	→	dog	(visual error)
ride	→	drived	(semantic error)
Patient V.O.			
hidden	→	hiding	(morphological substitution)
upward	→	upwards	(morphological insertion)
neutral	→	natural	(visual error)
Patient H.W.			
drainage	→	drains	(morphological substitution)
huge	→	big	(semantic error)

dysgraphia present written morphological errors co-occurring with phono-logical paragraphias (Bub and Kertesz 1982, Shallice 1981) and semantic errors (Patterson and Shewell 1987).

Setting aside for a moment those instances where segmental errors can result in the production of forms that coincidentally are related morphologically to the target (as when consonant cluster simplification at a peripheral stage of lex-ical processing derives *weld* [wɛld] from the intended *welds* [wɛldz]), morpho-logical paraphasias must be contrasted with whole-word substitutions in order to assess the possible involvement of disrupted mechanisms of morpheme composition or parsing. For example, Badecker and Caramazza (1987), Funnell (1987), and Pillon et al. (1991) argue that factors such as the relative frequency of an affixed word and its stem, semantic abstractness, and the visual similarity of lexically related forms can account for some patients' tendency to produce morphological errors on affixed words. If this were true in every patient, there would be little neuropsychological evidence for morphological composition as a normal (and disruptable) component of lexical production. What we discuss next are case studies that suggest that the picture is not all that bleak.

2 Errors of morphological composition: retrieval versus composition

Patient S.J.D. is an English-speaking patient who presents with an acquired lexical output impairment affecting spontaneous speech and a variety of single-word processing tasks such as reading and repetition (Badecker and Caramazza 1991). Morphological errors are the predominant error type in S.J.D.'s reading performance: S.J.D. also produced whole-word substitutions (e.g. reading *summit* for *summon*) and phonemic paraphasias (e.g. *shrilly* [šrɪli] → [šruli]). The fact that S.J.D. produced relatively few nonword phonemic paraphasias by comparison with the proportion of morphological errors (13 percent versus 65 percent of her reading errors, respectively) speaks strongly against the possibility that her morphological errors were merely the product of submorphemic, phonological errors. This possibility is also ruled out by the fact that she produced morphological errors (affix omissions and substitutions) in reading words like *bowled* [bold] and *links* [lɪŋks], but no comparable errors for their monomorphemic homophones *bold* [bold] and *lynx* [lɪŋks]. Had errors like *bowled* → *bowling* [bolɪŋ] arisen as the product of segmental substitutions (as opposed to morpheme substitutions), one should observe similar errors (e.g. *bold* → *bowls* [bolz]) for the monomorphemic items as well. Since errors like *bold* → *bowls* did not occur, it is implausible that the difficulty which S.J.D. encounters with affixed words could derive from whole-word phonological substitutions. Barring the use of ad hoc stipulations to derive such a pattern, there is no self-evident reason why the accessibility of whole-word forms should differ for monomorphemic words and precompiled representations for affixed words. At a minimum, though, this pattern indicates a selective difficulty in producing affixed forms.

Other features of her performance pattern reveal that S.J.D.'s morphological output errors could not be reduced to whole-word substitutions. The most striking of these was the production of illegal combinations of morphemes (e.g. *poorest* → "*poorless, the most poorless indians have very little money*"). If S.J.D.'s morphological paraphasias were simply a special case of whole-word misselection (analogous to the substitution of monomorphemic forms in her error *fluid* → *fluent*), then one would expect all of her affix insertion and substitution errors to consist of grammatically well-formed combinations. Instead, morphologically illegal forms like *youthful* → **youthly* were evident in her reading, repetition, writing to dictation, and spontaneous speech. This leaves sublexical, phonological substitutions as the only plausible alternative to an account that says that errors like *sinking* → *sinkly* arise from compositional procedures gone awry. The competing (nonmorphological) account is seriously undermined, though, by the facts that S.J.D. produced more illegal morphological paraphasias than phonological paraphasias, and that the phonological paraphasias she did produce for morphologically complex targets tended to affect either the entire word (i.e. the stem and suffix) or the stem only, a pattern that makes it difficult to view the morphological paraphasias as simply the chance outcome of phonological paraphasias.

Furthermore, both the legal and illegal combinations of morphemes in her insertion and substitution errors tended to involve inflectional and productive derivational affixes. A preference for inflection and productive derivation over nonproductive derivation would not be expected if mechanisms of word formation were not directly implicated in the generation of the morphological paraphasias. Hence, one conclusion that can be drawn from this case is that, in some patients, the production of morphological errors reflects an impairment to mechanisms that are devoted to morphological composition (and/or decomposition) in normal performance.

2.1 Does composition reflect a primary system or a back-up component?

The pattern of performance observed in the case of patient S.J.D. clearly points to compositional procedures as part of the normal lexical apparatus. Might one still worry, though, that the apparatus in question merely represents a set of back-up procedures that are available when the normal whole-word-based system falters (either because there is a temporary failure of retrieval, or because there is no entry for the target word in the first place)? While such an account is not without its advocates (e.g. Butterworth 1983), it is difficult to reconcile this view with certain facts of the case we have discussed. The central problem for this view is that the failures of a back-up system should be observed only when the primary system fails (in this case, the whole-word-based mechanisms hypothesized to operate over both the monomorphemic and affixed vocabularies). But unless there is some property of affixed words that can be shown to have an independent influence on the likelihood of producing an error, then the failures of the back-up system should be observable only in the range of cases in which the whole-word system would fail. In other words, if the back-up were entirely intact, then the performance on affixed words should be better than what one can get out of the whole-word system (because it should be able to do the back-up work it's there for). On the other hand, if the back-up system is completely impaired, then the level of performance will be entirely determined by the retained capacity of the whole-word system. The only chance of getting worse performance on affixed words than on monomorphemic words in such a system is if there are properties of affixed words that would make the whole-word system more susceptible to error on these words than on monomorphemic words, or if the input to such a system failed to preserve the morphosyntactic specification of marked forms.

S.J.D.'s performance on the affixed and unaffixed homophones discussed above (e.g. *bowled* and *bold*, *links* and *lynx*) bears on the likelihood of one such possible source of difficulty: namely, the properties of form that coincide with affixation. Given that these items were matched in form (and that the lists were matched for frequency, category, and length), this is not a candidate for a feature that would render a whole-word system more likely to fail for affixed words than for unaffixed words. This leaves the one lexical feature that this test did not control (since it will coincide by definition with the feature that was explicitly contrasted): the meaning that is encoded by the affixation. That is, one might suppose that it is not the affixation per se that makes the lexical system fail (because of a disruption to compositional procedures), but some feature of the content (e.g. the morphosemantic or morphosyntactic complexity) that accounts for the poorer performance of the lexical system on affixed words. This too can be excluded, though. If the input to the form-retrieval system were affected in such a way that the content associated with the morphology were not preserved, then this effect should be observed for both regular and irregular morphology (Badecker, to appear). On frequency- and length-matched lists of regularly inflected, irregularly inflected, and uninflected verbs (e.g. *walked*, *bought*, and *stand*, respectively), S.J.D. showed comparable performance on the uninflected and irregularly inflected verbs (90 and 92 percent correct, respectively), and significantly poorer performance on the regularly inflected items (60 percent correct; Badecker and Caramazza 1991). The account of normal processing that relegates compositional procedures to the status of a back-up system is seriously undermined by such performance.

2.2 *Jargonaphasia and word-formation mechanisms*

It is also possible to find evidence concerning processing of affixed words that does not crucially involve the production of morphological errors. Studies of

Table 20.2   Reported examples of neologistic jargon

... one of the nicest [fɛ́ndlowz]
... these little [trɛ́ftiz]
a lot of those [kɪ́stɪsis]
                    (Buckingham and
                         Kertesz 1976)

... put over two [baɪlz] that were [sneɪkt] in
I was [pleɪzd] to see the other [dakjumen]
                    (Butterworth and Howard 1987)

Yes, because I'm just *persessing* to one ...
... and I *persets* abowth abrow
                    (Caplan et al. 1972)

preserved inflectional capacity in patients who present with severe semantic and syntactic deficits have been proposed as evidence that mechanisms for inflectional morphology are functionally independent of the sentence-level mechanisms they must interact with (De Bleser and Bayer 1986). The classic cases of preserved inflection that motivate compositional mechanisms of inflection involve aphasic patients whose speech includes neologistic jargon. Examples of neologistic jargon are provided in table 20.2.

Several studies have reported patients whose neologisms cannot all be described as phonological deformations of a target word (e.g. Buckingham 1981, Butterworth and Howard 1987; Caplan et al. 1972). There is no evidence that, in every instance, abstruse neologisms require the retrieval of a phonological form from an output lexicon. One reason for holding this view is that in many instances the neologisms bear no phonological similarity to their target. In addition to being segmentally dissimilar, they may differ from a target form in the number of syllables and in stress pattern (Buckingham 1981). Nevertheless, the production of neologistic jargon often co-occurs with a preserved capacity to inflect words, and this capacity extends to neologisms as well.

In some cases, patients' use of inflections (on neologisms and on actual stems) will, on occasion, be grammatically inappropriate. However, of the five patients described by Butterworth and Howard (1987: 24), two never made inflectional errors on neologisms, and the remaining three were reported to have exhibited "good control of inflectional processes." For the latter, the number of inflections occurring in obligatory contexts (as well as the number of uninflected neologisms in syntactic contexts that excluded inflections) far outweighed the few cases where they failed to occur in contexts that required them or where they intruded ungrammatically. Regardless of their syntactic appropriateness, though, the very presence of the inflection on the nonlexical base forms suggests that the lexical system distinguishes stem and affix representations. In particular, inflected neologisms provide an additional form of evidence for the existence of mechanisms for morphological composition in the phonological output lexicon. (See also Semenza et al. 1990 for a discussion of three Italian-speaking patients who produce prefixed and derivationally suffixed neologistic forms.)

2.3 Composition and acquired dysgraphia

Evidence that affixed forms are composed in the lexical output system has been observed in various patterns of dysgraphic performance as well. In one such case, patient B.H. (Badecker et al. 1996), an acquired dysgraphia rendered certain stem forms irretrievable from the orthographic output lexicon. When B.H. could not spell words lexically, he resorted to a sublexical approach to spelling based on regular phonology–orthography correspondences. For example, he spelled *census* as *sensis*, and *benign* as *benine*. When asked to write affixed words for which he could not retrieve a stored form, though, there was clear evidence that the stem and affix spellings are differently derived. Sublexical spelling is implicated by the phonologically plausible errors made on the stem portion of the target, while retrieval of a stored form is implicated by the absence of such errors on the suffix portion of the target. That is, B.H. would spell *surfed* as *sourphed* (not as *sourpht*) and *cabooses* as *cabuses* (not as *cabusiz*). One can verify that the selective preservation of affix spellings is not merely apparent. For example, he would spell *wolfed* as *woulphed*, but *concoct* as *concauct*, not as *concauked*, as one might otherwise expect if the suffix spelling that he used were simply the most likely phonology–orthography mapping that his sublexical mechanisms would generate.

The pattern of errors that B.H. presented would not easily be explained if the lexical system were to store the affix as part of a whole-word representation of an inflected form. If as a consequence of the patient's deficit the hypothesized whole-word representation for a word (e.g. for *surfed*) could not be retrieved, and if instead a spelling could be generated only by using mechanisms whose input–output relations are specified in terms of regular phonology–orthography correspondences, then one would expect that these correspondences would derive just the sort of misspellings that were not observed (e.g. spelling *surfed* as *sourpht*). On the other hand, the interpretation is rather straightforward on the view that affixed forms like *surfed* are normally composed in the output system. If the stem is inaccessible to the retrieval mechanisms, but the (separately stored) affix form remains available, then the orthographic form of the stem, but not the affix, will need to be generated by some other means: in particular, by the rule-based mechanisms based on phonology–orthography correspondences. On this model, then, the rule-based spellings of stems can be combined with the lexically specified spellings of the inflectional affix in virtue of the compositional approach to the production of affixed forms that is taken even when both components of a complex form are retrieved from the lexicon.[1]

The role of morphological composition in the orthographic output system also finds motivation from cases of acquired dysgraphias that arise at a somewhat more peripheral processing stage: the level of the Graphemic Buffer (Badecker et al. 1990, Caramazza and Hillis 1990b). The general pattern of performance associated with a deficit at this processing level includes (a) spelling errors that can be construed as simple letter substitutions, deletions, insertions, and transpositions; (b) similar performance on both word and nonword targets, in both written and oral spelling tasks; (c) comparable performance in spontaneous writing, writing to dictation, and written naming tasks; and (d) effects for properties such as length (but not for lexical properties like grammatical category, lexical frequency, semantic abstractness, etc.). In one such case, that of patient D.H. (Badecker et al. 1990), the distribution of spelling errors was asymmetrically bow-shaped for monomorphemic words: D.H. produced few spelling errors at the beginnings of words, with most of his errors occurring to the right of the medial letters of the target. However, for suffixed words the error rate and error distribution were significantly different. D.H. misspelled fewer suffixed words than matched monomorphemic targets; and though the asymmetric distribution of errors that was characteristic of his performance on monomorphemic words was seen on the stem portion of the target, the letters that comprised the suffix portion of the target (e.g. E-D in *handed* and I-N-G in *walking*) were much less likely to be misspelled than the corresponding letters in monomorphemic words (like *wicked* and *awning*).

The contrast between D.H.'s performance on monomorphemic and suffixed words is easily accounted for on the following analysis of his dysgraphia. The likelihood of producing a spelling error is a function of the size of the lexical unit that is placed in the buffer, and the reason why suffixed words appear to be less susceptible to error is that (at the level of the deficit) these words are processed not as a single unit, defined in terms of the whole word, but as a sequence of two such units, defined in terms of their morphemic components.[2] This account is further supported by D.H.'s performance on prefixed and compound words. Prefixed and compound words were less likely to be misspelled than matched monomorphemic items; and when they were misspelled, the probability of an error for a particular letter position was clearly affected by the morphological structure of the target. Whereas frequency- and length-matched unaffixed controls for both types induced the characteristically asymmetric error distribution across the whole word, prefixed words induced fewer errors in the initial portion of the target than their controls, and the distribution of errors in compounds clearly exhibited the bimodal pattern one would expect if the whole word were processed as a concatenation of constituent stems (Badecker et al. 1990).[3]

The processing accounts we have offered in order to explain the performance patterns of D.H. and B.H. converge on a single model of orthographic processing. On this model, monomorphemic words are retrieved from the Orthographic Output Lexicon as whole-word units, while morphemic constituents of words like *farming*, *repay*, and *drugstore* are separately retrieved and then concatenated at the level of the Graphemic Buffer.[4] The selective preservation of suffix spellings in the case of B.H. derives from the fact that when attempting to spell an affixed word, a failure to retrieve a stored form for a lexical stem will not have as its necessary consequence that the affix spelling will also be irretrievable. The better performance on morphologically complex words than on monomorphemic items observed in the case of D.H. derives from the fact that this patient's deficit asymmetrically affects the probability of producing an error on the orthographic constituents that make up the (morpheme-sized) processing units that are deposited, and temporarily stored, in the Graphemic Buffer.

2.3.1 Productivity Productivity, the measure of a speaker's capacity to employ a particular Word Formation Rule in order to add new forms to the set of meaningful words, is a property of the lexical system that continues to receive much attention. (Cf. recent discussions in Anderson 1992, Baayen 1994, Baayen and Lieber 1991, Lieber 1992.) The predominance of a particular form for encoding a particular content has long been known to be a poor predictor of productivity (Aronoff 1976), and though there are properties of morphologically complex words that correlate most highly with the productivity of the rules that derive them – phonological transparency and semantic compositionality – it is still an open issue as to how the correlations are best understood (see Anderson 1992 and Aronoff 1976 for discussion). The present discussion will focus on neurolinguistic indications that the productivity of the morphology involved is a primary determinant as to whether the performance system uses compositional versus retrieval mechanisms for producing familiar, morphologically complex words.

In our earlier discussion of the legal and illegal morphological paraphasias produced by patient S.J.D., we indicated that the affixes that appeared in these paraphasias were inflections and productive derivations. We took the predominance of productive morphology in these paraphasias as one piece of support for the view that forms involving productive morphology may be processed compositionally, while forms involving nonproductive morphology must be listed in, and retrieved from, the lexicon in whole-word format. This processing distinction is further supported by evidence from acquired dysgraphia. When D.H. was asked to write productively derived words (e.g. *brightness*, *cloudless*), the distribution of errors showed a clear effect for the morphological structure of the target: the error rate increased from a low rate stem-initially to a high rate stem-finally, but then fell again to a very low rate at the beginning of the suffix region. By contrast, the distribution of spelling errors for derived words with nonproductive endings (e.g. *similarity*, *clearance*) showed no effect of the morphology of the target, and was in fact indistinguishable from the asymmetric distribution observed with monomorphemic targets (Badecker et al. 1990). This contrast offers a clear form of support for the view that productivity determines whether the output system takes a compositional approach to the production of morphologically complex words.

Recent studies of patients who present with acquired naming impairments – and in particular, patients who have difficulty naming objects with compound names – also bear on the role of productivity in determining how words are processed. Unlike derivation, where productive affixation will generally encode a fully transparent extension of the meaning of the base form, the mechanism of compounding, though it is productive, can result in forms that have largely unpredictable semantic properties. In general, the meaning–form relation is not entirely arbitrary (e.g. the meanings for *clothes* and for *pin* are not wholly unrelated to the meaning of *clothespin*), although the relation is typically idiosyncratic in the sense that it is not determined by the grammar. Compounds may differ from one another in terms of the WAY in which their whole-word meaning relates to the meanings of their constituent words (compare *fertility pill, nausea pill, garlic pill,* and *horse pill*) and also in the EXTENT to which these meanings are related (cf. *butterfly, butterball, buttercup, butter dish*). Hence, this particular type of word formation is interesting in that evidence for or against a compositional approach to the production of compounds can give us a tool to pry apart the effects of productivity from those of semantic predictability.

In a study of twelve unselected German-speaking aphasic patients, Hittmair-Delazer et al. (1992) found that their patients had a greater tendency to produce compound responses when naming objects that had compound names than when the objects had monomorphemic names, even when their responses were incorrect. Furthermore, a single case study of English-speaking patient C.S.S. has replicated this and other features of the group tendencies reported in the Hittmair-Delazer et al. (1992) group study. Perhaps one of the most notable features of C.S.S.'s performance with regard to evidence for a compositional approach to the production of compounds is his production of compound neologisms (e.g. naming a cheerleader as *gym master*, or a trash can as a *can trash*). These substitutions and misorderings of the constituents of the target form are analogous to illegal morphological paraphasias in the extent to which they implicate composition. Interestingly, C.S.S.'s compound neologisms are not limited to targets that can be thought to be semantically compositional (e.g. butterfly → *butter flower*, south paw → *south ball*, and sundial → *sunclock*). Hence, even when there is no clear parallel between the meaning of the compound target and its form, there is at least some evidence that these words are produced by retrieving constituent lexical items and a structural specification of the target form into which the two constituents must be fit. What this suggests is that morphological productivity may be the determining factor with regard to whether morphologically complex forms are composed in the processing system, even when the productivity of the word-formation type is paired with lexical idiosyncrasy regarding the meaning–form mapping.[5]

3 Inflection versus derivation

A case of acquired impairment which provides some indication of the morphological distinctions that are made in the language-processing system is that of patient F.S., an Italian-speaking patient who presented with a lexical impairment that resulted in morphological paraphasias in spontaneous speech and in single-word-processing tasks such as repetition (Miceli and Caramazza 1988). F.S. produced a substantial number of morphological substitution errors in a variety of tasks, but these errors predominantly affected the inflectional specification of a word (gender and number markers for nouns and adjectives; and tense, aspect, person, and number specifications of verbs). Derivational morphology was virtually unaffected. F.S.'s errors also included phonological paraphasias, but these can be distinguished from his inflectional substitutions in a relatively straightforward manner. For example, F.S.'s morphological paraphasias tended to result in the production of "citation forms" – that is, infinitival forms of verbs, singular forms for nouns, masculine singular forms for adjectives – regardless of whether the particular inflected forms were among the least frequent items of an inflectional paradigm.[6] Furthermore, the tendency to produce citation forms could not be reduced to a tendency to produce particular phonological shapes, since the preference for citation forms held constant even when the phonological form of the citation-form suffix varied. For instance, when F.S. repeated adjective forms, he exhibited a strong tendency to use the masculine singular form for those adjectives that allow a four-way inflectional contrast (masc. sg., masc. pl., fem. sg., fem. pl.), and the singular form for those adjectives which allow only a two-way contrast (sg. vs pl.). Notably, the maximally disfavored inflection for the former adjective type (fem. pl., as in *car-e*) was phonologically identical to the favored inflection for the adjectives showing a two-way contrast (sg., as in *fort-e*). Indications that these inflectional errors do not arise as simple whole-word substitutions derives from the fact that the misselected inflections that occurred in F.S.'s performance would occasionally result in the production of a morphologically illegal combination of stem and affix, as in the spontaneous speech error *studi-o* ('office', masc. sg.) → **studi-a* (*fem. sg.), where the contextually appropriate noun is inflected with the wrong gender ending; or the repetition error *mor-issimo* ('die', third conjugation inflection) → **mor-este* (second conjugation ending) (Badecker and Caramazza 1989). Hence, F.S.'s performance is significant both for the evidence it provides for morphological composition and for the motivation it provides for the lexical distinction between inflectional and derivational morphology.

Other cases of acquired language impairment have also exhibited inflection–derivation dissociations: the Finnish-speaking patients H.H. and J.S.[7] (Laine et al. 1994, 1995) and the English-speaking patients F.M. (Badecker, to appear) and P.B. (Badecker et al. 1995). It should not be assumed, however, that all impairments resulting in a disruption of inflection, but not derivation, are alike in their functional origins. Given that there are multiple ways in which derivation and inflection differ with respect to the language-processing system, current models of normal performance allow for a variety of deficits with a production and/or comprehension pattern that distinguishes these morphological types.

4 The nature of lexicality constraints: an open issue

As we have observed, it is not always the case that a patient's morphological paraphasias will result in potential word forms. S.J.D.'s *involveness* (for *involvement*) and F.S.'s *studia* (for *studio*) are clear instances of morpheme substitution that do not preserve lexicality at the level of morphotactics. Nevertheless, there does appear to be one lexicality constraint on morphological errors in spoken output: morphological paraphasias conform to the phonotactics of the language (Grodzinsky 1984, Miceli and Mazzucchi 1990). In languages such as English, morphological deficits often result in affix deletion errors (e.g. *farming* → *farm*). The occurrence of such errors is governed by the well-formedness of morphological "zero forms." In languages which lack zero forms, corresponding deletion errors are absent. Grodzinsky (1984) notes that Hebrew-speaking patients will produce inflectional substitutions like *kašarti* (tie, past tense) → *likšor* (tie, infinitive), but they will not simply omit the vocalic prosody that corresponds to the verb's inflection (*kšr*). However, evidence indicates that this constraint is not based merely on the unpronounceability (in some language-independent sense) of bare consonantal strings like *kšr*. For example, an English-speaking patient may produce morpheme-deletion errors of the form *farm-s* → *farm*, while an analogous error for an Italian-speaking patient (e.g. *fil-e* 'lines' → *fil*) does not occur. Here the phonological constraint on paraphasias exhibited by Italian aphasics must be attributed to conformity to a more abstract notion of phonotactic or morphological well-formedness than what one must invoke in the case of Semitic languages. Perhaps the constraints that are operative here are among the familiar variety of shape rules (e.g. a phonological word-edge constraint such as a condition that, in Italian, a word-final syllable must end in one of the vowels *a, e, i,* or *o*[8]); or perhaps they reflect the mechanisms that restrict, by one means or another, the occurrence of bound morphemes. For example, the fact that items in the open-class vocabulary bear morphosyntactic features that are spelled out by the morphological system, and the fact that there are no regular "zero form" options for the spelling out of these features in Italian (though there are in English) might jointly lead to the effects in question. The nature of the often observed, though poorly understood, lexicality constraints that govern aphasic production is a topic of inquiry that still awaits serious attention.

5 Morphological deficits in sentence comprehension and production

Several studies have documented cases of sentence comprehension impairment that strongly implicate morphological deficits. A case analogous to that of F.S.

(Miceli and Caramazza 1988) has been reported in which the patient, D.E., was found to be selectively impaired in processing inflections in normal speech comprehension (Tyler and Cobb 1987). For example, in a word-monitoring task, D.E. was sensitive to the contextual appropriateness of a word when the wrong derived form was used (as in *He was the most wasteful/*wastage/*wastely cook she had ever met*), but not when an inappropriate inflection intruded (as in *It often causes/*causing/*causely pain in my loose filling*). Given that different inflectional forms can often motivate diverging syntactic expectations (as when the contrast between *chasing* and *chased* signals the transitive/intransitive distinction in *The boy was chasing/chased . . .*), it is plain that D.E.'s sentence comprehension can be explained in part by this morphological impairment.[9]

In a similar study (Tyler et al. 1990), patient B.N. exhibited a more pervasive morphological impairment, in that his monitoring performance indicated an insensitivity to both syntactic ill-formedness, based on the use of inappropriate inflected or derived forms (the examples with *wastage* and *causing*), and lexical ill-formedness (the examples with **wastely* and **causely*). B.N. also failed to exhibit sensitivity to these morphological distinctions in a grammaticality judgment task. However, his lexical monitoring showed a strong effect for pragmatic, semantic, and syntactic appropriateness when the stem of a properly inflected form was varied (e.g. in the context *The crowd was very happy. John was playing/?burying/*drinking/*sleeping the guitar and . . .*). B.N.'s good performance on a lexical decision task (which included legal and illegal affixed forms like *wasteful* and *wastely* in the word and nonword stimuli respectively), along with his performance on a lexical gating task (Grosjean 1980), indicated that it was not impaired recognition of the phonological form of morphologically complex words that was implicated in his sentence-processing deficit. Instead, B.N. appears unable to integrate the syntactic and semantic information encoded in the inflectional and derivational affixes with the semantic (and grammatical) information encoded in lexical stems. It is not apparent whether this impairment arises out of a lexical impairment (i.e. to the mechanisms that derive syntactic and semantic information from affixes) or a deficit to sentence-processing mechanisms that normally exploit this lexical information. In either case, the contribution of the morphological deficit to BN's sentence-comprehension impairment appears well established.

Current theories of sentence production (e.g. M. F. Garrett 1982, 1984; Lapointe 1985) predict that morphological paraphasias (e.g. agreement errors) can result from deficits to sentence-processing mechanisms while single-word processing remains unimpaired. Two recent studies (Caramazza and Hillis 1989, Nespoulous et al. 1988) describe patients who are intact in single-word-processing tasks, but who exhibit selective deficits in processing grammatical morphemes in sentence-processing tasks. In the case of patient "Clermont" (Nespoulous et al. 1988), only free-standing grammatical morphemes were affected. Patient M.L. (Caramazza and Hillis 1989) produced some inflectional (morpholexical) substitutions in addition to omitting and substituting free-standing grammatical morphemes, although the proportion of such morphological agreement errors was small by comparison with the number of function word errors. While the presence of agreement errors in M.L.'s speech supports the hypothesis that "morphological deficits" can arise from damage to syntactic (nonlexical) processing components, a stronger case for this position can be envisioned. Studies which document contrasting patterns of inflectional impairment (e.g. Miceli et al. 1989) have provided some indications that grammatical agreement may be differentially affected (resulting e.g. in divergent error rates for subject–verb, noun–adjective, and determiner–noun agreement), although the relative contribution of lexical and syntactic deficits in most of the reported cases has not been established. Clearly this is one distinction that deserves greater attention.

ACKNOWLEDGEMENTS

This chapter contains some expanded material based on discussion in Badecker and Caramazza 1993. The writing of this paper was supported by NIH grant DC00366 to The Johns Hopkins University. We are grateful to Luigi Burzio and John McCarthy for their helpful comments on various issues raised in this paper.

NOTES

1   Independent considerations require the hypothesized routes of the spelling system to intersect at a point that accepts the output of both the orthographic lexicon and the nonlexical rule-based mechanisms. For discussion, see Caramazza et al. 1987, Hillis and Caramazza 1989, and Posteraro et al. 1988.

2   Note that composition at this level cannot be handled by simple concatenation, since there are several orthographic accommodations that must accompany affixation (e.g. consonant doubling as in *hit/hitting*, *e*-deletion as in *drive/driving*, etc.). For discussion of the mechanisms that might effect such accommodations at this processing stage, see Badecker 1996 and McCloskey et al. 1992.

3   For reasons that are unclear, the morphology-sensitive performance pattern observed in the case of D.H. is associated with the clinical features of attentional neglect (e.g. Hillis and Caramazza 1989): e.g. in a well-studied patient who presents with a deficit at the level of the graphemic buffer but does not exhibit signs of neglect, Italian-speaking patient L.B. (Caramazza et al. 1987), the pattern is not observed.

4   Note that this description is not meant to prejudge the issue of whether affix forms are retrieved from the lexicon in the same way that whole words or bound stems are retrieved (e.g. Lieber 1992, Selkirk 1982), or as the output of Word Formation Rules of the sort envisioned by Anderson (1992), Aronoff (1976), and others.

5 This is not to say, however, that composition in the lexical processing system is in all instances rule-derived. Whereas spellout rules that interpret morphosyntactic features would be appropriate in the case of regular inflection, the sort of compositional process evidenced in C.S.S.'s compound errors would be more aptly described in terms of a lexically driven process (e.g. the 'minor rules' of Stemberger 1985c).

6 By this term we mean the minimally marked members of the inflectional paradigm, a distinction that may have consequences throughout the grammar, which regularly serve as the base forms for the word-formation processes that derive other paradigm members. Burzio (1989) observed that phrase-level phonological processes can delete the vowel corresponding to the inflectional suffix of the citation form, but not any other. As an example, consider the four-ending adjective *buono* and the two-ending adjective *grande*:

buon ragazzo
(*buono ragazzo)   masc. sg.
*buon ragazza
(buona ragazza)   fem. sg.
*buon ragazzi
(buoni ragazzi)   masc. pl.
*buon ragazze
(buone ragazze)   fem. pl.

gran ragazzo
(*grande ragazzo)   masc. sg.
gran ragazza
(*grande ragazza)   fem. sg.
*gran ragazzi
(grandi ragazzi)   masc. pl.
*gran ragazze
(grandi ragazze)   fem. pl.

7 Patient J.S. is a bilingual subject (Finnish and Swedish) who presented with a dissociation between inflection and derivation in both languages.

8 This is not likely to be a satisfactory candidate on its own, given that there are a number of (albeit exceptional) forms that end in consonants (e.g. loan words like *golf* and *jeep*).

9 Patient D.E. was retested on these materials shortly after the study reported in Tyler and Cobb 1987, and on this occasion his monitoring performance failed to show the dissociation of inflection and derivation (Tyler 1992: ch. 12). On retest, D.E.'s monitoring performance failed to demonstrate sensitivity to morphologically inappropriate forms for both inflection and derivation. Tyler (p.c.) suggests that this difference may derive from the patient's over-familiarity with the testing materials (as evidenced by the overall faster reaction times in the retest).

21 Morphology in Word Recognition

JAMES M. MCQUEEN AND
ANNE CUTLER

1 Introduction

This chapter reviews the psycholinguistic literature on the representation and processing of morphological structure in the recognition of spoken and written words. To anticipate more than a little, this is how we will conclude: psychological morphology does not map neatly on to linguistic morphology. We will argue that the processing and representation of morphologically complex words are determined by performance factors, including order of occurrence of stems and affixes, transparency, productivity and frequency of usage. For this reason, linguistic distinctions – for example, between derivational and inflectional relations – may not map neatly on to processing distinctions.

In psycholinguistic descriptions of the mental lexicon it is common to distinguish between access representations and central representations. Access representations are modality-specific processing structures involved in the mapping of visual or auditory input on to the lexicon. They provide the link between more peripheral levels of processing and the central lexicon, and they code form information (orthographic or phonological). Central representations are modality-independent structures coding words' meanings and their syntactic and thematic roles. We will be concerned with the role of morphology at both the access and the central levels.

There are two core issues to be addressed in this chapter. The first concerns the representation of morphological structure in the central lexicon. Is the mental lexicon organized in a way which codes morphological relationships? For example, is the fact that two words share the same stem, or the same affix, coded in the lexicon? This is primarily a question of representation: what information about the internal structure of words is stored in long-term memory, and how? But it is also a question of processing. When a word and its morphology are recognized, does this involve contact with other entries (words and/or morphemes) in the lexicon?

The second issue is that of lexical access. What role does morphological structure play in the process of mapping perceptual information, from spoken or written input, on to the mental lexicon? Is morphological analysis necessary, optional or impossible prior to lexical access? Again, there are questions of both processing and representation: what type of morphological parsing might take place, and what form of access representations might be the product of such a process?

These two issues are in fact not independent. Underlying both is a question which is fundamental in many areas of psychology: the relative importance of rule-based processing and rote storage. Is it more 'efficient' to hold in memory only that which cannot be derived by rule and to be dependent on the smooth operation of such rules, or to store every piece of information and to be dependent on efficient access procedures and the availability of storage space? In the case of morphology, this question becomes one of whether morphologically complex words are decomposed into their component stems and affixes before access to a central lexicon, in which lexical entries are considered to be shared by the morphological derivatives of each stem (Taft and Forster 1975), or whether each word form in a language has a separate, undecomposed entry in the mental lexicon, with no morphological analysis of any word form prior to lexical access (Butterworth 1983). The former of these alternatives assumes that all morphology is completely transparent to the word-recognition system, the latter that it is all opaque. Between these extremes, as the following sections show, fall numerous intermediate positions.

2 Lexical representation of morphological structure

2.1 Are morphological relationships represented?

Words may be recognized faster if a morphologically related word has recently been processed; thus recognition of the 'target' *pour* in a lexical decision task (in which subjects judge whether a written or spoken item is a real word or not) is speeded by prior presentation of the 'prime' *pours* (Stanners et al. 1979a). This 'repetition priming' effect has been extremely influential in psycholinguistic studies of morphology. To be sure that it is a true morphological effect, however, one has to rule out alternative explanations invoking formal or semantic similarity. *Car* overlaps (both orthographically and phonologically) with *card* as much as it overlaps with *cars*; likewise, *sameness* and *same* have shared meaning, but to no greater extent than *equivalence* and *same*. A large body of research has been devoted to the question of whether morphological relationships are indeed represented independently of both formal and semantic relationships.

One such line of research has demonstrated that morphological effects pattern differently from effects of formal similarity. For instance, orthographic priming is absent where morphological priming occurs, both in brief visual recognition following list learning (Murrell and Morton 1974) and in repetition priming tasks (Feldman and Moskovljević 1987, Napps and Fowler 1987). Morphological priming is long-lived, while orthographic priming is very transient (cf. Napps 1989 with Napps and Fowler 1987). In the masked-priming paradigm, in which primes are presented very briefly and then immediately masked by the target, morphological priming is facilitatory, while orthographic priming is inhibitory (Drews and Zwitserlood 1995, Grainger et al. 1991). In unmasked lexical decision, in which the prime immediately precedes the target, orthographic priming is again inhibitory where morphological priming is facilitatory (Drews and Zwitserlood 1995, Henderson et al. 1984). Feldman and Moskovljević (1987) alternated the two alphabets of Serbo-Croatian (Roman and Cyrillic), and showed an effect of morphology in repetition priming which was just as large when visual similarity was very low (prime and target in different alphabets) as when visual similarity was high (prime and target in the same alphabets). A similar result has been obtained with Hebrew (Feldman and Bentin 1994), in which, due to vowel infixation, words sharing the same root morpheme can have different orthographic forms. Feldman and Bentin found equivalent morphological priming when prime and target either had the same or different orthographic structures.

All of these results suggest that there is a level of representation of morphological information independent from the representation of orthographic information. As, for example, Drews and Zwitserlood (1995) have argued, one way of conceptualizing these separate levels is to distinguish between more peripheral access representations, where entries overlapping in form inhibit each other, and central representations, where morphological relationships are coded.

In the auditory modality, morphological priming occurs when phonological priming is absent. Kempley and Morton (1982), assessing priming of words spoken in noise, found effects of regular inflectional overlap (*hedges – hedge*) but not phonological overlap (*pledge – hedge*). Emmorey (1989), in an immediate priming task (50 milliseconds between prime and target), found priming between morphological relatives (e.g. *submit – permit*), but no priming between purely phonological relatives (e.g. *balloon – saloon*). These results again suggest that form information (here, phonological form) is represented independently of morphological information.

Semantic priming, like form-based priming, also appears to have a different time course to morphological priming. L. Henderson et al. (1984) showed priming for morphological relatives when the prime preceded the target by both 1 and 4 seconds, but priming of semantic relatives (synonyms) at the 1-second interval only. Bentin and Feldman (1990) found semantic priming for written Hebrew with no intervening items between prime and target, but none with fifteen intervening items. When prime and target were morphologically related, there was priming at both lags, even when the prime and the target (derived from the same root) had only weak semantic association. Likewise, Emmorey (1989) showed priming between spoken words which were morphological relatives but not semantic associates (e.g. *submit-permit*). These results suggest that a model in which all morphological relationships in the lexicon are purely semantic (Butterworth 1983) is untenable. As Stolz and Feldman (1995) have argued, it appears that morphological effects cannot be reduced to either form-based effects (whether due to orthography or phonology) or effects of associative semantics.

2.2 Models of representation

How, then, is morphological information represented in the central lexicon? A number of alternative schemes have been proposed. One is that morphological relatives share a single lexical entry (e.g. Taft 1985, 1988). In this framework all morphological derivatives of a stem are listed fully within the same entry, but in morphologically decomposed form (Taft 1988). A related, shared-entry model is the Augmented Addressed Morphology (AAM) model for inflectional morphology (Caramazza et al. 1988; see also Chialant and Caramazza 1995). In this model, entries consist of stems positively linked to the inflectional suffixes with which they can combine, and (for irregular verbs) of stems negatively linked to suffixes with which they cannot combine.

Alternative accounts make the assumption that words have separate entries. One of these assumes that morphological relatives are linked together as 'satellites' under a main entry, the 'nucleus' (Feldman and Fowler 1987; Günther 1988; Lukatela et al. 1978, 1980; but see Kostić 1995 for problems with the satellite approach). Another type of separate-entries model envisages a network containing entries for words and, separately, for morphemes: lexical entries for morphologically related words are linked by a node which represents their shared-stem morpheme (S. Andrews 1986; Fowler et al. 1985; Grainger et al. 1991; Schreuder et al. 1990; Schriefers et al. 1991, 1992).

Schriefers et al. (1992), using the repetition-priming paradigm, provided evidence consistent with network models. Their study compared the size of priming effects between German inflectional and derivational forms, each form acting as both a prime and a target. The effects were asymmetrical: adjectival forms with the dative singular suffix *-em* primed suffixed relatives with *-e* and *-es* and their stem forms, but *-em* forms were themselves *not* primed by any of these three types. In network models, each word is represented as a processing node; when a word has been presented, its node has a high degree of activation. Each stem morpheme also has a node associated with it. The word nodes of all the morphological relatives of a given stem have bi-directional facilitatory connections to the stem node. The basis of the priming effect is that activation of a word node in a morphological cluster boosts the activation of the stem node, and, indirectly, the activation of connected word nodes. On the assumption that the facilitatory connections can vary in strength (such that a word node can prime a stem node more or less than that stem node can prime either that or other word nodes), these priming asymmetries (and similar results of Feldman and Fowler 1987 and Feldman 1991) can be accounted for. It is not yet clear, however, which processing or linguistic factors may determine the relative strengths of these associative connections.

These results seem problematic for decompositional models such as that of Taft (1988), since in such models stem access should produce the same amount of priming irrespective of the form in which the stem occurred. They also seem problematic for satellite models. For Serbo-Croatian, Lukatela et al. (1980; see also Feldman and Fowler 1987) operationally defined nominative singular nouns (because they were responded to most rapidly) as the nuclei around which were clustered other nominal inflected forms. There was, however, no clear nucleus in the German adjectives studied by Schriefers et al. (no one form stood out as having faster response times associated with it).

Grainger et al. (1991) also interpreted their finding of facilitatory morphological priming and inhibitory orthographic priming in the masked priming task in terms of a network, suggesting that inhibitory connections might exist between visually similar words (morphologically related or not), with negative priming operating alongside positive morphological priming. Schreuder et al. (1990) examined the processing of Dutch verbs using a partial priming technique (Jarvella et al. 1987), in which part of a word is briefly displayed prior to presentation of the complete word (for naming). Priming of whole words by either affixes or stems was found only for verbs with separable particles. Since these particles can be separated from their stem by several words when the verb is inflected, and since the meanings of the complex forms are often not predictable from the joint meanings of particle and stem, there is good reason to suppose that both particle and stem have separate but closely linked representations. Again, Schreuder et al. account for their results in terms of a network model. More recent research on the processing and representation of separable verbs in Dutch, using a grammaticality judgement task, has provided further support for a network approach, where 'morphological integration' nodes provide the links between separate representations for particles and stems (Frazier et al. 1993).

Other results support lexical representation of morphological structure. For example, Tyler and Nagy (1990) found that readers made fewer semantic errors and more syntactic errors in selecting paraphrases of sentences with suffixed than with matched non-suffixed words. They argued that a morphologically structured lexicon would give the reader immediate access to morphological relatives of a suffixed form, increasing the likelihood of accessing the appropriate semantics (hence the low semantic error rate), but also increasing the likelihood of misidentifying a suffixed form as one of its relatives (hence the high syntactic error rate). Using eye fixation time data, Holmes and O'Regan (1992) found gaze durations for both prefixed and suffixed words to be shortest when the first fixation on a word included the stem.

Laudanna et al. (1989, 1992) employed a stem homograph priming technique with Italian materials, in which pairs of words were presented (either simultaneously or sequentially) for lexical decision. Laudanna et al. (1989) showed that lexical decisions to pairs with homographic stems that were morphologically unrelated (e.g. *portare* 'to carry' and *porte* 'doors' with the stem *port-*) took longer than those to pairs with non-homographic stems (e.g. *collo* 'neck' and *colpo* 'blow' with the stems *coll-* and *colp-*), which in turn were slower than those to pairs where the stems were morphologically related (e.g. *porta* 'door' and *porte* 'doors'). Laudanna et al. (1992) replicated the inhibitory effect of orthographic overlap (relative to non-homographic controls) for word pairs sharing an inflectional stem (e.g. *mute* 'mute' and *mutarano* 'they changed' with the stem *mut-*), but did not find any effect for words sharing a homographic (but unrelated) derivational root (e.g. *mute* and *mutevole* 'changeable', where *mutevole* has the derivational root *mut-* but the inflectional stem *mutevol-*). Nevertheless, these authors also showed that derived words (e.g. *mutevole*) and inflected words (e.g. *mutarano*) were equally effective as primes for lexical decision on infinitival forms (e.g. *mutare* 'to change') in a priming experiment.

Laudanna et al. (1992) argue that words must therefore be represented in terms of their morphemic constituents, and that these constituents are inflectional stems and affixes, rather than derivational roots and affixes. They interpret their findings as evidence for their AAM model, in which lexical entries are morphologically decomposed (Caramazza et al. 1988). Lexical entries containing stems with the same orthographic structure (stem homographs) are considered to inhibit each other in order to resolve ambiguity. Morphological relatives facilitate each other through repeated access to the same stem. These results, however, can also be accommodated by network models, although they suggest that morpheme nodes should be based on inflectional stems rather than derivational roots, with inhibition between homographic stem nodes.

The data presented by Schriefers et al. (1992) also constrain network models. In addition to asymmetric inflectional priming, these authors obtained different patterns of priming for inflectional and derivational suffixes (of the same adjectival stems). Although not all priming effects were equal, both inflected and derived words primed, and were primed, by their stems, and inflected words primed other inflected words. However, there was no priming between derivational forms (e.g. *Röte, rötlich*). Feldman (1994) also compared inflectional and derivational priming in Serbian (the same language previously referred to as Serbo-Croatian). Although both inflectionally and derivationally related words produced facilitatory priming effects, those involving inflections were larger. The results for derivations thus contrast with the German findings. Further cross-linguistic experiments will be required before such differences can be explained. Nevertheless, it seems clear across several studies that inflectional priming is more robust than derivational priming.

Other results have indicated different patterns of priming dependent on the nature of the derivational relationship under test. Marslen-Wilson et al. (1994) used English materials in a cross-modal priming task (measuring lexical decision speed to written words, presented immediately after the offset of spoken word primes), and found that suffixed forms (e.g. *friendly*) primed and were primed by their stems, but that suffixed forms did not prime each other (e.g. *confession, confessor*). Derivationally prefixed forms (e.g. *unfasten, refasten*) primed and were primed by their stems, but, in contrast to suffixed forms, they also primed each other. Prefixed and suffixed forms sharing the same stem also primed each other (e.g. *distrust, trustful*).

Marslen-Wilson et al. argued that these results support a model in which lexical entries are morphologically decomposed, with affixes clustered around shared stem morphemes (their account is thus similar to the lexical component of Caramazza et al.'s (1988) AAM model). Priming takes place through repeated access to stems. All members of a cluster therefore prime each other. Suffixed forms do not prime each other, however, because additional inhibitory links between the suffixes in a cluster cancel out any benefit due to repeated access of the stem. Marslen-Wilson et al. justify these inhibitory connections on the grounds that during spoken word recognition, when the listener has only heard a stem, different suffixes of that stem are possible completions and should therefore all be activated. When evidence for one suffix arrives, the activation of incorrect suffixes needs to be suppressed – hence the inhibitory connections. No such connections are required between prefixes: a given prefix will not activate other prefixes of the same stem, so they need not be suppressed.

Although Marslen-Wilson et al.'s account is confined to derivational morphology, it suggests a more general way in which priming asymmetries (such as those reported for inflected words by Schriefers et al.) could be accommodated in shared-entry models (including their own model and Caramazza et al.'s AAM model). The basic claim would be that the shared entry does not consist of a simple listing of the affixes appropriate for a stem, but rather that the affixes are themselves structured processing units. In addition to the inhibitory connections postulated by Marslen-Wilson et al. for derivational suffixes, there could also be inhibition between inflectional suffixes. If the strengths of the connections between stems and affixes, and between affixes, were allowed to vary independently, then priming asymmetries between and within inflected and derived words could be explained. Such a model makes very similar predictions to those made by the network account proposed by Schriefers et al., where the strengths of connections between whole-word entries and their shared stems can vary.

An important constraint on the lexical representation of morphological information, both for network models and for internally structured shared-entry models, is that of semantic transparency. Marslen-Wilson et al. (1994) examined this issue explicitly. They asked subjects to rate the semantic related-ness of morphologically related word pairs, and found high estimates of re-latedness for pairs such as *confession – confessor*, which they then defined as transparent, and low estimates for pairs such as *successful – successor*, which they defined as opaque. The effects of morphological structure described above could be obtained only when the morphological relationship between stem and affixed form was transparent; that is, *friendly* primed *friend*, but *casualty* did not prime *casual*. In other words, morphological relationships in the mental lexicon, however they may be represented, cannot be defined purely on formal linguistic grounds. Most studies of derivational morphology have failed to control for semantic transparency/opacity; some of the variability of morphological effects in the literature may result from this lack of control (as pointed out by L. Henderson 1985, 1989, and by Marslen-Wilson et al. 1994). Note that although Emmorey (1989) did obtain priming between opaque forms (such as *submit – permit*), she employed a task in which both prime and target were presented auditorily (in contrast to Marslen-Wilson et al.'s cross-modal task). Furthermore, the morphological relationships between primes and targets tended to be less transparent in the Marslen-Wilson et al. study than in the Emmorey study.

Marslen-Wilson et al. also examined phonological transparency. They found as much priming in pairs such as *elusive – elude* and *serenity – serene* as in pairs such as *friendly – friend*. Fowler et al. (1985) and Downie et al. (1985) also found no effects of phonological transparency on the size of morphological priming effects. These results suggest that the locus of these effects is in the central lexicon, where representations have abstracted away from surface forms.

To summarize so far, the large priming literature indicates that morphological information is represented in the central lexicon. Recent research has shown that this includes detailed information on the relationships between the forms of a morphological family, more than just that they are related. This evidence therefore supports refined models of lexical organization: either those with separate entries for each word form which are linked with variable connections to entries representing their shared-stem morphemes (network models; Schriefers et al. 1992) or those with decomposed shared entries, with variable connections between stems and affixes, and between affixes (internally structured shared-entry models; Marslen-Wilson et al. 1994). As has often been pointed out (e.g. by Burani 1993), it can be difficult to distinguish between these alternative theoretical accounts.

It should be clear from the previous section that inflectional and derivational morphology could in principle be represented similarly in the lexicon, with semantic transparency of the morphological relationship being the main determinant of the strength of connections between related words. As Feldman (1994) has suggested, one reason why priming effects tend to be stronger for inflections than for derivations may be that inflectional relationships are in general more transparent than derivational relationships. There may be no need for a qualitative distinction in the way in which inflections and derivations are mentally represented.

Research on the representation of compounds leads to similar conclusions. Separate whole-word representations are often posited for compounds. Several authors (e.g. L. Henderson 1985; Sandra 1990, 1994) have argued that since the meanings of nominal compounds such as *blackbird* are not fully recoverable from their components, they require independent meaning representations in the central lexicon. These whole-word representations are usually considered to be linked in a network to representations of their component morphemes (see e.g. network accounts offered to explain the storage of Chinese compounds: Taft and Zhu 1995, Zhou and Marslen-Wilson 1994). When novel nominal compounds are encountered, they appear to be interpreted via activation of the meanings of their constituents (Coolen et al. 1991, 1993).

As in the account of inflections and derivations, semantic transparency also plays a role in the representation of compounds. Sandra (1990) has argued on the basis of a study of Dutch compounds that although semantically opaque compounds (like *blackbird*) have independent central representations, fully transparent compounds may lack such representations, and may be recognized on the basis of activation of their constituent morphemes. Zwitserlood (1994), again from a study of Dutch compounds, has proposed a multiple-level lexicon. In addition to access (form) representations, she proposes two further levels: a morphological level, where the relationships between compounds and their component morphemes are coded, even for fully opaque compounds like *klokhuis* (lit. 'clock-house', but meaning core, as of an apple); and a semantic level, where fully opaque compounds are not connected to their constituents.

A structured central lexicon, with morphological relationships coded in an activation network, is therefore the favoured account of the representation of all complex words: inflected, derived and compound forms. It appears, however, to be unnecessary to posit qualitatively different representational accounts for these different classes. Factors such as semantic transparency, which apply to all classes, appear to determine the strength and nature of the connectivity between morphemes.

3 Prelexical processing of morphological structure

3.1 Derivational morphology

As we pointed out earlier, questions of the structure of central lexical representations are closely bound to questions of lexical access. What is the nature of the pre-lexical processes and the lexical access representations via which the central representations are contacted during word recognition? An influential paper by Taft and Forster (1975) argued for an obligatory process of pre-lexical decomposition, whereby words are broken down into their constituent morphemes prior to lexical access. This decomposition model (and its modifications – Taft and Forster 1976, Taft 1979a; see also Taft 1979b, 1981, 1985, 1988; Taft et al. 1986) proposes that all affixes are detected and stripped from a word before lexical access is attempted using the remaining stem morpheme. *Revive*, for example, would be accessed via its stem, *vive*. Taft and Forster (1975) based their proposal on non-word interference effects in a lexical decision task in English; non-words were rejected more slowly when they were bound stems (e.g. *vive* from *revive*) than when they were pseudo-stems (e.g. *lish* from *relish*). Subjects also found it more difficult to reject prefixed non-words with real stems (e.g. *dejoice*) than prefixed non-words containing no real stem (e.g. *dejouse*). This second interference effect has been demonstrated in both the visual and the auditory modalities (Taft et al. 1986). Taft (e.g. 1985, 1988) proposed that stem morphemes are the access codes used in lexical lookup; in contrast to pseudo-stems, they cannot be rejected immediately because they succeed in making contact with a central lexical representation (but see also Taft 1994 for an alternative account based on interactive activation, in which pre-lexical prefix stripping is not required).

L. Henderson (1985) has argued, however, that data from processing of non-words may not reflect normal word recognition; rather, morphological decomposition of non-words may be attempted only when access based on whole-word representations fails to find a lexical entry. Experiments involving effects with real words avoid this problem. Consider a pair of words such as *misplace* and *misery*. Pre-lexical decomposition should, at least when these items are presented visually, strip *mis* from both words, delaying recognition of the pseudo-prefixed form *misery* (due to erroneous lookup of the false stem *ery*). Rubin et al. (1979) indeed found this pseudo-prefixation effect using a lexical decision task in English, but only when there were prefixed non-words in the experiment, not when there were no prefixed non-words. On the basis of this result, they argued that decomposition was only an optional strategy – not normally employed, but invoked by the presence of prefixed non-words. However, Taft (1981) has provided an explanation for the failure to find decomposition effects when prefixed non-words were absent: subjects were able simply to say 'yes' to any item beginning with a prefix. Any effect of decomposition would thus be masked. Taft (1981) also observed a pseudo-prefixation effect in a naming task when there were neither non-words nor truly prefixed words in the experiment. In this situation, strategic decomposition would be impossible; subjects were nevertheless slower to initiate the pronunciation of pseudo-prefixed words than non-prefixed words.

Bergman et al. (1988) also found pseudo-prefixation effects in lexical decision, in Dutch. L. Henderson et al. (1984), however, using a lexical decision task with a small proportion of potentially prefixed English words and non-words (thus avoiding the problem of strategic decomposition), found no difference in lexical decision latency between pseudo-prefixed words and monomorphemic control words; prefixed words were, if anything, responded to slightly more rapidly than both of the other word types.

Pseudo-affixation has also been studied with suffixes. Manelis and Tharp (1977) presented pairs of English suffixed forms (e.g. *bulky – dusty*) and pairs of pseudo-suffixed forms (e.g. *fancy – nasty*) in a lexical decision task in which subjects had to decide on the lexical status of both forms. They found no difference between these pairs. In addition, Henderson et al. (1984) and Bergman et al. (1988) both found no differences in lexical decision latencies for individually presented suffixed, pseudo-suffixed and monomorphemic control words.

However, Manelis and Tharp (1977) also tested mixed pairs of words (i.e. one suffixed and one pseudo-suffixed, e.g. *bulky – nasty*) and found that such pairs were responded to more slowly than the unmixed pairs. When pseudo-suffixed forms are paired with genuinely suffixed words, the processor may be misled into attempting their decomposition, increasing processing difficulty.

Bergman (1988) has argued that the fact that pseudo-prefixation effects are stronger than pseudo-suffixation effects can be accounted for by a left-to-right parsing process. If visual input is processed letter by letter, pseudo-prefixes will be recognized as prefixes, inducing a processing cost while the system recovers from its incorrect analysis. Pseudo-suffixes, on the other hand, are less problematic because they can be processed as a continuation of the stem.

Libben (1994) showed that lexical decisions to ambiguous novel compounds, like *busheater* (bus-heater or bush-eater) took longer than those to unambiguous compounds like *larkeater*. Libben argued that this result provided evidence for a decomposition process, and also suggested that parsing operates left-to-right. As further evidence for a decomposition procedure, Libben (1993) has shown that subjects are slower reading aloud morphologically illegal non-sense words like *rebirmity* (re- only attaches to verbs, while -ity only attaches to adjectives) than legal nonsense words like *rebirmize* (where the selectional restrictions of the affixes are compatible). This latter finding is open to the same criticism as the older non-word studies, however; it does not indicate that morphological decomposition is a necessary pre-lexical procedure in the recognition of words.

Two further paradigms which have been used recently also suggest that readers can use morphological information in processing written material. In the first, the segment-shifting task (Feldman et al. 1995), subjects are required to shift an underlined portion of one word (e.g. *hard<u>en</u>*) on to another word (e.g. *bright*), and then to say the resulting form (*brighten*). This task was found to be easier when the shifted portion was morphemic (e.g. *hard<u>en</u>*) than when it was non-morphemic (*gard<u>en</u>*). Similar results have been obtained in Hebrew, where affixes were infixed and no longer formed contiguous units (Feldman et al. 1995), and in Serbian (Feldman 1994). In the second paradigm (Beauvillain 1994), French subjects saw two French words, presented sequentially, and had to identify whether the second word was the same as the first. Parts of the words were presented in higher contrast. Judgements that the words were the same were faster when the high-contrast part corresponded to the stem of the word (e.g. **reflux** 'ebb') than when it did not (e.g. **reflet** 'reflection'). But again, although the data from both these tasks suggest that readers can take advantage of morphological information, they show neither that morphological parsing is obligatory nor that it is pre-lexical.

There is one particularly strong argument against mandatory pre-lexical decomposition of derived forms. An autonomous morphological parser, given an input which *could* be affixed, has to attempt decomposition on this form. For items which are not in fact morphologically complex, there will be a processing cost associated with recovery from the mis-parsing (this is the thinking behind the pseudo-affixation studies). Clearly, such a mechanism would be inefficient if the language it operated on contained a large number of pseudo-affixed forms. Schreuder and Baayen (1994) have shown that pseudo-prefixed forms occur frequently in both Dutch and English. In a corpus of Dutch text, around 30 per cent of words beginning with strings which could be prefixes were actually not prefixed, while the corresponding proportion for an English corpus was a staggering 80 per cent. Laudanna and Burani (1995) have shown that pseudo-prefixation rates in Italian are also very high. Baayen (1993) has shown, however, that high proportions of pseudo-suffixed forms do not occur.

These statistics suggest that mandatory pre-lexical decomposition of derivational prefixes would be highly inefficient. But they do not rule out decomposition completely. It may be the case that the recognition system is sensitive to the distributional properties of affixes. If so, decomposition may be more likely for prefixed forms where the orthographic string forming the prefix tends to occur only very rarely as a pseudo-prefix, and less likely when pseudo-prefixation is common for that string. Laudanna et al. (1994) performed multiple regression analyses on lexical decision data from prefixed Italian non-words, and found support for this hypothesis. Laudanna and Burani (1995) have also shown that other factors, such as prefix length and affix productivity, may determine how derived forms are processed. There is a very important point here: experiments which treat all affixes as alike may fail to reveal either clear or accurate results (Laudanna and Burani 1995, Sandra 1994). Lack of sufficient control of affix types (and indeed stem types) may account for some of the variability of previous results; it is to be hoped that tighter controls will be adopted in the future.

The balance of the evidence indicates that lexical access of derived forms does not *depend* upon morphological decomposition, but that decomposition can occur. Except for the Taft et al. (1986) non-word study, however, all studies described so far in this section have assessed visual word recognition. In spoken word recognition, there is evidence that prefixed words are not decomposed. Tyler et al. (1988) compared recognition performance on English prefixed words and their free stems (e.g. *amoral* and *moral*). In a gating task, in which listeners were asked to identify successively longer stretches of a word, Tyler et al. (1988) showed that the prefixed forms could be confidently identified earlier than the stems. There was a similar advantage for prefixed items over stems in both lexical decision and naming tasks when response time was measured from word onset. All these results support models of word recognition in which incoming information is processed continuously; they do not support discontinuous decomposition models, which predict processing costs associated with prefixation. Schriefers et al. (1991), avoiding some potential methodological confounds in the Tyler et al. study, also found that prefixed Dutch words were recognized earlier than their stems in a gating task. They used a phoneme monitoring task as well. They reasoned that if listeners use lexical knowledge in detecting target phonemes, and if lexical access depends on decomposition into stems and affixes, than detection of a phoneme in a stem should be equally fast whether the stem occurs in isolation or in a complex form. Subjects in fact detected target phonemes faster in prefixed words than in stems, suggesting that decomposition does not occur in the processing of spoken prefixed words.

3.2 *Inflectional morphology*

The picture that is emerging from the analysis of derivational morphology is that, at least in the visual modality, pre-lexical decomposition is an optional process. It is a strategy available to the language user, but it does not play a mandatory role in normal word recognition. Furthermore, it may be more likely to occur for some prefixes than for others. Is the picture the same for inflectional morphology?

Non-word interference effects have been obtained for inflected Italian words (Caramazza et al. 1988). Non-words composed of verbal stems with inappropriate inflections (e.g. *cantevi*, in which the first-conjugation verb root *cant-* occurs with the second-conjugation suffix *-evi*) were harder to reject than non-words composed either of genuine stems with illegal suffixes (e.g. *cantovi*) or of illegal stems with genuine suffixes (e.g. *canzevi*). These in turn were harder to reject than non-decomposable forms made from illegal stems and affixes (e.g. *canzovi*). Caramazza et al. argued that Taft's decomposition model would predict *cantovi* and *canzovi* to be equivalent, since both have an illegal suffix which cannot be stripped pre-lexically. They claimed, in contrast, that pre-lexical decomposition is non-mandatory. In their Augmented Addressed Morphology model, lexical access is achieved by two procedures operating in cascade, one based on whole-word forms (for known words) and one based on morphemes (for novel words). Caramazza et al. assume that the morphemic access procedure exercises an effect only when the whole-word procedure fails (e.g. when it is presented with non-words containing legal morphemes). Thus their model claims that morphological decomposition is optional to the same degree for inflected as for derived words.

Caramazza et al.'s study, however, given its non-word materials, is open to the same criticism as other non-word interference studies. Studies with real words suggest a different picture. For example, Stanners et al.'s (1979a) repetition-priming studies showed differences between derived and inflected words. Regularly inflected verbs primed later decisions on their bases as much as the base verbs primed themselves. Irregularly inflected verbs (e.g. *hung – hang*) and adjectival and nominal suffixed derivatives of verbs (e.g. *selective – select* and *appearance – appear*) were less efficacious as primes for the verbs than the verbs themselves. Stanners et al. (1979a) interpreted their results as evidence of pre-lexical decomposition of regularly inflected forms. They argued that the weaker priming for derived and irregularly inflected forms was due to the representation of morphological structure in the lexicon, while the equivalence of repetition priming and regular inflectional priming indicated a pre-lexical morphological process. The regular inflectional suffix on a verb like *pours* could be stripped pre-lexically, and the verb would then be recognized via the access code *pour*. If repetition-priming reflects repeated use of access codes, then the regular inflectional priming effect would indeed be predicted to be as large as the identical repetition effect.

However, it now seems clear that there are components of the priming effect which are not due to normal processes of lexical access, but instead are due to episodic memory processes (remembering that a prime occurred while processing the target) or to strategies adopted by subjects in response to the demands of the experimental task (see e.g. Fowler et al. 1985, Monsell 1985, Napps 1989). It is necessary to control for these factors before we can interpret any morphological effects. Fowler et al. (1985) provided these controls. In order to reduce episodic effects, the lag between first and second presentations of the critical word pairs (regular form–base and derived form–base pairs with matched base–base pairs) was increased from an average of nine intervening items (as in Stanners et al.'s design) to forty-eight; practice effects were also controlled. Under these conditions, both inflectional and derivational priming were statistically equivalent to repetition priming. With a similarly long lag condition, Stanners et al. (1979b) also found priming from prefixed words to stems to be equivalent to repetition priming. Furthermore, Fowler et al. compared derived and inflected forms in both the visual and auditory modalities. They found very little difference in the size of the priming effects for regular and irregular forms (irregular items were orthographically and/or phonologically opaque when compared to their stems, including some suppletive past-tense forms of verbs). These findings appear to undermine the pre-lexical decomposition account of regular inflectional priming, because they indicate that the priming effect is insensitive to surface-form transparency (see also Downie et al. 1985). Since irregular forms are not open to surface-form decomposition, the locus of the priming effect cannot be pre-lexical. Instead, it must be lexical. This is the position adopted by Fowler et al. (1985): that priming effects are due to the morphological structuring of the lexicon. This view is consistent with the results on central lexical representation reported in section 2.

A decomposition procedure for inflected forms predicts that under certain circumstances there may be a processing advantage for uninflected forms (but note that this is not a general processing advantage – overall, inflected forms are no more difficult to recognize than uninflected forms: Cutler 1983). Taft (1978) and McQueen et al. (1992) have shown that homophone pairs made up of a regularly inflected form and an uninflected form (e.g. *billed – build*) are more often recognized (written down in dictation) as the uninflected form, even when the inflected form is much more frequent (e.g. *based – baste*). This result suggests that the extra processing required in decomposition may delay recognition of the suffixed form. Jarvella and Meijers (1983) asked subjects to make same–different judgements on either the stems or the affixes of pairs of words. Subjects were faster to judge stems than inflections; Jarvella and Meijers argued that stem judgements were easier because they could be based on lexical representations of the stems, while inflection judgements were hard because they could not be based on independent representations of the inflected forms. Decomposition of inflected forms would prevent them having independent representations. It would also make them more difficult to remember: in a task where subjects had to recall lists of words, 17 per cent of the plurals in the lists were misremembered as their singular forms (Van der Molen and Morton 1979). Data from letter cancellation tasks is also consistent with the decomposition of inflected words; Smith and Sterling (1982; see also Drewnowski and Healy 1980) found that subjects were more likely to miss the letter *e* in affixes or pseudo-affixes than in other syllables. The fact that the effect appeared in both affixes and pseudo-affixes suggests a pre-lexical procedure which would be blind to the true status of a possible affix. Finally, Gibson and Guinet (1971) presented written words very briefly for identification. Fewer errors were made on inflectional endings than on non-inflectional endings, suggesting that the suffix acted as a separate unit in perception. This result again favours decomposition of inflected words.

In summary, the evidence for decomposition reviewed so far is stronger for inflectional than for derivational forms. Decomposition may be an optional strategy for derived words, available when normal access procedures fail. It would therefore appear that derived words have independent whole-word access representations. Inflected words may not have their own access representations, and access to the central lexicon for inflected forms may be via decomposition, leading to access representations of their component stems and affixes.

4 Frequency of occurrence

We have already seen that processing factors appear to determine the role of morphological information in word recognition. At the level of representation in the central lexicon, factors such as semantic transparency influence which morphological relationships are represented and how they are coded. During pre-lexical processing and lexical access, factors such as the likelihood of letter strings appearing as genuine prefixes may determine whether or not decomposition of derived forms takes place. One important processing factor, the frequency of occurrence of words, has so far been overlooked. Word frequency is treated separately, since its analysis has had implications both for lexical access and for central lexical representations. This body of work exploits the well-established finding of 'frequency effects' – lexical decisions are faster to high- than to low-frequency words.

Taft (1979b) manipulated independently surface frequency (the frequency of occurrence of any particular surface form) and combined stem frequency (the summed frequency of occurrence of a stem across all the inflected forms in which that stem occurs). He found that lexical decisions to inflected and uninflected words were faster both for higher combined stem frequency (when surface frequency was controlled) and for higher surface frequency (when stem frequency was controlled).

Taft's materials included both nouns and verbs; other studies, however, have examined frequency effects for each syntactic class separately. Burani et al. (1984) replicated Taft's results with Italian regular verbs: both combined stem frequency and surface frequency predicted lexical decision time of inflected forms. However, Katz et al. (1991) found that only surface frequencies, not combined stem frequencies, could predict lexical decision time for uninflected English verbs. (Their results for inflected English verbs are ambiguous: decision latencies for past-tense forms were predicted by surface frequency alone, but those for present participles were predicted by both surface and combined stem frequency.) Sereno and Jongman (1992) found surface frequency effects for both inflected and uninflected verbs, but they observed no effect of combined stem frequency for uninflected verbs (combined stem frequency effects in inflected verbs were not tested).

Although effects of combined stem frequency are fairly reliable for inflected verbs, the evidence is somewhat contradictory for uninflected verb forms. A similar pattern emerges for nouns. Sereno and Jongman (in press) used a set of nouns matched on combined stem frequency but differing on the relative frequency of their uninflected and inflected forms, such that one subgroup had higher-frequency singular forms and lower-frequency plurals (e.g. *river(s)*), while the other group had higher-frequency plurals and lower-frequency singular forms (e.g. *window(s)*). Surface frequency effects in lexical decision latency were observed for plurals (e.g. *windows* faster than *rivers*). Although there was a similar effect for singulars (e.g. *river* faster than *window*), this effect was not significant. For nouns matched on surface frequency of their singulars but differing in combined stem frequency, no effect of combined stem frequency was observed in lexical decisions regarding the uninflected nouns, while there was a non-significant trend for the plurals (high combined frequency plurals were responded to somewhat faster than low combined frequency plurals). The failure to find surface and combined stem frequency effects for uninflected nouns appears to contradict Taft's (1979b) results.

The results for both nouns and verbs are therefore somewhat inconclusive. The picture is little clearer for derivational morphology. Taft (1979b) found that lexical decisions regarding prefixed words, matched in terms of their surface frequency, were faster for those with higher combined root frequency than for those with lower combined root frequency (the summed frequency of occurrence of a root across all the derived and inflected forms in which that root occurs). Extending Taft's result, Burani and Caramazza (1987) found surface and combined root frequency effects for Italian suffixed derived words.

But Burani and Caramazza's finding appears to conflict with one reported by Bradley (1980). She found no effects of surface frequency for English suffixed words ending in *-ment*, *-er*, *-ness* and *-ion*, and effects of combined root frequency only for the first three of these types of word (i.e. she found no frequency effects whatsoever for words ending in *-ion*). As Burani and Caramazza note, however, Bradley's word lists contained a high proportion of items with the same suffix. This could have induced a decompositional strategy, and hence reduced surface frequency effects. Strategic decomposition, since it would depend on the detection of decomposable forms, would also produce the apparent effect of transparency which Bradley obtained: *-ion* suffixes alter pronunciation, spelling and stress (and therefore by implication impair detectability) of their roots, while *-ment*, *-er* and *-ness* do not.

Cole et al. (1989), in support of Burani and Caramazza, have also observed surface and combined root frequency effects for French suffixed words. However, in contradiction of Taft (1979b), they found no effect of combined root frequency for prefixed words. S. Andrews (1986) observed a reliable frequency effect in bisyllabic compound words, such that those with a high-frequency word in their first syllable were responded to, in lexical decision, more rapidly than those with low-frequency first syllables (replicating Taft and Forster 1976). But she found that stem frequency influenced the recognition of bisyllabic suffixed words only in the context of compound words. Andrews argued that this was evidence for strategic rather than mandatory decomposition. Finally, in the eye-fixation study mentioned earlier (Holmes and O'Regan 1992), it was found that gaze durations for prefixed words matched on surface frequency were longer for those with low-frequency stems than for those with high-frequency stems.

Clearly, the evidence from all these studies of morphological frequency effects is ambiguous. Certainly, the fact that there are combined frequency effects at all further supports claims that morphological information is used during word recognition; but not only are there differences in the patterns of results obtained, there are also differences in the way in which these results have been interpreted. Taft (1979b) argued that combined stem frequency effects occurred because the stem acts as the access representation for all words with that stem. However, these results are also consistent with any model in which morphological information is represented in the central lexicon and in which lexical entries are frequency-sensitive. If representations of stems are linked to those for whole-word forms in a cluster, either within a shared entry or in a network, then recognition of any word in that cluster should be sensitive both to combined stem frequency and its own surface frequency. For example, Burani and Caramazza (1987) interpreted their findings as support for the AAM shared-entry model.

One finding does suggest that combined stem frequency effects are due to the central representation of morphology. Kelliher and Henderson (1990) found combined frequency effects for irregular past-tense inflected verb forms of English such as *bought* and *shook*, matched on surface frequency; responses were faster on those with higher-frequency infinitive forms (e.g. *buy* is more frequent than *shake*). As Kelliher and Henderson point out, it was impossible to determine whether this was indeed an effect of infinitive form frequency, of combined paradigm frequency (summing over both regular and irregular inflected forms) or even of combined root frequency, since these measures are very highly correlated. Nevertheless, the result suggests that the recognition of inflected verbs is influenced by the frequency of occurrence of their morphological relatives. Furthermore, the demonstration of this effect on the recognition of *irregular* past-tense forms, since by definition these do not share the same form as their stems, indicates that the morphological combined frequency effect has its locus in the central lexicon.

The clearest evidence of combined stem frequency effects was seen for inflected forms (both nouns and verbs). This is consistent with the evidence supporting pre-lexical decomposition of inflected forms, reviewed in section 3. If an inflected form is decomposed, it will be recognized via contact with an access representation and a central representation of its stem. Since all inflections for a given stem would be recognized in this way, the lexical representations (if frequency-sensitive) would show combined stem frequency sensitivity.

Considering all the evidence on decomposition, therefore, it would appear that neither extreme theoretical position (all complex words decomposed or no decomposition at all) is tenable. Dual-route models, where some words are morphologically parsed prior to access via their constituent morphemes and others are accessed directly via whole-word representations, appear best suited to account for the data. Dual-route models do not suffer from the criticism that decomposition is inefficient given high proportions of pseudo-prefixation, since in these models decomposition is not obligatory. On the other hand, dual-route models can account for the evidence that decomposition, at least under certain circumstances, does occur.

One dual-route model is the AAM model (Caramazza et al. 1988). As previously discussed, in the original formulation of the model the parsing route was slower than the whole-word route, and its behaviour could be observed only during the processing of forms composed of known morphemes but lacking in whole-word representations (novel words or non-words). In more recent formulations (Chialant and Caramazza 1995), parsing may also operate for complex words which occur rarely, but which have high-frequency constituents; but parsing is still considered to be slower than whole-word access.

An alternative dual-route account has been offered by Schreuder and Baayen (1995; see also Frauenfelder and Schreuder 1992). In this model, there are two routes which operate in parallel; they race with each other, such that whichever route finishes first will be responsible for lexical access on a given occasion. In general, the parsing route tends to be slower than the whole-word access route, since it involves more computational steps; but the two routes are assumed to vary in their processing times, with overlapping distributions in their completion times. Access representations are considered to be sensitive to combined stem frequency through a process of activation feedback. For some forms (low-frequency transparent inflections), there may be no whole-word representations, so their recognition can only be achieved via the parsing route. But high-frequency inflected forms are able to develop their own whole-word access representations. The development of whole-word representations depends both on frequency and on the complexity of the computations performed during parsing. Words of high frequency whose morphological parsing is complex (and hence more time-consuming) are the most likely to have their own access representations (thus speeding up their recognition).

Lexical decision experiments examining the recognition of singular and plural nouns varying in their relative frequencies in both Italian (Baayen et al. 1997a) and Dutch (Baayen et al. 1997b) support the detailed predictions of the dual-route race model and challenge those of the AAM model. Baayen et al. argue that the data from Italian suggest that storage of full-form representations does not occur for forms with singular suffixes (whose parsing is considered to be less complex), but can occur for forms with plural suffixes (whose parsing is considered to be more complex). But, in keeping with the race model, the evidence also suggested that not all plurals have whole-word access representations: Baayen et al. argue that those with higher frequency of occurrence are more likely to have their own representations.

Word frequency effects therefore appear to inform the debate on morphological processing, particularly on the nature of morphological parsing. Although results for derived forms are rather unclear, those for inflected forms combine with other evidence to suggest that at least some inflections may be decomposed prior to lexical access. Note again, however, that there need not be a qualitative distinction made between inflections and derivations. Dual-route models suggest that morphological decomposition is attempted on all complex forms, but it is only likely to be responsible for normal word recognition on a subset of forms, according to constraints such as transparency, productivity and word frequency (low-frequency transparent forms involving productive affixes, such as noun plurals, may be the most likely candidates for normal parsing – a word such as *napes* may well be recognizable only via decomposition).

One final cautionary remark needs to be made about word frequency effects. Schreuder and Baayen (1997), in a study of the recognition of monomorphemic Dutch nouns, have found that at least in tasks requiring higher-level processing of visually presented words, the size of the morphological family of the noun (the number of different derived or compounded words containing the noun as a constituent) influenced performance. Nouns were responded to more rapidly in lexical decision if they came from larger families, and they elicited higher subjective familiarity ratings. There was no effect, however, of family frequency (the combined frequency of all members of the complete morphological family). The lack of control of family size may account for some of the previous variability in morphological frequency effects.

5 Conclusion

The evidence we have reviewed leaves no doubt that morphological information is represented in the mental lexicon in a quite detailed way. Moreover, the most recent evidence suggests that there is variability between the strengths of the connections between different members of a morphological family. Models which state that morphological relatives are simply linked are not sufficient. Network models (e.g. Schriefers et al. 1992) and internally structured shared-entry models (Caramazza et al. 1988, Chialant and Caramazza 1995, Marslen-Wilson et al. 1994) can both deal with the variability requirement. Access to morphologically structured lexical representations, on the other hand, need not involve morphological structure overtly; decomposition of derived forms may be an optional procedure, available when the normal whole-word access procedure fails. Here the evidence differs according to type of morphological relationship: regular inflectional forms may be decomposed, perhaps depending on their frequency of occurrence, but derived forms probably are not.

Of course, lexical representation and lexical access are not independent; they form part of a unified word recognition system. This system, we would argue, is structured for the processing of spoken language. (Thus it is unfortunate that so large a proportion of studies of morphology in recognition, like studies in many other areas of psycholinguistics, have been based on written materials.) As described above, Tyler et al. (1988) and Schriefers et al. (1991) have argued that lexical access of spoken words is a continuous process from the beginning of the word's presentation. In accounting for differences in priming between prefixes and suffixes, Marslen-Wilson et al. (1994) depend on this beginning-to-end assumption. The temporal nature of the speech input also forms the basis for Cutler et al.'s (1985) explanation of the bias towards suffix morphology in the world's languages; listeners prefer to process stems before affixes. Arguments have also been made for beginning-to-end processing in visual word recognition (Bergman 1988, Cole et al. 1989, Hudson and Buijs 1995).

Both network and decomposed shared-entry models are compatible with temporally continuous access. For network models, there are separate entries for each word form, so access would be direct to each entry. Effectively, any stem has multiple representations, one for each inflectional variant (in addition to its representation in the stem-morpheme node binding the entries together). Shared-entry models economize by representing each stem only once. Access for prefixed words would begin with contact being made with a representation of the prefix, and access of suffixed words would begin at a representation of the stem. But in both cases, decomposition would take place as more information arrived in a temporally continuous manner.

Given that the vast majority of inflections are suffixes, temporally continuous access is obviously consistent with the decomposition of inflected forms suggested by the evidence reviewed in sections 3 and 4. Initially, the stem portion of a word is mapped on to its lexical representation. When the suffix arrives, it can be mapped on to the representation of the inflected form. Suffixed words are therefore accessed via their stem. Decomposition is not delayed until contact has been made with a full form in the lexicon; it is achieved *before* the form has been identified. In this sense, decomposition takes place before word recognition. But it takes place *during* lexical access, not prior to it.

Temporally continuous processing has further implications. One is that it may underlie observed differences between prefixed and suffixed forms. Cole et al. (1989) argued that combined root frequency effects were detectable on suffixed but not prefixed words, because recognition of prefixed forms does not initially entail access to the stem. Root frequency thus has less opportunity to influence recognition time in prefixed words than in suffixed words. Another implication is that not only suffixed inflectional forms, but also suffixed derived forms – as long as they are sufficiently transparent – should be decomposed during lexical access. In other words, processing distinctions between inflectional and derivational morphology arise not from a categorical distinction between these types, but strictly from processing considerations: the relative ordering of stem and affix and the relative transparency of the relationships involved. Note that Marslen-Wilson et al.'s (1994) results suggest that it is *semantic* transparency, rather than phonological (or, by extension, orthographic) transparency, which determines whether a morphological relationship is lexically represented. This suggests that lexical representations are abstract: that they represent the underlying phonological structure of a morphological family, rather than each individual surface form.

A related factor which may determine morphological representation is productivity. Forms with highly productive affixes are more likely to be semantically transparent, and hence represented in a decomposed way. Badecker and Caramazza (MORPHOLOGY AND APHASIA) describe patients who show morphological errors (in production) on inflections and productive derivations but not on non-productive derivations. Finally, frequency of usage may determine the strength of connections between suffixes and their stems; for example, Schriefers et al. (1992) found the weakest priming for the low-frequency adjectival suffix -*em*.

The most important characteristic of the above list is that order of occurrence, transparency, productivity and frequency are all essentially performance factors. Processing factors, we would argue, underlie both our general conclusions: that lexical representations are morphologically structured, and that lexical access involves decomposition of some morphologically complex words but not of others. Clearly, there are likely to be differences across languages in the extent to which morphological structure is lexically represented. Here, again, it is particularly unfortunate that most of the evidence available is from English and other closely related languages. Speakers of languages with very transparent, productive or simple morphologies may have a much richer mental morphology than speakers of complex, opaque languages. Hankamer (1989) has convincingly argued for the necessity of morphological parsing in agglutinative languages such as Turkish (but see also Niemi et al. 1994 for related arguments concerning Finnish, another language with rich combinatorial morphology). Such cross-linguistic differences will be motivated, however, not by the nature of the morphological systems themselves, but rather by the processing considerations which determine the structure of the human word recognition system.

ACKNOWLEDGEMENTS

Much of the preparation of this chapter was carried out when both authors were at the MRC Applied Psychology Unit, Cambridge, where the first author was supported by the Joint Councils Initiative in Cognitive Science and HCI grant no. E304/148. We would like to thank Harald Baayen and Rob Schreuder for their comments on a previous version of this chapter.

22 Morphology in Language Production with Special Reference to Connectionism

JOSEPH PAUL STEMBERGER

Modern work on morphology in language production was begun by Meringer and Mayer (1895) and Meringer (1908). They observed that adult (and child) speakers of German occasionally regularize irregular verbs:

(1) (a) *erzieht*   for   *erzogen*   (infinitive *erziehen* 'educate')
     (b) *gedenkt*   for   *gedacht*   (infinitive *denken* 'think')
     (c) *heisste*   for   *hiess*   (infinitive *heissen* 'name')

After a long hiatus, MacKay (1970) brought attention back to these data, using them to argue that speakers actively use morphological rules to construct inflected forms, and that misapplication of those rules underlies the errors in (1). MacKay's work set the pattern for more recent work in several ways. First, most of it has focused on errors, rather than speed (reaction time). Second, most of it has focused on the question of whether speakers use morphological rules.

Early work was heavily based on linguistic theory, using the phonological and morphological concepts of linguistic theory and trying to demonstrate that they were psychologically real. Some researchers had no overt psychological theory of performance (e.g. Fromkin 1971), while others used a symbol-based serial theory of psychological processing in which it would be possible to instantiate a performance version of linguistic theory (e.g. M. F. Garrett 1975). G. S. Dell (1986) and Stemberger (1985b, c) introduced local connectionist models into research on morphology, but still focused on evidence for linguistic concepts such as rules. Rumelhart and McClelland (1986) brought distributed connectionist models into the picture, along with an attempt to eliminate rules from consideration. Researchers using symbolic models (e.g. Pinker and Prince 1988, Pinker 1991, Marcus et al. 1992) have argued that rules are necessary.

In this chapter, I explore the data and issues that have been brought up. First, I review the studies of the characteristics of morphology in language production. Given the focus of the field, most of this discussion addresses inflectional morphology. Next I review psychological models of morphology in language production, with an emphasis on connectionist models. A common theme is the question of whether there is any evidence that speakers use morphological rules during language production. I provide a summary of work thus far and comments about where the future will lead.

1 Empirical work on language production

Work on morphology in language production has focused heavily on errors. Much of it has to do with the expression of particular morphosyntactic features in a particular position in the syntactic structure. The phenomena can be typologized as follows:

(1) Right features, right place
    (1) wrong morphological pattern (regularization)
    (2) wrong base lexical item (and attendant agreement)
(2) Wrong features, right place
    (1) no affix when one should be there
    (2) an affix when none should be there
    (3) wrong affix (expressing the wrong features)
(3) Right features, wrong place
    (1) affix shifts, exchanges, anticipations, and perseverations
    (2) overtensing

Most of these error types occur with both inflectional and derivational affixes. A second area of interest is more overtly phonological (sections 1.4 and 1.5): when there is allomorphy, the allomorphy can be incorrect (right affix, wrong allomorph), or the allomorphy can be altered to accommodate a conditioning factor that was in error.

These errors provide information about several diverse areas. Errors where the wrong lexical item is present, or where the affix is expressed in the wrong syntactic position, reveal how syntax constrains the expression of morphosyntactic features. Getting an incorrect alternative pattern that expresses the same features has more to say about lexical processing. And allomorphy errors bear on the phonological processing of lexical items. As I discuss the phenomena, I briefly note what they reveal about processing. More details are provided in the later discussion of models of language production.

1.1 Right features, right place

1.1.1 Wrong morphological pattern: regularization and irregularization

Regularizations (as in (1) above in German) are commonly observed in English and other languages. In English, they have been observed with all inflectional affixes where irregulars are found: past tense, perfect aspect, present tense, and plurals.

(2) (a)   I carefully looked at 'em & *choosed – chose* that one.
     (b)   She's always *goed – gone* into these weird things.
     (c)   She goes and *do-s – does* that.
     (d)   ... but two *childs* – two *children* usually isn't.

Regularizations are easily obtained from adults in experimental tasks such as *morphonaming*, in which speakers are asked to produce a particular morphological variant of a word given a different morphological variant presented visually or auditorily (MacKay 1976; Bybee and Slobin 1982; Stemberger and MacWhinney 1986a, b). To derive such errors, there must be some mechanism by which morphological patterns can generalize. One such mechanism, rules, adds an affix to a base form, and is blocked by irregular forms (e.g. Aronoff 1976, Kiparsky 1982a). In regularizations, a speaker fails to access the irregular form and instead accesses the base; the addition of the regular suffix is then automatic.

In some cases, the irregular form is accessed, but there is a failure of blockage: the regular rule applies anyway, to yield a *partial* regularization.

(3) (a)   It *tooked* a while. 'took'
     (b)   ... he doesn't have any ... *lices.* 'lice'

Full regularizations as in (1)–(2) are more common than partial regularizations (MacKay 1976, Bybee and Slobin 1982, Stemberger 1985c). From this, we can infer that failure to access an irregular is more of a problem than failure of blockage. This does not derive from any independent principle, but must be stipulated as an empirical finding.

Less common, and receiving less attention in the literature, are *irregularizations*: when an irregular pattern generalizes to another word, whether that word is properly regular or irregular (but following a different pattern; Bybee and Slobin 1982):

(4) (a)   *cloamb*   'climbed'
     (b)   *crull*   'crawled'

(5) (a)   *flang*   'flung'
     (b)   *brung*   'brought'

There must be some means to generalize irregular patterns as well. One issue is whether regular and irregular patterns can be treated (and generalized) in a parallel fashion, differing primarily in terms of likelihood of generalization, or whether they are produced via different mechanisms.

There are strong phonological influences on both regularization and irregularization. Bybee and Moder (1983) reported that nonce forms are more likely to be irregular if they bear a family resemblance to known irregular verbs (often referred to as the *hypersimilarity effect*; the errors in (5) above rhyme with known irregulars like *rang* and *slung*, and so are more common than the errors in (4) above, which are far less common. Stemberger and MacWhinney (1986b) showed that regular verbs with base forms that rhyme with families of irregulars (e.g. *thank*, which rhymes with *drank*, *sank*, etc.) are more likely to be produced without the -*ed*, so that they appear to be irregular: *thank* rather than *thanked*. Daugherty and Seidenberg (1994) show that regulars whose base forms rhyme with the base forms of irregulars take longer to produce than other regular verbs, suggesting interference from these groups of irregulars. Overall, data suggest that regulars and irregulars are both considered as candidates for the pathway used for irregulars.

Stemberger (1993), Stemberger and Setchell (1994), and Marchman (1995) show that the relationship between the vowel of the base form and the vowel of the irregular past-tense form is important. Given any two phonemes involved in a phonological error, phoneme A (the recessive phoneme) tends to be mispronounced more as phoneme B (the dominant phoneme) than the reverse (see Stemberger 1992b for discussion of English vowels and the underlying mechanisms). If the dominant vowel is in the base form, there is a phonological bias for the vowel of the past-tense form to be mispronounced as the vowel of the base form. Given that mispronunciation, regularization often follows; regularizations like *falled* (/ɑː/ dominant over the /ɛ/ of *fell*), *sinked* (/ɪ/ dominant over the /æ/ of *sank* or the /ʌ/ of *sunk*), and *throwed* (/ow/ dominant over the /uː/ of *threw*) are common. By contrast, if the dominant vowel is in the past tense, regularizations are rarer: *getted* (/ɛ/ recessive to the /ɑː/ of *got*) and *see-ed* (/iː/ recessive to the /ɑː/ of *saw*). Stemberger (1994a) further found that phonological priming from the subject NP also affects regularizations: when subjects must take an NP like THE BALL and a verb like FALL (where the noun and base form of the verb rhyme) and construct a sentence in the past tense, regularizations like *falled* are common (between 6 and 11 percent of tokens, depending on the nature of the priming); but regularizations are much less common if the noun is phonologically unrelated (as in THE CONE and FALL; *c.* 4 percent of tokens in error) or if the noun rhymes with the past-tense form (as in THE BELL and FALL; *c.* 3 percent of tokens). Such effects reveal that the processing system considers both the base and past-tense forms when producing the past-tense form, and that factors that favor the vowel of the base form (dominance or priming) lead to the system failing to retrieve the correct irregular past-tense form. As discussed below, not all models predict such phonological effects.

1.1.2 Stranding and accommodation There are errors that occur that could be analyzed as either lexical or syntactic, in which a word is inserted into a sentence at the wrong place. For example, given a sentence with an embedded VP under the main VP (as in *wanted to watch*), the two verbs involved could be reversed. When this occurs, we commonly observe two phenomena: *stranding*, in which the morphological affixes remain at the place in the sentence where they belong, and *accommodation*, in which the misordered words take on the inflected form that is appropriate to their new locations in the sentence (M. F. Garrett 1976, 1980). In (6a), for example, when *sound* is anticipated, it leaves *-ing* behind and acquires *-s*.

(6) (a) It *sounds* up – *ends* up sounding like 'split'.
     (b) You just count *wheels* on a *light*. ('. . . *lights* on a *wheel*')

Stemberger (1985c) points out that these two phenomena are equally true of purely lexical errors, in which the wrong lexical item is accessed, since the form produced almost invariably has the inflected form appropriate to the syntactic context.

(7) That *understands* why he was that way. ('. . . *explains* why . . .')

Stemberger (1985c) also notes that there is one common exception to both stranding and accommodation: the plural *-s* affix often is exceptional, a fact that Stemberger attributes to the low level of syntactic constraints on plurality (8) and (9b) below.

(8) Your *teeth are* all red. ('Your *tongue is* all red.')

Stemberger argues that stranding and accommodation invariably occur when words of different syntactic categories are involved, but there can be exceptions when the two words are of the same category.

These facts are expected, given that we know from linguistic studies of syntax that inflections are often limited to particular positions in the sentence, such as tensed clauses, heads of NPs (but not nouns embedded in compounds), etc. They have no bearing on the issue of morphological rules, but reveal only that syntax constrains where inflections appear. If a word appears at an unexpected place in the sentence, it is subject to the constraints on that location in the sentence, so it loses any inflections that it would have had if it had appeared in its correct location, and takes on any inflections demanded by its erroneous syntactic position, with any irregularity appropriate to the word involved.

In syntactic environments in which one word agrees with another along some dimension, these lexical errors can lead to changes in other words. Stemberger (1985c) shows that changes in the subject (pro)noun can lead to changes of the verb from singular to plural or vice versa.

(9) (a) *You're* too good for *that*! (for *'That's* too good for *you!'*)
    (b) *Most cities are* true of *that*. (*'That's* true of *most cities.*)

Berg (1987), however, has shown that articles in German rarely accommodate to the gender and number of the displaced noun.

(10) Die wollen auch das *Welt* – das *Licht* der Welt erblicken.
    ('They want to see the (n.) world (f.) – light (n.) of day, too.')

Accommodation seems to be strong within a lexical item, but is less common in agreement with other words, which often agree with the word that they would have agreed with had the error not occurred.

1.2 Wrong features, right place

1.2.1 Base form errors In some cases, a speaker drops out inflections and produces the uninflected base (as found in English in singular nouns and in non-third-person present verb forms, infinitives, and imperatives).

(11) (a) They had cute little *mouse* on – *mice* on it.
    (b) Boy, that *draw* him out. – *Drew* him out.

1.2.2 Affix addition Stemberger (1985a) reports that speakers are more likely to drop affixes than to randomly add them. He argues that this is a frequency effect, since the base form in English is usually more frequent than any particular inflected form. One contrast is particularly interesting: in the present-tense forms of most verbs, speakers tend to drop the *-s* affix, substituting the (more frequent) plural for the singular; but with the irregular verb *to be*, most errors involve replacing the plural form *are* with the (more frequent) singular form *is*. While such errors are compatible with the notion of rules, they occur with irregularities as well (to an even greater extent than with regular affixes; Stemberger and MacWhinney 1986a), and reflect only lexical accessing errors. Congruent with this, Stemberger and MacWhinney (1986a) show that base form errors are more likely for low-frequency verbs, even for regulars (though there is a much larger frequency effect for irregulars than for regulars).

Prasada et al. (1990), using reaction-time data rather than error data, have argued that irregular forms show frequency effects, but regular forms do not. They argue that this difference suggests that regular and irregular forms are processed in fundamentally different ways, with the irregular forms showing more word-like properties than the regular forms. Daugherty and Seidenberg (1994) also report this difference, but show (via a connectionist simulation) that a single mechanism can handle the differences. (See below for further discussion.)

1.2.3 Wrong affix   Speakers sometimes produce forms with the wrong inflectional affix, given the meaning and/or the syntactic position of the word.

(12)   She has *paying – paid* $15 for a blouse.

This seems to be an accessing error, where either the wrong inflected form is accessed in the lexicon, or the wrong inflectional rule is applied.

1.3 Right features, wrong place

1.3.1 Affix shifts, exchanges, anticipations, and perseverations   Affixes can themselves be misordered: anticipated or perseverated, either being added to a word or replacing a different affix, being exchanged with another affix, or simply shifting so as to appear on the wrong word; these are rare but do exist (Stemberger 1985b, *contra* M. F. Garrett 1975).

(13)   (a)   I can't keep their *name straights*.   ('. . . *names straight*')
       (b)   . . . where the safe *part* of the *cities* are.   (. . . *parts* of the *city*)[1]
       (c)   . . . may take several years to be *masters*.   ('to be *mastered*')
       (d)   I *wind* up *rewroting* 12 pages.   ('I *wound* up *rewriting*')
       (e)   Rosa always *date shranks*.   ('*dated shrinks*')

                                                                    (Fromkin 1971)

Stemberger argued that such errors suggest that the affixes are separate morphemes, but the errors involving irregularities suggest rather that a syntactic error has been made, whereby the morphosyntactic features of the inflection are expressed in the wrong place in the sentence, in a way that violates the normal mapping rules of English syntax, rather than movement of affixes per se. Fromkin's example in (13e) suggests that shifts of features can even take place between words of different syntactic classes.

1.3.2 Overtensing   In some instances, the morphosyntactic features are erroneously expressed twice. In particular, verbs are normally inflected for tense, but are uninflected when embedded under an auxiliary or modal. In overtensing errors, the verb is erroneously inflected for tense.

(14)   (a)   Did you *found* her?   (for 'did you *find* her')
       (b)   Who does he *thinks* he is?   (for 'does he *think* he is')

Irregular verbs are more likely to be overtensed than regular verbs. Stemberger (1992a) has shown experimentally that this may be due to the vowel-changing nature of most irregular past-tense patterns versus the suffixation nature of regular patterns; perfect *-en* is much less often involved in overtensing than other irregulars. Stemberger further shows that overtensing is more common with low-frequency verbs than high-frequency verbs. Stemberger and Setchell (1994) have demonstrated that vowel dominance has an effect: verbs with the dominant vowel in the past tense are more likely to be overtensed. Apparently, the phonological bias to produce the vowel of the past-tense form combines with the semantic appropriateness of the error to make the error more likely.

1.4 Allomorphy

1.4.1 Accommodation to other errors   In many cases, an affix has multiple phonological realizations, depending on the phonological environment. The English -*ed* affixes have three allomorphs: /əd/ after /t/ and /d/, /t/ after other voiceless phonemes, and /d/ after other voiced phonemes. The -*s* affixes have /əz/ after strident phonemes, /s/ after other voiceless phonemes, and /z/ after other voiced phonemes. When phonological errors lead to a crucial change in the final segment of the base morpheme, the affix usually (but not always) takes on the appropriate shape for the new phonological environment.

(15) (a)   The infant *tucks* (/tʌks/) – *touches* (/tʌčəz/) the nipple.
      (b)   The Swedish got *gooed* (/uːd/) up – *goofed* (/uːft/) up.

This accommodation also is observed with the suppletive variants of the articles: *a* and /ðə/ before consonants versus *an* and /ði/ before vowels.

(16) (a)   ... gets 20 miles *an allon* – *a gallon*.
      (b)   Put *the* (/ðə/) *hoven* – put *the* (/ði/) *oven* on 'hot'.

The most extreme form of phonologically conditioned allomorphy in human languages is reduplication, in which the affix takes on consonants or vowels from the base form. Stemberger and Lewis (1986) investigated reduplication in Ewe, using an experimental task that combined morphonaming with phonological priming designed to lead to phonological errors, and found that the affix usually took on the form of the initial consonant and vowel of the base when that was in error.

(17) (a)   *haha fo*   (for *'fafa ho'*)
      (b)   *xaxa si*   (for *'sasa xi'*)

Phonological accommodation demonstrates that the *form* of the affix has not (usually) been finalized at the point in processing where phonological errors occur; allomorphy is determined either at the same time as or subsequent to phonological errors.

1.4.2 Wrong allomorphy   In some instances, the wrong allomorph appears.

(18)   Queen *Elizabeth'es* (/θəz/) – Queen *Elizabeth's* (/θs/) mother

Such errors are unusual, because incorrect allomorphs usually lead to a phonologically illegal sequence in the language (such as */kd/ or */čs/); speakers rarely produce illegal sequences (see Fromkin 1971) even in phonological errors. The allomorphs /əz/ and /əd/ are the only ones that are always legal, but even these rarely replace the other allomorphs, because /əz/ and /əd/ are low in frequency, and because these allomorphs require the addition of a syllable, something the phonological system is biased against (Stemberger and MacWhinney 1986a).

1.4.3 Affix checking   Base form errors are especially prevalent when there is a close phonological similarity between the base and the affix. Bases that end in /s/ and /z/ (like the nonsyllabic allomorphs of the *-s* affixes) tend to drop the *-s* affix. Bases that end in /t/ and /d/ (like the nonsyllabic allomorphs of the *-ed* affixes) tend to drop the *-ed* affix.

(19)   (a)   So we *test* 'em on it.   (for '. . . we *tested* 'em')
       (b)   It just *lose* something.   (for '. . . just *loses* something')

This is true of both adult speech (Bybee and Slobin 1982, Stemberger and MacWhinney 1986b), and child speech (Berko 1958, Bybee and Slobin 1982). MacWhinney (1978), Stemberger (1981), Bybee and Slobin (1982), and Menn and MacWhinney (1984) suggest that such errors arise because the base already appears to be inflected, and so the speaker does not add an "additional" inflection. Pinker and Prince (1988) suggest that it might be phonological dissimilation between the base and affix consonants (but see Stemberger 1981, Menn and MacWhinney 1984). Rumelhart and McClelland (1986) and Pinker and Prince (1988) suggest that it might be the overgeneralization of the no-change pattern of verbs like *hit* and *hurt*; but this is not the whole story, since such errors are also common with the *-s* affixes, where no-change irregulars do not exist.[2]

1.5 Derivational morphology and compounding

The bulk of studies of language production in normals has focused on inflectional morphology, but something is known about derivational morphology (MacKay 1978, 1979; Stemberger 1985c). The small number of studies is related to the fact that inflectional morphology is more frequent in spontaneous speech, so errors there are more noticeable.

1.5.1 Derivational morphology: base form/ wrong affix errors   As with inflectional morphology, derivational affixes can be left out, added, or replaced by an inappropriate affix.

(20)   (a)   It's not *mass* enough – *massive* enough for a sun.
        (b)   If you're *hunger* – *hungry*, you should've . . .

(21)   (a)   I'm Tony's *brother-in-law*.   (for 'Tony's *brother*')
        (b)   It was when they were first *marriaged* – *married*.

(22)   (a)   He was a *philosophist*, wasn't he?   (for 'a *philosopher*')
        (b)   It's an arbitrary *decidal*.   (for 'an arbitrary *decision*')

Inappropriate affixes are usually only inappropriate lexically; they represent a competing affix with the same meaning that simply cannot be used with that particular word; these might be called "regularizations," though it is often hard to determine which derivational affix is the "regular" one. With semantically transparent derivational affixes, loss errors are common, but addition errors are not (Stemberger 1985c). Apparently, the transparency of the semantics leads to the base form being a strong competitor which, because of its higher frequency, is more likely to win out when inappropriate (similar to the "hypernym problem" of Levelt 1989); but the derived form is unlikely to win out when it is inappropriate. With semantically opaque affixes, however, loss and addition errors are more balanced. Apparently, the differences in meaning between base and derived form lead to less semantic interference between them, so that the base is not activated as much when the derived form is appropriate, and vice versa; thus, substitution of one for the other is likely in either direction.[3]

Affixes can be anticipated or perseverated from a nearby word.

(23)   (a)   This longish *woodish* – longish wooden object is . . .
        (b)   . . . brood reduction and hatching *asynchrontion* – asynchrony.

1.5.2 Stranding and accommodation   As with inflections, derivational affixes can be left behind when a word is inserted into the wrong syntactic position in the sentence, whether regular or irregular (MacKay 1979, Stemberger 1985c).

(24)   . . . makes no pretense of *pretending* – of *preparing* you for . . .

This may be purely lexical, with the syntactic demands of a particular position in the sentence requiring a particular derived form. It should be noted that the *addition* of a derivational affix to render the correct part of speech seems to be uncommon, while the *loss* of a derivational affix to yield the right part of speech seems to be common. It appears that derivational affixes *require* that the words containing them be of a particular part of speech, and they can readily be eliminated when the word appears in the wrong syntactic position. However, errors rarely occur in which a derivational affix is added *solely* to change the part of speech of a word. The part of speech of a monomorphemic word in English is quite labile, and can change (e.g. from noun to verb, or vice versa) without the addition of any overt affix. If a monomorphemic word erroneously finds itself in a syntactic position requiring a different part of speech, it follows this no-affix pattern. This suggests that derivational affixes may be added partly for semantic or pragmatic reasons, and that syntax alone does not force the addition of derivational affixes.

1.5.3 Stress and vowel patterns   Fromkin (1971) first noted errors where the wrong stress and vowel patterns were present.

(25)   (a)   . . . inherent linguistic *suPERiority* in women.   (for *'superiORity'*)
         (b)   *ecoNOMists*   (for *'eCONomists'*)

(26)   (a)   Oakland gets all the *inDUStry*.   (for *'INdustry'*)
         (b)   . . . in the paper at the *secreTARy* jobs . . .   (for *'SECretary'*)

Fromkin interpreted these as demonstrating that the stress and vowel reduction rules posited for English by Chomsky and Halle (1968) were psychologically real. However, the exact details of how the errors occur were not given. Those in (25) seem reasonable, since an affix is simply ignored (thus shrinking the phonological domain of the rule, which entails a different resulting stress pattern). But it is unclear how the errors in (26) occur, where the rules act as if additional syllables were present.

Cutler (1980) (replicated by Stemberger 1985c) showed that such errors rarely occur unless the target has a derivationally related word with a different stress pattern. It seems as if speakers are "borrowing" the stress and vowel patterns from another form of the word. Cutler argues that suppletive stems are stored and retrieved without application of stress or vowel reduction rules (e.g. *econom-* as both /ˌiːkə'nɑm/ and /ˌiː'kɑnəm/), and that different suffixes choose different allomorphs. Stress errors arise when a suppletive stem is accessed that does not normally go with the suffix (or lack of a suffix) that is present in the target word. No one has yet proposed a stress-rule-based solution that accounts for the facts.

1.5.4 Compounding   Errors of compounding are rare. They are of two types. First, one member of a compound may be dropped, sometimes leading to a blend between the two parts of the compound.

(27)   (a)   This is *scotch.* – Hopscotch.
         (b)   How many *blerries* did you get?   (for *'blueberries'*)
         (c)   . . . a lot of Welch's *jape* commercials . . .   (for *'grape jam'*)

Second, the two words in the compound can be reversed (Meringer and Mayer 1895, Stemberger 1985c).

(28) (a) You were just closing the *lidboxes.* – The *boxlids.*
(b) That's a *busbike.* – I mean, a *bikebus.*

These errors implicate a processing of compounds that is vaguely syntax-like, with two positions available. Loss of a position (yielding a more frequent non-compound noun) leads to loss of the occupying noun, or to a word blend. Errors can occur in which the two nouns exchange their positions, just as errors occur in which any two nouns in a sentence are exchanged. In compound-noun reversals the stress is stranded (so that both the target and the error compounds have the same stress pattern; stress does not stay with the particular nouns, so that the stress pattern would change when the nouns exchange; the stranding of stress is also observed with true word exchanges (Stemberger 1985b). Lexical processing in compounds seems to engage some of the same mechanisms as lexical processing in general.

2 Morphology in models of language production

2.1 Rule-based models

There has been relatively little work on morphology in language production in nonconnectionist models that involves the building of explicit models. Fromkin (1971) assumed something roughly corresponding to morphology in linguistic theory, but gave few details about organization, how regularizations occur, etc. Cutler (1980) also assumes such a system, but focuses primarily on derivational affixes; she assumes that, for example, *-ity* and *-ness* are produced via rules, but that the bases to which they attach may be suppletive from the independent base word (i.e. /owpæs/ is suppletive from /owpeyk/ in *opacity*). Butterworth (1983) addresses regularizations: irregular forms and known regular forms are stored in the lexicon; if a speaker is unable to access a stored form (in error, or because the target word is a novel word), then the base form is accessed, and the regular inflectional rules of the language are applied. M. F. Garrett (1975, 1976) discusses morphology and stresses the difference between regular and irregular forms, but the details of the morphological component of the system are left unspecified. MacKay (1970, 1976, 1978, 1979) argues that rules are used for both regular and irregular forms, but provides little detail about the workings of the rule component.

Currently, the main psycholinguistic work in this area is being done by Pinker and his colleagues (Pinker 1991; Pinker and Prince 1988; Kim et al. 1991; Marcus et al. 1992, 1995), with a focus on language acquisition. Although the details of the model are still being worked out, the basic outline is clear.

There are two different ways in which inflected forms are processed, one path for irregulars and one for regulars.

Regular inflected forms are not stored in the lexicon at all (except at *very* early stages in language acquisition). The base form of the word is accessed. Then, the regular default rule is applied. The exact details of the rules have never been stated, but in English they are simple and concatenative (such as "add /d/ at the right edge of the base verb"). Rules are not sensitive to accidental phonological properties of the base word (though they *can* apply to words with only specific phonological characteristics, such as those that end in consonants).

There is a separate system to handle irregular words, set up in such a way that it has priority over the regular rule. The exact nature of this priority has not been spelled out. It could be serial priority: try the irregular system first to see if the word being processed is irregular; if it is irregular, bypass the regular system; if it isn't irregular, proceed to the regular system. It could be speed-of-processing priority: try both the regular and irregular systems, so that both a correct irregular like *chose* and the regularization *choosed are computed simultaneously, and select for production whichever pathway finishes first (a standard horse-race model); the irregular pathway would be faster for known irregular forms, so *chose* would usually win.

The irregular system is *not* one in which the irregular form is simply stored in the lexicon, either as an independent lexical entry or as a sub-entry under the base form. Instead, it is an associative network (much like a distributed connectionist model, on which see below). The reason for this is that some account must be given for hypersimilarity effects (section 1.1.1 above), and the symbolic processing model that is assumed apparently cannot compute such similarity naturally (though no details of the system are given, so this is uncertain). Because all verbs (regular or irregular) are checked for irregularity, regulars are subject to the same effects of similarity to families of irregular verbs (error rates and reaction times) as irregular forms (Daugherty and Seidenberg 1994). On occasion, an irregularization results, when an irregular pattern generalizes incorrectly. Note that a concession is made that connectionist models are needed to account for language production, but only for the irregular forms of a language. Bybee (1985, 1995a) disagrees with this concession, and provides a mechanism for accounting for these effects within a symbolic model (based on schema theory).

The standard linguistic account of irregular forms (e.g. Kiparsky 1982a) assumes that irregular forms are also produced via rules, but the rules are lexically bound (i.e. they apply only to words that are marked to undergo them). There is one argument against this: the lexical frequency effect, whereby error rates are higher on low-frequency words. A lexical frequency effect seems easy to derive as a lexical-accessing effect if irregulars are stored in the lexicon, but seems difficult to derive if all irregulars of the same pattern are produced via the same rule. The facts seem to demand lexical storage for irregulars rather than minor rules. However, this is not necessarily the case. If a verb has a feature such as [+æ-rule), that feature will be strong in frequent words and weak in infrequent words. If the mechanism responsible for applying irregular rules has a more difficult time reading the weak feature of the low-frequency verb, then low-frequency verbs would be more likely to be regularized. A lexical frequency effect is thus compatible with a system that uses rules for irregulars, and this is still a possibility (however unpopular).

None of the (nonconnectionist) rule-based accounts have really attempted to work out in detail how morphology works in a psychological processing model, or how most of the phenomena surveyed above are derived by the model. There has been a general feeling that this would not be difficult, but no one has actually attempted to do it.

2.2 *Connectionist models*

Within connectionism, one can distinguish several major types of models. Although there are many dimensions involved, the major division between classes of models lies in the way that information is represented. If a concept (semantic, lexical, etc.) is represented as a *single node*, then the representations are *local*; thus the word *dog* is represented with a discrete node in the system (McClelland and Rumelhart 1981, Dell 1986, Stemberger 1985b). If a concept is represented as a *pattern of activity* across *a set of nodes*, however, then the representations are *distributed*; there is no single node that corresponds to the word *dog*, but only a particular pattern of activation over a set of units that are used for all words (and each word has its characteristic pattern of activation). The local/distributed distinction is not that clear; as noted below, no local connectionist model has ever been truly local. However, the distinction is correlated with another very important factor: learning. There is no explicit learning algorithm for local connectionist models, while distributed models are linked to learning algorithms (such as back propagation). The field underwent a shift in the latter half of the 1980s from local to distributed models, primarily because it was judged important to have a model of learning.

There are other major dimensions that distinguish models, however, which cut across the local versus distributed distinction. The one that I consider the most important deals with the direction of flow of information. In local models, information flows in both directions between any two connected nodes. This means that there is no strict modularity between adjacent levels (though Dell and O'Seaghdha 1991 demonstrate that functionally there is modularity between levels that are not directly connected). Lexical and phonological processing are done simultaneously and interactively, with each influencing the other; such interactions dominated the local connectionism literature. Early distributed models, by contrast, were entirely unidirectional (or *nonrecurrent*). In language production models, information flowed from semantics, through the lexicon, to the phonology, and never in the reverse direction. More recently, *recurrent* models have been developed, in which lexical and phonological processing are intermixed.

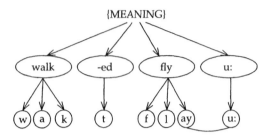

Figure 22.1 General rules within a local connectionist model.

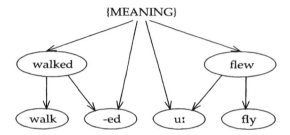

Figure 22.2 Lexically bound rules within a local connectionist model.

All varieties of connectionist models have a lot in common, and show many of the same behaviors. The current theoretical preference is for distributed models. However, in models of language production, local models are at this point more complete; their usefulness is limited primarily by the fact that there is no learning algorithm associated with them. Recurrent distributed models show many of the strengths of local models, and future morphology models will probably be of this type.

2.2.1 Local connectionist models All lexical and phonological elements are represented as discrete nodes and are activated simultaneously. For example, the node *walk* connects to the nodes /w/, /ɑː/, and /k/, and /k/ connects to the nodes [Dorsal], [-voice], [-continuant], etc. There are many schemes for encoding serial order (so that the words *cat*, *tack*, and *act*, which have identical sets of segments in different orders, can be distinguished; Rumelhart and McClelland 1981, Dell 1986); this issue goes far beyond morphology, and I will not address it here. Within a local model, it is possible to have something corresponding to a morphological rule: there may be a node for a suffix such as *-ed* (Stemberger 1985b, Dell 1986); if this node is activated along with the node for a verb, the verb is inflected for the past tense. Stemberger (1985b) distinguishes three positions: general rules (with nodes for affixes activated only by semantic/syntactic information, see figure 22.1), lexically bound rules (with the affix activated both by semantic/syntactic information and by lexical items, see figure 22.2), and non-rule-based representations (where inflected

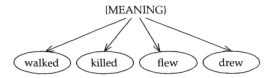

Figure 22.3   A rule-less local connectionist model.

forms are just stored as words; *walk* and *walked* are separate nodes, as are *tree* and *sky*, see figure 22.3). In theory, the three positions can be distinguished, but in practice, this is difficult, because they predict many of the same phenomena. Irregular patterns are lexically bound and cannot appear freely with just any word. This rules out only the general-rule approach. Regular patterns could in theory be instantiated in any of the three ways.

In local connectionist models, co-activated items reinforce each other. A co-activated base verb reinforces the syntactic slot with which it is associated, and thus indirectly reinforces any rule that is based on that slot. In the case of a lexically bound rule, the base verb also directly reinforces the rule. The amount of activation that a node passes is correlated with the frequency of the node: low-frequency nodes pass less activation than high-frequency nodes. Consequently, low-frequency elements provide less activation for all other connected nodes in the system, putting all other nodes at greater risk for error. Stemberger and MacWhinney (1986a) and Dell (1990) report that low-frequency words are more likely to undergo phonological speech errors than high-frequency words. This explains why low-frequency verbs (whether regular or irregular) are more prone to morphological errors: regularizations, base form errors, and overtensing errors (sections 1.1.1, 1.2.1, 1.3.2). Lexical frequency effects are compatible with any of the ways to store inflected forms.

If the system uses rules, generalization of patterns is easy to derive. The most frequent rule will tend to be accessed with most verbs, especially if it is not lexically bound. The less frequent (irregular) rules tend to be suppressed by the regular rule except under those circumstances where they get the most reinforcement. The most favorable circumstances include phonological reinforcement by groups of irregular verbs that take that rule: hence hypersimilarity effects (section 1.1.1). (Any hypersimilarity effects on regulars are swamped out by frequency effects, so it is not surprising that none have been detected.) Also favorable would be those situations where the past-tense vowel is dominant over the base vowel, so that it does not require as much activation to suppress the base vowel: the vowel-dominance effect. And phonological priming (as from the subject noun) should have an effect, positive or negative.

Local connectionist models do not require morphological rules. Inflected forms can be stored as words, parallel to any other word (fig. 22.3). The processing of known words is straightforward. Stemberger (1994b) discusses how generalization occurs via *gang effects*. Within local models, similarity between different lexical items leads to a group of partially activated nodes called a *gang*;

gangs form on the basis of both semantic and phonological similarities. Via inhibition between competing lexical items, nontarget words are kept at a low level of activation, but they still contribute small amounts of activation to the phonological level. In general, nontarget words contain sounds that cover the full spectrum of the phonological space of English, and activation from nontarget words has little effect on the output; different words cancel each other out, and just raise the level of noise in the system. However, if the words in a semantically based gang are correlated phonologically, then the effects are quite different. For example, if we consider 1,000 nontarget verbs that are past-tense forms, we would find that about 850 of them end in *-ed*, with the frequency of allomorphy being /d/ > /t/ > /əd/. Hundreds of words contribute a small amount of activation to /d/. The /d/ unit sums this activation, and the result is that /d/ gets more activation than any phoneme within the target word. However, when /d/ is unlikely because it creates a consonant cluster that is impossible in English (as in **walk-d*), it attains a lesser degree of activation, and the second most frequent past-tense pattern, /t/, wins. If neither /t/ nor /d/ is phonologically possible (as in **need-d* or **need-t*), then the third most frequent pattern, /əd/, wins. No irregular pattern has more than thirty exemplars, and so none gains enough activation to win – *unless* the irregular lexical item suppresses the regular gangs (which is usually the case in adults) or *unless* a phonologically based gang can also form, reinforcing a particular sequence of vowel + consonants that does not end in *-ed*; thus families that end in *ank* and *unk* can generalize to new forms, but only by supplementing semantic information with phonological information. The regular patterns are present in so many lexical items that phonological information is not needed for generalization; phonological effects are swamped out, and hypersimilarity effects are not observed with regular patterns. If the target irregular verb fails to suppress the regular gang, a regularization results; failure should be greatest for low-frequency verbs, whose phonological information is least well encoded. Failures decrease if phonological effects like vowel dominance favor the past-tense form.

Gangs give the lie to the characterization of local models as "local," as opposed to "distributed." All past-tense forms are processed whenever any past-tense form is processed, and together all these forms influence the output. One could say that the representation of any particular past-tense form is distributed across all the past-tense-form nodes in the system. Stemberger (1994b) raises an interesting possibility. How does a learner know when to add a new word to the system? Suppose that a new word is added only when the speaker would otherwise produce the wrong output. When regular gangs reach a certain size, they automatically cause generalization, so that the correct (regular) past-tense form is produced for less-frequent and novel verbs. The speaker would reach a point where new regular past-tense forms would not be added to the system, because the right output would arise without them. The gang comes to function as a distributed rule, and like a rule, the *-ed* pattern is relatively independent of any individual lexical item.

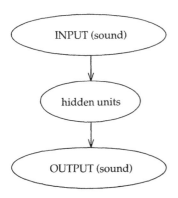

Figure 22.4 A nonrecurrent distributed connectionist model.

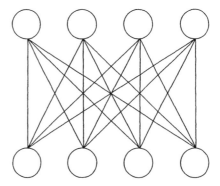

Figure 22.5 Connections between layers in a distributed model.

An important aspect of this model is the interaction between the lexical and phonological levels. Any phonological bias is predicted to affect morphology, including vowel dominance and priming. Additionally, the morphological system should tend to avoid outputs that contain less-frequent phonological patterns. Thus, there would be a tendency to avoid consonant clusters, to output words with fewer syllables, to favor high-frequency phonemes, etc. In this context, it is interesting that Clahsen et al. (1992) and Marcus et al. (1995) argue that for German the regular suffixes are perfect *-t* and plural *-s*, and that this would not be predicted on the basis of frequency. Perfect *-t* and *-en* are equally frequent as perfect suffixes for the 1,000 most frequent verbs of German (tied in both type and token frequency), so (morphological) frequency cannot explain why *-t* is the regular suffix for the perfect form, and not *-en*.[4] Plural *-s* is the least frequent plural suffix in German, but, they argue, is the regular suffix. However, phonological frequency may be relevant here. It happens that *-t* and *-s* are the only overt suffixes that (in general) do not add a syllable to the word; I note below that shorter words are more frequent than longer words in German. The predictions of connectionist models are unclear when two types of frequency conflict: high morphological frequency combined with low phonological frequency, versus low morphological frequency combined with high phonological frequency. German morphology may be an instance where phonological frequency outweighs morphological frequency in terms of which pattern is preferentially generalized; see below.

2.2.2 Distributed connectionist models I: nonrecurrent networks A typical nonrecurrent net is shown in figures 22.4 and 22.5. McClelland and Rumelhart (1986) developed the first nonrecurrent distributed model of morphology. The input was a distributed representation of the base word's pronunciation (e.g. /waːk/ *walk*, and /gow/ *go*), with all phonemes represented simultaneously. These were mapped directly onto an output representation of the pronunciation of the past-tense form (/waːkt/, /wɛnt/); all input nodes connected to all output nodes, as in figure 22.5. Both regular and irregular forms were stored in the same set of units and connections. The advantage of this model over local models was that there was an algorithm for learning (back propagation). The model produced regularizations, and (given family resemblance) irregularizations. Regularizations predominated, because the learning algorithms of distributed models extracted the most frequent pattern as the default one.

This was a primitive model (lacking even a layer of hidden units between the input and output layers), and has been heavily criticized, for example, by Pinker and Prince (1988). Most of the criticisms are of non-essential details, such as (a) the nature of the phonological units (wickel features) used to encode serial order, (b) the inability to differentiate homophones, (c) the temporal structuring of the training (done in an artificial way so that a U-shaped learning curve was derived), (d) the presence of a "teacher," disagreements over whether certain types of errors occur during acquisition, and (e) "cheating" by including standard aspects of linguistic representations in the input and output. (a) More recent models have used more conventional phonological representations (MacWhinney and Leinbach 1990, Plunkett and Marchman 1991, Hare and Elman 1992, Daugherty and Seidenberg 1994), and have derived similar results. (b) MacWhinney and Leinbach include semantic information, and have found that this allows the system to differentiate homophones (such as *ring – rang* vs. *wring – wrung* vs. *ring – ringed*) without compromising the system's ability to generalize patterns on a phonological basis. Marcus et al. (1995) have criticized the fact that MacWhinney and Leinbach used only a handful of semantic features, but this is a non-essential aspect of the model, deriving from limitations on the size of simulations; Marcus et al. admitted that the homophone problem can be solved in this way. (c) The artificial and incorrect way that Rumelhart and McClelland (1986) derived U-shaped learning is not a concern, because it now appears that U-shaped learning of the sort that had been assumed is unattested in children's acquisition of morphology (Marcus et al. 1992). (d) The "teacher" that told the system whether the output was correct or incorrect has been criticized, because children rarely get overt correction from adults. This is a misunderstanding of the nature of the "teacher," which is simply another cognitive subsystem, possibly the comprehension system. *All* models require some subsystem that can recognize that an error has occurred. (e) Although Pinker and Prince protested against outputs like *membled* as the past-tense form of *mail*, it should be noted that young children often pronounce words in ways that are quite different from adults (e.g. Priestly 1977, in which a child pronounced words such as *panda* /pandə/ as [pajan], and *dragon* /drægən/ as [dajak]), and all theories of acquisition probably predict that child forms like [mɛmbəld] for adult /meyld/ are possible.[5] This criticism is not based on any theory of language or of acquisition, and seems to lead to a position that would be unable to account for normal language acquisition. As a result, it cannot be taken as a failing of connectionist theories.

(f) Connectionist models often make the same assumptions about representations as linguistically based models. This is not a problem if we accept that all approaches to cognition have something of value to offer. It is no more "cheating" to include such analyses in connectionist models than it is to include them in symbolic models.

Current arguments about the feasibility of connectionist models concentrate on three issues: the lack of hypersimilarity effects for regular patterns, the role of semantics in determining whether a verb form is regular or irregular, and whether it must always be the most frequent morphological pattern that is the regular one. (a) As with non-rule-based local models, the most frequent pattern tends to generalize so readily that it is difficult to detect effects of factors like hypersimilarity or even lexical frequency (Daugherty and Seidenberg 1994). (b) The role of semantics is unclear. Kim et al. (1991) and Marcus et al. (1995) have maintained that semantic effects are irrelevant, and that symbolic rule-based deletion of features for irregularity (as when a verb is nominalized and then subsequently changed back into a verb, or when an irregular noun is made into a proper noun) are unaffected by how similar the resulting form is semantically to the regular verb or noun. They also maintain that metaphorical and semantic extensions of verbs and nouns always preserve the irregularity of the word. However, extensions of words always involve close semantic similarity, whereas denominal and deverbal verbs are usually more distant semantically. Kim et al. and Marcus et al. actually show that their predictions are incorrect: the probability that a denominal verb will be irregular is linearly correlated with the semantic similarity of the denominal verb to the prototypical usage of the homophonous verb. Thus, *sink* 'to put in a sink' (which has no semantic similarity to the usual verb *sink* 'to go down') has regular past *sinked*, but *fly* 'to hit a fly ball' (which is more similar to the usual verb *fly*, almost 'to cause a ball to fly high') has two equally acceptable past-tense forms, regular *flied* and irregular *flew*. The role of semantics is far from clear. And while it is possible to make the effects of semantics indirect (as in Kim et al.'s and Marcus et al.'s models, where they arise only during the process of learning lexical items), it remains possible that semantics has a direct effect.[6] (c) As noted above in the discussion of local models, it is an oversimplification to focus just on the frequency of the morphological pattern, ignoring the frequency of the phonological patterns that result. In some cases, a less frequent morphological pattern may be preferred because it creates the most frequent phonological pattern. When different measures of frequency conflict, predictions are not clear, for any connectionist model.

In relation to this last point, it should be noted that many nonrecurrent models (e.g. Rumelhart and McClelland 1986) do not predict that general phonological frequency in the language will affect morphological patterns. The reason is that such models have a special dedicated network, the sole purpose of which is to create past-tense forms. Such a network will pick up on statistical properties of past-tense forms only. If, however, the network produces all words (singular nouns, plural nouns, possessive nouns, infinitives,

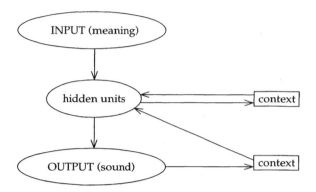

Figure 22.6   A recurrent distributed connectionist model.

present-tense forms, past-tense forms, progressive forms, adjectives, adverbs, etc.), then the statistics for all words will matter, not just the statistics of past-tense forms. In all probability, models cannot have subnetworks dedicated to particular morphological patterns. However, nonrecurrent networks do not require dedicated subnetworks (MacWhinney and Leinbach 1991), and so are still viable candidates for describing morphology in human languages.

2.2.3 Distributed connectionist models II: recurrent networks   Recent connectionist models are most often recurrent in nature: they contain loops that allow multiple passes through the system, with each pass corresponding to a phoneme (in models that generate the phonological output of words). Only a few models of morphology have been recurrent (e.g. Corina 1991), but this is likely to change. The basic structure of such a system is illustrated in figure 22.6 with the model of Dell et al. (1993), which was designed to address phonological processing; the model takes meaning as input and gives phonological features as output.[7] Each word is a pattern of activity across the meaning feature nodes and a pattern of activity across the phonological feature nodes, and these two layers are mediated by a layer of hidden units that maps the input onto the output. This model has two context layers to keep track of previous outputs.

Early distributed models, like local models, output all the segments of a word simultaneously. Recurrent models output a single segment at a time. The first pass through the system outputs the first segment of the word. The pattern of activity in the hidden units is saved in an *internal context* layer. The pattern of activity in the output layer is stored in an *external context* layer. Both context layers are then input into the hidden units on the second pass through the system, along with the *same* semantic pattern that was used during the first pass. That semantic pattern, in combination with context information about what was just produced, leads to the output of the second segment of the word on the second pass; without the context layers, the first phoneme would be output again. The pattern of activation in the hidden units and output units in the second pass are stored in the context units and input through the hidden units on the third pass, resulting in the third segment of the word. This continues until the system returns a null element that corresponds to the word boundary.

This recurrent model has interesting ramifications for morphology, especially for the regular/irregular distinction. First, the system can learn statistical probabilities between meaning units and phonological segments. Thus, it learns that there is a strong statistical correlation between the meaning {past tense} and a word-final /t/, /d/, or /əd/. Second, the system extracts statistical properties of a phonological nature as well, including *phonological constraints*. This phonological information can interact with morphology in predictable ways. The difference between the three allomorphs depends on phonological information contained in the context units; it is predictable from general phonological distribution patterns on voicing and sequences ending in /t/ and /d/ that are present even before any morphology is learned by the system. The correlation between any particular semantic unit and these final segments is small, and is equal for most input patterns; thus, the system will not tend to learn that a particular verb (like *walk*) takes -*ed*, but will learn that {past tense} maps onto -*ed*. The two local models in figures 22.1 and 22.2 above resemble this model; it is most like figure 22.2, in that there is input from both the meaning unit {past tense} and the /d/ output unit, and there is a lexical-item-specific component; but it approximates figure 22.1 in that the lexical-item-specific component for -*ed* is small. Unlike the distributed models with dedicated subnetworks for each inflectional category, this network outputs all morphological variants of the base word, including uninflected forms. As with local models, there is no mapping from the phonology of the base onto the phonology of the past tense.

Irregulars behave quite differently. Statistically, irregulars like *sang* and *fell* contain vowels that in general do not correlate with past tense any more than any other vowel (cf. base verbs such as *crack* and *rest*), and they fail to end in the -*ed* which correlates very strongly with past tense. The system must learn to output a vowel different from that of the base, as well as to suppress the final -*ed*. It learns both of these by being sensitive to the co-occurrence of elements in the semantic input; thus, given the co-occurrence of {past tense} and {fall}, the output will contain the vowel /ɛ/ but not the final consonant /d/. The final /d/ will also be suppressed using phonological context; given that the vowel /ɛ/ occurred with this semantic input, the system suppresses the final /d/, and outputs just /fɛl/.

Consider what happens when the system attempts to output the past tense of the word *fall*. The meaning maps onto /f/ in the first pass. In the second pass, in combination with the context units, the meaning of {fall} could map over onto either /ɑː/ (*fall, falls, falling, fallen*) or /ɛ/ (*fell*). Given that {past tense} is present, /ɛ/ will usually be accessed, but consider what happens if /ɑː/ is erroneously accessed. This will alter the information in the context units. This will not affect the phoneme accessed on the third pass, since /l/ appears in all forms of the word. However, the altered feedback makes the system less able to suppress the /d/ that is activated in the word-general meaning–form mapping. If this word-general mapping is weak, as in early speech, a base form error (*fall*) will usually result. If this mapping is strong, as later in learning, then the /d/ will not be suppressed, and a full regularization (*falled*) will usually result. Which output results depends on two things: the strength of the word-specific suppression of /d/ and the strength of the word-general mapping to /d/. In adults, the word-specific suppression is better learned, and base form errors are relatively more likely than they are in later child speech.

This system is capable of generalizing morphological patterns, whether inflectional or derivational, whether regular or irregular, using a single pathway. In fact, the system does not need to know that there are rules.[8] All that is necessary is the learning of particular lexical items, something that is present in all models of language.

This model is sensitive to a variety of factors, including the frequency of a pattern, but also including phonological factors. Marcus et al. (1995) have recently argued that connectionist models are inherently wrong, because frequency is irrelevant to the generalization of inflectional patterns in German. In fact, their own data require some frequency sensitivity (since Clahsen et al. 1992 are forced to normalize the competing noun-plural affixes for frequency in order to account for how affixes generalize in the speech of children with language disorders), but show that there are additional factors. Recurrent models, like local nets, intermix lexical and phonological processing, and do not predict that morphological frequency is the *only* factor that affects processing, just that frequency is *one* factor. For German, it appears that there is a preference for patterns that keep words short. Regular perfect *-t* and irregular perfect *-en* are about equally frequent as morphological markers of the perfect form, but *-t* generalizes preferentially because it leads to words with fewer syllables. Similarly, noun-plural *-s* generalizes more than expected when compared to the more frequent suffixes *-en*, *-er*, and *-e*, because those other suffixes add a syllable to the word and *-s* does not. The preference for shorter words may be based on frequency; Zipf (1935) reports that 49.8 percent of word tokens in German are monosyllabic, 22.9 percent are disyllabic, 12.9 percent are trisyllabic, and only 8.4 percent are longer. Frequency may be important here, but not the frequency of the morphological pattern.

This recurrent system is basically driven by meaning–sound mappings, just like the local model discussed above. It avoids the problems with the Rumelhart and McClelland model raised by Pinker and Prince (1988), Pinker (1991), Marcus et al. (1992, 1995), and Clahsen et al. (1992), in the same way that local models do. There is no basis for the claim that data from language production (whether of adults or of children) require the use of discrete inflectional rules and show that connectionist models (which lack such rules) are wrong in principle. Further, by highlighting the interactions of different sources of knowledge, connectionist models are inherently more likely to provide a non-arbitrary, non-stipulated *explanation* of why the facts are the way they are. Pinker's model requires us to accept that all the basic properties of morphology are random, due to the capricious nature of the genes that by chance have become a part of the human genetic endowment that controls the acquisition of language (e.g. Pinker 1991). One would hope that there is a more interesting reason for the basic properties of morphology than that.

3 Summary and conclusions

I have reviewed the types of morphological errors observed in language production in normal adults. Many of these phenomena derive from the way that syntax constrains morphology, and I did not dwell on them in the section of the chapter on models, since none of the models have addressed the syntax–morphology interface. But many phenomena concern the way that particular morphological patterns generalize, and all models have focused on that. Recent debates have focused on lexical frequency effects, semantic effects, and phonological effects of various types. We looked at three types of connectionist model: local, distributed nonrecurrent, and distributed recurrent. All can, in principle, handle the data that are currently known. However, extant non-recurrent models have included dedicated subnetworks for inflected forms, and seem unable to handle phonological priming effects from nouns to verbs. Local models have the drawback of lacking an explicit algorithm for learning, putting them at a disadvantage relative to distributed models (though symbolic models suffer from the same problem).

Connectionism is still a young field. Models, especially ones that have actually been implemented, are still quite primitive, and have addressed relatively small sub-areas of any cognitive domain. This is a reflection of the short time-span in which connectionist models have been addressing these questions, and of the great complexity of interactions in these models, rather than a limitation of the models per se. Basic issues concerning the organization of these models are still being worked out. Models will be in a state of flux for many years to come. Morphology is being addressed more and more frequently, both in modeling and in following up empirical predictions of models. Future models will focus even more on lexicon–phonology interactions. Whether they will ultimately be able to account for all the known facts without morphological rules remains to be seen. But any facts that ultimately derail this endeavor will be subtle in nature, and have yet to be found.

ACKNOWLEDGEMENT

This study was supported in part by NSF Research Grant #DBS-9209642 to the author.

NOTES

1 Note that the verb is plural *are*, and does not accommodate to *is*.

2 The four irregular present-tense singular forms of English (*is, has, does,* and *says*) all arguably end in the *-s* suffix.

3 Productivity is not the culprit here, since causative/inchoative *-en* (as in *redden*), which occurs in only a small number of words but is semantically transparent, is lost but never added.

4 The *-t* suffix is overwhelmingly more common than *-en* for less frequent verbs, but this is probably irrelevant. Young children generalize the *-t* suffix even when their lexicon is limited to the most frequent verbs.

5 All words containing a long vowel or diphthong followed by /l/ are often pronounced as two syllables by young children, and an onset is provided for the second syllable, e.g. mailed [meyːowd]. A harmonic onset is sometimes present, e.g. *piano* [pɪnænow]; a similar harmonic onset in *mailed* would yield [meymowd]. Other attested pronunciations in child phonology are intervocalic /m/ as [mb] and the simplification of diphthongs in closed syllables (such as before intervocalic [mb]); if we add in those two processes, *mailed* becomes [mɛmbod]. This is quite close to the "desired" output. Since no theory of phonology rules out such a pronunciation, it does not constitute a failing on Rumelhart and McClelland's model.

6 The mechanism is termed "short-circuiting." Semantic similarity leads a learner to conclude that a verb such as *fly* 'to hit a fly ball' is an extended use of the verb *fly* rather than a denominal verb based on the noun *fly* 'fly ball'. Any learner who (erroneously?) draws that conclusion will prefer the irregular past-tense form *flew*. Any learner who concludes that it is a denominal verb will prefer the regular past-tense form *flied*. Semantics has an effect only on learning in that model. It never has an effect on on-line processing of past-tense forms. However, the same predictions seem to be made whether semantics affects processing or learning. The only difference (so far untested) is the following: if semantics has a direct effect on processing, responses should be monomodal, with all speakers showing the same effect; if semantics has only an indirect effect, via learning, responses should be bimodal, reflecting the two different learning outcomes outlined above.

7 Dell's model uses two context layers. Corina (1991) used only internal context, and other models use only external context.

8 Rumelhart and McClelland (1986) make a similar claim, but their system actually needs to know that a dedicated subnetwork for each inflectional category is necessary.

Part V Morphological Sketches of Individual Languages

23 Archi (Caucasian – Daghestanian)

ALEKSANDR E. KIBRIK

Introduction

Archi is one of the twenty-six Daghestanian languages which, together with the three Nakh languages, makes up the North-East Caucasian family. Traditionally, Archi is assigned to the Lezghian group of Daghestanian languages, though its position there is somewhat isolated.

Archi is spoken in the central part of Daghestan and borders on Avar and Lak. Its 1,000 speakers live in a single village, Archi, situated 2,300 meters above sea-level. There is no dialectal differentiation. Archi is an unwritten language, and it is not taught in schools. However, it is the main means of everyday communication for all age-groups. Members of the older generation generally also know Avar and Lak, and middle-aged and younger speakers know Avar and Russian (primary education is conducted in Avar and middle school education in Russian).

There are a number of grammatical descriptions of Archi: Dirr 1908, Mikailov 1967, Xajdakov 1967, Kaxadze 1979, as well as the four-volume grammar compiled by the author and his collaborators (Kibrik et al. 1977a, b; Kibrik 1977a, b).

For reasons of space it is impossible to give an exhaustive account of Archi morphology, but to a certain extent those who do not read Russian can fill in the gaps by consulting Kibrik 1993. For this reason I shall concentrate primarily on those morphological phenomena in Archi which to my mind best reflect the general principles underlying the language, with its exceptionally rich paradigmatic resources. In addition, the sketch will acquaint the reader with a number of typologically unusual morphological categories, such as the verbal category of 'commentative' (with its 'double tense and mood'), the admirative, the system of spatial forms in nouns, 'double case marking' in the possessive locative and so on.

Archi (together with such familiar languages as Latin, Greek and Russian) is one of the large class of languages with rich paradigmatic morphology, in which a whole host of forms can be derived from a single root or stem. However, it has its peculiarities even within this class of languages. While in Russian a single noun produces about a dozen forms, the Archi noun produces more than eighty, and while a Russian verb root or stem gives rise to several hundred forms, in Archi it is more than a million (!). How does the language manage to generate such a record number of forms? What is the relationship between the measure of simplicity or complexity in a language and the size of its paradigms? To answer these and similar questions, let us look briefly at verbal and nominal inflection in Archi.

1 Verb inflection

The most striking features of Archi verbal morphology are the following:

(a) A distinction between dynamic and stative verbs (unlike dynamic verbs, the statives have no category of aspect, and therefore no infinitive (see below), imperative or prohibitive). Stative verbs include predicates with meanings such as *L'an* 'love', *sini* 'know', *k₀at* 'must', as well as words which would be adjectives in European languages, such as *libXI* 'shameful', *hiba* 'be good', *doI:z* 'be large'.

(b) A contrast between a closed class of simple dynamic verbs (roughly 150), whose basic form consists of a morphologically unanalysable root, and an open class of complex verbs, which are analytic complexes consisting of a non-inflecting and an inflecting part, where the inflecting part is one of the simple verbs – e.g. *anX as* 'fight' (lit. 'fight make') *ʕazab Los* 'torment' (lit. 'trouble give').

(c) An abundance of grammatical categories, including morphologically complex ones, many of which freely combine with each other.

(d) The productive formation of a variety of synthetic non-finite forms, with their own inventory of grammatical categories: participles, masdars and gerunds.

1.1 Finite forms

Finite verb forms are obligatorily marked for aspect, tense, mood, polarity, class and number, as well as the categories of continuality and inferentiality, co-occurring with a number of forms. In addition, the Archi verb may be marked for evidentiality with the categories commentative and admirative.

Aspectual and class/number markers are the most tightly attached to the root. They are the focus of a large number of inflectional irregularities. Thus, the 150 simple verbs enter into more than 30 distinct conjugation classes. For simplicity of exposition I shall restrict my discussion to the more regular types.

(For transcription conventions, see n. 1, and for abbreviations used only in this chapter, see appendix on pp. 473–4.)[1]

Dynamic verbs distinguish four aspects:

> durative (regular marker – discontinuous transfix -*r* . . . -*r*, e.g. 'to lie down' *aXa* ~ *a-r-Xa-r*, CONST:[2] 'Event P is prolonged and without result.'
>
> perfective (regular marker -*u* < *w, e.g. *aX-u* AOR < *aX-a-w): 'Event P takes place before the time of utterance and has a result.'
>
> potential (marker -*qi*, suffixed to the perfective marker, e.g. *aX-u-qi*, FUT): 'Event P may take place.'
>
> final (marker -*s* < **s̄*, e.g. *aXa-s*, INF): 'Event P must take place.'

Class-number markers (CNM) cross-reference the class and number of a noun in the nominative; that is, they function as agreement markers. Nouns distinguish four major and four minor classes (see section 2) and singular/ plural.

Class		Number	Class		Number
	SG	PL		SG	PL
I	w-/-w-	b-/-b-	V	w-/-w-	Ø-/-Ø-
II	d-/-r-	b-/-b-	VI	d-/-r-	Ø-/-Ø-
III	b-/-b-	Ø-/-Ø-	VII	b-/-b-	b-/-b-
IV	Ø-/-Ø-	Ø-/-Ø-	VIII	Ø-/-Ø-	b-/-b-

The CNM (usually) occupies a prefixal position in the durative and an infixal position (between the vowel and consonant of the root) in other aspects. For example, *w-a-r-Xa-r*, CONST 1 SG – *o-w-X-u*, AOR 1 SG[3] – *o-w-X-u-qi*, FUT 1 SG, *o-w-Xa-s*, INF 1 SG.

The category of tense has three meanings, which combine regularly with the aspectual meanings of the conjugated verb:

> neutral (zero marker): 'The aspectual meaning P is not related to the time of utterance.'
>
> present (formed analytically using the absolutive of the corresponding aspect and the auxiliary verb *i* 'be'): 'The aspectual meaning P is simultaneous with the time of utterance.'
>
> past (absolutive of the finite verb + auxiliary *edi* 'was'): 'The aspectual meaning P precedes the time of utterance.'

The durative and potential form the absolutive by suffixation of -*ši* (*arXar-ši*, DUR ABS, *aXuqi-ši*, POT ABS), the perfective, with -*li* (*aXu-li* PFTV ABS), the final is zero marked: *aXas-Ø*,[4] FIN ABS). In addition, the durative and perfective form the continual absolutive (marker -*mat*): *arXar-mat*, DUR CONTIN ABS, *aXu-mat*, PFTV CONTIN ABS. The continual absolutive adds the component 'continues to take place' to the standard aspectual meaning.[5]

Table 23.1   Tense-aspect forms of *aXas* 'lie down' (indicative, class III)

Aspect	Tense		
	Neutral (-Ø)	*Present (ABS + i)*	*Past (ABS + edi)*
Durative	b-a-r-Xa-r-Ø	b-a-r-Xa-r-ši b-i	b-a-r-Xa-r-ši e-b-di
(-r-r)	constative	1st present	1st imperfect
+iterative	——		b-a-r-Xa-r-si b-i-kir
			iterative
+contin.	——	b-a-r-Xa-r-mat b-i	b-a-r-Xa-r-mat e-b-di
		2nd present	2nd imperfect
Perfective	a-b-X-u-Ø	a-b-X-u-li b-i	a-b-X-u-li e-b-di
(-u)	aorist	1st perfect	1st pluperfect
+contin.	——	a-b-X-u-mat b-i	a-b-X-u-mat e-b-di
		2nd perfect	2nd pluperfect
Potentialis	a-b-X-u-qi-Ø	a-b-X-u-qi-ši b-i	a-b-X-u-qi-ši e-b-di
(-qi)	future	inceptive	past inceptive
Finalis	a-b-Xa-s-Ø	a-b-Xa-s b-i	a-b-Xa-s e-b-di
(-s)	infinitive	debitive	past debitive

Sixteen tense-aspect forms are available from the combination of aspect, tense and continuality categories (see table 23.1).

A further tense-aspect form is the iterative, also derived analytically from the durative absolutive by means of the auxiliary verb *ikir*[6] ('Event P repeatedly took place before the time of utterance'): *arXar-ši ikir* 'repeatedly lay down.'

Thus, the tense-aspect paradigm in the indicative contains seventeen basic elements. Their meanings are generally a straightforward composition of the meanings of their component categories. For example:

constative = 'event P is continuous, has no result, whatever the relation to the time of utterance':

(1)   godo-r ɬ-ann-a   iqlaw barsargat' b-a-r-sa-r.
      this-II[7] *woman-OBL.ERG always shawl.NOM III-wear-DUR.NEU*
      'This woman always wears a shawl.'

present 1 = 'event P is continuous, has no result and is simultaneous with the time of utterance':

(2)   to-w   buq'   b-e-r-k'u-r-ši   w-i.
      he-I.NOM grain.NOM III-clean-DUR-ABS I-be[8]
      'He is cleaning grain.'

aorist = 'event P took place and is finished':

(3) Xiᵗa te-jmaj   q'₀enn-ib lagum   Xab-u.
    then they-OBL.PL.ERG two-PL   song.ERG sing-PFTV.NEU
    'Then, the two of them started to sing a song.'

perfect 2 = 'event P is completed; the result of P has begun to take place and continues at the time of utterance':

(4) zon   šanRi-m-a-š   Xara: -si   ja-t
    I.NOM yesterday-OBL-IN-ABL from.behind-LAT this-IV
    biq'₀-m-a   q'o-w-di-mat⁹   w-i.
    place-OBL-IN.ESS sit-I-PFTV-CONTIN.ABS I-be
    'I have been sitting here since yesterday.'

inceptive = 'event P begins to occur at the time of utterance'/'Someone intends to perform some action':

(5) zari   buwa-ᵗe-ra-k   karRəra
    I.ERG mother-OBL.PL-CONT-LAT letter.NOM
    t'al=a-b-u-qi-ši¹⁰   b-i.
    send-III-PFTV-POT-ABS III-be
    'I intend to send a letter to my parents.'

debitive = 'at the time of utterance it is necessary that event P occur (at some time)':

(6) un   lagum   Xabu-s   i.
    you.ERG song.NOM sing-FIN IV-be
    'You should sing a song.'

The only form which is not used in the position of an independent predicate is the infinitive. It expresses the purpose of an action, or an action which must be performed.

(7) but'uᵗu-t č'at   Xo-t'u   hani wa-s   bo-s?
    other-IV word.NOM IV-find.PFTV-NEG that you-DAT say-FIN.NEU
    'Did you not find another word, which you might say?'

Forms denoting an event occurring before the time of utterance (i.e. past-tense and aorist forms) combine with the category of inferentiality, an evidential category (specifying the source of the information). The positive value of this category (marked with the suffix *-li*) is 'the speaker and/or hearer did not directly witness event P prior to the time of utterance'.

(8) to-w dase:ni   sin-t'u   uqIa-li¹¹   e-w-di-li.
    he-I somewhere know-NEG I.go.PFTV-ABS be-I-INFER
    'He went somewhere unknown.'

All tense-aspect forms (except the infinitive) combine with the category of polarity, whose positive value ('it is the case that P') is unmarked, and whose

Table 23.2 Partial paradigm of *aXas* 'lie down'

Category	+ polarity		– polarity
	I class	II class	I class
Indicative			
constative	w-a-r-Xa-r	d-a-r-Xa-r	w-a-r-Xa-r-t'u
present	w-a-r-Xa-r-ši w-i	d-a-r-Xa-r-ši d-i	w-a-r-Xa-r-ši w-i-t'u
1st imperfect	w-a-r-Xa-r-ši	d-a-r-Xa-r-ši	w-a-r-Xa-r-ši
	e-w-di	e-r-di	e-w-di-t'u
inferential 1st	w-a-r-Xa-r-ši	d-a-r-Xa-r-ši	w-a-r-Xa-r-ši
imperfect	e-w-di-li	e-r-di-li	e-w-di-li w-i-t'u
aorist	o-w-X-u	a-r-X-u	o-w-X-u-t'u
inferential	o-w-X-u-li	a-r-X-u-li	o-w-X-u-li w-i-t'u
aorist			
perfect	o-w-X-u-li w-i	a-r-X-u-li d-i	o-w-X-u-li w-i-t'u
future	o-w-X-u-qi	a-r-X-u-qi	o-w-X-o:-t'u
inceptive	o-w-X-u-qi-ši w-i	a-r-X-u-qi-ši d-i	o-w-X-u-qi-ši w-i-t'u
infinitive	o-w-Xa-s	a-r-Xa-s	——
debitive	o-w-Xa-s w-i	a-r-Xa-s	o-w-Xa-s w-i-t'u
Interrogative			
constative	w-a-r-Xa-r-a	d-a-r-Xa-r-a	w-a-r-Xa-r-t'u-ra
present	w-a-r-Xa-r-ši	d-a-r-Xa-r-ši	w-a-r-Xa-r-ši
	w-i-ra	d-i-ra	w-i-t'u-ra
Imperative	w-aXa	d-aXa	——
Prohibitive	——	——	w-a-r-Xa-r-(di)-gi
Optative	o-w-X-u-ťan	a-r-X-u-ťan	o-w-X-u-t'u-ťan

negative value ('it is not the case that P') is realized by the suffix *-t'u*. See the examples in table 23.2.

The majority of different moods are based on tense-aspect forms:

> indicative (the unmarked mood; for examples, see above and table 23.1) = 'Speaker believes that proposition P is true.' Combined with negation, the indicative means: 'It is the case that it is not the case that P.'
> interrogative (marker *-a/ra*): 'Speaker asks whether it is the case that P.'

(9) wa-ī-iš   ho:nu   Xer   b-i-ra?
     thou-SUPER-ABL some.kind.of use.NOM III-be-INTERR
     'Is there any use from you?'

> dubitative (marker *-čugu*, combines with all non-evidential forms): 'Speaker wants to know whether it is the case that P' or 'Speaker doubts whether it is the case that P'.

(10)   šanRi   barq   ba-sa-s   e-b-di-čugu.[12]
yesterday sun.NOM III-seize-FIN be-III-DUB
'I wonder whether there should have been a solar eclipse yesterday.'

(11)   e-b-di-čugu   šanRi   barq   ba-sa-s.
be-III-DUB   yesterday sun.NOM III-seize-FIN
'There should hardly have been a solar eclipse yesterday.'

In the second interpretation the verb in the dubitative form is fronted, and the intonation contour is falling.

approbative (marker *-di*, used in contrastive sentences and various types of conditional clause): 'Event P is true and speaker is positively disposed to P, but in addition to P there is another event contradicting it.'

(12)   zon   ja-b   meš̄-e   w-a-e-Xa-r-di,
I.NOM this-III mattress-OBL.IN.ESS I-lie-DUR.NEU.APPR
han   u-qi[13]   išik qIanna-t'u?
what IV.do.PFTV-POT.NEU here soft.NEU-NEG
'I may well lie on this mattress, but what will I do if it isn't soft?'

conjunctive (marker *-kini*): 'Speaker wants event P to be the case but doubts that P is the case.'

(13)   un   ošoš̄-ennu   olo-ma-ši[14]   w-a-rr-Li-r-kini!
thou.NOM sometimes-even we.GEN-LOC-LAT I-come-DUR.NEU-CONJ
'If only you would come to us just occasionally!'

possibilitive (derived analytically from the tense-aspect form of a lexical verb[15] (with obligatorily the evidentiality marker, if the given form combines with it, see above) and the auxiliary verb *Xos* 'to be situated', in the future *Xo-qi*): 'Speaker supposes that it is the case that P.'

(14)   to-w   X̄₀ak̄-a-ši
he.NOM-I forest-OBL.IN-LAT
quIa-li   Xu-qi.
I.go.PFTV.NEU-INFER be.situated.I.PFTV-POT.NEU
'He probably went into the forest.'

A number of moods are derived not from tense-aspect forms but from the root or the aspectual base, including:

imperative (derived only from dynamic verbs and usually coincides with the bare base form; the basic position of the class-number marker is prefixal, as in the durative): *w-aXa* 'lie down (sg.)'. Non-agentive verbs (which do not take an ergative subject) have a suffixal position for the plural marker (*-r*): *aXa-r*[16] 'lie down (pl.)'.

cohortative – a polite imperative, formed from the imperative by the addition of the marker -*su*: *w-aXa-su* 'do lie down'.

prohibitive (formed from the durative base with the marker -*(di)gi*): *w-a-r-Xa-r-(di)gi* 'don't lie down'.

optative (derived from the perfective base with the marker -*ĭan*, and having both a positive and a negative form): 'Speaker wants event P (not) to happen and presumes that the hearer wants this too.'

(15)   un   noL'-a-ši   uqIa-ĭan?
       thou.NOM home-OBL.IN-LAT I.come.PFTV-OPT
       'Shouldn't you be going home?'

Let us look finally at two evidential verb categories: the commentative and the admirative.

The commentative, which is a morphological means of expressing indirect speech, is derived from any finite verb form by suffixation of -*er*. Its meaning is: 'Someone A says that P,' where A is a person whose direct speech is introduced by means of the commentative form. For instance: *warXar*, CONST, 'he lies down' – *warXar-er* 'someone says that he lies down'; *warXargi*, PROH, 'don't lie down' – *warXarg-er* 'someone says: don't lie down'; *owXuqisi widi*, PRES, APPR 'he indeed is lying down' – *owXuqisi wid-er* 'someone says that he indeed is lying down'.

The commentative itself inflects for tense. The synthetic form realizes the neutral/present tense, while the past tense is formed analytically: *warXar-er-ši ewdi* 'someone said that he was lying down'. The past-tense form combines with inferentiality: *warXar-er-ši ewdi-li* 'apparently, someone said that he is lying down'. A number of marked mood types can also be formed from the commentative (where 'unmarked' refers to the indicative): for instance, *warXar-er-a*, INTERR, 'does someone say that he is lying down?'; *warXar-er-čugu*, DUB, 'it seems that someone says that he is lying down'. Thus, the categories of tense, mood and evidentiality can be realized twice: on the lexical verb and by the meaning of 'speaking'.

The admirative occupies an intermediate position between a fully and a partially grammaticalized analytical complex. Its meaning is: 'Someone becomes a witness to part of, or the result of, an event P.' The admirative is derived by combining the absolutive (in the durative, perfective or potential) or the infinitive of a lexical verb with the auxiliary verb *Xos*, lit. 'to find, discover', in one of the neutral tense forms (see table 23.3).

The forms of the admirative (especially the first two lines of the table) are structurally similar to the analytical forms of the present and past tense (cf. the auxiliary verb *i* – *edi*). It is also significant that negation, too, in the admirative is expressed on the auxiliary: *wirX̄ₒinši wit'u* 'he isn't working' – *wirX̄ₒinši Xut'u* 'they discovered that he isn't working'.

At the same time the auxiliary has its own addressee complement marked in the dative (the person who discovers that P):

Table 23.3 Formation of admirative

Verb form of Xos	Aspect of lexical verb			
	DUR	PFTV	POT	FIN
CONST	-ši + Xor -mat	-na + Xor -mat	-ši + Xor	-Ø + Xor
AOR	-ši + Xo -mat	-na + Xo -mat	-ši + Xo	-Ø + Xo
FUT	-ši + Xoqi -mat	-na + Xoqi -mat	-ši + Xoqi	-Ø + Xoqi
INF	-ši + Xos -mat	-na + Xos -mat	-ši + Xos	-Ø + Xos

(16) b-ez   qⅠin   e-b-ku-mat   bo-Xo-r
 III-I.DAT bridge.NOM fall-III-PFTV-CONTIN.ABS III-ADM-DUR
 'I discover that the bridge continues to be in a state of collapse.'

In this respect, *Xos* behaves like an independent lexical verb, rather than an auxiliary. Space does not permit discussion of the other interesting morphosyntactic properties of this construction.

1.2 Non-finite forms

The following are the non-finite verb forms: the masdar (deverbal nominal), participle (deverbal adjectival), gerund and absolutive (deverbal adverbial). While the finite verb forms make up the predicate of a main clause, the non-finite representations are used when the verb is the predicate of a dependent proposition: the verb is thereby transformed into that surface structure part of speech to which the syntactic node of the constituent expressing the given proposition relates. Consequently, there is every reason to consider these morphological processes as inflectional and to regard the derived representations as components of the verb's paradigm.

The masdar can be derived by suffixation of *-kul* from any tense-aspect form of the indicative (except for inferential forms), including negative and/or commentative forms (see table 23.4). In addition, it is possible to derive the masdar from the basic stem/root by means of the affix *-mul/t'i*[17] (with truncation of the right edge of the stem *-V#* or *Vn#* or *-bos#*). The class-number marker then occupies the prefix position (cf. the imperative). Examples:

Table 23.4   Examples of masdars and participles of the verb 'work'

Meaning	Finite form	Masdar	Participle
CONST, I	wir$\bar{X}_o$in	wir$\bar{X}_o$in-kul	wir$\bar{X}_o$in-nu
CONST, I, COMM	wir$\bar{X}_o$iner	wir$\bar{X}_o$iner-kul	wir$\bar{X}_o$iner-ɫu
IMPF-1, I	wir$\bar{X}_o$inši ewdi	wir$\bar{X}_o$inši ewdi-kul	wir$\bar{X}_o$inši ewdi-ɫu
INF, I	wir$X_o$mus	wir$X_o$mus-kul	wir$X_o$mus-du
AOR, II, NEG	dir$X_o$nit′u	dir$X_o$nit′u-kul	dir$X_o$nit′u-ɫu-r

> *aXas* 'to lie down' – stem *aXa* – masdar, III *b-aX-mul*
> *irX$_o$mus* 'to work' – stem *irX$_o$in* – masdar, I *w-irX$_o$-mul*
> *aI?-bos* 'to call' – stem *aI?-bo* – masdar[18] *aI?-t′i.*

The masdar, like any noun, has a full set of case inflections.

The participle is derived from any tense-aspect form of the indicative (including the commentative) by suffixation of *-ɫu*, after which follow the class-number markers, as with all adjectives; see table 23.3. The participle can also have the quantificational affix *-en*, which appears before the adjectivizing marker: e.g. *wir$\bar{X}_o$in-nu* 'working' – *wir$\bar{X}_o$in-en-nu* 'everyone who is working'.

Like all adjectives, the participle can be nominalized (by conversion), and inflects for case and number.

Gerunds are functionally equivalent to an adverbial subordinate clause expressing time, reason, purpose, condition, concession, contrast and place. They too are derived from finite tense-aspect forms (generally the indicative), including the commentative. At the same time particular types of gerunds may have specific restrictions (usually semantically motivated) on the set of basic forms (these restrictions are omitted for reasons of space). For examples of gerunds see table 23.5.

The absolutives are functionally similar to co-ordinate clauses: in one of the clauses (the communicatively backgrounded, peripheral clause) the verb appears in the absolutive form.[19] The absolutives are derived from aspectual stems (with or without negation) and express the meaning of simultaneity of the secondary and primary propositions; the meaning of simultaneity is here determined by a particular component of the aspectual meaning (e.g. simultaneity of result in the case of the perfective). Examples of absolutives are provided in table 23.6. As can be seen, positive and negative forms in the durative and potential are in complementary distribution (the negation of the durative is a form derived from the potential, which can be justified semantically). In the perfective the negative absolutive is formed by a cumulative affix *-t′aw* (which in general is untypical of Archi), and the positive has two forms, one in *-li*, the other in *-na*. The first is used when the proposition expressed in the main clause relates to the real world (referring to past or present), and the

Table 23.5 Examples of gerunds of the verb 'work' (class I)

Marker	Basic form	Gerund	Meaning
-ṭa	CONST	wirX̄oin-ṭa	when he works
	FUT, COMM	wirXoniqer-ṭa	when he says that he will work
-ejkun	CONST	wirX̄oin-ejkun	while he works
-ṭan	FUT	wirXoniqi-ṭan	before working
-kan	INF	wirXomu-l-kan	until he starts working
-m(u)Xur	PERF	wirXonili wi-mXur	when/because he worked
-e:rši	CONST	wirX̄oin-e:rši	on account of the fact that he works
-ḵut	INF	wirXomu-l-ḵut	in order not to work
-ḵus	PRES	wirX̄oinši wir-ḵus	to find out whether he is working
-enč' iš	INC	wirXoniqiši wi-nč'is	if he will work
-mat	INC	wirXoniqiši wi-mat	although he will work
-šaw	IMPF-1	wirX̄oinši ewdi-šaw	although he was working
-e:na	IMPF-1, INFER	wirX̄oinši ewdil-e:na	despite the fact that he was working
-ma	AOR	wirXoni-ma	where he worked
-ma-k	AOR	wirXoni-ma-k	to the place where he worked
-ma-š	AOR	wirXoni-ma-š	from the place where he worked

Table 23.6 Absolutives of the verb 'work'

Polarity/ continuality	Aspectual meaning			
	DUR	POT	FIN	PFTV
–NEG	wirX̄oin-ši	——	wirXomus-ši	wirXoni-li/na
+NEG	——	wirXona:-t' u-ši	wirXomus-t'u-ši	wirXoni-t'aw
+CONTIN	wirX̄oim-mat	——	——	wirXoni-mat
+NEG, +CONTIN	——	——	——	wirXoni-t'u-mat

second is used when speaking of hypothetical events (the main verb is in the potential aspect, the constative or the prohibitive). The continual absolutive is derived only from the durative and perfective (affix *-mat*). It adds the semantic component 'to begin and continue to take place'. The negative continual absolutive is possible from non-resultative verbs of instantaneous action (the example in table 23.6 is for illustration only).

1.3 The size of verb paradigms

As can be seen from the foregoing description, the Archi verb paradigm is rather large. Writing out all the verb forms would be involved, to say the least. For this reason it is necessary to describe the paradigm by means of the procedure which generates it, enumerating all the theoretically possible forms. Naturally, the majority of these forms exist solely as a theoretical possibility; only a tiny fraction of them are encountered in everyday speech with any frequency. However, under appropriate communicative, semantic and grammatical circumstances, any form with a licit assembly of semantic and grammatical categories can be constructed and will be perceived as entirely normal. It is therefore interesting to calculate the maximum number of theoretically available forms that can be derived from a single verb root. (Naturally, analytical forms are treated on a par paradigmatically with the synthetic forms.)

Since the number of forms is markedly increased by the class-number markers and the commentative, which enjoy the greatest freedom of co-occurrence, we will leave these forms, and also the case/number forms of deverbal nominals, out of our calculations in the first instance.

1.3.1 Forms excluding CNM and COMM

> Mood. In the indicative and interrogative there are 47 forms each (33 non-evidential ±negation and 14 evidential ±negation). The dubitative, approbative and conjunctive each have 33 forms. The possibilitive provides 23 forms. The irregular moods give a total of 7 forms. This comes to a total of 223 finite forms.
>
> The admirative (±negation) gives $24 \times 2 = 48$ forms. Taking evidentiality into consideration ($6 \times 2 = 12$), we get 60 forms for the admirative.
>
> The masdar may have 34 forms (33 are formed from tense-aspect stems and one from the root).
>
> The participles are derived from any of the 47 tense-aspect forms, and can be assigned the meanings of generality and class number[20] (five distinct class-number suffixes), that is $47 \times 2 \times 5 = 470$.
>
> The gerunds (taking into account co-occurrence restrictions on their derivation) number 929 forms.
>
> The absolutives have 9 forms.

Thus, the verb forms just listed total 1725 (= 223 + 60 + 34 + 470 + 929 + 9). However, the masdars can be inflected for 10 cases, which gives us 340 forms, and the participles take 22 cases: 470 × 22 = 10,340. Hence, if we take into consideration the case-marked forms of the deverbal nominals we get 12,405 forms (1725 + 340 + 10,340).

1.3.2 Forms with CNM

In calculating these forms, we must consider not the number of classes (8) and numbers (2), but the number of distinct class-number markers. In synthetic verb forms these do not exceed four, while in analytic forms with agentive verbs permitting double agreement, there are 16 (= 4 × 4).

Additional case-marked forms of the masdar and participles amount to 165,800, making a total for this type of 188,463.

1.3.3 Forms with COMM

The commentative can be formed from all personal forms and the admirative (=283), and itself has 9 personal forms, 10 gerunds, 1 absolutive, 7 masdars, 10 participles and 4 admiratives, a total of 41 forms, which gives 283 × 41 = 12,603.

Participles formed on the commentative give a further 283 × 10 × 22 = 62,260 case-marked forms, the masdars, 283 × 7 × 10 = 19,810, a total of 82,070 case-marked forms. In all, forms of the commentative without class-number markers come to 94,673.

The overall subtotal of forms without CNM is 12,405 + 94,673 = 107,078.

1.3.4 Forms with CNM and COMM

The commentative distinguishes 53 class-number forms, and can itself be formed from 3,832 class-number-marked forms (2,872 + 960), giving a total of 203,096 class-number forms with the commentative. Adding the class-number marked forms without the commentative (22,663), we obtain 225,729 distinct forms without case marking.

The case-marked participial forms from the commentative give 3,832 × 10 × 22 = 843,040 forms, the masdars 3,832 × 7 × 10 = 268,240. In all, the number of forms of the commentative (including class-number-marked and case-marked forms) is 1,314,376.

The number of corresponding forms without the commentative is 188,463. Thus, the grand total, which in principle can be derived from a single verb root is 1,502,839 – that is, more than one and a half million.

A summary of these facts is given in table 23.7.

2 Nominal inflection

The noun has the classificatory grammatical category of class (four basic and four minor classes,[21] number, case and localization. A characteristic feature of the nominal inflectional system of Archi (along with that of many other

Table 23.7   The number of forms derived from a single verb root

+/–COMM	–CNM		+CNM	
	without case forms	with case forms	without case forms	with case forms
–COMM	1,725	12,405	22,663	188,463
+COMM	12,603	94,673	203,096	1,314,376
+/–COMM	14,328	107,078	225,729	1,502,839

Daghestanian languages) is the asymmetry between two subsystems of the case system: a group of grammatical cases and a group of spatial cases. The latter form a regular system consisting of a combination of two categories, spatial and locational. In addition, the noun paradigms exhibit an opposition between a direct case (nominative) and oblique cases: the direct case generally identical to the number stem, the oblique cases formed regularly from the oblique stem.

2.1 General model for noun paradigms

The structure of the noun paradigm can be illustrated schematically as follows (cf. Kibrik 1991a):

$$\text{NOMSG} \quad = \text{DIRSTEM}_{sg} \rightarrow \text{DIRSTEM}_{pl} \quad = \text{NOMPL}$$

$$\text{OBLCASES} \leftarrow \text{OBLSTEM}_{sg} \qquad \text{OBLSTEM}_{pl} \rightarrow \text{OBLCASES}$$

The regular plural markers are *-mul/ťu* (depending on whether the stem ends in a consonant or a vowel), the oblique singular stem is *-li*,[22] and the oblique plural stem is *-(č)aj*. Thus, the properties of singular (direct stem) and nominative remain unmarked. Oblique case markers do not distinguish number: this property is realized cumulatively in the marker of the oblique stem.

2.2 Grammatical cases

There are ten grammatical cases in Archi (see table 23.8).
    Examples of the basic meanings:

(17)   to-w -mu   nesen Xuzen-ni -s   aL'   haɪršbo -qi.
        he-III-OBL.ERG now   master-OBL-DAT meat.NOM cook.PFTV-POT.NEU
        'Now he will cook the meat for the master.'

Table 23.8 Grammatical cases in Archi

Marker	Case	Case meaning
-∅	Nominative	A is the argument with which P occurs directly.
OBL + ∅	Ergative	(a) A is the animate argument which performs P.
		(b) A is the inanimate argument serving as the instrument/means of realizing P.
OBL + s	Dative	A is the argument with an interest in P.
OBL + n	Genitive	A is determinant of the NP node.
OBL + ɬu	Comitative	A is the argument together with which some other argument takes part in P.
OBL + Xur	Comparative	A is the argument which has a property to a lesser extent than some other argument.
OBL + L'əna	Permutative	A is the argument which takes part in P instead of another argument.
OBL + ši	Causal	A is the cause of event P.
OBL + qIiš	Partitive	A is the set of objects from which a particular subset is taken.
OBL + qIdi	Equative	An event P occurs in a manner typical of A.

(18) nac'-a -n cal -um-čaj naq'$_o$ caqI -u-li.
bird-OBL-GEN feather-PL-OBLPL.ERG ground.NOM cover-PFTV-INFER
'The bird's feathers covered the ground.'

(19) un hannum-mu-ɬu w-irX̄$_o$in -ši e-w-di?
thou.NOM who -OBL-COMIT I-work.DUR-ABS be-I-(be)
'Who did you work with?'

(20) zon uš -mu -Xur t'i -t'u.
I.NOM brother-OBL-COMP small.NEU-NEG
'I am not smaller than my brother.'

(21) w-is lah -a -L'əna lo t'al-w-a uɨa-w-u
I-I.GEN son-OBL-PERM son.NOM send-I-IMPER thou.GEN-I
'Send your own son in place of my son.'

(22) hiba-ɨu-t iq i-kul-ili-ši
be.good-ADJZR-IV day.NOM be-MASDAR-OBL-CAUSAL
nen k$_o$eki=šeki-s[23] oqIa.[24]
we.NOM walk-inf V-VI.PL.go.PFTV
'Since it was a nice day, we went for a walk.'

Table 23.9   Nominal spatial forms

Localization	Spatial case					
	essive	*ablative*	*lative*	*allative*	*terminative*	*translative*
IN	-a	-aš	-ak	-aši	-akana	-aXut
INTER	-qI	-qIaš	-qIak	-qIaši	-qIakana	-qIaXut
SUPER	-t	-ŧiš	-ŧik	-ŧiši	-ŧikana	-ŧiXut
CONT	——	-raš	-rak	-rši	-rakana	——
SUB	-L′	-L′aš	-L′ak	-L′aši	-L′akana	-L′aXut

(23)   jamu-r wiLa-r-u   lah-a-qIis   os t′inna tuX-du-r
       this-II   seven-II-(seven) girl-OBL-PART one slightly be.shy-ADJZR-II
       e-r-di-li.
       was-II-(was)-INFER
       'Of these seven girls, one was somewhat shy.'

(24)   te-jamj   L′an   nen   za-qIdi
       they-OBLPL.ERG want.NEU we.NOM REFL.OBLPL-EQU
       lagum   Xabu-s.
       song.NOM sing-FIN
       'They want us to sing in their fashion.'

2.3 Spatial forms

The system of spatial forms results from a combination of the sixth meaning of the category of locational case with the fifth meaning of the category of location. In all, twenty-eight forms are found, shown in table 23.9 (the locational CONT does not combine with two case meanings, the essive and the translative). For example (*č′ele* 'stone'):

č′ele-li-t   č′ele-li-ŧ-ik   č′ele-li-L′   č′ele-li-L′-iš
SUPER-ESSIVE   SUPER-LATIVE   SUB-ESSIVE   SUB-ABLATIVE
'on to the stone' 'on to the stone' 'under the stone' 'from under the stone'

A fragment of the nominal paradigm is shown in table 23.10.

The spatial forms are used principally to express a variety of spatial relationships of a position or direction of motion with respect to some reference point. The particular meanings of the localization determine either a contextual or a generic orientation with respect to the reference point, depending on the semantics of that reference point.

Table 23.10   Partial paradigm of the noun aɪnš 'apple'

Case	Sg.	Pl.
Nominative	aɪnš	aɪnš-um
Ergative	aɪnš-li	aɪnš-um-čaj
Dative	aɪnš-li-s	aɪnš-um-če-s
Genitive	aɪnš-li-n	aɪnš-um-če-n
Comitative	aɪnš-li-ɬu	aɪnš-um-če-ɬu
Comparative	aɪnš-li-Xur	aɪnš-um-če-Xur
Permutative	aɪnš-li-L'əna	aɪnš-um-če-L'əna
Partitive	aɪnš-li-qɪiš	aɪnš-um-če-qɪiš
In=essive	aɪnš-l-a	aɪnš-um-ča-j
In=ablative	aɪnš-l-a-š	aɪnš-um-če-j-š
In=lative	aɪnš-l-a-k	aɪnš-um-če-j-k
Super=essive	aɪnš-li-t	aɪnš-um-če-t
Super=ablative	aɪnš-li-t̄-iš	aɪnš-um-če-t̄-iš
Super=lative	aɪnš-li-t̄-ik	aɪnš-um-če-t̄-ik

The generic orientation is particularly important for the localizations IN and INTER, which for many nouns are in complementary distribution. The IN localization is possible with nouns denoting objects which have a volume and are capable of serving as containers (*k'adi* 'measure for flour', *noL'* 'house', *langar* 'tray') and objects covering a delimited area (*azbar* 'yard', *harq* 'roof', *qoq* 'back, spine'), or a delimited period of time (*nuɪbžal* 'week', *ʕummar* 'life(time)'). The localization INTER combines with nouns denoting substances (*diq'* 'soup', *eɪle* 'tin', *k'un* 'flour'), unarticulated aggregates of objects (*baɪk'i* 'pile', *Lon* 'herd, flock'), and types of fruit and plants (*mač* 'nettles', *arqɪut* 'nuts'). The generic localization SUPER is found with nouns denoting flat objects (*diwin* 'carpet', *qal* 'skin', *k'os* 'knife'), objects whose surface can be utilized (*kutuk* 'stump', *qɪin* 'bridge', *L'ili* 'saddle'), external body parts (*eXI* 'cheek', *nodo* 'forehead'), areas without any natural borders (*awlaq* 'steppe', *dunil* 'sky') and abstract concepts (*oq* 'wedding', *riši* 'elections'). The localizations SUB and CONT are generally only used contextually.

The essive refers to a spatial position which is given by the corresponding localization with respect to a reference point (LOCN):

> ablative – motion out of LOCN
> lative – motion into LOCN, implying attainment of that position
> allative – motion towards LOCN, not implying attainment of that position
> terminative – motion into LOCN but no further
> translative – motion along/across LOCN.

Table 23.11   Spatial postposition paradigms

Meaning of postposition	Spatial case				
	essive	lative	ablative	allative	translative
'between'	qI'on	qI'ana-k	qI'ana-š	qI'ana-ši	qI'ana-Xut
'on'	jat	jaī-ik	——	——	jaīi-Xut
'near'	——	ł₀a-k	ł₀a-š	ł₀a-ši	ł₀a-Xut
'under'	——	L'ara-k	L'ara-š	——	L'ara-Xut
'behind'	Xir	Xara-k	Xara-š	——	Xara-Xut
'in front of'	——	hara-k	hara-š	——	hara-Xut

In addition to the synthetic spatial case forms, postpositional constructions are used with similar meaning. These are comprised of the dative case of the noun and a spatial postposition. These postpositions, too, are inflected for spatial cases;[25] see table 23.11.

(25)   mul-li-s   jat   /mul-li-t   boXI
       mountain-OBL-DAT on-ESS/mountain-OBL-SUPER.ESS goat.NOM
       ob-sdi-li   b-i.
       stand.PFTV-III-ABS III-be
       'A (Caucasian) goat is standing on the mountain.'

As can easily be seen, the locational morphemes are related in form to the roots of the postpositions, which is evidence that they originate from postpositions.

Spatial forms can also be used with non-spatial meanings, such as external cause (IN-ESS), temporary possession (CONT-LAT, CONT-ABL), time (CONT-ESS) and so on. Examples are:

(26)   jasqi zon   Ler-kul-l-a   baIraj o-w-X-u.[26]
       today I.NOM be.hot-MASDAR-OBL-IN.ESS bathe-I-PFTV
       'Today I went for a swim because it was hot.'

(27)   to-w-mu   za-ra-š   X̄₀al-li-n   mec'e
       he-I-OBL.ERG I.OBL-CONT-ABL bread-OBL-GEN piece.NOM
       o-b-X̄a.
       take.PFTV-III
       'He took a piece of bread from me'.

In addition to this, the spatial forms can be used syntactically, by creating arguments to verbs which lexically govern those cases. For instance, the following verbs govern the super-essive: *ʃejb i* 'be guilty (subj.)', *qIes* 'ride (dir. obj.)', *L'ili elas* 'saddle (dir. obj.)', *wiX* 'believe (dir. obj.)', *šak* 'doubt (dir. obj.)', *mairš* 'envy (dir. obj.)'. The following govern the super-lative: *sak̄as* 'look at (something)', *oj-ačas* 'hear (dir. obj.)'; the sub-ablative: *L'inč'ar* 'be afraid of (something)', *Xustar-as* 'save (from something)'; the cont-allative: *barka-bos* 'congratulate (dir. obj.)', *k̥ač'et-bos* 'tell lies (to somebody)'.

2.4 The possessive locative

There is a highly idiosyncratic form in which the genitive form of an animate noun X combines with the locational *-ma* (cf. the identical temporal gerundive marker) to give the meaning 'region in space where X lives'. For instance, the noun *dos* 'friend' (genitive *dos-li-n*) gives the spatial case forms:

ESSIVE:	dos-li-m-ma	'at a friend's house, where a friend lives'
LATIVE:	dos-li-m-ma-k	'to a friend's house, to where a friend lives'
ABLATIVE:	dos-li-m-ma-š	'from a friend's house, from where a friend lives'

3 Conclusions

Our examination of the verbal and nominal paradigms has shown that the astronomically large number of forms does not mean that the morphology of Archi is unduly complex. The forms are not so much stored in the speaker's memory, as derived by fairly simple rules: each slot in the paradigm is the conjunction of the meanings of all the grammatical categories compatible with words of that part of speech.[27] Moreover, the co-occurrence restrictions on the meanings of categories are minimal, and, in general, are motivated semantically (which means that they, too, do not need to be memorized). At the same time, the rather large repertoire of grammatical categories themselves, many of which are, in addition, formally complex, affords the native speaker the opportunity to categorize reality in an extremely subtle fashion, using maximally simple (grammatical) means.

Furthermore, the question of simplicity/complexity must be viewed in relation to the structure of the language as a whole, not to specific levels. Thus, productive deverbal derivation (the masdars, participles and gerunds) facilitate a significant minimization of syntactical devices: clauses are embedded in NP-, AdjP- and AdvP- positions morphologically, by the nominalization, adjectivization or adverbialization of the head of the clause, its verb.[28] A similar picture is found with the functions of the spatial forms of nouns.

Abbreviations

ADJZR	adjectivizer
ADM	admirative

APPR	approbative mood
CNM	class-number marker
COMIT	comitative case
COMM	commentative
COMP	comparative case
CONJ	conjunctive mood
CONST	constative tense-aspect
CONT	'near'-localization
CONTIN	continous aspect
DEB	debitive mood
DIRSTEM	direct stem
DUB	dubitative mood
EQU	equative
ESS	essive case
FIN	finalis aspect
IMP	imperative mood
IN	'in'-localization
INCEP	inceptive tense-aspect
INFER	inferentiality
INTER	'between'-localization
INTERR	interrogative mood
LAT	lative case
LOCN	localization
NEU	neutral tense
OBL	oblique stem/case
OBLSTEM	oblique stem
OPT	optative mood
PART	partitive
PAST	past tense
PERF	perfect tense-aspect
PERM	permutative
PFTV	perfective aspect
POT	potential aspect
PROH	prohibitive mood
SUB	'under'-localization
SUPER	'over'-localization
TERM	terminative case

NOTES

1 Translator's note: I have retained Prof. Kibrik's transcriptions by and large, in order to facilitate comparison with other publications. His transcriptional conventions are as follows (IPA equivalents, where appropriate, are given in square brackets):

L   voiceless lateral affricate [tɬ]
ł   voiceless lateral fricative [ɬ]
X   voiceless uvular fricative [χ]

R   voiced uvular fricative [ʁ]
H   voiceless emphatic laryngeal [ħ]
ʕ   voiced emphatic laryngeal [ʕ]
ə   schwa [ə]
ŧ   fortis consonant
t'   ejective consonant [t']
t₀   labialized consonant [tʷ]
tI   pharyngealized consonant [tˤ]
aI   pharyngealized vowel [a]
a: long vowel [a:]

See also the main list of abbreviations at the beginning of this volume.

2   The aspect stem is identical to the tense-aspect form of the constative. Similarly, other aspect forms correspond to tense-aspect forms of the aorist, the future or the infinitive. See below.

3   a → o before w.

4   It is also possible to regard the analytic tense forms in the final as derived directly from the infinitive.

5   In conjunction with the perfective it has the meaning 'the result of event P continues to take place at the time of utterance'.

6   This is derived historically from *i* 'be' and *ker* 'become'.

7   Here and elsewhere SG is not specifically indicated.

8   In analytic forms of the verb a double nominative construction is possible, in which the lexical verb agrees with the patient and the auxiliary agrees with the agent.

9   The perfective is formed irregularly.

10   *t'al=as* 'send' is a complex verb with an adverbial component, *t'al* of unknown historical origin and a finite component *as* 'do, make'.

11   The verb 'to go, leave' with the irregular aspectual forms *qIe-s* 'FIN' – *oqIa* 'PFTV' – *XaŧI* 'POT'. The form *uqIa* derives from **o-w-qIa*.

12   Analytic form of the past debitive. The class-number prefix is given an epenthetic vowel, *-ba-*, because the root begins with a consonant.

13   The future *uqi* is derived from **a-u-qi*.

14   Special nominal form from personal nouns meaning 'region in space where the given person lives'; see section 2.4.

15   At the same time analytic forms of the present tense do not have the auxiliary verb *i* 'be', and forms of the neutral tense add the corresponding absolutive marker: i.e. the present and neutral tense coincide formally. Thus, from *wirX̄₀in*, CONST and *wirX̄₀inši wi*, PRES-I, the possibilitive takes the form *wirX̄₀inši X̄uqi*. In a number of cases (though by no means all!) the possibilitive coincides in shape with the admirative, but the constructions differ syntactically, since the admirative takes a Dative marked complement.

16   The controller for number agreement is the 2 pl. pronoun, which requires a zero formative (as does the 1 pl. pronoun); see n. 21.

17   The marker *-t'i* combines with complex verbs whose inflecting component is *-bos*, lit. 'to speak'.

18   This verb does not inflect for class.

19   The Daghestanian languages generally have a tendency to express co-ordinate relations by means of subordination. For this reason, the use of the Archi absolutive is wider than that of the gerund in European languages such as Russian: there is no co-referentiality constraint between the subjects of the matrix and embedded clauses, and, indeed, there need be no co-reference at all.

20   The class-number suffixes don't in general correspond to the verb prefixes/infixes inherited from the verb, since their controllers are different.

21   Classes are distinguished by agreement rules (on class-number markers, see above). Minor classes are generally not distinguished, though their behaviour in the plural is markedly different from that of the basic classes. The minor classes are semantically homogeneous. Firstly, two classes (V and VI) make up the first- and second-person masculine and feminine pronouns. In distinction to the nouns of classes I, II, which also denote male and female persons, these have a null marker for the plural rather than -*b*-, the usual marker for people. Class VII includes collective nouns for people. Unlike class III (with which class VII coincides in the singular), this class takes the marker -*b*- in the plural (which is characteristic of personal nouns, cf. classes I, II). Nouns in class VIII behave similarly. They denote people undifferentiated for sex (*lo* 'child', *adam* 'person'): in the singular they correspond to nouns in class IV (inanimates), while in the plural they correspond to personal nouns of classes I, II (marker -*b*-). Agreement for plural number with nouns from classes VII, VIII is semantically based, though there is no synchronic justification for the 'impersonal' agreements of the pronouns *nen* 'we' and *ž*₀*en* 'you (pl.)'. This phenomenon remains unexplained.

22   In fact a significant proportion of nouns form their plurals and oblique stems irregularly; see Kibrik and Kodzasov 1990: 283.

23   A verb with partial reduplication of the root.

24   On the null marker for Classes V, VI, see n. 21. This verb forms its perfect suppletively.

25   This fact, as well as the fact that spatial adverbs and locative gerunds (see above) also inflect for spatial cases, is evidence that this construction is common to a number of parts of speech, if we consider the spatial forms as entering into a single nominal paradigm. We might suppose that these forms (at least historically) are adverbial representations of the noun, where location fulfils the function of adverbial derivation. In that case, the spatial cases would characterize only the spatial adverbials. On the other hand, this interpretation is contradicted by situations in which the spatial forms are used as syntactic cases (see below).

26   Complex verb: *balraj aXas* 'to bathe', lit. 'lie down in a lake'.

27   In this connection, the following psychological fact is not without interest. When a native speaker is presented with a fairly cumbersome verb form, which fills 'exotic' slots in the paradigm, he will often deny that such a form is possible at first (since there is no such pre-compiled combination of category meanings in his memory), but then will radically change his grammaticality judgement: 'You can say that in such-and-such a context.' In other words, the verb paradigm is stored in the memory of an Archi speaker in a fundamentally different way from that in which a paradigm is stored in the memory of a Russian speaker, or, especially, an English speaker: viz. in the form of a deductive procedure, not as a fixed form.

28   To this one might add the semantic content of the grammatical cases, in that they code semantic roles (Factitive, Agent, Addressee, Instrument, Cause, Place, etc.), not syntactic relations (subject, direct object, indirect object); see Kibrik 1979a, 1991b. This, too, simplifies the syntax.

24   Celtic (Indo-European)

JAMES FIFE AND GARETH KING

1 Introduction

The Celtic languages, consisting of the Goidelic languages (Irish, Scots Gaelic and Manx) and the Brythonic languages (Welsh, Breton and Cornish), form a separate branch of the Indo-European family, though they are sometimes claimed to have special affinities with the Italic branch.

The Celtic languages present on the one hand examples of some very typical Indo-European morphological devices, particularly in the older forms of Celtic, like Gaulish and Old Irish. There we find many similarities in the format and meaning of complex declensions and conjugations reminiscent of Latin, Greek or Sanskrit. On the other hand, Celtic possesses a number of unusual morphological patterns which are so striking as to have prompted some linguists to posit profound substrate influences from languages such as Basque or Berber. For specific description of the languages comprising the family and their current status, see Ball and Fife (eds) 1993.

In this chapter we describe and illustrate some of the morphological devices of the Celtic languages which are typical of the family, but at the same time, rare or unique within Indo-European, or universally. Readers interested in the Indo-European morphological archetype should consult one of the handbooks on the subject (e.g. Lehmann 1993).

The discussion turns first to features which are shared by both branches of Celtic, followed by an examination of some more particular or typical to one branch.[1]

2 Common morphological features

The Celtic languages naturally have many morphological and other features which they share amongst themselves and with other branches of Indo-European.

But some of these stand out as typical for Celtic either in their uniqueness or in their degree of employment. We will discuss four such features below: mutation, conjugated prepositions, ablaut and determiner clitics.

2.1 *Mutation*

The system of mutation is perhaps the Celtic morphological trait *par excellence*. The term refers to a system of alternation to certain phonemes of a word in order to reflect grammatical information or function. Mutations are, as it were, a type of 'consonantal ablaut', by which consonants have different 'degrees' or manifestations which are exponents of certain grammatical categories.

Celtic has an intricate and active system of initial mutations. As the name implies, these involve a gradation to the initial phoneme of the word as a reflection of grammatical categories. The grammatical categories for which mutation is an (at least partial) exponent are central and ubiquitous in the languages: gender, case, objecthood, negation, person/number, relativization, subordination, tense/mood and word classes. In all these instances, Celtic languages use an alternation to the initial phoneme to express the relevant distinctions.

Turning first to the phonological side of the mutations, the alternations are simple and systematic. So much so that linguists have been tempted to treat them as a regular phonological rule. But the lack of any credible, consistent phonological trigger(s) forecloses this approach: mutations are assuredly morphosyntactic in nature (see Ball and Müller 1992 for further discussion of this point). It appears, however, that the mutations originally arose as a phonological sandhi phenomenon which eventually became thoroughly grammaticalized.

The phonological core of the system in both branches affects mostly the stop consonants, whereby the voiceless stops become either voiced or spirantized, and the voiced stops become either spirantized or nasalized. The languages divide up these basic processes in different ways, combining them variously or keeping them as separate mutations. For instance, in Irish there are two consonantal alternations which function as single grammatical units: one called 'Lenition' and another called 'Eclipsis'. The first of these mutations consists of the spirantizing effect, while the second combines the voicing and nasalizing effects. By way of contrast, Welsh can be described as consisting of three mutations: Soft (voicing and spirantizing), Spirant and Nasal mutations. Thus the two languages, while constructing their mutations from similar processes, combine them in different grammatical units. The languages also differ in the range of processes utilized: the nasal component is non-existent or sporadic in Cornish and Breton, but has developed differently in Scots Gaelic from Irish and Welsh. Many low-level variations are also manifest across the Celtic languages. However, the effects are fairly consistent, as can be seen from the diagrammatic presentation in (1) and (2) below.[2]

(1) Phonological components
    (a) [+voice]
    (b) [+continuant]
    (c) [+nasal]

(2) Combinations of components
    Irish, Scots Gaelic and Manx: Lenition (1b)
                                              Eclipsis (1a) + (1c)

    Welsh: Soft (1a) + (1b)
               Spirant (1b)
               Nasal (1c)
    Breton: Lenition (1a) + (1b)
               Spirant (1b)/(1a)
               Mixed (1a) + (1b)
    . Cornish: Lenition (1a) + (1b)
               Spirant (1b)

    The Goidelic languages are most consistent in having the same combination of the three components. In Brythonic, there is a basic voicing/spirantizing rule and a spirantizing rule (confined mostly to voiceless stops); only Welsh retains a true Nasal Mutation.

    To illustrate these changes as a system, the alternations for each mutation in Irish and Welsh are laid out in (3) and (4) below in orthographic and phonetic notation. Cf. (2).

(3) Irish
    Lenition
    p [p] → ph [f]   b [b] → bh [v]/[w]
    t [t] → th [h]   d [d] → dh [j]/[ɣ]
    c [k] → ch [x]   g [g] → gh [j]/[ɣ]

    m [m] → [v]/[w]   s [s] → sh [h]

    Eclipsis
    p → bp [b]   b → mb [m]
    t → dt [d]   d → nd [n]
    c → gc [g]   g → ng [ŋ]

(4) Welsh
    Soft Mutation
    p → b [b]   b → f [v]
    t → d [d]   d → dd [ð]
    c → g [g]   g → Ø

    m → f [v]   ll [ɬ] → l [l]   rh [r̥] → r [r]

Spirant Mutation
p → ph [f]
t → th [θ]
c → ch [x]

Nasal Mutation

p → mh [m̥]	b → m	
t → nh [n̥]	d → n	
c → ngh [ŋ̊]	g → ng [ŋ]	

(The alternates in the Irish Lenition are palatal vs non-palatal variants.) Thus the Irish word *caora* 'sheep' will, in certain grammatical contexts, also appear as *chaora* or as *gcaora*; likewise, Welsh *pen* 'head' will occur in context also as *ben*, *phen* and *mhen*.

It is apparent that there is significant congruence between the two branches of Celtic as regards the phonological effects of mutation. The morphosyntactic environments where the mutations appear are also similar across the family. While there are of course some uses of mutation particular to some languages, there are a number of triggers which are universal, or nearly so.

One of the most consistent instances of mutation is as a marker of gender, usually feminine gender. In all Celtic languages, it is a rule that feminine singular nouns are mutated following an article. Taking Irish and Welsh as examples, the nouns listed in (5a) and (5b) are grammatically feminine, as indicated in part by their mutating (Lenition in Irish, Soft Mutation in Welsh) following the definite (nominative) article in (5c) and (5d).

(5) (a) Irish: *bean* 'woman', *cearc* 'hen', *gealt* 'lunatic'
     (b) Welsh: *pont* 'bridge', *taith* 'trip', *desg* 'desk', *man* 'place'
     (c) *an bhean* 'the woman', *an chearc* 'the hen', *an ghealt* 'the lunatic'
     (d) *y bont* 'the bridge', *y daith* 'the trip', *y ddesg* 'the desk', *y fan* 'the man'

In a like fashion, feminine gender is also indicated by using the same mutation on adjectives following feminine nouns. Thus, just as a feminine noun mutates after the article, any adjective modifying a feminine noun takes mutation. Consider the examples from Breton in (6), using the feminine noun *merc'h* 'girl'.

(6) (a) *bras* 'big', *kentañ* 'first', *gwelloc'h* 'better', *plijus* 'pleasant', *trist* 'sad'
     (b) *ur verc'h vras* 'a big girl', *ar verc'h gentañ* 'the first girl', *ur verc'h welloc'h* 'the first girl', *ur verc'h blijus* 'the pleasant girl', *ur verc'h drist* 'the sad girl'

Another area where mutations apply universally in Celtic languages is in distinguishing person/number in possessive pronouns. Look at the systems in Irish and Welsh as examples:

(7)

	Welsh	Irish	
1SG	fy	mo	'my'
2SG	dy	do	'thy'
3SGMASC	ei	a	'his'
3SGFEM	ei	a	'her'
1PL	ein	ár	'our'
2PL	eich	bhur	'your'
3PL	eu	a	'their'

Each of these pronouns has a mutation effect associated with it which aids in distinguishing the possessor-antecedent. The mutation for each slot is given below:

(8)

	Welsh	Irish
1SG	Nasal	Lenition
2SG	Soft	Lenition
3SGMASC	Soft	Lenition
3SGFEM	Spirant	No mutation
1PL	No mutation	Eclipsis
2PL	No mutation	Eclipsis
3PL	No mutation	Eclipsis

Thus, overall, the singulars are distinguished from the plurals in each language by the fact that the singulars all use some form of mutation in Welsh and the plurals do not, while the plurals all use Eclipsis in Irish. This is especially important in the case of the third-person pronouns (in Welsh, despite the orthography in (7), the masculine and feminine singular and the plural are pronounced identically: [i]). Note then that the use of mutation is crucial in distinguishing which person is meant to be the possessor: it is precisely the mutation which disambiguates the forms in (9).

(9) (a) Irish: *teach*, Welsh: *tŷ* 'house'

  (b) *a theach* [ə h'ax] 'his house'
  a teach [ə t'ax] 'her house'
  a dteach [ə d'ax] 'their house'

  (c) *ei dŷ* [i di] 'his house'
  ei thŷ [i θi] 'her house'
  eu tŷ [i ti] 'their house'

This example shows the semiological centrality and importance of the mutation process to the Celtic languages.

Mutations are also found in uses analogous to case marking in other languages, for instance, in languages such as German or Russian, where different prepositions govern different cases. In the Celtic languages, the class of prepositions can be divided into different groups which reflect different mutation behaviours. All Celtic languages distinguish at a minimum a set of mutating prepositions from a set that does not mutate. In Breton, the prepositions *da* 'to' and *war* 'on' cause Lenition to the following noun: *da Vrest* 'to Brest'; however, the preposition *goude* 'after' does not mutate its object: *goude bloazh* 'after a year'. But in some languages the distinction is quite involved, as in Scots Gaelic and Welsh, leading to multiple classifications based on the available mutations: Scots Gaelic has eclipsing, leniting and non-mutating groups of prepositions; Welsh has leniting, spirantizing, nasalizing and non-mutating subclasses.

Another instance of case-like use of mutation is found in Welsh, where the object of an inflected verb occurs with Soft Mutation.

(10) (a) *ci* 'dog'

      (b) Gwelais gi neithiwr.
           saw-1SG dog last.night
           'I saw a dog last night.'

However, mutation does not occur everywhere we might expect accusative case marking (e.g. if the object noun phrase is topicalized), so the analogy to inflected case is not complete. But as regards the fundamental task of marking the transitive object in canonical cases, the Welsh object mutation acts in a way parallel to an objective case marking.

Mutation in verbs is also quite common. Mostly this is due to association with certain preverbal particles or complementizers. As with the possessive pronouns, in some cases these particles/complementizers are distinguished precisely by their mutation behaviour. So in literary Welsh we find an affirmative particle *fe* which causes Soft Mutation (11a), an interrogative particle *a* which likewise causes Soft Mutation (11b) and a negative particle *ni* which causes a mixed effect combining lenition and spirantization (11c). In spoken Welsh, the latter two particles do not appear, though their mutation effects remain. The examples use the verb *clywed* 'to hear'.

(11) (a) Fe   glywais gi neithiwr.
           AFFPRT heard.1SG dog last.night
           'I heard a dog last night.'

      (b) A   glywais gi neithiwr?
           INTPRT heard.1SG dog last.night
           'Did I hear a dog last night?'

      (c) Ni   chlywais gi neithiwr.
           NEGPRT heard.1SG dog last.night
           'I didn't hear a dog last night.'

Likewise in Irish, there are two relative/subordinating particles/comple-
mentizers. One is used when the antecedent is a direct relation in the relative
clause: that is, the subject or direct object. The other particle is used when the
antecedent is any other verbal argument or oblique case nominal: for example,
an adverb. Both of these particles are written *a* and are pronounced the same:
[ə]. Their important syntactic difference is conveyed totally by the difference
in mutation effects: the first particle uses Lenition and the second Eclipsis.
Consider (12), using *beidh* the future form of 'to be'.

(12) (a)   Sin é an fear a   bheidh anseo.
            this he the man DREL will.be here
            'This is the man who will be here.'

      (b)   Sin é an áit   a   mbeidh an fear ann.
            this he the place OREL will.be   the man there
            'This is the place the man will be.'

Adverbs too are subject to mutation effects. There is evidence, for instance,
that mutation is used as an indication of the class of adverbs, as when prepositions are mutated to mark their adverbial use. For example, the Welsh preposition *tros* 'over' is used adverbially in the form *drosodd*. Adverbs in any case
tend to become permanently marked with mutation. In Irish there are numerous root adverbs bearing Lenition: *thuas* 'above', *dháiríre* 'seriously', *choíchin*
'never', etc.

Mutation is an active part of derivational morphology. Whole classes of
compounds are distinguishable by their mutation behaviour, and sometimes
otherwise homophonous affixes are differentiated by their mutations. In Welsh
the group of forms called Proper Compounds differs from the Improper Compounds in that the former exhibit mutation, while the latter do not: *llaw* 'hand'
+ *morwyn* 'maid' → *llawforwyn* 'handmaiden' [proper] :: *gŵr* 'man' + *cath* 'cat'
→ *gwrcath* 'tomcat' [improper].

This brief sample of some of the common uses of mutation in Celtic gives
an idea of the pervasiveness and importance of the system of mutations in this
family. It is one of the most central and distinctive morphological traits of the
Celtic languages.

2.2 Conjugated prepositions

All Celtic languages share a morphological phenomenon virtually unique in
Indo-European, whereby pronouns used in conjunction with most simple prepositions appear as verb-like desinences. The Afro-Asiatic languages show
unexplained similarities in this regard. Morphologically, the structure of conjugated prepositions differs somewhat between Brythonic and Goidelic.

Of all the Celtic languages, modern spoken Welsh presents the most transparent conjugation pattern for prepositions. Although there is considerable formal variation, an underlying structure can be identified:

[preposition] + [(interposed element)] + [pronoun desinence]

The final desinences, with certain scope for vowel variation depending on the dialect, are:

(13)		SG	PL
1	*-a (i)*	*-on (ni)*
2	*-at (ti)*	*-och (chi)*
3MASC	*-o (fe)*	*-yn (nhw)*
3FEM	*-i (hi)*

Note the pronouns in parentheses: in spoken Welsh they are almost invariably used, except for 3 SG MASC and FEM, which are frequently omitted where context precludes ambiguity. Dialect variation gives different vowel quality to some persons, notably *-o-* for 1 and 2 SG, and conversely *-a-* for 1 and 2 PL.

With some prepositions, these desinences are added directly to the preposition: *wrth* 'by, to' – *wrtha i, wrthat ti, wrtho fe*, etc. With others, a consonantal element is interposed: *ar* 'on' – *arna i, arnat ti, arno fe*, etc. In some cases an entire extra syllable is interposed: *am* 'for, about' – *amdana i, amdanat ti, amdano fe*, etc. Note that in all cases the interposed element is invariable for person. In a few cases, the vowel of the preposition is changed with conjugation: *rhwng* 'between' – *rhyngddyn nhw* 'between them'. One preposition, *i* 'to, for', is anomalous, with the interposed element occurring in the third person only: *iddo fe* 'to him', but *i chi* 'to you'. Finally, a small number of prepositions do not conjugate at all, and are followed by the base form of the pronouns alone: e.g. *gyda* 'with' – *gyda fi, gyda ti, gyda fe*, etc. Welsh conjugated prepositions are examined in detail in G. King 1993.

Goidelic exhibits a broadly similar principle, though generally without the interposed consonant or syllable usually seen in Brythonic, and with the desinence alone indicating person – so Scots Gaelic *aig* 'at, with' + *mi* (1 SG) gives *agam*. But as in Brythonic there is a more obvious morphological relationship between desinences and their corresponding pronouns in the first and second persons than in the third person. Compare for Scots Gaelic:

(14)			desinences	pronouns
SG		1	*-m*	*mi*
	2	*-d/-t*	*t(h)u*
PL		1	*-(i)nn*	*sinn*
	2	*-(i)bh*	*sibh*

The third-person forms for most prepositions, on the other hand, are difficult to predict and harder to analyse: e.g. *air* 'on', 3 SG MASC *air*; *do* 'to', 3 PL *dhaibh*; *ann* 'in', 3 SGFEM *innte*. (The 3 SGFEM, however, is nearly always characterized by palatal articulation.) Indeed, for conjugated prepositions generally, Goidelic presents a far less regularized and more opaque morphological pattern than is found in Brythonic. Scots Gaelic prepositions *aig* 'at, with', *air* 'on', *bho* 'from', *do* 'to', *le* 'with', *mu* 'about' conjugate as follows:

(15) SG 1

(15)	SG	1	*agam*	*orm*	*bhuam*	*dhomh*	*leam*	*umam*
		2	*agat*	*ort*	*bhua(i)t*	*dhuit*	*leat*	*umad*
		3 MASC	*aige*	*air*	*bhuaithe*	*dha*	*leis*	*uime*
		3 FEM	*aice*	*oirre*	*bhuaipe*	*dhi*	*leatha*	*uimpe*
	PL	1	*againn*	*oirnn*	*bhuainn*	*dhuinn*	*leinn*	*umainn*
		2	*agaibh*	*oirbh*	*bhuaibh*	*dhuibh*	*leibh*	*umaibh*
		3	*aca*	*orra*	*bhuapa/ bhuatha*	*dhaibh*	*leotha/leo*	*umpa*

Note that the components of the conjugated prepositions in Goidelic are noticeably more 'fused' together or 'compacted' than is the case in Brythonic with its more readily segmentable formations described above, and this shows itself in greater distortion of the original elements.

2.3 *Ablaut (vowel gradation)*

Alongside their frequent use of mutations of consonants, Celtic languages also make extensive use of vowel gradations in their morphology. Between ablaut and mutation, Celtic appears to have a special penchant for morphological devices manifested on the subsegmental level – that is, through alteration of the stem rather than by addition of new morphs. Unlike mutations, however, the use of vowel gradation is not so unique, as it is also found elsewhere in Indo-European and other languages. Though not unusually Celtic, ablaut is still a major morphological device in these languages.

In talking about vowel gradation as part of a language's morphology, we are referring to the *synchronic* use of internal vowel changes as part of grammatical processes. Historically these alternations arose from a number of different phonological sources; they are not all vestiges of the proto-Indo-European system of ablaut *per se*.[3]

Examples of vowel gradations in Celtic are found frequently in the formation of noun plurals, as in Irish *ceann* 'head', pl. *cinn*, *fear* 'man', pl. *fir*, *muir* 'sea', pl. *mara*; Welsh *tŷ* 'house', pl. *tai*, and *car* 'car', pl. *ceir* (the last example showing that this is a productive device); Breton *ezel* 'member', pl. *izili*, and *dant* 'tooth', pl. *dent*.

In Irish the same device is used to reflect case: *cinn*, *fir* and *mara* are also the genitive singular forms of the nouns *ceann*, *fear* and *muir*.

Welsh has no case, but it uses ablaut to distinguish gender in determiners, as with the feminine and masculine forms for 'two' (*dwy* / *dau*) and 'this' (*hon* / *hwn*). Welsh also uses ablaut to reflect gender in adjectives: *dwfn* 'deep (masc.)' :: *dofn* 'deep (fem.)'; *bychan* 'small (masc.)' :: *bechan* 'small (fem.)'; *syml* 'simple (masc.)' :: *seml* 'simple (fem.)' Also in adjectives, Welsh manifests plurality fully or partially by vowel changes (in speech these are now used mostly as nominalizations): *tlawd* 'poor', pl. *tlodion*; *gwag* 'empty', pl. *gweigion*; *marw* 'dead', pl. *meirw*; *cadarn* 'strong', pl. *cedyrn*.

Literary Welsh has examples of vowel alternations taking part in the verbal paradigm. In some cases, as with the second-person plural future, the rule is universal (given an appropriate stem vowel): for example, *canu* 'to sing' :: *cenwch* 'you will sing'. However, ablaut is also used in certain cases to form the third-person singular present of various literary verb classes: for example, *galwaf* 'I call' :: *geilw* 'she calls'; *atebaf* 'I answer' :: *etyb* 'he answers'; *gadawaf* 'I leave' :: *geidw* 'he leaves'; *cysgaf* 'I sleep' :: *cwsg* 'she sleeps'; *profaf* 'I test' :: *prawf* 'he tests'.

2.4 Determiner clitics

'This' and 'that' (in a three-grade deictic system) are expressed in Celtic by clitics attached to the noun phrase. In all cases the definite article (W *y(r)*, Br *an*, Goidelic *an/am*) is required before the noun phrase when the determiner clitics are used, and all components of a complex noun phrase precede the clitics.

(16)		'this'	'that'	'that' (over there)

	'this'	'that'	'that' (over there)
Welsh (spoken):	*y . . . 'ma*	*y . . . 'na*	(*y . . . 'cw*)
Breton:	*an . . . -mañ*	*an . . . -se*	*an . . . -hont*
Goidelic:	*an . . . seo*	*an . . . sin*	*an . . . siud*

So, for example, Welsh:

(17)	*y lori 'ma*	'this lorry'
	y lori 'na	'that lorry'
	y lori fach 'na	'that little lorry'
	y lori fach goch 'na	'that little red lorry'.

All these clitic elements are invariable as to gender and number, and show a clear relationship to corresponding adverbs of location:

(18)	Welsh:	*yma* 'here'	*yna* 'there'	*acw* 'over there'
	Breton:	*amañ*	*aze*	*ahont*
	Irish:	*anseo*	*ansin*	*ansiúd*

Their clitic use is based on an underlying relative clause: that is, W *y llyfr 'ma* 'this book' < *y llyfr (sydd y)ma* 'the book (which is) here'.

An interesting situation exists in Welsh, where the literary construct language substitutes true demonstrative adjectives for the clitics of the spoken language (masc. in (a), fem. in (b)):

(19)			Spoken Welsh (clitics)	Literary Welsh (adjectives)
	(a)	this book	*y llyfr 'ma*	*y llyfr hwn*
		these books	*y llyfrau 'ma*	*y llyfrau hyn*
		that book	*y llyfr 'na*	*y llyfr hwnnw*
		those books	*y llyfrau 'na*	*y llyfrau hynny*
	(b)	this flag	*y faner 'ma*	*y faner hon*
		these flags	*y baneri 'ma*	*y baneri hyn*
		that flag	*y faner 'na*	*y faner honno*
		those flags	*y baneri 'na*	*y baneri hynny*

In the spoken language, the demonstrative adjectives given for literary Welsh above are used pronominally (e.g. *Beth ydy hwn?* 'What is this?'), and with minor rearrangements to accommodate non-concrete concepts. They are found in speech, however, in the pronominals *y rhain* 'these' and *y rheiny* 'those':

(20) (a)   *Faint yw'r rhain?*
            'How much are these?'

      (b)   *Gymera i'r rheiny.*
            'I'll have those'.

where *y rhain* = *y rhai hyn* 'these ones', and *y rheiny* = *y rhai hynny* 'those ones'. Yet even here it is not unusual to hear, at least for *y rheiny*, a clitic alternative *rheina* (= *y rhai 'na*): *Cymerwch reina!* 'Take those!'

3 Morphological devices in Goidelic

The features which are noteworthy particularly in the Goidelic branch of Celtic are the palatal/non-palatal opposition, verbal infixes and the pronominal supplement suffixes. In the following discussion of typically Goidelic morphological features, examples will be Scots Gaelic unless otherwise stated.

3.1 Palatal/non-palatal morphophonemic opposition

Initial consonant mutation is a phenomemon common to all the Celtic languages, and is discussed in section 2.1 above. The Goidelic languages, however, also exhibit final consonant mutation, characterized by a palatal/non-palatal opposition.

The consonant system of Old Irish was characterized, as a result of loss of non-stressed vowels, by a three-way opposition of articulation or 'quality': palatal – rounded – neutral. The quality of a consonant was determined by the type of vowel adjacent to it. *I* and *e* would palatalize an adjacent consonant, *u* would lend it a rounded articulation, and *a* and *o* would produce neither effect, leaving a neutral quality. With time, the distinction between neutral and rounded quality was lost, leaving a two-way opposition of neutral – palatal in most modern Goidelic dialects (some Irish dialects have rounded consonants, but these are a secondary development).

This two-way opposition, traditionally designated 'slender' (i.e. palatal) versus 'broad' (i.e. non-palatal), is the basis of a very rich consonantal inventory in mainstream Goidelic dialects today, reminiscent of East Slavonic languages, notably Russian, and producing in the case of Irish dialects a similar aural effect. But in Goidelic this essentially phonological opposition has been integrated into some of the most fundamental mechanisms of morphology, notably in the noun–adjective system.

The palatal/non-palatal consonant opposition is largely confined to word-final environments, with or without a following vocalic element. Hebridean Scots Gaelic exhibits a typical inventory of 'broad' and 'slender' pairs:

(21) (written)   d   t   g   c   dh/gh   ch   s   n   l   r
      broad: d   t   g   k   s   N/n   L   r
      slender: d′   t′   g′   k′   j   ç   N′   L′/l

with the remainder of the consonants lying outside this two-way system.

Orthography (both Irish and Scots Gaelic) gives the vowels a dual function: as indicators of vocalic phonemes in the normal way, but also (and this is by no means a secondary function) as indicators of consonant quality (i.e. whether the adjacent consonant is palatalized or not). In this function, as might be expected, the presence of *i* or *e* indicates a palatal consonant, with *-e* representing a following vowel. By default, the presence of any of the remaining vowels (*a, o* and *u*) indicates absence of palatal quality, and so vowels from these two groups cannot appear directly on either side of a consonant. This is the essence of the 'broad with broad, slender with slender' principle of modern Irish and Scots Gaelic orthography. So Scots Gaelic *snàthad* 'needle', gen. sg. *snàthaid* (representing phonetic [sNaːhəd], [sNaːhid′], with broad and slender *-d* respectively); *òg* 'young', comp. *òige* ([oːg], [oːg′ə]). Note that, for example, in the word *òige*, the initial vowel is the same, and the following *-i-* serves not to make a diphthong, but to show palatalization of the following *-g-*.

A number of grammatical functions make use of the broad–slender opposition, and in some cases the consonant quality determines a minimal pair. The following are examples of the main instances in modern Scots Gaelic where final consonant mutation has a morphological function. Note that it often appears in conjunction with a change of vowel.

3.1.1 Noun declension The palatal/non-palatal opposition comes into play in three main types of noun in Scots Gaelic.

(1) Masculine nouns whose base (i.e. nominative/accusative) form ends in a non-palatal consonant often palatalize to form the genitive singular:

(22) *bòrd* 'table'   *bùird* 'of a table'
cat 'cat'   *cait* 'of a cat'
each 'horse'   *eich* 'of a horse'
iasg 'fish'   *èisg* 'of a fish'
laoch 'hero'   *laoich* 'of a hero'

The palatalized form also functions as a vocative where needed, with preceding particle *a*: *Seumas* 'James', *a Sheumais!* 'James!'

(2) Feminine nouns ending in a non-palatal consonant may palatalize and add *-e* to form the genitive singular:

(23) *bròg* 'shoe'   *bròige* 'of a shoe'
bruach 'bank'   *bruaiche* 'of a bank'
muc 'pig'   *muice* 'of a pig'

This type of feminine retains the palatal consonant but drops the final *-e* to form the dative singular (used after prepositions): *leis a' bhròig* 'with the shoe'.

(3) Feminine nouns ending in a palatal consonant may depalatalize in the genitive singular and/or base plural, often in conjunction with one or more added syllables:

(24) *iuchair* 'key'   *iuchrach* 'of a key'   *iuchraichean* 'keys'
obair 'work'   *obraichean* 'works'

A few masculine nouns also depalatalize for the genitive singular and base plural, notably *athair* 'father', gen. sg. *athar*, pl. *athraichean*.

3.1.2 Comparison of the adjective The comparative/superlative (no morphological distinction in Scots Gaelic) is normally formed by palatalization + addition of *-e*:

(25) *caol* 'narrow'   *caoile* 'narrower'
òg 'young'   *òige* 'younger'
ùr 'new'   *ùire* 'newer'

and sometimes with vowel shift:

(26) *geal* 'white'   *gile* 'whiter'
gorm 'blue'   *guirme* 'bluer'
trom 'heavy'   *truime* 'heavier'

This is not a productive device, and is furthermore confined largely to monosyllables (but not exclusively – e.g. *fada* 'long', *faide*; *falamh* 'empty', *falaimhe*). In some dialects (e.g. East Sutherland) it has been almost entirely supplanted by analytic formations: for example, *nas trom* 'heavier', *as trom* 'heaviest' (Dorian 1978).

3.1.3 Formation of derived nouns
This involves mostly abstract nouns from adjectives. The final consonant is palatalized, and a vocalic element *-e* added – exactly the same principle, in fact, as to form the comparison of adjectives (see section 3.1.2 above). For example: *àrd* 'high' :: *àirde* 'height'; *geal* 'white' :: *gile* 'whiteness'. Sometimes an extra consonant intervenes between the root and the *-e*, but still with preceding palatalization: *lag* 'weak' :: *laigse* 'weakness'; *slàn* 'healthy' :: *slàinte* 'health'. This too is not a productive device, and seems largely confined to basic monosyllabic adjectives. Otherwise the termination *-achd* is the most common abstract-builder, with no effect on consonant quality.

3.1.4 Root (or stem form) of the verb
Scots Gaelic distinguishes for most verbs a verbal noun (VN), used in periphrastic constructions and as a true noun, and a verb stem, used with inflections – note that this includes a zero-desinence marking the preterite, singular imperative and dependent future. While there are many different formations for the verbal noun, a common pattern shows it with non-palatal final, and verb stem with palatal final:

(27)   VN   Stem

     ceannach(d)   *ceannaich*   'buy'
     cur   *cuir*   'put'
     falach   *falaich*   'hide'
     fuireach   *fuirich*   'wait'

This is not, however, a productive device in verb morphology, and many verbs do not make use of the broad–slender opposition in this way, or do so only in conjunction with other morphological devices, often an added syllable for the verbal noun.

The noun–adjective system of Irish dialects shows a broadly similar use of the palatal/non-palatal opposition. In some dialects, the opposition alone occasionally serves to distinguish between different persons of some inflected prepositions: for example, *thríbh* [hri:b'] 'through you (pl)' :: *thríothu* [hri:b] 'through them'. Some conservative Irish dialects use palatalization of the second consonant (or cluster) to distinguish the past autonomous/impersonal from a disyllabic VN in *-adh*. Examples from Mhac an Fhailigh 1968: VN *dúnadh* [du:nu:] 'close', past aut. *duineadh* [du:n'u:]; *losgadh* [Losgu:] 'burn', *loisgeadh* [Loʃg'u:].

3.2 Verbal infixes

Old Irish showed a propensity to verb prefixation unusual even by Indo-European standards, with semantic modification of a verbal root achieved by the addition of one or more preverbs, generally of prepositional origin; in addition, considerations of syntax as well as semantics frequently require use of an augment-like preverb *ro-*. This, in conjunction with the effects of a strong stress accent on the vowels in unstressed syllables and an orthography which, albeit unevenly, reflects this variable realization as well as internal sandhi, gives the Old Irish verbal system a complexity that defies brief summarization. Thurneysen (1970: §§512–818) and McCone (1987) give detailed treatments. As to the structural possibilities, which are of direct relevance to the question of pronoun infixation, two basic types may be identified:

(1) minimal verbs – that is, synchronically irreducible verb forms without preverbal elements: for example, (3 SG pres.) *berid* 'carries'.
(2) binary complex verbs – that is, an independent lexical unit comprising preverb + stressed main verb: for example, *as-beir* 'says' (< *as* + *berid*).

Both these types appear in two parallel conjugation patterns, depending on whether preverbs are added, since the addition of a syllable shifts the stress accent and so alters pronunciation. So, for example, the 3 SG absolute form of the minimal verb *berid* becomes *-beir* (conjunct form) when a preverb (e.g. *as-*) is added, here to form a binary complex. Binary complexes themselves appear in two conjugation patterns, depending on whether additional infixes or preverbs are used with them, so *as-béir* without further prefixation (the deuterotonic form, because the stress falls on the second syllable of the complex) becomes *-épir* (< **ess-ber*) when another preverb is added (the prototonic form).

As to the infixed elements themselves, they have two main uses:

(1) as direct object pronouns (occasionally indirect – almost always used with the verb 'be'); also used where the pronoun is the recipient of the action of a passive/autonomous verb.
(2) as subject or object relative markers.

In their basic forms, these pronouns are non-syllabic except for vocalic 3 SG MASC and NEUT (various mutation effects here omitted):

(28)

	SG	PL
1	*-m-*	*-n(n)-*
2	*-t-*	*-b-*
3 MASC	*-a-*	*-s-*
3 FEM	*-s-*	
3 NEUT	*-a-*	

These basic forms are used after preverbs and particles ending in a vowel; also occasionally where a final vowel has been lost. A series of expanded forms are used after preverbs ending in a consonant, in relative clauses and in a few other circumstances.

Examples with the 1 SG (basic) *-m-*, (expanded) *-dom-* (both causing Lenition):

(29)   *ad-cí* 'sees' :: *atom-chí* 'sees me'
     ni accai 'does not see' :: *nim accai* 'does not see me'
     ro-n-ánaic 'he reached' :: *ro-n-dom-ánaic* 'he reached me'
     intí do-eim 'he who protects' :: *intí do-dom-eim* 'he who protects me'
     for-comai 'preserve' :: *for-dom-chomaither* 'I am preserved'

The principle of infixation is so central to the verb system of Old Irish (note that the object pronouns exist only in infix or suffix form) that a technique developed for its use with minimal verbs as well. This involved a special semantically empty 'dummy' preverb *no-* used to create a binary complex suitable for infixation. For example, the use of an object pronoun (e.g. *-m-* 'me') with *fo-gaib* 'get' presents no structural problems, since this verb is a binary complex in any case: *fo-m-gaib* 'he gets me'; but 'he strikes me' requires *benaid* (conjunct *-ben*), a minimal verb which cannot of itself support an infixed pronoun, therefore *no-m-ben*. This empty *no-* is also routinely used, incidentally, with the imperfect indicative, secondary future and past subjunctive, whether an infixed pronoun is present or not.

True infixed pronouns have not survived into modern spoken Goidelic; nor have their particle-dependent counterparts in, for example, Middle Welsh. But suffixed pronouns remain in vestigial form in both branches of Celtic in the conjugated prepositions (see section 2.2 above).

3.3 Pronominal contrastive/emphatic suffixes

Irish and Scots Gaelic possess a set of enclitic particles that vary with person and are used in certain clearly defined circumstances. They convey either emphasis or contrast. Scots Gaelic forms for these suffixes are:

(30)

		SG	PL
1		*-sa*	*-ne*
2		*-sa*	*-se*
3 MASC		*-san*	*-san*
3 FEM		*-se*	

Some less conservative dialects have carried out morphological levelling and phonological simplification to various degrees, giving the allomorphs [sə] (after vowels) and [əs] (after consonants) for all persons.

The morphological environments where these clitics can be used are strictly limited. In Scots Gaelic they can be attached to (a) personal pronouns, (b) conjugated prepositions, (c) nouns preceded by possessive adjectives, and very occasionally to verb forms.

3.3.1 *With personal pronouns*

(31)

			base form	with clitic
SG	1		*mi*	*mise*
	2		*t(h)u*	*t(h)usa*
	3 MASC		*e*	*esan*
	3 FEM		*i*	*ise*
PL	1		*sinn*	*sinne*
	2		*sibh*	*sibhse*
	3		*iad*	*iadsan*

Note that 1 SG is *mise*, not **misa*. Generally, however, the clitics are invariable in Scots Gaelic, and as such are allowed to violate the general 'broad/slender' spelling convention. But some Irish dialects have allomorphs for some suffixes in conformity with the morphophonemic principle.

As well as for emphasis and contrast, the extended pronouns are especially common in copula sentences: for example, *Is mise a rinn sin* 'I (am the one who) did this'.

3.3.2 *With conjugated prepositions*
These personal forms of prepositions are characteristic of both Goidelic and Brythonic (see section 2.2 above), but in Goidelic the pronoun-type ending of the preposition in these circumstances allows the addition of the emphatic particle. So, for example:

aig 'at': 1 SG *agam* + clitic *agamsa*; 2 PL *againn* + clitic *againne*
do 'to': 1 SG *dhomh* + clitic *dhomhsa*; 3 SG FEM *dhi* + clitic *dhise*
le 'with' 1 PL *leinn* + clitic *leinne*; 3 PL *leotha* + clitic *leothasan*

(32) (a) Chan eil càil a   chuimhne <u>agamsa</u> air an fheadhainn sin.
    NEG be part its memory   with.1 SG.cl on the some   that
    'I don't remember anything at all about those.'

(b) Thoir <u>dhomhsa</u> e.
    give   to.1 SG.cl it
    'Give it to *me*.'

(c) Is <u>leinne</u>   an teilebhisean agus is <u>leothasan</u> an teip-chlàraidhear.
    be with.1PL.cl television   and   with.3PL.cl tape-recorder
    'The TV is *ours* and the tape-recorder is *theirs*.'

3.3.3 *With possessive adjectives*
Person is also implicit in the possessive adjectives, and for this reason a noun phrase comprising [possessive adj + noun (+ adjective)] can attract the emphatic clitics in Goidelic. So *làmh* 'hand' :: *do*

làmh-sa 'your hand'. In fact this straightforward usage is probably more characteristic of Irish dialects; a more complex situation exists in Scots Gaelic, where the possessive adjectives are in practice restricted to inalienable possession (kinship terms and parts of the body) and verbal nouns (see below), while being frequently supplanted in most other cases by a paraphrase involving the preposition *aig* 'at, with': so, instead of *ar baile* 'our town' we find *am baile againne*, literally 'the town with us'. But even here, note that the conjugated preposition can (and frequently does) appear with the emphatic clitic (here *-ne*).

Possessive adjectives have a further important use, in periphrastic verbal constructions of the common type: [verb 'be'] + *ag* 'at' + [verbal noun] in representing a pronoun object of the VN; and in these cases also the use of clitics is frequent. So VN *coimhead* 'watch(ing)' :: (*Bha e*) *gam choimhead-sa* '(He was) watching *me*' (*gam = ag + mo*, so lit. 'at my watching'). Similarly for other persons: for example, . . . *gar coimhead-ne* '. . . watching *us*', . . . *gan coimhead-san* '. . . watching *them*'.

The form and use of the contrastive/emphatic clitics in Irish dialects differ somewhat from Scots Gaelic:

(1)   Generally, there are more allomorphs, because the morphophonemic principle is more rigorously applied – so, for example, 1 SG *-sa* or *-se* depending on the articulation of the preceding syllable.

(2)   They may be used with synthetic verb forms: for example, *Dhéanfása praiseach de* 'You'd make a mess of it', . . . *ach táimse go maith* '. . . but *I* am well'. But synthetic verb forms are in any case more prevalent than in Scots Gaelic, which has replaced many by periphrastic constructions.

4 Morphological devices in Brythonic

We turn now to some traits characteristic of the Brythonic languages, but rarely or never found in Goidelic. The two features described are 'equative adjectives' and 'pronominal agreement clitics'.

4.1 Equative adjectives

A peculiar feature of the Celtic adjective/adverb is the appearance alongside the usual positive, comparative and superlative degrees of a form called the 'equative' degree of the adjective/adverb. Where the comparative and superlative express relative disparity in the possession of a certain quality, the equative in its main function asserts possession of an equal or comparable degree of the quality. As such, the equative forms can usually be translated 'as X [as]'.

While Irish possessed a sporadic equative inflection in its early stages (Lewis and Pedersen 1937: 182–3), it is in the Brythonic languages that we find the equative as a regular formation, where the construction has both analytic and synthetic versions.

The most widespread is the analytic formation, consisting of one of two particles before the positive form of the adjective; the particles are in Breton either *ken* or *mar*, in Cornish either *maga* or *mar*, and in Welsh either *cyn* or *mor*. The latter of each pair causes Lenition, as does Welsh *cyn*, but Breton *ken* causes no mutation, while Cornish *maga* causes hard mutation (Hemon 1975: 48; Lewis 1946: 21–2; Lewis and Pederson 1937: 183). This is the most productive form of the equative in all three languages, and is the usual form for derived or other polysyllabic adjectives/adverbs.

(33) (a)   Breton: *mat* 'good' :: *ker mat* 'as good'
       (b)   Cornish: *ker* 'dear' :: *mar ger* 'so dear'
       (c)   Welsh: *amddifad* 'destitute' :: *mor amddifad* 'so destitute'

Note that the final consonant of *ken* varies as part of a sandhi process with the following adjective in a manner similar to the forms of the article in Breton (see Hemon 1975: 48).

In some cases, however, the prefixed particle *ken / cyn* has coalesced with the adjective/adverb and formed a pseudo-prefix. Most of what would be considered irregular formations of the equative in these languages derive from this reanalysis of particle + stem. For example, the equative form of the Welsh adjective *drwg* 'bad' is *cynddrwg*. In some forms, the identity of the particle has become obscure: the equative of Welsh *hir* 'long' is *cyhyd*, using a nominal form as the stem. The obscurity in some cases led to doubling of the equative 'prefix', as in Cornish *kymmys* 'so much' occurring as *kekemys* (Lewis 1946: 21).

These instances of pseudo-prefixing are sporadic and uproductive. The equative inflectional pattern which can claim the greatest currency is one which involves suffixation of an element *-ed*, causing hard mutation (i.e. devoicing) on the last stop of the stem (usually the positive form of the adjective, though occasionally the comparative/superlative stem). This formation is not well-attested in Cornish or Breton, but is found throughout the history of Welsh. Some examples of the modern literary formation are given in (34) (see S. Williams 1959: 38–40).

(34) (a)   *byr* 'short', *dewr* 'brave', *gwlyb* 'wet', *tlawd* 'poor', *teg* 'fair', *hawdd* 'easy'
       (b)   *byrred* 'as short', *dewred* 'as brave', *gwlyped* 'as wet', *tloted* 'as poor', *teced* 'as fair', *hawsed* 'as easy'

Note the devoicing in the cases of *gwlyped*, *tloted* and *teced*. Although these adjectives/adverbs regularly form their equatives using the *-ed* suffix, they are still preceded by the particle *cyn* (also *mor* in the spoken versions). Thus, even at its greatest extent, the inflectional equative is one element of an analytic–synthetic construction, and only on rare occasions is it ever used on its own to express the equative.

This fact is no doubt related to the increasing tendency to replace the analytic–synthetic equative with the purely analytic form. As was noted, this is how Cornish and Breton have developed, and evidence tends to show that in Welsh too, except for certain common, irregular adjectives, the equative is usually formed spontaneously without any inflectional marking, using *mor* + the positive form of the adjective (see G. King 1993: 77).

4.2 Pronominal agreement clitics

We have introduced already the emphatic augments in Goidelic (section 3.3), which are partially distinctive for person and number. In Brythonic, the distinction is carried through to its logical extreme by using, in similar fashion to Goidelic, forms which appear virtually identical to the personal pronouns. Because of this, it may be more reasonable here to treat the clitic augments more as part of the agreement complex.

To see the congruence between these clitics and the independent pronouns, consider the data on the forms in Welsh and Breton given below.

(35) Independent pronouns

	Welsh	Breton
1 SG	*mi/fi*	*me*
2 SG	*ti*	*te*
3 SGMASC	*e/fe*	*eñ*
3 SGFEM	*hi*	*hi*
1 PL	*ni*	*ni*
2 PL	*chi*	*c'hwi*
3 Pl	*nhw*	*int*

(36) Agreement clitics

	Welsh	Breton
1 SG	*i/mi/fi*	*me*
2 SG	*ti/di*	*te/de*
3 SGMASC	*e/fe*	*eñ*
3 SGFEM	*hi*	*hi*
1 PL	*ni*	*ni*
2 PL	*chi*	*c'hwi/hu*
3 PL	*nhw*	*int*

The alternates given above are partly phonologically and partly dialectally conditioned. The sole significant divergence between the two sets is the fact that *i* in Welsh is found only as an agreement clitic, not as an independent pronoun. Unlike the Goidelic situation, Brythonic strongly equates the supplemental forms with the regular pronominal complex.

Despite this difference, Brythonic and Goidelic agree in broad outline on the environments where the augments are used. As in Goidelic, the agreement clitics in Brythonic occur as supplements in three main instances: with inflected verbs and prepositions and postnominally in the possessive complex. However, in Brythonic, the supplements are used far more frequently with the verb forms, but are never used to supplement other pronouns as in Goidelic (unless one were to consider the reduplicated pronouns of Welsh and Cornish as examples of this; see S. Williams 1959: 56–7; Lewis 1946: 29–30). Examples of these uses are given in (37); in each instance the clitic doubles the person and number of the inflection or possessive pronoun.

(37)　(a)　Inflected verb
　　　　　Welsh:　Wnes　　i erioed adduned.
　　　　　　　　　did-1 SG I never　vow
　　　　　　　　　'I never made a vow.'

　　　　　Breton:　Pe　laras　　eñ?
　　　　　　　　　what said-3 SG he
　　　　　　　　　'What did he say?'

　　　(b)　Inflected preposition
　　　　　Welsh:　amdanoch chi
　　　　　　　　　about.2 PL you
　　　　　　　　　'about you'

　　　　　Breton:　warnomp-ni
　　　　　　　　　on.1 PL　　we
　　　　　　　　　'on us'

　　　(c)　Nominal possession
　　　　　Welsh:　fy　ngwlad i
　　　　　　　　　my country I
　　　　　　　　　'my country'

　　　　　Breton:　ho　louzou c'hwi
　　　　　　　　　your remedy you
　　　　　　　　　'your remedy'

In (37a) the clitics *i* and *eñ* double the person and number of the endings *-es* and *-as*; in (37b) the same is true of the endings *-och* and *-omp*; in (37c) the clitics double the possessive adjectives/pronouns *fy* and *ho*.

The Brythonic forms also function similarly to the Goidelic augments: namely, for emphasis or contrast. Thus the forms in (37c) could be interpreted as '*my* country' or '*your* remedy'. However, unlike Goidelic, the Brythonic clitics have uses less informationally marked than contrast, amounting to something like 'switch reference'. That is, in Brythonic, the agreement clitics may turn up because a competing pronominal reference has occurred elsewhere in the discourse. For instance, in (38a), the use of the clitic after *brawd* does not indicate anything as strong as emphatic contrast; it simply means that the two instances of 3 SG FEM are non-co-referential. In (38b), the lack of the agreement clitic indicates the two 2 SG FEM are identical.

(38) (a) Fe   welodd hi ei brawd hi ddoe.
       PRT *saw.3 SG she her brother   yesterday*
       'She$_i$ saw her$_j$ brother yesterday.'

    (b) Fe welodd hi ei brawd ddoe.
       'She$_i$ saw her$_i$ brother yesterday.'

Thus, in Brythonic, the use of the supplemental clitic is much less marked, and the forms in (38) could occur in rather more neutral contexts than the corresponding Goidelic forms. Indeed, the de-marking of the agreement clitics has proceeded so far, particularly in Welsh, as to become the *un*marked option. This is especially the case with supplements to the verbal and prepositional inflections, the clitics being virtually obligatory in the spoken language (see G. King 1993).

Their use with the possessives is also nearly obligatory, but subject to the 'switch reference' function. For instance, the norm in spoken Welsh would be to use the agreement clitic in the possessive structure *ei gar e* in (39a), with no special emphasis or contrast. In (39b), however, we have a passive, whose structure requires that the possessor of the verbal noun *weld* be co-referential to the subject (see Fife 1992: 468–70). Accordingly, the agreement clitic is ungrammatical in (39b), since it would imply a switch in reference between the subject and the possessor.

(39) (a) Ces   i weld ei gar e ddoe.
       got-1 SG I seeing his car he yesterday
       'I got to see his car yesterday.'

    (b) Cafodd   e ei weld (*e) ddoe.
       *GOT-3 SG he his seeing (*he) yesterday*
       'He was seen yesterday.'

So natural has the use of augments become in spoken Welsh that they tend to supplant the pronouns in the possessive construction. Thus, in place of the canonical (40a), we find (40b) as an alternate (with no possessive pronoun, but just the Nasal Mutation it triggers), or even (40c), where both prenominal pronoun and mutation have been lost and only the clitic remains to mark the possession (though in this case using *fi*, which is ambiguously a clitic or independent pronoun; see A. Watkins 1976, Jones 1990, Tallerman 1991, for discussions of such forms).

(40) (a) fy nghap i
           my cap   *I*
           'my cap'

      (b) nghap i
           'my cap'

      (c) cap fi
           'my cap'

Although the version in (40c) is characteristic of child language, and would be considered substandard in adult speech, it is possibly an emergent structure, one further along in the evolution towards non-markedness for the agreement clitics. Because of such trends, the Brythonic use of these augments is starkly opposed to the informationally marked function of the comparable forms in Goidelic.

NOTES

1 It is important when discussing the Celtic languages to distinguish the spoken forms from the literary register, since in most cases the two are widely divergent (see e.g. Fife 1986). When constructions discussed here are largely confined to one form of the language, this is duly noted.

2 The loss of mutation is a common language-death phenomenon in the Celtic languages; see Dorian 1977, Dressler and Wodak-Leodolter 1977, Thomas 1984, Ball and Müller 1992. For illustration purposes, the discussion here assumes each language's mutation system in its current maximal range found in the literary language.

3 The situation is the same with regard to Modern English morphology's use of vowel alternations. Some of these arose from instances of 'true' ablaut, such as in *tell* :: *told*, but some alternations resulted from much later phonological changes which became grammaticalized, such as *man* :: *men*, which derives from a Germanic fronting (umlaut) rule triggered by a now-lost plural ending *-i̯. Some synchronic instances of vowel alternations in Celtic are likewise the result of later sound rules which have become phonologically opaque, though some represent original morphological alternations.

25 Chichewa (Bantu)

SAM A. MCHOMBO

Chichewa is a Bantu language spoken principally in the area of Africa lying in the Great Rift Valley. It is found in Malawi, where, since 1968, it has served as the national language; in Mozambique, Zambia, and Zimbabwe. Malcolm Guthrie in his classification of Bantu languages (1967–71) places this language in zone N in the unit N31. This language also goes by the name of "Chinyanja" in the region, except in Malawi, where the label "Chichewa" was adopted. In its morphological structure Chichewa is typical of the Bantu languages. It is a tone language, displaying characteristics of grammatical and lexical tone. It has the elaborate system of noun classification and the highly agglutinative and complex verbal morphology that characterize Bantu languages in general. In this chapter I will highlight some of the salient morphological aspects of Chichewa as a special case of the morphological organization of Bantu languages. Because of the immense interest that the verbal morphology holds for the description of Bantu languages, it will be useful to begin the discussion of Chichewa morphology by looking at the morphological organization of the verb.

1 The structure of the verb

The nucleus of the verbal morphology in Chichewa is the verb root or radical (VR), which supports a number of prefixes and suffixes which have different functions. In citation form every regular verb radical terminates with the suffix [a], which is referred to as the "final vowel." When it appears in a simple sentence, the VR must be prefixed with subject or person marker and tense/aspect marker. This may be illustrated by the example below:

(1)   chigawênga chi-ku-phwány-á maûngu.
       7-terrorist 7SM-pres.-smash-fv 6-pumpkins
       'The terrorist is smashing some pumpkins.'

The verb radical in this case is *phwany* 'smash', to which is attached the final vowel to create the verb *phwanya*. The subject marker *chi*, which duplicates the features of number and gender class of the noun *chigawênga* 'terrorist', which belongs to noun class 7 (see below for discussion of the noun classification system), and the tense marker *ku*, which marks present tense, are prefixed to the stem as required by the principles of sentence formation. The person markers in this language are *ndi-* (1st person sg.), *u-* (2nd sg.), *a-* (3rd sg. and pl.), *ti-* (1st pl.), and *mu-* (2nd pl.). Included in the tense–aspect markers are the following: *-ma-* (habitual or past progressive, depending on tone), *-a-* (perfective), *-na-* (past), *naa-* (remote past), *-dza-* (future). Some tense/aspect markers are realized simply by tone, as is the case with the immediate future. The simple construction given in (1) above can be expanded by the inclusion of an object marker that reflects the number and gender class features of the object noun phrase *maûngu* 'pumpkins', which belongs to noun class 6. The relevant object marker is *wa*, which is prefixed immediately before the verb stem, after the tense/aspect morpheme. This is given below:

(2)   chigawênga chi-ku-wá-phwány-a maûngu.
      7-terrorist 7SM-pres.-6OM-smash-fv 6-pumpkins
      'The terrorist is smashing them, the pumpkins.'

The presence of the subject and object markers has consequences for word order. For a start, the placement of the noun *chigawênga* in relation to the verb is free; that is, it may be either preverbal or postverbal. The noun *maûngu*, on the other hand, must occur adjacent to, and immediately after, the verb, unless the object marker (OM) is in position, in which case its position relative to the verb is free. When the subject and object markers are both present, all the various possible orderings of the words in sentence (2) yield perfectly grammatical results, and are synonymous. The results, besides the ones already given, are:

(3)   chi-ku-wá-phwány-a chigawênga maûngu
      chi-ku-wá-phwány-a maûngu chigawênga
      maûngu chi-ku-wá-phwány-a chigawênga
      maûngu chigawênga chi-ku-wá-phwány-a

The nouns *chigawênga* and *maûngu* can also be omitted without inducing ungrammaticality, as shown in (4) below:

(4)   chi-ku-wá-phwány-a.
      7SM-pres.-6OM-smash-fv
      'He (it) is smashing them.'

These facts raise a number of questions concerning the status of the subject and object markers in Chichewa and in other Bantu languages. In recent studies of Chichewa the object marker has been analyzed as an incorporated pronominal object (see Bresnan and Mchombo 1986, 1987). This explains the behavior of

the alleged object noun phrase (NP) which behaves in all relevant respects like
a topic element in the presence of the OM. This is to say that the evidence
points to its being outside the verb phrase, and it may actually be in a nonlocal
relationship to the verb. As a matter of fact, in other Bantu languages – for
example, Kikuyu – the OM and the postverbal agreeing NP do not co-occur
(cf. Bergvall 1985), suggesting that the object function is fulfilled by the OM. The
fact that the OM is in complementary distribution with the postverbal agreeing NP excludes its analysis as a grammatical agreement marker. The subject
marker (SM), on the other hand, has been analyzed by Bresnan and Mchombo
(1987) as functionally ambiguous between being a grammatical agreement
marker and an incorporated pronominal. This stems from the fact that it is
an obligatory element in the verbal morphology, which gives it the hallmarks
of agreement morphology; yet it is like a pronominal subject when the subject
NP is omitted. So far there has been hesitancy to analyze the SM simply as the
subject of the sentence. Implicit in this proposed analysis of the SM is the view
that the subject of the sentence should not be a bound morpheme. This view,
probably inspired by ideas rooted in traditional grammar, is one that could
be challenged, given the facts about Bantu languages. It appears that the SM
is analyzable as the subject of the sentence, and that perhaps it is best to so
analyze it. It does, after all, act as the relevant antecedent of the reflexive, a
typical characteristic of subject NPs. This point should perhaps be illustrated.

The reflexive in Chichewa is realized by the invariant morpheme -*dzi*-, which
appears in the OM slot. The reflexive observes the normal locality conditions
associated with bound anaphora in its binding properties: to wit, that it must
have an antecedent within the same simplex clause. The relevant antecedent
in this case is the subject of the clause. Consider the following:

(5) (a) Mkângo ú-ma-dzi-supûl-a.
          3-lion 3SM-hab.-reflex-bruise-fv
          'The lion always bruises itself.'

     (b) Mkângo u-ku-dzíw-á kutí kalú lu w-a-mv-a
          3-lion 3SM-pres.-know-fv that 1a-hare 1SM-perf.-hear-fv
          kutí ú-ma-dzi-supûl-a.
          that 3SM-hab.-reflex.-bruise-fv
          'The lion knows that the hare has heard that it bruises itself.'

In (5a) it is clear that the lion is the antecedent of the reflexive. The lion still
remains the antecedent of the reflexive in sentence (5b), despite the apparent
violation of the locality requirements. It turns out that the locality conditions
are satisifed because the reflexive is bound to the SM *u*, which, in turn, is
anaphorically linked to the NP *mkângo* 'lion'. Here is a case where the SM
is the relevant antecedent subject NP. Cases where the SM assumes the full
responsibilities of the subject NP could be readily proliferated. This seems to
suggest that the SM should be analyzed as the subject, a conclusion that Demuth

and Johnson (1989) have reached for Setswana, a Bantu language of Southern Africa. The possible extension of their proposal to Chichewa and other Bantu languages should reward investigation.

The subject and object markers and the tense/aspect marking do not exhaust the range of verbal prefixes. Negation, realized by the morpheme *si*, gets prefixed to the verb in the main clause. In a simple declarative sentence, the negative (NEG) morpheme is initial among the verbal prefixes. When the NEG is followed by a vowel, the *i* of *si* is dropped. This is illustrated by the following:

(6)   Mkângo s-ú-ku-wá-phwány-a maûngu.
      3-lion NEG-3SM-pres.-6OM-smash-fv 6-pumpkins
      'The lion is not smashing them, the pumpkins.'

The NEG is placed immediately after the SM in a subordinate clause, traditionally expressed in the subjunctive form. The subjunctive, normally signaled by the change of the final vowel to [e], can be found in sentential complementation, among other things. In this case, the NEG is realized by the morpheme *sa*. Note the following:

(7)   Kalúlú a-ku-fún-á kutí mkângo u-sa-phwány-é maûngu.
      1a-hare 1SM-pres.-want-fv that 3-lion 3SM-NEG-smash-subjun. 6-pumpkins
      'The hare wants that the lion not smash the pumpkins.'

Other elements that appear as verbal prefixes include modals – for instance, *-ngo-* 'just, merely' – as well as directional elements *-ka-* 'go' and *-dza-* 'come'. These are placed in the immediate pre-OM position, after the tense. This is shown by the following:

(8)   (a)   Mkângo s-ú-ná-ngo-wá-phwány-a maûngu . . .
            3-lion NEG-3SM-past-just-6OM-smash-fv 6-pumpkins . . .
            'The lion did not just smash them, the pumpkins . . .'

      (b)   Mkângo u-ku-ká-phwány-á máûngu.
            3-lion 3SM-pres.-go-smash-fv 6-pumpkins
            'The lion is going to smash some pumpkins.'

      (c)   Mkângo u-ku-dzá-phwány-á máûngu.
            3-lion 3SM-pres.-come-smash-fv 6-pumpkins
            'The lion is coming to smash some pumpkins.'

      (d)   Mkângo s-ú-na-ká-ngo-wá-phwány-a maûngu, . . .
            3-lion NEG-3SM-past-go-just-6OM-smash-fv 6-pumpkins . . .
            'The lion did not just go smash them, the pumpkins . . .'

Other verbal prefixes include the conditional form *-ka-* and *-sana-* 'before'. This latter induces the change of the final vowel to [e], putting it in the subjunctive. These are shown in the following:

(8) (e)   Mkângo u-ka-phwany-a maûngu, u-send-é nzímbe.
          3-lion 3SM-cond.-smash-fv 6-pumpkins, 3SM-peel-subjun. 9-sugar cane
          'If (when) the lion smashes pumpkins, it should peel the sugar cane.'

     (f)   Mkângo ú-sána-phwány-é maûngu u-b-é nzímbe.
          3-lion 3SM-before-smash-subjun. 6-pumpkins 3SM-steal-subjun. 9-sugar cane
          'Before the lion smashes pumpkins, it should steal the sugar cane.'

The conditional -*ka*- which, besides its position relative to the tense/aspect marker, is also tonally different from the directional -*ka*-, normally comes immediately after the SM and precedes the tense/aspect marker. The following illustrate this observation:

(8) (g)   Mkângo ú-ka-na-phwány-á maûngu, u-ka-ná-wá-dy-a.
          3-lion 3SM-cond.-past-smash-fv 6-pumpkins, 3SM-cond.-past-6OM-eat-fv
          'If the lion had smashed the pumpkins, it would have eaten them.'

These facts provide some insight into the functions of verbal prefixes in the Chichewa verbal morphology.

2 Suffixes

Perhaps the most engaging aspect of Bantu verbal morphology lies in the verbal suffixes. The suffixes, also known as "extensions" in Bantu linguistics, affect the number of NPs that the verb can "support" in the syntactic configuration. The suffixes can be conveniently subdivided into three groups: those which increase by one the number of NPs that can appear in the sentence, those which reduce by one the number of NPs the suffixed or extended verb can support, and those which do not alter the array of NPs. In correlation with these functions Guthrie (1962) classifies the extensions as O+, O−, and neutral (where O is really for 'object'). Typical examples of the O+ extensions are the causative and the applicative morphemes; the O− extensions are typified by the stative, the passive, and the reciprocal morphemes, and the neutral is shown by the reversive. The suffixes constitute argument-structure-changing morphology, and mark the verbal suffix domain as that of morphological processes which have functional unity. The extensions will be reviewed in the order given.

2.1 The causative

Causativization has received a lot of scholarly attention because of the range of problems associated with the description and analysis of the facts about causative constructions. The causative in Chichewa is realized by the morphs

-its- and *-ets-*, the choice of the morph being determined by vowel harmony (cf. Mtenje 1985, 1986). The causative morpheme is suffixed to the verb, with the result that there is a new NP introduced into the structure. Consider (9), which illustrates the causativization of an intransitive verb:

(9) (a) Chigawênga chi-ku-sék-a.
　　　　7-terrorist 7SM-pres.-laugh-fv
　　　　'The terrorist is laughing.'

　　(b) Kalúlú a-ku-sék-éts-a chigawênga.
　　　　1a-hare 1SM-pres.-laugh-caus.-fv 7-terrorist
　　　　'The hare is making the terrorist laugh.'

The presence of the causative suffix *-ets-* is accompanied by the introduction of a new NP *kalúlú* 'hare', into the structure, which becomes the grammatical subject. The causativization of a transitive verb is shown in (10) below, which is the causative of sentence (1) above:

(10) Mkângo u-ku-phwány-íts-a chigawéngá maûngu.
　　　3-lion 3SM-pres.-smash-caus.-fv 7-terrorist 6-pumpkins
　　　'The lion is making the terrorist smash pumpkins.'

In this sentence the presence of the suffix *-its-* is accompanied by the introduction of the NP *mkângo*. This NP would not otherwise have appeared in the construction, as shown below:

(11) *Mkango u-ku-phwany-a chigawenga maungu.
　　　**3-lion 3SM-pres.-smash-fv 7-terrorist 6-pumpkins*

The subject NP of the noncausative construction no longer appears as the subject in the causative construction. Chichewa provides two strategies for the realization of the subject of the noncausative sentence in cases where the input structure is transitive. It can appear either as the object NP, an in (10) above, or as an oblique, marked by *kwá*, as in (12) below:

(12) Mkângo u-ku-phwány-íts-a maûngu kwá chígawênga.
　　　3-lion 3SM-pres.-smash-caus.-fv 6-pumpkins by 7-terrorist
　　　'The lion is getting pumpkins smashed at the hands of (by) the terrorist.'

These two versions of the causative have semantic differences. First, when the causee surfaces as the object, the causative is "direct." In sentence (10) the lion must be making the terrorist smash the pumpkins. In sentence (12), on the other hand, the lion is merely having pumpkins smashed at the hands of the terrorist. The idea of direct force is not a necessary part of its interpretation. The causative is one of the valence-increasing operations. The other one that has received a lot of attention is the applicative.

2.2 *The applicative*

The applicative construction in Chichewa is typified by the suffixation of *-ir-* or *-er-* to the verb, which also introduces a new NP. Consider the following:

(13)   (a)   Kalúlú a-ku-phík-á maûngu.
            1a-hare 1SM-pres.-cook-fv 6-pumpkins
            'The hare is cooking pumpkins.'

       (b)   Kalúlú a-ku-phík-ír-a mkángó maûngu.
            1a-hare 1SM-pres.-cook-appl.-fv 3-lion 6-pumpkins
            'The hare is cooking (for) the lion some pumpkins.'

The most obvious difference between the causative and the applicative has to do with the semantic role and the grammatical function associated with the new NP. In causative constructions the new NP is agentive, and gets realized as the grammatical subject of the sentence. The applicative, on the other hand, introduces non-agentive NPs which are not directly associated with the subject function. In (13) above, the applied argument (NP), *mkângo*, is introduced as the direct object, and it is associated with the semantic role of beneficiary. The applicative construction is complex, in that the NP associated with the presence of the applied suffix can be associated with a number of semantic roles. We have already had an example of the benefactive-applicative, in which the applied argument is a beneficiary. The applicative is also used to introduce instrumentals as well as locatives into the range of arguments which the applicative can support. Note the following:

2.2.1 *Instrumental-applicative*

(14)   (a)   Kalúlú a-ku-phík-á maûngu ndí mkóndo.
            1a-hare 1SM-pres.-cook-fv 6-pumpkins with 3-spear
            'The hare is cooking pumpkins with (using) a spear.'

       (b)   Kalúlú a-ku-phík-íra mkôndo maûngu.
            1a-hare 1SM-pres.-cook-appl.-fv 3-spear 6-pumpkins
            'The hare is cooking pumpkins with a spear.'

In this the instrumental argument *mkóndo* behaves like the object on the applied verb *phik-ir-a*.

2.2.2 *Locative-applicative*

(15)   (a)   Kalúlú a-ku-phík-á maûngu pa chulu.
            1a-hare 1SM-pres.-cook-fv 6-pumpkins 16-on 7-anthill
            'The hare is cooking some pumpkins on the anthill.'

(b) Kalúlú a-ku-phík-ír-a pa chulu maûngu.
    1a-hare 1SM-pres.-cook-appl.-fv 16-on 7-anthill 6-pumpkins
    'The hare is cooking on anthill the pumpkins.'

In these examples the resultant sentences show some of the hallmarks of double object constructions (but see Alsina and Mchombo 1990, 1993, for important observations). The applicative is further utilized to introduce a reason or purpose NP, which has also been referred to as the "circumstantial" (cf. Hyman and Mchombo 1995). This is shown in the following sentence:

(16) Kalúlú a-ku-phík-ír-a njala maûngu.
     1a-hare 1SM-pres.-cook-appl.-fv 9-hunger 6-pumpkins
     'The hare is cooking the pumpkins for the sake of hunger.'

This sentence says that the hare is cooking the pumpkins because of hunger. There are constraints on word order in this case. The reordering of *maûngu* before *njala* yields ungrammatical results. Besides, the applied argument *njala* lacks the characteristics of a true object, according to the diagnostics given above. It cannot control the OM; neither can it be the subject under passivization. It is this ability to introduce NPs that have a wide range of semantic roles that has contributed to the interest in studies of the applicative in Bantu languages and in their relevance to matters of theoretical interest (cf. Bokamba 1976, 1981; Bresnan and Moshi 1990; Mchombo 1993).

It should be anticipated that the causative and the applicative can, and do in fact, co-occur. A particular co-occurrence restriction that Chichewa displays has to do with the ordering of the two suffixes. While applicativizing the causative is common, causativization of the applicative is rare. Consider the following:

(17) (a) Kalúlú a-ku-phík-íts-ír-a mkángó maûngu (kwá chígawênga).
         1a-hare 1SM-pres.-cook-caus.-appl.-fv 3-lion 6-pumpkins (by 7-terrorist)
         'The hare is getting pumpkins cooked for the lion (by the terrorist).'

     (b) *Kalulu a-ku-phik-ir-its-a mkango maungu.
         1a-hare 1SM-pres.-cook-appl.-caus.-fv 3-lion 6-pumpkins

There will be further comment below on constraints on verb stem morphotactics. At this juncture let us turn attention to the valence-reducing processes. These involve the passive, the stative, and the reciprocal, and they will be reviewed in that order.

2.3 *The passive*

The passive is marked by the suffix *-idw-* (and *-edw-*). It has the effect of 'demoting' the subject NP to the status of an oblique, marked as the object of the preposition *ndí*, while making the object NP the subject. The following is the passive of (13a) above:

(18)   Maûngu a-ku-phík-ídw-a (ndí kálúlú).
        6-pumpkins 6SM-pres.-cook-pass.-fv (by 1a-hare)
        'The pumpkins are being cooked (by the hare).'

The oblique NP can be omitted, as in English. The passive verb does not allow the occurrence of the OM, as shown by the following:

(19)   *Maungu a-ku-wa-phik-idw-a ndi kalulu.
        6-pumpkins 6SM-pres.-6OM-cook-pass.-fv by 1a-hare

The passive does interact with causatives and applicatives subject to a number of restrictions. For a start, the passive can apply to causative or applicative constructions, but occurrence of the causative or applicative suffixes after the passive suffix is uncommon, with minor exceptions. Thus, the following, which are the passives of the causative sentence (10) and of the applicative sentence (13b) respectively, are grammatical:

(20)   (a)   Chigawênga chi-ku-phwány-íts-idw-á maûngu (ndí mkângo).
               7-terrorist 7SM-pres.-smash-caus.-pass.-fv 6-pumpkins (by 3-lion)
               'The terrorist is made to smash pumpkins (by the lion).'

        (b)   Mkângo u-na-phík-ír-idw-á maûngu (ndí kálúlú).
               3-lion 3SM-past-cook-appl.-pass.-fv 6-pumpkins (by 1a-hare)
               'The lion was cooked pumpkins (by the hare).'

The passive can apply to causativized applicatives as well. Sentence (21) below is the passive of (17) above:

(21)   Mkângo u-ku-phík-íts-ir-idw-á maûngu (kwá chígawênga)
        3-lion 3SM-pres.-cook-caus.-appl.-pass.-fv 6-pumpkins (by 7-terrorist)
        (ndí kálúlú).
        (by 1a-hare)
        'The lion is getting pumpkins cooked for it (at the hands of the terrorist) (by (at the instigation of) the hare).'

Although the benefactive applicative can be passivized, other applicatives show some restrictions. For instance, the patient NP *maûngu* in the benefactive applicative cannot become the subject of the passive. Comparable restrictions apply to the instrumental applicative. The instrumental NP can be the subject of the passive of the instrumental applicative, but the patient NP may not. The reason applicative, on the other hand, is never passivizable. Consider the following, which is supposed to be the passive of 16 above:

(22) *Njala i-ku-phik-ir-idw-a maungu (ndi kalulu).
*9-hunger 9SM-pres.-cook-appl.-pass.-fv 6-pumpkins (by 1a-hare)

There are at least two cases where the applicative suffix may be attached to the passive. These have to do with the locative and reason applicatives. This is illustrated by the following:

(23) (a)   Maûngu a-ku-phík-ídw-ir-á njala.
          6-pumpkins 6SM-pres.-cook-pass.-appl.-fv 9-hunger
          'The pumpkins are being cooked for reasons of hunger.'

      (b)   Maûngu a-ku-phík-ídw-ir-á pa chulu.
          6-pumpkins 6SM-pres.-cook-pass.-appl.-fv 16-on 7-anthill
          'The pumpkins are being cooked on the anthill.'

The exact nature of the principles that regulate the co-occurrence restrictions among the verbal suffixes remains a topic of research interest (cf. Hyman and Mchombo 1995).

2.4 The stative

The stative suffix is signaled by the morpheme -*ik*- (and -*ek*-). It is very similar to the passive, in that it eliminates the subject NP and makes the object of the nonstative verb the subject.[1] However, this similarity between the two processes should not mask the many differences that separate them. For a start, unlike the passive, the stative does not allow the expression of the agentive NP, even as an oblique. As a matter of fact, the stative is marked semantically by the lack of any notion of agency. The stative predicates of the subject that it is in, or is entering or (has) entered, a particular state without the intervention of an agent. Consider the following:

(24)   Maûngu a-ku-phík-ík-a (*ndi kalulu).
        6-pumpkins 6SM-pres.-cook-stat.-fv (by 1a-hare)
        'The pumpkins are getting cooked (*by the hare).'

Secondly, the stative does not interact with the other suffixes as readily as the passive. For instance, statives of applicatives are not possible. Applicatives of the stative are possible, but in that case the applicative must be associated with either location, circumstantial (reason), or what may be termed the "maleficiary." This is the reading of something befalling someone. This is shown below:

(25) (a)   Maûngu a-a-phwany-ik-ir-á pa chulu.
          6-pumpkins 6SM-perf.-smash-stat.-appl.-fv 16-on 7-anthill
          'The pumpkins have got smashed on the anthill."

(b)   Maûngu a-a-phwany-ik-ir-á phûzo.
       6-pumpkins 6SM-perf.-smash-stat.-appl.-fv 5-spite
       'The pumpkins have got smashed out of spite.'

(c)   Maûngu a-a-chí-phwány-ik-ír-a (chigawênga).
       6-pumpkins 6SM-perf.-7OM-smash-stat.-appl.-fv (7-terrorist)
       'The pumpkins have got smashed on him (the terrorist).'

Thirdly, the stative differs from the passive in terms of what the semantic role of the subject NP must be. The passive can make the beneficiary, instrumental, locative, causee NPs the subject. The stative, on the other hand, appears to be confined to applying to transitive verbs which have agent and patient arguments. In other words, the subject NP in stative constructions is primarily associated with the patient role. The stative thus affects a proper subpart of the constructions that the passive applies to. The fact that the subject NP of the stative bears the patient role assimilates the construction to the unaccusativity phenomenon (cf. Mchombo 1992). In Bantu, the process of locative inversion has been analyzed as the hallmark of unaccusativity (cf. Bresnan and Kanerva 1989) exemplified in the sentence below:

(26)   Pa chulu pa-na-phwány-ídw-á máûngu.
        16-on 7-anthill 16SM-perf.-smash-pass.-fv 6-pumpkins
        'On the anthill were smashed some pumpkins.'

The stative participates in locative inversion too:

(27)   Pa chulu pa-na-phwány-ík-á máûngu.
        16-on 7-anthill 16SM-past-smash-stat.-fv 6-pumpkins
        'On the anthill got smashed some pumpkins.'

This raises the question of whether thematic information is relevant to the statement of morphotactic constraints in the verb stem. While the facts suggest that the response to this question should be in the affirmative, the issue will be left open here. Finally, we turn attention to the reciprocal.

2.5 *The reciprocal*

The reciprocal in Chichewa is marked by the suffix *-an-*. The verb appears with one NP which is plural in number. This is achieved either by having a subject NP that denotes a group or by having a coordinate structure in the subject position. Note the following:

(28)   (a)   Mikângo i-ku-phwány-an-a.
               4-lions 4SM-pres.-smash-recip.-fv
               'Lions are smashing one another.'

(b) Mbûzi ndí nkhôsa zi-ku-mény-an-a.
10-goats and 10-sheep 10SM-pres.-hit-recip.-fv
'Goats and sheep are hitting each other.'

The cases involving coordinate NPs normally introduce some problems because of the noun classification system that is characteristic of Bantu languages. In brief, the coordinate NP structure in the subject position must have an appropriate subject marker. While this is relatively easy in the example given above, because the coordinate nouns have been taken from the same class, problems arise when the nouns come from different gender classes with different number features and there is no simple strategy by which a unique SM for the coordinate structure may be determined (cf. Corbett and Mtenje 1987). In that case the strategy appealed to is that of extraposing all but the first conjunct, which then determines the shape of the SM. This yields some version of a comitative construction. Consider the following:

(29) (a) Mkango ndi kalulu ?-ku-pats-an-a mphatso.
3-lion and 1a-hare ?-pres.-give-recip.-fv 10-gifts
'The lion and the hare are giving each other gifts.'

(b) Mkângo u-ku-páts-án-a mphâtso ndí kálúlú.
3-lion 3SM-pres.-give-recip.-fv with 1a-hare
'The lion and the hare are giving each other gifts.'

In this sentence, the expression *ndí kálúlú* 'with the hare' is construed as going with the subject, *mkângo* 'lion'.

There is evidence that the reciprocal makes the verb intransitive or, at any rate, reduces by one the number of arguments the reciprocalized verb takes as its primary arguments. For instance, the reciprocalized verb cannot be passivized. Consider the following:

(30) *Mphatso i-ku-pats-an-idw-a ndi mkango ndi kalulu.
**9-gift 1SM-pres.-give-recip.-pass.-fv with 3-lion by 1a-hare*

Neither can it take the OM, which always bears the function of the direct object. This is shown in the following:

(31) *Mkango u-ku-i-pats-an-a ndi kalulu (mphatso).
**3-lion 3SM-pres.-9OM-give-recip.-fv with 1a-hare (9-gift)*

In brief, the reciprocal fails the simplest diagnostics of transitivity.

In its interaction with other suffixes, the reciprocal does not co-occur with the stative, or with the passive unless there is the intervention of the transitivizing affixes such as the applicative or the causative:

(32)   anyání a-na-mény-éts-an-í dw-a ndí míkângo.
        2-baboons 2SM-past-hit-caus.-recip.-pass.-fv by 4-lion
        'The baboons were made to hit each other by the lions.'

In its co-occurrence with the applicative (as with the causative in other languages), the reciprocal is constrained to appear after the applicative suffix, irrespective of the nature of the applicative argument. We get examples such as the following:

(33)   Mikângo í-ma-tung-ir-án-á má dzi.
        4-lions 4SM-hab.-draw-appl.-recip.-fv 6-water
        'Lions draw water for each other.'

However, note the following:

(34)   *Mikango i-ma-meny-an-ir-a pa chulu.
        **4-lions 4SM-hab.-hit-recip.-appl.-fv 16-on 7-anthill.*

Although this sentence is predicted to occur on the basis of semantic compositionality, it is bad because the reciprocal precedes the applicative. In order to meet the ordering constraints, either the appl–recip order is used, or, as in the case of the locative applicative, the reciprocal is repeated after the applicative to yield the form:

(35)   Mikângo í-ma-meny-an-ir-án-á pa chulu.
        4-lions 4SM-hab.-hit-recip.-appl.-recip.-fv 16-on 7-anthill
        'Lions hit each other on an anthill.'

The morphotactic constraints in the verb-stem suffixes seem to derive partly from syntactic/semantic considerations, where these may crucially involve thematic information, and in part from purely morphological factors, which, at this stage, are not very well understood (for some discussion see Hyman and Mchombo 1995). We will now have a look at an example of a suffix that does not alter the number of arguments.

2.6 The reversive

There is one very common suffix which does not affect the number of the arguments that the derived verb takes. This is the reversive *-ul-*, as shown in the following:

(36)   *tsek-a* 'shut'   *tsek-ul-a* 'open'
        v-al-a 'dress up'   *v-ul-a* 'undress'
        yal-a 'spread'   *yal-ul-a* 'remove something that is spread'

> *mat-a* 'stick' *mat-ul-a* 'remove something from surface'
> *mang-a* 'tie up' *mas-ul-a* 'untie'

(37) (a) Anyání a-ku-tsék-á zenêra.
       2-baboons 2SM-pres.-shut 5-window
       'The baboons are shutting the window.'

 (b) Anyání a-ku-tsék-úl-a zenêra.
       2-baboons 2SM-pres.-shut-rev.-fv 5-window
       'The baboons are opening the window.'

This suffix is no longer productive, and it appears only with a small set of verbs. In other words, it is not freely affixed to other verbs. For instance, there is the verb *kwer-a* 'climb up' whose antonym is not **kwel-ul-a*. There are even cases where it is conceivable that the *-ul-* that appears in them may have originally had to do with undoing, but where that aspect is no longer evident because the base form does not exist. These are suggested by words such as *gwed-ul-a* 'dismantle (e.g. a chair)' or *gum-ul-a* 'demolish (e.g. a building)'. There are no verbs **gwed-a* or **gum-a*.

There are other forms that may have originated as verbal suffixes: for example, *-am-*, found in some verbs which denote something about body posture or position, but which are completely unproductive in Chichewa and appear only in frozen forms. Indeed, the *-am-* suffix, sometimes referred to as the "positional extension," is found commonly in Bantu languages with a fixed set of verbal radicals that denote posture or body position. Chichewa affords such verbs as *wer-am-a* 'bend', *pol-am-a* 'stoop', *gad-am-a* 'lie on one's back', *yand-am-a* 'float', *pend-am-a* 'lean', *l-am-a* 'survive', *z-am-a* 'get stuck (e.g. a car in mud)'. This last one is tonally different from the rest, a fact that may be of some significance. There are cases where the notion of posture may be relatively abstract. Thus, there is the word *chat-am-a* 'keep quiet/shut up', which seems to be tenuously linked to this group. It probably has to do with the posture of the articulatory organs and the word *lung-am-a* 'be just', which has to do with mental disposition, rather than physical body posture. The *-am-* suffix, labeled the "stative" in past work on Bantu linguistics (cf. Dembetembe 1987, Meeussen 1967) is no longer isolable and productively attached to other verb stems in Chichewa.

3 Reduplication

One aspect of the verb stem that should be mentioned is that it is the part of the verb unit that gets reduplicated (cf. Mchombo 1991, Mtenje 1988). None of the verbal prefixes participate in this process. Thus, given an expression such as:

(38)   (a)   Anyání a-ma-mang-its-ir-án-á zisakasa kwá míkângo.
        2-baboons 2SM-hab.-build-caus.-appl.-recip.-fv 8-huts by 4-lions
        'The baboons get huts built for each other by (at the hands of) the
        lions.'

one gets the following reduplicated version to capture the idea of frequent or
repeated activity:

(b)   Anyání a-ma-[mang-its-ir-án-á]-[mang-its-ir-án-á]
        zisakasa kwá míkângo.
        'The baboons frequently get huts built for each other by the lions.'

The reduplication of the verb stem offers some evidence of the integrity of that
unit and suggests the presence of a more refined structure to the verbal morphology. The reduplication of the verb differs from that of nouns, in that in the
latter it applies to a prosodic structure. In Chichewa noun reduplication affects
only the last two syllables or the final foot of the noun (see Kanerva 1990 for
more details). This is shown in the following:

(39)   *mwamûna* 'man, male'   *mwamúnámuna* 'real or macho man'
        m-kâzi 'woman, female'   *mkázíkazi* 'cute and cultured woman'
        mu-nthu 'person'   *munthumúnthu* 'a real (humane) person'

It seems that in the case of the verb, the VR and the suffixes constitute a
prosodic unit which is also a grammatical entity and is the domain of a number
of linguistic processes. Besides the reduplication, it is the domain of vowel
harmony (cf. Kanerva 1990, Mtenje 1985) and of verb derivation (see Mchombo
1978). The verbal suffixes derive verb stems which are also the input to nominalization processes, as shown below. In many respects, derivational morphology in Chichewa is primarily suffixing, while inflectional morphology is
normally prefixal; and this holds, by and large, for nouns as well. The verb
stem is the unit that is the sister constituent to the OM, with which it forms
a higher unit which is referred to as the *macrostem* (see Hyman, in press) or
suprastem (Goldsmith and Sabimana 1985). The other prefixes are added to the
macrostem to form the larger construction. The prefixes to the verb stem appear
to fall into the category of inflectional morphemes, making the domain outside
the VS that of inflectional morphology.

4 Nominal derivation

The process of nominal derivation in Chichewa takes the verb stem as input.
The nominals are derived through the replacement of the final vowel [a]
by either [i] for agentive nouns or [o] for non-agentive nominals. Then an

appropriate gender-class prefix is added to obtain the noun. Consider the following examples:

(40) *phunzíts-a* 'teach'   *m-phunzits-i* 'teacher'
      sangalats-a 'amuse'   *m-sangalats-i* 'entertainer'
      lemb-a 'write'   *chi-lémb-o* 'script'
      tsek-a 'shut'   *chi-tsek-o* 'door'

That such nominalization takes the verb stem – that is, suffixed verbs – is readily demonstrated by the following:

(41) *kond-a* 'love'   *kond-an-a* 'love each other'   *chi-kond-an-o* 'mutual love'
      d-a 'hate'   *d-an-a* 'hate each other'   *m-d-án-i* 'enemy'
      kodz-a 'urinate' *kodz-er-a* 'urinate with'   *chi-kodz-er-o* 'bladder'
      fun-a 'want'   *fun-ir-a* 'wish for'   *chi-fun-ir-o* 'desire'

While the prefixes appear to add information concerning number and gender class, which is clearly inflectional, there are cases where they seem to straddle the border between inflection and derivation. This is to say that there are instances where the prefixes are also derivational. Consider the following:

(42) *kodz-a* 'urinate'   *m-kodz-o* 'urine'   *li-kodz-o* 'bilharzia'
      lemb-a 'write'   *m-lémbo* 'handwriting'   *chi-lémb-o* 'script'
      lang-a 'advise, punish'   *ma-lang-o* 'advice'   *chi-lang-o* 'punishment'

In these cases, the nominalizing suffix does not fully determine the meaning of the noun. Rather, the prefix plays a role in fixing the precise reading. The role of the prefix in deriving words is even more clear in the derivation of abstract nouns. Consider the modifier forms, *wisi* 'unripe', *kulu* 'big', *modzi* 'one', *kali* 'fierce'. From these the following abstract nouns are obtained through the prefixation of the class 14 marker *u*: *u-ŵisi* 'unripeness', *u-kûlu* 'magnitude', *u-môdzi* 'unity', *u-kâli* 'ferocity'. These raise questions relating to the delimitation of inflectional from derivational morphology. There is also what may be called 'manner nominalization' in Chichewa which involves the suffixation of *-idwe* or *-edwe* to the verb stem, and the prefixation of *ka* or *ma* to the result. The reading yielded is that of 'the manner of V-ing'. Note the following:

(43) *gumul-a* 'demolish'   *ka-gumul-idwe* 'the manner of demolishing'
      yendets-a 'drive'   *ka-yendets-edw-e* 'the manner of driving'
      lim-a 'cultivate'   *ma-lim-idwe* 'the manner of cultivating'

The nouns that have the *ka* prefix use the same prefix as the subject marker. Those that have the *ma* prefix pattern like class 6 nouns (see below), in that they have *a* as the subject marker. This is shown in the following:

(44) (a) Ka-gumul-idwe k-anú ká nyúmbá
      12-demolish-NOM 12SM-your 12SM-assoc. 9-house
      yá mkángo k-a-tí-khúmudwíts-a.
      9SM-assoc. 3-lion 12SM-perf.-1pl.-disappoint-fv
      'Your manner of demolishing the lion's house has disappointed us'.

    (b) Ma-lim-idwe anú á mundá wá mkángo
      6-cultivate-NOM 6SM-your 6-assoc. 3-garden 3SM-assoc. 3-lion
      a-a-tí-khúmudwíts-a.
      6SM-perf.-1st pl.-disappoint-fv
      'Your manner of tilling the lion's garden has disappointed us.'

5 Compounding

Another strategy by which nominals are derived is through compounding. The commonest form of compounding is that which takes a verb and its unmodified object noun or locative noun and creates a noun by adding an appropriate prefix. This is illustrated by the following:

(45) *ph-a dzuwa* 'kill the sun'   *ch-phadzuwa* 'beautiful woman'
      sw-a bumbu 'break vulva'   *chi-swabumbu* 'vulva-breaker (large penis)'
      tol-a nkhani 'pick up news'   *m-tolankhani* 'reporter'
      pal-a matabwa 'scrape timber'   *m-palamatabwa* 'carpenter'
      low-a m'malo 'enter in place'   *m-lowammalo* 'substitute, pronoun'
      gon-a m'bawa 'sleep in bar'   *chi-gonambawa* 'a drunk'

Cases of noun–noun compounding, while not impossible, are less common. Let us now look at the nominal morphology a little more closely.

6 The classification of nouns

The other main feature of Bantu languages is their system of noun classification. Nouns in Bantu languages traditionally display a bi-morphemic structure. A typical example is provided by the following:

(46) *chi-soti* 'hat'   *zi-soti* 'hats'
      m-kôndo 'spear'   *mi-kôndo* 'spears'

As these examples show, the nouns consist of a prefix and a stem. The prefix encodes information relating to number and gender, where the gender system is that of natural gender. The question of the basis for this classification of nouns still awaits a definitive response. The formal structure of the noun, which does have some bearing on its class membership, has relevance to the regulation of the agreement patterns of the languages. In brief, noun modifiers are marked for agreement with the class features of the head noun, and these features are also what are reflected in the SM and the OM in the verbal morphology. By way of illustration, consider the following:

(47) (a) chi-soti ch-ángá ch-á-tsópanó chi-ja
7-hat 7SM-my 7SM-assoc.-new 7SM-rel.pro.
chí-ma-sangaláts-á a-lenje.
7SM-hab.-please-fv 2-hunters
'That new hat of mine pleases hunters.'

(b) m-kóndó w-angá w-á-tsópanó u-ja
3-spear 3SM-my 3SM-assoc.-new 3SM-rel.pro.
ú-ma-sangaláts-á alenje.
3SM-hab.-please-fv 2-hunters
'That new spear of mine pleases hunters.'

In these sentences, the words in construction with the nouns are marked for agreement with that head noun (the actual agreement markers in these examples are *chi* and *u*. The '*i*' vowel in '*chi*' is elided when followed by a vowel, and the '*u*' is replaced by the glide '*w*' in a similar environment). It should be noted that in Chichewa the head noun precedes its modifiers within a noun phrase. The formal patterns that yield the singular and the plural forms are normally identified by a particular numbering system now virtually standard in Bantu linguistics. Consider the following data:

(48) *m-nyamá ta* 'boy'　　　　　*a-nyamá ta* 'boys'
　　 m-lenje 'hunter'　　　　　 *a-lenje* 'hunters'
　　 m-kâzi 'woman'　　　　　　*a-kâzi* 'women'

　　 m-kôndo 'spear'　　　　　　*mi-kôndo* 'spears'
　　 mú-nda 'garden'　　　　　 *mí-nda* 'gardens'
　　 m-kângo 'lion'　　　　　　 *mi-kângo* 'lions'

　　 tsamba 'leaf'　　　　　　　*ma-samba* 'leaves'
　　 duwa 'flower'　　　　　　　*ma-luwa* 'flowers'
　　 phanga 'cave'　　　　　　　*ma-panga* 'caves'

　　 chi-sa 'nest'　　　　　　　 *zi-sa* 'nests'
　　 chi-tósi 'chicken dropping'　*zi-tósi* 'chicken droppings'
　　 chi-pûtu 'grass stubble'　　 *zi-pûtu* 'grass stubble'

These classes show part of the range of noun classification that is characteristic of Bantu languages. The singular forms of the first group above constitutes Class 1, and its plural counterpart is Class 2. These classes tend to be dominated by nouns that denote animate things, although not all animate things are in this class. In fact, it also includes some inanimate objects. The next singular class is Class 3, and its plural version is Class 4. This runs on to Classes 5, 6, 7, and 8. There is also class 1a. This class consists of nouns whose agreement patterns are those of Class 1 but whose nouns lack the *m(u)* prefix found in the Class 1 nouns. The plural of such nouns is indicated by prefixing *a* to the word. The noun *kalulu* 'hare' whose plural is *akalulu* typifies this class. Each of these classes has a specific class marker and a specific agreement marker. Beginning with Class 2, the markers are, respectively, *a, u, i, li, a, chi, zi.* Class 1 is marked by *mu* for syllabic *m*), *u*, and *a*, depending on the category of the modifier. Consider the following:

(49)   m-lenje m-môdzi a-na-bwérá ndí mí-kôndo.
       1-hunter 1SM-one 1SM-past-come-fv with 4-spears
       'One hunter came with spears.'

In this, the numeral *môdzi* 'one' is marked with the agreement marker *m*, but the verb has *a* for the subject marker. The *u* is used with demonstratives and when the segment that follows is a vowel. This seems to apply to most cases, regardless of whether the vowel in question is a tense/aspect marker, an associative marker, or part of a stem, such as with possessives. Consider the following:

(50)   m-lenje w-ánú u-ja w-á nthábwala
       1-hunter 1SM-your 1 1SM-that SM-assoc. 10-humor
       w-a-thyol-a mi-kôndo.
       1SM-perf.-break-fv 4-spears
       'That humorous hunter of yours has broken the spears.'

In this sentence, the '*w*' is the glide that replaces '*u*' when a vowel follows, regardless of the function associated with that vowel. Although most of the nouns are bi-morphemic, there are a number of cases where a further prefix, which may mark either diminution or augmentation, is added to an already prefixed noun. This is shown in the following:

(51)   Ka-m-lenje k-ánú ka-ja k-á nthábwala
       12-1-hunter 12SM-your 12SM-that 12-assoc. 10-humor
       k-a-thyol-a ti-mi-kôndo.
       12SM-perf.-break-fv 13–4-spears
       'That small humorous hunter of yours has broken the tiny spears.'

In this sentence, the pre-prefixes *ka* for singular and *ti* for plural are added to nouns to convey the sense of diminutive size. These pre-prefixes then control the agreement patterns (cf. Bresnan and Mchombo 1995), which provides the rationale for regarding them as governing separate noun classes. One other significant point to be made is that locatives also control agreement patterns. Consider the following:

Table 25.1 Noun classes in Chichewa

Classes		Prefixes		Subject marker		Object marker	
SG	PL	SG	PL	SG	PL	SG	PL
1	2	m(u)-	a-	a-	a-	m(u)	wa
3	4	m(u)-	mi-	u-	i-	u	i
5	6	*li-	ma-	li-	a-	li	wa
7	8	chi-	zi-	chi-	zi-	chi	zi
9	10	*N-	*N-	i-	zi-	i	zi
12	13	ka-	ti-	ka-	ti-	ka	ti
14	6	u-	ma-	u	a	u	wa
	15	ku-		ku		ku	
	16	pa-		pa		pa	
	17	ku-		ku		ku	
	18	m(u)-		m(u)		m(u)	

(52)   Ku mudzi kw-ânu kú-ma-sangaláts-á alendo.
       17-at 3-village 17SM-your 17-hab.-please-fv 2-visitors
       'Your village (i.e. the location) pleases visitors.'

This gives such locatives the appearance of being class markers, and it has been argued that locatives in Chichewa are not really prepositions that mark grammatical case but, rather, class markers (for some discussion see Bresnan 1991).

The full range of noun classes for Chichewa is given in table 25.1. It should be noted that some classes are not present in this language. For instance Chichewa lacks Class 11, with prefix reconstructed as 'du' in proto-Bantu.

A few observations need to be made about some of these classes. The classes whose prefixes are asterisked normally lack the said prefix in the noun morphology. Samples of Class 5 nouns are given in (41) above. Most of the nouns in Classes 9 and 10 begin with a nasal, but there are no overt changes in their morphological composition that correlate with number. The number distinction is reflected in the prefixes rather than in the overt form of the noun. Examples of Class 9/10 nouns are *nyúmba* 'house(s)', *nthenga* 'feather(s)', *mphîni* 'tattoo(es)', *nkhôndo* 'war'. Class 15 consists of infinitive verbs. The infinitive marker *ku-* regulates the agreement patterns, just like the diminutives (Classes 12 and 13) and locatives. The infinitives are thus regarded as constituting a separate class, although, just as is the case with the locatives, there are no nouns that are peculiar to this class. This is exemplified by the following:

(53)   Ku-ímbá kw-ánu kú-ma-sangaláts-á alenje.
       15INF-sg. 15SM-your 15SM-hab.-please-fv 2-hunters
       'Your singing pleases hunters.'

7 Conclusion

In its morphological organization Chichewa is very typical of Bantu languages, most of which adhere very closely to the kind of nominal and verbal morphological patterns, as well as patterns of nominal derivation and compounding, exemplified by Chichewa. There are several questions of more theoretical significance that have not been addressed here or the discussion of which has been cursory at best, due to the limited scope of the chapter and the nature of its focus, on the structural patterns of this language. For more theoretical discussions of some of the issues touched upon slightly or even completely omitted here reference should be made to the works cited and to some of the references therein.

NOTE

1   This construction has also gone by a number of different labels. These have included such terms as "neuter," "neuter-passive," "quasi-passive," "neuter-stative," "metastatic-potential," "descriptive passive" (cf. Satyo 1985). In fact, in previous Bantu linguistic scholarship, the term "stative" has been applied to constructions involving the suffix -*am*- that is no longer productive in Chichewa (for recent illustration from Korekore, see Dembetembe 1987).

26 Chukchee (Paleo-Siberian)

IRINA A. MURAVYOVA

1 Introduction

Chukchee is a Paleo-Siberian language of the Chukchee–Kamchatkan stock, spoken by about 12,000 people living in the Far East of Russia, on the Chukotka peninsula and in some adjacent regions. Chukchee is considered a synthetic agglutinative language of the prefixal-suffixal type (Skorik 1961: 81). Chukchee has the following parts of speech: nouns, participles, adjectives, pronouns, numerals, verbs, adverbs, and also postpositions, particles, conjunctions and interjections. The syntactic and semantic functions of the major parts of speech are expressed chiefly by bound affixes (suffixes, prefixes, circumfixes), sometimes by derivational affixes (e.g. adjectivization with nouns), more rarely by analytic constructions (with nominal postpositions and auxiliary verbs). A special means of expressing grammatical functions is incorporation. (See appendix at end of chapter for abbreviations used only in this chapter.)

Chukchee words can reach considerable length. The root generally occupies a position in the middle of the word. The length of Chukchee words is increased by incorporation of a variety of types of element (see Skorik 1961, 1977):

ga-ŋəron-wet?at-arma-qaa-ta
COM-three-butt-strong-reindeer-COM
'with three butting strong reindeer'.

Chukchee has a great variety of phonological and morphonological processes that change considerably the shape of the original morphs. In order to understand the examples given below, the following changes should be taken into account (for more detailed rules see Bogoras 1922, Skorik 1961, Kenstowicz 1979):

(1) Numerous consonant assimilations and dissimilations.

(2) Vowel harmony. When *i, u, e* (recessive vowels) come together in one word with *e, o, a* (dominant vowels), the recessive vowels change into the corresponding dominant ones: *ga-reqoka-ma* (<*ga-riquke-ma*) 'with a polar fox'. Some morphemes having only *ə* (or no vowels at all) also cause this change, cf. *reqoka-lgən* 'polar fox (abs. sg.)'; we will mark such morphemes with an asterisk: *-lgən*(*).

(3) Epenthetic processes. An epenthetic schwa is introduced to break up inadmissible consonant clusters: *n-ə-wucq-ə-qin* (<*n-wucq-qin*) 'dark' (but with other morphemes *ə* may be a part of the original morph). In word forms we will attach the epenthetic *ə* to the previous morph or to a one-consonant morph: *nə-wucqə-qin*.

(4) Deletion processes. Most noun stems and some nominal affixes lose the final vowel in word-final position. We will write such vowels in brackets: *-in(e)*, 'adjectival suffix'. When two vowels come together, one of them is elided (except in reduplications and incorporatives): *g-iw-lin* (<*ge-iw-lin*) '/he/ said'.

2 Inflection

2.1 Nouns

Nouns are usually inflected for case and number, and in some situations (see section 2.1.2) for person and number. Nouns are not inflected when they are incorporated (see section 2.1.3).

2.1.1 Case-number marking on nouns
Chukchee has two numbers (sg., pl.), and nine principal cases: absolutive (nominative), ergative (ergative-instrumental), locative, dative (dative-directional), ablative, orientative, comitative-1, comitative-2 (or 'accompanying' case) and designative. The absolutive serves to express the grammatical subject of an intransitive verb and the grammatical object of a transitive verb. The ergative expresses the subject of a transitive verb and the instrument of an action. The orientative is used to express an object regarded as a point of orientation. The comitative-2 expresses the dependent comitative relation, with one of the participants playing a less active role (e.g. 'a bear with its cubs'). The comitative relation can also be expressed by means of the postposition *reen* 'together' (see section 2.8). The designative is used to express the subject-complement and object-complement.

Case and number markers are fused, and form two main patterns: pattern 1 and pattern 2. These are used to form three 'declensions' (Skorik 1961: 155), which reflect the difference between proper versus common nouns and human versus non-human nouns. These types are: (1) non-human common nouns (the 1st declension), pattern 1; (2) proper nouns (including names of domestic

Table 26.1 Noun declensions

	Pattern 1		Pattern 2	
	sg.	*pl.*	*sg.*	*pl.*
1 absolutive	-∅,-n/-nə, lgən(*)/-ləŋən/-tləŋən R, -ŋə	-t/-ti	=pattern 1	-ənti
2 ergative	-e/-te	-əne	-ərak	
3 locative	-k/-kə	-əne	-ərak	
4 dative	-gtə/-etə(*)	-əna	-ərəkə(*)	
5 ablative	-jpə/-gəpə/-əpə(*)	=pattern 1	-ərgəpə(*)	
6 orientative	-gjit	-gjit	-ərəgjit	
7 comitative-1	ge- . . . -e/-te	——	——	
8 comitative-2	ga- . . . -ma	ga- . . . -ma	ga- . . . -ərəma	
9 designative	-u/-nu	-ənu	-ənu	

The choice of the variants separated with '/' depends on the phonological type of the stem final (a vowel, a single consonant, a two-consonant cluster; see Skorik 1961).
Comitative-2 has plural forms only in the 3rd declension.

animals) and some kinship terms, pattern 2, with the obligatory expression of the singular/plural opposition; (3) all other common nouns (the 3rd declension), pattern 1 in the singular and pattern 2 in the plural, with the singular/plural opposition being expressed here optionally (i.e. the speaker may choose to use only pattern 1). These are illustrated in table 26.1.

The absolutive singular shows great variety in exponence. The markers are distributed morpholexically, and are listed here according to their productivity. The most frequent markers are -∅ (the zero ending) and -n. Nominal stems taking the zero ending undergo various phonological changes (see section 1). Examples are *ajkol-∅* (<*ajkola-∅*) 'bedding (abs. sg.)'; *qepəl-∅* (<*qepl-∅*) 'ball (abs. sg.)'; *məran-ləŋən* 'mosquito (abs. sg.)'; *nelg-ət* 'hides (abs. pl.)'; *qəpl-e* 'by a ball (erg.)'; *emnuŋ-kə* 'in the tundra (loc.)'; *jara-gtə* 'to the house (dat.)'; *kajŋ-epə* 'from a brown bear (abl.)'; *gətgə-gjet* 'orienting towards a lake'; *ge-tumg-e* 'with a friend (com.1)'; *ga-melgar-ma* 'with a gun (com.2)'; *Tutun-∅* 'Tutun (proper noun, abs. sg.)'; *Tutun-əne* 'Tutun (erg. sg.)'; *Tutun-ənu* 'in the role of Tutun (desg. sg.)'; *Tutun-ərak* 'at the Tutuns' (loc. pl.)'; *Toton-ərəkə* 'to the Tutuns (dat. pl.)'.

Some stems form the absolutive singular by means of reduplication (indicated in table 26.1 as 'R'). Reduplication consists in repeating the first closed syllable of the root: that is, CVC (including CəC) and VC; so: *nute-nut* 'country' (stem *nute-*); *qulgə-qul* 'fish-scale' (stem *qulg-*); *jəŋe-jəŋ* 'mist' (stem *jŋe-*); *ele-el* 'summer'.

Finally, there is a vocative form expressed by prolonging the last vowel and/or by adding a special ending, *-j*: *ŋewʔeen!* 'hey, wife! (voc.)', *Kopaa-j!* 'hey, Kopa! (proper name, voc.)'.

2.1.2 Person–number marking on nouns

A noun is marked for person and number when it is used as complement in the copular construction ('I am a reindeer-breeder'), as appositional attribute to an absolutive or ergative pronoun ('We reindeer-breeders went to the herd') or as addressee ('Hey you, reindeer-breeders!').

Person and number markers are fused to give the following patterns:

person	sg.	pl.
1	-jgəm/-igəm/-egəm	-muri
2	-jgət/-igət/-egət	-turi
3	= absolutive singular	= absolutive plural

Note: In the singular the choice between the morphs with *-j* and a vowel depends on the phonological shape of the stem and on vowel harmony. The endings for the first and second person originated from the corresponding personal pronouns (see section 2.4.1). Since the third person forms are homonymous with the case forms, they may be treated as non-person forms. Examples: *epe-jgəm* 'me, grandfather (1sg.)'; *ŋinqej-igət* 'thou, the boy (2sg.)'; *ənpənacgə-more* 'we old men (1pl.)'; *ənpənacg-ət* 'they, the old men (3pl. = abs. pl.)'.

2.1.3 Noun incorporation

Depending on the semantics, the dependent noun may be incorporated into a verbal or a nominal form without any category marking. In Chukchee the incorporated stem always precedes the head stem, and the whole compound is marked according to the grammatical class of the head, with prefixes preceding the incorporated stem.

When the head is a verb, the subject noun (with non-agentive, or unaccusative verbs), the direct object noun and the oblique object noun can be incorporated:

(1) (a) tirkə-tir Ø-amecat-Ø-gʔe.
         sun-ABS.SG 3SG.S.-appear-AOR-3SG.S
         'The sun appeared.'

     (b) Ø-terk-amecat-Ø-gʔe.
         3SG.S-sun-appear-AOR-3SG.S
         'The sun appeared.' (Lit. '/It/ sun-appeared.')

(2) (a) gəm-nan walə-Ø   tə-mne-Ø-gʔen.
         I-ERG   knife-ABS:SG 1SG.S-sharpen-AOR-3SG.O
         'I sharpened the knife.'

(b) gəm-∅ tə-wala-mna-∅-gʔak.
     I-ABS 1SG.S-knife-sharpen-AOR-1SG.S
     'I sharpened the knife.' (Lit. 'I knife-sharpened.')

(3) (a) ŋinqej-∅ gətg-etə ∅-qət-∅-gʔi.
          boy-ABS:SG lake-DAT 3SG.S-go-AOR-3SG.S
          'The boy went to the lake.'

     (b) ŋinqej-∅ ∅-gətgə-lqət-∅-gʔi.
          boy-ABS:SG 3SG.S-lake-go-AOR-3SG.S
          'The boy went to the lake.' (Lit. 'The boy lake-went.')

When the head is a noun, the attribute noun may be incorporated (without the relational adjective suffix; cf. section 2.3.3):

(4) (a) ŋinqej-in-∅   ewirʔ-ən
          boy-POSS-3SG clothes-ABS:SG
          'a/the boy's clothes'

     (b) ŋinqej-ewirʔ-ən
          boy-clothes-ABS:SG
          'a/the boy's clothes'

2.2 Participles

Participles, or 'participle-nouns' (Skorik 1961: 155), are considered a separate part of speech in Chukchee. All participles have the suffix -*lʔ* (with -*n* in the absolutive singular), and are derived from noun, adjective and verb stems: *milger-∅* 'a gun', *milgerə-lʔ-ən* 'the one having a gun'; *nə-gtiŋ-qin* 'beautiful', *gətiŋə-lʔ-ən* 'the one who is beautiful'; *iwini-k* 'to hunt', *iwini-lʔ-ən* 'the one who hunts, a hunter'.

Participles are inflected like nouns, but, unlike nouns, they may be used as attributes without any possessive or relative markers (cf. section 2.3.3): *milgerə-lʔ-ən ənpənacg-ən* 'the old man (abs. sg.) having a gun (abs. sg.)'. When the head is an oblique case form, participles, like adjectives (see section 2.3.3), may be either external or incorporated, depending on whether they are emphasized or not. When a participle is emphasized, it is expressed as a free word and agrees with its head in case and number; but, unlike an adjective, it has all the case forms without any restrictions: *milgerə-lʔ-etə ənpənacg-etə* 'to the old man (dat.) having a gun (dat.)'; compare the variant with incorporation *melgarə-lʔ-ənpənacg-etə* 'to the gun-having-old-man (dat.)'. When a participle has no head noun, it is used like an ordinary noun.

Negative participles are marked with *e-* . . . *kəlʔ[-in(e)]*, with the last part used only with the third person and in the absolutive: *e-milger-kəlʔin* 'the one who has no gun (3sg.)'. The circumfix *e-* . . . -*ke* is identical to that found with verbs (section 2.6.2) and when affixed to a noun stem gives the meaning 'without, lacking'.

Some participles have the marker *-cʔ* (which originated from *lʔ* by virtue of the historical alternation *l/c*): *mətlaŋen* 'five', *mətlaŋa-cʔ-ən* 'a "five" (figure)'.

2.3 Adjectives

2.3.1 General remarks   Adjectives in Chukchee form a peculiar grammatical class. Like other languages, Chukchee distinguishes between qualitative and non-qualitative (relational) adjectives, and these two classes have different morphological markers. In some grammars (e.g. Skorik 1961) qualitative adjectives are treated as separate parts of speech, 'words denoting quality state'. On the other hand, as non-qualitative adjectives are usually denominal, they are often treated as noun forms (Bogoras 1922, Skorik 1961). None the less, these two classes have very much in common, in both morphological and syntactic properties, so we will consider them as subclasses of one and the same part of speech.

All adjectives have markers that end in *-in(e)*, with the final vowel being lost in word-final position. Qualitative adjectives are marked with *n-* . . . *[-qin(e)]*, with the suffixal part *-qin(e)* used only for the third person (so it may be treated as a person marker): *n-erme-qin* 'strong'. Qualitative adjectives lose this marker when they are incorporated (see below).

Non-qualitative adjectives are usually denominal. The majority of them subdivide into two large groups:

(1)   possessive adjectives marked with *-in(e)* for nouns following pattern 1, *-ənin(e)* for singular nouns following pattern 2, *-ərgin(e)* for plural nouns following pattern 2 (see section 2.1.1): *uttu-ut* 'stick', *utt-in* 'wooden', *Tutun* (proper noun) *Tutun-ənin* 'belonging to Tutun, Tutun's', *ənpənacg-ən* 'an old man', *ənpənacg-ərgen* 'belonging to the old men';

(2)   relational adjectives marked with *-kin(e)*: *aŋqa-n* 'sea', *aŋqa-ken* 'related to the sea' (as in 'a sea bird'), *Tutun* (proper noun), *Tutun-kin* 'related to Tutun'.

Adjectives of these two groups do not lose their markers when they are incorporated (see below).

A further group of non-qualitative adjectives is marked with *ge-* . . . *[-lin(e)]* (with the suffixal part used only for the third person), used to describe the possessor of an object expressed by the nominal stem: *pojg-ən* 'a spear' – *ga-pojgə-len* 'the one supplied with a spear'.

When adjectives are not incorporated, they are usually marked for person and number, and in some instances for case and number.

2.3.2 Person and number marking on adjectives The adjectival person–number markers are almost identical to their nominal counterparts (cf. section 2.1.2):

person	sg.	pl.
1	-jgəm/-igəm/-egəm	-muri
2	-jgət/-igət/-egət	-turi
3	-∅	-t

The third-person markers are homonymous with the nominal number markers. In some types of adjectives they are combined with the suffixal part of the circumfixes, forming the following pairs of endings for the third person: *-qin-∅/ -qine-t, -lin-∅/-line-t*.

When used predicatively, adjectives always agree in person and number with the subject (there are no copular verbs in Chukchee): *ətlon-∅ n-erme-qin-∅* 'he /is/ strong', *ətr-i n-erme-qine-t* 'they /are/ strong', *mur-i emnuŋ-kine-muri* 'we /are/ from the tundra', *gəm-∅ ga-pojg-egəm* 'I /am/ supplied with a spear'. When adjectives are used as attributes, the first- and second-person markers appear only in the situations when the head noun is marked for person and number: *mur-i emnuŋ-kine-muri nəmətwal?ə-muri* 'We /are/ tundra (rel., 1pl.) dwellers (1pl.)'. In all other situations the third-person forms are used.

2.3.3 Case-number marking on adjectives and adjective incorporation
When an adjective is used attributively and the head noun is an absolutive case noun phrase (i.e. intransitive subject or object), the adjective is usually external and, as a rule, agrees in number with the head noun: *n-ilgə-qin-∅ qora-ŋə* 'a white (3sg.) reindeer (abs. sg.)' versus *n-ilgə-qine-t qora-t* 'white (3pl.) reindeer (abs. pl.)'. Possessive adjectives may not agree in number with the head noun: *ŋinqej-in-∅ jel?o-∅* 'the boy's (poss., 3sg.) uncle (abs. sg.)' versus *ŋinqej-in-∅ jel?o-nte* 'the boy's uncles (abs. pl.)'. In some cases attribute adjectives are incorporated without any obvious restrictions: *elgə-kojŋ-ən* 'white mug'.

When the head noun is not an absolutive case noun phrase, the adjective is usually incorporated. In this case a qualitative adjective loses its marker, but a relational adjective preserves its suffix: *n-ilgə-qin-∅ qora-ŋə* 'a white reindeer (abs. sg.)' versus *elgə-qora-ta* 'by a white reindeer (erg.)'; *aŋqa-kena-t galga-t* 'sea birds (abs. pl.)' versus *aŋqa-kena-galga-ta* 'by sea birds (erg.)'. Possessive adjectives are incorporated more rarely than other types of adjectives.

In the comitative-1 and comitative-2 forms, where there is a prefix, incorporation is obligatory: *nə-teŋ-qin-∅ tumgə-tum* 'a good friend (abs. sg.)' versus *ga-taŋ-tomgə-ma* 'with a good friend (com. 2)'. But if the case form has no prefix and the adjective is emphasized, it may be expressed as an external attribute. In such situations the adjective may be marked for case and number with the endings of pattern 1 (see section 2.1.1). This is more typical for relational adjectives and for the ergative and locative cases; possessive adjectives are not marked for case: *nə-mejəŋ-qine-k Ɂatw-ək* 'in the big (loc.) boat (loc.)', *emnuŋ-kine-k nəmnəm-ək* 'in the tundra (loc.) settlement (loc.)', *ənpənacg-en-Ø qora-ta* 'by the old man's reindeer (erg.)'.

When an adjective is used without a head noun, it is marked like an ordinary noun: *n-ilgə-qine-te* 'by the white one (erg.)', *epe-nine-k* 'at Grandpa's (loc.)', *amnoŋ-kena-gtə* 'to the one from the tundra (dat.)'.

2.3.4 Degrees of comparison   The comparative degree can be expressed by means of an analytic construction consisting of the adverbial form marked with *-ŋ(*)* and a participle of the auxiliary verb 'to be': *n-erme-qin* 'strong', *arma-ŋ wa-lɁ-ən* 'stronger' (lit. 'being stronger'). The superlative degree is expressed by means of the prefix *ənan-* attached to a participle marked with *-cɁ-* (see section 2.2): *nə-mejəŋ-qin* 'big', *ənan-majŋə-cɁ-ən* 'the biggest'.

2.4 Pronouns

2.4.1 Personal pronouns   Free pronouns for the first, second and third person, both singular and plural, occur in Chukchee. All personal pronouns are inflected for case. They cannot be incorporated. Personal pronouns follow pattern 1 (see section 2.1.1), but there is some divergence from the nominal case system as regards both realization and the set of cases.

The 1/2/3 person and singular/plural oppositions are expressed by different pronominal stems:

person	sg.	pl.
1	gəm-	mur-
2	gən-	tur-
3	ən-	ər-

These morphs are found only in the locative; in other cases the stems undergo various alternations. The absolutive singular is marked with *-Ø*, the absolutive plural with the pronominal pluralizer *-i*. Irregular absolutives are: *gət-Ø* 'thou', *ətlon-Ø* '(s)he, it', *ətr-i* 'they' (>*ərr-i* with geminated *r*). The ergative is marked with the pronominal marker *-nan*. In the ergative the second singular and third singular stems are reduced to *gə-* and *ə-* respectively, while the plural stems are augmented with *-gə*. Instead of the dative-directional case, the pronouns have two different cases: the dative, marked with *-ə(*)*, and the directional, marked with *-gtə*. In the dative, comitative-1, comitative-2 and designative cases all the stems are augmented with *-ək* (with variant *-əg*); in the directional, ablative and orientative they are augmented with *-əke*. Examples: *gə-nan* 'thou (erg.)', *torgə-nan* 'you (erg.)', *gəm-ək* 'at my place (loc.)', *gəmək-ə* 'to me (dat.)', *morəka-gtə* 'to us (dir.)', *ənəka-jpə* 'from him (abl.)', *gəməke-gjit* 'according to me, like me (orient.)', *g-ərək-e* 'with them (com.1)', *ga-gənəg-ma* 'together with thee (com.2)', *turək-u* 'as you (desg.)'.

2.4.2 *Possessive pronouns* Like nouns, personal pronouns have two types of adjectival derivatives:

> (1) possessive pronouns proper, derived by adding *-nin(e)* to the singular pronominal stems (the 2sg. and 3sg. stems are shortened as in the ergative), and *-gin(e)* to the plural stems: *gə-nin* 'thy (3sg.)', *ər-gin* 'their (3sg.)';
>
> (2) relational pronouns, derived by adding the suffix *-kin(e)* to the stem base augmented with *-ake*: *ənəke-kin* 'related to him (3sg.)', *murəke-kin* 'related to us (3sg.)'.

These derivatives are used like other adjectives (see section 2.3). When incorporated, possessive pronouns may preserve the possessive marker, but alongside this a special incorporative stem augmented with *-ək* may be used: *gəmək-kupre-te/gəm-nine-kupre-te* 'by my net (erg.)'.

2.4.3 *Interrogative pronouns* The principal interrogative pronouns correspond to 'who?' and 'what?'. When they express a person or an object, they are inflected like nouns (see section 2.1). The pronoun 'what?' follows pattern 1, with *rʔenut-∅* in the absolutive singular, *rʔenute-t* in the absolutive plural. In all other cases the stem *req-* used, with the phonologically regular alternant *rʔe-* when *-q* would occupy syllable-final position: *req-ək* 'in what place? (loc.)', *ga-rʔa-ma* 'with what? (com.2)'. The pronoun 'who?' follows pattern 2, with *meŋin-∅* in the absolutive singular and the stem *mik-* used in the absolutive plural and all other cases: *mik-ənti* 'who? (abs. pl.)'; *mik-əne* 'who? (erg.)'; *mek-əna* 'to whom? (dat.)'; *mik-ərak* 'at whom? (loc. pl.)'.

When the pronoun 'what?' is used attributively, it is always incorporated: *rʔa-wagərg-ən* 'what kind of life? (abs. sg)', *req-orw-ək* 'on what sledge? (loc.)'. Interrogative pronouns, like personal ones, have possessive and relational adjectival forms. Other interrogative words include *minkə* 'where?', *miŋkəri* 'how', *meŋko* 'from where?', *tite* 'when?', *tʔer* 'how many, how much?'. Like other numerals, the word *tʔer* may be incorporated (see section 2.5). Interrogatives can be used as relative pronouns.

2.4.4 *Demonstrative pronouns* Demonstrative pronouns specify a variety of spatial parameters. The principal demonstratives are: *ŋotqen(a)-* 'this' (incorporated form *ŋutin-*), *ənqen(a)-* 'that' (incorporated form *ənŋin-*), *ŋanqen(a)-* 'that far away'. Other degrees of distance are expressed iconically on the basis of the demonstrative *ŋanqen(a)-*: *ŋaanqen(a)-*, *ŋooqen(a)-*, *gaanqen(a)-*. Certain other demonstratives are derived from demonstrative particles.

Demonstratives are used like other adjectives (see section 2.3).

2.5 Numerals

The native Chukchee terms are based on finger counting. There are only eight original non-compound numerals, all others being either synthetic or analytic compounds (the latter are followed by the word *parol* 'addition'). The basic system is illustrated below:

1	ənnen	11	məngətken ənnen parol
2	ŋireq	15	kəlgənken(*)
3	ŋəroq	16	kəlgənken ənnen parol
4	ŋəraq	20	qlikkin
5	mətləŋen(*)	21	qlikkin ənnen parol
6	ənnan-mətləŋen	26	qlikkin ənnan-mətləŋen parol
7	ŋerʔa-mətləŋen	30	qlikkin məngətken parol
8	ŋərʔo-mətləŋen	35	qlikkin kəlgənken parol
9	ŋərʔa-mətləŋen	40	ŋireq-qlikkin
		100	mətləŋ-qlekken
		200	məngət-qlekken
		300	kəlgən-qlekken
		400	qlik-qlikkin

Like adjectives, in appropriate situations cardinal numerals may be marked for person and number (in the plural only). The third-person plural form is marked with *-ərgeri*. With analytic compounds the person marker is attached to the last word: *mur-i qlikkin ŋireq parol-more* 'there are twenty-two of us' (lit. 'we /are/ twenty-two'); adjectival markers used with the numerals are omitted before person markers: *ətr-i ŋerʔamətləŋ-ərgare* 'there are seven (of them)' (*ŋerʔamətləŋ-en* 'seven').

When a cardinal numeral is used attributively, it is either external or incorporated. A numeral is always incorporated when the head noun is an oblique case form. Some numeral stems undergo phonological changes. With analytic compounds only the last word is incorporated; the comitative prefix *ge-* is attached to the first word, the suffixal part *-te/-ma* to the last word: *ŋəron-pojg-a* 'by three spears (erg.)', *ge-qlikkin ŋəroq parol-tomg-a* 'with twenty-three friends (com.1)'.

Ordinal numerals are derived from the cardinal ones by means of the suffix *-qew*: *ənnen-qew* 'the first', *qlikkin ənnen parol-qaw* 'the twenty-first'. Ordinal numerals are used like adjectives. With the incorporated variant the rules are the same as with ordinal numerals: *ge-qlikkin ənnen parol-qaw-jatjol-a* 'with the twenty-first fox (com.1)'.

2.6 Verbs

2.6.1 Finite forms The following two morphological types of finite forms are found in Chukchee: canonical verbal forms and adjectival ones (see Skorik 1977).

2.6.1.1 Canonical verbal forms Canonical verbal forms express an action related to the moment of speech (see Nedjalkov 1993). They distinguish three principal moods: indicative, imperative and subjunctive. Each mood is characterized by an appropriate set of person–number markers; only the subjunctive mood has a separate marker, the prefix -ʔ-. Within each mood two classes of aspectual forms are distinguished: (1) imperfective forms marked with -rk- (-rkǝn in some grammars); (2) perfective forms that are not marked with -rk-, and thus have the zero marker. Additionally, there are forms expressing posteriority, or temporal sequence, marked with re- or re- . . . -ŋ (with morphophonemic suffixal variants -n, -g), that also distinguish imperfective/perfective forms. The posteriority forms are usually considered as future tenses of the indicative mood, but they can be also regarded as a separate mood.

The canonical verbal forms can be represented by the following tense–aspect–mood system (cf. also Nedjalkov 1993, Mel'čuk 1973, as well as discussion in Comrie 1979, 1980):

	indic. (non-fut.)	fut.	imper.	subjun.
impf.	Ø- . . . -rk	re- . . . -rk	Ø- . . . -rk	ʔ- . . . -rk
perf.	Ø- . . . -Ø	re- . . . -Ø/-ŋ	-Ø- . . . -Ø	ʔ- . . . -Ø

In the indicative mood the non-future imperfective forms are called Present (or Present-progressive), the perfective ones, Aorist; so in the examples given below we will mark -rk- as PRES, and -Ø-(-ŋ-) as AOR.

Besides tense–aspect–mood forms, there are also antipassive forms (see Kozinsky et al. 1988).

The usage and distribution of person–number markers used with canonical forms is complex. There are many zero affixes with different meanings, and many affixes are homonymous.

A canonical verbal form has a person–number prefix and a person–number suffix (including zero affixes) in word-initial and word-final positions respectively. An intransitive verb agrees in person and number with its grammatical subject; that is, it has a person–number circumfix. A transitive verb agrees in person and number with both its grammatical subject and grammatical object, so it is bi-personal: with some exceptions, it has a subject prefix and an object suffix. There are therefore two conjugational patterns, or two 'conjugations' (see Skorik 1977): one is for intransitives, the 'subject' conjugation, or pattern 1, the other is for transitives, the 'subject–object' conjugation, or pattern 2.

The following transitive forms diverge from the principle of subject–object marking given above: (1) where the subject is second-person singular or plural or third-person singular, the first-person singular object is expressed by means of the prefix *ine-* placed immediately before the stem; (2) with second-person subjects, the first-person plural object is expressed by means of the suffix -*tku* placed immediately after the stem. In these cases the verb is marked with a subject prefix and a subject suffix from pattern 1, as if it were intransitive. In

Table 26.2a   Pattern 1: subject prefixes (intransitive conjugation)

	indic.	fut.	imper.	subjunc.
1sg.	t-	t-	m-	t-
2sg.			q-	n-
3sg.			n-	n-
1pl.	mət-	mət-	mən-	mən-
2pl.			q-	n-
3pl.			n-	n-

Table 26.2b   Pattern 1: subject suffixes (intransitive conjugation)

	indic.		fut.		imper.		subjun.	
	pres.	aor.	pres.	aor.	pres.	aor.	pres.	aor.
1sg.	-n	-(gʔe)k	-n	-gʔe	-n	-(gʔe)k	-n	-(gʔe)k
2sg.	-n	-gʔi	-n	-gʔe	-n	-gi	-n	-(gʔe)n
3sg.	-n	-gʔi	-n	-gʔe	-n	-(gʔe)n	-n	-(gʔe)n
1pl.	-n	-mək	-n	-gʔe	-n	-mək	-n	-mək
2pl.	-tək	-tək	-tək	-tək	-tək	-tək	-tək	-tək
3pl.	-t	-(gʔe)t	-t	-t	-ənet	-ənet	-ənet	-ənet

The (*gʔe*) component may be omitted.

some verbal forms the connecting morph -*ni* is found before the final person–number marker; in some second-person imperative forms the connecting morph -*gə* is found in the same position.

For Chukchee person–number verbal markers see tables 26.2a, b, 26.3a, b. Subject circumfixes (pattern 1) are given here in two tables, because the distribution of the prefixal parts sometimes differs from that of the suffixal ones.

Examples:[1]

mət-Ø-kətgəntan-Ø-mək
1PL.S-INDIC-run-AOR-1PL.S   'we ran'

Ø-ra-kətgəntan-ŋə-tək
2PL.S-FUT-run-AOR-2PL.S   'you will run'

t-ʔə-kətgəntatə-rk-ən
1SG.S-SUBJ-run-PRES-1SG.S   'I would run'

mət-re-lʔu-tkə-ni-gət
1PL.S-FUT-see-PRES-CONN-2SG.O   'we will see thee'

Table 26.3a Pattern 2: subject prefixes
(transitive conjugation)

	indic.	*fut.*	*imper.*	*subjun.*
1sg.	t-	t-	m-	t-
2sg.			q-	n-
3sg.	Ø-/ne-	Ø-/ne-	n-/ʔən-	n-/nen-
1pl.	mət-	mət-	mən-	mən-
2pl.			q-	n-
3pl.	ne-	ne-	ʔən-	nen-

Of the two variants separated by '/' the second one is used
when the object outranks the subject on the following hierarchy:
1sg., pl > 2sg., pl. > 3sg. > 3pl. Otherwise the first variant is used
(except in situations where the object is expressed by the prefix
– see above).

Table 26.3b Pattern 2: object suffixes

	sg.	*pl.*
1	-gəm	-mək
2	-gət	-tək
3pres.	-n	-ənet/-ətkə
aor.	-[gʔe]n	-[gʔe]net/-ətkə

1 The (*gʔe*) component may be omitted.
2 The suffix *-ətkə* is used when the subject is 2pl.

Ø-Ø-lʔu-tku-rkə-ni-tək
2PL.S-INDIC-see-1PL.O-PRES-CONN-2PL.S   'you see us'

ne-Ø-lʔu-Ø-mək
3SG.S-INDIC-see-AOR-1PL.O   'he saw us'

nə-Ø-lʔu-Ø-ni-n
3SG.S-IMPER-see-AOR-CONN-3SG.O   'let him see it'

2.6.1.2 Adjectival verb forms   The adjectival forms denote an action not
related to the moment of speech (see Nedjalkov 1993). They display the same
imperfective/perfective opposition, but here it is expressed differently: (1)
imperfective adjectival forms (= Imperfect-Present, or Imperfect) are marked
with the circumfix *n- . . . [-qin(e)]*; (2) perfective adjectival forms (= Perfect) are
marked with *ge- . . . [-lin(e)]* (the suffixal parts of both markers are used only

with the third person). These markers are identical with those of qualitative and non-qualitative adjectives respectively (see section 2.3.1).

The adjectival forms take the same set of standard person–number markers as adjectives (see section 2.3.2). When a verb is intransitive, only the standard suffixes are used, and the suffix always codes the grammatical subject: *nə-kətgəntat-egəm*, IMPF-run-1SG.S, 'I run'. But when a verb is transitive, the prefix *ine-* and the suffix *-tku* are also used, and the standard person–number suffix may code either the subject or the object. With the Perfect forms the distribution is similar to the one observed for the canonical forms. When the object is expressed by means of *ine-* or *-tku*, the standard suffix codes the subject, but when there is no *ine-* or *-tku*, it codes the object. Examples are:

g-ine-lʔu-jgət
PERF-1SG.O-see-2SG.S   'thou saw me'

ge-lʔu-tku-jgət
PERF-see-1PL.O-2SG.S   'thou saw us'

ge-lʔu-muri
PERF-see-1PL.O   'he/they saw us'

With the Imperfect forms the distribution of *-tku* is the same, but the prefix *ine-* is used more widely:

nə-lʔu-tku-jgət
IMPF-see-1PL.O-2SG.S   'thou seest us'

n-ine-lʔu-muri
IMPF-2SG.O-see-1PL.S   'we see thee'

2.6.2 Non-finite forms

The Chukchee verb has several non-finite forms. The infinitive is marked with *-k/-kə*: *imti-k* 'to carry', *migciret-ək* 'to work'. The supine is marked with *-nwə*: *reŋa-nwə* 'in order to fly'. Action nominals are marked with the suffix *-gərg(*)*: *təle-k* 'to move', *təle-gərg-ən* 'movement'. Verbal participles (active) are marked with *-lʔ-* (see section 2.2): *təle-lʔ-ən* 'the one who moves, walks'. Relativized verbs are marked with *-kin* (cf. section 2.3): *əpaw-ken kojŋ-ən* 'mug for drinking'.

There is also a series of adverbial participles ('gerunds') with various meanings. Their markers are often identical with those of the case forms (see section 2.1.1 and Spencer 1991: 28–9): *piŋkutku-te* '(because of) having jumped' (cf. Erg.-instr.), *recqiw-ək* 'having entered' (cf. loc.), *rʔawo-jpə* 'having killed a whale' (cf. abl.), *ga-melgarətko-ma* 'shooting at somebody' (cf. com.2).

Negation with finite forms is expressed by means of the negative non-finite form marked with *e- . . . -ke*, which is sometimes accompanied by a negative particle and/or the auxiliary verb *it-ək* 'to be' for intransitives and *rət-ək* 'to keep, to have' for transitives in the appropriate form.

Negation with adverbial participles is expressed by means of *luŋ-* . . . *-e/-te: luŋ-tejk-e* 'without doing anything'.

2.6.3 *Verb incorporation* A verb modifying another verb can be incorporated into the head verbal form, as in (5):

(5) (a) galga-t   riŋe-te n-ekwet-qine-t.
  bird-ABS:PL fly-ADP IMPF-go-IMPF-3PL.S
  'The birds are going away, flying.'

  (b) galga-t nə-riŋe-ekwet-qine-t.
  bird-ABS:PL IMPF-fly-go-IMPF-3PL.S
  'The birds are going away, flying.' (Lit. 'fly-going')

There are also examples when a verb is incorporated into the head nominal form:

(6) tipʔejŋe-ŋewəcqet-Ø ənkə ga-twa-len-Ø.
  sing-woman-ABS:SG there PERF-be-PERF-3SG.S
  'The singing woman was there.'

2.7 Adverbs

Adverbs with qualitative adjective stems are marked with the circumfix *n- . . . -ʔew* (cf. section 2.3): *nə-jəq-qin* 'fast, rapid', *nə-jəq-ʔew* 'rapidly'. Other types of adverbs have various markers. The comparative degree is expressed with adverbs by means of the suffix *-ŋ(*)*: *jəq-əŋ* 'more rapidly'. The superlative degree is expressed by means of the prefix *ənan-* added to the form marked with *-ŋ*: *ənan-jəq-əŋ* 'most rapidly'.

In many instances an adverb modifying a verb is incorporated (without any inflections) into the head verb:

(7) (a) nə-tur-ʔew nə-tejkə-qine-t   nelgə-t.
  ADV-new-ADV IMPF-make-IMPF-3PL.O hide-ABS:PL
  '/They/ dressed the hides all over again.'

  (b) nə-tur-tejkə-qine-t nelgə-t.
  IMPF-new-make-IMPF-3PL.O hide-ABS:PL
  '/They/ dressed the hides all over again.' (Lit. 'newly-dressed')

2.8 Postpositions

Nominal postpositions such as *qaca* 'near', *cəmce* 'close to', *ʔattʔəjoca* 'in front of', *rəmagtə* 'behind', and others are used in Chukchee together with the locative form to specify the type of location: *gətg-ək qaca* 'near the lake (loc.)'. Postpositions may have some case forms: *gətg-ək qaca-gtə* 'to the place near (dat.) the lake (loc.)'. The postposition *reen* 'together' is used with the locative form to express the comitative meaning: *Rowt-əna reen* 'together with Rowten (proper name, loc.)'.

3 Derivational morphology

Chukchee has a great number of derivational affixes, and the boundary between inflection and derivation is sometimes unclear. Some derivational affixes originated from nominal and verbal roots used as second parts of compounds.

3.1 Nouns

Some productive nominal suffixes are used to specify different types of location. These affixes may be attached to any appropriate stem, and the derivatives have all case forms: *kuke-ŋə* 'cooking pot', *kuke-cəku-n* 'inside of cooking pot'; *miməl* 'water', *mimlə-cq-ən* 'surface of water'; *wəkw-ən* 'a stone', *wəkwə-geŋ-Ø* 'lower part of stone; place under a stone'.

Nouns may take the augmentative suffixes *-jŋ* and *-cg/-cəŋ* or the diminutive suffix *-qej*: *wala-jŋ-ən* 'big knife', *meməl-qej* 'little seal'. Prefixally, *qej-* is used to form the names of young of animals: *qej-umqə* 'bear cub'. Delimitative meaning is expressed by means of the prefix *em-*: *em-milute-t* 'only hares'. The prefixes *emqən-* 'every' and *gemge-* 'any' are used as quantifiers: *emqən-ŋinqej* 'every boy', *gemge-ŋewəcqet* 'any woman'. Collective nouns are marked with *-giniw* or *-mk*: *ʔatw-ʔat* 'boat', *ʔatwə-giniw* 'group of boats'; *ʔitu-ʔit* 'goose', *ʔitu-mk-ən* 'flock of geese'.

Other affixes used to derive nouns from nouns are: *jocg-* 'a receptacle': *wala-jocg-ən* 'knife sheath'; *-tʔul* 'piece of': *menigə-tʔul* 'piece of cloth'; *-curm* 'edge of': *aŋqa-corm-ən* 'seashore'; *-l(ə)qal* 'intended for': *ewirʔə-lqal* 'material for clothes'; *-ret* 'set of': *lili-ret* 'pair of mittens'; *-jan(w)* 'place full of something': *oonʔə-jan* 'place full of berries'; *ləgi-* 'true, original': *ləgi-ewirʔ-ən* 'true clothes (= Chukchee clothes)'; *təmŋe-* 'ordinary': *təmŋe-rərkə* 'an ordinary walrus'; *ewan-* 'the main': *ewan-nəm* 'the main settlement'; *e-... -ki* 'without': *e-gənnik-ki* 'place/person without animals' (cf. the negation circumfix for verbs, *e-... -ke*, section 2.6.2).

Some nominal stems are formed from nominal roots by means of reduplication: *nəmnəm* 'settlement' (stem *nəmnəm-*, root *nəm-*, cf. *nəmnəm-ək* 'loc.').

Nouns (and participles) can be derived from verb and adjective stems (see sections 2.2, 2.6.2). Instruments are derived from verbal stems by mean of the suffix *-ineŋ(e)*: *ejup-ək* 'to prick', *ejup-ineŋ* 'awl'. Abstract nouns can be derived from nominal stems by means of *-gərg(*)* (cf. section 2.6.2): *nə-ketgu-qin* 'strong', *katgo-gərg-ən* 'strength, power'. In some cases nouns derived from verbs have no obvious affix, *tejŋet-ək* 'to eat', *tejŋet-Ø* 'food'.

3.2 Verbs

Causatives are marked with the prefix *r-/-n-*, in most cases accompanied by a suffixal component *-et, -ew* or *-ŋet* (*r-* is the word-initial allomorph, *-n-* is used in word-medial position): *ekwet-ək* 'to go', *r-ekwet-ew-ək* 'to send'. Intransitives are marked with the prefix *-ine-* (sometimes accompanied by *-et*) or the suffix *-tku*: *rə-tenm-aw-ək* 'to prepare smthg.', *ine-n-tenm-aw-at-ək* 'to be engaged in preparations'. Iterative meanings are expressed by *-tku, -lʔet, -rʔu, -j(i)w*, amongst other suffixes: *rii-k* 'to touch', *rii-tku-k* 'to pull at'. Inceptives are formed by *-ŋŋo*: *wetgaw-ək* 'to speak', *wetgawə-ŋŋo-k* 'to begin speaking'. Reciprocal meaning is expressed by *walg-*: *lʔu-k* 'to see', *lʔu-walg-ək* 'to see each other'. Stativity is marked with *-twa*: *tenmaw-ək* 'to prepare', *tenmawə-twa-k* 'to be preparing'. The suffix *-cqiw* means 'to go to do something': *gite-k* 'to look at', *gite-cqiw-ək* 'to go to look at'.

Verbs can be derived from nouns by means of the suffixes *-tku, -et, -ew, -lʔet, -rʔu, -u*, amongst others. Examples: *walə* 'knife', *wala-tko-k* 'to cut with a knife'; *alpaŋŋ-ən* 'patch', *alpaŋŋ-at-ək* 'to patch'; *tumgə-tum* 'friend', *tumg-ew-ək* 'to become friends'; *ʔatw-ʔat* 'boat', *ʔatwə-lʔet-ək* 'to go out in a boat'; *piŋe-piŋ* 'snowfall', *piŋe-rʔu-k* 'to begin (of snowfall)'; *rʔew* 'whale', *rʔew-u-k* 'to kill whales'; *tekicg-ən* 'meat', *tekicg-u-k* 'to eat meat'.

Verbs are derived from adjective stems by means of the suffixes *-et, -ew* and *-twi*: *nə-watrə-qin* 'visible', *watr-et-ək* 'to be visible'; *n-ilgə-qin* 'white', *ilg-ew-ək* 'to appear white'; *nə-teŋ-qin* 'good', *teŋə-twi-k* 'to become good'.

3.3 Compounds

Besides regular incorporation structures, Chukchee has a good many compounds with idiomatic meaning: *piŋ-wətr-ən* 'flour' (= 'dust-looking'), *welwə-jeg-ət* 'Canadian skis' (lit. 'raven-skis').

Abbreviations

ADP	adverbial participle
ANT	antipassive
COM1/com.1	comitative-1
COM2/com.2	comitative-2
DESG/desg.	designative
DIR/dir.	directional

non-fut.   non-future
ORIENT/orient.   orientative
PART   participle
PERF/perf.   perfective
voc.   vocative

NOTE

1 The root of the verb is *kətgəntat-*. The
  alternation between the final /t/ and
  /n/ before a nasal is regular.

27 Hua (Papuan)

JOHN HAIMAN

Hua is a Papuan language of the Gorokan family, spoken by approximately 3,000 people in a dozen villages around the Lufa District Office in the Eastern Highlands of Papua New Guinea. Both the language itself and the immediate family to which it belongs (including Move, Yate, Kamano, Gimi, Asaro, Alekano, Fore, Siane, and Gende) are among the best known and most deeply studied non-Austronesian languages of the island of New Guinea: which is to say that there are at least a handful of descriptive articles on each of them, and in some cases a full-scale grammatical description. All of these are SOV predominantly suffixing and predominantly agglutinative languages characterized by an absence of grammatical gender and a striking degree of morphological regularity in their marking of nominal case and verbal tense, mood, and aspect, and subject–verb agreement. They are reminiscent in these respects of Turkish.

The Gorokan languages differ in the degree to which agglutinative expression of subject–verb agreement (invariable stem + personal desinence) has been replaced by a synthesis of these two morphemes. In Hua, it is impossible to make a morphological separation between stem and desinence, as the person and number of the subject of the verb are marked through a combination of vocalic ablaut affecting the final segment of the verb stem + an only partially specified personal desinence. Comparative evidence suggests that stem ablaut arose through vowel crasis, or gunah, the relatively unstable vowel chain sequence $/ \ldots V1 + V2 \ldots /$ (still comparatively well preserved in Gimi), being replaced by $/ \ldots V3 + \ldots /$. Nevertheless, it is impossible to posit phonologically plausible abstract underlying representations of the first type in a synchronic grammar of Hua. Rather, V3 is a person–number-sensitive derivative of V1, which belongs clearly to the verb stem, and the morph(eme) boundary between stem and desinence has shifted over one segment. Thus, contrast the Gimi and Hua cognate forms of 'you (sg.) do':

Gimi: ho + ane *do + 2sg. assertive*
Hua: ha + ne *do (2 person) + 2sg./1pl. assertive*

All of the Gorokan languages, in addition to marking subject–verb and (much more limited) object–verb agreement by verbal affixation, also exhibit exuberant morphological markings for different types of clause linkage in compound and complex sentences. There are a variety of devices for linking clauses, depending on whether they are invested with the same illocutionary force. For example, there is a characteristic subject–verb agreement-marking suffix roughly equivalent to our colon when an assertion is to be followed by a balancing assertion or a rhetorical question:

hi-va   *do (3 person) + colon 1sg./3sg./2, 3 pl.,*

another when an imperative is followed by an assertion, and another when an assertion is followed by an imperative.

When the marking clause and the following clause are in the same mood (or have roughly the same illocutionary force), then the verb of the nonfinal clause (or *medial*) in a compound sentence, in addition to marking the person and number of its subject, will also mark the person and number of the following verb.

Medial verbs are a notorious feature of many of the Papuan languages of the so-called trans-New Guinea phylum, and the distinction between medial and final verbs has been familiar to specialists since the appearance of Pilhofer's grammar of the Kate language in 1933.

A more recent discovery (Haiman 1976) is that in a somewhat smaller number of languages, including Hua, medial verbs may be of two types, coordinate and subordinate. Coordinate clauses are in the same tense and mood as the following clause and observe tense iconicity: that is, the events described in the prior clause occur before the events described in the subsequent clause. Subordinate medial clauses are invariably in the assertive/indicative mood (corresponding roughly to presuppositions), need not observe tense (iconicity, and need not be in the same tense as the following clause.

In addition to marking person and number of two subjects, *coordinate medial verbs alone* also indicate whether the following subject is or is not identical with its own. This is what is known as "switch-reference marking." Comparative evidence and typological universals allow us to reconstruct the origins of both medial verbs and the mechanism of switch reference with a fair amount of confidence.

There are a handful of morphological categories in all the Gorokan languages which are expressed by prefixes: on certain inalienably possessed nouns, the pronoun expressing the possessor:

d-vari   'my sweat';

on some transitive verbs, the pronoun expressing the human object (in the case of ditransitive verbs, this will be the indirect object):

d – mi   -e
me – give (non-first person) – 1, 3 sg., 2, 3 pl. assertive.

In Hua alone, for a fairly substantial number of verbal and nominal roots, these prefixes are infixed rather than prefixed, and comparative evidence from other languages and productive processes in Hua allow us to conjecture how infixation may have become established.

1 Nominal morphology

The superficial syllable structure of Hua is CV('), with the glottal stop as the only permitted final consonant. At a slightly more abstract level, the canonical syllable structure is C*V(C): underlying syllable-initial consonant clusters are broken up by the insertion of anaptyctic schwa, and the final consonant may be one of the three consonants /r, n, '/. Consequently, all syllabic morphemes in Hua end in open syllables, or at most in syllables closed by one of the consonants /r, n, '/.

1.1 The citation suffix

To some extent, the parts of speech are identifiable from their phonetic structure. Verb stems may end only in a vowel, in fact, one of the vowels /i, o, u/. Only nouns may end in /r, n/, and only before a single suffix /-a/, the "citation" suffix. This is an optional variant of the nominative case marker, and may occur only with monosyllabic roots or stems. The citation suffix may be followed by the predicate/exclamative marker /-e/ and no other suffix. When a nominal stem is itself polysyllabic, the citation suffix is disfavored. When the nominal stem is followed by any other suffix, the citation suffix cannot occur:

de-a-e	*man + cit. + pred.*	'Man!'
ar-a-e	*woman + cit. + pred.*	'Woman!'
mnin-a	*water + cit. + pred.*	'Water!'

Before any suffix other than the citation suffix, including zero, morpheme-final /r, n/ are realized as the glottal stop – hence the nominatives *de* 'man', *a'* 'woman', *mni'* 'water'.

As indicated, the citation suffix is hard to elicit or is rarely attested with polysyllabic stems:

okrumar-a	~	okruma'	'sky'
gian-a	~	gia'	'foot, leg'
ovu-a	~	ovu	'star',

but:

gasino'	'braid'
gana'	'younger brother'
atve	'taro'
ege	'banana, plantain'

In Hua (as in English) many proper nouns are derived from common nouns. All proper nouns, however, end in the glottal stop – hence the contrast *momoti* 'kind of wallaby' versus *momoti'* 'male name'.

The citation suffix is impossible to elicit with proper nouns. When they are used in the vocative, proper names lose the final glottal stop:

momoti – (o)   'Momoti!'

For practical purposes, all nonverbal syllabic stems in Hua end in either a vowel or the glottal stop. The contrast has consequences when these stems are followed by other morphemes, with two exceptions. The first we have already seen: the final glottal stop disappears in the vocative "case." In the second, before the possessive suffixes, a final glottal stop is apparently supplied.

1.2 The possessive suffixes

All nominal stems, whether or not they are inalienably possessed, may be followed by a possessive suffix marking the person and number of the possessor. The form of the possessive suffix (and of this suffix alone) is identical irrespective of whether the nominal stem ends in a vowel or the glottal stop.

The possessive suffixes, unlike other pronominal categories, distinguish second and third person not only in the singular, but also in dual and plural numbers:

Person	*Singular*	*Dual*	*Plural*
1	'di	ti'a	ti
2	ka	tti'a	ti
3	'a	'i'a	'i'

Thus *zur-a* 'house, home': 1sg. *zu'di*, 3sg. *zu'a*, 3pl. *zu'i'*, and *zu-a* 'work, garden': 1sg. *zu'di*, 3sg. *zu'a*, 3pl. *zu'i'*. (Most kin terms occur with an extension *-ma'* on the possessive suffix, thus *naru'ama'* 'his wife'.)

1.3 The case suffixes

No such neutralization occurs before other suffixes, such as the true case suffixes, which typically occur in two forms:

Case	Postvocalic	Postconsonantal
Benefactive	hi'	si'
Inessive	vi'	pi'
Allative	ro'	to'
Comitative	gi'	ki'

Thus, for *zura*: *zusi*' 'for the house', *zuto*' 'at the house', but for *zua*: *zuhi*' 'for the work', *zuro*' 'at work'. The forms in the right-hand column exemplify a general pattern of glottal stop absorption, whereby glottal stop + C1 yields a generally homorganic but less sonorant C2. (As a special case of this, a sequence of two glottal stops is pronounced as a single glottal stop.) The fact that the contrast between vowel- and consonant-final stems is neutralized before the possessive suffixes suggests that the latter may be analyzable as consisting of glottal stop + other material: thus 3sg. *'a* = ' + a, 2sg. *-ka* = ' + ga, etc. Then /zu + ' + ga/ 'your work' is indistinguishable from /zu' + ' + ga/ 'your house'.

Two other case suffixes are notable in that they distinguish singular and plural: these are the ergative and the genitive. The ergative case is irregular in the singular:

Case		Postvocalic	Postglottal
Ergative	sg.	mu'	'bamu'
	pl.	mi	'bi
Genitive	sg.	ma'	'ba'
	pl.	'i'	'i'

1.4 The personal pronouns

The personal pronouns are heteroclitic, in that they seem to be vowel-final with some affixes (among them the citation suffix *-a* and the comitative suffix *-gi*'), but glottal-stop-final with others (such as the benefactive suffix *hi*' and the allative suffix *-ro*'). The forms of the genitive and the ergative are irregular with personal pronouns, as well: the genitive is uniformly *-*', while the ergative agrees in both person and number with the personal pronoun. As is clear from the examination of any single column in table 27.1, the personal pronouns consist of various prefixes (identical with the prefixes which mark the person of the inalienable possessor) on a common stem *gai*, the meaning of which is uncertain. Thus 'I' is literally 'my *gai*', etc.

1.5 The possessive prefixes

Some (but not all) kin terms, effluviae, and body-part terms obligatorily mark possession with possessive prefixes identical with those which occur in the paradigm of personal pronouns. Thus *d-naru*' 'my wife', *k-gehu* 'your grandchild',

Table 27.1   Personal pronouns

	Citation	Benefactive	Ergative	Genitive
1sg.	dgai-a	dgai-si'	dgaivi'bamu'da	dgai-'
2sg.	kgai-a	kgai-si'	kgaivi'bamuga	kgai-'
3sg.	gai-a	gai-si'	gaivi'bamu'	gai-'
1du.	ra'agai-a	ra'agaisi'	ra'agaimuta'a	ra'agai-'
2/3du.	pa'agai-a	pa'agaisi'	pa'agaimita'a	pa'agai-'
1pl.	rgai-a	rgaisi'	rgaimuta	rgai-'
2/3pl.	pgai-a	pgaisi'	pgaimita	pgai-'

r-gia' 'our feet', *p-vari* 'their sweat', *p-gau* 'your vaginas'. With three kin terms, *e'gu'* 'elder brother', *i'ra'* 'mother', and *e'va'* 'father', the possessive prefix is irregularly infixed: thus *e'dgu'* (*e'-d- gu'*) 'my elder brother', *ikra'* (*i' -g – ra'*) 'your mother', *epva'* (*e' – p – va'*) 'their father'.

A number of kin terms and body parts, seemingly as inalienably possessed as any others, do not permit a possessive prefix at all. Among these are the kin terms *ba'de* 'boy, son', *a'ba'de* 'girl, daughter', *ete* 'husband', and the body parts *iko'* 'navel' and *aigi* 'anus', as well as the effluviae *vi* 'tears, urine' and *ai* 'feces'. Their inalienability is covertly marked, however, in the following way: with alienably possessed nouns, possession may be marked by either the possessive suffix or the expression possessor + genitive possessum, and the possessive suffix does not indicate inalienability at all. Thus 'my dog' can be either *dgai' kra*, 1sg. + genitive dog, or *kra -'di*, dog + 1sg., possessive. With inalienably possessed nouns, the possessive suffix is always obligatory. Thus *iko-'di* (**dgai'* iko') 'my navel', and so on. The same need to mark the possessor by an affix on inalienably possessed nouns is reflected in regular nouns when the possessor is 3sg. The pronoun prefix is nil, but this kind of non-expression is unacceptable: *d'za'* 'my hand, arm', but **0-za'* 'his/her hand'. Here the possessor again has to be indicated by the otherwise optional possessive suffix *za'a* 'his/her hand'.

1.6 Number marking

Except in personal pronouns and in the ergative case marker, number is not a fully grammaticalized category in nominal morphology. A handful of common human nouns have suppletive plurals:

	Singular	Plural
man	de	ve'de
woman	a'	a'de
person	gnu	naga'

Others form plurals by compounding or the addition of a collective affix like -*gi* 'group':

	Singular	Plural	
boy	ba'de	ba'de+ve'de	'boys'
bird	mna	mna+vza	'flock of birds'
sweet potato	bza	bza + vutavu	'pile of sweet potatoes'
Norope	Norope	Norope + gi	'Norope and his family'

1.7 The potential topic marker

Nominal expressions (including deverbal nominal expressions) may be marked as such by the addition of the potential topic marker -*mo* (postglottal -*'bo*), the distribution of which is somewhat complicated. First, the potential topic suffix may never co-occur with the citation suffix, even when this is functioning as nothing more than the redundant marker of the nominative case. One may say *vi-a toe* or *vi-mo toe* 'I cried, shed tears', but never **vi-a-mo toe*. This is the most evident constraint on the distribution of the suffix, leading one native language consultant to suggest that -*mo* occurred where words are joined together in an utterance, while the citation suffix tends to occur when words are uttered in isolation. But there are other constraints as well. The suffix is forbidden on nominal expressions acting as adjectives. That is, it cannot occur on nouns in the genitive case, nominal modifiers in the inessive or adressive/ allative cases, or on relative clauses:

dgai'	(*mo)	fu		'my pig'
fina + roga	(*mo)	de		'a fighting (lit. fight-at) man'
dmima'	(*mo)	fu		'the pig he gave me'

The suffix is also forbidden on nominal expressions which act as entire utterances. That is, it cannot occur on nouns in the vocative "case":

momoti (-o) (*mo) 'Momoti!'

And it is probably for this same reason that it never occurs on final finite verbs, and why it is listed here as an essentially nominal affix.

With nouns in other cases which are "acting as nouns" (not verbs or adjectives), the suffix is optional, though it is favored as a fattener (as is the citation suffix) on what would otherwise be monosyllabic words: one may say *dgai* or *dgai-a* or *dgai-mo* 'I', but the first occurs rarely. Similarly, one may say *dgaisi'* or *dgaisi'bo* 'for me', but both are common. (Recall that the citation suffix -*a* is impossible with any other suffix.)

Finally, the suffix -*mo* is virtually obligatory on one subordinate clause type, the conditional protasis (which would otherwise be identical with the relative clause):

d-mima-mo   'given that he gave it to me'

Within the limits of its permitted distribution, the potential topic suffix is virtually meaningless. It certainly cannot be translated as anything like "as for . . .", the way we might translate Japanese *wa* in some cases. For this, there exists an actual topic suffix -*ve*, which may follow the suffix -*mo*:

dgai-mo-ve   'as for me'

Nor can it be translated as the definite article (as the cognate etymon is translatable in Alekao or Asaro, for example; cf. Haiman 1992). Hua has no grammaticalized marking for definiteness at all.

2 Verbal morphology

The most striking fact about the Hua verb is that in all but the most common cases, it consists of a presumably nominal root followed by a verbalizer, the support verb *hu-* 'do': thus *zagita hu-* 'cook', *kori hu-* 'flee, be afraid', *fina hu-* 'fight'. Although the nominal stem in such compound verbs frequently has no independent existence, there are nevertheless three good reasons for analyzing it as a noun (and, in fact, an object noun). First, the nominal root is frequently found with the potential topic suffix -*mo*, here utterly meaningless, thus *fina-mo hu-* 'fight'. Second, the negative prefix *'a'* (*a*)-, which generally precedes the verb stem, comes between the nominal stem and the support verb; compare *'a'-d- gorai-* 'not -me- trick' with *kori – 'a- fu-* 'fleeing – not- do'. Finally, the subjects of semantically intransitive verbs of the form NP + *hu-* may occur in the ergative case.

The second most striking fact about Hua verbs, already touched on in the introductory paragraphs of this survey, is that the final vowel of the verb stem (which must be one of the vowels /i, o, u/) is subject to ablaut, depending on the person and number of its subject. There are, in fact, two person-marking ablauting rules of general validity, depending on the nature of the immediately following affix. Before we deal with these, some remarks on the structure of the verb phrase are in order.

Like other SOV languages, Hua has V + Auxiliary order, with personal or infinitival desinences following at the end of this complex. Auxiliaries marking aspect precede those marking tense and mood. Mood is marked by both auxiliaries and final desinences, and, in at least one case, by an invariable portmanteau of the two. Except in the case of the progressive aspect marker *bai-*, which is identical with the copula/existential verb "to be," the auxiliary verbs are distinct from lexical verbs. Some of the other common auxiliaries and auxiliary combinations are the following:

Perfective (past):	-ro-
Habitual:	-ro + hu-
Future	
(a) indicative:	-gu-
(b) subjunctive:	-su-
Avolitional:	-ro + gu- ~ ro + su-

(This last, clearly a combination of the perfective and one of the future auxiliaries, translates "it would be bad if . . ." in principal clauses, or "lest . . ." in subordinate clauses.)

Finite personal desinences are characterized by the peculiarity that they occur in three forms. Since there are seven persons in Hua, it follows that the desinences leave person and number systematically underspecified. Some examples of these "threefold desinences" are:

Person	Assertive	Interrogative	Exclamatory	Colon
1, 3sg., 2, 3pl.	e	ve	mane	va
dual	'e	've	'mane	'va
2sg, 1pl.	ne	pe	pane	pa

(It is notable that the glottal stop, where it functions as the characteristic mark of dual number, is impervious to the otherwise general rules of glottal-stop coalescence exemplified in the discussion of nominal morphology.)

Nonfinite desinences include the infinitives -'*di*' and -*gasi*', and the imperative -(*o*) (dual -'*o*, plural -(*h*)*o*).

2.1 The ablaut rules

The simplest and most general rule is that the final vowel of the verb or auxiliary stem immediately preceding the subjunctive auxiliary -*su*-, the invariable jussive portmanteau -*no*, and the invariable future medial portmanteau -*na*- is always fronted, irrespective of person and number of its subject. Stem-final /o, u/ change to /e, i/, while stem-final /i/ remains unchanged. The pattern is illustrated for the subjunctive only:

	Stem	Subjunctive			
be	bai-	bai-su-e	'let me be',	bai-si-e	'let him/her be'
eat	do-	de-su-e	'let me eat',	de-si-e	'let him/her eat'
do	hu-	hi-su-e	'let me do',	hi-si-e	'let him/her do'

The second rule is that the final vowel of the verb or auxiliary stem preceding any morpheme other than the subjunctive or one of the "threefold desinences" is fronted when its subject is nonfirst person and nonsingular. The pattern is illustrated with changes affecting the final vowel of the stem preceding the future indicative auxiliary -*gu*-:

		But:
do-gu-e	'I will eat'	
do-ga-ne	'You will eat'	
do-gi-e	'He/she will eat'	
do-gu-'e	'We two will eat'	

		de-ga-'e	'you two will eat' 'they two will eat'
do-gu-ne	'We will eat'		
		de-ga-e	'you all will eat' 'they will eat'

By the same rule, stem-final /u/ becomes /i/, but final /i/ is unaffected.

The most complex rule operates on the final vowel of the verb or auxiliary stem which immediately precedes one of the threefold personal desinences. If the desinence is 1sg., 1du., or 1pl. (*first* person), the stem vowel is backed: /i/ becomes /u/, and /o/ and /u/ remain unchanged. If the desinence is 2sg., 2, 3du., or 2, 3pl. (*second* person), the back vowels /o,u/ are lowered to /a/, while /i/ remains unchanged. If the desinence is 3sg. (*third* person), the back vowels /o,u/ are fronted, while the front vowel /i/ remains unchanged. The operation of the third rule is exemplified in the treatment of the future indicative auxiliary -*gu*- in the paradigm above, which immediately precedes the threefold assertive desinence -*e* (~'*e* ~*ne*).

Note that the alternation is not sensitive to the actual form of the personal desinence (e.g. the assertive -*e* does different work when it is 1sg., 2/3pl., and 3sg.), but to its "PERSON," and also to its identity as a threefold desinence with "unmarked (1, 3 sg., 2, 3pl.)," "dual (1, 2, 3du.)," and "other (2sg., 1pl.)" person forms. For example, the imperative personal desinences, which mark singular, dual, and plural, occur in three forms, but are not threefold desinences of this type. And they do not induce the complex rule, but the more simple two-way rule:

hu-(o)	'Do it!'		do-(o)	'Eat it! ([do])'
hi-'o	'You two do it!'		de-'o	'You two eat it!'
hi-o	'You all do it.'		de-ho	'You all eat it.'

2.2 Medial verbs

There are no clausal conjunctions in Hua. Instead, clause linkage is indicated by verbal affixes on the nonfinal or medial verbs (more generally: medial *predicates*, verbal or nominal) in compound sentences. The most common medial verb structure is the one which corresponds roughly to "and," which will be referred to as the "coordinate medial verb." Almost as common is the different

Table 27.2

Person	Present verb + medial desinence	Possible origin
1sg.	hu + ga +	*hu + e# ga
2sg.	ha + na +	*ha + ne# ga
3sg.	hi + ga +	*hi + e# ga
1du.	hu + 'ga +	*hu + 'e# ga
2/3du.	ha + 'ga +	*ha + 'e# ga
1pl.	hu + na +	*hu + ne# ga
2/3pl.	ha + ga +	*ha + e# ga

structure which may be translated as "given that . . . ," hereafter known as the "subordinate medial."

2.2.1 Coordinate medial verbs
Coordinate medial verbs occur with two sets of subject-marking desinences: the first, which mark agreement with the subject of the medial verb itself, are threefold desinences, inducing the complex ablaut rule in the immediately preceding verbal stem.

The unmarked (1, 3 sg., 2, 3pl.) form -ga is similar to the collective suffix -gi, the symmetrical phrasal conjunction . . . -gi . . . -gi 'both . . . and . . .', the comitative postposition -gi', and is also clearly cognate with etyma in other Gorokan languages, suggesting that it may have once been a clausal conjunction meaning "and" (cf. Haiman 1992). In addition, almost every phonological process that would be required to convert an inherited *verb + final desinence# "and" into verb + medial desinence is either active elsewhere in Hua, or is phonetically plausible on general typological grounds (Haiman 1987 and see table 27.2).

On the other hand, the second set of subject-marking desinences, which mark agreement with the subject of the following verb, are much more similar to the personal pronoun sets which we have already encountered as prefixes and suffixes. The contrasting paradigms of these medial and anticipatory desinences are presented in table 27.3.

The anticipatory desinences induce an ablaut alternation in the preceding *medial desinences*: final /a/ becomes /i/ before anticipatory desinences which are nonfirst person and nonsingular. Observe the contrast between hi – ga – ta, 3sg. did and we . . . , and hi – gi – ta, '3sg. did and you all/they . . .'. Co-occurrence of medial and anticipatory desinences on coordinate medial verbs signals that the subjects of medial and following verbs are distinct: hi – ga – na, 3sg. did and 3sg. . . . , will therefore be translated as 'he did and she . . .' for convenience, and structures like *hu – ga – 'da 'I did and I . . .' and *ha – na – ka 'You did and you . . .' are ungrammatical (although presumably ripe for exploitation by a Hua Pirandello, Rimbaud, Borges, or Kafka some day).

Table 27.3   Medial and anticipatory desinences

Person	Medial	Anticipatory
1sg.	ga	'da
2sg.	na	ka
3sg.	ga	na
1du.	'ga	ta'a
2/3du.	'ga	t(in)a'a
1pl.	na	ta
2/3pl.	ga	t(in)a

Where the subjects of medial and following verbs are identical, the medial verb consists of the verb plus auxiliary complex followed by the anticipatory desinence alone. (It is as if the medial desinences were gapped under identity.) The anticipatory desinences, since they are not threefold desinences, behave like all other morphemes which are not threefold desinences, and induce the two-way ablaut alternation in the immediately preceding verb stem. The pattern for same-subject medials is illustrated below with the paradigm for '... saw (perfective) them and ...':

1sg.	p- go – ro – 'da
2sg.	p -go – ro – ka
3sg.	p -go – ro – na
1dl.	p -go – ro – ta'a
2, 3dl.	p -g*e* – r*e* – ta'a
1pl.	p -go – ro – ta
2, 3pl.	p -g*e* – r*e* – ta

In general, coordinate medial verbs are possible whenever and only when the illocutionary force of medial and following clauses are the same. There are, however, some systematic relaxations of this constraint. First, the medial clause may be a content question, and the following clause may be an assertion, as in:

kzo' k – mi – ga – ka   da – ne?
who 2sg. give 3sg. 2sg. eat   2sg.
'Who gave it to you, that you ate it?'

Second, if the medial clause occurs in the future tense (the only acceptable future auxiliary in coordinate medial clauses being the subjunctive), it may be translated as a conditional protasis, and as such may freely co-occur with following clauses in any mood:

Table 27.4 Imperative desinences

Person	Medial imperative	Anticipatory imperative
1sg.	——	'di
2sg.	ga	——
3sg.	——	nu
1du.	——	ti'
2du.	'ga	——
3du.	——	ti'
1pl.	——	ti
2pl.	ga	——
3pl.	——	ti

k – mi – su – ga – ka   do   -(o)!
2sg. give fut. 1sg. 2sg. eat imper.   clamative
'If I give it to you, eat it!'

kmisugaka de – sa – pe?
          eat   fut. 2sg. interr.
'If I give it to you, will you eat it?'

Finally, a special form of the coordinate medial is used where the medial clause is an imperative and the following clause is assertive. The final assertive clause is frequently merely understood, as in the common formula of leave-taking:

bai – ga – 'di (ue)
stay 2   1sg.
'Stay! and I (am going).'

The imperative medial desinences, like the imperative final desinences, mark only number (all are second person), and induce the two-way ablaut alternation in the preceding stem. The anticipatory desinences are similar to the regular anticipatory desinences not only in their form (they differ only in their final vowel), but in their capacity to induce ablaut in the preceding medial desinence (see table 27.4). To see the ablauting of the medial desinence in operation, consider the contrast between *hu – ga – ti* 'Do it and we . . .' and *hu – gi – ti* 'Do it and they . . .'. The second-person form of the medial anticipatory desinence is lacking in all numbers: so it is impossible to use this construction to say things like "Seek, and ye shall find." It might seem logical to assume that the reason for this gap is that the co-occurrence of medial and anticipatory desinences in this form, as in the ordinary coordinate medial, would (incorrectly) signal the nonidentity of the subjects of the medial and following clause. Nevertheless, this plausible assumption is mistaken. One of the most remarkable things about the medial imperative, in fact, is that it can be used all by itself as a hortatory imperative: *u – ga – ti'* 'Go and we two . . .' or 'Let's you and me go' and *hu – ga – ti* 'Do and we all . . .' or 'Let's all do'. In this case, it is clear that the subject of the medial is included within the subject of the following (understood) verb. In ordinary medials, such referential overlap requires the use of a same-subject medial. One can no more say **hu – ga – ta* 'I did and we . . .' or **hu – na – da* 'We did and I . . .' than **hu – ga – da* 'I did and I . . .' or **hu – na – ta* 'We did and we . . .'. But in the medial imperative, this constraint is mysteriously relaxed.

2.2.2 *Subordinate medial verbs*   Nominal predicates may occur without a copula verb. When they do, they consist of the noun phrase followed by either the citation suffix or the potential topic particle, and the predicate suffix *-e* (the latter identical with the unmarked form of the assertive threefold desinence). Examples are:

dtir – a – e   '(Good) morning!'
bira ba'de – a – e   'You over there!'
fu – mo – e   'It's pork.'

Such predicates may be conjoined with the following clauses, and then occur in a medial form. Medialization of a nominal predicate is achieved by substituting invariable *-ga-* for the invariable final predicate suffix *-e* and adding the appropriate anticipatory desinences. What is noteworthy about the medialization of nominal predicates is that switch reference is not marked. The medial suffix *-ga-* is present whether the subject of the following clause is the same as or different from the "subject" (the only entity) of the medial clause:

ba'de-mo – ga – na   via   to – bai – e.
boy   p.t.   med. 3sg. tears shed prog. 3sg.
'Being a kid, he's crying.' (Presumably same subject)

fu – mo – ga – ta   do – ne.
pork p.t.   med. 1pl. eat   1pl.
'Since it's pork, we eat it.' (Different subject)

This neutralization of the same subject/different subject distinction is characteristic of verbs in subordinate medial clauses (which for this reason, among others, may be thought of as nominalizations).

The fundamental deverbalized nominal base of a subordinate medial clause consists of the verb plus auxiliary complex followed by the threefold conditional protasis desinence *-mamo* (~ *'mamo* ~ *pamo*). All combinations of auxiliary verbs are allowed except that the only permitted version of the future auxiliary in the subordinate medial clause is the indicative *-gu-*: *hi – mamo* 'given that 3sg. did . . .', *hu – gi – mamo* 'given that 3sg. will do . . .'. This base is then medialized in the same way as any other nominal predicate: *hu – ma[mo – ga] – na* 'given that I did, 3sg. . . .', *hu – ma[mo – ga] -'da* 'given that I did, I . . .'. An abbreviated form of the subordinate medial clause, apparently synonymous with the full form, elides the invariable morphemes *-mo* and *-ga-* (set in brackets in the examples above): *hu – ma – na* 'given that I did, 3sg. . . .', *hu – ma – 'da* 'given that I did, I . . .'. In both the full and abbreviated forms of the subordinate medial verb, stress is shifted to the *-ma* syllable.

The clumsy translations I have provided fail to make clear that the most striking semantic differences between coordinate and subordinate medial verbal clauses relate to the illocutionary and narrative autonomy of the subordinate medial clause. While coordinate medial clauses (subject to the relaxations noted) agree in mood with the clauses following them, subordinate medial clauses are invariably assertive and indicative; while coordinate medial clauses are in the same tense as the clauses following them, subordinate medial clauses need not be; and while coordinate medial clauses observe tense iconicity (and are thus often felicitously translated with subordinate conjunctions like "after . . ."), subordinate medial clauses do not have to do so. Both clause types are similar, however, in two fundamental ways.

First, if the first clause is assertive and the following clause is an imperative, there is a tendency to avoid the use of medial clauses entirely (except where the medial clause is a conditional protasis). The favored construction here is to use a final clause, followed by the invariable suffix *-ge*:

hepa ge   ha – ne – ge iro   – (o)!
bad   talk   do   2sg.   quit imper.   clamative
'You're talking nonsense: quit it!'

u – ro – ma(e) – ge bai   – o!
go   perf. 1sg.   stay imper.   clamative
'I'm leaving: you stay!' (Another formulaic leave-taking)

Second, use of the anticipatory desinence in many cases invites the *post hoc ergo propter hoc* inference. For this reason, medial clauses are often best translated by "if . . . then," "because," or "since." To express relations other than consequentiality, other clause-linking devices are sometimes needed.

2.2.3 Special uses of the same-subject medial
Before proceeding to a survey of these, however, we should take note of a class of cases (all involving same-subject medials) where medial verbs do *not* invite the propter hoc inference.

2.2.3.1 Manner adverbs   Hua lacks a separate category of adverbs of manner. These are expressed as same-subject medial verbs: *brgefi-e* '3sg. was quick', and *brgefu- na rgine-e* '3sg. came back quickly'. (One might suppose that this same structure is used more generally to indicate simultaneous activity. However, if simultaneity of two conceptually equally significant actions is to be emphasized, the structure of choice is V + *mo* V:

do – na rmi – e.
eat   3sg. go=down 3sg.
'S/he ate and went down.'

But

do – mo rmi   – e.
eat   go=down 3sg.
'S/he went down, eating.'

The suffix -*mo* is unique in itself undergoing the two-way ablaut alternation:

de – me rma   – e
eat   go=down 2, 3pl.
'You all/they went down eating.'

This property distinguishes it from the otherwise homophonous potential topic suffix -*mo*. It is cognate with the Gimi invariable same-subject marking medial suffix -*me* '-ing'.)

2.2.3.2 Lexicalizations In Hua, as in many Papuan languages, 'bring' and 'take' (and some other complex verbs) are lexicalized as a string of verbs: 'bring' is 'hold (same subject) + come', 'take' as 'hold (same subject) + go'.

2.2.3.3 Auxiliarization Finally, in Hua the line between Verb + Auxiliary and Same-subject medial verb # following verb is not absolutely fixed. (Note that the formal distinction between the two is the presence or absence of the anticipatory desinences on the first verb.) For example, the progressive aspect is occasionally expressed by Verb + SS *bai-* as well as by the more common V + *bai-* complex. Conversely, the anticipatory desinence tends to drop in frequently used V + SS # V collocations, making them look like V + Auxiliary constructions. One particularly significant structure where this is starting to occur is V + SS *to-*, where *to-* (reconstructible, on the basis of comparative evidence, as 'give', but in Hua meaning something more like 'put') functions as a transitivizer:

ehi – e   'S/he got up.'
ehi – (na) 0 – te (-e)   'S/he got him up.' ([ehite])
get=up 3sg. 3sg. put 3sg.

The possibility of elision of the SS suffix exists only where the transitivizing verb occurs without an audible prefix:

ehi   -na d – te -(e)   'S/he got me up.' ([ehinandte])
get=up 3sg. 1sg. put 3sg.

2.3 *Relative clauses and conditionals*

Relative clauses are prenominal. The clause-internal NP identical with the head is deleted, and in place of the final desinence, a relative desinence is used. The relative desinence may be either -'*di*', infinitive, or the threefold relative desinence -*ma*' (~'*ma*', ~ *pa*'). There may be a tendency to use the infinitive suffix (which cannot co-occur with either future auxiliary) to mark . habitual aspect and indefinite agents, but this is not an inflexible rule:

do – ma' -na
eat   1sg. thing
'what I ate'

do – 'di' – na
eat   inf.   thing
'food'

The relative desinence (unlike the homophonous genitive suffix) is a nominalizer, and relative clauses may occur with a variety of case affixes and the potential topic suffix when they are not performing an adjectival function as prenominal modifiers. Relative clauses followed by the inessive suffix -*vi*' translate 'while . . .' clauses; those followed by the allative/adessive suffix -*ro*' translate 'where . . .' clauses:

d -aumo vo – bau – ma – pi' u –re   – e.
1sg. eye lie   prog. 1sg. in. go perf. 3sg.
'While I was sleeping, s/he left.'

bau – ma – to' eno!
be   1sg. all. come=imper.
'Come to where I am!'

Relative clauses followed by the potential topic suffix -*mo* (the -*ma*' desinence unaccountably losing its final glottal stop here) may be thought of as nominative absolutes. They may occur in the nonfuture tense, in which case they may be translated as 'given that . . .' or 'when . . .'. In the future tense (with the subjunctive -*su*- the only permitted auxiliary), they are hypothetical conditionals:

a –   pamo k – go – e.
come 2sg.   2sg. see 1sg.
'When you came, I saw you.'

e –   sa – pamo k – go – gu – e.
come fut. 2sg.   2sg. see   fut.   1sg.
'If you come, I will see you.'

The hypothetical conditional protasis is regularly expressed with a coordinate future medial:

e –   sa – na – 'da k – go – gu – e.
come fut. 2sg. 1sg. 2sg. see   fut.   1sg.
'If you come, I'll see you.'

There are only three contexts in which the coordinate medial is impossible as a hypothetical protasis. The first, unremarkably, is where the subject of the second clause is identical with the subject of the medial clause (recall that co-occurrence of medial and anticipatory desinences signals different subjects in the two clauses). Here, the conditional or a same-subject conditional medial with a special auxiliary verb (?) -*to*- are required:

e-   sa – pamo d- go – ga – ne.
come fut. 2sg.   1sg. see   fut.   2sg.
'If you come, you will see me.'

o –   to – ka   d – go – ga – ne.
come ?   2sg. 1sg. see   fut.   2sg.
'If/when you come, you will see me.'

The second (remarkably), is where the conditional is *concessive*. The clearest and most unambiguous example of a concessive conditional (given the absence in Hua of a word like 'even') is a sentence of the form "whether X or not X, Y": the need for a conditional structure here and the impossibility of a coordinate medial at once underline the consequentiality of medial verbs with the anticipatory desinence, and the inconsequentiality of the regular conditional.

'ogue'   'a'ogue'   hi -sa – pamo dgaimo kge 'afu –   gu – e.
I'll come I won't   come do fut.   2sg.   I   worry   not=do fut.   1sg.
'Whether you come or not, I won't care.'

The third context where the true conditional is *de rigueur* is the counter-factual, as opposed to the hypothetical, conditional.

Counterfactual conditionals are morphologically distinct from given and hypothetical conditionals (which differ in Hua only through the presence or absence of the subjunctive future auxiliary). The counterfactual desinence is derived from an *irrealis* threefold desinence -*hine* (~'*hine* ~ -*sine*) which can be translated by 'almost . . .' or 'would have . . .': *kosa handaure – hine* 'I almost fell (but didn't)', *hepa namo do – sine* 'We would have eaten something bad.' The protasis of a counterfactual conditional will occur with the threefold desinence -*hipana* (~'*hipana* ~ *sipana*), while the apodosis will occur with -*hine*:

a – sipana k – go – hine.
come 2sg.   2sg. see   1sg.
'If you had come, I would have seen you.'

2.4 *The inconsequential*

Further highlighting the inconsequential nature of the unmarked hypothetical conditional in Hua is the interchangeability of the conditional desinence *-mamo* with another threefold desinence *-mana*. What is remarkable about this fact is that *-mana* occurs as a desinence on *final* verbs, in which case its most striking and widespread use is to signal that the act described in the verb was undertaken in vain, or without the consequences one would have expected:

hako – e.
seek   1sg.
'I looked for it.'

hako – mana – (o).
seek   1sg.   clamative
'I looked for it – in vain.'

One of the most philosophically interesting uses of this desinence in Hua is to signal speech which is responded to not by action, *but by other speech* (even where speech is the expected and desired response). It is easy to reconcile this with its fundamental use, given the common assumption that talk is cheap; but there is another frequent use of the inconsequential which does not follow from any familiar attitudes we may have.

Hua generally lacks complementizers like 'that', and uses the inconsequential (or the conditional) with verbs of knowing and perceiving, or even with verbs which lead up to acts of perception: it is then understood that the clause which follows a *-mana* clause represents the content of the perception:

ke – mana fi'a – ro' gnu – mo na   bai – mane!
look 3sg.   rack   on corpse p.t. there be   excl.3sg.
'S/he looked and (saw that) there was a corpse on the rack.'

The "complements" of verbs of perception in *-mana* tend to be high in factivity: the perceiver not only saw or heard whatever it was, but it was really so. For this reason, this structure is not favored for more subjective verbs of saying or thinking, the truth of whose complements is much more a matter of opinion.

2.5 *Modality*

A survey of the expression of modality in Hua may begin with a consideration of the syntax of the verb ( )*geta havi-* 'think, believe, opine', (lit. 'one's ear hear'). Although this may occur with the inconsequential *-mana* or the conditional *-mamo*, the favored structure for the verb of opinion is:

( )   geta havi + gasi'
possessor ear   hear   infinitive suffix

followed by the complement, which is understood to be low in factivity:

d- geta havi – gasi' abo   ri – e.
my ear   hear   inf.   woman take 3sg.
'I think he took a wife.'

This same structure also occurs with verbs of saying when it is emphasized that this is how the subject says it (but may not be what others would say or necessarily believe).

The internal structure of the *-gasi'* suffix (which otherwise occurs only infrequently) is unclear. It may be analyzable as bimorphemic, consisting of *-ga(')* + *hi'*, but the evidence for this analysis is scant. The former suffix *-ga'* occurs transparently in two rather marginal modal constructions: V + *ga' ktafu-* 'pretend to V' (*kta'* may be cognate with *gota* 'face') and V + *ga'* *afu-* 'not be permitted to V' (*'afu-* may be *'a'a* 'negative' + *hu-* 'do').

On the basis of comparative evidence from Kamano, a closely related language of the Gorokan family, *-ga'* may be identified as a component of the future indicative auxiliary *-gu-*, which may be historically derived from **ga'* + *hu-*. What now functions as the nonpermissive in Hua may be a frozen relic of the original negative of the future. The regular future negative differs only in the placement of the negative morpheme:

'a'a' + do – gi -e   <?? 'a'a + do – ga' = hi – e.
neg.   eat   fut. 3sg.
'S/he will not eat.'

do – ga 'a'a + hi – e   <?? do – ga' 'a'a + hi – e.
eat   ?   neg.   do   3sg.
'S/he may not eat.'

What makes this reconstruction implausible synchronically is that in present-day Hua there is nothing contingent, modal, or subjective about the *-gu-* future: it is flatly indicative.

There is a real dearth of modal expressions in Hua, most vividly attested by the fact that the pidgin borrowing *inap* 'be able' is the only abilitative morpheme in common use. But the major expression of subjectivity and uncertainty in the language is neither *-gasi'* nor *-ga'*, but the subjunctive auxiliary "verb" *-su-*, which clearly contrasts with *-gu-* in minimally contrasting expressions like

o – gi – e.
come fut. 3sg.
'S/he will come.'

e – si – e.
come subjun. 3sg.
'Let him/her come.'

But the contrast is suspended in various corners of Hua morphology. In questions, relative clauses, hypothetical protasis verbs, and coordinate medial verbs, only the subjunctive auxiliary is possible:

aigatoga vi – sa –   ne?   (*aigatoga u – ga – ne?)
where   go subjun. 2sg.
'Where will you go?'/'Where do you want to go?'

ve – su –   ma'   zu'bo   (*vo – gu – ma' zubo)
sleep subjun. 1sg.rel. house
'a house for me to sleep in'/'the house I will sleep in'

e – sa –   pamo   kgogue.   (*o – ga – pamo kgogue)
come subjun. 2sg.cond. I'll see you
'If you come, I'll see you.'

e – sa –   na – da kgogue   (*o – ga – na – da kgogue)
come subjun. 2sg. 1sg. I'll see you
'If you come, I'll see you.'/'You will come and I will see you.'

In the second person of the simple assertive future, and in subordinate medial verbs, only the indicative auxiliary is possible:

do – ga – ne.   (*de – sa – ne.)
eat fut. 2sg.
'You will eat.'

do – gi – [ma + mo] – ga – na . . .   (*de – si [ma – mo] ga – na)
eat fut. 3sg.rel. p.t.   med. 3sg.
'Given that he will eat, s/he. . . .'

In the avolitional, the two auxiliaries are in apparently free variation:

do – ro – gu –e   ~   do – re – su –   e
eat perf. fut. 1sg.   eat perf. subjun. 1sg.
'It would be bad if I ate.'

Finally, in the benefactive case of the relative clause, both futures are possible, and contrast in a quite idiosyncratic way. Relative clauses with the subjunctive auxiliary and the benefactive suffix -*hi'* are purpose clauses:

vi – su –   ma' – hi'   ([visumi'])
go   subjun. rel.1sg. ben.
'that I may go'

"Relative clauses" with the indicative future auxiliary and the same case ending are principal clauses, and signal that the speaker has said this before and is tired of repeating it:

u – gu – ma' – hi'   ([ugumi'])
go   fut.   1sg.rel. ben.
'(I've already told you that) I will go.'

A final glimpse of the morphological confusion in the expression of modality in Hua may be had by considering how to conjugate the idea of 'wanting to eat' in the absence of a verb meaning 'want':

Case	Assertive	Interrogative
1sg.	desumi' hue	——
2sg.	——	desape?
3sg.	"dogue" hie	desive?

In the first-person assertive, the purpose clause is followed by the verb *hu-* 'do' in the same person. The paradigm for this form is defective: utterly lacking in the second person, and in the interrogative, it exists in the third-person assertive, but only with the meaning of 'being about to', as in *ko' zesimi'hie* 'it's about to rain'. (No volition is attributed to the rain.) There is apparently no way to question oneself about one's own wants in Hua. In the second-person assertive, there is a gap: it is impossible to impute wants to one's interlocutor. It is possible to inquire about them, however, using the subjunctive. In the third-person assertive, it is possible to impute wants to someone by putting words into his/her mouth. Literally, the 3sg. form above means '"I will eat," s/he says.' The third-person interrogative is multiply ambiguous, but one of its meanings is 'does s/he want to eat?'

3 Systematic infixation

Personal pronoun prefixes occur on transitive verbs, in which cases they designate the human object:

d- verie.
me show
'They showed me.'

Table 27.5

Person	*hapai-* 'explain, tell'	*hamu'* 'namesake'
1sg.	ha-nd-apai-	ha-nd-amu'
2sg.	ha-g -apai-	ha- g-amu'
3sg.	hapai-	hamu'
1du.	ha-ra'a-pai-	ha-ra'a-mu'
	(also ra'a-ha-pai-	ra'a-hamu')
2/3du.	fa'apai-	fa'amu'
1pl.	ha-r -apai-	ha -r- amu'
2/3pl.	fapai-	famu'

r – gorai – ne.
1pl. trick 2sg.
'You tricked us.'

They also occur on inalienably possessed nouns, and indicate the identity of the possessor:

d- vari – a
my sweat cit.
'my sweat'

p – za' – 'bo
2, 3pl. hand, arm pt.
'their arms'

Several hundred nominal and verbal roots in Hua begin with the sounds [*ha*]. Those which are transitive verbs or inalienably possessed nouns will occur with their pronouns infixed or otherwise absorbed, as in the paradigms shown in table 27.5. In the 1du., a variant exists in which the pronoun is prefixed. The pronouns *p-* "2/3pl." and *pa'a-* "2/3du." are absorbed, and although there is no productive rule in present-day Hua of the form p + h → f, the rule is so plausible that it seems safe to assume prefixation here also. None of the neighboring closely related languages manifest anything similar to this pattern of infixation, which is what calls for some explanation.

It seems likely that what has occurred in Hua is a reinterpretation that is based on two structural facts about Hua and one striking ambiguity. The facts are, first, that there exists a widespread, mobile, meaningless unstressed prefix *ha-*, following which morpheme-initial /b, d/ are prenasalized. We thus observe variants like *bai'a ~ hambai'a* 'garden'. Second, there is a general rule which simplifies sequences of identical vowels: because of this rule, mono-syllabic nouns like *za* 'tree' never occur with the citation suffix *-a*, and the imperative of verbs like *do-* 'eat' never occur with the optional clamative suffix *-o*. Given these two facts, all words in initial [*ha . . .*] could be analyzed as having the structure /*ha + a . . .* /.

The striking ambiguity is provided by the fact that the third-person singular pronoun is nil. A form like /*hapai-*/ 'tell him/her' could therefore be interpreted as either 3sg. + *hapai-* (clearly the inherited form) or *ha* + 3sg. + *apai-* (with invisible infixation). Invisible metanalysis in one corner of the paradigm can bring about visible results elsewhere, by a mechanism familiar since at least Jespersen's discussion of doublets like *eft* and *newt*. Although we cannot account for why this reinterpretation (which is still only partial) occurred in Hua but in none of the other Gorokan languages, we can still be reasonably certain that it could not have happened in Hua without the three favoring factors listed here.

28 Malagasy (Austronesian)

EDWARD L. KEENAN AND
MARIA POLINSKY

1 Background

Malagasy is a West Austronesian language spoken by over 12 million people throughout the island of Madagascar. Its closest relatives (Dahl 1951) are the South-East Barito languages such as Maanjan in Kalimantan (Borneo). Dahl (1951, 1988) and Simon (1988) argue that around AD 400 the proto-Malagasy migrated north from Kalimantan, their language undergoing modest phonological influence from Sanscrit, then moved along the coast of the Indian Ocean, down the east coast of Africa, across the Mozambique Channel into the Comoro Islands, with significant Bantu influence on both phonology and syllable structure. Then they moved into the northern part of Madagascar, spreading thence throughout the island in two main dialect groups, Western and Eastern.

The earliest writing in Malagasy was in an Arabic script, but it was only with the formal adoption of a Latin script (minus C, Q, U, W and X) by King Radama I and the establishment of schools in the early 1820s that writing became widespread. The first Malagasy newspaper appeared in 1826. The large Richardson Malagasy–English dictionary appeared in 1885, and the standard, excellent Malagasy–French dictionary of Abinal and Malzac (henceforth A&M) appeared in 1888. By the late nineteenth century a tradition of high-quality grammar writing had been established, notably Cousins 1894, Ferrand 1903, Malzac 1926, Rajaobelina 1960, Rahajarizafy 1960, Rajemisa-Raolison 1971, and Rabenilaina and Razafindrakoto 1987, 1989.

Typologically Malagasy is both verb-initial and subject-final; it exhibits the major properties of head-initial languages: it is exclusively prepositional; complementizers and subordinate conjunctions precede their clause; adjectives, quantifiers, and possessors follow the noun, though definite articles and proper name articles precede, and demonstrative adjectives flank, the noun. NP objects follow verbs of all voices; prepositional phrases occur between direct objects and the subject. Negation is preverbal, and manner adverbs, homophonous with adjectives in simple cases, occur postverbally, often separating a transitive verb and its object. Yes–no question particles occur just before the subject. Temporal adverbs usually occur after the subject.

Morphologically Malagasy presents significant suffixing, but, as expected of head-initial languages (Greenberg 1966, Hawkins and Cutler 1988), is dominantly prefixing. There is some infixing and a little circumfixing.

Malagasy presents an extensive system of verb-based derivational morphology, specifically the same rich voicing system with the same functional load that we see in the languages of the Philippines and Sabah (N. Borneo). Any major NP of a clause – Agent, Theme, Patient, Benefactee, Instrument, etc. – can be presented as the subject (variously called "nominative," "external," or "in focus"); only the subject relativizes (and, with some qualifications, extracts). Imperatives also have distinctive voice morphology. Also in common with other West Austronesian languages, reduplication is prominent in Malagasy, feeding in particular the voicing and nominalization systems.

1.1 Phonology

Our study is based on "official Malagasy," the form of the language in which most newspapers and government documents are printed. It draws heavily on the Merina dialect spoken in and around the capital, Antananarivo, but has incorporated various elements from regional varieties. Rajaona (1977) provides an informative discussion of the historical morphology of Malagasy which draws significantly on dialect variation. Verin et al. 1969 is a glottochronological study of dialect relatedness.

Malagasy has a four-vowel system: /i/, /u/, /e/, and /a/, noted *i, o, e,* and *a* respectively in Malagasy orthography – which we use in this study, occasionally augmented with stress diacritics. Word-final /i/ is written *y*. The diphthongs *ai/ay* and *ao* (the latter often pronounced /o/) are frequent, *oi/oy* less so. The consonants are shown in table 28.1. *dz* is written *j*. *t'*, written *tr*, sounds much like the initial consonant in *church*, but the blade of the tongue just touches the upper part of the alveolar ridge, not the palate. *d'*, written *dr*, is the voiced counterpart of *tr*, but its point of articulation seems to be slightly lower.[1] The *s* and *z* are closer to š and ž than the corresponding English phonemes. The prenasalized consonants $^nC/^mC$ are graphed nC/mC or n-C/m-C, where the orthographic hyphen indicates a morpheme boundary. *h* is often not sounded, but can be in slow speech; and even in rapid speech surfaces as [k] or [g] in various derived forms (below). Voiceless prenasalized consonants do not occur word-initially. (Many words begin orthographically with *mp*- and a few with *nt*-, but the nasal is not heard.[2]) In other positions the nasal of a prenasalized stop is sounded, even when the stop itself is voiceless. In all cases (Keenan and Razafimamonjy 1996a, henceforth K&R 96a) the distinction between C and $^nC/^mC$ is phonemic: for example, *tápoka* 'dilute' versus *támpoka* 'suddenly', *éto* 'here' versus *énto* 'carry (imper.)', *atráno* 'be prepared (imper.)' versus *an-tráno* 'at home'.

Table 28.1 Consonants in Malagasy

	Bilabial	Labio-dental	Dental	Alveolar	Post-alveolar	Velar	Glottal
Stops	p, b ^{m}p, ^{m}b		t, d ^{n}t, ^{n}d			k, g ^{n}k, ^{n}g	
Fricatives		f, v		s, z			h
Affricates				ts, dz ^{n}ts, ^{n}dz	t^r, d^r ^{n}t^r, ^{n}d^r		
Nasals	m			n			
Lateral				l			
Trill				r			

Syllables are of the form (C)V, where V is a vowel or a diphthong, though some nonfinal consonant clusters are heard in borrowings: *repoblika* 'republic'. Borrowings of longer standing tend to assimilate to the (C)V pattern: *dokotera* 'doctor', but there is much individual variation. Arguably (Dahl 1988) the Malagasy (C)V syllable pattern is a result of the early Bantu contact. It is not shared by Malagasy's Austronesian relatives, and it was characteristic of East Bantu during the contact period.

Stress is phonemic. We write 'for main stress, ' for secondary stress, and leave unstressed syllables unmarked. Dipthongs do not occur preceding a syllable with main stress. Unstressed vowels other than *e*, especially word-finally, are often devoiced.

2 Morphology

The formation of words and phrases in Malagasy rides on the extensive and productive system of derivational morphology. We note first, however, a small amount of typologically interesting inflectional morphology. It occurs exclusively in deictic categories. There are no classical agreement phenomena, such as verbs agreeing with their arguments or nouns with their possessors. Nor are nouns inflected for number, class (gender), or case.

2.1 Inflectional morphology

Location names are obligatorily accompanied by a locative deictic which codes up to seven degrees of distance from the speaker as well as visible–nonvisible to speaker and past–nonpast. Contrast (1a, b):

(1) (a) Tsy eto an-tsekoly izy tompoko.
         not here at-school he Sir
         'He isn't here (close, non-past, visible) in school, Sir.'

    (b) Niakatra tany Antananarivo izy omaly.
         went + up there [far, past, non-visible] Antananarivo he yesterday
         'He went up to Antananarivo yesterday.'

The full, nonpast series marking relative distance from the speaker and visibility is given in (2), with main stress penultimate unless marked otherwise:

(2) NEAR   FAR

     etý   eto eo etsy eny eroa erý visible nonpast
     atý   ato ao atsy any aroa arý nonvisible nonpast

Clearly the initial *e-/a-* contrast triggers the visible versus nonvisible to speaker interpretation.[3] Moreover, these forms, along with interrogative *aiza?* 'where?', accept an active verbal prefix *-ank-* meaning 'goes here/there/where?' as in (3), yielding verbal forms that inflect internally for visibility and relative distance:

(3) (a) H + ank + eto izy   (b) N + ank + any izy
         fut. + act. + here he   *past + act. + there he*
         'He will come here.'   'He went there.'

    (c) M + ank + aiza ianao?
         pres. + act. + where you (sg.)
         'Where are you going?'

+ here and later marks morpheme boundaries and is not part of Malagasy orthography. To obtain the correct orthographic forms, erase + and concatenate. So *H + ank + eto* is *Hanketo*. Tense inflection on verbs is discussed later. The locative forms in (2) also combine with the root *hatra* to form binary locatives:

(4) Firy metatra hatreto ka hatrany?
     how + many meters from + here and up + to-there
     'How many meters is it from here to there?'

To form the past-tense series in (2), prefix the forms with *t-*, as in (5a). So here *t-* contrasts with *Ø-* in (5b). *t-* also marks past tense on some prepositions, notably the ubiquitous *amina* (accompaniment, instrument, source, goal, etc.):

(5) (a) N + iresaka t + amin-dRabe t + any Antsirabe izy.
         past + spoke past + with-Rabe past + there Antsirabe he
         'He spoke with Rabe in Antsirabe.'

    (b) H + iresaka Ø + amin-dRabe Ø + any Antsirabe izy
         Fut. + speak nonpast + with-Rabe nonpast + there Antsirabe he
         'He will speak with Rabe in Antsirabe.'

Verbal tense marking and that on locatives and prepositions must agree. Replacing any of the Ø's in (5b) with a *t-* results in ungrammaticality. *aoriana/ taoriana* 'after' and *aloha/taloha* 'before', both of which function as prepositions, adverbs, and subordinate conjunctions, also inflect for *past* with *t-*, as does the interrogative *Aiza* 'Where? (nonpast)' versus *Taiza* 'Where? (+past)'.

(6) (a) Aiza i Baholy no m + itoetra?
Where art Baholy Foc pres. + live
'Where does Baholy live?'

(b) T + aiza i Baholy no n + itoetra?
past + where art Baholy Foc past + live
'Where did Baholy live?'

Again, replacing the verbal past tense *n-* in (6b) with future *h-* is ungrammatical.

Returning to (2) we see that demonstrative determiners are built on the same seven member series using *i-* in the place of *e-/a-*:

(7) THIS   THAT   YONDER

   itý ito io itsy iny iroa irý

These forms normally flank the noun they specify (those in (2) may do so as well); sometimes they lack the postnominal copy, in which case, like definite articles, they reidentify something previously mentioned but not necessarily given in the nonlinguistic context.

(8) (a) itý bokin-dRabe itý
this book-of-Rabe this
'this book of Rabe's at hand'

(b) irý tanan-dehibe irý
yonder village-big yonder
'that large village very far away'

The demonstrative adjectives do not inflect for tense, but, unusually in Malagasy, they do for number, infixing a plural morpheme *-re-* after the initial *i-*.

(9) (a) io trano io   (b) ireo trano ireo
this house this   *these house these*
'this house'   'these houses'

   (c) iny trano iny   (d) ireny trano ireny
that house that   *those house those*
'that house (far)'   'those houses (far)'

Note that the noun itself does not inflect for number; only its demonstrative does. In fact *-re-* is the only number inflection in the entire language, and the only place it occurs besides the demonstratives is in the second-person pronoun: *ianao* (sg., nom.) versus *janareo* (pl., nom.). See table 28.2.

There are two other post *i-* infixes in the demonstratives, both somewhat less productive than *-re-*. The first is *-za-*, as in the adjectives/pronouns *izato*, *izao*, and *izany*, built from *ito, io,* and *iny*. The reference of these forms is not concrete and visible.[4]

(10) (a)   amin'izao fotoana izao
             prep'this time this
             'at the present time'

      (b)   Tsy tsara izany
             not good that (perhaps some general circumstance)
             'That isn't good.'

The second inserts a prenasalized dental following *i-* with a presentative meaning 'Here it/he/she is': *inty* from *ity, intsy* from *itsy, indro* from *io, indry* from *iry*, and 'Here they are': *indreo* from *ireo* and *indreny* from *ireny* (both with the *-re-* infix).

2.2 *Derivational morphology*

main language in madagascar

Words and phrases in <u>Malagasy</u> are built from roots by a large variety of morphological operations: affixing, reduplication, and incorporation. By roots, we mean expressions which are not derived from other expressions. Many roots are words, but a nontrivial number are not. Our presentation broadly follows the derivational complexity of expressions: (1) roots, (2) reduplication, (3) noun-based morphology, (4) verb-based morphology, and (5) generalized incorporation.

2.2.1 Roots   We use the several thousand roots in A&M together with the very many derived forms they present. Erwin (1996) presents an interesting alternative analysis of a sample of roots. We do not adopt that analysis here, as it lacks the extensive empirical coverage of A&M, but we will point out properties of A&M's "standard" analysis that motivate Erwin's proposals.

2.2.1.1 Prosodic properties of roots   These are crucial to understanding Malagasy morphology and concern stress and syllabicity (see K&R 96a). One stress-level distinction is phonemic both in roots and in derived forms, and in each root just one syllable carries the main stress.

(11) Roots   *tánana* 'hand', *tanána* 'village'; *lálana* 'path', *lalána* 'law'; *irý* 'there (far)', *íry* 'desire'; *áty* 'liver, interior', *atý* 'here' [close, not visible, nonpast]

Derived   *manása* 'is washing', *manasá* 'Wash! (imper.); *míditra* 'is entering', *midítra* 'is being stubborn, ill-behaved'

2.2.1.2 One-syllable roots   These are fairly numerous. Most are words. Those in (12) and (13) are grammatical morphemes, free standing in (12), bound in (13). Those in (14) are content words. (Stress marking on dipthongs is on the dominant vowel.)

(12)   *sa* 'or (in questions)'; *fa* 'that (complementizer), but'; *na* 'whether'; *i* and *ry* 'proper noun articles'; *sy* 'and (phrasal)'; *ny* 'definite article'; *no* 'focus particle'; *ho* 'future'; *ka* 'and so'; *ve, va* 'question particle'; *tsy* 'not'; *mba* 'in order to'; *ao* 'there + nonvisible'; *táo* 'there + nonvisible + past'; *sáo* 'lest'; *háy/káy* 'exclamation'

(13)   *-ko* 'my', *-náo* 'your (sg.)', *-ny* '3gen. (his, her, their)', *-náy* 'our (excl.)', *a-* 'passive', *ma-* 'adjective former'

(14)   *fe* 'thigh'; *fy* 'delicious'; *fo* 'heart'; *be* 'big, many, very'; *ra* 'blood'; *lo* 'rotten, spoiled'; *la* 'refusal', *mby* 'arrived'; *re* 'heard'; *ro* 'sauce'; *to* 'true, just'; *vy* 'metal'; *zo* 'rights'; *tsy* 'steel'; *py* 'a blink'; *ráy* 'father'; *ráy* 'grasp'; *fóy* 'abandoned'; *vóy* 'action of rowing'; *hóy* 'is said'; *tóy* 'like'; *ndre/ndry* 'interjection of surprise or pain'; *táy* 'excrement'; *máy* 'burnt, hurried'; *láy* 'tent'; *mbáy* 'step aside'; *váy* 'a boil'; *ndáo* 'let's go'; *jáy* 'pride'; *jáo* 'big, a big steer with long horns'

2.2.1.3 Two-syllable roots (as well as *n* > 2 syllable roots)   These overwhelmingly have penultimate main stress: *léla* 'tongue', *vády* 'spouse', *vítsy* 'few', *fótsy* 'white'. There are two sorts of exceptions: some borrowings: *zomá* 'Friday', *dité* 'tea' (< Fr. *du thé*), *diváy* 'wine' (< Fr. *du vin*), and some native roots, especially demonstratives, ending in /i/ or /i/-final diphthongs: *itý* 'this (near)', *intý* 'here is', *erý* 'there (far, visible, nonpast)', *izáy* 'that/comp.', *iráy* 'one', *iláy* 'the aforementioned'.

2.2.1.4 Three-syllable roots   These are usually stressed on the penultimate syllable (15), unless they end in one of the "weak" syllables: *-na/-ny*, *-ka*, *-tra* (16).

(15)   *omály* 'yesterday', *karáma* 'salary', *tanóra* 'young', *atsímo* 'south'

(16)   *tánana* 'hand', *tápaka* 'broken', *vóhitra* 'hill', *ídina* 'descend', *íditra* 'enter', *sásany* 'some', *tókony* 'should', *fárany* 'finally', *tápany* 'half'

Roots ending in a weak syllable and having antepenultimate stress will be called "weak roots."[5] They figure prominently (K&R 96a) in Malagasy morphology. While synchronically arbitrary, their behavior receives a historical account first presented and supported empirically by Dahl (1951: 105–15). Malagasy's close relatives, like Maanjan, present a variety of closed syllables. Dahl confirms that the shift to open syllables in Malagasy took place under Bantu influence when the Malagasy began settling in Madagascar. Certain word-final consonants, such as *h*, *s*, and *l*, were generally dropped, but words ending in *k*, *t*, *n*, and *r* added an *a* in conformity with the open-syllable pattern of Eastern Bantu. (Other changes also took place during this period, e.g. final *t* ⇒ *tr*.) We note that Erwin (1996) analyzes weak roots as consonant-final, lacking the final *-a*, which is later epenthesized (accompanied with certain consonant changes) in contexts in which the root is not suffixed or compounded.

Finally, there are a very few three-syllable roots with weak endings that are stressed penultimately (and so are not weak roots, as defined above):

(17)   *tanána* 'village', *lalána* 'law', *rehétra* 'all', *baríka* 'barrel' (< Fr. barrique)

2.2.1.5 Roots of four or more syllables   These assign secondary stress to every second syllable working back from the main stress. Within this group we distinguish: (1) borrowings: *làvarángana* 'verandah' (< Fr. 'la varangue'), *pàtalóha* 'pants' (< Fr. 'pantalon'); (2) words built from a root by the addition of a synchronically nonproductive) affix: *sarítaka* 'disorder' (prefix *sa-*), *sòmarítaka* 'preoccupied' (infix *-om-*); (3) frozen compounds: *àntsipíka* 'pocket knife' (< *ántsy* 'knife' + *píka* 'click'), *fàravòdilánitra* 'horizon' (< *fára* 'limit' + *vódy* 'posterior' + *lánitra* 'sky'); and (4), frozen reduplications where the base is no longer a root: *tàbatába* 'noise', *sàlasála* 'hesitation'. These reduplications are always of the form CV̀C'V' + CV́C'V', whereas productively formed reduplications have other shapes as well. Impressionistically, the secondary stress in frozen reduplications is stronger than that in the other types of *n*>3 syllable roots, but we know of no convincing way to show this, as these stresses are predictable from primary stresses and so are not phonemic.

2.2.1.6 Grammatical categories of roots   These are very unevenly instantiated. There are many nouns, some adjectives (*manga* 'blue', *fohy* 'short'), several passive verbs (below), and smatterings of numerals, prepositions, and adverbs. There are virtually no active verbs and no circumstantial verbs at all. Active verbs are morphologically derived from roots (nouns, adjectives, passives, or just bases which are not themselves words), and circumstantial verbs are derived from roots + active prefixes. Many nominals are morphologically derived from verbs. We turn now to these morphological operations.

2.2.2 Reduplication   This is formally defined in Keenan & Razafimamonjy 1996a, c. Here we summarize its main features. It applies to roots preserving their category: reduplicated nouns are nouns, adjectives are adjectives, passives are passives, and verb bases are verb bases. In addition there are two listable cases in which reduplication applies to derived active verbs yielding active verbs. The most common use of reduplication is to adjectival and verbal roots (whether passives or verbal bases). Its interpretation, as per our translations, is usually one of attenuation or diminution. Thus *fòtsifótsy* 'white white' means somewhat less white than simple *fótsy* 'white'. When applied to activity verbs, the result is sometimes frequentative: *mitény* 'speak' ⇒ *mitènitény* 'jabber'. Applied to nouns, which is less frequent, reduplication often has a pejorative effect: *latábatra* 'table' ⇒ *latàbatábatra* 'something approximating a table'. Also reduplication is used optionally without a weakening effect in the formation of comparatives.

(18) Faly (or falifaly) kokoa noho Rabe Rakoto   'Rakoto is happier than
    happy   *inten. against Rabe Rakoto*   Rabe'

To reduplicate an expression *d*, first copy the right-hand part of *d* to its right, beginning with the stressed syllable. Then combine *d* and its (partial) copy, the "reduplicant," according to the general rules of combination (called "Basic" in K&R 96a). We exemplify the range of core cases below.

Roots with final stress:[6]

(19)

root	reduplicant	derived form
bé 'big, numerous'	*bé*	*bèbé* 'fairly big, numerous'
ló 'rotten'	*ló*	*lòló* 'somewhat rotten'
ráy 'grasp'	*ráy*	*ràiráy* 'touch everything'
indráy 'again'	*ndráy*	*indràindráy* 'sometimes'
vovó 'barking'	*vó*	*vovòvó* 'bark occasionally'
lèhibé 'big'	*bé*	*lèhibèbé* 'biggish'

So in this case we just suffix the reduplicant to the root, reducing the main stress in the root to secondary. The main stress in the derived form is inherited from the reduplicant. This pattern of copying, stress reduction, and inheritance holds for all the other cases of reduplication as well, a point we shall not repeat.

Roots with penultimate stress:

(20)

root	reduplicant	derived form
fótsy 'white'	*fótsy*	*fòtsifótsy* 'whitish'
máimbo 'stinky'	*máimbo*	*màimbomáimbo* 'somewhat stinky'
háfa 'different'	*háfa*	*hàfaháfa* 'somewhat different'
hadíno 'forget'	*díno*	*hadìnodíno* 'forget a bit'
saláma 'healthy'	*láma*	*salàmaláma* 'fairly healthy'
àlahélo 'sadness'	*hélo*	*àlahèlohélo* 'little sadness'

Roots with antepenultimate stress:

If the reduplicant is vowel-initial, the final vowel of the root elides (henceforth we only translate reduplicated forms if their meaning is exceptional):

(21)   root   reduplicant   derived form

áloka 'shade'   *áloka*   *àlokáloka*
évotra 'bouncing back'   *évotra*   *èvotrévotra*
éntana 'baggage'   *éntana*   *èntanéntana*
ántitra 'old'   *ántitra*   *àntitrántitra*
ólika '(a) twist'   *ólika*   *òlikólika*

But if the first syllable of the reduplicant is consonant-initial, then the root endings *-ka* and *-tra* are deleted, and if the reduplicant begins with a continuant, it changes to its corresponding stop or fricative as given by the general correspondences in stop:

(22)   stop   f > p   s > ts   h > k   r > d^r v > b   z > dz   l > d

Henceforth "stop" will refer to the replacement of the consonants to the left of the > by the ones to the right, keeping any other consonants unchanged.

(23)   root   reduplicant   derived form

fántatra 'known'   *fántatra*   *fàntapántatra*
sóratra 'writing'   *sóratra*   *sòratsóratra*
héloka 'fault'   *héloka*   *hèlokéloka*
résaka 'conversation'   *résaka*   *rèsadrésaka*
várotra 'selling'   *várotra*   *vàrobárotra*
závatra 'thing'   *závatra*   *zàvajávatra*
lávitra 'far'   *lávitra*   *làvidávitra*

Finally, if a weak root ends in *-na/-ny*, drop *-na/-ny*, apply the stop to the initial consonant of the reduplicant, and then replace the resulting consonant by its prenasalized counterpart in table 28.1 if it has one, otherwise make no further change. This latter process will be called "nasal."

(24)   root   reduplicant   derived form

sítrana 'cured'   *sítrana*   *sìtrantsítrana*
sásany 'some'   *sásany*   *sàsantsásany* 'a few'
vélona 'alive'   *vélona*   *vèlombélona*
háingana 'quickly'   *háingana*   *hàingankáingana*
làvarángana 'verandah'   *rángana*   *làvaràngandrángana*
vòalóhany 'first'   *lóhany*   *vòalòhandóhany*
antóniny 'average'   *tóniny*   *antònintóniny*
másina 'holy'   *másina*   *màsimásina*

The examples in (19)–(24) cover the main cases of root reduplication. Three special cases (K&R 96c) should be mentioned: (1) a few vowel-initial reduplicants prefix a *k-*, reduplication then proceeding as for consonant-initial reduplicants:

(25)   root   reduplicant   derived form

      íditra 'enter'   *k + íditra*   *ìdikíditra*
      ádana 'slow'   *k + ádana*   *àdankádana*
      ídina 'descend'   *k + ídina*   *ìdinkídina*

(2) a certain number of two-syllable words with weak endings behave as weak roots with respect to stop and nasal, the derived forms tolerating stress clash:

(26)   *zátra* 'accustomed'   ⇒   *zàjátra* 'slightly accustomed'
      fóka 'absorb'   ⇒   *fòpóka* 'absorb a little'
      léna 'wet, fresh'   ⇒   *lèndéna* 'somewhat fresh'

(3) vowel elision is often optional, or does not take place at all with bisyllabic vowel-initial penultimately stressed reduplicants.

(27)   *óva* 'change'   ⇒   *òvaóva, òvóva*
      ívy 'spit'   ⇒   *ìviívy, ìvívy*
      ósa 'coward'   ⇒   *òsaósa*
      ázo 'understood, gotten'   ⇒   *àzoázo*
      ávo 'high'   ⇒   *àvoávo*

2.2.2.1 Domain of reduplication   This includes a considerable range of roots (and, erratically, two types of active verbs, discussed later). If a morphological operation applies to X, it also applies to the reduplication of X, the only systematic exceptions being reduplication itself and *tafa* prefixation, below. Even frozen reduplications do not reduplicate: *sàlasála* 'hesitation', but **sàlasàlasála*.[7] Also numerals do not reduplicate. We find no reason why, for example, *telotelo* 'three-three' could not mean 'about three'. Perhaps the existence of distributive numerals *tsitelotelo* 'in threes' which combine the prefix *tsi-* with a reduplicated numeral has preempted the bare reduplication of the numeral.

2.2.2.2 Reflection   Malagasy reduplication is similar to that in most (but not all) languages, in that material is copied to the side it is copied from (the right in Malagasy). But the copying may be either complete or partial, as determined by the stress pattern. So reduplication in Malagasy, in contrast to that of its many relatives, is not subject to a fixed-weight condition. It may copy one, two, or three syllables, according as main stress is final, penultimate, or antepenultimate.

Clearly CV-type templates (Marantz 1982) yield incorrect results in Malagasy. If we use a simple CV template, we miss the cases where n ≥ 2 syllables have been copied. If we use a CVCV template, we wrongly represent the words of two or more syllables with main stress on the last (*vovo, indray, lehibe*), as they copy only one syllable.

But equally, Malagasy reduplication is *prima facie* problematic for the Optimality Theoretic approach sketched in McCarthy and Prince (1995a). They assume that derived forms can be simply deconcatenated into a "base" and a reduplicant. It is natural to take the reduplicant as the copied part, as we have done. But McCarthy and Prince assert as a meta-constraint that Reduplicant–Base Identity universally outranks Reduplicant–Input Identity. This seems false for reduplications of weak roots in *-ka* and *-tra*, such as *tolo + tolotra*, with input *tolotra* 'offer', base *tolo*, and reduplicant *tolotra*. Even when the initial consonant of the reduplicant undergoes stop, as in *fanta + pantatra* from input *fantatra* 'known', we still find that Input–Reduplicant identity is better satisfied – it misses only the identity of initial consonant, *f* versus *p* – than Base–Reduplicant identity, which misses a final syllable and main stress correspondence. For all forms, reduplicants match the input with respect to main stress, and the input and the reduplicant always mismatch the base in that respect. So a proper Optimality Theoretic analysis of reduplication in Malagasy remains to be worked out.

3 Noun-based morphology

3.1 Nominal expressions

Noun-based morphology is constituted essentially by the formation of genitive expressions. They consist of a head bound in a complicated way to a following genitive NP. The binding draws significantly on stop and nasal, seen in reduplication. Head + NP$_{gen}$ is the major head-complement relation in Malagasy. It is used when (1) Head = Noun, and NP$_{gen}$ is its possessor; (2) Head = V[–active] and NP$_{gen}$ is its Agent Phrase; (3) Head = Preposition, and NP$_{gen}$ is its object; and (4) Head = Adjective, and NP$_{gen}$ is an Agent or (indirect) Cause. Our description follows Paul 1996a.

3.1.1 Genitive formation   Form Gen(w,w') from a head w and a following nominal w' (not a pronoun) as follows:

Case 1 w is not weak.

(1) If w' begins with a vowel, v, then prefix v with *n-* and concatenate, reducing any primary stresses in w to secondary ones. (The use of apostrophes and hyphens here and later is part of Malagasy orthography).

w	w'	Gen(w,w')
tráno 'house'	*andríana* 'noble'	*trànon'andríana* 'a noble's house'
akánjo 'clothes'	*ólona* 'person'	*akànjon'ólona* 'someone's clothes'
vóla 'money'	*i Váo* 'art name'	*vòlan'i Váo* 'Vao's money'

(2) If w' begins with a consonant, c, first apply stop to c and then nasal. Again, primary stresses in w reduce to secondary ones, a pattern common to all cases of genitive formation, which we shall not restate in each case that follows.

w	w'	Gen(w,w')
tráno 'house'	*soavály* 'horse'	*trànon-tsoavály* 'house for horses'
tráno 'house'	*bíby* 'animal'	*trànom-bíby* 'house for animals'
ráy 'father'	*Rabé* 'name'	*ràin-dRabé* 'Rabe's father' = /rai.^{n}d^{r}a.be/
aróso 'served'	*Rabé* 'name'	*aròson-dRabé* 'served by Rabe'
páiso 'peach''	*vazáha* 'foreigner'	*pàisom-bazáha* 'plum'
híta 'is seen'	*Rabé* 'name'	*hìtan-dRabé* 'seen by Rabe'
ázo 'received'	*Rasóa* 'name'	*àzon-dRasóa* 'received by Rasoa'
adála 'crazy'	*laláo* 'games'	*adàlan-daláo* 'crazed by games'
ré 'heard'	*ny záza* 'the child'	*rèn'ny záza* 'heard by the child' = /re.ni.za.za/
máty 'dead'	*ny jírika* 'the brigands'	*màtin'ny jírika* 'killed by the brigands'
jámba 'blind'	*ny vóla* 'the money'	*jàmban'ny vóla* 'blinded by the money'
tandrífy 'opposite'	*ny tráno* 'the house'	*tandrìfin'ny tráno* 'opposite the house'
imáso 'in view of'	*ny vahóaka* 'the public'	*imàson'ny vahóaka* 'in view of the public'

Despite the spelling of the last five examples, Malagasy has no geminate consonants.

In a few cases when the initial consonant of w' is one that does not change under stop or nasal, we find a morpheme *na* optionally separating w from w'. Gen(*trano* 'house', *miaramila* 'soldier') = *trano* (*na*) *miaramila* 'barracks'.

Case 2 w is weak.

(1) If w' begins with a vowel, then drop the final vowel of w and concatenate:

w	w'	Gen(w,w')
tóngotra 'foot'	*akóho* 'chicken'	*tòngotr'akóho* 'chicken's foot'
tóngotra 'foot'	*i Kóto* 'art name'	*tòngotr'i Kóto* 'Koto's foot'
sóroka 'shoulder'	*i Sóa* " "	*sòrok'i Sóa* 'Soa's shoulder'

sāsána 'washed'	*i Sóa* 'art name'	*sāsàn'i Sóa* 'washed by Soa'
vonóina 'killed'	*ólona* 'people'	*vonòin'ólona* 'killed by people'
áraka 'according to'	*ólona* "	*àrak'ólona* 'according to people'

(2) w' begins with a consonant.

(2.1) w ends in *-na* (or *-ny*[8]). Then *-na* is dropped, and Gen(w, w') is formed as in Case 1. This process may lead to ambiguities of analysis, as in the first example below.

w	w'	Gen(w,w')
vóla 'money'	*Rabé* 'name'	*vòlan-dRabé* 'Rabe's money'
vólana 'month'	*Rabé* 'name'	*vòlan-dRabé* 'Rabe's month'
órona 'nose'	*ólona* 'person'	*òron'ólona* 'a person's nose'
órona 'nose'	*sáka* 'cat'	*òron-tsáka* 'a cat's nose'
námana 'friend'	*Rabé* 'name'	*nàman-dRabé* 'friend of Rabe'
námana 'friend'	*ny talé* 'the boss'	*nàman'ny talé* 'friend of the boss'
ámina 'with'	*hafalíana* 'happiness'	*àmim-kafalíana* 'with happiness'
àoríana 'after'	*ny sakáfo* 'the mean'	*àorìan'ny sakáfo* 'after the meal'
táolana 'bones'	*bíby* 'animal'	*tàolam-bíby* 'bones of animals'
kapóhina 'is beaten'	*soavály* 'horse'	*kapòhin-tsoavály* 'beaten by a horse'
vonóina 'is hit'	*Rabé* 'name'	*vonòin-dRabé* 'is hit by Rabe'
sasána 'is washed'	*Rabé* 'name'	*sasàn-dRabé* 'is washed by Rabe'
lazáina 'is said'	*Rabé* 'name'	*lazàin-dRabé* 'said by Rabe'

As in reduplication, certain roots ending in *-na* (*-ka* or *-tra*, but never *-ny*) stressed on the penultimate behave as weak: e.g. *lena* 'moisten'; we have *len-dRabe* 'moistened by Rabe', and it reduplicates to *len-dena*. By contrast, *tena* 'body, self' is not weak: we have *tenan-dRabe* 'Rabe's body' (not *ten-dRabe), and it reduplicates to *tenatena*. But passives like *sasana* and *lazaina* formed by suffixing *-ina/-ana* to *laza* and *sasa* respectively, have penultimate stress (*ai* is a diphthong in *lazaina*). Genitive formation treats the passive form as if its main stress were still that of the root. Note that stress is antepenultimate in *kapohina* and *vonoina* (= /vo.no.i.na/; *oi* is not a diphthong here).

(2.2) w ends in *-ka* or *-tra*

(2.2.1) w' begins with the definite article *ny*. Then *-ka* $\Rightarrow$ *ky* and *-tra* $\Rightarrow$ *try*.

w	w'	Gen(w,w')
sóroka 'shoulder'	*ny záza* 'the child'	*sòroky ny záza* 'the child's shoulder'
tóngotra 'foot'	*ny fàrafára* 'the bed'	*tòngotry ny fàrafára* 'foot of the bed'

Table 28.2 Core pronouns

Person	NOM	ACC	GEN₁ / GEN₂
1sg.	áho	áhy	-ko / -o
2sg.	ianáo	anáo	-náo / -áo
3sg. or pl.	ízy	ázy	-ny / -ny
1pl., incl.	isíka	antsíka	-ntsíka / -tsíka
1pl., excl.	izaháy	anáy	-náy / -áy
2pl.	ianaréo	anaréo	-naréo / -aréo

It is the presence of the definite article /ni/, not simply the phonology of the initial syllable of the possessor that triggers *-ka* ⇒ *ky* and *-tra* ⇒ *try*. Thus, from *tapaka* 'broken' + *nify* 'tooth', one does not say **tapaky nify* 'broken toothed', but rather *tapa-nify* as in *Tapa-nify Rabe* 'Rabe has a broken tooth/is broken-toothed'.

(2.2.2) w' does not begin with *ny* 'the'. Then *-ka* and *-tra* are dropped, and stop applies (but nasal does not):

w	w'	Gen(w,w')
sóroka 'shoulder'	*záza* 'child'	*sòro-jáza* 'a child's shoulder'
tápaka 'broken'	*Rabé* 'name'	*tàpa-dRabé* 'broken by Rabe'
tóngotra 'foot'	*fàrafára* 'bed'	*tòngo-pàrafára* 'foot of a bed'
fántatra 'known'	*Rabé* 'name'	*fànta-dRabé* 'known by Rabe'

So genitive formation is sensitive both to prosodic properties of the head (weak vs nonweak) and to the internal syntactic structure of the possessor: namely, whether it begins with the definite article *ny*. Nominals governed by other articles, such as the proper-noun article *i* and the previously mentioned article *ilay*, behave like ordinary vowel-initial forms: *tranon'ilay olona* 'house of that (aforementioned) person'.

3.2 Pronominal genitives

Table 28.2 gives the core pronouns in all three cases. In addition, we note that Malagasy presents one third-person form *rizaréo* 'they distant' and several second-person singular familiar forms – *isé, ialáhy, indrý* – all of which behave like nouns in genitive formation.

The genitive forms are all morphologically dependent. All forms except first-person singular *-ko/-o* and third-person *-ny* carry their own stress, so after suffixation in these cases the main stress on the host reduces to secondary stress. *-ko/-o* and *-ny* do not induce stress shift. Those listed under GEN$_1$ suffix both to nonweak forms, as in (28), and to the root of weak forms ending in *-na*, as in (29).

(28) *tránoko* 'my house', *tranonáo* 'your (sg) house', *tránony* 'his/her/their house', *tranontsíka* 'our (incl.) house', *tranonáy* 'our (excl.) house'

(29) *sasána* 'washed': *sásako* 'washed by me', *sasanáo* 'washed by you (sg)', *sásany* washed by him/her/them', *sasantsíka* 'washed by us (incl.)', *sasanáy* 'washed by us (excl.)'.

The forms under GEN$_2$ combine somewhat idiosyncratically with weak heads ending in *-ka* or *-tra*.

(30) | person | *sóroka* 'shoulder' | *tóngotra* 'foot' |
| --- | --- | --- |
| 1sg. | sóroko | tóngotro |
| 2sg. | sorokáo | tongotráo |
| 3sg. or pl. | sórony | tóngony |
| 1pl., incl. | sorotsíka | tongotsíka |
| 1pl., excl. | sorokáy | tongotráy |
| 2pl. | sorokaréo | tongotraréo |

As (30) shows, genitive pronominals are similar to full NP genitives in distinguishing weak and nonweak heads and in distinguishing weak heads in *-na* from those in *-ka/-tra*.

Lastly, the genitive construction also sees some internal syntactic structure of pronouns: third-person pronominals are often augmented with a variety of forms that force a number distinction and give other information concerning the relation between referents of the pronoun. We have already seen [pronoun + demonstrative] such as *izy ireo, izy ireny,* etc. force a plural interpretation. But pronouns can be augmented with any of a large variety of kin terms: *izy mivady* 'they spouses', *izy mirahavavy* 'they sisters', *izy mianadahy* 'they siblings of different sexes', *izy mianaka* 'they parent and child' (more exactly a group representing two or more generations). These forms can be further modified with numerals: *izy telo mianadahy* 'they three siblings', or even *izy telo lahy* 'they three men'. We call these forms "augmented pronouns."

The genitive *-ny* cannot occur augmented. An augmented pronominal possessor in the third person occurs in the nominative form. In first-person plural, however, *-nay* can occur augmented.

(31) (a) *ny tranony mivady
       the house + 3 gen. spouses

(b) ny tranon'izy mivady
     the house'they spouses

(c) ny tranonay mivady
     the house + our spouses

Thus genitive formation distinguishes augmented and unaugmented pronouns, and within the augmented ones it makes person distinctions. The complete paradigms are still in need of investigation. But we note a last case of syntactic interest: coordinate pronouns count as augmented, and in the third person occur as nominatives:

(32) (a) *ny tranony sy Rasoa
   the house + his and Rasoa
   'his and Rasoa's house'

(b) ny tranon'izy sy Rasoa
   the house'he and Rasoa
   'his and Rasoa's house'

In first person the morphologically bound form may be used, but, as in co-ordinations generally, the first-person singular is presented as plural, in effect in agreement with the number of the entire coordination.

(33) (a) Niara-niresaka izahay sy Rasoa
   past + together-spoke we(excl.) and Rasoa
   'Rasoa and I (or we) spoke'

   (b) ny tranonay sy Rasoa
   the house + our(excl.) and Rasoa
   'my (our) and Rasoa's house'

4 Verbal morphology

We classify verbs according to the case (nominative, accusative, genitive) of their arguments. We call verbs "non-active" if they select a genitive complement and "active" otherwise. Actives and non-actives occur with about equal frequency (Keenan and Manorohanta 1996, hereafter K&M 96). Non-actives which are roots or are built by directly affixing roots will be called "passive." The other non-actives, called "circumstantial" (sometimes "relative") are built by suffixing roots + active prefixes. Active verbs are built by prefixing roots. Prefixes that apply directly to roots will be called "primary." "Secondary" prefixes apply to the result of applying primary ones. Tense marking, prefixal, applies after primary and secondary prefixes. There are two "tertiary" affixes which apply after tense marking (and themselves get tense-marked). Circumstantial verbs are built only from (tenseless) actives with either primary or primary and secondary affixes. A very few active verbs, which mostly behave as auxiliaries, are roots.

As we shall see, several morphological criteria correlate with whether a verb is passive, active, or circumstantial. (34) is a sample of these voices built from the root *rakotra* 'cover'. The rightmost NP in each S is, or is replaceable by, a nominative pronoun. It possesses many properties characteristically associated with subjects cross-linguistically (Keenan 1976, 1995; Polinsky 1995, 1996).

(34) (a)   no + rakofan'ny reniny t + amin'ny   (Passive)
           past + cover:pass. + gen.'the mother +
           bodofotsy izy.
           his past + with + gen.'the blanket 3:nom.
           'He was wrapped with a blanket by his mother.'

     (b)   n-aN-rakotra (nandrakotra) azy t + amin'ny   (Active)
           past-act.-cover   3:acc. past-with +
           bodofotsy ny reniny.
           gen.'the blanket the mother + his
           'His mother wrapped him with a blanket.'

     (c)   n + andrakofan'ny reniny azy ny bodofotsy.   (Circumstantial)
           past + act.-cover:pass.'the mother + his 3:acc. the blanket
           'The blanket was used by his mother to wrap him up.'

4.1 Passive verbs

4.1.1 Root passives   These are the second most frequent type of passive in texts (K&M 96). We have already given some examples: *re* 'heard', *azo* 'gotten, understood', *hita* 'seen', *fantatra* 'known'. A few others are *haino* 'listened to', *resy* 'defeated', *babo* 'captured', *simba* 'damaged', *sitrana* 'cured', *tadidy* 'remembered', *tratra* 'caught', *vaky* 'broken', *tsinjo* 'perceived from above', *tsapa* 'felt', *hadino* 'forgotten', *hay* 'is able to do', *very* 'lost', *voa* 'afflicted', *zaka* 'can be stomached'. Contrast the root passives in (35) with the derivationally more complex actives:

(35) (a)   haino + ko izy.
           listen-to + 1sg. (gen.) he (nom.)
           'He is/was listened to by me.'

     (a') n + i + haino   azy `   aho.
           past + act. + listen him (acc.) 1sg. (nom.)
           'I listened to him.'

     (b)   resi + ko izy.
           defeated-1sg. (gen.) he (nom.)
           'He was/is defeated by me.'

     (b') n + aN + resy (nandresy) azy aho.
           past + act. + defeat him (acc.) I (nom.)
           'I defeated him.'

We observe here that the genitive Agent suffixes directly to the verb root in the passives, whereas the active takes a prefix and a tense marker. When roots (of any sort) occur as predicates, they do not mark a distinction between present and past tense. Future is marked, with *ho,* even when the root is vowel-initial:

(36) (a)   Tsy azoko ianao.
            not understood + 1sg. (gen.) you (nom.)
            'You aren't/weren't understood by me.'

      (b)   Tsy ho azoko ianao.
            not fut. understood + 1sg. (gen.) you (nom.)
            'You won't be understood by me.'

Translating Malagasy passives by English passives often seems bizarre, as the English expression is often cumbersome or pragmatically marked, whereas the Malagasy one is natural. The only natural translation of "I didn't understand you" is (36a); the corresponding active verb, *mahazo*, doesn't have the sense of 'understand'.

Root passives reduplicate, as do other roots: *fantatra* ⇒ *fantapantatra* 'known a bit', *hadino* ⇒ *hadinodino* 'forgotten a bit'.

(37)   azoazoko ny teninao.
       understand (redup.) + 1sg. (gen.) the word + your
       'I understand your words somewhat.'

4.1.2 Suffix passives   These are the most common form of passives in texts. They present a range of morphological phenomena which are not fully understood, but are well documented by Rahajarizafy (1960). They are formed by suffixing the root with -(C)V*na*. The choice of vowel, /a/ or /i/, is determined by the verb root,[9] with /i/ the most frequent. An unpredictable "thematic" consonant C may be epenthesized, and when the verb root is weak, the consonant of -*na*, -*ka*, -*tra* may mutate as follows: *n* ⇒ *n* or *m*, *k* ⇒ *k*, *h*, or *f*, and *tr* ⇒ *t*, *r*, or *f*.

(38)   root   suffix passive   consonant mutation
                                                         or epenthesis

       hátona   *hatónina* 'be approached'   *n* ⇒ *n*
       tándrina *tandrémana* 'be paid attention to'   *n* ⇒ *m*
       dáka   *dakáina* 'be kicked'   *k* ⇒ *k*
       áraka   *aráhina* 'be followed'   *k* ⇒ *h*
       lélaka   *leláfina* 'be licked'   *k* ⇒ *f*   (mutation)
       fántatra *fantárina* 'be known, tested'   *tr* ⇒ *r*
       ávotra   *avótana* 'be redeemed'   *tr* ⇒ *t*
       rákotra   *rakófana* 'be covered'   *tr* ⇒ *f*
       fóno   *fonósina* 'be envelopped'   Ø ⇒ *s*
       tóhy   *tohízina* 'be continued'   Ø ⇒ *z*
       tsínjo   *tsinjóvina* 'be perceived from afar' Ø ⇒ *v*   (epenthesis)
       tény   *tenénina* 'be spoken about'   Ø ⇒ *n*
       dóka   *dokáfana* 'be flattered'   Ø ⇒ *f*

Note that main stress shifts one syllable to the right in all these cases, the typical case under (C)V*na* suffixation. Roots stressed on the last syllable are the exception. They do not shift stress, and they normally insert a thematic consonant (always, in the case of one-syllable roots): *la* ⇒ *lávina* 'be refused', *py* ⇒ *pízina* 'signaled by the eyes', *ray* ⇒ *ráisina* 'received', *to* ⇒ *tóvina* 'be obeyed'; *teté* ⇒ *tetévina* 'to have liquid dropped on drop by drop, *omé* ⇒ *oména* 'given' (note the exceptional absence of a pre-*na* vowel and thematic C; a thematic -*z*- does show up in the circumstantial forms). Also some two-syllable roots with penultimate stress and weak endings do not shift stress: *tána* ⇒ *tánana* 'be held', *fétra* ⇒ *férana* 'be determined', *táona* ⇒ *táomina* 'be transported' (see Rahajarizafy 1960: 34).

Stress shifting in the passives of weak roots with $n \geq 4$ syllables should create stress lapses: two unstressed adjacent syllables before a main stress, a pattern not found in unaffixed roots. But in fact speakers consulted endowed the initial syllable with a secondary stress, whence the stress pattern of the derived passives conformed to that of the roots: *sarítaka* ⇒ *sàritáhina* 'disordered', and *koróntana* ⇒ *kòrontánina* 'overthrown'.

In addition to consonantal changes, sometimes passive suffixation modifies the last vowel of the root: *i* ⇒ *e* is not uncommon: *voly* ⇒ *volena* 'be planted', *baby* ⇒ *babena* 'be carried on the back'. In these cases Erwin (1996) takes *e* as underlying, and applies *e* ⇒ *i* when the *e* is word-final. Probably more common with /i/ final roots is (1) -*ana* suffixed with hiatus: *vály* ⇒ *valíana* 'be responded to', *dídy* ⇒ *didíana* 'be cut', or (2) -*ina* suffixed and the two /i/ coalesce (vowel length is not phonemic): *fidy* ⇒ *fidína* 'chosen', *vídy* ⇒ *vidina* 'bought'. Rarely an epenthetic vowel appears: *tády* ⇒ *tadiávina* 'be sought', *ampó* ⇒ *ampóizina* 'be expected', *tsípy* ⇒ *tsipázana* 'have something thrown on', *óty* ⇒ *otázana* 'picked (of fruit)'. Note the loss of root-final /i/ in the last two cases.

Where R is a root to which -(C)V*na* suffixation applies, we write stem(R) for the result of modifying R by whatever stress and C and V changes (additions, mutations) appear in -(C)V*na* suffixation. See (38). Note that stem(R) is often consonant-final, so not a possible word in Malagasy.

A large-scale study is needed to determine what regularities there are in the vowel and consonant changes induced by passive suffixation and how best to represent them. On the "standard" (A&M) view presented here, lexical entries would have to consist, in effect, of root–stem pairs, in order to know what consonant mutations to apply and whether to insert a "thematic" consonant and, if so, which one of the five.

By contrast, Erwin (1996) would essentially identify a root R with stem(R), and derive unsuffixed forms by rule: the five epenthetic consonants would drop when root-final, and the consonant mutations above would be "undone" (e.g. word final -*t* ⇒ *tr*), followed by -*a* epenthesis, and stress would be moved back one syllable if possible. This has the effect of putting material unpredictable on the A&M analysis in the lexicon, and it explains the fact that imperatives of passives (discussed below) exhibit the same epenthetic consonants and consonant mutations as the suffix forms. We observe, theory neutrally:

(39) To form the imperative of a root R to which -(C)V*na* suffixation applies,
Step 1: form stem(R), then
Step 2a: suffix /i/ if the last syllable of stem(R) contains a /u/,
2b: suffix /i/ optionally if a syllable prior to the last one in stem(R) contains a /u/ and the last one does not contain a high vowel (/i/ or /e/)
Step 3: suffix /u/ in all other cases.

(40)

root R		stem(R)	suffix passive	imperative
tándrina	'pay attention'	tandrém	tandrémana	tandrémo
tóhy	'continue'	tohíz	tohízina	tohízo
tády	'remember'	tadiáv	tadiávina	tadiávo
vídy	'buy'	vidí	vidína	vidío
fántatra	'known'	fantár	fantárina	fantáro
sása	'wash'	sasá	sasána	sasáo
tápaka	'broken'	tapáh	tapáhina	tapáho
vóno	'hit/kill'	vonó	vonóina	vonóy
fóno	'wrap'	fonós	fonósina	fonósy
tólotra	'offer'	tolór	tolórana	tolóry
tsínjo	'see from afar'	tsinjóv	tsinjóvina	tsinjóvy
sóratra	'write'	sorát	sorátana	soráty / soráto
fólaka	'break/fold'	foláh	foláhina	foláhy
báby	'carry on back'	babé	babéna	babéo
vóly	'plant'	volé	voléna	voléo
omé	'give'	omé	oména	oméo
vónjy	'help'	vonjé	vonjéna	vonjéo

Thus 'Help me!' in Malagasy is *Vonjeo aho!* where *aho* 'I' is nominative. One might attempt to translate such sentences literally as '(May) I be helped (by you)!', which is pragmatically unrealistic as an order, but does get the voice right. It also makes clear that it is the addressee phrase that is omitted in Malagasy imperatives (as in English). That phrase will coincide with the nominative NP in active sentences, but with the genitive one in non-actives (of many sorts). Here are two examples:

(41) (a) Mba tolory vary ny vahiny.
prt. be offered (by you) rice the guest
'Please offer the guests some rice.'

(b) Voleo vary ity lohasaha ity.
be planted rice this valley this
'Plant this valley with rice.'

The final NP in each of these Ss is nominative. *ny vahiny* in (41a) can be replaced by the nominative pronoun *izy ireo* '3 dem. + pl.'. Also, though not usual, it is possible to add the genitive Agent to the imperative in contrastive circumstances. If Speaker wants to insist that it is just you, rather than you and others you represent he might say, in (41b), *Voleonao . . .* 'be planted by you (sg.)'.

The imperative data support Erwin's proposals, though there is one cause for pause: *f* arises as a mutation both from *k* and from *tr*, and further, it is one of the epenthetic consonants. Hence some listing of cases must be done to decide whether an instance of a root-final *-f* is to be dropped or become, after *-a* epenthesis, *-ka* or *-tra*. And the apparent irregularities with regard to epenthetic vowels and loss of final *-i* will have to be investigated. Still, these problems seem relatively minor.

More important is the interaction of Erwin's roots with other morphological operations. Prominent here are reduplication and the formation of circumstantial verbs.

4.1.2.1 Reduplication   On the standard A&M treatment, passive suffixation applies to reduplicated roots, both frozen, as in *karakara* ⇒ *karakaraina* 'is taken care of', and productive, as in *teny* ⇒ *teniteny* ⇒ *tenitenenina* 'is talked about some'. (42) is a sample of cases involving mutated and epenthetic consonants. They show that passive suffixation applies to a reduplicated A&M root triggering the same consonant mutation and epenthesis as with the unreduplicated root. They also show that reduplication (Red.) does not generally apply to passive forms.[10]

(42)	root R	stem(R)	Pass.(R)	Red.(R)	Pass.(Red.(R))	Red.(Pass.(R))
	tsínjo 'perceived'	tsinjóv	tsinjóvina	tsìnjotsínjo	tsìnjotsinjóvina	*tsinjòvinjóvina
	fántatra 'known'	fantár	fantárina	fàntapántatra	fàntapantárina	*fantàrintárina
	léfaka 'flexibility'	lefáh	lefáhina	lefadéfaka	lèfadefáhina	*lefàlefáhina
	vélona 'living'	velóm	velómina	vèlombélona	vèlombelómina	*velòmindómina
	anténa 'hope'	anténa	antenáina	antènaténa	antènatenáina	*antenàináina
	tólotra 'offer'	tolór	tolórana	tòlotólotra	tòlotolórana	*tolòrandórana
	tápaka 'cut'	tapáh	tapáhina	tàpatápaka	tàpatapáhina	*tapàhimpáhina
	ávotra 'redemption'	avót	avótana	àvotrávotra	avòtravótana	*avotavótana

These data are problematic if we take the stem (Erwin's roots) as the input to passive suffixation and reduplication. Reduplicating *tsinjov* must copy the first two syllables, since both are present in the correct output *tsinjotsinjovina*. But a complete copy of *tsinjov* is *tsinjovtsinjov*, with an unacceptable consonant cluster. We might invoke *CC, the ban on consonant clusters, to rule out this form (blocking *tsinjov* itself by *_C#, the ban on final consonants).

But *CC does both too much and too little. The first is seen in the next example, *fantatra*. Copying the stem yields *fantarfantar*, with a most offensive consonant cluster, *rf*. Eliminating the internal *r* by *CC, suffixing *-in* and applying *-a* epenthesis as per Erwin yields the incorrect **fantafantarina*. The problem is that we did not apply stop to the internal *f* to yield the correct *fantapantarina*. Nor is there any obvious phonotactic reason to do so: the internal sequence *tafa* is fine, as in *mitafa* 'chats' (< the root *tafa*) and *tafasiry* 'a chat'. The same problem arises with other weak roots that begin with consonants that undergo stop: e.g. eliminating the *-h* in copying *lefah* gives Red.(*lefaka*) = *lefalefahina*, not the correct *lefadelafina*.

The case where *CC does too little is given by the vowel-initial roots in (42). Copying *avot* just yields *avotavot*, which has no offensive consonant clusters. So some further constraint would have to be invoked to rule out *avotavotana*, not a word in Malagasy, but not phonotactically incorrect.

We do not claim that no analysis will integrate the facts of reduplication and suffix passives with Erwin's analysis of roots. We have just suggested one analysis. Others should be tried. But we move on, noting two further properties of suffix passives.

4.1.2.2 *Passive passives* Passive suffixation may apply to roots that are already passive. Sometimes there is a change in sense, as with *fantatra* 'known, understood', versus *fantarina* 'examined, tried to be understood'. And commonly the root passive just refers to a state, whereas the suffix form refers more to the process whereby the subject got into that state. Thus *vaky* 'broken' can be used when no agent is implied: *Vaky io* 'That is broken', whereas the suffix form *vakina* implies that the object went through the process of being broken, so an Agent is more naturally expected. (But genitive Agents can be directly attached to root passives, which is why we call them passive.)

4.1.2.3 *Tense* Suffix passives show a pattern of tense inflection common to all non-actives except roots. The future prefixes *ho* to consonant-initial verbs, *h-* to vowel-initial ones. The past prefixes *no* or *n-* under the same conditions. The present is unmarked:

(43) (a) nosasan-dRabe ny akanjo.   'The clothes were washed by Rabe.'
      (b) hosasan-dRabe ny akanjo.   'The clothes will be washed by Rabe.'
      (c) sasan-dRabe ny akanjo.   'The clothes are (being) washed by Rabe.'

Lastly, we note that passive *-ina* also applies, exceptionally, to a handful of active verbs to form a passive, and it applies productively to causative active verbs to form a passive. Examples are discussed in the section on active verbs.

4.1.3 *Prefix passives* These are morphological child's play compared to suffix ones. There are three such prefixes to consider: *a-*, *voa-*, and *tafa-*. We consider *a-* separately.

4.1.3.1 a-prefix passives   These are formed by prefixing the (A&M) root with *a-*. *a*-passives pattern with suffix ones rather than root ones, in that they focus attention on the process, rather than the result. They often differ from suffix passives with regard to the argument of the root that functions as their subject. (44a, b), from Rabenilaina 1987: 64, contrasts an *a*-passive with a suffix passive built from the same root, *lafika*. (44c) gives the corresponding active.

(44) (a)   alafik'i Soa ny atody akoho ny bozaka.
            pass. + place-under'by art. Soa the egg chicken the straw
            'The straw is put under the chicken eggs by Soa.'

      (b)   lafihin'i Soa bozaka ny atody akoho.
            place-under + pass.'art. Soa straw the egg akoho
            'The chicken eggs have straw put under them by Soa.'

      (c)   mandafika bozaka ny atody akoho i Soa.
            act. + place-under straw the egg chicken art. Soa
            'Soa puts straw under the chicken eggs.'

Subjects of *a*-passives are sufficiently often an instrument that Dez (1980b), following Rajaona (1972: 139–40, 148) identifies the *a*-voice as instrumental. But a more comprehensive characterization is that subjects of *a*-passives are "intermediaries" in an action or scene, as in (45). With ditransitive roots, typically *a*-passives are used with Theme subjects, and suffix passives with Goal subjects (46):

(45)   a + joro eo an-tokotany ny andry.
            pass.-set upright there loc.-courtyard the post
            'The post is set upright in the courtyard.'

(46) (a)   a + tolotra ny ray aman-dreny ny vodiakoho.
            pass.-offer the father-and-mother the signs of respect
            'Signs of respect are offered to one's parents.'

      (b)   tolor + ana vodiakoho ny ray aman-dreny.
            offer-pass. signs of respect the parents
            'One's parents are offered signs of respect.'

There are, however, two cases where *a*-passives do not contrast with suffix passives: (1) (vacuous), there are some roots with *a*-passives but no suffix passives: *atao* 'done' (< *tao*), *averina* 'be brought back' (< *verina*), and *ateraka* 'be born' (< *teraka*); (2) there are some nonvacuous cases where a given root admits both a suffix and an *a*-prefix passive taking arguments with the same semantic role: *asaritaka* and *saritahina* 'mixed up' from *saritaka*, and *afolaka* and *folahina* 'folded, sprained', from *folaka*. Often in these cases the two predicates differ somewhat in sense, but we do not know the extent or regularity of this variation.

Morphologically, *a*-prefixation does not alter the stress or phonological content of the root, and thus is in striking contrast with passive suffixation. Compare *afólaka* and *foláhina*, from *fólaka*. With the exception of *aN*-prefixation discussed below, all the (many) prefixes in Malagasy "protect" the identity of the root or stem they apply to. This is supportive of the account offered by Hawkins and Cutler (1988) for the cross-linguistic preference of suffixing over prefixing (and both over infixing).

Internal to Malagasy, *a*-prefixation is of interest in that it introduces two phonological patterns not present at the level of roots. First, it forms a hiatus with vowel-initial roots, rather than forming a diphthong: e.g. *ely* ⇒ *aely* 'dispersed' syllabifies as /a.e.li/, *itatra* ⇒ *aitatra* 'to be developed' syllabifies as /a.i.ta.tra/, and even *aakatra* from *akatra* 'go up' syllabifies to /a.a.ka.tra/. And from the root *oitra* 'action of raising up, as by a lever', which syllabifies as /o.i.tra/, we have *aoitra* = /a.o.i.tra/, a form with three adjacent syllables, none of which is consonant-initial – again a pattern that does not arise in root forms.

Second, *a*-prefixed forms tolerate a stress clash, as the *a*- seems to carry secondary stress. This stress is apparent in the cases of hiatus just cited, where, for example, in *aely* the initial *a* clearly has less stress than *e*, but more than *ly* (though judgments are less secure here). Equally, in the few cases where *a*- is prefixed to a root with main stress on its second syllable, it would naturally acquire a secondary stress in conformity with the pattern in roots. But even when prefixed to roots with initial stress, *a*- seems to have a secondary stress (recall our earlier caveat regarding the absence of simple tests to support claims of secondary stress). In such ordinary forms as *alatsaka* from *latsaka*, the main stress is on *la*, but the initial *a* has more stress then either *sa* or *ka*. Similar judgments obtain with *apetraka* 'be placed on something' and *atolotra* 'be offered to someone'. Thus morphologically derived forms tolerate both hiatus and stress clash, neither of which are present in the system of roots.

a-passives are identical to suffix ones with regard to their relation to reduplication, tense marking, and imperative formation. Thus *a*- applies to reduplicated roots: *tao* ⇒ *ataotao* 'done a bit', *petraka* ⇒ *apetrapetraka* 'placed'. Tense marking is *no-/n-* for past, as in (43), *ho-/h-* for future, and zero for present, exactly as with suffix passives.

And imperative formation follows the steps in (39), using the same consonant mutations, epenthetic consonants, and stress shift as do imperatives of suffix passives. For example, the consonant mutation *tr* ⇒ *r* is illustrated by the root *tolotra* 'offer', with suffix passive *tolorana* and imperative *tolory*, and prefix passive *atolotra*, imperative *atolory*. The epenthetic consonant *s* is seen in: *lefa* 'send, let go', with suffix passive *lefasana*, imperative *lefaso*, and prefix passive *alefa*, imperative *alefaso*. But we also get epenthetic consonants on *a*-passives which have no suffix passive counterpart: *tao* 'do' has no suffix passive, its prefix passive is *atao* 'be done', imperative *ataovy*, with epenthetic -*v*-, and ending -*y*, since the immediately preceding syllable contains a /u/.

a-prefixation and imperative suffixation interact to produce an "ungrammaticality"-type counterexample to Level Ordering in Malagasy (importing this hypothesis from English). Here, recall, *-ity* is stress shifting, and thus "level 1," and *un-* is not stress shifting, and thus "level 2," and so should occur outside any level 1 affixes. But for semantic and subcategorization reasons, we want to say that *-ity* has combined with *ungrammatical* rather than that *un-* has combined with the noun *grammaticality*, contradicting the claim that level 2 affixes apply after level 1 ones.

Consider now the following typical prefix/suffix passive contrast built from the root *róso* 'serve', stressed, as one sees, syllable-initially. (We translate the passive imperatives by actives in English in the interest of naturalness.)

(47)   (a)   Rosóana vary ny vahiny.   'The guests are served rice.'
              serve + pass. rice the guest

       (b)   Rosóy vary ny vahiny.   'Serve the guests some rice.'

(48)   (a)   Aróso ny vary.   'The rice is served.'
              pass. + serve the rice

       (b)   Arosóy ny vary.   'Serve the rice.'

Note that the nominative NP in (47b) is the Goal, just as in (47a), and the nominative in (48b) is the Theme, just as in (48a). Now, like *un-* in English, the passive *a-* prefix does not shift stress from the root, as seen in (48a). And, like *-ity* in English, imperative *-y* does shift stress, as is clear from (48b) and our many earlier examples. If Level Ordering applied in Malagasy, we should expect that passive *a-* would occur outside imperative *-y*. But this does not correspond to how we understand (48b). We understand (48b) to be the imperative of (48a): that is, the order to make (48a) true. And this just says that we form the imperative of the Theme (*a-*) passive: that is, apply *-y* suffixation after *a-* prefixation.

Thus it seems here (and later) that stress-shifting suffixes apply after stress-neutral prefixes, as in English *ungrammaticality*, just the order that Level Ordering blocks.

4.1.3.2 *voa-* and *tafa-* passives   These are formed by prefixing *vóa-* and *táfa-* to roots. *táfa-* is clearly disyllabic; *vóa* may be, but is often heard as /vo/. When prefixed, their primary stress reduces to secondary. Semantically and morphologically, the forms built from these affixes are more like root passives than like the suffixal or *a-*prefixal passives in focusing attention on the resultant state, not the process whereby that state was attained. They are both perfective in meaning, in that they imply that the action was completed. *voa-* passives focus on this final state, whereas *tafa-* passives emphasize that the resultant state was in some way unexpected. Sometimes the implication is "unintended," as though the action happened by itself without outside agency (in such cases it is not natural to use an Agent phrase); sometimes it is that the Agent was not expected to be able to bring about the result, in which case an Agent phrase is natural and the sense is that the Agent managed to bring about the result.

voa- and *tafa-* passives resemble root passives in not forming imperatives and in not marking present or past tense. Future is marked with *ho*. They are more tightly bound to the root than *a-* prefix passives, in that in some cases their final *-a* elides rather than forming a hiatus. Specifically, the *-a* of *tafa-* elides before *a-* and *i-*, but forms a hiatus before *e-*, as in *tafaely* 'dispersed', and *o-*, as in *tafaorina* 'built'. In cases like (49b, c) no external Agent is implied, and it would be unnatural to add one.

(49) (a)   tafa + iditra + ko (= tafiditro) ny omby.
         pass. + enter + 1sg. (gen.) the cow
         'I got the cows in.' (Lit. 'The cows were made-enter by me.')

     (b)   tafa + arina (= tafarina) ihany Rabe.
         pass. + put upright even so Rabe
         'Rabe managed to get up.'

     (c)   tafa + tsangana (= tafatsangana) tampoka aho.
         pass. + stand up   suddenly I
         'I stood up suddenly (in spite of myself).'

The *-a* of *voa-* often (but not always) elides before *a-*, as in *voa + araka = voaraka* 'followed'; otherwise we have a hiatus: *voaely* 'dispersed', *voaiditra* 'entered'.

tafa- creates stress lapses when applied to four-syllable weak verbs: *koróntana* ⇒ *tàfakoróntana*, *sarítaka* ⇒ *tàfasarítaka*. In such cases *voa-* tends to reduce to a monosyllable with secondary stress.

In many ways it is the *voa-* passive in Malagasy which most naturally translates passives from European languages. In part, this is due to its completive nature, and in part because *voa-* passives are often used without an Agent phrase. By contrast (K&M 96), suffix and *a-*prefix passives present an Agent phrase in the large majority of their occurrences. Further, in common with other languages of the Philippine type (Schachter 1976, Kroeger 1993, Keenan 1995), the Agent phrase with those passives presents several properties commonly associated with subjects of actives in European languages. Indicative here is that they can control, and be, missing Agents, as in (50b), a very common type of expression (see Keenan 1995 for other types of passive Agent control, and see Law 1995 for a study of these control properties).

(50) (a)   m + i + kasa h + aN + vaky (hamaky) io boky io ny mpianatra tsirairay.
         pres. + act. + intend fut. + act. + read that book that the student each
         'Each student intended to read that book.'

     (b)   kasain'ny mpianatra tsirairay ho vaky + ina (vakina) io boky io.
         intend + pass.'the student each fut. read + pass. that book that
         'That book was intended by each student$_i$ to be read (by him$_i$).'
         (Not 'Each student intended that the book be read (by someone).')

voa- and *tafa-* passives do appear to differ in one respect: *voa-* applies naturally to reduplicated roots, whereas *tafa-* does not, even when reduplication of
the root in other contexts is natural and when *tafa-* applies commonly to the
unreduplicated root.

(51) (a) *voalazalaza* 'said a bit' (< *laza* 'say'); *voadinidinika* 'glanced at'
           (< *dinika* 'study')

      (b) *verina* 'return': *verimberina, tafaverina,* but **tafaverimberina*
           latsaka 'fall': *latsadatsaka, tafalatsaka,* but **tafalatsadatsaka*
           tsangana 'stand': *tsangantsangana, tafatsangana,* but
           *tafatsangantsangana

4.1.4 Infixal passives
These are limited to a few forms and, at least in
official Malagasy, are not productive. They are formed by infixing *-in-* after
the initial consonant of the root, a pan-Austronesian phenomenon.

(52) *vaky* 'broken' – *vinaky* 'be broken'
      vidy 'bought' – *vinidy* 'be bought'
      tapaka 'broken' – *tinapaka* 'be broken'

Finally we note the existence of several suppletive passive–active pairs:

(53) active   passive

      maka   (< *aka*)   'takes'   *alaina*   'taken'
      mitondra (< *tondra*) 'carries' *entina*   'carried'
      mahalala (< *lala*)   'knows'   *fantatra* 'known'
      mivarotra (< *varotra*) 'sells'   *amidy*   'sold'

4.2 Active verbs

By contrast, active verbs are rarely roots; almost all are built by affixation of
roots. (54) lists the roots that function as active verbs. With one exception, they
are verbs of motion. Either they are degenerate in having no derived forms,
or they take an active prefix in the derived forms.

(54) active root   derived stem   derived nominalization

      tamy 'about to arrive' none
      mby 'arrived'   none

      tia 'like'   *-itia*   *fitia, fitiavana* 'love'
      avy 'come'   *-iavy*   *fihaviana* 'arriving'
      lasa 'gone'   *-ahalasana*   *fahalasana* 'leaving'
      tonga 'arrive'   *-ahatonga*   *fahatongavana* 'arrival'

tia occurs in clitic form *te-* or *ta-* when governing another verb (always in the future):

(55) te-hamaky (< h + aN + vaky) boky aho   'I want to read a book'
want-read   fut. + act. + read   book I

avy, *lasa*, and *tonga* are often used as auxiliaries:

(56) avy nisakafo izy ireo   'They just ate' (cf. 'Ils viennent
come past + act. + dine 3 dem. + pl.   de manger')

(57) lasa nanatrika (n + aN + atrika) fivoriana izy   'He went to a meeting'
gone attended meeting he

Moreover, *lasa* and *tonga*, whose use is quite common, also take genitive Agents, and thus also count as passive roots.

(58) (a)   lasako ny entanao.
           carried-by-me the packages-your
           'Your packages were carried off by me.'

     (b)   tonganay ny vata.
           brought-by-us the trunk
           'The trunk was brought by us.'

These roots, like roots in general, do not mark past or present. Only *avy* and *tonga* of the roots mentioned above naturally take future *ho*. *lasa* is inherently past.[11]

4.2.1 *Primary active verbs*   These are built by directly affixing – in fact, always prefixing – roots. The major, semantically neutral, such prefixes are *i-*, *aN-*, *a$_2$-* and *Ø-*, to which tense markers are prefixed. We illustrate the possibilities first, and then discuss two somewhat different analyses of the data that have been proposed.

(59) nipetraka (n + i + petraka) tany Antsirabe Rabe.
lived   past + i + sit   past + there Antsirabe Rabe
'Rabe lived in Antsirabe.'

Replacing *tany* with its nonpast variant *any*, the verb-initial *n-* can be replaced by *h-* to yield a future-tense interpretation and by *m-* to yield a present-tense interpretation.

(60) nametraka (n + aN + petraka) ny boky tao am-bata Rabe.
put   past + aN + sit   the book past + there at-trunk Rabe
'Rabe put the book(s) in the trunk.'

Again, the *n-* on the verb alternates with *h-* and *m-*, yielding as before future- and present-tense meanings, a fact that holds for the active expressions that follow as well.

(61)   (a)   natory (n + a_2 + tory) aho.
               saw past + a_2 + sleep I
               'I slept.'

    (b)   naka (n + ∅ + aka) ny satroko izy.
               took past + ∅ + take the hat + my he
               'He took my hat.'

i- and *aN-* prefixation are highly productive, whereas ∅- and a_2- prefixation apply to closed classes of roots. The roots in both the a_2- and ∅- classes are disjoint from any of the other classes, whereas many roots accept both *i-* and *aN-*.

The analysis of these affixes in traditional grammars and Rajaona 1972 is that the prefixes *i-*, *aN-*, a_2-, and ∅- are active voice designators, and the prefixes *h-*, *n-*, and *m-* are tense markers. On this view, the future and past marking, *h-* and *n-* (since the pre-tense prefixes begin with vowels and all the ∅- roots begin with vowels) are the same as for the non-active voices, but *m-* for present is peculiar to the active voice.

Builles (1988), however, proposes that present tense is unmarked in all voices, and that *m-* is specifically an active (or active–stative) voice marker whose privileges of occurrence are preempted by the future and past tense markers, whence it is overt only in the present tense. This analysis does not explain why the tense and voice markings are in complementary distribution, since, conceptually, tense can vary independently of voice. On the traditional view, the complementary distribution is expected: in simple cases a sentence is not expected to be simultaneously past and present, past and future, etc.

But Builles's analysis presents several advantages. First, of course, it accounts for the fact that *m-* shows up only in the active voice. Second, it accounts for the fact that *m-* is present in active imperatives.

(62)   (a)   *mipetraka* 'sits' ⇒ *mipetraha* 'sit down'
    (b)   *mametraka* 'place, put' ⇒ *mametraha vary eo* 'put rice here'
    (c)   *matory* 'sleeps' ⇒ *matoria* 'go to sleep'

On the tense interpretation *m-* is not expected to appear in imperatives, as they are not marked for tense in Malagasy. But the imperative ending *-a* is specific to actives (non-actives use *-o/-y*), so we expect *-a* forms to co-occur with *m-* if *m-* marks "active." See §4.2.2 for details on imperative formation.

Third, as we noted in (34), when an NP with an oblique role (Instrument, Location, Benefactee, etc.) is presented as subject, the verb goes into the cir-cumstantial form. On the traditional analysis, this form is built on the active form less its tense marker by suffixing (C)*ana* and shifting stress one syllable to the right. The C is the same epenthetic one that shows up in passives (if any) and active imperatives, and (C)*ana* resembles passive suffixes, but the first vowel is always /a/, never /i/, (recall that both are possible in passives, but /i/ is the overwhelming favorite). Some examples:

(63)

root	active (present)	circumstantial (present)
rákotra	*mandrákotra* 'covers'	*andrakófana*
pétraka	*mipétraka* 'sits'	*ipetráhana*
pétraka	*mamétraka* 'puts'	*ametráhana*
omé	*manomé* 'gives'	*anomézana*
sóratra	*manóratra* 'writes'	*anorátana*
íla	*míla* 'needs'	*ilána*
ánatra	*miánatra* 'studies'	*ianárana*
tóhy	*mitóhy* 'continues'	*itohízana*
vérina	*mivérina* 'returns (intr.)'	*iverénana*
vérina	*mamérina* 'brings back'	*amerénana*
tóry	*matóry* 'sleeps'	*atoríana*

On the traditional view, the circumstantial form includes the active prefix: *i-*, *aN-*, *a-*, and *Ø-*. But this morphology is what determines that the Agent (more generally, the highest-ranking semantic role in the grid determined by the root) will be presented as nominative. But suffixing circumstantial -(C)*ana* changes that. So on this view, circumstantial verbs present active affixes with no functional role, an unpleasant but not contradictory result.

A last, metalinguistic, observation lends further credence to Builles's analysis. Pedagogical grammars of Malagasy, while recognizing clearly that *m-* alternates with *n-* and *h-*, invariably give the active prefixes with the *m-* attached: *mi-*, *man-*, *ma-*, and *m-*.

Builles's analysis, then, supports several nontrivial generalizations. We shall not fully adopt it here, mainly because glossing examples that way makes it hard to match morphemes with the traditional analyses that the reader who follows up this article will doubtless consult. Equally, his analysis leaves open the glosses for the affixes *i-*, *aN-*, a_2, and *Ø-*. We turn now to these prefixes, drawing mainly on A&M, Rabenilaina 1987 and Rahajarizafy 1960.

4.2.1.1 *i-* This prefix is highly productive, and like *a-*, does not shift stress or alter the phonological content of the root it prefixes. A majority of *i*-verbs are intransitive: *mitsiky* 'smiles', *mijoro* 'is standing up', *mipoaka* 'explodes', *mifono* 'apologizes', *mihazakazaka* 'runs'. But many, including many common verbs, are transitive: *mifidy* 'chooses', *mividy* 'buys', *mikapoka* 'beats', *mijery* 'looks at', *mihaino* 'listens to', *mikarakara* 'takes care of'. And usually, unspecified object-deletion verbs are *i*-verbs: *Mifoka izy* 'He smokes' or *Mifoka sigara izy* 'He smokes cigars'. Similarly with *misotro* 'drinks' and *mihinana* 'eats'. We know of no case where *mi* + root is ditransitive.

A very small number of roots are built, historically, not productively, with the infix *-om-* (= /um/), and it is *i-* which combines with such roots to form verbs:

(64)   *tany* ⇒ *tomany* ⇒ *mitomany* 'cries'
       lano ⇒ *lomano* ⇒ *milomano* 'swims'
       hehy ⇒ *homehy* ⇒ *mihomehy* 'laughs'

4.2.1.2 aN-   This prefix, like *i-*, is a highly productive primary affix. Most commonly, *aN*-verbs are transitive: *mangataka* 'asks for' (< *hataka*), *mamono* 'hits, kills' (< *vono*), *manaikitra* 'bites' (< *aikitra*), *mamboly* 'plants' (< *voly*), *mandany* 'exhausts' (< *lany*). As far as we know, all primary ditransitive verbs are built with *aN-*: *manome* 'gives' (< *ome*), *manolotra* 'offers' (< *tolotra*), *manolo* 'substitutes' (< *solo*). But *aN-* also forms a significant number of intransitives: *mandeha* 'goes' (< *leha*), *mandihy* 'dances' (< *dihy*), *mandainga* 'tells lies' (< *lainga*), *mangetaheta* 'is thirsty' (< *hetaheta*), *mangovitra* 'shudders' (< *hovitra*), *mandohalika* 'kneels' (< *lohalika* 'knee'), *manjombona* 'is sad, cloudy' (< *jombona*), *ma(no)nofy* 'dreams' (< *nofy*). Also, many transitive *aN-* verbs can also be used intransitively: *loko* 'color' ⇒ *mandoko* 'paints X or engages in painting', *lositra* 'fleeing' ⇒ *mandositra* 'flees X, runs away'.

So, *contra* remarks in several grammars, we cannot treat *aN-* as a transitive verb-marker. None the less, the correlation of *aN* + root with two or more arguments is impressionistically greater than that of *i* + root with just one argument. Moreover, part of the motivation for the claim that *i-* forms intransitive verbs and *aN-* transitive ones is the fact that for many roots that take both, the *i*-verb is intransitive and the *aN*-one transitive: *latsaka* ⇒ *milatsaka* 'fall', versus *mandatsaka* 'drop'; *sasa* ⇒ *misasa* 'wash (oneself)', versus *manasa* 'wash something'; *seho* ⇒ *miseho* 'appear', versus *maneho* 'show'; *petraka* ⇒ *mipetraka* 'sit, reside', versus *mametraka* 'put'.

But even on a root-by-root basis, *i* + root does not always have lesser arity than *aN* + root. Rahajarizafy (1960: 192) lists over thirty roots in which both *i-* and *aN-* forms have the same valence. (65 and 66) exhibit a few in which the *i*-verb naturally takes inanimate objects, the *aN-* animate ones.

(65)   transitive: *tsongo* ⇒ *mitsongo* 'picks (e.g. flowers) by pinching' and *manongo* 'pinches (people)'; *tendry* ⇒ *mitendry* 'plucks (musical instrument)' and *manendry* 'touches with finger; points out, designates'; *fetsy* ⇒ *mifetsy* 'steals adroitly (something)' *mametsy* 'tricks, deceives (people)'

(66)   intransitive: *sidina* ⇒ *misidina*, *manidina* 'flies through the air'; *hozohozo* ⇒ *mihozohozo*, *mangozohozo* 'is weak, faltering'; *tsiry* ⇒ *maniry* 'grow (of plants)', *mitsiry* 'produce offshoots'

Morphologically, *aN-* prefixation is complex and shows several irregularities. Like other prefixes, it does not alter stress. But it does trigger mutation

or ellipsis of the initial consonant of the root it applies to. For an analysis see
Paul 1966a. Here we summarize the main points.

(67) aN- prefixation: we define by cases *aN-* + CVX, where CVX is a root, C
is any consonant or the empty symbol $\varnothing$, V is any vowel or diphthong,
X any string. Sometimes the syllabification is indicated to remind the
reader that syllabification overrides morpheme boundaries.

Case 1: if C is voiced and C $\neq$ /v/, then *aN-* + CVX = *a* + nasal(stop(C)) + VX

Examples:	root	derived present-tense form (prefixed with *m-*)	
	lány	*mandány* 'exhausts'	/ma.ⁿda.ni/
	dáka	*mandáka* 'kicks'	/ma.ⁿda.ka/
	gína	*mangína* 'is quiet'	/ma.ⁿgi.na/
	jómbona	*manjómbona* 'is cloudy, sad'	/ma.ⁿdzo.ᵐbo.na/
	róso	*mandróso* 'progresses, serves'	/ma.ⁿdʳu.su/
	záitra	*manjáitra* 'sews'	/ma.ⁿdzai.tʲa/
	ngídy	*mangídy* 'is bitter'	/ma.ⁿgi.di/
	nínina	*manínina* 'regrets'	/ma.ne.ni.na/
	mbómba	*mambómba* 'covers'	/ma.ᵐ.bo.ᵐba/

Note that in the last three cases the same derived form is obtained if the
prefix is taken simply to be *a-*, as is motivated by forms like *loto* $\Rightarrow$ *maloto* 'is
dirty' discussed below. In a few cases root initial /v/ also undergoes stop and
nasal: *voly* $\Rightarrow$ *mamboly* 'plants'. In one case a root initial /b/- optionally drops:
babo $\Rightarrow$ *mambabo* and also *mamabo* 'captures'.

Case 2: if C = $\varnothing$, k, s, ts, or t, then *aN-* + CVX = *an*VX

Examples:	root	derived present-tense form
	áloka	*manáloka* 'shades, protects'
	káikitra	*manáikitra* 'bites'
	sása	*manása* 'washes'
	tsáingoka	*manáingoka* 'removes'
	tólotra	*manólotra* 'offers'

Case 3: if C is f, p, or v, then *aN-* + CVX = *am*VX

Examples:	root	derived present-tense form
	fáfa	*mamáfa* 'sweeps'
	pétraka	*mamétraka* 'puts'
	vóno	*mamóno* 'hits, kills'
	fóno	*mamóno* 'wraps, envelops'

We could collapse cases 2 and 3, noting that when the initial consonant C of the root is lost, the shape of the nasal onset, /n/ or /m/, is the one appropriate to the prenasalized consonant resulting from applying stop to C. That is, we might characterize cases 2 and 3 as simply pursuing case 1 further: apply stop to C, then apply nasal, then drop the "C," retaining only the nasalization, now as a full segment.

Case 4: if C = h, then *aN*- + CVX = *an*VX if CVX = hety, hatona, etc. and *ang*VX if CVX = halatra, hataka, etc.

Examples: *aN*- + hety ⇒ *manety* 'cuts (hair)'; *aN*- + *halatra* ⇒ *mangalatra* 'steals'.

So whether *h* is lost or mutates to *g* and prenasalizes is decided just by listing the roots of each type. This completes the cases, as *aN*- does not apply to any roots beginning with /tʳ/, which we treat as voiceless.

However, the question of the form of *aN*-prefixation is more vexed than our analysis indicates. Like all the verb-forming affixes we consider, *aN*- does not apply to all roots. We make no attempt here to list the roots it (or any other Malagasy affix) does apply to. But we note that it does not apply to root adjectives like *tsara* 'good', *soa* 'pretty', or *kamo* 'lazy'. And we observe (present-tense) forms like *manatsara* 'improves', *manasoa* 'prettifies', and *manakamo* 'makes lazy'. So, as per traditional grammars, we assume the existence of a causative prefix *ana*-. But Andrianierenana (1966: 63), drawing on a large-scale study, observes that the choice of *aN*-prefixation versus *ana*-prefixation is largely determined by the choice of root: *manatsara*, **mantsara*, etc., whence it is not unreasonable to consider that there is just one prefixation process here. If so, it applies to many more roots than *aN*- above does, and in the absence of any conditioning factor, we must just list those for which the prefix takes the form *ana*- and those for which it takes the values we have given for *aN*- above.

A third option of analysis would be to derive forms like *manasoa* 'prettify' by applying *aN*- to *ha*-nominalizations like *hasoa* 'beauty', dropping the *h*-. This yields correct results for common adjectives which have *ha*- nominalizations, though *aN*- does not otherwise apply productively to nouns; but it leaves unanalyzed the many cases like *karama* 'salary' ⇒ *manakarama* 'hire' which have no *ha*- nominalization (**hakarama*).

Clearly, most, but not all, of the morphophonemic changes induced by *aN*-prefixation – namely, the application of stop and nasal – exist independently of *aN*-prefixation. But the consonant ellipsis cases do not. The voiceless consonants, such as *v*, *t*, *s*, *ts*, *k*, and *h*, could naturally have undergone stop and nasal. They clearly do in reduplication, and in one context that is phonologically identical to *aN*-prefixation, which we note aN_2. aN_2 functions as a prefix with a great range of uses: primarily, perhaps, it forms locatives (68); it is also widely used to form prepositions and adverbials (69); it combines with circumstantial nominalizations of verbs V to form adverbials "in the process of V-ing," and it functions as an accusative marker with certain types of NPs, as well as a possessive marker:

(68)   (a)   *Antsirabe* 'place name'   < aN_2- + *sira* 'salt' + *be* 'much'

        (b)   *Ambatolampy* 'place name'   < aN_2- + *vato* 'stone' +
                                                     lampy 'flat, big'

        (c)   *an'ala* 'in (the) forest'   < aN_2- + *ala* 'forest'

        (d)   *an-tsaha* 'in (the) fields, country'   < aN_2- + *saha* 'fields, countryside'

(69)   (a)   *ankoatra* 'beyond'   < aN_2- + *hoatra*, 'exceed'

        (b)   *ambadika* 'on the other side of'   < aN_2- + *vadika* 'the other side of'

        (c)   *an-tsoratra* 'in writing'   < aN_2- + *soratra* 'writing'

        (d)   *ampototra* 'at the source'   < aN_2- + *fototra* 'basis'

        (e)   *ankavia* 'to the left of'   < aN_2- + *havia* 'left'

(70)   Teo am-pisakafoana (aN_2- fisakafoana) izahay (raha niditra Rabe).
           past + there at-dining we (when entered Rabe)
           'We were dining (when Rabe came in).'

(71)   (a)   manaja an'i Soa/an-dRabe/azy aho.   'I respect Soa/Rabe/him.'
             respect acc.'art. Soa/acc.-Rabe/him I

        (b)   an'i Soa/an-dRabe/azy izany.   'That is Soa's/Rabe's/his.'
             acc.'art. Soa/acc.-Rabe/him izany

Cases like (69a, b, c) are particularly telling, as the active verb-former *aN*-applied to these roots triggers consonant ellipsis: *m* + *aN*- + *vadika* = *mamadika* 'turns over', *m* + *aN*- + *soratra* 'writing' = *manoratra* 'writes'. These facts confirm that the form of verbs derived from *aN*-prefixation is not determined just by the phonology of the prefix.

The irregularities in the behavior of *aN*-prefixation constitute one way in which the verbs it forms are treated like roots rather than derived forms. Specifically, on the definition we presented, certain /v/-initial roots like *voly* will have to be lexically marked as undergoing stop and nasal, whereas the more usual case is that root-initial *v*'s are deleted. Similarly, we shall have to lexically distinguish *h*-initial roots according to whether they drop or become /^{n}g/ under *aN*-prefixation.

Another respect in which verbs formed from *aN*-, henceforth *maN* verbs, behave like roots is that some of them undergo reduplication:

(72)

root R	m + aN-R	m + Red.(aN-(R))	m + aN-(Red.(R))
hóvitra	*mangóvitra* 'shivers'	*mangòvingóvitra*	**mangòvikóvitra*
lá	*mandá* 'refuses'	*mandàndá*	**mandàlá*
léha	*mandéha* 'goes'	*mandèhandéha*	**mandèhaléha*
lóa	*mandóa* 'pays, vomits'	*mandòandóa*	**mandòalóa*

In some cases reduplication applies either before or after *aN*- prefixation (but before *m*-prefixation), and in many cases (74), *aN*-prefixation applies only after reduplication.

(73) vóno   mamóno 'hits, kills'   manònomóno   mamònovóno
      láinga   mandáinga 'tells lies'   mandàingandáinga mandàingaláinga

(74) vélona   mamélona 'supports'   *mamèlomélona   mamèlombélona
      tóhy   manóhy 'continues'   *manòhinóhy   manòhitóhy
      vángy   mamángy 'visits'   *mamàngimángy   mamàngivángy
      fótotra   mamótotra 'deepens'   *mamòtomótotra   mamòtopótotra

4.2.1.3 a₂ This applies, as noted, to a closed class of roots, inducing no stress shifts, consonant mutations, or ellipsis. Most derived forms are stative, usually rendered by adjectives in English.

(75) root   present-tense derived form

      híta 'seen, found'   mahíta 'sees'
      tóry 'sleep'   matóry 'sleeps'
      tóky 'trust'   matóky 'trusts'
      lóto 'dirt'   malóto 'is dirty'
      ráry 'disease, sick'   maráry 'is sick'

The *m-* in these forms alternates with *h-* and *n-* for future and past, as expected. *a₂-* may apply to reduplicated roots: *matoritory* 'sleeps a bit', *malotoloto* 'a bit dirty'.

4.2.1.4 Ø- Malagasy has about twenty common roots which directly prefix the tense marker to the root to form verbs. We follow Malagasy grammarians in positing a zero prefix on the root. (76) is a partial list, which shows that, commonly, tense marking may apply either before or after reduplication. There is significant speaker variation in judgments:

(76) root R   Pres.(R)   Red.(Pres.(R))   Pres.(Red.(R))

      éty   méty 'agrees'   mètiméty   *mètiéty
      ísy   mísy 'exists'   mìsimísy   (*)mìsiísy
      ódy   módy 'goes home'   mòdimódy   mòdiódy
      ónina   mónina 'resides'   mònimónina   *moninónina
      ánana   mánana 'has'   mànamánana   *mànanánana
      áka   máka 'takes'   màkamáka   màkaáka/màkáka
      íno   míno 'believes'   mìnomíno   mìnoíno
      índrana   míndrana 'borrows'   mìndramíndrana   mìndraníndrana

4.2.1.5 aha- This is a primary active prefix which, in distinction to the basic prefixes above, is not semantically neutral, but rather abilitative or causative in sense. It combines with a bewildering variety of expressions, not all of which are roots. We classify cases below (see Phillips 1995 for further discussion).

aha- + root adjective: *gaga* 'surprised' ⇒ *mahagaga* 'surprises'; *finaritra* 'content' ⇒ *mahafinaritra* 'pleasing'; *menatra* 'ashamed' ⇒ *mahamenatra* 'shameful'. Usages here are often both transitive and intransitive:

(77) (a) mahagaga izany!
      surprising that
      'This is surprising!'

    (b) nahagaga ahy ny fitenin-dRabe.
        past + surprise me the manner-of-speech-of Rabe
        'Rabe's manner of speaking surprised me.'

aha- may apply to reduplicated roots: *maharikoriko* 'disgusting', *mahasosotsosotra* 'somewhat frustrating'; *mahataitaitra* 'somewhat startling'.

aha- + root passives: *fantatra* 'known' ⇒ *mahafantatra* 'knows'; *voa* 'attained, wounded' ⇒ *mahavoa* 'attains, wounds'; *resy* 'defeated' ⇒ *maharesy* 'defeats'; *zaka* 'handled' ⇒ *mahazaka* 'can handle'.

(78) ny tsy fahaizany no naharesy azy.
     the not ability-their foc. past + defeat 3(acc.)
     'It was their incompetence that defeated them.'

aha- + common noun N is either intransitive, meaning "constitutes N" (79a), or transitive, as in (79b). Mind-bogglingly, it also forms transitive verbs from pronouns (79c)!

(79) (a) ny fanahy no maha-olona.
      the spirit foc. makes-people
      'It is the mind/spirit that constitutes people.'

    (b) ny finoana an'i Jesosy no maha-fiangonana katolika
        the belief acc.-art. Jesus foc. makes-church catholic
        ny fiangonana katolika.
        the church catholic
        'It is the belief in Jesus that makes the Catholic Church the Catholic Church.'

    (c) Izany no maha-izy azy.
        that foc. makes-he him
        'That's what makes him him.'

aha- combines with the locative deictics discussed earlier to produce transitive verbs with tense marked twice:

(80) Nantsoiko izy. Izany no naha-teto azy.
     called-by-me he. That foc. past + make-past + here 3(acc.)
     'I called him. That's what brought him here.'

aha- also combines with a variety of derived expressions: (1) maha-te-h(o) + verb 'makes one want to verb', as indicated in (81); (2) a few *voa-* and a few *tafa-* passives, as indicated in (82); and (3) some predicates derived by NP Raising (Ralalaoherivony 1995), as indicated in (83):

(81)   m-aha-te-h-isotro ity ranomangalahala ity.
        pres.-cause-like-fut.-drink this water + clear this
        'This clear water makes one want to drink.'

(82) (a) izany no nahavoafidy (n + aha + voa + fidy) azy.
           that foc. past + make + pass. + choose 3(acc.)
           'That's what made him get elected.'

      (b) omaly no nahatafavoaka (n + aha + tafa + voaka) azy.
           yesterday foc. past + make + pass. + go-out 3(acc.)
           'It was yesterday that he was able to go out.'

(83) (a) vitsy ny mpanohana an'i Soa.
           few the supporters acc.'art. Soa
           'The supporters of Soa are few.'

      (b) vitsy mpanohana i Soa/izy.
           few supporters art. Soa
           'She/Soa has few supporters.'

      (c) izany no maha-vitsy mpanohana an'i Soa.
           that foc. makes-few supporters acc.'art. Soa
           'That's what makes Soa have few supporters.'

Phonologically, the initial vowel of *aha-* carries secondary stress when prefixed, and the final *-a* is retained, though in a few cases it fuses a stem-initial *a-*: *aha-* + *afa-po* (< *afaka* 'free' + *fo* 'heart') ⟹ *mahafa-po* 'satisfies'; *aha-* + *azo* ⟹ *mahazo* 'can'.

4.2.2 Imperatives
Imperatives of active verbs suffix the *m-* form with *-a*, apply consonant mutation and epenthesis, fuse the imperative *-a* with root-final /a/ if no epenthetic consonant intervenes, and shift stress one syllable to the right:

root R	active verb	active imperative
pétraka	*mipétraka* 'sits'	*mipetráha*
pétraka	*mamétraka* 'puts'	*mametráha*
sàlasála	*misàlasála* 'hesitates'	*misàlasalá*
dóka	*mandóka* 'flatters'	*mandokáfa*
róso	*mandróso* 'progresses'	*mandrosóa*

sása	*manása* 'washes (tr.)'	*manasá*
tólotra	*manólotra* 'offers'	*manolóra*
sóratra	*manóratra* 'writes'	*manoráta*
hátaka	*mangátaka* 'asks'	*mangatáha*
taó	*manaó* 'does'	*manaóva*
omé	*manomé* 'gives'	*manoméza*
rákotra	*mandrákotra* 'covers'	*mandrakófa*
vángy	*mamángy* 'visits'	*mamangía*
vóno	*mamóno* 'hits, kills'	*mamonóa*
fóno	*mamóno* 'wraps'	*mamonósa*
lóna	*mandóna* 'soaks'	*mandóma*
dóna	*mandóna* 'bumps, strikes'	*mandoná*
tóry	*matóry* 'sleeps'	*matoría*
ódy	*módy* 'goes home'	*modía*
íno	*míno* 'believes'	*minóa*
índrana	*míndrana* 'borrows'	*mindrána*

We observe that the *lona/dona* and *vono/fono* cases show that active imperatives cannot simply be directly formed from the present-tense active form. We must still know the underlying root. These facts support Erwin's analysis, as the relevant consonant would be present in his root. We note too the (possibly isolated) case of *ome*: its passive is just *omena* (either Theme or Goal is subject). But an epenthetic -*z*- appears in the active imperative (and the circumstantial form as well).

Imperative formation in -*a* + stress shift also applies to some adjectives, yielding forms sometimes more optative than imperative: *tsára* 'good' ⇒ *tsará* 'be good'; *máty* 'dead' ⇒ *matésa* 'die'.

We note, pending further consultant work, that active imperatives seem not to be productively formed from reduplicated forms. A&M list no cases. Here are speaker judgments on a few pragmatically plausible cases: *mamangivangy* 'visit a bit', but *?*mamangivangia*; *manaonao* 'do a bit', but *?*manaonaova*; *matoritory* 'is lightly sleeping', but *?*matoritoria* 'sleep a bit'. These judgments contrast with the generally accepted passive imperatives built from reduplicated roots: *vangivangio*, *ataotaovy*, etc.

Equally, imperatives from *aha*- verbs are in general unacceptable: *mahagága* 'is surprised', but *mahagagá; *mahaménatra* 'shameful', but *mahamenára. These facts are not surprising, given the normally abstract nature of "agents" of *maha*- verbs.

4.2.3 Secondary prefixes

These apply to the forms built by the primary prefixes discussed above. They are not semantically neutral in the way that most primary prefixes are, but are causative or reciprocal in meaning. We first review causatives, referring the reader to Randriamasimanana 1986 and Andrianierenana 1996 for extensive discussion.

4.2.3.1 Causatives: ank(a) This combines with actives built from a_2-. It induces no stress shift, consonant mutation, or ellipsis. The initial syllable of *ank(a)* carries a secondary stress in the forms it gives rise to.

(84) *héry* ⇒ *mahéry* 'is strong' ⇒ *mànkahéry* 'encourage, make strong'
      síaka ⇒ *masíaka* 'is nasty' ⇒ *mànkasíaka* 'makes nasty'
      ráry ⇒ *maráry* 'is sick' ⇒ *mànkaráry* 'makes sick'

Note that *ank(a)* takes the form *anka*- before a consonant, as in *mankahery*. (And of course the initial *m*- alternates with *h*- and *n*- for future and past, respectively).

We have also already seen a particular use of *ank*- with the locative deictics: *mankany* 'goes there', *mankaiza?* 'goes where?', etc. This use is not strictly causative in interpretation. There are also lexicalized, not strictly causative, cases: *fy* 'delicious' ⇒ *mankafy* 'find delicious, cherish'; *to* 'true, accepted' ⇒ *mankato* 'agree with, accept'.

4.2.3.2 Causatives: amp- This is the most productive causative prefix. It combines with actives built from *i*-, *aN*-, and ∅-. The derived roots may be of valency 1, 2, or 3. *h*- and *n*- replace the initial *m*- with the expected change in tense. All expressions with which *amp*- combines are vowel-initial, and the final consonant /^{m}p/ of *amp*- syllabifies with that vowel.

(85) *i*-: *mìhoméhy* 'laughs' ⇒ *màmpihoméhy* 'has/makes laugh'
      aN-: *manása* 'washes' ⇒ *màmpanása* 'has/makes wash'
      aN-: *manólotra* 'offers' ⇒ *màmpanólotra* 'has/makes offer'
      ∅-: *máka* 'takes' ⇒ *mampáka* 'has/makes taken'

In a few cases *amp*- combines with a_2- verbs: *matory* 'sleeps' ⇒ *mampatory* 'produces sleep'; *matahotra* 'fears' ⇒ *mampatahotra* 'makes afraid'.

amp- causatives form imperatives, as do other active verbs: *mampanáo* 'makes do' ⇒ *mampanáova* 'make do'; *mampanása* 'makes wash' ⇒ *mampanasá* 'make wash', etc. And *amp*- applies to reduplicated roots as expected: *manoratsoratra* ⇒ *mampanoratsoratra* 'make write a bit'. But, as with primary actives, imperatives are unnatural built from reduplicated forms: *?*mampanoratsoráta* 'make write a bit'.

Neither *amp*- nor *ank(a)*- combine with non-active verbs: *atolotra* 'be offered to', but **mampatolotra/*mankatolotra* 'makes offered to'; *voalaza* 'is said', but **mankavoalaza/*mampavoalaza*.

And in general *amp*- does not combine with verbs formed with the help of the causative prefixes *ana*-, *ank(a)*-, and *amp*- itself: *manasoa* 'makes pretty' ⇒ **mampanasoa* 'makes beautify'; *mampanasa* 'has wash' ⇒ **?mampampanasa* 'has make wash' (= X has Y make Z wash the clothes). The status of iterated *amp*- is somewhat unclear, in that there is nothing phonologically wrong with it, nor does it seem semantically unreasonable, especially when the initial verb is intransitive. Speakers understand what you are asking when you form and query such double causatives:

(86) (a)   mampandihy (m + amp + aN + dihy) ny ankizy Rabe
             makes-dance (pres. + Cause + act. + dance) the children Rabe
             'Rabe makes the children dance.'
             (better: 'Rabe acts so as to bring it about that the children dance')

      (b)   *?mampampandihy (m + amp + amp + aN + dihy)
             makes-make-dance (pres. + Cause + Cause + act. + dance)
             ny ankizy an-dRabe Rasoa.
             the children acc.-Rabe Rasoa
             'Rasoa has Rabe make the children dance.'

Nonetheless, double causatives like that in (86b) are not encountered in ordinary speech, and speakers do not really accept them, even though they can figure them out and pronounce them.

We have, however, found the odd example of an *amp-* causative formed from a *maha-* verb: (87) is from the Malagasy Constitution (*azy* refers to the President), and its initial verb [[*amp* + [*aha* + *fantatra*]] + *ina*] is the passive of the *amp-* causative of the *aha-* form of the passive root *fantatra* 'is known':

(87)   Ampahafantarina azy ny fifampiraharahana rehetra . . .
       cause + make + is-known + pass. him the negotiations all . . .
       'All the negotiations . . . are to be made known to him.'

Malagasy is a "double accusative" language, in that causatives of transitive verbs present, with some restrictions, two accusative NPs, the original direct object and the causee. Commonly, one of the two object NPs is indefinite, in which case, following the general pattern for ditransitive verbs, it occurs closest to the (derived) verb, and is not an accusative pronoun. Two accusative pronouns are disallowed:

(88) (a)   nanao farafara izy.   'He made (built) a bed.'
             made bed he

      (b)   nampanao farafara azy aho.   'I had him make a bed.'
             made-make bed him I

      (c)   *nampanao azy farafara aho.   'I had him make a bed.'
             makes-make him bed I

      (d)   *?nampanao azy azy aho.   'I had him make it.'

We noted earlier that *amp-* causatives form suffix passives. In the transitive case either accusative NP can be the subject of the passive, as Dez (1980b: 65) points out.

(89) (a)   nampanao farafara ahy Rabe.
             made-make bed me Rabe
             'Rabe made me make a bed.'

      (b)   nampanaovin-dRabe (n + amp + aN + tao + ina + Rabe(gen.))
             was made make by Rabe (past + cause + act. + make (rt) + pass. + Rabe)
             farafara aho.
             bed I
             'I was made to make a bed by Rabe.'

      (c)   nampanaovin-dRabe ahy io farafara io.
             is made make by Rabe me that bed that
             'That bed was made to be made by me by Rabe.'

Note that the verb forms in (89b) and (89c) are identical. This pattern is systematic with causatives of transitives in Malagasy. It is not typical of simple ditransitive verbs, where, as in (46), the two verb forms, *a-* prefix and *-CVna* suffix are used for Theme and Goal passives respectively. There is, however, one lexical exception: *ome* 'give', whose passive *omena* is unusual in having no vowel /i/ or /a/ in the passive suffix:

(90) (a)   manome vola ahy Rabe
             gives(act.) money me Rabe
             'Rabe gives me money.'

      (b)   omen-dRabe vola aho.
             give(pass.)-by-Rabe money I
             'I am given money by Rabe.'

      (c)   omen-dRabe ahy ilay vola.
             give(pass.)-by-Rabe me that money
             'That money is given to me by Rabe.'

There is one respect, however, in which the two accusatives exhibit syntactically distinct behavior: namely, in the control of reflexives. The reflexive pronoun *tena* 'self' (lit. 'body') is naturally anteceded by the causative subject when the initial verb is intransitive:

(91) (a)   mijaly Rabe.   (b)   mampijaly an-dRabe Rasoa.
             suffers Rabe   *makes-suffer acc-Rabe Rasoa*
             'Rabe suffers.'   'Rasoa makes Rabe suffer.'

      (c)   mampijaly tena Rasoa.
             makes-suffer self Rasoa
             'Rasoa makes herself suffer.'

But with causatives of transitives the only possibility for antecedents of *tena* is the Causee (92a).[12] This possibility is preserved under passive (92c).

(92)   (a)   nampamono tena$_{i,*j}$ an-dRabe$_i$ Rasoa$_j$.
             past + makes-hit/kill self acc.-Rabe Rasoa
             'Rasoa makes Rabe hit himself.'
             'Rasoa makes Rabe hit her'/'Rasoa makes herself hit Rabe.'

       (b)   *nampamono an-dRabe tena Rasoa.
             past + make-hit acc.-Rabe self Rasoa
             'Rasoa makes herself hit Rabe.'

       (c)   nampamonoin-dRasoa tena Rabe.
             past + make-hit + pass.-by-Rasoa self Rabe (nom.)
             'Rabe was caused to hit himself by Rasoa.'
             *'Rabe was caused to act in such a way that Rasoa hit herself.'

4.2.3.3 Reciprocals   These are built with the secondary affix *if-*. The positions that can be semantically bound by this morphology are studied in Keenan and Razafimamonjy 1996b. Here are some representative examples, with subject binding direct object in (93b), indirect object in (94), and the possessor of the direct object in (95):

(93)   (a)   m + aN + haja (= manaja) an-dRabe Rakoto.
           Pres. + act. + respect   *acc.-Rabe Rakoto*
           'Rakoto respects Rabe.'

       (b)   m + if + aN + haja (= mifanaja) Rabe sy Rakoto.
           pres. + recip. + act. + respect   *Rabe and Rakoto*
           'Rabe and Rakoto respect each other.'

(94)   mifanoratra (m + if + aN + soratra)   taratasy Rabe sy Rasoa.
           recip. + write (pres. + recip. + act. + write) letters Rabe and Rasoa
           'Rabe and Rasoa write each other letters.'

(95)   mifamantatra (m + if + aN + fantatra) toetra i Soa sy i Vao.
           rec. + know (pres. + rec. + act. + known) character art. Soa and art. Vao
           'Soa and Vao are getting to know each other's character.'

Such reciprocals form imperatives like other actives (suffix *-(C)a*, shift stress, . . .): *mifanorata taratasy*! 'write letters to each other', *mifamantara toetra* 'get to know each other's nature'. Reciprocal morphology combines with reduplicated actives:

(96)   nifanoratsoratra (n + IF + aN + Dup. (soratra)) taratasy Rabe sy Rasoa.
                 past + rec. + act. + Dup. (write) letter Rabe and Rasoa
     'Rabe and Rasoa wrote to each other sporadically.'

if- has two proper allomorphs: *ifamp-* and *ifank(a)-*. *ifamp-* is used (97a) with active verbs built from *i-* or *∅-* (very rarely a₂); *ifank(a)-* is used with active verbs built from *a₂-* or *aha-*.

(97) (a)   m + i + jery an-dRabe Rasoa.
       pres. + act. + look-at acc.-Rabe Rasoa
       'Rasoa is looking at Rabe.'

     (b)   m + ifamp + i + jery Rabe sy Rasoa.
       pres. + rec. + act. + look-at Rabe and Rasoa
       'Rabe and Rasoa are looking at each other.'

The occurrence of *amp* has no causative interpretation in (97b); it is purely epenthetic. Without it, **mifijery* is hopelessly ungrammatical.

(98) (a)   m + a + hita azy aho.
       pres. + a + see him I
       'I see him.'

     (b)   m + ifank + a + hita (= mifankahita) isika.
       pres. + rec. + a + see we (incl.)
       'We see each other.'

(99) (a)   m + aha + lala azy aho.
       pres. + pot./cause + know him I
       'I know him.'

     (b)   m + ifank + aha + lala (= mifankahalala) isika.
       pres. + rec. + pot./cause + know we (incl.)
       'We know each other.'

Again, absence of epenthetic *ank-* here is hopeless: **mifahita*, **mifahalala*. Henceforth we write IF for the reciprocal morpheme.

IF combines only with derived active verbs, never with roots or non-active verbs, even vowel-initial ones, which would not force an unacceptable consonant cluster: *atolotra* 'is offered' ⇒ **ifatolotra* 'is offered to each other'. On the other hand, IF does interact positively with (non-epenthetic) causative affixes.[13]

(100) (a)   nifandaka (n + IF + aN + daka) Rabe sy Rakoto.
        kicked each other (past + rec. + act. + kick) Rabe and Rakoto
        'Rabe and Rakoto are kicking each other.'

      (b)   nampifandaka (n + amp + IF + aN + daka)
        make-kick each other (pres. + cause + rec. + act. + kick)
        azy ireo aho.
        3:acc. dem. + pl. I
        'I made them kick each other.'

(101)   nampifanoratra (n + amp + IF + aN + soratra) taratasy an'i
                    (past + cause + rec. + act. + write) letter acc.'art.
        Be sy i Bao aho.
        Be and art. Bao I
        'I made Be and Bao write letters to each other.'

These causatives may be made imperatives (102a) and present suffix passives:

(102)   (a)   mampifanorata taratasy azy ireo.
              cause-each.other-make + imper. letter 3(acc.) dem. + pl.
              'Make them write each other letters.'

        (b)   nampifanoratana (n + amp + IF + aN + tao + ana + ko)
                          (past + cause + rec. + act. + do + pass.)
              taratasy izy ireo.
              letter 3(nom.) dem. + pl.
              'They were caused to write letters to each other.'

Reciprocals of causatives are also natural when formed from intransitive verb bases:

(103)   m + if + ana + soa Rabe sy Rasoa.
              pres. + rec. + cause + good Rabe and Rasoa
              'Rabe and Rasoa do each other good.'

(104)   (a)   m + a + siaka Rabe.
              pres. + a + nasty Rabe
              'Rabe is nasty.'

        (b)   m + anka + a + siaka (mankasiaka) azy aho.
              pres. + cause + a + nasty him I
              'I am making him nasty.'

        (c)   m + if + anka + a + siaka (mifankasiaka) Rabe sy Ranaivo.
              pres. + rec. + cause + a + nasty Rabe and Ranaivo
              'Rabe and Ranaivo are making each other nasty.'

(105)   nifampandihy (n + IF + amp + aN + dihy) i Bakoly sy i Vao.
                      past + rec. + cause + act. + dance art. Bakoly and art. Vao
              'Bakoly and Vao made each other dance.'

Interpretation of reciprocals of causatives of transitives is more variable across speakers, but certain cases seem acceptable to everyone:

(106)   (a)   nianatra (m + i + anatra) zavatra betsaka izy.
              studied   thing many he
              'He studied many things.'

(b)   nifampianatra (n + IF + amp + i + anatra) zavatra betsaka isika
      past + rec. + cause + act. + moral thing many we (incl.)
'We taught each other many things.'

4.2.4 Tertiary affixes   These form verbs from tensed verbs, and thus may
carry two tense markers. There are just two such affixes, *iha-* 'inchoative' and
iaraka- 'comitative'.

iha- combines with stative predicates P to form active verbs meaning "become
P little by little." P may be an adjectival root (107a), the odd noun (107b), or
an active stative verb built from *a-* or *aN-* (107c, d). Our data present no cases
of *iha-* combining with active verbs prefixed with *i-*, *∅-*, *aha-*, or any secondary
or other tertiary prefix.

(107)   (a)   *tsara* 'good' ⇒ *mihatsara* 'gradually becomes good'
        (b)   *vovoka* 'dust (noun)' ⇒ *mihavovoka* 'becomes dust'
        (c)   *madio* (*m + a + dio*) 'is clean' ⇒ *mihamadio* 'gradually becomes clean'
        (d)   *mangatsiaka* (*m + aN + hatsiaka*) 'is cold' ⇒ *mihamangatsiaka* 'becomes
              cold'

iha- does combine with reduplicated roots: *mihatsaratsara* 'becomes somewhat
good', *mihamadiodio* 'becomes a little cleaner', *mihamafimafy* 'becomes somewhat
stronger'. But we find essentially no forms derived from *miha-* verbs: e.g. no
imperatives (**mihatsará* 'become good', **mihamafía* 'become hard' (< *mafy* 'hard').
Nor (below) do *miha-* verbs have circumstantial forms.

But *miha-*verbs are complex in presenting double tense marking, though all
instances are ones in which the tense marking agrees:

(108)   n + iha + n + angatsiaka   'became cold'
        past + inch. + past + is cold

The comitative prefix *iaraka-* is basically an active verb (*i-* prefix, root *araka*
'following') (109a), which functions sometimes like a (tensed) preposition (109b),
and sometimes like a proper verbal prefix (109c).

(109)   (a)   niaraka izy ireo.
              past + i + following 3(nom.) dem. + pl.
              'They are together/going somewhere together.'

        (b)   Lasa niaraka tamin-dRabe izy.
              gone past-together past + with-Rabe he
              'He left with Rabe.'

        (c)   niara-nandeha (n + i + araka – n + aN + leha) t + any
                    (*past + act. + following – past + act. + go) past + there*
              Antsirabe izy sy Rabe.
              Antsirabe he and Rabe
              'He and Rabe went to Antsirabe together.'

As with *iha-*, tense is marked twice (109c), but not independently, in the main verb.

In distinction to *iha-*, *iaraka-* does not combine directly with roots, **miara-tsara* 'are good together', or with stative stems in general (such as typical *a₂*- or *aha-* verbs); but it does combine with activity verbs with *i-*, *aN-*, and *∅-* of any arity yielding an active activity verb of the same arity. It also combines with *amp-* causatives:

(110) *i-*:   *miasa* 'works'   ⇒ *miara-miasa* 'work together'
       aN-:   *manoratra* 'writes'   ⇒ *miara-manoratra* 'write together'
       ∅-:   *monina* 'resides'   ⇒ *miara-monina* 'reside together'
       amp-:   *mampianatra* 'teaches' ⇒ *miara-mampianatra* 'teach together'

Like *iha-*, *iaraka-* combines with reduplicated roots: *miara-mandehandeha* 'go a bit together'. And, like *miha-* verbs, *miaraka-* ones do not readily form complex derivatives. For example, they do not form independent imperatives; rather, the imperative form *miaráha* of *miaraka*, is used: *miaraha-mandeha* 'go together', but **miara-mandehana* 'go together'. Equally, transitive *miaraka-* verbs do not passivize: **miara-ampianarina* 'are taught together'.

4.3 Circumstantial forms of verbs

These are used when an oblique argument or adjunct of a verb is made the subject. See Keenan 1995, 1996, and Rajemisa-Raolison 1971: 111–18 for extensive discussion. Morphologically, circumstantial verbs appear to be built from active (tenseless) verbs by the suffixation of -(C)*ana* with stress shift, where C indicates the usual consonant mutation or epenthesis. Tense marking – *∅-*, *n-*, *h-* for present, past, and future respectively – follows the pattern for passives. Here, first, are some examples.

(111) (a) manao farafara amin'ity vy ity Rabe.   (active)
            makes bed with'this metal this Rabe
            'Rabe makes beds with this metal.'

       (b) anaovan-dRabe farafara ity vy ity.   (circumstantial)
            makes + circ. + Rabe bed this metal this
            'This metal is made beds with by Rabe.'

(112) (a) mividy mofo ho an'i Koto Rasoa.   (active)
            pres. + buy bread for'art. Koto Rasoa
            'Rasoa buys bread for Koto.'

       (b) ividianan-dRasoa mofo i Koto.   (circumstantial)
            buy + circ. + Rasoa (gen.) bread art. Koto
            'Koto will have bread bought for him by Rasoa.'

(113)   (a)   niarahaba anao tamin-kafaliana lehibe izahay.   (active)
                past + greeted you past + with-happiness great we (excl.)
                'We greeted you with great joy.'

         (b)   tamin-kafaliana lehibe no   (circumstantial)
                past + with + happiness great foc.
                niarahabanay anao.
                past + greet + circ. + 1pl. (excl., gen.) you
                'It was with great joy that we greeted you.'

Since only subjects can be relativized, a common use of circumstantial verbs is as relative clause modifiers of nouns (the relativizer *izay* is most usually absent).

(114)   (a)   ny vata (izay) nametrahan-dRabe ny vola
                the trunk (rel.) past + put + circ. + Rabe (gen.) the money
                'the trunk in which Rabe put the money'

         (b)   ny tanana nipetrahako taloha
                the village past + set + circ. + 1sg. (gen.) before
                'the village where I lived before'

All primary and secondary actives form a circumstantial verb as indicated (there are no roots which are themselves circumstantial verbs). In (114a, b) the root is *petraka* in both cases; as this root takes both *aN-* and *i-* prefixes, we have both circumstantial forms. Equally, causatives and reciprocals form circumstantials:

(115)   Betsaka ny zavatra nifampianarantsika
         many the things
         (n + IF + amp + i + anatra + ana + tsika).
         past + rec. + cause + act. + moral + circ. + 1pl. (incl., gen.)
         'Many were the things we taught each other.'

In (115) we have actually relativized the direct object of reciprocally-teach, not an oblique constituent. Reciprocal verbs do not passivize, and in such cases the circumstantial form is used. A simpler, non-causative example:

(116)   ny taratasy (izay) nifanoratan-dRabe sy Rasoa
         the letters (that) past + rec. + act. + write + circ. + Rabe and Rasoa
         'the letters that were written to each other by Rabe and Rasoa'

There are two other sorts of cases where a direct object of an active verb functions as the subject of a circumstantial one. The first, which is systematic, is when the referent of the direct object is understood as only partially affected. Compare (117a) and (b).

(117) (a) nihinana ny laoka tao am-bilany ny saka.
        past + i + eat the food past + there in-pot the cat
        'The cat ate (all) the food in the pot.'

    (b) nihinanan'ny saka ny laoka tao am-bilany.
        past + eat + circ. + the cat the food past + there in-pot
        'The cat ate some of the food in the pot.'

The second concerns a fair number of verbs that do not have a distinctive passive form, such as *mianatra* 'studies' and *manana* 'has' (and in fact all but one of the zero-prefix roots, most of which do not form transitive verbs).

(118) (a) ny teny vahiny nianaranao
        the language foreign past + study + circ. + 2sg. gen.
        'the foreign languages you studied'

    (b) Taiza no nianaranao?
        past + where foc. past + study + circ. + 2sg. gen.
        'Where did you used to study?'

It is of interest to note that the circumstantial *-ana* and passive *-ina* show up in minimal pairs in several cases, showing that they are not just phonological variants of each other. One case concerns those few verbs in which the passive is built from the active rather than from the underlying root:

(119) (a) nangataka (n + aN + hataka) vola azy Rabe.   (active)
              past + act. + beg money him Rabe
        'Rabe begged money from him.'

    (b) ny vola (izay) nangatahin-dRabe azy   (passive)
        the money (rel.) past + ask + pass.-Rabe 3.acc.
        'the money that Rabe asked him for'

    (c) ny antony (izay) nangatahan-dRabe vola azy   (circumstantial)
        the reason (rel.) past + ask + circ.-Rabe money 3.acc.
        'the reason that Rabe asked him for money'

A second type of minimal pair concerns the difference between passives and circumstantials of typical *amp-* causatives:

(120) (a) mampiasa (m + amp + i + asa) io angady io Rabe.
        makes-work that spade that Rabe
        'Rabe uses that spade.'

    (b) ny angady (izay) nampiasain-dRabe (n + amp + i + asa + ina-Rabe)
        the spade (rel.)   past + cause + act. + work + pass.-Rabe
        'the spade that was used by Rabe'

(c)   ny antony nampiasan-dRabe (n + amp + i + asa + ana-Rabe)
       the reason   past + cause + act. + work + circ.-Rabe
       io angady io
       that spade that
       'the reason that Rabe used that spade'

As we see, circumstantial verbs are derived from ones containing the primary (*i-*, *aN-*, *a-*, *Ø-*) and secondary (*ank(a)-*, *amp-*, *if-*) active affixes (though not the tertiary ones *iha-* and *iaraka-*). But, as with active imperatives, the choice or presence of epenthetic consonant varies with the root. Compare:

(121)
root	active present	active imperative	circumstantial present	circumstantial imperative
vóno 'hit, kill'	*mamóno*	*mamonóa*	*amonóana*	*amonóy*
fóno 'wrap'	*mamóno*	*mamonósa*	*amonósana*	*amonósy*
lóna 'soak'	*mandóna*	*mandóma*	*andómana*	*andómy*
dóna 'knock'	*mandóna*	*mandoná*	*andónana*	*andóny*
omé 'give'	*manomé*	*manoméza*	*anomézana*	*anomézo*
táo 'do'	*manáo*	*manáovy*	*anáovana*	*anáovy*
jéry 'look at'	*mijéry*	*mijeré*	*ijeréna*	*ijeréo*
ándry 'wait'	*miándry*	*miandrása*	*iandrásana*	*iandráso*
ráy 'receive'	*mandráy*	*mandráisa*	*andráisana*	*andráiso*

Clearly, the active indicative forms in the first two pairs above are identical, but their active imperatives and all their circumstantial (and passive) forms differ. So the input to circumstantial formation cannot just be the active indicative; it must include the sort of information that Erwin (1996) would build into the root.

Like both active and passive voice morphology, circumstantial morphology applies to stems that have been reduplicated:

(122) (a)   ny toerana nipetrapetrahanao (n + i + dup. (petraka)
              the location past + act. + dup. (live)
              + ana + nao)
              + *circ. + 2sg. gen.*
              'the place you stayed in for a bit'

       (b)   ny fomba nifanoratsoratanareo (n + IF + aN + dup. (soratra)
              the manner past + rec. + act. + dup. (write)
              + ana + nareo
              + *circ. + 2pl. gen.*
              'the manner in which you all wrote a bit to each other'

(c)   inona no hitsangantsangananareo (h + i + dup. (tsangana)
       what foc. fut. + act. + dup. (stand)
       + ana + nareo) any?
       + circ. + 2pl. (gen.) there
       'Why will you take a walk there?'

In general, the formation of circumstantial forms is highly productive and highly regular. The only, minor, idiosyncrasy we know of is that in a few cases the stem from which the active imperative and circumstantial forms are built contains a -*na* which does not surface in the passive (for those roots that form suffix passives).

(123)

active present	active imperative	passive suffix	circumstantial present	circumstantial imperative
mandéha 'goes'	*mandéhana*	——	*andehánana*	*andeháno*
mivídy 'buys'	*mividía, mividiána*	*vidína*	*ividiánana*	*ividiáno*
mifídy 'chooses'	*mifidía, mifidiána*	*fidína*	*ifidiánana*	*ifidiáno*

Circumstantial imperatives are formed on the passive pattern, suffixing -*o*/ -*y*, rather than -*a*, as in actives. And we restress that non-active (= passive and circumstantial) imperatives present a nominative NP, as in (124). The NP missing in imperatives is the addressee, and in non-actives that is the genitive Agent, not the nominative subject.

(124)   Mba ividiano satroka aho.
         part. buy + circ. + imper. hat 1sg. (nom.)
         'Please buy a hat for me.'

5 Verbal nominalizations

These are of two sorts. First, +human agent nominals are formed by prefixing *mp-* (pronounced /p/)[14] to tenseless active verbs of certain sorts, never to non-active verbs. *mp*-nominals do not mark number; their translations are given variously as singular or plural: *mandeha* 'goes' ⇒ *mpandeha* 'voyager'; *mihaino* 'listens' ⇒ *mpihaino* 'listeners'; *misolo* 'substitutes' ⇒ *mpisolo* 'replacement'; *mitsiky* 'smiles' ⇒ *mpitsiky* 'someone who is smiling'; *manoratra* 'writes' ⇒ *mpanoratra* 'writers'; *manolotra* 'offers' ⇒ *mpanolotra* 'offerers'. *mp-* also applies to ∅- prefix actives: *onina* ⇒ *monina* 'resides' ⇒ *mponina* 'inhabitants'; *aka* ⇒ *maka* 'takes' ⇒ *mpaka* 'takers'. But *mp-* does not apply naturally to *a*-prefix actives: *matoky* 'trusts' but *?*mpatoky* 'trusters'; *mahita* 'sees' but *?*mpahita* 'people who see' (cf. *mijery* 'look at' ⇒ *mpijery* 'spectators').

mp- also applies to secondary actives, both causatives – *mampianatra* 'teachers' ⇒ *mpampianatra* 'teacher', *mampivelona* 'makes-live' ⇒ *mpampivelona* 'mid-wife', *mankafy* 'finds delicious' ⇒ *mpankafy* 'delectors' – and to reciprocals – *mifanoratra* 'write each other' ⇒ *mpifanoratra* 'writers to each other', *mifanerasera* 'frequent each other' ⇒ *mpifanerasera* 'people who frequent each other'. *mp-* even combines with a few tertiary actives: *miara-miasa* 'work together' ⇒ *mpiara-miasa* 'co-workers'. And while several *mp-* nominals are lexicalized: *mpampianatra* 'teachers', *mpifankatia* 'lovers', *mp-* is used creatively. A *mpihaino* 'listener' can just be someone who is listening to something on some particular occasion; it need not be a habitual listener. Forms like *mpifampianatra* 'people who teach each other things' are readily interpreted in context, though the absence of professional mutual teachers makes the forms seem unusual out of context.

mp- does not combine with *iha-* verbs: *mihatsara* 'become good' but *?*mpihatsara* 'people who become good'. Nor does *mp-* combine with passives – *atolotra* 'is offered', but *?*mpatolotra* 'people who are offered' – or with circumstantials – *anolorana* 'circumstance of being offered', but *?*mpanolorana* 'people for/ because of whom things are offered'. *mp-* does combine with a variety of syntactically complex predicates:

(125)   (a)   iray tanana izy ireo.
        one village 3(nom.) dem. + pl.
        'They are from the same village.'

        (b)   ny mpiray tanana
        the nom-one village
        'people from the same village'

Arguably the predicate in (125a) is derived by NP (possessor) raising, illustrated in (126), and very widely used in Malagasy.

(126)   (a)   roa ny lelan'ny antsipika.
        two the tongue' of the pocketknife
        'The pocketknife has two blades.'

        (b)   roa lela ny antsipika.
        two tongue the pocketknife
        'The pocketknife is two-bladed.'

And the predicate in (127b) has been derived from that in (126a) by incorporation:

(127)   (a)   manana harena izy.   (b)   manan-karena izy.
        has wealth he   *has-wealth he*
        'He has some wealth.'   'He is wealthy.'

(c)   ny mpanan-karena
      the havers (of) wealth
      'the wealthy'

Further, *mp-* nominals built from (di)transitive verbs preserve the subcat-egorization of the verb. Thus they may take accusative complements (without, as in English, the need to insert a preposition to assign case):

(128) (a)   ny mpihaino azy
             the listener 3.acc.
             'the people listening to it/him'

       (b)   ny mpampianatra azy
             the teacher 3.acc.
             'the teacher of him' (= 'his teacher')

Note that (128b) contrasts with *ny mpampianany* (< *mpampianatra* 'teacher' + -*ny* 3(gen.)), which would translate as 'his teacher' but only in the sense of 'teacher that he hired, or in some other way possessed'. We note also that *mp-* nominals are not incompatible with a tensed interpretation of the underlying verb, even though the *mp-* has preempted the tense slot of the active verb:

(129) Mbola tsy nosamborina ny mpamono azy
       still not past + arrest + pass. the killer (of) him
       'His killer still hasn't been arrested.'

(130) Sosotra ny mpandeha tany Antsirabe fa ...
       frustrated the goers past + there Antsirabe because ...
       'The people who were going to Antsirabe were frustrated because ...'

Observe that certain lexical nouns also take both genitive and accusative complements:

(131) (a)   ny alahelon-dRasoa an-dreniny
             the sorrow'of Rasoa acc.-mother-3.gen.
             'Rasoa's grief over her mother'

       (b)   ny tahotr'i Koto azy
             the fear'art Koto 3.acc.
             'Koto's fear of him'

Agent nominals in Malagasy give rise to a bracketing paradox if *mp-* is required to combine just with words rather than with phrases. For then the morphological bracketing of (125b), (127b), and (128a) will be as in (132a, b, c) respectively:

(132) (a) [[mp + iray] tanana]   (b) [[mp + anana] + harena]
       (c) [[mp + ihaino] azy]

But in (132a) it is *iray tanana* that expresses the property shared by the referents of the nominal. And in (132c) the accusative pronoun satisfies the subcategorization requirements of *-ihaino* 'listen to'.

A second type of predicate-nominalizing operation in Malagasy consists of prefixing tenseless verbs with *f-*. Such forms are built both from active and from circumstantial verbs, but not from passive verbs.[15] *f-* nominals built from circumstantial verbs are by far the most common.

Applied to an active V, *f-* nominals sometimes have an instrument interpretation (not possible for *mp-* nominals): *manjaitra* 'sews' ⇒ *fanjaitra* 'needle', *mamaky* 'cuts' ⇒ *famaky* 'hatchet'. More productively, they have a "manner of V-ing" interpretation: *mandeha* 'goes' ⇒ *fandeha* 'manner of walking', *miteny* 'speaks' ⇒ *fiteny* 'manner of speaking'. Both instrument and manner interpretations are possible for a given form:

(133) (a) hafahafa ny fanjaitran'io olona io.
            different (dup.) the nom. + sew'this person this
            'This person sews in an unusual way.'

       (b) very ny fanjaitran'io olona io
            lost the needle'this person this
            'This person's needle is missing.'

Very widely used are *f-* nominals of circumstantial verbs. They refer to the abstract action or state expressed by the verb, or a contextually appropriate circumstance of that action or state, such as its place, time, or instrument.

(134) active present   f-nominalization of circumstantial
                                           form

       mátory 'sleeps'   *fatoríana* 'sleep'
       mánana 'possesses'   *fanánana* 'ownership, possessions'
       mandéha 'goes'   *fandehánana* 'departure, going'
       mámaky 'reads'   *famakíana* 'reading'
       miánatra 'studies'   *fianárana* 'studies'
       màmpiánatra 'teaches'   *fàmpianárana* 'instruction'
       mifànkatía 'love each other'   *fifànkatiávana* 'mutual love'
       mitsàngantsángana 'walks around' *fitsàngantsangánana* 'a walk'
       mahíta 'sees'   *fàhitána* 'sight, instrument of seeing'
       mivárotra 'sells'   *fivarrótana* 'shop, circumstance of
                                           selling'

       mifanáiky 'agree with each other' *fifanekéna* 'agreement, contract'
       mankató 'approve'   *fànkatoávana* 'ratification'
       mifàmpiràharáha 'work together'   *fifàmpiràharahána* 'negotiations'

As with *mp-* nominals, *f-* nominals preserve the subcategorization of their predicates:

(135) (a)   ny antony anajan-dRabe azy
             the reason respect (circ.)-Rabe 3.acc.
             'the reason Rabe respects him'

       (b)   ny fanajan-dRabe azy
             the nom.-respect + circ.-Rabe 3.acc.
             'Rabe's respect (for) him'

       (c)   tsy manaja tena Rabe.
             not respects (act.) self Rabe
             'Rabe doesn't respect himself.'

       (d)   ny tsy fanajan-dRabe tena.
             the not nom-respect + circ.-Rabe self
             'Rabe's not respecting himself.'

f- nominalizations of verbs contrast with the nominalized tensed forms. Tensed verbs in all voices may be construed with articles or demonstratives to form a derived nominal. Contrast (136a) with the *f-* nominal (136b). (136a) refers to a particular past event of Rabe's going to Antsirabe, whereas (136b) refers to Rabe's habitual trips, or just "his going" in the abstract.

(136) (a)   nahatezitra ahy ny nandehanan-dRabe tany Antsirabe omaly.
             angered me the past + go + circ.-Rabe past-there Antsirabe yesterday
             'Rabe's going to Antsirabe yesterday angered me.'

       (b)   mahasosotra ahy ny fandehanan-dRabe any Antsirabe.
             frustrates me the nom. + go + circ.-Rabe there Antsirabe
             'Rabe's going to Antsirabe frustrates me.'

In (136a) the past tense *n-* can be replaced by future *h-* or present *∅-*, making appropriate changes in the locatives and adverbials, with appropriate change in meaning.

6 Generalized incorporation

This is the last of the morphological processes we consider. Generalized Incorporation (Inc.) itself may fail to be a specifically morphological process, but it interacts with various of the processes already discussed in regular ways, and it utilizes essentially the same cluster of phonological alternations, stop and nasal, which characterized reduplication and were used significantly in genitive formation and *aN-* prefixation. A basic case of Inc. is the incorporation of objects into transitive verbs. We show below that all instances of stop apply, and under each case we give another example showing nasal:

f ⇒ p
    mihósotra 'anoints' + *fótaka* 'mud' ⇒ *mihòso-pótoka* 'anoints oneself with mud'
    mihínana 'eats' + *fáry* 'sugar cane' ⇒ *mihìnam-páry* 'eats sugar cane'

v ⇒ b
    mitóraka 'throws' + *váto* 'stone' ⇒ *mitòra-báto* 'throws stones'
    mánana 'has' + *vóla* 'money' ⇒ *mànam-bóla* 'has money, is wealthy'

s ⇒ ts
    matáhotra 'fears' + *sáka* 'cat' ⇒ *matàho-tsáka* 'fears cats'
    mánana 'has' + *sáina* 'mind' ⇒ *mànan-tsáina* 'is smart'

z ⇒ dz
    mangátaka 'asks for' + *závatra* 'thing' ⇒ *mangàta-jávatra* 'asks for a thing'
    mánana 'has' + *zánaka* 'child' ⇒ *mànan-jánaka* 'has children'

h ⇒ k
    manápaka 'cuts' + *házo* 'tree' ⇒ *manàpa-kázo* 'cuts trees'
    mánana 'has' + *haréna* 'wealth' ⇒ *mànan-karéna* 'is wealthy'

l ⇒ d
    mitárika 'leads' + *lálana* 'way, road' ⇒ *mitàri-dálana* 'leads the way'
    mihínana 'eats' + *làisóa* 'lettuce' ⇒ *mihìnan-dàisóa* 'eats lettuce'

r ⇒ dr
    mifóka 'absorbs' + *ráno* 'water' ⇒ *mifò-dráno* 'absorbs water'
    manándrana 'tries' + *ró* 'sauce' ⇒ *manàndran-dró* 'tastes sauce'

As is plain, the phonological alternations which arise under Inc. are all ones which occur in reduplication as well. Further, it is clear, as Donca Steriade (personal communication) points out to us, that these alternations are not arbitrary. Rather, they act to preserve the non-continuant nature of the consonant deleted under Inc. or Red. The main difference between Inc. and Red is that in Inc. the application of the phonological alternations is typically optional, although there may be some differences in meaning too (the incorporated form is more likely to have a generic or habitual interpretation).

Arguably, however, Inc applies at a later derivational level than reduplication. It applies to N + Adj. pairs, though even more optionally than for V + Object pairs:

(137)   *závatra* 'thing' + *rátsy* 'bad'   ⇒   *zàva-drátsy* 'bad thing'
    sátroka 'hat' + *fótsy* 'white'   ⇒   *sàtro-pótsy* 'white hat'
    tanána 'village' + *lehibé* 'big'   ⇒   *tanàn-dèhibé* 'big village'

More strikingly, Inc. applies to a predicate (often adjectival) and the possessee noun after NP (possessor) raising:

(138) (a)   rovitra ny vodin'ny harona. ⇒   rovi-body ny harona.
           torn the bottom'of-the basket   *torn-bottom the basket*
           'The bottom of the basket is torn.'   'The basket has a torn
                                                        bottom.'

      (b)   sarotra ny rafitr'io fehezan-teny io. ⇒
           difficult the structure'of-this sentence this
           'The structure of this sentence is difficult.'
           saro-drafitra io fehezan-teny io.
           difficult structure this sentence this
           'This sentence has a difficult structure.'

      (c)   miadana ny fandehan-dRasoa ⇒   miadam-pandeha Rasoa
           slow the going-by-Rasoa   *slow-going Rasoa*
           'Rasoa's manner of walking is slow.'   'Rasoa moves slowly.'

      (d)   lavitra tokoa ny lalana halehanay. ⇒
           far very the road fut. + pass. + go + 1pl.:gen., excl.
           'The road on which we go is very far.'
           lavi-dala-kaleha izahay.
           far-road-fut. + pass. + go 1pl.:nom., excl.
           'We have a long road to go.'

But Inc., and the stop + nasal changes that constitute it, do not apply every-where. In particular, they do not apply to intransitive verbs and their subjects:

(139)   'Rabe is eating' = *mihinana Rabe*, but **mihinan-dRabe*
        'Rabe is sitting' = *mipetraka Rabe*, but **mipetra-dRabe* 'Rabe is sitting'

So Inc. is sensitive to syntactic structure, and the stop + nasal combination clearly seems to apply at more than one level in the derivational history of an expression.

We conclude with three morphologically relevant properties of Inc. First, *mp-* nominals and circumstantial *f-* nominals incorporate their objects, just as the underlying verbs do. Thus, from the root *varotra*, we have the active verb *mivarotra* 'sells' and:

(140) (a)   *fivarotana* 'shop' + *fanafody* 'medicine' ⇒ *fivarotam-panafody*
           'pharmacy'
      (b)   *mpivarotra* 'seller' + *hena* 'meat' ⇒ *mpivaro-kena* 'meat-seller,
           butcher'

Note that it seems semantically natural to think that the object "medicine"/ "meat" forms a unit with the underlying verb, and that the nominalizing oper-ators apply to the verb + object complex. This seems particularly compelling when the incorporated V + object has an idiomatic interpretation:

(141)   *manapaka* 'cuts' + *hevitra* 'thought' ⇒ *manapa-kevitra* 'decides' ⇒ *fanapahan-kevitra* 'decision'

But morphologically circumstantial formation (-(C)*ana* suffixation) must precede Inc. Words like *fanafody* 'medicine' and *hena* 'meat' do not have circumstantial forms. If we suffixed (C)*ana* after Inc. applied, we would obtain the incorrect output (142):

(142)   *f-* nom. (Inc. (*mivarotra, fanafody*)) = *f-* nom(*mivaro-panafody*) = ****ivaro-panafodiana*

Similar claims hold for the more limited *ha-* . . . *-ana* nominalization of certain adjectives: for example, *tsara* 'good' ⇒ *hatsarana* 'goodness'. But semantically, predicates derived by NP (possessor) raising undergo this nominalizing process:

(143)   (a)   tsara fanahy Rabe.   (b)   ny hatsaram-panahin-dRabe
              good spirit Rabe   *the goodness-spirit-of + Rabe*
              'Rabe is a nice guy.'   'Rabe's niceness of character'

(144)   (a)   maranitra ny sain-dRabe   (b)   marani-tsaina Rabe.
              sharp the mind-of-Rabe   *sharp-mind Rabe*
              'The mind of Rabe is sharp.'   'Rabe is sharp-minded.'

        (c)   haranitan-tsain-dRabe
              sharpness-mind-of-Rabe
              'Rabe's sharpness of mind'

Second, we observe, unsurprisingly, that incorporation into *f-* nominals leads often to stress clashes:

(145)   *miála* 'removes' + *sásatra* 'tired'   ⇒   *miàla-sásatra* 'rests'
                                                 ⇒   *fialàn-tsásatra* 'rest period'
        míla 'seeks' + *hévitra* 'thought'   ⇒   *filàn-kévitra* 'council'

Third, Inc. iterates, at least within limits.

(146)   (a)   *miàra-mónina* 'live together' ⇒ *fiaràha-mónina* 'society', and
              ráfitra 'structure' + *fiaràha-mónina* ⇒ *ràfi-piaràha-mónina* 'social structure'

        (b)   *filàn-kévitra* 'council' + *filamínana* 'f-circ. (*milámina* "is in order")'
              ⇒ *filàn-kèvi-pilamínana* 'security council'

        (c)   *fétra* 'limit' + *fotóana* 'time' + *fiàsána* 'f-circ. (*miása* "works")'
              ⇒ *fè-potòam-piàsána* 'time limit for working/office holding'

In closing, consider briefly the motivation for the basic morphophonological changes we have observed in reduplication, genitive formation, *aN-* prefixation, and incorporation. The core of these changes is *-ka/-tra* deletion followed by stop and *-na* deletion followed by stop and then nasal. For convenience, call these changes "Basic."

Accepting the standard (A&M) roots, there does not seem to be much phonotactic motivation for Basic. The phonological combinations that would result from just concatenating the two expressions are not in general disallowed. This is most obvious in cases of Inc, where the incorporation of objects into verbs or adjectives into nouns is optional. For example, we have both *satroka fotsy* 'white hat' (lit. 'hat white') and *satro-potsy, manana vola* 'has money' and *manam-bola.*

However, adopting Erwin's (1996) analysis of roots, we can find some phonotactic motivation for Basic. On that analysis, weak roots are consonant-final, ending in *-k, -t, -r, -f, -m,* or *-n.* Combining such roots, or their prefixed derivatives, with consonant-initial objects, possessors, or (partial) copies of themselves would produce consonant clusters, not in general tolerated. Dropping the final consonant of a root would avoid the cluster. Perhaps the optional character of Inc on this view can be accounted for by allowing it to apply both before and after *-a* epenthesis. And perhaps the occasional differential behavior of homophones can be accounted for by deriving them from different roots. For example, from K&R 96a we note that bisyllabic *saina* 'mind' behaves as weak, and *saina* 'flag' (?< Fr. *enseigne* 'sign') does not, plausible on Erwin's view if the root form of *saina* 'mind' is just *sain*, whereas the root form of *saina* 'flag' is *saina.*

(147) *saina* 'mind' + *zaza* 'child' ⇒ *sain-jaza* 'a child's mind'
       saina 'flag' + *fotsy* 'white' ⇒ *saina fotsy* 'white flag', **saim-potsy*

This idea is appealing, but most of the analysis remains to be worked out. Consider in more detail what is involved with a concrete example: *latsaka* 'fallen, flows' + *ranomaso* 'tears' ⇒ *latsa-dranomaso* 'cried', as in

(148) (a) latsaka ny ranomasony.   (b) latsa-dranomaso izy.
            fell the tears + his   *fell-tears he*
            'His tears were falling.'   'He was crying.'

Taking the root to be *latsaka*, we observe that the sequence *latsaka ranomaso* is phonotactically acceptable. Indeed, the relevant portion occurs in *Latsaka Ranona* 'Ranona fell'. And the crucial juncture, *ka + ra*, is a sequence that occurs word-internally elsewhere: *mikarakara* 'takes care of', *karakaraina* 'is taken care of'.

But on Erwin's analysis, the root would just be *latsak*. And concatenation with *ranomaso* yields the consonant cluster $k + r$.[16] Dropping the *-k* is one way of avoiding the cluster. But there are others. For example, we could drop the initial *r-* of *ranomaso* (unexpected on the account given by Hawkins and Cutler 1988). Or, more plausibly, we could insert a vowel following *-k*, something which is done anyway on Erwin's analysis, and which is independently motivated: borrowings may accept various consonant clusters, but a borrowed word which is consonant-final usually has a vowel added, most normally /a/, or /i/, as in *dokotera* 'doctor' or *Kristy* 'Christ'.

But most problematic is why the initial consonant of *ranomaso* should mutate when *-k*. If it remained /r/, we would have an internal sequence *tsa + ra = tsara* which is good (in fact, *tsára* is the root adjective 'good'). And in general the ban on consonant clusters does not suffice to account for the consonant mutations in stops. However, as indicated earlier, these mutations are better understood as an effect of preserving the noncontinuant property of the consonant deleted.

NOTES

1   More study is needed to determine the precise points of articulations of *t'* and *d'* and the prenasalized counterparts, as well as possible idiolectal variability. We note that Domenichini-Ramiaramanana (1977: 23) classifies these phonemes as retroflex.

2   There is one exception: *ntaolo* 'the ancients' Rajaona (1977) provides evidence that this word derives historically from one containing an initial vowel /u/.

3   Characterizing the semantics of these forms solely in terms of distance from the speaker is a simplification. For example, *any* and its demonstrative correspondent *iny* in (7) are used as a kind of not-too-close default. *ao* is often used when the notion of 'inside' is intended. And certain point of view shifts can change "distance from Speaker" to "distance from Hearer."

4   We note also the form *rizareo* 'they', which appears to contain both *-za-* and *-re-*. The source of the initial *r* is not clear. Perhaps it arises from the free morpheme *ry* (= /ri/)

which can indicate plural when combining with proper nouns: *ry Rabe* 'the Rabes'.

5   We differ from standard analyses in counting as weak, roots ending in *-ny* with antepenultimate stress. Several of these appear to be historically formed from a two-syllable root or a weak three-syllable one by adding the third-person genitive suffix *-ny*, which does not carry or shift stress: *sásaka* 'half' + *ny* = *sásany* 'some', *tápaka* 'cut' + *ny* = *tápany* 'half', *fára* 'end' + *ny* = *fárany* 'finally', *rámbo* 'tail' + *ny* = *rámbony* 'last in rank', *fahéfatra* 'fourth' + *ny* = *fahéfany* 'a quarter', aN + *lány* 'side, end' + *ny* = *an-dániny* 'on the one hand', *vóa* + *lóha* 'head' + *ny* = *vòalóhany* 'at first'. But others, like *tókony* 'should', *ántony* 'reason, cause', and *antóniny* 'average, so-so', are hard to assimilate to this pattern.

6   The forms *indray* and *lehibe* are historically complex, but are now treated both syntactically and semantically as roots. Specifically, we don't get their meaning

compositionally as a function of the meanings of their parts.

7 Malagasy presents many frozen reduplications of the form (CV)⁴, such as *midràdradrádra* 'laments' and *mifòfofófo* 'blows (wind)'. But the stress pattern shows that they are not the result of two applications of reduplication to a monosyllabic root. If they were, then the first application to *fó* would be *fòfó*, as we see in *bèbé*, and the second application would then yield (*mi*)*fofòfó*, which in fact is unattested.

8 In fact, the relatively few weak roots ending in *-ny* rarely head a possessive construction, so only *-na* is considered here.

9 Rahajarizafy (1960: 190) lists thirteen roots which accept both an *-ana* and an *-ina* suffix with somewhat different meanings: e.g. the root *velatra* yields both *velarana* and *velarina*:

(i) Novelaran-dRabe tsihy
     opened up-by-Rabe mat
     ny vahiny.
     the guest
     'Rabe opened up a mat for the guest.'

(ii) Novelarin-dRabe ny
     opened up-by-R the
     hevitr'izany teny izany.
     idea'that word that
     'Rabe explained the meaning of that word.'

10 There were two cases in our data where both passive of a reduplicated root (as expected) and reduplication of a derived passive were accepted:

root R	stem
sóratra 'write'	sorát
fóno 'wrap'	fonós

Red.(R)	Pass.(R)
sòratsóratra	sorátana
fònofóno	fonósina

Pass.(Red.(R))	Red.(Pass.(R))
sòratsorátana	soràtandrátana
fònofonósina	fonòsinósina

Note that the expected forms, Pass.(Red.(R)) do present stress lapses, whereas the novel forms, Red.(Pass.(R)) do not. Perhaps we are witnessing change in progress, motivated by *Lapse.

11 Though it does enter frames like *Efa ho Verb*, meaning "about to Verb": e.g. *Efa ho lasa izy* 'He is about to leave'.

12 One speaker found causatives of transitives quite generally bad. But her judgments regarding the possible antecedents of *tena* 'self' in (92a, c) were strongly supportive of our claims here.

13 All speakers accept causatives of intransitive reciprocal verbs, as in (100b). The one speaker who objected to causatives of transitives in simple cases objected to causatives of transitive reciprocals (101) as well.

14 It seems (Rajaona 1977) that historically the *mp-* was preceded by a vowel, which would have supported the prenasalization.

15 There is one lexical exception: *faleha* < *f-* aleha = a + leha 'where one habitually goes'.

16 This cluster does occur in a few borrowings, e.g. *kristianina* 'Christian'.

29 Qafar (East Cushitic)

RICHARD J. HAYWARD

Introduction

The language described in this chapter is spoken by at least three million people who call themselves 'Qafar', though earlier European writers and travellers usually referred to them as 'Dankali' or 'Danakil'. The Qafar inhabit that vast tract of land which stretches from the Red Sea coast south and west as far as the scarplands of the Ethiopian plateau, an area generally referred to as the 'Danakil Depression'. With the exception of narrow belts of luxuriant jungle along the banks of rivers, such as the Awash and the Mille, which descend into the Depression, the country is largely desert; though even quite short spells of rain can resurrect grass and other seasonal plant life. Although Qafar living in large coastal towns such as Djibouti and Assab and those on the Red Sea coast who live by fishing have clearly abandoned pastoralism as a way of life, the majority of Qafar remain pastoralists, and this is strongly reflected in the lexicon of their language.

The Qafar language belongs to the Northern Lowland (Saho–Qafar) division of East Cushitic, a sub-family of Cushitic whose two best-known members are Somali and Oromo. At a remoter level of genetic affinity, Cushitic is classified, along with Semitic, Omotic, Berber, Chadic and Egyptian, as a family of the Afro-Asiatic phylum.

Although generally not so well known as Somali or Oromo, Qafar has not escaped the attention of linguists, the first descriptions having appeared as long ago as the 1880s (Reinisch 1886, Colizza 1887). More recently, a number of works have been published on aspects of the language, the most comprehensive of these being Bliese 1981 and Parker and Hayward 1985.

In company with most Ethiopian languages, Qafar exhibits strongly head-final syntax. Qafar is a consistently right-headed language; complements, modifiers, and specifiers all precede their heads. This is exemplified in (1).[1]

(1) VP   *ħán nake* (milk he-drank-milk) '(He) drank milk'; *núm lih yabta*
            (person with she-talks) '(She) is talking to someone'; *inkínnak baye*
            (entirely he-got-lost) 'Altogether/entirely lost'

     NP   *yí toobokoytih ina* (my brother-gen. mother) 'mother of my brother';
            woó ʕari (that house) 'that house'; *nabá num* (great/old person) 'big/
            great/old man'; *tiḍḍigillé boddina* (it-was-broken tooth) 'tooth that
            was broken'

     AP   *nabám xeera* (very tall/long) 'very tall/long'

     PP   *gíta-t* (road-on/in) 'on/in the road'; *daʕaár-ak* (wadi-from) 'from the
            wadi'; *yó-llih* (me-with) 'with me'

As we might expect from the syntactic order, Qafar is predominantly a
suffixing language. However, there are some obvious relics of an ancient
Afro-Asiatic feature in the form of a class of verbs with subject agreement
and valency-changing derivational morphology attached prefixally. Other
Afro-Asiatic legacies show up in aspects of the morphology that are 'nonconcatenative': that is, have infixal and reduplicative properties. Cleft constructions based on free relatives are frequent in Qafar, as in most other Ethiopian
languages where they generally function as devices for contrastive focalization.
Another prominent areal characteristic shared by Qafar is the extensive use of
direct speech, together with the development of a type of compound involving
the quotative verb 'to say'.

From the point of view of morphological behaviour Qafar words fall into
three broad sets, which may conveniently be labelled 'nominals', 'verbals',
'indeclinables'. On account of their morphological behaviour, what are adjectives semantically are included within a special inflectional class of stative verbals. Where not expressed by postpositional phrases, adverbial concepts fall
under either the nominal or the verbal categories. Numeral quantifiers pattern
like nominals, while most non-numeral quantifiers join the aforementioned set
of statives.[2]

1 Nominals

The class of nominals are characterized by the following properties: (a) they
are subcategorized for gender, which requires control of agreement in the
verb; (b) they may be assigned distinct case forms; (c) they may show formal
variation for up to three number categories. Prototypical nominals are, or
course, nouns. Personal pronouns and a few Wh-words and numerals also fit
comfortably into the nominal category. A few nominals have to be regarded
as dependent, in so far as they never occur as free-standing items, even in
citation.

1.1 Nouns

There is no phonological shape common to the stems of underived nouns; some terminate in consonants, others in vowels, and stems may range from one to five syllables in length. It is nevertheless the case that the great majority of nominal stems are monosyllabic or bisyllabic.

1.1.1 Gender
Nouns are subcategorized for the control of masculine (m.) or feminine (f.) gender in the verb;[3] for example:

(2)   *yí boddin biyaakit-áh.*[4]
      My teeth (m.) hurt-3m.sg-impf.   'My teeth hurt.'

      yí amo biyaakit-t-áh.
      My head (f.) hurt-3f.sg.-impf.   'My head hurts.'

Gender is also a determinant for the marking of case. Except in the case of sexually differentiable animates, it is not possible to relate gender to any inherent semantic properties. There are, however, such regular correlations between the phonological form of a nominal and its gender that gender need never be marked lexically; thus (a) all feminine nominals are vowel-final in their basic case (i.e. absolutive case, cf. section 1.1.4) form; and (b) all feminine nominals are unaccented. It may only be inferred from these statements, however, that any consonant-final or any accented nominal will be masculine, for the properties of consonant finality and bearing of accent do not always coincide; and it should be noted that while all accented vowel-final nominals are masculine, not all consonant-final nominals are accented. Typical nominals are illustrated in (3).

(3)   masculine: (i)   *ʕåri* 'house'; *waåmu* 'male ostrich'; *sóḍa* 'mistake'
                    (ii) *kålam* 'throat'; *gûbun* 'venomous snake sp.'; *ḍållaħ* 'cockroaches'
                    (iii) *nahar* 'chest, front'; *musut* 'comb'; *kumakum* 'snails'
      feminine: *dale* 'wound'; *kaʕalso* 'washing'; *waaga* 'doubt'

There is a further strong correlation between gender and the occurrence of certain vowels in final position; thus, final mid-vowels occur only in feminine nouns, while final high vowels tend to occur in masculine nouns; nouns in final *a* can be of either gender: for example, *amo* (f.) 'head'; *saare* (f.) 'type of song'; *koðri* (m.) 'saddle'; *mûlħu* (m.) 'bitterness'; *ħaḍa* (f.) 'tree'; *gîta* (m.) 'way, road'.

1.1.2 Number
There are two marked categories of number: plural (pl.) and singulative (sgt.). There is also an unmarked 'base' form. In some cases the base form refers to a mass or a collective entity – for example, *ḍågo(o)r* 'hair'; *wadar* 'goats, flock of goats' – but in other cases the base form is either generic in reference or indeterminate in referring to one item or many – for example, *feera* 'finger(s)' as in *yí feera biyaakitta* 'My finger(s) hurt(s)'. In contrast to the base form, a singulative form will always refer to a single individual, while a

plural form will refer to a number of individual entities – for examples, *faroosa* (pl.) 'horses', cf. *faras* 'horse', or (in the case of the base form having collective reference) it may refer to a number of collective entities – for example, *ḍagorta* (sgt.) 'single hair'; *wadaariyowa* (pl.) 'flocks of goats'. While all three forms occur for some nouns (e.g. *guruf* 'beehive(s)', *gurufta* (sgt.) 'a single beehive', *gurufwa* (pl.) 'beehives'), for others either a singulative or a plural may not be in use. Occasionally, a base form itself may be lacking, and the plural is built upon the singulative – for example, *baadônta* (sgt.) 'bell', *baadontitte* (pl.) 'bells', *baadon* ??. The fact that a singulative may effectually replace the base form, whereas the plural form may not, suggests that the relationship of these two forms *vis-à-vis* the base form is not symmetrical. This suggestion is strengthened by the fact that some singulatives have come to have idiosyncratic meanings that would require lexical listing, which, again, is not true of plurals – for example, *daroyta* 'loaf of bread', cf. *daro* 'grain'; *amôyta* 'headman, chief', cf. *amo* 'head'.

The great majority of singulatives involve suffixation of *-yta* to the base form. If the base form is consonant-final, the *y* of the suffix undergoes truncation, and if the final vowel of the base form is *a*, the vowel of the suffix dissimilates to *o* in the case of feminine nouns and to *u* in the case of masculine nouns – for example, *tooboko* (f.) 'siblings', *toobokôyta* (m.) 'brother', *toobokoyta* (f.) 'sister'; *gade* (f.) 'type of reed', *gadeyta* (f.) 'single blade of reed'; *dåħul* (m.) 'calves', *daħulta* (m.) 'bull calf', *dahulta* (f.) 'cow calf'; *ʃåday* (m.) 'tree species', *ʃadayto* (f) 'twig of *ʃåday* tree'; *båsal* (m.) 'onion(s)', *basåltu* (m.) 'single onion'. There are, however, some exceptions to this statement about singulative formation: for example, *gennaʃta* 'palm, sole', cf. *gênna(a)ʃ*; *baddiyta* 'eastwind from the sea', cf. *bad* 'sea'; *ilmônta* 'bastard', cf. *îlmu*.

The preceding examples also illustrate another feature of singulatives: namely, that the gender of a singulative may not be the same as that of its base form; indeed, in the case of collectives denoting animates, it is common to find a pair of singulatives which distinguish male and female individuals.

There is a bewildering variety of plural shapes, and great difficulty is experienced in attempting to establish patterns of formal relationship between base forms and plurals.[5] Plural forms are not used with great frequency, and speakers may often disagree in their judgements about what is the appropriate plural for a given base form. Broadly speaking, plural formation itself seems to be of two distinct types. One type, the 'external' plural, involves simple suffixation to the base form. The other type (the 'internal' plural) involves processes of stem-internal lengthening and of what has usually been regarded as reduplication. Not infrequently, we encounter plurals exhibiting a mixture of these two.

External plurals are formed by two main suffixed plural formatives *-itte* and *-wa*. Plurals in *-itte* occur commonly for vowel-final masculine nouns, where the suffix replaces the final vowel: for example, *fîlla* (m.) 'neck' – *fîllitte* (f.); *bågu* (m.) 'belly' – *bagitte* (f.); *gînni* (m.) 'demon' – *ginnitte* (f.); *gårba* (m.) 'stomach' – *garbitte* (f.). There are, however, numerous exceptions: for example, *barkuma* (f.) 'headrest' – *barkumitte* (f.); *bar* (m.) 'night' – *baritte* (f.). Plurals in *-wa* occur commonly for consonant-final (masculine) nouns: for example, *ʃarum* (m.) 'belt, strap' – *ʕarumwa* (f.); *baayu(u)r* (m.) 'irrigation canal' – *baayurwa* (f.); *damum* (m.) 'tip, end' – *damumwa* (f.); *danan* (m.) 'donkey' – *danawa*[6] (f.). But once again, there are numerous exceptions: for example, *ʕeéla* (m.) 'well' – *ʕelwa* (f.); *dabeéla* (m.) 'billy-goat' – *dabelwa* (f.).

When considering internal plurals, it is less helpful to concentrate on the many kinds of base form: plural form relationships than to recognize that internal plurals themselves actually conform to a relatively small set of target shapes, which is the approach adopted here. Just three types are selected for illustration.

(a) Plurals terminating in the target shape -CVVCa, where VV represents a long counterpart of the last vowel of the base form, and the final C represents the final (third) consonant of the base form; where a base form lacks a third consonant, the final consonant is 'copied'/'reduplicated':[7] for example, *duʕur* (m.) 'fool' – *duʕuura* (f.); *ħaagid* (m.) 'affair, matter' – *ħaagiida* (f.); *minin* (m.) 'eyebrow' – *miniina* (f.); *gide* (f.) 'amount' – *gideeda* (f.); *mago* (f.) 'debt' – *magooga* (f.); *beʕra* (m.) 'steer' – *beʕeera* (f.); *bírta* (m.) 'metal' – *biriita* (f.).

The matter is further complicated by a constraint disallowing the low vowel, *a*, from occurring in two consecutive syllables in internal plural forms. (Actually this constraint is attested elsewhere in Qafar morphology, though it is clearly not part of the general phonology.) This results in dissimilation of the penultimate long vowel of the plural to *oo* if the preceding vowel is low. Where a penultimate long *aa* does not undergo dissimilation, the final *a* will dissimilate to *i*: for example, *gafan* (m.) 'sandbank' – *gafoona* (f.); *taama* (m.) 'work' – *taamooma* (f.); *gárba* (m.) 'stomach' – *garooba* (f.); *booha* (m.) 'hole' – *boohaahi* (f.); *gúra* (m.) 'left hand' – *guraari* (f.).

(b) Plurals terminating in the target shape -CVVCi. Apart from the final *i*, this pattern is in all respects like that described under (a): for example, *gaafo* (m.) 'gap in teeth' – *gaafoofi* (f.); *maaʕo* (m.) 'food' – *maaʕooʕi* (f.). Here too the operation is complicated by dissimilation to avoid successive syllables containing *a*: for example, *lafa* (m.) 'bone' – *lafoofi* (f.); *dala* (m.) 'gourd' – *dalooli* (f.).

(c) Plurals targetting the shape CVCaáCiC. Such 'broken' plurals occur mainly, though not quite exclusively, with Semitic loan words. Apart from the fact that the base forms nearly always contain an internal cluster, they are not of a uniform shape: for example, *sandug* (m.) 'box' – *sanaádig* (m.); *bismaar* (m.) 'nail' – *bisaámir* (m.); *busʕado* (f.), *busʕádu* (m.) 'Soemmering's gazelle' – *busaáʕid* (m.); *balbala* (f.) 'verandah' – *balaábil* (m.).

1.1.3 Plural, gender and agreement

Inspection of the preceding forms demonstrates that very frequently plurals do not have the same gender as their base form counterparts. It is, of course, clear that the correlation between phonological shape and gender referred to in section 1.1.1 is what governs this. Change of gender between singular and plural, sometimes termed 'polarity', has been long noted for Arabic, and is known also from other Cushitic languages, such as Somali.[8]

The Qafar verb paradigm does not distinguish 3m.pl. and 3f.pl. forms, and the gender agreement in verbs having plural nouns as subjects is expressed in

3m.sg. and 3f.sg. verb forms. In other words, in the case of noun subjects there is gender (but not number) agreement. In fact, virtually the only lexical item requiring number agreement in the verb is the 3pl. personal pronoun *óson* 'they'.[9]

1.1.4 Case Like many other languages of the region, Qafar has a case system in which the unmarked absolutive form of the noun occurs as head in NPs functioning as complements of verbs or clitic postpositions. Heads of some subject NPs exhibit a marked nominative case form. The system, however, is not an ergative one, for when nominative case marking occurs, it does so with intransitive as well transitive verbs. All nouns have at least one distinct genitive form. In addition, nouns which are consonant-final in the absolutive exhibit a further form when functioning as nominal predicates. The details are taken up in the next three paragraphs.

For the majority of nouns the absolutive and nominal predicate forms are identical. Unless otherwise stated, all examples of nominals cited in isolation throughout this chapter are absolutive forms. However, when functioning as simple nominal predicates (i.e. not as complements of an overt copula), consonant-final nouns appear with a final vowel. The quality of this vowel is predictable in terms of the last stem vowel. Where this is rounded, *u* is added; where it is a front vowel, *i* is added; otherwise, the vowel added is *a*.[10] For example:

(4) *áh roóbu* 'This is rain';[11] cf. *nanú rób fanḍa* 'We want rain'.
    áh debéni 'This is a beard'; cf. *anú debén liyóh* 'I have a beard'.
    wóh danána 'That is a donkey'; cf. *yangulí danán yibbiḍe* 'A hyena seized a donkey'.

Overt nominative marking occurs only with vowel-final masculine nouns, in which a suffix *-i* replaces the terminal vowel. Such a noun also undergoes 'de-accentuation', which means that any phrasal high tone for which it might happen to be the locus, associates by default with the final syllable of the word – the suffix in this case. Consonant-final nouns never take *-i*, but will, if accented, undergo de-accentuation. Feminine nouns show no nominative marking: for example, *awkí yemeetéh* 'A/the boy has come', cf. *áwka* (m.) 'boy (abs.)'; *yangulí umáh* 'The hyena is bad', cf. *yangúla* (m.) 'hyena (abs.)'; *oggól mámeʕe* 'Consent is not good', cf. *óggol* (m.) 'consent, agreement (abs.)'; *awká temeetéh* 'A/the girl has come', cf. *awka* (f.) 'girl (abs.)'; *gadlá mámeʕe* 'Sleeping sickness is not good', cf. *gadla* (f.) 'sleeping sickness (abs.)'.

As the general syntactic typology would predict, the genitive precedes its head. In terms of case marking, two situations need to be distinguished: what may conveniently be referred to as 'indefinite' and 'definite' genitives. The distinction hinges upon whether or not the head of the genitive phrase is itself preceded by a modifying element, such as a determiner, relative clause, quantifier or its own genitive NP. Indefinite genitives lack any such modifier, and inflection is realized according to the following rules:

(a) Polysyllabic consonant-final nouns (all masculine) undergo de-accentuation, if lexically accented, but show no other change: for example, *aʕán iba* '(a) frog's leg(s)', cf. *åʕan* 'frog (abs.)'; *danan iba* '(a) donkey's leg(s)', cf. *danan* 'donkey (abs.)'.

(b) Monosyllabic consonant-final nouns (all unaccented) suffix *-ti*: for example, *ħantí dala* '(a) milk gourd', cf. *ħan* 'milk (abs.)'.

(c) Vowel-final masculine nouns undergo de-accentuation and replace the final vowel with *-i*: for example, *kutí ḍagor* '(a) dog's fur', cf. *kûta* 'dog (abs.)'.

(d) Feminine nouns (all vowel-final) suffix an underspecified consonant which receives phonological content from the initial consonant of the following (head) noun; in the event that the following noun is vowel-initial, the features for *h* (the default consonant of the language) are supplied: for example, *sagággaysa* '(a) cow's horn', cf. *saga* 'cow (abs.)', *gaysa* 'horn (abs.)'; *sagáḍḍaylo* '(a) cow's offspring', cf. *saga* 'cow (abs.)', *ḍaylo* 'offspring (abs.)'; *sagáhiba* '(a) cow's leg(s)', cf. *saga* 'cow (abs.)', *îba* 'leg (abs.)'.

The definite genitive is realized by suffixation of *-ih* to masculine nouns, which also replaces any final vowel. In the case of feminines, an *-h* is suffixed to the final vowel: for example, *yí dananih iba* 'my donkey's leg(s)', cf. *danan* 'donkey (abs.)'; *woó kutih ḍagor* 'that dog's fur', cf. *kûta* 'dog (abs.)'; *laʕín ħanih suruy* 'the smell of warm milk', cf. *ħan* 'milk (abs.)'; *rabté barrah baḍa* 'the son of the woman that died', cf. *barrá* 'woman (abs.)'.

1.2 Pronouns

In terms of the three defining criteria of inflection (cf. section 1), certain sets of pronouns fall within the nominal category. Thus the personal pronouns distinguish number for all persons, but gender only for the third person singular. They also have distinct case forms in subject and possessor functions, though suppletion is extensive. For example:

(5)

Case	1sg.	2sg.	3m.sg.	3f.sg.	1pl.	2pl.	3pl.
absolutive:	yoo	koo	kåa	te(e)t	nee	si(i)n	ke(e)n
nominative:	anu	atu	ûsuk	is	nanu	îsin	ôson
genitive:	yi	ku	kay	tet	ni	sin	ken

A handful of items which might traditionally be regarded as pronouns fit easily within the morphological paradigm of nominals. The list includes the two Wh-words, 'what?' and 'who?': for example, *akíttu* (m.), *akitto* (f.) 'another, the other one'; *gersíttu* (m.), *gersitto* (f.) 'a / the next one'; *hebélu* (m.), *hebelo* (f.) 'so-and-so'; *tíya* (m.), *tiya* (f.) 'a / the thing, something'; *íyya* (m.) 'who?'; *maħa* (f) 'what?'.

1.3 Numerals

The nominal character of cardinal numerals is evidenced both by their being subcategorized for gender (e.g. *nammay* (m.) 'two'; *sido(o)ħ* (m.) 'three'; *tåban* (m.) 'ten', etc.[12]) and number, where the two forms for 'one' clearly show a type of singulative morphology (viz. *inkitto* (f.), *inkîttu* (m.), cf. *inîki* (counting form)), and higher basic cardinal numerals form reduplicative plurals (e.g. *nammammay* 'twos', cf. *nammay*; *sidoddo(o)ħ* 'threes', cf. *sido(o)ħ*; *tabåbban* 'tens', cf. *tåban*). With regard to case, a few numerals have the *-i* nominative (e.g. *inkitt-i* (m.) 'one', cf. *inkîttu* (abs.); *labaatann-i* 'twenty', cf. *labaatånna* (abs.); *alf-i* 'thousand', cf. *ålfi* (abs.). Moreover, the special forms assumed by numerals in attributive function is interpretable as a form of genitive case morphology (e.g. *nammá saga* 'two cows', cf. *nammay* (abs.); *kooná ʕari* 'five houses', cf. *konoy* (abs.); *baħrá ruga* 'eight calves', cf. *baħåar* (abs.), etc.[13] Finally, it may be observed that with the exception of 'one', the absolutive forms are all consonant-final and their counting forms behave manifestly like predicative nominals (cf. section 1.1.4): for example, *feréyi* 'four', cf. *ferey* (abs.); *konóyu* 'five', cf. *konoy* (abs.); *tábana* 'ten', cf. *tåban* (abs.).

The commonest formation of ordinal numerals pairs masculine and feminine forms: for example, absolutive: *nammahayto* (f.), *nammahåytu* (m.) 'second'; *leħeyhayto* (f.), *leħeyhåytu* (m.) 'sixth', cf. *leħey* 'six (abs.)'.

1.4 Dependent nominals

There is a small set of commonly occurring nominals that never appear alone: that is, they only ever occur as heads of expanded NPs. In the case of some of them, the choice of modifying element is severely restricted, either semantically or syntactically. In spite of their dependent status, these items inflect for case, and control gender agreement in an entirely nominal way: for example, *måra* (m.) 'people'; *waʕådi* (m.) 'time'; *ikke* (f.) 'place'; *gide* (f.) 'amount'; *inna* (f.) 'likeness'. The vowel-initial members of this set usually cliticize on to the preceding modifier element: for example, *á tiya wókkel háys* 'Put this thing there' (where *wókkel* < *woo ikke-l* that place-in); *úsuk silaytínna le* 'He is like the wind' – that is, 'He is fast' (where *silaytínna* < *silaytí inna* 'wind-gen. likeness').

2 Verbals

Description of the verb system from the point of view of morphology poses several distinct problems. First, there is the problem that although a discussion of the two main inflectional classes ought in some sense to be a relatively

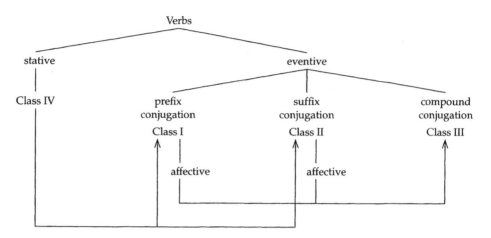

Figure 29.1

lower-order object in the hierarchy of things to be considered, it turns out that class membership affects the allomorphy not only of inflection but of derivation as well. Secondly, a formation which creates an 'affective' verb category has probably to be seen from an inflectional point of view as constituting a third class. It takes as its input (among other items) any verb, simple or derivationally complex, from either of the two main classes. On a relatively superficial inspection, the formation could be considered as part of the inflection of these verbs; yet in so far as the formation (a) behaves differently according to whether the base verb is transitive or intransitive, and (b) also has the capacity to create verbs from non-verbal items, it appears to belong more with lexeme building than with lexeme inflection; a more detailed, properly exemplified account appears below. A third problem concerns the 'stative' verbs. Earlier it was stated that Qafar has no adjectives, and that the items that do the semantic work of adjectives behave morphologically like verbs in having agreement and tense morphology when in predicative function. Nevertheless, the morphological elements concerned are distinct enough to warrant speaking about a fourth inflectional class. Stative verbs inflect neither for aspect nor for mood, as other verbs do. The question here is simply: Is it correct to classify these items as verbs in the first place? Most statives may furnish input to word-formation processes creating 'eventive' (i.e. non-stative) verbs, some belonging to Class I, others to Class II. The schema in figure 29.1, furnishes a simple overview of the issues just described. In the diagram, simple lines indicate classificatory divisions, and arrow-headed lines indicate cross-class derivational links.

For ease of presentation the morphological basis for distinguishing four inflectional classes is considered first.

2.1 The inflectional classes

As the names in figure 29.1 suggest, Classes I and II are most obviously distinguished in terms of prefixal versus suffixal morphology. This distinction manifests itself in person and gender agreement, cf. (6), and in class-maintaining derivational morphology, cf. (7).

(6)   Class I   Class II

	Class I		Class II	
3m. sg. perf.	*y-eeḍegeh*	'he knew'	*fak-eh*	'he opened'
3f. sg. perf	*t-eeḍegeh*	'she knew'	*fak-t-eh*	'she opened'
1pl. perf.	*n-eeḍegeh*	'we knew'	*fak-n-eh*	'we opened'

(7)

	Class I stems		Class II stems	
basic stem	*-eeḍeg-*	'know'	*fak-*	'open'
passive stem	*-im-iḍḍig-*	'be known'	*fakk-iim-*	'be opened'
causative stem	*-iys-iḍḍig-*	'make known'	*fak-siis-*	'get sthg. opened'

Equally diverse in the two classes are the basic mechanisms for marking (perfect and imperfect) aspect and certain mood distinctions, where Class I employs ablaut (sometimes in addition to suffixation), while Class II makes use of suffixation only. For example:

(8)

	Class I		Class II	
3m. sg. perf.	*yeeḍeg-e*	'he knew'	*fak-e*	'he opened'
3m. sg. impf.	*yaaḍig-e*	'he knows'	*fak-a*	'he opens'
3m. sg. jussive.	*yaaḍág-ay*	'let him know!'	*fák-ay*	'let him open!'
2sg. imper.	*iḍig*	'know!'	*fak*	'open!'

However, prefixing versus suffixing, and ablaut versus suffixing allomorphy is not pursued rigorously throughout the two classes, and many inflectional and derivational categories are realized identically. In general in Qafar morphology suffixation has to be seen as the typological default. Thus, plural agreement for second and third persons is expressed by identical suffixes in both classes. For example:

(9)

	Class I		Class II	
2pl. perf.	*teeḍege-n*	'you(pl.) knew'	*fakte-n*	'you(pl.) opened'
2pl. impf.	*taaḍige-n*	'you(pl.) know'	*fakta-n*	'you(pl.) open'
3pl. perf.	*yeeḍege-n*	'they knew'	*fake-n*	'they opened'
3pl. impf.	*yaaḍige-n*	'they know'	*faka-n*	'they open'

Numerous examples similar to this could be adduced. On the other hand, primary marking of negation in main verbs is prefixal in all verb classes, cf. section 2.3.6.

The third class of eventive verbs consists of a compound formation in which an invariable base (termed here a 'particle') is followed by one or other of the verbs *-eḍħ-* or *hay-*, which in this function are enclitic and lexically bleached – though, when functioning independently, they have the meanings 'say' and 'do, put' respectively. Inflection takes place entirely by means of *-eḍħ-* or *hay-*. Both these verbs exhibit inflectional idiosyncrasies: *-eḍħ-*, for example, has suppletive stem morphology for various cells of the paradigm, and since each of the two stems involved belongs to a different primary class, compounds based on *-eḍħ-* have 'hybrid' (Class I × Class II) inflectional behaviour.[14] The idiosyncrasies of *hay-* are only at the level of morphophonology. Because the peculiarities of *-eḍħ-* and *hay-* are carried over into the inflection of the compounds in which they participate, a new inflectional class is created. For example,

(10)

	Class IIIa		Class IIIb	
1sg. perf.	*sígga-eḍħe*	I became strong	*sígga-hee*	I strengthened
2sg. perf.	*sígga-inte*	you became strong	*sígga-hayte*	you strengthened
1pl. perf.	*sígga-inne*	we became strong	*sígga-hayne*	we strengthened
2sg. imper.	*sígga-inḍiħ*	become strong!	*sígga-hay*	make (it) strong!

One obvious question that arises is: Why should this be treated simply as one class? On the basis of the sort of argumentation just employed in establishing Class III as a distinct class, ought we not to treat members of the compound conjugation based on *-eḍħ-* and members of the compound conjugation based on *hay-* as belonging to two separate classes? One argument for the unifying classification is that the selection of *-eḍħ* or *hay-* is not an arbitrary matter. It relates to the formation of intransitive and transitive verbs respectively; the examples in (10) show this: *sígga* is an underived (primitive) particle, and the transitivity of the compound verbs *sígga-eḍħ-* and *sígga-hay-* depends entirely on which of the two compounding verbs has been chosen. This suggests that the formation of these compounds is functionally analogous to processes in the derivational morphology which create verbs with differing argument structures; see sections 2.2.2–2.2.4.[15]

The strongest evidence in favour of a unitary treatment, however, is the fact that a Class III verb can be formed (potentially at least) from any verb (simple or derived) belonging to Classes I or II. A 'particle' is formed (apparently from the imperative stem) to which *-eḍħ-* or *hay-* attaches, just as in the case of a primitive particle such as *sígga*. There are two differences, however, in the case of deverbative compounds. First, the selection of *-eḍħ-* or *hay-* now depends on whether the particle is derived from an intransitive or a transitive verb; thus, *ḍóʕʕa-eḍħ-* derives from the intransitive *ḍooʕ-* 'perspire', while *usgúdda-hay-* derives from the transitive *-usguud-* 'slaughter'. Secondly, compound verbs based lexically on derived (deverbative) particles are semantically distinct from their base counterparts of Class I or II. The precise nature of this difference is difficult to pin down. Often the compound form denotes a diminution of the event or action expressed in the base counterpart, but in other cases it may denote simply that the speaker is employing a rather dramatic style. Considerably more research will be necessary in order to reach a proper appreciation of the semantics and sociolinguistic functions of these forms; as a temporary measure, I have simply labelled them as 'affective'. However, the point to note here is that the availability of such affective forms for any verb of Class I or II could even suggest that they be treated as (a formally neutralized) part of the inflectional paradigm of those classes. The occurrence, however, of verbs such as *sígga-eḍḥ-*, formed from primitive particles, argues against such an analysis.

Verbs of Class IV denote states of being, and in addition to typical adjectival concepts (e.g. *meʕ-e* 'be good', *um-a* 'be bad', *ʕas-a* 'be red, be new', *kaḍḍ-a* 'be big/great/old'[16]), they include *kiħn-a* 'love, be happy/pleased', *niʕb-a* 'hate, dislike', *l-e* 'have', *sinn-i* 'be without', *kinn-i* 'be' (copula) and *hinn-a* 'not be' (negative copula). The relatively small stock of simple stative verbs is augmented by a large number of compounds consisting of a nominal together with one of the simple statives: for example, *gabá-gibd-i* 'be stingy' (lit. 'hand is tough'), *makó-l-e* 'be bent/dishonest' (lit. 'it has a bend',) *másu-ʕunḍ-a* 'be skinny/shrimpy' (lit. 'stature is small').[17]

Like verbs of all classes, statives heading independent clauses require the prefix *må-* in negation; otherwise, however, suffixation is the norm in this class too. Agreement in the 'present state' paradigm has a distinct set of realizations and there is a common third-person singular form where gender of the subject is not distinguished. The full paradigm of the present state is given in (12), alongside the imperfect aspect paradigm[18] of a typical Class II verb. (Both paradigms express predicate focus; cf. section 2.3.7.)

(11)		Class IV		Class II	
	1sg.	*nibd-iyoh*	'I am awake'	*duf-ah*	'I push'
	2sg.	*nibd-itoh*	'you are awake'	*duf-tah*	'you push'
	3m. sg.	*nibd-ah*	'he is awake'	*duf-ah*	'he pushes'
	3f. sg.	*nibd-ah*	'she is awake'	*duf-tah*	'she pushes'
	1pl.	*nibd-inoh*	'we are awake'	*duf-nah*	'we push'
	2pl.	*nibd-itoonuh*	'you are awake'	*duf-taanah*	'you push'
	3pl.	*nibd-oonuh*	'they are awake'	*duf-aanah*	'they push'

2.2 *Derivation*

Verb derivation is highly productive. Once the inflectional class membership, the argument structure, and certain semantic properties of a base lexeme are taken into account, verbs are seen to fit into regular patterns of derivation. Such regularity, however, does not always extend to allomorphy, and there is very considerable irregularity in the case of the ancient Class I derived verbs. The highest degree of predictability with regard to derivation within the verbal system is seen in the fact that every basic intransitive verb has a derived transitive counterpart.[19] If we omit various minor patterns, five main formations are readily recognized.

Inchoativization is the derivation of eventive verbs from statives. Inchoative derivatives belong to Class I or II, though the selection of which it will be is not predictable: for example, *ʃunḍ-a* 'be small/young' – *-uʃunḍuy-* (I) 'become small'; *meʃ-e* 'be good' – *-emʃ-* (I) 'become good'; *dat-a* 'be black' – *dattoow-* (II) 'become black'; *lab-i* 'be male' – *labboow-* (II) 'become male, become hard'; *kurdudin-i** 'be round' – *kurdudinit-* (II) 'become round'. (The number following the stems above and in other examples that follow indicates class membership. An asterisk following a base stem indicates that that form itself is derived.)

Transitivization is the derivation of transitive verbs from basic intransitives as well as from inchoativized verbs. Such verbs require that the agent introduced into their argument structure is expressed as subject: for example, *faħ-* (II) 'boil (intr.)' – *faħis-* (II) 'boil (tr.); *-ifriħ-* (I) 'feel glad/happy' – *iyfirriħ-* (I) 'gladden'; *-uʃunḍuy-** (I) 'become small' – *-usʃunḍuy-* (I) 'diminish (tr.)'; *dattoow-** (II) 'become black' – *dattoys-* (II) 'blacken (tr.)'.

Causativization is the derivation of causative verbs from basic intransitives (including inchoativized verbs) and transitives. Causatives require that the controlling agent (causee) introduced be expressed as subject:[20] for example, *ḍaam-* (II) 'buy, sell' – *ḍamsiis-* (II) 'cause to buy/sell; get bought/sold'; *faħ-* (II) 'boil (intr.)' – *faħsiis-* (II) 'cause to boil; get boiled'; *dattoow-** (II) 'become black' – *dattoysiis-* (II) 'cause to blacken; get sthg blackened'; *-ukkuʃ-* (I) 'pick up, carry' – *-uysukuʃ-* (I) 'cause to pick up, etc.; get picked up'; *-eʃess-** (I) 'indicate' – *-eʃessiis-* (I) 'cause to indicate, get indicated'.

Passivization is the derivation of passives from basic transitives, transitivized and (rarely) causativized verbs.[21] Passives require that the patient be expressed as subject. The agent is almost always suppressed – though see note 20. For example, *fiy-* (II) 'sweep' – *fiyyiim-* (II) 'be swept'; *admis-** (II) 'tan' – *admisim-* (II) 'be tanned'; *-eħet-* (I) 'chew' – *-emħett-* (I) 'be chewed'; *massoys-** (II) 'cause to get ready; get made ready' – *massoysim-* (II) 'be made ready'.

Autobenefactivization is the derivation of forms indicating that the action denoted by the verb is performed for the benefit of the subject. Autobenefactives can be derived from any verb, basic or derived providing the thematic role expressing the subject is capable of volitional action: for example, *ab-* (II) 'do, make' – *abbaasit-* (II) 'do/make f.o.b.'[22]; *digir-* (II) 'play' – *digirit-* (II) 'play f.o.b.'; *-idħiḍ-* (I) 'sew' – *-iḍḍiħiḍ-*[23] (I) 'sew f.o.b.'; *faħis-** (II) 'boil (tr.)' – *faħsit-* (II) 'boil f.o.b.'; *ʃaddoysiis-** (II) 'cause to whiten; get sthg whitened' – *ʃaddoysiisit-* (II) 'get sthg whitened f.o.b.'.

2.2.1 Denominal verbs Some of the actual affixes employed in the above processes have homophonous counterparts which serve to form verbs from nouns. Thus, alongside the transitivizing *-is* we find a denominalizing *-is*, as in *amris-* 'command', cf. *ǎmri* 'order'; *ʃadayis-* brush teeth with twig from an *ʃadayto* tree'; *giiris-* 'swim', cf. *giíru* 'floating'; and alongside autobenefactivizing *-it*, we find a denominalizing *-it*, as in *gosonit-* 'catch a cold', cf. *goson* 'common cold'; *sanit-* 'have a nosebleed', cf. *san* 'nose'. Likewise, alongside inchoativizing *-oow*, we find a denominalizing *-oow*, as in *dirabboow-* 'become a liar', cf. *dîrab* 'lie'; *marroow-* 'encircle', cf. *maro* 'circle'.

It is quite common to find derived verbs for which there is no (extant) simple stem base. Such verbs are often 'deponent' in the sense of having passive (if Class I) or autobenefactive (if Class II) morphology while functioning as simple intransitives. Moreover, they very frequently occur coupled with a cognate lexeme having transitivized morphology, the two together furnishing an intransitive: transitive 'complementary pair', which reflects the core organization of the verb lexicon. Thus Class I: *-embeḍ-* 'be used up' and *-esbeḍ-* 'use/ finish up'; *-enkett-* 'gather (intr.)' and *-eskett-* 'gather (tr.)'; *-onkonoonoħ-* 'glow' and *oykonoonoħ-* 'cause to glow'; and Class II: *ugut-* 'get up' and *ugus-* 'rouse'; *summit-* 'suffer poisoning' and *summis-* 'poison'; *firʃit-* 'convulse' and *firʃis-* 'make convulse'. The need for this same fundamental pairing is clearly reflected in the existence of the two series of compound verbs of Class III; cf. section 2.1.

2.3 *Inflectional categories*

Leaving aside agreement, eventive verbs of Classes I, II and III carry inflections for a great many categories, the most obvious of these being aspect, mood, subordinate clause role and polarity. In addition to these categories, which are typically marked on the verb lexeme itself, there are a variety of periphrastic constructions furnishing systems of tense and modality. Finally, the verb is the locus of a rather simple but highly important scheme of focus-marking morphology. The following sections will offer a brief overview of these categories and their expression.

2.3.1 Aspect It can be generalized that the perfect : imperfect dichotomy is expressed by a phonological opposition of *a* : non-*a* in the morphology; witness the imperfect : perfect ablaut patterns of the typical Class I verbs *-abbiḍ-* : *-ibbiḍ-* 'seize, hold', *-ard-* : *-erd-* 'run', *-akm-* : *-okm-* 'eat', *-abl-* : *-ubl-* 'see',[24] and the uniformity of suffixes in Class II *nak-a* : *nak-e* 'drink milk', *fiil-a* : *fiil-e* 'comb', etc., and in the hybrid features of Class IIIa verb forms such as *gúmma-aḍħ-* : *gúmma-eḍħ-* 'become dazzled' (1sg. forms), *gúmma-int-a* : *gúmma-int-e* 'become dazzled' (2sg. forms).[25]

The Class IV statives do not distinguish aspect so much as tense; see section 2.3.3.

2.3.2 Mood Since the indicative, jussive and requestive carry a marker in at least one class, while the imperative never does, there are grounds for considering the latter to be the unmarked mood. The indicative is marked only in Class I, where a -*e* suffix appears in both the perfect and imperfect: for example, *yubl-e* : *yabl-e* 'he saw/sees'. All eventive verbs share the same suffixal marking for jussive and requestive. As in many languages, the jussive (oblique command) and imperative moods display a paradigm complementarity with regard to person,[26] and the requestive is confined to the first person. In (13) these points are illustrated with Class I -*erd*- 'run' and Class II *nak*- 'drink milk'.

(12)

	1sg.	2sg.	3m. sg	3f. sg.	1pl.	2pl.	3pl.
requestive	*ardóò*				*nardóò*		
	nakóò				*naknóò*		
imperative		*eréd*				*eréda*	
		nák				*náka*	
jussive	*árday*		*yárday*	*tárday*	*nárday*		*yardoónay*
	nákay		*nákay*	*náktay*	*náknay*		*nakoónay*

Stative verbs do not show any inflection for mood.

2.3.3 Tense In general tense is expressed by means of a periphrastic construction in which the second ('auxiliary') verb component is -*en*, a verb which in independent function is the locative existential verb. -*en* is unique in behaving as a Class I verb (albeit somewhat irregular) with regard to inflection, while at the same time displaying the reduced paradigm typical of statives.[27] The *a* : non-*a* contrast, which marks imperfect : perfect aspect in eventive verbs, distinguishes a present : past distinction in the case of -*en* and in those periphrastic paradigms in which it appears. With both components of the construction engaged in the selection of the *a* : non-*a* feature, the language is furnished with perfect and imperfect present and past tenses. This is exemplified in (13), where only 3m. sg. and 3f. sg. forms are shown for Classes I and II.[28] (The forms assumed by the 'main' (lexical) verb will be considered below in section 2.3.5.)

(13)

		past		present	
perf.		*yerdeh yen*	'he had run'	*yerdeh yan*	'he has run'
		terdeh ten	'she etc.'	*terdeh tan*	'she etc.'
		nakeh yen	'he had drunk milk'	*nakeh yan*	'he has drunk milk'
		nakteh ten	'she etc.'	*nakteh tan*	'she etc.'
impf.		*árduk yen*	'he was running/ used to run'	*yardeh yan*	'he is running/ runs'
		árduk ten	'she etc.'	*tardeh tan*	'she etc.'
		nákak yen	'he was drinking milk/ used to drink milk'	*nakah yan*	'he is drinking milk/ drinks milk'
		nákak ten	'she etc.'	*naktah tan*	'she etc.'

The unmarked base form of a stative verb expresses a 'present state' – for example, *ḍeeriyoh* 'I am tall', *ḍeeritoh* 'you are tall' – while a form structurally analogous to the imperfect past of eventive verbs expresses a 'past state' – for example, *ḍeéruk en* 'I was tall', *ḍeéruk ten* 'you were tall'.

2.3.4 Modal forms

Qafar has a great variety of forms expressing modalities such as anticipation, probablility, intention, factual condition, contrafactual condition, etc. Many of them are periphrastic, and many of them show distinctions of aspect expressed in the ways described above. In the interests of brevity, just one of these, the anticipatory, will be considered.

The anticipatory denotes an event that the speaker expects to happen, and can readily be translated by a 'future' tense. It has a periphrastic structure, and inflects by means of the stative verb *l-e*, which in independent function would normally be translated as 'have'. Perfect and imperfect anticipatory paradigms are constructed on the model of the past- and present-tense formations, though here *sug-* occurs, rather than *-en*. For example:

		Simple anticipatory	Perfect anticipatory	Imperfect anticipatory
(14)				
	1sg.	*ardé-liyo*[29]	*erdéh sugé-liyo*	*árduk sugé-liyo*
		'I shall run'	'I shall have run'	'I shall be running'
	3m. sg.	*ardé-le*	*yerdéh sugé-le*	*árduk sugé-le*
		'he will run'	'he will have run'	'he will be running'
	1sg.	*naké-liyo*	*nakéh sugé-liyo*	*nákak sugé-liyo*
		'I shall drink milk'	'I shall have drunk milk'	'I shall be drinking milk'
	3m. sg.	*naké-le*	*nakéh sugé-le*	*nákak sugé-le*
		'he will drink milk'	'he will have drunk milk'	'he will be drinking milk'

2.3.5 Lexical base forms

The leftmost (lexical) element occurring throughout the wide variety of periphrastic paradigms is almost always one of five forms: (1) the simple perfect – for example, *yerdéh, nakéh*; (2) the simple imperfect – for example, *yardéh, nakáh*; (3) the imperfect participle ('K-participle', cf. Parker and Hayward 1985: 256), which is invariant – for example, *árduk, nákak*; (4) what has been termed the 'E-form' (cf. ibid. 286), which is an invariant form terminating in *-e* that is devoid of any aspectual significance – for example, *ardé, naké* (elsewhere it often has a distinctly nominal character in functioning as a complement for a particular set of verbs); (5) what has been termed the 'U-form' (cf. ibid.) – for example, *árdu* – which terminates in *-u*, and must derive historically from the East Cushitic 'subjunctive/optative', which, unlike the E-form, shows full agreement morphology. What all these forms have in common is that in complex sentences (whether we think of coordination or subordination) they can occur in the non-final clause. Qafar lacks a distinct non-final conjoining ('converb') form, which is so typical of the Ethiopian Semitic languages; simple perfect and imperfect forms fulfil this role. The imperfect participle, E-form and U-form never occur sentence-finally; it is not surprising, therefore, that they have undergone a high degree of grammaticalization in these periphrastic paradigms.

Simple perfects and imperfects appear not only in the various tense paradigms (cf. section 2.3.3) and in aspectually distinct forms of the anticipatory (cf. section 2.3.4), but also in various conditional modalities (e.g. *yardék* 'if he runs', *yardéh sugek* 'if he has run'). The imperfect participle occurs in present-tense paradigms. The E-form occurs in the various anticipatory paradigms and in both the protasis and apodosis of contrafactual conditionals (e.g. *ardínnay*[30] 'if he had run', *ardé ḍaaḍe* 'he would have run'), but its role, *par excellence*, is in forming negatives for subordinate clause verbs; cf. section 2.3.6. The U-form is the lexical base in the 'intentive' (e.g. *yárdu waa* 'he is intending to run', the 'probable' (e.g. *yárdu takkeh* 'he may run') and the 'purposive' (e.g. *yárduh* 'that he run') paradigms.

2.3.6 Negation   East Cushitic languages generally have distinct strategies for negative marking in independent and dependent clauses (including relative clauses). In Qafar the former always requires the prefix *må-*, though other suffixal elements may occur in various paradigms.[31] For example (the verb *gúmma-eḍḥ-* 'become dazzled' has been selected to represent Class III):

(15)

		Affirmative	Negative
<u>perfect</u>	Class I	*yerdéh*	*márdinna*
'he ran/has	Class II	*nakéh*	*mánakinna*
run', etc.	Class III	*gúmma-iyyéh*	*gúmma-máḍḥinna*
<u>present state</u>	Class IV	*nibdáh*	*mánibda*
'he is awake'			
<u>impf. past</u>	Class I	*árduk yen*	*árduk mánanna*
'he was	Class II	*nákak yen*	*nákak mánanna*
running', etc.	Class III	*gúmma-áḍḥuk yen*	*gúmma-áḍḥuk mánanna*
<u>past state</u>	Class IV	*nibduk yen*	*nibduk mánanna*
'he was awake'			

Dependent clauses (including) relatives, however, employ a periphrasis involving the verb *way-*, which as a free lexeme means 'lack, miss'. For example:

(16)

		Affirmative	Negative
<u>conditional</u>[32]	Class I	*yerdék*	*ardé weék*
'if he runs', etc.	Class II	*nakék*	*naké weék*
	Class III	*gúmma-iyyék*	*gúmma-adḥé weék*
<u>purposive</u>	Class I	*yárduh*	*ardé wáyuh*
'that he run', etc.	Class II	*nákuh*	*naké wáyuh*
	Class III	*gúmma-íyyuh*	*gúmma-adḥé wáyuh*

Some stative verbs come in antonymic pairs, and may make use of lexical negation alongside the regular morphological negation, but only in the case of *kinn-i* 'be' and *hinn-a* 'not be' is this obligatory.

2.3.7 Focus The majority of affirmative verbs marked for aspect or tense that have been cited as examples in the preceding pages have terminated in *-h* preceded by a vowel associated with a (phonological) phrasal high tone. Such forms are always required when there is predicate focus, which probably represents the unmarked or neutral situation. When, however, some NP or PP constituent is focused – as, for example, in a Wh-word question or in a sentence responding to one – the focused item occurs immediately preceding the verb and forms a single phonological phrase with it. This is signalled by the association of the high tone with the focused item rather than with the verb, and by dropping the terminal *-h*. This is illustrated in (17) in a comparison of Yes/No and Wh-word questions and their responses.

(17)   predicate focus   other focus

    ʕáli tubléè? 'Did you see Ali?'   *iyyá tuble?* 'Who did you see?'
    yeéy, ubléh 'Yes, I saw (him).'   *ʕáli uble* 'I saw Ali.'

2.4 Nominalizations

There are a number of regularly formed nominalizations. Some of these have already been considered in section 2.3.5. Most Class I verbs have nominalizations which refer to the verbal event; such a nominalization involves a prefix *m-* together with a pervading vocalism in *a* – for example, *m-ambada* 'getting up', cf. *-imbid-* 'get up'; *m-andaʕa* 'swallowing', cf. *-unduʕ-* 'swallow'. But there is variation of both form and meaning – for example, *m-argaade* 'type of dance', cf. *-irgid-* 'dance in line'; *m-abraka* 'hollow formed by rolling', cf. *-ubruk-* 'roll'. Class IV verbs form nominalizations fairly regularly in *-iina* and *-aane* – for example, *kaḍḍ-iina* 'being big'; *maʕ-aane* 'being good'. For Class II a number of recurrent patterns exist on a lexically determined basis (in *-itto*, *-to*, *-ta*, *-o* and *-a*, etc.), but the only perfectly general formation here has the suffix *-íyya*, and this exists for Class I too: for example, *geḍ-íyya* 'going'; *faḥis-íyya* 'boiling (tr.)', etc. The *-íyya* form is rather gerund-like, and its meaning is perfectly predictable. Complements of transitive verbs are expressed as genitive NPs of their *-íyya* form counterparts – for example, *sarí kaʕalisiyya míyaaḍiga* (clothes-gen. washing neg.-he-knows) 'He doesn't know laundry-work'; *yí ʕarih ḍisiyyi gidíbuk suge '*(my house-gen. building-nom. expensive-being 3m. sg.-was) 'Building my house was expensive'.

Possibly the most important nominalization from a syntactic point of view is the M-nominalization considered in section 3.3.3.

3 Indeclinables

Words that lack nominal or verbal morphology – indeed, that lack any inflectional morphology at all – comprise a highly heterogeneous group and from a syntactic viewpoint possess no uniting factor at all. Omitting consideration of the rag-bag of 'interjections' (items such as *yeey* 'Yes', *baleey* 'No', *aleya* 'Hey!', etc.), the following sets deserve to be distinguished: determiners, particles and clitics.

3.1 Determiners

There are no 'articles' in Qafar, but there are three pairs of deictic determiners: namely, *a ~ ta* 'this, these – near to speaker'; *ama ~ tama* 'this, these/ that, those – near to addressee'; *woo ~ too* 'that, those – distant from speaker and addressee'.[33] None of these forms shows any agreement in gender, number or case with its head – the *t*-initial forms are simply variants. In addition, there is an assortment of indeclinable words with determiner-like functions – for example, *inni* 'my own',[34] *ninni* 'our own', *issi* 'you/his/her own', *sinni* 'your (pl.)/their own', *anni* 'which?', *aki* '(an)other', *uli* '(a) certain', *gersi* 'the next', *kúlli* 'every', *gidiidin* 'the entire/complete'.

Pronouns are derivable from some of the determiners by suffixation of *-h* (e.g. *ah, amah, woh, innih, issih*). These derivative pronouns, however, are as morphologically inert as their bases.

3.2 Particles

Particles resemble clitics in being phonologically dependent, but go further than clitics in being dependent upon particular words with which they must co-occur. They exist only in combination with verbs in the (Class III) compound conjugation, cf. section 2.1. 'Primitive' – that is, non-deverbative, particles are often onomatopoeic, and the same root may also sometimes turn up in derived nominals or verbals – for example, *tutúh-eɖħ-* 'whisper', cf. *tutuħto* 'whispering'; *kúʕ-eɖħ-* 'cry out', cf. *kuʕ-ta* 'shout, cry'; *firíg-eɖħ-* 'move convulsively', cf. *firg-o* 'convulsive movements', *firg-it-* 'move convulsively'.

3.3 Clitics

On functional grounds three sets of clitics are distinguishable: postpositions, conjunctions and the M-nominalizer.

3.3.1 Postpositions The four postpositions are all single-consonant forms. In view of the fact that there are only four of them, each has to cover a range of distinct meanings, though we can easily denote their core meanings: namely, *-l* 'locative', *-k* 'ablative', *-t* 'instrumental', *-h* 'allative, dative, benefactive'. For example, *gíta-l* 'on the road/way', *ʕaléh-amo-l* 'on top of the mountain', *gaantá-k* 'from the encampment', *yó-k* 'from/than me', *ħádda-t* 'with a stick', *baabúr[u]-t* 'by car', *addá-h* 'to the interior', *keén[i]-h* 'for them'. Certain verbs obligatorily require postpositional complements headed by particular postpositions, though the semantic reason for the choice is sometimes far from obvious; thus, 'say to' requires *-k* (e.g. *káa-k innéh* 'we said to him'); 'reply to' requires *-l* (e.g. *káa-l gaħséh* 'I replied to him'). When these postpositions attach to a consonant-final nominal, an epenthetic vowel is inserted (shown in preceding examples within square brackets) which harmonizes qualitatively with the vowel of the preceding syllable, as in predicative nominals, cf. section 1.1.4.

Although there are no 'relative pronouns' in Qafar for relativizations based on NPs, there is a set of pro-forms corresponding to each of the postpositions, which function in relative clauses: namely, *elle* (cf. *-l*), *edde* (cf. *-t*), *akak, kak* (cf. *-k*) and *akah* (cf. *-h*). For example, *ħán elle hee ayni* 'the container in which he put the milk', *leé akak bahne ʕeela* 'the well from which we bring water'.

3.3.2 Conjunctions Both *-kee* and *-y* function in conjoining NPs; they cliticize onto the left-hand conjunct. *-y* tends to occur as the non-final conjunction when the conjuncts exceed two in number. Attachment of either element is assocated with lengthening of a final vowel – for example, *lubakwaá-kee kabaaʕá* 'lions and leopards'; *lubakwaáy, kabaaʕaáy yangulwá* 'lions, leopards and hyenas'.

The conjunction *-y* seems to be acquiring the additional role of a topic marker, for it commonly appears on pre-sentential items that furnish foregrounding.

All types of independent clause, except those in which the verbs are indicative affirmative, may be conjoined by means of a clitic *-ay* attached to the non-final conjunct(s) – for example,[35] *eréd-ay káah waris* 'Run and tell (to) him!', *maámaatinn[ay] mágedinna* 'He did not come and did not go', *yí saro máʕas[ay], máʕad[oy], mádata* 'My cloth is neither red, white, nor black'.

Two other common and important clitics concerned with disjunction are discussed in Parker and Hayward (1985: 292).

3.3.3 M-nominalizer(s) Nominalizing morphology has already received some attention (cf. section 2.4), but the most ubiquitous form remains to be considered.

In one set of forms having a final clitic *-m* we can clearly identify a complementizer-like function. This is illustrated in the following sentences: *umá num kinni-m akkaléh* (bad man he-is-M I-opine) 'I think that he is a bad man'; *úsuk yoó yuble-m aadigeħ* '(he me he-saw-M I-know) 'I know that he saw me'; *lubák aggifé wee-m naaminéh* '(lion he-not-killing-M we-believe) 'We believe that he did not kill the lion'. M-nominalizations also appear as complements of verbs that would take an infinitival complement in English – for example, *nanú gendá-m fandéh* (we we-go-M we-wanted) 'We wanted to go'; *yamaaté-m káak faden* (he-comes-M him-from they-wanted) 'They wanted him to come'; *giirissá-m duddáh* (she-swims-M she-is-able) 'She can swim'; *á taama aba-m efferéh* (this work I-do-M I-am-unable) 'I am unable to do this work'. In all cases the clause terminating in *-m* looks formally like a relative clause, which suggests that *-m* occurs where we might expect a nominal. The impression of 'nominalness' is strengthened by noting that when appearing in subject function, clauses terminating in *-m* control feminine gender in the verb – for example, *úsuk rabé waa-m nét ħelta.* (he he-not-dying-M us-to 3f.sg.-seems) 'It seems to us that he is not dying'; *káa ħatna-m nél tingiddibéh* (him we-help-M us-on 3f.sg.-presses) 'We ought to help him'. 'Free' relative clauses are extremely common in the language. Formally these are M-nominalizations of relative clauses the verbs of which carry feminine agreement – for example, *neé tássa-hayta-m mangóh* (us 3f.sg-makes-happy-M it-is-much) 'The things that make us happy are many'; *yí toobokoyta taadige-m íyyay* (my brother 3f.sg.-knows-M who-is?) 'Who is it knows my brother?'. The thoroughly nominal character of *-m* is further affirmed by the fact many constructions involve attaching postpositional clitics to it – for example, *sinám takmee-m[i]-k meysinnáh* (people 3f.sg.-eats-M-from we-fear) 'We fear that which eats people'.[36]

NOTES

1   The transcription employed here for Qafar does not follow that adopted in *An Afar – English – French Dictionary*, which accepted the proposals made by Dimis and Reedo (1976a, b). In some respects that orthography is far from optimal, and it is likely that it will be revised in the near future. With this is mind, the present study adheres closely to IPA usage, although double letters are employed to represent geminate consonants and long vowels. The name of the language itself, however, retains its orthographic spelling, in which the voiced pharyngeal fricative is represented by 'Q'. Upper-case letters will not be employed in Qafar examples. On account of an absolutely general process of contraction of long vowels in closed syllables, underlying long vowels are masked in the citation forms of some consonant-final nouns; such long vowels are indicated here, but the second vowel letter is placed in parenthesis. An acute accent denotes high tone, which occurs once per phonological phrase, and is associated at some point in the syntax. In most recent works on Qafar, high tone is only marked on vowel moras where the unpredictable property of lexical accent requires it. The default location of high tone in unaccented or de-accented words is on the final vowel mora of the first word in the phonological phrase, and, being predictable, is not usually marked.

Nevertheless, in the present study it has, as a convenience to readers, been marked wherever it occurs within a phonological phrase, though it has not been marked in unaccented words cited in isolation. Accent, which is a lexical property of some words and affixes is indicated (where appropriate) by a superscript circle above the vowel mora where it is hypothesized to occur. Detailed accounts of the segmental and tonal accent phonology appear in Hayward 1974 and Hayward 1991 respectively.

2 Although this study attempts to provide an overview of the main morphological features of the language, limitations of space have made it necessary to omit some aspects. The interested reader should consult Bliese 1981 and Parker and Hayward 1985 for further detail and exemplification.

3 There is no formal expression of agreement within the NP; nor, in general, is the selection of anaphoric pronouns controlled by gender considerations.

4 In the examples adduced here morphological boundaries are indicated by hyphenation (where possible), but it will be indicated only where it is relevant to the point under discussion.

5 Bliese's (1967, 1981) attempts to reduce plural formation to more manageable proportions represent a *tour de force* within a classical Generative Phonology framework.

6 Also *dananitte* and *danoona*.

7 To relate the base and plural forms in such manifestly 'non-concatenative' morphology would seem to call for something along the lines of Prosodic Morphology, an approach in which consonantal and vocalic melodies are segregated on separate tiers and mapped onto prosodic templates of various types (see McCarthy and Prince, PROSODIC MORPHOLOGY). It would be most satisfactory in the present instance to see the root-final melody element as spreading on to the final C position in the template; the terms 'copy' and 'reduplicate' are, accordingly, rather misleading. In both (a) and (b) types of internal plural there are cases where a consonant cluster in the stem remains intact: e.g. *mablo : mabloola* council(s), court(s); *gadma : gadmoomi* vixen(s), etc. These would call for special attention in a sustained analysis.

8 Corbett and Hayward (1987) present, *inter alia*, an analysis of the polarity phenomenon in the East Cushitic language Bayso.

9 Aspects of Qafar plural agreement phenomena are analysed in Corbett and Hayward 1987.

10 Language comparison suggests that this vowel may be a relic of an earlier copula.

11 The vowel length alternation in this noun results from the closed-syllable contraction process referred to in n. 1.

12 Due to the fact that all cardinal numerals are consonant-final in their absolutive forms, they all have masculine gender. The only exception to this is 'one', which is not consonant-final, and has masculine and feminine forms, e.g. *inkitto* (f.), *inkîttu* (m.).

13 From these examples it will be observed that with attributive numerals nouns appear in base rather than plural forms.

14 All forms of the paradigm based on the first person singular or on the imperative make use of reflexes of the E. Cushitic root *-d'eħ- 'say', while all other forms employ a somewhat disguised form of the E. Cushitic root *-i/en 'say, be'.

15   There is a rather special parallel with the 'complementary pairs' referred to in that section.

16   The vocalic ending of the common third-person ending is included in stems of statives when cited since, as the examples here show, the quality of this vowel varies, and, indeed, is a lexically determined feature.

17   Cf. English 'small of stature', 'hard of heart', etc. For discussion of these, see Hayward 1978, 1996.

18   This paradigm is the nearest match semantically.

19   Consideration of passivization as basically an 'intransitivizing' strategy would furnish the reverse side of this organizational scheme.

20   When the patient is expressed as the object, a causative resembles a passive in suppressing expression of the agent immediately concerned in an action. If pressed, native speakers allow an expression of the agent in sentences like this, but usually only by means of a postpositional phrase involving periphrasis – e.g. *Acmàd gabat* 'by the hand of Ahmad' (lit. 'Ahmad's hand-by').

21   There seems to be a morphologically determined constraint here, however, for I have found no clear cases of passives derived from transitivized verbs of Class I.

22   'f.o.b.' is an abbreviation for 'for one's own benefit'.

23   The autobenefactive formative in Class I often involves an underspecified consonantal prefix, which receives phonetic content by means of leftward spreading from the first stem consonant.

24   It is clear from these examples that on grounds of predictability the vocalism of the perfect has generally to be seen as lexically significant. The fact that such a generalized pattern can be abstracted is on account of the fact that the suffix conjugation (Class II) originated as a periphrastic construction in which the second element was a monosyllabic prefix conjugation verb which happened to have *e* as its vocalism in the perfect.

25   Class IIIb verbs are based inflectionally entirely on the Class II verb *hay-*, which shows some peculiarities: e.g. *gúmma-haa/ gúmma-hee* 'it dazzles/it-dazzled', but in general *hay-* does follow the inflectional pattern of Class II.

26   Unlike many of the Ethiopian Semitic languages, East Cushitic languages provide no grounds for including jussive and imperative in a single paradigm.

27   It should be noted, however, that a dialect alternative exists, in which the auxiliary *sug-* functions in an identical way to *-en. sug-* is an entirely regular Class II verb with regard to inflection.

28   Class III(a) verbs behave entirely as would be predicted: e.g. *gúmma-eḍheh en* 'I had become dazzled', *gúmma-inteh ten* 'you had become dazzled', etc.

29   As a modal verb the 1sg. form *liyo* usually undergoes contraction to *-yyo*, viz. *ardéyyo*. A similar contraction occurs with 2sg. and 1pl. forms, viz. *ardé-lito > ardétto*, *ardé-lino > ardénno*.

30   < *ardé innay*.

31   Such elements commonly contain a component deriving from the stative verb *hinn-a* 'not to be'.

32   The expression of the conditional (and many other forms) is not possible for stative verbs; the nearest equivalent expression requires the substitution of the stative lexeme by its eventive counterpart – in this case Class II

-*imbid*- 'wake up, become alert', thus: *yimbidék* 'if he wakes up'.

33 In addition to the primary function of spatial indexing, these forms seem to have acquired a secondary function in indexing close, intermediate and remote time.

34 It will be recalled that what would usually be regarded as 'possessive determiners' fall into the personal pronoun paradigm morphologically, cf. section 1.2.

35 On account of long vowel contraction in closed syllables, the *a* of the conjunction is not in evidence with vowel-final conjuncts. Clauses in which the verbs are indicative affirmative are simply juxtaposed, and an intonation of non-finality is associated with every verb except the last.

36 Vowels in square brackets are again epenthetic. It is not clear whether the -*m* clitic discussed here should or should not be identified morphologically with another nominalizing element -*m* ~ -*im* which attaches to NP modifiers (genitive NPs, relative clauses, numerals) and creates a nominalization having the meaning 'ones/things of X', where X is the modifier in question (e.g. *káy-im* 'his ones/things'). From a syntactic point of view, there would appear to be little merit in identifying them, and the allomorphy of this second clitic would require resolution; but given the wide range covered by the first clitic anyway, and given the possibility of an autonomous morphology, the task of uniting them in some insightful way remains a challenge.

30 Slave (Northern Athapaskan)

KEREN RICE

Athapaskan languages are of great interest to the linguist concerned with morphology, presenting numerous intricate and complex problems. As a sketch is limited in space, in-depth discussion of all the morphological problems raised by languages of this family is impossible. My goal here is to focus on a small set of the problems raised for theories of morphology by a single Athapaskan language, Slave.[1] I do not present definitive analyses, but rather outline analyses which, I hope, will provide linguists interested in the problems of languages of this family with direction for further research.

The structure of the Athapaskan word, especially of the verb, is complex, and has received the lion's share of attention from early times (e.g. Golla 1970; Hoijer 1946; F-K. Li 1930, 1946; Morice 1932; Sapir and Hoijer 1969) to more recent times (e.g. Cook 1984, 1989; Hargus 1988, 1991; Kari 1976, 1989, 1990, 1992, 1993; McDonough 1990; Randoja 1989; K. Rice 1989; Speas 1986, 1990, 1991b; Tenenbaum 1977; Wright 1983, 1986). In this sketch, I too focus on the structural properties of words, examining some problems of the noun briefly and some problems of the verb in greater detail.

Athapaskan languages have been analysed as exhibiting a range of quite unusual structural properties, some of which are listed in (1):

(1) (i) A template, or position-class analysis, appears to be required for both the noun and the verb.

(ii) Inflectional morphemes appear to be ordered linearly inside derivational morphemes in both the noun and the verb.

(iii) Phonological rule domains are apparently arbitrary and unrelated to morphosyntactic properties, and must be stipulated in lexical entries.

(iv) Discontinuous dependencies between morphemes exist within the verb.

(v) Two positions for subject markers are found within the verb.

In the following sections, I examine some of these structural properties in nouns (section 1) and verbs (section 2), suggesting ways in which they might be reconciled with theoretical ideas about the nature of morphological structure.

1 Nouns

The noun system of Athapaskan languages has received remarkably little attention in the literature (for some exceptions, see Hargus 1988, K. Rice 1989, Young and Morgan 1987), probably due to the extreme complexity of the verb. However, nouns too are interesting in many ways, and are worthy of brief discussion.

1.1 Background

Nouns in Slave can be divided into a number of categories based on structural properties (see K. Rice 1989). The nouns of concern here are stem nouns and compounds. Stem nouns consist, as their name implies, of a stem alone. These nouns often have related verb stems (2), but need not (3). They are generally monosyllabic (2, 3), although they may have a vocalic suffix -ε (4).[2,3]

(2) dzéh   'gum'   -dzég-ε   'be gummy, sticky' (H)
    shį   'song'   d-shį   'sing' (SS, B)
    seh   'saliva'   -seh   'spit'
    t'éh   'charcoal' -t'éh   'cook (imperfective)'
    tsih   'ochre'   -tsil-e   'be red'
    xáh   'club'   -xáh   'club'

(3) ʔah   'snowshoe'
    mbeh   'knife' (SS)
    tthah   'carrot' (SS)
    du   'island' (B, H)

(4) t'er-ε   'girl' (B, H)
    ts'al-ε 'frog'
    lug-ε   'fish' (H)

Compounds of two types exist. The first, which I will term 'possessive compounds', have meanings of the following sorts: belonging to, used by, used for, associated with, consisting of. Some examples are given in (5). The second type of compound, which I term 'non-possessive compounds', have a uniform meaning, N2 made out of N1. This type is exemplified in (6). I have written compounds as two words for ease of distinguishing the morphemes involved.

(5) ta ghú   'white cap'   ta 'water' + ghu 'tooth' + ɛ́ 'possession'

tɛh t'ǫ́   'water lily'   tɛh 'water' + t'ǫ́ 'plant'

dlǫ bɛ́rɛ́   'cheese'   dlǫ 'mouse' + bɛ́r 'food' + ɛ́ 'possession' (H)

tɬ'á ʔe   'pants'   tɬ'á 'bottom' + ʔe 'clothing'

mɛ́h dǫ   'food bag in grouse'   bɛ́h 'stomach' + dǫ 'storage area' (SS)

jíyɛ́ tú   'wine, juice'   jíyɛ́ 'berry' + tu 'water' + 'possession'

sa dzɛ́ɛ́   'watch, clock'   sa 'sun' + dzé 'heart' + ɛ́ 'possession'

tɬį tɬ'ulɛ́   'dog harness'   tɬį 'dog' + tɬ'ul 'rope' + ɛ́ 'possession'

(6) kwe gohkwį   'stone axe'   kwe 'stone' + gohkwį 'axe' (B)

satsǫ́ xóo   'wire snare'   satsǫ́ 'metal, wire' + xóo 'snare' (SS)

xa tɛnɛ   'basket'   xa 'root' + tɛn + 'container' + ɛ suffix

fe shíh   'stone mountain'   fe 'stone' + shíh 'mountain' (H)

ʔɛ́dhɛ́h thɛ   'leather belt'   ʔɛ́dhɛ́h 'hide, leather' + thɛ 'belt' (SS)

dɛchį ɬuh   'wooden spoon'   dɛchį 'wood' + ɬuh 'spoon' (SS)

1.2 A boundaries problem: the distribution of stem-initial fricatives

While the structure of the nouns is generally straightforward and amenable to many theories of morphology, they do present some problems. The one that I address here concerns the distribution of voiced and voiceless fricatives in noun stem-initial position. These fricatives exhibit voicing alternations in this position. Strictly phonological analyses that have been given to account for the voicing alternations (e.g. Cook 1984 on Sarcee, Kari 1976 on Navajo) are empirically inadequate. In this section I follow work by K. Rice 1988, 1991c, in suggesting that voicing alternations in nouns are attributable to the presence of a morph consisting simply of the feature [voice], an autosegment that indicates that a stem is inflectable.[4]

I begin with a survey of the distribution of voiced and voiceless stem-initial fricatives, leaving aside possessed compounds, which are discussed in section 1.3.

It is generally said in the Athapaskan literature that voiceless stem-initial fricatives occur in absolute initial position and following a voiceless segment in Athapaskan languages with voicing alternations; see, for example, Cook 1984 on Sarcee and Kari 1976 on Navajo.

The first of these observations is definitely borne out: alternating fricatives are voiceless word-initially.[5] This can be seen in (7), showing forms which contrast stem-initial fricatives in absolute initial position with stem-initial fricatives following the possessive prefix sɛ 'my.'

(7) non-possessed   possessed

    ʂeh   'saliva'   sɛ-zeg-ɛ́   'my saliva' (H)

    shį   'song'   sɛ-*zh*in-ɛ́   'my song' (SS, B)

    thɛ   'belt'   sɛ-*dh*ɛ-ɛ́   'my belt' (SS)

    ɬuh   'spoon'   sɛ-luz-ɛ́   'my spoon' (SS)

    ʂa   'sun, month'   sɛ-za-á   'my sun, month' (SS, B)

    xay   'year'   sɛ-*gh*ay-ɛ́   'my year, age' (H)

The second of these observations is not borne out, however: voiced fricatives occur in noun stem-initial position when the noun follows a voiceless segment, as in (8), as well as when it follows a voiced segment, as in (7).[6]

(8) *shį*   'song'   sah *zh*in-ɛ́   'bear's song' (SS, B)

    sah   'bear'

    ʂo   'frost'   dah zo   'frost on tree'

    dah   'above'

    sah   'bear'   tɛh za-á   'polar bear' (H)

    tɛh   'water'

Forms such as those in (8) illustrate that voicing alternations are not phonologically transparent in nouns, as a voiced fricative occurs whenever a segment precedes, regardless of whether that segment is voiced or voiceless. These forms indicate that a solution to the problem of the environment for fricative voicing alternations must be sought somewhere other than in the phonology.

Given the surface opacity of voicing alternations in nouns, K. Rice (1988, 1991c, 1992a) proposes that the source of the stem-initial voicing is an autosegment of the form [voice], a morpheme which appears in a branching construction, as a kind of stem joiner. The following examples fully illustrate the distribution of voiced fricatives in Slave nouns.

(9)   The initial fricative of a noun is voiced when preceded by a possessor, pronominal or nominal:

    xay 'winter, year' sɛ-*gh*ay-ɛ́ 'my age'   dɛnɛ *gh*ay-ɛ́ 'the man's age' (H)

    shį 'song'   sɛ-*zh*in-ɛ́ 'my song'   sah *zh*in-ɛ́   'the bear's song' (SS, B)

(10)   The initial fricative of the second noun of a possessive type compound is voiced:

    sah *gh*ú 'bear tooth'   cf. xu 'tooth' (sah 'bear')

    kwí *gh*a 'head hair'   cf. xa 'hair' (kwí 'head') (B)

    tɛh za-á 'polar bear'   cf. ʂah 'bear' (tɛh 'water') (H)

(11)   The initial fricative of a noun is voiced when preceded by a derivational prefix:

    dah zo 'frost on tree'   cf. ʂo 'frost' (*dah* 'above')

K. Rice (1988, 1991c) argues on the basis of data such as those in (9)–(11) that a morpheme [voice] is inserted when the construction is branching. While this explanation provides an account of the data illustrated so far, it is problematic in two ways, one of which will be considered immediately, the second of which will be discussed in section 1.3.

First, consider the second compound type, that with the meaning N2 made of N1. Such compounds present a difficulty, because, despite the branching construction, they nevertheless have a voiceless fricative beginning the second noun. Some examples, repeated from (6), are given in (12).

(12)   dɛchį ɬuh   'wooden spoon' (SS)
       ʔɛdhɛ́h thɛ   'leather belt' (SS)

The phonology of this compound type has received some attention in the literature, with attempts made to provide boundary-type accounts for the failure of voicing. K. Rice (1985a) argues that the compound type is phrasal, and thus escapes the criterion of branching construction. However, evidence for the phrasal nature of the compounds is weak. Hargus (1988) argues that compounds are formed at two levels in the Lexical Phonology of Sekani, another language of the Athapaskan family, with this type of compound created after voicing has ceased to apply; this account is problematic in requiring a loop to account for embedding properties of compounds. These accounts, while providing adequate descriptions, raise theoretical problems associated with boundaries (e.g. Selkirk 1980a) and loops (e.g. Sproat 1985).

An alternative structural analysis is available, one that appeals to the semantics of the compounds. A systematic semantic difference between the two compound types is found: those of the first type involve a possessive relationship, with N1 being the possessor of N2. This is not true of the second type, which have the meaning N2 made out of N1.

One characteristic often associated with possession is inflection. It is not unreasonable to think that an inflectional element might be involved in possessive constructions, including compounds of the first type. In fact, inflection may be overt in possessive constructions, and can be present in what seem to be compounds rather than phrases. An example is given in (13), where *go*, glossed 'areal', is required in the possessive construction.

(13)   kóɛ̨ gofít'a   'roof'   kóɛ̨ 'house' + go- areal agreement + fí 'head' + t'a
                              'top' (H)

Compounds of the second type do not exhibit a possessive relationship, and no reason exists to think that they involve inflection. For instance, the second noun of such a compound is never inflected. This suggests that compounds of the first type have roughly the structure in (14a), while those of the second type have the structure in (14b), where I = inflection.[7]

(14) (a)   (b)

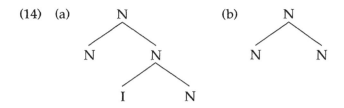

If this is the case, then the morpheme [voice] can be functionally identified: it must be present when inflection, null or specified, is present. Inflection is required in the possessive construction, and thus voicing is found in compounds of the first type; it is not present in the non-possessive compounds of the second type.

One type of boundary problem, that which arises from the arbitrary assignment of structure to compounds, can be solved if [voice] signals inflection, rather than being inserted in a purely structurally defined environment. The structures for the two types of compound differ, but the difference correlates with meaning differences.

1.3 A structural problem: the marked distribution of fricatives in compounds

In the possessive constructions examined so far, a stem-initial fricative is voiced, leading to the generalization that the voicing is produced by an autosegment which associates to a stem-initial fricative. When a wider range of possessed forms is examined, there is reason to reconsider this hypothesis about the distribution of [voice]. The need for this can be seen by considering the following forms, in which voicing does not occur.

(15)   A stem-initial fricative is voiceless when it is the initial consonant of a possessed compound:

łéh-t'é	'bread'	sɛ-łéh-t'é	'my bread'	-léz-ɛ́	'flour'
łeh 'flour' + t'é 'charcoal'					(SS)
sa-dzé	'clock, watch'	s-sadzéɛ́	'my clock'	-za-á	'month'
sa 'sun' + -dzé-ɛ́ 'heart, possessed form'					(SS, B)
sah-dhɛh	'bearskin'	sɛ-sah-dhɛh	'my bearskin'	-za-á	'bear'
sah 'bear' + thɛh 'skin'					(SS)

(16)   A stem-initial fricative is voiceless when it is the initial consonant of a possessed deverbal noun:

shɛ́ts'ɛye   sɛ-shɛ́ts'ɛyé   'meal' (cf. shɛ́ts'ɛye 'one eats') shɛ́ 'food' (incorporate that does not appear independently)

xede   sɛ-xedé   'word, language' (cf. -de 'talk') (H)

The initial consonants of the noun stems in (15) are subject to voicing, as is shown by the possessed forms in the last column. As the morphemes in the verbs in (16) do not typically appear on their own in an inflected form, it is impossible to know what their patterning would be if they did appear independently of the verb.

The discussion so far would suggest that the stem-initial fricatives should be voiced in the forms in (15) and (16) as the possessive construction is involved.[8] This construction involves inflection, and I have suggested that the presence of [voice] correlates with the presence of inflection in nouns. The absence of [voice] is thus surprising.

When the forms in which the initial fricative of the inflected noun is voiced are compared with those in which it is voiceless, a striking property stands out: when the fricative is voiceless, the word in question is polysyllabic. In the examples in (15) and (16), the word is also at least bimorphemic. However, this need not be the case. Bisyllabic monomorphemic stems, while rare, exist in Slave. When a bisyllabic monomorphemic noun is possessed, a stem-initial fricative fails to voice, as in (17).

(17) xɛníh 'raft'   sɛ-xɛníh   'my raft'
      xɛwi   'pus'   sɛ-xɛwi   'my pus'
      xali   'small sled'   sɛ-xali   'my small sled' (H)
      súhga 'sugar'   sɛ-súhga   'my sugar'

A generalization is available: voicing fails to affect the initial of a monomorphemic stem of more than one syllable.

While [voice] marks inflection, occasions arise in which this morpheme is disallowed: namely, when the stem is not of the normal monosyllabic shape. This unusual condition makes one suspect that its absence is not random. Instead, it suggests a prosodic condition on the distribution of [voice] in nouns. When the cases in which the stem with the voiced initial fricative appears and those in which the voiceless initial stem appears are compared, a systematic difference is observable: the voiceless initial stem is found whenever more than one syllable is involved, while the voiced initial stem occurs when the inflected item is monosyllabic (save the possessive suffix). In K. Rice 1991c, I argue on phonological and morphological grounds that this two-syllable construction forms a prosodic domain of the minimal word. The distribution of [voice] can be stated as follows:

(18) (a) [Voice] is present when inflection is found with nouns (and postpositions).
      (b) [Voice] is present only at a juncture within a minimal word.

In the possessive construction, the possessor and the noun form a single minimal word, and [voice] can be present. In the type-2 compounds, two minimal words are found, and [voice] does not appear between them. In bisyllabic nouns, the stem itself forms a minimal word, and in the possessed form [voice] cannot be present, as it appears only internally to the minimal word, not at an edge.

[Voice] marks that a stem is inflectable; it is not present under the prosodic conditions that the unit with which it is associated forms a minimal word. It thus occurs at a juncture within a minimal word, but not at the edge of a minimal word.

1.4 An ordering problem: diminutive/augmentative and possession

A claim that is often made is that inflection is ordered outside derivation in word formation. In Slave, a striking counterexample is found in the noun system, with an inflectional suffix that marks a possessive construction appearing linearly inside the diminutive and augmentative morphemes. Slave nouns have diminutive (zha, ah) and augmentative (cho) forms, as in the examples in (19).

(19) ʔah   'snowshoe'   ʔah-cho   'hunting snowshoe' (B, SS)
      téh   'mat'   téh-zha   'small mat'

The diminutive and augmentative morphemes follow the noun stem.

A problem arises when possessed diminutives and augmentatives are considered. These forms include an inflectional possessive marker -ɛ́, which is ordered linearly inside the diminutive and augmentative markers, as in (20).

(20) -ʔah-ɛ́-cho   'hunting snowshoe, possessed form' (SS)
      -tél-ɛ́-zha   'small mat, possessed form'

These constructions appear to be highly problematic, since inflection is ordered linearly inside derivation.

Facts indicate that the diminutive/augmentative suffixes are not part of the minimal word. Recall that when a minimal word is possessed, voicing of a stem-initial fricative fails to occur. In possessed diminutive and augmentative forms, voicing is found, as in (21).

(21) non-possessed   possessed

      shį-ah   -*zh*in-ɛ́-ah   'small song, ditty' (SS)
      ɬuh-cho   -*l*uz-ɛ́-cho   'tablespoon' (SS)

Assuming the conclusion of the previous section, that voicing is prohibited when the stem is a minimal word, the suffixes in question cannot form part of the minimal word.

The minimal word provides an elegant solution to this problem. It appears that the possessive suffix has a bipartite environment. First, it attaches to a noun that is inflected. This condition, while necessary, is not sufficient, since it would place the suffix on the outside of the diminutive and the augmentative. The prosodic condition corrects this: in addition to attaching to an inflected noun, this suffix must attach to the minimal word. The inflectional suffix then has a well-defined position environment. While it normally appears at a word edge, in those cases where a derivational suffix that is not integrated with the stem into the minimal word occurs, the inflectional suffix appears to be infixed between the stem and the augmentative/diminutive. The infixation is not genuine, however, but merely a consequence of suffixation to the prosodic word.[9]

1.5 Summary

While the noun has not been the object of intensive study, it has properties of interest. First, it indicates that the notion 'inflectable' is important in the language for determining the distribution of a morpheme. Second, it shows that in addition to morphosyntactic conditions on morpheme placement, prosodic conditions may also be required.

2 The verb

2.1 Background

The structure of the Athapaskan verb has been the topic of enormous study (see references in the second paragraph of the chapter). The verb is complex, and presents a myriad of problems for most theories of word structure. In this section I summarize a traditional view of the verb; this serves as a background against which to examine a number of the areas of study.

The Athapaskan verb is traditionally thought to consist of a single word, composed of a stem and a number of prefixes. The stem itself is complex, consisting of a root followed by a suffix that indicates mode and aspect.[10] The order of prefixes is determined by a template, or position-class model. Thus, morphemes occur in a fixed order, and are lexically marked for the position in which they occur. In addition, each morpheme is lexically marked for phonological boundary type. A template for Slave is given in (22). The template includes verb-prefix positions, boundary types and a labelling of the traditional inflection/derivation categorization of morphemes in the position.

(22)   preverb#distributive#iterative#incorporate#direct object %deictic

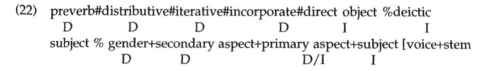

(22)   preverb#distributive#iterative#incorporate#direct object %deictic
         D   D   D   D   I   I
         subject % gender+secondary aspect+primary aspect+subject [voice+stem
                   D   D   D/I   I

A brief description is in order. Several phonological boundaries are indicated. The symbol '#' represents a strong boundary type, marking what are traditionally called 'disjunct morphemes'.[11] The second symbol, '+', indicates a regular boundary type. It separates what are traditionally called 'conjunct morphemes', a span that includes some items considered to be derivational and others considered to be inflectional. The third symbol '%' is associated with the direct objects and deictic subjects. These morphemes are intermediate in phonological pattering between the disjunct and the conjunct. Finally, the symbol '[' separates the voice morpheme and verb stem from the remainder of the verb.

I will briefly describe the content of each position, beginning at the right edge.

The stem is obligatory, supplying the major event, action or state.

The morpheme labelled 'voice' is traditionally called the classifier. It productively marks voice or valency, but is lexicalized in many cases. For example, while transitivity is often marked by a morpheme *h* (*ł) in this position (e.g. łánįwɛ 's/he died' (B) with a null voice marker versus O łánįhwhɛ 's/he killed O' (B) with the *h* voice marker), there are transitive verbs that do not include this morpheme (e.g. ráyɛrɛyįtá 's/he kicked him/her' (H), with a null voice marker), and the morpheme may be present in intransitives (e.g. k'ɛhtłóh 'it (meat, fish) is soft' (SS), whɛhchú 'cloth-like object is located' (B), with *h*).

The subject holds overt morphemes marking person and number: first-person singular, second-person singular, first-person dual/plural, and second-person dual/plural.

Primary aspect indicates the primary aspect of the verb – imperfective, perfective or optative – while secondary aspect marks aspects that combine with the primary aspects; these include inceptive, semelfactive, conative, transitional and others (see Cook 1989 for a similar distinction). What I term 'primary aspect' is often divided into two positions, conjugation and mode (e.g. K. Rice 1985c, Rice and Hargus 1989). Perfective and optative are overtly marked in primary aspect position, while imperfective is unmarked. The morphemes called 'conjugation markers' are found in every verb form (they have overt forms *y*, *n*, *w*; a null form is considered present if there is no overt morpheme present). Each verb requires a particular conjugation pattern, or set of conjugation markers, for the imperfective, perfective and optative. Conjugation pattern is determined in two different ways, both of which are linked to semantic properties of the verb. First, verbal lexical entries fall into a range of semantically defined classes called verb theme categories (i.e. categories that unify the verb themes, or underlying lexical entries; see below). If the verb surfaces as an inflected lexical entry, the conjugation pattern is decided by the semantics of the verb theme category. For instance, verbs of motion require the conjugation pattern *n* imperfective, *n* perfective, *n* optative, while those involving sustained actions over time require ∅ imperfective, *y* perfective, ∅ optative. Second, preverbs and secondary aspectual morphemes are conjugation choosers, and determine the conjugation pattern for a verb. Again, the semantics of the conjugation chooser is linked to the particular choice of conjugation marker. For example, the adverb *dah* 'up on to a horizontal surface' requires *w* imperfective, *w* perfective, *w* optative conjugation marking; the adverb *ká* 'out from inside' requires ∅ imperfective, *y* perfective, ∅ optative conjugation marking; and the secondary aspectual marker *d* 'inceptive' requires ∅ imperfective, *w* perfective, ∅ optative conjugation marking. The iterative and distributive also select conjugation patterns.

The conjugation–primary aspect–subject portion of the verb combines in ways that are not always predictable. For instance, the first-person singular subject has the form *h* except in the perfective of ∅ and *h* voice-element verbs, where it is *i*. While it is possible to assign the morpheme *h* the meaning 'first-person singular subject', the morpheme *i* includes more than one meaning: namely, first-person singular subject/perfective primary aspect. The optative is predictably *u* or *wo-* except when the conjugation marker is *n* or *w*, when it is *'wo* or *wo* (the acute accent indicates that a high tone falls on the vowel of the preceding syllable). Other morphemes show similar patterns. While the second-person singular is regularly nasalization in certain environments, in ∅ and *h* voice-element perfectives it has the form *ne* in these environments. The third person exhibits similar allomorphy, with an unusual form in the perfective of ∅ and *h* voice-element verbs. *n* and *w* conjugation optatives also display unexpected patterns. The non-systematic combinations of conjugation–primary aspect–subject suggest that in at least some cases this stretch of the verb should be treated as a single unit, or portmanteau morph, with complex meaning, as proposed, for instance, by Anderson 1982 for Georgian and by E. Williams 1981b for Latin.

Gender morphemes, generally viewed as derivational prefixes, include *d* 'fire', *d* 'benefactive', *d* 'by mouth', *n* 'mind, feeling', *n* 'water', *y* 'dual subject'. These morphemes marked gender historically. Some are productive; for instance, *d* 'by mouth' occurs in a wide range of verbs having to do with noise; examples include 'whistle', 'snore', 'burp', 'sit', 'bark', 'cough', 'squeak', 'ask', 'whine, fuss', 'argue', 'defend (help with words)', 'walk laughing, crying, etc.', 'joke (tease with words)', 'win with words'. Others occur in restricted circumstances. For example, *n* occurs in verbs meaning 'handle unspecified object (water) on object; wash' and 'handle in water'. Without *n*, the meaning of the verb does not include the concept of water. The prefix *y* is found in certain verbs with a dual subject (e.g. 'dual arrive'); however, it is not generally found even when the stem requires a dual subject. I also include under the rubric of 'gender' morphemes which always occur with a particular verb stem; these are usually termed thematic in the Athapaskan literature, and are part of the underlying representation of the lexical item. For instance, the basic lexical entry for the verb 'handle singular object (uncontrolled)' includes the morpheme *y*, with every derivative based on this lexical entry requiring this morpheme.

While in general, gender precedes secondary aspect, as in (22), the ordering may be overridden by phonological constraints. In Slave, the ordering of these morphemes is *u, y* gender, *d, n, y* secondary aspect, *í*. See Hargus 1988 on Sekani, Kari 1989 on Ahtna, Kari 1993 on several Alaskan languages, K. Rice 1989 on Slave, and Speas 1986, Wright 1986 and McDonough 1990 on Navajo.

The so-called deictic subjects are two in number. The morpheme *ts'* indicates a human subject unspecified for number, while the morpheme *k/g* (the form varies depending on dialect) indicates a human plural.

Direct-object morphemes mark the person and number of the direct object.

The disjunct complex consists of three major categories. Incorporates are of two types: internal arguments, including both objects and subjects (K. Rice 1991a, Rice and Saxon 1994), and some adverbials. The meaning of the verb with an incorporate differs in systematic ways from the meaning of the verb without it; see Axelrod 1990 and K. Rice 1991a for discussion.

Two quantificational adverbs are found in Slave. The distributive can quantify the subject, the object, the location or the event. The iterative quantifies the event or object, indicating that an action is habitual or repeated, depending on other morphemes present within the verb. These are divided into two positions in most Athapaskan literature.

Preverbs, traditionally called incorporated postpositions and adverbs, represent oblique relations and manner. See Kari 1989, 1990, and K. Rice 1991b for details. Typical meanings of preverbs include 'around', 'away', 'up on to', 'out of', 'across', 'to a point', 'into fire', 'into air', in half', 'to pieces', 'excess'. While the meanings of many of these morphemes are transparent, with some the meaning is defined only in combination with the verb stem. Preverbs can be intransitive or transitive, and more than one is possible in a particular verb word.

The minimal lexical entry of a verb is generally considered to be a 'verb theme' rather than a stem (or root). 'Verb theme' is a technical term referring to the stem, a voice element (perhaps null), and whatever other morphemes are required with that stem; these may be preverbs and gender morphemes. Some verb themes are given in (23).

(23) (a) d-dǫ   'drink'
         voice–stem

     (b) d-l-wɛ́   'sg. fall' (H)
         gender–voice–stem

Word formation involves several distinct stages. In the first stage, a level called the 'verb base' is formed. At this level, derivational affixes are added to the verb theme. These include preverbal, gender and secondary aspectual items. Some sample bases formed on the themes in (23) are given in (24). Verb words are also shown; this is the base plus inflectional items; see the discussion below.[12]

(24) (a) verb theme   d-dǫ   'drink (object)'
           verb word   hɛdǫ   's/he drinks (object)'
           verb base   tɛ-d-d-dǫ   'drink to excess'
                         preverb – sec. asp.
                         – voice – stem
           verb word   tɛdɛ́hdǫ   's/he drank to excess' (H)
           verb base   n-d-dǫ   'get full of (food)'
                         sec. asp. – voice – stem
           verb word   ʔɛnɛ́hdǫ   's/he is full (of food)' (SS)

      (b) verb theme   d-l-wɛ́   'fall'
                         gender – voice – stem
           verb base   ká-d-d-l-wɛ́   'fall out'
                         preverb – gender – asp.
                         – voice – stem
           verb word   kádɛdɛ́hwɛ́   'she/he/it fell out' (H, B)
           verb base   tɛh-d-l-wɛ́   'fall into water'
                         preverb – gender –
                         voice – stem
           verb word   tɛdɛ́wɛ́   's/he fell into water' (H, B)
           verb base   ch'a-tthí-d-l-dhɛ́   'fall and bump on head'
                         preverb – 'head' – gender
                         – voice – stem
           verb word   zhɛch'atthídɛ́dhé   's/he$_i$ fell and bumped
                                                          his/her$_i$ head' (SS)

At the final stage of word formation, the verb word is produced. At this level, inflectional affixes are present (e.g. subject, object markers, conjugation and primary aspect[13]), and the formation of the verb word is complete. (See Kari 1979, 1990, 1992, for a far more highly articulated model of word formation in Ahtna, an Athapaskan language of Alaska.)

This traditional model of word formation includes three levels commonly assumed in word formation (although with unusual names in the Athapaskan literature): verb theme (basic lexical entry), verb base (verb minus inflection), and verb word (inflected verb). Such a model of word formation is proposed to account for paradigmatic properties of the Athapaskan verb. It results in making Athapaskan verb formation like word formation in other languages, with derivational morphology preceding inflectional morphology.

Given this model of word formation and the boundaries in (22), it is evident that word formation and phonology do not take place in tandem, as the phonological domains are not defined until the verb word is formed (see Hargus 1986 for comments). Because of this lack of isomorphism between word formation and phonology, the Athapaskan literature recognizes two models of the verb. One (theme, base, word) accounts for morphological structure, allowing for derivation to precede inflection. The second (boundaries) accounts for the phonological structure of the verb. This second type of structure is coded as boundary symbols (or some other diacritic) on the lexical entry of the affixes.

With this background, I am ready to turn to some of the theoretical problems posed by the Athapaskan verb. The issues that I raise are, I believe, problems that must be dealt with by any theory of morphology. However, the solutions that I frame are basically within a government-binding framework. My basic proposal is that the traditional verb word is a syntactic rather than a lexical unit. If this is the case, then some of the apparently odd properties of the verb given in (1) take on a different complexion, and the verb is far less unusual typologically than it initially appears to be.

2.2 An ordering problem: the ordering of inflection and derivation

It is often proposed as a linguistic universal that inflection, defined as what is relevant to the syntax, appears outside derivation (e.g. Anderson 1982, 1988b). Athapaskan languages are often cited as counterexamples, with derivation appearing outside inflection. In this section I examine this problem, suggesting that the concern is misplaced with respect to Slave. When the overall structure of the verb is considered, the generalization can be drawn that clearly inflectional material does occur outside derivational material. In this section I restrict discussion to the traditional conjunct morphemes, ignoring disjunct material (see section 2.6).

To reiterate, the conjunct portion of the verb is generally assigned a structure similar to that in (25). The labels I (inflectional) and D (derivational) represent the word-formation category in which the position class is usually thought to fall.

(25)   direct object – deictic subject – gender – secondary aspect –
       I   I   D/I   D
      primary aspect – subject
        D/I   I

Given the labels in (25), inflection and derivation appear to be hopelessly intermingled, with apparently no generalizations about their ordering available.

While (25) appears to present an insoluble ordering problem, the criteria used for labelling morphemes as inflectional or derivational are not generally addressed in the Athapaskan literature. Thus, before turning to the details of the Slave verb, I establish criteria to distinguish inflection. Morphemes can be established as inflectional in several ways. First, inflectional items are syntactically active, while lexical items are not.[14] In determining which items are syntactically active, I follow Anderson (1982, 1988b), who argues that syntactically active items show configurational, agreement, inherent (e.g. gender) and phrasal properties. Second, inflectional items are obligatory, or paradigmatic, being marked each time a category to which they apply appears (Anderson 1982; Bybee 1985: 27). Lexical items, on the other hand, are not obligatory in this sense. Third, inflectional items can combine to form portmanteau morphemes with more than one element of meaning in a single entry. Lexical items do not combine with each other or with inflectional items (see Anderson 1988b). Finally, inflectional classes are normally closed classes, while lexical classes tend to be open.

These criteria can be used to establish the following categories in Slave: the traditional disjunct morphemes are lexical items (I call them this rather than derivational, as I suggest that the verb is a syntactic phrase rather than a lexical word; see section 2.4), and the traditional conjunct morphemes are inflectional items.

In the following discussion, I review the evidence for this categorization.

2.2.1 *Pronominal subject agreement*   Saxon (1986) argues that the pronominal elements of Dogrib, a language closely related to Slave, represent inflection: in particular, agreement between a noun phrase and the clausal element upon which it depends syntactically. The primary evidence for this is that subject marking is obligatory, being present whether a specified noun is present or absent. The evidence adduced by Saxon for pronominal subjects representing agreement in Dogrib is found in Slave: these morphemes are obligatory, and function paradigmatically. In addition, as discussed in section 2.1, the subject markers combine with aspect morphemes to yield portmanteau forms, another diagnostic of their inflectional nature. See also Rice and Saxon 1994 for discussion.

2.2.2 *Primary aspect*   Anderson (1982) points out that tense/aspect play an important role syntactically, so one might expect these morphemes to be of syntactic relevance. There are reasons in Slave to consider primary aspect morphemes as inflectional. First, co-occurrence restrictions exist between primary aspect and aspectual category-assigning morphemes which follow the verb: if the verb stem is optative, then the optative morpheme must be present in primary aspect position, and so on. Second, co-occurrence restrictions exist with other postverbal material. For instance, an imperfective verb combines with the postverbal particle *gha* to yield a future. The optative combines with the postverbal *sáná* to give a prohibitive meaning. If the postverbal particles are higher predicates (K. Rice 1989), it is possible to view this as selection of primary aspect by a higher verb, a configurational property. Third, primary aspect is an obligatory part of the verb, again an indication that it is inflectional. Finally, the subject and primary aspect morphemes combine to form portmanteau morphs, suggesting that each of the components is inflectional.

2.2.3 *Conjugation*   Although I have treated primary aspect and conjugation together, I will briefly discuss the inflectional status of conjugation. Two facts suggest the inflectional nature of these morphemes: first, they are obligatory; second, they combine with primary aspect and subject in unpredictable

ways, suggesting that a single morpheme may include the meaning conjugation, primary aspect and subject. Again, since inflectional morphemes form portmanteaus only with other inflectional items, this suggests that these morphemes must be inflectional.

2.2.4 Secondary aspect These morphemes show co-occurrence restrictions with temporal adverbs that are clearly outside the verb, and they are required in order to yield the particular meaning. For instance, the inceptive, which marks a point in time, does not occur with an adverb indicating a span of time. In addition, some of these morphemes combine in unexpected ways phonologically with the conjugation markers and subject pronouns. These combinations can be treated as portmanteau morphs, providing evidence for their inflectional nature.

2.2.5 Gender The morphemes that I have labelled 'gender' are normally considered to be derivational. These items have some non-local correlates, as discussed in section 2.1, in that dependencies between them and verbal arguments exist. Given this, they appear to be inflectional. In addition, they show the same unpredictable patterns of combination, with subject, conjugation and primary aspect as secondary aspect morphemes. While these morphemes have non-local properties, they are not found with every verb that has a particular item as an argument. The gender morphemes appear to have been productively inflectional historically, showing regular agreement with a verbal argument; however, it is not clear that this is the case synchronically. I consider gender morphemes to be inflectional, understanding that problems exist with this definition.

The two non-disjunct classes yet to be discussed are deictic subject and direct object. I postpone discussion of these until section 2.5. Additionally, there are two disjunct morphemes whose semantics might suggest that they have inflectional properties: the distributive and the iterative. These do not meet the criteria for inflection; see section 2.6. Finally I have not discussed the voice morphemes. In their productive use, these supply argument structure; in their non-productive use, they are listed as part of the lexical entry. As argument structure is determined by the verb, they appear to be part of the lexical entry in this way as well.

If the conclusions of this section are correct, the problem that I began with – that inflection and derivation are intermingled in the conjunct span of the verb – disappears: the morphemes in this portion of the verb all function inflectionally.

2.3 An ordering problem: the need for a template for the conjunct morphemes

I have suggested that the conjunct morphemes (with deictic subject and direct object yet to be considered) are inflectional, in that they exhibit configurational properties, are obligatory, and can enter into portmanteau formations. I now address the ordering of these elements, examining whether it is a language-particular property or follows from more general principles.

Two perspectives have been proposed in the Athapaskan literature on the ordering of the conjunct morphemes, One, elucidated in the greatest depth by Kari (1989, 1990, 1992, 1993), is that the ordering of elements is stipulated by a template. Kari argues that a template accounts for the rigidity of the ordering and the idiosyncrasies of ordering of gender and aspect. He argues that the conjunct morphemes divide into three major zones: a qualifier zone, a conjugation zone and a subject zone. The first two of these zones are complex in structure, containing several positions whose ordering is again stipulated by the template. The second proposal, that of Speas (1991b) and K. Rice (1993, forthcoming) attempts to provide a semantically based account of the ordering of conjunct morphemes for Navajo and Slave, respectively. It is this model that I shall pursue; however, see note 15 for discussion of how the models may be more compatible than originally appears.

If the ordering of morphemes is predictable, there must be a principle that determines the ordering. In this section I assume that the order of morphemes is a reflection of scopal properties (e.g. Baker 1988a, Speas 1991b, K. Rice 1993). I return to discussion of this in more detail in section 2.6.

With this hypothesis in mind, I turn to an examination of the ordering of the inflectional elements in Slave. I use the term 'scope' in the following discussion; by this I mean something similar in nature to Bybee's (1985) term 'relevance to the verb'.

When the position of the verb stem (as well as of direct object and number) is ignored, the following order of conjunct morphemes is found.

(26)   gender – secondary aspect – conjugation/primary aspect – subject

The subject morpheme, which occurs on the right edge of the inflectional complex in Slave, can be viewed as being relevant to an entire sentence (e.g. Speas 1991b); if ordering is a consequence of scope, one might expect to find it appearing on an edge. It is also not relevant to the verb (see Bybee 1985), another reason why it might be at an edge away from the verb (see below).

Aspect may be seen as having scope over the verb, being relevant to the verb in a way that the subject generally is not. Properties of the predicate can affect primary aspect and conjugation: for instance, preverbs and quantificational adverbs play a role in conjugation choice; some verb stems include inherent number, which can have an affect on conjugation choice as well.

Primary aspect is required, while secondary aspect is not, and some secondary aspects occur with a restricted range of primary aspects; it thus appears that primary aspect has scope over secondary aspect. Secondary aspect, like primary aspect, has relevance to the verb; for instance, adverbial and preverb types can affect secondary aspect.

Gender generally represents concord with non-agentive thematic roles, or non-subjects, so it is not unreasonable to think of this morpheme as having scope over the direct object, but not over other inflectional material.

Based on these criteria, the overall ordering of the Slave inflectional morphemes appears to be a consequence of their scopal properties.[15] Strikingly, the order of elements found in Slave does not appear to be unique to Slave, or to the Athapaskan family. In work on the ordering of inflectional elements, Speas (1991b) examined six languages (English, French, Modern Greek, Finnish, Basque, Navajo), and found the morpheme order in (27) to be similar across languages.[16]

(27)   subject agreement – tense – aspect – object agreement – voice – verb

The languages that Speas discussed do not have gender, so the models are not directly comparable. However, it is notable that the order of Slave inflectional elements may not be unique to this language, but may be found cross-linguistically. If this is true, a language-particular statement of scopal relationships is unnecessary and the order of inflectional items in Slave follows from a theory of ordering that is part of universal grammar.

2.4 A structural problem: the structure of the inflectional complex

I now turn to the structure of the verb. A controversial question concerns the structure of the inflectional complex and the position of the stem. Speas (1991b) and K. Rice (1993) argue that inflectional categories project phrasally in Navajo and Slave respectively, following work by Chomsky (1988) and Pollock (1989). Their reasoning is that since inflectional morphemes are syntactic in nature, they should be accessible to the syntax; this is achieved by making them syntactic, rather than lexical, objects. Most other Athapaskan linguists (e.g. Hargus 1988; Kari 1990, 1992; McDonough 1990; Randoja 1990) propose that all word formation is lexical. This hypothesis has to deal with the syntactic accessibility issue; access to inflection can be achieved in other ways than through phrasal projections; an alternative involves percolation conventions (see e.g. Lieber 1992).

I adopt a version of the syntactic position. I assume, following, for example, Anderson (1992) and Chomsky (1993), that inflectional items are available to the syntax as features, and, with Anderson (1992), that the morphological form is supplied post-syntactically. Some evidence for this comes from the existence of portmanteau forms. In the aspect–conjugation–mode span of the verb, some morphs consist of a single component of meaning (e.g. first-person singular), while others contain more than one component of meaning (e.g. first-person singular perfective). Portmanteau patterning is suggestive of post-syntactic insertion, as otherwise rules are required to provide just these affixes with their surface form. The fact that there are phonological or templatic criteria that override the basic syntactic/semantic ordering of gender/secondary aspect also suggests that more than principles of syntax alone are at work. Syntactic ordering tends to be determinable by a set of principles, principles that do not predict the actual orderings of the gender and secondary aspect morphemes that occur.

Given this, the inflectional complex (ignoring for the moment deictic subjects) has the syntactic structure in (28).

(28)

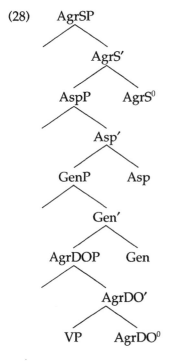

(28) provides full structure; post-syntactically, strictly adjacent positions (e.g. primary aspect–subject, gender–aspect–subject) may be spelled out as a portmanteau form. Portmanteau morphs combine meanings of adjacent positions only, never non-adjacent ones (e.g. secondary aspect–subject when there is an intervening overt primary aspect).[17]

Of interest is the comparison of (28) with the surface order of morphemes in (22). This comparison shows that morpheme order in the verb matches c-command relations in clause structure, with left-to-right ordering reflecting a lower-to-higher hierarchical arrangement.

Having examined the internal structure of the inflectional complex, I now focus on VP-internal structure. I suggest, following Rice and Saxon 1994, that a Slave sentence has the structure shown in (29). The two VP-internal NPs represent subject and object arguments; see K. Rice 1993; Rice and Saxon 1991, 1994; and Saxon and Rice 1993 for arguments that all subject NPs originate in a VP-internal subject position in Athapaskan languages. In addition, the VP houses preverbs and quantificational adverbs.

(29)

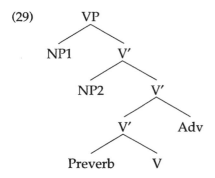

The major discrepancy between (22) and (28/29) is the position of the verb stem, the syntactic head of VP. This positioning of the verb is appropriate (see K. Rice 1993). While the verb originates within the VP, this is not its surface position: it is in the rightmost position in the verb in the surface form. I take the positioning of the verb to be the major idiosyncrasy of the verb structure in the language, and derive the surface placement of the verb stem by verb raising. I will assume that raising works in the following way.[18] The verb raises from its position in the VP to the lowest functional head, AgrDO. This affixes to the verb by prefixing it. This unit then raises to the next functional head; it then affixes to the left of the verb stem, producing the order AgrDO–Gen–V. Again the unit raises, and again affixation is to the verb stem. In this manner, the tree in (30) results.

(30)

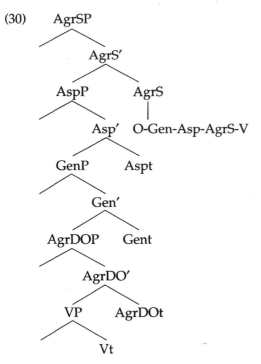

See K. Rice 1993 for additional discussion, and Speas 1991b for further discussion of ordering problems raised by the Navajo verb.

2.5 A duplication problem: two subject positions

So far, I have ignored two morpheme types: direct object and deictic subject. In this section, I attempt to deal with these through an examination of another problem: the need for the two subject positions, labelled 'subject' and 'deictic subject', in (22). I will suggest, following Rice and Saxon 1994, that the content of these positions is actually rather different: the subjects are, as discussed in section 2.1, agreement markers that indicate person and number; the deictic subjects, on the other hand, mark number but not person.

2.5.1 Inflection revisited   A major area of debate in the Athapaskan literature concerns whether pronominal elements have the status of agreement, or inflection, or of arguments. Saxon (1986) argues that all pronominals represent agreement, while nouns are arguments. Sandoval and Jelinek (1989) argue that all pronominals are arguments, while nouns are adjuncts. Speas (1990) argues that most pronominal elements are agreement, but that at least one object pronoun is an argument. Tuttle (1993) proposes that object pronominals are arguments; she takes no position on subjects. Rice and Saxon (1994) argue that all subject pronominal elements are inflectional, but differ with respect to the type of inflection that they represent. Thus, a wide range of opinions is represented in the literature.

I follow Rice and Saxon (forthcoming) in the view that the pronominals fall into two inflectional classes: agreement and number. The first- and second-person subjects (section 2.2) and the first- and second-person objects (section 2.6) represent agreement, or AgrS, while the deictic subjects k/g and ts' (this section) and the third-person objects (section 2.6) are categorized as number, or Num.

Before examining the arguments for the division between agreement and number, I consider briefly the semantics of the different subject morphemes. The first- and second-person subjects are marked for features of person and number. In addition, they are human, specific and definite. The third-person subjects are more diverse in nature. In addition to the two deictic subjects, it is generally said that third-person singular in Athapaskan languages is marked by a null morpheme. Rice and Saxon (1994) assign the following features to these forms:

(31)   k/g   ts'   ∅

	k/g	ts'	∅
Number	plural	± plural	± plural
Gender	human	human	± human
Specificity	specific	non-specific	specific
Definiteness	± definite	± definite	± definite

Rice and Saxon (1994) provide several arguments for treating first- and second-person subjects as agreement and third-person subjects as number. As they point out, third person becomes a misnomer for these subjects, as they do not represent person, but are unmarked for person; I continue to use the term 'third person', recognizing that it is not appropriate. In the following discussion, I review some of Rice and Saxon's arguments for treating third-person subjects as a category different from subject agreement.

Rice and Saxon argue that first- and second-person subjects and third-person subjects differ in their paradigmatic properties. First- and second-person subjects are obligatorily overtly marked, and depend on syntactic properties of the clause. This can be seen in the examples in (32), where the subject agreement markers are italicized.

(32) (a) (sį) jǫ ná*h*dɛ́   'I live here' (SS)
           1sg. here 1sg.S.live
           *(sį) jǫ nádɛ́

      (b) (nį) jǫ nán*ɛ*dɛ́   'you (sg.) live here'
           2sg. here 2sg.S.live

      (c) (naxį) jǫ ná*í*dɛ́   'we live here'
           1pl. here 1pl.S.live

      (d) (naxį) jǫ ná*a*hdɛ́   'you (pl.) live here'
           2pl. here 2pl.S.live

The emphatic subject pronouns are optional, as indicated by the parentheses. In the presence of any given pronoun, only a single verb form is possible. It is impossible to impose an interpretation of, for instance, speaker as subject on a verb without first-person singular subject agreement, as is shown in (a).[19] This is a prototypical property of agreement: it represents a relationship between the inflectional item and a noun.

Deictic subjects have different paradigmatic properties: they are not obligatory in the same sense that the first- and second-person subject inflections are. For instance, the three sentences in (33) have approximately the same meaning.

(33) (a) dɛnɛ jǫ nádɛ́   'people live here' (SS)
           people here live

      (b) dɛnɛ jǫ ná*ts'ɛ*dɛ́   'people live here'
           people here ts'.live

      (c) dɛnɛ jǫ ná*g*ɛdɛ́   'people live here'
           people here g.live

The verb in (33a) contains neither of the number morphemes, but nevertheless can receive a third-person plural interpretation; the verb in (33b) is marked with the unspecified subject prefix *ts'*, and that in (33c) with the third-person plural human subject prefix *g*. Cook (1996) and Saxon (1993) provide discussion of the semantic and discourse contexts of occurrence of these affixes in closely related languages. Rice and Saxon (1994) suggest that these morphemes, like the subject agreement morphemes, depend on syntactic properties of the clause and are obligatory; the understanding of their semantics and discourse properties is inadequate at this time. The morpheme *ts'* appears to include the speaker, while *k/g* indicates that a group, rather than individuals, are important. What is important here is that the third person, unlike the first and second person, does not require an obligatory overt marker.

Further examples illustrate in slightly different ways that *k/g* is not required for a third-person plural interpretation. In Slave, some verb stems are found which have inherent in their meaning that the theme of the verb is plural; the verb stem *de* in (34) is one example. When *k/g* is present, the subject is necessarily third-person plural and human; in the absence of *k*, a non-human interpretation is also allowed.

(34) rį́kɛrénįde   'they landed (human)' (H)
     k.pl.land
     rírénįde   'they landed (human, non-human)' (H)
     pl.land

The different paradigmatic status of the deictic subjects from the first- and second-person subjects can also be seen in examples from texts where alternations between these morphemes are found. For example, in (35), the first occurrence of the verb 'kill' has the unspecified subject *ts'*, while the second has the plural affix *k-*.

(35) ʔɛyi gots'ɛ ʔɛkúhnį́ɛ ɬɛts'ɛgǫ dzá ʔagǫt'ɛ gots'ɛ
     that from then   ts'.kill   bad it is   and
     k'áts'ɛlɛht'inɛkɛ sį́i dɛnɛ kɛghǫ
     Chipewyan   foc. person pl.kill
     'In those days, they killed each other and it was bad. The Chipewyan killed people.' (B)

While first- and second-person inflection has strictly syntactic conditions determining its presence, this is not true of inflection for third person: an overt marking may be present, but just which one is determined by semantic and contextual factors.

A second difference between first- and second-person subjects on the one hand and third-person subjects on the other can be seen in conjoined clauses. With first-person subjects, the relationship between the pronominal inflection and its specifier NP is one of agreement; with third-person subjects, the relationship is not one of agreement, but rather of mutual elaboration of semantic properties.

Slave is a pro-drop language, as can be seen in the examples in (32). The use of a pronominal subject is optional, and these subjects, when present, are necessarily interpreted as emphatic or contrastive. These pronouns enter into coordinate constructions in an interesting way. In the examples in (36), the first sentence of each set has a noun phrase consisting of a noun and a pronoun as subject. The second example illustrates that the pronoun can be dropped in this context, just as it is when it is the sole subject. That the subject involves a conjoined phrase is made clear from the presence of the conjunction. The final example of each set illustrates that if the conjunction too is absent, ill-formedness results. If first- and second-person subjects represent agreement, this is not surprising: the verb has plural subject agreement, but the NP with which it agrees is overtly singular. Without the conjunction, the NP is not second person.

(36) (a) Simon hɛ́ nị̃ hɛ́ juice náahdí   'you and Simon buy juice'
            and 2sg.and   2pl.S.buy   (B)
          Simon hɛ́ juice náahdí
          *Simon juice náahdí

     (b) Ann sɛnị̃ hǫ gok'ɛríʔe lɛ́t'ɛ hít'ị̃   'Ann and I have the same
            1sg. and   jacket   like   1pl.S.have jacket' (H)
          Ann hǫ gok'ɛríʔe lɛ́t'ɛ hít'ị̃
          *Ann gok'ɛríʔe lɛ́t'ɛ hít'ị̃

The deictic subjects pattern otherwise: in this case, there is no agreement between a subject NP and the verb. In the example in (37), the subject noun phrase necessarily has a real-world singular referent, yet has a verb which contains the plural subject marker k/g. The meaning that obtains is one in which the subject is a group defined by the named individual.

(37) sɛtá   názɛ́ɬɛkɛdɛ́htɬa 'my father and he went hunting' (SS)
     1sg.father k.dual go hunting

The specifier–head relationship is clearly quite different for agreement and number inflection.

I have argued, following Rice and Saxon 1994, that the two positions traditionally identified as subject inflection are both inflectional, but that two types of inflection are involved, agreement with first- and second-person subjects and number otherwise. I now return to the question first raised in section 2.2: the ordering of subject agreement and number. Ritter (1995), in a study of Hebrew, proposes that two subject categories are required in that language: agreement for first- and second-person subjects and number for the so-called third-person subjects. Ritter argues that these categories are layered with subject agreement above aspect and number below it. The hierarchical ordering of agreement and number relative to each other is thus identical in Hebrew and Slave.

The structures proposed for Slave in (38) summarize the discussion so far.

(38)

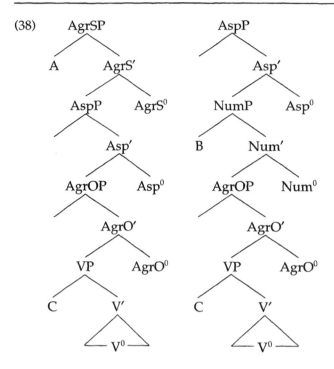

In first- and second-person contexts, subject agreement, AgrS, is found, while in 'third person' contexts, number, Num, occurs instead. If this is correct, then the mystery of two subject positions is revealed: the apparent splitting of subject inflection in the Athapaskan verb between two morphological positions is not so unusual, as these two positions house different morphological categories: they do not both represent agreement, as has often been assumed; rather, one is agreement, and the other number. It further appears that the ordering of agreement and number may reflect a universal property. If this is correct, then the ordering of the categories in the Slave verb is not an idiosyncrasy of the language that requires stipulation, but instead represents a cross-linguistic tendency to position number and agreement differently.

2.6 *The status of objects*

The inflectional nature of object pronouns has yet to be considered. While it is generally assumed that these pronouns are inflectional (e.g. in traditional treatments, Saxon 1986), Tuttle (1993) has argued that they are arguments. I have left these until last amongst the inflectional items, because the insight into subjects helps us to understand some of the properties of objects. I will propose that subjects and objects are parallel in nature: both are inflectional, and both show a split between first and second person on the one hand and third person on the other.

First- and second-person objects are identical in patterning to first- and second-person subjects: they are obligatory; in their absence, a reading of object as first or second person is not possible. These facts are shown by the examples in (39), forms with a first-person singular object. (39a) is a simple sentence with a first-person singular object, *s*. (39b) illustrates how if this morpheme is absent, a reading of object as first-person singular cannot be obtained. (39c) and (39d) differ from (39a) and (39b) in that an overt object, *sɛnį*, 'first person singular' is present. The pronominal inflection is required, even in the presence of this overt pronoun.

(39) (a) rá*s*ɛrɛyįht'u   's/he punched me' (H)
          1sg.O.punched

   (b) *rárɛyįht'u   (on reading 's/he punched me')

   (c) sɛnį rá*s*ɛrɛyįht'u   'it's me that s/he punched'
          1sg. 1sg.O.punched

   (d) *sɛnį rárɛyįht'u
          1sg. punched

Third-person objects differ in their paradigmatic patterning from first- or second-person objects. These must be divided into two different types: anaphors and non-anaphors.

The anaphors fall into two categories: reflexive anaphors and disjoint anaphors (see Saxon 1984, 1986; Rice and Saxon 1991). The anaphors are all specific in reference. The reflexive *ʔɛdɛ* is used when the subject and object are co-referential (see K. Rice 1989 for details). The reflexive clearly does not mark person, as it is used to mark co-referentiality regardless of person of the subject.

A disjoint anaphor (the name is due to Saxon 1984), *zh/y*, is used only when the subject is third-person specific and when the object is a non-co-referential third-person-specific form. It occurs only when no object noun is present, as in (40). In the first form of each data set, an object pronoun is present; in the remaining forms a nominal object occurs, and there is no object pronoun. The anaphor is italicized.

(40) (a) Mary ná*zh*ɛnįįtá   'Mary kicked him/her/it (sg./pl.)' (SS)
          Mary John nánįįtá   'Mary kicked John'
          Mary tthe nánįįtá   'Mary kicked the stone/s'
              stone

   (b) Mary gá*y*urɛhtɛ   'Mary taught him/her' (H)
          Mary ts'ǫ́dani gáhurɛhtɛ 'Mary taught the child'
              child

While the disjoint anaphor is not present when a nominal object appears in the sentences in (40), there is one condition under which a disjoint anaphor and a nominal object may co-occur: when the nominal object is third-person plural human. The plural disjoint anaphoric form is *go*. Like the subject *k/g*, it may or may not be present in a sentence.

(41)   ts'ǫ́danikɛ kágodenézhú   's/he chased the children out' (B)
       child.pl.   *go.chased out*
       ts'ǫ́danikɛ kádenézhú   's/he chased the children out'

When it is present, it necessarily implies a human object; if it is absent, the object may be human or non-human.

(42)   łagonįhdé   'they killed them (human)' (B, SS)
       łanįhdé   'they killed them (human/non-human)'

The object form *go* marks that the object is human, plural, specific and non-co-referential with the subject. The semantics of this morpheme closely parallels that of *k/g* except for the anaphoricity, a property that cannot be found in subjects. While *y/zh* is simply disjoint anaphoric and specific, *go*, in addition to being a specific disjoint anaphor, includes number and gender in its meaning. The disjoint anaphoric pronouns, then, do not mark person, since they are not obligatorily present in third-person contexts; they instead indicate number, gender and specificity.

Sentences with third-person direct objects and first- and second-person subjects remain to be considered. In this context, a third-person non-human object never has an overt marker (43a); a third-person human object may be marked by *b/m*, but need not be (43b). The semantic and discourse conditions under which *b/m* is found remain to be explored.

(43)   (a)   nániita   'I kicked him/her/it' (B)
             nábɛniita   'I kicked him/her'

       (b)   gáhurɛhtę   'I taught him/her' (H)
             gáburɛhtę   'I taught him/her'

Third-person plural human specific objects may be marked by *ku/ki/gi/go* (form differs depending on dialect).

(44)   (a)   ts'ɛkunįwa   'you (sg.) wake them up' (H, B)

       (b)   t'erɛ ts'ɛkunįwa   'you (sg.) wake the girl up' (H, B)
             girl

       (c)   t'erɛ ts'ɛnįwa   'you (sg.) wake the girl up' (H, B)

The form *b/m* marks animacy alone when it is an object. *ku*, and its other dialect forms, in addition to indicating gender, also marks plural number; both indicate specificity.

The semantics of the third-person direct objects is summarized in (45). The unspecified object *ʔɛ* is included for completeness.

(45)

	zh/y	go	b/m	ku	ʔɛ
	anaphoric	anaphoric	anaphoric	non-anaphoric	non-anaphoric	non-anaphoric
number	± plural	plural	non-plural	plural	± plural
gender	± human	human	human	human	non-human
specificity	specific	specific	specific	specific	non-specific

These pronouns are similar to the third-person subjects. In both cases, the third persons have a different paradigmatic status than do the first and second persons: while the sense of first and second person can be conveyed only by the overt presence of a morpheme, the sense of third-person object does not require the appearance of a morpheme. The object morphemes thus fall into two different categories, agreement and number, just as the subject morphemes do.

Further facts indicate a split between first- and second-person objects and third-person objects, and provide additional evidence for just first and second persons indicating agreement. Just as co-ordination facts differ for subjects, depending upon whether a first or second person or a third person is involved as a conjunct, so they do for objects. This can be seen by comparing the examples in (46) and (47). In (47), with a first person involved in the co-ordination, the pronoun can be dropped (46b), but the conjunction is required (46c); in (47), with a third-person plural reading, the stated NP is overtly singular, and the conjunction is not needed. The object form *raxe* marks both a first-person plural and a second-person plural object.

(46) (a) Mary sɛnį hɛ́ raraxɛrɛyįht'u 's/he punched Mary and
            1sg. and 3 hit 1pl./2pl.   me/you' (H)

      (b) Mary hɛ́ raraxɛrɛyįht'u   's/he punched Mary and
            and 3 hit 1pl./2pl.   me/you' (H)

      (c) *Mary raraxɛrɛyįht'u   (okay as 'Mary punched
            3 hit 1pl./2pl.   you (pl.)/us')

(47)   sɛtá   rágorɛyįht'u   'I punched my father and him/
         1sg.father 1sg.hit 3pl.   her/them' (H)

In (46), the conjunction is required to yield the interpretation in (46a, b), while in (47) no conjunction is necessary.

Objects, like subjects, then, are of two types. First and second persons include features of person and number, and exhibit syntactic properties of agreement. The so-called third persons may be either anaphoric or non-anaphoric; in addition, they are marked for features of number, gender and specificity. The fact that they are not obligatory for third-person interpretation suggests that they are unmarked for person. The syntactic patterning in conjunction of first- or second-person object forms shows properties of agreement, just as with subjects; the patterning of the third-person forms is not one of agreement, but of elaboration.

First- or second-person subjects and third-person subjects clearly appear in two different positions in the verb, being separated by other inflectional material. The evidence discussed in this section suggests that the objects should have structure parallel to that of the subjects, which trees as in (48).

(48)   first and second persons   'third' persons

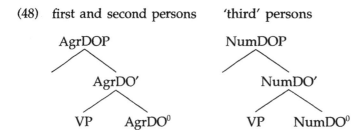

The additional evidence from morpheme ordering that argues for two subject positions is not available for objects, since objects are traditionally thought to occupy only a single position in the verb template.

2.7 An ordering problem: the need for a template for the disjunct morphemes

So far I have discussed the conjunct complex. I have suggested (i) that the traditional divisions of morphemes into categories of inflection and derivation requires rethinking, with some of the traditional derivation being considered as inflection; (ii) that pronouns do not form a single inflectional category, but non-third-person pronominals represent agreement, while deictic third-person pronominals represent number; (iii) that the verb originates as head of the VP, and moves to provide a host to the inflectional complex. Given this view of the verb, several traditional problems receive an explanation.

In this section I turn to the need for a template within the remaining portion of the verb, the disjunct complex. I suggest that the need for a template is again overstated, and that basic principles of semantics provide a means of predicting the order in which disjunct morphemes appear. I begin by proposing an overall structure for the verb phrase.

The verb phrase has the structure in (49), expanded from (29).

(49)

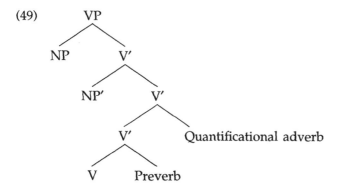

Some of this structure was introduced in section 2.3. The primary purpose of this section is to discuss the overall ordering of the remaining material.

Before turning to this, however, it is necessary to address briefly two other issues. First, the inflectional/lexical status of VP-internal elements has not been established. The lexical status of all VP-internal material is obvious with the exception of the quantificational adverbs. These elements are aspectual in nature, and one might think that they should be regarded as inflectional. But they fail the test of obligatoriness, as is shown for the iterative in (50) and the distributive in (51).

(50) nidídhah   's/he picked up plural objects' (SS)
     ninadídhεh, nidídhεh   's/he picked up plural objects repeatedly'

(51) nánεyihkwa   'I whipped it' (y conjugation) (B)
     náyánεhkwa, nánεhkwa   'I whipped each one' (w conjugation)

On the first line of each data set, a form without a quantificational adverb is shown. On the second line, two forms are given, one with the adverb (*na* iterative, *yá* distributive), the other without it, but with the same meaning. In both cases, there are further differences between the forms on the two lines. With the iterative, a different stem form is required, and this is the major signal of iterativity. In the distributive form, the change in conjugation and aspect is the primary signal of distributivity; the distributive morpheme serves only to reinforce this. The morphemes themselves, then, are not paradigmatic.

Second, in (49) the adverbs and preverbs are daughters of V' rather than of V. This syntactic status is clearest for the quantificational adverbs. The iterative quantifies the action with many verbs; for instance, with the stem 'go' it means 'go again'. However, it can also quantify an object. In a predicate such as 'I ate an apple', if the iterative is present, it refers to the apple, specifying that the speaker ate another apple. Thus, depending on the semantics of the predicate, the iterative can refer to material outside the verb word itself. This is different from the semantics of a prefix such as *re-* in English, which refers just to the verb. Arguments are more difficult to establish for the preverbs, but do exist. Many of the preverbs need not be part of the verb word, but can be independent of it, being included within the verb word when they are strictly subcategorized for. This might suggest that they are phrasal- rather than word-level elements. In addition, preverbs can be transitive. A phrasal structure better allows for this property, perhaps, than a lexical structure would.

Having established these preliminaries, I turn to the ordering of elements within the disjunct portion of the verb. The common analysis of the disjunct complex, like the rest of the verb, proposes that a template orders the morphemes. While templates, or position classes, have been proposed both traditionally (e.g. Lounsbury 1953 on Oneida; Sapir and Hoijer 1967 on Navajo) and recently (e.g. Bessler et al. 1993 and Bonet 1991 on Romance; Kari 1989 on Ahtna and Navajo; Kari 1992 on Ahtna; Kari 1993 on Tanaina; Simpson and Withgott 1986 on Central Australian languages), they have also been the target of criticism (e.g. McDonough 1990 and Speas 1990, 1991b on Navajo; Myers 1987 on Shona; K. Rice 1991b, 1993, on Slave). In this section I suggest that evidence for position classes in the disjunct complex of the Slave verb is weak. Rather, the basic ordering follows from the semantic principle of scope discussed in section 2.3, where morphemes of greater scope appear higher in the tree than morphemes within their scope. While the template is a useful descriptive device, it has little reality beyond this.

Recall that in the Slave verb template, the morphemes of the disjunct complex occur in a fixed order, summarized again in (52).

(52)   preverb – quantificational adverb – incorporate

If the morphemes are ordered by a template, one might expect to find random variation in the ordering of the position classes across the languages of a family; one would additionally expect there to be no general principle that orders the morphemes. These predictions are not borne out when the languages of the Athapaskan family are examined. I will concentrate on the evidence that can be garnered from Slave alone (see Rice K. 1991b, forthcoming, for discussion of comparative evidence).

One prediction of a template is that position classes should be rigidly ordered within a language, with no variation allowed, except by phonologically motivated metathesis. Unexpectedly for this hypothesis, some variability in the ordering of position classes is found in several Athapaskan languages (see ibid.). This variability is seen in Slave when the position of the iterative with respect to incorporates is examined. While generally incorporates appear at the right edge of the disjunct complex, this is not invariably the case: there are some verbs in which the position of the iterative is variable, being allowed to the right or the left of the incorporate. Some examples are given in (53). *na* is the iterative; it precedes or follows the incorporate (*dze* 'heart' in (53a) and *ła* 'rope' in (53b)). Forms are from Howard 1990.

(53)   (a)   dahdze*na*łéts'ɛdɛtthɛ   'start in fright, be startled repeatedly' (SS)
                dah*na*dzełéts'ɛdɛtthɛ

   (b)   naɬana?ɛts'ɛdɛtɬɛ   'drag, lead (rope, animal on leash)
          nanaɬa?ɛts'ɛdɛtɬɛ   repeatedly' (SS)

The existence of a template presupposes a rigidity of ordering that should not be violable; the examples in (53) show that this absolute ordering is not actually found.

Perhaps a more important reason for rejecting a template is the fact that the ordering both within and between constituents within the disjunct complex appears to correlate with semantic properties of the morphemes involved. In the remainder of this section, I suggest that the major ordering properties of disjunct morphemes need not be stipulated, but are a consequence of semantic properties. I suggest the following principle, a principle alluded to in the discussion of the ordering of inflectional elements in section 2.3.

(54)   When one morpheme is in the scope of another, the morpheme of greater scope must be higher in the tree than the morpheme within its scope.

By this, I mean that, given two morphemes that can be construed as being related in some way, the more general one will appear higher in the tree than the more specific one.

While I am making this proposal with respect to ordering in Slave, it is perhaps a particular instantiation of a general principle, that D-structure hierarchical relations are a reflection of scope (cf. Baker 1988a, Brunson 1989, Jackendoff 1972, McCawley 1988, Speas 1984, for discussion of the relationship between scope and word order).

Having set out the basic proposal, I turn to the facts of Slave, beginning with a discussion of the treatment of the preverb-verb as a unit, and then examining higher-level ordering. The preverb–stem unit is often considered to be a lexical entry or a result of an early level of word formation (see e.g. Kari 1979, 1990, 1992; Randoja 1989; Sapir and Hoijer 1967; Speas 1984; and discussion in section 2.1). This is because the preverbs modify the meaning of the stem, providing either a systematic or an idiosyncratic change in meaning to the stem. Consider, for example, the preverb in (55).

(55)   kádįtɬa   'you (sg.) go out'
        ká   'out' (preverb)
        tɬa   'sg., dual go on land' (stem)

In this example, the preverb restricts the meaning of the verb stem, expressing something about the direction of movement.

Another indication that the preverb-verb forms an integral unit is that modification of the preverb alone is not possible, but the preverbs modify the meaning of the verb stem alone. A parallel argument has been used in English to argue for verb-particles as units in a phrase like 'strike out the batter', where the particle 'out' can be viewed as incorporated into the verb, as it cannot be modified. When the particle appears after the object, it can be modified, as in 'strike the batter right out'. The difference between Slave and English is that morphemes in preverb position are always incorporated in Slave, while in English incorporation is optional. The fact that the preverb is the closest item to the stem is consistent with its patterning.

Assuming that the preverb and verb form a unit, the ordering of preverbs and quantificational adverbs is predictable: quantificational adverbs are higher than preverbs.

The adverbs modify the preverb–verb complex, not just the stem, as argued for explicitly in Kari 1979, 1990, 1992, and Randoja 1989, and widely assumed in the literature. For instance, consider the Slave iterative form in (56).

(56)   kǫdįtła   'you (sg.) go back out'

In this example, the iterative morpheme, which surfaces here as nasalization and raising of the vowel of the preverb *ká*, indicates that the entire action of going out is repeated, suggesting that the iterative has scope over the action as a whole, not just over the verb stem. The example in (57) illustrates this with the distributive adverb.

(57)   tehętła   's/he went into water'
       teyáhtła   's/he went into water over and over'

The entire action of going into water is repeated, not just the going.

The adverbs thus have scope over the preverb-verb, in that they modify the meaning of the complex, not just the meaning of the stem. Given scopal ordering, one expects the adverbs to appear higher than the preverbs.

Combinations of preverbs within a single verb word are possible in Slave, as shown in (58). Numbers following a gloss refer to page numbers in Howard 1990; other data are from K. Rice 1989.

(58)   (a)   tɛkáyįya   's/he got out of water' (tɛh 'water' +
                                          ká 'out of') (H)
               -t'áhkáts'ɛdíle   'unharness, take out of harness (e.g. dog
                                          team)' (315) (t'áh 'into' + ká 'out of')
               tɛhk'ɛts'ɛnɛtah   'look around in water, feel around in water
                                          with stick' (393) (tɛh 'water' + k'ɛ 'on')

       (b)   O k'ɛnínįdhah   's/he put pl. O back together' (k'e 'on' +
                                          ní 'terminative')
               łɛníts'įʔa   'fold' (9) (łɛ 'in half' + ní 'terminative')
               -k'ɛnídagodɛnįʔǫ   's/he accused, blamed' (34) (k'ɛ 'on' +
                                          ní 'terminative')

	-dáhká?ɛts'ɛdɛchu	'open (e.g. container)' (67) (dáh 'close' + ká 'open')
	sɛ́ɛ́níɛnits'įhthi	'think over, get straightened out in mind' (148) (sɛ́ɛ́ 'good, right' + ní 'terminative')
	xǫníagots'įhthi	'get married, establish home' (182) (xǫ 'spouse' + ní 'terminative')
	łaáníts'įtsɛ́h	'kill with spear' (567) (łáá 'dead' + ní 'terminative')
(c)	kátáhtłah	's/he got out on shore' (ká 'out of' + tá 'to shore') (SS)
	łǫdahɛtłɛ	's/he is dancing in circle' (łǫ 'circle' + dah 'up and down')
	nałǫts'ɛ́d?éh	'turn in circles on water' (42) (na 'continuative' + łǫ 'circle')

Within the preverbs too, the ordering of morphemes appears to be predictable. The forms in (58a) show that preverbs specifying location precede those specifying direction, source and position. For example, *tɛh* 'water' is a location and *ká* 'out (of)' specifies a direction; *tɛh* specifies the location and *k'ɛ* the location. The relational items share properties with postpositions, following their object.

The forms in (58b) suggest that a more specific preverb precedes a more general preverb. For instance, in 'kill with spear', the second preverb indicates termination of an activity, and the first indicates the manner of termination: namely, death. The same pattern is found in 'think over'; here the second preverb again indicates termination, while the first specifies the type of ending: namely, in something being good or straightened. The example 'accuse, blame' is similar: the verb without *k'ɛ* indicates coming to an end of a verbal action; the preverb *k'ɛ* then indicates the goal of this activity. In these cases, then, the first preverb delimits the domain defined by the second.

Some verbs show somewhat different patterning. In some cases, it is difficult to identify whether one of the preverbs is more general than the other. Examples in (58c) include 'out to shore' and 'circle up and down'. More work on the semantics of such constructions is required. If the preverbs are equivalent in scope or generality, bearing no particular relationship to one another, their ordering properties must be determined by other factors (e.g. is the reverse ordering possible; if so, are the interpretations identical?).

The order of preverbs does not appear to be random, but is a consequence of general semantic properties, where a more specific preverb precedes a more general preverb.

The placement of quantificational adverbs shows the greatest variability across the family. This is perhaps not surprising, given the considerable variation in the placement of adverbs cross-linguistically. For instance, Jackendoff (1972) notes that an English adverb such as 'frequently' may occur in a range of positions without having discernible effect on the meaning of a sentence. He suggests a possible account of the variable placement of sentential adverbs: such adverbs are transportable, or can be placed in various positions in the sentence. Jackendoff shows that VP adverbs do not show the same privileges of occurrence as sentential adverbs.

This analysis of transportability may provide insight into the position of the iterative. As shown in (44), the iterative exhibits some freedom in its position. In fact, it may even occur more than once in a particular verb, as (59) illustrates.

(59)   góhdǫkǫʔɛts'ɛdetsɛ   'break into, through, repeatedly' (574) (SS)

In this case, the nasalization on *dá* and *ká* are the surface realization of the iterative. The adverb 'sprinkles' itself over the preverbs.

While the iterative is variable in position, it occurs to the right of the preverbs. Perhaps it can be considered to be a transportable adverb, and thus can be found in more than one position within the VP. It is subject to the constraints of scopal ordering, however, meaning that it must be to the right of the preverbs.

Within the adverbs themselves, I have suggested that the ordering is distributive-iterative. I make this suggestion based on forms such as (60), where *yá* distributive precedes *nǫ* iterative.

(60)   łéyánǫhtsɛ   'I break each customarily' (B)
       O yánaníhshe   's/he grows plural object again' (B)
       sɛyiyánǫwɛta   's/he kicked me customarily' (H)
       níyánǫgokɛhwhɛ   'they each returned' (B)

In fact, the ordering of the distributive and iterative is not straightforward in Slave. While *na* iterative clearly follows *yá* distributive in the examples in (60), a closer examination indicates that not only the iterative *na* follows the distributive. More generally, any low-toned disjunct morpheme *na* must follow the distributive. This is shown in (61).

(61)   nahk'á   'I sharpen it' (B, SS)
       yánǫhɛ́hk'á   'I sharpen each' (B)

Assuming that *na* here is a preverb, not the iterative, any disjunct morpheme of the form *na* follows the distributive, making it difficult to determine if there is a semantically based ordering relationship between the distributive and the iterative. They are clearly adjacent, but their overall ordering is possibly determined by phonological, rather than meaning, factors.

In Slave, incorporated stems occur within the verb, generally at the right edge of the disjunct complex. Saxon and Rice (1993) argue that such stems originate in VP-internal positions (B, C in (38)) and fail to move to A, external subject position. They are then incorporated by head movement.

2.8 Summary

The full structure that I have proposed for the Slave verb ((28)/(29)) is strikingly like that of the template that is generally given, but differs in two ways: first by the placement of the verb stem, and second by the position of the incorporated stems. I have argued that the template provides a convenient descriptive tool; the ordering of the elements is actually largely a consequence of scopal properties and thus follows from principles of universal grammar combined with language particular statements concerning directionality.

2.9 A locality problem: discontinuous constituents

Athapaskan languages illustrate another problem: they are rife with discontinuous constituents. As discussed in section 2.1, the basic lexical entry of a verb obligatorily includes a voice element and a stem. I assume that the voice element combines with the stem lexically, with voice and transitivity alternations determined in the lexicon (see section 2.1). The minimal lexical entry of a verb is thus as in (62).

(62)   voice – root $]_v$

More complex lexical entries exist, as illustrated in section 2.1, with other morphemes occurring within a verb theme. In such cases, the meaning is defined on the entry as a whole, not on individual morphemes. For instance, in the theme *n-h-ji* 'scare', it is not possible to assign meanings to the individual elements of the theme. In such structures, the assumption made in the Athapaskan literature has been that these are single words (see e.g. Kari, Randoja, Rice, Speas, Wright and many others). However, an alternative solution is available. Di Sciullo and Williams (1987), in a study of English phrasal idioms, suggest that these idioms are syntactic objects that are listed in the lexicon. The idioms are like words, in that their meanings are non-compositional, but differ from words in being phrasal. I propose that the discontinuous verb themes in Slave entries should be considered as comparable to English phrasal idioms. (63) gives an example.

(63) $[[h]_{voice} [ti]]_v [zha]_N$ 'preach, bark'

Each morpheme is labelled for category. When this unit is inserted into the larger syntactic structure, the morphemes are correctly placed. No further stipulation of position is required, as it is a consequence of phrasal structure, which itself follows from scopal properties.

Lexical entries can also include gender material and direct objects. For instance, the verb 'scare' has a gender morpheme, and 'tell a lie' a direct object that must occur with the stem. I have labelled the direct object as a pronoun. The fact that the verb is transitive determines that the pronoun is an object rather than a subject.

(64)   [h]$_{voice}$ [ji]$_v$ [n]$_{gender}$ 'scare'
       [ts'i]$_v$ [go]$_{Pro}$ '(tell a) lie'

By treating discontinuous verb themes as idioms, the benefits achieved by the analysis proposed here can be maintained. Slave may be unusual in the number of phrasal idioms it has, but the construct is not in and of itself unexpected. Adverbial material and gender-type classes are often lexicalized. The apparent discontinuous dependencies are, I suggest, historically motivated, but synchronically frozen, with the forms listed as phrasal idioms.

2.10 An isomorphism problem: deriving the phonological structure

So far I have addressed issues of morphosyntactic structure, rather than phonological structure. The interface between these two components is an important one to consider for Athapaskan languages. In most accounts of languages of this family, it is assumed that a boundary is associated with each lexical entry, with the morphosyntactic structure and the phonological structure being autonomous. Kari (1990), for instance, proposes that a boundary is associated with each lexical entry. The entire string of lexical items is formed through processes of derivation and inflection, with morphemes being interdigitated amongst each other. At the end of the morphological derivation, a form that serves as underlying representation is produced. I suggest an alternative: that boundaries are not listed lexically, but rather that the phonological structure can be derived directly from the morphosyntactically given structure (see K. Rice 1993 for a slightly different analysis).

The phonology of Slave divides the verb word into several distinct units, as indicated by the boundaries in (22). Limitations of space prevent me from presenting arguments for the boundaries; see Hargus 1988 on Sekani; Kari 1976 on Navajo; Kari 1975 on Navajo and Tanaina; Kari 1990 on Ahtna; F-K. Li 1946 on Chipewyan; McDonough 1990 on Navajo; Randoja 1989 on Beaver; K. Rice 1989, 1992b, 1993, on Slave; and many others for justification of these domains within the verb word in a number of Athapaskan languages.

The following phonological domains are required.

(65)   (a)   The traditional verb word is a domain for the purposes of the phonology.
       (b)   Each lexical item, or morpheme traditionally identified as disjunct, forms a domain.
       (c)   The traditional conjunct items form a domain.

(d)   The direct object and deictics are intermediate in patterning, sometimes patterning with conjunct morphemes, sometimes with disjunct morphemes, and sometimes on their own.

I will characterize these domains in an informal way. Recall the structure of
the verb that results from verb raising, repeated in (66).

(66)   [[[Pre] [Adv] [Inc]]$_{vp}$ [[AgrDO Num Asp2 Asp1 AgrS] [V]]]

The output of the syntax defines certain domains directly. First, the largest
domain, the traditional verb word, is the maximal functional projection, in
this case AgrSP. Within this, the VP-internal material forms a domain, as does
the remainder of the material. Second, each major category lexical item (noun,
verb, preverb, adverb) forms a unit on its own; in addition, the inflectional component is a unit. These phonological units thus parallel directly the syntactic
structure. Within the inflectional word, AgrDO and Num are intermediate in
their phonological patterning: these, I suggest, form words in this component,
and are uniquely recognizable as the pronominal forms. The phonological
domains are summarized in (67).

(67) $X^{max.}$ (X is a functional head)
phrasal units within $X^{max.}$
word-level units
pronominals

Consider, for instance, a verb with a preverb, AgrDO, Asp2, Asp1, AgrS and
V. This unit has the derived syntactic structure in (68).

(68)   [[Pre]$_{vp}$ [[[AgrDO] [Asp2] [Asp1] [AgrS]] [V]]]

The only discrepancy between the structure defined by the syntax and the
domains required for the phonology comes within the inflectional component,
where Asp2, Asp1 and AgrS form a single span.

While this discussion of the phonology is brief, the approach to the phonological domains is one that promises to be revealing, leading, if successful, to
the elimination of boundary type as part of the underlying entry of a Slave
word. It appears that while the lexically stipulated boundary types are a useful descriptive device, they have no linguistic reality.

3 Summary

In this sketch I have touched briefly on a range of problems introduced by the
noun and the verb in Slave. I have suggested that in both cases, analyses that

are more in keeping with those of other languages may be more appropriate than has often been believed to be the case. In the noun, the apparent ordering paradox of inflection inside derivation disappears when prosodic information as well as morphosyntactic information is allowed as part of a lexical entry. In the verb, the major ordering of constituents can be determined through an appeal to a principle that derives ordering through scopal relations between morphemes. I have also suggested that the apparently anomalous two subject positions in the Slave verb are not arbitrary, but are a consequence of the fact that they represent two different inflectional categories. Finally, I have suggested that the frequently proposed lack of isomorphism between the model required for word formation and that required for the phonology is an artefact of the analysis rather than a true fact of the language; the phonological domains derive in a straightforward way from the morphosyntactic structure, referring only to information that is independently required for the morphology and the syntax.

ACKNOWLEDGEMENTS

Thank you to Leslie Saxon, E.-D. Cook and Andrew Spencer for many comments that have improved the quality of this chapter.

NOTES

1 Languages of the Athapaskan family are found in three discontinuous groups: Apachean, spoken in the South-west of the United States; Pacific Coast Apachean, consisting of a number of languages (many now extinct) spoken on the Pacific coast of the United States; and northern Athapaskan, consisting of a number of languages spoken in Canada and Alaska. The spelling 'Athapaskan' is the official spelling of the language family adopted by the Canadian government, while the spelling 'Athabaskan' is suggested by the Alaska Native Language Centre. The word Slave is pronounced [slévi]. This language is composed of a dialect complex, with the major dialects being Alberta Slavey, South Slavey, Bearlake, Hare and Mountain. Data in this paper are drawn from South Slavey (SS), Bearlake (B) and Hare (H) ([hær]), and are, where appropriate, labelled as to dialect when the particular phonological form represents a single dialect. The major dialect differences are phonological; the facts discussed here are the same across the dialects. See K. Rice 1989 for discussion of dialect differences. An updated and more in-depth study of the issues raised in this chapter is to be found in Rice, forthcoming.

2 I use the standard orthography for Slave with one exception. I use <e> to represent [e] and <ɛ> to represent [ɛ]; the orthography employs <ə> and <e> respectively. The following correspondences should be noted: sh = [ʃ], zh = [ʒ], gh = [ɣ], th = [θ], dh = [ð], wh = [w̥]. An acute accent marks high tone; absence of an accent indicates low tone. A hook under a vowel represents nasalization. The symbols d, dz, dl, g, etc. represent voiceless unaspirated stops and t, ts, tɬ, k, etc. represent voiceless aspirated stops, following Athapaskan tradition. C' is an ejective consonant. The laterals pattern with the fricatives in Slave. The symbol ɬ is thus a voiceless lateral fricative, and l a voiced lateral fricative.

3 A small number of bisyllabic monomorphemic nouns exists; see section 1.3.

4 See Cook 1984 on Sarcee; Cook 1989 on Chilcotin; Hargus 1988 on Sekani; Kari 1976 on Navajo; Kari 1990 on Ahtna; Krauss 1965, 1969 on proto-Athapaskan; Leer 1979 on proto-Athapaskan; K. Rice 1988, 1991c, 1992a on Slave for various perspectives on voicing alternations.

5 There are some stems with non-alternating voiced fricatives: for example, zhah 'snow', la 'work', zo 'marten' (H), zǫ 'only'.

6 In Slave verbs, stem-initial fricatives *are* voiceless following a voiceless segment and voiced following a voiced segment, hence showing phonological transparency.

7 Some comments are in order. First, I ignore the possessive agreement suffix illustrated in many of the forms in (7)–(10). There is some evidence, largely phonological, that it is outside possessive structure. Whether it is a head or not requires further investigation. Second, as

the structures in question are compounds, I assume that they are lexically formed. This suggests that the structure which houses the [voice] autosegment, labelled I in (14a), is available lexically. This is turn suggests that this inflectional item can have lexical as well as syntactic properties. The consequence of this is that the strict identification of inflection as syntactic must be weakened, although the configurational properties that identify an item as inflectional are present.

8 In some Athapaskan languages (e.g. Carrier, Koyukon), noun-stem-initial fricatives are voiced in possessed compounds as well as in the other environments in which the voiced alternant occurs in Slave.

9 In some forms, a diminutive or augmentative has become lexicalized and forms part of the minimal word with the stem. This can be seen in two ways. First, the inflectional suffix is on the right edge rather than internal, and second, the voiceless form of a noun-stem-initial fricative occurs. These effects can be seen in the following forms: tɬį 'dog', -lįɛ 'dog, possessed form'. The uninflected stem historically began with a voiceless lateral fricative. While restructuring to a lateral affricate has occurred, the possessive form reflects the old alternation. In possessed compound forms, the initial of this stem fails to voice: thus -tɬįtɬ'ulɛ 'dog harness, possessed form'. An augmentative form of this word exists which has not the expected meaning of 'large dog', but rather an idiosyncratic meaning: 'horse'. In this form, the inflectional suffix is exterior to the augmentative, and the affricate,

rather than the voiced fricative, appears: for example, tłįcho 'horse', -tłįchoé 'horse, possessed form'.

10 These terms are used idiosyncratically in the Athapaskan literature, and should not be equated with the usual definitions. 'Mode' refers to morphemes which mark aspectual categories of imperfective and perfective, the modal category of optative, and the tense category of future. 'Aspect' also refers to what is traditionally thought of as aspect: morphemes marking concepts such as inceptive, terminative, semelfactive and conative.

11 The template in (22) is somewhat different from that proposed by Kari 1976, 1990. Kari places a single disjunct boundary between the incorporate and the direct object as part of the template, and uses + boundary between the disjunct morphemes themselves.

12 It is claimed that themes can include disjunct as well as conjunct morphemes (e.g. K. Rice 1989 on Slave). However, a search of the South Slavey verb lexicon (Howard 1990) fails to reveal any real cases of this. A commonly cited example is the form *ya-ti* 'preach, bark'. However, *ya*, an incorporate meaning 'word', does not appear in all bases involving this root, suggesting that the theme does not include this morpheme.

13 There is dispute about where conjugation and primary aspect are added.

14 See n. 7, however, where it is pointed out that not all inflectional items can be considered to be syntactic. The possessive agreement marker discussed in section 2 has configurational properties, but in compounds these are lexical rather than syntactic.

15 As discussed in section 2.1, phonological properties also enter into the ordering of gender and secondary aspect. Interestingly, there may be less of a difference between the two hypotheses for ordering of conjunct elements than initially appears. Under both hypotheses, the ordering qualifier (gender/secondary aspect) – conjugation (primary aspect) – subject is found. This overall order, I have argued, is established by semantics. The difference between the hypotheses comes in the subordering within the qualifier zone, where Kari argues that the ordering is strictly by template, while I have suggested that the ordering is a combination of semantics factors with a template. It thus seems that a hypothesis that combines features of the two hypotheses, with semantics providing first-degree ordering and a template providing second-degree ordering, would be in order.

16 This ordering is similar to that found by Bybee (1985) in her survey of morpheme ordering in fifty languages; however, Bybee's survey is based on surface morpheme order and Speas's on a more abstract underlying order, so they are not directly comparable.

17 McDonough (1990) proposes for Navajo that the conjunct component is formed in the lexicon and forms an inflectional stem. Specifically, she argues that subject and primary aspect form a portmanteau; the positions that I have labelled 'secondary aspect' and 'gender' (and also deictic subject and direct object) are prefixed to this unit. The inflectional stem and verb stem compound in the lexicon, forming a verb word. Her hypothesis is overly restrictive in forcing regular as well

as irregular morphology to be considered as single morphs, and faces several phonological problems in that predicted phonological characteristics are not always found and non-predicted ones are.

18 Thank you to Lisa Travis for this suggestion.

19 The so-called direct discourse verbs (K. Rice 1989, Saxon 1986) allow for an interpretation where a first-person singular subject marks that the subject of a lower clause is co-referential with the subject of the higher clause.

31 Wari' (Amazonian)

DANIEL L. EVERETT

1 Introduction

The purpose of this chapter is to provide an overview of inflectional and derivational morphology in Wari', a Chapacuran language spoken along the Brazil–Bolivia border, in the state of Rondônia, Brazil. This is only the second published study ever made of a Chapacuran language, the only other surviving languages of this family being (apparently) More (spoken in Bolivia) and 'Oro Win, spoken by a group of approximately forty individuals living among the Wari'.[1] Wari' is divided into eight close and mutually intelligible dialects, each spoken by a separate cultural subgroup (cf. Vilaça 1992 for details). The dialect described here is that of the 'Oro Nao' (lit. 'The bats').[2]

The chapter is organized as follows. First, I offer a brief overview of Wari' syntax and phonology. I will next provide an overview of word classes in Wari'. Next, I discuss inflectional morphology. Finally, I describe the very interesting derivational morphology of Wari', arguing that some derivational processes in Wari' follow the syntax. Given the space limitations of this volume, I am only able to provide the briefest overview of Wari' morphology here. The reader is advised to consult Everett and Kern (1997, henceforth EK) for more details.

2 An overview of Wari' syntax and phonology

2.1 Phonology

In this section I discuss only those elements of Wari' phonology absolutely crucial to the understanding of Wari' morphology: the phonemic inventory and the rules of vowel harmony and stress placement. For a fuller discussion of Wari' phonology, the reader is referred to EK.

2.1.1 Phonemic inventory The phonemes of Wari' are as follows (with orthographic symbols given in quotes when these differ from the phonemic symbol): /p/, /t/, /k/ 'c' before /a/, /o/, and /ü/; 'qu' before /e/ and /i/; /kʷ/ 'cw' /ʔ/ '''', /tš/ 'x'; /h/, /hʷ/ 'hw'; /m/, /mʔ/ 'm''; /n/, /nʔ/ 'n''; /r/ 'r'; /w/, /y/ 'j'; /i/, /e/, /ö/, /a/, /o/, /ü/ 'u'; /eⁱ/ 'ei'; /aⁱ/ 'ai'; /oⁱ/ 'oi'; /iᵒ/ 'io'.[3]

2.1.2 Vowel harmony The types of vowel harmony most relevant to us here are the following (all of which are word-internal only).

All consecutive tense front mid-vowels are laxed when the final /e/ precedes a nonglottal plosive.

(1)

$$
\text{Ce(Ce)}^{n}\text{Ce} \qquad \text{C} \qquad \rightarrow \qquad \text{Ce(Ce)}^{n}\text{Ce} \qquad \text{C}
$$

$$
\text{[ATR]} \begin{bmatrix} \text{−cont} \\ \text{+place} \end{bmatrix} \qquad\qquad \text{[ATR]} \begin{bmatrix} \text{−cont} \\ \text{+place} \end{bmatrix}
$$

The next type of vowel harmony is seen in the fact that all nonlow vowels become [ü] when preceding a [ü] in the same word, and there is no intervening /a/:

(2)

$$
[\ldots (\text{V})^{n} \text{ C V (C)}] \qquad \rightarrow \qquad [\ldots (\text{V})^{n} \text{ C V (C)}]
$$

$$
\text{[−low]} \begin{bmatrix} \text{+rd} \\ \text{+high} \\ \text{+front} \end{bmatrix} \qquad\qquad \text{[−low]} \begin{bmatrix} \text{+rd} \\ \text{+high} \\ \text{+front} \end{bmatrix}
$$

The rules of vowel harmony are important, since they operate only internal to (grammatical) words. As mentioned below, they operate within verbs and nouns, but not between verbs and verbal inflectional clitics (VICs) or nouns and nominal inflectional clitics (NICs).

2.2 Syntax

2.2.1 Basic constituent order Wari' is a VOS language: that is, the verb always precedes direct (and indirect) objects, which in turn precede the subject. However, there are two fundamentally different types of sentences in Wari', both of which maintain the VOS order, but in different contexts. These are verb-initial and COMP-initial sentences. These sentences differ primarily in the relative positions of the verb and the tense marker(s), as well as in agreement patterns and whether or not there is an overt element in COMP (i.e. a nonverbal element in sentence-initial position). Consider the examples below:

2.2.1.1 Verb-initial sentences

(3) Quep na   -in xirim te   pane   ta.
     do   3sg.:rp/p-3n. house father:1sg. rem.:past emph.
     'My father made a house long ago.'

(4) Quep xucucun   hwijima' ma'.
     do   reflexive:3pl.m. children that:prox.:hearer
     'The children fought each other.'

(5) To' xima   -on   womi -um ta.
     hit 2sg.:irr. -3sg.m. cotton -2sg. emph.
     'You should wash (lit. hit) your clothes.'

(6) Ten   ta   wao'.
     weave pass.:3sg. type of basket
     'Baskets are woven.'

2.2.1.2 COMP-initial sentences

These differ from simple V-initial sentences in three ways: (i) there is a COMP(lementizer) or 'operator' word in sentence-initial position; (ii) an INFL(ectional) morpheme usually follows the operator/COMP word. This morpheme combines tense and agreement, like postverbal VICs, but its 'φ-features' (cf. Everett 1996) are governed by COMP, rather than the subject or object directly, as with VICs; the INFL morpheme also precedes the verb; (iii) the inflectional morphemes following the verb (the VIC) are tenseless, *unless* the COMP refers to a masculine or feminine *subject*.

(7) Ma'   co   tomi na?
     that:prox.:hearer INFL:m/frp/p speak 3sg.:rp/p
                                          VIC
     'Who is speaking?'

(8) Ma' co tomi' ca?
                   3sg.m.
                   VIC
     'Of whom is he speaking?'

Notice the lack of tense on the VIC in (8), (9), and (11), where a *nonsubject* is questioned.

(9) Ma'   ca   para 'aca ca   pije ma'?
     that:prox.:hearer INFL:nrp/p why cry 3sg.m. child that:prox.:hearer
     'Why is the child crying?'

(10) 'om   ca   mao ca.
     not:exist INFL:nrp/p go(sg.) 3sg.m.
     'He did not go.'

(11) Cain'   xi   xirao' ta'?
     that:n.:distal INFL:irr. write 1sg.
     'How shall I write?'

We can account for several of the differences between C-initial and V-initial sentences if we assume that the C-word is in COMP, the INFL word agrees with COMP (presumably because it has been moved to the head of COMP, C^0 (cf. Everett 1996), and that tense must be located on the second X^0-level constituent of the clause.[4]

2.2.2 Agreement

There are four principal points at which agreement appears in Wari' constituent structure: following COMP, following the verb, following possessed nouns, and on the preposition. Agreement morphemes, along with their phonological/grammatical host, can all be the target of rules of the derivational morphology, so it is important to provide a careful introduction of these prior to taking up the morphology proper. I will review VICs, NICs, *-xi* suffixes, and C^0/INFL morphemes, in that order.

2.2.2.1 VICs   *Subject agreement*: The subject always triggers agreement on the postverbal, *verbal inflectional clitic*, VIC. Objects may also trigger agreement on the VIC, although the conditions under which object agreement occurs are more complex. Subject agreement is illustrated in (12):[5]

(12) (a)   Mao   na   'orowao'.
         go(sg.) 3sg.:rp/p masc. name
         'Orowao went.'

     (b)   Mao na.
         'He went.'

     (c)   'om   ca   mao ca.
         not:exist INFL:nrp/p go(sg.) 3sg.m.
         'He did not go.'

     (d)   Mao 'ina.
         go(sg.) 1sg.:rp/p
         'I went.'

The only case I am aware of in which subject agreement may be omitted is when the subject is third person and the object is first person, although even in this case, subject agreement is not prohibited from occuring:

(13) (a) Tapa′ na   -pa′ wina-∅.
           burst 3sg.:rp/p -1sg. head-1sg.
           'My head is hurting me' (lit. 'Bursting to me').

      (b) Tapa′ pa′ wina-∅.
           'My head is hurting.'

(14) (a) ′om   na   -parut.
           not:exist 3sg.:rp/p -1pl. excl.
           'We do not have any.' (Lit. 'It does not exist to us.')

      (b) ′om parut.
           'We do not have any.' (Lit. 'It does not exist to us.')

Object agreement: This is partially determined by semantic role, definiteness, and Wh-movement, in addition to grammatical function. As with the subject, third-person direct object may be referenced by a pronoun and vic, or NP and vic, or just one member of either of these two pairs:

(15) (a) To′ na   -on   'Orowao'.
           hit 3sg.:rp/p -3sg.m. masc. name
           'He hit Orowao.'

      (b) To′ na -on co   ma′.
                       masc. that:prox.:hearer
           'He hit him.' (Lit. 'That masculine one near you.')

      (c) To′ na-on.
           'He hit him.'

      (d) To′ na 'Orowao'.
           'He hit Orowao.'

      (e) To′ na.
           'He is hitting.'

However, unlike subject agreement, object agreement can indicate the definiteness of the object:

(16) (a) Pa′ ma   hwam?
           kill 2sg.:rp/p fish
           'Did you kill a/the fish?'

      (b) Pa′ ma-on hwam?
                 -3sg.m.
           'Did you kill the/a fish?'

In (16), the articles are listed in order of preference, so that (16b) has a preferred definite reading, and (16a) has a preferred indefinite reading.

The VIC agrees with the direct object, which is the NP (overt or covert) to the immediate right of a transitive verb (in most cases). As EK describes it, the direct object and subject are the only NPs that may be moved, either via NP or Wh-movement. However, the NP which manifests the grammatical function of direct object is determined according to the semantic/thematic hierarchy in (17) (cf. EK for details):

(17) Goal > Circumstance > Theme/Patient > Instrument > Location > Time

I will illustrate here only the fact that Circumstance takes precedence over Theme/Patient for mapping to the direct object position, since that is the only really surprising part of the hierarchy in (17).

(18) (a) Mam to' 'ina   -in ca   xain ne
           instr. hit 1sg.:rp/p-3n. INFL:nrp/p hot   poss.:1sg.
           con   womi-u.
           prep.:3sg.m. cotton-1sg.
           'I washed my clothes with a fever.'

      (b) *Mam to' 'ina   -on   womi -u pain
           instr. hit 1sg.:rp/p-3sg.m. cotton-1sg. prep.:3n.
           ca   xain ne.
           INFL:nrp/p hot poss.:1sg.
           'I washed my clothes with a fever.'

In addition, an NP outside the subcategorization frame of the verb, not introduced by a preposition, may be referenced on the object position of the VIC as an "ethical dative" (as is common in Romance languages, for example; cf. Everett 1996). Any additional (nonsubject) arguments can only be expressed as PPs:

(19) Noc nana -pa' con   panxi-ta'.
      dislike 3pl.:rp/p-1sg. prep.:3sg.m. son   -1sg.
      'They dislike my son.' (Lit. 'They dislike to me my son.')

In this example, we would have expected agreement with the theme, *panxita'* 'my son', but instead, agreement is with '1p' 'me'. Another example of this "ethical dative" is found in (20):

(20) To' cat ne   xe.
      hit break 2sg.:1sg.:rf fire/firewood
      'Cut me some firewood.'

Also in (20), we would have expected agreement with *xe* 'firewood' as the theme of *to' cat* 'hit/break' (= 'cut'). It might be that ethical dative agreement could be subsumed under what we have already said about CIRCUMSTANCE, if the ethical dative is considered a circumstance of the action. In any case, these examples are sufficient to show that object agreement is not as simple as subject agreement.

Anti-agreement effects: Wh-moved objects, unlike subjects, may never trigger agreement on the VIC. This, coupled with the fact that only NPs potentially referenceable (in a given clause) on the VIC may be moved, results in an anti-agreement effect in which verbs of clauses with Wh-moved objects may only agree with their subjects:

(21) (a)   Querec ma   -on   wijam.
             see   *2sg.:rp/p-3sg.m. enemy*
             'You saw the enemy (= non-Wari').'

      (b)   Ma'   wijam co   querec ma?
             that:prox.:hearer enemy INFL:m/frp/p see   2sg.
             'Which enemy (= non-Wari') did you see?'

      (c)   *Ma'   wijam co   querec ma-on?
             that:prox.:hearer enemy INFL:m/frp/p see   2sg.-3sg.m.
             'Which enemy (= non-Wari') did you see?'

This completes our brief overview of Wari' syntax and phonology. We are now ready to turn to the morphology proper.

3 Wari' Morphology Proper

3.1 Word classes

In EK the following word classes are identified: nouns (subdivided into *-xi'* and non-*xi'* nouns), pronouns (subdivided into emphatic and demonstrative pronouns), verbs (subdivided into modificational and nonmodificational verbs), a preposition (only one in the language), inflectional clitics (subdivided into nominal (NICs) vs verbal inflectional clitics (VICs)), particles, INFL morphemes, COMP words, and ideophones.

3.1.1 Nouns Nouns are distinguishable from other word classes by the following criteria: (i) they may bear possessive suffixes or have NICs cliticized to them; (ii) they may be followed by any of the spatial/temporal demonstratives; (iii) they may appear as subject or object of a verb (in particular, only nouns may govern agreement on the VIC); (iv) they may appear as complement of (the) preposition; (v) they may occur in sequence with another noun in a possessive NP.

Table 31.1   Demonstrative pronouns

	prox. to speaker	*prox. to hearer*	*distal*
masc. sg.	co cwa'	co ma'	co cwain
fem. sg.	cam cwa'	cam ma'	cam cwain
neuter	'i ca'	'i ma'	'i cain
plural	caram cwa'	caram ma'	caram cwain
	seen/not heard	*recently absent*	*long absent*
masc. sg.	co paca'	co pacara ne	co pacara pane
fem. sg.	cam paca'	cam pacara ne	cam pacara pane
neuter	('i paca')	'i cara ne	'i cara pane
plural	caram paca'	caram pacara ne	caram pacara pane

3.1.2 Pronouns   There are two classes of pronouns: demonstrative and emphatic (there are no personal pronouns). The demonstrative pronoun is in fact a subclass of nouns, satisfying three of the syntactic distributional criteria for nouns: (i) it may appear as subject or object of the verb; (ii) it may be the complement of a preposition; (iii) it may be the possessor of an NP. However, *un*like other nouns, a pronoun cannot be suffixed by a possessive morpheme or be followed directly by an NIC, nor can it be followed by a demonstrative. Both types of pronouns are illustrated in the tables and examples which follow:

3.1.2.1 Demonstrative pronouns   Demonstrative pronouns occur only in the third person. They are listed in table 31.1. Note especially the separate dimensions of spatial and temporal proximity in the demonstrative pronoun paradigm.

Demonstratives may also be used as personal pronouns. They may appear in apposition to emphatic pronouns (22), or in subject (23), or verbal object position (24). They may *not* appear as object of a preposition, as in (25).

(22)   Wirico   **co cwa'**   co   pa' na   -in   mijac pane.
        emph:3sg.m.   m. this:m/f   INFL:mfrp/p   kill   3sg.:rp/p-3n.   pig   rem.:past
        'He himself, this masculine one, was the one who killed the pig.'

(23)   Maqui' na   **co ma'**.
        come   3sg.:rp/p m   that:prox.:hearer
        'He came.' (Lit. 'That masculine one near you came.')

(24)   Querec na   -m   **cam ma'**   Xijam.
        see   3s:rp/p-3sg.f.   f.sing.   that:prox.:hearer   masc.:name
        'Xijam saw her.' (Lit. 'Xijam saw that feminine one.')

(25) *Mi na   -m   con   hwam   cam cwa'.
      give 3sg.:rp/p-3sg.f. prep:3sg.m. fish(masc.) f.   this:m/f
      'The man gave her the fish.'

3.1.2.2 Emphatic pronouns   Emphatic pronouns may occur in any person or number, except that neuter gender in emphatic pronouns, like neuter gender throughout the language, does not inflect for number.[6] Emphatic pronouns may not occur in a verbal argument position. However, third-person emphatic pronouns may occur in apposition to a subject NP. Third-person emphatic pronouns can appear only in apposition to a verbal object NP in coordinate structures, and in this case must follow the first conjunct. First- and second-person emphatic pronouns can only appear in lists of names which clarify participants (26), or in isolation, as answers to questions (27). Emphatic pronouns, in rare cases in discourse, may be verbalized (28).

(26)   Ji'am xi'   jowin   pain   ca'   ma' 'urut Jimain
          hunt 1pl. incl.:rf monkey:species prep:3n. this:n. that:prox.:hearer
          'urut Jimain Hwara' Waji,   Wem Xao, wata'.
          1pl. excl:rp/p m.:name m.:name emph.:1sg.
          ' "We will (go) hunting for *jowin* monkey," we (said), Jimain Hwara' Waij, We Xao, and I.'

(27) (a) Ma'   wari' ma'   quem?
           that:prox.:hearer person that:prox.:hearer ref.
           'Who is it?'

      (b) Wata'.
           emph:1sg.
           '(It is) I.'

(28)   Ma' **wirico**   na   Pinom ma'.
          exist emph.:3sg.m. 3sg.:rp/p m.:name that:prox.:hearer
          'There was Pinom.'

Emphatic pronouns are as follows:

1sg.	wata'
2sg.	wum
3sg.m.	wirico
3sg.f.	wiricam
3sg.n.	je
1pl. incl.	wari'
1pl. excl.	warut
2pl.	wahu'
3pl.m.	wiricoco
3pl.f.	wiricacam

3.1.3 Verbs Verbs are distinguished by (i) their potential to be compounded with another verb or verbal modifier and (ii) their ability to be followed directly by vics.[7] There are two subclasses in addition to the main verbs discussed in EK. These are pre- and postverbal modifiers, which can appear only when compounded with another verb. Some modifiers may appear in either pre- or postverbal positions, although there are usually (slight to significant) meaning changes associated with the different positions. As discussed below, there is a highly productive set of derivational processes for forming verbs from other lexical classes.

3.1.4 Preposition There is a single preposition in the language, inflected (often suppletively) for person, number, and, in the case of the third person, gender (cf. (18), (19), and (26) above).

1sg.	pata'
2sg.	pum
3sg.m.	con
3sg.f.	cam
3n.	pain
1pl. incl.	pari'
1pl. excl.	parut
2pl.	pahu'
3pl.m.	cocon
3pl.f.	cacam

3.1.5 Inflectional clitics (vics and nics) Another morphological class is formed by the inflectional clitics: what EK refer to as vics (*verbal inflectional clitics*) and nics (*nominal inflectional clitics*). vics must follow the verb, and nics must follow non-*xi* possessor nouns. nics form a separate prosodic unit for purposes of stress and vowel harmony from the noun. The set of nics is given below.

1sg.	ne
2sg.	nem
3sg.m.	nucun
3sg.f.	nequem
3sg.n.	nein
1pl. incl.	nexi'
1pl. excl.	nuxut
2pl.	nuhu'
3pl.m.	nucucun
3pl.f.	nequequem

As shown in the examples below, nics may occur with or without a possessive NP:

(29)   nanacam' nucun.
       fish:species poss.:3sg.m.
       'his **nanacam'** fish.'

(30)   xirim nucun   Mirin.
       house poss.:3sg.m. m.:name
       'Mirin's house.'

VICs must follow the verb. Like NICs, VICs form a separate prosodic unit. In the case of VICs this prosodic independence is perhaps more interesting due to the fact that VICs are composed of *both* object and subject agreement. That is, the VIC forms a prosodic word, although it is morphosyntactically composed exclusively of affixes, without a *root*.[8] Cf. section 2.2.2.1 above for examples.

3.1.6 Particles   There is a very small class of clitics/particles which occur in or near sentence-final position, used to mark pragmatic information, such as gender of audience, emphasis, doubt on the part of the speaker, and temporal information (usually taking the entire sentence into its scope). (Cf. EK 2.1.8.1.6 for more details.)

These clitic forms behave like separate prosodic words, although their status as distinct grammatical words is difficult to determine. I have assumed here that they are words both morphologically and prosodically, although this assumption may need to be modified or abandoned after further study.

3.1.7 INFL morphemes   EK label five second-position clitics as INFL(ection) morphemes. These five express tense and, in two cases, gender. They are *co* 'masculine/feminine realis past/present', *ca* 'neuter realis past/present, *iri* 'realis past/present', *ta* 'realis future', and *xi* 'irrealis'. An INFL morpheme's gender features are governed by the gender of the COMP word (i.e. a sentence-initial word indicating mood or subordination). An INFL morpheme co-occurs with a tense VIC if and only if the COMP morpheme references a masculine/feminine subject:

(31)   Ma'   co   tomi' na?
       that:prox.:hearer INFL:m/frp/p speak 3sg.:rp/p
       'Who is speaking?'

(32)   Ma'   ca   querec ca?
       that:prox.:hearer INFL:nrp/p see   3sg.m.
       'What did he see?'

(33)   Ma'   xi'   'awin na   -in cwa'?
       that:prox.:hearer INFL:irr take   3sg.rp/p-3n. this:m/f
       'Who shall take it?'

Table 31.2 COMP words

Declarative only		*Interrogative only*	
mo	'conditional'	ma'	'general inter.'
'ac	'resemblance'	mon	'masculine inter.'
'ane	'contraexpectation'	mam	'feminine inter.
		main	'neuter inter.'
		cain	'distal inter.'
Both[9]			
'om	'negation'		
je	'affirmation/interrogation'		
'pain	subordination/distant past'		

(34) Ma'   co   tomi' ca?
      that:prox.:hearer INFL:m/frp/p speak 3sg.m.
      'Of whom is he speaking?'

(35) Ma'   wari' co   mao   na?
      that:prox.:hearer person INFL:m/frp/p go (sg.) 3sg.rp/p
      'What person went?'

3.1.8 COMP words EK points out that Wari' makes a fundamental distinction between COMP-initial and non-COMP-initial sentences, a distinction which applies to both matrix and embedded clauses. The COMP words select for specific INFL morphemes and are always sentence-initial. Some COMP words can appear only in declarative sentences, others only in interrogatives, and still others in either (see table 31.2). Examples are found in (36) and (37):

(36) Ma   -in ca   mao   ca?
      that:prox.:hearer -n. INFL:nrp/p go(sg.) 3sg.m.
      'Where did he go?'

(37) Mo   xi   pi'am cacama.
      conditional INFL:irr sleep   3pl.f.
      'If they slept'

The analysis of EK proposes that many of the COMP word distinctions listed above result from SPEC-head agreement within the COMP phrase.

3.1.9 Ideophones Wari' has a relatively large number of ideophones, discussed in detail in EK. These, according to the traditional definition, are onomatopoeically based, but may be inflected like any other word of the same major class.

3.2 *Inflectional morphology*

Possessive marking is handled by NICS (cf. 3.1.5 above) or via a set of suffixes indicating inalienable possession (what EK calls *-xi* suffixes). The latter are illustrated in (38):

(38)   (a)   'ara-con
             bone-3sg.m.
             'his bone/leg'

       (b)   wina-hu
             head-2pl.
             'your head'

       (c)   *at nucun
             bone poss.:3sg.m.
             'his bone/leg'

Example (38c) is ungrammatical because an inalienably possessed noun can only take one of the *-xi* suffixes, not a NIC.

Other distinctions among NPs are made by word order, prepositional marking, and agreement with the VIC. Objects precede the subject NP; oblique NPs (those which are neither subjects nor direct or indirect objects) follow the subject. The direct object and subject NPs trigger VIC agreement, although this is obligatory only for subjects (see below). The indirect object is preceded by the appropriately inflected form of the preposition (cf. second part of section 2.2.2.1 above for semantic criteria in determining which NP will be the direct vs indirect object).

Definiteness is indicated (loosely) by verbal agreement (39), or with demonstrative pronouns (40). A VIC need not agree with the object, unless the object is definite, in which case it must:

(39)   (a)   Cao' 'ina   hwam.
             eat   1sg.:rp/p fish
             'I ate fish.'

       (b)   Cao' ina   -on   hwam.
             eat   1sg.:rp/p-3sg.m. fish
             'I ate (*the*) fish.' ((*the*) is required if **hwam** is to be interpreted as definite)

Demonstratives usually only follow the last noun in the clause or a noun in isolation, indicating that they prefer utterance-final position.

(40) tarama' cwa'
      man   this
      'this man'

3.3 Derivational morphology

Wari' makes generous use of zero-derivation and compounding for word formation, deriving verbs from nominals and sentences and deriving nouns from sentences, subsentential constituents, verbs, and relative clauses. These are exemplified in the following subsections.

3.3.1 Zero-derivation Various kinds of words are derived from other syntactic constituents with no affixal morphology, and hence are labeled as *zero-derivation* by EK: for example, from sentences:

(41) [$_{S3}$ [$_{V3}$ [$_{V2}$ [$_{V1}$ [$_{S2}$ [$_{S1}$ Pan'   'am   ta']   tara]]ma']]
                              fall(sg.) be:lost 1sg.:rf 3sg.:rf that:prox.:hearer
      ina   -on   xa'].
      1sg.:rp/p-3sg.m. younger:brother:1sg.
      'I thought my younger brother was going to get lost.' (Lit. '"I will probably get lost, he will probably (say)," I (thought) (of) my younger brother.')

In (41), the derivation is as follows: first we begin with the sentence *pan' am ta'* 'I get lost', which undergoes zero-derivation to form a verb. This derived verb is then inflected by the addition of the VIC *tara*. This new sentence itself then undergoes zero-derivation and is compounded with the particle, *ma'*. The resultant predicate is then inflected by the VIC *ina-on*, which is in turn followed by *xa'* 'younger brother', the object of V3.

Verbs may also be formed via zero-derivation from nominals: for example, from pronouns. We already saw in 3.1.2.2 above that emphatic pronouns may undergo zero-derivation to form a verb. Nouns may also undergo zero-derivation, with different results semantically, according to the type of noun which undergoes the process.

They may also be formed from nouns and nouns + NICs. If the input noun is in the first person (whether the noun is a *-xi* noun or a noun followed by a NIC), the resultant verb is active, often taking an agentive or volitional subject. When a non-first-person form of the noun serves as input to verb derivation, the result is either a descriptive predicate or, in compound forms, an adverbial-like translation of the denominalized portion of the compound. Some examples are given below.

(42) capija-xi' (citation form)
      mouth-1pl. incl.
      'our mouth'

(43)   capija -∅   na   panxi-ca   'Orowao.
         mouth -1sg. 3sg:rp/p child-3sg.m. m.:name
         'Orowao's son talks (i.e. is talkative).'

(44)   wijima-xi
         'our smallness'

(45) (a) Ma'   co   wijima -∅   na   -em?
           that:prox.:hearer INFL:m/frp/p smallness-1sg. 3sg.:rp/p-2sg.
           'Who gave birth to you?'

      (b) Cut   wijima -in 'ina   -in.
           take (pl.) smallness-3n. 1sg.:rp/p-3n.
           'I took a little bit.'

In these examples, especially the last pair, we see that the form of the input noun can drastically affect the semantics of the output verb.

Nouns can be formed by various types of constituents. For example, consider (46):

(46)   Hohot na   ca   mixein ne.
       okay   3sg.:nrp/p INFL:nrp/p lie   poss.:1sg.
       'My lying is OK.'

In this example, the noun 'lying' is formed from the verb, *mixein* 'lie', plus the INFL morpheme *ca* 'neuter realis past/present'. Such examples are interesting, of course, since they both provide insight into Wari' constituent structure, and are important clues to the structure of the clause in Universal Grammar. This is so since they indicate that INFL and the verb form a constituent (cf. EK for detailed argumentation that the INFL morpheme really does correspond to INFL in GB-theoretic terms).

3.3.2 Compounding
Compounding is easily the most productive process for deriving subtypes of verbs. EK analyzes the leftmost member of the compound as the semantic "core" and head of the compound. Other members are added in a rather iconic fashion, meaning that their relative ordering reflects the relative ordering of the individual events in the real world. Up to five verb roots have been found in a compound verb structure:

(47)   Pan' corom mama' pin 'awi nana.
       fall enter go(pl.) completely completely 3pl.:rp/p
       'They all fell into the water.'

3.3.3 Reduplication
Wari' has a number of different reduplication strategies, from reduplication of the entire word to partial reduplication. INFL morphemes

are almost in complementary distribution with reduplication in the sense that INFL morphemes are usually omitted in the context of a(n immediately governing) reduplicated verb. Cf. EK (317ff) for more details. Only a few examples are given here.

(48) (a) wac 'cut' (sg.)
     (b) wawac 'cut' (pl.)

(49) (a) cao' 'eat' (sg.)
     (b) cacacao' 'eat' (pl.)

(50) (a) cat 'break' (sg.)
     (b) caracat 'break' (pl.)

(51) (a) hwet 'appear' (sg.)
     (b) hwerehwet 'appear' (pl.)

(52) (a) capija-∅
          mouth -1sg.
          'my mouth'

     (b) capija capija 'talkative person'

NOTES

1 This language was previously known only to New Tribes missionaries working among the Wari'; I discovered its existence only in March 1994.

2 The other subgroups are the *'Oro 'Eo* 'The burpers', the *'Oro 'At* 'The bones', the *'Oro Jowin* 'The jowin monkeys', the *'Oro Waram* 'The waram monkeys', the *'Oro Waram Xijein* 'The other waram monkeys', the *'Oro Cao 'Orowaji* 'The eaters of green things', and the *'Oro Mon* 'The feces' (these are all names accepted by the members of the relevant subgroups and are not understood as derogatory). The Wari' have practiced endo-cannibalism (eating their own dead) and exo-cannibalism (eating their enemies) for their known history. Aparecida Vilaça (anthropologist, *Museu Nacional*, Rio de Janeiro) believes that this no longer takes place, although Barbara Kern, who has lived with the Wari' for thirty-two years, believes that in the absence of foreigners, endo-cannibalism is still practiced on people whose cause of death is poorly understood. (This, of course, has nothing whatsoever to do with Wari' morphology, but is fascinating enough culturally to warrant mention here, given that the people and language have never been discussed before in the linguistic literature.)

3 In EK, the diphthongs are incorrectly given as underlyingly nasalized. This unnecessary complication of the

phonemic inventory can be avoided if we simply posit a rule nasalizing both members of a diphthong.

4   The alternative would be to say simply that tense must be suffixed onto the first grammatical word. However, this would require us to analyze VICs as suffixes and INFL as a suffix on COMP. At this point in my analysis, I do not like either of these consequences, so I will stick to the analysis in the text.

5   EK points out that vowel harmony does not cross from the verb to the VIC, although it does operate within VICs and verbs independently.

6   Note that the 1pl. incl. form of the demonstrative is used as the name of the entire culture-language group by the people themselves.

7   Superficially, this diagnostic does not seem to work when following a *verbalized sentence*, since, as we will see below, a VIC may in fact appear after any word type which can occur at the end of a sentence. However, the criterion in the text refers to abstract syntactic boundaries, not merely the phonologically adjacent word, as in $[_v [_s \ldots NP \ldots]_s]_v$ VIC. In this example, the VIC directly follows V, not S or NP.

8   The reader is referred to EK, 269ff for a more complete listing and discussion of VICs.

9   Cf. EK 29ff for more details.

32 Warumungu (Australian – Pama-Nyungan)

JANE SIMPSON

1 Introduction

Warumungu is a language spoken by a few hundred people in the central part of the Northern Territory of Australia around Tennant Creek. The speakers have suffered greatly from the invasion of their country and their dispossession. Through some successful land claims, they have regained some of this country, and many continue to work to overcome the tragic effects of the invasion on their families, health, culture and language. The language is undergoing rapid change (as are many surviving Australian languages), and the morphology used by younger speakers differs greatly from that used by older speakers. The analysis here is based largely on analysis of older speakers' speech as in Hale 1959 and Heath 1977. (For annotated list of abbreviations used in this chapter, see appendix at end of chapter.)

Warumungu is a Pama-Nyungan language.[1] It is both a neighbour and a close relative of Warlpiri, whose morphology has been widely discussed (e.g. K. Hale 1973b, 1982, 1983; Nash 1986). Like Warlpiri and many other Pama-Nyungan languages, Warumungu is a suffixing language (although new verbs may be formed by compounding 'preverbs' with the verb root). Phonologically, Warumungu is set apart by the presence of three realizations of stops. Grammatically, it is a language with an Ergative-Absolutive case-marking system, but with subject–object cross-referencing by pronominal clusters. Word order is reserved mostly for pragmatic functions, while the main grammatical functions are expressed by nominal suffixes and pronominal clusters.

It is not possible to give a complete morphological description of Warumungu here. I shall focus instead on some aspects of the phonology and functions of word formation that seem interesting. These include:

morphophonological properties

    (i)   a fortis–lenis distinction in part distinctive and in part conditioned morphologically and phonologically. This interacts with a syllable-counting choice of case-suffix allomorph, and with verb reduplication.

    (ii)   complete vowel assimilation for most case suffixes

word formation properties

    (i)   a slot-and-filler (template) structured pronominal cluster
    (ii)   reduplication to indicate aspect, the form of which varies according to tense and conjugation
    (iii) portmanteau verb inflection indicating associated motion, tense and aspect
    (iv) derivational case

morphosyntactic properties

    (i)   the representation of grammatical functions by the interaction of pronominal clusters and case suffixes
    (ii)   the areal feature of using the ALLATIVE case suffix to represent location in a transitive sentence and a suffix homophonous with the ERGATIVE to represent location in an intransitive sentence

There are six principal classes of morphemes: nominals, preverbs, verb roots, bound pronouns, particles and suffixes.

Nominals form an open class that also contains several closed subclasses: demonstratives, genitive pronouns and predicative nouns. Nominal roots are always two or more syllables long, and may appear uninflected. Predicative nouns have more restricted possibilities for inflection. Nominal roots can be used to stand for things, or as predicates, whether as adjectives, secondary predicates or as the main predicate in a verbless sentence.

Verb roots form a semi-closed class (probably not more than a hundred or so), falling into four main conjugations. Verb roots may be one, two or, arguably, three syllables long. Verbs never appear uninflected. New verbs are formed productively by suffixing one of several bound verb roots to nominals or preverbs. Inflected verbs can only act as predicates in finite clauses; they have to be nominalized to appear as predicates in non-finite clauses. With one or two exceptions, verb roots are rigidly either transitive or intransitive.

Preverbs form an open class whose members have a status indeterminate between being free and bound. They attach loosely to verbs, although some preverbs may sometimes act as nominals in taking case suffixes. Preverbs may be one or more syllables long. If monosyllabic, their vowel is lengthened. They differ from regular words in permitting a wider range of final consonants, including stops.

Pronouns are a closed class. Non-subject pronouns are always bound (in a template structure), while subject pronouns may sometimes be free. Subject pronoun roots are all disyllabic. The boundaries and inflections of non-subject pronouns are not clear, but most non-subject pronoun roots are also disyllabic. Pronominal clusters always start with /a/.

Particles are a closed class. They do not inflect. They include both free particles (which are two or more syllables long) and enclitic particles (which may be monosyllabic). I represent the latter with a plus (+) boundary.

Suffixes include affixes attaching to nouns and verbs. I represent them with a hyphen (-) boundary. They may be monosyllabic, and the range of consonants appearing morpheme-initially is wider than those which can occur word-initially.

2 Phonology

2.1 Inventory

Warumungu has a typical Australian three-vowel system: /i/, /a/ and /u/. Each can be long, written 'aa', 'iyi' or 'ii', and 'uwu' or 'uu'. It has a typical Australian consonant system, with five places of articulation, and the usual manner possibilities. The existence of a second stop series is the only unusual feature. Table 32.1 shows allophones (in square brackets) and the orthographic representation in boldface.[2] Free-standing words are two or more syllables long, with the exception of a few words with long vowels: /piyi/ 'burnt-out country'. Borrowed English monosyllables are given long vowels: /yaat/ 'yard', /joop/ 'shop'. The minimum word structure is: (C)V(V)C(C)V(C).[3] Thus, consonant clusters cannot appear word-initially or word-finally.[4] They can, however, start bound morphemes: e.g. the verb suffix /-rrkarl/ FUTURE.AWAY.

Primary stress is assigned to the first syllable of a morpheme of two or more syllables. In a monomorphemic word of four or more syllables, secondary stress is assigned to alternating syllables: Wárumùngu. In complex words the primary stress on a morpheme is weakened following a primary stress: /ngáppa/ 'water', /ngápa-kàjji/ 'water' LEST. Reduplications, even frozen ones, act as complex words for stress assignment: /kíjji-pàkkarla-pàkkarla/ 'hawk species' (neither /kijji/ nor /pakkarla/ seem to have independent meaning).

Monosyllabic suffixes form units with the preceding syllables for stress assignment. Thus a trisyllabic word with a monosyllabic suffix acts like a quadrisyllabic monomorphemic word: /pápulù-kku/ 'house' DATIVE, while a two-syllable suffix retains its stress: /pápulu-kkùna/ 'house' ALLATIVE/ LOCATIVE. All preverbs (whether one or more syllables long) have primary stress, and the stress on the initial syllable of the verb is weakened to secondary stress: /púu-wàngka-n/ 'moo-talk' PRES = 'to bellow'.

Word-initially, most sounds can appear, with a few exceptions. The following are relevant here:

Table 32.1 Phonetic chart

	bilabial	apico-alveolar	apico-post alveolar	lamino-palatal[a]	dorso-velar
stop ~					
long voiceless	[pː] **pp**	[tː] **tt**	[ʈː] **rtt**	[cː~c̺ː] **jj**	[kː] **kk**
short voiceless	[p] **pp**	[t] **tt**	[ʈ] **rtt**	[c~c̺] **jj**	[k] **kk**
short voiced	[p~b] **p**	[t~d] **t**	[ʈ~ɖ] **rt**	[c~ɟ~c̺~ɟ̺] **j**	[k~g] **k**
nasal	[mː ~m] **m**	[nː~n~dn[b]] **n**	[ɳː~ɳ] **rn**	[ɲ~ɳ̺ː~ɲ~ɳ̺] **ny**	[ŋ~ɳ] **ng**
lateral	[lː~l~dl] **l**	[lː~ɭ] **rl**	[ʎː~ʎ~ʎ̺~ʎ̺] **ly**		
flap	[ɾ~r] **rr**				
semivowel	[w] **w**	[ɻ] **r**	[y] **y**		

Notes:

[a] Lamino-dentals are sometimes used instead of these.

[b] The very oldest speakers occasionally pre-stopped alveolar nasals and laterals instead of lengthening them.

(i)   There is no contrast in voice or length. Stops are phonetically short and usually voiced, although initial /k/ may be voiceless. Bound morphemes, however, show a voicing alternation: for example, /-kkari ~ -kari/ ([-kaɹi]~[-gaɹi]) RELATIVE suffix.

(ii)   There is no contrast between apico-alveolars and apico-postalveolars. They are written as /n/, /l/ and /t/. Bound morphemes, however, retain this distinction: for example, /-rni-~-rnti-~-rti-/ CAUSATIVE suffix, /-ntti~-ntta~-nttu/ ERGATIVE/LOCATIVE allomorph.

Word-finally, vowels are most common. Some sonorant consonants can occur: flaps, laterals and non-peripheral nasals. A handful of words have phonetically short and voiceless final stops.

Length and voicing of stops are distinctive word-medially, as Heath (1977) observes. That is, long voiceless stops contrast with short voiced stops: /api/ [abi] 'go' FUTURE, /lappi/ [lap:i] 'chest', /wajjingkarr/ [wac:iŋgaɻ] 'echidna', /wajirrki/ [waɟiɽgi] 'vegetation'. Short voiceless stops alternate predictably with short voiced stops in the initial position of certain suffixes, depending on the number of morae in the stem: [babulu-kuna] 'house' ALL/LOC, and [manu-guna] 'country' ALL/LOC.[5] Voiceless stops do not contrast with each other in length. The contrast can be seen as a fortis–lenis distinction, with the actual phonetic realization of fortis depending on the position in the word.

In a disyllabic word $C_1VC_2(C_3)$, C_2 is normally long if a nasal or lateral,[6] and voiceless and long if a stop. In a disyllabic word $C_1VC_2C_3V(C_4)$ the cluster C_2C_3 is normally long,[7] and C_3 is voiceless if a stop.

jana	[ɟan:a]	'high'
jala	[ɟal:a]	'mouth'
makku	[mak:u]	'flesh'
wankka	[wan.k.a]	'I don't know'
lirrppi	[liɽ.p.i]	'fingernail, claw'

Like pre-stopping and fortition in other Pama-Nyungan languages (Jaeger 1983, McKay 1980, Henderson 1992, Hercus 1972), fortition here is a manifestation of primary stress in the minimal word, a way of making the stressed syllable heavy. However, there are lexical exceptions.

Exceptions			Regular		
turtu	[ɖuɖu]	'sleep'	wurttu	[wuʈ:u]	'wind'
apan	[aba-n]	'go' PRES	apparr	[ap:aɻ]	'language'
yarnti	[yaɳɖi]	'one'	parnttarr	[baɳ.ʈ.aɻ]	'crack'
lurnku	[luŋgu~lu:ŋgu]	'kingfisher'	jurnkku	[ɟuɳ.k.u]	'nape'
yungga	[yuŋga]	'lie'	lungkku	[luŋ.k.u]	'lightning'
warlji	[waʎɟi]	'own, family'	waljji	[waʎ.c.i]	'bloodwood'

Some, but not all, of these are traceable to earlier monosyllables, [luuṇ+gu],[8] or reduplications of monosyllables, [ḍuu+ḍuu].

Here I use the orthographic convention of double consonants for fortis (long or short) stops (but not for nasals and laterals), and single consonants for lenis stops.

2.2 Major phonological processes

These include the following:

2.2.1 Vowel coalescence   In a sequence of two vowels, the first vowel is normally deleted, and the second may be lengthened. This coalescence is virtually obligatory inside words, /kumpp(u)-(y)ilppi/ [kump:i:lp:i] 'big' EXCESS = 'too big'. It is optional across word boundaries. If the second word starts with a semi-vowel, it is usually deleted too.

(1)   Kilyirr-(i) + ajj(u)   (y)ungka-n jina.   [kiʎiɾac:uŋgan]
      sun-ERG/LOC + me burn-PRES foot.ABS
      'The sun is burning my foot.' [KH[9]:SN:7]

2.2.2 Alveolar and postalveolar alternation   Following an alveolar flap an apico-alveolar is realized as an apico-postalveolar: /paki-nnyi/ 'spear' PAST.PUN, /marri-rnnyi/ 'call' PAST.PUN. (A similar phenomenon of neutralizing apical distinctions following a trill is found in Warlpiri (Nash, p.c.).)

2.2.3 Nasal + stop cluster dissimilation   Certain sequences of nasal + stop and nasal + stop in the same word are sometimes subject to dissimilation: /yarnti/ 'one' ABSOLUTIVE, /yarni-njji~yarnti-jji~yarnti-njji/ 'one' ERGATIVE/ LOCATIVE. This is an areal phenomenon, more strongly manifested in Mudburra (McConvell 1988).

2.2.4 Vowel assimilation   Vowel assimilation can be complete (between nominals and certain case suffixes).[10]

nanttu	nantu-ngku	[nandu-ŋgu]	'humpy' ERG/LOC
marla	marla-ngka	[maḷa-ŋga]	'shade' ERG/LOC
kartti	karti-ngki	[gaḍi-ŋgi]	'man' ERG/LOC

I shall write the vowel in such suffixes as V, /-ngkV/.

Partial vowel assimilation is found in pronoun clusters, and between verbs and some suffixes. Elements showing partial vowel assimilation have underlyingly high vowels (/i/ or /u/) in their initial syllables. If the final vowel of the root is high, then the suffix assimilates to it. If the final vowel is low, then the suffix appears in its underlying form; for example:

nyi-njjirra   'sit' FUTURE.HITHER
ngu-njjurra   'lie' FUTURE.HITHER
ja-njjirra   'stand' FUTURE.HITHER

2.2.5 Fortis–lenis alternations   The most striking morphophonological process (first systematically analysed in Heath 1977) concerns associations of stress, segment length, mora and voice, which appear as several fortis–lenis alternations, including:

(a)   a predictable alternation in disyllabic stems between long voiceless stops and short voiced stops depending on the affixation of certain suffixes (case suffixes, reduplication, some pronominal cluster parts, and, arguably, some verb inflectional suffixes): for example, [nan.t.u.] 'humpy', 'hut', [nandu-gu] 'humpy' DAT.

(b)   a strong tendency for the onset of the third syllable in three-syllable words to be lenis, /payinti/ [bayindi] 'now'. This includes those created by vowel coalescence: /murrkka/ [muɾ.k.a] 'hair', /murrkkalki/ [muɾkalgi] 'headband' (with ASSOCIATIVE derivational suffix /-alkki/). Contrast this with /payintalkki/ [bayindalki] 'new'.

(c)   arising from (b), is the predictable alternation of the initial stops of the case suffixes, /papulukku/ [babuluku] 'house' DATIVE, /manuku/ [manugu] 'country' DATIVE, as well as some reduplicated verbs: /pakkil/ [bak:il] 'spear' FUTURE, /pakkakil/ [bakagil] 'spear' FUTURE.CONTINUOUS.

(d)   a less predictable alternation involves the initial consonants of some verb suffixes, which depend partly on verb class and partly on root length.

paki-n-jirra	'cook' FUTURE.HITHER	L conjugation
nyi-n-jjirra	'sit' FUTURE.HITHER	R conjugation (1-syllable root)
mana-n-jjirra	'seek' FUTURE.HITHER	R conjugation

3 Word formation

Word-formation possibilities in Warumungu include compounding, suffixation, reduplication, and template (for pronouns).

3.1 Compounding

3.1.1 Noun compounding   Nouns may compound with other nouns to form nouns. Such forms are not common in our data. The order matches the preferred order in syntactic noun phrases: namely, head modifier.

jala-jirrppa	mouth-quiet	'bird sp.', 'Little Corella'
lappi-pulyurrulyurru	chest-red	'bird sp.', 'Port Lincoln Parrot'

I list a few types of compound:

kujjarra yarnti two-one	'three'	**coordinate**
parrakurl ngapa-kari billy can water-REL	'quart-pot'	**noun and derived noun**
jina-kari parrkkama-nj(i)-alkki foot-REL grasp-NOM-ASSOC	'horseshoe tongs'	**two derived nouns**
ngappa kangkurr-kangkurr water immersed-immersed	'rainy/wet weather'	**noun and preverb**
kárlampi-jùrrujùrru creek-?	'vine sp.'	**noun and frozen form**

3.1.2 Preverb–verb compounds

Preverb-verb compounding is very productive. Combining members of the open class of preverbs with the closed class of verb roots is one of the main ways Warumungu expresses different kinds of verbs.

The most productive preverbs are those that quantify an argument of the verb, and those that describe how an action is performed, or the resultant state from that action. (Whether a state, manner or a resultant state is described depends on the verb as well.)

Medium

kangkurr-wanppa-	immersed-fall	'swim'
kangkurr-ngarapu-	immersed-throw	'throw in water'
kangkurr-ngu-	immersed-lie	'float'

Direction

palyal-ngarapu-	out-throw	'spill'
palyal-parta-	out-start	'rise, to get up'

Manner

wuruly-para-	hiding-take	'steal'
wuruly-nyirri-	hiding-put	'hide'
wuruly-kura-	hiding-run	'take lover'
wuruly-wangka-	hiding-talk	'backbite'
wililik-ngu-	hanging-lie	'hang' (intr.)
wililik-nyirri-	hanging-put	'hang' (tr.)
wililik-juku-	hanging-carry	'carryhanging'

Result

mulymuly-jajja-	hole-eat	'eat into holes (e.g. clothes moth)'
muly-kupu-	hole-cook	'burn a hole in something'

Quantifier

lalkki-nyi-	separate-sit	'sit separately'
lalkki-para-	separate-take	'each take'
lalkki-apa-	separate-go	'split up, go'

Some preverbs may add Dative arguments, as in (2), in which the verb /pakanta/ normally takes only an Absolutive object. Otherwise preverbs do not affect the argument structure of the verb they attach to, with a few exceptions, as in (3).

(2) Land Council-jji apparr anyungkku pakanta pakarli-kkina,
    Land Council-ERG word.ABS we.pl.incl.NS poke-PRES paper-ALL
    kaji-paka-nta anyungkku, anyinginyi-kki manu-ku.
    benefit-poke-PRES we.pl.incl.NS we.pl.incl.GEN-DAT country-DAT
    'As for Land Council it writes stuff on paper for us, it writes it for our benefit for our country.' [JS:HNJ:86n][11]

(3) Wirnkkalki laarr-ngarapu-njjan.
    dingo.ABS ?-throw-PRES
    'Dingoes howl together.' [JS:BNN:nd]
    [from *ngarapu* 'throw', which normally takes ergative subject, absolutive object]

3.2 Suffixation

Suffixation is a prominent feature of Warumungu morphology. It is used both for derivation and for inflection. With respect to morphophonological processes, suffixes are of two types: those that are involved in fortis–lenis alternations (and vowel assimilation), and those that are not. The latter behave more like compounds. The division corresponds roughly to the division between inflection and derivation. I discuss them in turn.

3.2.1 Inflection

3.2.1.1 Noun inflection – Case   Case suffixes fall into two types based on their meanings. 'Semantic case suffixes' are those with meanings akin to English prepositions: for example, /-ngara/ ABLATIVE 'from', /-kVna/ ALLATIVE/LOCATIVE 'to, at, in', /-kajji/ LEST 'for fear of', as in (4), etc. A subclass of these, 'derivational case suffixes', act more like derivational affixes (see section 3.2.1.2).

'Grammatical case suffixes' are those which express grammatical relations (subject, object, indirect object), like /karriny-ji/ in (4). A noun without a case suffix is interpreted as having Absolutive case – /nanttu/ in (4) and /wangarri/ in (5) – or as being the main predicator, or as agreeing with some argument with Absolutive case – /kumppu/ and /pulyurrulyurru/ in (5).

(4)   <u>Karriny-ji</u> +ajjul nyirri-njina   <u>nanttu</u>, <u>ngapa-kajji</u>.
      people-ERG +3pl.S put-PAST.CONT humpy, water-LEST
      'The people were erecting humpies for fear of the rain.' [JS:PND:RS]

(5)   Nyirri-nyi   +ama <u>wangarri</u> <u>kumppu</u> <u>pulyurrulyurru</u>.
      place-PAST.PUN +he   rock ABS big.ABS   red.ABS
      'He placed a big red hill.' [JS:PND:RS]

The inflectional case suffixes generally show two main types of allomorphy: vowel assimilation (triggered by the final vowel of the stem) and a fortis–lenis alternation (triggered by whether or not the stem has two morae). Aside from these, the Ergative/Locative case has a range of allomorphs. All three processes are illustrated below:

'humpy'	[nan.t.u]	[nandu-ŋgu]	'house'	[babulu]	[babulu-cu]
'shade'	[mal:a]	[mala-ŋga]	'dog'	[gunaba]	[gunaba-ca]
'man'	[gaṭ:i]	[gaḍi-ŋgi]	'woman'	[giṛiji]	[giṛiyi-nti]

I discuss each in turn.

The vowels of most case suffixes assimilate in place entirely to the final vowel of the stem to which the suffixes attach. Non-alternating case suffixes all have /a/ as their first vowel.

	stem		
kartti 'man'	ngappa 'water'	manu 'country'	
karti-ki	ngapa-ka	manu-ku	**Dative**
karti-kina	ngapa-kana	manu-kuna	**Allative/Locative**
karti-ngki	ngapa-ngka	manu-ngku	**Ergative/Locative**
karti-kajji	ngapa-kajji	manu-kajji	**Lest**
karti-ngara	ngapa-ngara	manu-ngara	**Ablative**

Presumably this vowel assimilation was involved in the merger of an original locative /*-ngka/ with an ergative /*-ngki~-ngku/.[12]

The Ergative has several allomorphs, depending on whether the stem has two morae on what the final segment is, and on whether there is a nasal stop cluster in the stem (see table 32.2). The allomorphy is undergoing change in the speech of younger speakers.

Forms like /ngapa-kapurtu-njul/ (as opposed to /ngapa-ngka/ and the unattested */ngapa-kapurtu-njju/) show that the allomorphy selection is sensitive to certain morpheme boundaries. Other suffixes – for example, the derivational case suffix /-jangu/ – create words which are treated as plain polysyllabic words: /ngapa-jangu-njju/.

Among older speakers, only a few bisyllables take the irregular allomorphy. They include frozen reduplications, /turtu/ 'sleep'. These are sometimes realized with a long vowel (and so pattern with /kaarnu/ in having three morae), but often there is no phonetic long vowel. Some speakers have alternations, as with /lurnkkurr/ and /kirriji/ in table 32.2. The fortis–lenis alternation in the stem is quite regular for older speakers: if the speaker uses the two-mora allomorph, the medial consonant of the stem is lenited, but the same speaker will not lenite the medial consonant if using the three-mora allomorph.

Younger speakers seem to be generalizing the three-mora pattern, at the expense of the other patterns. They also rarely use the stem fortis–lenis alternations.

stem	meaning	older speaker	younger speaker
kilyirr	'sun'	[giʎiɽ-i]	[giʎiɽ-iɲci]
marttan	'stone knife'	[maḍan-da]	[maṭan-ca]
yingal	'scared'	[yiŋal-iɲci]	[yiŋal-ca]
pulkka	'old person'	[bulga-ŋga]	[bulga-ɲɟa]

3.2.1.2. *Verb inflection*   Verbs fall into four major conjugations, labelled according to their future form: the Ø, Y, L and R conjugations. The Y, L and R have monosyllabic members which behave slightly differently. Verbs are inflected for tense, aspect and mood. They also have portmanteau inflections which include associated motion. The conjugations differ with respect to transitivity and with respect to fortis–lenis alternations (see table 32.3).

The Ø conjugation consists mostly of intransitive verbs. One form, wanppan/ 'fall' PRES shows a rigidly fortis consonant. Otherwise stem-medial consonants are lenis. Suffix-initial consonants are all lenis, with the exception of one irregular transitive form, /jajjan/ 'eat' PRES, in which the /jj/ is analysable sometimes as part of the stem and sometimes as part of the suffix: /jaji/ 'eat' FUT, / janyi~ jajanyi/ 'eat' PAST.PUN, /jajjina/ 'eat' PAST.CONT, /jajakurn/ 'eat' ADMON.

The Y conjugation consists of transitive verbs. It shows some fortis–lenis alternation in suffix-initial consonants: /para-njan/ 'get' PRES, /wuru-njjan/ 'hit' PRES *with thrown object*.

The L conjugation consists of strongly transitive verbs. This is the only conjugation with a consistent fortis–lenis alternation in stem form, /pakanta/ 'spear' PRES, /pakkil/ FUT. Suffix-initial consonants are lenis, except for some suffixes after the one monosyllabic L-conjugation root, /ku-/ 'have'.

The R conjugation, the largest conjugation, contains both transitive and intransitive verbs, and three monosyllabic stance verbs. It shows fortis–lenis alternation in some suffix-initial consonants. Some forms, like /ngattanta/ 'find' PRES, show rigidly fortis consonants.

Table 32.2 Ergative allomorphy

ERGATIVE allomorphs	Type of noun stem	Phonetic	Translation	Spelling of stem
	Two morae			
-ngkV	V-final	[maɭa-ŋga]	'leaf'	marla
		[waʎɟi-ŋgil]	'bloodwood'	waljji
-V	rr-final	[abaɾ-a]	'language'	apparr
		[luŋgu-u]	'rib'	lurnkkurr
-tV	n-final	[gayin-di]	'boomerang'	kayin
-rtV	rn-final	[gaɾin-ɖi]	'blood' (written /karrirnti/)	karrirn
-jV	ny-final	[ɟaɾaɲ-ɟa]	'tongue'	jarany
-injji	l-final	[yiɲal-iɲci]	'scared'	yingal
	Three or more morae			
-njjV~jjV[a]	V-final	[makuɾa-ɲca]	'cold.weather'	makkurra
		[giɽiʎi-ci]	'woman' (younger speakers)	kirriji
		[mayibaʈula-nca]	'mountain devil' (lizard sp.)	mayiparttula
		[gaaṇu-ɲcu]	'boy'	kaarnu
	l-final	[gililgiḻil-ci]	'galah' (bird sp., frozen redup.)	kirlilkirlil
	rr-final	[waɾagu-cu]~		
		[waɾagu-ɲcu]	'hole'	warakurr

	irreg. bisyllables	[yaɲi-ɲci]~[yaɳḍi-ci]	'one'	yarnti
		[walji-(ɲ)ci] [luŋkur-cu]	'own' 'rib'	warlji lurnkkurr
-ntti	-ji ~ -nyi final three-syllable	[giṛiyi-nti]	'woman'	kirriji
-nttu	-ju final three-syllable	[gambawu-ntu]	'father'	kampaju
-ttV	n-final (alternates with -jV)	[waḷugun-tu]~[waḷugun-cu]	'fire'	warlukun
-jjV	n-final polysyllable, or after nasal stop cluster	[gaḷambi-ci]	'creek'	karlampi
irregular grammatical morphemes				
-njil		[gulalgi-ɲɟil]	'middle'	kulalki
-njul		[ɲaba-gabuḍu-ɲɟul]	'water-without'	ngapa-kapurtu
-ul	on dual	[buḷuɳu-guɟuṛu-ul]	'child-two'	purlungu-kujjurr

Note:

a I have not found a way of predicting when the forms with and without /n/ will appear.

Table 32.3 Typical tense inflections, organized by conjugation

Conjug. and gloss	Future	Present	Past punctual	Past continuous	Admonitive	Nominal stem[a]
Ø 'go'	api	apa-n	api-nyi	api-na	apa kurn	api-ji-
Ø 'fall'	wanppi	wanppa-n	wanppi-nyi	wanppi-na	wanppa-kurn	wanppi-ji-
Ø 'eat'	jaji	jajja-n	ja-nyi~jaja-nyi	jajji-na	jaja-kurn	ja-ji-
Y 1-syll. 'see'	nya-yi	nya-njan	nya-nyi	nya-njina	nya-ngkkurn	nya-nji~nya-njji-
Y 2-syll. 'get'	pari	para-njan	pari-nyi	pari-njina	para-ngkurn~para-ngkkurn (rare)	pari-nji-
Y 2-syll. 'throw'	wuru	wuru-njan	wuru-nyu	wuru-njuna~wuru-njina	wuru-ngkkurn	wuru-nju-
Y 2-syll. 'sing out'	kula-yi[b]	kula-njan	kula-nyi	kula-njina	kula-ngkurn	kula-nji-
Y 3-syll. 'leave'	pangkali	pangkala-njan	pangkala-nyi	pangkala-njina	pangkala-ngkkurn	pangkala-nji-
L 1-syll. 'have'	kumul	ku-nta	ku-nnyu~ku-nyu	ku-yina~ku-yuna	ku-nkkurn	ku-nju~ku-nju-
L 2-syll. 'spear'	pakkil	paka-nta	paki-nnyi~paki-nyi	paki-njina	paka-nkurn	paki-nji-
R 1-syll. 'sit'	nyii-ni	nyi-nta	nyi-nyi~nyi-nnyi~nyi-nni[c]	nyi-yina	nyi-nkkurn	nyi-nji~nyi-njji-
R 2-syll. 'seek'	mana-rri	mana-nta	mana-nyi~mana-nmi	mana-yina	mana-nkkurn	mana-nji-

Notes:

[a] The nominal participial stem can never appear without a following suffix.

[b] Some speakers treat this as an R-conjugation verb.

[c] These forms with /-nn-/ have only been heard from older speakers.

Speakers show some variation in inflection forms, because the system is quite complex, involving choice of conjugation and the interaction between fortis–lenis alternations in stems and suffixes.

An important inflectional category in Warumungu and nearby languages such as Arrernte (Wilkins 1989, 1993) and Kaytetye (Koch 1984) is 'associated motion'. The motional forms are extremely common, and can be added to any simple verb stem. They form portmanteau affixes with tense and aspect. The four categories are motion/direction towards deictic centre, motion/direction away from deictic centre, 'setting off' and neutral. They can indicate direction, or they can include a motion component:

(6) Ngalanya yuwaji ngunjjirranta   kajunu.
    this   *road.ABS lie-PRES.AWAY north*
    'This road goes north.' [KH:GB:43]

(7) Wangarri +ajju wanppi-rrajina
    money.ABS +1sg.NS fall-PAST.CONT.AWAY
    'The money fell out of my pockets as I was walking along'
    [JS:RT:12-8-92]

They can also be used for projected deictic centres:

(8) Wangki-nyi   +ama '. . . Panupurtta +arn(i)+a   **parti-rrkarl.**'
    say-PAST.PUN +3sg.S   *that.way*   *+1sg.S+FUT set.off-FUT.AWAY*
    Jung(a)+arnp(a) +ama **parti-rrarni**.
    true+indeed   *+3sg.S set.off-PAST.PUN.AWAY*
    'He said, "I will set off away that way." Sure enough he set off away.'
    [JS:PND:RS]

In the narrative in which (8) and (9) occur, the speaker (snake) says he will go away from the current place of speaking (deictic centre). The AWAY suffix is used. The narrator takes the snake's point of view, and also uses the AWAY suffix to report the snake leaving the projected deictic centre. In (9), the snake tells the two boys to come inside him, using the HITHER suffix. This time the narrator uses the neutral form to report the boys going inside the snake.

(9) Wangki-ny(i) +apulu, '**Jarrpi-jirra**   +akkul kantu.'
    say-PAST.PUN +3du.O enter-FUT.HITHER +2du.S inside
    Jung(a) +arnp(a) +awul **jarrpi-nyi**.
    true + indeed   *+3du.S enter-PAST.PUN*
    'He said to them two, "You two come inside." Sure enough they went inside (his mouth).' [JS:PND:RS]

As can be seen from the examples, the associated motion forms vary for different tenses and moods. Table 32.4 shows a typical L-conjugation paradigm.

Table 32.4   Paradigm for L-conjugation verb /pakki-l/ 'spear'

Associated motion

Tense	neutral	hither	away, while going along away	setting.out
future	pakki-**l**	paki-**n-jirra**	paki-**nti-(rr)-karl**	paki-**nti-(rr)-parti**
imperative	pakki-**l+a**	paki-**n-jirra**	paki-**nti-(rr)-karl+a**	paki-**nti-(rr)-part+a**
present	paka-**nta**	paki-**nti-rr-apa-n**	paki-**nti-rr-a-nta**	paki-**nti-(rr)-parta-n**
past punctual	paki-**nyi~** paki-**nnyi~** paki-**nni**	paki-**nti-(rr)-ka-rni** ~paki-**nji-(rr)-ka-rni**	paki-**nti-rr-a-rni**	paki-**nti-(rr)-parti-nyi**
past continuative	paki-**njina**	paki-**nti-rr-a-jina**	*gap in paradigm*	paki-**nti-(rr)-parti-na**
admonitive	paka-**nkurn**	paki-**nti-(rr)-pun-kkurn**	paki-**nti-rr-arn-kkurn**	paki-**nti-(rr)-parta-kurn**
optative/irrealis	paka-**nnga(ri)**	paki-**nti-(rr)-pun-nga(ra)**	paki-**nti-rr-arn-nga(ra)**	paki-**nti-(rr)-parta-nga(ra)**

Notes:

(i)   Boldface indicates the ending. Hyphens in the boldfaced elements indicate commonality of form, and only occasionally do these hyphenated forms have a clearly associated meaning.

(ii)   Parentheses around (rr) indicate that some speakers omit this before a following consonant.

(iii)   The imperative clitic /a/ is represented with a plus boundary sign +.

(iv)   The blank in the table for PAST CONTINUOUS AWAY appears to be a genuine gap in the paradigm.

A summary of the different endings is given in table 32.5. The choice between the fortis /-jjirra/ and the lenis /-jirra/ depends on verb class. Forms shown above beginning /-rrC/ (e.g. /-rrkarl/) become /-rriC/ for R-conjugation verbs (including the monosyllabic verbs of that conjugation). Some verb classes show special augments between the nuclear root and the suffixes above which begin with /-rr/ (augments are /-nji-/ and /-nti-/).

3.2.2 *Derivation*   Derivational suffixes fall into two main types, those that create words of a different category from the stem to which they attach, and those that create words of the same category as the stem to which they attach.

3.2.2.1 Category-changing   Category-changing suffixes create denominal verbs and deverbal nouns. New verbs can be created from nouns by suffixing one of three bound verb roots of the R conjugation. The bound verb root /-ji-/ (INCHOATIVE) creates intransitive verbs, which are often, but not always, inchoative.

Table 32.5 Suffixes for motional verb forms

	hither	*away*	*setting.out*
future	-jjirra~ -jirra	-rrkarl	-rrparti
imperative	jjirra~ jirra	rrkarl + a	rrpart + a
present	-rrapan	-rranta~-jjirra(r)nta ~-jirra(r)nta	-rrparta-n
past punctual	-rrkarni	-rrarni	-rrparti-nyi
past continuative	-rrajina	———	-rrparti-na
admonitive	-rrpunkkurn	-rrarnkkurn	-rrparta-kurn
optative /irrealis	-rrpunnga(ra)	-rrarnnga(ra)	-rrparta-nga(ra)

yingal	'afraid'	yingal-ji-	'to become afraid'
English	'lead'	lead-ji-	'to lead (intr.)'
English	'work'	work-ji-	'to work (intr.)'

Transitive factitive or causative verbs (CAUSATIVE) can be formed from nominals by suffixing the bound verbs /-rni-~-ni-~-ti-~-rti-~-rnti-/ or /-mu-/:

yingal	'afraid'	yingal-mu-	'to make afraid'
piliyi	'good'	piliyi-rni-	'to make'
English	'tease'	tijim-ni-[13]	'to tease'
English	'read'	readim-mu-	'to read'

Neither of these bound verbs show fortis–lenis alternations; nor do the stems when they are attached: for example, /kumppu-ji-/ big-INCHO 'grow up'.

New verbs can also be created by suffixing one of the monosyllabic stance verbs: /turtu/ 'sleep', /turtu-ngu-/ 'to sleep'. The reason for analysing these as suffixation, rather than as a preverb–verb compound, is that, whereas regular compounding has no effect on the conjugation of the verb, in these cases the resulting verb may act like a polysyllabic R-conjugation verb (suffixing), or like a monosyllabic R-conjugation verb (compounding). Thus the FUTURE of /ngu-/ 'to lie' is /nguunu/, while the FUTURE of /turtu-ngu-/ is /turtu-ngu-rru/ (polysyllabic) or /turtu-nguunu/ (monosyllabic).

All deverbal nouns are formed on verb stems consisting of verb plus a nominalizing marker whose form is /-ji-~-ju-~-nji-~-nju-~-njji-~-njju-/, depending on the conjugation of the verb, the number of syllables and the final vowel of the verb root. These deverbal noun stems are used with derivational suffixes as nouns (10, 11), and with nominal inflectional suffixes as the base for various tenseless participial clauses (12). However, unlike nouns, deverbal noun stems can never appear in isolation.

(10)   miyili-kkari <u>nya-nj(i)-alkki</u>
       eye-REL   see-NOM-ASSOC
       'spectacles'

(11)   wangka-<u>j(i)-ara</u>
       talk-NOM-INTENS
       'one who talks too much'

(12)   Watti + ankkul api-nyi   Barunga-kkana
       far + 1plexcS   go-PAST.PUN Barunga-ALL
       festival-kku <u>nya-njji-ki</u>.
       festival-DAT see-NOM-DAT
       'We went far to Barunga to see the festival.'   [JS:PND:86]

The nominalizing suffix has no effect on the stem verb. The nominalizing suffix itself is sometimes voiceless after monosyllabic verb stems (12). However,
if the suffix /-alkki-/ is attached, the nominalizing suffix is usually voiced
(10).[14]

   Nominalized verbs are used to form non-finite clauses. The suffix indicates
what is the controller. Thus the Allative/Locative suffix shows control by the
object of the matrix clause.

(13)   Pina-ny(i)   +ajurnu <u>wina-njji-kina</u>+karn.
       hear-PAST.PUN +3pl.NS sg.-NOM-ALL/LOC+now
       'He heard them singing then.'   [JS:PND:RS]

3.2.2.2 Category-maintaining morphology   While Warumungu has no formally distinct class of adjectives as opposed to nouns, some derivational affixes
create nominals that denote entities, and others create nominals which focus
on having a particular property. Thus /nginngin/ 'thievingly' is used as a
preverb or as an action nominal describing how an action is carried out. When
suffixed with /-yilppi/ EXCESSIVE it means 'thief', /nginngin-yilppi/. On the
other hand, /kurlppu/ 'honey, sugar' denotes a thing, but when suffixed with
/-jangu/ HAVING, /kurlppu-jangu/ denotes a property, 'sweet'. These properties can in turn be used to denote things: /yurrkkurlu/ 'snake', /yurrkkurlu-
jangu/ snake-HAVING 'Aboriginal doctor'.

   Suffixes like /-jangu/ have been called 'derivational case' markers because
while they can create new words, they can also show agreement, including
double case marking:[15]

(14)   ... wanga-nta +ama karlkkurr nyayi-jangu-njju
       ...cut-PRES+3sg.S   grass.ABS   what-HAVING-ERG
       nipi-nipi-jangu-njju.
       scissors-HAVING-ERG
       'She cuts the grass with something, with scissors.'[JS:PND]

Their meanings do not distinguish them clearly from semantic case suffixes. Phonologically, however, they behave differently. These suffixes do not trigger fortis–lenis alternations in the noun to which they attach; nor do they themselves have voiceless allomorphs, as the lack of contrast between the stems and endings of /kurlppu-jangu/ and /yurrkkurlu-jangu/ shows.

3.3 Reduplication

Warumungu uses both total and partial reduplication. Total reduplication is common on nouns, and can act like the case suffixes that cause fortis–lenis alternation:

pulkka 'old man'   pulka-pulkka 'old people'

Partial reduplication is uncommon on nouns,[16] is probably prefixing, and does not seem to show the same fortition alternation.

ngarnkka	'fast'	ngarnkkarnkka	'very fast'
pulyurr(u)-	'red' (preverb)	pulyurrulyurru	'red'
marluka	'old person'	marlarluka	'old people'

Partial reduplication on verbs is complex. In meaning it appears to express a continuative aspect. If the verb complex includes a preverb, then the usual strategy is to reduplicate the preverb, not the verb. The form of reduplication differs according to the tense and to the conjugation, but the most significant difference in form is between the FUTURE (and the IMPERATIVE which is based on it) and the other tenses (see table 32.6).

Reduplication strategies for different conjugations and roots of different numbers of syllables constitute an area where speakers diverge in interesting ways.

3.4 Template

Pronouns fall into two types, those that represent direct arguments of the verb with functions such as subject, object and indirect object, and those which represent adjunct or oblique functions. The latter act like nouns; the former are obligatory, acting sometimes like agreement markers (17), and sometimes like full pronouns, albeit restricted in position (15) and (16). They occur initially or after the first major constituent (verb, noun phrase, etc.), and only rarely later in the clause (17):

(15) Warakurr-kkuna +ajjul kupu-nta kuyu   puliki.
      hole-ALL   +3pl.S cook-PRES meat.ABS bullock.ABS
      'They cook beef in an earth oven.' [JS:BN:Cooking]

Table 32.6 Verb reduplication forms

	Non-future type		
1			
Ø conjugation PAST CONTINUOUS	partina	partartina	'set out' intr.
L conjugation PRESENT	pakanta	pakkal-pakanta[a] ~pakal-pakanta	'spear'
Y conjugation PAST CONTINUOUS	kulanjina	kulakulanjina	'sing out'
R conjugation PAST CONTINUOUS	manayina	manamanayina	'seek'
2	**Future type**		
Ø conjugation FUTURE	parti	partarti	'set out' (intr.)
L conjugation FUTURE	jarrpi	jarrpapi (common)~jarrparrpi	'enter' (intr.)
	jarrppi-l	jarrppapil~jarrpapil (common)~jarrpparrpil	'enter' (tr.)
	pakki-l	pakkakil~pakakil	'spear'
	wangi-l	wangingil <sic>	'cut'
	kuppu-l	kuppupul~kupupul	'cook' (tr.)
	nyirri-l	nyirrirlirl	'put'
	kunul~kunurl (PRES kunta)	kununul~kununurl	'have'
R conjugation FUTURE	kura-ri	kuranani	'run'
	nyii-ni (PRES nyinta)	nyinini	'sit'
Y conjugation IMPER	kula-y+a	kulayay+a~kulanan+a[b]	'sing out'
Y conjugation FUTURE	nya-yi (PRES nyanjjan)	nyayayi~nyaayi	'see'
	pari (PRES paranjan)	parari	'get'

Notes:

[a] A linking /l/ is often found in reduplication in Australian languages. It may reflect a conjugation marker (Patz 1982), transitivity (Koch 1984), or may have no clear function (Alpher 1973, 1991; Breen 1974, Kirton 1978, Wilkins 1989).

[b] This verb is sometimes also treated as an R conjugation verb.

(16) Narra-warinyi   +<u>arni</u>.
      ground-INHABITANT +1sg.S
      'I am a ground-dweller.' [JS:PND:88w]

(17) Disco-kina   pika-pikka +<u>ajjul</u> warlan-ja-nta.
      Disco-ALL/LOC children.ABS +3pl.S dance-stand-PRES
      'At the disco the children dance.' [JS:PND: young speaker's Warumungu]

All non-null pronouns start with /a/.[17] The third-person singular subject pronoun is either null or realized as /ama/ (18), a form which does not otherwise
take part in the pronominal cluster system but resembles a demonstrative. The
third-person singular object pronoun is null (a paradigmatic zero) (19).

(18) Palyupalyu   +<u>ama</u> purluju kumppu, munkku   kumppu.
      blue.tongue.lizard.ABS +3sg.S head.ABS big.ABS stomach.ABS big.ABS
      'The blue tongue lizard has a big head, and a big stomach.' [JS:HNJ:86n]

(19) Purrumu-rra!
      touch-IMPER
      'Touch it!'

Pronouns occur either as enclitics (with reduced stress on the initial syllable)
in pronominal clusters, or occasionally as phonologically independent words
(with full stress on the initial syllable). There is no major formal difference
between bound pronominal clusters and 'independent' pronominal forms,
except that since the former all begin in the vowel /a/, the latter may add
an initial epenthetic /y/[18] – hence the interjection /yangi/! 'Hey you!' (2sg.
/angi/). This epenthesis is regular for the second-person singular form, but is
rare for the other pronouns.
   Like many Australian languages, Warumungu uses one pronominal form
for transitive and intransitive subjects (whether the verb requires of its subject
Ergative case (20) or Absolutive case (17)), and another form for objects (whether
the verb requires of its object Absolutive case (21) or Dative case (22)), although
if the object is third-person singular Dative, there is a special form (23).

(20) Warra+ajjul kunta   wangarri-kari,[19] wakkapi-njji.
      not +3pl.S   have-PRES money-REL,   many-ERG
      'Many of them don't have bankbooks.' [JS:PND]

(21) Ngatta-nyi+karn   +<u>ajurnu</u> akinyi   karriny.
      find-PAST.PUN +now +3pl.NS his.ABS people.ABS
      'He found his people then.' [JS:PND:RS]

(22) Yama +<u>ajurnu</u> jarti-ki+karn   pikapikka-ka ngu-nngara.
      leave +3pl.NS other-DAT+now children-DAT lie-OPT+FUT
      'Some should be left for the other children.' [JS:PND 24/6/86]

Table 32.7 Pronominal clusters (1)

	Subject	Subject + 3sg. dative	Subject + reflexive	Subject + reflexive dative
1sg.	arni	arnakku	arnajju	arnaju-kku(l)
1du.incl.	ayil	ayilikki	ayilirni	ayilirni-kki(l)
1du.excl.	ajjil~ajil	ajilikki	ajirni	ajirni-kki(l)
1pl.incl.	anyul	anyulukku	anyurnu ~anyulurnu	anyurnu-kku(l)
1pl.excl.	ankkul~angkkul	ankulukku ~angkulukku	ankurnu ~angkurnu	ankurnu-kku(l) ~angkurnu-kku(l)
2sg.	angi	angakku	angurnu ~angkurnu	angurnu-kku(l)
2du.	amppul	ampulukku	ampurnu ~ampulurnu	ampurnu-kku(l)
2pl.	a(rr)kkul	a(rr)kulukku	a(rr)kurnu	a(rr)kurnu-kku(l)
3sg.	(ama)	aku	awurnu	awurnu-kku(l)
3du.	awul	awulukku	awulurnu	awulurnu-kku(l)
3pl.	ajjul	ajulukku	ajurnu~ajulurnu	ajurnu-kku(l)

Note: /angkurnu/ and /ajulurnu/ have only been heard from younger speakers.

(23)   Kujjarra-yarnti+karn +<u>aku</u>   ngu-nngar+a
        two-one.ABS+now   +3sg.DAT lie-OPT+FUT
        kiwari-ki ala-ka+nya.
        child-DAT that-DAT+EMPH
        'That child will have three left then.' [JS:PND 13/11/86]

If a sentence has both a subject pronoun and non-subject pronoun these form an inseparable group, a 'pronominal cluster', which is sometimes impossible to divide into recognizable subject and non-subject morphemes.

(24)   Kupu-njuna   +<u>arnajurnu</u> kantirri   marnukuju-jangu.
        cook-PAST.CONT +1sg.S.3pl.NS bread.ABS grape-HAVING.ABS
        'I used to cook them bread with sultanas.' [JS:PND]

A form such as /árnajùrnu/ has primary stress on the first syllable and secondary stress on the third syllable (see table 32.7).

The reflexive and reflexive Dative are illustrated below. Observe that the subject of a sentence with a reflexive object receives Ergative case just as it would if the object were not reflexive (25). The reflexive can represent an Absolutive object as in (25) or a Dative argument as in (26), in which the verb /wangka-/ normally takes an Absolutive subject and a Dative non-subject.

(25) Napurrula-jja +<u>awurnu</u>   karrju-nyu   blanketi-jji.
     Napurrula-ERG +3sg.S.REFL cover-PAST.PUN blanket-ERG
     'Napurrula covered herself with a blanket.' [JS:BN:C3.2:29]

(26) Kina   +awurnu   wangka-n.
     alone.ABS +3sg.S.REFL talk-PRES
     'He talks to himself.'   [JS:PND:88n]

(27) Kartti-l   +<u>awurnu-kkul+a</u>   kayin.
     trim-FUT +3sg.S.REFL.DAT+FUT boomerang.ABS
     'He will trim a boomerang for himself.'   [JS:BN:C3.2:12]

(27) illustrates another feature of Warumungu pronominal clusters: an element representing FUTURE tense (/a/) or IRREALIS mood (/aparn/) can attach to the clusters.[20]

There is no point in trying to create pronominal clusters by a binary-branching structure with a head. Rather, an exocentric word structure rule, or a position class template is needed.

Position 1	Position 2	Position 3	Position 4
Subject	Non-subject Reflexive	Dative Dative-reflexive Inversion marker	Future Irrealis

While the first four forms[21] could be analysed as having some sort of case marker for non-subject, the last two forms cannot be so analysed. In these the /-ngkki/ seems best analysed as an inversion marker: 'reverse the assignment of grammatical functions'. This suggests that the action of a third person on a first person is considered more marked than the reverse (Silverstein 1976).

Pronouns also have special GENITIVE (GEN) forms. These consist of nouns formed by suffixing /-nyi/ or /-nginyi/ to non-subject pronouns /ajju, ajjinyi/, with two exceptions: 1 dual inclusive, which is formed on the root for the subject and REFLEXIVE, and the third-person singular pronoun, which is formed on the DATIVE of the third-person singular /aku/, (the third-person singular non-subject pronoun is otherwise a zero morpheme). /-nginyi/ is added if there is an augment in the non-subject form: for example, /ampu-kku/ 3sg.S – 2du.NS, /ampi-ngi-nyi/ 2du. GEN, and for third person non-singular forms (see Mylne 1996 for an alternative analysis).

These genitive pronouns act like nouns, in that they appear anywhere in the sentence and take noun-type case suffixes. With Absolutive or Ergative case, they modify the element acting as subject or object (28). With other case suffixes, they may modify some other element (29), or they may fill the role themselves (30).

Table 32.8 Pronominal clusters (2)

	1st person non-subject	2nd person non-subject	3rd person non-subject
1st pers.subj.			
1sg.-S->NSsg.			arri
1sg.S->NSdu.			arnapulu
1sg.S->NSpl.		arnangkku arnampukku ~arnapukku arnturrkku	arnajurnu ~arnajunu
1du.excl.-S->NSsg.		ajilirnkki ~ajilinkki	ajil
1du.incl.-S->NSsg.			ayil
1pl.excl.S->NSsg.		ankulurnkku	ankkul
1pl.incl.S->NSsg.			anyul
1pl.excl.S->NSpl.		alkurntukku~alkutukku	ankuljarni
1pl.incl.S->NSpl.			anyuljarni
2nd pers.subj.			
2sg.S->NSsg.	angajju~anganjju		angi
2sg.S->NSdu.	angajikki		angapulu
2sg.S->NSpl.	angankku		angajurnu ~angajunu
2du.S->NSsg.	ampulajji		amppul
2pl.S->NSpl.	akularnkki		akuljarni
3rd pers.subj.			
3sg.S->NSsg.	ajju	angku	(ama)
3sg.S->NSdu.	ajikki (1 excl. object)	ampukku	apulu

3sg.S->NSdu.	ayingkki (1 incl. object)		ajurnu ~ ajunu
3sg.S->NSpl.	ankku (excl.)	arrkku	
3sg.S->NSpl.	anyungkku (incl.) ~anyukku		
3du.S->NSsg.	awulajji	awulurnkku ~awulunkku	awul
3pl.S->NSsg.	ajulajji	ajulurnkku	ajjul
3pl.S->NSpl.	ankuljarni-ngkki (excl.)	ajurntulkku ~ajultukku	ajuljarni
3pl.S->NSpl.	anyuljarni-ngkki (incl.)		

Notes:

1 3pl.S->NSpl. means a third-person plural subject acting on a plural non-subject.

2 The table shows an absence of dual pronouns combined with either dual or plural pronouns, so-called 'dual neutralization'. (The form /awulupulu/ has been heard from a younger speaker, for a third-person dual object, but it was unclear in context whether the subject was singular or dual.) The plural is used instead of the dual when such situations arise. (Hale (1973b) compares different strategies for dual neutralization in Eastern Warlpiri, Warumungu and Yuendumu Warlpiri. See also McConvell 1980.)

Wuru-nyu   akuljarni   'you two shot them two'   or   'you mob shot them two'
shot-PAST.PUN   or   'you two shot all of them'   or   'you mob shot all of them'

3 The table also shows that, while the first part of the pronominal cluster is normally made up of the subject pronoun and the second of the non-subject, there are some forms for which this is not true:

3sg.S 1du.incl.NS   ayingkki
3sg.S 1pl.incl.NS   anyungkku
3sg.S 1du.excl.NS   ajikki
3sg.S 2du.NS   ampukku
3pl.S 1pl.incl.NS   anyuljarningkki~anyuljarnikki (cf. anyuljarni: 1pl.incl.S 3pl.NS)
3pl.S 1pl.excl.NS   ankuljarningkki~ankuljarnikki (cf. ankuljarni: 1pl.incl.S 3pl.NS)

Table 32.9 Formation of genitive pronouns

Person	Base	Genitive
1sg.	ajju (non-subj.)	ajjinyi
1du.incl.	ayil (subj.)	ayilinginyi
	ayi-ngkki (non-subj.)	
	ayil-irni (refl.)	
1du.excl.	aji-kki (non-subj.)	ajinginyi
1pl.incl.	anyu-ngkku (non-subj.)	anyinginyi
1pl.excl.	ankku (non-subj.)	ankkinyi
2sg.	angku (non-subj.)	angkinyi
2du.	ampu-kku (non-subj.)	ampinginyi
2pl.	arrkku (non-subj.)	arrkkinyi
3sg.	aku (DAT)	akinyi
3du.	apulu (non-subj.)	apilinginyi
3pl.	ajurnu (non-subj.)	ajurnunginyi

(28)   Karnanti   <u>akinyi</u>,   kampaju   <u>akinyi</u>   +angkuljarnikki
       mother.ABS his.ABS, father.ABS his.ABS +1pl.excl.3pl.S.INVERT
       kili+karn   api-karni   karlampi-kkina.
       angry+now go-PAST.PUN.HITHER creek-ALL/LOC
       'His mother and father angrily came to us to the creek.' [KH:SN:73]

(29)   Kartungunyu-kk(u)   +aku   <u>akinyi-kki</u>   kartti
       wife-DAT   +3sg.DAT his-DAT   man.ABS
       kujuwa-ji-nyi
       bereaved-INCHO-PAST.PUN
       'A man is bereaved of his wife.' [JS:MNM:C3.1:21]

(30)   *Ajjinyi-ngara* pari-njirrarni.
       my.ABL   take-PAST.PUN.AWAY.
       'He took it away from me.' [KH:SN:21]

Annotated abbreviations

ABL	ABLATIVE	semantic case suffix
ADMON	ADMONITIVE	verb inflectional suffix
ALL	ALLATIVE	semantic case suffix, switch reference marker
ASSOC	ASSOCIATIVE	derivational suffix on nouns and nominalized verbs

AWAY	away from deictic centre	associated motion, part of portmanteau verb suffixes
ABS	ABSOLUTIVE	interpretation of lack of marking on nouns as grammatical case on subject of intransitive sentence, object of transitive sentence.
CONT	CONTINUOUS	aspect, marked by suffix or reduplication on verbs
DAT	DATIVE	grammatical case suffix marking object, semantic case suffix marking indirectly affected participants and directions
du.	dual	number feature of pronominals
EMPH	EMPHATIC	clitic attaching to demonstratives
ERG	ERGATIVE	grammatical case suffix marking subject of transitive sentence, semantic case suffix marking Locative and Instrument
excl.	exclusive	feature of first-person plural pronominals, 'excluding Hearer'
EXCESS	EXCESSIVE	derivational suffix on nouns, 'too much'
FUT	FUTURE	verb inflectional suffix; clitic attaching to pronominal clusters and optative verb inflection
GEN	GENITIVE	form of pronoun
HAVING		derivational case suffix on nouns
HITHER	towards deictic centre	associated motion, part of portmanteau verb suffixes
IMPER	IMPERATIVE	clitic attaching to verb inflected for FUTURE
incl.	inclusive	feature of first person plural pronominals, "including Hearer"
intr.	intransitive	property of verb root
INCHO	INCHOATIVE	bound verb attaching to nouns to create derived intransitive verbs
INHABITANT		derivational case suffix on nouns
INTENS	INTENSIFIER	suffix attaching to nominalized verbs, 'do something too much'
INVERT	INVERSION	suffix attaching to pronominal clusters inverting subject and non-subject
LEST		semantic case suffix on nouns
LOC	LOCATIVE	interpretation of ERGATIVE in intransitive sentences and ALLATIVE in transitive sentences
NOM	NOMINALIZER	nominalising verb suffix
NS	NON-SUBJECT	property of pronominal clusters
OPT	OPTATIVE	verb inflectional suffix
PAST.PUN	PAST PUNCTUAL	verb inflectional suffix
pl.	plural	number feature of pronominals
PRES	PRESENT	verb inflectional suffix
REFL	REFLEXIVE	feature of pronominals

REL	RELATIVE	semantic/grammatical case suffix on nouns linking nouns together
S	SUBJECT	property of pronominal clusters
sg.	singular	number feature of pronominals
tr.	transitive	property of verb root

ACKNOWLEDGEMENTS

Material in this paper comes from unpublished grammars and field-notes by Kenneth Hale (1959), Jeffrey Heath (1977), Prithrindra Chakravarti (1967), and from material given by many Warumungu, in particular B. Nabarula, R. P. Narrurlu, V. S. Narrurlu, K. F. Napanangka, E. G. Nakamarra, R. T. Nakamarra, and the late P. N. D., H. N. J. and M. N. M. I thank them all. I thank Ken Hale, Jeffrey Heath and David Nash for discussion.

NOTES

1 Warumungu's exact genetic relationship to other subgroups of Pama-Nyungan is still being debated. It is surrounded by great language diversity. To the south are Arandic languages (Kaytetye and Alyawarr), to the north and west the Ngumbin-Yapa languages Warlpiri, Warlmanpa and Mudburra, to the east Wakaya, and to the north and north-east the non-Pama-Nyungan languages Jingilu and Wambaya. It is most clearly related to the Ngumbin-Yapa languages, and to the Arandic languages. However, Warumungu and its neighbours share many properties which cannot be classified as clearly arising from shared inheritance or from areal diffusion. Diffusion and convergence of grammar are undoubtedly helped by the fact that many Warumungu people are multilingual, and have relations who identify with different languages.

2 Warumungu people have been using the spelling system given in table 32.1 since 1983. In this paper I shall use // to enclose forms given in this spelling system.

3 I have found no clear examples of long vowels past the first syllable of a morpheme.

4 Inside monomorphemic words, the following clusters are possible ('peripheral' refers to bilabial and velar, and 'non-peripheral' to the remainder):

    (i)   all homorganic nasal stop clusters

    (ii)   homorganic lamino-palatal lateral stop clusters

    (iii) heterorganic clusters: non-peripheral nasals followed by peripheral stops or peripheral nasals

(iv) heterorganic lateral clusters: laterals followed by peripheral stops or /m/ or /w/ (the latter two are rare)

(vi) heterorganic flap clusters: flaps followed by peripheral stops or nasals, or palatal stops

(vii) heterorganic stop clusters: non-peripheral stop (usually /j/) followed by /p/. These are very rare, and are found mostly in names for birds. These names are often onomatopoeic and/or shared with other languages.

5 Literate speakers tend not to write this distinction, a tendency reinforced by their preference for writing suffixes of more than one syllable (and hence with a stress on their first syllable) as separate words: /papulu kuna/, but /papuluku/ ('house' DAT).

6 Length of nasals and laterals is not marked in the orthography because it seems predictable.

7 It is hard to attribute length to one segment or the other by ear, hence the transcription convention C.C. for long clusters and C: for single long consonants.

8 Compare Warlpiri /lurnpa/ 'kingfisher', where /-pa/ is the usual augment for making consonant-final stems conform to the vowel-final word structure constraint.

9 The initials in square brackets refer to the source: KH: K. Hale's field-notes: speaker XX; JS: YY, J. Simpson's field-notes: speaker YY.

10 From now on forms in square brackets will be semi-phonetic, for showing voicing alternations.

11 [JS:HNJ:86n] refers to the source in my notes.

12 Warlpiri separates the two: ergative /-ngki ~ -ngku/ and locative /-ngka/. Roughly, Warumungu uses the ergative for location in an intransitive sentence, the allative for location in a transitive sentence, as do some neighbouring languages. However, the coalescence of the two case functions apparently has different sources in different languages (Wambaya: Nordlinger 1993; Wakaya: Breen 1974; Alyawarra: Yallop 1977).

13 Transitive English verbs borrowed into Warumungu have the Kriol transitive marker /-im/ included.

14 This alternation has not been adequately analysed, but it may reflect a tendency towards dissimilation of sequences of fortis/ lenis stops, a phenomenon found in Ngalakgan (Brett Baker, work in progress).

15 Double case marking is a widespread phenomenon in Australian languages (Dench and Evans 1988). Warumungu does not show as much as Warlpiri (K. Hale 1982, Nash 1986, Simpson 1991). Part of the function of double case marking is fulfilled by the existence of different case markers to indicate location in transitive and intransitive sentences.

16 *marlarluka* may be a borrowing from languages further north in which this form appears and in which this type of reduplication is more productive, e.g. Wambaya (Nordlinger 1993), Mangarayi (Merlan 1982).

17 This suggests reanalysis from agreement markers following an original verb suffix or auxiliary ending in /a/, such as the Warlpiri /ka/ PRESENT and /lpa/ PAST IMPERFECT.

18 Some younger speakers reanalyse the bound pronouns as nouns, inflecting subject pronouns for Ergative: /arni-njji/ for /arni/.

19 The examples here are spelled in accordance with speakers' preferences for not marking the fortis–lenis distinction suffix-initially.

20 This is an areal feature, more pronounced in Jingilu (Chadwick 1975) and Wambaya (Nordlinger 1993).

21 The forms /arnampukku/ and /angajikki/ suggest that for /ajikki/ and /ampukku/ at least /kki/ and /kku/ should be treated either as part of the stem of the non-subject pronoun or as suffixes marking non-subject.

References

Abinal, and Malzac, (RR.PP) (1888). *Dictionnaire malgache-français.* Paris: Éditions maritimes et d'outre-mer.

Ackema, P. (1995). *Syntax below zero.* Utrecht: Utrecht University, OTS Research Institute for Language and Speech.

Ackema, P. and Schoorlemmer, M. (1994). The middle construction and the syntax–semantics interface. *Lingua,* 93, 59–90.

—— (1995). Middles and nonmovement. *Linguistic Inquiry,* 26, 173–97.

Ackerman, F. (1992). Complex predicates and morphological relatedness: the locative alternation in Hungarian. In Sag and Szabolcsi (eds), 55–84.

Addis, K. (1993). Paradigm trimming in Basque. *Linguistics,* 31, 431–74.

AHD (1992). *The American heritage dictionary of the English language,* 3rd edn. Boston: Houghton Mifflin Company.

AIATSIS. Australian Institute of Aboriginal and Torres Strait Islander Studies.

Akhtar, R. N. (1992). Punjabi compounds: a structural and semantic study. Unpub. M.Litt. diss., University of Strathclyde.

Akmajian, A., Steele, S. and Wasow, T. (1979). The category AUX in universal grammar. *Linguistic Inquiry,* 10, 1–64.

Aksu-Koç, A. A. and Slobin, D. I. (1986). A psychological account of the development and use of evidentials in Turkish. In W. Chafe and J. Nichols (eds), *Evidentiality: the linguistic coding, of epistemology,* Norwood, N.J.: Ablex, 159–67.

Allen, B. J., Gardiner, D. B. and Frantz, D. G. (1984). Noun incorporation in Southern Tiwa. *International Journal of American Linguistics,* 50, 292–311.

Allen, M. (1978). Morphological investigations. Ph.D. diss., University of Connecticut.

Alpher, B. (1973). Son of ergative. Ph.D. diss., Cornell University.

—— (1991). *Yir-Yoront lexicon: sketch and dictionary of an Australian language.* Berlin: Mouton de Gruyter.

Alsina, A. (1992). On the argument structure of causatives. *Linguistic Inquiry,* 23, 517–56.

—— (1993). Predicate composition: a theory of grammatical function alternations. Ph.D. diss., Stanford University.

Alsina, A. and Mchombo, S. A. (1990). The syntax of applicatives in Chichewa: problems of a theta theoretic asymmetry. *Natural Language and Linguistic Theory,* 8, 493–506.

—— (1993). Object asymmetries in the Chichewa applicative construction. In Mchombo (ed.), 17–46.

Alsina, A., Bresnan, J. and Sells, P. (eds) (1997). *Complex predicates*, Stanford, Calif.: CSLI.

Andersen, H. (1973). Abductive and deductive change. *Language*, 49, 765–93.

—— (1980). Morphological change: towards a typology. In J. Fisiak (ed.), *Historical morphology*, The Hague: Mouton, 1–50.

Anderson, S. R. (1971). On the role of deep structure in semantic interpretation. *Foundations of Language*, 7, 387–96.

—— (1977a). Comments on the paper by Wasow. In Culicover et al. (eds), 361–77.

—— (1977b). On the formal description of inflection. In *Papers from the 13th annual regional meeting of the Chicago Linguistic Society*, 15–44.

—— (1982). Where's morphology? *Linguistic Inquiry*, 13, 571–612.

—— (1985a). Inflectional morphology. In Shopen (ed.), 150–201.

—— (1985b). Typological distinctions in word formation. In Shopen (ed.), 3–56.

—— (1988a). Morphological change. In Newmeyer (ed.), 324–62.

—— (1988b). Morphological theory. In Newmeyer (ed.), 146–91.

—— (1992). *A-morphous morphology*. Cambridge: Cambridge University Press.

—— (1993). Wackernagel's revenge: clitics, morphology, and the syntax of second position. *Language*, 69, 68–98.

Andrews, J. R. (1975). *Introduction to classical Nahuatl*. Austin: University of Texas Press.

Andrews, S. (1986). Morphological influences on lexical access: lexical or nonlexical effects? *Journal of Memory and Language*, 25, 726–40.

Andrianierenana, C. L. (1996). Morphological causatives in Malagasy. In Pearson and Paul (eds), 58–75.

Anisfeld, M. and Tucker, G. R. (1967). English pluralization rules of six-year-old children. *Child Development*, 38, 1201–17.

Anshen, F. and Aronoff, M. (1981). Morphological productivity and phonological transparency. *Canadian Journal of Linguistics*, 26, 63–72.

—— (1988). Producing morphologically complex words. *Linguistics*, 26, 641–55.

Antinucci, F. and Miller, R. (1976). How children talk about what happened. *Journal of Child Language*, 3, 167–89.

Anttila, R. (1972). *An introduction to historical and comparative linguistics*. New York: MacMillan Publishing Co.; revised and expanded edition published 1988, Amsterdam: J. Benjamins.

—— (1977). *Analogy*. The Hague: Mouton.

Anttila, R. and Brewer, W. A. (1977). *Analogy: a basic bibliography*. Amsterdam: J. Benjamins.

Aoun, J. (1985). *A grammar of anaphora*. Cambridge, Mass.: MIT Press.

Archangeli, D. (1983). The root CV-template as a property of the affix: evidence from Yawelmani. *Natural Language and Linguistic Theory*, 1, 348–84.

—— (1984). Underspecification in Yawelmani phonology and morphology. Ph.D. diss., Massachusetts Institute of Technology.

—— (1991). Syllabification and prosodic templates in Yawelmani. *Natural Language and Linguistic Theory*, 9, 231–84.

Aronoff, M. (1976). *Word formation in generative grammar*. Cambridge, Mass.: MIT Press.

—— (1982). Potential words, actual words, productivity and frequence. In *Proceedings of the thirteenth international congress of linguists*, 163–71.

—— (1988). Head operations and strata in reduplication: a linear treatment. In Booij and van Marle (eds), 1–15.

—— (1994). *Morphology by itself.* Cambridge, Mass.: MIT Press.

Aronoff, M., Arsyad, A., Basri, H. and Broselow, E. (1987). Tier configuration in Makassarese reduplication. In *Papers from the 23rd annual regional meeting of the Chicago Linguistic Society, part two: parasession on autosegmental and metrical phonology,* 1–15.

Ashton, E. O. (1944). *Swahili grammar.* London: Longman Group Ltd.

—— (1947). *Swahili grammar,* 2nd edn. Harlow, Essex: Longman.

Auger, J. and Janda, R. D. (1994). Clitics as affixes and the process morphology of romance verbs. Paper presented at the Linguistic Society of America annual meeting, Boston, January 1994.

Austin, P. (1981). *A grammar of Diyari, South Australia.* Cambridge: Cambridge University Press.

Axelrod, M. (1990). Incorporation in Koyukon Athapaskan. *International Journal of American Linguistics,* 56, 179–95.

Baayen, R. H. (1992). Quantitative aspects of morphological productivity. In G. Booij and J. van Marle (eds), *Yearbook of morphology 1991,* Dordrecht: Kluwer, 109–49.

—— (1993). On frequency, transparency and productivity. In G. Booij and J. van Marle (eds), *Yearbook of morphology 1992,* Dordrecht: Kluwer, 227–54.

—— (1994). Productivity in language production. *Language and Cognitive Processes,* 9, 447–69.

Baayen, R. H. and Lieber, R. (1991). Productivity and English derivations: a corpus-based study. *Linguistics,* 29, 801–43.

Baayen, R. H., Burani, C. and Schreuder, R. (1997a). Effects of semantic markedness in the processing of regular nominal singulars and plurals in Italian. In G. Booij and J. van Marle (eds), *Yearbook of morphology 1996,* Dordrecht: Kluwer.

Baayen, R. H., Dijkstra, T. and Schreuder, R. (1997b). Singulars and plurals in Dutch: evidence for a parallel dual-route model. *Journal of Memory and Language,* 37, 94–117.

Badecker, W. (1996). Representational properties common to phonological and orthographic output systems. *Lingua,* 99, 55–84.

—— (to appear). Levels of morphological deficit: indications from inflectional regularity. *Brain and Language.*

Badecker, W. and Caramazza, A. (1987). The analysis of morphological errors in a case of acquired dyslexia. *Brain and Language,* 32, 278–305.

—— (1989). A lexical distinction between inflection and derivation. *Linguistic Inquiry,* 20, 108–16.

—— (1991). Morphological composition in the lexical output system. *Cognitive Neuropsychology,* 8, 335–67.

—— (1993). Disorders of lexical morphology in aphasia. In G. Blanken, J. Dittmann, H. Grimm, J. Marshall and C.-W. Wallesch (eds), *Linguistic disorders and pathologies: an international handbook,* Berlin: Walter de Gruyter, 181–6.

Badecker, W., Hillis, A. and Caramazza, A. (1990). Lexical morphology and its role in the writing process: evidence from a case of acquired dysgraphia. *Cognition,* 35, 205–43.

Badecker, W., Rapp, B. and Caramazza, A. (1995). A modality-neutral lexical deficit affecting morpho-syntactic representations. Paper presented at the 33rd annual meeting of the Academy of Aphasia, San Diego, Calif., 5–7 Nov. 1995; abstract in *Brain and Language,* 51, 83–4.

—— (1996). Lexical morphology and the two orthographic routes. *Cognitive Neuropsychology,* 13, 161–75.

Bagemihl, B. (1991). Syllable structure in Bella Coola. *Linguistic Inquiry*, 22, 589–646.

Baker, M. (1985). The mirror principle and morphosyntactic explanation. *Linguistic Inquiry*, 16, 373–416.

—— (1988a). *Incorporation: a theory of grammatical function changing*. Chicago: University of Chicago Press.

—— (1988b). Morphology and syntax: an interlocking independence. In Everaert et al. (eds), 9–32.

—— (1988c). Theta theory and the syntax of applicatives in Chichewa. *Natural Language and Linguistic Theory*, 6, 353–68.

—— (in press). Thematic roles and syntactic structure. In L. Haegeman (ed.), *Handbook of generative syntax*, Dordrecht: Kluwer.

Baker, M., Johnson, K. and Roberts, I. G. (1989). Passive arguments raised. *Linguistic Inquiry*, 20, 219–52.

Ball, M. and Fife, J. (eds) (1993). *The Celtic languages*. London: Routledge.

Ball, M. and Müller, N. (1992). *Mutation in Welsh*. London: Routledge.

Bánhidi, Z., Jókay, Z. and Szabó, D. (1965). *Learn Hungarian*, 4th edn. Budapest: Tanykönyvkiadó.

Barbosa, P. (1996). Clitic placement in European Portuguese and the position of subjects. In Halpern and Zwicky (eds), 1–40.

Barlow, A. R. (1960). *Studies in Kikuyu grammar and idiom*. Edinburgh: Foreign Mission Committee of the Church of Scotland.

Barlow, M. (1988). A situated theory of agreement. Ph.D. diss., Stanford University. Published 1992, New York: Garland.

—— (1991). The agreement hierarchy and grammatical theory. In *Proceedings of the 17th annual meeting of the Berkeley Linguistics Society*, 17, 30–40.

Barlow, M. and Ferguson, C. A. (eds) (1988). *Agreement in natural language: approaches, theories and descriptions*. Stanford, Calif.: CSLI.

Bat-El, O. (1989). Phonology and word structure in modern Hebrew. Ph.D. diss., UCLA.

Bates, D. (1988). Prominence relations and structure in English compound morphology. Ph.D. diss., University of Washington.

Bates, D. and Carlson, B. (1992). Simple syllables in Spokane Salish. *Linguistic Inquiry*, 23, 653–9.

Bates, E., Friederici, A. and Wulfeck, B. (1987). Grammatical morphology in aphasia: evidence from three languages. *Cortex*, 23, 545–74.

Bayer, S. and Johnson, M. (1995). Features and agreement [Online]. Available: http://xxx.lanl.gov/list/cmp-lg/9506007 [June 1995].

Bazell, C. E. (1949). On the problem of the morpheme. *Archivium Linguisticum*, 1, 1–15.

—— (1952). The correspondence fallacy in structural linguistics. *Studies by Members of the English Department, Istanbul University*, 3, 1–41.

Beard, R. (1966). The suffixation of adjectives in contemporary literary Serbo-Croatian. Ph.D. diss., University of Michigan.

—— (1976). A semantically based model of a generative lexical word-formation rule for Russian adjectives. *Language*, 52, 108–20.

—— (1981). *The Indo-European lexicon*. Amsterdam: North-Holland.

—— (1988). On the separation of derivation from morphology: toward a lexeme/morpheme-based morphology. *Quaderni di Semantica*, 9, 3–59.

—— (1990). The nature and origins of derivational polysemy. *Lingua*, 81, 101–40.

—— (1991). Decompositional composition: the semantics of scope ambiguities and 'bracketing paradoxes'. *Natural Language and Linguistic Theory*, 9, 195–229.

—— (1993). Simultaneous dual derivation in word formation. *Language*, 69, 716–41.

—— (1995). *Lexeme–morpheme Base Morphology*. Albany: State University of New York Press.

Beauvillain, C. (1994). Morphological structure in visual word recognition: evidence from prefixed and suffixed words. *Language and Cognitive Processes*, 9, 317–39.

Becker, D. A. (1971). Case grammar and German *be-*. *Glossa*, 5, 125–45.

Belić, A. (1958). *O jezickoj prirodi i jezickom razvitku. Knjiga I*. Beograd: Nolit.

Bell, C. R. V. (1953). *The Somali language*. London: Longmans, Green and Co.

Belletti, A. (1990). *Generalized verb movement: aspects of verb syntax*. Torino: Rosenberg and Sellier.

Belletti, A. and Rizzi, L. (1988). Psych-verbs and θ theory. *Natural Language and Linguistic Theory*, 6, 291–352.

Bennett, P. R., Biersteker, A., Gikonyo, W., Hershberg, S., Kamande, J., Perez, C. and Swearingen, M. (1985). *Gikuyu ni Kioigire: essays, texts, and glossaries*. Madison: African Studies Program of the University of Wisconsin–Madison.

Bennis, H. and Haegeman, L. (1984). On the status of agreement and relative clauses in West-Flemish. In W. de Geest and Y. Putseys (eds), *Sentential complementation*, Dordrecht: Foris, Bentin, S. and Feldman, L. B. (1990). The contribution of morphological and semantic relatedness to repetition priming at short and long lags: evidence from Hebrew. *Quarterly Journal of Experimental Psychology*, 42A, 693–711.

Benton, R. (1971). *Pangasinan reference grammar*. Honolulu: University of Hawaii Press.

Berent, G. (1980). On the realization of trace: Macedonian clitic pronouns. In C. Chvany and R. Brecht (eds), *Morphosyntax in Slavic*, Columbus: Slavica, 150–86.

Berg, T. (1987). The case against accommodation: evidence from German speech error data. *Journal of Memory and Language*, 26, 277–99.

Bergman, M. W. (1988). The visual recognition of word structure: left-to-right processing of derivational morphology. Ph.D. diss., University of Nijmegen.

Bergman, M. W., Hudson, P. T. W. and Eling, P. A. T. M. (1988). How simple complex words can be: morphological processing and word representations. *Quarterly Journal of Experimental Psychology*, 40A, 41–72.

Bergvall, V. (1985). A typology of empty categories for Kikuyu and Swahili. In G. Dimmendaal (ed.), *Current approaches to African linguistics*, vol. 3.

Berko, J. (1958). The child's learning of English morphology. *Word*, 14, 150–77.

Berman, R. A. and Clark, E. V. (1989). Learning to use compounds for contrast: data from Hebrew. *First Language*, 9, 247–70.

Bessler, P., Cummins, S., Nadasdi, T. and Roberge, Y. (1993). The lexicon–syntax interface. In C. Dyck (ed.), *Toronto Working Papers in Linguistics*, 12, 1–12.

Bhat, D. N. S. (1977). Multiple case roles. *Lingua*, 42, 365–77.

Bierwisch, M. (1967). Syntactic features in morphology: general problems of so-called pronominal inflection in German. In *To honour Roman Jakobson: essays on the occasion of his seventieth birthday*, The Hague: Mouton, 239–70.

Black, H. A. (1991). The optimal iambic foot and reduplication in Axininca Campa. *Phonology at Santa Cruz*, 2, 1–18.

—— (1993). Constraint-ranked derivation: a serial approach to optimization. Ph.D. diss., University of California at Santa Cruz.

Blake, B. (1990). *Relational grammar*. London: Routledge.

Bliese, L. (1967). Selected problems in noun morphology in the Aussa dialect of Afar. Unpub. M.A. diss., University of Texas at Austin.

—— (1981). *A generative grammar of Afar*. Arlington: Summer Institute of Linguistics and the University of Texas at Arlington.

Bloom, L., Lifter, K. and Hafitz, J. (1980). Semantics of verbs and the development of verb inflection. *Language*, 56, 386–412.

Bloomfield, L. (1933). *Language*. New York: Henry Holt.

—— (1946). Algonquian. In *Linguistic structures of Native America*, The Viking Fund publications in anthropology, 6. New York: The Viking Fund; repr. 1971 by Johnson Reprint Corporation, New York.

—— (1962). *The Menomini language*. New Haven, Conn.: Yale University Press.

Boase-Beier, J. and Toman, J. (1986). Theta-role assignment in German. *Folia Linguistica*, 20, 319–40.

Bochner, H. (1984). Inflection within derivation. *Linguistic Review*, 3, 411–21.

—— (1992). *Simplicity in generative morphology*. Berlin: Mouton de Gruyter.

Bock, K. and Miller, C. A. (1991). Broken agreement. *Cognitive Psychology*, 23, 45–93.

Bogoras, W. (1917). *Koryak texts*, American Ethnological Society Publications, 5. Leiden: Brill.

—— (1922). Chukchee. In F. Boas (ed.), *Handbook of American Indian languages*, pt 2, Washington: Government Printing Office, 631–903.

Bokamba, E. (1976). On the syntax and semantics of derivational verb suffixes in Bantu languages. In F. Ingeman (ed.), *Mid-America Linguistic Conference Papers*, Lawrence: University of Kansas Press.

—— (1981). Aspects of Bantu syntax. MS, University of Illinois, Urbana–Champaign.

Bonet, E. (1991). Morphology after syntax: pronominal clitics in Romance. Ph.D. diss., Massachusetts Institute of Technology.

Booij, G. (1988). The relation between inheritance and argument linking: Deverbal nouns in Dutch. In Everaert et al. (eds), 57–73.

—— (1993). Against split morphology. In G. Booij and J. van Marle (eds), *Yearbook of morphology 1993*, Dordrecht: Kluwer, 27–49.

Booij, G. and van Marle, J. (eds) (1988). *Yearbook of morphology 1*. Dordrecht: Foris.

—— (1990). *Yearbook of morphology 3*. Dordrecht: Foris.

Booij, G. and Rubach, J. (1987). Postcyclic versus postlexical rules in Lexical Phonology. *Linguistic Inquiry*, 18/1, 1–44.

Borer, H. (1984a). *Parametric syntax*. Dordrecht: Foris.

—— (1984b). The Projection Principle and rules of morphology. In *Proceedings of the 14th meeting of the North-Eastern Linguistic Society*, 16–33.

—— (1988). On the morphological parallelism between compounds and construct. In Booij and van Marle (eds), 45–66.

—— (1991). The causative-inchoative alternation: a case study in parallel morphology. *Linguistic Review*, 8, 119–58.

—— (1994). The projection of arguments. In E. Benedicto and J. Runner (eds), *UMass Occasional Papers in Linguistics*, 17, Amherst: University of Massachusetts, GLSA, 1–29.

—— (1995). Deconstructing the construct. In K. Johnson and I. G. Roberts (eds), *Papers in memory of Osvaldo Jaeggli*, Dordrecht: Kluwer.

—— (in press). Deriving passive without theta roles. In S. Lapointe (ed.), *Morphological interfaces*, Stanford, Calif.: CSLI.

Börjars, K., Chapman, C. and Vincent, N. (1996). Paradigms, periphrases and pro-drop: a feature-based account. In G. Booij and J. van Marle (eds), *Yearbook of morphology 1996*, Dordrecht: Kluwer, 155–80.

Borowsky, T. (1986). Topics in the lexical phonology of English. Ph.D. diss., University of Massachusetts, Amherst.

Botha, R. P. (1981). A base rule theory of Afrikaans synthetic compounding. In M. Moortgat, T. Hoekstra and H. van der Hulst (eds), *The scope of lexical rules*, Dordrecht, Foris, 1–77.

Bowe, H. J. (1990). *Categories, constituents and constituent order in Pitjantjatjara*. London and New York: Routledge.

Bowerman, M. (1974). Learning the structure of causative verbs: a study in the relationship of cognitive, semantic, and syntactic development. *Papers and Reports on Child Language Development*, 13, 148–56.

Bradley, D. (1980). Lexical representation of derivation relation. In M. Aronoff and M.-L. Kean (eds), *Juncture*, Saratoga, Calif.: Anma Libri, 37–55.

Brecht, R. D. (1985). The form and function of aspect in Russian. In M. S. Flier and R. D. Brecht (eds), *Issues in Russian morphosyntax*, Columbus, Ohio: Slavica, 9–34.

Breen, G. (1974). Wakaya grammar informant: Willy Clegg. Copy at AIATSIS, Canberra.

Brekle, H. E. (1986). The production and interpretation of ad hoc nominal compounds in German: a realistic approach. *Acta Linguistica*, 36, 39–52.

Bresnan, J. (1982a). Control and complementation. *Linguistic Inquiry*, 13, 343–434.

—— J. (ed.) (1982b). *The mental representation of grammatical relations*. Cambridge, Mass.: MIT Press.

—— (1982c). The passive in lexical theory. In J. Bresnan (ed.), (pp. 3–86). Cambridge, MA: MIT Press.

—— (1991). Locative case vs. locative gender. In *Proceedings of the 17th annual meeting of the Berkeley Linguistics Society*, 53–68.

—— (1995). Locative inversion and the architecture of UG. MS, Stanford University.

—— (1996). Lexical-functional syntax. MS, Stanford University.

Bresnan, J. and Kanerva, J. M. (1989). Locative inversion in Chichewa: a case study of factorization in grammar. *Linguistic Inquiry*, 20, 1–50.

Bresnan, J. and Mchombo, S. A. (1986). Grammatical and anaphoric agreement. In *Papers from the 22nd annual regional meeting of the Chicago Linguistic Society, parasession on pragmatics and grammatical theory*, 278–97.

—— (1987). Topic, pronoun, and agreement in Chichewa. *Language*, 63, 741–82.

—— (1995). The lexical integrity principle: evidence from Bantu. *Natural Language and Linguistic Theory*, 13, 181–254.

Bresnan, J. and Moshi, L. (1990). Object asymmetries in comparative Bantu syntax. *Linguistic Inquiry*, 21, 147–85; also in S. A. Mchombo (ed.), 1993b, 47–91.

Broadbent, S. (1964). *The Southern Sierra Miwok language*. Berkeley: University of California Press.

Bromberger, S. and Halle, M. (1988). Conceptual issues in morphology. MS, MIT.

Broselow, E. (1982). On the interaction of stress and epenthesis. *Glossa*, 16, 115–32.

Broselow, E. and McCarthy, J. (1983). A theory of internal reduplication. *Linguistic Review*, 3, 25–88.

Brousseau, A.-M. (1988). *Triptique sur les composés. Les noms composés en français, fongbe et haitien en regard des notions de tête et de percolation*. Montreal: Groupe de recherche sur le créole haitien, UQAM.

Brown, D., Corbett, G., Hippisley, A., Fraser, N. and Timberlake, A. (1996). Russian noun stress and network morphology. *Linguistics*, 34, 1–55.

Brown, R. (1973). *A first language: the early stages*. Cambridge, Mass.: Harvard University Press.

Browne, W. (1974). On the problem of enclitic placement in Serbo-Croatian. In R. Brecht and C. Chvany (eds), *Slavic transformational syntax*, Michigan Slavic Materials, 10, Ann Arbor: Dept. of Slavic Languages and Literatures, University of Michigan, 36–52.

—— (1975). Serbo-Croatian enclitics for English-speaking learners. In R. Filipovic (ed.), *Contrastive analysis of English and Serbo-Croatian*, Zagreb: Institute of Linguistics, 105–34.

Brunson, B. (1989). Thematic dependencies and government. Paper presented at the fifth meeting of the Eastern States conference on Linguistics.

Bub, D. and Kertesz, A. (1982). Evidence for lexico-graphic processing in a patient with preserved written over single word naming. *Brain*, 105, 697–717.

Buck, C. D. (1928). *A grammar of Oscan and Umbrian*. Boston: Ginn and Co.

Buckingham, H. (1981). Where do neologisms come from? In J. Brown (ed.), *Jargonaphasia*, New York: Academic Press, 39–62.

Buckingham, H. and Kertesz, A. (1976). *Neologistic jargonaphasia*. Amsterdam: Swets and Zeitlinger.

Builles, J.-M. (1988). La voix agento-stative en malgache. In *Etudes d'Océan Indien*, 9, Paris: INALCO.

Burani, C. (1993). What determines morphological relatedness in the lexicon? Comments on the chapter by Tyler, Waksler, and Marslen-Wilson. In G. Altmann and R. Shillcock (eds), *Cognitive models of speech processing*, Hillsdale, N.J.: Erlbaum, 141–59.

Burani, C. and Caramazza, A. (1987). Representation and processing of derived words. *Language and Cognitive Processes*, 2, 217–27.

Burani, C., Salmaso, D. and Caramazza, A. (1984). Morphological structure and lexical access. *Visible Language*, 18, 342–52.

Burzio, L. (1989). Prosodic reduction. In C. Kirschner and J. DeCesaris (eds), *Studies in Romance linguistics*, Amsterdam: J. Benjamins, 51–68.

Butterworth, B. (1983). Lexical representation. In B. Butterworth (ed.), *Language production*, vol. 2, London: Academic Press, 257–94.

Butterworth, B. and Howard, D. (1987). Paragrammatisms. *Cognition*, 26, 1–37.

Bybee, J. (1985). *Morphology: a study of the relation between meaning and form*. Amsterdam: J. Benjamins.

—— (1988). Morphology as lexical organization. In Hammond and Noonan (eds), 119–41.

—— (1991). Natural morphology, the organization of paradigms and language acquisition. In T. Huebner and C. A. Ferguson (eds), *Crosscurrents in second language acquisition and linguistic theories*, Amsterdam: J. Benjamins, 67–92.

—— (1995a). Diachronic and typological properties of morphology and their implications for representation. In L. B. Feldman (ed.), *Morphological aspects of language processing*, Hillsdale, N.J.: Lawrence Erlbaum Associates, 225–46.

—— (1995b). Regular morphology and the lexicon. *Language and Cognitive Processes*, 10, 425–55.

Bybee, J. and Moder, C. (1983). Morphological classes as natural categories. *Language*, 59, 251–70.

Bybee, J. and Newman, J. E. (1995). Are stem changes as natural as affixes? *Linguistics*, 33, 633–54.

Bybee, J. and Slobin, D. I. (1982). Rules and schemas in the development and use of the English past tense. *Language*, 58, 265–89.

Bynon, T. (1990). Pronoun and verb agreement in typological and diachronic perspective. *SOAS Working Papers in Linguistics and Phonetics*, 1, 97–111.

—— (1992). Pronominal attrition, clitic doubling and typological change. *Folia Linguistica Historica*, 13, 27–63.

Campbell, L. (1991). Some grammaticalization changes in Estonian and their implications. In Traugott and Heine (eds), 1991a, 285–99.

Caplan, D., Keller, L. and Locke, S. (1972). Inflection of neologisms in aphasia. *Brain*, 95, 169–72.

Caramazza, A. (1984). The logic of neuropsychological research and the problem of patient classification in aphasia. *Brain and Language*, 21, 9–20.

Caramazza, A. and Hillis, A. (1989). The disruption of sentence production: some dissociations. *Brain and Language*, 36, 625–50.

—— (1990a). Levels of representation, co-ordinate frames, and unilateral neglect. *Cognitive Neuropsychology*, 7, 391–445.

—— (1990b). Where do semantic errors come from? *Cortex*, 26, 95–122.

Caramazza, A., Laudanna, A. and Romani, C. (1988). Lexical access and inflectional morphology. *Cognition*, 28, 297–332.

Caramazza, A., Miceli, G., Villa, G. and Romani, C. (1987). The role of the graphemic buffer in spelling: evidence from a case of acquired dysgraphia. *Cognition*, 26, 59–85.

Cardinaletti, A. (1992). On cliticization in Germanic languages. *Rivista di grammatica generative*, 17, 65–99.

Cardinaletti, A. and Roberts, I. G. (to appear). Clause structure and X-Second. In G. Horrocks and W. Chao (eds), *Levels of representation*, Dordrecht: Foris.

Carey, S. (1994). Does learning a language require the child to reconceptualize the world? *Lingua*, 92, 143–67.

Carlson, B. F. (1989). Compounding and lexical affixation in Spokane. *Anthropological Linguistics*, 31, 69–82.

Carpenter, K. (1991). Later rather than sooner: Extralinguistic categories in the acquisition of Thai classifiers. *Journal of Child Language*, 18, 93–113.

Carrier, J. and Randall, J. H. (1992). The argument structure and syntactic structure of resultatives. *Linguistic Inquiry*, 23, 173–234.

Carstairs, A. (1987). *Allomorphy in inflexion*. London: Croom Helm.

—— (1988). Some implications of phonologically conditioned suppletion. In Booij and van Marle (eds), 67–94.

—— (1991). Inflection classes: two questions with one answer. In Plank (ed.), 213–53.

Carstairs, A. and Stemberger, J. (1988). A processing constraint on inflectional homonymy. *Linguistics*, 26, 601–17.

Carstairs-McCarthy, A. (1991). Inflection classes: two questions with one answer. In Plank (ed.), 213–53.

—— (1992). *Current morphology*. London: Routledge.

—— (1994). Inflection classes, gender, and the Principle of Contrast. *Language*, 70, 737–88.

—— (in press). Uses for junk: a new look at inflection classes. In W. U. Dressler, H. C. Luschützky, O. E. Pfeiffer and J. R. Rennison (eds), *Progress in morphology*, Berlin: Mouton de Gruyter.

Carter, R. J. (1976). Some constraints on possible words. *Semantikos*, 1, 27–6.

—— (1988a). Compositionality and polysemy. In Levin and Tenny (eds), 167–204 (originally written in 1984).

—— (1988b). Some linking regularities. In Levin and Tenny (eds), 1–92 (originally written in 1976).

Cazden, C. B. (1968). The acquisition of noun and verb inflections. *Child Development*, 39, 433–48.

Chadwick, N. (1975). *A descriptive study of the Djingili language*. Australian Aboriginal Studies Regional and Research Studies. Canberra: Australian Institute of Aboriginal Studies.

Chakravarti, P. (1967). A report on WaRumunu. Copy at AIATSIS, Canberra.

Chambers, J. K. and Shaw, P. A. (1980). Systematic obfuscation of morphology in Dakota. *Linguistic Inquiry*, 11, 325–36.

Chantraine, P. (1973). *Morphologie historique du grec*, (2nd edition). Paris: Editions Klincksieck.

Chen, M. (1987). The syntax of Xiamen tone sandhi. *Phonology Yearbook*, 4, 109–49.

Chialant, D. and Caramazza, A. (1995). Where is morphological and how is it represented? The case of written word recognition. In Feldman (ed.), 55–76.

Chiang, W-Y. (1992). The prosodic morphology and phonology of affixation in Taiwanese and other Chinese languages. Ph.D. diss., University of Delaware.

Chomsky, N. (1970). Remarks on nominalization. In R. Jacobs and P. Rosenbaum (eds), *Readings in transformational grammar*, Waltham, Mass.: Ginn and Co., 184–221.

—— (1980). *Rules and representations*. Oxford: Blackwell Publishers.

—— (1981). *Lectures on government and binding*. Dordrecht: Foris.

—— (1986). *Barriers*. Cambridge, Mass.: MIT Press.

—— (1988). *Some notes on economy of derivation and representation*, MIT Working Papers in Linguistics, 10. Cambridge, Mass.: MIT Press.

—— (1993). A minimalist program in linguistic theory. In Hale and Keyser (eds), 1–37.

—— (1995a). Bare phrase structure. In G. Webelhuth (ed.), *Government and binding theory and the Minimalist Program*, Oxford: Blackwell Publishers, 383–439.

—— (1995b). *The Minimalist Program*. Cambridge, Mass.: MIT Press.

Chomsky, N. and Halle, M. (1968). *The sound pattern of English*. New York: Harper and Row.

Chung, S. and Timberlake, A. (1985). Tense, aspect, and mood. In Shopen (ed.), 202–58.

Churchward, C. M. (1953). *Tongan grammar*. Oxford: Oxford University Press.

Clahsen, H. and Hansen, D. (1993). The missing agreement account of specific language impairment: evidence from therapy experiments. *Essex Research Reports in Linguistics*, 2, 1–36.

Clahsen, H. and Rothweiler, M. (1993). Inflectional rules in children's grammars: evidence from German participles. In G. Booij and J. van Marle (eds), *Yearbook of morphology 1992*, Dordrecht: Kluwer, 1–34.

Clahsen, H., Rothweiler, M., Woest, A. and Marcus, G. F. (1992). Regular and irregular inflection in the acquisition of German noun plurals. *Cognition*, 45, 225–55.

Clark, E. V. (1982). The young word-maker: a case study of innovation in the child's lexicon. In E. Wanner and L. R. Gleitman (eds), *Language acquisition: the state of the art*, Cambridge: Cambridge University Press, 390–425.

—— (1987). The principle of contrast: a constraint on acquisition. In MacWhinney (ed.), 1–33.

—— (1990). The pragmatics of contrast. *Journal of Child Language*, 17, 417–31.

—— (1993). *The lexicon in acquisition*. Cambridge: Cambridge University Press.

—— (1996). Early verbs, event-types, and inflections. In J. H. V. Gilbert and C. E. Johnson (eds), *Children's language*, vol. 9, Hillsdale, N.J.: Lawrence Erlbaum, 61–73.

Clark, E. V. and Berman, R. A. (1984). Structure and use in the acquisition of word formation. *Language*, 60, 547–90.

—— (1987). Types of linguistic knowledge: interpreting and producing compound nouns. *Journal of Child Language*, 14, 547–67.

Clark, E. V. and Clark, H. H. (1979). When nouns surface as verbs. *Language*, 55, 767–811.

Clark, E. V. and Cohen, S. R. (1984). Productivity and memory for newly formed words. *Journal of Child Language*, 11, 611–25.

Clark, E. V. and Hecht, B. F. (1982). Learning to coin agent and instrument nouns. *Cognition*, 12, 1–24.

Clark, E. V., Gelman, S. A. and Lane, N. M. (1985). Noun compounds and category structure in children. *Child Development*, 56, 84–94.

Clark, E. V., Hecht, B. F. and Mulford, R. C. (1986). Acquiring complex compounds: affixes and word order in English. *Linguistics*, 24, 7–29.

Cohn, A. (1989). Stress in Indonesian and bracketing paradoxes. *Natural Language and Linguistic Theory*, 7, 167–216.

Cole, J. F. (1991). Phrasal reduplication in Bengali. To appear in *Proceedings of the third Leiden conference of junior linguists*, Leiden: University of Leiden.

Cole, P., Beauvillain, C. and Segui, J. (1989). On the representation and processing of prefixed and suffixed derived words: a differential frequency effect. *Journal of Memory and Language*, 28, 1–13.

Colizza, G. (1887). *La lingua Afar nel nord-est dell'Africa: grammatica, testi e vocabolario.* Vienna:

Collinge, N. E. (1985). *The laws of Indo-European.* Amsterdam: J. Benjamins.

Coltheart, M. (1980). Deep dyslexia: a review of the syndrome. In Coltheart et al. (eds), 22–47.

Coltheart, M., Patterson, K. and Marshall, J. (eds) (1980). *Deep dyslexia.* London: Routledge and Kegan Paul.

Comrie, B. (1975). Polite plurals and predicate agreement. *Language*, 51, 406–18.

—— (1976). The system of causative constructions: cross language similarity and divergencies. In Shibatani (ed.), 1976a, 261–312.

—— (1979). The animacy hierarchy in Chukchee. In P. Clyne, W. Hanks and C. Hofbauer (eds), *Papers from the 15th annual meeting of the Chicago Linguistics Society: the elements: a parasession on linguistic units and levels*, 322–9.

—— (1980). Inverse verb forms in Chukchee. Evidence from Chukchee, Koryak and Kamchadal. *Folia Linguistica Historica*, 1/1, 64–74.

—— (1985). Causative verb formation and other verb-deriving morphology. In Shopen (ed.), 309–48.

—— (1992). Siberian languages. In W. Bright (ed.), *International encyclopedia of linguistics*, New York: Oxford University Press, 429–32.

Comrie, B. and Corbett, G. (eds) (1993). *The Slavonic languages.* London and New York: Routledge.

Condoravdi, C. (1989). The middle: where semantics and morphology meet. Student Conference in Linguistics, 1. *MIT Working Papers in Linguistics*, 11, 16–30.

—— (1990). Sandhi rules of Greek and prosodic theory. In S. Inkelas and D. Zec (eds), *The phonology–syntax connection*, Chicago: University of Chicago Press, 63–84.

Cook, E-D. (1984). *A Sarcee grammar.* Vancouver: University of British Columbia Press.

—— (1989). Chilcotin tone and verb paradigms. In Cook and Rice (eds), 145–98.

—— (1996). Third-person plural subject prefix in Northern Athapaskan. *International Journal of American Linguistics*, X, 86–110.

Cook, E-D. and K. Rice (eds) (1989). *Athapaskan linguistics. Current perspectives on a language family*, Trends in linguistics, state-of-the-art reports, 15. Berlin: Mouton de Gruyter.

Coolen, R., van Jaarsveld, H. J. and Schreuder, R. (1991). The interpretation of isolated novel nominal compounds. *Memory and Cognition*, 19, 341–52.

—— (1993). Processing novel compounds: evidence for interactive meaning activation of ambiguous nouns. *Memory and Cognition*, 21, 235–46.

Corbett, G. (1979). The agreement hierarchy. *Journal of Linguistics*, 15, 203–24.

—— (1983). *Hierarchies, targets and controllers: agreement patterns in Slavic.* London: Croom Helm.

—— (1991). *Gender.* Cambridge: Cambridge University Press.

—— (1994). Agreement. In R. E. Asher (ed.), *Encyclopedia of language and linguistics*, vol. 1, Oxford: Pergamon Press, 54–60.

—— (1995). Agreement (research into syntactic change). In J. Jacobs, A. von Stechow, W. Steinefeld and T. Vennemann (eds), *Syntax: an international handbook of contemporary research*, vol. 2 Berlin: Walter de Gruyter, 1235–44.

Corbett, G. and Hayward, R. J. (1987). Gender and number in Bayso. *Lingua*, 73, 1–28.

Corbett, G. and Mtenje, A. (1987). Gender agreement in Chichewa. *Studies in African Linguistics*, 18, 1–38.

Corbin, D. (1987). *Morphologie dérivationnelle et structuration du lexique.* Tübingen: Niemeyer.

Corina, D. P. (1991). Towards an understanding of the syllable: evidence from linguistic, psychological, and connectionist investigations of syllable structure. Ph.D. diss., University of California at San Diego.

Cousins, W. E. (1894). *A concise introduction to the study of the Malagasy language.* Antananarivo, Madagascar: Press of the London Missionary Society.

Croft, W. A. (1991). *Syntactic categories and grammatical relations.* Chicago: University of Chicago Press.

Crowhurst, M. (1991a). Demorafication in Tübatulabal: evidence from initial reduplication and stress. In *Proceedings of the 21st meeting of the North-Eastern Linguistic Society*, 49–64.

—— (1991b). Minimality and foot structure in metrical phonology and prosodic morphology. Ph.D. diss., University of Arizona, Tucson.

Culicover, P., Wasow, T. and Akmajian, A. (eds) (1977). *Formal syntax.* New York: Academic Press.

Cutler, A. (1980). Errors of stress and intonation. In V. A. Fromkin (ed.), *Errors in linguistic performance*, New York: Academic Press.

—— (1983). Lexical complexity and sentence processing. In G. B. Flores d'Arcais and R. J. Jarvella (eds), *The process of language understanding*, New York: Wiley, 43–79.

Cutler, A., Hawkins, J. A. and Gilligan, G. (1985). The suffixing preference: a processing explanation. *Linguistics*, 23, 723–58.

Dahl, O-C. (1951). *Malgache et maanjan: une comparaison linguistique.* Oslo: Egede-Instituttet.

—— (1988). Bantu substratum in Malagasy. *Etudes d'Océan Indien*, 9, 91–132. Translation of Dahl, 1954. Le substrat bantu en malgache.

Dai, J. (1990). Historical morphologization of syntactic structures: evidence from derived verbs in Chinese. *Diachronica*, 7, 9–46.

Daugherty, K. and Seidenberg, M. S. (1994). Beyond rules and exceptions: a connectionist approach to inflectional morphology. In S. D. Lima, R. L. Corrigan and G. K. Iverson (eds), *The reality of linguistic rules*, Amsterdam: J. Benjamins, 353–88.

Davies, W. D. (1986). *Choctaw verb agreement and universal grammar.* Dordrecht: Reidel.

Davis, H. and Demirdash, H. (1995). Agents and events. Paper presented at GLOW 1995, Tromsoe.

De Bleser, R. and Bayer, J. (1986). German word formation and aphasia. *Linguistic Review*, 5, 1–40.

—— (1990). Morphological reading errors in a German case of deep dyslexia. In Nespoulous and Villard (eds), 32–59.

Declerck, R. (1979). Aspect and the bounded/unbounded (telic/atelic) distinction. *Linguistics*, 17, 761–94.

Decroly, O. and Degand, J. (1913). Observations relatives au developpement de la notion du temps chez une petite fille. *Archives de Psychologie*, 13, 113–61.

De Groot, C. (1984). Totally affected. Aspect and three-place predicates in Hungarian. In C. De Groot and H. Tommola (eds), *Aspect bound: a voyage into the realm of Germanic, Slavonic and Finno-Ugrian aspectology*, Dordrecht: Foris, 133–51.

DeLancey, S. (1991). The origins of verb serialization in Modern Tibetan. *Studies in Language*, 15, 1–23.

Dell, F. and Elmedlaoui, M. (1992). Quantitative transfer in the nonconcatenative morphology of Imdlawn Tashlhiyt Berber. *Journal of Afroasiatic Languages*, 3, 89–125.

Dell, G. S. (1986). A spreading activation theory of retrieval in sentence production. *Psychological Review*, 93, 283–321.

—— (1990). Effects of frequency and vocabulary type on phonological speech errors. *Language and Cognitive Processes*, 5, 313–49.

Dell, G. S. and O'Seaghdha, P. G. (1991). Mediated vs. convergent lexical priming in language production: comment on Levelt et al. *Psychological Review*, 98, 604–14.

Dell, G. S., Juliano, C. and Govindjee, A. (1993). Structure and content in language production: a theory of frame constraints in phonological speech errors. *Cognitive Science*, 17, 149–95.

Dembetembe, N. C. (1987). *A linguistic study of the verb in Korekore.* Harare: University of Zimbabwe.

Demuth, K. (1988). Noun classes and agreement in Sesotho acquisition. In Barlow and Ferguson (eds), 305–21.

Demuth, K. and Johnson, M. (1989). Interaction between discourse functions and agreement in Setawana. *Journal of African Languages and Linguistics*, 11, 21–35.

Dench, A. and Evans, N. (1988). Multiple case-marking in Australian languages. *Australian Journal of Linguistics*, 8, 1–47.

De Reuse, W. J. (1992). A bibliography on incorporation and polysynthesis in native American and paleosiberian languages. *Kansas Working Papers in Linguistics*, 17, 277–308.

Dez, J. (1980a). *La syntaxe du malgache.* Paris: Librairie H. Champion.

—— (1980b). *Structures de la langue malgache: elements de grammaire a l'usage des francophones.* Paris: Publications Orientalistes de France.

Di Sciullo, A. M. and Williams, E. (1987). *On the definition of word.* Cambridge, Mass.: MIT Press.

Dimis and Reedo (1976a). *Qafar afak: yabti-rakiibo.* Paris: L'Imprimerie Parisienne de la Runion.

—— (1976b). *Qafar afih baritto.* Paris: L'Imprimerie Parisienne de la Runion.

Dimmendaal, G. J. (1983). *The Turkana language.* Dordrecht: Foris.

—— (1987). Drift and selective mechanisms in morphological change: the Eastern Nilotic case. In A. G. Ramat, O. Carruba and G. Bernini (eds), *Papers from the 7th international conference on historical linguistics*, Amsterdam: J. Benjamins, 193–210.

Dirr, A. M. (1908). Arčinskij jazyk. In *Sbornik materialov dlja opisanija mestnostej i plemen Kavkaza*. Vyp. 39. Tbilisi.

Dobrovie-Sorin, C. (1990). Clitic doubling, wh-movement and quantification in Romanian. *Linguistic Inquiry*, 21/3, 351–97.

Domenichini-Ramiaramanana, B. (1977). *Le malgache: essai de description sommaire*. Paris: SELAF.

Donaldson, T. (1980). *Ngiyambaa: the language of the Wangaaybuwan*. Cambridge: Cambridge University Press.

Dorian, N. (1977). A hierarchy of morphophonemic decay in Scottish Gaelic language death: the differential failure of lenition. *Word*, 28, 96–109.

—— (1978). *East Sutherland Gaelic*. Dublin: Institute for Advanced Studies.

Doron, E. and Rappaport Hovav, M. (1991). Affectedness and externalization. In *Proceedings of the 21st meeting of the North-Eastern Linguistic Society*, 81–94.

Downie, R., Milech, D. and Kirsner, K. (1985). Unit definition in the mental lexicon. *Australian Journal of Psychology*, 37, 141–55.

Downing, P. (1977). On the creation and use of English nominal compounds. *Language*, 55, 810–42.

Dowty, D. R. (1979). *Word meaning and Montague grammar*. Dordrecht: Reidel.

—— (1991). Thematic proto-roles and argument selection. *Language*, 67, 547–619.

Dowty, D. R., Wall, R. and Peters, S. (1981). *Introduction to Montague semantics*. Dordrecht: Reidel.

Drabbe, P. (1955). *Spraakkunst van het Marind*, Studia Instituti Anthropos, 11 (cited from Foley, 1986).

Dressler, W. U. (1982). Zum Verhältnis von Wortbildung und Textunguistik. In J. Petöfi (ed.), *Text vs. sentence continued*, Hamburg: Buske, 96–106.

—— (1987). Subtraction in a polycentristic theory of Natural Morphology. In E. Gussmann (ed.), *Rules and the lexicon*, Lublin: Redakcja Wydawnictw Katolickiego Uniwersytetu Lubelskiego, 67–78.

Dressler, W. U. and Kiefer, F. (1990). Austro-Hungarian morphopragmatics. In Dressler et al. (eds), 69–77.

Dressler, W. U. and Merlini-Barbaresi, L. (1993). *Morphopragmatics*. Berlin: Mouton de Gruyter.

Dressler, W. U. and Wodak-Leodolter, R. (1977). Language preservation and language death in Brittany. *International Journal of the Sociology of Language*, 12, 33–44.

Dressler, W. U., Mayerthaler, W., Panagl, Oswald and Würzel, W. U. (1987). *Leitmotifs in Natural Morphology*. Amsterdam: J. Benjamins.

Dressler, W. U., Luschützky, H. C., Pfeiffer, O. E. and Rennison, J. R. (eds), (1990). *Contemporary morphology*. Berlin: Mouton de Gruyter.

Drewnoski, A. and Healy, A. F. (1980). Missing -ing in reading: letter detection errors on word endings. *Journal of Verbal Learning and Verbal Behavior*, 19, 247–62.

Drews, E. and Zwitserlood, P. (1995). Morphological and orthographic similarity in visual word recognition. *Journal of Experimental Psychology: Human Perception and Performance*, 21, 1098–1116.

Ellis, A. and Young, A. (1988). *Human cognitive neuropsychology*. Hove and London: Lawrence Erlbaum.

Elman, J. L. (1990). Finding structure in time. *Cognitive Science*, 14, 213–52.

Emmorey, K. D. (1989). Auditory morphological priming in the lexicon. *Language and Cognitive Processes*, 4, 73–92.

Emonds, J. (1978). The verbal complex V'-V in French. *Linguistic Inquiry*, 9, 49–77.

—— (1985). *A unified theory of syntactic categories*. Dordrecht: Foris.

Erwin, S. (1996). Quantity and moras: an amicable separation. In Pearson and Paul (eds), 2–30.

Esper, E. A. (1925). *A technique for the experimental investigation of associative interference in artificial linguistic material*, Language Monographs, 1. Philadelphia: Linguistic Society of America.

—— (1973). *Analogy and association in linguistics and psychology*. Athens, Ga.: University of Georgia Press.

Everaert, M., Evers, A., Huybregts, R. and Trommelen, M. (eds) (1988). *Morphology and modularity*. Dordrecht: Foris.

Everett, D. L. (1987). Pirahã clitic doubling. *Natural Language and Linguistic Theory*, 5, 245–76.

—— (1990). Clitic doubling, reflexives, and word order alternations in Yagua. *Language*, 65/2, 339–72.

—— (1996). *Why there are no clitics*. Dallas, Tex.: SIL-UTA.

—— and Kern, B. (1997). *Wari': the Pacaas Novos language of Western Brazil*. London: Routledge.

Ewen, R. (1979). A grammar of Bulgarian clitics. Unpublished Ph.D. diss., University of Washington.

Fabb, N. (1984). Syntactic affixation. Ph.D. diss., Massachusetts Institute of Technology.

—— (1988). Doing affixation in the GB Syntax. In Everaert et al. (eds), 129–45.

Fabri, R. (1993). *Kongruenz und die Grammatik des Maltesischen*. Tübingen: Niemeyer.

Fagan, S. M. B. (1988). The English middle. *Linguistic Inquiry*, 19, 181–203.

—— (1992). *The syntax and semantics of middle constructions*. Cambridge: Cambridge University Press.

Feldman, L. B. (1991). The contribution of morphology to word recognition. *Psychological Research*, 53, 33–41.

—— (1994). Beyond orthography and phonology: differences between inflections and derivations. *Journal of Memory and Language*, 33, 442–70.

Feldman, L. B. (ed.) (1995). *Morphological aspects of language processing*. Hillsdale, N.J.: Erlbaum.

Feldman, L. B. and Bentin, S. (1994). Morphological analysis of disrupted morphemes: evidence from Hebrew. *Quarterly Journal of Experimental Psychology*, 47A, 407–35.

Feldman, L. B. and Fowler, C. A. (1987). The inflection noun system in Serbo-Croatian: lexical representation of morphological structure. *Memory and Cognition*, 15, 1–12.

Feldman, L. B. and Moskovljević, J. (1987). Repetition priming is not purely episodic in origin. *Journal of Experimental Psychology: Learning, Memory, and Cognition*, 13, 573–81.

Feldman, L. B., Frost, R. and Pnini, T. (1995). Decomposing words into their constituent morphemes: evidence from English and Hebrew. *Journal of Experimental Psychology: Learning, Memory, and Cognition*, 21, 947–60.

Ferguson, C. A. and Slobin, D. I. (eds) (1973). *Studies of child language development*. New York: Holt, Rinehart and Winston.

Ferrand, G. (1903). *Essai de grammaire malgache*. Paris: Ernest Leroux.

Fife, J. (1986). Literary vs. colloquial Welsh: problems of definition. *Word*, 37, 141–51.

—— (1992). *The semantics of the Welsh verb*. Cardiff: University of Wales Press.

Fillmore, C. J. (1970). The grammar of hitting and breaking. In R. Jacobs and P. Rosenbaum (eds), *Readings in English transformational grammar*, Waltham, Mass.: Ginn and Co., 120–33.

Finer, D. (1985). Reduplication and verbal morphology in Palauan. *Linguistic Review*, 6, 99–130.

Flier, M. S. and Timberlake, A. (eds) (1985). *The scope of Slavic aspect*. Columbus, Oh.: Slavica.

Foley, W. A. (1986). *The Papuan languages of New Guinea*. Cambridge: Cambridge University Press.

Foley, W. A. and Van Valin, R. D. Jr. (1984). *Functional syntax and universal grammar*. Cambridge: Cambridge University Press.

Fontana, J. M. (1993). Phrase structure and the syntax of clitics in the history of Spanish. Unpublished Ph.D. diss., University of Pennsylvania.

Forchheimer, P. (1953). *The category of person in language*. Berlin: de Gruyter.

Fowler, C. A., Napps, S. E. and Feldman, L. B. (1985). Relations among regular and irregular morphologically related words in the lexicon as revealed by repetition priming. *Memory and Cognition*, 13, 241–55.

Frantz, D. G. (1971). *Toward a generative grammar of Blackfoot*. Norman, Okla.: Summer Institute of Linguistics.

Frauenfelder, U. H. and Schreuder, R. (1992). Constraining psycholinguistic models of morphological processing and representation: the role of productivity. In G. Booij and J. van Marle (eds), *Yearbook of morphology 1991*, Dordrecht: Kluwer, 165–83.

Frazier, L., Flores d'Arcais, G. B. and Coolen, R. (1993). Processing discontinuous words: on the interface between lexical and syntactic processing. *Cognition*, 47, 219–49.

Freeland, Lynn S. (1951). *The language of the Sierra Miwok*. Memoir 6 of the International Journal of American Linguistics. Bloomington, Ind.: Indiana University Press.

Freeze, R. (1992). Is there more to V2 than meets the I? In *Proceedings of the 22nd meeting of the North-Eastern Linguistic Society*, 151–64.

Freidin, R. (1978). Cyclicity and the theory of grammar. *Linguistic Inquiry*, 9/4: 519–49.

Fromkin, V. A. (1971). The non-anomalous nature of anomalous utterances. *Language*, 47, 27–52.

Fukui, N., Miyagawa, S. and Tenny, C. L. (1985). *Verb classes in English and Japanese: a case study in the interaction of syntax, morphology and semantics*, Lexicon Project Working Papers, 3. Cambridge, Mass.: Center for Cognitive Science, MIT.

Fulmer, S. L. (1991). Dual-position affixes in Afar: an argument for phonologically driven morphology. In *Proceedings of the 9th West Coast conference on Formal Linguistics*, 189–203.

Funnell, E. (1987). Morphological errors in acquired dyslexia: a case of mistaken identity. *Quarterly Journal of Experimental Psychology*, 39A, 497–539.

Garrett, A. (1990). The syntax of Anatolian pronominal clitics. Ph.D. diss., Harvard University.

Garrett, M. F. (1975). The analysis of sentence production. In G. Bower (ed.), *Psychology of learning and motivation*, vol. 9, New York: Academic Press, 133–77.

—— (1976). Syntactic processes in language production. In R. J. Wales and E. Walker (eds), *New approaches to language mechanisms*, Amsterdam: North-Holland, 231–56.

—— (1980). The limits of accommodation. In V. A. Fromkin (ed.), *Errors in linguistic performance: slips of the tongue, ear, pen, and hand*, New York: Academic Press, 263–71.

—— (1982). Production of speech: observations from normal and pathological language use. In A. Ellis (ed.), *Normality and pathology in cognitive functions*, London: Academic Press, 19–76.

—— (1984). The organization of processing structure for language production: applications to aphasic speech. In D. Caplan, A. Lecours and A. Smith (eds), *Biological perspectives on language*, Cambridge, Mass.: MIT Press, 172–93.

Gazdar, G., Klein, E., Pullum, G. and Sag, I. (1985). *Generalized phrase structure grammar*. Oxford: Blackwell Publishers.

Gebert, L. (1988). Universal hierarchy of topicality and Soali syntax. In M. Bechhaus-Gerst and F. Serzisko (eds), *Cushitic-Omotic: papers from the international symposium on Cushitic and Omotic languages*, Hamburg: Buske, 591–604.

Ghomeshi, J. and Massam, D. (1994). Lexical/syntactic relations without projection. *Linguistic Analysis*, 24, 175–217.

Gibson, E. J. and Guinet, L. (1971). Perception of inflections in brief visual presentations of words. *Journal of Verbal Learning and Verbal Behavior*, 10, 182–9.

Givón, T. (1976). Topic, pronoun and grammatical agreement. In C. N. Li (ed.), 149–88.

Goldberg, A. (1995). *Constructions*. Chicago: University of Chicago Press.

Goldsmith, J. and Sabimana, F. (1985). The Kirundi verb. MS, University of Chicago and Indiana University.

Golla, V. (1970). Hupa grammar. Ph.D. diss., University of California at Berkeley.

Goodglass, H. (1976). Agrammatism. In H. and H. Whitaker (eds), *Studies in neurolinguistics*, vol. 1, New York: Academic Press, 237–60.

Goodman, B. (1988). Takelma verbal morphology. In *Proceedings of the 18th meeting of the North-Eastern Linguistic Society*, 156–74.

—— (1994). The integration of hierarchical features into a phonological system. Ph.D. diss., Cornell University.

Grainger, J., Cole, P. and Segui, J. (1991). Masked morphological priming in visual word recognition. *Journal of Memory and Language*, 30, 370–84.

Greenberg, J. H. (1966a). *Language universals*. The Hague: Mouton.

—— (1966b). Some universals of grammar with particular reference to the order of meaningful elements. In J. H. Greenberg (ed.), *Universals of language*, 2nd edn, Cambridge, Mass.: MIT Press, 73–113.

Grimshaw, J. (1982). On the lexical representation of Romance reflexive clitics. In Bresnan (ed.), 87–148.

—— (1986). A morphosyntactic explanation for the mirror principle. *Linguistic Inquiry*, 17, 745–9.

—— (1990). *Argument structure*. Cambridge, Mass.: MIT Press.

—— (1993). Semantic structure and semantic content in lexical representation. MS, Rutgers University.

Grimshaw, J. and Mester, A. (1988). Light verbs and theta-marking. *Linguistic Inquiry*, 19, 205–32.

Grimshaw, J. and Vikner, S. (1993). Obligatory adjuncts and the structure of events. In Reuland and Abraham (eds), 143–55.

Grodzinsky, Y. (1984). The syntactic characterization of agrammatism. *Cognition*, 16, 99–120.

Gropen, J., Pinker, S., Hollander, M. and Goldberg, R. (1991). Affectedness and direct objects: the role of lexical semantics in the acquisition of verb argument structure. *Cognition*, 41, 153–95; also in Levin and Pinker (eds), 1992, 153–95.

Grosjean, F. (1980). Spoken word recognition processes and the gating paradigm. *Perception and Psychophysics*, 28, 267–83.

Gruber, J. S. (1965). Studies in lexical relations. Ph.D. diss., Massachusetts Institute of Technology.

Guerssel, M., Hale, K., Laughren, M., Levin, B. and White Eagle, J. (1985). A cross-linguistic study of transitivity alternations. In *Papers from the parasession on causatives and agentivity*, Chicago Linguistic Society, University of Chicago, 48–63.

Guillaume, P. (1927). Le développement des éléments formels dan le langage de l'enfant. *Journal de Psychologie*, 24, 203–29.

Günther, H. (1988). Oblique word forms in visual word recognition. *Linguistics*, 26, 583–600.

Guthrie, M. (1962). The status of radical extensions in Bantu languages. In M. Guthrie (ed.), *Collected papers on Bantu linguistics*, London: Gregg International Publishers.

—— (1967–71). *Comparative Bantu*. Farnsborough: Gregg International Publishers.

Gvozdanović, J. (1991). Syncretism and the paradigmatic patterning of grammatical meaning. In Plank (ed.), 133–60.

Haegeman, L. (1992). *Generative syntax: theory and description. A case study from West Flemish*. Cambridge: Cambridge University Press.

Hagège, C. (1978). Lexical suffixes and incorporation in mainland Comox. *Forum Linguisticum*, 4, 241–5.

Haiman, J. (1976). Presuppositions in Hua. In *Papers from the 12th annual meeting of the Chicago Linguistic Society*, 258–70.

—— (1987). On some origins of medial verb morphology in Papuan languages. *Studies in Language*, 11, 347–64.

—— (1992). *Hua–English dictionary*. Wiesbaden: Harrassowitz.

Hale, K. (1959). Warumunu notes. Copy at AIATSIS, Canberra.

—— (1973a). Deep-surface canonical disparities in relation to analysis and change: an Australian example. In T. A. Sebeok (ed.), *Current trends in linguistics*, vol. 11: *Diachronic, areal, and typological linguistics*, The Hague: Mouton, 401–58.

—— (1973b). Person marking in Walbiri. In S. Anderson and P. Kiparsky (eds), *A Festschrift for Morris Halle*, New York: Holt, Rinehart and Winston, Inc., 308–44.

—— (1982). Some essential features of Warlpiri main clauses. In S. Swartz (ed.), *Papers in Warlpiri grammar: in memory of Lothar Jagst*, Berrimah, Australia: Summer Institute of Linguistics, 217–315.

—— (1983). Warlpiri and the grammar of non-configurational languages. *Natural Language and Linguistic Theory*, 1/1, 5–47.

Hale, K. and Lacayo Blanco, A. (1989). *Diccionario elemental del Ulwa (Sumu Meridional)*. Cambridge, Mass.: Center for Cognitive Science, MIT.

Hale, K. and Keyser, S. J. (1986). *Some transitivity alternations in English*, Lexicon Project Working Papers, 7. Cambridge, Mass.: Center for Cognitive Science, MIT.

—— (1987). *A view from the middle*, Lexicon Project Working Papers, 10. Cambridge, Mass.: Center for Cognitive Science, MIT.

—— (1992). The syntactic character of thematic structure. In Roca (ed.), 107–43.

—— (1993). On argument structure and the lexical expression of syntactic relations. In Hale and Keyser (eds), 53–110.

—— (1997). On the complex nature of simple predicators. In Alsina et al. (eds).

Hale, K. and Keyser, S. J. (eds) (1993). *The view from building 20: essays in linguistics in honor of Sylvain Bromberger*. Cambridge, Mass.: MIT Press.

Hale, M. (1987). Notes on Wackernagel's law in the language of the Rigveda. In C. Watkins (ed.), *Studies in memory of Warren Cowgill*, New York: Walter de Gruyter, 38–50.

—— (1996). Deriving Wackernagel's law: prosodic and syntactic factors determining clitic placement in the language of the Rigveda. In Halpern and Zwicky (eds), 165–98.

Hall (Partee), B. (1965). Subject and object in English. Ph.D. diss., Massachusetts Institute of Technology.

Halle, M. (1973). Prolegomena to word formation. *Linguistic Inquiry*, 4/1, 3–16.

—— (1989). An approach to morphology. In *Proceedings of the 20th meeting of the North-Eastern Linguistic Society*, 150–84.

Halle, M. and Marantz, A. (1993). Distributed morphology and the pieces of inflection. In Hale and Keyser (eds), 111–76.

Halle, M. and Vergnaud, J.-R. (1987). *An essay on stress*. Cambridge, Mass.: MIT Press.

Halpern, A. L. (1992). Topics in the placement and morphology of clitics. Ph.D. diss., Stanford University.

—— (1995). *On the placement and morphology of clitics*, Dissertations in Linguistics. Stanford, Calif.: CSLI.

Halpern, A. L. and Fontana, J. M. (1994). X^0 and X^{max} clitics. In *Proceedings of the 12th West Coast conference on formal linguistics*, 251–66.

Halpern, A. L. and Miller, P. (1993). Phrasal inflection vs. postlexical cliticization: the English possessive marker 's. MS, Ohio State University and University of Lille.

Halpern, A. L. and Zwicky, A. M. (eds) (1996). *Approaching second*. Stanford, Calif.: CSLI.

Hammond, M. and Noonan, M. (eds) (1988). *Theoretical morphology: approaches in modern linguistics*. San Diego, Calif.: Academic Press.

Hamp, E. P., Householder, F. W. and Austerlitz, R. (eds) (1966). *Readings in linguistics*, vol. 2. Chicago: University of Chicago Press.

Hankamer, J. (1989). Morphological parsing and the lexicon. In Marslen-Wilson (ed.), 392–408.

Harada, S. I. (1976). Honorifics. In M. Shibatani (ed.), *Japanese generative grammar*, New York: Academic Press, 499–561.

Hare, M. and Elman, J. L. (1992). A connectionist account of English inflectional morphology: evidence from language change. *Proceedings of the 14th annual conference of the Cognitive Science Society*, Hillsdale, N.J.: Erlbaum, 265–70.

Hargus, S. (1986). Phonological evidence for prefixation in Navajo verbal morphology. In *Proceedings of the 5th West Coast conference on formal linguistics*, 53–67.

—— (1988). *The lexical phonology of Sekani*. New York: Garland.

—— (1991). The disjunct boundary in Babine-Witsu Wit'en. *International Journal of American Linguistics*, 57, 426–45.

Harner, L. (1975). Yesterday and tomorrow: development of early understanding of the terms. *Developmental Psychology*, 11, 864–5.

Harris, A. C. (1978). Number agreement in modern Georgian. In B. Comrie (ed.), *Classification of grammatical categories*, Edmonton: Linguistic Research Inc., 75–98.

—— (1994). Ergative-to-nominative shift in agreement: Tabassaran. In H. I. Aronson (ed.), *Linguistic studies in the non-slavic languages of the Commonwealth of Independent States and the Baltic republics*, Chicago: Chicago Linguistic Society, 113–31.

Harris, J. W. (1991). The form classes of Spanish substantives. In G. Booij and J. van Marle (eds), *Yearbook of morphology 1991*, Dordrecht: Kluwer, 65–88.

Harrison, S. P. (1976). *Mokilese reference grammar*. Honolulu: University Press of Hawaii.

Haspelmath, M. (1990). The grammaticization of passive morphology. *Studies in Language*, 14, 25–72.

—— (1993). *A grammar of Lezgian*. Berlin: Mouton de Gruyter.

Hauge, K. (1976). *The word order of predicate clitics in Bulgarian*, Meddelelser, Slavisk Baltisk Institut, 10. Oslo: Universitetet i Oslo.

Hawkins, J. A. and Cutler, A. (1988). Psycholinguistic factors in morphological asymmetry. In J. A. Hawkins (ed.), *Explaining language universals*, Oxford: Blackwell Publishers, 280–317.

Hayes, B. (1985). Iambic and trochaic rhythm in stress rules. In *Proceedings of the 13th annual meeting of the Berkeley Linguistics Society*, 429–46.

—— (1987). A revised parametric metrical theory. In *Proceedings of the 17th meeting of the North-Eastern Linguistic Society*, 274–89.

—— (1989a). Compensatory lengthening in moraic phonology. *Linguistic Inquiry*, 20, 253–306.

—— (1989b). The prosodic hierarchy in meter. In P. Kiparsky and G. Youmans (eds.), *Rhythm and meter*, Orlando, Fla.: Academic Press, 201–60.

—— (1995). *Metrical stress theory: principles and case studies*. Chicago: University of Chicago Press.

Hayes, B. and Abad, M. (1989). Reduplication and syllabification in Ilokano. *Lingua*, 77, 331–74.

Hayward, R. J. (1974). The segmental phonemes of Afar. *Bulletin of the School of Oriental and African Studies, University of London*, 37, 385–406.

—— (1978). The stative conjugation in Afar. *Annali dell'Istituto Orientale di Napoli*, 38/1, 1–39.

—— (1979). Bayso revisited: some preliminary linguistic observations – II. *Bulletin of the School of Oriental and African Studies, University of London*, 42, 101–32.

—— (1988). In defence of the skeletal tier. *Studies in African Linguistics*, 19, 131–72.

—— (1991). Tone and accent in the Qafar noun. *York Working Papers in Linguistics*, 15, 117–37.

—— (1996). Compounding in Qafar. *Bulletin of the School of Oriental and African Studies, University of London*, 59/3, 525–45.

Hayward, R. J. and Corbett, G. G. (1988). Resolution rules in Qafar. *Linguistics*, 26, 259–79.

Hayward, R. J. and Orwin, M. (1991). The prefix conjugation in Qafar-Saho: the survival and revival of a paradigm – Part I. *African Languages and Cultures*, 4, 157–76.

Hazout, I. (1990). Verbal nouns: theta-theoretical studies in Hebrew and Arabic. Ph.D. diss., University of Massachusetts, Amherst.

—— (1995). Action nominalization and the lexicalist hypothesis. *Natural Language and Linguistic Theory*, 13, 355–404.

Healey, A., Isoroembo, A. and Chittleborough, M. (1969). Preliminary notes on Orokaiva grammar. *Papers in New Guinea Linguistics*, 9, 33–64.

Heath, J. (1977). Warramunga grammatical notes. Warramunga English wordlist. Warramunga texts. Field tapes 65, 66. Copy at AIATSIS, Canberra.

Heine, B., Claudi, U. and Hünnemeyer, F. (1991). From cognition to grammar – Evidence from African languages. In Traugott and Heine (eds), 1991a, 149–87.

Hemon, R. (1975). *A historical morphology and syntax of Breton*. Dublin: Institute for Advanced Studies.

Henderson, J. (1992). Pre-stopped nasals in Arandic languages. Paper presented at Australian Linguistic Institute, Sydney.

Henderson, L. (1985). Toward a psychology of morphemes. In A. W. Ellis (ed.), *Progress in the psychology of language*, vol. 1, 15–72.

—— (1989). On mental representation of morphology and its diagnosis by measures of visual access speed. In Marslen-Wilson (ed.), 357–91.

Henderson, L., Wallis, J. and Knight, D. (1984). Morphemic structure and lexical access. In H. Bouma and D. Bouwhuis (eds), *Attention and performance*, 10 Hillsdale, N.J.: Erlbaum, 211–26.

Hercus, L. (1972). The pre-stopped nasal and lateral consonants of Arabana-Wanganuru. *Anthropological Linguistics*, 14, 293–305.

Hetzron, R. (1972). Phonology in syntax. *Journal of Linguistics*, 8, 251–65.

Hewitt, B. G. (1979). *Abkhaz*. Amsterdam: North-Holland.

Hewitt, M. (1992). Vertical maximization and metrical theory. Ph.D. diss., Brandeis University.

—— (1994). Deconstructing foot binarity in Koniag Alutiiq. MS, University of British Columbia, Vancouver.

Hewitt, M. and Prince, A. (1989). OCP, locality, and linking: the N. Karanga verb. In E. J. Fee and K. Hunt (eds), *Proceedings of the 8th West Coast conference on Formal Linguistics*, 176–91.

Higginbotham, J. (1985). On semantics. *Linguistic Inquiry*, 16, 547–621.

Hill, J. and Zepeda, O. (1992). Derived words in Tohono O'odham. *International Journal of American Linguistics*, 58, 355–404.

Hillis, A. and Caramazza, A. (1989). The graphemic buffer and attentional mechanisms. *Brain and Language*, 36, 208–35.

Hinnebusch, T. (1979). Swahili. In T. Shopen (ed.), *Languages and their status*, Philadelphia: University of Pennsylvania Press, 209–93.

Hittmair-Delazer, M., Andree, B., Semenza, C. and Benke, C. (1994). Naming by German compounds. *Journal of Neurolinguistics*, 8, 27–41.

Hock, H. H. (1976). Review article on Anttila, 1972. *Language*, 52, 202–20.

—— (1991). *Principles of historical linguistics*, 2nd edn, revised and updated. Berlin: Mouton de Gruyter.

—— (1992). What's a nice word like you doing in a place like this? Syntax vs. phonological form. *Studies in the Linguistic Sciences*, 22/1, 39–87.

—— (1996). Who's on first? Toward a prosodic account of P2 clitics. In Halpern and Zwicky (eds), 199–270.

Hockett, C. (1958). Two models of grammatical description. In M. Joos (ed.), *Readings in linguistics*, 2nd edn, Chicago: University of Chicago Press, 386–99.

Hoeksema, J. (1985). *Categorial morphology*. New York: Garland.

—— (1986). Some theoretical consequences of Dutch complementizer agreement. In *Proceedings of the 12th Meeting of the Berkeley Linguistics Society*, 147–58.

—— (1987). Relating word structure and logical form. *Linguistic Inquiry*, 18, 119–26.

Hoekstra, T. (1984). *Transitivity*. Dordrecht: Foris.

—— (1988). Small clause results. *Lingua*, 74, 101–39.

Hoekstra, T. and Mulder, R. (1990). Unergatives as copular verbs: locational and existential predication. *Linguistic Review*, 7, 1–79.

Hoekstra, T. and Roberts, I. G. (1993). Middle constructions in Dutch and English. In Reuland and Abraham (eds), 183–220.

Hofmann, T. R. (1982). Lexical blocking. *Journal of the Faculty of Humanities, Toyama University*, 5, 239–50.

Hoijer, H. (1946). Chiricahua Apache. In H. Hoijer (ed.), *Linguistic structures of native America*, New York: Viking Fund, 55–85.

Holmes, V. M. and O'Regan, J. K. (1992). Reading derivationally affixed French words. *Language and Cognitive Processes*, 7, 163–92.

Hook, P. E. and Joshi, D. M. (1991). Concordant adverbs and postpositions in Gujarati. *Indian Linguistics*, 52, 1–14.

Hopkins, A. W. (1988). Topics in Mohawk grammar. Ph.D. diss., City University of New York.

Hopper, P. J. and Traugott, E. C. (1993). *Grammaticalization*. Cambridge: Cambridge University Press.

Horn, L. R. (1984). Towards a new taxonomy for pragmatic inference: Q-based and R-based implicature. In D. Schiffrin (ed.), *Meaning, form and use in context*, Georgetown: Georgetown University Press, 11–42.

—— (1988). *A natural history of negation*. Chicago: University of Chicago Press.

—— (1993). Economy and redundancy in a dualistic model of natural language. In M. Vilkuna and S. Shores (eds), *Yearbook of the Linguistic Association of Finland*.

Hout, A. van (1992). Linking and projection based on event structure. MS, Tilburg University.

—— (1996). *Event semantics of verb frame alternations*. Tilburg: TILDIL Dissertation Series, 1996–1.

Howard, P. (1990). *A dictionary of the verb of South Slavey*. Yellowknife, Northwest Territories, Canada: Department of Culture and Communication, Government of the Northwest Territories.

Huddleston, R. (1975). Homonymy in the English verbal paradigm. *Lingua*, 37, 157–76.

Hudson, P. T. W. and Buijs, D. (1995). Left-to-right procession of derivational morphology. In Feldman (ed.), 383–96.

Hulst, H. van der (1984). *Syllable structure and stress in Dutch*. Dordrecht: Foris.

Hulst, H. van der and Smith, N. (eds) (1984). *Advances in nonlinear phonology*. Dordrecht: Foris.

Hyman, L. M. (1980). Babanki and the Ring group. In L. M. Hyman and J. Voorhoeve (eds), *Les classes nominales dans le bantou des grassfields*, Paris: Société d'études linguistiques et anthropologiques de France, 225–58.

—— (1985). *A theory of phonological weight*. Dordrecht: Foris.

—— (in press). Conceptual issues in the comparative study of the Bantu verb stem. In *Proceedings of the 21st African Linguistics Conference*, Amsterdam: J. Benjamins.

Hyman, L. and Mchombo, S. A. (1995). Morphotactic constraints in the Chichewa verb stem. In *Proceedings of the 21st annual meeting of the Berkeley Linguistics Society, parasession on the place of morphology in a grammar*, 350–64.

Ingram, D. (1978). Typology and universals of personal pronouns. In J. H. Greenberg, C. A. Ferguson, and E. A. Moravcsik (eds), *Universals of human language*, vol. 3: *Word structure*, Stanford, Calif.: Stanford University Press, 213–47.

Inkelas, S. (1990). *Prosodic constituency in the lexicon*. New York: Garland.

—— (1993). Nimboran position class morphology. *Natural Language and Linguistic Theory*, 11, 559–624.

Itô, J. (1989). A prosodic theory of epenthesis. *Natural Language and Linguistic Theory*, 7, 217–60.

—— (1991). Prosodic minimality in Japanese. In *Papers from the 26th annual meeting of the Chicago Linguistic Society, parasession on the syllable in phonetics and phonology*, 213–39.

Itô, J. and Mester, R.-A. (to appear). Weak layering and word binarity. *Linguistic Inquiry*.

Jackendoff, R. S. (1972). *Semantic interpretation in generative grammar*. Cambridge, Mass.: MIT Press.

—— (1975). Morphological and semantic regularities in the lexicon. *Language*, 51, 639–71.

—— (1978). Grammar as evidence for conceptual structure. In M. Halle, J. Bresnan and G. Miller (eds), *Linguistic theory and psychological reality*, Cambridge, Mass.: MIT Press, 201–28.

—— (1983). *Semantics and cognition*. Cambridge, Mass.: MIT Press.

—— (1987). The status of thematic relations in linguistic theory. *Linguistic Inquiry*, 18, 369–411.

—— (1990). *Semantic structures*. Cambridge, Mass.: MIT Press.

—— (1996). Conceptual semantics and cognitive linguistics. *Cognitive Linguistics*, 7, 93–129.

Jaeger, J. J. (1983). The fortis/lenis question: evidence from Zapotec and Jawony. *Journal of Phonetics*, 11, 177–89.

Jaeggli, O. A. (1982). *Topics in Romance syntax*. Dordrecht: Foris.

—— (1986a). Passive. *Linguistic Inquiry*, 17, 587–622.

—— (1986b). Three issues in the theory of clitics: case, doubled NPs and extraction. In H. Borer (ed.), *Syntax and semantics 19: the syntax of pronominal clitics*, New York: Academic Press, 15–42.

Jake, J. L. (1980). Object verb agreement in Tigre. In C. W. Kisseberth, B. B. Kachru and J. L. Morgan (eds), *Studies in the linguistics sciences*, vol. 10, Urbana, Ill.: Department of Linguistics, University of Illinois, 71–84.

Jakobson, R. (1932). Zur Struktur des russischen Verbums. In *Charisteria V. Mathesio oblata*, Prague: Cercle Linguistique de Prague, 74–83.

—— (1939). Le signe zéro. In *Mélanges de linguistiques offerts à Charles Bally*, Geneva: Georg, 143–52.

—— (1966). Beitrag zur allgemeinen Kasuslehre: Gesamtbedeutungen der russischen Kasus. *Travaux du Cercle Linguistique de Prague*, 6, 240–88 (1936); repr. in E. Hamp, F. Householder and R. Austerlitz (eds) (1966), 158–74. English translation: Contribution to the general theory of case: general meanings of the Russian cases. In L. R. Waugh and M. Halle (eds), *Roman Jakobson: Russian and Slavic grammar: studies 1931–1981*, Berlin: Mouton, 59–103.

Janda, R. D. (1982). Of formal identity and rule-(un)collapsability: on lost and found generalizations in morphology. In *Proceedings of the 1st West Coast conference on formal linguistics*, 1, 179–97.

—— (1983). Two Umlaut-heresies and their claim to orthodoxy. *Coyote Papers, Working Papers in Linguistics*, 4, 59–71. University of Arizona.

—— (1990). Frequency, markedness, and morphological change: on predicting the spread of noun-plural -s in modern High German and West Germanic. In *Proceedings of the 7th Eastern States conference on linguistics*, 136–53.

—— (1994). Checking-theory, syntactic feature-geometry, and the structure of IP. In *Proceedings of the 12th West Coast conference on formal linguistics*, 319–37.

—— (1995). From agreement affix to subject 'clitic' – and bound root: -mos > -nos vs. (-)nos(-) and nos-otros in New Mexican and other regional Spanish dialects. In A. Dainora et al. (eds), *Papers from the Parasession on Clitics, 31st Regional Meeting of CLS*, 20–2 April 1995, 118–39.

Janda, R. D. and Kathman, D. (1992). Shielding morphology from exploded INFL. In *Papers from the 28th annual regional meeting of the Chicago Linguistic Society, parasession on the cycle in linguistic theory*, 141–57.

Janda, R. D. and Joseph, B. (1986). One rule or many? Sanskrit reduplication as fragmented affixation. *Ohio State University Working Papers in Linguistics*, 34, 84–107.

Jarema, G. and Kehayia, E. (1992). Impairment of inflectional morphology and lexical storage. *Brain and Language*, 43, 541–64.

Jarvella, R. J. and Meijers, G. (1983). Recognizing morphemes in spoken words: some evidence for a stem-organised mental lexicon. In G. B. Flores d'Arcais and R. J. Jarvella (eds), *The process of language understanding*, New York: Wiley, 81–112.

Jarvella, R. J., Job, R., Sandström, G. and Schreuder, R. (1987). Morphological constraints on word recognition. In A. Allport, D. G. MacKay, W. Prinz and E. Scheerer (eds), *Language perception and production: relationships between listening, speaking, reading, and writing*, London: Academic Press, 245–62.

Jeffries, L. and Willis, P. (1984). A return to the spray paint issue. *Journal of Pragmatics*, 8, 715–29.

Jensen, J. T. and Stong-Jensen, M. (1984). Morphology is in the lexicon! *Linguistic Inquiry*, 15, 474–98.

Job, R. and Sartori, G. (1984). Morphological decomposition: evidence from crossed phonological dyslexia. *Quarterly Journal of Experimental Psychology*, 36A, 435–58.

Jones, M. (1990). Variation in the use of pronouns in verbnoun phrases and genitive phrases in child language. In M. Ball et al. (eds), *Celtic linguistics*, Amsterdam: J. Benjamins, 53–76.

Joseph, B. D. (1983). *The synchrony and diachrony of the balkan infinitive: a study in areal, general, and historical linguistics*. Cambridge: Cambridge University Press.

—— (1988). Pronominal affixes in Modern Greek: the case against clisis. In *Papers from the 24th annual meeting of the Chicago Linguistic Society*, 24, 203–15.

—— (1990). *Morphology and universals in syntactic change: evidence from medieval and modern Greek*. New York: Garland.

—— (1992). Yet more on -gate words: a perspective from Greece. *American Speech*, 67, 222–3.

—— (1996a). Where can grammatical morphemes come from? Greek evidence concerning the nature of grammaticalization. Paper presented at 7th meeting of the Formal Linguistic Society of the Midwest, Ohio State University, May 1996.

—— (to appear). Textual authenticity: evidence from medieval Greek. In S. Herring, P. van Reenen and L. Schoesler (eds), *Textual parameters in ancient languages*, Amsterdam: J. Benjamins.

Joseph, B. D. and Janda, R. D. (1988). The how and why of diachronic morphologization and demorphologization. In Hammond and Noonan (eds), 193–210.

Joseph, B. D. and Smirniotopoulos, J. C. (1993). The morphosyntax of the modern Greek verb as morphology and not syntax. *Linguistic Inquiry*, 24, 388–98.

Joseph, B. D. and Wallace, R. (1984). Latin morphology: another look. *Linguistic Inquiry*, 15, 319–28.

Kager, R. (1989). *A metrical theory of stress and destressing in English and Dutch*. Dordrecht: Foris.

—— (1992). Shapes of the generalized trochee. In *Proceedings of the 11th West Coast conference on formal linguistics*, 298–303.

—— (1993). Alternatives to the iambictrochaic law. *Natural Language and Linguistic Theory*, 11, 381–429.

Kaisse, E. (1982). Sentential clitics and Wackernagel's law. In *Proceedings of the 1st West Coast conference on formal linguistics*, 1–14.

—— (1985). *Connected speech: the interaction of syntax and phonology.* Orlando, Fla.: Academic Press.

Kanerva, J. (1987). Morphological integrity and syntax: the evidence from Finnish possessive suffixes. *Language*, 63, 498–521.

—— (1990). *Focus and phrasing in Chichewa phonology.* New York: Garland.

Karcevskij, S. (1929). Du dualisme asymmetrique du signe linguistique. *Travaux du Cercle Linguistique de Prague*, 1, 88–93.

Kari, J. (1975). The disjunct boundary in the Navajo and Tanaina verb prefix complexes. *International Journal of American Linguistics*, 41, 330–45.

—— (1976). *Navajo verb prefix phonology.* New York: Garland.

—— (1979). *Athabaskan verb theme categories: Ahtna*, Alaska Native Language Center Research Papers, 2. Fairbanks: Alaska Native Language Center.

—— (1989). Affix positions and zones in the Athapaskan verb complex: Ahtna and Navajo. *International Journal of American Linguistics*, 55/4, 424–54.

—— (1990). *Ahtna dictionary.* University of Alaska Press.

—— (1992). Some concepts in Ahtna Athabaskan word formation. In M. Aronoff (ed.), *Morphology now*, Albany: State University of New York Press, 107–31.

—— (1993). Diversity in morphological order in several Alaskan Athabaskan languages: notes on the gh-qualifier. In *Proceedings of the 19th annual meeting of the Berkeley Linguistics Society*, 50–6.

Karlsson, Fred (1987). *Finnish grammar*, 2nd edn. Helsinki: Werner Sörderström Osakeyhtiö.

Karmiloff-Smith, A. (1979). *A functional approach to child language.* Cambridge: Cambridge University Press.

Kathol, A. (forthcoming). Agreement and the syntax–morphology interface in HPSG. In R. Levine and G. Green (eds), *Readings in HPSG*, Cambridge: Cambridge University Press.

Katz, L., Rexer, K. and Lukatela, G. (1991). The processing of inflected words. *Psychological Research*, 53, 25–32.

Kaufman, E. (1974). Navajo spatial enclitics: a case for unbounded rightward movement. *Linguistic Inquiry*, 5/3, 507–33.

Kaxadze, O. I. (1979). *The Archi language and its relation to other Daghestan languages* (in Georgian). Tbilisi: Mecniereba.

Kayne, R. (1975). *French syntax.* Cambridge, Mass.: MIT Press.

—— (1984). Unambiguous paths. In R. Kayne, *Connectedness and binary branching*, Dordrecht: Foris, 129–63.

—— (1990). Romance clitics and PRO. In *Proceedings of the 20th meeting of the North-Eastern Linguistic Society*, 20, 255–302.

—— (1991). Romance clitics, verb movement, and PRO. *Linguistic Inquiry*, 22/4, 647–86.

—— (1994). *The antisymmetry of syntax.* Cambridge, Mass.: MIT Press.

Kazizis, K. and Pentheroudakis, J. (1976). Reduplication of indefinite direct objects in Albanian and Modern Greek. *Language*, 52/2, 398–403.

Kean, M.-L. (1978). The linguistic interpretation of aphasic syndromes: agrammatism in Broca's aphasia, an example. *Cognition*, 5, 9–46.

Keenan, E. L. (1976). Towards a universal definition of subject. In Li (ed.), 303–33.

—— (1978). On surface form and logical form. In B. B. Kachru (ed.), *Linguistics in the seventies: directions and prospects*, Urbana, Ill.: Department of Linguistics, University of Illinois, 163–203.

—— (1995). Predicate–argument structure in Malagasy. In C. Burgess, K. Dziwirek and D. Gerdts (eds), *Grammatical relations: theoretical approaches to empirical questions*, Stanford, Calif.: Stanford University, CSLI, 178–216.

—— (1996). Morphology is structure: a Malagasy test case. In Pearson and Paul (eds), 92–112; also to appear in I. Paul, V. Phillips and L. Travis (eds), *Problems in Austronesian morphology and syntax*, Dordrecht: Kluwer.

Keenan, E. L. and Manorohanta, C. (1996). A quantitative study of voice in Malagasy. MS, UCLA.

Keenan, E. L. and Razafimamonjy, J. P. (1996a). Malagasy morphology: basic rules. In Pearson and Paul (eds), 31–47.

—— (1996b). Reciprocals in Malagasy. Paper presented at the 3rd annual meeting of the Austronesian formal linguistics association, Los Angeles, April 1996.

—— (1996c). Reduplication in Malagasy. Paper presented at the 3rd annual meeting of the Austronesian formal linguistics association, Los Angeles, April 1996.

Kehayia, E., Jarema, G. and Kadziela, D. (1990). Cross-linguistics study of morphological errors in aphasia: evidence from English, Greek and Polish. In Nespoulous and Villard (eds), 140–55.

Kelliher, S. and Henderson, L. (1990). Morphologically based frequency effects in the recognition of irregularly inflected verbs. *British Journal of Psychology*, 81, 527–39.

Kempley, S. T. and Morton, J. (1982). The effects of priming regularly and irregularly related words in auditory word recognition. *British Journal of Psychology*, 73, 441–54.

Kenny, A. (1963). *Action, emotion, and will.* London: Routledge and Kegan Paul.

Kenstowicz, M. (1979). Chukchee vowel harmony and epenthesis. In *Papers from the 15th annual meeting of the Chicago Linguistic Society: the elements: a parasession on linguistic units and levels*, 402–12.

Keyser, S. J. and Roeper, T. (1984). On the middle and ergative constructions in English. *Linguistic Inquiry*, 15, 381–416.

—— (1994). Antisymmetry and leftward movement in morphology. MS, MIT and University of Massachusetts, of paper presented at the 1995 GLOW conference, Tromsoe.

Kibrik, A. E. (1972). O formal'nom vydelenii soglasovatel'nyx klassov v arčinskom jazyke. *Voprosy jazykoznanija*, 1, 124–31.

—— (1977a). *Opyt strukturnogo opisanija arčinskogo jazyka*, vol. 2: *Taksonomičeskaja grammatika*. Moscow: Izdatel'stvo moskovskogo universiteta.

—— (1997b). *Opyt strukturnogo opisanija arčinskogo jazyka*, vol. 3: *Dinamičeskaja grammatika*. Moscow: Izdatel'stvo moskovskogo universiteta.

—— (1979a). Canonical ergativity and Daghestan languages. In F. Plank (ed.), *Ergativity: towards a theory of grammatical relations*, New York: Academic Press, 61–78.

—— (1979b). *Materialy k tipologii èrgativnosti: 2. Lakskij jazyk, 3. Čiragskij jazyk.* Moscow: Institut russkogo jazyka AN SSSR.

—— (1991a). Organizing principles for nominal paradigms in Daghestan languages: comparative and typological observations. In Plank (ed.), 225–74.

—— (1991b). Semantically ergative languages in typological perspective. In R. A. Dooley and J. S. Quakenbush (eds), *Working Papers of the Summer Institute of Linguistics*, 35, University of North Dakota Press, 67–90.

—— (1993). Archi. In R. Smeets (ed.), *Indigenous languages of the Causasus*, vol. 3, North-East Caucasus, Delmar, NY: Caravan Books, 297–365.

Kibrik, A. E. and Kodzasov, S. V. (1988). *Sopostavitel'noe izucenie dagestanskix jazykov. Glagol.* Moscow: Izdatel'stvo moskovskogo universiteta.

—— (1990). *Sopostavitel'noe izučenie dagestanskix jazykov. Imja. Fonetika.* Moscow: Izdatel'stvo moskovskogo universiteta.

Kibrik, A. E. and Seleznev, M. G. (1982). Sintaksis i morfologija glagol'nogo soglasovanija v tabasaranskom jazyke. In *Tabasaranskie ètjudy: Materialy Dagestanskoj èkspedicii 1979*, Moscow: Izdatel'stvo moskovskogo universiteta, 17–33.

Kibrik, A. E., Kodzasov, S. V., Olovjannikova, I. P. and Samedov, D. S. (1977a). *Arčinskij jazyk. Teksty i slovari.* Moscow: Izdatel'stvo moskovskogo universiteta.

—— (1977b). *Opyt strukturnogo opisanija arčinskogo jazyka. Tom 1. Leksika. Fonetika.* Moscow: Izdatel'stvo moskovskogo universiteta.

Kiefer, F. (1970). *Swedish morphology.* Stockholm: Skriptor.

—— (1973). *Generative Morphologie der Neufranzösischen.* Tübingen: Max Niemeyer Verlag.

Kim, J., Pinker, S., Prince, A. and Prasada, S. (1991). Why no mere mortal has ever flown out to center field. *Cognitive Science*, 15, 173–218.

King. G. (1993). *Modern Welsh: a comprehensive grammar.* London: Routledge.

King, R. (1969). *Historical linguistics and generative grammar.* Englewood Cliffs, N.J.: Prentice-Hall.

Kiparsky, P. (1968). Linguistic universals and linguistic change. In E. Bach and R. Harms (eds), *Universals in linguistic theory*, New York: Holt, Rinehart and Winston, 170–202.

—— (1971). Historical linguistics. In W. O. Dingwall (ed.), *A survey of linguistic science*, College Park: University of Maryland Linguistics Program, 576–648.

—— (1982a). From cyclic phonology to lexical phonology. In H. van der Hulst and N. Smith (eds), *The structure of phonological representations*, pt 1, Dordrecht: Foris, 130–75).

—— (1982b). Lexical morphology and phonology. In I.-S. Yang (ed.), *Linguistics in the morning calm*, vol. 1 Seoul: Hanshin Publishing Co., 3–91.

—— (1982c). Lexical phonology and morphology. MS, MIT.

—— (1986). The phonology of reduplication. MS, Stanford University.

—— (1992). Catathesis. MS, Stanford University.

—— (1997). Remarks on denominal verbs. In Alsina et al. (eds).

Kirchner, R. (1993). Edgemost*. Electronic communication of April 14 to Prince, Smolensky, and McCarthy: Internet.

Kirton, J. F. (1978). Yanyuwa verbs. In J. F. Kirton, R. K. Wood, L. A. Hercus, C. S. Street, H. P. Kulampurut, D. Buchanan and B. Charlie (eds), *Papers in Australian Linguistics*, 11, Canberra: Pacific Linguistics, 1–52.

Klavans, J. (1980). Some problems in a theory of clitics. Ph.D. diss., University College London. (Distributed 1982 by IULC, Bloomington, Ind.)

—— (1982). Configuration in non-configurational languages. In *Proceedings of the 1st West Coast conference on formal linguistics*, 292–306.

—— (1983). The morphology of cliticization. In *Papers from the 19th annual meeting of the Chicago Linguistic Society, from the parasession on the interplay of phonology, morphology and syntax*, 103–21.

—— (1985). The independence of syntax and phonology in cliticization. *Language*, 61, 95–120.

Klima, E. and Bellugi, U. (1979). *The signs of language.* Cambridge, Mass.: Harvard University Press.

Koch. H. (1984). The category of 'associated motion' in Kaytej. *Language in Central Australia*, 1, 23–34.

Kok, A. de (1985). *La place du pronom personnel régime conjoint en francais: une étude diachronique.* Amsterdam: Rodopi.

Kontra, Miklos (1992). Hungarians turned gateniks in 1990. *American Speech*, 67, 216–22.

Koptjevskaja-Tamm, M. and Muravyova, I. A. (1993). Aljutor causatives, noun incorporation, and the Mirror Principle. In B. Comrie and M. Polinsky (eds), *Causatives and transitivity*, Amsterdam: J. Benjamins, 287–313.

Kostić, A. (1995). Information load constraints on processing inflected morphology. In Feldman (ed.), 317–44.

Kozinsky, I. S., Nedjalkov, V. P. and Polinskaja, M. S. (1988). Antipassive in Chukchee: oblique object, object incorporation, zero object. In M. Shibatani (ed.), *Passive and voice*, Amsterdam: J. Benjamins, 651–706.

Kratzer, A. (1994). The event argument. MS, University of Massachusetts, Amherst.

Krauss, M. (1965). Eyak: a preliminary report. *Canadian Journal of Linguistics*, 10, 167–87.

—— (1969). On the classification in the Athapascan, Eyak and the Tlingit verb. *Supplement to International Journal of American Linguistics*, 35/4, 49–83.

Krauss, M. (ed.) (1985). *Yupik Eskimo prosodic systems*. Fairbanks: Alaska Native Language Center.

Kroeber, A. L. (1909). Noun incorporation in American languages. In F. Heger (ed.), *Proceedings of the 16th International Congress of Americanists*, Vienna and Leipzig: Hartleben, 569–76.

—— (1911). Incorporation as a linguistic process. *American Anthropologist*, 13, 577–84.

Kroeger, P. (1989a). Discontinuous reduplication in vernacular Malay. Paper presented at the 15th annual meeting of the Berkeley Linguistics Society.

—— (1989b). On the nature of reduplicative templates. MS, Stanford University.

—— (1993). *Phrase structure and grammatical relations in Tagalog*. Stanford, Calif.: Stanford University, CSLI.

Kuczaj, S. A., II (1977). The acquisition of regular and irregular past tense forms. *Journal of Verbal Learning and Verbal Behavior*, 16, 589–600.

—— (1979). Evidence for a language learning strategy: on the relative ease of acquisition of prefixes and suffixes. *Child Development*, 50, 1–13.

Kuroda, S-Y. (1988). Whether we agree or not: a comparative syntax of English and Japanese. *Lingvisticae Investigationes*, 12, 1–47.

Kuryłowicz, J. (1936). Dérivation lexical et dérivation syntaxique; contribution à la théorie des parties du discours. *Bulletin de la Société de Linguistique de Paris*, 37, 79–92.

—— (1945–9). La nature des procès dits 'analogiques'. *Acta Linguistica*, 5, 121–38; repr. in Hamp et al. (eds), 1966, 158–74.

Labov, W. (1981). Resolving the neogrammarian controversy. *Language*, 57, 267–308.

—— (1994). *Principles of linguistic change*, vol. 1: *Internal factors*. Oxford: Blackwell Publishers.

Laidig, W. D. and Laidig, C. J. (1990). Larike pronouns: duals and trials in a Central Moluccan language. *Oceanic Linguistics*, 29, 87–109.

Laine, M., Niemi, J., Koivuselkä-Sallinen, Ahlsén, E. and Hyönä, J. (1994). A neurolinguistic analysis of morphological deficits in a Finnish–Swedish bilingual aphasic. *Clinical Linguistics and Phonetics*, 8, 177–200.

Laine, M., Niemi, J., Koivuselkä-Sallinen and Hyönä, J. (1995). Morphological processing of polymorphemic nouns in a highly inflected language. *Cognitive Neuropsychology*, 12, 457–502.

Laka, I. (1990). Negation in syntax: on the nature of functional categories and projections. Ph.D. diss., Massachusetts Institute of Technology.

Lamontagne, G. (1989). Suffix-triggered variation in Southern Sierra Miwok. MS, University of Massachusetts, Amherst.

Landau, B. (1994). Where's what and what's where: the language of objects in space. *Lingua*, 92, 259–96.

Langacker, R. W. (1976). *Non-distinct arguments in Uto-Aztecan*. Berkeley University of California Press.

Langacker, R. W. and Munro, P. (1975). Passives and their meaning. *Language*, 51, 789–830.

Lapointe, S. G. (1980). A theory of grammatical agreement. Ph.D. diss., University of Massachusetts, Amherst.

—— (1985). A theory of verb form use in the speech of agrammatic aphasia. *Brain and Language*, 24, 100–55.

—— (1988). Toward a unified theory of agreement. In Barlow and Ferguson (eds), 67–87.

—— (1990). EDGE features in GPSG. In *Papers from the 26th annual meeting of the Chicago Linguistic Society*, 221–35.

—— (1991). Constraints on autolexical analyses. *Linguistic Analysis*, 18, 123–55.

Lasnik, H. (1994). Verbal morphology: Syntactic Structures meets the Minimalist Program. MS, University of Connecticut, Storrs.

Laudanna, A. and Burani, C. (1985). Address mechanisms to decomposed lexical entries. *Linguistics*, 23, 775–92.

—— (1995). Distributional properties of derivational affixes: implications for processing. In Feldman (ed.), 345–64.

Laudanna, A., Badecker, W. and Caramazza, A. (1989). Priming homographic stems. *Journal of Memory and Language*, 28, 531–46.

—— (1992). Processing inflectional and derivational morphology. *Journal of Memory and Language*, 31, 333–48.

Laudanna, A., Burani, C. and Cermele, A. (1994). Prefixes as processing units. *Language and Cognitive Processes*, 9, 295–316.

Law, P. (1995). On grammatical relations in Malagasy control structures. In C. Burgess, K. Dziwirek and D. Gerdts (eds), *Grammatical relations: theoretical approaches to empirical questions*, Stanford, Calif.: Stanford University, Center for the Study of Language and Information, 271–89.

Lee, B. (1991). Prosodic structures in Takelma phonology and morphology. Ph.D. diss., University of Texas, Austin.

Lee, K. (1975). *Kusaiean reference grammar*. Honolulu: University Press of Hawaii.

Leer, J. (1979). *Proto-Athabaskan verb stem variation, part one: phonology*, Alaska Native Language Center Papers, no. 3. Fairbanks: Alaska Native Language Center.

—— (1985a). Evolution of prosody in the Yupik languages. In Krauss (ed.), 135–57.

—— (1985b). Prosody in Alutiiq. In Krauss (ed.), 77–133.

Lees, R. (1960). *The grammar of English nominalization*. The Hague: Mouton.

Lehmann, C. (1982). Universal and typological aspects of agreement. In Seiler and Stachowiak (eds), 201–67.

Lehmann, W. (1993). *Theoretical bases of Indo-European linguistics*. London: Routledge.

Leitner, G. (1973). Zur Derivation in einer generativen Grammatik. In A. ten Cate and P. Jordens (eds) *Linguistische Perspektiven*, Tübingen: Max Niemeyer, 130–48.

Lema, J. and Rivero, M. L. (1989). Long head movement: ECP vs. HMC. In *Proceedings of the 20th meeting of the North-Eastern Linguistic Society*, 333–47.

Levelt, C. (1990). Samoan reduplication. MS, University of Leiden.

Levelt, W. J. M. (1989). *Speaking: from intention to articulation*. Cambridge, Mass.: MIT Press.

Levi, J. N. (1978). *The syntax and semantics of complex nominals*. New York: Academic Press.

Levin, B. (1993). *English verb classes and alternations: a preliminary investigation*. Chicago: University of Chicago Press.

—— (1994). Approaches to lexical semantic representation. In D. Walker, A. Zampolli and N. Calzolari (eds), *Automating the lexicon I*, Oxford: Oxford University Press, 53–91.

Levin, B. and Pinker, S. (eds) (1992). *Lexical and conceptual semantics*. Oxford: Blackwell Publishers.

Levin, B. and Rapoport, T. (1988). Lexical subordination. In *Papers from the 24th annual meeting of the Chicago Linguistic Society*, 275–89.

Levin, B. and Rappaport, M. (1986). The formation of adjectival passives. *Linguistic Inquiry*, 17, 623–62.

Levin, B. and Rappaport Havav, M. (1992). The lexical semantics of verbs of motion: the perspective from unaccusativity. In Roca (ed.), 247–69.

—— (1995). *Unaccusativity: at the syntax–lexical semantics interface*. Cambridge, Mass.: MIT Press.

Levin, B. and Tenny, C. (eds) (1988). *On linking: papers by Richard Carter*, Lexicon Project Working Papers, 25. Cambridge, Mass.: Center for Cognitive Science, MIT.

Levin, J. (1983). Reduplication and prosodic structure. MS, Massachusetts Institute of Technology.

Levin, L. (1986). Operations on lexical forms: unaccusative rules in Germanic languages. Ph.D. diss., Massachusetts Institute of Technology.

Levy, Y. (1983). The acquisition of Hebrew plurals: the case of the missing gender category. *Journal of Child Language*, 10, 107–22.

Lewis, H. (1946). *Llawlyfr Cernyweg Canol* (Handbook of Middle Cornish). Gaerdydd: Gwasg Prifysgol Cymru.

Lewis, H. and Pedersen, H. (1937). *A concise comparative Celtic grammar*. Gottingen: Vandenhoek and Ruprecht.

Li, C. N. (ed.) (1976). *Subject and topic*. New York: Academic Press.

Li, F-K. (1930). *Mattole, an Athapaskan language*, University of Chicago Publications in Anthropology, Linguistics Series. Chicago: University of Chicago Press.

—— (1946). Chipewyan. In H. Hoijer (ed.), *Linguistic structures of native America*, Viking Fund Publications in Anthropology, New York: Viking, 398–423.

Li, Y-F. (1990). On V–V compounds in Chinese. *Natural Language and Linguistic Theory*, 8, 177–207.

Libben, G. (1993). Are morphological structures computed during word recognition? *Journal of Psycholinguistic Research*, 22, 535–44.

—— (1994). How is morphological decomposition achieved? *Language and Cognitive Processes*, 9, 369–91.

Liberman, M. and Prince, A. (1977). On stress and linguistic rhythm. *Linguistic Inquiry*, 8, 249–366.

Liddell, S. K. and Johnson, R. E. (1986). American Sign Language compound formation processes, lexicalisation, and phonological remnants. *Natural Language and Linguistic Theory*, 4, 445–513.

Lieber, R. (1980). On the organization of the lexicon. Ph.D. diss., Massachusetts Institute of Technology. Reproduced by Indiana University Linguistics Club, 1981.

—— (1981). *The organization of inflection*. Bloomington: Indiana University Linguistics Club.

—— (1983). Argument linking and compounds in English. *Linguistic Inquiry*, 14, 251–85.

—— (1984). Consonant gradation in Fula: an autosegmental approach. In M. Aronoff and R. T. Oehrle (eds), *Language sound structure*, Cambridge, Mass.: MIT Press.

—— (1987). *An integrated theory of autosegmental processes.* Albany: State University of New York Press.

—— (1992). *Deconstructing morphology: word formation in syntactic theory.* Chicago: University of Chicago Press.

Lodge, K. R. (1979). The use of the past tense in games of pretend. *Journal of Child Language*, 6, 365–9.

Lounsbury, F. (1953). The method of descriptive morphology. In M. Joos (ed.), *Readings in linguistics*, Washington, D.C.: American Council of Learned Societies, 379–85.

Lowenstamm, J. and Kaye, J. (1986). Compensatory lengthening in Tiberian Hebrew. In L. Wetzels and E. Sezer (eds), *Studies in compensatory lengthening*, Dordrecht: Foris, 97–132.

Lukatela, G., Gligorijević, B., Kostić, A. and Turvey, M. T. (1980). Representation of inflected nouns in the internal lexicon. *Memory and Cognition*, 8, 415–23.

Lukatela, G., Mandić, Z., Gligorijević, B., Kostić, A., Savić, M. and Turvey, M. T. (1978). Lexical decision and inflected nouns. *Language and Speech*, 21, 166–73.

Lunt, H. G. (1974). *Old Church Slavonic grammar.* The Hague: Mouton.

Lyons, C. (1990). An agreement approach to clitic doubling. *Transactions of the Philological Society*, 88, 1–57.

Lyons, J. (1968). *Introduction to theoretical linguistics.* Cambridge: Cambridge University Press.

MacKay, D. G. (1970). Spoonerisms: the structure of errors in the serial order of speech. *Neuropsychologia*, 8, 323–50.

—— (1976). On the retrieval and lexical structure of verbs. *Journal of Verbal Learning and Verbal Behavior*, 15, 169–82.

—— (1978). Derivational rules and the internal lexicon. *Journal of Verbal Learning and Verbal Behavior*, 17, 61–71.

—— (1979). Lexical insertion, inflection, and derivation: creative processes in word production. *Journal of Psycholinguistic Research*, 8, 477–98.

MacWhinney, B. (1975). Rules, rote, and analogy in morphological formations by Hungarian children. *Journal of Child Language*, 2, 65–77.

—— (1978). *The acquisition of morphophonology*, Monographs of the Society for Research in Child Development, 43 (serial no. 174).

MacWhinney, B. (ed.) (1987). *Mechanisms of language acquisition.* Hillsdale, N.J.: Lawrence Erlbaum.

MacWhinney, B. and Leinbach, J. (1991). Implementations are not conceptualizations: revising the verb learning model. *Cognition*, 40, 121–57.

Malzac, R. P. (1960). *Grammaire malgache*, 4th edn. Paris: Société d'éditions géographiques, maritimes et coloniales (1st edn 1926).

Mańczak, W. (1958). Tendances générales des changements analogiques. *Lingua*, 7, 298–325, 387–420.

Manelis, L. and Tharp, D. A. (1977). The processing of affixed words. *Memory and Cognition*, 5, 690–5.

Manning, C. M. (1992). *Romance is so complex.* Stanford, Calif.: Technical Report, Stanford University: Center for the Study of Language and Information.

Manzini, M. R. (1992). Second position dependencies. Paper presented at the 8th Workshop on Germanic Syntax, Tromsoe.

—— (1994). Triggers for verb-second: Germanic and Romance. *Linguistic Review*, 11/3–4, 299–314.

Marais, G. F., Brinkman, U., Clahsen, H., Wiese, R., Woest, A. and Pinker, S. (1993). *German inflection: the exception that proves the rule*, MIT Center for Cognitive Science Occasional Paper, 47. Cambridge, Mass.: MIT Press.

Marantz, A. (1982). Re reduplication. *Linguistic Inquiry*, 13/3, 435–82.

—— (1984a). *On the nature of grammatical relations*. Cambridge, Mass.: MIT Press.

—— (1984b). Tagalog reduplication is affixation, too. Paper presented at the LSA, Baltimore.

—— (1988). Clitics, morphological merger, and the mapping to phonological structure. In Hammond and Noonan (eds), 253–70.

—— (1989). Clitics and phrase structure. In M. Baltin and A. Kroch (eds), *Alternative conceptions of phrase structure*, Chicago: University of Chicago Press, 99–116.

Maratsos, M. P. (1993). Artifactual overregularizations? In E. V. Clark (ed.), *Proceedings of the 24th annual Child Language Research Forum*, Stanford, Calif.: Stanford University, Center for the Study of Language and Information, 39–48.

Maratsos, M. P., Gudeman, R., Gerard-Ngo, P. and DeHart, G. (1987). A study in novel word learning: the productivity of the causative. In MacWhinney (ed.), 89–113.

Marchand, H. (1967). Expansion, transposition, and derivation. *La Linguistique*, 1, 13–26.

—— (1969). *The categories and types of English word-formation*, 2nd edn. Munich: C. H. Beck'sche Verlagsbuchhandlung.

Marchman, V. (1995). Children's productivity in the English past tense: the role of frequency, phonology, and neighborhood structure. MS, University of Wisconsin, Madison.

Marcus, G. F., Brinkmann, U., Clahsen, H., Wiese, R., Woest, A. and Pinker, S. (1995). German inflection: the exception that proves the rule. *Cognitive Psychology*, 29, 189–256.

Marcus, G. F., Pinker, S., Ullrnan, M., Hollander, M., Rosen, T. J. and Xu, Fei (1992). *Overregularization in language acquisition*, Monograph of the Society for Research in Child Development, 57 (serial no. 228).

Mardirussian, G. (1975). Noun incorporation in universal grammar. In *Papers from the 11th regional meeting of the Chicago Linguistic Society*, 383–9.

Markman, E. M. (1989). *Categorization and naming in children*. Cambridge, Mass.: MIT Press.

—— (1994). Constraints on word meaning in early language. *Lingua*, 92, 199–227.

Marr, D. and Vaina, L. (1982). Representation and recognition of the movements of shapes. *Proceedings of the Royal Society of London*, B 214, 501–24.

Marslen-Wilson, W. (ed.) (1989). *Lexical representation and process*. Cambridge, Mass.: MIT Press.

Marslen-Wilson, W., Tyler, L. K., Waksler, R. and Older, L. (1994). Morphology and meaning in the English mental lexicon. *Psychological Review*, 101, 3–33.

Matthews, P. H. (1972). *Inflectional morphology: a theoretical study based on aspects of Latin verb conjugations*. Cambridge: Cambridge University Press.

—— (1974). *Morphology*, 1st edn. Cambridge: Cambridge University Press.

—— (1991). *Morphology*, 2nd edn. Cambridge: Cambridge University Press.

Mayerthaler, W. (1981). *Morphologische Natürlichkeit*. Wiesbaden: Athenaion.

—— (1988). *Morphological naturalness*, trans. Janice Seidler. Ann Arbor: Karoma Press (trans. of Mayerthaler, 1981).

McCarthy, J. (1979). Formal problems in Semitic phonology and morphology. Ph.D. diss., Massachusetts Institute of Technology.

—— (1981). A prosodic theory of nonconcatentive morphology. *Linguistic Inquiry*, 12, 373–418.

—— (1984a). Prosodic structure in morphology. In M. Aronoff and R. Oehrle (eds), *Language sound structure*, Cambridge, Mass.: MIT Press, 299–317.

—— (1984b). Speech disguise and phonological representation in Amharic. In van der Hulst and Smith (eds), 305–12.

—— (1989). Linear order in phonological representation. *Linguistic Inquiry*, 20, 71–99.

—— (1993). Template form in Prosodic Morphology. In *Papers from the 3rd annual Formal Linguistics Society of Mid-America conference*, 187–218.

McCarthy, J. and Prince, A. (1986). Prosodic Morphology. MS, University of Massachusetts and Brandeis University.

—— (1988). Quantitative transfer in reduplicative and templatic morphology. In Linguistic Society of Korea (ed.), *Linguistics in the morning calm*, vol. 2, Seoul: Hanshin Publishing Co., 3–35.

—— (1990a). Foot and word in prosodic morphology: the Arabic broken plurals. *Natural Language and Linguistic Theory*, 8, 209–82.

—— (1990b). Prosodic morphology and templatic morphology. In M. Eid and J. McCarthy (eds), *Perspectives on Arabic linguistics: papers from the second symposium*, Amsterdam: J. Benjamins, 1–54.

—— (1991a). Linguistics 240: prosodic morphology. Lectures and handouts from 1991 LSA Linguistic Institute Course, University of California, Santa Cruz.

—— (1991b). Prosodic minimality. Paper presented at University of Illinois Conference on the Organization of Phonology.

—— (1993a). Generalized alignment. In G. Booij and J. van Marle (eds), *Yearbook of morphology 1993*, Dordrecht: Kluwer, 79–153.

—— (1993b). Prosodic morphology I: constraint interaction and satisfaction. MS, University of Massachusetts, Amherst, and Rutgers University.

—— (1994a). The emergence of the unmarked: optimality in prosodic morphology. In Mercè Gonzàlez (ed.), *Proceedings of the 24th annual meeting of the North-Eastern Linguistic Society*, 333–79.

—— (1994b). Prosodic morphology: an overview. Paper presented at the Utrecht Workshop on Prosodic Morphology.

—— (1995a). Faithfulness and reduplicative identity. In L. Beckman, L. Walsh Dickey and S. Urbanczyk (eds), *Papers in optimality theory*, UMass. Occasional Papers, 18, Amherst: GLSA UMass., 252–384.

—— (1995b). Prosodic morphology. In J. Goldsmith (ed.), *Handbook of phonology*, Oxford: Blackwell Publishers, 318–66.

McCawley, J. D. (1988). *The syntactic phenomena of English*, vol. 2. Chicago: University of Chicago Press.

McClelland, J. L. and Rumelhart, D. E. (1981). An interactive activation model of context effects in letter recognition: part 1. An account of basic findings. *Psychological Review*, 88, 375–407.

McCloskey, M., Badecker, W., Goodman-Schulman, R. and Aliminosa, D. (1992). The structure of output orthographic representations: evidence from a case of acquired dysgraphia. *Cognitive Neuropsychology*, 11, 341–92.

McClure, W. T. (1994). Syntactic projections of the semantics of aspect, Ph.D. diss., Cornell University.

McCone, K. (1987). *The early Irish verb*. Maynooth: An Sagart.

McConvell, P. (1978). Hierarchical variation in pronominal clitic attachment in the Eastern Ngumbin languages. In S. A. Wurm (ed.), *Australian linguistic studies, papers in Australian linguistics 13, Pacific linguistics A.59*, Canberra: Pacific Linguistics, 31–117.

—— (1988). Nasal cluster dissimilation and constraints on phonological variables in Gurindji and related languages. *Aboriginal Linguistics* vol. 1.

—— (1996). *The functions of split-Wackernagel clitics systems: pronominal clitics in the Ngumpin languages (Pama-Nyungan family, Northern Australia)*. In Halpern and Zwicky (eds), 299–332.

McDonough, J. (1990). Topics in the phonology and morphology of Navajo verbs. Ph.D. diss., University of Massachusetts, Amherst.

McKay, G. R. (1975). Rembarnga: a language of central Arnhem Land. Ph.D. Diss., Australian National University.

—— (1980). Medial stop gemination in Rembarrnga: a spectrographic study. *Journal of Phonetics*, 8, 343–52.

McNally, L. (1990). Multiplanar reduplication: evidence from Sesotho. In *Proceedings of the 9th West Coast conference on formal linguistics*, 331–46.

McQueen, J., van Ooijen, B. and Cutler, A. (1992). Are regular and inrregular inflections represented in the same way in the lexicon? Paper presented at the Oxford meeting of the Experimental Psychological Society, April 1992.

Mchombo, S. A. (1978). A critical appraisal of the place of derivational morphology within transformational grammar, considered with primary reference to Chichewa and Swahili. Ph.D. diss., School of Oriental and African Studies, University of London.

—— (1980). Dative and passive in Chichewa: an argument for surface grammar. *Linguistic Analysis*, 6, 97–113.

—— (1991). Reciprocalization in Chichewa: a lexical account. *Linguistic Analysis*, 21, 3–22.

—— (1992). A formal analysis of the stative construction in Bantu. *Journal of African Languages and Linguistics*, 13.

—— (1993). Reflexive and reciprocal in Chichewa. In Mchombo (ed.), 181–208.

Mchombo, S. A. (ed.) (1993). *Theoretical aspects of Bantu grammar*. Stanford, Calif.: Stanford University, CSLI.

Mchombo, S. A. and Mtenje, A. D. (1983). Noncyclic grammar. *Linguistic Analysis*, 11, 219–36.

Mchombo, S. A. and Ngalande, R. M. (1980). Reciprocal verbs in Chichewa: a case for lexical derivation. *London University Bulletin of the School of Oriental and African Studies*, 43, 570–5.

Meillet, A. (1897). *Recherches sur l'emploi du génitif-accusatif en vieux slave*. Paris:

Mel'čuk, I. A. (1973). Model' sprjaženija v aljutorskom jazyke (A model for Alutor conjugation). Moscow: Institut russkogo jazyka, Akademija Nauk.

—— (1986). Toward a definition of case. In R. D. Brecht and J. S. Levine (eds), *Case in Slavic*, Columbus, Oh.: Slavica, 35–85.

Menn, L. and MacWhinney, B. (1984). The repeated morph constraint. *Language*, 60, 519–41.

Meringer, R. (1908). *Aus dem Leben der Sprache*. Berlin: Behrs Verlag.

Meringer, R. and Mayer, M. (1895). *Versprechen und Verlesen*. Stuttgart: Geschensche Verlag.

Merlan, F. (1976). Noun incorporation and discourse reference in modern Nahuatl. *International Journal of American Linguistics*, 42, 177–91.

—— (1982). *Mangarayi*. Amsterdam: North-Holland.

Mester, R.-A. (1990). Patterns of truncation. *Linguistic Inquiry*, 21, 478–85.

Meeussen, A. (1967). Bantu grammatical reconstructions. *Annales du Musée Royal de l'Afrique Centrale*, Série 8, *Sciences Humaines*, 61, 81–121.

Mey, J. L. (1989). Valentie en interferentie in morfologie en discourse: een pragmatische studie. *Journal of Pragmatics*, 13, 881–97.

Mhac an Fhailigh, E. (1968). *The Irish of Erris, Co. Mayo*. Dublin: Institute for Advanced Studies.

Miceli, G. and Caramazza, A. (1988). Dissociation of inflectional and derivational morphology. *Brain and Language*, 35, 24–65.

Miceli, G. and Mazzucchi, A. (1990). Agrammatism in Italian: two case studies. In L. Menn and L. Obler (eds), *Agrammatic aphasia: a cross-language narrative sourcebook*, Amsterdam: J. Benjamins, 717–816.

Miceli, G., Silveri, M., Romani, C. and Caramazza, A. (1989). Variation in the pattern of omissions and substitutions of grammatical morphemes in the spontaneous speech of so-called agrammatic patients. *Brain and Language*, 36, 447–92.

Mikailov, K. Š. (1967). *Arčinskij jazyk*. Maxachkala.

Mikeš, M. (1967). Acquisition des catégories grammaticales dans le langage de l'enfant. *Enfance*, 20, 289–98.

Miller, D. G. (1993). *Complex verb formation*. Amsterdam: J. Benjamins.

Miller, P. (1992). *Clitics and constituents in phrase structure grammar*. New York: Garland.

Miner, K. L. (1986). Noun stripping and loose incorporation in Zuni. *International Journal of American Linguistics*, 52, 242–54.

—— (1989). A note on noun stripping. *International Journal of American Linguistics*, 55, 476–7.

Mitchell, E. (1991). Evidence from Finnish for Pollock's theory of IP. *Linguistic Inquiry*, 22, 373–9.

Mithun, M. (1984). The evolution of noun incorporation. *Language*, 60, 847–94.

—— (1986). On the nature of noun incorporation. *Language*, 62, 32–7.

—— (1989). The acquisition of polysynthesis. *Journal of Child Language*, 16, 285–312.

—— (1991). The development of bound pronominal paradigms. In W. P. Lehmann and H.-J. Jakusz Hewitt (eds), *Language typology 1988: typological models in reconstruction*, Amsterdam: J. Benjamins.

Mohanan, K. P. (1982). Lexical phonology. Ph.D. diss., Massachusetts Institute of Technology. (Distributed by Indiana University Linguistics Club.)

—— (1986). *The theory of lexical phonology*. Dordrecht: Reidel.

Monsell, S. (1985). Repetition and the lexicon. In A. W. Ellis (ed.), *Progress in the psychology of language*, vol. 2, 147–95.

Montgomery, M. and Bailey, G. (1991). In which: a new form in written English? *American Speech*, 66, 147–63.

Moortgat, M., van der Hulst, H. and Hoekstra, T. (eds) (1981). *The scope of lexical rules*. Dordrecht: Foris.

Moravcsik, E. (1978a). Agreement. In J. Greenberg, C. Ferguson and E. Moravcsik (eds), *Universals of human language*, vol. 4: *Syntax*, Stanford, Calif.: Stanford University Press, 331–74.

—— (1978b). On the case marking of objects. In J. H. Greenberg (ed.), *Universals of human language*, vol. 4: *Syntax*, Stanford, Calif.: Stanford University Press, 249–90.

—— (1978c). Reduplicative constructions. In J. Greenberg, C. Ferguson and E. Moravcsik (eds), *Universals of human language*, vol. 3: *Word structure*, Stanford, Calif.: Stanford University Press, 297–334.

Morice, A. G. (1932). *The carrier language*. Vienna: Verlag der Internationalen Zeitschrift 'Anthropos' Mödling bei Wien, St Gabriel, Osterreich.

Morin, Y.-C. (1996). The simplicity and acquisition of defective paradigms: a historical perspective. Presented at the 7th International Morphology meeting, Vienna, February 1996.

Mtenje, A. D. (1985). Arguments for an autosegmental analysis of Chichewa vowel harmony. *Lingua*, 66, 21–52.

—— (1986). Issues in the nonlinear phonology of Chichewa. Ph.D. diss., University College London.

—— (1988). On tone and transfer in Chichewa reduplication. *Linguistics*, 26, 125–55.

Mulford, R. C. (1985). Comprehension of Icelandic pronoun gender: semantic versus formal factors. *Journal of Child Language*, 12, 443–53.

Murrell, G. A. and Morton, J. (1974). Word recognition and morphemic structure. *Journal of Experimental Psychology*, 102, 963–8.

Mutaka, N. and Hyman, L. (1990). Syllable and morpheme integrity in Kinande reduplication. *Phonology*, 7, 73–120.

Myers, S. (1987). Tone and the structure of words in Shona. Ph.D. diss., University of Massachusetts, Amherst.

Mylne, T. (1996). The "inversion marker" in Warumungu. MS, Department of English, University of Queensland.

Napps, S. E. (1989). Morphemic relations in the lexicon: are they distinct from semantic and formal relationships? *Memory and Cognition*, 17, 729–39.

Napps, S. E. and Fowler, C. A. (1987). Formal relationships among words and the organisation of the mental lexicon. *Journal of Psycholinguistic Research*, 16, 257–72.

Nash, D. (1986). *Topics in Warlpiri grammar*. New York: Garland.

Nedjalkov, V. P. (1993). *Tense–aspect–mood forms in Chukchi*, Eurotype Working Papers, Series VI, no. 4.

Nedjalkov, V. P. and Silnitsky, G. G. (1973). The typology of morphological and lexical causatives. In F. Kiefer (ed.), *Trends in Soviet theoretical linguistics*, Dordrecht: Reidel, 1–32.

Nespor, M. and Vogel, I. (1986). *Prosodic phonology*. Dordrecht: Foris.

Nespoulous, J.-L. and Villard, P. (eds) (1990). *Morphology, phonology and aphasia*. Berlin: Springer-Verlag.

Nespoulous, J.-L., Dordain, M., Perron, C., Ska, B., Bub, D., Caplan, D., Mehler, J. and Lecours, A. (1988). Agrammatism in sentence production without comprehension deficits: reduced availability of syntactic structures and/or grammatical morphemes? A case study. *Brain and Language*, 33, 273–95.

Nevis. J. A. (1984). A non-endoclitic in Estonian. *Ohio State University Working Papers in Linguistics*, 29, 139–47.

—— (1986). Decliticization and deaffixation in Saame: Abessive taga. In B. D. Joseph (ed.), *Studies on language change*, Ohio State University Working Papers in Linguistics, 34, Columbus: Ohio State University Department of Linguistics, 1–9.

—— (1988). *Finnish particle clitics and general clitic theory*. New York: Garland.

Nevis, J. A., Joseph, B. D., Wanner, D. and Zwicky, A. M. (1994). *A bibliography of clitics: 1892–1991*. Amsterdam: J. Benjamins.

Newman, Stanley (1944). *The Yokuts language of California*. New York: Viking Fund Publications in Anthropology.

Newmark, L., Hubbard, P. and Prifti, P. (1982). *Standard Albanian. A reference grammar for students*. Stanford, Calif.: Stanford University Press.

Newmeyer, F. J. (ed.) (1988). *Linguistics: the Cambridge survey*, vol. 1: *Linguistic theory: foundations*. Cambridge: Cambridge University Press.

Nichols, J. (1985). The directionality of agreement. In *Proceedings of the 11th annual meeting of the Berkeley Lingustics Society*, 273–86.

—— (1992). *Linguistic diversity in space and time*. Chicago: University of Chicago Press.

Nicolaci-da-Costa, A. and Harris, M. (1983). Redundancy of syntactic information: an aid to young children's comprehension of sentential number. *British Journal of Psychology*, 74, 343–52.

Niemi, J., Laine, M. and Tuominen, J. (1994). Cognitive morphology in Finnish: foundations of a new model. *Language and Cognitive Processes*, 9, 423–46.

Nivens, R. (1992). A lexical phonology of West Tarangan. In D. Burquest and W. Laidig (eds), *Phonological studies in four languages of Maluku*, Dallas: Summer Institute of Linguistics.

Nolan, K. and Caramazza, A. (1982). Modality-independent impairments in word processing in a deep dyslexic patient. *Brain and Language*, 16, 237–64.

Nordlinger, R. (1993). A grammar of Wambaya. M.A. diss., University of Melbourne.

Noske, M. (1991). Metrical structure and reduplication in Turkana. In M. L. Bender (ed.), *Proceedings of the 4th Nilo-Saharan linguistics colloquium*, Hamburg: Helmut Buske Verlag, 245–62.

Noyer, R. R. (1994). Mobile affixes in Huave: optimality and morphological well-formedness. In *Proceedings of the 12th West Coast conference on formal linguistics*, 67–82.

—— (in press). Impoverishment theory and morphosyntactic markedness. In S. G. Lapointe (ed.), *Morphological interfaces*. Stanford, Calif.: Stanford University, CSLI.

Oates, L. F. (1964). *A tentative description of the Gunwinggu language* (of Western Arnhem Land), Oceania Linguistic Monograph, 10. Sydney: University of Sydney Press.

Omar, M. K. (1973). *The acquisition of Egyptian Arabic as a native language*. The Hague: Mouton.

Ó Siadhail, M. (1989). *Modern Irish. Grammatical structure and dialectal variation*. Cambridge: Cambridge University Press.

Oswalt, R. L. (1986). The evidential system of Kashaya. In W. Chafe and J. Nichols (eds), *Evidentiality: the linguistic coding of epistemology*, Norwood, N.J.: Ablex, 29–45.

Ouhalla, J. (1991). *Functional projections and parametric variation*. London: Routledge.

Parker, E. M. and Hayward, R. J. (1985). *An Afar–English–French dictionary* (with grammatical notes in English). London: School of Oriental and African Studies, University of London.

Patterson, K. (1980). Derivational errors. In Coltheart et al., 286–306.

—— (1982). The relation between reading and phonological coding: further neuropsychological observations. In A. Ellis (ed.), *Normality and pathology in cognitive functions*, London: Academic Press, 77–111.

Patterson, K. and Shewell, C. (1987). Speak and spell: dissociations and word-class effects. In M. Coltheart, R. Job and G. Sartori (eds), *Cognitive neuropsychology of language*, London: Lawrence Erlbaum Associates, 273–94.

Patz, E. (1982). A grammar of the Kuku-Yalanji language of North Queensland. Ph.D. diss., Australian National University.

Paul, I. (1996a). The active marker and nasals in Malagasy. In Pearson and Paul (eds), 49–57.

—— (1996b). The Malagasy genitive. In Pearson and Paul (eds), 76–91.

Payne, D. (1981). *The phonology and morphology of Axininca Campa*. Arlington, Tex.: Summer Institute of Linguistics.

Payne, J. (1989). Pamir languages. In R. Schmitt (ed.), *Compendium linguarum iranicarum*, Wiesbaden: Reichert, 417–44.

—— (1995). Inflection postpositions in Indic and Kashmiri. In F. Plank (ed.), *Double case: agreement by Suffixaufnahme*, New York: Oxford University Press, 283–98.

Pearson, M. and Paul, I. (eds) (1996). *The structure of Malagasy*, vol. 1, UCLA Occasional Papers in Linguistics, 17. Los Angeles: Dept of Linguistics, UCLA.

Perlmutter, D. (1971). *Deep and surface structure constraints in syntax*. New York: Holt, Reinhart and Winston.

—— (1988). The split morphology hypothesis: evidence from Yiddish. In Hammond and Noonan (eds), 79–100.

—— (1992). Pervasive word formation patterns in a grammar. Paper presented at the 18th meeting of the Berkeley Linguistics Society.

Perlmutter, D. and Postal, P. (1984). Impersonal passives and some relational laws. In D. Perlmutter and Carol Rosen (eds), *Studies in relational grammar*, Chicago: University of Chicago Press.

Pesetsky, D. (1979). Russian morphology and lexical theory. MS, MIT.

—— (1985). Morphology and logical form. *Linguistic Inquiry*, 16, 193–246.

—— (1995). *Zero syntax*. Cambridge, Mass.: MIT Press.

Phillips, V. (1995). Up-rooting the prefix *maha-* in Malagasy. Paper presented at the 2nd annual meeting of the Austronesian Formal Linguistics Association, Montreal, March 1995.

Pierrehumbert, J. and Beckman, M. (1988). *Japanese tone structure*. Cambridge, Mass.: MIT Press.

Pilhofer, G. (1933). *Grammatik der Kâte Sprache aus Neuguinea. Zeitschrift für Eingeborenen-Sprachen*, Bieheft 14.

Pillon, A., de Partz, M.-P., Raison, A.-M. and Seron, X. (1991). L'orange, c'est le frutier de l'orangine: a case of morphological impairment? *Language and Cognitive Processes*, 6, 137–67.

Pinker, S. (1989). *Learnability and cognition: the acquisition of argument structure*. Cambridge, Mass.: MIT Press.

—— (1991). Rules of language. *Science*, 253, 530–5.

Pinker, S. and Prince, A. (1988). On language and connectionism: analysis of a parallel distributed processing model of language acquisition. *Cognition*, 28, 73–194.

—— (1991). Regular and irregular morphology and the psychological status of rules of grammar. In *Proceedings of the 17th annual meeting of the Berkeley Linguistics Society*, 230–51.

Pintzuk, S. (1991). Phrase structures in competition: variation and change in Old English word order. Ph.D. diss., University of Pennsylvania.

Plank, F. (1979). The functional basis of case systems and declension classes: from Latin to Old French. *Linguistics*, 17, 611–40.

—— (1980). Encoding grammatical relations: acceptable and unacceptable non-distinctness. In J. Fisiak (ed.), *Historical morphology*, The Hague: Mouton, 289–325.

—— (1986). Paradigm size, morphological typology, and universal economy. *Folia Linguistica*, 20, 29–48.

—— (1996). Patterns of suppletion in inflection. Paper presented at the 7th International Morphology Meeting, Vienna, February 1996.

Plank, F. (ed.) (1991). *Paradigms: the economy of inflection*. Berlin: Mouton de Gruyter.

—— (1995). *Double case: agreement by Suffixaufnahme*. New York: Oxford University Press.

Platzack, C. and Holmberg, A. (1989). The Role of Agr and finiteness in Germanic VO languages. *Working Papers in Scandinavian Syntax*, 43, 51–76.

Plunkett, K. and Marchman, V. (1991). U-shaped learning and frequency effects in a multi-layered perception: implications for child language acquisition. *Cognition*, 38, 43–102.

Polinskaja, M. S. and Nedjalkov, V. P. (1987). Contrasting the absolutive in Chukchee. *Lingua*, 71, 239–69.

Polinsky, M. S. (1990). Subject incorporation: evidence from Chukchee. In K. Dziwirek, P. Farrell and E. Mejías-Bikandi (eds), *Grammatical relations: a cross-theoretical perspective*, Stanford, Calif.: Stanford University, CSLI, 349–64.

—— (1995). The existential construction in Malagasy. MS, Dept. of Linguistics, University of Southern California.

—— (1996). Incorporation in Malagasy. MS, Dept. of Linguistics, University of Southern California.

Pollard, C. and Sag, I. (1988). An information-based theory of agreement. In *Papers from the 24th annual meeting of the Chicago Linguistic Society*, 236–57.

—— (1994). *Head-Driven Phrase Structure Grammar*. Chicago: University of Chicago Press.

Pollock, J.-Y. (1989). Verb movement, Universal Grammar, and the structure of IP. *Linguistic Inquiry*, 20, 365–424.

Poser, W. (1982). Why cases of syllable reduplication are so hard to find. MS, Massachusetts Institute of Technology.

—— (1984). Hypocoristic formation in Japanese. In *Proceedings of the 3rd West Coast conference on formal linguistics*, 218–29.

—— (1985). Cliticization to NP and Lexical Phonology. In *Proceedings of the 4th West Coast conference on formal linguistics*, 262–72.

—— (1989). The metrical foot in Diyari. *Phonology*, 6, 117–48.

—— (1990). Evidence for foot structure in Japanese. *Language*, 66, 78–105.

Postal, P. M. (1969). Anaphoric islands. In *Papers from the 5th annual meeting of the Chicago Linguistic Society*, 205–39.

—— (1979). *Some syntactic rules in Mohawk*. New York: Garland.

—— (1982). Some Arc Pair Grammar descriptions. In P. Jacobson and G. K. Pullum (eds), *The nature of syntactic representation*, Dordrecht: Reidel, 341–425.

Posteraro, L., Zinelli, P. and Mazzucchi, A. (1988). Selective impairment of the graphemic buffer in acquired dysgraphia. *Brain and Language*, 35, 274–86.

Prasada, S., Pinker, S. and Snyder, W. (1990). Some evidence that irregular forms are retrieved from memory but regular forms are rule-generated. Paper presented at the annual meeting of the Psychonomic Society, New Orleans, 23–5 November.

Prentice, D. J. (1971). *The Murut languages of Sabah*, Pacific Linguistics, Series C, no. 18. Canberra: Australian National University Press.

Priestly, T. M. S. (1977). One idiosyncratic strategy in the acquisition of phonology. *Journal of Child Language*, 4, 45–65.

Prince, A. (1980). A metrical theory for Estonian quantity. *Linguistic Inquiry*, 11, 511–62.

—— (1991). Quantitative consequences of rhythmic organization. In *Papers from the 26th annual meeting of the Chicago Linguistic Society, parasession on the syllable in phonetics and phonology*, 355–98.

Prince, A. and Smolensky, P. (1991). Notes on connectionism and harmony theory in linguistics. Technical Report CU-CS-533–91, Boulder, Colo.: Department of Computer Science, University of Colorado.

—— (1993). Optimality Theory: constraint interaction in generative grammar. MS, Rutgers University and University of Colorado, Boulder.

Progovac, L. (1996). Serbian/Croatian clitics: the mystery of the second position. In Halpern and Zwicky (eds), 411–28.

Prokosch, E. (1938). *A comparative Germanic grammar*. Baltimore: Linguistic Society of America.

Pullum, G. K. (1984). How complex could an agreement system be? In *Proceedings of the 1st Eastern States conference on linguistics*, 79–103.

Pullum, G. K. and Zwicky, A. M. (1992). A misconceived approach to morphology. In D. Bates (ed.), *Proceedings of the 10th West Coast conference on formal linguistics*, 387–98.

Pusch, L. R. (1972). Bemerkungen über partitive and holistische Konstruktionen im Deutschen und Englischen. In G. Nickel (ed.), *Reader zur kontrastiven Linguistik*, Frankfurt: Athenäum Fischer Taschenbuch, 122–35.

Pustejovsky, J. (1991a). The generative lexicon. *Computational Linguistics*, 17, 409–41.

—— (1991b). The syntax of event structure. *Cognition*, 41, 47–81; also in Levin and Pinker (eds), 1992, 47–81.

—— (1995). *The generative lexicon*. Cambridge, Mass.: MIT Press.

Rabenilaina, R.-B. (1987). *Lexique-grammaire du malgache*. Autananarivo, Madagascar: FOFIPA.

Rabenilaina, R.-B. and Razafindrakoto, A. (1987). *Ny fitsipiky ny teny*, Taona, 10. Antananarivo, Madagascar: FOFIPA.

—— (1989). *Ny fitsipiky ny teny*, Taona, 11. Antananarivo, Madagascar: FOFIPA.

Radanović-Kocić, V. (1988). The grammar of Serbo-Croatian clitics: a synchronic and diachronic perspective. Unpublished Ph.D. diss., University of Illinois at Urbana–Champaign.

Rahajarizafy, A. (R. P.) (1960). *Essai de grammaire malgache*. Antananarivo, Madagascar: Imprimérie Catholique.

Rainer, F. (1988). Towards a theory of blocking: the case of Italian and German quality nouns. In Booij and van Marle (eds), 155–85.

Rajaobelina, P. (1960). *Gramera Malagasy Salohy*. Tananarive: Presses Luthériennes.

Rajaona, S. (1972). *Structure du malgache*. Fianarantsoa: Ambozontany.

—— (1977). *Problèmes de morphologie malgache*. Fianarantsoa: Ambozontany.

Rajemisa-Raolison, R. (1971). *Grammaire malgache*. Fianarantsoa: Ambozontany (1st edn 1959).

Ralalaoherivony, B. (1995). Incorporation and Raising from NP in Malagasy. MS, Dept. of Linguistics, UCLA.

Ramsden, H. (1963). *Weak-pronoun position in the early Romance languages*. Manchester: Manchester University Press.

Randoja, T. (1990). The phonology and morphology of Halfway River Beaver. Ph.D. diss., University of Ottawa.

Randriamasimanana, C. (1986). *The causatives of Malagasy*. Honolulu: University of Hawaii Press.

Rappaport, M. and Levin, B. (1988). What to do with θ roles. In W. Wilkins (ed.), *Syntax and semantics 21: thematic relations*. New York: Academic Press, 7–36.

Reinisch, L. (1886). *Die Afar-Sprache*. Repr. from Sitzungsberichte der Kaiserlichen Akademie der Wissenschaften, Phil. – Hist. Classe 91, 93, 94. Vienna: Karl Gerold's Sohn.

Reuland, E. and Abraham, W. (eds) (1993). *Knowledge and language*, vol. 2: *Lexical and conceptual structure*. Dordrecht: Kluwer.

Rice, C. (1988). Stress assignment in the Chugach dialect of Alutiiq. In *Papers from the 24th annual meeting of the Chicago Linguistic Society*, 304–15.

Rice, K. (1985a). Noun compounds in Dene. *Journal of the Atlantic Provinces Linguistic Association*, 6/7, 55–72.

——— (1985b). On the placement of inflection. *Linguistic Inquiry*, 16, 155–61.

——— (1985c). The optative and *s- and *n- conjugation marking in Slave. *International Journal of American Linguistics*, 51, 282–301.

——— (1988). Continuant voicing in Slave (northern Athapaskan): the cyclic application of default rules. In Hammond and Noonan (eds), 371–88.

——— (1989). *A grammar of Slave*. Berlin: Mouton de Gruyter.

——— (1991a). Intransitives in Slave (Northern Athapaskan): arguments for unaccusatives. *International Journal of American Linguistics*, 57, 51–69.

——— (1991b). Predicting the order of the disjunct morphemes in the Athapaskan languages. *Toronto Working Papers in Linguistics*, 10, 99–121.

——— (1991c). Prosodic constituency in Hare (Athapaskan): evidence for the foot. *Lingua*, 82, 201–45.

——— (1992a). Blocking and privative features: a prosodic account. *Linguistic Review*, 9, 359–93.

——— (1992b). On deriving rule domains: the Athapaskan case. In *Proceedings of the 10th West Coast conference on formal linguistics*, 417–30.

——— (1993). The structure of the Slave (Northern Athapaskan) verb. In S. Hargus and E. Kaisse (eds), *Studies in Lexical Phonology. Phonetics and Phonology*, vol. 4, San Diego, Calif.: Academic Press, 145–71.

——— (forthcoming). *Scope and morpheme order in the Athapaskan verb*. Cambridge: Cambridge University Press.

Rice, K. and Hargus, S. (1989). Conjugation and mode in Athapaskan languages: evidence for two positions. In Cook and Rice (eds), 265–315.

Rice, K. and Saxon, L. (1991). A structural analysis of *y- in Athapaskan. Paper presented at the Athapaskan Linguistics Conference, Santa Cruz, California, July 1991.

——— (1994). The subject positions in Athapaskan languages. In H. Harley and C. Phillips (eds), *The morphology–syntax connection*, MIT Working Papers in Linguistics, Cambridge, Mass.: MIT Press, 22, 173–95.

Richardson, J. (1885). *A new Malagasy–English dictionary*. Antananarivo: London Missionary Society.

Riley, K. and Parker, F. (1986). Anomalous prepositions in relative clauses. *American Speech*, 61, 291–306.

Ritter, E. (1995). On the syntactic category of pronouns and agreement. *Natural Language and Linguistic Theory*, 13, 405–43.

Rivas, A. (1978). A theory of clitics. Unpublished Ph.D. diss., Massachusetts Institute of Technology.

Rivero, M. L. (1990). The location of nonactive voice in Albanian and Modern Greek. *Linguistic Inquiry*, 21, 135–46.

——— (1993). Bulgarian and Serbo-Croatian yes–no questions: V0 raising to -li vs. -li Hopping. *Linguistic Inquiry*, 24/3, 567–75.

Rizzi, L. (1982). *Issues in Italian syntax*. Dordrecht: Foris.

Rizzi, L. and Roberts, I. G. (1989). Complex inversion in French. *Probus*, 1, 1–30.

Roberts, I. G. (1985). Agreement parameters and the development of English modal auxiliaries. *Natural Language and Linguistic Theory*, 3, 21–58.

—— (1987). *The representation of implicit and dethematized subjects*. Dordrecht: Foris.

—— (1991). Excorporation and minimality. *Linguistic Inquiry*, 22, 209–18.

Robertson, J. (1975). A syntactic example of Kuryłowicz's Fourth Law of Analogy in Mayan. *International Journal of American Linguistics*, 41, 140–7.

Robins, R. H. (1959). In defence of WP. *Transactions of the Philological Society*, 57, 116–44.

Roca, I. M. (ed.) (1992). *Thematic structure: its role in grammar*. Dordrecht: Foris.

Rodrigues, A. D. (n.d.). Estrutura do Tupinambá. MS, Universidade Estadual de Campinas, Brazil.

Roeper, T. (1988). Compound syntax and head movement. In Booij and van Marle (eds), 187–228.

Roeper, T. and Siegel, M. (1978). A lexical transformation for verbal compounds. *Linguistic Inquiry*, 9, 199–260.

Rohrbacher, B. (1994). The Germanic VO languages and the full paradigm: a theory of V to I raising. Ph.D. diss., University of Massachusetts, Amherst.

Rosen, C. (1984). The interface between semantic roles and initial grammatical relations. In D. M. Perlmutter and C. Rosen (eds), *Studies in relational grammar*, vol. 2, Chicago: University of Chicago Press, 38–77.

Rosen, S. T. (1989a). Argument structure and complex predicates. Ph.D. diss., Brandeis University, Waltham, Mass.

—— (1989b). Two types of noun incorporation: a lexical analysis. *Language*, 65, 294–317.

Ross, J. R. (1967). Constraints on variables in syntax. Ph.D. diss., Massachusetts Institute of Technology. (Reproduced by the Indiana University Linguistics Club, 1968.)

Rubach, J. (1984). *Cyclic and lexical phonology: the structure of Polish*. Dordrecht: Foris.

—— (1993). *The lexical phonology of Slovak*. Oxford: Clarendon Press.

Rubin, G. S., Becker, C. A. and Freeman, R. H. (1979). Morphological structure and its effect on visual word recognition. *Journal of Verbal Learning and Verbal Behavior*, 18, 757–67.

Rudes, B. (1980). On the nature of verbal suppletion. *Linguistics,* 18, 655–76.

Rumelhart, D. and McClelland, J. (1986). On learning the past tenses of English verbs. In D. Rumelhart and J. McClelland (eds), *Parallel distributed processing: explorations in the microstructure of cognition*, vol. 1, Cambridge, Mass.: Bransford Books, 216–71.

Ruwet, N. (1972). *Théorie syntaxique et syntaxe du Français*. Paris: Editions du Seuil.

Sadock, J. M. (1980). Noun incorporation in Greenlandic: a case of syntactic word formation. *Language*, 56, 300–19.

—— (1985). Autolexical syntax: a proposal for the treatment of noun incorporation and similar phenomena. *Natural Language and Linguistic Theory*, 3, 379–440.

—— (1986). Some notes on noun incorporation. *Language*, 62, 19–31.

—— (1991). *Autolexical syntax: a theory of parallel grammatical representations*. Chicago: University of Chicago Press.

Saeed, J. I. (1987). *Somali reference grammar*. Wheaton, Md.: Dunwoody Press.

—— (1993). Adpositional clitics and word order in Somali. *Transactions of the Philological Society*, 91, 63–93.

Saffran, E., Schwartz, M. and Marin, O. (1980). Evidence from aphasia: isolating the components of a production model. In B. Butterworth (ed.), *Language production*, vol. 1: *Speech and talk*, New York: Academic Press, 221–41.

Sag, I. A. and Szabolcsi, A. (eds) (1992). *Lexical matters*. Stanford, Calif.: Stanford University, Center for the Study of Language and Information.

Salmons, J. C. (1994). Umlaut and plurality in Old High German. Some problems with a Natural Morphology account. *Diachronica*, 11/2, 213–29.

Sandoval, M. and Jelinek, E. (1989). The bi-construction and pronominal arguments in Apachean. In Cook and Rice (eds), 379–406.

Sandra, D. (1990). On the representation and processing of compound words: automatic access to constituent morphemes does not occur. *Quarterly Journal of Experimental Psychology*, 42A, 529–67.

—— (1994). The morphology of the mental lexicon. Internal word structure viewed from a psycholinguistic perspective. *Language and Cognitive Processes*, 9, 227–69.

Sapir, E. (1911). The problem of noun incorporation in American languages. *American Anthropologist*, 13, 250–82.

—— (1921). *Language*. New York: Harcourt, Brace and World.

—— (1922). The Takelma language of southwestern Oregon. In F. Boas (ed.), *Handbook of American Indian languages*, pt 2, 1–296.

Sapir, E. and Hoijer, H. (1967). *The phonology and morphology of the Navaho language*, University of California Publications in Linguistics, 50. Berkeley: University of California Press.

Satyo, S. C. (1985). Topics in Xhosa verbal extensions. Ph.D. diss., University of South Africa, Pretoria.

Saussure, F. de (1959). *Course in general linguistics*, trans. W. Baskin. New York: McGraw-Hill.

Sauvageot, A. (1951). *Esquisse de la langue hongroise* (Sketch of the hungarian language). Paris: Klincksieck.

Saxon, L. (1984). Disjoint anaphora and the binding theory. In *Proceedings of the 3rd West Coast conference on formal linguistics*, 3, 242–51.

—— (1986). The syntax of pronouns in Dogrib: some theoretical consquences. Ph.D. diss., University of California at San Diego.

—— (1993). A personal use of the Athapaskan 'impersonal' *ts'e-*. *International Journal of American Linguistics*, 59, 342–54.

Saxon, L. and Rice, K. (1993). On subject–verb constituency: evidence from Athapaskan languages. In *Proceedings of the 11th West Coast conference on formal linguistics*, 434–50.

Scalise, S. (1984). *Generative morphology*. Dordrecht: Foris.

Schachter, P. (1973). Constraints on clitic order in Tagalog. In A. Gonzalez (ed.), *Parangal Kay Cecilio Lopez*, Philippine Journal of Linguistics, Special Monograph Issue, 4, 214–31.

—— (1976). The subject in Philippine languages: topic, actor, actor-topic, or none of the above? In C. N. Li (ed.), 491–518.

—— (1985). Parts-of-speech systems. In T. Shopen (ed.), *Language typology and syntactic description*, vol. 1, Cambridge: Cambridge University Press, 3–61.

Schadeberg, T. C. (1984). *A sketch of Swahili morphology*. Dordrecht: Foris.

Schäufele, S. (1991). Single-word topicalization in Vedic prose: a challenge to government and binding? In H. Hock (ed.), *Studies in Sanskrit Syntax*, Delhi: Motilal Banarsidass, 153–75. (Paper read at the First Sanskrit Syntax Symposium, Eighth South Asian Languages Analysis Roundtable, University of Illinois, Urbana, 30 May 1986.)

Schilling-Estes, N. and Wolfram, W. (1994). Convergent explanation and alternative regularization patterns: were/weren't leveling in a vernacular English variety. *Language Variation and Change*, 6, 273–302.

Schlindwein, D. (1988). The phonological geometry of morpheme concatenation. Ph.D. diss., University of Southern California.

—— (1991). Reduplication in lexical phonology: Javanese plural reduplication. *Linguistic Review*, 8, 97–106.

Schlyter, S. (1978). German and French movement verbs: polysemy and equivalence. In K. Gregersen (ed.), *Papers from the 4th Scandinavian conference of linguistics*, Odense: Odense University Press, 349–54.

—— (1981). De- à/von-zu avec les verbes de mouvement cursifs et transformatifs. In C. Schwarze (ed.), *Analyse des prépositions*. Tübingen: Niemeyer, 171–89.

Schreuder, R. and Baayen, R. H. (1994). Prefix stripping re-revisited. *Journal of Memory and Language*, 33, 357–75.

—— (1995). Modeling morphological processing. In Feldman (ed.), 131–54.

—— (1997). How complex simplex words can be. *Journal of Memory and Language*, 37, 118–39.

Schreuder, R., Grendel, M., Poulisse, N., Roelofs, A. and Voort, M. van der (1990). Lexical processing, morphological complexity and reading. In D. A. Balota, G. B. Flores d'Arcais and K. Rayner (eds), *Comprehension processes in reading*, Hillsdale, N.J.: Erlbaum, 125–41.

Schriefers, H., Friederici, A. and Graetz, P. (1992). Inflectional and derivational morphology in the mental lexicon: symmetries and asymmetries in repetition priming. *Quarterly Journal of Experimental Psychology*, 44A, 373–90.

Schriefers, H., Zwitserlood, P. and Roelofs, A. (1991). The identification of morphologically complex spoken words: continuous processing or decomposition? *Journal of Memory and Language*, 30, 26–47.

Schuhmacher, W. W. (1989). More on -gate. *American Speech*, 64, 380.

Schultink, H. (1961). Produktiviteit als morphologische fenomeen. *Forum der Letteren*, 2, 110–25.

Schwartz-Norman, L. (1976). The grammar of 'content' and 'container'. *Journal of Linguistics*, 12, 279–87.

Schwyzer, E. (1939). *Griechische Grammatik* (Greek grammar), vol. 1. Munich: C. H. Beck'sche Verlagsbuchhandlung.

Scott, Graham (1978). The Fore language of Papua New Guinea. Canberra: Department of Linguistics, Research School of Pacific Studies, Australian National University. (cited from Foley, 1986).

Segui, J. and Zubizaretta, M.-L. (1985). Mental representation of morphologically complex words and lexical access. *Linguistics*, 23, 759–67.

Seiler, H. and Stachowiak, F. J. (eds) (1982). *Apprehension: Das sprachliche Erfassen von Gegenständen: II: Die Techniken und ihre zusammenhang in Einzelsprachen*. Tübingen: Narr.

Selkirk, E. O. (1980a). Prosodic domains in phonology: Sanskrit revisited. In M. Aronoff and M.-L. Kean (eds), *Juncture*, Saratoga, Calif.: Anma Libri, 107–29.

—— (1980b). The role of prosodic categories in English word stress. *Linguistic Inquiry*, 11, 563–605.

—— (1982). *The syntax of words*. Cambridge, Mass.: MIT Press.

—— (1984). *Phonology and syntax*. Cambridge, Mass.: MIT Press.

Semenza, C., Butterworth, B., Panzeri, M. and Ferreri, T. (1990). Word formation: new evidence from aphasia. *Neuropsychologia*, 28, 499–502.

Sereno, J. A. and Jongman, A. (1992). The processing of inflectional morphology in English. Paper presented at the 5th annual CUNY conference on human sentence processing, March 1992.

—— (in press). Processing of English inflectional morphology. *Memory and Cognition*.

Serzisko, F. (1982). Numerus/Genus-Kongruenz und das Phänomen der Polarität am Beispiel einiger ostkuschitischer Sprachen. In Seiler and F. J. Stachowiak (eds), 179–200.

Shallice, T. (1981). Phonological agraphia and the lexical route in writing. *Brain*, 104, 413–29.

Shapiro, M. (1990). On a universal criterion of rule coherence. In Dressler et al. (eds), 25–34.

Shaw, P. A. (1985). Modularisation and substantive constraints in Dakota Lexical Phonology. *Phonology Yearbook*, 2, 171–200.

—— (1987). Non-conservation of melodic structure in reduplication. In *Papers from the 23rd annual regional meeting of the Chicago Linguistic Society, parasession on autosegmental and metrical phonology*, 291–306.

—— (1992). Templatic evidence for the syllable nucleus. In *Proceedings of the 23rd annual meeting of the North-Eastern Linguistic Society*, 463–77.

Shibatani, M. (1976). *The grammar of causative constructions: a conspectus*. In Shibatani (ed.), 1–40.

—— (1985). Passives and related constructions. *Language*, 61, 821–48.

Shibatani, M. (ed.) (1976). *Syntax and semantics*, vol. 6: *The grammar of causative constructions*. New York: Academic Press.

Shibatani, M. and Kageyama, T. (1988). Word formation in a modular theory of grammar: a case of post-syntactic compounds in Japanese. *Language*, 64, 451–84.

Shopen, T. (ed.) (1985). *Language typology and syntactic description*, vol. 3: *Grammatical categories and the lexicon*. Cambridge: Cambridge University Press.

Short, D. (1993). Slovak. In Comrie and Corbett (eds), 533–92.

Siegel, D. (1978). The adjacency constraint and the theory of morphology. In *Proceedings of the 8th annual meeting of the North-Eastern Linguistic Society*, 189–97.

—— (1979). *Topics in English morphology*. New York: Garland.

Siewierska, A. and Bakker, D. (1996). The distribution of subject and object agreement and word order type. *Studies in Language*, 20, 114–61.

Silverstein, M. (1976). Hierarchy of features and ergativity. In R. M. W. Dixon (ed.), *Grammatical categories in Australian languages*, Canberra: Australian Institute of Aboriginal Studies, 112–71.

Simões, M. C. P. and Stoel-Gammon, C. (1979). The acquisition of inflections in Portuguese: a study of the development of person markers on verbs. *Journal of Child Language*, 6, 53–67.

Simon, P. (1988). *Ny Fiteny Fahizany* (Reconstitution et periodisation du malgache ancien jusqu'au XIVème siècle). Paris: Institut des Langues et Civilisations Orientales.

Simpson, J. (1991). *Warlpiri morphosyntax: a lexicalist approach*. Dordrecht: Kluwer.

Simpson, J. and Heath, J. (1982). Warumungu sketch grammar. MS, Massachusetts Institute of Technology and Harvard University. Copy at AIATSIS, Canberra.

Simpson, J. and Withgott, M. (1986). Pronominal clitic clusters and templates. In H. Borer (ed.), *Syntax and semantics*, vol. 19: *The syntax of pronominal clitics*, Orlando, Fla.: Academic Press, 149–74.

Skorik, P. Ja. (1961). *Grammatika Čukotskogo jazyka*, vol. 1. Moscow and Leningrad: Izdatel'stvo Akademii Nauk.

—— (1977). *Grammatika Čukotskogo jazyka*, vol. 2. Moscow and Leningrad: Izdatel'stvo Akademii Nauk.

Skousen, R. (1989). *Analogical modeling of language*. Dordrecht: Kluwer.

Sloan, K. (1991). Syllables and templates: evidence from Southern Sierra Miwok. Ph.D. diss., Massachusetts Institute of Technology.

Slobin, D. I. (1973). Cognitive prerequisites for the acquisition of grammar. In Ferguson and Slobin (eds), 173–208.

Slobin, D. I. (ed.) (1985). *The crosslinguistic study of language acquisition*, vols 1 and 2. Hillsdale, N.J.: Lawrence Erlbaum.

—— (1992). *The crosslinguistic study of language acquisition*, vol. 3. Hillsdale, N.J.: Lawrence Erlbaum.

—— (1997). *The crosslinguistic study of language acquisition*, vol. 4. Hillsdale, N.J.: Lawrence Erlbaum.

Smith, C. S. (1991). *The parameter of aspect*. Dordrecht: Kluwer.

Smith, J. R. (1981). Inwhich: A New Case Form? *American Speech*, 56, 310–11.

Smith, N. (1985). Spreading, reduplication, and the default option in Miwok nonconcatenative morphology. In van der Hulst and Smith (eds), 363–80.

—— (1986). Reduplication, spreading and/or empty suffix slots in Sierra Miwok associative morphology. In Hans Bennis and F. Beckema (eds), *Linguistics in the Netherlands 1986*, Dordrecht: Foris, 235–43.

Smith, N. and Hermans, B. (1982). Nonconcatenatieve woordvorming in het Sierra Miwok. *Glot*, 5, 263–84.

Smith P. T. and Sterling, C. M. (1982). Factors affecting the perceived morphemic structure of written words. *Journal of Verbal Learning and Verbal Behavior*, 21, 704–21.

Smolensky, P. (1993). Harmony, markedness, and phonological activity. Handout from talk presented at Rutgers Optimality Workshop I, Rutgers University.

Smyth, H. W. (1956). *Greek grammar*, rev. edn. Cambridge, Mass.: Harvard University Press.

Speas, M. (1984). Navajo prefixes and word structure typology. In M. Speas and R. Sproat (eds), *MIT Working Papers in Linguistics*, 7, 86–109.

—— (1986). Adjunctions and projections in syntax. Ph.D. diss., Massachusetts Institute of Technology.

—— (1990). *Phrase structure in natural language*. Dordrecht: Kluwer.

—— (1991a). Functional heads and inflectional morphemes. *Linguistic Review*, 8, 389–417.

—— (1991b). Functional heads and the Mirror Principle. *Lingua*, 84, 181–214.

—— (1994). Null arguments in a theory of economy of projection. In E. Benedicto and J. Runner (eds), *UMass Occasional Papers in Linguistics*, 17. Amherst: University of Massachusetts, GLSA.

Spencer, A. (1988a). Arguments for morpholexical rules. *Journal of Linguistics*, 24, 1–29.

—— (1988b). Bracketing paradoxes and the English lexicon. *Language*, 64, 663–82.

—— (1991). *Morphological theory: an introduction to word structure in generative grammar*. Oxford: Blackwell Publishers.

—— (1992). Nominal inflection and the nature of functional categories. *Journal of Linguistics*, 28, 313–41.

—— (1995). Incorporation in Chukchi. *Language*, 71, 439–89.

—— (1996). Agreement morphology in Chukotkan. Paper presented at the 7th International Morphology meeting, Vienna, February 1996.

Sportiche, D. (1988). A theory of floating quantifers and its corollaries for constituent structure. *Linguistic Inquiry*, 19, 425–49.

Spring, C. (1990). Implications of Axininca Campa for Prosodic Morphology and reduplication. Ph.D. diss., University of Arizona, Tucson.

Sproat, R. (1985). On deriving the lexicon. Ph.D. diss., Massachusetts Institute of Technology.

—— (1988). Bracketing paradoxes, cliticizaton and other topics: the mapping between syntactic and phonological structure. In Everaert et al. (eds), 339–60.

—— (1992). Unhappier is not a bracketing paradox. *Linguistic Inquiry*, 23, 347–52.

—— (1993). Morphological non-separation revisited: a review of Lieber's *Deconstructing morphology*. In G. Booij and J. van Marle (eds), *Yearbook of morphology 1992*, Dordrecht: Kluwer, 235–58.

Stafford, R. (1967). *The Luo language*. Nairobi: Longmans.

Stang, C. (1966). *Vergleichende Grammatik der baltischen Sprachen*. Oslo: Universitetsforlaget.

Stanners, R. F., Neiser, J. J., Hernon, W. P. and Hall, R. (1979a). Memory representation for morphologically related words. *Journal of Verbal Learning and Verbal Behavior*, 18, 399–412.

Stanners, R. F., Neiser, J. J. and Painton, S. (1979b). Memory representation for prefixed words. *Journal of Verbal Learning and Verbal Behavior*, 18, 733–43.

Steele, S. (1976). On the count of one. In A. Juilland (ed.), *Linguistic studies offered to Joseph Greenberg*, vol. 3, Anma Libri, Saratoga, Calif., 591–613.

—— (1978). Word order variation: a typological study. In J. Greenberg, C. Ferguson and E. Moravcsik (eds), *Universals of human language*, vol. 4: *Syntax*, Stanford, Calif.: Stanford University Press, 585–623.

—— (1990). *Agreement and anti-agreement: a syntax of Luiseño*, Studies in Natural Language and Linguistic Theory, 17. Dordrecht: Kluwer.

Steele, S., Akmajian, A., Demers, R., Jelinek, E., Kitagawa, C., Dehrle, R. and Wasow, T. (1981). *An encyclopedia of Aux: a study of cross-linguistic equivalence*. Cambridge, Mass.: MIT Press.

Steever, S. B. (1988). Tamil and the Dravidian languages. In B. Comrie (ed.), *The world's major languages*, London: Croom Helm, 725–46.

Stemberger, J. P. (1981). Morphological haplology. *Language*, 57, 791–817.

—— (1985a). Bound morpheme loss errors in normal and agrammatic speech: one mechanism or two? *Brain and Language*, 25, 246–56.

—— (1985b). An interactive activation model of language production. In A. Ellis (ed.), *Progress in the Psychology of Language*, vol. 1, London: Lawrence Erlbaum, 143–86.

—— (1985c). *The lexicon in a model of language production*. New York: Garland.

—— (1992a). Overtensing, regularity, and the unreality of rules. Paper presented at the 33rd annual meeting of the Psychonomics Society, St Louis.

—— (1992b). Vocalic underspecification in English language production. *Language*, 68, 492–524.

—— (1993). Vowel dominance in overregularization. *Journal of Child Language*, 20, 503–21.

—— (1994a). Phonological priming and irregular past: for whom the bell telled. Paper presented at the 35th annual meeting of the Psychonomic Society, St Louis, November 1994.

—— (1994b). Rule-less morphology at the phonology–lexicon interface. In R. Corrigan, G. Iverson and S. Lima (eds), *The reality of linguistic rules*, Amsterdam: J. Benjamins, 147–69.

Stemberger, J. P. and Lewis, M. (1986). Reduplication in Ewe: morphological accommodation to phonological errors. *Phonology Yearbook* 3, 151–60.

Stemberger, J. P. and MacWhinney, B. (1986a). Form-oriented errors in inflectional processing. *Cognitive Psychology*, 18, 329–54.

—— (1986b). Frequency and the lexical storage of regularly inflected forms. *Memory and Cognition*, 14, 17–26.

—— (1988). Are inflected forms stored in the lexicon? In Hammond and Noonan (eds), 101–16.

Stemberger, J. P. and Setchell, C. M. (1994). Vowel dominance and morphological processing. MS, University of Minnesota and SUNY, Buffalo.

Steriade, D. (1980). Clitic doubling in the Romanian wh constructions and the analysis of topicalization. *CLS*, 16, 282–97.

—— (1988a). Greek accent: a case for preserving structure. *Linguistic Inquiry*, 19, 271–314.

—— (1988b). Reduplication and syllable transfer in Sanskrit and elsewhere. *Phonology*, 5, 73–155.

—— (1990). *Greek prosodies and the nature of syllabification*. New York: Garland.

Stolz, J. A. and Feldman, L. B. (1995). The role of orthographic and semantic transparency of the base morpheme in morphological processing. In Feldman (ed.), 109–29.

Stonham, J. T. (1990). Current issues in morphological theory. Ph.D. diss., Stanford University.

—— (1994). *Combinatorial morphology*. Amsterdam: J. Benjamins.

Stowell, T. (1981). Origins of phrase structure. Ph.D. diss., Massachusetts Institute of Technology.

Stump, G. T. (1980). An inflectional approach to French clitics. In A. Zwicky (ed.), *Clitics and ellipsis*, Ohio State University Working Papers in Linguistics, 24, 1–54.

—— (1990a). Breton inflection and the split morphology hypothesis. In R. Hendrick (ed.), *Syntax and semantics*, vol. 23: *The syntax of the modern Celtic languages*, San Diego, Calif.: Academic Press, 97–119.

—— (1990b). La morphologie bretonne et la frontière entre la flexion et la dérivation. *La Bretagne linguistique*, 6, 185–237.

—— (1991). A paradigm-based theory of morphosemantic mismatches. *Language*, 67, 675–725.

—— (1992). On the theoretical status of position class restrictions on inflectional affixes. In G. Booij and J. van Marle (eds), *Yearbook of morphology 1991*, Dordrecht: Kluwer, 211–41.

—— (1993a). How peculiar is evaluative morphology? *Journal of Linguistics*, 29, 1–36.

—— (1993b). On rules of referral. *Language*, 69, 449–79.

—— (1993c). Position classes and morphological theory. In G. Booij and J. van Marle (eds), *Yearbook of morphology 1992*, Dordrecht: Kluwer, 129–80.

—— (1993d). Reconstituting morphology: the case of Bantu preprefixation. *Linguistic Analysis*, 23, 169–204.

—— (1993e). Review of Lieber, 1992. *Journal of Linguistics*, 29, 485–90.

—— (1995a). Stem formation, stem indexing, and stem choice. MS, University of Kentucky.

—— (1995b). The uniformity of head marking. In G. Booij and J. van Marle (eds), *Yearbook of morphology 1994*, Dordrecht: Kluwer, 245–96.

—— (1997). "Template" morphology and inflectional morphology. In G. Booij and J. van Marle (eds), *Yearbook of morphology 1996*, Dordrecht: Kluwer.

Suñer, M. (1988). The role of agreement in clitic-doubled constructions. *Natural Language and Linguistic Theory*, 6/3, 391–434.

Sussex, R. (1980). On agreement, affixation and enclisis in Polish. In C. Chvany and R. Brecht (eds), *Morphosyntax in Slavic*, Columbus, Oh.: Slavica, 187–203.

Szymanek, B. (1989). *Introduction to morphological analysis*. Warsaw: Panstwowe wydawnictwo naukowe.

Taft, M. (1978). Evidence that auditory word perception is not continuous: the DAZE effect. Paper presented at the the 5th Australian Experimental Psychology Conference, La Trobe University, May 1978.

—— (1979a). Lexical access via an orthographic code. The Basic Orthographic Syllabic Structure (BOSS). *Journal of Verbal Learning and Verbal Behavior*, 18, 21–39.

—— (1979b). Recognition of affixed words and the word frequency effect. *Memory and Cognition*, 7, 263–72.

—— (1981). Prefix stripping revisited. *Journal of Verbal Learning and Verbal Behavior*, 20, 289–97.

—— (1985). The decoding of words in lexical access: a review of the morphographic approach. In D. Besner, T. G. Waller and G. E. Mackinnon (eds), *Reading research: advances in theory and practice*, vol. 5, 83–123.

—— (1988). A morphological-decomposition model of lexical representation. *Linguistics*, 26, 657–67.

—— (1994). Interactive-activation as a framework for understanding morphological processing. *Language and Cognitive Processes*, 9, 271–94.

Taft, M. and Forster, K. I. (1975). Lexical storage and retrieval of prefixed words. *Journal of Verbal Learning and Verbal Behavior*, 14, 630–47.

—— (1976). Lexical storage and retrieval of polymorphemic and polysyllabic words. *Journal of Verbal Learning and Verbal Behavior*, 15, 607–20.

Taft, M. and Zhu, X. (1995). The representation of bound morphemes in the lexicon: a Chinese study. In Feldman (ed.), 293–316.

Taft, M., Hambly, G. and Kinoshita, S. (1986). Visual and auditory recognition of prefixed words. *Quarterly Journal of Experimental Psychology*, 38A, 351–86.

Tallerman, M. (1991). The directionality of head subcategorization in Welsh. In J. Fife and E. Poppe (eds), *Studies in Brythonic word order*, Amsterdam: J. Benjamins, 311–27.

Talmy, L. (1975). Semantics and syntax of motion. In J. P. Kimball (ed.), *Syntax and semantics*, vol. 4, New York: Academic Press, 181–238.

—— (1976). Semantic causative types. In Shibatani (ed.), 43–116.

—— (1985). Lexicalization patterns: semantic structure in lexical forms. In Shopen (ed.), 57–149.

—— (1988). Force dynamics in language and thought. *Cognitive Science*, 12, 49–100.

Tateishi, K. (1989). Theoretical implications of the Japanese musician's language. In *Proceedings of the 8th West Coast Conference on Formal Linguistics*, 384–98.

Taylor, A. (1990). Clitics and configurationality in Ancient Greek. Unpublished Ph.D. diss., University of Pennsylvania.

—— (1992). Second position clitics. Paper presented at 1992 Winter meeting of the LSA, Philadelphia.

—— (1996). A prosodic account of clitic position in Ancient Greek. In A. L. Halpern and A. M. Zwicky (eds), *Approaching second: second position clitics and related phenomena*, Stanford, Calif.: CSLI. 477–503.

Tegey, H. (1978). *The grammar of clitics: evidence from Pashto (Afghani) and other languages.* Kabul: International Center for Pashto Studies.

Tenenbaum, J. (1977). Morphology and semantics of the Tanaina verb. Ph.D. diss., Columbia University.

Tenny, C. L. (1987). Grammaticalizing aspect and affectedness. Ph.D. diss., Massachusetts Institute of Technology.

—— (1992). The aspectual interface hypothesis. In Sag and Szabolcsi (eds), 1–27.

—— (1994). *Aspectual roles and the syntax–semantics interface.* Dordrecht: Kluwer.

Thomas, P. (1984). Variation in South Glamorgan consonant mutation. In M. Ball and G. Jones (eds), *Welsh phonology*, Cardiff: University of Wales Press, 208–36.

Thomas-Flinders, T. (ed.) (1981). *Inflectional morphology: introduction to the extended word-and-paradigm theory*, Occasional Papers in Linguistics, 4. Los Angeles: UCLA Department of Linguistics.

Thomason, S. G. and Kaufman, T. (1988). *Language contact, creolization, and genetic linguistics*. Berkeley: University of California Press.

Thurneysen, R. (1970). *A grammar of Old Irish*, trans. D. A. Binchy and Osborn Bergin. Dublin: Dublin Institute for Advanced Studies.

Tiersma, P. (1978). Bidirectional leveling as evidence for relational rules. *Lingua*, 45, 65–77.

Timberlake, A. (1988). Case agreement in Lithuanian. In Barlow and Ferguson (eds), 181–99.

Tissot, R., Mounin, G. and Lhermitte, F. (1973). *L'agrammatisme*. Paris: Dessart.

Titov, E. G. (1971). *Sovremennyj amxarskij jazyk*. Moscow: Nauka.

Toman, J. (1983). *Wortsyntax: Eine Diskussion ausgewählter Probleme deutscher Wortbildung*. Tübingen: Niemeyer.

—— (1985). A discussion of coordination and word-syntax. In J. Toman (ed.), *Studies in German grammar*, Dordrecht: Foris, 407–32.

—— (1986). A (word-)syntax for participles. *Linguistische Berichte*, 105, 367–408.

Traugott, E. C. and Heine, B. (eds) (1991a). *Approaches to grammaticalization*, vol. 1: *Focus on theoretical and methodological issues*. Amsterdam: J. Benjamins.

—— (1991b). *Approaches to grammaticalization*, vol. 2: *Focus on types of grammatical markers*. Amsterdam: J. Benjamins.

Travis, L. (1984). Parameters and the effects of word order variation. Ph.D. diss. Massachusetts Institute of Technology.

Trépos, P. (1957). *Le pluriel breton*. Brest: Emgleo Breiz.

Trudgill, P. (1990). *The dialects of England*. Oxford: Blackwell Publishers.

Tsujimura, N. (1996). *An introduction to Japanese linguistics*. Oxford: Blackwell Publishers.

Tuttle, S. (1993). The status of object markers in Salcha Athabaskan. MS.

Tyler, L. K. (1992). *Spoken language comprehension: an experimental approach to disordered and normal processing*. Cambridge, Mass.: MIT Press.

Tyler, L. and Nagy, W. (1990). Use of derivational morphology during reading. *Cognition*, 36, 17–34.

Tyler, L. K., Behrens, S., Cobb, H. and Marslen-Wilson, W. (1990). Processing distinctions between stems and affixes: evidence from a non-fluent aphasic patient. *Cognition*, 36, 129–53.

Tyler, L. K. and Cobb, H. (1987). Processing bound grammatical morphemes in context: the case of an aphasic patient. *Language and Cognitive Processes*, 2, 245–62.

Tyler, L. K., Marslen-Wilson, W., Rentoul, J. and Hanney, P. (1988). Continuous and discontinuous access in spoken word recognition: the role of derivational prefixes. *Journal of Memory and Language*, 27, 368–81.

Van der Molen, H. and Morton, J. (1979). Remembering plurals: unit of coding and form of coding during serial recall. *Cognition*, 7, 35–47.

Van Valin, R. D., Jr (1990). Semantic parameters of split intransitivity. *Language*, 66, 221–60.

—— (1993). A synopsis of role and reference grammar. In R. D. Van Valin, Jr (ed.), *Advances in Role and Reference Grammar*, Amsterdam: J. Benjamins, 1–164.

Vendler, Z. (1957). Verbs and times. *Philosophical Review*, 56, 143–60; also in Z. Vendler, *Linguistics in philosophy*, Ithaca, N.Y.: Cornell University Press, 1967, 97–121.

Verin, P., Kotak, C. and Gorlin, P. (1969). The glottochronology of Malagasy speech communities. *Oceanic Linguistics*, 81/1, 26–83.

Verkuyl, H. J. (1972). *On the compositional nature of the aspects*. Dordrecht: Reidel.

—— (1993). *A theory of aspectuality*. Cambridge: Cambridge University Press.

Verschueren, J. (1987). *Pragmatics as a theory of linguistic adaptation*. Antwerp: IPRA Working Document 1.

Vigliocco, G., Butterworth, B. and Semenza, C. (1995). Constructing subject–verb agreement in speech: the role of semantic and morphological factors. *Journal of Memory and Language*, 34, 186–215.

Vilaca, A. (1992). *Comendo Como Gente*. Rio de Janeiro: ANPOCS, Universidade Federal do Rio de Janeiro.

Vinay, J.-P. and Darbelnet, J. (1958). *Stylistique compareé du Français et de l'Anglais*. Paris: Didier.

Vincent, N. (1974). Analogy reconsidered. In J. M. Anderson and C. Jones (eds), *Historical linguistics* (Proceedings of the 1st International Conference on Historical Linguistics), vol. 2, Amsterdam: North-Holland, 427–45.

Volek, B. (1987). *Emotive signs in language and semantic functioning of derived nouns in Russian*. Amsterdam: J. Benjamins.

Voorhoeve, C. L. (1965). *The Flamingo Bay dialect of the Asmat language*. The Hague: Martinus Nijhoff.

Wackernagel, J. (1892). Uber ein Gesetz der Indogermanischen Wortstellung [On a law of Indo-Germanic syntax]. *Indogermanishe Forschungen*, 1, 333–436.

Walinska de Hackbeil, H. (1986). The roots of phrase structure: the syntactic base of English morphology. Ph.D. diss., University of Washington.

Wang, W. S.-Y. (1969). Competing changes as a cause of residue. *Language*, 45, 9–25.

Wanner, D. (1987). *The development of Romance clitic pronouns from Latin to Old Romance*. Berlin: Mouton de Gruyter.

Warburton, I. P. (1973). Modern Greek verb conjugation: inflectional morphology in a transformational grammar. *Lingua*, 32, 193–226.

Warren, B. (1978). *Semantic patterns of noun–noun compounds*. Göteborg: Acta Universitatis Gothoburgensis.

Wasow, T. (1977). *Transformations and the lexicon*. In Culicover et al. (eds), 327–60.

Watkins, A. (1976). The Welsh personal pronoun. *Word*, 28, 146–65.

Watkins, C. W. (1962). *Indo-European origins of the Celtic verb*. Dublin: Dublin Institute for Advanced Studies.

—— (1985). *The American heritage dictionary of Indo-European roots*. Boston: Houghton Mifflin Co.

Watkins, M. H. (1937). *A grammar of Chichewa*, Language Dissertations, 24. Baltimore: Linguistic Society of America.

Waxman, S. (1994). The development of an appreciation of specific linkages between linguistic and conceptual organization. *Lingua*, 92, 229–57.

Weeda, D. (1987). Formal properties of Madurese final syllable reduplication. In *Papers from the 23rd annual regional meeting of the Chicago Linguistic Society, parasession on autosegmental and metrical phonology*, 403–17.

—— (1992). Word truncation in prosodic phonology. Ph.D. diss., University of Texas, Austin.

Weimer, H. and Weimer, N. (1970). Reduplication in Yareba. *Papers in New Guinea Linguistics*, 11, 37–43.

—— (1975). A short sketch of Yareba grammar. In T. E. Dutton (ed.), *Studies in languages of Central and South-Eastern Papua*, Pacific Linguistics, series C, no. 29, Canberra: Australian National University Press.

Weist, R. M., Wysoska, H., Witkowska-Stadnik, K., Buczowska, E. and Konieczna, E. (1984). The defective tense hypothesis: on the emergence of tense and aspect in child Polish. *Journal of Child Language*, 11, 347–74.

Werner, H. and Kaplan, B. (1963). *Symbol formation. An organismic–developmental approach to language and the expression of thought*. New York: Wiley and Sons.

Whitney, W. D. (1889). *Sanskrit grammar*, 2nd edn. Cambridge, Mass.: Harvard University Press.

Wienold, G. (1995). Lexical and conceptual structures in expressions for movement and space: with reference to Japanese, Korean, Thai, and Indonesian as compared to English and German. In U. Egli, P. E. Pause, C. Schwarze, A. von Stechow and G. Wienold (eds), *Lexical knowledge in the organization of language*, Amsterdam: J. Benjamins, 301–40.

Wierzbicka, A. (1983). The semantics of case marking. *Studies in Language*, 7, 247–75.

—— (1984). Diminutives and depreciatives. *Quaderni di Semantica*, 5, 123–30.

Wiese, R. (1996). Phonological vs. morphological rules: on German umlaut and ablaut. *Journal of Linguistics*, 32, 113–35.

Wilkins, D. P. (1986). Particle/clitics for criticism and complaint in Mparntwe Arrernte (Aranda). *Journal of Pragmatics*, 10, 575–96.

—— (1989). Mparntwe Arrernte (Aranda): studies in the structure and semantics of grammar. Ph.D. diss., Australian National University (to appear, Oxford University Press).

—— (1993). *The semantics, pragmatics and diachronic development of 'associated motion' in Mparntwe Arrernte*, Buffalo Working Papers in Linguistics. Buffalo: State University of New York Press.

Willett, T. (1988). A cross-linguistic survey of the grammaticization of evidentiality. *Studies in Language*, 12, 51–97.

Williams, E. (1980). Predication. *Linguistic Inquiry*, 11, 203–38.

—— (1981a). Argument structure and morphology. *Linguistic Review*, 1, 81–114.

—— (1981b). On the notions 'lexically related' and 'head of a word'. *Linguistic Inquiry*, 12, 245–74.

—— (1994a). Remarks on lexical knowledge. *Lingua*, 92, 7–34.

—— (1994b). *Thematic relations*. Cambridge, Mass.: MIT Press.

—— (1996). Three models of the morphology–syntax interface. Paper presented at the 7th International Morphology meeting, Vienna, February 1996.

Williams, J. (1991). A note on echo word morphology in Thai and the languages of South and South-East Asia. *Australian Journal of Linguistics*, 11, 107–12.

Williams, S. (1959). *Elfennau gramadeg Cymraeg*. Caerdydd: Gwasg Prifysgol Cymru.

Wilson, P. M. (1985). *Simplified Swahili*. Harlow: Longman Group UK Ltd.

Winters, M. (1995). J. Kuryłowicz: the so-called laws of analogy, trans. and introduced. *Diachronica*, 12, 113–45.

Wolfart, H. C. (1973). Plains Cree: a grammatical study. *Transactions of the American Philosophical Society*, 63/5, 1–90.

Wolfart, H. C. and Caroll, J. F. (1981). *Meet Cree: a guide to the Cree language*, 2nd edn. Edmonton: University of Alberta Press.

Woodbury, A. (1985). Meaningful phonological processes: a consideration of Central Alaskan Yupik Eskimo prosody. MS, University of Texas, Austin.

—— (1987). Meaningful phonological processes: a consideration of Central Alaskan Yupik prosody. *Language*, 63, 685–740.

—— (1996). On restricting the role of morphology in autolexical syntax. In E. Schiller and E. Steinberg (eds), *Autolexical theory: ideas and methods*, Trends in Linguistics, Studies and Monographs, 85, Berlin and New York: Mouton de Gruyter, 319–66.

Woodbury, H. (1975). Onondaga noun incorporation: some notes on the interdependence of syntax and semantics. *International Journal of American Linguistics*, 41, 10–20.

Wright, M. (1983). The CV skeleton and verb prefix phonology in Navajo. In *Proceedings of the 14th annual meeting of the North-Eastern Linguistic Society*, 461–77.

—— (1986). Mapping and movement of partial matrices in Navajo. In *Proceedings of the 17th annual meeting of the North-Eastern Linguistic Society*, 685–99.

Wunderlich, D. (1993). Funktionale Kategorien im Lexikon. In F. Beckmann and G. Heyer (eds), *Theorie und Praxis des Lexikons*, Berlin: de Gruyter, 54–73.

—— (1994). Towards a lexicon-based theory of agreement. *Theoretical Linguistics*, 20, 1–25.

Wurzel, W. U. (1984). *Flexionsmorphologie und Natürlichkeit. Ein Beitrag zur morphologischen Theoriebildung*. Berlin: Akademie Verlag.

—— (1987). Paradigmenstrukturbedingungen: Aufbau und Veränderung von Flexionsparadigmen. In A. G. Ramat, O. Carruba and G. Bernini (eds), *Papers from the 7th International Conference on Historical Linguistics*, Amsterdam: J. Benjamins, 629–44.

—— (1989). *Inflectional morphology and naturalness*. Dordrecht: Kluwer. (English trans. of Würzel, 1984.)

Xajdakov, S. M. (1967). *Arčinskij jazyk*. In *Jazyki narodov SSSR*, vol. 4. Moscow: Nauka.

Yallop, C. (1977). *Alyawarra, an aboriginal language of Central Australia*, Australian Aboriginal Studies Regional and Research Studies. Canberra: Australian Institute of Aboriginal Studies.

Yin, Y.-M. (1989). Phonological aspects of word formation in Mandarin Chinese. Ph.D. diss., University of Texas, Austin.

Yip, M. (1982). Reduplication and CV-skeleta in Chinese secret languages. *Linguistic Inquiry*, 13, 637–62.

—— (1983). Redundancy and the CV-skeleton. MS, Brandeis University.

—— (1991). Prosodic morphology of four Chinese dialects. *Journal of East Asian Linguistics*, 1, 1–35.

—— (1992). Reduplication with fixed melodic material. In *Proceedings of the 22nd annual meeting of the North-Eastern Linguistic Society*, 459–76.

Young, R. and Morgan, W. (1987). *The Navajo language: a grammar and colloquial dictionary*, rev. edn. Albuquerque: University of New Mexico Press.

Zaenen, A. (1993). Unaccusativity in Dutch: integrating syntax and lexical semantics. In J. Pustejovsky (ed.), *Semantics and the lexicon*, Dordrecht: Kluwer, 129–61.

Zec, D. (1988). Sonority constraints on prosodic structure. Ph.D. diss., Stanford University.

Zec, D. and Inkelas, S. (1991). The place of clitics in the prosodic hierarchy. In *Proceedings of the 10th West Coast conference on formal linguistics*, 505–19.

Zhou, X. and Marslen-Wilson, W. (1994). Words, morphemes and syllables in the Chinese mental lexicon. *Language and Cognitive Processes*, 9, 393–422.

Zipf, G. K. (1935). *The psychobiology of language*. Boston: Houghton Mifflin.

Zubizarreta, M.-L. (1985). The relation between morphophonology and morphosyntax: the case of Romance causatives. *Linguistic Inquiry*, 16, 247–90.

—— (1987). *Levels of representation in the lexicon and in the syntax*. Dordrecht: Foris.

Zwart, J.-W. (1993a). Clues from dialect syntax: complementizer agreement. In W. Abraham and J. Bayer (eds), *Dialektsyntax*, Linguistische Berichte, special issue 5, 246–70.

—— (1993b). Verb movement and complementizer agreement. In J. D. Bobaljik and C. Phillips (eds), *MIT Working Papers in Linguistics, 18, Papers on Case and Agreement I*, Cambridge, Mass.: MIT, 297–340.

—— (1996). Clitics, scrambling and head movement in Dutch. In Halpern and Zwicky (eds), 579–612.

Zwicky, A. M. (1977). On clitics. Bloomington: Indiana University Linguistics Club.

—— (1985). How to describe inflection. In *Proceedings of the 11th annual meeting of the Berkeley Linguistics Society*, 372–86.

—— (1986a). Agreement features: layers or tags? *Ohio State University Working Papers in Linguistics*, 32, 146–8.

—— (1986b). The general case: basic form versus default form. In *Proceedings of the 12th annual meeting of the Berkeley Linguistics Society*, 305–14.

—— (1986c). German adjective agreement in GPSG. *Linguistics*, 24, 957–90.

—— (1987). Suppressing the Zs. *Journal of Linguistics*, 23, 133–48.

—— (1989). Idioms and constructions. In *Proceedings of the 5th annual meeting of the Eastern States conference on linguistics*, 547–58.

—— (1990). Inflectional morphology as a (sub)component of grammar. In Dressler, et al. (eds), 217–36.

—— (1991). Systematic versus accidental phonological identity. In Plank (ed.), 113–31.

—— (1992). Jottings on adpositions, case inflections, government, and agreement. In D. Brentari, G. N. Larson and L. A. MacLeod (eds), *The joy of grammar: a festschrift in honour of James D. McCawley*, Amsterdam: J. Benjamins, 369–83.

—— (1993). Heads, bases and functors. In G. Corbett, N. Fraser and S. McGlashan (eds), *Heads in grammatical theory*, Cambridge: Cambridge University Press, 292–315.

Zwicky, A. M. and Pullum, G. K. (1983a). Cliticization vs. inflection: English n 't. *Language*, 59, 502–13.

—— (1983b). Phonology in syntax: the Somali optional agreement rule. *Natural Language and Linguistic Theory*, 1, 385–402.

—— (1987). Plain morphology and expressive morphology. In *Proceedings of the 13th annual meeting of the Berkeley Linguistics Society*, 330–40.

Zwitserlood, P. (1994). The role of semantic transparency in the processing and representation of Dutch compounds. *Language and Cognitive Processes*, 9, 341–68.

Subject Index

Author Index